FINDING BIGFOOT™

Meet the *Finding Bigfoot* team:
Cliff Barackman, James "Bobo" Fay,
Ranae Holland, and Matt Moneymaker!

ANIMAL PLANET

FINDING BIGFOOT™

EVERYTHING YOU NEED TO KNOW

BY MARTHA BROCKENBROUGH

FEIWEL AND FRIENDS
NEW YORK

A Feiwel and Friends Book
An Imprint of Macmillan

Printed in the United States of America by Worzalla, Stevens Point, Wisconsin.
For information, address Feiwel and Friends,
175 Fifth Avenue, New York, N.Y. 10010.

Library of Congress Cataloging-in-Publication Data Available

ISBN: 978-1-250-04089-3 (hardcover)
2 4 6 8 10 9 7 5 3 1

ISBN: 978-1-250-04090-9 (paperback)
2 4 6 8 10 9 7 5 3

Book design by April Ward

Feiwel and Friends logo designed by Filomena Tuosto

First Edition: 2013

mackids.com

CONTENTS

I AM IN LOVE WITH MONSTERS. Always have been.

My first memories of bigfoot go back to when I was four or five years old. My dad, who is the best father you could ever ask for, joined something called the Indian Guides with me. We had to choose "little" and "big" Indian Guide names, and I almost went for Bigfoot. But even then, I was picky about words and didn't like how "Little Bigfoot" and "Big Bigfoot" sounded.

I've always been interested in these animals, though. They fascinate a lot of people because of what they represent: an archetype that gives us clues about our own origins. They also represent the monster in the human condition. And as much as we like the comforts of home, a lot of us want to be able to survive in the wild as a bigfoot does—that's why all those survivor shows are so successful.

While I didn't start searching for a real sasquatch until I was older, I'd always had a strong connection to the outdoors. Growing up in California, I'd go camping a lot with my family, especially in Sequoia National Park. We'd go looking for animal footprints. I never thought I'd see a bigfoot track, though. Back then, I thought the animal was a Pacific Northwest thing.

As I got older and started coming into my own self, I became even more drawn to weird things, as normal people bore me to tears. I like freaks and weirdos. I might look totally normal, and I have the dubious honor of being Bobo Fay's most normal friend (and his parents love me because it means there's hope for their boy). But I'm a pretty weird guy under it all. I was kicked out of the Boy Scouts because I didn't fall into line like I was supposed to.

In college, I rediscovered my fascination with bigfoot when I came across a collection of papers by cultural and physical anthropologists. They talked about stone heads depicting apes found on the Columbia River. These things were 1,000 years old, long before white men first visited the continent. What's more, there are no apes in North America. So what might these have represented? Furthermore, every Native American tribe has something like sasquatches as part of their mythology, even if they don't call them that. These animals are thrown in there with other real creatures: bears, foxes, and wolves. That's too big of a coincidence.

I was also impressed with the way physical anthropologists analyzed the Sierra Sounds, concluding that human beings aren't capable of producing noises like those. And there was Grover Krantz's convincing reconstruction of a sasquatch foot based on the tracks of a crippled specimen found in Bossburg, Washington.

I got hooked on the subject after that. I devoured every book in the library on it, and I started realizing that holy smokes, these things might be real! It wasn't so much a single piece of evidence that persuaded me, but rather, it was the consistency and internal congruency of all the data that had been gathered. People have been describing animals that look like bigfoot and act like bigfoot for centuries or more.

Bigfoot is real. But don't just take my word for it. Read this book. Consider the evidence. Look at the tracks. It's true that bigfoot doesn't yet have academic acceptance, but that's mostly a matter of ignorance, by which I mean ignoring data and evidence.

Even better, go look for bigfoot yourself. My favorite way to seek it is to sit in the woods and just listen. I calm my mind and bring a sense of awareness. I'm grounded when I'm out there in the woods. To search for bigfoot is to find . . . yourself.

I'm a professional teacher, and teachers are learners. My life is bigfoot now, and the only answer I have for why is that I love it. I didn't choose it. It chose me. I am in this for life.

—*Cliff Barackman*

PEOPLE SAY BIGFOOT DOESN'T EXIST.

That sasquatch is a legend. That we can forget about finding a yeti. It's a common misperception that all of these animals have been proven to be hoaxes, that "Bigfoot" was just some guy playing tricks on a Northern California road crew. But those doubters don't know what the stars of *Finding Bigfoot* know....

They don't know about the tracks...

About the noises and shining eyes in the woods at night...

About the deer carcasses with strangely snapped-off bones...

That long before the name "bigfoot" was applied to describe a creature that left giant tracks in the earth, human beings from around the world have been telling stories about an enormous, bipedal ape—a hairy, wild, and stunningly elusive mystery.

But thanks to Animal Planet's hit documentary show, which is entering its fourth fascinating season, people are starting to find out there is real science behind the possibility of the animal best known as bigfoot.

One key to the show's success is its four intrepid stars: Bigfoot Field Research Organization president Matt Moneymaker, researchers James "Bobo" Fay and Cliff Barackman, and skeptical scientist Ranae Holland.

These tireless searchers have covered vast territory, ranging from the shaggy woods of the Pacific Northwest to the nearly impenetrable jungles of Indonesia, taking viewers places they can only dream of visiting. The foursome brings an incredible depth of knowledge to their pursuit. They know what these animals like to eat, where they're most likely to be spotted, how they're likely to behave, and what sets them apart from other animals. They also know how to sniff out phonies and false leads.

What's more, the team is thorough in its search. They study photos and videos. They re-create sightings in the field, no matter how remote the territory. They use incredibly sophisticated technology, from night-vision cameras to drones, as well as clever techniques such as glow-in-the-dark powder. And they're not afraid to put their own bodies on the line, whether they're blasting sasquatch calls or waiting in the dark alone, hoping for a close encounter with the most elusive primate the world has ever known.

Without a doubt, if and when this team proves the existence of a giant North American ape, they will rewrite scientific history and satisfy a curiosity that has gripped humankind since we were telling stories around fire pits and painting our legends in caves.

You can follow the team both on the show and in this book, which shares the show's most mind-boggling encounters, historical and scientific background, new developments in sasquatch science, a collection of some of the strongest bigfoot evidence yet gathered, and practical advice you can put to use in your own adventures in finding bigfoot. It's enough to make even the most hardened skeptic take another look, and for people already fascinated by the creature, it's all the information you've ever wanted and so much more.

Chapter One
DOES BIGFOOT EXIST?

THE CASE FOR CRYPTIDS

Some people believe we know everything there is to know about this world. People who believe every inch of land has been conquered, every drop of ocean explored. And while it's true that adventurers have made their way around the globe, mapping the edges of oceans and continents, the heights of the mountains, the depths of the rivers and lakes, it's also true that scientists learn new things every day. What's more, we find new animals all the time.

Since 2012, for example, we have discovered all sorts of previously unknown creatures, including monkeys, frogs, sharks, and lizards—even primates. Would you believe there is such a thing as a poisonous spider with hooklike claws on each of its legs? A group of people exploring a cave in bigfoot Country—southern Oregon—stumbled across this family of spiders deep in the throat of a cave in 2012. The *Trogloraptor marchingtoni* was the first family of native North American spiders to be found in more than a century.

That same year, a Louisiana State University snake expert named Christopher Austin followed strange chirping noises while he was inside a

Papua New Guinea forest. It turns out a frog the size of the housefly, the world's tiniest vertebrate, was responsible for the singing. (The same professor has found several other species that hadn't yet been recognized by science, including other frogs, lizards, and parasites.)

There was a new primate recognized around the same time: the lesula monkey, a wise-looking creature with a grayish brown beard. This one was found in 2007 living as a school administrator's pet in the Democratic Republic of the Congo. Researchers studied its DNA to conclude it was an unrecognized species. It's already endangered because it's being hunted for its meat. It's only the second new kind of African monkey to be recognized in twenty-eight years, and it might have died out before scientists learned of its existence.

While most of these newly discovered creatures are small or live in remote places, history is full of animals once called legend that turned out to be real. The list of animals known by reputation first and recognized by science later includes gorillas, giant pandas, Komodo dragons, bonobos, megamouth sharks, giant geckos, and the okapi, a short-necked giraffe relative.

Here are a few especially important finds:

THE GIANT PANDA

This fuzzy creature was unknown outside of China until 1869, when a French missionary named Père Jean-Pierre Armand David described one that had been killed on a hunt. Westerners have been enthralled with pandas ever since. Today, they're exceedingly rare; only about 1,590 exist in the wild. But they could be an incredibly important species. Early in 2013, a component in giant panda blood was found to kill deadly bacteria six times faster than other antibiotics.

This is crucial because certain types of infections have become resistant to drugs we already have. If you think of your immune system as an army, and the drugs as bullets, drug resistance turns those once-effective bullets into soap bubbles. The panda blood could be an important key in fighting those tough and terrible infections.

And don't worry—scientists figured out how to re-create the panda substance in a lab. They decoded a panda's DNA and synthesized the substance, which is called cathelicidin-AM and probably helps keep the pandas healthy in the wild. Pandas aren't the only animals that have these disease-fighting powers. The same group of scientists found similar compounds in the slime of snails and certain amphibians.

THE GIANT SQUID

The giant squid is a literary legend. Vikings told tales of the terrible kraken, a sea monster big enough to wrap its tentacles around a ship and pull it below the waves. The *Odyssey*, an ancient poem, has a scary bit about a monster named Scylla that may well have been a giant squid.

But these creatures aren't just legends. In 2004, researchers in Japan shot the first-ever images of a live giant squid—nearly three thousand years after Homer wrote the *Odyssey*. That's a really long time for people to know about an animal without actually seeing a live specimen. The squids aren't the size of islands, but researchers found one squid that was fifty-nine feet long with eyes the size of dinner plates. There's a chance even bigger specimens are gliding beneath the waves.

Another animal, the saola (pronounced SOW-la), sometimes called the Asian unicorn because of its parallel sharp-tipped horns, was found in 1992 in north central Vietnam. Since then, scientists have observed this animal only four times; and none live in captivity. The saola is so rare that it is considered critically endangered, according to the World Wildlife Fund.

AN EXTINCT FISH—FOUND!

And then there's the coelacanth [SEE-luh-canth]. According to the fossil record, many species of this ancient fish lived between 360 million years ago and 80 million years ago. Then they went extinct, around the time that dinosaurs did.

This is why it was so very surprising when, in

1938, a self-trained naturalist named Marjorie Courtenay-Latimer found a coelacanth on a fishing dock. She brought it to a professor, who identified it by its distinctive shape and lobed fins. With that, a once-extinct fish was miraculously and officially back among the living, having somehow survived in secret in the Comoros Islands in the western Indian Ocean.

Equally surprising, in 1997, yet another variety was found in northern Sulawesi in Indonesia—nearly six thousand miles away from the islands in the western Indian Ocean where Courtenay-Latimer's fish was found. These two species of coelacanth are believed to be the only survivors of a once-varied type of fish, for now at least.

They're unique in many ways. For example, their skulls have a hinge that lets them open their mouths superwide. They also have a "rostral organ" in their noses that is part of an electrosensory system. This works like an extra sense, allowing them to feel electromagnetic energy (sharks can do this, too). And they have fleshy, lobed fins that have bones inside of them, sort of like limbs.

Bigfooters love to offer up these examples as proof that bigfoot is a scientific possibility. Like the giant squid of legend, hairy two-legged creatures have appeared in folklore and stories around the world for ages. Like the coelacanth, there's a fossil record for similar creatures (hirsute human-like species that walk on two feet). And, as with the panda, there are real benefits to finding these mysterious creatures, wherever they might be hiding.

There's a controversial field of science that specializes in the study of "hidden" animals. It's called "cryptozoology," a word invented in the late 1950s by Bernard Heuvelmans, a zoologist. The word itself sounds pretty out there, but its meaning is straightforward: *crypto* means "hidden" and *zoology* means the "study of animals." It's related to paleontology, the study of prehistoric life, and both use reconstructions and evidence to build pictures of animals that haven't been seen or are no more. In addition to bigfoot, another famous cryptid, or hidden animal, is the Loch Ness Monster.

SPOTTED!
"It Was Kind of Creepy"

Howie Dagg lives in Hydaburg on Prince of Wales Island in Alaska. He and a neighbor had taken his truck out into the woods for a hike, hoping to relax and unwind after school. At first, they didn't even notice the tracks.

But then he got a closer look.

"I stopped and one of the tracks had toes, big toes in it," he said. "I stopped and we took some pictures . . . it was kind of creepy."

What's more, he and his friend felt as if they were being watched. Still, he felt skeptical, so he pushed on. Were they really bigfoot prints? He followed the trail all the way up the mountain.

At the top, where the road was choked with trees, he noticed a lot of branches had been snapped off about seven feet off the ground—a classic bigfoot sign.

The sun dipped behind the hill and it started to get dark, and that's when Howie's neighbor got scared, calling the creature a Gogit, which is a term used to describe a hairy giant in parts of Prince of Wales. Howie also had the willies, so they left.

The photos they took that day show prints 17.3 inches long and about 6.5 inches wide, the sort that might belong to a large male Sasquatch.

IS BIGFOOT REAL?

The truth is, no one knows for sure, although many people have strong opinions on the matter. We can only be absolutely certain there is such a creature as bigfoot when we have found one.

Otherwise, bigfoot remains a theoretical possibility. A theory is an explanation of something based on observations, experiments, and reasoning. When formed with care, theories are scientifically valid—even if they are not proven, and even when they apply to things we haven't seen.

Take black holes, for example. These are spots in space, big and small, where matter has been compressed (this can happen when a star dies). The compression of matter makes for an incredibly strong gravitational pull—a pull so strong nothing can escape it, not even light.

No one has ever seen a black hole (they're invisible!). No one has ever been inside one. But we can form theories about their existence because of careful, repeatable observations that have been made. As we learn more about physics, we might someday adjust our understanding and definition of black holes. But no one calls scientists crazy for believing such a thing exists because there is enough evidence to make it a reasonable thing to believe in.

Scientists ask questions, make observations, come up with smart guesses, devise experiments to test them, and consider the results thoughtfully. And that's exactly what you can do when it comes to bigfoot. There's nothing wrong with a healthy dose of skepticism. That's how scientists get smarter. And open minds are the only ones that can learn new things.

THE ARGUMENTS FOR BIGFOOT

Plenty of smart people believe bigfoot is alive and well and hiding from humanity. What makes them so sure there's a bigfoot when others say there's no such creature? It comes down to four things:

Folklore. One of the oldest surviving works of literature, *The Epic of Gilgamesh*, describes a hairy wild man named Enkidu. Similar tales of a hairy wild man who lives in the forest are part of many cultures around the world. Ancient cave paintings in California depict a Hairy Man and his family, and stories that go along with them sound very much like bigfoot tales. If no such animal exists, why would these stories be so common?

EVIDENCE PHOTO

Eyewitness accounts. Thousands

of people in the United States have reported seeing bigfoot. People in Canada have sasquatch sightings. In Nepal, people claim to have seen yetis. In Indonesia, a smaller version of a hairy man-like creature that walks on two feet is known as the Orang Pendek. There's also the Australian yowie. Many people who've had encounters are respected community members, including police officers and judges, who have a lot to lose by lying. If they're not lying, what did they see?

Physical evidence. Although no

one has found the body of a bigfoot, people have seen what they consider to be physical evidence. Footprints are among the best-known forms of evidence. The Bigfoot Field Research

Organization (BFRO), for example, has collected more than seven hundred suspected Bigfoot prints. Many that come from different areas are strikingly similar in size and overall proportions.

Other physical evidence includes hair samples, some of which has not been identified as belonging to other known animals. Does it belong to bigfoot? We can only know for sure when there is a known specimen of Bigfoot to test against. bigfooters have also gathered what they believe are blood and stool samples.

And finally there are twisted-off branches, animal carcasses with cleanly broken bones, and clumps of sticks arranged into sleeping nests, all of which are considered evidence of the creature's presence in the woods.

Photos, video, and audio recordings. There are photographs, the famous Patterson-Gimlin film, thermal video recordings, and audio recordings said to be multiple bigfoots communicating with one another.

When you combine all of this evidence, believers say, you have a compelling picture of a large, hairy, bipedal animal that lives in remote forests and swamps.

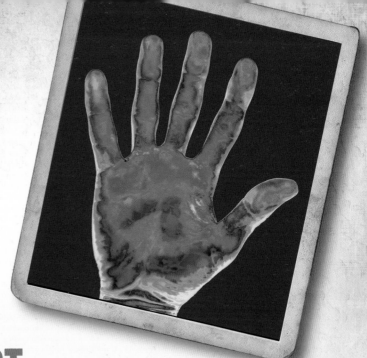

BUILDING A BIGFOOT FROM A TRACK: ZADIG'S METHOD

In many ways, bigfoot hunters have to think like detectives, taking bits of information they have to make a picture of the animal as a whole. When you go through a process like this with the natural world, you use something called Zadig's Method, taking signs that are visible and deducing as much information as possible.

Baron Georges Cuvier, who created the modern field of paleontology, observed that if you saw a cloven hoof print, you could project a lot of information about the animal. For example, it would be a ruminant, meaning it is a mammal that chews

plant material, softens it in the first part of its stomach, and then regurgitates it for a bit more chewing. But that's not all.

"This single track therefore tells the observer about the kind of teeth, the kind of jaws, the haunches, the shoulder, and the pelvis of the animal which has passed," he wrote in 1834.

This is what bigfoot believers are trying to do, and many people believe the evidence of bigfoot that has been gathered to date justifies the continued search.

THE ARGUMENTS AGAINST BIGFOOT

Bigfoot has an army of doubters. Their best argument is that people have been looking unsuccessfully for bigfoot for decades and, lately, even using sophisticated equipment such as cameras that can detect heat. If there really were such a creature, all those dedicated searchers using that great technology would have found proof.

That's a hard argument to counter, although die-hard squatchers will tell you the evidence they have gathered is proof. But if we define proof of bigfoot as an actual bigfoot, dead or alive (preferably alive, for the sake of the bigfoot), then we are about eight hairy feet and six hundred fifty pounds shy of certainty. Likewise, a DNA sequence confirmed by independent laboratories would also work as proof. Unless scientific standards relax, which isn't likely, you'd certainly need a holotype—a physical example of a Bigfoot, a Bigfoot body part, or DNA—for an official species to be named.

There are other arguments, as well.

What does a bigfoot eat?

Some people say there isn't enough food in places like the forests of the Pacific Northwest to support a bigfoot. That would be true if bigfoot eats a diet similar to gorillas, which are believed to survive on large quantities of plants and fruits, with the occasional insect thrown in. But even with known animals such as gorillas, we don't necessarily know everything there is to know about their diets.

For example, a study in 2010 raised the possibility that western lowland gorillas secretly eat meat. The study found DNA in their poop that came from monkeys and duikers (a small forest-dwelling antelope). The gorillas might have hunted or scavenged this meat, the study said. That would be a new and surprising find. We do have to stay somewhat skeptical, though—a good practice for scientists studying evidence. Other things could explain the DNA in the gorilla droppings. First, the ants that the gorillas ate might have fed on carcasses of these animals. The ants had the DNA in their bodies, and when the gorillas ate the ants, they got a secondhand dose. Second, the monkeys and duikers could have licked or otherwise come in contact with the feces. (Yuck!)

The point, though, is that it's possible bigfoot's diet extends beyond the salad bar. Two other great apes, chimpanzees and bonobos, do eat meat. Likewise, bigfooters argue the creatures are omnivores, living on plants as well as deer and other animals consumed by predators at the top of the food chain, such as cougars, wolves, and bears.

Questions about habitat

A trickier argument is that everywhere else in the world, large apes live in tropical habitats. The Pacific Northwest and Canada, two bigfoot and sasquatch hotspots, are anything but hot when it comes to the weather. It doesn't mean bigfoot is impossible in such climates. But it does make them different from the world's other apes. There are primates that buck this tropical trend, though. The Japanese macaque, *Macaca fuscata*, is found in the same latitude as northern California. Those monkeys even survive snowy winters (which is why they're known informally as snow monkeys).

The agony of the feet

Many skeptics believe there are other explanations for the evidence the bigfoot believers have gathered. A huge footprint, for example, might actually be multiple footprints. If you stepped in wet sand and then moved your foot down and made a new print, you might be able to create what looks like a very long foot. When this happens, it's called a "double-stepped" footprint. Likewise, a bear footprint in the snow that's melted or sublimated (evaporated without melting first) might look larger than the original print.

A plague of hoaxes

Finally, bigfoot hoaxes have done a lot of damage to the cause. There are many accounts of people faking tracks well enough to convince experts, only to reveal the shenanigans afterward. Other hoaxers have frozen ape suits and dressed up in costume for a misleading run through the woods.

A cast of possible bigfoot footprint

The many high-profile hoaxes over the years have swirled like drops of black ink in a cup of milk, discoloring the whole pursuit for many sensible people.

SPOTTED!
A Flying Piece of Wood from "Out of Nowhere"

Nyna Fleury drives a cab in Alaska's Prince of Wales Island, making regular trips back and forth during the night. On one of those wee-hours trips, she had a passenger with her.

"Out of nowhere, this piece of wood comes flying at us," she said. "It hit the front end of the car and cracked my windshield all the way across."

Something big had to have thrown it because the impact shook her entire van. Nyna wanted to stop, but her frightened passenger urged her on.

She returned to investigate the next day and found the piece of wood. It smelled putrid. She looked up into a nearby tree and saw a pair of big green eyes looking at her from inside a "humongous" body.

There's no way it was a bear, she said.

"It's a strange story," Bobo Fay said, "but sasquatches are strange animals. They do weird things."

BRINGING SCIENCE TO THE SEARCH

For bigfoot to become an official species, we need concrete evidence that can be examined systematically and thoroughly. We also need a theory that explains why, despite a lot of searching, no one has ever found bigfoot, a skeleton, or even a few remaining bones that once belonged to the creature.

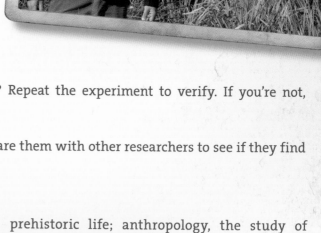

Cliff Barackman has advice for bigfooters about how to take a scientific approach to the search: Follow the scientific method. Here's how that model of thinking works:

1. Ask a question.

2. Research. Look for evidence and other clues that could point to an answer.

3. Take a guess at an answer. This guess is called a hypothesis.

4. Create an experiment to see if your hypothesis could be right.

5. Execute the experiment. Were you right? Repeat the experiment to verify. If you're not, start again at step 2.

6. Write your experiment and results, and share them with other researchers to see if they find the same thing.

The goal of these observations—or any scientific observations, really—is to establish a set of reliable facts. Using those, we can then conduct further research. It's sort of like building with LEGOs. You start with a foundation and keep adding to that, removing blocks or theories that have been disproved with additional observations and experiments.

Many people in traditional science are so skeptical of bigfoot they don't even bother to consider new evidence. But this doesn't mean science itself is a jerk. Science can be a bigfooter's best friend. Many kinds of science can potentially come into play: paleontology, the study of prehistoric life; anthropology, the study of human behavior and cultures; kinesiology, the study of human movement; primatology, the study of primates; and of course genetics and wildlife biology.

Generally speaking, the more you know about science, the more opportunities and insight you will have in life. When it comes to bigfoot specifically, the more you know about what sort of animal bigfoot might be, the more you know about how and where a bigfoot might live. That insight gives you a better chance at encountering a bigfoot at last.

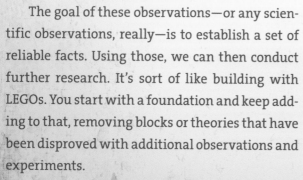

IS BIGFOOT SCIENTIFICALLY POSSIBLE? MAYBE!

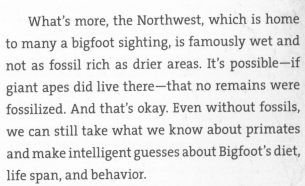

To establish that bigfoot is a possibility, scientists might first pose a "continuity test." If an animal like bigfoot has been alive at any point, it has to be a link somewhere in the evolutionary chain. Complex animals don't just magically appear. They are the offspring and relatives of animals that have come before them.

Going from the descriptions of bigfoot given by people who've had encounters and by Native American "hairy man" tales, we can take an educated guess that bigfoot is an ape-like primate. Primates are in a category of animals, called an order, that includes monkeys, apes, and humans, as well as other mammals.

Although North America's fossil record includes primates, and although giant mammals flourished on the continent, there isn't at this point any fossil evidence for giant apes in North America. We have paleontological evidence of plenty of amazing, huge mammals, including giant sloths, woolly mammoths, and saber-toothed cats. But no apes, at least not in the fossil record. Asia has fossil apes. South America has fossil monkeys. So it's a troubling blank spot.

But this isn't as devastating for bigfoot's case as it might sound. We know there are apes in Africa, which means there had to be earlier forms, too. Even so, it still took scientists ages to dig up fossil ancestors for African apes.

What's more, the Northwest, which is home to many a bigfoot sighting, is famously wet and not as fossil rich as drier areas. It's possible—if giant apes did live there—that no remains were fossilized. And that's okay. Even without fossils, we can still take what we know about primates and make intelligent guesses about Bigfoot's diet, life span, and behavior.

And, because we are arming ourselves with science, we can eliminate some of the goofier Bigfoot lore, which claims they are space alien scouts or able to disappear into a different dimension magically at will. People are of course free to believe what they want, but it's best for any serious bigfooter to focus on theories that are grounded in verifiable observations.

Using science, we can also pinpoint where bigfoot might be most likely to live: a habitat that has enough food and other resources. We can examine evidence, including footprints, hair, and other biological samples, as well as sounds, pictures, and videos.

And we can share our research with other seekers, such as the Bigfoot Field

Researchers Organization. Even though much of the scientific world has rejected the possibility of Bigfoot, real scientists are—to this day—opening their laboratories to evidence gathered in the field. Late in 2012, for example, the Oxford-Lausanne Collateral Hominid Project at the University of Oxford in the United Kingdom invited people to do just this. A professor of human genetics there requested samples—especially hair—suspected to belong to Bigfoot for DNA analysis. It's exciting to see a partnership between universities and Bigfoot investigators in the field. If anything will get us closer to finding bigfoot, it's teamwork such as this.

FAMOUS FANS OF BIGFOOT

Bigfoot has many famous fans.

Theodore "Teddy" Roosevelt became the twenty-sixth president of the United States—and also the youngest—when he took office after the assassination of President William McKinley. He led an exciting and sometimes sad life. His first wife, Alice, and his mom died on the same day in 1884. Understandably heartbroken, he spent the next two years mostly riding horseback on his ranch, which was in the Badlands of the Dakota Territory.

His book, *The Wilderness Hunter*, was published in 1893, and included a story about a hunter in Idaho who'd been attacked by a hairy monster. Bigfooters sometimes point to this incident as a sighting.

Another famous fan was Mark Twain, who wrote books such as *The Adventures of Tom Sawyer*, *The Adventures of Huckleberry Finn*, and *The Prince and the Pauper*, and who also argued for simplified spelling rules that would have saved you a lot of studying if people had actually listened to his ideas.

Twain once wrote a pretend interview with bigfoot, whom he called "the mysterious 'wild man' out there in the West." He said he felt sorry for bigfoot, whose life had been one of suffering, disappointment, and exile. This doesn't necessarily mean he thought there was such a thing as sasquatch, but rather, that he liked the idea of the creature and thought it represented something true about human beings and the shabby way we sometimes treat one another.

Daniel Boone, the American frontier explorer, actually claimed to have shot a bigfoot when he was in the Kentucky forest that now bears his name. He described his quarry as a ten-foot-tall ape, which he called a yahoo. It's hard to tell if this is a true story or a tall (and hairy) tale.

The actor Jimmy Stewart, most famous for playing George Bailey in *It's a Wonderful Life*, might not have been a believer in bigfoot, but he helped play a role in an abominable snowman mystery in 1959. A yeti hunter named Peter Byrne had visited the Pangboche monastery in Nepal to

James Stewart

study what was supposedly a yeti hand. Byrne's own fingers were a bit sticky, and he replaced a phalanx and thumb bone from the yeti hand with human bones. Then he met with Stewart and his wife, Gloria, in Calcutta and passed the stolen bones on to the Hollywood star, who smuggled them to London. Ultimately, experts deemed the bones to be human. Weirdly shaped. But human, after all.

Bigfoot's most famous modern friend, though, might be the actor Matt LeBlanc, who played Joey on the TV show *Friends*. He's told interviewers he's a fan of bigfoot and the search for the creature, and Ellen DeGeneres even gave him his own bigfoot statue. (Don't worry—it wasn't life-size. He'd never fit that in a suitcase!)

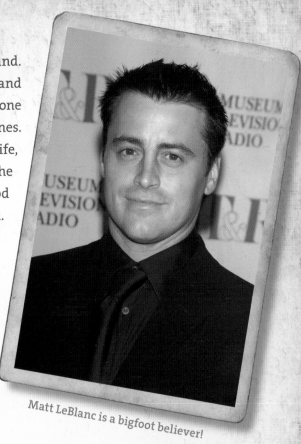

Matt LeBlanc is a bigfoot believer!

SPOTTED!
Screams from All Sides

Osh Lang-Edenshaw rode his four-wheeler as far into the woods near Hydaburg, Alaska, as he could before parking it and heading into the backcountry on foot. It was early in the morning and the twelve-year-old boy had planned to do a little solo hunting. He was tracking a deer, maybe a bit farther into the wilderness than he should have.

"It kept going," he said, "and I got to the point where I thought I should turn around. And as soon as I turned around, I heard those loud screams coming in three directions, and I just froze."

Thirty feet away from him stood a creature the *Finding Bigfoot* team estimated to be as big as nine feet tall in a reenactment.

"I looked right in its eyes," he said. "The most terrifying sight I've ever seen in my life." Shaken, he looked down and closed his eyes. When he opened them again a few seconds later, he heard heavy thumps. The screams from other creatures continued.

"It was just a flashback of my life," he said. "I honestly thought I was gonna die. It was bad."

Chapter Two
A LOOK AT THE EVIDENCE

THE BEST EVIDENCE FOR BIGFOOT

Over the years, people have cataloged all sorts of evidence for bigfoot, including prints made by feet, hands—and even a couple of bottoms. Evidence includes audio recordings of sasquatch shrieks and video recordings of squatches on the move.

Although no evidence is as compelling as an actual bigfoot, the best that's been gathered over the years is fascinating and guarantees you'll always have something meaty to talk about with your friends at lunch. As mystery meat goes, bigfoot is much more palatable than what they serve in the cafeteria.

Note: There is no evidence whatsoever anywhere to suggest school cafeterias serve bigfoot meat in their food.

THE HAIRY MAN PICTOGRAPHS

Plenty of people believe bigfoot is a made-up creature, a hoax from the 1950s meant to pull the legs of gullible loggers.

Even if every sighting of a bigfoot since then is a hoax, it's hard to explain Painted Rock. This is a five-hundred- to one-thousand-year-old archaeological site in California's Sierra Nevada range. The Yokut tribal members who lived there were called the People of Painted Rock (O-ching'-i-ta), which shows how significant the site was to their culture.

Anthropologists believe this cave art was meant to explain the origin of human beings and our various traits. The pictures show a hairy man family with two parents and a child. He looks a lot like bigfoot, with shaggy hair, a big, human-like body, and a ridge on top of his head known as a sagittal crest. The traditional Yokut stories describe the creature as a nocturnal hunter that knocks on wood, whistles, and eats both animals and plants—the same as many modern accounts.

White people first described the site in 1889, and a tribal elder living there identified the creatures depicted as hairy man long before any of the famous California bigfoot sightings occurred. While it is true that no fossils of North American

apes have been found, it's hard to dismiss the significance of ancient pictures of apes in Native American sites, especially when these pictures are meant to explain how human beings came to walk on two feet. Tribal lore is full of real animals these people witnessed: crows, eagles, lizards, owls, coyotes, condors. So if they did not see a hairy man, what inspired this creature?

What's more, First Nations art includes ceremonial masks and carved stones that resemble apes. What would their model be if there were no North American apes?

As fascinating as these paintings are, so are the parallels between First Nations lore and real behavior of apes in the wild. Kathy Moskowitz Strain, an archaeologist for the U.S. Forest Service, has written about the pictographs and the accompanying tales in a book called *Giants, Cannibals & Monsters: Bigfoot in Native Culture*. As typical narratives go, parents warn their kids not to swim in the river at night, lest they run into bigfoot. They also warn that a hungry bigfoot who can't find other animals to eat might choose to dine on children— something chimpanzees have been known to do in the wild when they can't find enough food in the forest.

SPOTTED!
"Honored" by bigfoot

Brenda Leask, her cousin, and her aunt were out deer hunting, and her cousin had just blown a deer call when a tall, hairy creature stepped out from behind a tree.

"It was so big," she said, estimating its height at over eight feet. "I couldn't believe what I just saw." Momentarily stunned into silence, she and her cousin finally acknowledged what had just happened.

"We were there about five minutes," she said, "and we told my aunt, 'We've got to go.'"

But it wasn't a traumatic experience. Leask is a member of the Tlingit tribe and her clan's history is tied to the sasquatch itself. "You feel honored to have had this creature show itself to you. It was such a profound moment in my life."

BOSSBURG TRACKS

A little town in Stevens County, Washington, has played a big part in the hunt for bigfoot evidence. Its name is Bossburg, and it lies on the east bank of the mighty Columbia River, not too far south of the Canadian border. It's a ghost town now, and it was never big—just eight hundred people at its peak.

But it was an interesting place to be late in 1969, when the first of some very curious bigfoot tracks appeared. A couple of things made them stand out. First, they were near a garbage dump—an unusual thing for a normally reclusive bigfoot. Second, these footprints revealed something sad and stunning: Although the left foot was normal for a Squatch, measuring seventeen inches long and seven inches wide, the creature that made them had a deformed right foot.

The bum foot gave the creature its nickname: Cripplefoot, as well as an explanation for what it might be doing so close to people. Because it was injured or deformed, it couldn't make its way in the wilderness. It also gave scientists a reason to take a close look at the prints, which were extremely detailed. One toe was so bent, for example, that it hardly left an impression in the soil. A pair of bumps on the outside edge of the foot revealed the bones there might have been broken.

John Napier, a famous primate expert from the Smithsonian Institution, believed the deformity almost guaranteed the tracks were authentic. "It's very difficult to conceive of a hoaxer so subtle, so knowledgeable—and so sick—who would deliberately fake a footprint of this nature," he said. "I suppose it is possible, but it is so unlikely that I am prepared to discount it."

They also intrigued Grover Krantz, a professor of physical anthropology at Washington State University and the first academic to seriously investigate the possibility of bigfoot. Based on the deformity, Krantz figured out the anatomy of a sasquatch foot, and from there, how heavy bigfoot might be based on its foot.

In an article in *Northwest Anthropological Research Notes* from the spring of 1972, Krantz pointed out differences in human and Sasquatch feet.

In general, the sasquatch foot differs from man's in having greatly enlarged ankle bones, especially the heel, very short metatarsals, and a more nearly equal set of toes. These characteristics are all logical requirements for an otherwise human foot adapted to a body weight of five hundred pounds or more. These characteristics are also evident in preserved footprints.

Bigfoot footprint cast

In all, lifelong sasquatch hunter René Dahinden found 1,089 of these footprints, and whatever creature made them had to step twice over a barbed wire fence forty-three inches high—something a human would have a hard time doing.

Even today, they're among the favorite pieces of evidence that persuade bigfoot seekers the creature is out there, even though the experts studying them back in the day didn't agree on every point. Napier, the Smithsonian expert, thought the tracks showed bigfoot had a human-like foot. Krantz did not.

What makes the tracks a tricky piece of evidence, though, are a couple of hoaxes that happened around the same time and place. It doesn't necessarily mean the tracks are phony. People could have capitalized on them to profit from hoaxes of their own. But they made the tracks smell a bit fishy as a result. (See Chapter 9.)

BIGFOOT WITNESS PHOTO

THE PATTERSON-GIMLIN FILM

For some, Friday, October 20, 1967, is the biggest day in bigfoot history. Roger Patterson and Bob Gimlin had left Patterson's home state of Washington, where the two were shooting a movie about bigfoot. They heard of some tracks in California and went to check them out—but the rain had beaten them there and washed the footprints away. It was disappointing, to be sure, but the two men decided to make the best of it. They set up camp and rode into the Bluff Creek area on horseback, taking footage of the beautiful fall scenery as they rode.

That afternoon, their horses freaked out.

Roger took a tumble. And that's when he saw it, sixty to eighty feet away. A bigfoot.

The *Los Angeles Times*'s *West Magazine* described what he saw:

> Its head was very human, though considerably more slanted, and with a large forehead and wide, broad nostrils. Its arms hung almost to its knees when it walked. Its hair was two to four inches long, brown underneath, lighter at the top, and covering the entire body except for the face around the nose, mouth, and cheek. And it was female.

Patterson jumped up, turned on his camera, and ran toward the creature. Gimlin stood with his gun ready (although he apparently had no plans to shoot unless it was necessary). Patterson captured footage until his film ran out. Too spooked to reload, they took plaster casts of prints that were fourteen and a half inches, and so deep Gimlin had to jump off a fallen tree to make similar impressions with his cowboy boots. They sent the film to a town in Washington called Yakima to be developed, and when they met with other committed Bigfoot researchers (including John Green and René Dahinden—see Chapter 5), people agreed they had all the proof they needed. Patterson, who was sort of a schemer in his business dealings, even refrained from selling the movie to the highest bidder because he was warned it would lead to ridicule and rejection.

The footage, which lasts about one minute, is imperfect. The first few seconds show nothing but the ground rushing by, because Patterson is running. When he finally tilts the camera up toward "Patty," the name people have given the creature on the film, it's shaky at first. The footage does get more stable and shows a tall, hairy creature with a pointed head stride by, glance over her right shoulder, and turn toward the woods.

Supporters of the movie say the footage would be impossible to fake. Not only would such a costume have been too sophisticated to fake at the time—the chest and shoulders of the animal are too broad to be human, the arms are too long, and muscles are visible moving under the fur. They also say her gait isn't human and is too swift to be faked. Both men involved believed what they'd seen was real and not someone in a suit.

Bob Titmus, a taxidermist who studied and collected many suspected bigfoot tracks over the years, visited the site after the footage was shot and took casts of ten footprints. He noted each one was different. The toes moved. The way they gripped the soil varied. They showed different weight placement. In short, they hadn't been made by a rigid, carved template. They appeared to him as if they'd been laid down by a walking creature.

But, as it's turned out, the movie hasn't been universally acknowledged as slam-dunk scientific sasquatch proof.

For starters, the footage is low quality and brief, because Patterson used most of his film taking nature shots. What's more, he didn't know the film speed (which determines the sensitivity to light) he used for taking the movie, which is a piece of information you need to have to know whether a human in a costume could have taken those steps. There's been quite a bit of debate about the f-stop the camera had been set at. Scientists such as Idaho State University's Jeffrey Meldrum and the late Grover Krantz have made strong cases that it was shot at a speed that would make it impossible for humans to fake the footage, but others remain unconvinced.

Since then, it's been studied many times over the years, with mixed results. John Napier, the anatomist and anthropologist who was the director of primate biology at the Smithsonian Institution, dissected the footage in a book called *Bigfoot*.

"There is little doubt that the scientific evidence taken collectively points to a hoax of some kind," he wrote.

He spotted several problems: a person could have walked that way, the center of gravity is more human than ape, and the length of the steps didn't match up with the footprints Patterson and Gimlin found.

Frank Beebe, a naturalist and the illustrator at the Royal British Columbia Museum, raised other questions. Even though the animal has breasts, she walks like a man. She also has a distinct sagittal crest—that's the pointy part on the

SAGITTAL CREST

top of her head. Animals that eat leaves, like gorillas, have heads like these because the strong muscles required for chewing low-calorie, fiber-filled leaves connect to the skull. To digest all this fiber, these animals also have long intestines and a big belly to house these guts. Patty doesn't.

On the whole, Beebe found the movie "rather good, very interesting," even if it wasn't ultimately persuasive, he wrote in his notes. "It just could be genuine and the darn thing for real, although the chance, indeed, the likelihood of a hoax is very high."

Another critic, David Daegling, author of *Bigfoot Exposed,* also objected to the sagittal crest, saying only male primates have these. Other experts dispute this, saying these are more noticeable in males, but that some female primates have them.

Scientists at the American Museum of Natural History and the University of British Columbia ruled the movie a fake. So did Bernard Heuvelmans, a scientist and explorer known as the father of cryptozoology. His reason? Patty has curving buttocks and apes don't. The counterargument: Apes aren't bipedal and don't need a muscular bottom to keep their torsos upright, as a two-footed walker such as sasquatch does.

All these objections aside, the film hasn't been universally rejected by scientists. In 1994, Russian scientists from the Darwin Museum in Moscow endorsed the movie.

What's more, no one has definitively proved the film is a hoax. And certainly for bigfoot believers, the movie is just what it looks like: proof that sasquatch are out there, just waiting to be found.

SPOTTED!
Sasquatch with a Sweet Tooth

Mike Greene is a bigfooter from North Carolina. He's worked with the Bigfoot Field Researchers Organization and other groups for about twenty years, but never hit pay dirt until he started coming to a particular campground.

The night he had his encounter, the campground was empty. He'd put up his tent and was sacked out until three o'clock in the morning, when a plopping noise woke him up.

"It sounded like somebody dropping a water balloon on the floor," he said.

Then the wheezing Darth Vader breaths started—right over his tent.

"And then something cuffed the top of the tent and I whacked the side of the tent back and it ran off."

He heard a rustling noise below and figured the creature was watching him. So he decided to grab his tripod and camera from the car, which was parked about eighty-five feet away. He mounted his thermal camera and drove off, waited two hours, and then returned.

The camera battery was dead, but he'd captured a blurry thermal image of a creature stealing a candy bar from a stump.

SIERRA SOUNDS

Alan Berry was a geologist, Vietnam veteran, and former newspaper reporter who wrote about his bigfoot encounters in the Sierra Mountains. He'd been visiting a remote deer hunters' camp and had become aware of "a 'presence' . . . of several creatures who were crafty enough to avoid observation, but freely vocalized and whistled, several times . . . and left big prints of bare feet around in the snow and pine mat."

He'd heard of similar strange experiences by other hunters. So he brought what was then a state-of-the-art Sony portable tape recorder and some plaster of Paris to capture evidence of this elusive creature.

On his first visit, nothing happened, although he did see some old footprints that he dismissed as a joke by other hunters.

The second time in, things were different.

"As dusk became dark night, something approached camp from a ridge above, rapping on wood or rocks as it came, and when it arrived, two voices that I could discern . . . vocalized, and the sounds carried through the trees as I have never heard human voices carry ever before or since.

"And it whistled," he wrote, "a clear, beautiful whistle like a bird might make, between its kind, and at one point back and forth and with us."

He recorded the exchange and cast several footprints. He looked around for evidence it was all a hoax, including in other hunters' belongings. But he came home stumped.

Experts have found the recordings to be intriguing.

The tapes hadn't been altered, prerecorded, or rerecorded, and the vocal range went beyond what an average human male could produce, according to a presentation by Dr. R. Lynn Kirlin, a professor of electrical engineering at the University of Wyoming. Kirlin made this presentation at an "Anthropology of the Unknown" symposium at the University of British Columbia.

Later, a retired U.S. Navy linguistics expert named R. Scott Nelson listened to the tapes. Nelson spent his career as a cryptolinguist—someone trained to recognize coded language. He's convinced the recordings have captured a real language.

On Bigfootsounds.com, he wrote:

We have verified that these creatures use language by the human definition of it. The months of hard work that we have put into the study of the Berry/Morehead tapes are finally coming to fruition. The analysis is finished, although I am still working on parts of the final write-up such as frequency count tables, morpheme lists, etc.

I believe that the study of these tapes will never (and should never) end. With the recognition and acceptance that these creatures do indeed speak and understand a complex language, a greater effort will be made to collect voice recordings and our analysis of the language will improve. Now that we have a precedent and techniques established for this study, this process will certainly become easier.

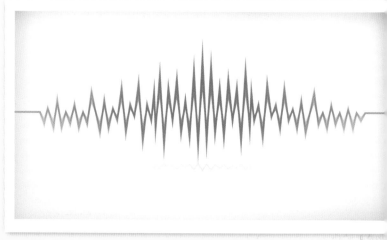

Here's an example of a frequency wave.

JACOBS PHOTOGRAPHS

Technology has improved since the days when people measured bigfoot tracks with pieces of cardboard. Cameras are more sophisticated than ever. It's possible to set them up in the woods so that they take pictures when something passes by. These are called "trail cameras," and on rare occasions, they capture fascinating evidence.

The Jacobs Photographs might be the most famous of suspected bigfoot pictures captured by trail camera. They were taken in 2007 by a hunter named Rick Jacobs, who'd set up the camera in the Allegheny National Forest in northwest Pennsylvania.

The pictures, lit by an invisible infrared flash, depict a smallish, hairy creature bent toward the ground, almost as though it's walking on all fours.

Some people have dismissed it as a "mangy

This trail camera is the eyes of the forest!

though, wildlife photography is a difficult business. The images we often see in documentaries and on television are very often staged in conditions that don't occur naturally, making us expect to see any animal we wish in high-definition video. But it's much harder than this, and plenty of animals we *know* to exist are rarely photographed in the wild. One example is the wolverine, a member of the weasel family that looks a bit like a four-foot, sixty-pound bear, and is known to rove some of the same habitat a sasquatch is thought to occupy.

For now at least, it is worth paying close attention to what's captured by trail cameras—one good shot could change everything about people's willingness to accept the possibility of Bigfoot.

bear," but bigfoot researchers disagree. The camera also took pictures of bear cubs, and these look quite different. People have analyzed the pictures and compared the arm and leg length of bears with that of primates, and concluded the creature was built more like a primate than a bear.

The images are important for a couple of reasons, Cliff Barackman says. "The first reason is they're close and fairly clear. There are very few if any good photographs of juvenile sasquatches. Another reason the Jacobs Photographs are important is because it actually shows that sasquatches can be captured by trail cameras. . . . It's encouraging to people like me."

Despite the improvement in technology,

A real wolverine doesn't quite resemble the X-Men character, does it?

SKOOKUM CAST

Not all famous sasquatch prints come from the creature's feet. Many people believe that in 2000, a male bigfoot left a body print in the muddy Skookum Meadow of the Gifford Pinchot National Forest in Washington State. This print—made into what is called the Skookum Cast—was found by Matt Moneymaker and other members of the

Bigfoot Field Researchers Organization.

It happened on September 22, 2000, a briskly cold clear day. Frost covered the ground, and members of the team were checking fruit traps they'd baited with melons, apples, and peanuts. A report on their Web site explains how they'd done all sorts of other things designed to attract a bigfoot, broadcasting squatch calls, playing tapes of children playing and babies crying.

At nine o'clock in the morning, three team members checked the traps. Three of six apples were missing at one of the sites, which was surrounded by old tracks of elk, deer, bears, and coyotes. That's when the team members noticed an unusual impression at the edge of a muddy pool.

"Then suddenly it dawns what animal caused it," the field notes said.

They alerted base camp and everyone came to check out the print. They agreed an animal sat down at the edge of the mud and leaned toward the fruit, using its left forearm for support. It grabbed the fruit with its right hand. People wondered right away why the bigfoot didn't just bend over for the fruit. One explanation readily sprang to mind—that the creature didn't want to leave tracks. It was also possible that the animal was being cautious and sitting to observe the situation, especially because the muddy site was near the camp.

"If these animals have been avoiding confrontations with humans for thousands of years, might this behavior—avoidance of leaving distinctive footprints—be an ancient survival strategy?" the report said.

This stealth behavior seems unique to sasquatch, the report said.

Several experienced sasquatch field researchers in the group noted that they had likely seen this behavior before—track patterns suggesting the animals did not want to leave obvious tracks behind. . . . This is in contrast to most other large mammals, which usually don't make special efforts, or take special paths, to avoid leaving tracks behind. We also noted that in cases where lots of clear sasquatch tracks have been found, the locations were usually in very remote areas that saw little to no human traffic—such as Bluff Creek in the late 1950s.

The researchers made a cast using more than two hundred pounds of plaster. The whole thing is huge: more than three-and-a-half feet by five feet long. That same expedition netted investigators' voice recordings and blurry seventeen-inch footprints.

Afterward, a team of scientists and bigfoot researchers examined the cast, including Jeffrey Meldrum, a professor at Idaho State University; Dr. Grover Krantz, a retired physical anthropologist from Washington State University; Dr. John Bindernagel, a Canadian wildlife biologist; John Green, a retired Canadian journalist and author; and Dr. Ron Brown, exotic animal handler and health care administrator.

Idaho State University issued a press release about the find, quoting Meldrum: "While not definitively proving the existence of a species of North American ape, the cast constitutes significant and compelling new evidence that will hopefully stimulate further serious research and investigation into the presence of these primates in the Northwest mountains and elsewhere."

The cast is unique because it's the only imprint believed to represent a partial bigfoot body. Searchers have found hands, knuckles—even bigfoot butt prints—but this was the first time they'd snagged a body, and the dimensions of it suggested it was forty to fifty percent bigger than a six-foot-tall human. A careful cleaning revealed hair impressions on the creature's bottom and thighs, as well as a longer fringe of hair on the forearm. The heel had fingerprint-like skin ridges, Meldrum noted. It looked like other sasquatch footprints. He could also make out a heel, ankle, and Achilles tendon that looked like the hundreds of other alleged sasquatch footprints he'd studied.

The Achilles tendon and big rump are things you'd find on creatures that walk upright, something that led Daris Swindler, a University of Washington primate anatomist who studied the cast, to say, "In my opinion, the Skookum body cast is that of an upright descendant of Gigantopithecus [an extinct giant ape]" (see Chapter 3).

But that wasn't all. A biomedical research scientist named Dr. Wolf Henner Fahrenbach studied hair samples from the scene and on the

cast. Most were deer, elk, coyote, and bear. But one hair—based on characteristics of other samples collected in Sasquatch sightings—was distinctly primate. Its owner? According to Fahrenbach, sasquatch.

Again, not everyone agrees with this interpretation, but the fact remains that well-trained experts are convinced.

SPOTTED!

The Long Arm of the Law Not Long Enough

Rural northern Georgia is lush, a mix of small farming communities surrounded by vast tracts of national forest. The Chattahoochee National Forest has a reputation for being a bigfoot hotspot. The region even has petroglyphs—rock paintings—by early Native Americans that show them interacting with a bigfoot-like creature.

So it was not a surprise to the *Finding Bigfoot* team that a Georgia State patrol car captured what appears to be Sasquatch footage on its dashboard camera.

Mary Scott was a passenger in the car on the night it happened. It was late and the road was empty.

"We were coming this way about fifty-five miles an hour," she said. "It's pitch black, so it seemed like we were doing a hundred.

"All of a sudden with no notice whatsoever, this very tall, very furry, very fast creature comes from that side of the road," she said.

The trooper braked, turned around, and put on his flashing lights. They both jumped out of the car. He drew his gun and identified himself, but to no avail.

"Whatever it was, was gone," she said.

NEW YORK BABY SASQUATCH

Just what was that creature swinging nimbly from a tree branch in the Catskill Mountains in 1997?

In a short video that's been dubbed "New York Baby Bigfoot" footage, sharp-eyed viewers can make out what appears to be a large figure move beneath a tree to give a smaller creature a boost into the high branches, where it swings around like some sort of ape.

The footage was captured by accident on private land that used to be an apple orchard and still has a few fruit-bearing trees growing. The cameraman, Doug Pridgen, was sitting around a campfire at a music festival shooting footage of his friends. Pets weren't allowed at the festival. People who'd brought dogs (and parrots and iguanas, apparently) were turned away, so it seems unlikely anyone could've smuggled in a gibbon, which is an ape about the size of the creature on the film.

The *Finding Bigfoot* team tried to re-create the footage, but Cliff Barackman wasn't nimble enough to ape the ape.

"I've spent a lot of time around gymnastics in general," he said. "My ex-wife was a gymnastics instructor. I've seen it again and again. The best gymnasts in the world, they cannot duplicate what I've seen in that video. So what we have here is either a case of a pet ape or a sasquatch, possibly an adult and a juvenile."

Gregg Dancho, director at Connecticut's Beardsley Zoo, agreed the footage is neither bear nor human.

It's clearly something that's brachiating through the trees, hanging like a monkey. People don't realize how big our wild areas are. People have a tendency of thinking, you know, the United States, we're all closed in and there's not many wild areas. When you actually go out in the woods you see how much, how big these areas are, so I wouldn't be surprised if something's out there that hasn't been discovered yet. I would not be surprised at all.

(That said, Dancho stated later in a Connecticut newspaper interview that he does not believe in bigfoot.)

THE LONDON TRACKWAY

In February 2012, a man named Max Roy was taking a walk in London, Oregon, when a passerby told him about some bigfoot tracks. Roy went to check them out and took photos, but felt a bit spooked, so he went home. He couldn't get them out of this mind, though, so he got in touch with a bigfooter named Toby Johnson, who inspected the tracks for himself and immediately contacted Cliff Barackman.

"I was definitely interested in the find, especially after seeing one of Max's photographs of the prints in the ground," Cliff said. "I instructed him what to document, and how to cast all four prints."

Cliff couldn't check them out by himself, though. The next day, he had to teach students about how he uses the scientific method. That's when he got another call from Johnson. It wasn't

Bigfoot footprint cast alongside a dollar bill gives perspective to the print size.

mold. Cliff's Web site has photos of each footprint cast, in addition to detailed notes about their depth, shape, and how closely they correlate to other suspected bigfoot tracks.

The tracks are a unique event in bigfoot history because so many were found and cast at one time. Cliff is still studying the prints to see what they might reveal. But they remain his most important piece of evidence.

It is, by far, the most significant thing I've been directly involved with. The casts and photographs from the event continue to astound me. I have spent countless hours poring over the minute details of the casts and pictures taken at the site, and I continually learn more from them at every inspection.

It's not just me, either. Every bigfooter that has seen the casts has walked away from inspecting them with the impression that these are probably the real deal.

just four tracks. It was more than a hundred. As soon as Cliff finished teaching, he set out for London and asked a friend to meet him with two hundred pounds of Hydrocal to take casts of the prints.

They eventually cast 72 of the 122 found. They also photographed the series, which appears to show feet in motion through the mud, as opposed to static prints made by a hoaxer with a rigid

SPOTTED!

"This Creature Has Opened My Door"

Carolyn Bridges and her husband, Bill, live in Florida, home to thick forests, treacherous swamps, and stories of a foul-smelling creature called the skunk ape.

One night, a horrible growl ripped Carolyn out of sleep. "I was spooked and I touched Bill and kind of [shook] him and he doesn't move," she said. "I'm kind of in shock here because this thing sounded monstrous."

And it sounded close. As close as her porch.

When she checked the next day, she was in for a shock.

"Here was a huge handprint," she said. The thumb and fingers were huge and long, she said. The attached arm was wide and greasy and left a hairy print on the window.

"It looked similar to a human but it was . . . just too large," she said. "And I'm thinking, 'Oh my God, this creature has opened my door.'"

Chapter Three

BIGFOOT AROUND THE WORLD

ARE THEY ALL THE SAME SPECIES?

People all around the world have seen creatures whose description more or less matches that of Bigfoot. Eyewitness accounts of a hair-covered wild man can be found on every continent except Antarctica, according to a book by famous bigfoot hunter Ivan Sanderson, *Abominable Snowmen: Legend Come to Life*. These wild men are called many different things—sasquatch, skunk ape, yeti, yowie—but could they possibly be the same animal?

There are many similarities between these hidden creatures, from the way they look and behave to the strange sounds they make. Without examples of the creatures, though, it's hard to say whether and how they might be related, and when they went from one species to two or more.

Remember the coelacanth? That's the fish everyone thought was extinct until 1938. The other variety of this living fossil is a *separate species*. The two split apart from each other millions of years ago, according to a doctoral student at the University of California–Berkeley who examined the DNA in tissues from the Indonesian and Indian Ocean varieties. They're related—just not the same creature, which is why they have different names.

At this point, we can't know whether the various wild man creatures spotted around the world might be related, or whether they are related to apes or hominids (human relatives who walk on two feet). The best thing to do is continue to make observations and learn as much as we can about animals and their classifications in general.

HOW LIVING THINGS ARE ORGANIZED

You've probably heard the word *species* before. To be of the same species, two individuals have to share enough characteristics to breed offspring. So, two dogs (even if they are different breeds) are members of the same species. They can have puppies! Hooray! But a dog and a cat, alas, cannot.

There are some tricky exceptions to this. For example, a female horse and a male donkey can produce an offspring called a mule, even though they are different species with a different number of chromosomes. Generally, mules can't reproduce, and hybrids that can't reproduce can't be classified as a species. (Less well-known is the hinny, which comes from a male horse and a female donkey.)

But it's not all about breeding. Species can also be defined based on their DNA, their internal and external physical characteristics (called "morphology"), and their "ecological niche," which depends on where it lives, what it eats, and how it behaves to survive.

So there's actually quite a lot of information you need to have to determine exactly what species an animal belongs to, and even with known animals, researchers sometimes make observations that lead them to reclassify animals. For example, as recently as 2012, a group of Western chimpanzees have been observed hunting with spears, living in caves, and playing in water—things so un-chimp-like, some experts are wondering whether they're another species.

What's more, species is just one level of the organizational system scientists use to understand the relationships living things have to one another. It's entirely possible that bigfoot, yetis, and other wild man creatures are as distinct from one another as humans are from chimpanzees.

WHAT GROUPS WOULD BIGFOOT FIT INTO?

The organization system starts with "kingdom," which includes all animals. Each category below divides animals further into groups (and there's a separate system for plants).

Kingdom: All animals.

Phylum: *Chordata.* Bigfoot, great apes, and human beings (*Homo sapiens sapiens*) would be in this group together.

Class: *Mammalia.* Bigfoot, humans, and the great apes are also mammals.

Order: *Primate.* Bigfoot, humans, and the great apes are also primates.

Family: *Hominidae.* Humans and the great apes are all in the same family. Bigfoot would most likely be classified here.

Genus: Human beings are in the genus *Homo.* The apes split off here into different groups. Would bigfoot? We don't know.

Species: Humans are *sapiens* (which means "wise"). The apes, meanwhile, split further into species (and some into subspecies).

Memory Trick

You can remember the classification categories with this handy sentence: Kings Play Chess On Fridays, Generally Speaking.

While we don't know exactly where a bigfoot would fit in the system, it's reasonable to assume we'd share classifications all the way down to the genus level, which is where we split from apes. Humans are the only species left with the *Homo* genus, although others, including *Homo neanderthalensis, Homo erectus,* and *Homo habilis,* once walked the planet. And remember that bit about donkeys and horses sometimes producing offspring? *Homo sapiens sapiens* and *Homo neanderthalensis* did just this, which shows why the "what's a species" question can sometimes require a long answer. According to a paper written by a Swedish evolutionary biologist named Svante Pääbo, everyone who is not of African descent has a tiny bit of Neanderthal DNA—between one and four percent. Wherever bigfoot might fit in, it's reasonable to assume that there could be separate species of bigfoot—yetis, orang pendeks, and so on—just as there are two species of gorilla (plus a number of subspecies). The bigger question, and one we can't answer without an actual bigfoot to study, is whether the creature is an ape or a hominid.

Based on suspected bigfoot footprints that have been collected, we do know its footprints aren't apelike. Apes have thumb-like toes. But bigfoot tracks are also unlike human ones—they are broader and have longer heels and toes, no arches, and a more flexible mid-foot (see Chapter 8).

Interestingly, their toe length as a percentage of the overall foot length compares with *Australopithecus afarensis*, an early bipedal hominid, according to Jeff Meldrum, author of *Sasquatch: Legend Meets Science,* and an expert in anatomy and walking and the evolution of feet. So at least in this regard, bigfoot has feet more like a hominid's than an ape's, which is fascinating because scientists believe all other hominids besides humans—*Homo sapiens*—are extinct. If it turns out bigfoot is a hominid that only looked extinct, like the coelacanth, a lot of textbooks will have to be rewritten.

SPOTTED!

"I Dare You to Look Out the Window"

Mark Stanislawski's family had a rabbit at their Oregon campground they always figured attracted bigfoot. Some time later, he and a couple of friends thought they'd do a little experiment to lure a sasquatch closer.

They might have gotten more than they bargained for.

They hung a cage six feet above the ground, suspending the rabbit inside. Then they put a glow stick on its cage, knowing that if anything passed, they'd be able to see it.

"I'm looking out the window and I seen him pass through the camp," Mark said. "And so I told my friend Steve here, 'I dare you to look out the window.'"

Steve did. The rabbit was going nuts, running around really fast in the cage, "like something's out there."

And then he saw it—a huge hand slowly move in front of the cage. The next morning, when they went back, they found tracks. Another friend who was in the Bigfoot Field Researchers Organization showed them how to make a cast and how to measure the length of the stride using a piece of fishing line.

Whatever had scared the rabbit during the night had a fifty-three-inch stride. Just like a bigfoot's.

HOW DO LIVING THINGS EVOLVE?

So how is it that species change and turn into different organisms, anyway? Evolution. Over time, living things change. This happens across generations, not within them—a really important thing to keep in mind. Some people dismiss evolution because they find it hard to believe that monkeys can turn into people. This sort of monkey business doesn't happen, of course. But over time, changes in living things *do* occur.

All sorts of things can bring these changes about. Changes in climate can mean certain characteristics give a survival advantage, whether that characteristic is size, color, ability to metabolize certain foods, or any number of things. Over time, characteristics that are disadvantageous will disappear, because the animals that have it don't survive to reproduce and pass the traits along.

Sometimes environmental changes can be abrupt. Let's say something permanently separates one group of animals from another. This happened in 1995 to a group of fifteen iguanas that rode out Hurricane Marilyn by floating on top of uprooted trees until they reached Anguilla, an island in the Caribbean. Over time, if these iguanas survive, they might adapt to the climate on their new home. Iguanas that are especially well suited to the environment—let's say they're a nicely disguised color—might have more offspring, passing along the traits that served them well as they reproduce. After a number of generations, they might change enough so that they look like a new species.

And of course, sometimes these changes are gradual. Over a very long time, the continents move apart or land bridges might be covered by water. What once was a single species of animals might over many generations develop enough differences between them that they become two species.

ABOMINABLE SNOWMAN

The abominable snowman didn't always have such an exciting name. British explorers who said they spotted him in Tibet called him a wild man. And the natives had their own names for the creature. You might have heard the Nepalese name, *yeti*. This isn't a specific name for one animal, though. It's kind of like the word "bird," which can refer to ducks and eagles and pigeons and all sorts of things (or monster, which might mean a werewolf, vampire, wendigo, or zombie).

There are three basic types of yeti:
- A big, ferocious, bear-like "*dzuteh-a*"
- A small, monkeyish wild man called "*the-lma*"
- A half human, half animal called "*met-teh*"

As a human-like animal, the meh-teh sounds most like the Himalayan version of bigfoot. Bigfoot scholars believe the first time the creature was mentioned in print was in 1832. An Englishman named B. H. Hodgson lived in the court of Nepal and heard stories from native hunters about a furry, tailless demon who walked on two feet. At the time, the sensible Hodgson thought it was probably an orangutan.

Almost sixty years later, in 1889, a lieutenant-colonel and surgeon in the British Army named L. A. Waddell happened upon mysterious tracks in northwest Sikkim. He thought they belonged to the yeti.

Then, in 1900, we had the first Westerner's sighting of a yeti. William Hugh Knight, a member of the Royal Society Club, a sort of scientific advisory board, described the creature he saw as just under six feet tall, "stark naked in the bitter cold," and kind of pale yellow with matted hair on its head, a bit on its face, splayed feet and huge hands.

All of this is classic bigfoot evidence: stories from natives, footprints, sightings. And yet none of it was absolute proof.

Two decades passed and Westerners began to look at Mount Everest, the world's tallest mountain, as an irresistible challenge. In 1921, Lieutenant Colonel C. K. Howard-Bury was in charge of a mission to scout a path to the mighty mountain. On Lhakpa La, a Tibetan mountain pass almost four miles above sea level, they found something totally unexpected: tracks that seemed human.

Howard-Bury had native porters with him. These people thought right away that the tracks must belong to the wild man of the snows. Howard-Bury, more of a stuffy British sort, thought such talk was poppycock, the sort of bogeyman story your mom and dad might tell you to scare you into your best behavior. He figured the tracks were wolf prints that had been stepped on more than once, making them look larger and like something else. But he did send word of the discovery to a newspaper columnist.

This is where the abominable snowman accidentally got its name. Howard-Bury told the columnist that the track belonged to what the natives called a *metoh kangmi*. A *kangmi* is a "snow man." *Metoh* means "wild man," so the words together translate as "wild man of the snow."

But the columnist, a man named Henry Newman, messed up the words. Instead of *metoh*, he translated the word *metch*, which means "filthy" in Tibetan. He dubbed the creature that made the tracks the "abominable snowman," which was so intriguing that word spread from Tibet to India to England and then to the United States, as newspapers picked it up (that's how things went viral before there was the Internet).

People really started to wonder what was up there on that snowy peak. Interest in climbing Mount Everest stayed strong. But it took many years before anyone succeeded. In 1951, a famous British climber named Eric Shipton was trying to find a path that led to the mountaintop. As they crossed an icefall to the head of the Menlung Glacier through knee-deep snow untouched by human feet, Shipton found something strange.

"Where the snow covering the ice was thin . . . was a well-preserved impression of the creature's foot." The print had three wide toes and a broad thumb. Shipton's team followed the prints across a crevasse, a deep crack in a glacier. It looked as though the creature had jumped and used its toes to grip onto the other side, he wrote.

Curious, the climbers followed the footprints for about a mile before they lost them. Shipton took pictures, using his boot and an ice pick to show the scale of these strange tracks. The experience was sort of a creepy one. It gave him the feeling that the creature was lurking "somewhere in the moonlit silence."

When Shipton wrote about his trip for the London *Times*, which printed a photo in the Dec. 7, 1951, edition, people were intrigued. Many other publications wrote articles and Hollywood made movies (including *The Abominable Snowman of the Himalayas*). No one was quite sure what it was. Britain's Natural History Museum theorized langurs—long-tailed Asian monkeys—had left the tracks. Others said they might have been left by monks wearing snowshoes (or no shoes). An anthropologist at Johns-Hopkins University, William Straus, guessed it was a Himalayan red bear, but a biologist named Lawrence Swan countered that those animals are only in the eastern Himalayas, where these tracks were laid in the west.

One name of the Himalayan chain—Mahalangur Himal—is intriguing. It means mountains (himal) of the great apes (langur). Was the truth of the presence of giant apes on the remote, snowy peak hidden in the name of the mountain range itself?

The Himalayan red bear.

ABOMINABLE SNOWMAN TRACKS DEBUNKED?

After he climbed Mount Everest in 1953, Edmund Hillary was a star. He was also curious about the yeti said to live on the mountain he'd conquered. It made a good deal of sense to him, now that he'd mastered the world's largest mountain, to go in search of its most mysterious inhabitant. In a *New York Times Magazine* article, he said, "I believe there is sufficient evidence to warrant a closer search for the maker of these tracks."

So, in 1960, he set out to see whether he might find the creature. The expedition was serious and well funded, with twenty-two scientists and mountaineers, six Sherpas, one hundred fifty porters, and even a journalist named Desmond Doig, who later created a comic strip called *Bing: The Abominable Snow-Baby*.

They left Katmandu, Nepal, on September 13, 1960, in search of tracks and other evidence. When they returned home, they were convinced the yeti did not exist.

What happened?

It was a number of things. First, remember those strange, long tracks Eric Shipton saw?

They figured out a scientific explanation for them. At high altitudes, it's very cold and snow doesn't melt. Instead, it goes straight from a solid form to water vapor. This is called sublimation.

When an animal makes a footprint in the snow, part of the print might be exposed to sunlight, while part remains in shadow. The part that sees sunlight sublimates. In doing so, it gets longer and wider. If only part of the print is exposed to sunlight, it will stretch unevenly, looking like a different sort of print. But because there is no melting, the edges stay crisp, making the track look freshly laid.

One big clue for the team was that the tracks in a particular area always faced the same direction. The Sherpas had an explanation for this—that the yeti could turn its feet around to fool anyone who might be following it. But this explanation is complicated and sounds a bit made-up. It also depends on some unusual feet. Sublimation

is a simpler explanation that works and can be demonstrated.

Occam's razor is a scientific principle that says the best explanation for something is the one that requires the fewest assumptions. Scientists are fond of this principle. It helps them create good hypotheses—educated guesses about something—and then devise experiments that let them test whether their guesses are true. This methodical process replaces assumptions with patterns and behaviors that can be observed by independent witnesses.

Guessing that a yeti has feet that can swivel around in many directions isn't something that can be observed until we have a yeti on hand, so it can't be tested and proved or disproved until then. But you can make a footprint in the snow in Nepal and watch what happens when the sun hits part of it. Other people can check your work. This gives reliable, trustworthy results.

What's more, Hillary's team considered more than footprints. There were the yeti scalps sometimes displayed in villages. Were they real or not?

The team figured out how to make a serow pelt (that's a goat-antelope native to the region) look like a yeti scalp. It was convincing enough that it even fooled one of the people who worked on the fake. In exchange for renovating a monastery and fund-raising for a school for the locals, the team sent back one of these yeti scalps and a so-called yeti skin for analysis. Scientists matched the skin to the skin and fur of a blue bear, which is a known native of the region. Bristles from the scalp, meanwhile, were found to be from an animal related to the pelt.

With that, Hillary was convinced the yeti was merely a legend, and he was so popular and respected that many people took his word for it, although believers still remained unconvinced and did their best to point out flaws with the research and the expedition.

SPOTTED!
"You Could Hear the Footsteps"

Casey Skodje and Shane Hamre were bow hunting in the dense woods just outside of Yacolt in southwest Washington State, prime Bigfoot country.

"On the way in, we kept hearing random noises," Shane said. "It started off like sticks breaking every once in a while." The noises got louder over time. "I could hear something physically walking."

His buddy Casey said, "You could hear it brushing through the bushes, but you could hear the footsteps, too."

Shane turned around and walked backward, pointing his gun into the darkness of the woods. He yelled at it. "If you're a person, you better identify yourself, otherwise you're gonna get shot!"

No one said a word. From the evidence, Cliff theorizes that they were being escorted out of the area by none other than a sasquatch.

SASQUATCH

Canadian folklore is full of stories of wild men. Very often, these creatures were nocturnal and hairy (but not always). Sometimes, they stole young women away. Other times, they helped young men who'd been cast out. Some could speak. Some could only whistle. Strangely, some had spiked toes or legs that wouldn't bend (which meant they could only run downhill).

In 1929, a Canadian teacher named John Burns wrote

a story about these creatures for the magazine *Maclean's*. He named the creature sasquatch, and he helped form a consistent image for the furry monster out of folklore. Many of the details are consistent with aspects the *Finding Bigfoot* team hears from people describing their own encounters with squatches:

- They're about eight feet tall;
- They're covered with dark hair;
- They're uncivilized; and
- They throw rocks.

A few details, though, aren't commonly reported but still made it into his article:

- They can speak and have magical powers; and
- They covet women (Burns told one story of a woman who was abducted by a sasquatch and then gave birth to a baby who died a few hours later).

In 1941, a First Nations woman named Jeannie Chapman lived in Ruby Creek with her family. One day her child told her a big cow was coming, so she glanced out the window. What she saw was no cow. As soon as the creature worked its way into their storage shed, she took her children and fled to the Ruby Creek station. Chapman's husband and other men found footprints and a broken barrel of salted salmon when they checked out the scene. The Bellingham, Washington, sheriff's station investigated and opened a file on the case. Coincidentally, Burns covered the sighting as a journalist—but he thought it was a bear.

Years later, a newspaper owner named John Green was aware of sasquatch, but chalked it up to legend. Then he met a man named René Dahinden in 1956. Dahinden had heard of the yeti in Nepal and hoped to find the Canadian equivalent. The next year proved to be a turning point. The town of Harrison Hot Springs offered $600 for a civic project to help celebrate its centennial. Someone proposed a sasquatch hunt. They rejected the idea and bought a furnace for the new community hall (adults can be so boring), but people went nuts about the sasquatch idea.

Pretty soon, Green figured out that local people really did take the creature seriously, and it appealed to his curiosity as a journalist to find out more. He brought evidence he found to a zoologist at Provincial Museum, and eventually hired Dahinden to be a reporter on his newspaper staff.

Over the years, Green branched out his research to include bigfoot, interviewing people who'd claimed they had sightings, including Albert Ostman, a retired logger who said he'd been taken captive and lived with a sasquatch family for days before he used a can of snuff to make a wily escape. Green also wrote several books and followed the trail of bigfoot for decades without giving up.

BIGFOOT

There are more bigfoots hidden in the forests of North America than there are pandas in the wild, according to estimates of the Bigfoot Field Researchers Organization, which estimates there are 2,000 to 6,000 of the hairy creatures roaming free.

Bigfoot folklore is old. The Hoopa Indians, who live on a reservation near Humboldt County, tell tales of giant wild men, "creek devils" and "O-mah," which are huge, hairy, smelly monsters. There are also ancient cave paintings (see page 15). And a Pacific Northwest tribe called the Tsimshian [CHIM-she-un] has carved stone sculptures depicting ape-like creatures. This is stunning, given North America has no native apes. It's hard to imagine what might have inspired the artwork if there wasn't some creature Native Americans had seen.

But bigfoot didn't really become big, so to speak, until 1958.

That was the year a logging company worker in northern California named Jerry Crew, who was by all accounts reliable, hard-working, and religious, hopped on his bulldozer for another day's

When does bigfoot have a capital B?

The creature whose footprints Jerry Crew found in 1958 is the one that inspired the name Bigfoot. When you're talking about this particular animal, you use a capital letter. When you're talking about bigfoot as a species, you use a little "b."

work when he found big, man-like footprints all around him. It was late summer, August 27, to be exact. He found more tracks in September and took his evidence to a taxidermist who said he could capture better detail if he took a casting of the print. So Crew did just that and brought back a sixteen-inch track.

A newspaper columnist from the *Humboldt Times*, Andrew Genzoli, was curious. He'd received a letter about the tracks and, one day when he had a bit of extra space in his column, he ran the letter. A reporter on the newspaper staff, Betty Allen, started writing news articles about the mysterious find. Then, in October, Genzoli met with Crew, who had his picture taken with the cast for the paper.

Genzoli called the creature Bigfoot, and he wrote about its effect on the road crew. "The men are often convinced that they are being watched. However, they believe it is not an unfriendly watching." Rather, the creature was more of an invisible

That's one big footprint.

supervisor, stopping by daily to inspect their work. They measured the space between footprints, and Genzoli wrote that Bigfoot appeared to have a fifty-inch stride that stretched to ten feet as it ran.

His column was a sensation. Genzoli got more than 2,500 letters. A game show called *Truth or Consequences* offered a thousand-dollar reward to anyone who could explain the origin of the tracks. People wondered if it was an ape. Or a bear. Swedish people with large feet. A race of giants living in the mountains (this rumor got pretty wild—these giants were said to be lost relatives of the Atlanteans).

All along, Jerry Crew believed they were real, even as newspapers duked it out with one another. One of Crew's bosses, Ray Wallace, even threatened to sue anyone who called the tracks a hoax. But here's the surprising part. After Wallace died in 2002, his son said Wallace had made the tracks himself. When Wallace's obituary ran in *The Seattle Times*, it even contained the quote "Bigfoot is dead."

Was it Wallace all along? Bigfooters were convinced the tracks were real. John Green, the Canadian newspaper editor who studied sasquatch for much of his career, drove two thousand miles to California to see what the big deal was. His map was unreliable and he got lost, and the roads were dusty, but his journey was successful in one regard because he found tracks. Looking at them was remarkable, he wrote.

"I had never expected there would be anything to see." He was glad his wife was there with him because it helped her be understanding as he endured this decades-long quest. He thought the tracks he'd found were genuine, and noted their similarity to the ones from the Ruby Creek incident so many years earlier. How could separate people faking both sets of tracks manage to come up with something so similar?

Meanwhile, members of the Bigfoot Field Researchers Organization carry on the work, but with the advantages of modern technology. The group has a database with thousands of bigfoot sightings submitted by users. The sightings paint a picture of a hairy, nocturnal animal that ranges between seven and ten feet tall, weighs around six hundred fifty pounds, and has flat feet and body odor.

SKUNK APE

Far from the Pacific Northwest, in the opposite corner of the country, in an entirely different sort of environment, lives the skunk ape. This devastatingly smelly, seven-foot-tall hairy creature resides in the boggy places in Florida, Louisiana, and eastern Texas, where more than a million and a half acres of impenetrable forests and swamps provide these elusive beasts with plenty of privacy and protein.

"The edges of the canals in Florida provide a number of food resources for skunk apes," Matt Moneymaker says. "There are fish and reptiles and birds, and these canals run for miles like highways across the Everglades."

But that's not all that's on a skunk ape menu. They're also believed to eat deer, wild hogs, alligators, and even swamp apples, Moneymaker says. "That's how they're able to survive in such an unforgiving environment."

ARE SKUNK APES BIGFOOTS? OR A SEPARATE ANIMAL?

This isn't something that can be determined without specimens of each creature. Like bigfoot, the skunk ape is hairy, but has been described as smaller, with more hair that is lighter in color, sort of a reddish black, according to the Skunk Ape Research Headquarters in Ochopee, Florida. The headquarters also reports that male skunk apes are six to seven feet tall, weighing in at more than four hundred fifty pounds—so, large, but not bigfoot big. Females, meanwhile, run five to six feet tall and weigh up to two hundred fifty pounds.

As with bigfoots and yetis, stories of skunk apes stretch back in time, often before white explorers arrived. The Miccosukee Seminole nation in southern Florida tell stories of a tall, hairy man. And the first newspaper reference dates back to 1850 in a story about a wild man covered in hair spotted by Arkansas farmers. Since then there have been a couple of notable sightings: one in 1977 in which the man who had the encounter described its stench.

"It stunk awful," Charlie Stoeckman said. "Like a dog that hasn't been bathed in a year and suddenly gets rained on."

In another notable encounter that happened in 2000, a man driving near Trout, Louisiana, claimed to have hit a man in a fur coat with his car . . . but they never found the victim. For sure he hit something, though. His car was badly damaged.

Witnesses have described the odor of a skunk ape as rotten eggy. Some theorize that these creatures hide in alligator dens, absorbing the smell of swamp gas or rotting animals. Skunk apes no doubt sweat in the hot Florida weather. And, says Dave Shealy, who runs the Skunk Ape Research Center with his brother Jack, skunk apes don't bathe.

SKUNK APE BAIT

The Skunk Ape Research Headquarters has a warning for those of you who'd put out bait trying to catch a specimen: reconsider. The more bait you put out for these rare creatures, the less likely they are to be able to feed themselves. What's more, leaving food on the side of the road makes it more likely they will be hit by cars. It's also not legal to do in national parks or state-owned preserves.

If you have permission from a private property owner to leave out a little skunk ape bait, though, dry beans make the best bait, followed by deer liver, and then corn, rice, or dog food.

If you opt for deer liver, make sure you keep it safe by keeping it cold until you've chosen a bait site, and only put out bait if you've spotted a skunk ape and want to lure it. Otherwise, you're just feeding buzzards, which love the stuff.

If you opt for dry beans, lima beans are the most popular choice. Making sure you choose a dry spot (because moisture will rot the beans), clear a ten-foot-square area with a rake. Cover it evenly with a pound of large, dry lima beans.

You can use wet beans, too. Prepare these by soaking a pound of beans overnight in eight cups of water. Then dump the pile in the center of the ten-foot area that you've cleared of debris, or hang it in a pot from a tree limb in the middle of this same space.

The sour smell of the wet beans is believed to be appealing to skunk apes. After five days or so, you have to remove your wet beans.

And if a skunk ape takes the bait, keep it quiet. This will protect the animal from unscrupulous sorts who might want to come in and shoot the creature.

Mmm . . . skunk ape bait!

Is It Wrong to Shoot a Bigfoot?

The only definitive proof of a bigfoot, sasquatch, skunk ape, or yeti is an actual animal to study. While bigfoot searchers have gathered many footprints and other examples of evidence, science requires an actual animal or part thereof to be officially declared a species. What if the only way to prove bigfoot exists is to kill it? Some bigfoot seekers over the years have argued that this approach is ethical. It's worth sacrificing one to prove the animal exists. Others think it's a terrible idea to kill such a rare creature. Doing so could put an already rare species at risk. In considering your own answer to this question, think about how you'd feel if you purposely killed the last animal of its kind on the planet. Would it be worth it to prove one existed—only to make it disappear forever?

SHOOT A BIGFOOT, GO TO JAIL?

In Skamania County, Washington, an ordinance passed in 1969 makes it illegal to kill a bigfoot. Anyone who hunted bigfoot and committed a "willful and wanton slaying" could be convicted of a felony, fined up to $10,000, and sent to jail for up to five years. The law was softened a bit in 1984. Now, bigfoot hunting is a gross misdemeanor punishable with a $1,000 fine and up to a year in the clink.

In 2012, a bigfooter in New York tried to get the state's Department of Environmental Conservation to pass a similar no-hunting law, but the state declined, saying "no program or action in relation to mythical animals is warranted."

SPOTTED!
"It Just Ripped up There So Quick"

Northern California's Humboldt County is a Bigfoot hotbed, but is most famous for being the location where Roger Patterson and Bob Gimlin filmed "Patty," believed to be a female Bigfoot walking by Bluff Creek in the Six Rivers region.

Serene White had a similar encounter one afternoon.

Dead battery, she thought. She'd left the music on in her boom box. No big deal. She'd go back up to the top of the road and meet her uncle with a charger.

As she walked back down to the river, a friend who was with her said, "Hey, do you hear that?"

It sounded like something drinking. And then, quick as a flash, whatever it was took off. "It just ripped up there so quick," she said, pointing to the hillside on the riverbank. It passed through a wall of thicket like it was nothing. "I remember being freaked out because if that thing can go up there that quick, how quick could it get to me?"

She's seen bear and deer before, and neither could travel that swiftly. What's more, neither came close to the size of the mystery creature.

"It was huge," she said. With the *Finding Bigfoot* team, she estimated its size to be nine feet tall.

What could it possibly have been?

"I think Serene saw a sasquatch," Matt Moneymaker said.

GIGANTOPITHECUS

Fossils form only when conditions are just right—most living things die and decay without a trace. But when an animal dies in a way that allows its bones to be replaced with minerals over a period of time, it turns into a fossil. This can happen when a body is buried in sediment and covered with seawater, when it's entombed without oxygen, and when there's not too much heat or pressure put on it.

The fossil record isn't complete by any stretch. Some experts estimate we might only have five percent of primate species that made it through this process. Another way of looking at it: We have no record of most animals that have walked the planet. This also means there are a lot of possible big-foot ancestors that we don't know about.

One of the rare possibilities we do know about is Gigantopithecus, a primate species that might have gone unrecognized except for a bit of luck on the part of a paleontologist named Ralph von Koenigswald. In 1935, he was in China searching for dragon bones, which is what the Chinese believed the fossilized teeth and bones of long-vanished animals to be. He came back with something cooler than a dragon bone: a massive ape tooth. The thing was stunning, twice as big as a gorilla's tooth. He named it *Gigantopithecus blacki*.

Then, in 1950, an Italian expedition to China found an entire Gigantopithecus jawbone. Findings of this humongous ape are rare, and the only proof we have that such a massive ape once lived. In all, there are just a few jaws (and hundreds of single teeth).

It would be really nice to have a skull or even a full skeleton. But by observing the shapes of the teeth and quality of the enamel, which were similar to early hominids that walked upright on two feet, scientists can use Zadig's method to guess what these creatures might have been like and what they ate. They theorize these creatures were nine-foot-tall apes that—according to the fossil record—disappeared from the planet about 100,000 years ago. This means they were alive at the same time as *Homo sapiens sapiens* (that's human beings to you and me).

With the limited fossil evidence, it's hard to tell how the Gigantopithecus might have traveled around—on all fours or on two feet. This is the sort of thing you can tell by looking at a skull or the bones of a pelvis, legs, knee joints, and foot

bones, none of which we have at this point. But in all likelihood, it was too big to swing from the trees. It either walked on two or four legs.

The leading bigfoot expert, Jeffrey Meldrum, a professor of anatomy and anthropology at Idaho State University, believes it's possible bigfoot is some form of Gigantopithecus that made its way from East Asia on a land bridge that every so often linked Asia and North America. Humans managed to cross the sea this way. And if Sasquatch or its ancestors made it to North America this way, it would also explain in part why there isn't a fossil record that shows the emergence of giant apes. If they didn't evolve in North America but instead traveled there, you wouldn't find ancestor species. Also, its giant body and thick tooth enamel might have equipped it to survive in the colder north.

Average-sized monkey skull. The Gigantopithecus would be much larger!

MORE PUZZLE PIECES THAT FIT

The sasquatch's supersize also makes sense from a scientific standpoint, Meldrum has argued. Other animals living closer to poles are bigger than their relatives in tropical climates. Polar bears, for example, can weigh almost 1,500 pounds. But the spectacled bear found in tropical South America tops out at around 300 pounds.

This is called Bergmann's rule, by the way—the tendency of animals living in the north to be

bigger. Being big helps them hold on to body heat better. It also gives them more room for big bellies, which house the kind of intestines an animal needs to break down the coarser food in northern latitudes.

What's more, Gigantopithecus isn't the only ape that might be linked to sasquatch. Meldrum wrote in his book, *Sasquatch: Legend Meets Science*, that the Miocene era (about twenty-three million

to about five million years ago) offered a huge variety of the apes.

"For a time, Earth truly was 'a planet of the apes,'" he said.

What if the descendants of those apes are alive today, living in stealth in the wilderness? It's not a totally oddball idea. Remember the coelacanth. Everyone thought this fish had been gone for millions of years when someone found a living example.

THE YOWIE

In the late 1700s in Australia, early white settlers thought the Aborigines were trying to scare them off with tales of a "Narcoonah," a wild man living in the forests. But then, in 1790, newspapers carried reports of the first yowie sighting by a white man in a small town that is now known as Sydney. During the next century, this sort of thing happened more frequently, and from all around the vast continent.

The creatures have been described as intelligent, smelly, broad-shouldered, and powerfully built upright walkers that weigh between five hundred and eight hundred pounds, and as with the North American bigfoot, are believed to be nocturnal omnivores. Witnesses have seen them swiping chicken and other livestock, as well as fruit, road kill, and garbage.

They're also reclusive, but signs of their presence might include snapped and bent trees, trails, and strangely woven branches.

A BIGFOOT BY ANY OTHER NAME

One of the most compelling things about bigfoot is that people all around the world tell similar stories about the creature. If bigfoot doesn't exist, how do you explain these stories? Of course, not everyone calls the creature bigfoot or sasquatch, two names we're most familiar with.

Here are a few of the many other names that have been used to describe bigfoot-like creatures.

Wild man: China
The Alma: Mongolia
Metoh-Kangmi: Tibet
Snow Person, Forest Creature: Russia
Ba'oosh: Tsimshian (CHIM-she-un) tribe of the Pacific Northwest
Chie-tanka: Lakota or Western Sioux
Chiha-tanka: Dakota or Eastern Sioux
Rugaru: Turtle Mountain Ojibwa nation in North Dakota
S-cwene'y'ti: Colville Indians

Orang Pendek: Indonesia
Yeren: China
Woodbooger/Beast of Gum Hill: southwest Virginia
Kushtaka, also known among the Tlingit people as Water Devil because the creature was often seen near the water hunting fish
Knobby: a creature in the Carpenter's Knob area of North Carolina
La Llorona: Louisiana (the word is Spanish for "crying woman")

TIMELINE:
BIGFOOT, YETI, AND SASQUATCH

500–1,000 years ago: Bigfoot pictograms made in Painted Rock

1832: Englishman B. H. Hodgson reports native Nepalese hunters are talking about a furry, tailless demon that walks on two feet.

July 4, 1884: A young sasquatch dubbed "Jacko" is captured on the Fraser River in Vancouver. A newspaper reports it (but the story dies out there).

1889: Lieutenant-Colonel L. A. Waddell sees mysterious footprints in Himalaya.

1896: Del Norte County newspaper article describes a wild man that was about seven feet high, with a bulldog head, short ears, and long hair. This wild man had a shrill soprano voice that sounded like a terrified woman.

1924: A miner named Fred Beck reports that apes armed with rocks had attacked his camp. The *Portland Oregonian* carries a news story about it. (Beck claims to have shot the creature.)

1924: Albert Ostman claims to have been kidnapped by a family of sasquatches (he signed an affidavit in 1957 swearing it was true).

1929: John Burns writes an article about sasquatches for a Canadian magazine.

1935: Ralph von Koenigswald finds a Gigantopithecus tooth in China.

1941: Jeannie Chapman sees a sasquatch outside her home in Ruby Creek, British Columbia.

Nov. 8, 1951: Mountain climber Eric Shipton photographs what appears to be yeti tracks on the Menlung Glacier in the Himalayas.

1955: A highway worker named William Roe wanders into the mountains on a break and meets a shapely female sasquatch who was stripping leaves from a branch with her teeth. He follows a trail of her poop to her nest, but decides she looks too human to shoot.

1958: Jerry Crew finds Bigfoot tracks.

August 28, 1967: Journalist John Green gets a call about fresh bigfoot tracks; a cultural anthropologist views the tracks and is the first representative of a scientific institution in North America sent to study tracks.

October 20, 1967: Patterson-Gimlin shoots footage of what appears to be a female bigfoot walking along Bluff Creek in Humboldt County, California.

April 1, 1969: Skamania County, Washington, makes it illegal to kill a bigfoot there after a sighting.

September 22, 2000: A suspected bigfoot body print is found in the Skookum Meadow area of Washington State's Gifford Pinchot Forest.

February 11, 2012: London Trackway is discovered in Oregon.

BIGFOOT WITNESS PHOTO

Chapter Four
HOME SMELLY HOME

HOW TO SPOT A BIGFOOT DWELLING

*If the people are away, they always
know when [bigfoots] are coming
very near by their strong smell,
which is most intolerable.*

—A letter from Rev. Elkanah Walker to the American Board
of Commissioners for Foreign Missions, 1840

The more you know about an animal—what it eats, how it travels, where it's likely to live—the better chance you have of finding a sample of one. This is why bigfoot researchers have pondered where a sasquatch sleeps at night.

In a cave? In a hole? In hollow trees? Certainly all are possible.

But to get to the best possible answer for this question, some bigfoot researchers have turned to the gorilla for clues. Along with bonobos, chimpanzees, and orangutans, gorillas are great apes. They're not as big as bigfoot. They don't walk on two feet (at least not most of the time). But they are a large, hairy primate that

has managed to elude scientists for many years. Their behavior and sleeping habits could provide valuable clues in the hunt for bigfoot.

Gorillas sleep in nests. When they choose an area to bed down, one of the criteria they use is whether it has enough material for them to make their beds. And while there isn't a single method of building a gorilla nest, they usually take bent and broken vines, twigs, leaves, and branches to form an individual sleeping area (although baby gorillas share one with their mamas for the first three or so years). The nest keeps the gorilla off the ground and provides a bit of safety as they sleep by making them

less likely to tumble out of a tree or down a slope as they doze.

They build nests at least once a day, in part because they move around looking for vegetation to eat. If they stayed in one place, they'd literally eat themselves out of house and home. Another reason they might move, though, is that fresh bedding makes it less likely parasites will have a chance to set up shop.

The adults in the gorilla troop build their first nest of the day after their morning's foraged meal. (The kids get to play.) They nap in these nests, wake up for more eating, and then build a new nest for nighttime, never using the same nest twice. Gorilla researchers love finding nests of gorilla troops, because they can tell all sorts of information about the animals—how many, what they're doing—just from this single set of clues.

The same goes for bigfooters. They keep their eyes peeled for sleeping quarters—for clumps of sticks and branches that appear to have been twisted off and arranged in such a way that a sasquatch would have a soft, protected place to sleep, even if it's just used once.

CLOSE-UP: A BIGFOOT NEST AND HOW IT WAS MADE

In 2001, what some believe are three bigfoot nests in various stages of construction were found on private property near Sonora, California. Two nests were unfinished, but one looked as though it had been recently used, according to Kathy Moskowitz Strain, an anthropologist and USDA forest worker, who found the site and wrote an article about it for the Bigfoot Field Researchers Organization.

According to her report, the nests were in an

area with plenty of water and vegetation, including black oak, interior live oak, Jeffrey pine, manzanita, and bracken fern. The area also had a stream that was a tributary of the Stanislaus River, as well as a native deer herd, which meant plenty of food and water.

According to the USDA Forest Service records, there are no identified Native American sites and the area is not used for recreation. In other words, it's decent sasquatch territory: private and graced with food and water. Only its proximity to people makes it somewhat less desirable, Moskowitz said.

Moskowitz also found fresh, fourteen-inch Bigfoot tracks nearby, and the three nests were built near one another. The complete one was 1.3 meters high, 1.6 meters wide, and 1.9 meters long, and was made from live oak and Jeffrey pine. Its doorway opened to the northwest. The "padding" inside appeared matted from recent use.

Moskowitz waited a few months to be sure the nest was abandoned, and measured a 213-by-30-centimeter body imprint in it. She also took it apart to understand how it had been made. It looked as though a twelve-foot live oak tree had been bent over and secured with a heavy rock to create a dome. Then, fifteen Jeffrey pine branches, each an average of seven feet long, were stripped of smaller limbs and woven into the branches of the bent oak. Holes were filled in with smaller sticks. Then the interior was padded in three layers. The top was made of three centimeters of fresh moss, bracken ferns, and oak leaves. Below that came four centimeters of dead and decaying leaves. The bottom three centimeters were old moss, bracken fern fronds, and soil.

"Overall, the nest had a spongy, soft consistency," she wrote in her report.

"None of the layers had any apparent smell, other than that of dead and decaying organic material. No rocks or sticks were noted."

She combed through those layers, hoping to find evidence such as bones, teeth, hairs, and blood, but didn't find anything, and microscopic examination showed plant materials, seeds, and insect casings. She didn't find any direct evidence this was a bigfoot nest, but based on its similarities to other nests reported in books by John Bindernagel and Grover Krantz, the overall evidence suggested a lone sasquatch had built and briefly occupied this little refuge in the woods.

OTHER FAVORITE BIGFOOT HANGOUTS

Some bigfooters theorize the animals live in caves, which helps the creature avoid human detection. For certain, people claim to have had encounters in caves.

"I get excited when I see a cave because I've heard so many reports of people encountering a squatch in a cave," Bobo Fay says. "This is perfect squatch habitat."

There are a few scientific reasons bigfoot seekers think the animals could well be hiding out in caves.

BIG EYES: Many reports of bigfoot say the creature's eyes shine at night. This is common among nocturnal creatures. (See Chapter 6 for more information about eye shine and what causes it.) Bigfoot is also said to have large eyes. As with the giant squid, these large eyes would make for better vision in low light.

BIG SMELL: Caves are wet and dank. A furry animal living in such a spot would stink. (If you've ever gotten a whiff of wet dog, then you can imagine a fraction of the odor a much larger, much dirtier bigfoot might produce.)

STRATEGIC SOUNDS: Bigfoots are said to howl and knock. This might be their version of echolocation—using sound and listening to their echoes to navigate and hunt. Bats, whales, and even some blind humans are known to use this technique.

Matt

SPOTTED!

"You Guys Have Got to Check This Out"

Ben Mills's parents were off on a hike with each other in the Marble Mountain range of Humboldt County, leaving Ben and his brother Scott alone at the campsite. But not for long, Ben said.

The parents hightailed it back to the camp and said, "You guys have got to check this out."

The family set out for a strange sort of hut his parents had discovered. There were strange things about it.

"It looked like there were some claw marks. The limbs themselves were broken. There were no saw marks," Ben said.

Matt Moneymaker says this sounds like a possible Bigfoot nest.

"Bigfooters speculate that sasquatches build these type of nests from materials in the surrounding environment, to both protect themselves from the elements and to hide from humans during the day."

As Ben's dad was capturing video of the structure, Ben saw a little speck walking toward them. Its arms looked abnormally long. Its back appeared hunched, which he first thought was a backpack. But it was so tall.

"Then it disappeared," he said. The whole thing was odd . . . that there was someone there alone, the way the creature moved. After the *Finding Bigfoot* team staged a reenactment, Cliff Barackman was convinced it was no hiker they'd seen. He said, "I see no reason to discount that it's a sasquatch."

A PEEK AT SOME CAVES IN NORTH AMERICA

North America has many large caves. For example, Mammoth Cave in Kentucky is the largest known cave in the world, with more than 390 miles that have been explored. The name really describes it—the next biggest cave we know about is only a quarter the size of Mammoth Cave, which might even have more to it than we've been able to measure. The Green River in Kentucky carved Mammoth Cave over a period of ten million years, and all sorts of interesting critters live there—from eyeless fish to white cave spiders. So why not a bigfoot?

Carlsbad Caverns in New Mexico also took millions of

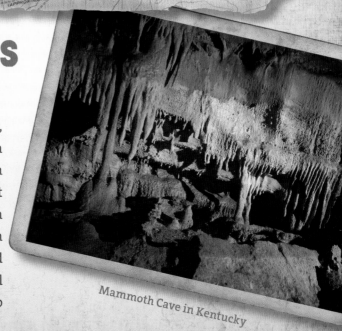

Mammoth Cave in Kentucky

years to form, and are also so big they haven't been fully explored. They're really cool—there are three different underground levels, a four-thousand-foot-long cavern (called Big Room), and even a natural stone structure that looks like a tumbling waterfall of rock.

In Washington State, near an active volcano named Mount St. Helens, there's also a spectacular cave made from a tube of lava. It's got a very provocative name: Ape Cave. Nearby is Ape Canyon, and bigfoot has been spotted in both places. There was even a fight reported in 1924 between some miners and a family of bigfoots.

But the "Ape" in the place names are not necessarily a Bigfoot reference. Instead, the Mount St. Helens tourist Web site says this name might come from a troop of Boy Scouts who explored it

Mount St. Helens

in the 1950s.

They were the Mount St. Helens Apes. It's also possible the area was named for early loggers and foresters, who were sometimes called "brush apes."

That said, if bigfoot ever is definitely found to be living in the area, the maps won't have to be changed, will they?

SPOTTED!
Nobody Messes with Tinman

Rodney "Tinman" Mitchell lives on the Hoopa Reservation, a place long linked to bigfoot.

When he had his encounter with the creature, it was nighttime. The sky was moonless, so it was dark. But he knew something was out there.

"My dogs were barking like crazy," he said. "I shined my light right through here and I heard a big snap."

Not one to put up with trespassers or tomfoolery, he blasted two rounds into the night. Then something huge jumped eight feet out of a tree.

"He jumped right into my light and went down over the hill," Tinman said. "I was so nervous and shook up that I couldn't even figure out how to get the bullet out of the chamber. And I was, like, just fumbling it."

That's when he realized he needed to get himself back in his house. He figures the creature he saw—no way was it someone in a suit—weighed about four hundred pounds and was around six feet tall.

"I could just see his muscles right through here," Tinman said. "He just looked stocky, you know."

There's one more reason Tinman knows it wasn't a person in a suit.

"Nobody messes around here because they know I'll shoot them," he said. "I mean, it's as simple as that."

WHAT YOU MIGHT FIND (AND SMELL) INSIDE A BIGFOOT NEST

If bigfoots are like gorillas, they do not use their nests for long. Remember, gorillas make two nests a day. If bigfoots follow a similar pattern, we should not expect to find sturdy housing intended to last. Likewise, we shouldn't expect to find much evidence beyond the twisted-off, woven branches and arranged bedding.

Nor should we expect to find any sort of tools or decorations. Apes and some monkeys have been observed using tools, but bigfoot is generally not believed to use tools, although there have been sightings of sasquatches using sticks to dig. The theory about why tools aren't found in suspected bigfoot nests is that these creatures don't need to use tools.

Still, there's one thing you can expect to find in a bigfoot nest: a certain odor. Many people who've encountered bigfoot describe a distinctive aroma, either of feces or rotting meat. And one variety, the skunk ape, is named for its distinctive methane smell—think cow farts.

Branches make great gorilla tools.

HOW TO MAKE A BIGFOOT BED

Bigfoots need sleep, just like you. And according to the people who've dedicated their lives to finding the elusive creature, bigfoots prefer beds. Matt Moneymaker has studied every aspect of the animal's behavior and preferences. It's a detail many people ignore.

"But this is a very important thing for understanding how sasquatch live, where they'll go, what they like, and what they don't like."

He believes a good spot for a bigfoot bed is in a secluded area, where people won't stumble across it.

"A place full of pine needles that's in the sunlight," he says. That's what a squatch will like.

He's even built a sasquatch bed by piling up leaves and sun-dried pine needles until he has a thick, mattress-like construction that gives bigfoot a few insulated inches between its body and the ground. And he thinks it's a pretty comfortable way to sleep. "I'm feeling just right here," he says, feeling his mother-nature mattress. "I can hang here for hours."

Sasquatch Snack Attack:
HOW TO EAT LIKE BIGFOOT AND MAKE YETI SPAGHETTI

WHAT DOES BIGFOOT EAT?

Anything goes at the sasquatch snack bar. Bigfoot is an omnivore, which means both plants and animals are on the menu. In the wooded areas in which they are said to live, they might find everything from nuts and berries to rabbits, crawdads, fish, and deer. "Jacko," the suspected juvenile sasquatch found in British Columbia in 1884, was fed berries and milk.

In setting up bait stations, the *Finding Bigfoot* team has left out apples, bacon, peanut butter, doughnuts, bagels, and . . . gag . . . raw liver.

For fun, you might try packing yourself a Bigfoot lunch to take to school. Assuming you're not allergic to peanut butter (and you aren't planning to eat near anyone who is), you might pack yourself a peanut butter bagel with a sliced apple, a container of blueberries, and a carton of milk.

Bigfoot-Inspired Recipes for You to Cook

You'll work up a big appetite hunting for bigfoot. You can keep your belly full from breakfast until dinner with these delicious recipes that are easy enough for you to make—and something your whole family will enjoy.

Yeti Spaghetti is a creamy, white mountain of pasta flavored with lots of garlic and Parmesan cheese, so you will be good and stinky after eating it.

Yeti Spaghetti

1/2 pound dry fettuccine pasta

3 to 4 tablespoons unsalted butter

1 tablespoon of chopped garlic

2/3 cup finely grated Parmesan cheese

Black pepper

1/2 cup cream

1. Boil a big pot of water. Add a pinch of salt and your dry pasta. (You can use fresh pasta, but if you do, don't drop it in the water until your sauce is cooked.)

2. Melt the butter in a saucepan set over low heat. Cook the garlic for about three minutes. Then stir in the cream. Keep stirring this mix over very low heat (don't let it boil) until your pasta is cooked.

3. When your noodles are done, lift them out of the pot and put them into the sauce. Don't pour them out to drain—you want them to be dripping a bit with water. Turn on the heat under the saucepan to medium. Twirl the noodles around in your sauce. Then add half the cheese and twirl again. Once the cheese is mixed in, add the rest. You might need a couple of spoons of the pasta water if it gets dry.

4. Serve at once. If you want to get fancy, you can sprinkle a tad of nutmeg on top and call it mountain dust.

This recipe makes enough for four people. Or for one yeti.

Bigfoots are believed to have a special fondness for peanut butter and bacon, which is why this Bigfoot-Long Sandwich might just be the ultimate squatch lunch.

Bigfoot-Long Sandwich

One twelve-inch baguette

Six to eight pieces of bacon

Peanut butter

* Optional: honey or pickles (but not both—Bigfoot is an omnivore but not crazy)

1. Cook the bacon in a skillet set over medium-high heat, turning it every so often so it gets uniformly crispy. You might need a grown-up's help with this.

2. Put a piece of paper towel on a big plate and drain the bacon there once it's cooked.

3. Slice your baguette in half.

4. Cover both sides generously with peanut butter.

5. If you're using honey or pickles, put them on top.

6. Add the bacon, close your sandwich, and enjoy!

This is enough sandwich for two to four people. Or one bigfoot.

Butternut Squatch Soup

One butternut squash

One onion

Four cups of chicken broth

Two tablespoons of butter or olive oil

Salt and pepper to taste

1. Preheat your oven to 400 degrees.
2. Ask an adult to slice the squash in half (squash are really hard and cutting them is kind of a chore).
3. Put the squash on a cookie sheet, cut side up, and roast it about 45 minutes until the insides are soft.
4. Take it out of the oven and let it cool.
5. As it cools, dice one onion into small cubes. Put two tablespoons of butter or olive oil into a soup pot and cook the onion in it over medium heat until the cubes get soft and clear. You don't want to use such high heat that they turn brown.
6. Scoop out the soft, roasted butternut squash. Put it into the pot with the cooked onion. Gently stir in the chicken broth. Bring it to a boil, and then simmer for about 15 minutes, stirring as you go. Season it with salt and pepper until it tastes good. Serve!

This makes enough soup for four people. Or one sasquatch.

Abominable Snowcones

One box of cake mix—any flavor you like.

Two dozen flat-bottomed ice cream cones

Two dozen cupcake liners

One tub of vanilla frosting

1. Preheat your oven to 350 degrees.
2. Make the cake batter according to the recipe on the box.
3. After lining each indentation with a cupcake liner, pour the batter into a muffin tin until each reservoir is two-thirds full. Put an ice cream cone upside down over each one—the cake will rise into the spot.
4. Bake for 16 to 22 minutes.
5. Let your snowcakes cool. Don't be in a rush or your frosting will get melty.
6. Peel off the papers. Frost and then top with a sprinkling of sugar so it looks like sparkling snow.

This makes enough cupcakes for a party of twenty-four or so. Or one yeti.

SPOTTED!
"One of the Scariest Things Ever"

Kristy Aho and her husband, Dale, were hunting grouse in the woods of Minnesota. Their prey took off and Dale got off his four-wheeler and followed it. As soon as he walked in the woods, he passed a sasquatch.

"That's when it jumped and ran away," he said.

Kristy swears it's true. "I seen it, the whole side of it come through this little clearing, every time it took a step, the two of us were just shaking, my heart almost stopped."

The creature was seven and a half or eight feet tall and covered in long, dark-brown hair that you could see through all the way to its skin. "I knew what it was right away," Kristy said, "but I, I didn't wanna believe it, and it was one of the scariest things ever."

Chapter Five
FAMOUS BIGFOOT HUNTERS

THE *FINDING BIGFOOT* FOUR

Cliff Barackman

Cliff Barackman has loved both music and science since he was a boy growing up in Long Beach, California. Now, talk of bigfoot sightings is music to his ears—and it has been since he was in college, when he first realized the animal might be more than just a legend.

He read lots of books in his college library and came to believe bigfoot is biologically possible. He brought that knowledge with him to the great outdoors and on his first bigfoot expedition—to the famous Bluff Creek area in 1994—he found possible bigfoot tracks, damaged trees, and hair that looked squatchy. He's been hooked ever since.

Cliff is especially interested in footprint casts and has one of the biggest collections of them in the country. They're a great form of physical evidence in support of sasquatch, and Cliff is a big believer in gathering and analyzing data (he's the best at math in the bunch). He also used to be a teacher and is great at explaining complicated things about bigfoot in ways everyone can understand.

He's still interested in music, by the way—he studied jazz guitar in college and sometimes plays gigs around his adopted hometown of Portland, Oregon.

Matt Moneymaker

Matt is the founder and president of the Bigfoot Field Researchers Organization (BFRO). He's a lifelong bigfoot fan, starting when he was just an eleven-year-old kid watching a number of documentaries in the 1970s. As a college student at the University of California–Los Angeles, he started talking with bigfoot researchers in the United States and Canada.

And then, in 1987, his life changed forever. He found his first track in the mountains of Ventura County, California. After that, life took him from the West Coast to the Midwest in the early 1990s, but he never left his interest in bigfoot behind. He learned about the many bigfoot sightings Ohio farmers had made in the previous decade, and then had his own first encounter in 1994, as he camped overnight in a swampy wildlife refuge south of Kent, Ohio.

In 1996, just as regular people started using the Internet regularly for the first time, Matt founded the BFRO, which helped connect researchers around the Web site and blog. The BFRO publishes and investigates reports of sightings by eyewitnesses, and they have a Web site you can visit and explore for all sorts of information about the creatures, as well as sightings that have been made.

In 2000, he organized the BFRO's first big expedition, to a place called Skookum Meadows in Washington State, where a team found what is believed to be a bigfoot body print. He coproduced television programming about bigfoot and also organized trips where researchers would seek out the creature all around the country. He still does this today, in addition to his work on *Finding Bigfoot*.

Matt has popularized many new techniques in sasquatch hunting:

- He helped promote the use of sound blasting and howling to find bigfoot and the first to record "the Ohio howl," a long, moaning noise believed to have been made by a large, male sasquatch.

- He was the first to connect piles of dead deer with bigfoot, after Mennonite farmers in Ohio pointed out the strange stashes to him.

- He was the first to formally present a paper on knocking sounds made by bigfoots at a 1992 International Society of Cryptozoology conference at Rutgers University.

- He organized the first public expeditions to gather observations and evidence in various parts of North America.

- His organization was the first to debunk the "Georgia Bigfoot Body" hoax in the summer of 2008.

Ranae Holland

She's come a long way since her girlhood in Sioux Falls, South Dakota. Now she's a research biologist and field biologist who regularly works for the National Oceanic and Atmospheric Administration.

But even when she was a kid, Ranae Holland was interested in bigfoot. It was during the 1970s that she and her dad used to cozy up and watch bigfoot movies and documentaries together, so sasquatch has a special place in her heart even if she can't quite wrap her brain around believing the creature exists.

That's right. Ranae Holland *doesn't* believe in bigfoot. But that doesn't stop her from tromping through the woods with the team in search of evidence.

Her role is to help the guys think critically and ask themselves what other explanations could account for the sightings that people have reported. It's sometimes a tough spot to be in,

being the only skeptic surrounded by some of the most passionate squatchers in the world.

But Ranae loves helping people think critically by considering evidence, asking questions about it, and coming up with credible explanations. She also loves being in the outdoors. Camping, hiking, fishing, and kayaking are some of her favorite activities. Mix in bigfoot and real science, and she's as happy as could be.

James "Bobo" Fay

James "Bobo" Fay grew up surfing sasquatch-size waves in Manhattan Beach, California. By the time he was in college, though, he'd left the beach behind for the woods of northern California, where he hoped to find bigfoot.

After college, he worked as a logger on Native American crews with the same goal in mind. He hoped to learn enough about their legends that he'd finally experience some sightings out in the wild. That day came in 2001, when he was on an investigation with John Freitas, a veteran bigfoot researcher. The experience rocked his world.

Bobo is a big guy. He's six feet, four inches tall, which makes him a great stand-in for bigfoot

when the team is reenacting sightings. This important research technique lets witnesses re-create what they saw, helping understand the creature's size and behavior. This can help the team validate or rule out a sighting.

Bobo is also accomplished at making bigfoot calls.

Today, when he's not with the *Finding Bigfoot* crew, he works as a commercial fisherman out of Eureka, California. He also does odd jobs that can bring him closer to bigfoot.

BIG NAMES IN BIGFOOT HISTORY

Over the years, many people have devoted their lives to finding bigfoot. Here are some of the most notable:

Tom Slick

Tom Slick was a man with an aptronym—a last name that suited him. Born to a wealthy family that made its money in the oil business, he was a bit like a character out of a movie: a brash Texan who founded an airline, hung out with the eccentric billionaire Howard Hughes, advocated for world peace, and funded scientific research institutions he hoped would revolutionize the stodgy science frontier.

He thought the yeti was the missing link between humans and apes (even though anthropologists and biologists are already well aware of many species linking humans to earlier primate forms).

In 1957, Slick traveled to the Himalayas' Arun Valley in search of the yeti, interviewing people who said they'd had encounters. They found track and samples of yeti scat, and the experience whetted their appetites for a bigger hunt that would be covered by the *New York Journal-American*, something Slick thought of as "the Ultimate Quest." He was confident enough they'd snag a yeti that he bet a friend $1,000 he'd have one in hand within a month (although he didn't go on the second mission himself—he had people for those things). He lost the bet, but his team estimated there were four thousand small yetis living in the Himalayas. In all, he spent $100,000 on three yeti hunts, expecting the abominable snowman would someday soon be found.

Slick also funded the Pacific Northwest Expedition to find bigfoot. It started in 1959, again with high hopes. But the searchers didn't trust each other or get along well, and the discovery didn't happen during his lifetime. On Sunday, October 6, 1962, his private plane crashed near Dell, Montana. Slick and his pilot died.

SPOTTED!
Seeking Wisdom from the First Nations

In their search for sasquatch, the *Finding Bigfoot* team is willing to try anything, including a traditional cleansing ceremony with members of the Stoney-Nakoda tribe in the Canadian Rockies.

Lenny Wesley, a tribe member, explained how they would burn ten different types of medicinal plants in a sacred smoke ceremony meant to help the foursome cleanse themselves and tap into the power of sasquatch.

"What you see is not just hiking trails," Lenny said. "There's more beyond those mountains. There's power."

It's a sort of a sixth sense that lets the bigfoot researchers tap into the creature's power and follow it wherever it might lead, a technique they recognized as unusual, but one worth respecting as they walked the Stoney-Nakoda land.

John Green

This newspaperman originally thought stories about a sasquatch were hooey, and when a Swiss man named René Dahinden stopped by Green's newspaper office to inquire about sightings in 1956, he told the man as much.

It's understandable. Green was the son of a Canadian cabinet minister and a lumber heiress. He grew up in cities. But, knowing newspaper readers always enjoy interesting stories, he put a bit in the paper about Dahinden's interest in a North American yeti. That's when people he respected talked about the Ruby Creek incident from 1941, where a giant, hairy creature broke into a woman's storage lean-to and scared her out of her wits.

He put his journalistic mind to work, interviewing the son of the sheriff's deputy who had investigated the sighting. The deputy, who had since passed away, had been thorough. He'd made sketches and casts of the footprints. A lawyer and former magistrate had also interviewed witnesses and taken sworn affidavits (signed documents used as evidence in court). You can be convicted of a crime called perjury if you lie in one, so this was evidence Green took seriously, concluding there was maybe something to this sasquatch thing after all.

In 1958, when Jerry Crew reported the Willow Creek footprints, Green and his wife visited. June Green found one as soon as she stepped out of their car.

John Green told an interviewer at a University of British Columbia alumni magazine, "What particularly impressed me was the similarity between the outline of these tracks and the tracings I had of one of the Ruby Creek footprints."

Later, he was instrumental in the famous

Patterson-Gimlin film, which is said to show a female bigfoot walking beside a creek. Green brought Roger Patterson to the Bluff Creek area of northern California where the film was shot. Patterson said he captured his famous footage a month later.

After the movie touched off a bigfoot craze, Green—always methodical—started a database of sightings. He recorded four thousand of them, stopping when his database technology grew out of date. He wrote many books about the lengthy search and estimated he sold 250,000 of them. His most famous is probably one he wrote in 1978, called *Sasquatch: The Apes Among Us*. He did all this while raising four children, being a

competitive sailor, and holding local political office. He also founded the World Sand Sculpture Contest, which paved the way for record-setting sculptures in sand. (Look them up online—they're really incredible.)

He was never discouraged by the media reports that Ray Wallace had faked those 1958 tracks that made so many people believe in Bigfoot, even if the news widely reported that Bigfoot "died" with Ray Wallace in 2002.

"The fact is that the tracks exist, and no human being has yet proven to be able to replicate the tracks of the depth recorded. I'd like to know what's making the bloody tracks," Green told the alumni magazine.

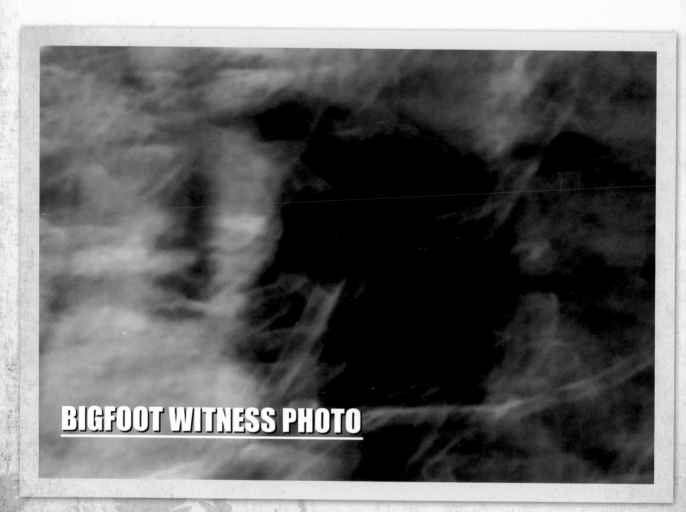

BIGFOOT WITNESS PHOTO

Bob Titmus

By trade, Bob Titmus was a taxidermist, someone who specializes in stuffing dead animals and making them appear lifelike. But the real work of his life was the search for bigfoot. In 1958, after Jerry Crew found Bigfoot tracks in the Bluff Creek area, Titmus taught Crew how to make plaster casts of footprints. Not long after that, Titmus and a friend found slightly smaller sasquatch tracks that made people think more than one creature was afoot.

He also was the first leader of the Pacific Northwest Expedition to find bigfoot, which was funded by the millionaire Tom Slick. After he moved to British Columbia, Titmus collected a ton of tracks (plus knee- and handprints). Finally, he cast the tracks at the site of the Patterson-Gimlin encounter.

Many believe footprints are the best evidence for bigfoot we have.

SPOTTED!
There Is No "P" in Bigfoot

Keith Hamilton is an experienced outdoorsman. He hunts, fishes, camps, hikes—if you can do it in the woods, he's a pro.

But one night as he was settling into sleep inside his tent in a patch of wilderness a forty-minute hike from the trailhead, he heard something unusual . . . heavy footsteps.

"I heard it slowly coming closer and closer to me," he said.

And then the truly strange happened. He heard a sound, a stream of liquid hitting his tent. It was raining steadily outside, but this particular noise sounded different. So he opened the flap of his tent five or six inches to investigate.

That's when he saw it.

"A figure that was about twice the width of my shoulders," he said. "The hair on my neck just stood up, because this is not normal."

And what was the creature doing?

Peeing. A lot.

Keith describes it as a "strong, steady stream." His theory is that the bigfoot was urinating on his tent to mark it.

He had time to see the creature's full upper torso, shoulders, and head. Based on a re-creation, the *Finding Bigfoot* team estimates it to be an eight-foot-tall male.

No word on how Keith cleaned his tent, but after his sighting, he was hooked on sasquatch hunting.

René Dahinden

Intrigued by tales of the Himalayan yeti, René Dahinden heard about sasquatch when he was working on a farm in Alberta, Canada. Finding the North American version became his life's work. He worked alongside John Green do to this, and hunted bigfoot for fifty years, even choosing the pursuit over his wife and family. He also cowrote a book called *Sasquatch/Bigfoot: The Search for North America's Incredible Creature* in 1973.

Over the years, he collected hundreds of footprint casts that he took with him on his travels. He also interviewed legions of people who claimed to have encountered bigfoot and had choice words for skeptics who didn't think footprints mattered.

"If anyone finds this kind of evidence immaterial," he said, while holding a heavy plaster casting, "let me strike his head with it."

The pipe-smoking Dahinden wasn't a fan of university-educated scientists.

"Those clodhoppers!" he once told a magazine reporter. "Science is the pursuit of the unknown. Now maybe the scientists think there is nothing unknown, since they know it all, and therefore they don't have to pursue it. I don't know, it looks like the scientists get up every morning and pray, 'Please God, let me go through another day without a new thought.'"

He was equally scornful of people who faked evidence and encounters.

Dahinden bought the rights to show the Patterson-Gimlin film, and he created a sensation in Moscow when he showed it to a roomful of scientists, but he never made much money showing it, and he supported himself by gathering the lead out of spent shotgun shells at a gun range, gathering hundreds of pounds of it using his bare hands.

Before he died, he admitted some disappointment and possibly even doubt with his lifelong quest. "You know, I've spent over forty years—and I didn't find it. I guess that's got to say something."

Look closely. Can you see bigfoot?

Peter Byrne

When he was a child in Ireland, Peter Byrne's father used to tell him bedtime stories about the yeti. As a young man, Byrne spent years in the Himalayas, and later—once he was convinced by bigfoot tracks and Native American lore—he traveled across five continents in search of bigfoot. He led three major trips in the Pacific Northwest.

He later helped launch the Bigfoot Information Center in The Dalles, Oregon, during the 1970s, and the Bigfoot Research Project in the Hood River in the 1990s. The second project, which lasted five years, seemed to have a better chance for success because of its prime location near the Cascade Mountains. They used better technology, including remote sensors. They had a hotline for sightings and a helicopter.

They didn't find a bigfoot, but they did find several sets of huge footprints, along with eyewitness reports. They also found a giant, nine-foot-by-four-foot bed of moss, "which one of the creatures almost certainly constructed and in which it slept," he reported.

All these years later, he's still continuing what he calls The Great Search. His goal at this point is to extract DNA because "scientists will accept absolutely nothing less as evidence."

Ivan Sanderson

Ivan Sanderson was a Scottish explorer who became an American citizen and one of bigfoot's biggest boosters, even though he wasn't always taken seriously. His big idea was to turn the study of bigfoot into a science called ABSMery. He didn't like the term abominable snowman, so he took letters from it and married it to a suffix that gave the study a bit more respectability.

He was a follower of an early twentieth-century writer named Charles Fort, who collected articles and other tidbits about things that science couldn't explain, and in 1965, he started the Society for the Investigation of the Unexplained, which published its own *Pursuit Magazine.* In addition to many articles, he wrote *Abominable Snowmen: Legend Come to Life*, which was published in 1961.

When Sir Edmund Hillary dismissed the yeti as mere legend, Sanderson was one of the many who objected. Later, Tom Slick paid him to hire John Green, René Dahinden, and other serious bigfoot seekers.

In addition to bigfoot, Sanderson was also interested in UFOs and wrote a book called *Invisible Residents: The Reality of Underwater UFOs*, which speculated, among other things, whether long-ago alien visitors had built themselves underwater docking bases. For some people, this sort of interest and theory discredits his interest in sasquatch.

Roger Patterson and Bob Gimlin

This duo is famous for shooting the first film footage of a bigfoot. In October 1967, they took a break from making a movie about the creature in Washington State, and traveled down to Humboldt County, California, to check out a new set of tracks that had been reported. The rain washed them away before the men arrived, but on a horseback ride one afternoon in the Bluff Creek area, they rounded a bend and spotted something astounding: a furry creature with a human-like head, long arms, and obvious female body parts. They filmed the creature, and the resulting clip has been held up as both a hoax and the holy grail of the bigfoot search.

Patterson, who died of cancer in 1972, was a bit of a scoundrel who had hoped to make a lot of money from the movie, which did not help his credibility. But Gimlin never made any grand attempt to capitalize on the incident, nor was he characterized as anything less than an honest man.

Paul Freeman

One of the most controversial figures in bigfoot history was a man named Paul Freeman, who in 1982 was going about his job as a United States forest ranger when he found bigfoot tracks near Walla Walla, Washington. He also had a sighting and straightaway contacted a biologist and the state's border patrol. Ultimately, there was no official government report about it.

Depending on whom you talk to, Freeman was either a truly gifted bigfoot seeker—he found many footprints—or a persistent hoaxer. Anthropologists like Grover Krantz and Jeff Meldrum were on Freeman's side. They found the dermal ridges on the tracks to be persuasive, and Meldrum even bought Freeman's track collection in order to study it. Other people, especially Dahinden, thought Freeman found too many tracks to be credible.

Whatever the case, before his death in 2003, he found many footprints, handprints, and even a bigfoot buttock-print. He also captured what he claimed was video of bigfoot, which you can search for online.

Daniel Perez

This devoted bigfoot scholar is author of *Bigfoot at Bluff Creek*, the definitive account of the Patterson-Gimlin film; *Bigfoot Notes*, a bibliography of the many things that have been written about the creature; and editor and publisher of the *Bigfoot Times*, a monthly newsletter that is considered essential reading for bigfooters.

Perez also founded the Center for Bigfoot Studies and has one of the biggest collections of books and bigfoot files anywhere.

Wolf Henner Fahrenbach

This Berlin-born scientist earned his doctorate in zoology from the University of Washington and a postdoctoral fellowship in anatomy at Harvard Medical School. He also ran the electron microscope lab at the Oregon Regional Primate center for thirty years and has expertise in everything ranging from insect morphology to cell biology.

In short, he's a scientist with fantastic credentials—but unlike the scientific mainstream, he's a firm believer that the Patterson-Gimlin film is genuine.

Fahrenbach has written many scientific articles about sasquatch and its body size, and is an expert in identifying suspected sasquatch hair. As recently as 1999, he identified a dozen hair samples he believes belong to the creature.

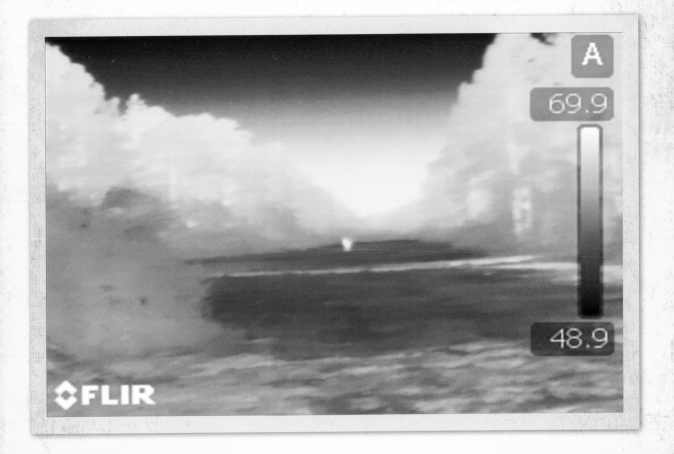

THE ABSMery AND INTERNATIONAL SOCIETY OF CRYPTOZOOLOGY

Over the years, people fascinated by hidden animals—cryptids or cryptozoids—have tried to be organized in their approach to finding animals such as bigfoot and the Loch Ness Monster, a massive, dinosaur-like creature believed to inhabit one of Scotland's largest, deepest freshwater lakes. Their goal was to turn the study of these animals into a proper science.

Ivan Sanderson kicked off the first of these, naming it the ABSMery. Supporters didn't end up finding bigfoot or making much of a scientific contribution, but it did give the creature more attention. Sanderson wrote many articles about wild men and published them in a magazine called *Fantastic Universe*, which was printed from 1953 to 1960. (He didn't only write about wild men. One of his articles was titled "What Pilots a UFO?")

Later came the International Society of Cryptozoology, which was set up in 1982 in

Washington, D.C. Unlike the ABSMery, the ISOC focused on gathering and evaluating evidence for all "unverified animals." By this, they meant ones that had been encountered or had left tracks or other evidence, but had not yet been recorded by scientists. They also included creatures that were no longer thought to be living but actually were, a category that would include something like the Loch Ness Monster.

Bernard Heuvelmans, who coined the term cryptozoology, was the group's president. The organization used an image of an okapi on its logo, honoring an animal that looks like it was built from parts of a zebra and a giraffe and had been thought to be a local central African legend until 1901, when a British explorer sent a pelt home to London. From 1982 to 1996, the ISOC published a journal called *Cryptozoology*. Alas, the group ran out of funding in 1998.

BIGFOOT FIELD RESEARCHERS ORGANIZATION

While the International Society of Cryptozoology was headed toward extinction, the Bigfoot Field Researchers Organization was just taking off. The organization, started by Matt Moneymaker, is focused exclusively on bigfoot-type creatures, and its members approach the topic scientifically by collecting physical evidence from suspected bigfoot habitats and doing their best to understand what the evidence can reveal. They also aim to do no harm to bigfoot, so, unlike certain hunters, would not kill a bigfoot to prove the creature exists.

Unlike earlier groups, the BFRO was born in a time of sophisticated technology. A centerpiece is their database of bigfoot sightings. It's a great place to figure out where you should start your own search for bigfoot (see Chapter 6 for more information on that). You can search for sightings by region, and you can also look for the most recent reports. If you're into even more technology, you can install Google Earth and zoom in on sightings, viewing the actual topography from above.

You can also join the BFRO yourself, but it's not easy. The first thing you have to do is join one of their four-day expeditions, which are scheduled around the United States and Canada. There is a $300 to $500 fee, and you have to be over twenty-one or traveling with someone at least that old. You also have to be an experienced camper (although you can in some cases get a motel room). After you've successfully completed one of their expeditions, a member has to recommend you.

If this sounds like too much, you can report sightings to their database. Be warned that they don't look kindly on hoaxers. But if you did go camping and saw tracks, gathered other evidence such as hair, or encountered a bigfoot, you can visit the site to report what you saw or found, when you saw it, where you were, and whether there was anyone else with you. They'll also ask you for your contact information in case one of their volunteer researchers needs to get in touch with you for more information.

SPOTTED!
Things That Go Thud in the Night

Sisters Lonni Olson and Donna Ross are new to the pursuit of bigfoots. A series of strange incidents that happened when they were camping in the woods left them rattled.

It started at three o'clock in the morning; after a long night of searching, Donna had lain down in her tent. Something went thud outside.

"I sat up immediately and I took a look around," she said.

The next morning, when she investigated by daylight, she found a rock nearby. But that wasn't all.

Lonni said there were indentations in the ground. "Not footprints, per se, but the grass had absolutely been stepped on."

The next night, around nine thirty or ten o'clock, just as the sun was setting, they heard a tree knock and some growls, a deep, guttural sound that affects you like no other.

"It's hard to explain," Lonni said, "because it kind of goes through your body."

The experience has them convinced that sasquatch turned the tables on them—turning the hunters into the hunted.

PRO TECHNIQUES

Want to search for Bigfoot like a professional? You might try using one of the *Finding Bigfoot* team's techniques. Some require special equipment, but many are relatively simple.

Vocalizing and knocking:
Bigfooters believe the creatures communicate with each other by whistling, making loud whooping and shrieking noises, and by knocking rocks against trees. You can do the same to see if you get a response. To practice your bigfoot call, you might go to BigfootSounds.com and listen to the samples.

Projecting audio:
If you have a portable music player with speakers, you can blast sounds that might be interesting to a curious Sasquatch. The *Finding Bigfoot* team has projected the sounds of a crying baby, for example.

Glow sticks and bait:
The *Finding Bigfoot* team once suspended a bunny in a cage from a tree. Then they hung glow sticks that would move if anything disturbed the cage. (Don't worry—the bunny was fine.) Instead of using live bait, you might try putting food in the cage and seeing if a bigfoot goes for it.

A Ghillie suit:
This is a sort of hair- and leaf-covered camouflage suit used by some hunters and snipers to disguise themselves in the woods. It was originally invented by Scottish hunters, but was then used for military reasons in World War I. The *Finding Bigfoot* team has used a Pied Piper kind of technique with a Ghillie suit, making themselves visible with lights as they try to lure a sasquatch into traveling alongside them in the woods. You would want to be very careful with this method. Instead of using it as camouflage, which can be dangerous, combine it with lights and noise to call attention to yourself.

Piles of food and glow-in-the-dark powder:
You can use fresh fruit, peanut butter, Zagnut bars, bacon, raw liver, or other favorite bigfoot treats for this. Just set out a pile of food somewhere squatchy, sprinkle glow-in-the-dark powder on top, and follow the footprints wherever they lead you. (You can buy this powder at science supply stores.)

MORE ADVANCED TECHNIQUES AND EQUIPMENT

The Dark Man Technique

is recommended for grown-ups only. To use it, one person sits alone in the woods with no lights or electronics whatsoever. The goal is that a sasquatch will pass by.

Use a drone camera

if, say, your family just won the lottery. These expensive, lightweight flying contraptions can be guided by remote control. The *Finding Bigfoot* team used one during the first season of the show.

Thermal imagers

detect anything that gives off heat, turning it white on the screen. You can tell if whatever you've picked up is wearing clothing (bigfoot travels in the buff), and you can also gauge its size. If you spot a nine-foot creature on your thermal imager, you're on to something. If you want to get super-fancy, you might borrow a vehicle built by the FLIR Corporation, which comes equipped with a thermal camera that can pick up anything from a hundred meters to nine miles away.

"I've literally dreamed about things like this a thousand times," Bobo Fay said when the *Finding Bigfoot* team took a spin in one.

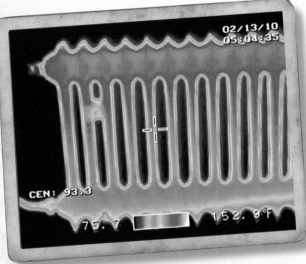

This radiator is HOT.

What about a blimp?

One team of bigfoot researchers tried to raise $355,000 to build the ultimate stealth sasquatch tracking and recording device. The Falcon Project would have sent a blimp up to patrol forests at night with a high-definition thermal camera, silently sending back images from remote areas likely to be home to bigfoot. They unfortunately fell short of their fund-raising goal by a maddening $343,135.

SCIENTISTS FOR SASQUATCH

Your average scientist will probably be squeamish about sasquatch. It's not because he or she is afraid of coming across one but, rather, because no one has for absolute certain encountered one despite a lot of looking. Logically speaking, the longer it takes anyone to find a bigfoot, a body, or a set of bones, the less likely it is that such a creature exists to be found. To some scientists, it seems silly to continue looking.

Scientists are also kind of clubby. They follow one another's work, share information, compete, and collaborate to push the frontiers of what is known and understood. If you're a scientist who believes something different from the mainstream, it can harm your reputation in the same way eating something really different for lunch at school might (say, freshly cooked tarantula seasoned with salt, sugar, and a whiff of garlic, which is apparently delicious, like soft-shelled crab).

Not every scientist has been scared off of the pursuit of bigfoot, though. When a body print called the Skookum Cast was found, the renowned chimpanzee expert Jane Goodall said it was worth studying. She surprised a lot of people when she told a National Public Radio inter-

Jane Goodall, chimp expert.

viewer she was certain large undiscovered primates like yeti and sasquatch exist.

"I've talked to so many Native Americans who've all described the same sounds—two who have seen them," she said in the September 27, 2002 interview.

She later seemed to backpedal just a bit in a *National Geographic* interview, where she said, "I'm fascinated and would actually love them to exist."

Some scientists, however, have done even more than hope for bigfoot.

Grover Krantz

Back in the 1960s, when people got a little wild and when the University of California at Berkeley was a wilder spot than most, one student stood out for being perhaps the wildest of them all. His name was Grover Krantz and he became a campus legend for holding parties that lasted all night—and all the next day.

In addition to the parties, he was also known

for having smart conversations and unusual ideas. One of his hobbies growing up was collecting the skeletons of animals. In college, he wrote a paper about the small differences between coyote and dog bones. Despite all the partying, he did graduate and got a master's degree at Berkeley, but an argument with a professor stopped him short of getting his doctorate. He later finished that at the University of Minnesota, with a PhD dissertation titled "The Origin of Man."

It must have been fun watching Krantz work. For one experiment, he wore a fake eyebrow ridge for six months so he could figure out what the structure did for *Homo erectus,* an extinct species of upright-walking hominid that lived from 1.8 million to 300,000 years ago, spreading from Africa to Spain, Georgia, India, China, and Java.

He became a professor at Washington State University, where he taught and studied evolution, with a special focus on skeletons. He published books and articles that focused on the anatomy of bigfoots based on tracks, making observations about things that separated bigfoot prints and tracks from human ones.

For example, he did not believe there was any evidence bigfoot had opposable thumbs, which would mean they also lack something called a thenar pad. On your hand, that's the fleshy part at the base of your thumb.

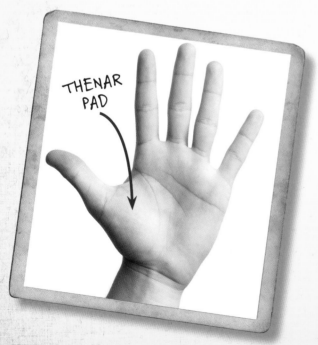

THENAR PAD

He also thought sasquatch feet and human feet were differently proportioned. Sasquatch toes are all one length. Their feet are flat with a long heel and relatively short forefoot. And the balls of their feet appear in some prints to be split in two. He was the first scientist to establish this with tracks, his fans say. He also noted skin ridges, sort of like fingerprints, on some tracks. Called "dermatoglyphs," these were different from the prints of humans and other animals.

He definitely got people's attention. With certain tracks, other researchers agreed there was something notable. A set of tracks in the snow called the Cripplefoot tracks had been made by a creature that could spread its toes, according to a professor at the University of Groningen. And a fingerprint expert at Scotland Yard said the prints were "probably real." Krantz also gave his expert opinion on the authenticity of important bigfoot evidence, such as the Patterson-Gimlin film and the Skookum body print.

Krantz was protective of his research. According to the book *Bigfoot: The Life and Times of a Legend* by Joshua Blu Buhs, Krantz wrote notes in code and had a couple of secret methods he believed allowed him to separate authentic footprints from the hoaxes, although apparently one determined hoaxer in 1996 made a fake that fooled him by pouring mud into a box of cat litter, shaping a print, and marking it to look like it had toenails and scars. After Krantz said it was the real thing, the construction worker revealed his fakery. Instead of admitting he was fooled, Krantz tried to argue that the construction worker was only pretending it was fake so he could later embarrass Krantz by saying it was real—not a very likely scenario.

Krantz believed that bigfoot was a surviving Gigantopithecus and even proposed a scientific name for the creature, *Gigantopithecus blacki*, although that was rejected because there was no actual body to study. (He didn't give up, trying again with another name and a research paper published on naming a creature using footprint evidence. Both were rejected.)

After Krantz died from pancreatic cancer on Valentine's Day in 2002, he began his last lessons for students. He donated his body to the University of Tennessee's "body farm." Scientists there study how quickly bodies decompose, which is useful for people investigating suspicious deaths (you can work backward to figure out when a person might have died based on the state of the body).

Then, in 2003, his bones were sent to the Smithsonian—the same place he sent the bones of his giant dog, a beloved Irish wolfhound named Clyde. They're on display there together.

Carleton Coon

Carleton Coon was an anthropologist who taught at Ivy League universities. Although he specialized in prehistoric farming communities as well as contemporary tribal societies, he had a keen interest in wild men and he had some ideas about what they might be—intelligent primates living in secret in remote lands.

In an essay called "Why There Has to Be a Sasquatch," he wrote:

It is easier to say what they are not than what they are. They are not Neanderthals. Neanderthals had beaky noses and brains bigger than those of most men alive today. They had fire and flaked sophisticated tools. They were not dropped out of flying saucers. It is unlikely that they are the unaltered descendants of our ancestors. They are fellow primates. They are smarter than we are in the sense that they can live without modern inventions, in apparently every climate, even deserts, if the latter are within walking distance of mountains and water. It is less costly and easier to find out what they are than it is to dig up our fossil ancestors, and possibly theirs, in lands now torn by war and seething with newfound national pride. If we don't destroy the atmosphere, it may be they who have the better chance to survive, if it is true that the meek shall inherit the earth.

John Napier

John Napier was the director of the Primate Biology Program at the Smithsonian Institution in Washington, D.C. He wrote a book called *Bigfoot, The Yeti and Sasquatch in Myth and Reality*, and was one of the rare mainstream scientists who took the time to consider evidence of bigfoot. He believed it was reasonable to devote a small amount of the money spent on scientific research toward unsolvable, outrageous, and offbeat topics.

This didn't make him a believer by any stretch, but he was at least willing to investigate, and he weighed in on some of the biggest bigfoot findings of the twentieth century.

He was one of the people who helped debunk the Minnesota Iceman of 1969 (see Chapter 9), and described how, early on, he was legitimately excited to see this find.

"In those early days this seemed a very exciting prospect," he said. "I drafted a rather pompous press release indicating that although the Institution was somewhat skeptical, it was open-minded enough to cooperate fully in the investigation."

He also reviewed the Patterson-Gimlin film, which he thought was probably a hoax. But he believed that indirect evidence of bigfoot, especially footprints, held enough interest that sasquatch couldn't be dismissed outright.

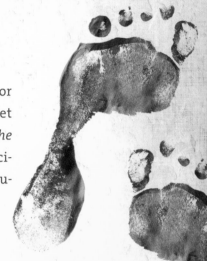

Roderick Sprague

Roderick Sprague was an anthropologist at the University of Idaho and editor of *Northwest Anthropological Research Notes*, the rare scholarly journal that let people submit articles about sasquatch. With Grover Krantz, he also edited *The Scientist Looks at Sasquatch*, a two-volume collection of articles written by scientists about various aspects of bigfoot research, including how you can calculate their weight from a footprint.

Jeffrey Meldrum

Jeffrey Meldrum is the academic heir to Gordon Krantz. A professor of anatomy and anthropology at Idaho State University, he's a tireless and creative researcher who believes that the evidence gathered to date about bigfoot demands scientists to keep pursuing the truth—even if it's unpopular.

He was eleven years old when he first saw the Patterson-Gimlin film, a subject he covered thoughtfully in his book, *Sasquatch: Legend Meets Science*. He also has a huge collection of footprint casts (more than two hundred), some of which look like hoaxes, but others that show all sorts of things that convince him they're real: musculature, skin impressions, and even "pressure ridges" caused by sasquatch's flexible foot bending in the middle.

Although his fellow scientists aren't jumping on the bigfoot bandwagon, they respect his expertise and dedication.

"He does bring more scientific rigor to this question than anyone else in the past, and he does do state-of-the-art footprint analysis," David R. Begun, a paleoanthropologist at the University of Toronto, told *Scientific American* magazine in 2007.

Meldrum also edits *The Relict Hominoid Inquiry*, a free online journal that publishes papers about possible relict hominoids—ancient forms of humans believed still to be alive and undiscovered. The papers are peer reviewed, which means other scientists have looked at them and determined they are responsible scholarship. (You can read it online here: www.isu.edu/rhi)

John Bindernagel

Since 1963, John Bindernagel, a PhD scientist, has been searching for bigfoot. In 1998, he wrote *North America's Great Ape: The Sasquatch*. He has collected tracks and heard alleged sasquatch sounds that reminded him of a chimpanzee's whoop.

Chapter Six
READY, SET, SQUATCH!

PREPARING FOR YOUR OWN
BIGFOOT EXPEDITION

So you've decided to set out and find bigfoot for yourself. This puts you in excellent company. Smart, adventurous people from around the world have been seeking proof of bigfoot for ages, turning up all sorts of tantalizing and fascinating clues in the woods, in swamps, and atop the world's highest mountains. Over the years they've cataloged footprints, hair samples, and handprints. They've stolen bones, studied curiously mangled deer, and pored over audio recordings of mysterious shrieking animals.

What hasn't been found, though, is definitive proof: a bigfoot skeleton or a living specimen.

But that doesn't mean *you* won't be the one to make history. The famous French biologist Baron Georges Cuvier was completely wrong in 1852 when he said, "There is little hope of discovering new species" of large animals. At that time, Westerners thought gorillas were mythical creatures. We know today these species are as real as peanut butter sandwiches, a food bigfoot would probably like, given the creature's apparent fondness for peanut butter. (Various bigfoot researchers have left peanut butter products and entire jars of the spread as bait, according to Matt

Moneymaker. One bigfoot seeker even left out a Zagnut bar and it disappeared at the same time a thermal camera recorded a sasquatch-shaped figure swiping the treat from a stump, much to the excitement of bigfoot fans. Could Zagnut be a sasquatch's favorite candy bar? Maybe!)

At any rate, new species are discovered all the time—maybe even someday by you.

If you are going to find a bigfoot, you have to be smart about it. You have to know what to bring, where to look, and how to gather your evidence. Also? Getting a parent's approval is essential. But don't worry. We've got you covered.

WHERE TO LOOK

In each place there have been bigfoot sightings, the elusive creature is called something different: sasquatch, yeti, skunk ape, yowie. No matter what the giant primate is called, though, there have been sightings around the world.

Your best bet for spotting your own sasquatch might be someplace close to home. For sure, your parents are more likely to go for that as your next family trip instead of, say, Indonesia or Nepal. It's a good idea for a first-time bigfooter to be practical and get some experience before heading off to the world's most remote and exotic places.

Here's a chart of bigfoot hotspots in the United States. Which one is closest to your home?

STATE	SIGHTINGS	MOST RECENT	LAST POSTED
Washington	554	Feb-13	Nov-12
California	426	Aug-12	Oct-10
Florida	236	Feb-13	Dec-12
Oregon	232	Nov-12	Aug-12
Ohio	230	Feb-13	Aug-11
Illinois	210	Feb-13	Dec-12
Texas	193	Sep-12	Nov-11
Michigan	164	Feb-13	Nov-12
Colorado	113	Feb-13	May-12
Georgia	109	Feb-13	May-12
Missouri	102	Dec-12	Sep-12
New York	101	Jul-11	Sep-10
Pennsylvania	100	Oct-12	Mar-12
Kentucky	90	Jan-13	Nov-12
Oklahoma	86	Nov-12	Apr-12
Tennessee	85	Jan-12	Oct-11
West Virginia	85	Jan-13	Nov-12
Arkansas	82	Jan-13	Sep-12
North Carolina	79	Mar-12	Jan-12
Indiana	73	Jul-12	Jul-11
Arizona	71	Feb-13	Oct-12
Idaho	67	Jul-11	Nov-09
Utah	67	May-12	Dec-08
Alabama	65	Jun-12	Apr-11
Wisconsin	64	Feb-13	Sep-13

STATE	SIGHTINGS	MOST RECENT	LAST POSTED
Iowa	61	Jan-13	Oct-12
Minnesota	55	Oct-12	Aug-11
Virginia	53	Jan-13	Oct-12
South Carolina	51	Nov-11	Feb-12
New Jersey	46	Aug-10	Jul-10
Louisiana	40	Apr-11	Feb-10
New Mexico	40	Oct-11	Jan-12
Montana	38	Feb-13	Nov-12
Kansas	36	Feb-13	Jun-12
Maryland	32	Dec-12	May-11
Wyoming	28	May-10	Mar-10
Alaska	23	Aug-10	Jan-13
Mississippi	21	Sep-12	Oct-10
Massachusetts	19	Apr-12	Mar-12
South Dakota	17	Aug-11	Jun-08
Nebraska	14	Jun-11	Aug-08
Maine	13	Mar-04	Feb-04
New Hampshire	10	Nov-09	Jun-09
Connecticut	8	Jul-09	May-09
Nevada	8	Apr-09	Feb-05
North Dakota	6	Dec-10	Aug-05
Vermont	6	Jan-06	Oct-05
Rhode Island	5	Dec-11	Nov-11
Delaware	3	Dec-12	Jan-04

TOTAL SIGHTINGS: 4317

GETTING PERMISSION

If you tell your parents, "I'm going to find bigfoot. Smell ya later!" they're likely to grab you by the straps of your backpack and pull you back indoors. This is not because parents exist to stomp your dreams into tiny bits. No, one of their jobs is to keep you safe. Your parents can actually be your best bigfoot-hunting allies. Here's how to get them on your side.

Tell your parents you're interested in studying primate evolution. Almost any word that comes after "studying" is going to fill your parents with glee. But "primate evolution"? That's irresistible. (And in case they ask, *primates* are large mammals, including apes, chimps, and humans. *Evolution* describes the way generations of living things change and grow more complex over time.)

Explain that they don't even need to believe in bigfoot to be fans of the creature. This way, if your parents are skeptics, you can give them a way to rationalize the trip to their curious friends, relatives, and neighbors.

Remind them that hands-on learning is the most effective. Something like this is called "field study." Again, there's that *study* word!

It will be a fun, affordable trip for the whole family. Even if you'd rather go by yourself, forget it. If you're going to be serious about your sasquatch search, you're going to have to cover a lot of ground and this means you need an adult to drive you. But they don't need to worry that this will be a budget buster, because you'll be sleeping in a tent instead of a hotel. Bigfoot doesn't hang out at the Holiday Inn—not even at the complimentary waffle bar.

WHAT **NOT** TO SAY

Bigfoot is mostly nocturnal so we'll have to stay up all night. Break it to them gently later, like when you're already en route to the woods. Tell them to think about all the stars they'll get to see.

Sasquatches are super-strong and can throw heavy objects long distances. Definitely don't quote Bobo Fay, who says, "It's a known fact sasquatches throw rocks. Any sasquatch researcher will agree to that and [sasquatches]'ll do it to protect their feeding areas. We've got over a thousand reports in the BFRO database of rocks being thrown in conjunction with bigfoot activity." Although the *Finding Bigfoot* team and other experts have heard accounts of tire-size logs and basketball-size rocks being launched at people, there aren't a lot of reports of people being injured this way, so you can keep this tidbit to yourself. Likewise, there is no need to mention that bigfoots like brushing up against tents, behavior often reported by people who claim to have encountered bigfoots, including members of the *Finding Bigfoot* team. Information like this will just scare your poor parents.

Sasquatches are more likely to approach women, who are smaller and therefore less threatening, according to members of the *Finding Bigfoot* team, which in the past has had their resident skeptic, Ranae Holland, raise a ruckus in the hopes a sasquatch would show its face (it didn't work, but then again, Ranae is six feet tall and in great physical shape). Anything that suggests your mom is the most likely to have an encounter will flip her wig, and not in a good way. Didn't we already tell you not to freak out your parents?

Bigfoot poop can be huge. According to the BFRO, a potential sample spotted in Florida's Rock Springs State Park contained segments that were up to eleven inches long. Yes, it is a fascinating thing to note. But it's the sort that tends to cancel out all the positive effects of the word *study*.

PACKING YOUR GEAR

Expert hikers recommend a list of ten things you should have with you when you venture into the wilderness. Even if you aren't planning to be out overnight, you should always have this gear with you in the woods because you never know what might happen. Here's what you need for any outdoor adventure, in addition to sturdy shoes and weather-appropriate clothes:

☐ 1. navigation device (map and compass or GPS)

☐ 2. sun protection (sunglasses and sunscreen)

☐ 3. extra clothes

☐ 4. a headlamp and/or flashlight

☐ 5. first-aid supplies (also bug repellant and bear spray)

☐ 6. stuff to make fire (waterproof matches/lighter/candles)

☐ 7. tools—a Swiss Army knife, duct tape, a whistle, walkie-talkies

☐ 8. extra food

☐ 9. extra water

☐ 10. a tent or tarp

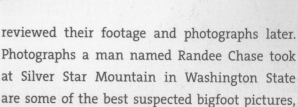

There's also special gear you'll need just for your bigfoot expedition.

At the top of the list? **A camera.** Few of the thousands of bigfoot sightings in the United States were made by people equipped with one. If you don't own one, see if you can borrow one. Your school might even have one you can check out with permission from a science teacher or librarian.

Not only can you use the camera—still and video are good—to capture photographic evidence of a bigfoot, you can also record the terrain for review, just in case you missed something the first time around. What's more, some of the most famous images and videos were shot accidentally. The people who captured them didn't know what they had until they reviewed their footage and photographs later. Photographs a man named Randee Chase took at Silver Star Mountain in Washington State are some of the best suspected bigfoot pictures, and they were pretty much shot by accident.

Many bigfooters prefer video cameras because they can record the creature's howls, moans, rock taps, and other sounds they're known to make. If you capture footage, experts can also use it to stage reenactments and better understand the nature of what you caught on your video.

What else belongs in your bigfoot expedition kit? All sorts of things you can use to gather evidence, including samples of hair, footprints, and even poop.

Dental Stone, Hydrocal, or similar material to take casts of footprints. Plaster of Paris works too, but the experts like Dental Stone better because it's harder.

A bowl. This is to mix the plaster and water in.

A magnifying glass. This you can use to examine small things, such as hair samples.

Tweezers. Use these to pick up the hair.

Plastic bags in several sizes. Use these to store hair and other evidence.

Latex gloves. More than one pair, please. Remember . . . you might be gathering poop, known to researchers as "scat."

A tape measure. Use this to measure the length of tracks you find, the distance between them, and the height of twisted-off branches that might be signs of passing bigfoots.

Binoculars. If you see a possible bigfoot in the distance, these will come in handy.

A field journal. Any notebook you can hold in your hand will do. It's probably best to have one that you use just for bigfoot expeditions, so it doesn't get cluttered with other things. You can use the notebook to record all sorts of observations: what you saw, what you heard, and what you smelled (Bigfoot is said to stink to high heaven. For more on bigfoot body odor and what might cause it, check out Chapter 8). It's also important to write down *when* you had these observations. Take notes about other animals you observed and even things you didn't see that you expected to, just to have a well-rounded record.

A "scale item." When you take a picture of a bigfoot track, put something next to it for scale. The mountain climber Eric Shipton used his ax. You could use a can of soda or something else that can be measured and gives a later viewer a quick idea of the track's size. (But don't forget to take measurements and make a cast.)

Why study SCAT?

Poop is gross, but it's also a treasure trove of information that reveals what a creature eats and whether it's in good health. Bigfoots are omnivores, which means they eat meat and plants. You might find seeds, plant parts, or even hair and bones in its droppings. Likewise, if you find the droppings of animals bigfoots are believed to eat (such as deer), then you know a food supply exists that makes it possible for the area to support a sasquatch.

Some extra-fancy things you can bring if you're an extra-fancy person

Illuminated pushpins. If you're tracking bigfoot at night, you can mark your route with thumbtacks that light up.

A parabolic listening device. This is spy gear—it's a shallow bowl, sort of like a miniature TV satellite dish with a microphone attached. (You can make one yourself. A couple of Web sites tell you how. Use the keywords "parabolic listening device instructions.")

A GPS device. You can use it to mark your route and record the exact location of evidence you gather and see.

Night-vision goggles. Think of how handy these would be on Halloween, too.

This is what peering through night-vision goggles looks like.

The Finding Bigfoot crew . . . in thermal vision!

Professional equipment serious sasquatch hunters use

Thermal cameras: These are sensitive to body heat given off by living creatures. Experts look at the shape of the readings and determine the animal it most likely belongs to.

Trail cameras: These can detect motion and photograph passing animals.

Drone planes: These unmanned flying devices are equipped with cameras and can travel to areas too remote for humans.

Bobby Greffrath was driving in the Catskills when he saw something lying in the road: a grocery bag, and from the looks of it, there was a box of cereal inside. He swerved to avoid it . . . and then something darted behind his car.

He glanced in his rearview mirror and saw a massive, hairy thing.

"So I keep driving," he said, "and as I turned the corner there's something—an over-seven-foot-tall creature walking on two feet right on the side of the road."

The creature stepped behind a tree and darted into some tall grass. Bobby was dumbfounded and acutely aware that he was the only human around.

"I didn't know what to make of it," he said. "I've never seen something like that walk on two feet before. I was alone, and I just didn't know what to do."

The *Finding Bigfoot* team's verdict: a squatch sighting.

WHAT to LOOK FOR:
TELLTALE SASQUATCH SIGNS

While it would be great fun to stroll through the woods and happen upon a bigfoot napping in a glade of ferns, that's not exactly likely to happen. Think of yourself as a detective hunting for clues big and small.

FOOTPRINTS: They call the creature bigfoot for a reason. The best footprints can be found in muddy areas, so keep your eyes peeled. A study of more than seven hundred prints by Dr. W. Henner Fahrenbach, PhD, showed the average length is just over fifteen inches. Footprints are very important clues, too. Researchers can tell all sorts of things about animals by the prints they leave behind, not only how big they are, but also whether they walk upright—and sometimes even what they eat.

NESTS: These aren't just for the birds. Large primates such as gorillas make nests, and bigfoot is believed to do the same. Look for sticks and branches that have been twisted off and arranged into clumps. Some believe bigfoots dig holes and conceal them with branches, as well. The nests are said to be smelly.

HAIR SAMPLES: Bigfoot sheds, and these hairs are some of the best evidence a field researcher can gather, because scientists who study genetics can test them. Sometimes, this is disappointing. In 2005, for example, hair samples gathered in Canada turned out to have come from a bison. But other samples haven't been matched to any known animal. Intriguing! Bobo Fay says utility poles are a great place to look for evidence because animals use them as scratching posts.

SCAT:
Not only are bigfoot droppings super-size, they can potentially be full of all sorts of interesting things, including plants, hair, eggs, and larvae. Although there are no scat samples tied to Bigfoot with 100 percent certainty, sasquatch hunters leave no stone unturned when it comes to the pursuit. Many have gathered samples of suspicious droppings, which are said to have an "eye-watering" odor, according to an article by a biologist in *Beautiful British Columbia Magazine*.

The BFRO says the droppings can be up to four inches wide and three feet long, and they're shaped like sausages. Witnesses have watched bigfoot do its business, wipe itself, and then lick its hand. So yes, the whole scat business is disgusting. But this is science. It's not for wimps.

BROKEN BRANCHES:
Sasquatches are said to twist branches off, perhaps as trail markers. If you see twisted-off branches, particularly big ones out of reach of human hands, you might have just found a bigfoot path.

EYE SHINE:
At night, bigfoot's eyes are said to reflect light. Look for the shine to be much brighter than human eyes.

Why do some animals' eyes GLOW at night?

Some animals have a special reflective surface behind their retinas. This extra inner-eye mirror helps them see better at night. And it's kind of a backup plan. When light hits the eye, it's supposed to hit something called a photoreceptor. But if it misses, this reflective surface—called a *tapetum lucidum*—acts like a mirror. It bounces the light back to the photoreceptor for one more try.

Many animals have tapetum lucida: cats and dogs, deer, cattle, and horses. Humans, apes, squirrels, pigs, kangaroos, and many other primates *don't* have them—even though bigfoot is said to, according to many eyewitness accounts, including members of the *Finding Bigfoot* team. If a bigfoot or sasquatch is found, no doubt the presence of a tapetum lucidum in a hominid would be of great interest to scientists.

HOW TO MAKE A CAST

Your best bet at finding a good footprint is to look near soft, damp soil. Just as you do, Bigfoot gets thirsty, so if you can find a river or creek, it's worth looking closely for prints.

When you find one you like, clean it up a bit. Remove any twigs, leaves, or pebbles, but be careful not to mess up the print. Even if you're not sure it's good enough to preserve, err on the side of caution.

"When in doubt, cast it," Cliff Barackman says.

Mix your Hydrocal with water, following the instructions on the package. You'll want to mix slowly so you don't get a lot of bubbles in it. Let it sit a moment until the bubbles stop rising. Then tap the side of the bowl gently, just to make sure you've gotten rid of all of them.

Once your mixture is smooth, pour it gently into the print. Now comes the hard part: waiting. It will take at least thirty minutes, and even then, your print will be very fragile, so wait longer if you can stand it. While you're waiting, you can write field notes or look for more prints nearby, making sure to measure the distance between them if you find a second or third.

Are there power lines nearby?

Don't forget to look for power lines. Sasquatches are often seen around them, Cliff Barackman notes—and with good reason. "Power lines represent one of the few places that sunlight reaches the forest floor, and therefore gives us rise to highly nutritious plants that deer and other herbivores need to survive."

The Sasquatches, in turn, hunt the deer and other herbivores.

WRITING GOOD FIELD NOTES: A GUIDE

There's no such thing as "sloppy copy" in field notes. You're not supposed to rewrite them more legibly at some date in the distant future, when your hand has stopped cramping or when it's stopped raining. Field notes are supposed to be the very document you wrote when you were making your observations. Some field notes have become really famous, like the ones Charles Darwin took on his voyage to the Galapagos Islands. If you spot a bigfoot, your notes will be *invaluable*, which means they will be worth so much money no one can put a price tag on them.

Also, take your time to make your handwriting legible, or you might be very sad when you look at your notes a few weeks later and can't figure out what you were writing about. One expert tip: Write your notes *before* you collect your sample. That way, you aren't trying to juggle your notepad and a giant sack of bigfoot evidence.

FIVE THINGS TO INCLUDE IN EVERY ENTRY

Number each sample separately. Write the number in the notebook and on your plastic bag. Sharpie works best for this, but it will stain your clothes, so be careful and put the cap on tightly.

Describe the sample. What does it look like? What does it smell like? How big is it?

Identify where you found it. The more accurate you can be, the better. This is where a GPS device can be very handy.

Describe your surroundings. Are you by a river? Surrounded by trees? On a mountain slope? What kinds of plants are growing nearby? You can shoot a photo or video to accompany your description.

You should also note the date, time, location (with GPS coordinates if you have them), the weather, and the names of the people you're with.

Sample #17: Three possible sasquatch hairs. All medium brown, approximately three inches long, one of which is covered in mud or possible scat. Found on a telephone pole in Bluff Creek area of Humboldt Forest. Telephone pole was next to a stand of mixed vegetation, including Redwoods and ferns.

Date: April 28, 2013

Time found: 3:47 p.m.

Witnesses: Corey, Sean, and Rick

GPS Coordinates: 32.8400° N, 117.2769° W

SPOTTED!
An "In Tents" Experience

Robert Boyd and his girlfriend had found the perfect campsite off a trail in New York's gently sloping, thickly wooded Catskill Mountains. He'd just pitched his tent when the footsteps began: distinctive, heavy thuds that stopped just out of the range of his vision.

He ducked inside the tent and something started throwing objects, first on one side of the tent, then on another. It got scarier from there.

"Next thing I know, the tent is being pushed in," he said. The pushing motion was down and sideways, a common pattern, according to Cliff Barackman.

What's more, Robert said, someone—or something—on two legs was doing it. There's "no, no way" it was a four-legged creature, or quadruped.

The footsteps "were loud. They sounded heavy. They sounded very deliberate . . . definitely bipedal." And they were louder than Cliff's reenactments.

Even though Robert didn't see a sasquatch that night as he was huddled in his tent, all signs point to the presence of one, Cliff said. "Most of the time, people don't see them."

IF YOU SEE BIGFOOT

Stay calm! As Bobo Fay puts it, "Don't point at it, you don't run at it . . . just . . . film it."

As you record your sighting with your camera, take care not to make a lot of noise that would spook the sasquatch. If it sees you back, don't look straight at its eyes, because this is the sort of thing that animals perceive as a challenge. Just stay calm and quiet, and move slowly. You might even sit down and pretend to eat a snack or pick fleas out of your pelt. Don't even think about running. The bigfoot is probably extremely fast and has a longer stride than you, which means it can cover more ground more quickly.

Afterward, once you are in a safe location, fill out your field guide with everything you can remember, and then report the sighting to the Bigfoot Field Researchers Organization.

WHEN YOU GET HOME

If you got really lucky and saw a bigfoot or found evidence, hurrah! If you didn't make a sighting, don't feel bad. Even bigfoot researchers who have been at this for decades don't always hit the jackpot. But what separates you from almost everyone else in the world is that you tried. If you have evidence such as hair samples or footprint casts, you can share these with your fellow bigfooters. Save all your research. And as soon as you feel ready for more adventure, you can try again.

Persistence is everything. "There's no more important trait to a bigfooter than perseverance," Cliff Barackman says, "because skill comes with perseverance."

THREE
SASQUATCH SIGHTINGS

"This is getting creepy"

Troy, North Carolina, is a small town with a big legend: that its streets are paved with gold. It's kind of true—the fill dirt used beneath the pavement came from a gold mine, and a few sharp-eyed sorts have found nuggets. Since 1978, though, another kind of hunt has become even more thrilling.

Everything changed for this little hamlet on the edge of the Uwharrie National Forest in 1978, when Bigfoot sightings began in a flurry. Soon, locals were obsessed with the creature that seemed to be secretly living alongside them, sparking all sorts of speculation and gossip. "What could it be?" people wondered.

Kevin Green doesn't wonder what the mystery creature is. He's convinced it's a sasquatch—and one that guards its turf jealously.

The night Kevin saw a bigfoot, he and his buddies were camping. They'd just lit a crackling fire and were making their dinner when the first of a volley of rocks was launched from the woods.

"We tried to ignore it," he said. This proved impossible. "The rocks were just pelting, like flying through the air, at us."

They were like baseballs, he said, and all through the night, the rocks kept coming. His friend Brad was sleeping when one struck the tent's wall. It was unsettling, to say the least.

"I remember he said, 'One just hit my tent. This is getting creepy. I want to go home.'"

It got scarier from there as they heard a low growl coming from the direction of the rocks. Now, Kevin is left with the unforgettable impression he'd been trespassing in bigfoot's habitat, upsetting the creature. "They were just like mad at us for getting in their way," he said.

"They see these eyes, and they have a different glow"

Central Oregon is a place of spectacular beauty: farmland, former logging towns, mossy woods, and rolling mountains. It's also the heart of Bigfoot country in the Pacific Northwest. Since 1950, Oregon has been home to almost 1,300 bigfoot sightings, many of which are concentrated within the Willamette Valley. The Willamette National Forest consists of more than one and a half million acres of pristine woodlands, run through with 1,500 miles of rivers, lakes, and streams that can support a great deal of wildlife.

Rusty Carroll and Brady Berglund were fishing in central Oregon's Molalla River when someone hurled a rock at them. Then the screaming started.

"We hear two . . . screams coming in from the opposite direction," Rusty said.

Their pal Nolan, who was fishing with them that evening, held up a light and slowly scanned the banks of the river.

"Hey, guys," he said. "Look at this."

The trio saw a pair of glowing, amber-colored eyes glide slowly behind a tree on the opposite riverbank. The mysterious eyes were the most amazing hue.

"I've never really seen anything that color," Brady said. "It's tough to explain." What's more, the eyes were large, round, and spaced far apart. "It looked like it was floating almost, the way those eyes moved through the woods."

They took pictures. When they went back the next day to take a cast of the footprint, they found another and measured the animal's stride with a piece of fishing line: a whopping fifty-three inches. Given the smooth gait of the creature they saw, this could only have been made by an animal with extremely long legs (a shorter creature taking such big steps would have lurched up and down more). The friends felt sure they'd seen a bigfoot.

But they weren't quite right. It wasn't *one* sasquatch they encountered that night on the riverbank, the *Finding Bigfoot* team believes. It was two—the screams they heard were from the other, calling out to its hairy companion in the darkness.

A giant at the edge of the cemetery

Ryan Harris's family lives near a cemetery in Washington State. He patrols the edge of his family's land quite a bit, looking for animals as well as vandals and thieves. That's what he was doing one night when he noticed something on the right-hand side of the road. It didn't look quite right, so he stopped his car and flicked on the high-beam headlights.

"I watched just for a few seconds and it seemed to move a little bit," he said. "And the next thing I know, it takes a step into the road— one step halfway across the road, next step it was off in the brush on the left-hand side of the road."

This creature that could cross a road in two strides was bipedal. It had grayish-brown, matted fur. It was probably seven feet tall. And in all Ryan's years of patrols, he'd never seen anything like it.

"I've seen every animal there is to see in these woods," he said. "I've seen bear. I've seen cougar. Nothing has ever given me the feeling that this gave me."

It made the hairs on the back of his neck stand up. His body shook. His heart raced. He was afraid—overwhelmingly so.

"As soon as I got my composure back I, I went through in my head many times, *What did I just see?*" he said. "I know that it stood on two legs, and was larger than myself, and walked across the road in two steps."

Could it be a prankster in a sasquatch suit? He doubts it. Why would an extraordinarily large human dress up at nine thirty or ten o'clock at night and goof around on the edge of Ryan's property? And there was no way a human could cross a road that wide in just two steps, he said. (When Bobo reenacted it on behalf of the *Finding Bigfoot* team, it took him three, and he was really trying.)

"There's not in my mind any way that a human could possibly do that," Ryan said. "It was definitely not, in my mind, a human."

Chapter Seven
BIGFOOT SPOTTED

BIGGEST HOTSPOTS IN NORTH AMERICA

People used to keep track of all the bigfoot sightings by hand. Now, though, we can use computers and databases to get a better idea of where a bigfoot is most likely to be found. The best of these is the one kept by the Bigfoot Field Research Organization, which keeps records of sightings in the United States and Canada. If you see one, you can go online and report it using their form. A volunteer might even contact you for more information.

The database has more than 4,300 sightings in the United States, and nearly 300 in Canada. Some states and provinces report more sightings than others.

THE TOP TEN STATES FOR BIGFOOT

Where are you most likely to see bigfoot? Based on a percentage of overall sightings, these ten states have had more sightings than any others.

Washington: almost 13 percent of bigfoot sightings occur here
California: almost 10 percent of bigfoot sightings occur here
Florida: about 5.5 percent of bigfoot sightings occur here
Oregon: about 5.4 percent of bigfoot sightings occur here
Ohio: about 5.3 percent of bigfoot sightings occur here
Illinois: about 5 percent of bigfoot sightings occur here
Texas: about 4.5 percent of bigfoot sightings occur here
Michigan: about 4 percent of bigfoot sightings occur here
Colorado: about 2.6 percent of bigfoot sightings occur here
Georgia: about 2.6 percent of bigfoot sightings occur here

The numbers change a little when you factor in how populated the state is. For example, Oregon, which has fewer residents than Florida and Ohio, has more bigfoot sightings per capita, so it moves up the list. Here's how many sightings these top ten states have had per 100,000 residents. The higher the ratio of sightings to population, the more likely *you* are to have your own. (We rounded these numbers just a bit to keep them manageable.)

Washington: 8 per 100,000 residents

Oregon: 6 per 100,000 residents

Wyoming: 5 per 100,000 residents

West Virginia: 4.5 per 100,000 residents

Idaho: 4.2 per 100,000 residents

Montana: 3.8 per 100,000 residents

Alaska: 3.2 per 100,000 residents

Arkansas: 2.8 per 100,000 residents

Utah: 2.4 per 100,000 residents

Oklahoma: 2.2 per 100,000 residents

THE FIVE **WORST** AREAS FOR BIGFOOT SIGHTINGS

If you *don't* want to see a bigfoot, you might travel to Vermont, Rhode Island, or Delaware. Sightings are so rare in those states that they represent less than one-tenth of a percentage of the total reports. In fact, Delaware might have to update its official state slogan from "We're first!" to "We're third-to-last . . . in bigfoot sightings!"

You are even less likely to see bigfoot in Washington, D.C.—which makes sense because a sasquatch wouldn't be caught dead in a suit and tie. There have been zero sightings in the nation's capital. Likewise, no bigfoots have been seen in Hawaii. It actually might seem worrisome if they have, because how would a bigfoot have traveled from the mainland to the islands, which have never been connected to the continental United States or Asia by a land bridge?

IN CANADA

If you want to see a sasquatch up north, the best place to be is in British Columbia—just north of the Washington State border. Quebec, on the other hand, is *not* the place to see a sasquatch. Here's how it breaks down by province:

British Columbia: about 44 percent of sasquatch sightings
Ontario: about 24 percent of sightings
Alberta: about 13 percent of sightings
Manitoba: about 11 percent of sightings

From there, sasquatch sightings **REALLY** drop off:

New Brunswick: about 2 percent
Saskatchewan: about 2 percent
Yukon: less than 2 percent
Quebec: less than 2 percent

Less than **2%**

44% **13%** **2%** **11%**

24%

Less than **2%**

2%

Certain provinces and territories— Newfoundland and Labrador, Prince Edward Island, Nova Scotia, Nunavut, and the Northwest Territories—reported no sightings at all.

TYPES OF SIGHTINGS

There are three types of bigfoot sightings in the Bigfoot Field Researchers Organization database: Class A, Class B, and Class C.

But these aren't like school grades. A sighting doesn't get an A for being interesting, or if the person who saw it seems like he or she is definitely telling the truth. Rather, it has to do with how certain we can be that the sighting was of bigfoot and not something else.

Class A: This is the most certain type of sighting. If a witness got a clear look at a bigfoot and can rule out any other animal, or if there are well-documented footprints that can't be attributed to any other animal, then squatch hunters consider this a Class A sighting.

It doesn't have to be in person. The Jacobs Photographs (see Chapter 2), taken by trail camera, show a creature with limbs too long to be a baby bear. Bigfooters have ruled that animal and others out, so the sighting gets the top rating.

Class B: Let's say you were far away, or you had your bigfoot encounter at night. Or let's say you didn't see a bigfoot, but heard vocalizations. This kind of sighting is a Class B, because there's a potential for misidentification.

Experts don't look at Class B reports as less valuable or credible, and sometimes they can be so detailed they're quite compelling. For example, a former police officer took a hunting trip to Mud Spring on South Dubakella Mountain in Trinity County, California, in 1998. He described squatchy sounds in great detail on the BFRO Web site. You might include this level of detail if you ever make a report to the organization:

The whole area was extremely quiet, even in late afternoon/dusk when many animals begin to venture out. I saw only two ravens and a couple blue jays, the entire time I was there. No squirrels, no deer, and no noise.

As many of you know, the forest has solitude but is far from silent.

I had made a small fire that evening. I do not normally make a fire when backpacking, but because I had a fire ring available, a plentiful supply of deadwood, and it had been years since my last trip, I decided to enjoy one.

I turned in at about 2150 hours [9:50 PM], and was asleep within minutes.

At about 2230 hours [10:30 PM] . . . I was awakened by the sound of a large snapping branch. It was not a branch falling, and the branch gave a cracking noise that made it sound like it was a thick branch. Even though my eyes snapped open with the sound, I just lay in my sleeping bag listening. I didn't move.

Then with my head close to the ground resting on my ground pad, I heard it. Not the clop of *hooves or the padding of paws, but the dull, vibrating thud of footsteps! I nearly defecated in my sleeping bag. I was keenly aware of what I was hearing, and I could feel the adrenaline in my veins.*

The footsteps were to the northeast of my tent, when first detected. My hearing was trained in that direction because that is the same direction I heard the branch snap, too. I estimated them to be ten to twenty feet away, judging from the vibration and sound. Two more steps and the thing making them was in front of my tent, about five to ten feet away. Then the footsteps faded to the southwest with two more footsteps.

I was lying there scared to death, thinking about what I was going to do, when all of a sudden, my pots down at the kitchen moved and clanged together! I was not imagining anything now, and knew it was not a dream! I grabbed my headlamp and illuminated my tent, trying to drive off my visitor.

After I waited about two minutes, I looked out my tent and saw nothing. I pulled on my boots and walked to my kitchen area. There I found my nested cookware pots un-nested, and spread out. What ever un-nested those pots had thumbs!

Class C: The final category is for second- and third-hand reports. So if someone told you a story about their sighting, or if it was a "friend of a friend" kind of tale, or even a story with sources that can't be traced, this would count as a Class C report. The BFRO does keep them in their archives but only rarely makes them public unless they happened before 1958, the year the "Bigfoot" name was attached to sightings in the media.

SPOTTED!
Bigfoot Versus the Biker

In 1974, Bud Garcia was out riding his ten-speed bicycle in Rhode Island when he noticed one of his brakes had come loose. He stopped to fix it—and that's when he heard a series of loud footsteps.

"That's where I see it step out," he said, "this white gorilla. And it chased me right down the road."

But before the creature caught him, it pivoted and leapt over a wall and into a thatch of brush and tall grass. Bud spied on the six-foot creature, noting its pointed head, broad shoulders, big arms, and barrel chest.

He thought it was a gorilla, but Matt Moneymaker thinks otherwise. In southern Ohio during the 1980s, there were numerous sightings of a white bigfoot. Likewise in the mountains behind Big Sur, California. And it's probably an old one, he says. After all, elderly bigfoots get gray hair—just like we do.

BIGFOOT TRAP

Why don't people just build a bigfoot trap and catch one already? People have, and what is believed to be the world's first and only bigfoot trap still stands in southern Oregon.

An organization called the North American Wildlife Research Team built the trap in 1974, near a spot where a miner had spied what appeared to be bigfoot tracks in his garden. The trap stands in a fairly remote site in the Rogue River National Forest, near the Oregon-California border, though it can be reached by the Collings Mountain hiking trail.

As traps go, this one's huge—over eight feet tall and roughly ten feet square. Its sides are wood, and on one end a gate of green steel slides down to contain an unlucky sasquatch.

For years, the North American Wildlife Research team baited and monitored the trap. But all they ever caught were bears. Now the trap no longer works and is mostly an item of curiosity for tourists.

GPS INFO FOR THE TRAIL AND TRAP
#943 TRAILHEAD GPS
N 42°03.073' W 123° 07.903'

BIGFOOT TRAP GPS
42.056567, -123.137233

Chapter Eight
THE SCIENCE OF SASQUATCH

It is not uncommon for them to come in the night and give three whistles. Then the stones will begin to hit the houses. The people are troubled with their nocturnal visits.

—A letter from Rev. Elkanah Walker to the American
Board of Commissioners for Foreign Missions, 1840

When it comes to established animals, it's possible to know all sorts of interesting facts about them. For example, an African elephant can be up to eleven feet tall, weigh between 7,000 and 13,200 pounds, and live sixty to seventy years in dense forests and on open plains. They also eat plants and try to avoid humans, their top predator.

When it comes to cryptids, we have to take our best guesses about their behaviors, habitats, diets, and life spans. These aren't blind guesses, though. We use evidence we find, other observations we make, and facts about similar animals to build a reasonable picture.

Here's the best thinking about where bigfoot might live, what the creature might eat, and how it might behave.

Habitat

Although bigfoot sightings have occurred in most states and in many Canadian provinces, most sightings tend to be in remote, forested regions with plenty of sources of protein. They also require sources of water.

Bigfoot is believed to make use of certain human technology, though—power lines in particular. They're not powering their nests, though. They're traveling.

As Matt Moneymaker puts it, "Power lines are significant because sasquatches travel along power line routes. They can walk along them at night. They know they're not gonna run into any people. It's really kind of their highway."

But it's not just that. Where power lines have been built, trees have been removed. This changes the environment in a way that helps bigfoots, Cliff Barackman says. "Power lines represent one of the few places that sunlight reaches the forest floor and therefore gives us rise to highly nutritious plants that deer and other herbivores need to survive. And as it turns out, Sasquatches are hunting the deer and other herbivores."

Diet

Bigfoots are omnivores, which means they eat plants and animals. (See How They Hunt, What They Eat, p. 111.)

Social organization

Unlike gorillas, chimpanzees, and bonobos, which live in groups, a sasquatch is a more solitary creature—possibly like orangutans, which are occasionally seen in groups of two or three when there's enough food to go around. Some bigfooters do believe the creatures live in small family groups. (One famous bigfoot encounter even involved a man named Albert Ostman, who claimed he was kidnapped by a family of bigfoots—a mom, a dad, and two kids.) Bigfooters also believe these nocturnal animals communicate with each other by shrieking, whistling, and knocking tree trunks.

Sasquatches wouldn't be seen in groups like these—they're believed to be more solitary creatures.

SPOTTED!
Father-Son Sasquatch Sighting?

Chris Patterson and his father, Jeff, had followed a trail through a dense, deciduous forest tall enough to block out much of the sun's light. As they stood in the semidarkness, they heard a noise. Jeff switched on his camera.

There, on the embankment just ahead of them, stood a large dark creature.

"It almost seemed like it was looking right directly at me," Jeff said. "And then it reached out and grabbed a tree and he just started pulling on the tree."

They could hear the roots crack, and instinct took over. They were too close to this creature, whatever it was. Jeff reached out, grabbed Chris by the arm, and the two took off.

"This creature was tearing down this tree," Chris said. "I thought we better get out of there in a hurry."

The two feel there's no chance it was a hoaxer in a costume, which fit like real skin. "It was form fitting," Jeff said.

When the *Finding Bigfoot* four visited later, they found the lower half of the tree the animal had torn at. Bobo was able to reenact the tree shaking, which means Chris and his dad couldn't rule out the possibility that it was a human, but the location itself felt like a prime habitat—good enough for the team to investigate further.

BEHAVIOR AROUND HUMANS:
ARE THEY DANGEROUS?

Of all the thousands of sasquatch sightings over the years, there have been hardly any reports of attacks on humans. It's not uncommon for a bigfoot to chuck rocks at people, to make scary sounds, or to brush its hand along tents.

But actual attacks are almost unheard of. There was the incident in Teddy Roosevelt's book where a human was killed. There's an old Native American tale, echoed in a similar early-twentieth-century account, that claims a bigfoot abducted a woman, who later gave birth to a half-bigfoot baby that died shortly afterward.

But in modern times, no sasquatch has been accused of harming a human. Eyewitnesses say the animals retreat when they are spotted—especially when someone shines a bright light.

While they aren't harmful to humans, this isn't the case for animals, though. Wildlife such as deer, elk, raccoons, beavers, ducks, and rodents are on the bigfoot menu. The same goes for livestock. Sasquatches are believed to swipe chickens, rabbits, and pigs when given the chance. And, according to the Bigfoot Field Researchers Organization, aggressive dogs have been found dead and surrounded by bigfoot tracks.

BIGFOOT BY THE NUMBERS:

SIZE: The average height is seven feet, ten inches, according to measurements from eyewitness reports and projections based on footprint length. The biggest bigfoots are believed to be taller than ten feet.

WEIGHT: The average weight is about six hundred fifty pounds, but they might grow to be over a thousand pounds, based on some of the largest footprints.

FOOT LENGTH: Of more than seven hundred footprints collected over a fifty-year period, the average length is fifteen and a half inches. Tiny bigfoot prints as small as four inches have been seen, all the way up to twenty-seven-inch whoppers. The "median" length is sixteen inches. How is this different from the average? It means half of the footprints are longer and half are shorter.

The *Finding Bigfoot* team measuring possible bigfoot strides.

SKIN COLOR: Varied, from black to charcoal to browns and red-browns. It's lighter on their palms and soles.

HAIR COLOR: Generally dark, including black, brown, and reddish. But gray-white hair has been spotted on older bigfoots. Can range from matted to glossy and clean. Females are reportedly cleaner. Hair can range from three inches to two feet long.

"Sasquatches basically look like a combination of human and ape," Cliff Barackman says. But because of their long lives and their low reproductive rate, there are going to be a lot of differences between two different bigfoots, he says—just as there are between two different people.

WHAT DO BIGFOOT BABIES LOOK LIKE?

According to reports gathered by the BFRO, bigfoot babies are something only a mother could love. One eyewitness claims to have seen a small and "ugly" bigfoot baby. Baby bigfoots are believed to be born weighing about four pounds after a gestation period of about nine months.

Young sasquatches are typically born between the months of February and May, grow rapidly, and stay with their mothers until they are about ten years old and six feet tall.

Sometimes, young offspring are found in remote areas with lots of food nearby. "Native Americans have told me on several occasions that sasquatches drop off their juveniles in certain areas I call nurseries," Cliff says. "These nurseries have some things in common, such as an abundance of food and plenty of places to hide."

A BIGFOOT'S BODY: WHAT IT'S LIKE

No one knows for sure what bigfoot's skeleton might look like, but the late bigfoot scholar Grover Krantz thought it might be a relict giant ape named *Gigantopithecus blacki*, the humongous ape that lived in southern China (see Chapter 3 for more on this creature).

Krantz reconstructed a skull based on the partial jawbone that is among the only fossil evidence of this mammoth ape. It shows a big-eyed creature with a ridge of bone running from the front to the back of the skull, otherwise known as a sagittal crest. The creature's mouth and squarish, human-like teeth protrude (but less than an ape's), and its spine runs straight down from the skull, as with other bipedal animals.

Eyewitnesses have told the BFRO the creature has a heavy brow ridge, prominent cheekbones, and a square jaw. Bigfoots also have a flat nose, thin lips, and human-like ears that are usually covered by hair.

Is Bigfoot HAIRY everywhere?

According to the Bigfoot Field Researchers Organization's data, Sasquatches have hair just about everywhere, but the lengths vary. It's long on the head and ears, but short on the face (although some male Bigfoots sport mustaches and beards). Their forearm hair is long. Both males and females have hairy chests, and their private parts are similarly obscured. Their lower legs are like hairy bell-bottoms, and they have hairy butts.

"Bigfoots in general are covered in hair from head to toe, except for maybe the palms of their hands and the soles of their feet, and the tips of their noses," Matt Moneymaker says.

Continuing down the body, bigfoots have powerful neck and back muscles, which is why one might turn its body along with its head to glance over its shoulder (the Patterson-Gimlin film's most famous frame depicts this). Its shoulders are wider than human ones—about 40 percent of its body height, as opposed to 25 to 30 percent that you tend to see in people. Bigfoots don't have great posture. They lean forward about fifteen degrees.

They have big, broad chests. According to some experts, Patty in the Patterson-Gimlin film measures sixty inches around—and she was on the small side. The average sasquatch would measure sixty-five to seventy-five inches around. Male waists are said to taper more than female waists, although female hips are somewhat wider. Neither males nor females tend to have big bellies (except during pregnancy).

Their arms are very long and strong, and their slouch makes them look even longer. Some people report seeing hands hanging down around their knees. Those hands, of course, are also big and broader than human hands, although sasquatch fingers and especially their thumbs appear shorter and lack the thenar pad—that muscle at the base of your thumb. They have fingernails, not claws. Unsurprisingly, they have muscular legs, especially about the calves.

An actual bigfoot skeleton would tell a lot about how the creature came to be bipedal, and whether it followed a similar path to humans, or whether upright walking evolved independently. No bones about it, such a specimen would be a treasure for bigfoot enthusiasts.

A CLOSE-UP OF THE FOOT

If there's any one piece of bigfoot evidence that has excited people for decades, it's the footprint. The famous newspaper picture of Jerry Crew holding a big plaster cast made many people curious.

There's just one thing: How do we know the tracks are real?

It's true that thousands of footprints have been observed, and many have been cast in plaster and meticulously measured. It's also true that many of those reveal fingerprint-like ridges, scarring, and other things that leave some people convinced the tracks are real. For plenty of people, they are the consistent and compelling piece of evidence that makes sasquatch worth studying.

"Something is making those . . . tracks!" is what bigfoot searcher René Dahinden said about them. The search for their source was enough to

drive him to continue looking his whole life, even though it cost him his marriage and he died disappointed.

But there's one thing you can't get around. Without a bigfoot to use for comparisons and measurement, we don't know for sure what a bigfoot track looks like. There's just no way to avoid the fact that we're *assuming* these giant footprints that have been found all around the world are, in fact, bigfoot tracks. It is, after all, one possible explanation for them. The other is that they are all the result of hoaxes.

Of the two explanations, the former—that bigfoot left the tracks—is more persuasive to many people. How and why would so many hoaxers have left tracks? How would they independently create so many similar prints?

No matter what, there are several reasons to

study the tracks. For one thing, it's fun. What's more, it's a great way to learn about anatomy. And it's possible that we can make smart guesses about the rest of bigfoot's body—its size, its weight, the mechanics of its walk—using the footprints and what they reveal.

But there are limits to what the tracks can tell us. We have to remember two things: (1) that as scientific evidence, the tracks alone don't constitute proof that bigfoot is making them; and (2) anything we base on the tracks might not necessarily be correct, so we have to think of size and body projections as the best possible guess instead of as fact.

WHAT SOME OF THE BEST AND MOST FAMOUS TRACKS LOOK LIKE

In 1982, a Grays Harbor, Washington, Sheriff's deputy named Dennis Heryford took five notable casts of a fifteen-inch track. They're two inches wide and six inches deep, and they show features bigfoot seekers admire, including toenails and tendons, as well as dermal ridges and bunions. The tracks were found in clusters by more than one person, and they even had hair samples that Heryford sent to a laboratory for examination. One was found to belong to a human, but another had a "non-human root," and did not "resemble known human or primate hairs on file."

People who study these tracks believe they are evidence of an unknown animal. People who haven't seen the tracks for themselves often dismiss them, in part because hoaxers have been featured in the newspaper holding crudely carved molds they used to make fake tracks.

But many bigfoot tracks don't appear to have been made by a mold. Instead, they show what looks like a foot in motion. The toes are in different positions. The heel imprints are different depths. A partial imprint might indicate the sasquatch was running. Some tracks even show detail of the skin texture—fingerprint-like marks called dermatoglyphs—as well as healed scars.

Not all experts in bipedal walking agree on what the footprints signify. Some are of the mind that there is no bigfoot and all tracks are hoaxes. Others, though, like Professor Jeffrey Meldrum of Idaho State University, have pored over hundreds of tracks and made some fascinating observations about bigfoot feet. In a paper he wrote about alleged sasquatch footprints and how they might affect the creature's walk, he argued the following:

They are *not* enlarged human feet.

If you could put your feet in a magical enlarger and then leave a bunch of tracks on a muddy riverbank, the prints would be big, but not bigfoot prints. Bigfoot and human feet differ in several key ways:

Bigfoot has flat feet.

Human feet tend to have what's called a longitudinal arch. Unless you have flat feet, this means the bottom of your foot has an upward curve that runs from your foot's ball to its heel. You use your toes to push off from the ground when you're walking. Bigfoot feet don't work this way. Instead, a bigfoot foot has a more flexible midtarsal joint. In footprints, this shows up as a ridge across the footprint, created when the exceptionally bendy sasquatch foot presses the soil below it into a ridge.

Some bigfoot tracks have a "double ball."

On the inside of your own footprint, just below the toes, the ball of your foot curves out a bit. On bigfoot, there are sometimes two curves. This doesn't mean bigfoot has extra foot bones, but rather, that its flexible foot creases when it's bent. Bigfoot feet have thick pads of fat on their soles, which form this scallop shape. If you fold your hand in half, you might see the fleshy bit between your thumb and fingers do this same thing.

Bigfoot has long toes.

They're actually long, of course. They're also *relatively* long. In other words, they take up a bigger percentage of the overall foot than human toes do. Although they're longer in this way than human toes, they aren't as long as the toes of early bipedal hominid known as *Australopithecines*.

*He is both spirit and real being,
but he can also glide through the forest,
like a moose with big antlers,
as though the trees weren't there.*

— Oglala Lakota Medicine Man Pete Catches (as told to author Peter Matthiessen in the book *In the Spirit of Crazy Horse*)

"A Creature That Was Immensely Huge"

Chief Little Soldier lives on the Munsee Delaware Indian Reservation in Cambridge, Ohio. He's been aware of strange sights and sounds since 1998—occurrences that remind him of ancient stories told by his people.

He had his first sasquatch encounter when he was putting in trail markers. A branch broke. Something caught his eye.

"I saw a creature that was immensely huge looking back at me," he said. "It took off down the side of the ravine."

He gave chase, but had no hope of catching up with such a swift creature.

Making a sighting didn't scare him, though.

"It gave me a feeling of peace," he said. "It's kind of hard to explain, and it was kind of exciting at the same time."

BIGFOOT: A GRACEFUL CREATURE

Sasquatch has big feet, but it hasn't stopped the creature from moving with stunning grace, according to eyewitnesses. Instead of having bobbing heads, like human beings, they move with surprising smoothness.

As Bobo Fay puts it: "A common observation amongst witnesses when they see one, it looks like it's gliding like it's almost a human on a bicycle. You see the legs moving, but the shoulders and head hold fairly steady."

It might be smooth, but it's not a noiseless walk, according to Cliff Barackman. When a bigfoot roams the woods at night, it stirs up rodents, which attracts owls, he said. This is why bigfoot and owls are often found near each other. (Same with coyotes, who like to dine on sasquatch leftovers.)

It's also less like a human walk than you might think.

"The way a sasquatch walks seems to be very similar to a human being," Cliff explains. "But as it turns out, it's very different." Sasquatch footprints tend to line up in a "tightrope walk . . . one foot in front of the other."

They do this by swinging their leg out to the side and putting it down in front, something you can observe by watching the Patterson-Gimlin film. And instead of locking their knees, bigfoots are believed to keep them bent as they walk, minimizing their upper-body movement. Scientists call this a "compliant gait."

Jeffrey Meldrum, who specializes in the way animals move, has analyzed hundreds of suspected sasquatch footprints, comparing the shapes of the bones and the length of the toes and heels, to understand how bigfoot might walk and how it's different from a human walk.

People stride on stiff legs, striking the heel first and pushing off on the toe. We have relatively short toes that help propel us forward. Our feet are arched and not too flexible, leading to an efficient stride that doesn't tax the muscles too much.

Sasquatches, on the other hand, have flat, flexible feet and toes long enough to grab things. The flexibility of the foot helps propel a sasquatch forward (instead of the toes). From an evolutionary standpoint, it makes sense, Meldrum says.

"This would be an efficient strategy for negotiating the steep, broken terrain of the dense montane forests of the Pacific and Intermountain West, especially for a bipedal hominoid of considerable body mass," he writes in a report evaluating suspected sasquatch footprints and what they tell us about the way these creatures move. "The dynamic signatures of this adaptive pattern of gait are generally evident in the footprints examined in this study."

One thing that's up for debate is whether it's physically possible for humans to walk this way. If it's not, bigfoot-seekers argue, then the Patterson-Gimlin film couldn't possibly be a hoax.

Grover Krantz, the late professor of physical anthropology at Washington State University, said there was no way a person could walk like this. But Ranae Holland and others who've studied the subject disagree.

People can adopt a compliant gait when they aren't allowed to extend their knees or hips all the way as they walk. According to David Daegling, who wrote the book *Bigfoot Exposed*, people walking this way don't bob their hips, shoulders, and heads. And while you'd think you'd walk more slowly doing this, you can actually walk *faster*. The only catch is, it's tiring so you get worn out quickly. He tested this at Yale University, confirming it with a researcher at Duke University who studies the way people walk.

You can try it yourself—it's a walk many kids have been known to use when they are told not to run in the hallways at school. Or it's how you might walk if you were wearing a full diaper. In any case, it's safest to say that people *can* fake at least certain aspects of a bigfoot walk.

What's harder to explain are the eyewitness stories that describe bigfoot crossing a road in two steps, or the footprints that indicate a stride length outside the normal human range, and more within the range that a creature in the seven- to nine-foot range might make.

This is why it's worth it to keep looking, taking excellent care in your field notes to measure the distance between tracks, and to count how many steps it takes any bigfoots you witness to make it from one landmark to the next.

HOW THEY HUNT, WHAT THEY EAT

Unlike gorillas, chimpanzees, orangutans, and bonobos, bigfoots don't inhabit a tropical environment—at least not everywhere there have been sightings. In the mossy woods of the Pacific Northwest, for example, there's not a lot of edible plant matter. Certainly not enough to feed a creature this size.

But that's fine, bigfooters say. Unlike the gorilla, which is believed by most to exist on a great deal of fruit and plant matter, bigfoots are more like chimpanzees, which eat plants and meat.

Deer is a primary food source for the creatures, according to Matt Moneymaker. And bigfoot has a specific way of hunting, something noted by Mennonite farmers in eastern Ohio in the early 1990s. These creatures are believed to immobilize a deer by breaking one of its legs, Moneymaker says. That way, the animal can't run off.

"He breaks the leg and snaps it and twists it to disable it," Moneymaker says, "and then it pulls out the guts, the intestines, and goes after the liver."

This is why the *Finding Bigfoot* team pays special attention to deer carcasses it finds in the woods. If there's one with a foreleg that's been snapped clean and there's no other way to explain the injury, such as

tooth marks on the bone, it's a suspected sasquatch kill.

Depending on where a bigfoot lives, though, it might also eat crayfish, fish, or even duck.

"There's been a few instances that I know of for sure where squatches have come under geese and ducks and will swim under in a pond or a lake, come underneath them and just grab them—just yank them right down," Bobo Fay says.

Bigfoots aren't picky, as you might have guessed from the way they go after deer. They'll go after anything people leave out, including birdseed, cat food, and dog kibble.

Searchers step it up a bit when they're putting out bait. Favorite things to leave are piles of fruit and peanuts. But they'll even put out entire jars of peanut butter. And of course who can forget the bigfoot that is believed to have swiped a Zagnut bar, a candy made from peanut butter and toasted coconut? (See Chapter 5 for more about that incident.)

But that's not all. Bigfoot is believed to have a taste for a certain smoky breakfast staple.

"Bacon is a known squatch attractor," Bobo says. He likes to cook a bit when there's a light breeze going, "just to get the smell out."

Bobo always eats a piece first, to show any quietly observing sasquatches that he isn't out to poison them. Then he throws the rest into the bushes for any passing bigfoots to enjoy. You do have to be careful when you're using bacon bait. Bigfoot isn't the only creature that likes it—bears do, too.

SHARP SENSES

Dian Fossey and Jane Goodall are famous for their work observing gorillas and chimpanzees. These women were anything but overnight successes. In order to get close enough to these apes to study them, they had to track the creatures with great patience for months.

In part, it took this long just to start their research because apes see and hear much better than humans. Hearing is important in the jungle, where plants and vines make it hard to see things that are far away. This fine-tuned sense allowed Fossey's gorillas and Goodall's chimps to detect the scientists long before the scientists detected them—and it's likely that Goodall and Fossey finally got close to the animals once the animals were so accustomed to seeing them that they no longer cared to hide.

Bigfoot experts believe sasquatch hearing is similarly sharp.

"Sasquatches depend on their hearing to know where each other are at any given time," Cliff Barackman says. It's a communication and possibly warning system. "Sasquatches rely mostly on hearing to find if something is nearby, so it was trying to communicate something, possibly that we were there, to another sasquatch."

DO THE EYES HAVE IT?

Whether bigfoot sees in color would be a very interesting thing to determine. Scientists need to study an animal's actual eyes to know whether it can see in color. If an animal's eye has a type of cell called cones, then it should be able to see at least some colors.

Diurnal animals—ones that are awake during the day and asleep at night—tend to be the ones that see in color. Nocturnal primates—animals that are active at night and asleep during the day—don't have as much use for color vision. To understand why this is true, think about how

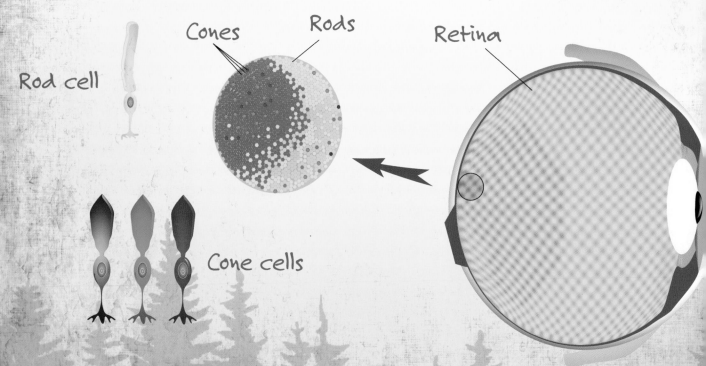

Rod cell

Cones   Rods

Retina

Cone cells

you see at night. Even if there's enough light to see a little bit, it's hard to tell what color things are. Your eyes need relatively bright light to pick out colors.

Humans and apes, which are diurnal, have eyes that allow for "trichromatic" vision. This means we have cones that let us distinguish between red, green, and blue (unless we're color-blind). Owl monkeys, the only truly nocturnal monkey species, have monochromatic. They can only see black and white and the tones in between.

So is bigfoot more like humans and apes, or more like nocturnal monkeys? It's hard to say. In truth, there aren't a lot of nocturnal primates. At best, we can only guess how bigfoot sees. And if the animals truly are nocturnal, chances are, bigfoot's world is black and white (and gray).

WHAT'S THAT SMELL?

According to the BFRO, about 10 to 15 percent of people who encounter bigfoot have been socked by a terrible odor. Gorillas have been known to produce a "fear smell" from certain underarm glands when they are threatened, so it's possible the sasquatch stench is a similar thing.

There's another aspect to smell, though—and that's how strong their sense of it is. Compared with humans, gorillas have a strong sense of smell. If you get sweaty walking through the jungle in search of a gorilla, it can smell you. Likewise, a male gorilla can tell by the smell when a female gorilla is ready to conceive a baby.

If a bigfoot's nose is like the next biggest ape's, chances are its nose knows people are near, which is perhaps why they're so elusive. They smell us coming and hide.

ENEMIES OF BIGFOOT

Bigfoot is an apex predator. This means it eats other animals, and that it doesn't have to worry a lot about being eaten by other animals, although it does share its habitat with bears, cougars, and other apex predators.

Threats to bigfoot are similar to threats to bears, cougars, wolves, and the like: other apex predators, including . . . humans. Although most people interested in bigfoot wouldn't dream of shooting one, there have been cases where people claimed to have done so.

Other dangers are development and environmental degradation, which is why it's important to preserve wild spaces and protect air and water quality in general. And then of course there's old age and disease, which will eventually take bigfoots that manage to survive other animals.

Making bigfoot calls can help lure the beasts out.

IS THEIR LANGUAGE REAL?

People who've had encounters with bigfoots have long reported consistent descriptions of the sounds the creatures make. It's a wide variety of noises, including screeches and howls, whistling sounds, and knocking noises. If you hear these noises when you're out squatching, one of the creatures might be nearby. If you hear another animal, though, it also might be a bigfoot because the animals are good mimics.

"They might imitate an owl. They could imitate a coyote, too. So even if that does sound very much like a coyote, it's possible that it was a bigfoot . . . imitating that to be able to call out to each other, while still trying to kind of mask their identity," Matt Moneymaker says. They do this to confuse whoever is in earshot.

SPOTTED!

A Hairy Go-Round at the Merry-Go-Round

It was 1984, and Lorena Cunningham was with her kids at a playground in Sharon, Ohio. Her children were sick of the swings and had just moved over to the merry-go-round when there was a crashing noise in the woods.

Lorena looked toward the sound. "This big, hairy creature was looking down at me," she said. "I was paralyzed with fright."

The seven- to eight-foot bigfoot she claims she saw experienced no such fear.

"It seemed to be at ease and curious," she said. "It was watching me and watching the children. It seemed to be interested. . . . I could see it looking at us."

Matt Moneymaker thinks Lorena might have seen a female sasquatch in this rare, day-time sighting. The she-squatch was curious about Cunningham's family.

BUT IS IT LANGUAGE?

It's one thing to make sounds. It's another thing to be capable of meaningful speech. Some people believe sasquatches do have their own language, though. One expert in 2010 transcribed what he calls the Sasquatch Phonetic Alphabet.

R. Scott Nelson, the author of this amazing alphabet, worked for many years as a military cryptologic linguist, which means he was responsible for listening to foreign communications (even coded ones), recognizing important signs, translating, and transcribing them. In short, he's an expert in recognizing language—even ones he doesn't speak. When his son was researching Bigfoot sounds for a school project, Nelson overheard a recording of the Sierra Sounds (see page 21) and recognized them as an actual language.

Intrigued, he spent a good deal of time listening to the sounds, observing, among other things, that sasquatches are fast talkers. Their speech flows at twice the rate of any known language.

Nelson devised the phonetic alphabet so listeners would have a consistent way to write down the sounds that are overheard. Eventually, this system might enable us to translate the sounds into language we understand (something he called "the recovery of the sasquatch language").

Nelson has advice if you overhear suspected sasquatch sounds. Record them in your field journal and be sure to keep track of the following:

- how many bigfoots were present;
- how many were talking;
- whether they were talking to each other;
- what their emotional states seemed to be at each point in the conversation; and
- whether anything sounded like a question or a command.

SPOTTED!
A Biologist and a Believer

Nick Maione, a Rhode Island biologist, was trekking through the state forest and working on his tracking skills. As he crawled along some rocks, he heard a snap.

"I looked—I saw a bigfoot. It went right around the corner," he said. "I mustered the courage, and I followed it."

He was close behind, only about one hundred twenty feet away, and he speculated that he'd woken the creature up from a nap, because until that moment, the woods had been silent, as had he.

The walking, bipedal creature made a great deal of noise but did not turn to look at Nick. Nonetheless, he's certain of what he saw.

"I'm a believer," he said. "This was a bigfoot."

DO OTHER ANIMALS HAVE LANGUAGE?

If sasquatch does have language, the creature won't be alone in this. Not only have certain animals learned to speak with humans, researchers believe many animals communicate with each other using languages native to their species.

ANIMALS THAT ARE FAMOUS FOR SPEAKING "HUMAN"

Koko the gorilla understands something like two thousand words in English. She can't speak them because her vocal cords aren't set up that way, but she can reply using some of the thousand American Sign Language gestures she knows. Including her own gorilla tongue, this means Koko knows three languages, which she uses to communicate things as abstract as emotions. (Another gorilla she lived with, Michael, knew six hundred words.) And she's quite a talker. She initiates most conversations with the humans who work with her, and can put together statements made of three to six words.

An African gray parrot named Alex, meanwhile, learned one hundred fifty words. The night before he died at age thirty-one, he told his handler, "You be good. See you tomorrow. I love you." He was also a crack mathematician who could count up to eight and add sums up to six, in addition to being able to put numbers in order from one through eight using labels in English.

THE CHALLENGES IN TRANSLATING "ANIMAL"

Scientists are trying hard to decode the languages used by many species, including dolphins, elephants, wolves, and chimps. It's no easy thing, though. Dolphins, for example, make all sorts of sounds, including clicks and whistles. One theory holds that they use a "sonopictorial" language, which embeds images into sound waves. When the waves bounce off objects, the dolphins understand the images being expressed in sound. Researchers at speakdolphin.com created a device that makes sound waves visible, and found that dolphins could recognize images broadcast 86 percent of the time.

Surprisingly, prairie dog is one language that a retired biology professor from Northern Arizona University has succeeded in cracking. Constantine Slobodchikoff, the professor, has reported that prairie dogs give each other detailed warning calls when a potential predator is near. For example, they say something different when a heavy, tall human in a blue T-shirt is near than they do when a short, thin person in green approaches.

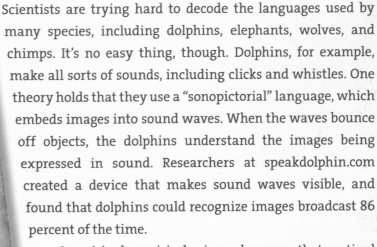

Chapter Nine
BIGGEST BIGFOOT HOAXES

Not every fake bigfoot or yeti sighting is a hoax. For example, in March of 1986, an experienced hiker was in the Himalayas when he saw a creature with a "large and squarish" head and a dark body covered in hair. It didn't move. He also observed a line of strange tracks that appeared to lead up to this mysterious animal. He photographed it, and bigfoot experts who analyzed it concluded it was a genuine, undoctored picture of a yeti.

The hiker, Anthony Woolridge, was experienced and would know what he'd seen, so people were eager to believe him. But the next year, when researchers went back to the spot to do more investigation, they found the yeti was actually a rock outcropping.

This was a case of a mistake. No one was trying to trick anyone else. But people really wanted to believe Woolridge had seen a yeti, and so they did. If such a thing can happen accidentally, consider how much more susceptible people are to believing hoaxes—people's intentional attempts to trick others into believing something.

These pranks might seem funny at the time, but most people don't end up laughing for long. Someone tramping through the woods in a bigfoot suit could accidentally get shot by a hunter. In 2012, a man wearing a kind of hairy-looking camouflage costume called a Ghillie suit was hit by two cars driven by teenagers in Montana. His friends told police he was trying to make people think they'd seen a sasquatch. Tragically, he died.

Ghillie suits, like this one, make you undetectable.

It's also cruel to mislead and waste the time of people who've devoted their lives to finding bigfoot. They take this work seriously. Imagine how you would feel if someone took the thing that meant the most to you and turned it into a joke. It also ruins the credibility of a group of people who really are trying to investigate something scientifically.

There is one thing about bigfoot, though, that stands separate from all the hoaxes. John Green, the journalist who spent his career seeking the animal, said, "If you establish at any point that even one report is accurate, then you have an animal. And, if you have an animal, then you have literally thousands of animals."

In other words, people can pull all the bigfoot hoaxes they want. If we someday find an animal, then bigfoot exists—and there can't be just one.

CARDIFF GIANT

While no one claimed the Cardiff Giant was bigfoot (the term hadn't been invented yet), when this ten-foot stone man was "discovered" on October 16, 1869, in Cardiff, New York, he became a truly big deal. Thousands of people traveled to a farm to pay fifty cents each to see the stone colossus, which was said to be an example of the giants referred to in the Bible.

Some people were fooled. A journalist describing the effect the giant had on some onlookers said it took their breath away and made them look awestruck. No matter how it affected these early witnesses, this stone man wasn't a real giant. It was a sculpture made by stonecutters. A tobacco salesman named George Hull had paid the stonecutters and the farmer a total of $2,600 to create and house the giant.

Hull had taken some pains with his project.

He found the stone in Montana and paid to ship it to Chicago, where stonecutters set to work, using Hull's body as their model. It was fairly detailed (you could see ribs and other bits), and Hull himself used a sponge, water, and sand to make the giant look as though he were an ancient being.

Hull's efforts to make his giant seem real were for nothing—at least from a scientific standpoint. A paleontologist from Yale University inspected it and pronounced it an obvious hoax because the chisel marks were visible.

But something surprising happened after this: People didn't care. They kept paying to see it.

The fake giant became so popular that P. T. Barnum, the circus owner who allegedly said, "There's a sucker born every minute," had a plaster copy made. That one became even more popular than the original.

This just shows how much people want to believe in fantastic things. Even when presented with evidence to the contrary, they'll still go along with it—just for fun.

Oh, and about that P. T. Barnum quote about suckers? He never said it. It's just another thing people like to believe.

THE MINNESOTA ICEMAN

In the late 1960s and early 1970s, a retired Air Force pilot named Frank Hansen had something pretty cool in his trailer: a frozen wild man dubbed "The Minnesota Iceman." Hansen took it to carnivals and fairs, charging people a quarter for a peek.

It's not clear where Hansen got his supposed sasquatch. At a critical moment, the story kept changing. . . .

It came from a rich, mysterious owner!

It was discovered in the seas of Siberia!

It attacked him in the woods and he killed it in self-defense!

But before all that, when the frozen wild man was entertaining Midwestern fairgoers, Bernard Heuvelmans, the father of cryptozoology, examined it for a period of days with Ivan Sanderson, the founder of the ABSMery. Impressed, these two notables were ready to declare it real. Not only did Sanderson say he could smell it rotting through the cracks in the ice, Heuvelmans was ready to identify it as a previously unknown species.

His name for the creature was *Homo pongoides*, and the way he described it in *The Bulletin of the Royal Institute of Natural Sciences of Belgium* was convincing. The wild man they nicknamed Bozo looked like a six-foot-tall man covered from head to toe in hair, he wrote. His skin was waxy white and cadaverish, like a Caucasian man who hadn't seen much sun. His broken left arm was twisted behind his head, while his right lay against his body, the palm pressed against his belly.

But it was Bozo's face that was most surprising, Sanderson wrote in a magazine called *Argosy*. Both eyes seemed to be missing. One was blown out. Bozo had a wide, flat nose, "rather like that of a Pekinese dog." Sanderson was insistent the thing was real. "Then again, you may well be able to fool me, I fully admit," he wrote. "But I defy anybody to fool Bernard Heuvelmans in a case like this."

Sanderson asked John Napier at the Smithsonian to investigate, and this is when things took a strange turn. Hansen's story about the origins of the creature changed. Then he took a "vacation," and during that time, someone allegedly replaced the original Iceman with a

fake made out of latex. The Smithsonian weighed in harshly after their investigation turned up the company that had made just such a suit for Hansen.

"The Smithsonian Institution . . . is satisfied that the creature is simply a carnival exhibit made of latex rubber and hair . . . the 'original' model and the present so-called 'substitute' are one and the same."

And so ended the saga. Or so everyone thought. Early in 2013, someone claiming to have the rubber suit put it and a nonworking freezer up for sale on eBay with an asking price of $20,000. It sold—for how much, they don't say. Nor do they say where the suit is going, so the mystery might live on a while longer.

SQUATCHCICLE, PART II

In 2008, a couple of guys in Georgia—later joined by a Las Vegas promoter—created the biggest bigfoot hoax in modern times, again with what they claimed was a frozen sasquatch.

A press release sent to reporters beforehand promised DNA evidence and photos of the beast. Judging by some of the claims in the press release, it's no wonder many people were excited. They claimed they'd found a seven-foot seven-inch creature that weighed more than five hundred pounds, looked part human and part ape, was male with reddish hair and blackish-gray eyes, and was in possession of two arms, two legs, and the usual number of fingers and toes. Its feet measured sixteen and three-quarters inches long, and were flat and human-like. And it was an upright walker (as were the other specimens sighted the day this one was discovered).

So where'd they get it? According to their tall tale, the two men, Matthew Whitton and Rick Dyer, had been on a June hike in the woods of Georgia when a creature began to follow them. In all, they saw three other bigfoot-like creatures before they found the prize, the body of a seven-foot-seven sasquatch near a stream. Tom Biscardi, the Vegas promoter, said he'd inspected the body before it was frozen and was certain it was authentic, according to the *National Geographic* news Web site.

Some people's flags went up right away, because Biscardi had been involved in an earlier bigfoot hoax. But Whitton was especially persuasive because he was a police officer on leave from his job as he recovered from being shot in the hand while he arrested someone, which is probably why reporters from respected media outlets, including CNN, went to the infamous press conference on August 15, 2008.

Whitton pretended the whole thing had been a happy accident. "We were not looking for bigfoot . . . we wouldn't know what we were doing if we did," he said. "I didn't believe in bigfoot at the time . . . but you've got to come to terms with it and realize you've got something special. And that's what it was."

They even showed reporters photographs of a sasquatch that had been allegedly following them.

Although there were skeptics all along, lots of people were very excited to see the creature.

Loren Coleman, a well-known cryptozoologist, posted pictures on the cryptomundo blog a few days before the press release. The photos depict a chocolate-brown, furry beast with white teeth and a protruding tongue. They also reveal a knot of pale pink guts on the creature's belly.

He wrote, "The body doesn't look exactly like people thought it would, because the Patterson-Gimlin bigfoot has been the model in our minds. However, this looks as if it is an actual apelike primate. Indeed, the gorilla-like facial features, the alleged lack of canines, and the grinding surfaces shown in the teeth *suggest* a bulky vegetarian with a mixture of higher primate characteristics."

You can hear the mix of optimism and

SPOTTED!

"I'd Never Seen Anything Like It Before"

Kirsten Jorgensen was cranking tunes on her Game Boy as she took a quick trip down the hill to the mailbox. That's when she noticed something out of the corner of her eye. The Virginia teen turned to look, "and I was, like, 'Oh my gosh! There's something standing there watching me.'"

She ran up the hill screaming. As soon as she got to the house, she caught her breath and burst into tears. "I'd never seen anything like it before."

skepticism in that post. Afterward, on an entry outlining many more details of the ways Biscardi in particular had tried to trick him, Coleman wrote, "I was ninety-nine percent sure this was a hoax. However, I honestly admitted that I had a tiny bit of hope that perhaps some of the most unreliable people around had come up with a body."

Other scientifically minded bigfoot hunters were turned off immediately. Matt Moneymaker told *Scientific American* that the pictures looked like "a Halloween costume in a box." Jeffrey Meldrum, the professor at Idaho State University, said pretty much the same thing, and that his previous contact with Biscardi made the whole thing seem made-up.

THE RAY WALLACE SAGA

When Ray Wallace died in 2002, *The Seattle Times* wrote an article that said, "The reality is, bigfoot just died."

The reporter was quoting Ray Wallace's son, Michael, who claimed his father had made the original tracks in 1958 that Jerry Crew discovered—the very tracks that made bigfoot a household name in the United States.

Wallace couldn't help himself, his relatives said. "He'd been a kid all his life. He did it just for the joke and then he was afraid to tell anybody because they'd be so mad at him," his nephew Dale Lee Wallace said.

For sure, Wallace did some things that make him *seem* like a prankster. For example, in 1960 he claimed to have caught a young bigfoot. He offered it to Peter Byrne for a million dollars. Byrne, who led several bigfoot-seeking expeditions in the Pacific Northwest, counter-offered $5,000 for a peek. They couldn't make a deal. Later, Wallace told Byrne the baby bigfoot was eating him into the poorhouse (his food of choice: Kellogg's Frosted Flakes by the hundred-pound bag), but he never did get the money and claims to have released the animal.

He moved from California to Toledo, Washington, where he ran a roadside zoo and entertained himself by writing fifty-page letters to his old hometown newspaper, the *Klamity Kourier*, detailing tales of bigfoots who befriended cougars, spoke in their own language, and lived in abandoned gold mines. He also made bigfoot movies and took supposed pictures of the creature in the wild, eating elk and frogs, among other things.

One of his claims to the newspaper: "Bigfoot used to be very tame, as I have seen him almost every morning on the way to work," he wrote in 1969. "I would sit in my pickup and toss apples out of the window to him. He never did catch an apple, but he sure tried."

After his death, his family produced a pair of carved alder wood feet—the ones they said gave life to the whole bigfoot myth. And for a lot of people, that was proof enough that there is no bigfoot.

There's just one problem, though. Most bigfoot tracks that have been cast don't match those wooden templates, so anyone dismissing bigfoot on the basis of Ray Wallace's family confessions is missing out on a great deal of research. It's possible that he was a hoaxer *and* that there is also such an animal we think of as bigfoot.

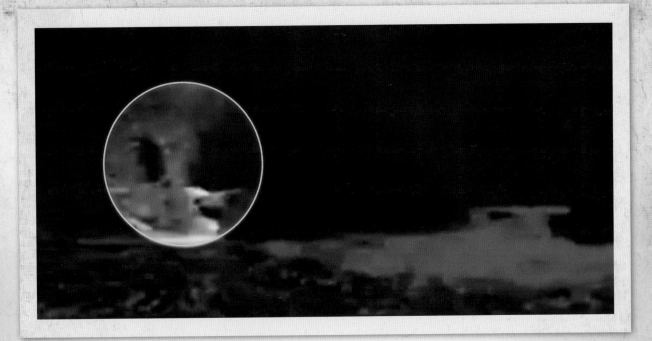

RANT MULLENS

One of the earliest bigfoot hoaxers might just be a man named Rant Mullens, who claimed he started fooling people with giant footprints in 1924, long before the name "bigfoot" was even coined.

In that early incident, a gold miner named Fred Beck said that apes armed with rocks had attacked his camp. The *Portland Oregonian* carried an article about the "Ape Canyon" incident, which Beck later described at length. Beck and his crew had seen mysterious tracks during their work. "We knew no known animal could have made them: The largest measured nineteen inches long."

They considered leaving, but everyone was excited about the prospect of finding gold, so they soldiered on. And then one night, their cabin came under attack. Someone or something was pelting them with rocks. The attack lasted all night. In the morning, when things ended, Beck looked outside.

"It was not long before I saw one of the ape-like creatures, standing about eighty yards away near the edge of Ape Canyon. I shot three times, and it toppled over the cliff, down into the gorge, some four hundred feet below."

Was it a bigfoot attack?

Well, fast-forward fifty-eight years to when Rant Mullens took credit for the Ape Canyon attack. There are persuasive photographs of him showing feet he carved. He also admitted to providing similar ones to Ray Wallace, who was linked to the Bluff Creek Bigfoot tracks that inspired many people to seek bigfoot. And he said he sold fake feet for fifty years, any of which could be still out there, being used.

But knowing there are guys like Rant Mullens out there doesn't deter experts like Jeffrey Meldrum. He's spent his career studying footprints and, in the real ones, he sees things that could only be made by a living foot interacting with the soil beneath.

CRAZY CLAIMS

You'll remember that science follows certain rules. For something to be a scientific theory, you need to be able to make observations. You need to turn these observations into a hypothesis—an educated guess about something. You need to test this hypothesis with an experiment that proves or disproves your hypothesis, and that other people can repeat. This part is vital, and it's why certain ideas about bigfoot have been unhelpful in advancing understanding of the creature.

In the 1980s, for example, a woman named B. Ann Slate cowrote a book with one of the men who recorded the Sierra Sounds. In part, the book considered the possibility that bigfoot might be an advance guard for an incoming alien invasion. It's an, uh, interesting idea. But how on earth would one test it? The idea continues to circulate today. A cable TV host, Dr. Franklin Ruehl, has written for *The Huffington Post* making the same case (and you can watch him on YouTube saying, "May bigfoot be with you. Yes! Yes! Yes!").

Another man with unusual ideas, Jon-Erik Beckjord, had a similarly unprovable theory that explained why no one had ever managed to kill a sasquatch, and why they were so hard to spot. It's because they live "between dimensions" and can fade out through wormholes, possibly to parallel universes.

SPOTTED!
The Last Hunting Trip

Jeff Boling, a police officer and hunter from southwest Virginia, was up before dawn walking along a ridge when he heard something coming through the high grass.

"I could tell it was like a man," he said, describing the serpentine path it made alongside him. Eventually, it walked out of earshot—and into plain view. That's when he realized it wasn't a man after all. It was a bigfoot. His life hasn't been the same since.

"It was November of 1993," he said, "and to this day, I have not hunted anymore."

THE CRIPPLEFOOT CONUNDRUM

One of the most confounding episodes in bigfoot history has to be the "Cripplefoot" incident, because it's a mix of the believable and the nutty, the rational and the rascally.

In November 1969, a butcher near the small eastern Washington town of Bossburg found some mysterious tracks near a garbage dump. People had been spotting sasquatches in the area, so the tracks were an instant source of curiosity. And they were interesting: One foot looked messed up, possibly drawing bigfoot close to people and their castoffs because it could not survive in the wild.

Before long, some of the most notable names in bigfoot history had gathered to study the tracks: René Dahinden, Bob Titmus, and Ivan Marx (who lived nearby). After the initial discovery of tracks, they did their best to find more—or the creature that made them. A few weeks later, they came upon a series of 1,089 tracks in the snow. More experts arrived, including Roger Patterson. They searched without luck into January, all the while wondering if the tracks were a hoax.

Things started to get strange after that. A local prospector said he'd trapped a live bigfoot in an abandoned mineshaft. He at first offered to sell it. Later, he offered to sell a frozen sasquatch foot. (No one ever saw either.) After that, Ivan Marx produced what he claimed was footage of the Cripplefoot after it was hit by a train. His claim was undermined, though, by reports that he'd been seen shopping for fur earlier that month in Spokane, Washington. The footage also didn't hold up to scrutiny.

But here's the kicker.

The tracks themselves were convincing to experts, including Professor Grover Krantz, John Napier of the Smithsonian, and later, to Jeffrey Meldrum, the professor at Idaho State University.

Meldrum wrote that you could see evidence of movement in the tracks. "In some instances, the toes are sharply curled, leaving an undisturbed ridge of soil behind toe tips resembling peas in a pod. In other instances the toes are fully extended," he wrote in a paper analyzing them.

This isn't the sort of thing you'd expect a hoaxer to do, or to even know was possible. In Napier's book, *Bigfoot: The Yeti and Sasquatch in Myth and Reality*, he wrote, "It is very difficult to conceive of a hoaxer so subtle, so knowledgeable— and so sick—who would deliberately fake a footprint of this nature. I suppose it's possible, but it is so unlikely that I am prepared to discount it."

And Krantz was even more emphatic when he talked with a television reporter. "If someone faked [these footprints] with all the subtle hints of anatomy design, he had to be a real genius, an expert at anatomy, very inventive, an original thinker. He had to outclass me in those areas, and I don't think anyone outclasses me in those areas, at least not since Leonardo da Vinci. So I say such a person is impossible, therefore the tracks are real."

PAUL FREEMAN

Paul Freeman is a controversial figure in the big-foot world. He found many, many tracks. The one-time U.S. Forest Service worker also captured suspected bigfoot video. But old-school bigfooters like Titmus and Dahinden thought he was nothing but a hoaxer.

He gained a certain respectability, though, when scholars like Krantz and Meldrum took serious interest in the bigfoot casts he tracked. Meldrum was initially skeptical. But when he went out to look at some tracks in the Blue Mountains area of southeastern Washington, he was blown away. The line of prints he observed in wet, silty soil had all the characteristics of prints made by a living foot.

"These are all the features that make it come to life in my mind and began to cause me to set aside my skepticism," he told a reporter for the *Yakima Herald*. "While it's clearly from the same foot, in one instance the toes are tightly flexed and it's gripping the soil on a slight incline . . . in one extended and splayed, the first three toes sunken into the soil but the fourth and fifth don't quite leave a mark."

One print even showed a rock that had pressed into the soft sole of the foot. Another showed how the creature's toes had wrapped around a larger rock. Meldrum cast the prints, ready to conclude they were still a hoax. Later, an expert in primate handprints examined the casts and found scars and dermal ridges. The expert, Jimmy Chilcutt, concluded they were real—and belonged to a mysterious, nonhuman primate.

SPOTTED!
Moonshine and Bigfoot

Brandon and Leslie White have an old cabin in the mountains of Kentucky. It's remote—surrounded by a thousand acres of wilderness—the perfect place to slow-cook ribs and raccoon, play bluegrass tunes on the fiddle, and maybe even brew up some moonshine, a potent kind of liquor made of fermented cornmeal.

Everything changes at night, though. That's when the sasquatches come out.

"In the middle of the night they come around here knocking and banging," Brandon said. "You can hear them, I don't know, it sounds like they're kind of talking. But it ain't nothing I ever heard before."

But it doesn't end with bigfoot banter.

"They throw rocks," Leslie said. A couple of times a month, the cabin is pelted.

HOW TO SPOT A FAKER

The history of bigfoot hoaxes can teach us a few things. For example, if someone is offering to sell you peeks at a bigfoot, a captured bigfoot, or bigfoot body parts, you're wise to be suspicious. Real bigfooters are interested in finding the animal for the sake of science, not profit. It's a question of credibility, which is diminished when people are obviously out for a buck.

The same thing applies when the *Finding Bigfoot* team interviews witnesses. They ask questions designed to make sure the witnesses can be trusted. If the alleged bigfoot that's been spotted isn't behaving in a typically squatchy way, that makes the story seem less credible. Similarly suspicious are bigfoot tracks that are uniform or spaced incorrectly—a bigfoot walks in a single-file gait and has a step length of around five feet.

There are also telltale clues with videos that alert them to hoaxes. Genuine videos aren't short, Bobo Fay says. If a video is just a couple of seconds, if it's shaky, if it includes just a quick pan of some creature, it's probably a hoax.

"When it's a real video, people keep filming. When they're kind of, like, trying to keep it as brief as possible, that's an indicator sign for a possible hoax."

You also want to see telltale sasquatch signs when you're looking at a video, Cliff Barackman says. Is the posture right for a squatch? Does it have butt muscles? It should, he says, "because that's a physical trait that is absolutely necessary for bipedal walking."

That said, even hoax videos are worth studying. Matt Moneymaker puts it like this: "Investigating potentially hoax videos is important also because you can't become an expert on bigfoot videos unless you become very familiar with both legit footage and hoax footage."

Chapter Ten
EXTRAS

Certain questions about bigfoot come up again and again. Here are answers to the most common of them.

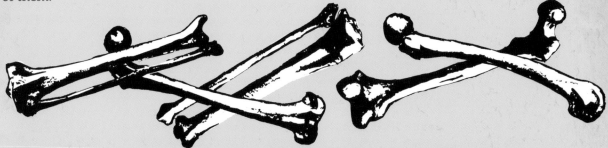

WHERE ARE THE BIGFOOT BONES?

A bigfoot skeleton—or even part of one—could be used as proof of the animal's existence. So far, though, no one has come forward with any bones. People who reject the possibility of bigfoot use this as an argument for their cause. No bones, no bigfoot.

Not so fast, though, bigfooters argue. For one thing, fossils are very rare, particularly in wet environments like Washington State, where many of the sightings have been made. For another thing, bigfoots themselves are rare, with perhaps only two to six thousand in all of North America, according to estimates of the Bigfoot Field Researchers Organization. For someone to stumble across exceedingly rare bigfoot remains in a remote part of the world would also be an unlikely event, especially given Mother Nature's propensity to absorb dead animals back into the soil, assisted by animals such as porcupines, which eat bones.

But the main reason we haven't found bigfoot bones is that we haven't been looking for them, the BFRO says. "No one should expect remains of such an elusive species to be found, collected, and identified without some effort."

HOW DID BIGFOOT GET HERE FROM THE HIMALAYAS?

We don't know for sure that's where bigfoot came from, although it is a logical theory, for a couple of really good reasons:

First, we know that Asia was home to giant apes. One species in particular, *Gigantopithecus blacki*, is often offered up as a potential bigfoot relative.

Second, we also know that during the last Ice Age, between 70,000 and 11,000 years ago, a land bridge connected Asia and North America. This is how early humans made their way to the New World. If bigfoot *is* related to Asian apes, this would be the most reasonable means of getting to North America.

HOW MANY BIGFOOTS ARE OUT THERE?

No one knows for sure. But the Bigfoot Field Researchers Organization estimates there are between two thousand and six thousand bigfoots in North America.

The animals are only rarely spotted, which means—no surprise—that they're rare. But there needs to be a certain number of them to sustain the population. The BFRO thinks about three hundred would be a minimum.

But there have been many more sightings than that, so the number is probably higher. When wildlife biologists are trying to gauge the size of an animal population, they use a principle called the "observability factor." For every single animal you see, there might be four others of the same species. That would give you an observability factor of four to one.

What's the observability factor for bigfoot? It's hard to say for sure, but the BFRO estimates based on the four thousand credible sightings recorded since the 1960s, it's reasonable to guess at their two to six thousand bigfoot figure. Grover Krantz, a professor of physical anthropology, concurred, basing his population estimate in the "low thousands" on the number of prints that had been collected and the average life expectancy of a sasquatch.

Rosie Caldwell was on the porch of her Kentucky home, making a phone call in the dark. She wasn't happy about it.

"I'm a scaredy cat," she said, "so I went to turn the porch light on."

But it wasn't working. So she fetched a bulb, and as she was changing it, she saw something.

"I saw a huge, seven- to eight-foot creature just strolling by," she said. "It turned and looked at me while it was walking." The creature had sloped shoulders and it swung its arms as it moved.

Terrified, she dropped everything and ran into the basement. "After I got in the house," she said, "I called my dad."

"I think I saw a bigfoot," she told him.

He rushed over. They went to look for it, but whatever mysterious creature she'd seen had disappeared right into the woods.

HOW MANY TYPES OF BIGFOOTS ARE THERE?

Without having even a single bigfoot specimen to examine, no one can say for sure if the creature is the same as the Florida Skunk Ape, the Himalayan Yeti, the Indonesian Orang Pendek, or the Australian Yowie.

Given the distance that separates the Pacific Northwest from Florida, Nepal, Indonesia, and Australia, though, as well as the differences in the creatures' appearances and behaviors that witnesses have described, it would be reasonable to expect them to be different species, at least.

HOW AGGRESSIVE ARE THEY?

Before people knew much about gorillas, the animals had a reputation of being aggressive, chest-thumping menaces. In reality, their nickname among wildlife biologists is "gentle giants."

We haven't been able to observe sasquatches as closely, but in all of the thousands of sightings in the past sixty years or so, there hasn't been a single human death or serious injury caused by bigfoot. Compared with other apex predators, bigfoots seem downright tame. For example, since 1890, twenty people have been killed by cougars in North America. Bears are even deadlier. Since 2000, thirty-four people have been killed by either black or brown bears.

WHAT DOES BIGFOOT EAT?

Bigfoot is an omnivore, which means it eats plants and other animals. Wherever it lives, it needs protein and water. In the Pacific Northwest, deer, elk, and rodents are sources of protein. In Florida, the skunk ape is believed to eat deer and wild hogs, as well as snakes, alligators, and swamp apples.

Many bigfooters put out bait for the animals, hoping to get a peek. Favorite bait items include bacon, raw liver, peanut butter, and candy bars, which means bigfoot and truck drivers like the same foods (just kidding—we aren't up on our truck driver research).

IS THERE TRUE EVIDENCE THAT IT EVEN EXISTS?

There is evidence but not proof. Evidence has been found in the form of footprints, hair, scat, and encounters—some of which have been recorded in pictures and video. People don't always agree on their interpretations of this evidence, but there is evidence for sure. To have proof of bigfoot, we would need a body or part of a body. To date, that has not happened.

IS BIGFOOT AS BROWN AS A BEAR?

Eyewitnesses have described seeing bigfoot with all sorts of different hair colors—black, brown, reddish—even gray and white streaks in more senior sasquatches. Their skin is dark, either brown or black, although it's lighter on their palms and soles, witnesses have reported.

HOW TALL IS A SASQUATCH?

When it comes to determining the average size for humans, researchers can simply measure a number of people and work it out from there. There are complications—some populations are taller than others. But there are people readily available for measurement.

It's not so with sasquatches. So how did researchers come up with seven foot ten as the average height of a bigfoot? Two ways: using landmarks for measurements, and making projections based on the size of their feet.

Seven foot ten is the average, though. Some are even taller. Based on footprint size, the biggest are believed to top ten feet.

They are correspondingly heavy. As height increases, weight goes up *exponentially*, because the volume of the body is greater. Think of it this way. A cube measuring two feet on a side has a volume of eight. A cube measuring three feet on a side has a volume of twenty-seven. The average squatch tips the scales at six hundred fifty pounds. Jumbos might weigh over a thousand pounds, based on some of the largest footprints.

Here's James "Bobo" Fay demonstrating
the massive height of bigfoot.

SPOTTED!
"It Was Built Like . . . a Rock"

Phil Ramos was hunting in the Morgan-Monroe State Park, a 24,000-acre tract in southern Indiana. He sat by a tree for a moment and heard a twig snap. His hunter's instincts kicked in. He spotted its massive head and shoulders, trained his gun on it, and watched it follow the tree lines before cutting into the woods.

"I got a good look at it. It was tall. I would say at least ten, twelve feet," he said. "It was built like . . . a rock." Scared stiff at the time, he told no one of the sighting but his wife. And he never went back to that spot in the woods.

After Bobo visited the spot, he was a believer. "After being at the site with Phil and having him recount his story, relive his story, there's no doubt in my mind this dude is . . . telling the truth. This guy really saw and experienced what he says he did. I believe the guy a hundred percent."

HOW DOES SASQUATCH SURVIVE IN THE MOUNTAINS?

Like any wild animal, sasquatches are adapted to survive in the habitats where they've been seen. As with other apex predators, they feed on smaller animals. As omnivores, they also eat plants. They also need water.

IS SASQUATCH CURIOUS?

Many sasquatch sightings describe the animals peering into windows, visiting barns, and investigating loud sounds such as chainsaws, explosions, and playing children. Some have even been said to observe humans for hours. For the most part, though, their curiosity seems balanced by their desire to remain hidden away.

For sure, humans are more curious about sasquatches than they are about us.

HOW LONG DO THEY LIVE?

Gorillas in the wild live about thirty-five to forty years. In captivity, they live a bit longer—up to fifty years or so. Writing for the International Society of Cryptozoology in 1998, W. Henner Fahrenbach calculated a similar life expectancy based on the size of a sasquatch and its nine-month gestation period. Some animals do live longer, he wrote. Those are the old-looking creatures that people have reported seeing, old and wrinkled with rotten teeth and hair that looks like "goat dreadlocks."

WHAT CLIMATE DOES BIGFOOT PREFER?

Judging by where Bigfoot is most often seen, the thickly forested, temperate rain forests of Washington State are their favorite habitat. Almost 13 percent of all sightings occur there. That said, sightings have been reported in every state except for Hawaii. No sightings have been made in Washington, D.C., either.

WOULD BIGFOOT EAT A HUMAN?

There are no reports of human consumption by bigfoot. President Teddy Roosevelt wrote a book that contained a story of a fatal attack by a sasquatch-like animal, but even then, the victim—who had a broken neck—wasn't eaten. Or even nibbled on.

HOW MANY PEOPLE HAVE SEEN BIGFOOT?

No one knows! But the Bigfoot Field Researchers Organization database lists more than 4,300 sightings. Almost certainly there are many more than that. Not everyone who sees bigfoot reports it to the database. And many people who see bigfoot never tell anyone, because they're afraid of being ridiculed.

WHAT PERCENTAGE OF AMERICANS BELIEVE IN BIGFOOT?

An Angus Reid Public Opinion poll in 2012 found that almost 30 percent of Americans believe in bigfoot. Democrats are more likely to say bigfoot is "probably real," and men are more likely than women to believe.

30% BELIEVE

70% DON'T BELIEVE

WHAT DO YOU DO IF YOU SEE A BIGFOOT?

Remember that bigfoot is a wild animal. Staring at wild animals can be perceived as threatening, so as tempting as it might be to goggle away, it would be better for you to sit down and look unthreatening. Have a snack. Pretend to pick fleas out of your friend's hair.

Then, slowly remove your camera if you have one and slyly snap some pictures or capture video. Do your best to make observations and not scare it off, and then write a really great entry in your field journal.

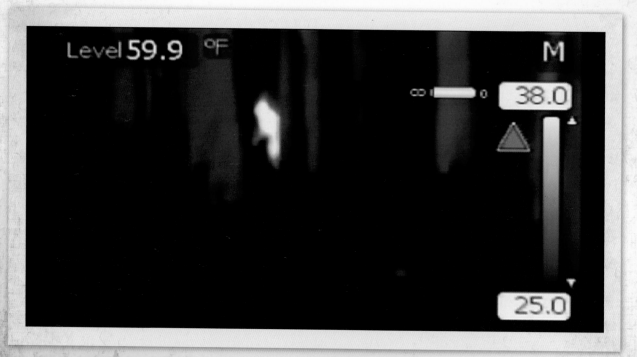

IS IT A BOY OR A GIRL?

We talk about "Bigfoot" as though there is just one. But of course, there couldn't possibly be just one. A bigfoot can be male or female. One of the most famous—the one in the Patterson-Gimlin film—had female body parts. Her fans named her Patty.

WAS BIGFOOT EVER CAPTURED ON FILM?

Some of the best evidence for bigfoot is on film (go back and look at Chapter 2, if you haven't). So, yes. There are plenty of people who believe they have photographed and filmed bigfoot. The most famous of all bigfoot films is the Patterson-Gimlin film (see page 18). It has been reviewed many times by experts and no one has proved it authentic or faked, although there are people who firmly believe it's one or the other.

You can look up the movie on YouTube and decide for yourself. There's also a Facebook group called FB/FB (for Facebook/Find Bigfoot), and people there analyze footage. They've posted many, many videos and photographs.

IS CHEWBACCA A BIGFOOT?

Chewbacca was a Wookiee, and while he certainly looks like a bigfoot and talks like a bigfoot, he isn't—at least according to George Lucas, who created the character.

He also said the name Wookiee came from a line one of his actors made up during the shooting of *THX 1138*, a sci-fi movie that came before *Star Wars*: "I think I just wan over a wookiee on the expressway."

But the personality of Chewbacca is based on Lucas's loyal, brave dog, Indiana.

HOW DOES BIGFOOT MOVE AROUND WITHOUT BEING SPOTTED?

There have been some wackadoodle theories about that. One of the most outlandish is that bigfoot travels through wormholes to other dimensions.

More reasonable theories: bigfoot is nocturnal. Humans aren't equipped to see particularly well at night. Bigfoots are also rare and live in remote areas, two other factors that make them harder to see. As with many animals, they will have evolved characteristics that camouflage them—dark fur that blends in with the shadows of the forest, for example.

And, some researchers believe, they don't want to be seen. Jeffrey Meldrum, author of *Sasquatch: Legend Meets Science*, said there is evidence that chimpanzees obscure their tracks and take other measures to avoid detection. Perhaps bigfoot does the same.

HAVE A BIGFOOT MOVIE NIGHT

Let's say you and your friends are into bigfoot, big-time. After a long day of research, you can unwind together with any number of famous bigfoot movies while you eat Zagnut bars.

Here are some you might like.

Legend of Boggy Creek

This movie, from the early 1970s, is a docudrama—it's meant to look real. This is definitely the most famous of all bigfoot movies, and it is based on events that really happened in Fouke, Arkansas, where a smelly, seven-foot monster was killing chickens and scaring people half to death. (There's a sequel called *Boggy Creek II: And the Legend Continues*.)

Harry and the Hendersons

For a bit more comedy, this movie is about a man who runs into bigfoot (literally), brings him home, discovers him to be a true friend—and then has to protect him from a hunter.

Sasquatch: The Legend of Bigfoot

This one's about seven men who venture into the wilds of northwest Canada. It's another one that looks like a documentary, though it's not. There are, however, simulated bear attacks (done using a trained grizzly and a Tootsie Roll).

The Sasquatch Gang

A group of friends find sasquatch footprints in the woods, and while a team investigates, some neighborhood dummies try to make money from the sasquatch. This one's rated PG-13 for some crude humor, so keep that in mind.

Not Your Typical Bigfoot Movie

For an actual documentary, you might try *Not Your Typical Bigfoot Movie*, an award-winning production about two real bigfooters in an economically depressed Ohio town. It's a story about bigfoot on one level, but also about big dreams and the meaning of friendship.

SPOTTED!
Too Fast to Hunt

In the northeast corner of Utah, near where the borders of Wyoming and Idaho intersect, are mountain ranges thick with deer and elk, which the *Finding Bigfoot* team believes to be a staple of the Sasquatch diet.

It's also a favorite spot for hunters such as Bryce Chestnut, who was in the region for the second time, walking along a hillside, when he heard branches breaking and crashing sounds coming from a nearby ravine.

He put his binoculars to his face, looked down, and saw something black race by.

"I could see it was on two legs," he said. "It came running through this brush and crashed into this clearing, went over the top and was gone into the trees."

By the time he'd grabbed his rifle, the creature was gone. But he has no doubt what he saw. "The only thing it can be in my mind is bigfoot."

BIGFOOT JOKES

How do you keep a bigfoot from smelling?
Plug her nose!

Why did the sasquatch cross the road?
So he could eat the chicken.

Knock, knock.
Who's there?
Squatch.
Squatch who?
Gesundheit!

Bigfoot and the Easter Bunny had a race. Who won?
Bigfoot, silly. The Easter Bunny doesn't exist!

Why did the world's fastest runner refuse to race bigfoot?
Because he was afraid of defeet.

What did bigfoot do to the mosquito?
She squatched it.

What car does bigfoot want to drive?
A toe truck.

Why did the bigfoot talk back?
Because she was a sass Squatch.

What sport is bigfoot best at?
Tracks-in-field.

How did the yeti know what time it was?
She checked her sasq-watch.

MORE BOOKS TO READ

Bigfoot
by Stephen Krensky
Lerner Publications, 2007
This is a compact book about bigfoot that covers lots of interesting facts. It's a straightforward introduction to the topic.

Bigfoot Exposed: An Anthropologist Examines America's Enduring Legend
by David J. Daegling
Altamira Press, 2005
Daegling does not believe bigfoot exists. He uses his background as an anthropologist to examine evidence for the creature—especially tracks and the gait displayed in the Patterson-Gimlin film—to form counterarguments to the claims made by Grover Krantz, Jeffrey Meldrum, and other colleagues who find the evidence of bigfoot to be compelling. This is a good book to read to understand how the same evidence can be read in different ways.

Bigfoot: The Life and Times of a Legend
by Joshua Blu Buhs
University of Chicago Press, 2009
This book has a lot of great information about bigfoot, the history of the creature, and the attempts that have been made to find one. Another skeptic, Buhs argues that bigfoot is a legend with particular appeal to society's least powerful men.

Giants, Cannibals & Monsters: Bigfoot in Native Culture
by Kathy Moskowitz Strain
If you're interested in learning a lot about Native American tales about bigfoot, this book is a great choice. If there truly were no North American apes, you will wonder what on earth might have inspired these stories.

In Search of Sasquatch
by Kelly Milner Halls
This book is full of great information from people seriously pursuing sasquatches: cryptozoologists, linguists, anthropologists, biologists, and more. There's a particularly interesting section on bigfoot in folklore. The author has written other books about cryptids, so if you're interested in more about undiscovered animals, you might check out her work.

Sasquatch: Legend Meets Science
by Jeffrey Meldrum
Jeffrey Meldrum is one of the nation's leading bigfoot researchers. He's a professor at Idaho State University, an expert in bipedalism and foot morphology, and a tireless seeker of the facts about bigfoot. This book is full of detailed and compelling arguments about the creature, and it also rebuts some arguments made by people who think bigfoot is nothing more than legend.

Bigfoot: The Yeti and Sasquatch in Myth and Reality
by John Russell Napier
Dutton, 1973
This book is one you'll probably have to find in a library, as it's decades old. But it's important for the historical record. John Napier was one of the world's leading primate researchers. He wrote about the Patterson-Gimlin film, which he believed was probably a hoax, but concluded that there was no way to prove that conclusively.

Sasquatch: The Apes Among Us

by John Green
Hancock House Pub, 2006
John Green is a journalist who's spent his whole life collecting stories of bigfoot encounters. He worked closely with every significant bigfoot seeker of the last several decades, and he's written several books about bigfoot. This one is considered the definitive account. It's hard to come by, but you might find a copy at your library.

The Scientist Looks at the Sasquatch

(Volumes I and II)
by Grover Krantz and Roderick Sprague
University Press of Idaho, 1977 and 1979
These books are collections of articles by anthropologists about bigfoot. Because they are by scientists for scientists, they are not light reading and have lots of nitty-gritty detail. But if you want to know how anthropologists go about their work, you might go to a library and check one or both of these out.

HELPFUL WEB SITES

You can go online to learn more about bigfoot, examine footprint casts and pictures, watch videos believed to be of the creature, report sightings, and stay current with the latest news. Here are some good places to start:

Animal Planet | Finding Bigfoot

animal.discovery.com/tv-shows/finding-bigfoot
Find plenty of information about the show, exclusive videos, data on sightings and tracks, as well as a place where you can share your own evidence.

Bigfoot Lunch Club

bigfootlunchclub.com
When there's bigfoot news or research, the Bigfoot Lunch Club is likely to have it.

Bigfoot Field Researchers Organization

BFRO.net
This is Matt Moneymaker's group, and their Web site has information on thousands of sightings, plus insight about bigfoot gained from analyzing the many sightings that have occurred. It's a great place to start your research and report sightings.

Bigfoot Information Project

bigfootproject.org

Go here for interviews with top researchers and investigators.

Bigfoot Sounds

bigfootsounds.com
Listen to excerpts of the Sierra Sounds, a famous exchange of what is believed to be multiple bigfoots talking.

North American Bigfoot

northamericanbigfoot.com
This is Cliff Barackman's blog. He has field notes from the *Finding Bigfoot* show. It also links to his main site, CliffBarackman.com, where you can report encounters, look at his huge collection of casts, read articles, and watch instructional videos.

Bigfoot Books

bigfootbooksblog.blogspot.com
This is the blog of a Willow Creek, California, bookstore that specializes in sasquatch literature.

Bigfoot Encounters

bigfootencounters.com

You'll find news, sightings, articles, and scholarly musings about all aspects of bigfoot.

Bigfoot Times

mcclean.org/bigfoottimes/index.html

A variety of information about bigfoot, from news to new books to events. It's managed by longtime bigfoot scholar Daniel Perez.

Crypto Zoo News

cryptozoonews.com

Longtime bigfoot and general cryptid expert Loren Coleman gives regular updates about bigfoots and other undiscovered animals.

Facebook Finding Bigfoot

facebook.com/FindBigfoot

This Facebook group posts pictures and videos and offers analysis of them.

THE SMITHSONIAN ON THE YETI

What does the foremost Museum of Natural History in the United States have to say about the yeti? A lot, as it turns out. Here's a form letter the museum sent in 1988 in response to the many inquiries people had about the creatures:

The Museum of Natural History often receives requests for information concerning the "abominable snowman," "yeti," "sasquatch," or "bigfoot," and other unknown creatures said to exist in certain mountain regions of the world, particularly the Himalayas, western Canada, and northwestern United States. Though the term "abominable snowman" can refer to all these creatures, generally the terms "snowman" and "yeti" refer to an Asiatic creature, while "sasquatch" and "bigfoot" refer to North American creatures.

The actual existence of a "snowman" has not been definitely proven. Most evidence submitted so far is based on photographs of previously unknown animal tracks, unusual scats (dung), and some hair samples. Among the many explanations offered on the basis of the above evidence, one that has appealed greatly to the popular imagination, is that the animal in question is a huge, human-like ape, or possibly a surviving race of early man. Because of its terrifying aspect, the animal, supposedly of Himalayan origin, came to be called "abominable snowman"; it is this intriguing name that is probably responsible for such widespread interest in these creatures in various parts of the world.

Many zoologists who have reviewed the evidence have come to the conclusion that the tracks of the Himalayan "snowmen" were really made

by bears, monkeys, or other already known animals. A few disagree, saying there is little similarity. The tracks attributed to the sasquatch of the northwestern United States are much more human-like but of vast proportions (fifteen to eighteen inches in length). With the large publicity the "snowman" has received in recent years, many popular articles of little scientific value have been written. Some of these are convincing to read, but they are mostly based on circumstantial evidence of "sightings," tracks, hair, scats, and some doubtful pelts and skull caps.

While most scientists believe the likelihood of the existence of such a creature is small, they keep an open mind, as scientists should. One cannot prove anything on the basis of negative evidence, and the only satisfactory proof that an animal fitting the description of the "snowman" exists would be either to capture one and study it or to find undisputed skeletal evidence. Only these kinds of finds would result in the universal recognition of the "snowman" by all scientists.

Below is a list of references through which you can pursue this topic further:

Byrne, Peter. *The Search for Bigfoot: Monster, Myth or Man?* Washington, D.C.: Acropolis Books Ltd., 1975. (Summary of the evidence collected over the years by a believer in the "snowman's" existence.)

Halpin, Marjorie and Michael M. Ames, eds. *Manlike Monsters on Trial: Early Records and Modern Evidence.* Vancouver: University of British Columbia Press, 1980. (Explores Sasquatch-like creatures and summarizes reports of sightings.)

Hillary, Edmund and Desmond Doig. *High in the Thin Cold Air.* New York: Doubleday and Co., 1963. (The famous Mount Everest climber recounts searches for the "snowman" in the Himalayas.)

Izzard, Ralph. *The Abominable Snowman Adventure.* Toronto: Modder and Stoughton, 1954. (Concerns the search for the "snowman" in the Himalayas.)

Napier, John. *Bigfoot: The Yeti and Sasquatch in Myth and Reality.* New York: E. P. Dutton, 1973. (An eminent primatologist discusses his views on the possibility of the "snowman's" existence. Concludes no hard evidence exists though allows for some soft evidence.)

Sanderson, Ivan T. *Abominable Snowmen: Legend Come to Life; The Story of Sub-Humans on Five Continents from the Early Ice Age Until Today.* Philadelphia and New York: Chilton Co., 1961. (Sifts the accumulated evidence for and against the "snowman's" existence rather thoroughly. For a critical comment on this book, see Carleton S. Coon's review in the January 1962 issue of *Natural History* magazine.)

Sprague, Roderick and Grover S. Krantz, eds. *The Scientist Looks at the Sasquatch.* (*Anthropological Monographs of the University of Idaho*, no. 3.) Moscow: The University of Idaho Press, 1977. Collection of articles first published in *Northwest Anthropological Research Notes.*)

Suttles, Wayne. "On the Cultural Track of the Sasquatch," *Northwest Anthropological Research Notes.* 6(1):65 90, 1972. (Discusses Native American views of the Sasquatch. Article also in Sprague.)

PUBLIC INFORMATION OFFICE
DEPARTMENT OF ANTHROPOLOGY
SMITHSONIAN INSTITUTE

PHOTO CREDITS

They comb forests, study nests, and track footprints of the notorious creature known as bigfoot. They are the team of *Finding Bigfoot*.

ACKNOWLEDGMENTS

About ten years ago, I almost didn't receive an email that would change my life.

Troublesome Internet monkeys had rerouted the message to my junk mail folder, and I was just about to click the delete button when I noticed an interesting subject line: literary agent?

As it turns out, the email was from Erin Niumata, who'd read my educational humor column on Encarta, loved it, and thought I had a book in me. Over the years, Erin has given me endless encouragement, support, and great advice. She was also correct in her diagnosis. It was a book in there. Or two! And perhaps many more, which beats intestinal parasites every time.

Thanks, also, to my other literary agent, Jill Corcoran, for being a mom and a sister and a friend . . . and also very fierce about the details.

I'm grateful to the team at Feiwel and Friends for knowing I was the right writer for this book, and for doing such a beautiful job with the design and packaging. Special thanks to Anna Roberto and Jean Feiwel for their terrific support.

To the kids in Ms. Monroe's class at Hamlin Robinson School in Seattle, your questions made a huge difference. Thank you, Tyler, Sam, Kellen, Lee, Sophie, Emily, Isabella, Lucy, Vanessa, David, Luke, Matthew, and Kyle.

To my writing friends, most especially Sean Beaudoin, Kevin Emerson, and Cat Patrick. You turn this solitary slog into a hilarious adventure. More, please.

To Adam, Lucy, and Alice for your love, patience, and willingness to listen to all of my bigfoot jokes. I promise I'll stop . . . eventually. To Graham and Rosie, you are good dogs.

And finally, thank you to everyone seeking sasquatches, both literal and metaphorical. To chase after something while others doubt takes courage. Whatever your dream is, keep after it.

—*Martha Brockenbrough*

INDEX

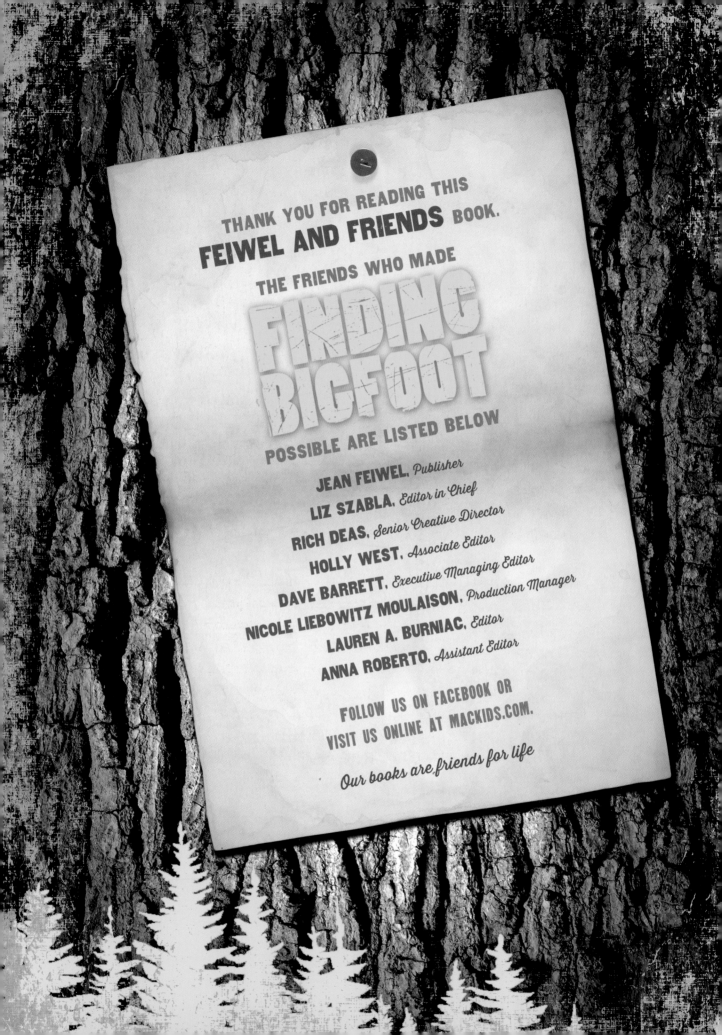

Improve Your Grade!

Self-Study Companion Website resources included with any new book.

Access to MyNutritionLab, including assignments and eText, sold separately.

Get help with exam prep!
REGISTER NOW!

Registration will let you:

See It!

- View the engaging new Cooking 101 videos covering a wide range of essential skills
- Access 20 topical *ABC News* videos on current nutrition issues and trends

Do It!

- Connect with NutriTools interactive activities to experiment with different food options and learn first-hand nutrition skills
- Interact with online versions of key text features like Nutrition Label Activities

www.pearsonhighered.com/thompsonmanore

TO REGISTER

1. Go to www.pearsonhighered.com/thompsonmanore
2. Select your book cover.
3. Click "See It" in the left navigation menu.
4. Click "Register."
5. Follow the on-screen instructions to create your login name and password.

Your Access Code is:

Note: If there is no silver foil covering the access code, it may already have been redeemed, and therefore may no longer be valid. In that case, you can purchase access online using a major credit card or PayPal account. To do so, go to www.pearsonhighered.com/thompsonmanore click on "Buy Access," and follow the on-screen instructions.

TO LOG IN

1. Go to www.pearsonhighered.com/thompsonmanore
2. Select your book cover.
3. Click "See It" in the left navigation menu.
4. Enter your login name and password.
5. Click "Log In."

Hint:
Remember to bookmark the site after you log in.

Technical Support:
http://247pearsoned.custhelp.com

W9-CDA-133

Nutrition
is all about
LIFE!

Making Concepts
Relevant to REAL LIFE

Unique features throughout the book help
students make connections between essential concepts
and their own lives by discovering new foods, learning about important nutrition
milestones, eating right, and staying actively engaged with their nutritional choices.

FOODS YOU DON'T KNOW YOU LOVE YET

Star Fruit

There's a new "star" in the fruit galaxy—the star fruit! Also known as carambola, the star fruit is native to the Philippines, Indonesia, India, and Sri Lanka. As it thrives in warm, humid conditions, star fruit are now grown in the United States in Florida and Hawaii. Its name reflects its unique shape, with ridges running down its sides, which cause it to look like a star when cut in cross section. There are both tart and sweet types of star fruit, and they taste like a combination of lemons, pineapples, and plums. Star fruit are an excellent source of water and vitamin C, and they are naturally low in fat and sodium. To enjoy star fruit, no peeling is necessary—simply wash them, remove any damaged areas, slice crosswise to get the star shape, and enjoy!

NEW! Foods You Don't Know You Love Yet

This feature appears throughout the text, highlighting unusual or up-and-coming foods making inroads into the American diet. Users looking for greater diversity in their food choices will find this new feature an exciting addition to cross-cultural content. Featured foods, highlighted with appealing photos, include quinoa, kefir, and star fruit, as well as more familiar foods with newly discovered nutritional benefits.

NEW! Nutrition Milestones

This new column feature appears in every chapter and highlights key developments in nutrition history, emphasizing links between the past and what we know and do nutritionally today.

NUTRITION
MILESTONE

In 1782, the French chemist Antoine Lavoisier invented a device that could measure the heat produced by chemical reactions, including those taking place in an animal. He called his device a *calorimeter*, from the Latin word *calor*, meaning "heat." Using his calorimeter, Lavoisier made the first measurements of the energy (thermal energy, or heat) produced by the consumption of various types of foods. Today, we measure this heat in units called Calories.

Eating Right All Day

Breakfast
Grapefruit juice instead of sweetened coffee!

Lunch
Vegetable soup instead of chicken noodle!

Dinner
Spring rolls instead of sweet & sour pork!

Snack
Grapes instead of M&Ms!

NEW! Eating Right All Day

This visual planning feature uses an engaging breakfast/lunch/snack/dinner format to highlight content in the micro- and macronutrient chapters, with distinctive graphics and appetizing photos designed to help users get more of a particular nutrient in their diets.

What Can I Do Today?

Now that you've read this chapter, try changing these three things:

- At mealtimes today, select nourishing foods. Take smaller portions. Eat slowly. Savor each bite.

- Take better care of your GI tract! If you smoke, stop. If you drink alcohol, do so in moderation. Keep up your fluids throughout the day, and stay active.

- If you're experiencing GI pain, unexplained weight loss, or problems with bowel function, make an appointment with your healthcare provider or student health services center. Do it today!

NEW! What Can I do Today?

This end-of-chapter feature includes three bulleted points underscoring key content, prompting readers to take action.

Applying Concepts to **REAL LIFE**

The **Third Edition** emphasizes ways that students can bring good nutrition into their own lives, demonstrated through several robust media resources.

NEW! Cooking 101 Videos

All new Cooking 101 videos, presented by Dr. Anne-Marie Gloster, R.D., are available on the Companion Website and on MyNutritionLab® and cover a wide range of nutritional topics important to students, including the basics of stocking a kitchen and using inexpensive and simple ingredients to build a great meal.

NEW! Cooking 101 Glossary

The dedicated Cooking 101 Glossary, available in the Do It section of MyNutritionLab and the Companion Website, also provides tips for selecting and storing produce, and how to handle and prepare foods safely, among many others!

ABC News Video Clips

Created in partnership with *ABC News*, these 35 clips, each 4–15 minutes long, are a great way to promote critical thinking and spark interesting classroom discussion.

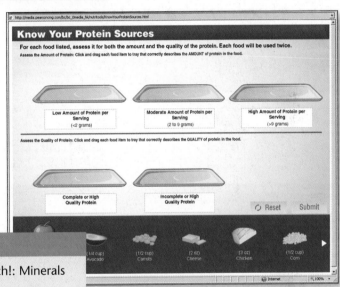

NutriTools

NutriTools Include:

- Build-a-Meal
- Build-a-Salad
- Build-a-Sandwich
- Build-a-Pizza
- Know Your Calcium Sources
- Know Your Iron Sources
- Know Your Carbohydrate Sources
- Know Your Fat Sources
- Know Your Protein Sources
- Let's Go to Lunch!: Fat-Soluble Vitamins

- Let's Go to Lunch!: Minerals
- Let's Go to Lunch!: Water-Soluble Vitamins
- Metabolism
- Mineral Functionality
- Vitamin Functionality
- Nutrients: Vitamin or Mineral?
- Food Label: What is Required?
- Digestion and Absorption
- Find the Carbohydrates

NEW! NutriTools

19 new NutriTools interactive activities are available on the companion website and on MyNutritionLab.® The Build-a-Sandwich, Build-a-Pizza, Build-a-Salad, and Build-a-Meal activities allow students to combine and experiment with different food options and learn firsthand how to build healthier meals. NutriTools activities include assignable and gradable questions on MyNutritionLab.

See Concepts in **REAL LIFE**

Trusted partner

MyNutritionLab® delivers engaging, dynamic learning opportunities—focused on instructor learning objectives and responsive to each student's progress—with improved registration and instructor support.

- Quick Start Videos demonstrate MyNutritionLab basics for instructors giving just-in-time help.

- Dedicated instructor and student support via Internet chat at http://247pearsoned.custhelp.com or dedicated customer service line at 800-677-6337.

Engaging experience

MyNutritionLab provides a one-stop spot for accessing a wealth of preloaded content and tools, while giving you the ability to customize your course as much (or as little) as you'd like.

NEW! *ABC News* Videos

These videos bring nutrition topics to life and are available on the Instructor Resource DVD, MyNutritionLab, and the Companion Website.

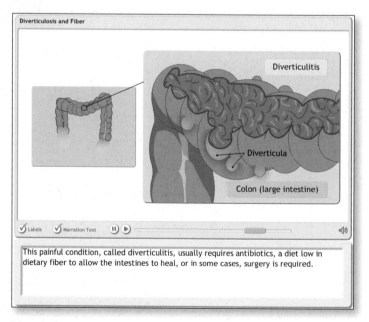

Nutrition Animations

40 Nutrition Animations explain the big picture concepts with assignable quizzes.

MyNutritionLab®

The new MyNutritionLab from Pearson has been designed and refined with a single purpose in mind: to help educators create that moment of understanding with their students. The MyNutritionLab system helps instructors maximize class time with customizable, easy-to-assign, and automatically graded assignments that motivate students to learn outside of class and arrive prepared for lecture. By complementing your teaching with our engaging technology and content, you can be confident your students will arrive at that moment—the moment of true understanding.

Proven results

MyNutritionLab has a consistently positive impact on the quality of learning in higher education personal health instruction. MyNutritionLab can be successfully implemented in any environment—lab-based, hybrid, fully online, traditional—and demonstrates the quantifiable difference that integrated usage of these products has on student retention, subsequent success, and overall achievement.

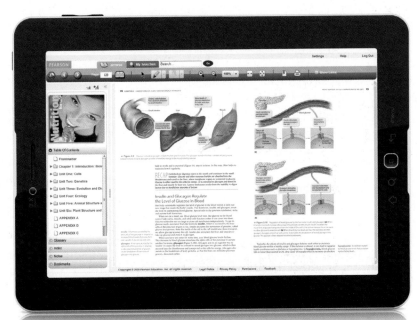

Pearson eText

Pearson eText is easy for students to read. Users can create notes, highlight text in different colors, create book marks, zoom, click hyperlinked words and phrases to view definitions, and view in single page or two-page view. Pearson eText also links students to associated media files, enabling them to view an animation as they read the text.

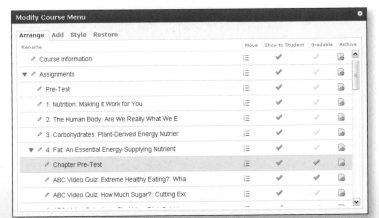

NEW! Quizzing

Instructors can lessen their prep time and simplify their lives with preloaded quiz and test questions (specific to the textbook) that they can assign and/or edit, a gradebook that automatically records student results from assigned tests, and the ability to customize the course as much (or as little) as desired. Over 150 pre-built, publisher created assignments are easily assignable and gradable.

Instructor and Student RESOURCES

For Instructors

MyNutritionLab
or
MyNutritionLab® with MyDietAnalysis
www.mynutritionlab.com

MyLab Instructor Access Kit
978-0-321-81554-5 • 0-321-81554-8

Printed Test Bank
978-0-321-78801-6 • 0-321-78801-X

Instructor Manual
978-0-321-78779-8 • 0-321-78779-X

Instructor Resource DVD
978-0-321-78777-4 • 0-321-78777-3

MyDietAnalysis
www.mydietanalysis.com

Companion Website
www.pearsonhighered.com/thompsonmanore

For Students

MyNutritionLab with MyDietAnalysis Standalone Access Card
978-0-321-78769-9 • 0-321-78769-2

MyNutritionLab Standalone Access Card
978-0-321-78774-3 • 0-321-78774-9
or
www.mynutritionlab.com

MyDietAnalysis
www.mydietanalysis.com
or
978-0-321-73390-0 • 0-321-73390-8

Companion Website
www.pearsonhighered.com/thompsonmanore

Food Composition Table
978-0-321-66793-9 • 0-321-66793-X

Eat Right!
978-0-8053-8288-4 • 0-8053-8288-7

Nutrition
for Life

Third Edition

Nutrition
for Life

Third Edition

Janice Thompson, PhD, FACSM
University of Bristol
University of New Mexico

Melinda Manore, PhD, RD, FACSM
Oregon State University

PEARSON

Boston   Columbus   Indianapolis   New York   San Francisco   Upper Saddle River
Amsterdam   Cape Town   Dubai   London   Madrid   Milan   Munich   Paris   Montreal   Toronto
Delhi   Mexico City   São Paulo   Sydney   Hong Kong   Seoul   Singapore   Taipei   Tokyo

Executive Editor: Sandra Lindelof
Project Editor: Susan Scharf
Development Director: Barbara Yien
Developmental Editor: Laura Bonazzoli
Assistant Editor: Meghan Zolnay
Editorial Assistant: Briana Verdugo
Executive Media Producer: Liz Winer
Assistant Media Producer: Annie Wang
Senior Managing Editor: Deborah Cogan
Associate Production Project Manager: Megan Power
Design Manager: Derek Bacchus
Interior and Cover Design: Gary Hespenheide
Art Editor: Kelly Murphy

Production Management and
    Composition: S4Carlisle Publishing Services
Illustrators: Precision Graphics
Associate Director of Image Management/
    Image Vendor Strategy: Travis Amos
Photo Researcher: Jessica Bruah
Image Rights and
    Permissions Manager: Donna Kalal
Manufacturing Buyer: Stacey Weinberger
Executive Marketing Manager: Neena Bali
Text Printer: Courier Kendallville
Cover Printer: Lehigh-Phoenix Color/Hagerstown
Cover Photo Credit: Ariwasabi/Shutterstock

Credits and acknowledgments borrowed from other sources and reproduced, with permission, in this textbook appear on the appropriate page within the text [or on p. CR-1].

Library of Congress Cataloging-in-Publication Data
Thompson, Janice, 1962-
    Nutrition for life / Janice Thompson, Melinda Manore. — 3rd ed.
        p. cm.
    Includes bibliographical references and index.
    ISBN-13: 978-0-321-77435-4 (student ed.: alk. paper)
    ISBN-10: 0-321-77435-3 (student ed.: alk. paper)
1. Nutrition—Textbooks. I. Manore, Melinda, 1951- II. Title.
TX354.T46 2013
613.2—dc23
                        2011029810

1 2 3 4 5 6 7 8 9 10 11–**CRK**–15 14 13 12 11
Manufactured in the United States of America.

ISBN 10:   0-321-77435-3 (Student edition)
ISBN 13: 978-0-321-77435-4 (Student edition)

ISBN 10:   0-321-78775-7 (Instructor's Review copy)
ISBN 13: 978-0-321-78775-0 (Instructor's Review copy)

"To our moms—your consistent love and support

are the keys to our happiness and success.

You have been incredible role models."

"To our dads—you raised us to be independent,

intelligent, and resourceful. We miss you and

wish you were here to be proud of, and to

brag about, our accomplishments."

Janice Thompson, PhD, FACSM

University of Bristol

University of New Mexico

Janice Thompson earned a PhD from Arizona State University in exercise physiology and nutrition. Her research focuses on designing and assessing the impact of nutrition and physical activity interventions to reduce the risks for obesity, cardiovascular disease, and type 2 diabetes in high-risk populations. She also teaches nutrition and research methods courses and mentors graduate research students.

Janice is a Fellow of the American College of Sports Medicine (ACSM) and recently served as Vice President of ACSM. She is also a member of the American Society for Nutrition (ASN), the British Association of Sport and Exercise Science (BASES), The Nutrition Society in the United Kingdom, and the European College of Sports Science (ECSS), where she serves as a member of the Scientific Committee. Janice won an undergraduate teaching award while at the University of North Carolina, Charlotte. In addition to *Nutrition: An Applied Approach*, Janice co-authored the Pearson textbooks *Nutrition: An Applied Approach*, with Melinda Manore, and *The Science of Nutrition*, with Melinda Manore and Linda Vaughan. Janice loves traveling, yoga, hiking, and cooking and eating delicious food. She likes almost every vegetable except canned peas and believes chocolate should be listed as a food group.

Melinda Manore, PhD, RD, CSSD, FACSM

Oregon State University

Melinda Manore earned a PhD in human nutrition with a minor in exercise physiology at Oregon State University (OSU). She is the past chair of the Department of Nutrition and Food Management at OSU and is currently a professor in the Department of Nutrition and Exercise Sciences. Prior to her tenure at OSU, she taught at Arizona State University for 17 years. Melinda's area of expertise is nutrition and exercise, especially the role of diet and exercise in health, the nutrient needs of active people, weight control, and chronic disease prevention. A particular area of emphasis is on the nutritional needs of active women and girls across the life cycle.

Melinda is an active member of the American Dietetic Association (ADA). She is a current Fellow of the American College of Sports Medicine (ACSM), and a past Vice-President. She is the past chair of the ADA Research Committee and the Research Dietetic Practice Group, and she served on the ADA Obesity Steering Committee. She is an active member of SCAN, a nutrition and exercise practice group of ADA. Melinda is also a member of the American Society of Nutrition (ASN) and the Obesity Society. She is also the past chair of USDA's Nutrition and Health Planning and Guidance Committee. Melinda is the past nutrition column author and associate editor for ACSM's *Health and Fitness Journal* and *Medicine and Science in Sports and Exercise*, and she serves on the editorial boards of numerous research journals. She has won awards for excellence in research and teaching. She also co-authored the Pearson textbooks *Nutrition: An Applied Approach*, with Janice Thompson, and *The Science of Nutrition*, with Janice Thompson and Linda Vaughan. Melinda is an avid walker, hiker, and former runner who loves to cook and eat great food. She is now trying her hand at gardening and birding.

WELCOME TO *NUTRITION FOR LIFE*, THIRD EDITION!

Why We Wrote the Book

You stop at the convenience store for a snack. Blaring across the front of a bag of chips is the banner *No Trans Fats!* while a bag of pretzels claims *Now with Whole Grains!* What do these claims really mean, you wonder, and why should you care? You buy the chips and take them to a party, where a football game is on TV. It's half-time and an athlete is pushing some new protein supplement. A friend comes up and offers you a can of something called *Action!* "It's this new high-energy drink," he explains. But then your roommate snickers, "Yeah, and the caffeine in it disintegrates your bones! You know, they've banned that stuff in France!"

No doubt about it, nutrition is a hot topic, but do you ever wind up with information overload? Everybody claims to be an expert, but what's their advice based on? Is it reliable? How do you navigate through the endless recommendations and arrive at a way of eating that's right for *you*—one that energizes you, allows you to maintain a healthful weight, and helps you avoid disease and promote good health?

We Wrote This Book to Help You Answer These Questions

Nutrition for Life began with the conviction that students would benefit from an engaging, accurate, and clear textbook that links essential nutrition content to their own health, and encourages them to make nutrition part of their everyday life. As authors and educators, we know that students have a natural interest in their body, their health, their weight, and their success in sports and a range of life activities. By demonstrating how nutrition relates to these interests, *Nutrition for Life*, Third edition, empowers students to reach their personal health and nutritional goals. We use multiple strategies to capture students' interest, from highlighting how nutrients are critical to health, to discussing the vitamins and minerals based on their clear functions within the body, to a variety of special features and activities that bring nutrition to life. Throughout the text, material is presented in a lively narrative style that consistently links the essential facts to students' lifestyles and goals. Information on current topics and research keeps the inquisitive spark alive, illustrating that nutrition is very much a "living" science, and the source of ongoing debate, research, and interest. We present nutritional basics in an easy-to-read, friendly narrative and with engaging features that reduce students' apprehensions and encourage them to apply the information directly to their lives. We've also ensured that the organization and flow of the content and the art work together to provide a learning resource that is enjoyable to engage with for both instructors and students.

As educators, we are both familiar with the myriad challenges of presenting nutrition information in the classroom, and we have included tools in the book and ancillary materials that will assist instructors in successfully meeting these challenges. Through broad instructor and student support with print and media supplements, we hope to contribute to the excitement of teaching and learning about nutrition: a subject that affects all of us, one so important and relevant that correct and timely information can make the difference between health and disease.

Features of *Nutrition for Life*

The following features are integrated throughout *Nutrition for Life*, Third edition, to help you learn, study, and apply all the fascinating concepts of nutrition to your own life. As you read through each chapter, be sure to look at the feature boxes and work through their activities, complete the margin journaling features, and test your knowledge with the Review Questions. You can also find more information, resources, and self-quizzing activities on the book's Companion Website, available at www.pearsonhighered.com/thompsonmanore.

- **Where I'm Starting From . . .** and **Where I'm at Now . . .** are margin journaling features designed to help you assess how your real-life practices relate to the nutrition information provided in the chapter. Fill out "Where I'm starting from . . ." before you read the chapter, and complete "Where I'm at now . . ." once you've finished it.

- **Test Yourself questions** are located at the beginning of each chapter. These targeted prompts will help you dispel common myths about nutrition. The answers can be found at the end of each chapter.

- **What About You?** feature boxes help you figure out where you stand with regard to important nutrition issues. This feature, appearing in most chapters, provides self-assessment prompts and exercises that enable you to determine whether your diet and lifestyle are as healthful as they could be, and whether you should be concerned about any particular nutrition-related issues.

- **Game Plan** feature boxes offer detailed strategies for adopting healthful eating and lifestyle changes. They have been updated and reconfigured in this edition into a consistent checklist format, making it even easier to follow the recommended tips and guidelines.

- **Nutrition Label Activities** will show you how to evaluate the labels from actual food products, so that you can make educated decisions about the foods you consume. Updated for this edition, these activities have been made even more interactive, providing hands-on practice that you can apply when you do your own food shopping. Answers to Nutrition Label Activities, when applicable, can be found on the Companion Website.

- **Nutrition Myth or Fact?** feature boxes provide the facts behind the hype surrounding many current nutrition and dietary issues. They dispel common misconceptions and show you how to critically evaluate information you encounter every day from the Internet, media sources, and your peers.

- **Highlight** feature boxes provide deeper background into topics you'll recognize from the Internet, mass media, and popular culture, including issues such as sports beverages, alternative sweeteners, and fad diets. Highlight boxes review the facts and theories surrounding widely-discussed subjects and help you sort out the core issues they relate to.

- **Nutri-Case** scenarios follow the stories of five recurring and diverse characters (Hannah, Theo, Liz, Judy, and Gustavo) from varying backgrounds and with different nutritional needs. One Nutri-Case study appears in each chapter, exploring the effects of nutritional choices and challenges that each character faces. Some of them are probably similar to challenges that you also have grappled with. By prompting you to help the characters make the most sensible choices, these cases help you apply the information you've learned to your own life.

- **Healthwatch** sections found throughout the text are special subject areas designed to highlight the health effects of various and key nutrients and foods, illuminating the consequences of diet on your health.

- **Recaps** are placed strategically throughout each chapter to clearly review and highlight the key points, helping you to grasp the full concepts in easily understood terms.

- **Organization of vitamins and minerals** is unique in this book. Traditionally, students are taught vitamins and minerals content by memorizing each nutrient, along with its deficiency and toxicity symptoms. We've found that, with that approach, students quickly forget the information and don't truly understand why these nutrients are important, and how they affect the body. In *Nutrition for Life*, Third edition, we organize the vitamins and minerals based on their *functions* inside your body, giving you a framework for understanding why they're important, what they do, and what happens when you don't get enough—or get too much!—of each one. This breakthrough approach has enjoyed enormous success and popularity from students and instructors alike.

- **Art, photos, and tables** in this edition have been updated and designed to take you clearly through your body's processing of nutrients. Figures are constructed to show step-by-step what happens to the food you eat, as well as which foods are good sources of key nutrients. Photos illustrate various conditions created by deficiency and toxicity, and identify foods that you may not immediately think of as good sources for specific nutrients.

- **Review Questions** at the end of each chapter help you assess your retention and understanding of the material covered in each chapter. Answers to Review Questions appear at the end of the book.

- **Web Links** at the end of each chapter identify additional web-based resources for further information and study.

- **References,** located in this edition at the end of the book, provide students with references to all of the research used within the chapters.

New to the Third Edition

For this edition, our goal was to make the book even more practical and relevant to students in applying the information to their own lives. We also wanted to include more material on how to evaluate nutrition information, and to provide the most up-to-date and accurate nutrition information currently available.

Eating Right All Day is an engaging new visual planning feature with a breakfast/lunch/snack/dinner format that appetizingly highlights content in the micro- and macronutrient chapters. Also new to this edition is **Foods You Don't Know You Love Yet**, a topical "emerging foods" feature that brings readers' attention to exciting new foods they may not yet be familiar with (and which pack a surprising nutritional punch), or more common foods they may have overlooked or underestimated in the past. **What Can I Do** *Today?* appears at the end of each chapter and spurs students to think in active, concrete ways about three key things they can do right now to incorporate their new nutritional knowledge into making their lives healthier. **Nutrition Online** icons appear throughout each chapter, directing students to web links, videos, podcasts, and other useful online and new media resources. **Nutrition Milestones** is another new feature in every chapter that highlights key developments in nutrition history and provides insights into how the science of nutrition evolves and applies to their everyday life.

In addition to these exciting new features in this edition, we have modified or expanded many of the existing features to be even more practical, often appearing as worksheets or checklists that students can work through. The design and art programs have been updated with dynamic colors to add to visual clarity and interest. In order to provide a focused and easy-to-use text, we've moved the chapter summaries, See for Yourself, and answers to Nutrition Label Activity prompts onto our Companion Website.

Also, now included in the media package for *Nutrition for Life* are new **Cooking 101 videos**, organized by chapter, covering basic skills, creative ideas, and recipe approaches that students can use in their daily life.

The visual summary of features in the front of the book provides an overview of these and other important features in the third edition. For specific changes to each chapter, please see below.

Chapter 1

- Revised and updated Test Yourself questions

- Updated Figure 1.2 with the addition of a 2006 obesity map

- Deleted content on *Healthy People 2010* and content on the Canadian and UK guidelines for healthy eating

- Deleted first edition Table 1.6 (sample diets across four levels of energy intake) and revised the text to reinforce this concept

- Deleted the MyPyramid Tracker figure (first edition Figure 1.11)

- Increased coverage of ethnic/religious/cultural influences on why people eat as they do
- Added a new box feature: What About You? Do You Eat in Response to External or Internal Cues?
- Added a new Figure 1.9 that illustrates using a hand to estimate portion sizes
- Expanded information on how to evaluate nutrition sources and information and added new Highlight: Research Study Results: Whom Can You Believe? feature box
- Added a new Nutri-Case about Hannah as a young adult attending college

Chapter 2

- Revised Test Yourself question 1
- Moved hypothalamus information into the main physiology section
- Added a margin definition of *satiation*
- Added information on celiac disease and on gluten allergy
- Replaced the introductory story
- Included a new Judy Nutri-Case about hunger and satiation
- Added a new Nutrition Label Activity: Recognizing Common Allergens in Foods feature box
- Added a new What About You?: How Well Do You Treat Your GI Tract? feature box
- Updated the Review Questions

Chapter 3

- Expanded the discussion of fiber and included definitions of *soluble* and *insoluble fiber*
- Converted first edition Table 3.4 (fiber content of common foods) to Figure 3.11 to more clearly illustrate food sources of carbohydrates
- Converted first edition Table 3.5 (comparison of two high-carbohydrate diets) to Figure 3.12 to provide a more reader-friendly comparison of two types of high-carbohydrate diets
- Deleted first edition Figure 3.11 (nutrients in whole-grain, enriched, and unenriched breads)
- Simplified the mathematical calculations contained in the Nutrition Label Activity
- Reformatted the Nutrition Label Activity feature box to make it more interactive, encouraging students to "fill in the blanks" and providing the correct answers to allow self-testing of acquired knowledge
- Added a Theo Nutri-Case about wanting to eat carbohydrates after a basketball game
- Added a Hannah Nutri-Case about eating a low-carb diet

Chapter 4

- Clarified the discussion of the distinction between high cholesterol and high blood triglycerides
- Clarified the section on adipose tissue and fat storage
- Added content on omega-3's and eicosanoids and their roles in the body
- Clarified the section on fat metabolism
- Moved the introduction to the essential fatty acids from the Why Do We Need to Eat Fats? section to the What Are Fats? section
- Updated the information and references on fats and cancer
- Revised the Highlight and What About You? feature boxes on blood lipids to help students relate to them more

Chapter 5

- Revised and updated the Test Yourself questions
- Clarified the coverage of the function of proteins in fluid and electrolyte balance
- Added information on transport proteins
- Updated the Highlight boxes on high-protein diets, soy, and mad cow disease
- Replaced first edition Table 5.2 (complementary food combinations) with new Figure 5.4
- Deleted the What About You? feature box on how to calculate one's protein intake and replaced it with journaling activities at the beginning and end of the chapter

Chapter 6

- Expanded the information on vitamin A and the prescription drug Accutane
- Updated recent recommendations related to cancer, diet, and physical activity
- Expanded the information on food sources of vitamins in Tables 6.1 and 6.2 and Figure 6.1
- Added Figure 6.13 on phytochemicals
- Deleted first edition Table 6.4 (B-vitamin food sources) and added food source figures for B-vitamins (Figures 6.12–6.14, 6.16–6.18)
- Revised Figure 6.11 to show only one breakfast cereal
- Added information on phytochemicals and functional foods
- Replaced first edition Table 6.5 with updated Figure 6.13 covering health claims and food sources of phytochemicals
- Deleted first edition Table 6.6 (groups likely to benefit from vitamin supplementation) and condensed this information into bulleted text
- Updated and expanded the information related to the recent controversy on increasing vitamin D recommendations
- Added a Hannah Nutri-Case about vitamin C powder

Chapter 7

- Added a short paragraph on trace minerals of uncertain status
- Revised the content on myoglobin
- Revised the statements about osteoclasts for accuracy
- Added content about sodium and calcium being involved in muscle contraction and relaxation
- Added menopause to the discussion of age as a risk factor for osteoporosis
- Checked tables and narrative to ensure that food sources that are mentioned have good bioavailability
- Updated the Nutrition Myth or Fact?: Do Zinc Lozenges Help Fight the Common Cold? feature box
- Revised the osteoporosis-risk quiz to be more appropriate for younger readers
- Added a Judy Nutri-Case about trying to reduce her sodium intake

Chapter 8

- Added a discussion of the terms *intracellular fluid* and *extracellular fluid*
- Updated the recommendations regarding fluid intake
- Strongly emphasized the importance of water in the All Beverages Are Not Created Equal section

- Replaced first edition Table 8.1 (water content of foods) with Figure 8.3
- Added brief discussions on energy drinks, fortified waters, and the environmental concerns of using bottled water
- Updated the discussion on the various complications related to maternal consumption of alcohol during pregnancy
- Added a Theo Nutri-Case on alcohol consumption

Chapter 9

- Added more emphasis on tools for portion control, discussed in the section on behavioral strategies
- Added information on cultural and economic factors influencing weight loss
- Added more information on strategies for losing weight (including behavioral modification, portion control, setting realistic goals, and various weight-loss plans)
- Added a brief section called Set Realistic Goals and another called Eat Smaller Portions of Lower-Fat Foods
- Added information on weight management after weight loss and the National Weight Control Registry
- Added Figure 9.11 (photos of good vs. bad fast-food meals)
- Included information on more weight-management drugs, such as Orlistat and Alli, and the dangers of dieter's tea and other over-the-counter drugs
- Reorganized the dieting section
- Added a Nutrition Myth or Fact?: Does It Cost More to Eat Right? feature box

Chapter 10

- Updated the information on ergogenic aids and emphasized how supplements are not regulated in the same way as drugs/medications
- Replaced first edition Table 10.2 with new Figure 10.3 on using the FIT principle to achieve cardiorespiratory and musculoskeletal fitness and flexibility
- Replaced first edition Table 10.7 (signs and symptoms of dehydration) with new Figure 10.9
- Integrated the section A Sound Fitness Program Is Fun into the section on variety and consistency of physical activity
- Reduced the size and revised the content of first edition Table 10.5 (nutrient composition of various foods and sports bars) to become new Table 10.4
- Added new Figure 10.6 on the relative contributions of ATP-CP, carbohydrate, and fat to activities of various durations and intensities
- Added a discussion of changing trends in lifestyle contributing to low levels of physical activity in the section Most Americans Are Inactive

Chapter 11

- Condensed the sections Why Is Nutrition Important Before Conception? and Why Is Nutrition Important During Pregnancy?
- Deleted first edition Figures 11.1 and 11.3 on embryonic and placental development
- Condensed the sections What Are a Toddler's Nutrient Needs? and What Are a Child's Nutrient Needs? to rely more on Table 11.4 for this information
- Deleted the discussion called Obesity: A Concern Now from the toddler section
- Deleted the discussion called Body-Image Concerns from the toddler section
- Added a Nutrition Myth or Fact?: Is Breakfast the Most Important Meal of the Day? feature box

- Deleted the section on nutrition for middle-aged adults
- Slightly expanded Table 11.5 on nutrient considerations and condensed the narrative on micronutrient recommendations, referring readers to the table for specific data
- Expanded the discussion called Interactions Between Medications and Nutrition and added a discussion of supplement use among older adults; also added Table 11.6 on drug–nutrient interactions
- Changed the opening story to focus on obesity and diabetes in a family

Chapter 12

- Reorganized the section called How Can You Prevent Foodborne Illness?
- Moved Table 12.3 on preservatives to the section on food additives and updated it to be a bit more comprehensive
- Added new Figure 12.12 on bioaccumulation
- Updated the Test Yourself questions and answers
- Updated the opening story with current information about foodborne illness outbreaks
- Condensed the Highlight feature box on genetically modified foods.
- Moved the content from the first edition Highlight feature box on sustainable food production into the text narrative
- Revised the What About You? feature box on actions contributing to global food security to be more succinct

Appendices and Back Matter

- Previous Appendix A (The Nutrient Value of Foods) has been dropped from the text and is now available as a fuller stand-alone print supplement called the Food Composition Table
- A new Appendix A has been added, The USDA Food Guide Evolution, which provides an overview of the development of the USDA nutritional recommendations in light of the recent 2011 switch from MyPyramid to MyPlate and the USDA Food Patterns guidelines
- Available on the Companion Website is a new online appendix, the Cooking 101 Glossary, with adaptations from the *Eat Right! Healthy Eating and Beyond* print ancillary, including recipes, shopping lists, tips for eating on a budget, and essential cooking terms and concepts
- The 2010 Dietary Guidelines are posted on the inside front cover of the text. Located on the inside back cover, and in adjoining back pages of this text, are the current Tolerable Upper Intake Levels (ULs) for Vitamins and Elements (minerals), and the Dietary Reference Intakes (DRIs) for Macronutrients, Vitamins, and Elements (minerals)

ACKNOWLEDGMENTS

It is always eye opening to write a textbook and realize how many people actually contribute to the final, completed product!

We would like to thank the fabulous staff at Pearson Higher Education for their incredible support and dedication to this book. Frank Ruggirello, Publisher, committed extensive resources to ensuring the quality of this text, and his support and enthusiasm helped us maintain the momentum we needed to continue to enhance this project. Our Acquisitions Editor, Sandy Lindelof, encouraged us to be authors and provided unwavering support and guidance throughout the entire process of writing and publishing this book. We could never have written this text without the exceptional writing and organizational skills of Laura Bonazzoli, our Developmental Editor. Laura's energy, enthusiasm, and creativity significantly enhanced the quality of this textbook. Susan Scharf, our dedicated Project Editor, kept us sane and focused with her excellent editorial skills. Meghan Zolnay, Assistant Editor, provided sterling editorial and administrative support, which we would have been lost without, and Briana Verdugo, Editorial Assistant, managed endless critical details and tasks with grace and aplomb.

We also extend our deep gratitude to our wonderful contributor, Linda Vaughan, who expertly developed and enhanced the fluids and life cycle chapters in this and the previous editions. We would also like to gratefully acknowledge Carole Conn of the University of New Mexico, for her contributions to the first edition and her efforts and research on global nutrition issues.

Multiple talented players helped build this book in the production and design process as well. Deborah Cogan and Megan Power at Pearson, with Tiffany Timmerman and the skilled team at S4Carlisle Publishing Services, kept manuscripts moving through the production process and expertly tracked every minute detail. Travis Amos supervised the art and photo programs, and Jessica Bruah researched photos. Gary Hespenheide, with the excellent guidance of Derek Bacchus, created a beautiful interior text and cover design.

We can't go without thanking the marketing and sales teams, especially Neena Bali, Executive Marketing Manager, who has worked so hard to get this book out to those who will benefit most from it.

Our goal of meeting instructor and student needs could not have been realized without the strong team of educators and editorial staff who worked on the substantial supplements for *Nutrition for Life*. Pat Longoria adroitly updated and revised the comprehensive Test Bank, and Linda Fleming authored the wonderful Instructor Manual. Michelle Wu, guided by the inestimable Liz Winer, ably headed up the coordination and development of the Companion Website. Annie Wang coordinated the media components, and Miriam Adrianowicz masterfully guided the development of the IR-DVD and its assets. Special thanks go to Dr. Anne-Marie Gloster (University of North Carolina, Greensboro) for contributing her considerable talents and body of knowledge to the creation of the terrific new Cooking 101 videos.

Finally, we would also like to acknowledge the many colleagues, friends, and family members who helped us along the way. Janice would especially like to thank her family and friends, who have been so wonderful throughout her career. She also thanks her colleagues and students, who continue to challenge her and contribute significantly to her deep enjoyment of teaching and nutrition-related research. Melinda would specifically like to thank her husband, Steve Carroll, for the patience and understanding he has shown through this process—once again. He has learned that there is always another chapter due! Melinda also thanks her family, friends, and professional colleagues for their support and attentive listening through this whole process. They have all helped make life a little easier during this incredibly busy time.

BRIEF CONTENTS

CONTENTS

Chapter 3
Carbohydrates:
Plant-Derived Energy Nutrients
67

Chapter 4

Fats: Essential Energy-Supplying Nutrients 97

Chapter 5

Proteins: Crucial Components of All Body Tissues

129

Chapter 6

Vitamins:
Micronutrients with Macro Powers 155

Chapter 10

Nutrition and Physical Activity: Keys to Good Health

295

Chapter 11

Nutrition Throughout the Life Cycle 325

Chapter 12

Nutrition Issues: The Safety and Security of the World's Food Supply

369

Appendices

1

Nutrition: Making It Work for You

Miguel hadn't expected that college life would make him feel so tired. After classes, he just wanted to go back to his dorm room and sleep. Plus, he had been having difficulty concentrating and was worried that his first-semester grades would be far below those he'd achieved in high school. Scott, his roommate, had little sympathy. "It's all that junk food you eat!" he insisted. "Let's go down to the organic market for some real food." Miguel dragged himself to the market with Scott but rested at the juice counter while his roommate went shopping. A woman wearing a white lab coat approached him and introduced herself as the market's staff nutritionist. "You're looking a little pale," she said. "Anything wrong?" Miguel explained that he had been feeling tired lately. "I don't doubt it," the woman answered. "I can see from your skin tone that you're anemic. You need to start taking an iron supplement." She took a bottle of pills from a shelf and handed it to him. "This one is the easiest for you to absorb, and it's on special this week. Take it twice a day, and you should start feeling better in a day or two."

Miguel purchased the supplement and began taking it that night with the meal his roommate prepared. He took it twice the next day as well but didn't feel any better. After 2 more days on the supplement, he visited the university health clinic, where a nurse drew some blood for testing. When the results of the blood tests came in, the physician told him that his thyroid gland wasn't functioning properly. She prescribed a medication

Nutrition Online icons are located throughout the chapter, directing you to web links, videos, podcasts, and other useful online resources.

and congratulated Miguel for catching the problem early. "If you had waited," she said, "it would only have gotten worse, and you could have become seriously ill." Miguel asked if he should continue taking his iron supplement. The physician looked puzzled. "Where did you get the idea that you needed an iron supplement?"

Like Miguel, you've probably been offered nutrition-related advice from well-meaning friends and self-professed "experts." Perhaps you found the advice helpful, or maybe, as in Miguel's case, it turned out to be all wrong. Where can you go for reliable advice about nutrition? What exactly *is* nutrition, anyway? And how does our diet influence our health? In this chapter, we'll explore these questions and help you begin to design a diet that works for you.

What Is Nutrition, and Why Is It Important?

If you think that the word *nutrition* means pretty much the same thing as food, you're right—partially. But the word has a broader meaning that will gradually become clear as you make your way in this course. Specifically, **nutrition** is the science that studies food and how food nourishes our body and influences our health. It encompasses how we consume, digest, metabolize, and store nutrients and how these nutrients affect our body. Nutrition science also studies the factors that influence our eating patterns, makes recommendations about the amount we should eat of each type of food, and addresses issues related to food safety and the global food supply. You can think of nutrition, then, as the discipline that encompasses everything about food.

Thousands of years ago, people in some cultures believed that the proper diet could cure criminal behavior, cast out devils, and bring us into alignment with the divine. Although modern science has failed to find evidence to support these claims, we do know that proper nutrition can help us improve our health, prevent certain diseases, achieve and maintain a healthy weight, and maintain our energy and vitality. Think about it: if you eat three meals a day, then by this time next year, you'll have had more than a thousand chances to influence your body's functioning! Let's take a closer look at how nutrition supports health and wellness.

Nutrition Is One of Several Factors Supporting Wellness

Wellness can be defined in many ways. Traditionally considered simply the absence of disease, wellness is now described as a multidimensional state of being that includes physical, emotional, and spiritual health **(Figure 1.1)**. Wellness is not an end point in our lives but is an active process we work on every day.

In this book, we focus on a critical aspect of wellness: physical health, which is influenced by both our nutrition and our level of physical activity. The two are so closely related that you can think of them as two sides of the same coin: our overall state of nutrition is influenced by how much energy we expend doing daily activities, and our level of physical activity has a major impact on how we use the nutrients in our food. Several studies have even suggested that healthful nutrition and regular physical activity can increase feelings of well-being and reduce feelings of anxiety and depression. In other words, wholesome food and physical activity just plain feel good!

A Healthful Diet Can Prevent Some Diseases and Reduce Your Risk for Others

Nutrition appears to play a role—from a direct cause to a mild influence—in the development of many diseases **(Figure 1.2)**. Poor nutrition is a direct cause of deficiency diseases such as scurvy and pellagra. Scurvy is caused by a deficiency of

nutrition The scientific study of food and how food nourishes the body and influences health.

wellness A multidimensional, lifelong process that includes physical, emotional, and spiritual health.

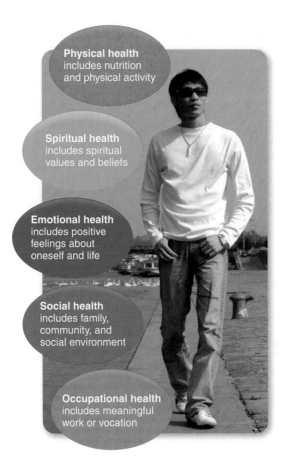

Physical health
includes nutrition
and physical activity

Spiritual health
includes spiritual
values and beliefs

Emotional health
includes positive
feelings about
oneself and life

Social health
includes family,
community, and
social environment

Occupational health
includes meaningful
work or vocation

Figure 1.1 Many factors contribute to wellness. Primary among these are a nutritious diet and regular physical activity.

vitamin C, whereas pellagra is a result of a deficiency of niacin, one of the B-vitamins. Early nutrition research focused on identifying the missing nutrient behind such diseases and on developing guidelines for nutrient intakes that are high enough to prevent them. Over the years, nutrition scientists successfully lobbied for fortification of foods with the nutrients of greatest concern. These measures, along

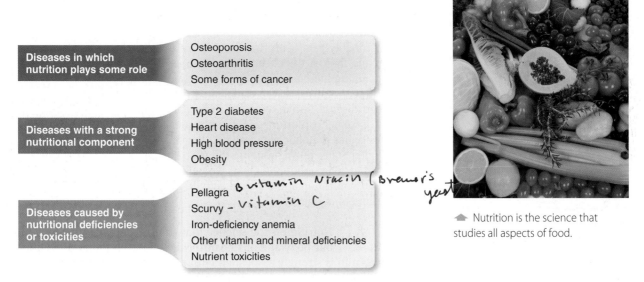

Diseases in which
nutrition plays some role

Osteoporosis
Osteoarthritis
Some forms of cancer

Diseases with a strong
nutritional component

Type 2 diabetes
Heart disease
High blood pressure
Obesity

Diseases caused by
nutritional deficiencies
or toxicities

Pellagra B vitamin Niacin (Brewer's yeast
Scurvy – Vitamin C
Iron-deficiency anemia
Other vitamin and mineral deficiencies
Nutrient toxicities

Nutrition is the science that studies all aspects of food.

Figure 1.2 The relationship between nutrition and human disease. Whereas nutritional factors are linked only marginally to the diseases at the top, they are strongly linked to the development of the diseases in the middle row, and they directly cause the diseases in the bottom row.

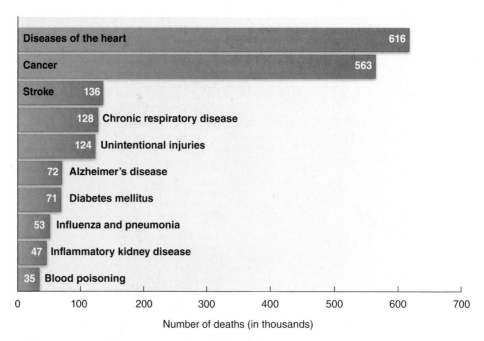

Diseases of the heart — 616
Cancer — 563
Stroke — 136
128 Chronic respiratory disease
124 Unintentional injuries
72 Alzheimer's disease
71 Diabetes mellitus
53 Influenza and pneumonia
47 Inflammatory kidney disease
35 Blood poisoning

0 100 200 300 400 500 600 700
Number of deaths (in thousands)

Figure 1.3 Of the ten leading causes of death in the United States in 2007, three—heart disease, stroke, and diabetes—are strongly associated with poor nutrition. In addition, nutrition plays a more limited role in the development of some forms of cancer.
Data from Centers for Disease Control and Prevention, NCHS. FastStats. Deaths and Mortality. www.cdc.gov/nchs/fastats/deaths.htm.

1994
No Data | <10% | 10%–14% | 15%–19% | 20%–24% | 25%–29% | ≥30%

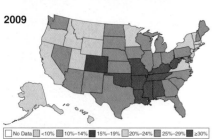
2009
No Data | <10% | 10%–14% | 15%–19% | 20%–24% | 25%–29% | ≥30%

Figure 1.4 These diagrams illustrate the increase in obesity rates across the United States from 1994 to 2009. Obesity is defined as a body mass index greater than or equal to 30, or approximately 30 lb overweight for a 5′4″ woman.
Graphics from Centers for Disease Control and Prevention, U.S. Obesity Trends 1985 to 2009. www.cdc.gov/obesity/data/trends.html.

with a more abundant and reliable food supply, have almost completely wiped out the majority of nutrient-deficiency diseases in developed countries. However, they are still major problems in many developing nations.

In addition to directly causing disease, poor nutrition can have a more subtle influence on our health. For instance, it can contribute to the development of brittle bones (a disease called *osteoporosis*), as well as to the progression of some forms of cancer. These associations are considered mild; however, poor nutrition is also strongly associated with three chronic diseases that are among the top ten causes of death in the United States (**Figure 1.3**). These are heart disease, stroke, and diabetes.

It probably won't surprise you to learn that the primary link between poor nutrition and mortality is obesity. That is, obesity is fundamentally a consequence of consuming more energy than is expended. At the same time, obesity is a well-established risk factor for heart disease, stroke, type 2 diabetes, and some forms of cancer. Unfortunately, the prevalence of obesity has dramatically increased throughout the United States during roughly the past 20 years (**Figure 1.4**). Throughout this text, we will discuss in detail how nutrition and physical activity affect the development of obesity.

Want to see how the prevalence of obesity has changed in the United States year-by-year for the past 25 years? Watch the changing obesity maps at www.cdc.gov/obesity/data/trends.html.

RECAP Nutrition is the science that studies food and how food affects our body and our health. Nutrition is an important component of wellness and is strongly associated with physical activity. One goal of a healthful diet is to prevent nutrient-deficiency diseases, such as scurvy and pellagra; a second goal is to lower the risk for chronic diseases, such as type 2 diabetes and heart disease.

What Are Nutrients?

A spoonful of peanut butter may seem as if it is all one substance, but in reality most foods are made up of many different chemicals. Some of these chemicals are not useful to the body, whereas others are critical to human growth and function. These latter chemicals are referred to as **nutrients.** The following are the six groups of nutrients found in the foods we eat **(Figure 1.5)**:

- carbohydrates
- fats (types of lipids)
- proteins
- vitamins
- minerals
- water

Carbohydrates, Fats, and Proteins Are Macronutrients That Provide Energy

Carbohydrates, fats, and proteins are the only nutrients in foods that provide energy. By this we mean that these nutrients break down and reassemble into fuel that

SIX GROUPS OF ESSENTIAL NUTRIENTS

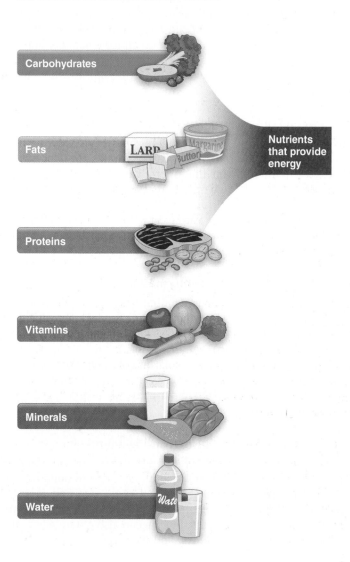

◀ **Figure 1.5** The six groups of essential nutrients found in the foods we consume.

nutrients Chemicals found in foods that are critical to human growth and function.

our body uses to support physical activity and basic functioning. Although taking a multivitamin and a glass of water might be beneficial in other ways, it will not provide you with the energy you need to do your 20 minutes on the stair-climber! The energy nutrients are also referred to as **macronutrients.** *Macro* means "large," and our body needs relatively large amounts of these nutrients to support normal functioning. Macronutrient needs are measured in grams, metric units of weight. Grams are small: ¼ teaspoon of sugar weighs about 1 gram.

Alcohol is a chemical found in food, and it provides energy. Nevertheless, it is not technically considered a nutrient because it does not support body functions or the building or repair of tissues. In fact, the alcohol in beverages is technically classified as a narcotic drug.

Nutrition scientists describe the amount of energy in food as units of *kilocalories* (*kcal*). A kilocalorie is the amount of heat required to raise the temperature of 1 kilogram of water (the weight of about 1 quart of water) by 1 degree Celsius. *Kilo-* is a prefix used in the metric system to indicate 1,000; so a kilocalorie is technically 1,000 calories. However, for the sake of simplicity, food labels use the term *Calories* to indicate kilocalories. Thus, if the wrapping on an ice cream bar states that it contains 150 Calories, it actually contains 150 *kilo*calories. In this textbook, we use the term *kilocalories* as a unit of energy; we use the term *Calories* when discussing food labels or for everyday usage.

Carbohydrates Are a Primary Fuel Source

Carbohydrates are the primary source of fuel for our active body, particularly for the brain. They provide 4 kcal per gram. Many carbohydrates are *fiber rich*; that is, they contain nondigestible parts of plants that offer a variety of health benefits. Many are also rich in *phytochemicals*, plant chemicals that are thought to reduce our risk for cancer and heart disease.

Carbohydrates encompass a wide variety of foods. Grains and vegetables contain carbohydrates, as do fruits, legumes (including lentils, dry beans, and peas), seeds and nuts, and milk and other dairy products.

Fats Provide More Energy Than Carbohydrates

Fats are also an important source of energy for our body, especially during rest and low-intensity activity. Because they pack together tightly, fats yield more energy per gram than carbohydrates, 9 kcal versus 4 kcal. Dietary fats come in a variety of forms. Solid fats include such foods as butter, lard, and margarine. Liquid fats are referred to as *oils* and include vegetable oils, such as corn, canola, and olive oils. You've probably heard about a fatty substance called *cholesterol*, which is present in animal foods such as meats and egg yolks. Cholesterol is synthesized in our body, so we don't need to consume it; thus, it's not an essential nutrient.

Proteins Support Tissue Growth, Repair, and Maintenance

Although **proteins** can provide energy (4 kcal per gram), they are not a primary source of energy for our bodies. Proteins play a major role in building new cells and tissues, maintaining the structure and strength of bone, repairing damaged structures, and assisting in many body functions. Meats and dairy products are primary sources of proteins for many Americans, but we can also obtain adequate amounts from nuts and seeds, legumes, vegetables, and whole grains.

Carbohydrates are the primary source of fuel for our body, particularly for our brain.

macronutrients Nutrients that our bodies need in relatively large amounts to support normal function and health. Carbohydrates, fats, and proteins are macronutrients.

carbohydrates The primary fuel source for our bodies, particularly for the brain and for physical exercise.

fats An important energy source for our body at rest and during low-intensity exercise.

proteins Macronutrients that the body uses to build tissue and regulate body functions. Proteins can provide energy but are not a primary source.

Vitamins and Minerals Are Micronutrients

Vitamins and minerals are referred to as **micronutrients** because we need relatively small amounts of them (*micro-* means "small") to support normal health and body functions.

Vitamins Assist in Regulating Body Functions

Vitamins are compounds that contain the substance carbon and assist us in regulating the processes of our body. For example, vitamins play a critical role in building and maintaining healthy bone, blood, and muscle tissue; supporting the immune system so we can fight illness and disease; and maintaining healthy vision. Contrary to popular belief, vitamins do not provide energy (kilocalories); however, vitamins do play an important role in assisting our body with releasing and using the energy found in carbohydrates, fats, and proteins.

A vitamin's ability to dissolve in water versus fat affects how it is absorbed, transported, stored, and excreted from our body. Thus, nutrition experts classify vitamins into two groups (Table 1.1):

- water soluble
- fat soluble

Because our body cannot synthesize most vitamins, we must consume them in our diet. Both water-soluble and fat-soluble vitamins are essential for our health and are found in a variety of foods, from animal products, nuts, and seeds to fruits and vegetables. Many vitamins break down upon prolonged exposure to heat and/or light, which explains why vitamin supplements are not sold in clear bottles.

Minerals Are Not Broken Down During Digestion

The sodium in table salt, the calcium in milk, and the iron in red meat are all examples of minerals essential to human health and functioning. **Minerals** are substances that

- do not contain carbon,
- are not broken down during digestion, and
- are not destroyed by heat or light.

Thus, all minerals maintain their structure no matter what environment they are in. This means that the calcium in our bones is the same as the calcium in the milk we drink, and the sodium in our cells is the same as the sodium in table salt. Among their many important functions, minerals assist in fluid regulation and energy production, are essential to the health of our bones and blood, and help rid our body of harmful chemicals. They are classified into two groups, according to the amounts we need in our diet and how much of the mineral is found in our body (Table 1.2):

- major minerals
- trace minerals

Major minerals earned their name from the fact that we need to consume at least 100 milligrams (mg) per day in our diet and because the total amount found in our

◆ Fat-soluble vitamins are found in a variety of fat-containing foods, including dairy products.

micronutrients Nutrients needed in relatively small amounts to support normal health and body functions. Vitamins and minerals are micronutrients.

vitamins Micronutrients that contain carbon and assist us in regulating the processes of our body. They are classified as water soluble or fat soluble.

minerals Micronutrients that do not contain carbon, are not broken down during digestion and absorption, and are not destroyed by heat or light. Minerals assist in the regulation of many body processes and are classified as major minerals or trace minerals.

major minerals Minerals we need to consume in amounts of at least 100 mg per day and of which the total amount in our body is at least 5 grams.

TABLE 1.1	Overview of Vitamins	
Type	**Names**	**Characteristics**
Fat soluble	A, D, E, and K	Soluble in fat Stored in the human body Toxicity can occur from consuming excess amounts, which accumulate in the body
Water soluble	C, B vitamins (thiamin, riboflavin, niacin, vitamin B_6, vitamin B_{12}, pantothenic acid, biotin, and folate)	Soluble in water Not stored significantly in the human body Excess is excreted in urine Toxicity generally only occurs as a result of vitamin supplementation

TABLE 1.2	Overview of Minerals	
Type	**Names**	**Characteristics**
Major minerals	Calcium, phosphorus, sodium, potassium, chloride, magnesium, sulfur	Needed in amounts greater than 100 mg/day in our diet Amount present in the human body is greater than 5 grams (5,000 mg)
Trace minerals	Iron, zinc, copper, manganese, fluoride, chromium, molybdenum, selenium, iodine	Needed in amounts less than 100 mg/day in our diet Amount present in the human body is less than 5 grams (5,000 mg)

Peanuts are a good source of the major minerals magnesium and phosphorus, which play important roles in the formation and maintenance of our skeleton.

body is at least 5 grams (5,000 mg). **Trace minerals** are those we need to consume in amounts less than 100 mg per day, and the total amount in our body is less than 5 grams (5,000 mg). Food sources of major and trace minerals are varied and include meats, dairy products, fruits and vegetables, and nuts.

Water Supports All Body Functions

Water is a nutrient vital for our survival. We consume water in its pure form; in juices, soups, and other liquids; and in solid foods, such as fruits and vegetables. Adequate water intake ensures the proper balance of fluid both inside and outside our cells and assists in the regulation of nerve impulses, muscle contractions, nutrient transport, and excretion of waste products.

RECAP The six essential nutrient groups found in foods are carbohydrates, fats, proteins, vitamins, minerals, and water. Carbohydrates, fats, and proteins are macronutrients, and they provide our body with the energy necessary to thrive. Vitamins and minerals are micronutrients that do not provide energy but are essential to human functioning. Adequate water intake ensures the proper balance of fluid both inside and outside our cells.

What Is a Healthful Diet?

A **healthful diet** provides the proper combination of energy and nutrients. It has four characteristics: it is adequate, moderate, balanced, and varied. Whether you are young or old, overweight or underweight, healthy or coping with illness, if you keep in mind these characteristics of a healthful diet, you will be able to select foods that provide you with the optimal combination of nutrients and energy each day.

A Healthful Diet Is Adequate

An **adequate diet** provides enough energy, nutrients, and fiber to maintain a person's health. A diet may be inadequate in many areas or only one. For example, many people in the United States do not eat enough vegetables and therefore are not consuming enough of many of the important nutrients found in vegetables, such as fiber-rich carbohydrate, vitamin C, beta-carotene, and potassium. Other people may eat only plant-based foods. Unless they supplement or use fortified foods, their diet will be inadequate in a single nutrient, vitamin B_{12}.

A Healthful Diet Is Moderate

Moderation refers to eating the right amounts of foods to maintain a healthy weight and to optimize the functioning of our body. People who eat too much or too little of certain foods may not be able to reach their health goals. For example, some people

trace minerals Minerals we need to consume in amounts less than 100 mg per day and of which the total amount in our body is less than 5 grams.

healthful diet A diet that provides the proper combination of energy and nutrients and is adequate, moderate, balanced, and varied.

adequate diet A diet that provides enough energy, nutrients, and fiber to maintain a person's health.

moderation Eating the right amounts of foods to maintain a healthy weight and to optimize our body's functioning.

A diet that is adequate for one person may not be adequate for another. A woman who is lightly active may require fewer kilocalories of energy per day than a highly active male, for example.

drink 60 fluid ounces (three 20 oz bottles) of soft drinks every day. Drinking this much contributes an extra 765 kcal of energy to a person's diet. To avoid weight gain from these kilocalories, most people would need to reduce their food intake, probably by cutting out healthful food choices. Consuming soft drinks in moderation keeps more energy available for nourishing foods.

A Healthful Diet Is Balanced

A **balanced diet** is one that contains the combinations of foods that provide the proper balance of nutrients. As you will learn in this course, our body needs many types of foods in varying amounts to maintain health. For example, fruits and vegetables are excellent sources of fiber, vitamin C, beta-carotene, potassium, and magnesium. Meats are not good sources of these nutrients, but they are excellent sources of protein, iron, zinc, and copper. By eating a proper balance of healthful foods, we can be confident that we are consuming enough of the nutrients we need.

A Healthful Diet Is Varied

Variety refers to eating different foods each day. In many communities in the United States, there are thousands of healthful foods to choose from. By trying new foods on a regular basis, we optimize our chances of consuming the multitude of nutrients our body needs. In addition, eating a varied diet prevents boredom and avoids getting into a "food rut."

RECAP A healthful diet provides adequate nutrients and energy in moderate amounts. A healthful diet also includes an appropriate balance and a wide variety of foods.

How Can You Design a Diet That Works for You?

Now that you know what the six classes of nutrients are, you are probably wondering how much of each you need each day. To answer this question for yourself, you need to know the current recommended nutrient intakes.

balanced diet A diet that contains the combinations of foods that provide the proper proportion of nutrients.

variety Eating different foods each day.

⬆ Knowing your daily Estimated Energy Requirement (EER) is a helpful way to maintain a healthy body weight.

Dietary Reference Intakes (DRIs)
A set of nutritional reference values for the United States and Canada that apply to healthy people.

Estimated Average Requirement (EAR) The average daily nutrient intake level estimated to meet the requirement of half of the healthy individuals in a particular life stage and gender group.

Recommended Dietary Allowance (RDA) The average daily nutrient intake level that meets the nutrient requirements of 97% to 98% of healthy individuals in a particular life stage and gender group.

Use the Dietary Reference Intakes to Figure Out Your Nutrient Needs

The lists of dietary standards in both the United States and Canada are called the **Dietary Reference Intakes (DRIs).** These standards identify the amount of a nutrient you need to prevent deficiency disease, but they also consider how much of this nutrient may reduce your risk for chronic disease. The DRIs also establish an upper level of safety for some nutrients.

The DRIs consist of six values **(Figure 1.6):**

- The **Estimated Average Requirement (EAR)** represents the average daily nutrient intake level estimated to meet the requirement of half of the healthy individuals in a particular life stage or gender group.[1] As an example, the EAR for iron for women between the ages of 19 and 30 years represents the average daily intake of iron that meets the requirement of half of the women in this age group.
- The **Recommended Dietary Allowance (RDA)** represents the average daily nutrient intake level that meets the nutrient requirements of 97% to 98% of healthy individuals in a particular life stage and gender group.[1] For example, the RDA for iron is 18 mg per day for women between the ages of 19 and 30 years. This amount of iron will meet the nutrient requirements of almost all women in this age category. Scientists use the EAR to establish the RDA. In fact, if an EAR cannot be determined for a nutrient, then this nutrient cannot have an RDA. When this occurs, an Adequate Intake value is determined for a nutrient.
- The **Adequate Intake (AI)** value is a recommended average daily nutrient intake level based on estimates of nutrient intake by a group of healthy people.[1] These estimates are assumed to be adequate and are used when the evidence necessary to determine an RDA is not available. Numerous nutrients have an AI value, including calcium, vitamin D, vitamin K, and fluoride.
- The **Tolerable Upper Intake Level (UL)** is the highest average daily intake likely to pose no risk of adverse health effects. As intake of a nutrient increases in amounts above the UL, the potential for toxic effects and health risks increases. Note that there is not enough research to define the UL for all nutrients.
- The **Estimated Energy Requirement (EER)** is the average energy (kcal) intake that is predicted to maintain energy balance in a healthy adult. This recommendation considers a person's level of physical activity: the EER for an active person is higher than the EER for an inactive person, even if all other factors (age, gender, etc.) are the same.
- The **Acceptable Macronutrient Distribution Range (AMDR)** is a range of intakes for carbohydrate, fat, and protein that is associated with reduced risk for chronic disease and provides adequate levels of essential nutrients. The AMDR is expressed as a percentage of total energy or as a percentage of total Calories **(Table 1.3).**

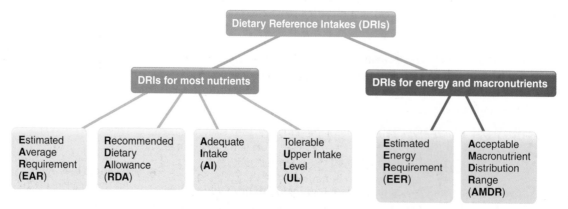

⬆ **Figure 1.6** The Dietary Reference Intakes (DRIs) for all nutrients. Note that the Estimated Energy Requirement (EER) only applies to energy (kilocalories), and the Acceptable Macronutrient Distribution Ranges (AMDRs) only apply to the macronutrients and alcohol.

TABLE 1.3	Acceptable Macronutrient Distribution Ranges (AMDRs) for Healthful Diets
Nutrient	**AMDR***
Carbohydrate	45–65%
Fat	20–35%
Protein	10–35%

*AMDR values expressed as percent of total energy or as percent of total kilocalories.
Data from *Dietary Reference Intakes for Energy, Carbohydrates, Fiber, Fat, Fatty Acids, Cholesterol, Protein, and Amino Acids*. Reprinted with permission from the National Academy of Sciences, courtesy of the National Academies Press. Copyright © 2005, National Academy of Sciences.

(Note: Many of the DRI values are listed in tables on the inside front and back covers of this book and in adjoining back pages; they are also reviewed with each nutrient as it is introduced throughout this text. To determine your nutrient needs using those tables, find your life stage group and gender in the left-hand column; then look across to see each nutrient's value that applies.) Using the DRI values in conjunction with diet-planning tools such as the Dietary Guidelines for Americans, discussed next, will help ensure a healthful and adequate diet.

Follow the Dietary Guidelines for Americans

The **Dietary Guidelines for Americans** are a set of principles developed by the U.S. Department of Agriculture and the U.S. Department of Health and Human Services to promote health, reduce the risk for chronic diseases, and reduce the prevalence of overweight and obesity among Americans through improved nutrition and physical activity.[2] They are updated approximately every 5 years. The 2010 Dietary Guidelines for Americans include twenty-three recommendations for the general population, but you don't have to remember all twenty-three! Instead, they encourage you to focus on the following four main ideas.

Balance Calories to Maintain Weight

Consume adequate nutrients to promote your health while staying within your energy needs. This will help you maintain a healthful weight. You can achieve this by controlling your Calorie intake; if you are overweight or obese, you will need to consume fewer Calories from foods and beverages. At the same time, increase your level of physical activity and reduce the time that you spend in sedentary behaviors, such as watching television and sitting at the computer.

An important strategy for balancing your Calories is to consistently choose nutrient-dense foods and beverages—that is, foods and beverages that supply the highest level of nutrients for the lowest level of Calories. **Figure 1.7** (on page 12) compares 1 day of meals that are high in **nutrient density** to meals that are low in nutrient density. As you can see in this figure, skim milk is more nutrient dense than whole milk, and a peeled orange is more nutrient dense than an orange soft drink. This example can assist you in selecting the most nutrient-dense foods when planning your meals.

Consume Fewer Foods and Food Components of Concern

The Dietary Guidelines suggest that we reduce our consumption of the following foods and food components. Doing so will help us maintain a healthy weight and lower our risks for chronic diseases.

Sodium   Excessive consumption of sodium, a major mineral found in salt, is linked to high blood pressure in some people. Eating a lot of sodium also can cause some people to lose calcium from their bones, which can increase their risk for bone loss and bone fractures. Although table salt contains sodium and the major mineral chloride, much of the sodium we consume in our diet comes from processed and prepared foods. Key recommendations include keeping your daily sodium intake below 2,300 milligrams (mg) per day. This is the amount in just 1 teaspoon of table salt! If you are African American; you have high blood pressure, diabetes, or chronic

▲ Being physically active for at least 30 minutes each day can reduce your risk for chronic diseases.

Adequate Intake (AI) A recommended average daily nutrient intake level based on observed or experimentally determined estimates of nutrient intake by a group of healthy people.

Tolerable Upper Intake Level (UL) The highest average daily nutrient intake level likely to pose no risk of adverse health effects to almost all individuals in a particular life stage and gender group.

Estimated Energy Requirement (EER) The average dietary energy intake that is predicted to maintain energy balance in a healthy adult.

Acceptable Macronutrient Distribution Range (AMDR) A range of intakes for a particular energy source that is associated with reduced risk for chronic disease while providing adequate intake of essential nutrients.

Dietary Guidelines for Americans A set of principles developed by the U.S. Department of Agriculture and the U.S. Department of Health and Human Services to assist Americans in designing a healthful diet and lifestyle.

nutrient density The relative amount of nutrients per amount of energy (or number of Calories).

A Day of Meals: Low vs. High Nutrient Density

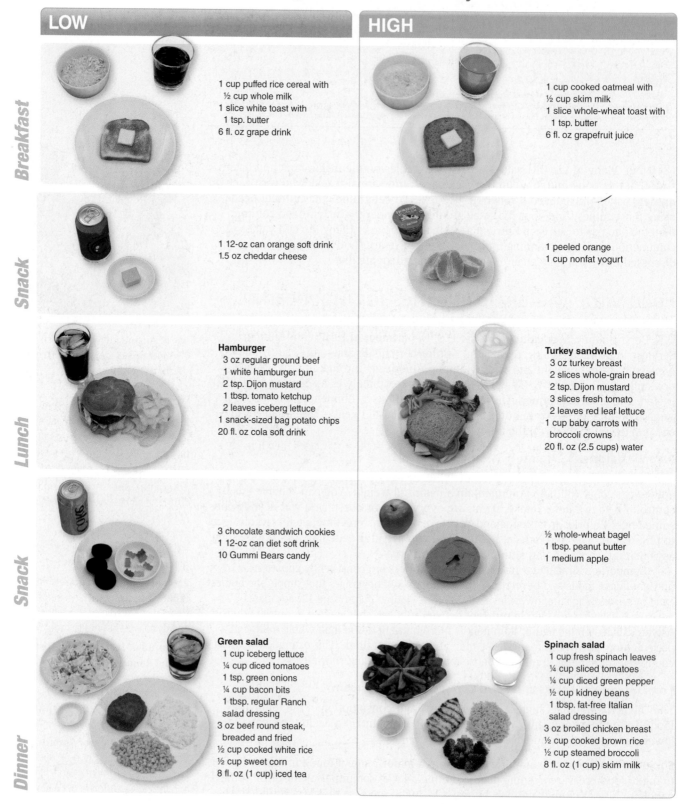

LOW

Breakfast
1 cup puffed rice cereal with
½ cup whole milk
1 slice white toast with
1 tsp. butter
6 fl. oz grape drink

Snack
1 12-oz can orange soft drink
1.5 oz cheddar cheese

Lunch
Hamburger
3 oz regular ground beef
1 white hamburger bun
2 tsp. Dijon mustard
1 tbsp. tomato ketchup
2 leaves iceberg lettuce
1 snack-sized bag potato chips
20 fl. oz cola soft drink

Snack
3 chocolate sandwich cookies
1 12-oz can diet soft drink
10 Gummi Bears candy

Dinner
Green salad
1 cup iceberg lettuce
¼ cup diced tomatoes
1 tsp. green onions
¼ cup bacon bits
1 tbsp. regular Ranch
salad dressing
3 oz beef round steak,
breaded and fried
½ cup cooked white rice
½ cup sweet corn
8 fl. oz (1 cup) iced tea

HIGH

1 cup cooked oatmeal with
½ cup skim milk
1 slice whole-wheat toast with
1 tsp. butter
6 fl. oz grapefruit juice

1 peeled orange
1 cup nonfat yogurt

Turkey sandwich
3 oz turkey breast
2 slices whole-grain bread
2 tsp. Dijon mustard
3 slices fresh tomato
2 leaves red leaf lettuce
1 cup baby carrots with
broccoli crowns
20 fl. oz (2.5 cups) water

½ whole-wheat bagel
1 tbsp. peanut butter
1 medium apple

Spinach salad
1 cup fresh spinach leaves
¼ cup sliced tomatoes
¼ cup diced green pepper
½ cup kidney beans
1 tbsp. fat-free Italian
salad dressing
3 oz broiled chicken breast
½ cup cooked brown rice
½ cup steamed broccoli
8 fl. oz (1 cup) skim milk

Figure 1.7 A comparison of 1 day's meals containing foods low in nutrient density to meals with foods high in nutrient density.

kidney disease; or you are over age 50, you should aim for a daily sodium intake below 1,500 mg. Some ways to decrease your sodium intake include the following:

- Eat fresh, plain frozen, or canned vegetables without added salt.
- Limit your intake of processed meats, such as cured ham, sausage, bacon, and most canned meats.
- When shopping for canned or packaged foods, look for those with labels that say "low sodium."
- Add little or no salt to foods at home.
- Limit your intake of salty condiments, such as ketchup, mustard, pickles, soy sauce, and olives.

Fat   Fat is an essential nutrient and therefore an important part of a healthful diet; however, because fats are energy dense, eating a diet high in total fat can lead to overweight and obesity. In addition, eating a diet high in cholesterol and saturated fat (a type of fat abundant in meats and other animal-based foods) is linked to an increased risk for heart disease. For these reasons, less than 10% of your total daily Calories should come from saturated fat, and you should try to consume less than 300 mg per day of cholesterol. You can achieve this goal by replacing solid fats, such as butter and lard, with vegetable oils, as well as by eating meat less often and fish or vegetarian meals more often. Finally, replace full-fat milk, yogurt, and cheeses with low-fat or nonfat versions.

Sugars   Limit foods and beverages that are high in added sugars, such as sweetened soft drinks and fruit drinks, cookies, and cakes. These foods contribute to overweight and obesity, and they promote tooth decay. Moreover, doughnuts, cookies, cakes, pies, and other pastries are typically made with unhealthful fats and are high in sodium.

Alcohol   Alcohol provides energy, but not nutrients. In the body, it depresses the nervous system and is toxic to liver and other body cells. Drinking alcoholic beverages in excess can lead to serious health and social problems; therefore, those who choose to drink are encouraged to do so sensibly and in moderation: no more than one drink per day for women and no more than two drinks per day for men, and only by adults of legal drinking age. Adults who should not drink alcohol are those who cannot restrict their intake, women of childbearing age who may become pregnant, pregnant and lactating women, individuals taking medications that can interact with alcohol, people with certain medical conditions, and people who are engaging in activities that require attention, skill, or coordination.

Consume More Healthful Foods and Nutrients

Another goal of the Dietary Guidelines is to encourage people to increase their consumption of healthful foods rich in nutrients, while keeping their Calorie intake within their daily energy needs. Key recommendations for achieving this goal include the following:

- Increase your intake of fruits and vegetables. Each day, try to eat a variety of dark-green, red, and orange vegetables, along with beans and peas.
- Make sure that at least half of all grain foods—breads, cereals, pasta, etc.—that you eat each day are made from whole grains.
- Choose fat-free or low-fat milk and milk products, which includes milk, yogurt, cheese, and fortified soy beverages.
- When making protein choices, choose protein foods that are lower in solid fat and Calories, such as lean cuts of beef or skinless poultry. Try to eat more fish and shellfish in place of traditional meat and poultry choices. Also choose eggs, beans and peas, soy products, and unsalted nuts and seeds.
- Choose foods that provide an adequate level of dietary fiber as well as nutrients of concern in the American diet, including potassium, calcium, and vitamin D. These nutrients help us maintain healthy blood pressure and reduce our risks for certain diseases. Healthful foods that are good sources of these nutrients include fruits, vegetables, beans and peas, whole grains, and low-fat milk and milk products.

Follow Healthy Eating Patterns

There is no one healthy eating pattern that everyone should follow. Instead, the recommendations made in the Dietary Guidelines are designed to accommodate diverse

When grocery shopping, try to select a variety of fruits and vegetables.

Eating a diet rich in whole-grain foods, such as whole-wheat bread and brown rice, can enhance your overall health.

90% 🔋

GAME PLAN

Ways to Incorporate the Dietary Guidelines into Your Daily Life

People experience a wide range of reactions when reading the Dietary Guidelines for Americans. Some feel satisfied that they are already following them, but many people see one or more areas where their behaviors could improve. If that sounds like you, and

you'd like to make some changes, we recommend you start small. Substitute just one of these actions for your regular behavior each week, and by the time you finish this course, you'll have made the Dietary Guidelines for Americans part of your healthy life!

If You Normally Do This . . .	Try Doing This Instead . . .
Watch television when you get home at night	Do 30 minutes of stretching or lifting of hand weights in front of the television
Drive to the store down the block	Walk to and from the store
Go out to lunch with friends	Take a 15- to 30-minute walk with your friends at lunchtime 3 days each week
Eat white bread with your sandwich	Switch to a bread made from whole grains
Eat white rice or fried rice with your meal	Eat brown rice or wild rice
Choose cookies or a candy bar for a snack	Choose a fresh peach, apple, pear, orange, or banana for a snack
Order french fries with your hamburger	Order a green salad with low-fat salad dressing on the side
Spread butter or margarine on your white toast each morning	Spread fresh fruit compote or peanut butter on whole-grain toast
Order a bacon double cheeseburger at your favorite restaurant	Order a grilled chicken sandwich with lettuce and tomato
Drink sugared soft drinks to quench your thirst	Drink water with a slice of lemon, diet soft drinks, or iced tea
Eat potato chips with your favorite sandwich	Eat baby carrots or slices of sweet red pepper dipped in low-fat ranch dressing

cultural, ethnic, traditional, and personal preferences and to fit within different individuals' food budgets. Still, the Guidelines offer several flexible templates you can follow to build your healthy eating pattern, including the USDA Food Patterns and the Mediterranean diet (both discussed shortly).

Building a healthy eating pattern also involves following food safety recommendations to reduce your risk for foodborne illnesses, such as those caused by microorganisms and their toxins. The four food safety principles emphasized in the Dietary Guidelines are

- *Clean* your hands, food contact surfaces, and vegetables and fruits;
- *Separate* raw, cooked, and ready-to-eat foods while shopping, storing, and preparing foods;
- *Cook* foods to a safe temperature; and
- *Chill* (refrigerate) perishable foods promptly.

Another important tip is to avoid unpasteurized juices and milk products and raw or undercooked meats, seafood, poultry, eggs, and raw sprouts.

The *Game Plan* feature box (on page 14) provides examples of how you can change your current diet and physical activity habits to meet some of the recommendations in the Dietary Guidelines.

RECAP The goals of the Dietary Guidelines for Americans are to promote health, reduce the risk for chronic diseases, and reduce the prevalence of overweight and obesity among Americans through improved nutrition and physical activity. This can be achieved by eating whole-grain foods, fruits, and vegetables daily; reducing intake of foods with unhealthful fats and cholesterol, salt, and added sugar; eating more foods rich in potassium, dietary fiber, calcium, and vitamin D; keeping foods safe to eat; and drinking alcohol in moderation, if at all.

The USDA Food Patterns

As just mentioned, you can use the U.S. Department of Agriculture (USDA) Food Patterns to design healthy eating patterns. The visual representation of the USDA Food Patterns is called **MyPlate (Figure 1.8)**. MyPlate, which was released in May 2011, is an interactive, personalized guide that you can access on the Internet to assess your current diet and physical activity level and to plan appropriate changes. MyPlate replaces the previous MyPyramid graphic (see Appendix A). While many variations of MyPyramid will continue to be displayed and referenced until new MyPlate versions can be developed, MyPlate is the now the primary food icon intended to help Americans make better food choices; it illustrates how to

- eat in moderation to balance calories,
- eat a variety of foods,
- consume the right proportion of each recommended food group,
- personalize their eating plan,
- increase their physical activity, and
- set goals for gradually improving their food choices and lifestyle.

MyPlate encourages people to eat a variety of fruits.

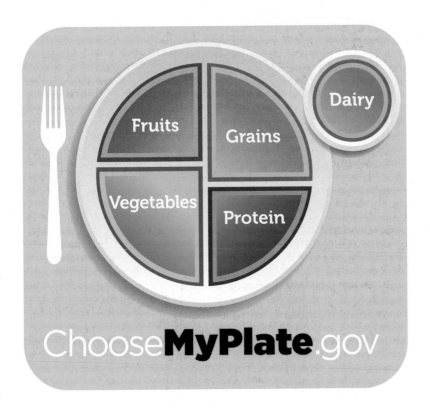

Figure 1.8 The USDA MyPlate graphic. MyPlate is an interactive food guidance system based on the 2010 Dietary Guidelines for Americans and the Dietary Reference Intakes from the National Academy of Sciences. Eating more fruits, vegetables, and whole grains and choosing foods low in fat, sugar, and sodium from the five food groups in MyPlate will help you balance your Calories and consume a healthier overall diet.

Food Groups in the USDA Food Patterns

The food groups emphasized in the USDA Food Patterns are grains, vegetables, fruits, dairy, and protein foods. The food groups are represented in the plate graphic with segments of five different colors. **Figure 1.9** illustrates each of these food groups and

Grains

Make half your grains whole. At least half of the grains you eat each day should come from whole-grain sources.

Eat at least 3 oz of whole-grain bread, cereal, crackers, rice, or pasta every day.

Whole-grain foods provide fiber-rich carbohydrates, riboflavin, thiamin, niacin, iron, folate, zinc, protein, and magnesium.

Vegetables

Vary your veggies. Eat a variety of vegetables and increase consumption of dark-green and orange vegetables, as well as dry beans and peas.

Eat at least 2½ cups of vegetables each day.

Vegetables provide fiber and phytochemicals, carbohydrates, vitamins A and C, folate, potassium, and magnesium.

Fruits

Focus on fruits. Eat a greater variety of fruits (fresh, frozen, or dried) and go easy on the fruit juices.

Eat at least 1½ cups of fruit every day.

Fruits provide fiber, phytochemicals, vitamins A and C, folate, potassium, and magnesium.

Dairy Foods

Get your calcium-rich foods. Choose low-fat or fat-free dairy products, such as milk, yogurt, and cheese. People who can't consume dairy foods can choose lactose-free dairy products or other sources, such as calcium-fortified juices and soy and rice beverages.

Get 3 cups of low-fat dairy foods, or the equivalent, every day.

Dairy foods provide calcium, phosphorus, riboflavin, protein, and vitamin B_{12} and are often fortified with vitamins D and A.

Protein Foods

Go lean with protein. Choose low-fat or lean meats and poultry. Switch to baking, broiling, or grilling more often, and vary your choices to include more fish, processed soy products, beans, nuts, and seeds. Legumes, including beans, peas, and lentils, are included in both the protein and the vegetable groups.

Eat about 5½ oz of lean protein foods each day.

These foods provide protein, phosphorus, vitamin B_6, vitamin B_{12}, magnesium, iron, zinc, niacin, riboflavin, and thiamin.

Figure 1.9 Food groups of the USDA Food Patterns.

provides more detailed information on the nutrients they provide and recommended servings each day.

The Concept of Empty Calories

One concept emphasized in the USDA Food Patterns is that of **empty Calories.** These are Calories from solid fats and/or added sugars that provide few or no nutrients. The USDA recommends that you limit the empty Calories you eat to a small number that fits your Calorie and nutrient needs depending on your age, gender, and level of physical activity. Foods that contain the most empty Calories for Americans include cakes, cookies, pastries, doughnuts, soft drinks, fruit drinks, cheese, pizza, ice cream, sausages, hot dogs, bacon, and ribs. High-sugar foods, such as candies, desserts, gelatin, soft drinks, and alcoholic beverages, are called *empty Calorie foods.* However, a few foods that contain empty Calories from solid fats and added sugars also provide important nutrients. Examples are sweetened applesauce, sweetened breakfast cereals, regular ground beef, and whole milk. To reduce your intake of empty Calories but ensure you get adequate nutrients, choose the unsweetened, lean, or non-fat versions of these foods.

Number and Size of Servings in the USDA Food Patterns

The USDA Food Patterns also helps you decide *how much* of each food you should eat. The number of servings is based on your age, gender, and activity level. A term used when defining serving sizes that may be new to you is **ounce-equivalent (oz-equivalent).** It is defined as a serving size that is 1 ounce, or is equivalent to an ounce, for the grains and meats and beans sections. For instance, both a slice of bread and ½ cup of cooked brown rice qualify as ounce-equivalents.

What is considered a serving size for the foods recommended in the USDA Food Patterns? **Figure 1.10** (on page 18) identifies the number of cups or oz-equivalent servings recommended for a 2,000-Calorie diet and gives examples of amounts equal to 1 cup or 1 oz-equivalent for foods in each group. As you study this figure, notice the variety of examples for each group. For instance, an oz-equivalent serving from the grains group can mean one slice of bread or two small pancakes. Because of their low density, 2 cups of raw, leafy vegetables, such as spinach, actually constitute a 1-cup serving from the vegetables group. Although an oz-equivalent serving of meat is actually 1 oz, ½ oz of nuts also qualifies. One egg, 1 tablespoon of peanut butter, protein and ¼ cup cooked legumes are also considered 1 oz-equivalents from the protein group. Although it may seem inconvenient to measure food servings, understanding the size of a serving is crucial to planning a nutritious diet. **Figure 1.11** (on page 19) shows you a practical way to estimate serving sizes using just your own hand.

No nationally standardized definition for a serving size exists for any food. Thus, a serving size as defined in the USDA Food Patterns may not be equal to a serving size identified on a food label. For instance, the serving size for crackers suggested in the USDA Food Patterns is three to four small crackers, whereas a serving size for crackers on a food label can range from five to eighteen crackers, depending on the size and weight of the cracker.

For food items consumed individually, such as muffins, frozen burgers, and bottled juices, the serving sizes in the USDA Food Patterns are typically much smaller than the items we actually buy and eat. In addition, serving sizes in restaurants, cafés, and movie theaters have grown substantially over the past 30 years (**Figure 1.12**, page 19). This "super-sizing" phenomenon, now seen even at home, indicates a major shift in accepted eating behaviors. It is also an important contributor to the rise in obesity rates around the world. A recent study[3] reported that the discrepancy between USDA serving sizes and the portion size of many common foods sold outside the home is

 Think you understand the relationship between portion sizes and the physical activity necessary to avoid weight gain? Find out by taking the National Heart, Lung, and Blood Institute's *Portion Distortion Quiz* at http://hp2010.nhlbihin .net/portion.

empty Calories Calories from solid fats and/or added sugars that provide few or no nutrients.

ounce-equivalent (oz-equivalent) A term used to define a serving size that is 1 ounce, or equivalent to an ounce, for the grains section and the protein foods section of MyPlate.

Serving Size Examples: 1 cup of 1 Oz-Equivalent

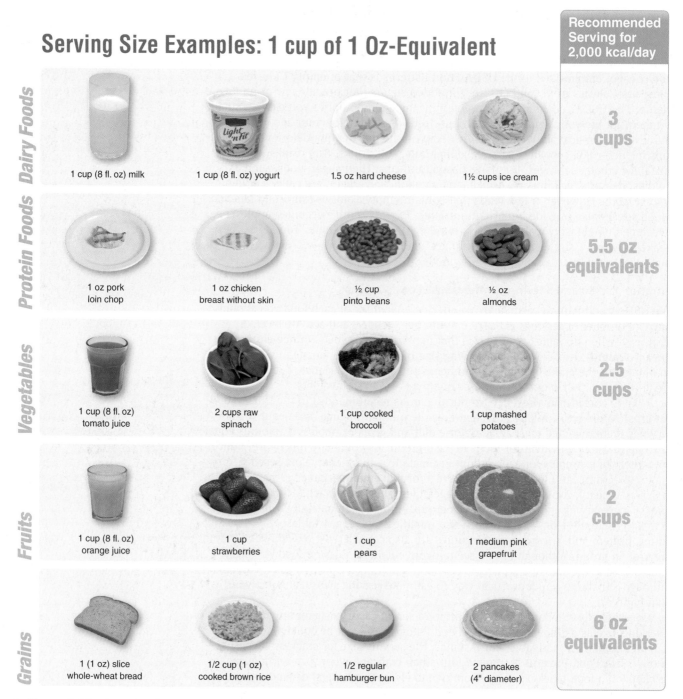

Recommended Serving for 2,000 kcal/day
Dairy Foods
1 cup (8 fl. oz) milk — 1 cup (8 fl. oz) yogurt — 1.5 oz hard cheese — 1½ cups ice cream	**3 cups**
Protein Foods
1 oz pork loin chop — 1 oz chicken breast without skin — ½ cup pinto beans — ½ oz almonds	**5.5 oz equivalents**
Vegetables
1 cup (8 fl. oz) tomato juice — 2 cups raw spinach — 1 cup cooked broccoli — 1 cup mashed potatoes	**2.5 cups**
Fruits
1 cup (8 fl. oz) orange juice — 1 cup strawberries — 1 cup pears — 1 medium pink grapefruit	**2 cups**
Grains
1 (1 oz) slice whole-wheat bread — 1/2 cup (1 oz) cooked brown rice — 1/2 regular hamburger bun — 2 pancakes (4" diameter)	**6 oz equivalents**

⬆ **Figure 1.10** Examples of serving sizes for foods in each food group of MyPlate for a 2,000-Calorie food intake pattern. Here are some examples of household items that can help you estimate serving sizes: 1.5 oz of hard cheese is equal to four stacked dice, 3 oz of meat is equal in size to a deck of cards, and half of a regular hamburger bun is the size of a yo-yo.

staggering—chocolate chip cookies are seven times larger than USDA standards, a serving of cooked pasta in a restaurant is almost five times larger, and steaks are more than twice as large.[4] Thus, when using diet-planning tools, such as the USDA Food Patterns, learn the definition of a serving size for the tool you're using and *then* measure your food intake to determine whether you are meeting the guidelines. If you don't want to gain weight, it's important to become informed about portion size.

Ethnic Variations of MyPyramid

As you know, the population of the United States is culturally and ethnically diverse, and this diversity influences our food choices. Foods that we may typically consider a part of an Asian, a Latin American, or a Mediterranean diet can also fit into a healthful diet. As previously mentioned, the MyPlate graphic is replacing MyPyramid; however, MyPlate graphics have not yet been developed for various ethnic diets. Still, you can easily incorporate foods that match your specific ethnic, religious, or other lifestyle preferences into your own personal MyPlate. You can also use one of the many ethnic and cultural variations of the previous USDA Food Guide Pyramid. These include the Latin American Diet Pyramid and the Asian Diet Pyramid, shown in **Figure 1.13** (page 20). There are also variations for Native Americans, African Americans, and many others.[5] These variations illustrate that anyone can design a healthful diet to accommodate his or her food preferences.

Of these variations, the Mediterranean diet has enjoyed considerable popularity. Does it deserve its reputation as a healthful diet? Check out the ***Nutrition Myth or Fact?*** box (page 21) to learn more.

Want to assess the quality of your overall diet? Or to learn whether you need more of any nutrient—or less? Use the USDA MyPyramid Tracker at www.mypyramidtracker.gov.

A woman's palm is approximately the size of 3 ounces of cooked meat, chicken, or fish

(a)

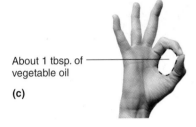

A woman's fist is about the size of 1 cup of pasta or vegetables (a man's fist is the size of about 2 cups)

(b)

About 1 tbsp. of vegetable oil

(c)

⬆ **Figure 1.11** Use your hands to help estimate serving sizes of common foods.

⬆ To avoid unwanted weight gain, it's important to understand the role of portion control.

20 Years Ago   **Today**

3-inch diameter, 140 Calories   6-inch diameter, 350 Calories

(a) Bagel

8 fluid ounces, 42 Calories   16 fluid ounces, 350 Calories

(b) Coffee

⬆ **Figure 1.12** Examples of increases in food portion sizes over the past 20 years. **(a)** A bagel has increased in diameter from 3 inches to 6 inches; **(b)** a cup of coffee has increased from 8 fl. oz to 16 fl. oz and now commonly contains Calorie-dense flavored syrup as well as steamed whole milk.

▶ **Figure 1.13** Ethnic variations of healthy eating plans. **(a)** The Latin American Diet Pyramid. **(b)** The Asian Diet Pyramid.

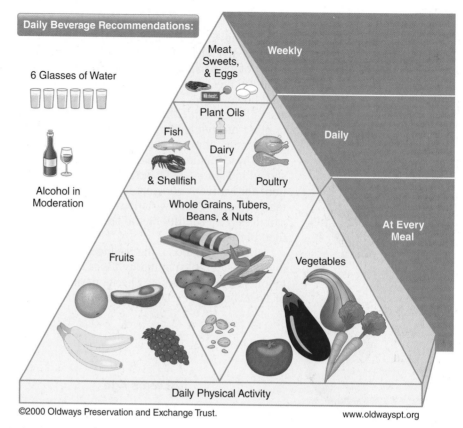

(a) Latin American Diet Pyramid

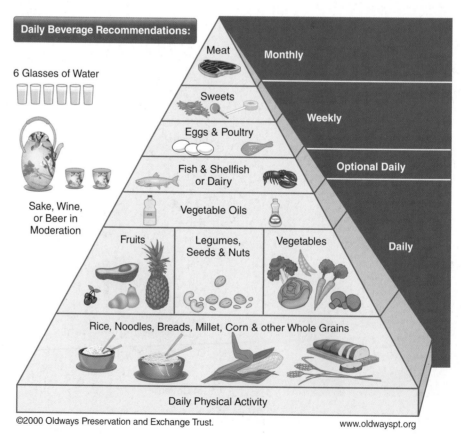

(b) Asian Diet Pyramid

NUTRITION MYTH OR FACT?

The Mediterranean Diet: Just Another Fad?

A Mediterranean-style diet has received significant attention in recent years, as the rates of cardiovascular disease in many Mediterranean countries are substantially lower than the rates in the United States. These countries include Portugal, Spain, Italy, France, Greece, Turkey, and Israel. Each country has unique dietary patterns; however, they share the following characteristics:

- Meat is eaten monthly, and eggs, poultry, fish, and sweets are eaten weekly, making the diet low in saturated fats and refined sugars.
- The fat used predominantly for cooking and flavor is olive oil, making the diet high in monounsaturated fats.
- Foods eaten daily include grains, such as bread, pasta, couscous, and bulgur; fruits; beans and other legumes; nuts; vegetables; and cheese and yogurt. These choices make this diet high in fiber and rich in vitamins and minerals.

Figure 1.14 illustrates the Mediterranean Diet Pyramid. Its similarities to the USDA Food Patterns include suggestions for daily physical activity and a daily intake of whole grain breads, cereals, other grains, fruits, and vegetables. It is different from the USDA Food Patterns in that it includes the daily consumption of beans, other legumes, and nuts and less frequent consumption of meat, fish, poultry, and eggs. Cheese and yogurt, rather than milk, are the primary dairy sources. A unique feature of the Mediterranean diet is the consumption of wine and olive oil daily.

Interestingly, the Mediterranean diet is not lower in fat; in fact, about 40% of the total energy in this diet is derived from fat, which is much higher than the dietary fat recommendations made in the United States. However, the majority of fat in the Mediterranean diet is from plant oils, which are more healthful sources than the animal fats found in the U.S. diet, making the Mediterranean diet more protective against cardiovascular disease. Thus, far from being a fad diet, the Mediterranean Diet is an excellent example of a healthy eating pattern that you can follow.

Figure 1.14 The Mediterranean Diet Pyramid.
Copyright ©2009 Oldways Preservation & Exchange Trust. www.oldwayspt.org. Reprinted by permission.

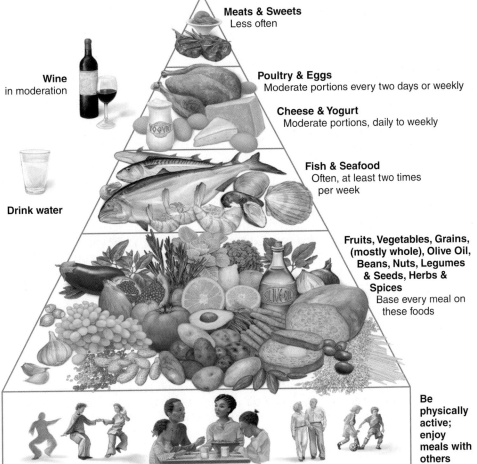

Meats & Sweets
Less often

Wine
in moderation

Poultry & Eggs
Moderate portions every two days or weekly

Cheese & Yogurt
Moderate portions, daily to weekly

Fish & Seafood
Often, at least two times per week

Drink water

Fruits, Vegetables, Grains, (mostly whole), Olive Oil, Beans, Nuts, Legumes & Seeds, Herbs & Spices
Base every meal on these foods

Be physically active; enjoy meals with others

Illustration by Geoge Middleton © 2009 Oldways Preservation and Exchange Trust www.oldwayspt.org

RECAP The USDA Food Patterns can be used to plan a healthful, balanced diet that includes foods from the grains group, vegetables group, fruits group, dairy group, and protein foods group. As defined in the USDA Food Patterns, serving sizes typically are smaller than the amounts we normally eat or are served, so it is important to learn the definitions of serving sizes when using the USDA Food Patterns to design a healthful diet. There are many ethnic and cultural variations of the USDA Food Patterns. This flexibility enables anyone to design a diet that meets the goals of adequacy, moderation, balance, variety, and nutrient density.

Read Food Labels

If you want to take control of your food choices, then it's essential to read food labels. That's because food labels give you the facts behind the hype. The U.S. Food and Drug Administration (FDA) requires all food manufacturers to include complete nutrition information on labels of all packaged foods. Besides fresh produce and meats, which are unpackaged or minimally packaged, the only products exempt from the labeling requirement are foods, such as coffee and most spices, that contain insignificant amounts of all nutrients.

Keep in mind that the current nutrition labeling system used in the United States is evolving. The FDA is planning to revise current regulations, so that food labels provide information that is clearer to consumers and more consistent with recent updates in the Dietary Guidelines. Possible changes under consideration include more concise and consistent front-of-package information, more appropriate information on number of servings contained within the entire package of food, less complex ingredient information, and tighter regulation of health claims made by manufacturers. The following sections describe what is currently required on food labels.

Five Components Must Be Included on Food Labels

Five primary components of information must be included on food labels **(Figure 1.15)**:

1. *A statement of identity:* The common name of the product or an appropriate identification must be prominently displayed on the label.
2. *The net contents of the package:* This information accurately describes the quantity of the food product in the entire package. This information may be listed as weight (e.g., grams), volume (e.g., fluid ounces), or numerical count (e.g., four bars).
3. *Ingredient list:* The ingredients must be listed by their common name, in descending order by weight. This means that the first product listed in the ingredient list is the predominant ingredient in that food.
4. *The name and address of the food manufacturer, packer, or distributor:* This information can be used to contact the company.
5. *Nutrition Facts Panel:* This panel is the primary tool to assist you in choosing more healthful foods. Let's take a closer look at the components of the Nutrition Facts Panel.

How to Read and Use the Nutrition Facts Panel

Figure 1.16 (on page 24) shows an example of a **Nutrition Facts Panel.** This part of the label includes a variety of information that is useful when designing a healthful diet. Let's start at the top of the panel and work our way down.

1. *Serving size and servings per container:* The FDA has defined serving sizes based on the amounts people typically eat for each food. However, keep in mind that the serving size listed on the package may not be the same as the amount you eat. You must factor in how much of the food you eat when determining the amount of nutrients that this food contributes to your actual diet.
2. *Total Calories and Calories from fat per serving:* By looking at this section of the label, you can determine if this food is relatively high in fat. For example, one serving of the food on this label contains 320 total Calories, of which 90 are from

Nutrition Facts Panel The label on a food package that contains the nutrition information required by the FDA.

▲ **Figure 1.15**   The five primary components that are required for food labels.
Data from Food Label © Con Agra Foods.

fat. This means that this food contains approximately 28% of its total Calories as fat, making it relatively low in fat.

3. *List of nutrients:* Those nutrients listed toward the top, including total fat, saturated fat, cholesterol, and sodium, are generally nutrients that we strive to limit in a healthful diet. Some of the nutrients listed toward the bottom are those we try to consume more of, including fiber, vitamins A and C, calcium, and iron.

4. **The percent daily values (%DV):** This information tells you how much a serving of food contributes to your overall intake of nutrients listed on the label. Because we are all individuals with unique nutritional needs, it is impossible to include nutrition information that applies to each person consuming this food. Thus, the FDA used standards based on a 2,000-Calorie diet when defining the %DV. You can use these percentages to determine whether a food is high or low in a given nutrient, even if you do not consume a 2,000-Calorie diet each day. For example, if you are trying to consume more calcium, you might compare the labels of two different brands of fortified orange juice: you read that one contains 10% DV for calcium in an 8 oz serving, whereas the other contains 25% DV for calcium in an 8 oz serving. Thus, you can make your choice between these products without having to know anything about how many Calories you need.

5. *Footnote:* The footnote includes an explanatory note and a table with Daily Values for a 2,000- and 2,500-Calorie diet. This table, which may not be present on the package if the size of the food label is too small, is always the same because the information refers to nutrients, not to a specific food. Fort instance, it states that someone eating 2,000 Calories should strive to eat less than 65 g of fat per day, whereas a person eating 2,500 Calories should eat less than 80 g of fat per day.

Think you understand how to read the Nutrition Facts Panel? Take an interactive quiz and find out at www.extension.iastate .edu/healthnutrition/ nutrition/diet/nutrition _label.htm.

percent daily values (%DV) Information on a Nutrition Facts Panel that tells you how much a serving of food contributes to your overall intake of nutrients listed on the label. The information is based on an energy intake of 2,000 Calories per day.

Figure 1.16 The Nutrition Facts Panel contains a variety of information to help you select more healthful food choices.

Nutrition Facts

Serving Size: 3.5 oz
Servings Per Container about 4

Amount Per Serving	
Calories 320	
Calories from Fat 90	

	% Daily Value
Total Fat 10g	15%
Saturated Fat 3.5g	18%
Trans Fat 1g	
Cholesterol 20mg	7%
Sodium 890mg	37%
Total Carbohydrate 44g	15%
Dietary Fiber 2g	8%
Sugars 4g	
Protein 13g	16%

Vitamin A 4%	●	Vitamin C 0%	
Calcium 15%	●	Iron 15%	

*Percent Daily Values are based on a 2,000 calorie diet. Your daily values may be higher or lower depending on your calorie needs:

		Calories	2,000	2,500
Total Fat	Less than		65g	80g
Sat. Fat	Less than		20g	25g
Cholest.	Less than		300mg	300mg
Sodium	Less than		2,400mg	2,400mg
Total Carb			300g	375g
Fiber			25g	30g
Protein			50g	65g

1. Serving size and servings per container

2. Calories and Calories from fat per serving

3. List of nutrients and
4. % Daily Values

5. Footnote for Daily Values

Food Labels Can Contain a Variety of Claims

Have you ever noticed a food label displaying a claim such as "This food is low in sodium" or "This food is part of a heart-healthy diet"? The claim may have influenced you to buy the food, even if you weren't sure what it meant. Let's take a look.

The FDA regulates two types of claims that food companies put on food labels: nutrient claims and health claims. Food companies are prohibited from using a nutrient or health claim that is not approved by the FDA.

The Daily Values on the food labels serve as a basis for nutrient claims. For instance, if the label states that a food is "low in sodium," the food must contain 140 mg or less of sodium per serving. **Table 1.4** defines the terms approved for use in nutrient claims.

The FDA also allows food labels to display certain claims related to health and disease (**Table 1.5**, page 26). The claims listed are backed up with significant scientific agreement as to their validity. If current scientific evidence about a particular health claim is not convincing, the label may have to include a disclaimer, so that consumers are not misled.

In addition to nutrient and health claims, labels may also contain structure–function claims. These claims can be made without approval from the FDA. Although these claims can be generic statements about a food's impact on the body's structure

TABLE 1.4   U.S. Food and Drug Administration (FDA)–Approved Nutrient-Related Terms and Definitions

Nutrient	Claim	Meaning
Energy	Calorie free	Less than 5 kcal per serving
	Low Calorie	40 kcal or less per serving
	Reduced Calorie	At least 25% fewer kcal than reference (or regular) food
Fat and cholesterol	Fat free	Less than 0.5 g of fat per serving
	Low fat	3 g or less fat per serving
	Reduced fat	At least 25% less fat per serving than reference food
	Saturated fat free	Less than 0.5 g of saturated fat **AND** less than 0.5 g of *trans* fat per serving
	Low saturated fat	1 g or less saturated fat and less than 0.5 g *trans* fat per serving **AND** 15% or less of total kcal from saturated fat
	Reduced saturated fat	At least 25% less saturated fat **AND** reduced by more than 1 g saturated fat per serving as compared to reference food
	Cholesterol free	Less than 2 mg of cholesterol per serving **AND** 2 g or less saturated fat and *trans* fat combined per serving
	Low cholesterol	20 mg or less cholesterol **AND** 2 g or less saturated fat per serving
	Reduced cholesterol	At least 25% less cholesterol than reference food **AND** 2 g or less saturated fat per serving
Fiber and sugar	High fiber	5 g or more fiber per serving*
	Good source of fiber	2.5 g to 4.9 g fiber per serving
	More or added fiber	At least 2.5 g more fiber per serving than reference food
	Sugar free	Less than 0.5 g sugars per serving
	Low sugar	Not defined; no basis for recommended intake
	Reduced/less sugar	At least 25% less sugars per serving than reference food
	No added sugars or without added sugars	No sugar or sugar-containing ingredient added during processing
Sodium	Sodium free	Less than 5 mg sodium per serving
	Very low sodium	35 mg or less sodium per serving
	Low sodium	140 mg or less sodium per serving
	Reduced sodium	At least 25% less sodium per serving than reference food
Relative claims	Free, without, no, zero	No or a trivial amount of given nutrient
	Light (or lite)	This term can have three different meanings: (1) a serving provides ⅓ fewer kcal than or half the fat of the reference food; (2) a serving of a low-fat, low-Calorie food provides half the sodium normally present; or (3) lighter in color and texture, with the label making this clear (for example, light molasses)
	Reduced, less, fewer	Contains at least 25% less of a nutrient or kcal than reference food
	More, added, extra, or plus	At least 10% of the Daily Value of nutrient as compared to reference food (may occur naturally or be added). May only be used for vitamins, minerals, protein, dietary fiber, and potassium.
	Good source of, contains, or provides	10% to 19% of Daily Value per serving (may not be used for carbohydrate)
	High in, rich in, or excellent source of	20% or more of Daily Value per serving for protein, vitamins, minerals, dietary fiber, or potassium (may not be used for carbohydrate)

*High-fiber claims must also meet the definition of low fat; if not, then the level of total fat must appear next to the high-fiber claim.
Data from U.S. Food and Drug Administration. 2009. Food Labeling Guide. Available at http://www.fda.gov/Food/GuidanceComplianceRegulatoryInformation/GuidanceDocuments/FoodLabelingNutrition/FoodLabelingGuide/default.htm.

and function, they cannot refer to a specific disease or symptom. Examples of structure–function claims include "Builds stronger bones," "Improves memory," "Slows signs of aging," and "Boosts your immune system." It is important to remember that these claims can be made with no proof, and thus there are no guarantees that any benefits identified in structure–function claims are true about that food. Thus, just because something is stated on the label doesn't guarantee it is always true!

TABLE 1.5 U.S. Food and Drug Administration–Approved Health Claims on Labels

Disease/Health Concern	Nutrient	Example of Approved Claim Statement
Osteoporosis	Calcium	Regular exercise and a healthy diet with enough calcium help teens and young adult white and Asian women maintain good bone health and may reduce their high risk for osteoporosis later in life.
Coronary heart disease	Saturated fat and cholesterol Fruits, vegetables, and grain products that contain fiber, particularly soluble fiber Soluble fiber from whole oats, psyllium seed husk, and beta glucan soluble fiber from oat bran, rolled oats (or oatmeal), and whole oat flour Soy protein Plant sterol/stanol esters Whole-grain foods	Diets low in saturated fat and cholesterol and rich in fruits, vegetables, and grain products that contain some types of dietary fiber, particularly soluble fiber, may reduce the risk for heart disease, a disease associated with many factors.
Cancer	Dietary fat Fiber-containing grain products, fruits, and vegetables Fruits and vegetables Whole-grain foods	Low-fat diets rich in fiber-containing grain products, fruits, and vegetables may reduce the risk for some types of cancer, a disease associated with many factors.
Hypertension and stroke	Sodium Potassium	Diets containing foods that are a good source of potassium and that are low in sodium may reduce the risk for high blood pressure and stroke.*
Neural tube defects	Folate	Healthful diets with adequate folate may reduce a woman's risk of having a child with a brain or spinal cord defect.
Dental caries	Sugar alcohols	Frequent between-meal consumption of foods high in sugars and starches promotes tooth decay. The sugar alcohols in [name of food] do not promote tooth decay.

*Required wording for this claim. Wordings for other claims are recommended model statements but not required verbatim.
Data from U.S. Food and Drug Administration. 2009. Food Labeling Guide. Available at http://www.fda.gov/Food/GuidanceComplianceRegulatoryInformation/GuidanceDocuments/FoodLabelingNutrition/FoodLabelingGuide/default.htm.

NUTRI-CASE GUSTAVO

"Until last night, I hadn't stepped inside of a grocery store for 10 years, maybe more. But then my wife fell and broke her hip and had to go to the hospital. On my way home from visiting her, I remembered that we didn't have much food in the house, so I thought I'd do a little shopping. Was I ever in for a shock. I don't know how my wife does it, choosing between all the different brands, reading those long labels. She never went to school past sixth grade, and she doesn't speak English very well, either! I bought a frozen chicken pie for my dinner, but it didn't taste right. So I got the package out of the trash and read all the labels, and that's when I realized there wasn't any chicken in it at all! It was made out of tofu! This afternoon, my daughter is picking me up, and we're going to do our grocery shopping together."

Given what you've learned about FDA food labels, what parts of a food package would you advise Gustavo to be sure to read before he makes a choice? What other advice might you give him to make his grocery shopping easier? Imagine that, like Gustavo's wife, you have only limited skills in mathematics and reading. In that case, what other strategies might you use when shopping for nutritious foods?

RECAP The ability to read and interpret food labels is important for planning and maintaining a healthful diet. Food labels must list the identity of the food, the net contents of the package, the contact information for the food manufacturer or distributor, the ingredients in the food, and a Nutrition Facts Panel. The Nutrition Facts Panel provides specific information about Calories, macronutrients, and selected vitamins and minerals. Food labels may also contain FDA-approved claims related to nutrients and health, but body structure and function claims can be made without approval from the FDA.

Whom Can You Trust to Help You Choose Foods Wisely?

Over the past few decades, the public has become more and more interested in understanding how nutrition affects health. One result of this booming interest has been the publication of an almost overwhelming quantity of nutritional information and claims on television infomercials; on websites; in newspapers, magazines, and journals; on product packages; and via many other forums. Most of us do not have the knowledge or training to interpret and evaluate the reliability of this information and thus are vulnerable to misinformation.

Throughout this text we provide information and activities to help you become a more educated consumer regarding nutrition. As you may know, **quackery** is the misrepresentation of a product, program, or service for financial gain. For example, a high-priced supplement may be marketed as uniquely therapeutic when, in fact, it is only as effective as much less expensive alternatives that are commonly available. Many manufacturers of such products describe them as "patented," but this means only that the product has been registered with the U.S. Patent Office, for a fee. It provides no guarantee of the product's effectiveness or its safety. So the question for a consumer of nutrition information would be, Is this a legitimate product or service, or is it quackery? Armed with the information in this book, plus plenty of opportunities to test your knowledge, you will become more confident when trying to evaluate nutrition claims. Let's start by identifying *trustworthy* sources of nutrition information.

Trustworthy Experts Are Educated and Credentialed

The following is a list of the most common groups of health professionals who provide reliable and accurate nutrition information.

- Registered dietitian (RD): A registered dietitian (RD) is someone who possesses at least a baccalaureate (bachelor's) degree and has completed a defined content of coursework and experience in nutrition and dietetics, and who meets the eligibility requirements of the Commission on Dietetic Registration.[6]

For a list of registered dietitians in your community, visit the American Dietetic Association at www.eatright.org.

- Licensed dietitian: A licensed dietitian is someone who meets the credentialing requirement of a given state in the United States to engage in the practice of dietetics.[5] Each state in the United States has its own laws regulating dietitians.
- Nutritionist: This term generally has no definition or laws regulating it. In some cases, it refers to a professional with academic credentials in nutrition who may also be an RD.[6] In some states, these professionals are called licensed nutritionists (LN). In other cases, the term *nutritionist* may refer to anyone who thinks he or she is knowledgeable about nutrition. In the chapter-opening scenario, how might Miguel have determined whether the "nutritionist" was qualified to give him advice?
- Professional with an advanced degree (a master's degree [MA or MS] or doctoral degree [PhD]) in nutrition: Many people hold an advanced degree in nutrition

◆ Medical doctors may have limited experience and training in the area of nutrition, but they can refer you to a registered dietitian (RD) or a licensed dietitian to help you meet your dietary needs.

quackery The promotion of an unproven remedy, such as a supplement or other product or service, usually by someone unlicensed and untrained.

and have years of experience in a nutrition-related career. For instance, they may teach at a community college or university or work in a fitness or healthcare setting. Unless these individuals are licensed or registered dietitians, they are not certified to provide clinical dietary counseling or treatment for individuals with disease. However, they are reliable sources of information about nutrition and health.

- Physician: The term *physician* encompasses a variety of healthcare professionals. A medical doctor (MD) is educated, trained, and licensed to practice medicine in the United States. However, MDs typically have very limited experience and training in the area of nutrition, as medical students in the United States are not required to take any nutrition courses. If you require a dietary plan to treat an illness or a disease, most MDs will refer you to an RD or LN. In contrast, an osteopathic physician, referred to as a doctor of osteopathy (DO), may have studied nutrition extensively, as may a naturopathic physician, a homeopathic physician, or a chiropractor. Thus, it is prudent to determine a physician's level of expertise rather than assuming that he or she has extensive knowledge of nutrition.

Government Sources of Information Are Usually Trustworthy

Many government health agencies address the problem of nutrition-related disease in the United States. These organizations are publicly funded, and many provide financial support for research in the areas of nutrition and health. A few of the most recognized and respected of these government agencies are discussed here.

The Centers for Disease Control and Prevention Protects the Health and Safety of Americans

The *Centers for Disease Control and Prevention (CDC)* is considered the leading federal agency that protects the health and safety of people in the United States. The CDC is located in Atlanta, Georgia, and works in the areas of health promotion, disease prevention and control, and environmental health.

The National Institutes of Health Is the World's Leading Medical Research Agency

The *National Institutes of Health (NIH)* is the world's leading medical research center, and it is the focal point for medical research in the United States. The NIH is one of the agencies of the Public Health Service, which is part of the U.S. Department of Health and Human Services. The NIH has many institutes, such as the National Cancer Institute and the National Center for Complementary and Alternative Medicine, that focus on a broad array of nutrition-related health issues. NIH headquarters are located in Bethesda, Maryland.

Professional Organizations Provide Reliable Nutrition Information

There are a number of professional organizations whose members are qualified nutrition professionals, scientists, and educators. These organizations publish cutting-edge nutrition research studies and educational information in journals that are accessible in most university libraries. The following are some of these organizations.

- The American Dietetic Association (ADA): This is the largest organization of food and nutrition professionals in the United States and the world. The ADA publishes a professional journal called the *Journal of the American Dietetic Association*. The Canadian equivalent is Dietitians of Canada.
- The American Society for Nutrition (ASN): The ASN is the premier research society dedicated to improving quality of life through the science of nutrition.

The ASN publishes two professional journals, the *Journal of Nutrition* and the *American Journal of Clinical Nutrition (AJCN)*.

- The American College of Sports Medicine (ACSM): The ACSM is the leading sports medicine and exercise science organization in the world. *Medicine and Science in Sports and Exercise* is the professional journal of the ACSM.

If you aren't sure whether the source of your information is reliable or can't tell whether the results of a particular study apply to you, how do you find out? What if two studies seem sound but their findings contradict each other? The next section explains how you can become a more informed and critical consumer of nutrition-related research.

RECAP The most common groups of health professionals who provide reliable and accurate nutrition information include registered dietitians, licensed dietitians, licensed nutritionists, professionals with an advanced degree in nutrition, and some physicians. The term *nutritionist* is not a guarantee that the individual has any training in nutrition. The Centers for Disease Control and Prevention is the leading U.S. federal agency that protects citizen's health and safety. The National Institutes of Health is the leading medical research agency in the world.

Research Study Results: Whom Can You Believe?

"Reduce your fat intake! Make sure at least 60% of your diet comes from carbohydrates!"

"Eat more protein and fat! Carbohydrates cause obesity!"

Do you ever feel overwhelmed by the abundant and often conflicting advice in media reports related to nutrition? If so, you're not alone. In addition to the "high-carb, low-carb" controversy, we've had mixed messages about the effectiveness of calcium supplements in preventing bone loss, high fluid intake in preventing constipation, and high fiber intake in preventing colon cancer. And after decades of warnings that coffee and tea could be bad for our health, it now appears that both contain chemicals that can be beneficial! When even nutrition researchers don't seem to agree, whom can we believe?

Nutrition is a relatively young science: the U.S. Congress first funded research into human nutrition in 1894. At that time, vitamins were unknown, and the role of minerals in the body was unclear.[7] Moreover, discoveries in nutrition rely in part on the discoveries of other relatively young sciences, such as biochemistry and genetics. New experiments are being designed every day to determine how nutrition affects our health, and new discoveries are being made. Viewing conflicting evidence as essential to the advancement of our understanding may help you feel more comfortable with the contradictions. In fact, controversy is what stimulates researchers to explore unknown areas and attempt to solve the mysteries of nutrition and health.

In addition, it's important to recognize that media reports rarely include a thorough review of the research findings on a given topic. Typically, they focus only on the most recent study. Thus, one report on the nightly news should never be taken as absolute fact on any topic. To become a more educated consumer and informed critic of nutrition reports in the media, you need to understand the research process and how the results of different types of studies should be interpreted. So let's take a closer look.

Research Involves Applying the Scientific Method

The *scientific method* is a multistep process that involves observation, experimentation, and development of a theory **(Figure 1.17**, page 30**)**. Its standardized procedures minimize the influence of personal prejudices on our understanding of natural phenomena. Thus, this method is used to perform quality research studies in any discipline, including nutrition.

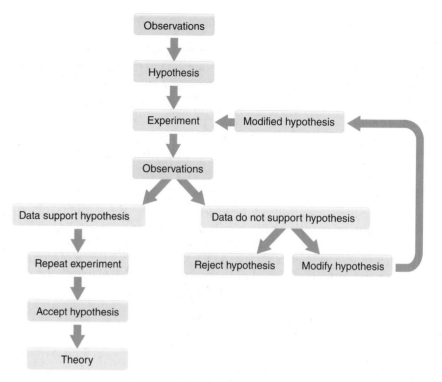

Figure 1.17   The scientific method, which forms the framework for scientific research. A researcher begins by making an observation about a phenomenon. This leads them to ask a question. A hypothesis is generated to explain the observation. The researcher then conducts an experiment to test the hypothesis. Observations are made during the experiment, and data are generated and documented. The data may either support or refute the hypothesis. If the data support the hypothesis, more experiments are conducted to test and confirm support for the hypothesis. A hypothesis that is supported after repeated testing may be called a theory. If the data do not support the hypothesis, the hypothesis is either rejected or modified and then retested.

Observation of a Phenomenon Starts the Research Process

The first step in the scientific method is observing and describing a phenomenon. As an example, let's say you are working in a healthcare office that caters to mostly elderly clients. You have observed that many of the elderly have high blood pressure, but there are some who have normal blood pressure. After talking with a large number of elderly clients, you notice a pattern developing in that the clients who report being more physically active are also those having lower blood pressure readings. This observation leads you to question the relationship that might exist between physical activity and blood pressure. Your next step is to develop a *hypothesis,* or possible explanation for your observation.

A Hypothesis Is a Possible Explanation for an Observation

A hypothesis states an assumption you want to test. It is also sometimes referred to as a research question. In this example, your hypothesis would be something like "Regular physical activity lowers blood pressure in elderly people." You must generate a hypothesis before you can conduct experiments to determine what factors may explain your observation.

Experiments Are Conducted to Test Hypotheses

An *experiment* is a scientific process that tests a research question, or hypothesis. In the case of your hypothesis, we could design a variety of research studies to determine the impact of regular physical activity on blood pressure in elderly people.

Later in this section, we will review the different types of research that can be done to assist us in answering your question.

A well-designed experiment attempts to control for factors that may coincidentally influence the results. In the case of your research study, it is well known that weight loss can reduce blood pressure in people with high blood pressure. Thus, in performing your experiment on the effects of exercise on blood pressure, you would want to control for weight loss. You could do this by making sure people eat enough food, so that they do not lose weight during your study, and by weighing them regularly to verify weight maintenance.

It is important to emphasize that one research study does not prove or disprove a hypothesis. Ideally, multiple experiments are conducted over many years to thoroughly examine a hypothesis. Science exists to allow us to continue to challenge existing hypotheses and expand what we currently know.

A Theory May Be Developed After Extensive Research

If multiple experiments do not support a hypothesis, then the hypothesis is rejected or modified. On the other hand, if the results of multiple experiments consistently support a hypothesis, then it is possible to develop a theory. A *theory* represents a hypothesis or group of related hypotheses that have been confirmed through repeated scientific experiments. Theories are strongly accepted principles, but they can be challenged and changed as a result of applying the scientific method. Remember that, centuries ago, it was theorized that the earth was flat. People were so convinced of this that they refused to sail beyond known boundaries because they believed they would fall off the edge. Only after multiple explorers challenged this theory was it discovered that the earth is round. We continue to apply the scientific method today to test hypotheses and challenge theories.

Various Types of Research Studies Tell Different Stories

You have just learned how the scientific method is applied to test a hypothesis. Establishing nutrition guidelines and understanding the role of nutrition in health involves constant experimentation. Depending on how the research study is designed, we can gather information that tells us different stories. Let's explore the different types of research conducted and what they tell us.

Animal Versus Human Studies

In many cases, studies involving animals provide preliminary information that assists scientists in designing human studies. Animal studies also are used to conduct research that cannot be done with humans. For instance, researchers can cause a nutrient deficiency in an animal and study its adverse health effects over the animal's life span, but this type of experiment with humans is not acceptable. Drawbacks of animal studies include ethical concerns and the fact that the results may not apply directly to humans.

Over the past century, animal studies have advanced our understanding of many aspects of nutrition, from micronutrients to obesity. Still, some hypotheses can only be investigated using human subjects. The three primary types of studies conducted with humans include observational studies, case-control studies, and clinical trials.

Observational Studies

Observational studies are used in assessing nutritional habits, disease trends, or other health phenomena of large populations and determining the factors that may influence these phenomena. However, these studies can only indicate *relationships* between factors; they do not suggest that the data are linked by cause and effect. For instance, smoking and low vegetable intake appear to be related in some studies, but this does not mean that smoking cigarettes causes people to eat fewer vegetables, or that eating fewer vegetables causes people to smoke.

Case-Control Studies

Case-control studies are more complex observational studies with additional design features that allow scientists to gain a better understanding of things that may influence disease. They involve comparing a group of individuals with a particular condition (for instance, 100 elderly people with high blood pressure) to a similar group without this condition (for instance, 100 elderly people with normal blood pressure). This comparison allows the researcher to identify factors other than the defined condition that differ between the two groups. For example, researchers may find that 75% of the people in their normal blood pressure group are physically active but that only 20% of the people in their high blood pressure group are physically active. Again, this would not prove that physical activity prevents high blood pressure. It would merely suggest a significant relationship between these two factors.

Clinical Trials

Clinical trials are tightly controlled experiments in which an intervention is given to determine its effect on a particular disease or health condition. Interventions may include medications, nutritional supplements, controlled diets, or exercise programs. In clinical trials, people in an experimental group are given the intervention, and people in a control group are not. The responses of the two groups are compared. In the case of the blood pressure experiment, researchers could assign one group of elderly people with high blood pressure to an exercise program and assign a second group of elderly people with high blood pressure to a program where no exercise is done. Over the next few weeks, months, or even years, researchers could measure the blood pressure of the people in each group. If the blood pressure of those who exercised decreased and the blood pressure of those who did not exercise rose or remained the same, the influence of exercise on lowering blood pressure would be supported.

Two questions important to consider when evaluating the quality of a clinical trial are whether the subjects were randomly chosen and whether the researchers and subjects were *blinded*:

- *Randomized trials.* Ideally, researchers should *randomly* assign research participants to intervention groups (who get the treatment) and control groups (who do not get the treatment). Randomizing participants is like flipping a coin or drawing names from a hat; it reduces the possibility of showing favoritism toward any participants and ensures that the groups are similar on the factors or characteristics you are measuring in the study. These types of studies are called *randomized clinical (controlled) trials.*
- *Single- and double-blind experiments.* If possible, it is also important to *blind* both researchers and participants to the treatment being given. A *single-blind experiment* is one in which the participants are unaware of or *blinded* to the treatment they're receiving, but the researchers know which group is getting the treatment and which group is not. A *double-blind experiment* is one in which neither researchers nor participants know which group is really getting the treatment. Double blinding helps prevent the researcher from seeing only the results he or she wants to see, even if these results do not actually occur. In the case of testing medications or nutrition supplements, the blinding process can be assisted by giving the control group a placebo. A *placebo* is an imitation treatment that has no effect on participants; for instance, a sugar pill may be given in place of a vitamin supplement. Studies like this are referred to as *double-blind randomized clinical trials.*

Use Your Knowledge of Research to Evaluate Media Reports

How can all of this research information assist you in becoming a better consumer and critic of media reports? By having a better understanding of the research process and types of research conducted, you are more capable of discerning the truth or fallacy within media reports. One of the most important points to consider when examining any media report is the issue of conflict of interest.

Conflict of Interest

You probably wouldn't think it strange to read an ad from your favorite brand of ice cream encouraging you to "Go ahead. Indulge." It's just an ad, right? But what if you were to read about a research study in which people who ate your favorite brand of ice cream improved the density of their bones? Could you trust the study results more than you would the ad?

To answer that question, you'd have to investigate several more:

- Who conducted the research, and who paid for it?
- Was the study funded by a company that stands to profit from certain results?
- Are the researchers receiving goods, personal travel funds, or other perks from the research sponsor, or do they have investments in companies or products related to their study?

If the answer to any of these questions were yes, a *conflict of interest* would exist between the researchers and the funding agency. Whenever a conflict of interest exists, it can seriously compromise the researchers' ability to conduct impartial research and report the results in an accurate and responsible manner. That's why, when researchers submit their results for publication in scientific journals, they are required to reveal any conflicts of interest they may have that could be seen as affecting the integrity of their research. In this way, people who review and eventually read and interpret the study are better able to consider if there are any potential researcher *biases* influencing the results. A bias is any factor—such as investment in the product being studied or gifts from the product manufacturer—that might influence the researcher to favor certain results.

Recent media investigations have reported widespread bias in studies funded by pharmaceutical companies testing the effectiveness of their drugs for medical treatment. In addition, journals in both the United States and Europe have been found less likely to publish negative results (that is, study results suggesting that a therapy is not effective). We also know that clinical trials funded by pharmaceutical companies are more likely to report positive results than are trials that were independently financed.[8,9] This has serious implications: if ineffectiveness and side effects are not fully reported, healthcare providers may be prescribing medications that are ineffective or even harmful.

The seriousness of this issue has inspired researchers around the world to demand a global system whereby all clinical trials are registered and all research results are made accessible to the public. The development of such a system would allow for independent review of research data and work toward ensuring that healthcare decisions were fully informed. As a first step, the U.S. Food and Drug Administration in 2009 launched a Transparency Initiative with the goal of making useful and understandable information about FDA activities and decision making available to the public.

To learn more about the FDA Transparency Initiative, go to www.fda .gov/AboutFDA/ Transparency/ TransparencyInitiative/ default.htm.

Other Issues in Evaluating Research

In addition to the considerations noted above, make sure you investigate the following.

- Who is reporting the information? Is it an article in a newspaper, in a magazine, or on the Internet? Many people who write for popular magazines and newspapers are not trained in science and are capable of misinterpreting research results. But even trained scientists and physicians can misreport research results for financial gain. For instance, if the report is published on the website of a healthcare provider who sells the product or service that was studied, you should be skeptical of the reported results.

To become a more educated consumer and informed critic of nutrition reports in the media, you need to understand the research process and how study results should be interpreted.

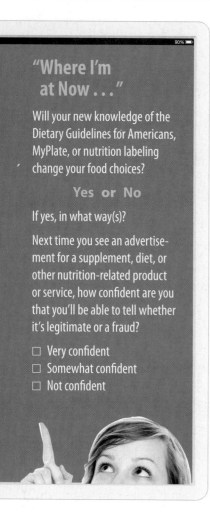

• Is the report based on reputable research studies? Did the research follow the scientific method, and were the results reported in a reputable scientific journal? Ideally, the journal is peer-reviewed; that is, the articles are critiqued by other specialists working in the same scientific field. A reputable report should include the reference, or source of the information, and should identify researchers by name. This allows the reader to investigate the original study and determine its merit. Examples of reputable journals include the *American Journal of Clinical Nutrition, Journal of Nutrition, Journal of the American Dietetic Association, New England Journal of Medicine,* and *Journal of the American Medical Association* (*JAMA*).

• Is the report based on testimonials about personal experiences? Are sweeping conclusions made from only one study? Be wary of personal testimonials, as they are fraught with bias. In addition, one study cannot answer all of our questions or prove any hypothesis, and the findings from individual studies should be placed in their proper perspective.

• Are the claims in the report too good to be true? Are claims made about curing disease or treating a multitude of conditions? If something sounds too good to be true, it probably is. Claims about curing diseases or treating many conditions with one product should be a signal to question the validity of the report.

Throughout this text, we provide information to assist you in evaluating research studies and marketing statements about nutrition-related products and services. Armed with this knowledge, you can feel more confident when trying to determine what to buy and whom to trust.

COOKING 101

What's the best way to stock your fridge and pantry? How can you build a fast, tasty, and nutritious meal from a simple shopping list? What's the best way to store your fruits and veggies? Answers to these and other pressing cooking and food preparation questions can be found in our new Cooking 101 videos, available on the Companion Website at **www.pearsonhighered.com/thompsonmanore**.

Chapter Review

What Can I Do Today?

Now that you've read this chapter, try making these three changes:

- Read the Nutrition Facts Panel of your favorite snacks and change your usual selections to ones that are lower in sodium, total fat, or saturated fat.

- Log on to the MyPlate website (see Web Links for the url) and design a healthy food plan that will help you maintain your present weight or lose weight.

- Follow the Mediterranean diet for one full day and see how you like it!

Test Yourself ANSWERS

1. **T** Although nutrition guidelines recommend that we consume these types of foods only occasionally, they can be included in moderation as part of a healthful diet.

2. **F** Not all nutrients provide energy; the primary energy sources for our body are carbohydrates and fats.

3. **F** Calories are a measure of the energy in foods. More precisely, a kilocalorie is the amount of heat required to raise the temperature of 1 kilogram of water by 1 degree Celsius.

4. **F** A diet that is adequate, moderate, balanced, and varied may not require supplementation. However, certain individuals may need to supplement based on specific health concerns.

5. **F** The top nutritional guidelines published in the United States, the 2010 Dietary Guidelines for Americans, state that moderate alcohol consumption can be part of a healthful diet for adults of legal drinking age. Moderate alcohol consumption is defined as no more than one drink per day for women and two drinks per day for men.

 NutriTools

Check out the Companion Website at www.pearsonhighered.com/thompsonmanore, or use MyNutritionLab.com, to access interactive animations, including

- Food Label: What Is Required?
- Build-a-Meal
- Build-a-Salad

Review Questions

1. Which of the following foods contains all six nutrient groups?
   a. strawberry ice cream
   b. an egg-salad sandwich
   c. creamy tomato soup
   d. all of the above

2. An adequate diet
   a. provides enough energy to meet minimum daily requirements.
   b. provides enough of the energy, nutrients, and fiber necessary to maintain a person's health.
   c. provides a sufficient variety of nutrients to maintain a healthy weight and to optimize the body's functioning.
   d. contains combinations of foods that provide healthful proportions of nutrients.

3. The Dietary Guidelines for Americans recommend which of the following?
   a. choosing and preparing all foods without salt
   b. consuming two alcoholic beverages per day
   c. being physically active each day
   d. consuming a fat-free diet

4. MyPlate recommends
   a. drinking a variety of fruit juices each day.
   b. eating more dark-green and orange vegetables.
   c. consuming at least one 8 oz glass of whole milk each day.
   d. baking, broiling, or frying meats.

5. The Nutrition Facts Panel on packaged foods provides information about the micronutrients
   a. vitamin A, sodium, potassium, and calcium.
   b. vitamin A, vitamin C, sodium, iron, and calcium.
   c. vitamin C, sodium, and calcium.
   d. No micronutrient information is included on the Nutrition Facts Panel.

6. True or False? Fat-soluble vitamins provide energy.

7. True or False? The Recommended Dietary Allowance represents the average daily intake level that meets the requirements of almost all healthy individuals in a given life stage or gender group.

8. True or False? Alcohol can be part of a healthful diet.

9. True or False? Eating a variety of foods ensures that your diet is healthful.

10. True or False? The serving size listed on a Nutrition Facts Panel is based on the amount people typically eat of that food.

Answers to Review Questions are located at the back of this text.

Web Links

www.fda.gov
U.S. Food and Drug Administration (FDA)

www.cnpp.usda.gov/dietaryguidelines.htm
2010 Dietary Guidelines for Americans

www.chooseMyPlate.gov
The USDA's MyPlate Home Page

www.eatright.org
American Dietetic Association (ADA)

www.cdc.gov
Centers for Disease Control and Prevention (CDC)

www.nih.gov
National Institutes of Health (NIH)

www.nutrition.org
American Society for Nutrition (ASN)

www.acsm.org
American College of Sports Medicine (ACSM)

www.naaso.org
Obesity Society

2 The Human Body: Are We Really What We Eat?

Nutrition Online

icons are located throughout the chapter, directing you to web links, videos, podcasts, and other useful online resources.

Two months ago, Andrea's lifelong dream of becoming a lawyer came one step closer to reality: she moved out of her parents' home in the Midwest to attend law school in Boston. Unfortunately, the adjustment to a new city, new friends, and her intensive coursework has been more stressful than she'd imagined, and Andrea has been experiencing insomnia and exhaustion. What's more, her always "sensitive stomach" has been getting worse: after almost every meal, she gets cramps so bad she can't stand up, and twice she has missed classes because of sudden attacks of pain and diarrhea. She suspects that the problem is related to stress and wonders if she is going to experience it throughout her life. She is even thinking of dropping out of school if that would make her feel well again.

Almost everyone experiences brief periods of abdominal pain, diarrhea, or other symptoms of gastrointestinal distress from time to time. Such episodes are usually caused by food poisoning or an infection, such as influenza. But do you know anyone who experiences these symptoms periodically for days, weeks, or even years? If so, has it made you wonder why? What are the steps in normal digestion and absorption of food, and at what points can the process break down?

We begin this chapter with a look at some of the factors that make us feel as if we want to eat. We'll then take a tour of the cells, tissues, and organs of the human body, focusing on their function within the digestive system. Finally, we'll discuss some common disorders that affect this system.

Why Do We Want to Eat What We Want to Eat?

You've just finished eating at your favorite Thai restaurant. As you walk back to the block where you parked your car, you pass a bakery window displaying several cakes and pies, each of which looks more enticing than the last, and through the door wafts a complex aroma of coffee, cinnamon, and chocolate. You stop. You know you're not hungry, but you go inside and buy a slice of chocolate torte and an espresso, anyway. Later that night, when the caffeine from the chocolate and espresso keeps you awake, you wonder why you succumbed.

Two mechanisms prompt us to seek food: hunger and appetite. **Hunger** is a physiologic drive for food that occurs when our body senses that we need to eat. The drive is *nonspecific*; when you're hungry, a variety of foods could satisfy you. If you've recently finished a nourishing meal, then hunger probably won't compel you toward a slice of chocolate torte. Instead, the culprit is likely to be **appetite,** a psychological desire to consume *specific* foods. It is aroused when environmental cues—such as the sight of chocolate cake or the smell of coffee—stimulate your senses, triggering pleasant emotions and memories.

People commonly experience appetite in the absence of hunger. That's why you can crave cake and coffee even after eating a full meal. On the other hand, it is possible to have a physiologic need for food yet have no appetite. This state, called *anorexia,* can accompany a variety of illnesses from infectious diseases to mood disorders. (Anorexia is detailed in Chapter 9.) It can also occur as a side effect of certain medications, such as the chemotherapy used in treating cancer patients. Although the following sections describe hunger and appetite as separate entities, ideally the two states coexist: we seek specific, appealing foods to satisfy a physiologic need for nutrients.

The Hypothalamus Prompts Hunger in Response to Various Signals

Because hunger is a physiologic stimulus that drives us to find food and eat, we often feel it as a negative or unpleasant sensation. The primary organ producing that sensation is the brain. That's right—it's not our stomach but our brain that tell us when we're hungry. The region of brain tissue responsible for prompting us to seek food is called the **hypothalamus (Figure 2.1)**. It's located above the pituitary gland in the forebrain, a region that regulates many types of involuntary activity. The hypothalamus triggers feelings of either hunger or satiation (fullness) by integrating signals from three sources: nerve cells, chemicals called *hormones,* and the amount and type of food we eat. Let's review these three types of signals.

The Role of Nerve Cells

One important signal comes from nerve cells lining the stomach and small intestine that detect changes in pressure according to whether the organ is empty or distended with food. The cells relay these data to the hypothalamus. For instance, if you have not eaten for many hours and your stomach and small intestine do not contain food, these data are sent to the hypothalamus, which in turn prompts you to experience the sensation of hunger.

The Role of Hormones

Hormones are chemical messengers that are secreted into the bloodstream by one of the many *glands* of the body. The presence of different hormones in the blood helps regulate body functions. Insulin and glucagon are two hormones responsible for maintaining blood glucose levels. Glucose is our body's most readily available fuel supply. It's not surprising, then, that its level in the blood is an important signal affecting hunger. When we have not eaten for a while, our blood glucose levels fall, prompting a change in the level of insulin and glucagon. This chemical message is

hunger A physiologic sensation that prompts us to eat.

appetite A psychological desire to consume specific foods.

hypothalamus A brain region where sensations such as hunger and thirst are regulated.

hormone A chemical messenger that is secreted into the bloodstream by one of the many glands of the body.

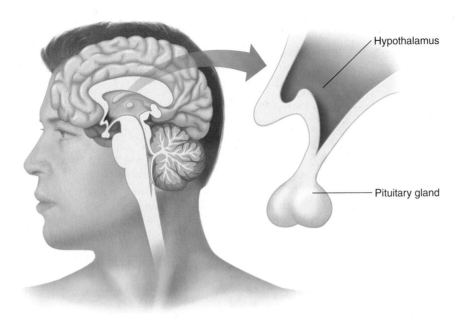

Figure 2.1 The hypothalamus triggers hunger by integrating signals from nerve cells throughout the body, as well as from messages carried by hormones.

relayed to the hypothalamus, which then prompts us to eat in order to supply our body with more glucose.

After we eat, the hypothalamus picks up the sensation of a distended stomach, other signals from the gut, and a rise in blood glucose levels. When it integrates these signals, we have the experience of feeling full, or *satiated*. However, as we have noted, even though our brain sends us clear signals about hunger, most of us become adept at ignoring them and eat when we are not truly hungry.

In addition to insulin and glucagon, a variety of other hormones and hormone-like substances signal the hypothalamus to cause us to feel hungry or satiated. So it's not surprising that many nutrition researchers are exploring the role of hormones in weight management.

The Role of the Amount and Type of Food

Although the reason behind this observation is not fully understood, researchers have long recognized that foods containing protein have the highest satiety value.[1,2] This means that a ham and egg breakfast will cause us to feel satiated for a longer period of time than will pancakes with maple syrup, even if both meals have exactly the same number of Calories.

Another factor affecting hunger is how bulky the meal is—that is, how much fiber and water is within the food. Bulky meals tend to stretch the stomach and small intestine, which sends signals back to the hypothalamus telling us that we are full, so we stop eating. Beverages tend to be less satisfying than semisolid foods, and semisolid foods have a lower satiety value than solid foods. For example, if you were to eat a bunch of grapes, you would feel a greater sense of fullness than if you drank a glass of grape juice.

Our body feels hunger when we haven't eaten for many hours or our blood glucose is low.

RECAP In contrast to appetite, hunger is a physiologic sensation triggered by the hypothalamus in response to cues about stomach and intestinal distention and the levels of certain hormones and hormone-like substances. High-protein foods make us feel satiated for longer periods of time, and bulky meals fill us up quickly, causing the distention that signals us to stop eating.

Food stimulates our senses.

Environmental Cues Trigger Appetite

Whereas hunger is prompted by internal signals, appetite is triggered by aspects of our environment. The most significant factors influencing our appetite are sensory data, social and cultural cues, and learning (Figure 2.2).

The Role of Sensory Data

Foods stimulate our five senses. Foods that are artfully prepared, arranged, or ornamented, with several different shapes and colors, appeal to our sense of sight. The aromas of foods such as freshly brewed coffee and baked goods can also be powerful stimulants. Much of our ability to taste foods actually comes from our sense of smell. This is why foods are not as appealing when we have a stuffy nose due to a cold. Certain tastes, such as sweetness, are almost universally appealing, whereas others, such as the astringent taste of spinach and kale, are quite individual. Texture, or "mouth feel," is also important in food choices, as it stimulates nerve endings sensitive to touch in our mouth and on our tongue. Even our sense of hearing can be stimulated by foods, from the fizz of cola to the crunch of pretzels.

The Role of Social and Cultural Cues

In addition to sensory cues, our brain's association with certain social events, such as birthday parties and holiday gatherings, can stimulate our appetite. At these times, our culture gives us permission to eat more than usual or to eat "forbidden" foods. Even when we feel full, these cues can motivate us to accept a second helping.

For some people, being in a certain location, such as at a baseball game or a movie theater, can trigger appetite. Others may be triggered to eat when they engage in certain activities, such as watching television or studying. Many people feel an increase or a decrease in appetite according to whom they are with; for example, they may eat more when at home with family members and less when out on a date.

In some people, appetite masks an emotional response to an external event. For example, a person might experience a desire for food rather than a desire for emotional comfort after receiving a failing grade or arguing with a close friend. Many people crave food when they're frustrated, worried, or bored or when they're at a gathering where they feel anxious or awkward. Others subconsciously seek food as a "reward." For example, have you ever found yourself heading out for a burger and fries after handing in a term paper?

Figure 2.2 Appetite is a drive to consume specific foods, such as popcorn at the movies. It is aroused by social and cultural cues and sensory data and is influenced by learning.

WHAT ABOUT YOU?

Do You Eat in Response to External or Internal Cues?

Whether you're trying to lose weight, gain weight, or maintain your current weight, you might find it intriguing to keep a log of the reasons behind your decisions about what, when, where, and why you eat. Are you eating in response to internal sensations telling you that your body needs food, or in response to your emotions, your situation, or a prescribed diet? Keeping a "cues" log for 1 full week would give you the most accurate picture of your eating habits, but even logging 2 days of meals and snacks should increase your cue awareness.

Each day, every time you eat a meal, snack, or beverage other than water, make a quick note of the following:

- *When you eat:* Many people eat at certain times (for example, 6 PM) whether they are hungry or not.
- *What you eat, and how much:* Do you choose a cup of yogurt and a 6 oz glass of orange juice or a candy bar and a 20 oz cola?
- *Where you eat:* home, watching television; on the subway; and so on.
- *With whom you eat:* Are you alone or with others? If with others, are they eating as well? Have they offered you food?
- *Your emotions:* Some people overeat when they are happy, others when they are anxious, depressed, bored, or frustrated. Still others eat as a way of denying feelings they don't want to identify and deal with. For some, food becomes a substitute for emotional fulfillment.
- *Your sensations—what you see, hear, or smell:* Are you eating because you just saw a TV commercial for pizza, smelled homemade cookies, or the like?

- *Any dietary restrictions:* Are you choosing a particular food because it is allowed on your current diet plan? Or are you hungry for a meal but drinking a diet soda to stay within a certain allowance of Calories? Are you restricting yourself because you feel guilty about having eaten too much at another time?
- *Your physiologic hunger:* Finally, rate your hunger on a scale from 1 to 5 as follows:

  1 = you feel uncomfortably full or even stuffed

  2 = you feel satisfied but not uncomfortably full

  3 = neutral; you feel no discernible satiation or hunger

  4 = you feel hungry and want to eat

  5 = you feel strong physiologic sensations of hunger and need to eat.

After keeping a log for 2 or more days, you might become aware of patterns you'd like to change. For example, maybe you notice that you often eat when you are not actually hungry but are worried about homework or personal relationships. Or maybe you notice that you can't walk past the snack bar without going in. This self-awareness may prompt you to change those patterns. For instance, instead of stifling your worries with food, you could write down exactly what you are worried about, including steps you can take to address your concerns. And the next time you approach the snack bar, you could check with your gut: are you truly hungry? If so, then purchase a healthful snack, maybe a piece of fruit or a bag of peanuts. If you're not really hungry, then take a moment to acknowledge the strength of this visual cue—and then walk on by.

The Role of Learning

Pigs' feet, anyone? What about blood sausage, stewed octopus, or snakes? These are delicacies in various cultures. Would you eat grasshoppers? If you'd grown up in certain parts of Africa or Central America, you might. That's because your preference for particular foods is largely a learned response. The culture in which you are raised teaches you what plant and animal products are appropriate to eat. If your parents fed you cubes of plain tofu throughout your toddlerhood, then you are probably still eating tofu.

That said, early introduction to foods is not essential: we can learn to enjoy new foods at any point in our life. For instance, many immigrants adopt a diet typical of their new home, especially when their traditional foods are not readily available. This happens temporarily when we travel: the last time you were away from home, you probably sampled a variety of dishes that are not normally part of your diet.

⬆ Our preference, or distaste, for certain foods is something we learn from our culture.

Food preferences also change when people learn what foods are most healthful. Since the first day of your nutrition class, has your diet changed at all? Chances are, as you learn more about the health benefits of specific types of carbohydrates, fats, and proteins, you'll start incorporating more of these foods in your diet.

We can also "learn" to dislike foods we once enjoyed. For example, if we experience an episode of food poisoning after eating undercooked scrambled eggs, we might develop a strong distaste for all types of eggs. Many adults who become vegetarians do so after learning about the treatment of animals in slaughterhouses: they might have eaten meat daily when young but no longer have any appetite for it.

Now that you understand the differences between appetite and hunger, as well as the influence of learning on food choices, you might be curious to investigate your own reasons for eating what and when you do. If so, check out the self-assessment box **What About You?** (page 41).

RECAP   In contrast to hunger, appetite is a psychological desire to consume specific foods. It is triggered when external stimuli arouse our senses, and it often occurs in combination with social and cultural cues. Our preference for certain foods is largely learned from the culture in which we were raised, but our food choices can change with exposure to new foods or through new learning experiences.

Are We Really What We Eat?

You've no doubt heard the saying that "you are what you eat." But is this scientifically true? To answer that question, and to better understand how we digest and process foods, we'll need to look at how our body is organized (**Figure 2.3**).

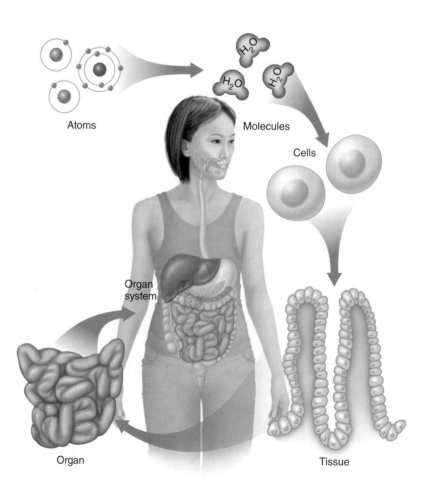

▶ **Figure 2.3** The organization of the human body. Atoms bind together to form molecules. The cells of our body are constructed using molecules made from the foods we eat. Cells join to form tissues, one or more types of which form organs. Body systems, such as the gastrointestinal system shown here, are made up of several organs, each of which performs a discrete function. The human organism has 11 such organ systems.

Atoms Bond to Form Molecules

Like all substances on Earth, our body is made up of *atoms*. Atoms are the smallest units of matter, and they cannot be broken down by natural means. Atoms almost constantly bind to each other in nature to form groups called *molecules*. For example, a molecule of water is composed of two atoms of hydrogen and an atom of oxygen, which is abbreviated H_2O.

Every bite of food we eat is composed of molecules. The actions of digestion break food down into molecules small enough to be easily transported in the bloodstream. From there, these food molecules cross into our cells to help build the structures of our body and provide the energy we must have to live.

Molecules Join to Form Cells

Whereas atoms are the smallest units of matter and make up both living and nonliving things, **cells** are the smallest units of life. That is, cells can grow, reproduce themselves, take in nutrients, and excrete wastes. The human body is composed of billions of cells that are continually being replaced. To support the construction of new cells, we need a steady supply of nutrient molecules to serve as building blocks. All cells, whether of the skin, bones, or brain, are made of the same basic nutrient molecules, which are derived from the foods we eat. Nutrient molecules also provide the fuel that cells need to perform their functions in the body.

Cells Are Encased in a Membrane

The contents of a cell are enclosed by a **cell membrane** (Figure 2.4). This thin, outer coat defines the cell's boundaries. Cell membranes are *semipermeable:* some molecules can easily flow through them, whereas others cannot. This quality enables the cell membrane to act as a gatekeeper, controlling what goes into and out of the cell.

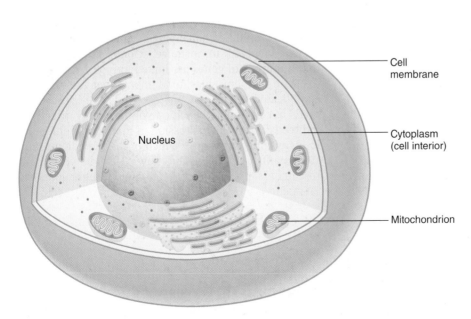

Nucleus

Cell membrane

Cytoplasm (cell interior)

Mitochondrion

▲ **Figure 2.4** Representative cell of the small intestine, showing the cell membrane, the cytoplasm, the nucleus, and several mitochondria.

cell The smallest unit of matter that exhibits the properties of living things, such as growth, reproduction, and the taking in of nutrients.

cell membrane The boundary of an animal cell that separates its internal cytoplasm, nucleus, and other structures from the external environment.

NUTRITION MYTH OR FACT?

Nutrigenomics: Personalized Nutrition or Pie in the Sky?

Agouti mice are normally yellow, obese, and prone to cancer and diabetes. When agouti mice breed, these traits are passed on to their offspring. Look at the picture of the agouti mice on this page; do you see a difference? The mouse on the right is obviously brown and of normal weight, but what you can't see is that it hasn't inherited its parents' susceptibility to disease. What caused this dramatic difference?

In 2000, researchers found that, when they changed the mother's diet just before conception, they could "turn off" the agouti gene, and any offspring born to that mother would appear normal.[3] A *gene* is a segment of DNA, a substance in cells that—by directing the assembly of proteins—is responsible for passing on traits from parents to offspring. The diet that the researchers fed the mother was high in a chemical that attached to the agouti gene and disabled it. This study was one of the first to link a change in diet to a genetic modification, and it led to the emerging science of *nutrigenomics*.

Nutrigenomics is a scientific discipline studying the interactions between genes, the environment, and nutrition.[4,5] It proposes that foods can act as a switch in body cells, turning on some genes and turning off others. When a gene is activated, it instructs the cell to create a protein that will show up as a characteristic or an ability, such as yellow fur or a tendency to store fat. When a gene is switched off, the cell will not create that protein, and the organism's form or function will differ. In addition, evidence suggests that diet can affect gene function not only in the exposed organism but also in his or her offspring.[3–5]

It's an intriguing theory—and certain common observations support it. For example, nutrition researchers have long noted that some people will lose weight on a specific diet and exercise program, whereas others following the same program will not.[5,6] The varying results are now thought to depend to a certain extent on how the foods in that diet affect the study participants' genes. Evidence from population studies also supports

⬆ With only a change in diet, inbred agouti mice (left) gave birth to young mice (right) that differed not only in their appearance but also in their susceptibility to disease.

nutrigenomics. For example, when different ethnic groups are exposed to a Western diet, the percentage of type 2 diabetes increases in some populations significantly more than in others.[4] Researchers have also found that, when one generation experiences a food surplus during critical periods of reproductive development, their offspring are more likely to develop diabetes.[3]

One promise of nutrigenomics is that it can help people improve their health through diet alone.[4] For example, some researchers are studying how leafy green vegetables may turn on an important gene that suppresses cancerous tumors.[7] Another promise of nutrigenomics is personalized nutrition. In the world of nutrigenomics, you would provide a tissue sample for genetic analysis. Then, your healthcare provider would tailor a diet to your genetic makeup. This "personalized diet" would identify foods you should eat and foods you should avoid in order to turn on beneficial genes and turn off genes that may be detrimental.

One challenge in making nutrigenomic therapies a reality is determining what foods turn on or off specific genes in specific people. Genetic pathways are extremely complicated, and turning on a gene may have a beneficial effect on one body function but a harmful effect on another. Individual factors, such as age, gender, and lifestyle, also may affect how different foods interact with these different genes. Even emotional and social factors may play a role.[8] In addition, dietary intervention to prevent or treat chronic diseases would be challenging because multiple genes may be involved: for instance, scientists have determined that hundreds of genes are linked to type 2 diabetes.

Even by themselves, food interactions are extremely complicated because, in any one meal, we consume hundreds of compounds. Each one of these may directly or indirectly affect the expression of many different genes in many different ways.[8] Which of the ingredients consumed affect what gene and how? It will be years before researchers are capable of mapping out these complex interactions.

Cells Contain Fluid and Tiny Structures That Support Life

Enclosed by the cell membrane is a fluid called **cytoplasm.** Floating in the cytoplasm are many tiny structures that accomplish some surprisingly sophisticated functions. For instance, cells that have high energy needs, such as muscle cells, contain lots of

cytoplasm The fluid within an animal cell, enclosed by the cell membrane.

mitochondria. You can think of mitochondria as a cell's "powerhouse," because they produce energy from food molecules. Nearly all body cells have a *nucleus*, where genetic information, in the form of DNA (deoxyribonucleic acid), is located. DNA contains the instructions that cells use to assemble proteins. Segments of DNA, called genes, code for the manufacture of structural proteins—components of the body's tissues—and functional proteins involved in everything from immunity to digestion. Reflecting our growing understanding of the importance of genetics in human health, a new field of research called *nutrigenomics* is seeking to uncover links between our genes, our environment, and our diet. Some even claim that our diet should be personalized to our unique DNA! But is the idea of personalized nutrition just wishful thinking? Find out in the **Nutrition Myth or Fact?** feature box (page 44).

Cells Join to Form Tissues, Organs, and Systems

Cells of a single type, such as muscle cells, join together to form **tissues** (see **Figure 2.3**). Several types of tissues join together to form **organs,** which are sophisticated structures that perform a unique body function. The stomach is an organ, for example, as is the small intestine.

Organs are further grouped into **systems** that perform integrated functions. For example, the gastrointestinal system is responsible for digesting food, absorbing nutrients, and excreting food wastes. The stomach is one organ of the gastrointestinal system. It holds and partially digests a meal, but it can't perform all the functions of the gastrointestinal system by itself. These functions require several organs working together, as we'll see shortly. Finally, many organ systems together make up the human **organism**, that is, a complete living being that can function independently of other living beings.

RECAP Atoms, the smallest units of matter, group together to form molecules. Digestion breaks down food into molecules small enough to be easily absorbed into the body and transported to cells. The smallest units of life, cells are encased in a cell membrane, which acts as a gatekeeper. Cells of the same type join together to make tissues. Different tissues combine to form different kinds of organs. Body systems, such as the gastrointestinal system, depend on many different organs to carry out their functions. Many systems are present in an organism.

What Happens to the Food We Eat?

When we eat, the food is digested, then the useful nutrients are absorbed, and finally the waste products are eliminated. Here are some useful definitions for these three steps:

- **Digestion** is the process by which foods are broken down into their component molecules, either mechanically or chemically.
- **Absorption** is the process of taking the products of digestion through the wall of the intestine.
- **Elimination** is the process by which the undigested portions of food and waste products are removed from the body.

The processes of digestion, absorption, and elimination occur within the **gastrointestinal (GI) tract,** a long tube beginning at the mouth and ending at the anus: if held out straight, an adult GI tract would be close to 30 feet in length (**Figure 2.5**, page 46). It is composed of several distinct organs, including the mouth, the esophagus, the stomach, the small intestine, and the large intestine. These organs work together to process foods but are kept somewhat separated by muscular **sphincters,** which are tight rings of muscle that open when a nerve signal indicates that food is ready to pass into the next section. The nerves serving the GI tract are known as *enteric nerves.*

tissue A sheet or other grouping of like cells that performs like functions— for example, muscle tissue.

organ A body structure composed of two or more tissues and performing a specific function—for example, the esophagus.

system A group of organs that work together to perform a unique function—for example, the gastrointestinal system.

organism A complete and independent living being.

digestion The process by which foods are broken down into their component molecules, both mechanically and chemically.

absorption The physiologic process by which molecules of food are taken from the GI tract into the body.

elimination The process by which the undigested portions of food and waste products are removed from the body.

gastrointestinal (GI) tract A long, muscular tube consisting of several organs: the mouth, esophagus, stomach, small intestine, and large intestine.

sphincter A tight ring of muscle separating organs of the GI tract that opens in response to nerve signals, indicating that food is ready to pass into the next section.

Figure 2.5 An overview of the gastrointestinal (GI) tract. The GI tract begins in the mouth and ends at the anus and is composed of numerous organs.

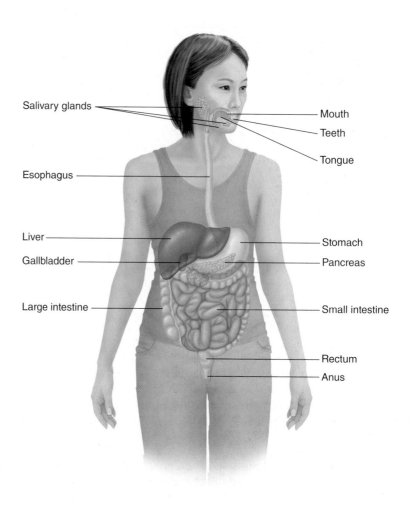

Salivary glands

Esophagus

Liver

Gallbladder

Large intestine

Mouth

Teeth

Tongue

Stomach

Pancreas

Small intestine

Rectum

Anus

Digestion of a sandwich starts before you even take a bite.

saliva A mixture of water, mucus, enzymes, and other chemicals that moistens the mouth and food, binds food particles together, and begins the digestion of carbohydrates.

salivary glands A group of glands found under and behind the tongue and beneath the jaw that release saliva continually as well as in response to the thought, sight, smell, or presence of food.

Enteric nerves can often work independently; in other words, they don't need to relay signals produced within the GI tract to the brain for interpretation or assistance. One of their most important functions is to regulate the secretion of digestive juices, mucus, and water by glands located all along the GI tract. These substances promote gastrointestinal functioning, as described next.

Imagine that you eat a turkey sandwich for lunch today. It contains two slices of bread spread with mayonnaise, some turkey, two lettuce leaves, and a slice of tomato. Let's travel along with the sandwich and see what changes it undergoes within your GI tract.

Digestion Begins in the Mouth

Believe it or not, your body starts preparing to digest food even before you take your first bite. In response to the sight, smell, or thought of food, the nervous system stimulates the release of digestive juices that help prepare the GI tract for the breakdown of food. Sometimes we even experience some involuntary movement of the GI tract, commonly called "hunger pangs."

Now it's time to take that first bite and chew. Chewing is very important because it moistens the food and mechanically breaks it down into pieces small enough to swallow **(Figure 2.6)**. The tough lettuce fibers and tomato seeds are also broken open. Thus, chewing initiates the mechanical digestion of food.

As our teeth cut and grind the different foods in the sandwich, more surface area is exposed to the digestive juices in our mouth. Foremost among these is **saliva,** which we secrete from our **salivary glands.** Saliva not only moistens food but also

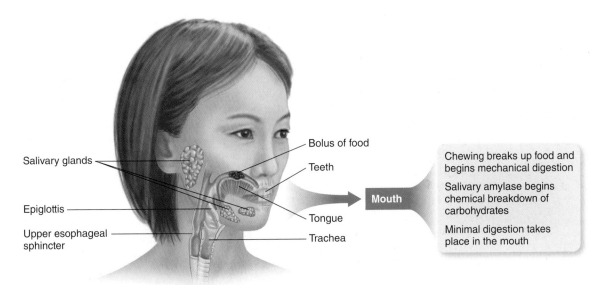

Salivary glands

Epiglottis

Upper esophageal
sphincter

Bolus of food

Teeth

Tongue

Trachea

Mouth

Chewing breaks up food and
begins mechanical digestion

Salivary amylase begins
chemical breakdown of
carbohydrates

Minimal digestion takes
place in the mouth

Figure 2.6 Where your food is now: the mouth. Chewing moistens food and mechanically breaks it down into pieces small enough to swallow, while salivary amylase begins chemical digestion of carbohydrates.

begins the process of chemical digestion. Saliva contains *amylase,* a chemical that begins to break apart carbohydrate molecules. Saliva also contains other components, such as antibiotics that protect the body from germs entering the mouth and keep the oral cavity free from infection.

Salivary amylase is the first of many *enzymes* that assist the body in digesting and absorbing food. Because we will encounter many enzymes on our journey through the GI tract, let's discuss them briefly here. **Enzymes** are chemicals, usually proteins, that induce chemical changes in other substances to speed up body processes. Imagine them as facilitators: a chemical reaction that might take hours to occur independently can happen in seconds with the help of one or more enzymes. Digestion—as well as many other biochemical processes that go on in the body—could not happen without them. By the way, enzyme names typically end in -*ase* (as in amylase), so they are easy to recognize as we discuss the digestive process. A few of the many digestive enzymes active in the GI tract are identified in **Table 2.1**.

In reality, very little digestion occurs in the mouth. We don't hold food in our mouth for long, and very few of the enzymes needed to break down food are present in saliva. Salivary amylase starts the digestion of carbohydrates, but this ends when food reaches the stomach. That's because the acidic environment of the stomach destroys this enzyme.

TABLE 2.1 Some Digestive Enzymes and Their Actions

Site of Production	Enzyme	Site of Action	Primary Action
Mouth	Salivary amylase	Mouth	Digests carbohydrates
Stomach	Pepsin	Stomach	Digests proteins
	Gastric lipase		Digests lipids
Pancreas	Proteases	Small intestine	Digest proteins
	Pancreatic lipase		Digests lipids
	Pancreatic amylase		Digests carbohydrates
Small intestine	Variety of peptidases	Small intestine	Digest proteins
	Lipase		Digests lipids
	Sucrase		Digests sucrose
	Maltase		Digests maltose
	Lactase		Digests lactose

enzymes Chemicals, usually proteins, that act on other chemicals to speed up body processes.

The Esophagus Transports Food into the Stomach

Now that our sandwich is soft and moist, it's time to swallow **(Figure 2.7)**. Most of us take swallowing for granted, but it's a very complex process. As the bite of sandwich moves to the very back of the mouth, the brain is sent a signal to raise the soft palate. This temporarily closes the openings to the nasal passages, preventing aspiration of food or liquid into the sinuses. The brain also receives a signal to close off the *epiglottis*, a tiny flap of tissue that is like a trapdoor covering the entrance to the trachea ("windpipe"). The epiglottis is normally open, allowing us to breathe freely. When it closes during swallowing, food and liquid cannot enter the trachea. Sometimes this protective mechanism goes awry—for instance, when we try to eat and talk at the same time and food or liquid "goes down the wrong way." When this happens, we experience the sensation of choking, and we cough until the offending food or liquid is expelled.

> To view a step-by-step animation of the complex process of swallowing, visit www.linkstudio.info/images/portfolio/medani/Swallow.swf.

As the trachea closes, the *upper esophageal sphincter* opens. This allows food to pass from the back of the throat into the **esophagus,** the muscular tube that propels food toward the stomach **(Figure 2.8)**. It does this by contracting two sets of muscles: inner sheets of circular muscle squeeze the food, while outer sheets of longitudinal muscle push food along. Together, these rhythmic waves of squeezing and pushing are called **peristalsis.** We will see shortly that peristalsis occurs throughout the GI tract.

Gravity also helps food move down the esophagus. Together, peristalsis and gravity can transport a bite of food from the mouth to the opening of the stomach in 5 to 8 seconds. At the end of the esophagus is another sphincter muscle, the *gastroesophageal sphincter* (*gastro-* indicates the stomach; also called the *lower esophageal sphincter*), that is normally tightly closed. When food reaches the end of the esophagus, this sphincter relaxes to allow it to pass into the stomach. In some people, this sphincter is continually somewhat relaxed. Later in the chapter, we'll discuss this disorder and why it causes the unpleasant sensation of heartburn.

esophagus   Muscular tube of the GI tract connecting the back of the mouth to the stomach.

peristalsis   Waves of squeezing and pushing contractions that move food in one direction through the length of the GI tract.

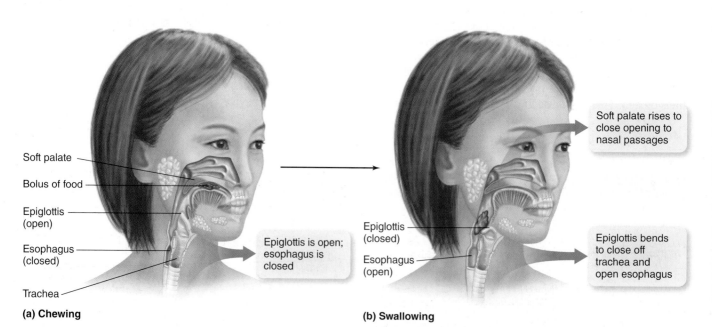

(a) Chewing

Soft palate
Bolus of food
Epiglottis (open)
Esophagus (closed)
Trachea

Epiglottis is open; esophagus is closed

(b) Swallowing

Soft palate rises to close opening to nasal passages

Epiglottis (closed)
Esophagus (open)

Epiglottis bends to close off trachea and open esophagus

Figure 2.7   Chewing and swallowing are complex processes. **(a)** During the process of chewing, the epiglottis is open and the esophagus is closed so that we can continue to breathe as we chew. **(b)** During swallowing, the epiglottis closes so that food does not enter the trachea and obstruct our breathing. Also, the soft palate rises to seal off our nasal passages to prevent aspiration of food or liquid into the sinuses.

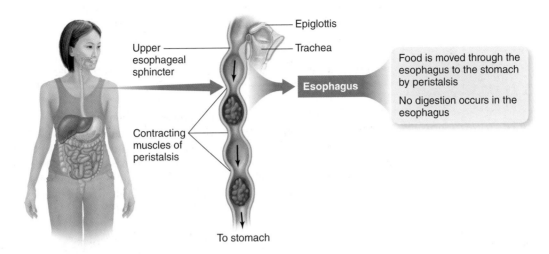

Figure 2.8 Where your food is now: the esophagus. Peristalsis, the rhythmic contraction and relaxation of muscles in the esophagus, propels food toward the stomach. Peristalsis occurs throughout the GI tract.

The Stomach Mixes, Digests, and Stores Food

The J-shaped **stomach** is a saclike organ that can expand in some people to hold several cups of food **(Figure 2.9)**. Before any food reaches the stomach, the brain sends signals, telling it to be ready for the food to arrive. The stomach gets ready for your sandwich by secreting **gastric juice,** which contains several important compounds, including *hydrochloric acid (HCl)* and the enzyme *pepsin*, which together start to break down proteins, and the enzyme *gastric lipase*, which begins to break down fats. The stomach also secretes *mucus*, which protects its lining from being digested by the hydrochloric acid and pepsin.

In addition to chemical digestion, the stomach performs mechanical digestion, mixing and churning the food until it becomes a liquid called **chyme.** Enzymes can access this liquid chyme more easily than solid food.

Although most absorption occurs in the small intestine, the stomach lining does begin absorbing a few substances. These include water, some minerals and some fats, and certain drugs, including aspirin and alcohol.

stomach A J-shaped organ where food is partially digested, churned, and stored until released into the small intestine.

gastric juice Acidic liquid secreted within the stomach that contains hydrochloric acid, pepsin, and other chemicals.

chyme Semifluid mass consisting of partially digested food, water, and gastric juices.

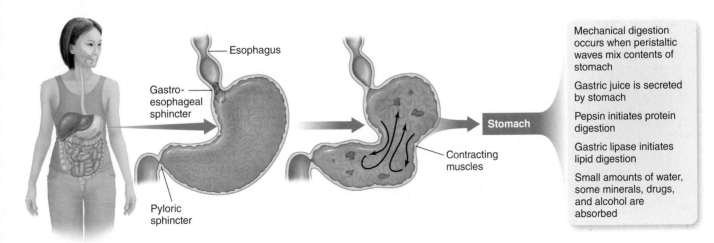

Figure 2.9 Where your food is now: the stomach. In the stomach, the protein and fat in your sandwich begin to be digested. Your meal is churned into chyme and stored until released into the small intestine.

Another of your stomach's jobs is to store your sandwich until the next part of the digestive tract, the small intestine, is ready for it. Remember that the stomach can hold several cups of food. This amount would overwhelm the small intestine if it were released all at once. Instead, food stays in your stomach about 2 hours before it is released a little at a time, as chyme, into the small intestine. Regulating this release is the *pyloric sphincter*.

RECAP Chewing initiates mechanical and chemical digestion. During swallowing, our nasal passages close and the epiglottis covers the trachea. The esophagus is a muscular tube that transports food from the mouth to the stomach via rhythmic waves called peristalsis. The stomach secretes gastric juice, which begins the breakdown of proteins and fats, as well as mucus to protect its lining. It mixes food into chyme, which is released into the small intestine through the pyloric sphincter.

Most Digestion and Absorption Occurs in the Small Intestine

The **small intestine** is the longest portion of the GI tract, accounting for about two-thirds of its length. However, at only an inch in diameter, it is comparatively narrow. The small intestine is composed of three sections (**Figure 2.10**):

* The first section is the *duodenum*. It is connected via the pyloric sphincter to the stomach.
* The *jejunum* is the middle portion of the small intestine.
* The *ileum* is the last portion. It is connected to the large intestine at another sphincter, called the *ileocecal valve.*

small intestine The largest portion of the GI tract, where most digestion and absorption take place.

Most digestion and absorption takes place in the small intestine. Here, food is broken down into its smallest components, molecules that the body can then absorb into its internal environment. Ahead, we identify a variety of *accessory organs*

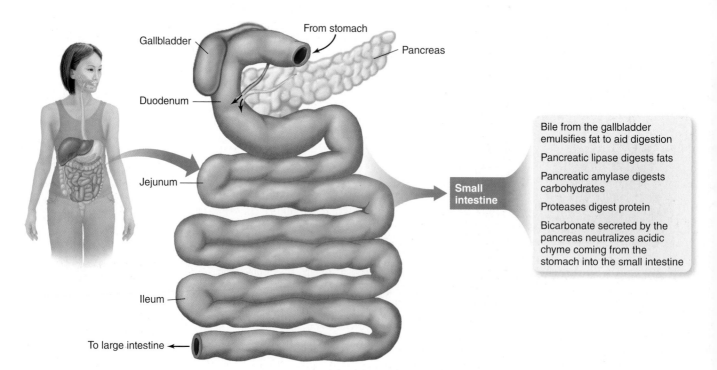

Gallbladder
From stomach
Pancreas
Duodenum
Jejunum
Ileum
To large intestine

Small intestine

Bile from the gallbladder emulsifies fat to aid digestion

Pancreatic lipase digests fats

Pancreatic amylase digests carbohydrates

Proteases digest protein

Bicarbonate secreted by the pancreas neutralizes acidic chyme coming from the stomach into the small intestine

Figure 2.10 Where your food is now: the small intestine. Here, most of the digestion and absorption of the nutrients in your sandwich takes place.

(organs that assist digestion but are not part of the gastrointestinal tract), enzymes, and unique anatomical features of the small intestine that allow for maximal absorption of most nutrients.

The Gallbladder and Pancreas Aid in Digestion

As the fat from the turkey and mayonnaise enters the small intestine, an accessory organ, the **gallbladder,** contracts. The gallbladder is located beneath the liver (see Figures 2.5 and 2.10) and stores a greenish fluid produced by the liver called **bile.** Contraction of the gallbladder sends bile into the duodenum. Bile then *emulsifies* the fat—that is, it breaks it up into smaller particles that are more accessible to digestive enzymes. If you've ever noticed how a drop of liquid dish soap breaks up a film of fat floating at the top of a basin of greasy dishes, you understand the function of bile.

The **pancreas,** an accessory organ located behind the stomach, manufactures, holds, and secretes digestive enzymes (see Figures 2.5 and 2.10). These enzymes include pancreatic amylase, which breaks down carbohydrates; lipase, which breaks down fats; and proteases, which break down proteins (see Table 2.1). The pancreas is also responsible for manufacturing hormones that are important in the conversion of food into energy. Finally, the pancreas secretes bicarbonate—a base—into the duodenum, where it neutralizes the acidity of the chyme entering from the stomach.

Now the macronutrients in your sandwich have been processed into a liquid that contains molecules small enough for absorption. This molecular "soup" continues to move along the small intestine via peristalsis, encountering the absorptive cells of the intestinal lining all along the way.

A Specialized Lining Enables the Small Intestine to Absorb Food

The lining of the small intestine is especially well suited for absorption. If you looked at it under a microscope, you would notice that it is heavily folded **(Figure 2.11,** page 52). Within these folds are small, finger-like projections called *villi,* whose constant movement helps them encounter and trap nutrient molecules. Covering the villi are even tinier, hairlike structures called *microvilli.* The microvilli form a surface somewhat like the bristles on a hairbrush and are often referred to as the *brush border.* Together, these absorptive features increase the surface area of the small intestine by more than 500 times, allowing it to absorb many more nutrients than it could if it were smooth.

Nutrients enter the body by passing through the cells of the brush border. Once inside the villi, the nutrients encounter *capillaries* (tiny blood vessels) and a *lacteal,* which is a small lymphatic vessel. These vessels soak up the final products of digestion and begin their transport.

Intestinal Cells Readily Absorb Vitamins, Minerals, and Water

The turkey sandwich you ate contained several vitamins and minerals in addition to the protein, carbohydrate, and fat. These vitamins and minerals are not really "digested" the same way that macronutrients are. Vitamins do not have to be broken down because they are already small enough to cross into brush border cells, whereas minerals are already the smallest possible units of matter.

Finally, a large component of food is water, and, of course, you also drink lots of water throughout the day. Water is absorbed along the entire length of the GI tract because it is a small molecule that can easily pass through the cell membrane. However, as we will see shortly, a significant percentage of water is absorbed in the large intestine.

gallbladder A sac of tissue beneath the liver that stores bile and secretes it into the small intestine.

bile Fluid produced by the liver and stored in the gallbladder that emulsifies fats in the small intestine.

pancreas Gland located behind the stomach that secretes digestive enzymes.

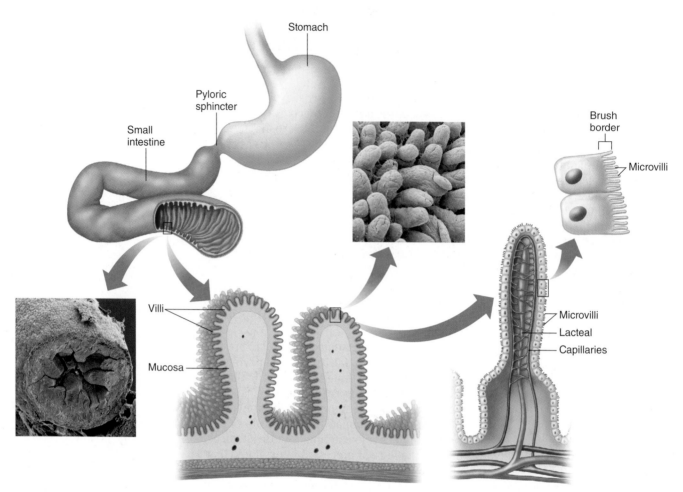

🔺 **Figure 2.11** Absorption of nutrients occurs via the specialized lining of the small intestine. The lining of the small intestine is heavily folded and has thousands of finger-like projections called villi. The cells covering the villi end in hairlike projections called microvilli, which together form the brush border. These features significantly increase the absorptive capacity of the small intestine.

Blood and Lymph Transport Nutrients

Our body has two main fluids that transport nutrients (including water) and waste products throughout the body. These fluids are blood and lymph. Blood travels through the cardiovascular system, and lymph travels through the lymphatic system **(Figure 2.12)**.

As blood travels through the GI tract, it picks up the nutrients that were absorbed through the villi of the small intestine and then carries them to the liver for processing. The waste products picked up by the blood as it circulates around the body are filtered and excreted by the kidneys.

The lymphatic vessels pick up most fats and fat-soluble vitamins and transport them in lymph. These nutrients eventually enter the bloodstream at an area near the heart where the lymphatic and blood vessels join together.

The Liver Regulates Blood Nutrients

liver The largest organ of the GI tract and one of the most important organs of the body. Its functions include production of bile and processing of nutrient-rich blood from the small intestine.

Most nutrients absorbed from the small intestine enter the *portal vein*, which carries them to the **liver.** Another accessory digestive organ, the liver is a triangular wedge that rests almost entirely within the protection of the lower rib cage, on the right side of the body (see Figure 2.5). The liver is the largest digestive organ; it is also one of the most important organs in the body, performing more than 500 discrete functions. One of these functions is to receive the products of digestion and then release into

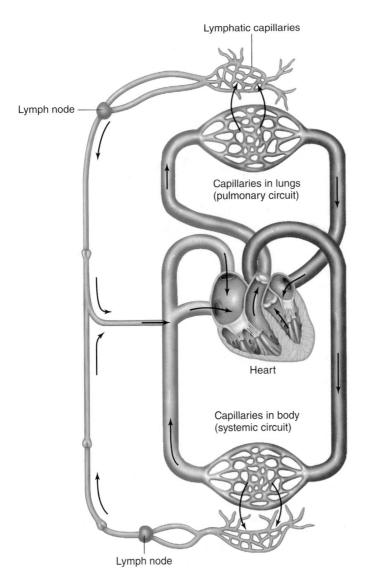

Lymphatic capillaries

Lymph node

Capillaries in lungs
(pulmonary circuit)

Heart

Capillaries in body
(systemic circuit)

Lymph node

◆ **Figure 2.12** Blood travels through the cardiovascular system to transport nutrients and fluids and pick up waste products. Lymph travels through the lymphatic system and transports most fats and fat-soluble vitamins.

the bloodstream those nutrients needed throughout the body. The liver also plays a major role in processing, storing, and regulating the blood levels of the energy nutrients.

Have you ever wondered why people who abuse alcohol are at risk for damaging their liver? It's because another of its functions is to filter the blood, removing potential toxins, such as alcohol and other drugs. The liver can filter the blood of alcohol at the rate of approximately one drink per hour. When someone exceeds this rate, the liver becomes overwhelmed by the excessive alcohol, which damages its cells. With chronic alcohol abuse, scar tissue forms. The scar tissue blocks the free flow of blood through the liver, so that any further toxins accumulate in the blood. This can lead to confusion, coma, and even death.

Another important job of the liver is to synthesize many of the chemicals the body uses in carrying out digestion. For example, the liver synthesizes bile, which, as we just discussed, is then stored in the gallbladder until needed to emulsify fats.

◆ Water is readily absorbed along the entire length of the GI tract, especially in the large intestine.

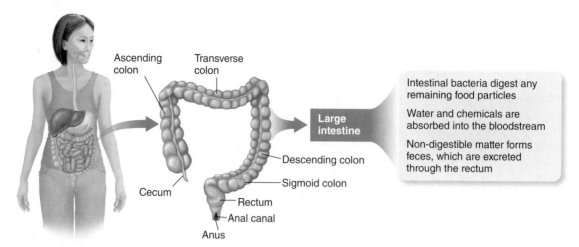

Ascending colon

Transverse colon

Large intestine

Intestinal bacteria digest any remaining food particles

Water and chemicals are absorbed into the bloodstream

Non-digestible matter forms feces, which are excreted through the rectum

Descending colon

Sigmoid colon

Cecum

Rectum

Anal canal

Anus

Figure 2.13 Where your food is now: the large intestine. Most water absorption occurs here, as does the formation of food wastes into feces. Peristalsis propels the feces to the body exterior.

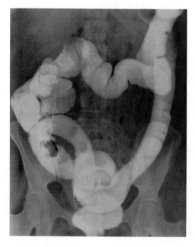

The large intestine is a thick, tubelike structure that stores the undigested mass leaving the small intestine and absorbs any remaining nutrients and water.

large intestine Final organ of the GI tract consisting of the cecum, colon, rectum, and anal canal and in which most water is absorbed and feces are formed.

The Large Intestine Stores Food Waste Until It Is Excreted

The **large intestine** is a thick, tubelike structure that frames the small intestine on three and a half sides **(Figure 2.13)**. It begins with a sack of tissue called the *cecum*. From the cecum, it continues up the right side of the abdomen as the *ascending colon*. The *transverse colon* runs across the top of the small intestine, and then the *descending colon* comes down on the left side of the abdomen. The *sigmoid colon* is the last segment and extends from the bottom left corner to the *rectum*. The rectum ends in the *anal canal,* which is just over an inch long.

What has happened to your turkey sandwich? When any undigested and unabsorbed food components and water in the chyme finally reach the large intestine, they mix with intestinal bacteria. These bacteria are normal and helpful residents, as they finish digesting any remaining particles left from your sandwich. In fact, the bacteria living in the large intestine are so helpful that, as discussed in the **Highlight** feature box (page 55), many people consume them deliberately!

No other digestion occurs in the large intestine. Its main functions are to store the chyme for 12 to 24 hours and during that time to absorb chemicals and water from it, leaving a semisolid mass called *feces.* Weak waves of peristalsis move the feces through the colon, except for one or more stronger waves each day that force the feces more powerfully toward the rectum for elimination.

To view an animation of the process of digestion, visit http://www.health .howstuffworks.com/ human-body/systems/ digestive/adam-200142 .htm.

RECAP Most digestion and absorption occurs in the small intestine with the help of bile, which emulsifies fats, and pancreatic enzymes that break down carbohydrates, fats, and proteins. The lining of the small intestine contains villi and microvilli that trap and absorb nutrients. The liver processes all nutrients absorbed from the small intestine. Bacteria in the large intestine assist with digestion of any remaining digestible food products. The large intestine stores chyme, from which it absorbs water and any other remaining nutrients, leaving a semisolid mass, called feces, which is then eliminated from the body.

HIGHLIGHT
Probiotics: What Are They, and Should You Eat Them?

The last time you ate a cup of creamy, fruity yogurt, did you think about the fact that you were also eating *bacteria*? Don't worry—these microorganisms won't harm you; they'll help your body to function. They are one of a group of substances called *probiotics*: live microorganisms found in, or added to, fermented foods that optimize the bacterial environment of the large intestine.

Interest in probiotics was sparked in the early 1900s with the work of Elie Metchnikoff, a Nobel Prize–winning scientist. Dr. Metchnikoff linked the long, healthy lives of Bulgarian peasants with their consumption of fermented milk products, such as yogurt. Subsequent research identified the bacteria in fermented milk products as the factor that promoted health. These bacteria were given the name *probiotics,* meaning "pro-life."

In the United States, foods that contain probiotics include fortified milk, yogurt, and a creamy beverage called *kefir,* which is made from fermented milk. Probiotics are also sold in supplement form. The bacterial species most frequently used in these foods and supplements are *Lactobacillus* and *Bifidobacterium.*

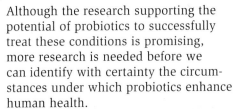
Probiotics can be found in yogurt and other fermented milk products.

When a person consumes a product containing probiotics, the bacteria adhere to the intestinal wall for a few days, exerting their beneficial actions. Because their activity is short-lived, they probably need to be consumed on a daily basis to be most effective. The exact means by which probiotics benefit human health is currently being researched. One theory is that they increase the number and activity of immune cells that help us fight infections. However, although they appear to improve immune function, there is still limited research on how this occurs.[9,10]

The following are some health problems that may be successfully treated with probiotics:[11-13]

- Diarrhea caused by certain infectious microorganisms or associated with the use of antibiotic medications
- Infections in children in daycare
- Traveler's diarrhea
- Irritable bowel syndrome (IBS) and inflammatory bowel diseases
- Infection from *Helicobacter pylori,* which is the bacterium associated with conditions such as peptic ulcers, gastritis, and gastric cancer
- Lactose intolerance (inability to digest milk sugar)
- Allergy risk in infants
- Eczema in children
- Urinary and genital tract infections in women

Although the research supporting the potential of probiotics to successfully treat these conditions is promising, more research is needed before we can identify with certainty the circumstances under which probiotics enhance human health.

It is important to remember that, in order to be effective, a minimum number of bacteria must be present in foods. Although the exact number of bacteria is not known, it is estimated that a daily dose of at least 1 billion to 10 billion bacteria is needed to be effective.[14] To put this in perspective, commercial yogurts meeting the National Yogurt Association Standards contain 100 million live and active cultures per gram. So a 1-cup serving (8 oz, or 227 grams) of yogurt contains more than 22 billion bacteria, or more than the estimated effective dose.

Bacteria live only for a short time. This means that foods and supplements containing probiotics have a limited shelf life and must be properly stored and consumed within a relatively brief period of time to confer maximal benefit. In general, refrigerated foods containing probiotics have a shelf life of 3 to 6 weeks, whereas the shelf life for supplements containing probiotics is about 12 months. However, because the probiotic content of refrigerated foods is much more stable than that of supplements, the more perishable forms may be a better health bet.

Now that you know a little more about probiotics, will you be adding them to your daily diet?

HEALTHWATCH

What Disorders Are Related to Digestion, Absorption, and Elimination?

Considering the complexity of digestion, absorption, and elimination, it's no wonder that sometimes things go wrong. Let's look at some GI tract disorders and what you can do if any of these problems affect you.

Belching and Flatulence Are Common

Many people complain of problems with belching and/or flatulence (passage of intestinal gas). The primary cause of belching is swallowed air. Eating too fast, wearing improperly fitting dentures, chewing gum, sucking on hard candies or a drinking straw, and gulping food or fluid can increase the risk for swallowing air. To prevent or reduce belching, avoid these behaviors.

Although many people find *flatus* (intestinal gas) uncomfortable and embarrassing, its presence in the GI tract is completely normal, as is its expulsion. Flatus is a mixture of many gases, including nitrogen, hydrogen, oxygen, methane, and carbon dioxide. Interestingly, all of these are odorless. It is only when flatus contains sulfur that it causes the embarrassing odor associated with flatulence.

Foods most commonly reported to cause flatus include those rich in fibers, starches, and sugars, such as beans, dairy products, and some vegetables. The partially digested carbohydrates from these foods pass into the large intestine, where they are acted upon by bacteria, producing gas. Other food products that may cause flatus, intestinal cramps, and diarrhea include products made with the fat substitute olestra, sugar alcohols, and quorn (a meat substitute made from fungus).

Since many of the foods that can cause flatus are healthful, it is important not to avoid them. Eating smaller portions can help reduce the amount of flatus produced and passed. In addition, some preventive products, such as Beano, can offer some relief. These over-the-counter supplements contain alpha-galactosidase, an enzyme that digests the complex sugars in gas-producing foods. Although flatus is generally normal, some people have malabsorption diseases that cause painful bloating and require medical treatment. Some of these disorders are described later in this section.

Gastroesophageal Reflux Is Due to Backflow of Stomach Acid

When you eat food, your stomach secretes hydrochloric acid (HCl) to start the digestion process. In some people, the gastroesophageal sphincter becomes irritated or overly relaxed. In either case, the result is that HCl seeps back up into the esophagus **(Figure 2.14)**. Although the stomach is protected from HCl by a thick coat of mucus, the esophagus does not have this coating. Thus, the HCl burns it. When this happens, a person experiences a painful sensation in the center of the chest. The clinical name for this condition is *gastroesophageal reflux (GER)*, but it is commonly called *heartburn*. People often take over-the-counter "antacids" to neutralize the hydrochloric acid, thereby relieving the pain. A nondrug approach is to repeatedly swallow: this action causes any acid within the esophagus to be swept down into the stomach, eventually relieving the symptoms.

Gastroesophageal reflux disease (GERD) is a more painful type of GER that occurs more than twice per week. GERD affects about 19 million Americans and, like GER, occurs when HCl flows back into the esophagus. Although people who experience occasional GER usually have no structural abnormalities, many people with GERD have an overly relaxed esophageal sphincter or damage to the esophagus itself. Symptoms of GERD include persistent acid regurgitation and burning pain in the central chest. Some people have GERD without heartburn and instead experience trouble

gastroesophageal reflux disease (GERD) A more painful type of gastroesophageal reflux that occurs more than twice per week.

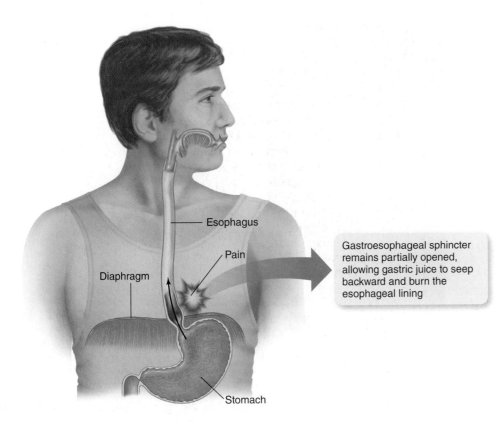

Esophagus

Pain

Diaphragm

Gastroesophageal sphincter remains partially opened, allowing gastric juice to seep backward and burn the esophageal lining

Stomach

◀**Figure 2.14** In gastroesophageal reflux, acidic gastric juices seep backward through an open or relaxed sphincter into the lower portion of the esophagus, burning its lining. The pain is felt in the center of the chest, over the heart.

swallowing, burning in the mouth, the feeling that food is stuck in the throat, and/or hoarseness in the morning.[15]

The exact causes of GERD are unknown. However, a number of factors may contribute, including cigarette smoking, alcohol use, overweight, pregnancy, lying down after a meal, and certain co-existing medical conditions, including a *hiatal hernia,* in which the upper part of the stomach lies above the diaphragm muscle. Certain foods may trigger episodes, but the precise offenders vary for different people, from caffeine to chocolate to fatty foods to onions. Controlling any contributing factors—for instance, by avoiding lying down for 3 hours after a meal—can prevent or reduce symptoms. The individual's healthcare provider may recommend taking an antacid before meals or taking one of several over-the-counter and prescription medications now available to treat GERD.

An Ulcer Is an Area of Erosion in the GI Tract

A **peptic ulcer** is an area of the GI tract that has been eroded away by a combination of hydrochloric acid and the enzyme pepsin **(Figure 2.15**, page 58). In almost all cases, it is located in the stomach area (*gastric ulcer*) or the part of the duodenum closest to the stomach (*duodenal ulcer*). It causes a burning pain in the abdominal area, typically 1 to 3 hours after eating a meal. In serious cases, eroded blood vessels bleed into the GI tract, causing vomiting of blood and/or blood in the stools, as well as anemia. If the ulcer entirely perforates the tract wall, stomach contents can leak into the abdominal cavity, causing a life-threatening infection called *peritonitis.*

For decades, physicians believed that experiencing high levels of stress, drinking alcohol, and eating spicy foods were the primary factors responsible for ulcers. But in 1982, Australian gastroenterologists Robin Warren and Barry Marshall detected the same species of bacterium in the majority of their ulcer patients' stomachs.[16] Treatment with an antibiotic effective against the bacterium, *Helicobacter pylori* (*H. pylori*), cured the ulcers. It is now known that *H. pylori* plays a key role in the development of most peptic ulcers. The hydrochloric acid in gastric juice kills most bacteria, but *H. pylori* is unusual in that it thrives in acidic environments. Approximately

▲ Although the exact causes of gastroesophageal reflux disease (GERD) are unknown, smoking and being overweight may be contributing factors.

peptic ulcer An area of the GI tract that has been eroded away by the acidic gastric juice of the stomach. The two main causes of peptic ulcers are an *H. pylori* infection or use of nonsteroidal anti-inflammatory drugs.

◗ **Figure 2.15** Ulcer formation.
(a) The *Helicobacter pylori* bacterium plays a key role in the development of most peptic ulcers. **(b)** A peptic ulcer.

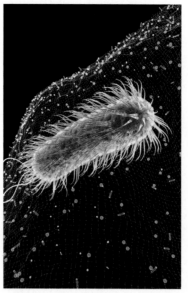

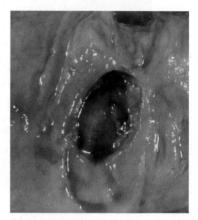

(a) The *Helicobacter pylori* (*H. pylori*) bacterium plays a key role in the development of most peptic ulcers.

(b) A peptic ulcer.

40% of people have this bacterium in their stomach, but most people do not develop ulcers. The reason for this is not known.[17]

Prevention of infection with *H. pylori*, as with any infectious microorganism, includes regular hand washing and safe food-handling practices. Because of the role of *H. pylori* in ulcer development, treatment usually involves antibiotics and acid-suppressing medications. Special diets and stress-reduction techniques are no longer typically recommended because they do not reduce acid secretion. However, people with ulcers should avoid specific foods they identify as causing them discomfort.

Although most peptic ulcers are caused by *H. pylori* infection, some are caused by prolonged use of nonsteroidal anti-inflammatory drugs (NSAIDs); these drugs include pain relievers such as aspirin, ibuprofen, and naproxen sodium. They appear to cause ulcers by suppressing the secretion of mucus and bicarbonate, which normally protect the stomach from its acidic gastric juice. Ulcers caused by NSAIDs use generally heal once a person stops taking the medication.[18]

RECAP Gastroesophageal reflux (GER) is caused by seepage of gastric juices into the esophagus. Gastroesophageal reflux disease (GERD) is a more painful type of GER that occurs more than twice per week. A peptic ulcer is an area of erosion of the stomach lining caused by gastric juices.

Some People Experience Disorders Related to Specific Foods

You check out the ingredients list on your energy bar, and you notice that it says "Produced in a facility that processes peanuts." The package on your microwave dinner cautions "Contains wheat, milk, and soy." Why all the warnings about these foods? The reason is that, to some people, consuming these foods can be dangerous, even life threatening. To learn more about product labeling for potential food offenders, see the **Nutrition Label Activity** (page 59).

Disorders related to specific foods can be clustered into three main groupings: food intolerances, food allergies, and a genetic disorder called celiac disease. We discuss these separately.

NUTRITION LABEL ACTIVITY
Recognizing Common Allergens in Foods

The U.S. Food and Drug Administration (FDA) requires food labels to clearly identify any ingredients containing protein derived from the eight major allergenic foods.[19] Manufacturers must identify "in plain English" the presence of ingredients that contain protein derived from

- milk,
- eggs,
- fish,
- crustacean shellfish (crab, lobster, shrimp, and so on),
- tree nuts (almonds, pecans, walnuts, and so on),
- peanuts,
- wheat, and
- soybeans.

Although more than 160 foods have been identified as causing food allergies in sensitive individuals, the FDA requires labeling for only these eight foods because together they account for over 90% of all documented food allergies in the United States and represent the foods most likely to result in severe or life-threatening reactions.[19]

These eight allergenic foods must be indicated in the list of ingredients; alternatively, adjacent to the ingredients list, the label must say "Contains" followed by the name of the food. For example, the label of a product containing the milk-derived protein casein would have to use the term *milk* in addition to the term *casein*, so that those with milk allergies would clearly understand the presence of an allergen they need to avoid.[19] Any food product found to contain an undeclared allergen is subject to recall by the FDA.

Look at the ingredients list from an energy bar, shown below, and try the following questions:

- **Which of the FDA's eight allergenic foods does this bar definitely contain? _____**
- **If you were allergic to peanuts, would eating this bar pose any risk to you?**

  Yes or No

- **If you were allergic to almonds, would eating this bar pose any risk to you?**

  Yes or No

(Answers can be found on the Companion Website at www.pearsonhighered.com/thompsonmanore.)

Ingredients: Soy protein isolate, rice flour, oats, milled flaxseed, brown rice syrup, evaporated cane juice, sunflower oil, soy lecithin, cocoa, nonfat milk solids, salt.
Contains soy and dairy. May contain traces of peanuts and other nuts.

Food Intolerance

A **food intolerance** is a cluster of GI symptoms (often gas, pain, and diarrhea) that occurs following consumption of a particular food. The immune system plays no role in intolerance, and although episodes are unpleasant, they are usually transient, resolving after the offending food has been eliminated from the body. An example is lactose intolerance. It occurs in people whose bodies do not produce sufficient quantities of the enzyme lactase, which is needed for the breakdown of the milk sugar lactose. People can also have an intolerance to wheat, soy, and other foods, but as with lactose intolerance, the symptoms pass once the offending food is out of the person's system.

Food Allergy

A **food allergy** is a hypersensitivity reaction of the immune system to a particular component (usually a protein) in a food. This reaction causes the immune cells to release chemicals that cause either limited or bodywide inflammation. Although they are much less common than food intolerances, food allergies can be far more serious. Approximately 30,000 consumers require emergency room treatment and 150 Americans die each year because of allergic reactions to foods.[19]

You may have heard stories of people being allergic to foods as common as peanuts. This is the case for Liz (see the Nutri-Case at the end of this discussion). She was out to dinner with her parents, celebrating her birthday, when the dessert cart came around. The caramel custard looked heavenly and was probably a safe choice, but she asked the waiter, just to be sure that it contained no peanuts. He checked with the chef, then returned and assured her that, yes, the custard was peanut-free—but within minutes of consuming it, Liz's skin became flushed and she struggled to breathe. As her parents were dialing 911, she lost consciousness. Fortunately, the

food intolerance A cluster of GI symptoms that occurs following consumption of a particular food but is not caused by an immune system response.

food allergy An inflammatory reaction caused by an immune system hypersensitivity to a protein component of a food.

◆ For some people, eating a meal of grilled shrimp with peanut sauce would cause a severe allergic reaction.

paramedics arrived within minutes and were able to resuscitate her. It was subsequently determined that, unknown to the chef, the spoon that his prep cook had used to scoop the baked custard into serving bowls had been resting on a cutting board where he had chopped peanuts for a different dessert. Just this small exposure to peanuts was enough to cause a severe allergic reaction in Liz.

How can a food that most people consume regularly, such as peanuts, shellfish, eggs, or milk, cause another person's immune system to react so violently? In Liz's case, a trace amount of peanut stimulated immune cells throughout her body to release their inflammatory chemicals. In some people, the inflammation is localized, so the damage is limited. For instance, some people's mouth and throat itch when they eat cantaloupe, whereas others develop a rash whenever they eat eggs. What made Liz's experience so terrifyingly different was that the inflammation was widespread, affecting essentially all of her body systems and sending her into a state called *anaphylactic shock*. Left untreated, anaphylactic shock is nearly always fatal, so many people with known food allergies carry with them a kit containing an injection of a powerful stimulant called epinephrine. This drug can reduce symptoms long enough to buy the victim time to get emergency medical care.

Physicians use a variety of tests to diagnose food allergies. Usually, the physician orders a skin test, commonly known as a "scratch test," in which a clinician swabs a small amount of fluid containing the suspected allergen onto the patient's skin, then lightly scratches or pricks the area so that the fluid seeps under the patient's skin. After 15 to 20 minutes, the clinician checks the area: redness and/or swelling indicates that the patient is allergic to the substance. However, people can have a positive skin response yet not have any problems when the substance is consumed.[20] Thus, some physicians will perform a blood test, in which a sample of the patient's blood is tested for the presence of unique proteins called *antibodies* that the immune system produces in a person with an allergy. But once again, the presence of antibodies does not necessarily mean the person will react to consumption of the food. The

---

NUTRI-CASE LIZ

"I used to think of my peanut allergy as no big deal, but ever since my experience at that restaurant last year, I've been pretty obsessive about it. For months afterward, I refused to eat anything that I hadn't prepared myself. I do eat out now, but I always insist that the chef prepare my food personally, with clean utensils. Shopping is a lot harder, too, because I have to check every label. The worst, though, is eating at my friends' houses. I have to ask them whether they keep peanuts or peanut butter in their homes. Some of them are really sympathetic, but others look at me as if I'm a hypochondriac!

I wish I could think of something to say to them to make them understand that this isn't something I have any control over."

What could Liz say in response to friends who don't understand the cause and seriousness of her food allergy? Do you think it would help Liz to share her fears with her doctor and discuss possible strategies? If so, why? In addition to shopping, dining out, and eating at friends' houses, what other situations might require Liz to be cautious about her food choices?

only test that can definitively establish the presence of a food allergy is an *oral challenge*, in which the patient consumes the suspected food and the healthcare provider monitors the reaction. When challenges are performed, only about one-third of suspected foods are found to cause allergies.[20]

Beware of e-mail spam, Internet websites, and ads in popular magazines attempting to link a vast assortment of health problems to food allergies. Typically, these ads offer allergy-testing services for exorbitant fees, then make even more money by selling "nutritional counseling" and sometimes supplements and other products they say will help you cope with your allergies. If you experience symptoms that cause you to suspect you might have a food allergy, consult an MD.

Celiac Disease

Celiac disease, also known as *celiac sprue* or *gluten-induced enteropathy*, is a digestive disease that severely damages the lining of the small intestine and interferes with absorption of nutrients.[21] As in food allergy, the body's immune system causes the disorder. However, because there is a strong genetic predisposition to celiac disease, with the risk now linked to specific gene markers, it is also classified as a genetic disorder.[21] Once thought to be a rare disorder, celiac disease is now known to occur in about 1 of 133 Americans.

In celiac disease, the offending food component is a protein called *gluten*, which is found in wheat, rye, and barley. Note, however, that celiac disease is not the same as a gluten allergy: many people believe they are allergic to gluten because they experience symptoms (a runny nose, a skin rash, and so on) when they eat wheat products, but they do not have the intestinal damage characteristic of celiac disease. That is, when people with celiac disease eat gluten, their immune system triggers an inflammatory response that erodes the villi of the small intestine. If the person is unaware of the disorder and continues to eat gluten, repeated immune reactions cause the villi to become greatly decreased. As a result, the person becomes unable to absorb certain nutrients properly—a condition known as *malabsorption*. Over time, malabsorption can lead to malnutrition (poor nutrient status).

Symptoms of celiac disease can mimic those of other intestinal disturbances, so the condition is often misdiagnosed. Some of the symptoms include fatty stools (due to poor fat absorption); frequent stools, either watery or hard; cramping; anemia; pallor; and weight loss. Other puzzling symptoms do not appear to involve the GI tract. These include an intensely itchy rash called *dermatitis herpetiformis*, osteoporosis (poor bone density), infertility, seizures, anxiety, depression, and fatigue, among others.[21]

Diagnostic tests for celiac disease include a variety of blood tests that screen for the presence of immune proteins called antibodies, or for the genetic markers of the disease. However, the "gold standard" for diagnosis is a biopsy of the small intestine showing atrophy of the intestinal villi. Because long-term complications of undiagnosed celiac disease include an increased risk for liver disease and for cancer of the small intestine, early diagnosis can be life-saving. Unfortunately, celiac disease is thought to be widely underdiagnosed and misdiagnosed in the United States.[21]

Currently, there is no cure for celiac disease. Treatment is with a special gluten-free diet that excludes all forms of wheat, rye, and barley. The diet is challenging, but many gluten-free foods are now available, including breads, pasta, and other products made from corn, rice, soy, and even garbanzo bean flours.

RECAP Food intolerance is a condition in which a person experiences gastrointestinal discomfort following consumption of certain foods, but the symptoms are not prompted by the immune system. In contrast, both food allergies and celiac disease are caused by an immune response. Food allergies cause inflammation, which results in localized problems (such as skin rash) or systemic problems (such as life-threatening anaphylactic shock). Celiac disease is a genetic disorder that causes damage to the intestinal villi following consumption of gluten, a protein found in wheat, rye, and barley.

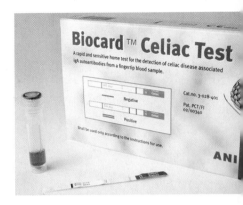

A simple blood test can identify celiac disease.

For people with celiac disease, corn is a gluten-free source of carbohydrates.

celiac disease A genetic disorder characterized by an inability to absorb a protein called gluten. This causes an inflammatory immune response that damages the lining of the small intestine.

FOODS YOU DON'T KNOW YOU LOVE YET

Job's Tears

One grain on the "no" list for people with celiac disease is barley, a popular ingredient in soups and stews. Fortunately, a pleasing, gluten-free barley substitute called Job's tears is available in many Asian markets and natural food stores, where you might find it labeled as Asian barley. Job's tears, the seeds of an Asian grass, are the color of pearl barley but much larger, with a brown groove splitting the seed on one side. Cooked Job's tears have a sweet taste somewhat like corn. They can be used in any recipe calling for barley, including soups and stews, or served on their own as a side dish instead of rice. They can even be cooked as a gluten-free breakfast porridge.

Diarrhea Results When Food Is Expelled Too Quickly

Diarrhea is the passage of loose, watery stools, often three or more times a day. Other symptoms may include cramping, abdominal pain, bloating, nausea, fever, and bloody stools. Diarrhea is usually caused by an infection of the gastrointestinal tract, a chronic disease, stress, food intolerances, reactions to medications, or a bowel disorder.[22]

Acute diarrhea lasts less than 3 weeks and is usually caused by an infection from bacteria, a virus, or a parasite. Chronic diarrhea is usually caused by allergies to cow's milk, celiac disease, irritable bowel syndrome, or some other disorder. Whatever the cause, diarrhea can be harmful because the person can lose large quantities of water and minerals, such as sodium, and become severely dehydrated. Diarrhea is particularly dangerous in infants and young children. In fact, each year millions of children worldwide die from dehydration caused by diarrhea. Oral rehydration with specially formulated fluids can reverse dehydration and allow for the introduction of yogurt, rice, banana, and other mild foods.

A condition referred to as *traveler's diarrhea* has become a common health concern because of the expansion in global travel. The accompanying *Game Plan* (page 63)provides tips for avoiding traveler's diarrhea.

Constipation Results When Food Wastes Are Expelled Too Slowly

Constipation is typically defined as a condition in which no stools are passed for 2 or more days; however, it is important to recognize that many people normally experience bowel movements only every second or third day. Thus, the definition of constipation varies from one person to another. In addition to being infrequent, the stools are difficult to pass and usually hard and small.

diarrhea A condition characterized by the frequent passage of loose, watery stools.

constipation A condition characterized by the absence of bowel movements for a period of time that is significantly longer than normal for the individual. When a bowel movement does occur, stools are usually small, hard, and difficult to pass.

GAME PLAN
Tips for Avoiding Traveler's Diarrhea

Diarrhea is the rapid movement of fecal matter through the large intestine, often accompanied by large volumes of water. *Traveler's diarrhea* (also called *dysentery*), which is experienced by people traveling to regions where clean drinking water is not readily available, is usually caused by viral or bacterial infections. Diarrhea represents the body's way of ridding itself of the invasive agent. The large intestine and even some of the small intestine become irritated by the microbes and the body's defense against them. This irritation leads to increased secretion of fluid and increased peristalsis of the large intestine, causing watery stools and a higher-than-normal frequency of bowel movements.

⬆ When traveling in developing countries, it is wise to avoid food from street vendors.

People generally get traveler's diarrhea from consuming water or food that is contaminated with fecal matter. Travelers to developing countries are at increased risk; however, hikers and others traveling in remote regions anywhere are at risk if they drink untreated water from lakes, rivers, and streams.

Traveler's diarrhea usually starts a few days after exposure. Symptoms include fatigue, lack of appetite, abdominal cramps, and watery diarrhea. In some cases, you may also experience nausea, vomiting, and low-grade fever. Usually, the diarrhea passes within 4 to 6 days, and people recover completely. What can you do to prevent traveler's diarrhea? The following tips should help.[22]

☐ Drink only brand-name bottled beverages, including water, wine, beer, and sodas. Use bottled water even for brushing your teeth. In general, it is smart to assume that all local water, even if bottled, is unsafe.

☐ Wipe the bottle or can clean before drinking the beverage.

☐ Avoid foods and beverages exposed to or cleaned with local water, as well as beverages containing ice (freezing does not kill all bacteria).

☐ To render local water safe, boil it for several minutes. Beverages such as tea and coffee made with boiled water are safe.

☐ Avoid drinking unpasteurized milk and eating raw or rare meat, poultry, fish, or shellfish. Avoid raw vegetables, including salad greens. Do not eat raw fruits unless they've been washed in boiled or bottled water, then peeled. Do not eat fruits without peels, such as berries.

☐ Avoid eating food purchased from street vendors, as well as any cooked food that is no longer hot in temperature.

☐ Prior to traveling to a high-risk country, discuss your trip with your physician for current recommendations for prevention and treatment.

☐ If you do suffer from traveler's diarrhea, drink a specially formulated oral rehydration solution to help replenish vital nutrients; these solutions are available in most countries at local pharmacies and stores. Antibiotics may also be needed to kill the bacteria. Once treatment is initiated, the diarrhea should cease within 2 to 3 days. If the diarrhea persists for more than 10 days after the initiation of treatment, or if there is blood in your stools, you should see a physician immediately to determine the cause and avoid serious medical consequences.

Many people experience temporary constipation at some point in their life in response to a variety of causes. Often, people have trouble with it when they travel, when their schedule is disrupted, if they change their diet, or if they are on certain medications. Neural factors are thought to be responsible in some people, as explained in the following discussion of irritable bowel syndrome. Treatment with a short course of laxatives or bowel stimulants is often effective. Many healthcare professionals recommend increasing the consumption of fruits, vegetables, whole-grain foods (such as oatmeal), and fluids as well as increasing the amount of physical activity.

Irritable Bowel Syndrome Causes Intense Pain After Eating

Irritable bowel syndrome (IBS) is a bowel disorder that interferes with normal functions of the colon. Symptoms include abdominal cramps, bloating, and either constipation or diarrhea. Approximately one in six Americans has symptoms of IBS, and it is more commonly diagnosed in women than men.[23] IBS first appears in about 50% of people before the age of 35.

Although no definitive cause of IBS is known, recent studies indicate that the syndrome may arise from an abnormality in the way the brain interprets information from the colon or from abnormal functioning of a chemical called *serotonin*, which transmits messages within the nervous system—including the enteric nervous system. In the brain, serotonin is thought to influence mood, but in the colon, where 95% of the body's serotonin is found, it is associated with bowel movement, motility, and sensation, including pain sensation.[23] Researchers also theorize that IBS may be initiated by a GI infection. In some cases, undiagnosed celiac disease is determined to be the initiating factor.

Whatever the cause, normal peristalsis appears to be disrupted. In some people with IBS, food moves too quickly through the colon and fluid cannot be absorbed fast enough, which causes diarrhea. In others, the movement of the colon is too slow and too much fluid is absorbed, leading to constipation.

Emotional and physiologic stress is currently thought to contribute to symptoms of IBS. Foods linked to physiologic stress include caffeinated beverages, alcohol, dairy products, wheat, large meals, and certain medications. Treatment options include medications that treat diarrhea or constipation, as well as antispasmodics and antidepressants. Lifestyle changes are important and include stress management, regular physical activity, and dietary strategies such as eating smaller meals with increased fiber and fluids, especially plain water.

> For a video providing ten tips for preventing episodes of irritable bowel syndrome (IBS), visit www.youtube.com/watch?v=67bus9nD1AU.

At this point, you might be wondering whether Andrea, in our chapter opener, has IBS. Without a full medical examination, it's impossible to say. That's because IBS and celiac disease can present with very similar symptoms. In fact, some researchers are now advising that all patients with symptoms suggestive of IBS be screened for celiac disease.[24]

RECAP   Diarrhea is the frequent passage of loose or watery stools, whereas constipation is the failure to have a bowel movement for 2 or more days or within a time period that is normal for the individual. Irritable bowel syndrome (IBS) causes abdominal cramps, bloating, and constipation or diarrhea. The causes of IBS are unknown; however, both physiologic and emotional factors may play a role.

irritable bowel syndrome (IBS) A bowel disorder that interferes with normal functions of the colon. IBS causes abdominal cramps, bloating, and constipation or diarrhea.

COOKING 101

Balanced meals help keep your digestive system on track! Learn how to create delicious meals, using only a few simple ingredients, that will boost your nutrients by viewing our new Cooking 101 videos, available on the Companion Website at www.pearsonhighered.com/thompsonmanore.

Chapter Review

What Can I Do Today?

Now that you've read this chapter, try making these three changes:

- At mealtimes today, select nourishing foods. Take smaller portions. Eat slowly. Savor each bite.

- Take better care of your GI tract! If you smoke, stop. If you drink alcohol, do so in moderation. Keep up your fluids throughout the day, and stay active.

- If you're experiencing GI pain, unexplained weight loss, or problems with bowel function, make an appointment with your healthcare provider or student health services center. Do it today!

Test Yourself ANSWERS

1. Ⓕ Your brain, not your stomach, is the primary organ responsible for telling you when you are hungry.

2. Ⓣ Although there are individual variations in how we respond to food, the entire process of digestion and absorption of one meal usually takes about 24 hours.

3. Ⓣ Certain bacteria are normal and helpful residents of the large intestine, where they assist in digestion. They also appear to protect the tissue lining the intestinal walls and

may improve immune function. Food products and supplements containing these bacteria are called *probiotics*.

4. Ⓣ Most ulcers result from an infection of the bacterium *Helicobacter pylori*. Contrary to popular belief, ulcers are not caused by stress, alcohol, or spicy foods.

5. Ⓕ Irritable bowel syndrome is a relatively common disease that often appears prior to age 35.

**NutriTools** Check out the Companion Website at www.pearsonhighered.com/thompsonmanore, or use MyNutritionLab.com, to access interactive animations, including

- Digestion and Absorption
- Metabolism

Review Questions

1. Enzymes are
   a. chemical messenger molecules released from glands.
   b. chemicals that help speed up body processes.
   c. acids found in the cell nucleus that instruct cells in the building of proteins.
   d. acids that begin the breakdown of proteins in the mouth.

2. Bile is a greenish fluid that
   a. is stored by the pancreas.
   b. is produced by the gallbladder.
   c. breaks down proteins.
   d. emulsifies fats.

3. The region of brain tissue that is responsible for prompting us to seek food is the
   a. pituitary gland.
   b. pancreas.
   c. hypothalamus.
   d. thalamus.

4. Heartburn is caused by
   a. seepage of gastric acid into the esophagus.
   b. seepage of gastric acid into the cardiac muscle.

   c. seepage of bile into the chest cavity.
   d. seepage of salivary amylase into the stomach.

5. Most digestion of carbohydrates, fats, and proteins takes place in the
   a. mouth.
   b. stomach.
   c. small intestine.
   d. large intestine.

6. True or False? Atoms are the smallest units of life.

7. True or False? Nutrients absorbed through the cells of the brush border are transported to the liver.

8. True or False? The nerves of the GI tract are collectively known as the enteric nervous system.

9. True or False? Vitamins and minerals are digested in the small intestine.

10. True or False? Undiagnosed irritable bowel syndrome increases the risk for cancer of the small intestine.

Answers to Review Questions are located at the back of this text.

Web Links

www.digestive.niddk.nih.gov
National Digestive Diseases Information Clearinghouse (NDDIC)

www.foodallergy.org
Food Allergy and Anaphylaxis Network (FAAN)

www.americanceliac.org/cd.htm
American Celiac Disease Alliance

www.csaceliacs.org
Celiac Sprue Association—National Celiac Disease Support Group

www.ibsassociation.org
Irritable Bowel Syndrome Association

3
Carbohydrates: Plant-Derived Energy Nutrients

Jasmine skipped school again today. When her Mom asked her why, she said she had a headache. That is only partly true: her real "headache" is the thought of explaining to her friends why, all of a sudden, she can't have the sodas and snacks they've always consumed at school. She and her friends admit they're overweight, but they've always had fun together, so their weight hasn't bothered them. Jasmine doesn't want her friends to find out that things are different now—that she has to change her diet, exercise regularly, and lose weight. She doesn't want to admit that she's just been diagnosed with the same disease her grandmother has: type 2 diabetes.

Does consuming soft drinks and other sugary foods lead to diabetes, or, for that matter, to obesity or any other disorder? Several popular diets, including The Zone Diet, Sugar Busters, and Dr. Atkins' New Diet Revolution, claim that refined carbohydrates can be harmful to your health.[1-3] Is this true? If you typically drink three or four soft drinks a day, plus snack on candy and other sweets, should you change your ways? Are carbohydrates a health menace, and is one type of carbohydrate as bad as another?

In this chapter, we explore the differences between simple and complex carbohydrates and learn why some carbohydrates really are better than others. You'll learn how the body breaks down carbohydrates and uses them for fuel and find out how much carbohydrate you

Nutrition Online icons are located throughout the chapter, directing you to web links, videos, podcasts, and other useful online resources.

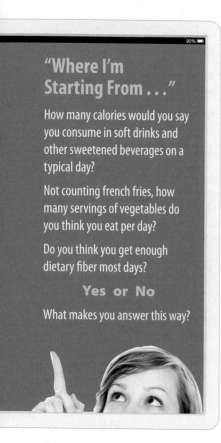

"Where I'm Starting From..."

How many calories would you say you consume in soft drinks and other sweetened beverages on a typical day?

Not counting french fries, how many servings of vegetables do you think you eat per day?

Do you think you get enough dietary fiber most days?

Yes or No

What makes you answer this way?

should eat each day. We'll end the chapter with a look at diabetes, a serious health problem that occurs when the body loses its ability to process the carbohydrates we eat. One form, type 2 diabetes, used to be considered a disease of older people but is now increasingly diagnosed in overweight and obese teens and young adults in the United States.

What Are Carbohydrates?

As we mentioned in Chapter 1, **carbohydrates** are one of the three macronutrients. They are an important energy source for the entire body and are the preferred energy source for nerve cells, including those of the brain. We will say more about their functions shortly.

The term *carbohydrate* literally means "hydrated carbon." You know that water (H_2O) is made of hydrogen and oxygen and that, when something is said to be hydrated, it contains water. The chemical abbreviation for carbohydrate is CHO. These three letters stand for the three components of a molecule of carbohydrate: carbon, hydrogen, and oxygen.

Most Carbohydrates Come from Plant Foods

We obtain carbohydrates mainly from plant foods, such as fruits, vegetables, and grains. Plants make the most abundant form of carbohydrate, called glucose, through a process called **photosynthesis.** During photosynthesis, the green pigment of plants, called chlorophyll, absorbs sunlight, which provides the energy needed to fuel the manufacture of glucose. As shown in **Figure 3.1**, water absorbed from the earth by the roots of plants

carbohydrate One of the three macronutrients, a compound made up of carbon, hydrogen, and oxygen. It is derived from plants and provides energy.

photosynthesis The process by which plants use sunlight to fuel a chemical reaction that combines carbon and water into glucose, which is then stored in their cells.

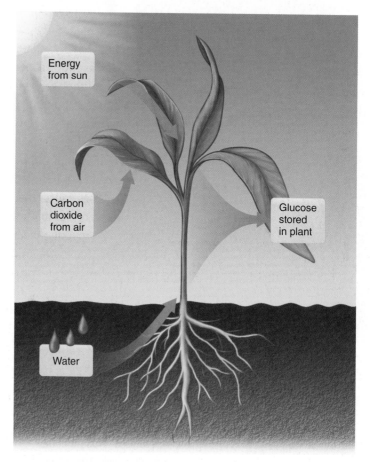

Energy from sun

Carbon dioxide from air

Glucose stored in plant

Water

⬆ **Figure 3.1** Plants make carbohydrates through the process of photosynthesis. Water, carbon dioxide, and energy from the sun are combined to produce glucose.

combines with carbon dioxide present in the leaves to produce glucose. Plants continually store glucose and use it to support their own growth. Then, when we eat plant foods, our body digests, absorbs, and uses the stored glucose.

The only nonplant sources of carbohydrates are foods derived from milk. For instance, breast milk, cow's milk, cheese, and ice cream all contain a carbohydrate called lactose.

Simple Carbohydrates Are Sugars

Carbohydrates can be classified as *simple* or *complex*. These terms describe carbohydrates based on the number of molecules of sugar present. Simple carbohydrates contain either one or two molecules, whereas complex carbohydrates contain hundreds to thousands of molecules.

Simple carbohydrates are commonly called *sugars*. Six sugars are common in our diet. Three of these are called **monosaccharides** because they consist of only a single sugar molecule (*mono* means "one," and *saccharide* means "sugar"). The other three sugars are **disaccharides** and consist of two molecules of sugar joined together (*di* means "two").

The Three Monosaccharides Are Glucose, Fructose, and Galactose

Glucose, *fructose*, and *galactose* are the three monosaccharides in our diet **(Figure 3.2)**. Because plants manufacture **glucose,** it probably won't surprise you to discover that glucose is the most abundant sugar in our diet and in our body. Glucose does not generally occur by itself in foods; instead, it is usually attached to other sugars in larger molecules. In our body, glucose is the preferred source of energy for the brain, and it is a very important source of energy for all cells.

Fructose, the sweetest natural sugar, is found in fruits and vegetables. Fructose is also called *fruit sugar*. In many processed foods, it comes in the form of *high-fructose corn syrup*. This syrup is made from corn and is used to sweeten many common foods including soft drinks, desserts, candies, and jellies.

Galactose does not occur alone in foods. It joins with glucose to create lactose, one of the three most common disaccharides.

The Three Disaccharides Are Lactose, Maltose, and Sucrose

The three most common disaccharides found in foods are *lactose*, *maltose*, and *sucrose* (Figure 3.2). **Lactose** (also called *milk sugar*) is made up of glucose and

In our body, glucose is the preferred source of energy for the brain.

simple carbohydrate A monosaccharide or disaccharide, such as glucose; commonly called *sugar*.

monosaccharide The simplest of carbohydrates; consists of one sugar molecule, the most common form of which is glucose.

disaccharide A carbohydrate compound consisting of two sugar molecules joined together.

glucose The most abundant sugar molecule; a monosaccharide generally found in combination with other sugars. The preferred source of energy for the brain and an important source of energy for all cells.

fructose The sweetest natural sugar; a monosaccharide that occurs in fruits and vegetables. Also called *fruit sugar*.

galactose A monosaccharide that joins with glucose to create lactose, one of the three most common disaccharides.

lactose A disaccharide consisting of one glucose molecule and one galactose molecule; also called *milk sugar*. Found in milk, including human breast milk.

Monosaccharides

Disaccharides

Glucose	+	Galactose	→	Lactose	Glucose + galactose; also called milk sugar
Glucose	+	Glucose	→	Maltose	Glucose + glucose; maltose molecules join in food to form starch molecules
Glucose	+	Fructose	→	Sucrose	Glucose + fructose; found in sugarcane, sugar beets, and honey

Figure 3.2 Galactose, glucose, and fructose join together to make the disaccharides lactose, maltose, and sucrose.

NUTRITION MYTH OR FACT?
Is Honey More Nutritious Than Table Sugar?

Liz's friend Tiffany is dedicated to eating healthful foods. She advises Liz to avoid white sugar and to eat foods that contain honey, molasses, or raw sugar. Like many people, Tiffany believes these sweeteners are more natural and nutritious than refined table sugar. How can Liz sort sugar fact from fiction?

Remember that sucrose consists of one glucose molecule and one fructose molecule joined together. From a chemical perspective, honey is almost identical to sucrose, as honey also contains glucose and fructose molecules in almost equal amounts. However, enzymes in the "honey stomachs" of bees separate some of the glucose and fructose molecules, with the result that honey looks and tastes slightly different than sucrose. As you know, bees store honey in combs and fan it with their wings to reduce its moisture content. This also alters the appearance and texture of honey.

Honey does not contain any more nutrients than sucrose, so it is not a more healthful choice than sucrose. In fact, per tablespoon, honey has more calories (energy) than table sugar. This is because the crystals in table sugar take up more space on a spoon than the liquid form of honey, so a tablespoon

contains less sugar. However, some people argue that honey is sweeter, so you use less.

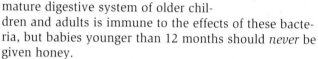

It's important to note that honey commonly contains bacteria that can cause fatal food poisoning in infants. The more mature digestive system of older children and adults is immune to the effects of these bacteria, but babies younger than 12 months should *never* be given honey.

Are raw sugar and molasses more healthful than table sugar? Actually, the "raw sugar" available in the United States is not really raw. Truly raw sugar is made up of the first crystals obtained when sugar is processed. Sugar in this form contains dirt, parts of insects, and other by-products that make it illegal to sell in the United States. The raw sugar products in American stores have actually gone through more than half of the same steps in the refining process used to make table sugar.

Molasses is the syrup that remains when sucrose is made from sugarcane. Molasses is darker and less sweet than table sugar. It does contain some iron, but this iron does not occur naturally; it is a contaminant from the machines that process the sugarcane!

The truth is, no added sugars contain many nutrients that are important for health. This is why highly sweetened products are referred to as "empty calories."

---

galactose. Interestingly, human breast milk has a higher amount of lactose than cow's milk and therefore tastes sweeter.

Maltose (also called *malt sugar*) consists of two molecules of glucose. It does not generally occur by itself in foods but, rather, is bound together with other molecules. As our body breaks these larger molecules down, maltose results as a by-product. Maltose is also the sugar that is fermented during the production of beer and liquor products. Contrary to popular belief, very little maltose remains in alcoholic beverages after the fermentation process; thus, alcoholic beverages are not good sources of carbohydrate.

Sucrose is composed of glucose and fructose. Because sucrose contains fructose, it is sweeter than lactose or maltose. Sucrose provides much of the sweet taste found in honey, maple syrup, fruits, and vegetables. Table sugar, brown sugar, powdered sugar, and many other products are made by refining the sucrose found in sugarcane and sugar beets. Are naturally occurring forms of sucrose more healthful than manufactured forms? The ***Nutrition Myth or Fact?*** box above investigates the common belief that honey is more nutritious than table sugar.

Complex Carbohydrates Are Polysaccharides

Complex carbohydrates, the second major type of carbohydrate, generally consist of long chains of glucose molecules. The technical name for complex carbohydrates is **polysaccharides** (*poly* means "many"). Complex carbohydrates exist in foods as

maltose A disaccharide consisting of two molecules of glucose. Does not generally occur independently in foods but results as a by-product of digestion. Also called *malt sugar.*

sucrose A disaccharide composed of one glucose molecule and one fructose molecule. It is sweeter than lactose or maltose.

complex carbohydrate A nutrient compound consisting of long chains of glucose molecules, such as starch, glycogen, and fiber.

polysaccharide A complex carbohydrate consisting of long chains of glucose.

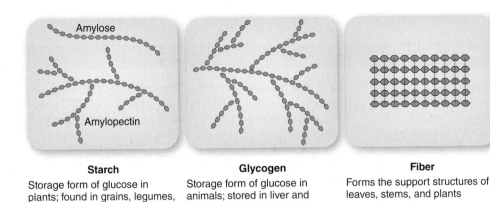

Starch
Storage form of glucose in plants; found in grains, legumes, and tubers

Glycogen
Storage form of glucose in animals; stored in liver and muscles

Fiber
Forms the support structures of leaves, stems, and plants

Figure 3.3 Polysaccharides include starch, glycogen, and fiber.

either starches or fiber. A third complex carbohydrate, glycogen, is not obtained from our diet **(Figure 3.3)**. Let's look at each of these three types.

Starch Is a Polysaccharide Stored in Plants

Plants store glucose not as single molecules but as polysaccharides in the form of **starch.** Excellent food sources include grains (wheat, rice, corn, oats, and barley), legumes (peas, beans, and lentils), and tubers (potatoes and yams). Our cells cannot use starch molecules exactly as they occur in plants. Instead, our body must break them down into the monosaccharide glucose, from which we can then fuel our energy needs.

Fiber Is a Polysaccharide That Gives Plants Their Structure

Fiber is the nondigestible part of plants that forms leaves, stems, and seeds. Like starches, fiber consists of long polysaccharide chains. The body easily breaks apart the chains in starches; however, the bonds that connect fiber molecules are not easily broken. This means that most forms of fiber pass through the digestive system without being broken down and absorbed, so fiber contributes little or no energy to our diet. However, fiber offers many health benefits, which we will discuss shortly.

Nutrition experts and food producers use several terms to distinguish among different types of fiber. We discuss these terms here, as they're important for understanding the contribution of fiber to our health.

Dietary vs. Functional Fiber Fiber that occurs naturally in foods is called **dietary fiber.** In a sense, you can think of dietary fiber as the plant's "skeleton." Good food sources of dietary fiber include fruits, vegetables, seeds, legumes, and whole grains. We often hear the recommendation to eat *whole* grains, but is grain ground into flour and baked into bread still whole? Maybe, maybe not! So what does the term *whole grain* really mean? Find out in the *Highlight* feature box (page 72).

Another type of fiber, called **functional fiber,** is manufactured and added to foods and fiber supplements. Examples of functional fiber sources you might see on nutrition labels are cellulose, guar gum, pectin, and psyllium.

Total fiber is the sum of dietary fiber and functional fiber in a particular food. On the Nutrition Facts Panel, the term *Dietary Fiber* actually represents the total amount of fiber in that food, and it includes the dietary fiber that occurs naturally in addition to any functional fiber that may have been added.

Soluble vs. Insoluble Fiber Fiber can also be classified, according to its chemical and physical properties, as soluble or insoluble. **Soluble fibers** dissolve in water. They are also *viscous*, which means they form a gel when wet. Although the digestive tract cannot independently digest soluble fibers, they are easily digested by bacteria present in the colon. Soluble fibers are typically found in citrus fruits, berries, oat products, and beans. Research suggests that consuming soluble fibers regularly

Tubers, such as these sweet potatoes, are excellent food sources of starch.

starch A polysaccharide stored in plants; the storage form of glucose in plants.

fiber The nondigestible carbohydrate parts of plants that form the support structures of leaves, stems, and seeds.

dietary fiber The type of fiber that occurs naturally in foods.

functional fiber The nondigestible forms of carbohydrate that are extracted from plants or manufactured in the laboratory and have known health benefits.

total fiber The sum of dietary fiber and functional fiber.

soluble fibers Fibers that dissolve in water.

HIGHLIGHT
What Makes a Whole Grain Whole?

Grains are grasses that produce edible kernels. A kernel of grain is the seed of the grass: if you were to plant a kernel of barley, a blade of grass would soon shoot up. Kernels of different grains all share a similar design. As shown in the **Figure 3.4**, they consist of three parts:

- The outermost covering, called the *bran*, is very high in fiber and contains most of the grain's vitamins and minerals.

- The *endosperm* is the grain's midsection and contains most of the grain's carbohydrates and protein.

- The *germ* sits deep in the base of the kernel, surrounded by the endosperm, and is rich in healthful fats and some vitamins.

Whole grains are kernels that retain all three of these parts.

The kernels of some grains also have a *husk* (hull): a thin, dry coat that is inedible. Removing the husk is always the first step in milling (grinding) these grains for human consumption.

People worldwide have milled grain for centuries, usually using heavy stones. A little milling removes only a small amount of the bran, leaving a crunchy grain suitable for cooked cereals. For example, cracked wheat and hulled barley retain much of the kernel's bran. Whole-grain flours are produced when whole grains are ground and then recombined. Because these hearty flours retain a portion of the bran, endosperm, and germ, foods such as breads made with them are rich in fiber and a wide array of vitamins and minerals.

With the advent of modern technology, processes for milling grains became more sophisticated, with seeds being repeatedly ground and sifted into increasingly finer flours, retaining little or no bran and therefore little fiber and few vitamins and minerals. For instance, white wheat flour, which consists almost entirely of endosperm, is high in carbohydrate but retains only about 25% of the wheat's fiber, vitamins, and minerals. In the United States, manufacturers of breads and other baked goods made with white flour are required by law to enrich their products with vitamins and minerals to replace some of those lost in processing. However, enrichment replaces only a handful of nutrients and leaves the bread low in fiber.

When choosing breads, crackers, and other baked goods, look for whole wheat, whole oats, or similar whole grains on the ingredient list. This ensures that the product contains the fiber and micronutrients that nature packed into the plant's seed.

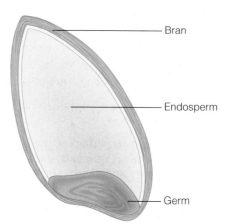

◄ Figure 3.4 A whole grain includes the bran, endosperm, and germ.

---

reduces the risks for cardiovascular disease and type 2 diabetes by lowering blood cholesterol and blood glucose levels.

Insoluble fibers are those that do not typically dissolve in water. These fibers are usually not viscous and typically cannot be easily digested by bacteria in the colon. Insoluble fibers are generally found in whole grains, such as wheat, rye, and brown rice, as well as in many vegetables. These fibers are not associated with reducing cholesterol levels but are known for promoting regular bowel movements, alleviating constipation, and reducing the risk for a disorder called diverticulosis (discussed later in this chapter).

insoluble fibers Fibers that do not dissolve in water.

fiber-rich carbohydrates A group of foods containing either simple or complex carbohydrates that are rich in dietary fiber. These foods, which include most fruits, vegetables, and whole grains, are typically fresh or only moderately processed.

Fiber-Rich Carbohydrates Materials written for the general public usually don't refer to the carbohydrates found in foods as complex or simple; instead, resources such as the *Dietary Guidelines for Americans 2010* emphasize eating **fiber-rich carbohydrates,** such as fruits, vegetables, and whole grains.[4] This term is important because fiber-rich carbohydrates are known to contribute to good health, but not all complex carbohydrate foods are fiber-rich. For example, potatoes that have been processed into frozen hash browns retain very little of their original fiber. On the other hand, some foods rich in simple carbohydrates (such as fruits) are also

Carbohydrate Use by Exercise Intensity

Light
12.5% Carbohydrate
87.5% Fat

Moderate
45% Carbohydrate
55% Fat

Intense
67% Carbohydrate
33% Fat

⬆ **Figure 3.6** Amounts of carbohydrate and fat used during light, moderate, and intense exercise.
Romijn, J. A., E. F. Coyle, L. S. Sidossis, A. Gastaldelli, J. F. Horowitz, E. Endert, and R. R. Wolfe. 1993. Regulation of endogenous fat and carbohydrate metabolism in relation to exercise intensity and duration, from the American Journal of Physiological Endocrinology and metabolism, vol. 265, no. 3, Sept. 1993. Copyright © 1993 the American Physiological Society. Reprinted by permission.

stools. A great deal of pressure must be generated in the large intestine (colon) to pass hard stools. This increased pressure weakens intestinal walls, causing them to bulge outward and form pockets **(Figure 3.7)**. Feces and fibrous materials can get trapped in these pockets, which become infected and inflamed. Diverticulosis is a painful condition that must be treated with antibiotics or surgery.

Other health benefits of eating fiber-rich carbohydrates include:

- Reduced overall risk for obesity. Eating a high-fiber diet causes a person to feel fuller, which may help people eat less and maintain a more healthful weight.
- Reduced risk for heart disease. Fiber can delay or block the absorption of dietary cholesterol into the bloodstream.

⬆ When we exercise or perform any other activity that causes us to breathe harder and sweat, we begin to use more glucose than fat.

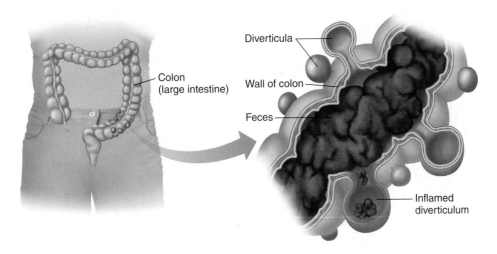

Diverticula

Colon (large intestine)

Wall of colon

Feces

Inflamed diverticulum

◀ **Figure 3.7** Diverticulosis occurs when bulging pockets form in the wall of the large intestine (colon). These pockets become infected and inflamed, demanding proper treatment.

- Decreased risk for type 2 diabetes. Fiber absorbs water, expands in the large intestine, and slows the movement of food through the upper part of the digestive tract. In slowing digestion, fiber also slows the release of glucose into the blood and may thereby lower the risk for type 2 diabetes (discussed in detail later in this chapter).

RECAP Carbohydrates are an excellent energy source while we are at rest and during exercise, and they provide 4 kcal of energy per gram. Carbohydrates are necessary in the diet to "spare" body protein. Complex carbohydrates contain fiber and phytochemicals that can reduce the risk for obesity, heart disease, diabetes, colon cancer, and other health problems.

What Happens to the Carbohydrates We Eat?

Because glucose is the form of sugar that our body uses for energy, the primary goal of carbohydrate digestion is to break down polysaccharides and disaccharides into monosaccharides, which can then be converted to glucose. (Chapter 2 provided an overview of digestion). Here, we focus in more detail on the digestion and absorption of carbohydrates. **Figure 3.8** provides a visual tour of carbohydrate digestion.

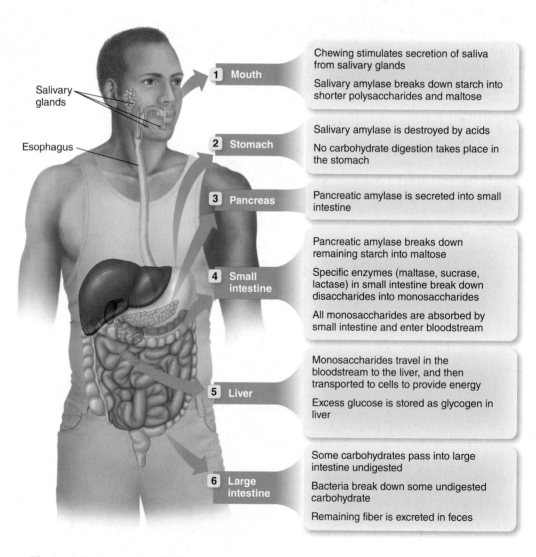

Salivary glands

Esophagus

1 Mouth

Chewing stimulates secretion of saliva from salivary glands

Salivary amylase breaks down starch into shorter polysaccharides and maltose

2 Stomach

Salivary amylase is destroyed by acids

No carbohydrate digestion takes place in the stomach

3 Pancreas

Pancreatic amylase is secreted into small intestine

4 Small intestine

Pancreatic amylase breaks down remaining starch into maltose

Specific enzymes (maltase, sucrase, lactase) in small intestine break down disaccharides into monosaccharides

All monosaccharides are absorbed by small intestine and enter bloodstream

5 Liver

Monosaccharides travel in the bloodstream to the liver, and then transported to cells to provide energy

Excess glucose is stored as glycogen in liver

6 Large intestine

Some carbohydrates pass into large intestine undigested

Bacteria break down some undigested carbohydrate

Remaining fiber is excreted in feces

Figure 3.8   An overview of carbohydrate digestion and absorption.

Digestion Breaks Down Most Carbohydrates into Monosaccharides

Carbohydrate digestion begins in the mouth (Figure 3.8, step 1). The starch in the foods you eat mixes with your saliva during chewing. Saliva contains an enzyme called **salivary amylase,** which breaks starch into smaller particles and eventually into the disaccharide maltose.

As the mass of chewed and moistened food (called the *bolus*) leaves the mouth and enters the stomach, all digestion of carbohydrates stops. This is because the acid in the stomach inactivates most of the salivary amylase enzyme (Figure 3.8, step 2).

The majority of carbohydrate digestion takes place in the small intestine. As the contents of the stomach enter the small intestine, an enzyme called **pancreatic amylase** is released by the pancreas into the small intestine (Figure 3.8, step 3). This enzyme digests any remaining starch into maltose. Additional enzymes (maltase, sucrase, and lactase) in the mucosal cells that line the intestinal tract work to break down disaccharides into monosaccharides (Figure 3.8, step 4). All monosaccharides are then absorbed into the mucosal cells lining the small intestine, from which they enter the bloodstream.

In some people, the small intestine does not produce enough of the enzyme lactase, which is necessary to break down the disaccharide lactose, found in milk products. People with this condition, called **lactose intolerance,** cannot digest dairy foods properly. Lactose intolerance should not be confused with a milk allergy: people who are allergic to milk experience an immune reaction to the proteins found in cow's milk. Lactose intolerance is not caused by an immune response but, rather, by an enzyme deficiency.

Symptoms of lactose intolerance include intestinal gas, bloating, cramping, nausea, diarrhea, and discomfort after eating dairy foods. Not everyone experiences these symptoms to the same extent. Some people can digest small amounts of dairy products, whereas others cannot tolerate any. Many people can tolerate specially formulated milk products that are low in lactose, while others take pills or use drops that contain the lactase enzyme when they eat dairy products. Some lactose-intolerant people can also digest yogurt and aged cheese, as the bacteria (or molds) used to ferment these products break down the lactose during processing.

Milk products, such as ice cream, are hard to digest for people who are lactose intolerant.

The Liver Converts All Monosaccharides into Glucose

After they are absorbed into the bloodstream, monosaccharides travel to the liver, where any nonglucose monosaccharides are converted to glucose (Figure 3.8, step 5). If needed immediately for energy, the liver releases glucose into the bloodstream, which carries it throughout the body to provide energy to cells. If the body has no immediate demand for glucose, it is stored as glycogen in the liver and muscles. The liver can store 70 grams (280 kcal) of glycogen, and our muscles can normally store about 120 g (480 kcal) of glycogen. Between meals, the body draws on liver glycogen reserves to maintain blood glucose levels and support the needs of cells, including those of the brain, spinal cord, and red blood cells **(Figure 3.9).**

The glycogen stored in our muscles provides energy to the muscles during intense exercise. Endurance athletes can increase their storage of muscle glycogen from two to four times the normal amount through a process called *glycogen loading,* also known as *carbohydrate loading* (see Chapter 10).

Fiber Is Excreted from the Large Intestine

We do not possess enzymes that can break down fiber. Thus, fiber passes through the small intestine undigested and enters the large intestine, or colon. Once in the large intestine, bacteria break down previously undigested carbohydrates, including soluble fiber, causing the production of gas and a few fatty acids. The cells of the large intestine use these fatty acids for energy. The fiber remaining in the colon adds

salivary amylase An enzyme in saliva that breaks starch into smaller particles and eventually into the disaccharide maltose.

pancreatic amylase An enzyme secreted by the pancreas into the small intestine that digests any remaining starch into maltose.

lactose intolerance A disorder in which the body does not produce sufficient lactase enzyme and therefore cannot digest foods that contain lactose, such as cow's milk.

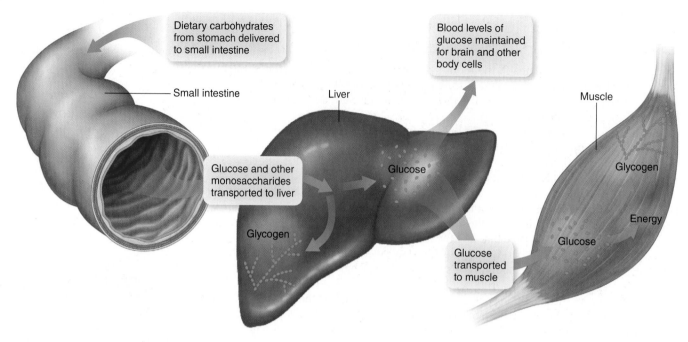

Figure 3.9 Glucose is stored as glycogen in both the liver and in muscle. The glycogen stored in the liver maintains blood glucose between meals; muscle glycogen provides immediate energy to the muscle during exercise.

bulk to stools and is excreted (Figure 3.8, step 6) in feces. In this way, fiber helps to maintain bowel regularity.

RECAP Carbohydrate digestion starts in the mouth and continues in the small intestine. Glucose and other monosaccharides are absorbed into the bloodstream and travel to the liver, where nonglucose sugars are converted to glucose. Glucose is either used by the cells for energy, or is converted to glycogen and stored in the liver and muscle for later use. Lactose intolerance results from the inability to digest lactose due to insufficient amounts of lactase.

Insulin and Glucagon Regulate the Level of Glucose in Blood

Our body continually regulates the level of glucose in the blood within a fairly narrow range that meets the body's needs. Two hormones, insulin and glucagon, assist the body in maintaining blood glucose. Special cells in the pancreas synthesize, store, and secrete both hormones.

When we eat a meal, our blood glucose level rises. But glucose in the blood cannot help nerve, muscle, and other cells function unless it can cross into them. Glucose molecules are too large to cross cell membranes independently. To get in, glucose needs assistance from the hormone **insulin,** which is secreted by the beta cells of the pancreas **(Figure 3.10a)**. Insulin increases the movement of proteins, called *glucose transporters*, from the inside of the cell to the cell membrane; these transporters allow glucose to enter the cell. Insulin also stimulates the liver and muscles to take up glucose and store it as glycogen.

When you have not eaten for some time, your blood glucose levels decline. This decrease in blood glucose stimulates the alpha cells of the pancreas to secrete another hormone, **glucagon** (Figure 3.10b). Glucagon acts in an opposite way to insulin: it causes the liver to convert its stored glycogen into glucose, which is then secreted into the bloodstream and transported to the cells for energy. Glucagon also assists in the breakdown of body proteins, so that the liver can stimulate *gluconeogenesis*, discussed earlier.

insulin A hormone secreted by the beta cells of the pancreas in response to increased blood levels of glucose; facilitates uptake of glucose by body cells.

glucagon A hormone secreted by the alpha cells of the pancreas in response to decreased blood levels of glucose; causes breakdown of liver stores of glycogen into glucose.

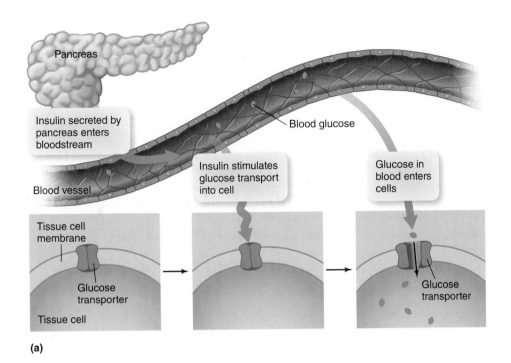

(a)

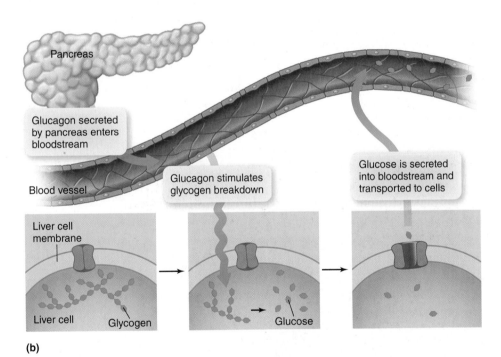

(b)

◀ **Figure 3.10** Regulation of blood glucose by the hormones insulin and glucagon. **(a)** When blood glucose levels increase after a meal, the pancreas secretes insulin. Insulin increases the movement of glucose transporters from the inside of the cell to the cell membrane; these transporters allow glucose to enter the cell. **(b)** When blood glucose levels are low, the pancreas secretes glucagon. Glucagon enters liver cells, where it stimulates the breakdown of stored glycogen into glucose. This glucose is then released into the bloodstream.

Typically, the effects of insulin and glucagon balance each other to maintain blood glucose within a healthy range. If this balance is altered, it can lead to negative health conditions such as diabetes or hypoglycemia. In **hypoglycemia,** blood glucose falls to lower-than-normal levels. One cause of hypoglycemia is excessive production

hypoglycemia A condition marked by blood glucose levels that are below normal fasting levels.

of insulin, which lowers blood glucose too far. The symptoms usually appear about 1 to 3 hours after a meal and include nervousness, shakiness, anxiety, sweating, irritability, headache, weakness, and rapid or irregular heartbeat. Although many people believe they experience these symptoms, true hypoglycemia is rare. People with diabetes can develop hypoglycemia if they inject too much insulin, or when they exercise and fail to eat enough carbohydrates. It can also be caused by a pancreatic tumor, liver infection, or other underlying disorder.

RECAP Two hormones, insulin and glucagon, are involved in regulating blood glucose. Insulin lowers blood glucose levels by facilitating the entry of glucose into cells. Glucagon raises blood glucose levels by stimulating gluconeogenesis and the breakdown of glycogen stored in the liver. Hypoglycemia is a condition characterized by lower-than-normal blood glucose level.

The Glycemic Index Shows How Foods Affect Our Blood Glucose Levels

The **glycemic index** is a measurement of the potential of foods to raise blood glucose levels. Foods with a high glycemic index cause a sudden spike in blood glucose. This in turn triggers a surge in insulin, which may be followed by a dramatic drop in blood glucose. Foods with a low glycemic index cause low to moderate fluctuations in blood glucose. When foods are assigned a glycemic index value, they are often compared with the glycemic effect of pure glucose.

The glycemic index of a food is not always easy to predict. **Figure 3.11** ranks certain foods according to their glycemic index. Do any of these rankings surprise you? Most people assume that foods containing simple sugars have a higher

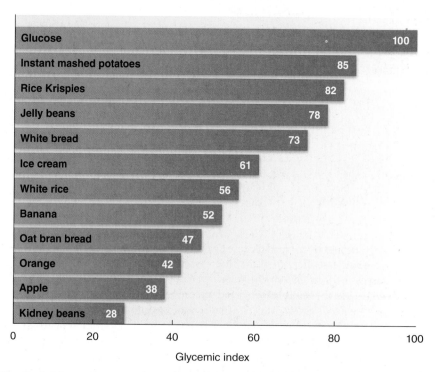

glycemic index A value that rates the potential of a given food to raise blood glucose and insulin levels.

◄ **Figure 3.11** Glycemic index values for various foods as compared with pure glucose.
Data from Foster-Powell, K., S. H. A. Holt, and J. C. Brand-Miller. 2002. International table of glycemic index and glycemic load values. *Am. J. Clin. Nutr.* 76: 5–56.

glycemic index than starches, but this is not always the case. For instance, compare the glycemic index for apples and instant potatoes. Although instant potatoes are a starchy food, they have a glycemic index value of 83, whereas the value for an apple is only 36! Nutritious, low-glycemic-index foods include beans and lentils, fresh vegetables, and whole-wheat bread.

The **glycemic load** of a food is the amount of carbohydrate it contains multiplied by its glycemic index value (number). Some nutrition experts believe that the glycemic load is a better indicator than the glycemic index value of the effect of food on a person's glucose response, because it factors in both the glycemic index and the total grams of carbohydrate in the food that is consumed. For instance, raw carrots have a relatively high glycemic index but very little total carbohydrate and thus have a low glycemic load. Therefore, a serving of raw carrots is unlikely to cause a significant rise in glucose and insulin.

Why do we care about the glycemic load? Meals with a lower glycemic load are a better choice for someone with diabetes, for instance, because they will not trigger dramatic fluctuations in blood glucose. Even among healthy people, consuming a low-glycemic-load diet may help maintain healthy blood glucose levels and reduce the risk for heart disease and colon cancer, because low-glycemic-load foods generally contain more fiber and help decrease fat levels in the blood.

An apple has a lower glycemic index (36) than a serving of white rice (56).

> To find out the glycemic index and glycemic load of over 100 foods, visit www.health.harvard.edu/newsweek/Glycemic_index_and_glycemic_load_for_100_foods.htm.

RECAP The glycemic index is a value that indicates the potential of foods to raise blood glucose and insulin levels. The glycemic load of a food is the amount of carbohydrate it contains multiplied by its glycemic index value (number).

How Much Carbohydrate Should We Eat?

Carbohydrates are an important part of a balanced, healthy diet. The Recommended Dietary Allowance (RDA) for carbohydrate is based on the amount of glucose the brain uses.[5] The current RDA for carbohydrate for adults age 19 and older is 130 grams per day. It is important to emphasize that this RDA does not cover the amount of carbohydrate needed to support daily activities; it covers only the amount of carbohydrate needed to supply adequate glucose to the brain.

As we mentioned earlier (in Chapter 1), carbohydrates and the other macronutrients are also assigned an Acceptable Macronutrient Distribution Range (AMDR). This is the intake range associated with a decreased risk for chronic diseases. The AMDR for carbohydrates is 45% to 65% of total energy intake. **Table 3.1** (page 82) compares the carbohydrate recommendations from the Institute of Medicine with the Dietary Guidelines for Americans related to carbohydrate-containing foods.[4,5] As you can see, the Institute of Medicine provides specific numeric recommendations, whereas the Dietary Guidelines for Americans are general suggestions for foods high in whole grains and fiber, and low in refined grains and added sugars. Most health agencies agree that most of the carbohydrates you eat each day should be fiber rich and unprocessed. Eating the recommended amount of whole grains and fruits and vegetables every day will ensure that you get enough fiber and other complex carbohydrates that your body needs.

Eating the recommended amount of whole grains, vegetables, and fruit each day ensures that you'll get enough fiber and other complex carbohydrates in your diet.

glycemic load The amount of carbohydrate contained in a given food, multiplied by its glycemic index value.

TABLE 3.1 Dietary Recommendations for Carbohydrates

Institute of Medicine Recommendations*	Dietary Guidelines for Americans†
Recommended Dietary Allowance (RDA) for adults 19 years of age and older is 130 grams of carbohydrate per day.	Increase vegetable and fruit intake.
	Eat a variety of vegetables, especially dark-green and red and orange vegetables and beans and peas.
The Acceptable Macronutrient Distribution Range (AMDR) for carbohydrate is 45% to 65% of total daily energy intake.	Consume at least half of all grains as whole grains. Increase whole-grain intake by replacing refined grains with whole grains.
Added sugar intake should be 25% or less of total energy intake each day.	Limit the consumption of foods that contain refined grains, especially refined-grain foods that contain solid fats, added sugars, and sodium.
	Reduce intake of sugar-sweetened beverages.
	Monitor intake of 100% fruit juice for children and adolescents, especially those who are overweight or obese.

*Data from Dietary Reference Intakes for Energy, Carbohydrates, Fiber, Fat, Fatty Acids, Cholesterol, Protein, and Amino Acids (Macronutrients). © 2005, National Academy of Sciences, courtesy of the National Academies Press, Washington, DC.
†U.S. Department of Agriculture and U.S. Department of Health and Human Services. 2010. *Dietary Guidelines for Americans, 2010.* 7th ed. Washington, DC: U.S. Government Printing Office.

⬆ Foods with added sugars, such as candy, have lower levels of vitamins, minerals, and fiber than foods that naturally contain simple sugars.

added sugars Sugars and syrups that are added to food during processing or preparation.

nutritive sweeteners Sweeteners, such as sucrose, fructose, honey, and brown sugar, that contribute calories (energy).

non-nutritive sweeteners Manufactured sweeteners that provide little or no energy; also called *alternative sweeteners.*

acceptable daily intake (ADI) An estimate made by the Food and Drug Administration of the amount of a non-nutritive sweetener that someone can consume each day over a lifetime without adverse effects.

RECAP The RDA for carbohydrate is 130 grams per day; this amount is only sufficient to supply adequate glucose to the brain. The AMDR for carbohydrate is 45% to 65% of total energy intake.

Most Americans Eat Too Much Refined Carbohydrate

The average carbohydrate intake in the United States is approximately 50%. This means that Americans consume carbohydrates as roughly one-half of all the foods they eat. And for some people, much of their total carbohydrate consumption consists of simple sugars. Where does all this sugar come from? Some sugar comes from healthful food sources, such as fruits and milk. Some comes from foods made with refined grains, such as soft white breads, saltine crackers, and pastries. Much of the rest comes from *added sugars*. **Added sugars** are sugars and syrups that are added to foods during processing or preparation.[5] For example, many processed foods include high-fructose corn syrup (HFCS), an added sugar.

The most common source of added sugars in the U.S. diet is sodas and soft drinks; we drink an average of 40 gallons per person each year. Consider that one 12 oz cola contains 38.5 grams of sugar, which is almost 10 teaspoons. If you drink the average amount, you are consuming more than 16,420 grams of sugar (about 267 cups) every year. That's a lot of sugar! Other common sources of added sugars include cookies, cakes, pies, fruit drinks, fruit punches, and candy. Even many nondessert items, such as peanut butter, yogurt, and even salad dressing, contain added sugars.

If you want a quick way to figure out the amount of sugar in a processed food, check the Nutrition Facts Panel on the box for the line that identifies "Sugars." You'll notice that the amount of sugar in a serving is identified in grams. Divide the total grams by 4 to get teaspoons. For instance, one national brand of yogurt contains 21 grams of sugar in a half-cup serving. That's more than 5 teaspoons of sugar! Doing this simple math before you buy may help you choose between different, more healthful versions of the same food.

Added sugars are not chemically different from naturally occurring sugars. However, foods and beverages with added sugars do have lower levels of vitamins, minerals, and fiber than fruits and other foods that naturally contain simple sugars. That's why most healthcare organizations recommend that we limit our consumption of added sugars.

Most of us love sweets but want to avoid the extra calories and tooth decay that go along with them. That's why foods with alternative sweeteners have become dietary staples. But what are alternative sweeteners, and are they safe to consume?

Remember that all carbohydrates contain 4 kcal of energy per gram. Because sweeteners such as sucrose, fructose, honey, and brown sugar contribute calories (energy), they are called **nutritive sweeteners.** Other nutritive sweeteners include the *sugar alcohols,* such as mannitol, sorbitol, isomalt, and xylitol. These are popular in sugar-free gums and mints, because they do not support the bacteria that cause tooth decay. However, at 2 to 4 kcal of energy per gram, they are not calorie free.

Alternative Sweeteners Are Non-Nutritive

A number of other products have been developed to sweeten foods without promoting tooth decay and weight gain. Because these products provide little or no energy, they are called **non-nutritive,** or *alternative,* **sweeteners.**

Limited Use of Alternative Sweeteners Is Not Harmful

Research has shown alternative sweeteners to be safe for adults, children, and people with diabetes. Women who are pregnant should discuss the use of alternative sweeteners with their healthcare provider. In general, it appears safe for pregnant women to consume alternative sweeteners in amounts within the Food and Drug Administration (FDA) guidelines.[6] These amounts, known as the **acceptable daily intake (ADI),** are estimates of the amount of a sweetener that someone can consume each day over a lifetime without adverse effects.

Many Alternative Sweeteners Are in Our Foods

Alternative sweeteners available on the market today include saccharin, acesulfame-K, aspartame, sucralose, neotame, and stevia.

Discovered in the late 1800s, *saccharin* is about 300 times sweeter than sucrose. More than 20 years of scientific research have shown that saccharin is not related to bladder cancer in humans. Based on this evidence, in May 2000 the National Toxicology Program of the U.S. government removed saccharin from its list of products that may cause cancer. Saccharin is used in foods and beverages and as a tabletop sweetener. It is sold as Sweet'N Low in the United States.

Acesulfame-K (acesulfame potassium) is marketed under the names Sunette and Sweet One. It is a calorie-free

⬆ Contrary to reports claiming severe health consequences related to consumption of alternative sweeteners, major health agencies have determined that these products are safe for us to consume in moderation.

sweetener that is 175 times sweeter than sugar. It is used to sweeten gums, candies, beverages, gelatins, and puddings. The taste of acesulfame-K does not change when it is heated, so it can be used in cooking.

Aspartame, also called Equal and NutraSweet, is one of the most popular alternative sweeteners currently in use. Although aspartame contains 4 kcal of energy per gram, it is 200 times sweeter than sucrose. Thus, it ends up contributing almost no energy. Although there are numerous claims that aspartame causes headaches and dizziness, and can increase a person's risk for cancer and nerve disorders, studies do not support these claims.[7,8] A significant amount of research has been done to test the safety of aspartame: **Table 3.2** (page 84) shows how many servings of aspartame-sweetened foods have to be consumed to exceed the ADI. People with the disease *phenylketonuria (PKU)* should not consume aspartame at all.

Sucralose is marketed under the brand name Splenda. It is 600 times sweeter than sucrose and is stable when heated, so it can be used in cooking, and it has been approved for use in many foods.

Neotame is an alternative sweetener that is 7,000 to 13,000 times sweeter than sugar. Manufacturers use it to sweeten a variety of products, such as beverages, dairy products, frozen desserts, and chewing gums.

Stevia was approved as an alternative sweetener by the FDA in 2008. It is produced from the stevia plant, native to South America. Stevia is 200 to 300 times sweeter than sugar, and it is currently used to sweeten beverages. Stevia is also called Rebiana, Reb-A, Truvia, and Purevia.

Using Artificial Sweeteners Does Not Necessarily Prevent Weight Gain

Remember that to prevent weight gain, you need to balance the total number of calories you consume against the number you expend. If you're expending an average of 2,000 calories a day and you consume about 2,000 calories a day, then you'll neither gain nor lose weight. But if, in addition to your normal diet, you regularly indulge in "treats," you're bound to gain weight, whether they are sugar free or not. Consider the calorie count of these artificially sweetened foods:

One cup of nonfat chocolate frozen yogurt with artificial sweetener	199 calories
One sugar-free chocolate cookie	100 calories
One serving of no-sugar-added hot cocoa	55 calories

Does the number of calories in these foods surprise you? *Remember, sugar free doesn't mean calorie free.* Make it a habit to check the Nutrition Facts Panel to find out how much energy is really in your food!

TABLE 3.2	The Amount of Food That a 50-lb Child and a 150-lb Adult Would Have to Consume Each Day to Exceed the ADI for Aspartame	
Food	**50 lb Child**	**150 lb Adult**
12 fl. oz carbonated soft drink	7	20
8 fl. oz powdered soft drink	11	34
4 fl. oz gelatin dessert	14	42
Packets of tabletop sweetener	32	97

Data from International Food Information Council. 2003. Food safety and nutrition information. Sweeteners. Everything you need to know about aspartame. www.foodinsight.org/Resources/Detail.aspx?topic=Everything_You_Need_to_Know_About_Aspartame.

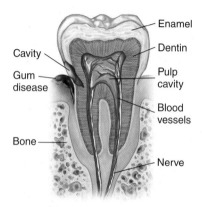

Figure 3.12 Eating simple carbohydrates can cause an increase in cavities and gum disease. This is because bacteria in the mouth consume simple carbohydrates present on the teeth and gums and produce acids, which eat away at these tissues.

To prevent weight gain and tooth decay, many people choose sugar-free versions of soft drinks, jams, flavored yogurts, desserts, chewing gum, and other foods. These products are typically made with alternative sweeteners. The *Highlight* feature box (page 83) identifies the most common alternative sweeteners in use today and examines the controversy about their safety.

The Atkins Diet, the Sugar Busters Diet, and many other diet plans blame sugar for many of our health problems, from tooth decay to hyperactivity to obesity. Does sugar deserve its bad reputation? Let's examine the facts behind the accusations.

Sugar Causes Tooth Decay

Simple carbohydrates, both naturally occurring and in processed foods, play a clear role in dental problems because the bacteria that cause tooth decay thrive on them. These bacteria produce acids that eat away at tooth enamel and can eventually cause cavities and gum disease (Figure 3.12).

Eating sticky foods that cling to teeth, such as caramels, crackers, pretzels, breads, sugary cereals, marshmallows, and licorice, and sipping sweetened beverages over a given time period, increase the risk for tooth decay. This means that people shouldn't slowly sip soda or juice, and babies should not be put to sleep with a bottle in their mouth unless it contains water. As we have seen, even breast milk contains sugar, which can slowly drip onto the baby's gums. As a result, infants should not be routinely allowed to fall asleep at their mother's breast.

To reduce your risk for tooth decay, brush your teeth after every meal and especially after drinking sugary drinks or after eating candy and other sticky foods. Drinking fluoridated water and using a fluoride toothpaste will also help protect your teeth.

NUTRI-CASE HANNAH

"Last night, my mom called and said she'd be late getting home from work, so I made dinner. I made vegetarian quesadillas with flour tortillas, canned green chilies, cheese, and sour cream, plus a few baby carrots on the side. Later that night, while I was studying, I got really hungry, so I raided a package of sugar-free cookies. They're sweetened with sorbitol and taste just like real cookies! I ate maybe three or four, but I didn't think it was a big deal because they're sugar-free. Then when I checked the package label this morning, I found out that each cookie has 90 Calories! It bummed me out—until those cookies, I'd been making really healthy choices!"

Without knowing the exact ingredients in Hannah's dinner, would you agree that, prior to the cookies, she'd been "making really healthy choices"? Why or why not? How might she have changed the ingredients in her quesadillas to increase their fiber content? And if the cookies were sugar-free, how can you explain the fact that each cookie still contained 90 Calories?

There Is No Proven Link Between Sugar and Hyperactivity in Children

Although many people believe that eating sugar causes hyperactivity and other behavioral problems in children, there is little scientific evidence to support this claim. Some children actually become *less* active shortly after a high-sugar meal! However, it is important to emphasize that most studies of sugar and children's behavior have only looked at the effects of sugar a few hours after ingestion. We know very little about the long-term effects of sugar intake on the behavior of children. Behavioral and learning problems are complex issues, most likely caused by a multitude of factors. Because of this complexity, the Institute of Medicine has stated that, overall, there currently does not appear to be enough evidence to suggest that eating too much sugar causes hyperactivity or other behavioral problems in children.[5] Thus, a Tolerable Upper Intake Level for sugar has not been set.

High Sugar Intake Can Lead to Unhealthful Levels of Blood Lipids

Many low-carbohydrate diet plans claim that North Americans' overconsumption of simple sugars is partly responsible for our high rates of heart disease. Is this claim valid? There is research evidence suggesting that consuming a diet high in simple sugars can lead to unhealthful changes in blood lipids. (You will learn more about blood lipids, including cholesterol and lipoproteins, in Chapter 4). Briefly, higher intakes of simple sugars are associated with *increases* in blood lipids that contribute to heart disease, and *decreases* in blood lipids that are considered protective against heart disease.[5,9] Although there is not enough scientific evidence currently to state with complete confidence that eating a diet high in simple sugars causes heart disease, it's prudent for people at risk for heart disease to eat a diet low in simple sugars.

High Sugar Intake Does Not Cause Diabetes but May Contribute to Obesity

There is no scientific evidence that eating a diet high in sugar causes diabetes. In fact, studies examining the relationship between sugar intake and type 2 diabetes report either no association between sugar intake and diabetes or a decreased risk for diabetes with increased sugar intake.[10] However, people who have diabetes nonetheless need to moderate their intake of sugar and closely monitor their blood glucose levels.

There is somewhat more evidence linking sugar intake with obesity. For example, a recent study found that overweight children consumed more sugared soft drinks than did children of normal weight.[11] Another study found that, for every extra sugared soft drink a child consumes per day, the risk for obesity increases by 60%.[12] We also know that, if you consume more energy than you expend, you will gain weight. It makes intuitive sense that people who consume extra energy from high-sugar foods are at risk for obesity, just as people who consume extra energy from fat or protein gain weight. In addition to the increased potential for obesity, another major concern about high-sugar diets is that they tend to be low in nutrient density because eating high-sugar foods tends to replace eating more nutritious foods.

The relationship between sugared soft drinks and obesity is highly controversial. Over the past 30 years, obesity rates have increased dramatically for adults and children, and one lifestyle factor that has been blamed for these rising obesity rates is *high-fructose corn syrup* (HFCS). HFCS is made by converting the starch in corn to glucose, then converting some of the glucose to fructose, which is sweeter. Unfortunately, fructose is metabolized differently than glucose, and its absorption doesn't stimulate the pancreas to release insulin. Since insulin inhibits food intake, we're more likely to continue eating when insulin isn't released. Also, whereas glucose can enter brain cells and stimulate signals telling us that we're full, fructose can't. If we don't feel full, we're likely to continue eating or drinking.

Some researchers suggest that these differences are associated with increased energy intake—which can lead to overweight and obesity. They point out that HFCS is the only caloric sweetener used in soft drinks, and it represents more than 40% of the caloric sweeteners added to other foods and beverages in the United States.

Not all researchers agree that HFCS is an important factor in obesity. The rates of overweight and obesity are rising around the world, and many countries experiencing this epidemic don't use HFCS as a sweetener. Some experts believe that rising obesity rates are not due to HFCS specifically, but to increased consumption of total energy from super-sizes of beverages, snack foods, and desserts sweetened with any of a variety of sugars, not to mention our increasingly sedentary lifestyle.

To watch a CBS News video on the HFCS controversy, visit www.cbsnews.com/video/watch/?id=6213315n.

RECAP Added sugars include sucrose, high-fructose corn syrup, and other sugars and syrups added to foods during processing or preparation. Sugar causes tooth decay but does not appear to cause hyperactivity in children. Higher intakes of simple sugars are associated with increases in the blood lipids that are associated with heart disease. Diets high in sugar cause unhealthful changes in blood sugar but do not cause diabetes. The relationship between added sugars and obesity is controversial.

⬆ Whole-grain foods provide more nutrients and fiber than foods made with enriched flour.

Most Americans Eat Too Little Fiber-Rich Carbohydrate

Do you eat enough fiber-rich carbohydrates each day? If you are like most people in the United States, you eat only about 2 servings of fruits or vegetables daily, which is far below the amount recommended in the USDA Food Plans. Do you eat whole grains and legumes every day? Many people eat lots of breads, pastas, and cereals, but most don't consistently choose whole-grain products. As we explained earlier, whole-grain foods have a lower glycemic index than simple carbohydrates; thus, they prompt a more gradual release of insulin and result in less severe fluctuations in both insulin and glucose. Whole-grain foods also provide more nutrients and fiber than foods made with enriched flour.

Table 3.3 defines the terms commonly used on nutrition labels for breads and cereals. Read the label for the bread you eat—does it list *whole-wheat* flour or just *wheat* flour? Although most labels for breads and cereals list wheat flour as the first ingredient, this term actually refers to enriched white flour, which is made when wheat flour is processed. Don't be fooled—becoming an educated consumer will help you select whole grains instead of processed foods.

TABLE 3.3	Terms Used to Describe Grains and Cereals on Nutrition Labels
Term	**Definition**
Brown bread	Bread that may or may not be made using whole-grain flour. Many brown breads are made with white flour with brown (caramel) coloring added.
Enriched (or fortified) flour or grain	Enriching or fortifying grains involves adding nutrients back to refined foods. In order to use this term in the United States, a minimum amount of iron, folate, niacin, thiamin, and riboflavin must be added. Other nutrients can also be added.
Refined flour or grain	Refining involves removing the coarse parts of food products; refined wheat flour is flour in which all but the internal part of the kernel has been removed. Refined sugar is made by removing the outer portions of sugar beets or sugarcane.
Stone ground	Refers to a milling process in which limestone is used to grind any grain. Stone ground does not mean that bread is made with whole grain, as refined flour can be stone ground.
Unbleached flour	Flour that has been refined but not bleached; it is very similar to refined white flour in texture and nutritional value.
Wheat flour	Any flour made from wheat; includes white flour, unbleached flour, and whole-wheat flour.
White flour	Flour that has been bleached and refined. All-purpose flour, cake flour, and enriched baking flour are all types of white flour.
Whole-grain flour	A grain that is not refined; whole grains are milled in their complete form, with only the husk removed.
Whole-wheat flour	An unrefined whole-grain flour made from whole-wheat kernels.

We Need at Least 25 Grams of Fiber Daily

How much fiber do we need? The Adequate Intake for fiber is 25 grams per day for women and 38 grams per day for men, or 14 grams of fiber for every 1,000 kcal per day that a person eats.[5] Most people in the United States eat only 12 to 18 grams of fiber each day, getting only half of the fiber they need. Although fiber supplements are available, it is *best to get fiber from food* because foods contain additional nutrients, such as vitamins and minerals.

Eating the amounts of whole grains, vegetables, fruits, nuts, and legumes recommended in the USDA Food Patterns will ensure that you eat adequate fiber. **Figure 3.13** (page 88) lists some common foods and their fiber content. Think about how you can design your own diet to include high-fiber foods.

It is also important to drink more water as you increase your fiber intake, as fiber binds with water to soften stools. Inadequate water intake with a high-fiber diet can result in hard, dry stools that are difficult to pass through the colon. Thus, eating a high-fiber diet without consuming adequate water can result in constipation.

Can you eat too much fiber? Excessive fiber consumption can lead to problems such as the following:

Eating Right All Day

Breakfast
Oatmeal instead of sugary cereal!

Lunch
Bean soup instead of pizza!

Dinner
Sweet potato instead of French fries!

Snack
Fresh Fruit instead of a candy bar!

- Intestinal gas and bloating.
- Dehydration: because fiber binds with water, it causes the body to eliminate more water, so a very-high-fiber diet can result in dehydration.
- Reduced absorption of certain nutrients: because fiber binds many vitamins and minerals, a high-fiber diet can reduce the absorption of important nutrients, such as iron, zinc, and calcium.
- Malnutrition in groups such as children, some elderly, the chronically ill, and other at-risk populations: in these groups, excess fiber intake can lead to malnutrition because they feel full before they have eaten enough to provide adequate energy and nutrients.

Do you want to increase the amount of fiber you consume each day? If so, it's important to go slowly, giving your system time to adjust to the increased bulk in your new diet. Otherwise, you might experience some of the symptoms of excessive fiber consumption. To avoid stressing your body, check out the *Game Plan* feature box (page 90) for tips on increasing your fiber intake one step at a time.

Shopper's Guide: Hunting for Fiber

Figure 3.14 (page 89) compares the food and fiber content of two diets: one high in fiber-rich carbohydrates and one high in refined carbohydrates. Here are some hints for selecting healthful carbohydrate sources:

Brown rice is a good food source of dietary fiber.

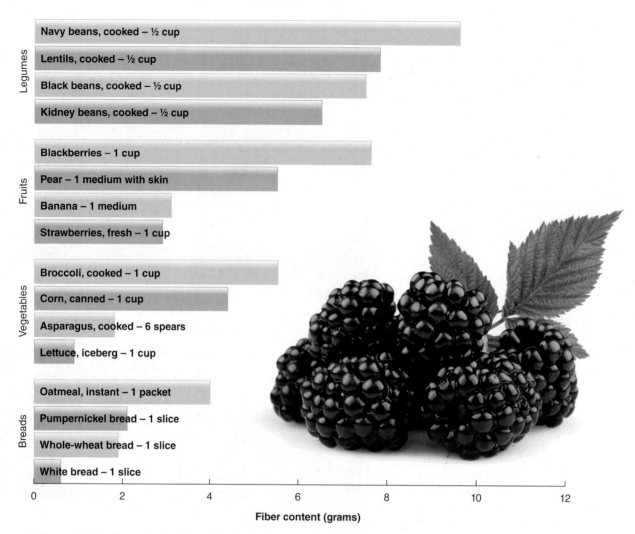

Figure 3.13 Fiber content of common foods. *Note:* The Adequate Intake for fiber is 25 grams per day for women and 38 grams per day for men.

Data from U.S. Department of Agriculture, Agricultural Research Service. 2010. USDA National Nutrient Database for Standard Reference, Release 23. Nutrient Data Laboratory Home Page, www.ars.usda.gov/ba/bhnrc/ndl.

Check to make sure that canned fruits are packed in their own juices, not syrup.

- Select breads and cereals made with whole grains, such as wheat, oats, barley, and rye (make sure the label says *whole* before the word *grain*). Choose foods that have at least 2 to 3 grams of fiber per serving.
- Buy fresh fruits and vegetables whenever possible. When appropriate, eat foods such as potatoes, apples, and pears with the skin left on.
- Frozen vegetables and fruits can be a healthful alternative when fresh produce is not available. Check frozen selections to make sure there is no extra sugar or salt added.
- Be careful when buying canned fruits and vegetables, as many are high in sodium and added sugar. Foods that are packed in their own juice are more healthful than those packed in syrup.
- Eat legumes frequently; every day if possible. Canned or fresh beans, peas, and lentils are excellent sources of complex carbohydrates, fiber, vitamins, and minerals. Add them to soups, casseroles, and other recipes—it's an easy way to eat more of them. If you're trying to consume less sodium, rinse canned beans to remove extra salt, or choose low-sodium alternatives.

To see a vast menu of high-fiber choices for each meal of the day, and find out how much fiber the foods you eat provide, visit the Fiber-o-Meter at www.webmd.com/diet/healthtool-fiber-meter.

A Day of Meals: Two High-Carb Diets

High in Refined Carbs

Breakfast

1½ cups Fruit Loops cereal
1 cup skim milk
2 slices white bread toasted,
  with 1 tbsp. light margarine
8 fl. oz fresh orange juice

Lunch

McDonald's Quarter Pounder
1 large order French fries
16 fl. oz cola beverage
30 jelly beans

Snack

1 cinnamon raisin bagel
  (3½-inch diameter)
2 tbsp. cream cheese
8 fl. oz low-fat strawberry yogurt

Dinner

1 whole roasted chicken breast
2 cups mixed green salad
2 tbsp. ranch salad dressing
1 serving macaroni and cheese
12 fl. oz cola beverage
Cheesecake (1/9 of cake)

Snack

2 cups gelatin dessert
  (cherry flavored)
3 raspberry oatmeal no-fat
  cookies

Nutrient Analysis
4012 kcal
60% of energy from carbohydrates
25% of energy from fat
15% of energy from protein
18.5 grams of dietary fiber

High in Fiber-Rich Carbs

Breakfast

1½ cups Cheerios
1 cup skim milk
2 slices whole-wheat toast
  with 1 tbsp. light margarine
1 medium banana
8 fl. oz fresh orange juice

Lunch

Tuna sandwich
  2 slices whole-wheat bread;
  ¼ cup tuna packed in water,
  drained; 1 tsp. Dijon mustard;
  2 tsp. low-calorie mayonnaise
2 carrots, raw, with peel
1 cup raw cauliflower
1 tbsp. peppercorn ranch
  salad dressing
8 fl. oz low-fat blueberry yogurt

Snack

3 cups nonfat popcorn

Dinner

½ chicken breast roasted
1 cup brown rice, cooked
1 cup cooked broccoli
Spinach salad
  (1 cup chopped spinach,
  1 whole egg white, 2 slices
  turkey bacon, 3 cherry
  tomatoes, and 2 tbsp. creamy
  bacon salad dressing)
2 baked apples (no added sugar)

Snack

(No Snack)

Nutrient Analysis
2150 kcal
60% of energy from carbohydrates
22% of energy from fat
18% of energy from protein
38 grams of dietary fiber

Figure 3.14 Comparison of two high-carbohydrate diets. *Note:* Diets were analyzed using Food Processor Version 7.21 (ESHA Research, Salem, OR).

90% ▭

GAME PLAN

Tips for Increasing Your Fiber Intake One Step at a Time

Gradually increasing your fiber intake gives your gastrointestinal organs time to adjust to the increased bulk in your diet. This is especially important if you've been eating a very-low-fiber diet (fewer than 10 grams of fiber per day) for many years. Here's how to increase your fiber intake one step at a time:

Step 1 Incorporate just one of the strategies listed below each day for 1 week.

Step 2 Make sure you drink plenty of fluids. The best way to make sure you're well hydrated is to track your output: if your urine is clear to pale yellow, you're getting enough fluid.

Step 3 Keep a record of your total daily fiber intake and of how you're feeling.

Step 4 If you adjust well to the increased fiber, then go ahead and incorporate two strategies a day the following week.

Step 5 Continue until you reach your optimal daily fiber intake.

Here are some strategies to choose from:

☐ Switch from a low-fiber breakfast cereal to one that has at least 4 grams of fiber per serving.

☐ Switch to whole-grain bread for morning toast or lunchtime sandwiches. Two slices of whole-grain bread provide 4–6 grams of fiber. (Check the Nutrition Facts Panel of the whole-grain bread you're using.)

☐ For a midmorning snack, mix 1–2 tablespoons of bran or whole ground flaxseed meal (4 grams of fiber) into a cup of low-fat yogurt. These products are available at most health-food stores and many large supermarkets.

☐ Instead of chips with your sandwich, have a side of carrot sticks or celery sticks (approximately 2 grams of fiber per serving).

☐ For an afternoon snack, choose an apple or a pear, with the skin on (approximately 5 grams of fiber).

☐ Eat 1 serving of beans or other legumes at dinner (approximately 6 grams of fiber).

☐ Don't forget the vegetables! A cup of boiled chopped okra or beet greens provides about 4 grams of fiber, and acorn squash a whopping 9 grams! Raw veggies are fiber-rich, too, so a large salad is a good source of fiber.

☐ For dessert, switch from cookies, cake, or ice cream to a serving of fresh, frozen, or dried fruit. A half cup of fresh or frozen blackberries or raspberries provides 4–5 grams of fiber, and a single ounce of dried mixed fruit (prunes, apricots, etc.) provides 2 grams.

☐ For an evening snack, try a mixture of plain, air-popped popcorn, peanuts, and raisins: 1 cup of popcorn (1 gram of fiber) with 1/4 cup of peanuts (3 grams) and 1/4 cup of raisins (2 grams) provides a total of 6 grams of fiber.

If you incorporate these strategies and experience diarrhea, constipation, or excess intestinal gas, then your body may not be adjusting well to the increased fiber. Try cutting the serving size or incorporating a strategy only every other day. And make sure to drink plenty of fluids! Try this for 2 weeks; then increase gradually again.

RECAP The Adequate Intake for fiber is 25 grams per day for women and 38 grams per day for men. Most Americans eat only half of the fiber they need each day. Foods high in fiber include whole grains and cereals, fruits, and vegetables. The more processed the food, the less fiber it is likely to contain.

HEALTHWATCH

What Is Diabetes, and Why Has It Become a Public Health Concern?

Diabetes is a serious chronic disease in which the body can no longer regulate glucose within normal limits and blood glucose levels become dangerously high or fall dangerously low. These fluctuations in glucose injure tissues throughout the body. If not controlled, diabetes can lead to blindness, seizures, kidney failure, nerve disease, amputations, stroke, and heart disease. In severe cases, it can be fatal.

Approximately 18 million people in the United States—6% of the total population—are diagnosed with diabetes. It is speculated that another 5.7 million people have the disease but don't know it. There are two main forms of diabetes: type 1 and type 2. Some women develop a third form, *gestational diabetes,* during pregnancy; we discuss this in more detail later in this text (Chapter 11).

Figure 3.15 shows the percentage of adults with diabetes from various ethnic groups in the United States.[13] As you can see, type 2 diabetes is more common in African Americans, Hispanic/Latino individuals, American Indians, and Alaska Natives. It is also more common in older adults than in younger adults and children.

In Type 1 Diabetes, the Body Does Not Produce Enough Insulin

Approximately 10% of people with diabetes have **type 1 diabetes,** in which the body cannot produce enough insulin. When people with type 1 diabetes eat a meal and their blood glucose rises, the pancreas is unable to secrete insulin in response. Glucose levels soar, and the body tries to expel the excess glucose by excreting it in the urine. In fact, the medical term for the disease is *diabetes mellitus* (from the Greek *diabainein,* "to pass through," and Latin *mellitus,* "sweetened with honey"), and frequent urination is one of its warning signs (see **Table 3.4** for other symptoms). If blood

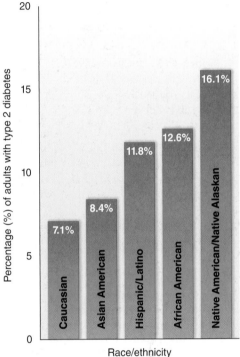

◀ **Figure 3.15** The percentage of adults from various ethnic and racial groups with type 2 diabetes.
Data from The National Diabetes Information Clearinghouse [NDIC]. 2011. National diabetes statistics. National Institutes of Health [NIH] Publication No. 11-3892. http://diabetes.niddk.nih.gov/dm/pubs/statistics/index.htm.

TABLE 3.4	Symptoms of Type 1 and Type 2 Diabetes
Type 1 Diabetes	**Type 2 Diabetes***
Frequent urination	Any of the type 1 symptoms
Unusual thirst	Blurred vision
Extreme hunger	Cuts/bruises that are slow to heal
Unusual weight loss	Tingling/numbness in the hands or feet
Extreme fatigue	Recurring skin, gum, or bladder infections
Irritability	

*Some people with type 2 diabetes experience no symptoms.
Copyright © 2011, The American Diabetes Association, from www.diabetes.org. Modified with permission from the American Diabetes Association.

diabetes A serious, chronic disease in which the body can no longer regulate glucose.

type 1 diabetes The form of diabetes in which the body cannot produce enough insulin.

Figure 3.16 Monitoring blood glucose typically requires pricking a finger each day and measuring the blood using a device called a glucometer.

glucose levels are not controlled, a person with type 1 diabetes will become confused and lethargic and have trouble breathing. This is because the person's brain is not getting enough glucose to function properly.

Uncontrolled diabetes can lead to *ketoacidosis*, a condition that occurs when inadequate glucose levels prompt the body to break down stored fat for energy. The fuels produced from fat breakdown, called ketones, are acidic. Their production therefore raises the level of acidity of the blood (a condition called *acidosis*). Any form of acidosis—including ketoacidosis—interferes with basic body functions and damages many body tissues; left untreated, the ultimate results are coma and death.

The cause of type 1 diabetes is unknown, but it may be an *autoimmune disease.* This means that the body's immune system attacks and destroys its own tissues—in this case, the beta cells of the pancreas.

Most cases of type 1 diabetes are diagnosed in adolescents around 10 to 14 years of age, although the disease can appear in younger children and adults. It occurs more often in families, so siblings and children of people with type 1 diabetes are at greater risk.

The only treatment for type 1 diabetes is daily insulin injections. Insulin is a hormone composed of protein, so it would be digested in the small intestine if taken as a pill. People with type 1 diabetes must monitor their blood glucose levels closely, using a device called a *glucometer,* and must give themselves injections of insulin several times a day to maintain their blood glucose levels within a healthful range **(Figure 3.16)**.

NUTRITION
MILESTONE

1921 By the late 19th century, scientists knew there was a link between the pancreas and diabetes. Experiments had shown that, without a pancreas, an otherwise healthy animal would develop the disease quickly. Still, no one knew how to treat diabetes: nutritional therapies ranged from low-carbohydrate diets to starvation. For children, a diagnosis of diabetes was essentially a death sentence. Then, in 1921, Canadian surgeon Frederick Banting had an idea. He and his medical assistant removed the pancreas from a dog, thereby inducing diabetes. They then injected the diabetic dog with secretions extracted from a cluster of cells in the pancreas called the islets of Langerhans. They called this extraction *isletin*. A few injections of isletin a day cured the dog of diabetes. They then purified the substance—which we now call insulin—and repeated their experiment several times before trying it on a 14-year-old boy dying of diabetes. The injection reversed all signs of the disease in the boy. Banting published a paper on his research in 1922 and received a Nobel Prize the following year.

In Type 2 Diabetes, Cells Become Less Responsive to Insulin

In **type 2 diabetes,** body cells become *resistant,* or less responsive, to insulin. This type of diabetes develops progressively, meaning that the biological changes resulting in the disease occur over a long period of time.

In most cases, obesity is the trigger for a cascade of changes that eventually result in the disorder. Specifically, the cells of many obese people exhibit a condition called *insulin insensitivity* (or, *insulin resistance*). The pancreas attempts to compensate for this by secreting more insulin. Over time, a person who is insulin insensitive will have to circulate very high levels of insulin to use glucose for energy. Eventually, this excessive production of insulin becomes insufficient for preventing a rise in fasting blood glucose. The resulting condition is referred to as **impaired fasting glucose,** meaning glucose levels are higher than normal but not high enough to indicate a diagnosis of type 2 diabetes. Some health professionals refer to this as *pre-diabetes*, since people with impaired fasting glucose are more likely to develop type 2 diabetes. Ultimately, the pancreas becomes incapable of secreting such excessive amounts of insulin, and the beta cells stop producing the hormone altogether.

type 2 diabetes The form of diabetes in which body cells progressively become less responsive to insulin, or the body does not produce enough insulin.

impaired fasting glucose Fasting blood glucose levels that are higher than normal but not high enough to lead to a diagnosis of type 2 diabetes; also called *pre-diabetes*.

As noted, obesity is the most common trigger for type 2 diabetes. But many other factors also play a role. For instance, relatives of people with type 2 diabetes are at increased risk, as are people with a sedentary lifestyle.

A cluster of risk factors referred to as the *metabolic syndrome* is also known to increase the risk for type 2 diabetes. The criteria for metabolic syndrome are

> To download a family history tree that you can fill out to determine your family history of diabetes, visit www.heart.org/HEARTORG/GettingHealthy/HealthierKids/ActivitiesforKids/My-Family-Health-Tree_UCM_312356_Article.jsp.

- a waist circumference of or greater than 35 inches (88 cm) for women, and 40 inches (102 cm) for men,
- elevated blood pressure,
- unhealthful levels of certain blood lipids, and
- abnormally high blood glucose levels.

Increased age is another risk factor for type 2 diabetes; most cases develop after age 45, and 23% of Americans 60 years and older have diabetes. Once commonly known as *adult-onset diabetes,* type 2 diabetes in children was virtually unheard of until recently. Unfortunately, the disease is increasing dramatically among children and adolescents, posing serious health consequences for them and their future children.[13] In a 2004 study, more than 6% of U.S. college students were found to have pre-diabetes.[14] And every year, 3,700 Americans under age 20 are newly diagnosed with full-blown type 2 diabetes.[13]

◆ Actress Halle Berry has type 2 diabetes.

Lifestyle Choices Can Help Control or Prevent Type 2 Diabetes

Type 2 diabetes can be treated in a variety of ways. Losing weight, establishing healthful eating patterns, and exercising regularly can control the symptoms in many people. More severe cases may require oral medications, such as pills. These drugs work in one of two ways: they improve the sensitivity of body cells to insulin, or reduce the amount of glucose the liver produces. However, if a person with type 2 diabetes can no longer secrete enough insulin, the patient must have daily injections of insulin just like a person with type 1 diabetes.

FOODS YOU DON'T KNOW YOU LOVE YET

Dhal

Have you heard of dhal? If you enjoy foods from India, Pakistan, Nepal, Sri Lanka, or Bangladesh, you've probably tried it. If not, it's time to find out about this healthy dish! Dhal (also spelled *dal, dahl,* or *daal*) is a spicy dish traditionally made with lentils, dried peas, or beans that have been stripped of their outer hull. The processed legumes themselves are also referred to as dhal. They've been used in foods since prehistoric times and are high in protein and fiber, with a low glycemic index.

Like dry beans, most varieties of dhal are cooked slowly in water for 30–60 minutes. A variety of spices, as well as tomatoes, onions, and other vegetables, can be added, and the resulting fragrant dish—the consistency of a thick soup—is typically served with rice or breads, such as chapatti or naan.

90%

WHAT ABOUT YOU?

Calculate Your Risk for Type 2 Diabetes

To calculate your risk for developing type 2 diabetes, circle your answers to the following questions:

▶ I am overweight.	YES/NO
▶ I am sedentary (I exercise fewer than three times a week).	YES/NO
▶ I have a close family member with type 2 diabetes.	YES/NO
▶ I am a member of one of the following groups	YES/NO
• African American	
• Hispanic American (Latino)	
• Native American	
• Pacific Islander	
▶ I have had gestational diabetes, or I gave birth to at least one baby weighing more than 9 lb.	YES/NO
▶ My blood pressure is 140/90 or higher, or I have been told that I have high blood pressure.	YES/NO
▶ My cholesterol levels are not normal. (See a fuller discussion of cholesterol in Chapter 4.)	YES/NO

The more "yes" responses you give, the higher your risk of developing type 2 diabetes. You cannot change your ethnicity or your family members' health, but you can take steps to maintain a healthful weight and increase your physical activity. For tips, see Chapters 9 and 10.

Data from The National Diabetes Information Clearinghouse (NDIC). http://diabetes.niddk.nih.gov.

People with diabetes should follow most of the same dietary guidelines recommended for those without diabetes. One difference is that people with diabetes may need to eat less carbohydrate, and slightly more fat or protein, to help regulate their blood glucose levels. Typically, a registered dietitian develops an individualized diet plan based on each patient's responses to foods.

In addition, people with diabetes should avoid alcoholic beverages, which can cause hypoglycemia. The symptoms of alcohol intoxication and hypoglycemia are very similar. The person with diabetes, his or her companions, and healthcare professionals may confuse these conditions; this can result in a potentially life-threatening situation.

Although there is no cure for type 2 diabetes, many cases could be prevented or have their onset delayed. We cannot control our family history, but we can use the following strategies to decrease our risk:

- Eat a balanced diet with plenty of whole grains, fruits, legumes, and vegetables.
- Exercise regularly: moderate daily exercise may prevent the onset of type 2 diabetes more effectively than dietary changes alone.[15]
- Maintain an appropriate body weight: studies show that losing only 10 to 30 lb can reduce or eliminate the symptoms of type 2 diabetes.[16]

What's your risk of developing diabetes? Check out *What About You?* feature box (shown above) to find out.

RECAP Diabetes is a serious disease that results in dangerously high levels of blood glucose. In type 1 diabetes, the pancreas cannot secrete sufficient insulin, so insulin injections are required to manage the disease. Type 2 diabetes develops over time and may be triggered by obesity: body cells are no longer sensitive to the effects of insulin, or the pancreas no longer secretes sufficient insulin for the body's needs. Supplemental insulin, usually in the form of injections, may or may not be needed. Diabetes causes tissue damage and increases the risk for heart disease, blindness, kidney disease, and amputations. Many cases of type 2 diabetes could be prevented or delayed by eating a balanced diet, getting regular exercise, and maintaining a healthful body weight.

COOKING 101

Rice, grains, and pasta aren't the only foods that contain carbs. Vegetables, fruits, and many sauces also contain this essential nutrient! Learn how to cook pasta and more with our new Cooking 101 videos, available on the Companion Website at www.pearsonhighered.com/thompsonmanore.

"Where I'm at Now ..."

Now that you've read this chapter, would you say you've been getting enough fiber most days?

Yes or No

Do you plan to increase your intake of fiber-rich carbohydrates?

Yes or No

Do you plan to decrease your intake of simple carbohydrates?

Yes or No

What other changes—if any—do you plan to make in your food choices?

Chapter Review

What Can I Do Today?

Now that you've read this chapter, try making these three changes:

- Eat more high-fiber foods with each meal—including fruits, vegetables, legumes, and whole-grain cereals and breads.

- Drink fewer sweetened beverages and more water with every meal to reduce your energy intake and help with digesting the higher amount of fiber you are eating.

- Brush your teeth more often throughout the day, particularly after eating sweet foods or sticky, starchy foods. This will reduce your risk for dental caries.

Test Yourself ANSWERS

1. **F** The term *carbohydrate* refers to both simple and complex carbohydrates. The term *sugar* refers to the simple carbohydrates: monosaccharides and disaccharides.

2. **F** There is no evidence that diets high in sugar cause hyperactivity in children.

3. **T** Our brain relies almost exclusively on glucose for energy, and our body tissues use glucose for energy both at rest and during exercise.

4. **F** At 4 kcal per gram, carbohydrates have less than half the energy of a gram of fat. Eating a high-carbohydrate diet will not cause people to gain body fat unless their total diet contains more energy (calories) than they expend. In fact, eating a diet high in complex, fiber-rich carbohydrates is associated with a lower risk for obesity.

5. **T** Contrary to recent reports claiming severe health consequences related to the consumption of alternative sweeteners, major health agencies have determined that these products are safe for most people to consume in moderation.

 **NutriTools**

Check out the Companion Website at www.pearsonhighered.com/thompsonmanore, or use MyNutritionLab.com, to access interactive animations, including

- Build-a-Sandwich
- Find the Carbohydrates
- Know Your Carbohydrate Sources

Review Questions

1. The glycemic index rates
   a. the acceptable amount of alternative sweeteners to consume in 1 day.
   b. the potential of foods to raise blood glucose and insulin levels.
   c. the risk of a given food for causing diabetes.
   d. the ratio of soluble to insoluble fiber in a complex carbohydrate.

2. Carbohydrates contain
   a. carbon, nitrogen, and water.
   b. carbonic acid and a sugar alcohol.
   c. hydrated sugar.
   d. carbon, hydrogen, and oxygen.

3. The most common source of added sugar in the American diet is
   a. table sugar.
   b. white flour.
   c. alcohol.
   d. sweetened soft drinks.

4. Glucose, fructose, and galactose are
   a. monosaccharides.
   b. disaccharides.
   c. polysaccharides.
   d. complex carbohydrates.

5. Obesity is thought to be a common trigger of
   a. hypoglycemia.
   b. type 1 diabetes.
   c. type 2 diabetes.
   d. lactose intolerance.

6. True or False? Children and teens with diabetes most often have type 1 diabetes.

7. True or False? High-fructose corn syrup is both a simple carbohydrate and a refined carbohydrate.

8. True or False? A person with lactose intolerance is allergic to milk.

9. True or False? Plants store glucose as glycogen.

10. True or False? Salivary amylase breaks down starches into galactose.

Answers to Review Questions are located at the back of this text.

Web Links

www.eatright.org
American Dietetic Association

www.ada.org
American Dental Association

www.diabetes.org
American Diabetes Association

www2.niddk.nih.gov
National Institute of Diabetes and Digestive and Kidney Diseases (NIDDK)

4

Fats: Essential Energy-Supplying Nutrients

Test Yourself

Are these statements true or false? Circle your guess.

1. T F Dietary cholesterol is not required because our body makes all the cholesterol it needs.

2. T F Fat is an important fuel source during rest and exercise.

3. T F Fried foods can be high in unhealthful fats even if fried with vegetable shortening.

4. T F Certain fats protect against heart disease.

5. T F High-fat diets are a primary cause of cancer.

Test Yourself answers can be found at the end of the chapter.

Shivani moved with her parents to the United States from India when she was 6 years old. Although slender compared to her American friends, Shivani was healthy and energetic, and loved riding her bike around her new suburban neighborhood. But by the time Shivani entered high school, her weight had caught up to that of her American classmates. Now a sophomore in college, she is struggling with obesity.

Shivani explains, "In India, the diet is mostly rice, lentils, and vegetables. Many people are vegetarians, or they eat only fish and poultry. Breakfast is usually fruit and yogurt, not eggs and sausage. And for most families, desserts are only for special occasions. When we moved to America, I wanted to eat like all the other kids: hamburgers, french fries, ice cream, cookies . . . I gained a lot of weight, and now my doctor says I weigh too much, my blood pressure is high, and I need to have a cholesterol test to see if I'm at risk for heart disease. It freaks me out thinking that some day I might have a heart attack! I wish I could start eating like my relatives back in India again, but they don't serve rice and lentils in the cafeteria."

What causes heart disease, and how can you calculate your risk? Is a high-fat diet always to blame? Can a low-fat diet prevent it? When was the last time you heard anything good about dietary fat? If Shivani were your friend and you noticed her regularly eating high-fat foods, would you say anything about it? If so, what would you say?

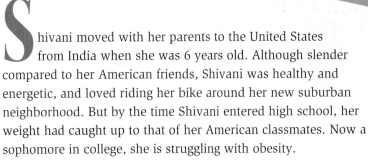

Nutrition Online

icons are located throughout the chapter, directing you to web links, videos, podcasts, and other useful online resources.

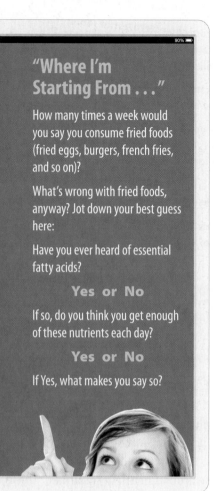

Although some people think of dietary fat as something to be avoided, a certain amount of fat is absolutely essential for good health. In this chapter, we'll discuss the function of fat in the human body and help you distinguish between beneficial and harmful types of dietary fat. You'll also learn about how much fat you need in your diet, and about the relationship between different types of dietary fat and the risks for heart disease and other disorders.

What Are Fats?

Fats are just one form of a much larger and more diverse group of substances called **lipids** that are distinguished by the fact that they are *insoluble* (do not dissolve) in water. Think of a salad dressing made with vinegar and olive oil—a lipid. Shaking the bottle *disperses* the oil but doesn't *dissolve* it: that's why it separates back out again so quickly. Lipids are found in all sorts of living things, including plants, animals, and human beings. In fact, their presence on your skin explains why you can't clean your face with water alone: you need some type of soap to break down the insoluble lipids before you can wash them away.

We consume lipids in either of two forms: fats, such as butter, which are solid at room temperature, and oils, such as olive oil, which are liquid at room temperature. In this chapter, we focus on three types of lipids found in foods:

- triglycerides
- phospholipids
- sterols

Most of the fat we eat (95%) is in the form of triglycerides, which is the same way most of the fat in our body is stored. In addition, the types of triglycerides we choose to eat can have a significant impact—positive or negative—on our health. So although this chapter discusses phospholipids and sterols briefly, our main focus is on triglycerides. Also, because most people are familiar with the term *fats,* we will use that term generically throughout this book whenever we're discussing triglycerides, whether we're referring to solid fats or liquid oils.

Triglycerides Can Contain Saturated or Unsaturated Fatty Acid Chains

As reflected in the prefix *tri,* a **triglyceride** is a molecule consisting of *three* fatty acids attached to a *three*-carbon glycerol backbone. **Fatty acids** are long chains of carbon atoms bound to each other as well as to hydrogen. They are classified as acids because they contain an acid group at one end of their chain. **Glycerol,** the backbone of a triglyceride molecule, is an alcohol composed of three carbon atoms. One fatty acid chain attaches to each of these three carbons to make the triglyceride **(Figure 4.1)**.

You've probably heard the recommendation that you should reduce your intake of saturated and *trans* fatty acids, and increase your intake of unsaturated and essential fatty acids. All of these are components of triglycerides, so why are some better than others? The difference lies mainly in how their carbon atoms are bound to hydrogen. As we explain next, this simple factor varies their shape and their effect in our body quite dramatically.

Saturated Fats Contain the Maximum Amount of Hydrogen

An atom of carbon has four "attachment sites." It will be unstable until it has bonded to four other atoms—that is, until all four of its attachment sites are filled. In fatty acids, two of these four sites are typically bound to adjacent carbon atoms. These bonds form the carbon chain.

lipids A diverse group of organic substances that are insoluble in water; lipids include triglycerides, phospholipids, and sterols.

triglyceride A molecule consisting of three fatty acids attached to a three-carbon glycerol backbone.

fatty acids Long chains of carbon atoms bound to each other as well as to hydrogen atoms.

glycerol An alcohol composed of three carbon atoms; it is the backbone of a triglyceride molecule.

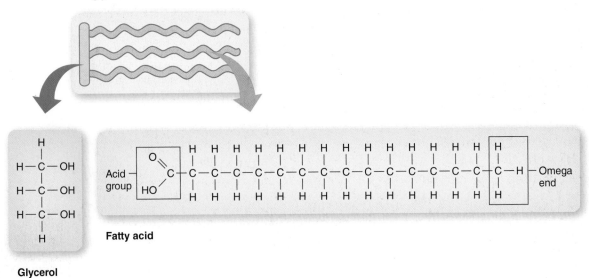

Figure 4.1 A triglyceride consists of three fatty acid chains attached to a three-carbon glycerol backbone.

In saturated fatty acids, the two remaining attachment sites are always filled by hydrogen atoms:

$$H - \overset{\displaystyle H}{\underset{\displaystyle H}{C}} - H$$

Thus, the saturated fatty acid chain is simply a long chain of carbon atoms bonded to other carbon atoms (two attachment sites) and to hydrogen atoms (two more attachments sites). You can see this in the long chain shown at the top of **Figure 4.2** (page 100). When you look at this chain, notice how regular it is.

In contrast, look at the chain in middle part of Figure 4.2a. At one point, it has a *double bond* between adjacent carbon atoms. (Chemists indicate double bonds between atoms with two parallel lines, like an equal sign [C = C]). This double bond fills two attachment sites, one of which would otherwise be filled by hydrogen. Notice that each of the carbons at this site has just one hydrogen attached, not two. Thus, the total amount of hydrogen is lower in a fatty acid chain with one or more double carbon bonds.

A fatty acid with no double carbon bonds, like the top figure in Figure 4.2a, is referred to as a **saturated fatty acid (SFA).** This is because the chain is *saturated* with hydrogen: it has the maximum amount of hydrogen bound to it. Some foods that are high in saturated fatty acids are butter, lard, cream, whole milk, many cheeses, beef, coconut oil, and palm oil.

Double carbon bonds give fatty acids chains a "kink" wherever they occur. Molecules of saturated fat have no such bonds, so they always form straight, rigid chains. This quality allows them to pack together densely in fats like butter and lard. To understand why, it might help to imagine a box of toothpicks. Have you ever noticed how many toothpicks are packed into a small box? A hundred? More? But if you were to break a bunch of toothpicks into V shapes anywhere along their length, how many could you then fit into the same box? It would be very few because the bent toothpicks would jumble together, taking up much more space. Like straight toothpicks, saturated fatty acid chains can pack together tightly (Figure 4.2b). That is why saturated fats, such as the fat in meats and butter, are solid at room temperature.

Does the straight, rigid shape of the saturated fats we eat have any effect on our health? Absolutely! Research over the past twenty years has shown that diets high in

Some fats, such as olive oil, are liquid at room temperature.

saturated fatty acid (SFA) A fatty acid that has no carbons joined together with a double bond; these types of fatty acids are generally solid at room temperature.

Fatty acids

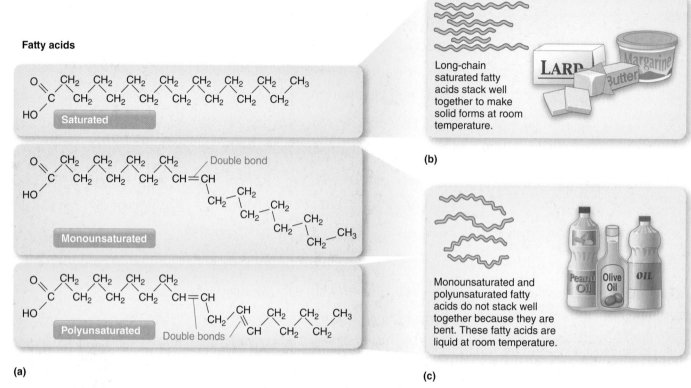

◀ **Figure 4.2** Examples of levels of saturation among fatty acids and how these levels of saturation affect the shape of fatty acids. **(a)** Saturated fatty acids are saturated with hydrogen, meaning they have no carbons bonded together with a double bond. Monounsaturated fatty acids contain two carbons bound by one double bond. Polyunsaturated fatty acids have more than one double bond linking carbon atoms. **(b)** Saturated fats have straight fatty acids packed tightly together and are solid at room temperature. **(c)** Unsaturated fats have "kinks" wherever there is a double bond. These kinks prevent them from packing tightly together, and they are liquid at room temperature.

saturated fatty acids increase our risk for heart disease. We'll discuss the relationship between saturated fats and heart disease in more detail later in this chapter.

Unsaturated Fats Contain Less Hydrogen

Within a chain of carbon atoms, if two carbons are double-bonded to each other, then hydrogen is excluded at this point in the chain. This lack of hydrogen at *one* part of the molecule results in a **monounsaturated fatty acid (MUFA)** (*mono-* means "one"). See the middle example in Figure 4.2a. If the fatty acid chains have *more than one* double bond, they contain even less hydrogen and are referred to as **polyunsaturated fatty acids (PUFAs);** *poly-* means "many." An example is shown at the bottom of Figure 4.2a.

Both MUFAs and PUFAs are usually liquid at room temperature, because their double carbon bonds produce kinks in their chains. So, like broken toothpicks, they cannot pack together tightly (Figure 4.2c). Foods that are high in MUFAs are olive oil, canola oil, and cashew nuts. Foods that are high in PUFAs include canola, corn, and safflower oils. As we discuss later, both types have important health benefits and should be consumed in moderation every day.

As shown in **Figure 4.3**, foods typically contain a variety of fatty acids. For example, animal fats provide approximately 40% to 60% of their energy from saturated fats but also provide some unsaturated fats. Most plant fats provide 80% to 90% of their energy from monounsaturated and polyunsaturated fats. For this reason, diets higher in plant foods (fruits and vegetables) will usually be lower in saturated fats than diets high in animal products.

monounsaturated fatty acid (MUFA) A fatty acid that has two carbons in the chain bound to each other with one double bond; these types of fatty acids are generally liquid at room temperature.

polyunsaturated fatty acids (PUFAs) Fatty acids that have more than one double bond in the chain; these types of fatty acids are generally liquid at room temperature.

Essential fatty acids

Linoleic acid

Alpha-linolenic acid

🔺 **Figure 4.3** The two essential fatty acids: linoleic acid (omega-6 fatty acid) and alpha-linolenic acid (omega-3 fatty acid).

RECAP Three lipids are found in foods: triglycerides, phospholipids, and sterols. Triglycerides, or fats, are the most common. They are made up of a glycerol backbone attached to three fatty acid chains. Saturated fatty acids are solid at room temperature and are plentiful in butter, lard, whole milk, and beef. A diet high in saturated fats increases the risk for heart disease. Monounsaturated and polyunsaturated fatty acids are liquid at room temperature and are plentiful in vegetable oils, nuts, and many fish. They have important health benefits and should be consumed in moderation daily.

Both Saturated and *Trans* Fats Are Harmful to Health

For several years, food companies from McDonald's to Dunkin' Donuts have been reformulating their recipes to remove *trans* fats from their foods. But what's behind all the fuss? What are *trans* fats, and why are they harmful?

The type of unsaturated fatty acid that occurs most commonly in nature is kinked, as we just described. In contrast, *trans* fats are rigid, just like saturated fats. These fats occur rarely in nature; extremely small amounts are found only in dairy foods, beef, and lamb. In contrast, they are abundant in margarines, commercial frying fats, shortenings, and any processed foods or fast foods made with these products. Health concerns about *trans* fats began to arise with research that linked high-*trans*-fat diets with heart disease and early death.

The trouble began in the late 1800s, when food manufacturers identified the need for a fat that could be produced cheaply and abundantly from vegetable oils, that could be sold in a solid form, and that resisted "going bad" (rancidity). (As you may

🔺 Walnuts and cashews are high in monounsaturated fatty acids.

The FDA has ruled that *trans* fatty acids, or *trans* fat, must be listed as a separate line item on Nutrition Facts Panels for most foods and some dietary supplements. Research shows that diets high in *trans* fatty acids can increase the risk for cardiovascular disease.

know, most fats and oils cannot be stored for long without going rancid.) They developed a process called **hydrogenation,** in which pressurized hydrogen is inserted into the double carbon bonds in the unsaturated fatty acid chains of vegetable oils. Hydrogenation straightens out the chains, making the liquid fat more solid at room temperature—as well as more saturated. In addition, the extra hydrogen helps the fat resist rancidity. Hydrogenated fats are also easier to mold or shape into food products; for example, they make margarines spreadable and help pie crusts keep their shape without crumbling.

Research has shown that *trans* fats are more detrimental to our health than saturated fats because they change the way our cell membranes function and reduce the removal of cholesterol from the blood. For these reasons, the 2010 *Dietary Guidelines for Americans* and the Institute of Medicine recommend keeping consumption of *trans* fats to an absolute minimum.[1,2] In addition, because of concerns related to *trans* fatty acid and heart disease, the U.S. Food and Drug Administration (FDA) now requires food manufacturers to list the amount of *trans* fatty acids per serving on the Nutrition Facts Panel. In response to such pressures, many food manufacturers have begun offering many products that are free of *trans* fatty acids, and they clearly state this claim on the label. However, there's a catch: some products labeled as having "zero" *trans* fats in fact still contain them! That's because the (FDA) allows products that have less than 1 gram of *trans* fat per serving to claim that they are *trans* fat free. So, even if the Nutrition Facts Panel states 0 grams *trans* fat, the product can still have ½ gram of *trans* fat per serving. If you're determined to keep *trans* fats out of your diet, check the ingredients list: if it states that the product contains *partially hydrogenated oils*, that means it contains *trans* fats.

In recent years, legislators and food policy organizations in the United States have been lobbying for the labeling of *trans* fats on restaurant menus, and even for the total elimination of artificial *trans* fats from some restaurant foods. These efforts have already had some success: in 2008, 2 years after New York City's Board of Health began a campaign to phase out *trans* fats in restaurant food, a study reported that 98% of New York eating establishments were no longer using them.[3] But many public health authorities argue that, in order to improve public health, we need to make sure that restaurants don't simply substitute saturated fats. They need to switch to plant oils and similar healthful unsaturated fats to decrease the dining public's risk for heart disease.

Despite the process of hydrogenation, *trans* fats are still less saturated than saturated fats. So margarine is still a better choice than butter, right? The **Nutrition Myth or Fact?** feature box (page 103) explores this question.

Essential Fatty Acids Protect Our Health

Although many people think that all dietary fats should be avoided, we actually must consume certain fats for our survival and optimal functioning. These **essential fatty acids (EFAs)** are incorporated into the many phospholipids in our body (described shortly) and are needed to make a number of important biological compounds called *eicosanoids*. In the body, eicosanoids help regulate some key functions, including gastrointestinal tract motility, blood clotting, the expanding and contracting of our blood vessels to regulate blood pressure, the permeability of our blood vessels to fluid and large molecules, and the regulation of inflammation—just to name a few. Since they play an important role in regulating biological processes, we need a balance of the various eicosanoids and thus a balance of EFAs. For example, we need just the right amount of blood clotting at the right time—too much results in excessive blood clotting, and too little can cause excessive bleeding.

The two EFAs are linoleic acid and alpha-linolenic acid (Figure 4.3). They are called "essential" because they must be consumed in the diet; our body cannot make them.

Linoleic Acid

Linoleic acid is found in vegetable and nut oils, such as sunflower, safflower, corn, soy, and peanut oils. If you eat lots of vegetables or use vegetable oil–based

hydrogenation The process of adding hydrogen to unsaturated fatty acids, making them more saturated and therefore more solid at room temperature.

essential fatty acids (EFAs) Fatty acids that must be consumed in the diet because they cannot be made by our body. The two essential fatty acids are linoleic acid and alpha-linolenic acid.

linoleic acid An essential fatty acid found in vegetable and nut oils; also known as omega-6 fatty acid.

NUTRITION MYTH OR FACT?
Is Margarine More Healthful Than Butter?

Your toast just popped up! Which topping will you use: butter or margarine? Butter is 65% saturated fat: 1 tablespoon provides 30 grams of cholesterol! In contrast, corn oil margarine is just 2% saturated fat, with no cholesterol. But how much *trans* fat does that margarine contain? And which is better—the more natural and more saturated butter or the more processed and less saturated margarine?

You're not the only one asking this question. Until recently, vegetable-based oils were hydrogenated to make margarines. These products were filled with *trans* fats that could increase the risk for heart disease, as well as harm cell membranes, weaken immune function, and inhibit the body's natural anti-inflammatory hormones. Some margarines also contained harmful amounts of toxic metals, such as nickel and aluminum, as by-products of the hydrogenation process. These are among some of the reasons researchers began warning consumers against using margarines years ago.

So does that mean that the saturated-fat, cholesterol-rich butter is the better choice? A decade ago, that may have been true, but, over the last 10 years, food manufacturers have introduced "*trans* fat free margarines and

spreads" that contain no cholesterol or *trans* fats, and low amounts of saturated fats. The American Heart Association advises that consumers choose these *trans* fat free margarines over butter.[4] Other groups point out that such manufactured products are still "non-foods" and recommend choosing unprocessed nut butters (peanut, walnut, cashew, and almond butters) instead. Although they are still about as high in Calories as butter, these alternatives are rich in essential fatty acids and other heart-healthy unsaturated fats.

Remember, a label claiming that a margarine has zero *trans* fat or *trans* fatty acids doesn't guarantee that the product is actually free of them. You'll need to look for margarines with no "partially hydrogenated" oil in them: that's the only way to know that your spread is entirely free of *trans* fatty acids.

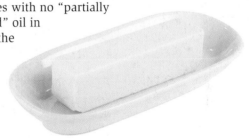

margarines or vegetable oils, you're probably getting adequate amounts of this essential fatty acid in your diet. In the body, linoleic acid is transformed into arachidonic acid, which is in turn used to make compounds that regulate body functions such as blood clotting and blood pressure.

Linoleic acid is often referred to as *omega-6 fatty acid*. In order to understand the reason for this name, you need to know that chemists call the final carbon in a fatty acid chain the *omega carbon* (Omega [Ω] is the last letter in the Greek alphabet). In the fatty acid illustrated in Figure 4.1, the omega end is shown. *Omega-6* refers to the sixth carbon in a fatty acid chain when counting back from the omega carbon. In omega-6 fatty acids, the end-most double carbon bond occurs at this carbon. You can see this in Figure 4.3. The body cannot make fatty acids with double carbon bonds this close to the omega end of the chain, and so linoleic acid is an essential fatty acid.

Alpha-Linolenic Acid

The second essential fatty acid is **alpha-linolenic acid,** an *omega-3 fatty acid*, which was officially recognized as essential in 2005 with the establishment of an RDA.[2] However, research suggesting that alpha-linolenic acid was essential began as early as the 1980s.[5] Its outermost double carbon bond is even further along the chain, at the omega-3 carbon. In addition, its many double carbon bonds make this fatty acid highly kinked and therefore highly fluid. Alpha-linolenic acid is found mainly in leafy green vegetables, flaxseeds and flaxseed oil, soy oil and foods, canola oil, and fatty fish and fish oils.

You may have seen news reports about the health benefits of the omega-3 fatty acids found in many fish. Two of these fatty acids, **eicosapentaenoic acid (EPA)** and **docosahexaenoic acid (DHA),** are found in especially high amounts in cold-water fish, such as wild salmon, sardines, and tuna, where their high degree of unsaturation helps

alpha-linolenic acid An essential fatty acid found in leafy green vegetables, flaxseed oil, soy oil, fish oil, and fish products; an omega-3 fatty acid.

eicosapentaenoic acid (EPA) A type of omega-3 fatty acid that can be made in the body from alpha-linolenic acid and found in our diet primarily in marine plants and animals.

docosahexaenoic acid (DHA) A type of omega-3 fatty acid that can be made in the body from alpha-linolenic acid and found in our diet primarily in marine plants and animals; together with EPA, it appears to reduce our risk for a heart attack.

◀ Salmon is high in omega-3 fatty acid content.

keep the fish cell membranes flexible even in extremely cold temperatures. Research indicates that EPA and DHA protect against heart disease.[6] These fatty acids play a role in improving the function of blood vessels. They also reduce inflammation, blood clotting, blood pressure, irregularities in the heartbeat, and the triglycerides level in blood, all of which are associated with a reduction in heart disease.[7] **Figure 4.4** has an overview of some major food sources of all types of dietary fats.

Getting enough of these essential fatty acids is important for health. Because the omega-6 and omega-3 fatty acids are metabolized by the same enzymes, their ratio has also been an issue of concern. But a large body of research suggests that it is more important to get adequate amounts of these fatty acids in your diet than to attempt to consume some precise balance between the two types.[8] By consuming adequate amounts of these EFAs, you can reduce the negative health impact of saturated and *trans* fatty acids. Dietary recommendations for the EFAs are discussed later in this chapter.

NUTRITION
MILESTONE

In 1935, J. A. Urquhart, a physician working among the Inuit people of the Arctic Circle in Canada, reported that, in 7 years of serving this population, he had encountered no cases of heart disease, diabetes, or cancer. Over the next 50 years, studies from other researchers working among Inuit groups in Canada and Greenland continued to report similar surprising findings: how could the Inuit—whose diets were made up of as much as 75% fat—have such extremely low rates of heart disease? The key, the researchers soon discovered, was in the *type* of fat the Inuit consume. The cold-water fish and sea mammals, such as seal, walrus, and whales, that are staples of the Inuit diet are very low in saturated fats, high in monounsaturated fats, and particularly rich in polyunsaturated omega-3 fatty acids—particularly EPA and DHA.

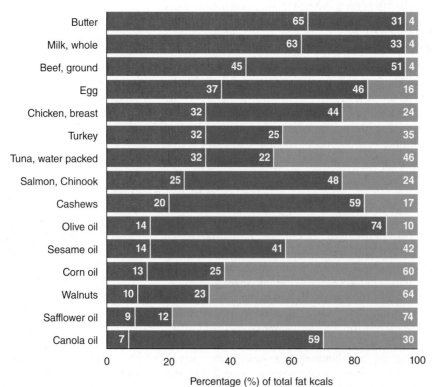

Key:
- Saturated fatty acids
- Monounsaturated fatty acids
- Polyunsaturated fatty acids

◀ **Figure 4.4** Major sources of dietary fat.

RECAP Consuming of high levels of saturated fatty acids and *trans* fatty acids is associated with an increased risk for heart disease. In contrast, essential fatty acids are critical to our health. The body cannot synthesize EFAs, so we must consume them. Research suggests that two omega-3 EFAs—EPA and DHA—protect against heart disease.

Phospholipids Combine Lipids with Phosphate

Along with the triglycerides just discussed, two other types of fats—phospholipids and sterols—are present in the foods we eat. **Phospholipids** consist of a glycerol back-bone bound to two fatty acids. In place of the third fatty acid found in triglycerides, phospholipids have a compound that contains *phosphate,* a chemical that is soluble (dissolves) in water **(Figure 4.5)**. This substitution of a phosphate compound makes phospholipids soluble in water, a property that enables them to assist in transporting fats in our bloodstream (blood is about 50% water). Also, as shown in Figure 4.5, phospholipids are an important component of the outer membrane of every cell in the body and thus help regulate the transport of substances into and out of our cells.

Phospholipids are present in peanuts, egg yolk, and some processed foods with dispersed fats, such as salad dressings. However, because our body manufactures them, they are not essential for us to include in our diet.

Sterols Have a Ring Structure

Sterols are also a type of lipid found both in foods and in the body, but their multiple-ring structure is different from that of triglycerides or phospholipids **(Figure 4.6a**, page 106). Sterols are found in both plant and animal foods and are also produced in the body.

Cholesterol is the most commonly occurring sterol in our diet (Figure 4.6b). Cholesterol is found only in the fatty part of animal products, such as butter, egg yolks, whole milk, meats, and poultry. Egg whites, skim milk, and lean meats have little or no cholesterol. Dietary cholesterol (cholesterol that comes from foods) has a bad reputation because it is found mainly in foods high in saturated fatty acids, which can increase our blood cholesterol levels. As you will read later in this chapter, elevated blood cholesterol levels suggest an increased risk for cardiovascular disease.

We don't need to consume cholesterol in our diet because our body continually produces it, mostly in the liver and intestines. This continuous production (or *synthesis*) is vital because cholesterol is part of every cell membrane, where it works with fatty acids to help

> Concerned about the saturated fat and cholesterol in the meat you eat? Use this guide to choosing the leanest cuts of beef at www .mayoclinic.com/health/cuts-of-beef/MY01387.

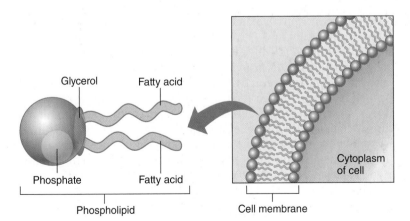

Figure 4.5 Structure of a phospholipid. Phospholipids consist of a glycerol backbone attached to two fatty acids and a compound that contains phosphate. They are an important component of our cell membranes and are found in certain foods, such as peanuts, egg yolks, and some processed foods that contain dispersed fats.

phospholipid A type of lipid in which a fatty acid is combined with another compound that contains phosphate; unlike other lipids, phospholipids are soluble in water.

sterol A type of lipid found in foods and the body that has a ring structure; cholesterol is the most common sterol that occurs in our diet.

Figure 4.6 Sterol structure.
(a) Cholesterol and other sterols are lipids that contain multiple ring structures. **(b)** Cholesterol is the most commonly occurring sterol in the diet. It is found in meats, fish, egg yolks, and dairy products.

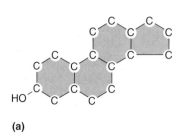

(a)

(b)

maintain cell membrane integrity. Cholesterol is particularly plentiful in the neural cells that make up the brain, spinal cord, and nerves. The body also uses cholesterol to synthesize several important sterol compounds, including sex hormones (estrogen, androgen, and progesterone), adrenal hormones, bile, and vitamin D. Thus, despite cholesterol's bad reputation, it is absolutely essential to human health.

RECAP Phospholipids combine two fatty acids and a glycerol backbone with a phosphate-containing compound that makes them soluble in water. They help transport fats in our bloodstream and are found in the cell membrane. Sterols have a multiple-ring structure; cholesterol is the most commonly occurring sterol in our diet.

Dietary fat provides energy.

Why Do We Need to Eat Fats?

Dietary fat provides energy and helps our body perform some essential internal functions.

Fats Provide Energy

Dietary fat is a primary source of energy. Fat provides 9 kcal per gram, while carbohydrate and protein provide only 4 kcal per gram. This means that fat is much more energy-dense. For example, just 1 tablespoon of butter or oil contains about 100 kcal, whereas it takes 2.5 cups of steamed broccoli or 1 slice of whole-wheat bread to provide 100 kcal.

When we are at rest, approximately 30% to 70% of the energy used by our muscles and organs comes from fat.[9] The exact amount of fat you burn when you are at rest depends on how much fat you eat in your diet, how physically active you are, and whether you are gaining or losing weight.

Fat is also a major energy source during physical activity. In fact, one of the best ways of losing body fat is through regular aerobic exercise. During exercise, the body begins to break down fat stores to fuel the working muscles. The amount and source of the fat used depend on your level of fitness; the type, intensity, and duration of the exercise; and what and how much you've eaten before you exercise. Because the body has only a limited supply of stored carbohydrate (as glycogen) in muscle tissue, the longer you exercise, the more fat you use for energy.

Fats Store Energy for Later Use

The longer you exercise, the more fat you use for energy. For example, cyclists in long-distance races use stores of fat for energy.

Our bodies store extra energy as fat in our *adipose tissue,* which then can be used for energy at rest, during exercise, or during periods of low energy intake. Adipose tissue provides the body with an energy source even when we choose not to eat (or are unable to eat), when we are exercising, and while we are sleeping. Our body has relatively little stored carbohydrate—only enough to last about 1 to 2 days—and there is no place that our body can store extra protein. We cannot consider our muscles and organs as a place where "extra" protein is stored! For these reasons, although we don't want too much stored adipose tissue, some is essential to keep the body going.

Fats Enable the Transport of Fat-Soluble Vitamins

Dietary fat enables the transport of the fat-soluble vitamins. These are vitamins A, D, E, and K. Vitamin A is important for vision, vitamin D helps maintain bone health, vitamin E prevents and repairs damage to cells, and vitamin K is important for blood clotting and bone health. Without an appropriate intake of dietary fat, our body can become deficient in these important vitamins.

◄ Adipose tissue pads our body and protects our organs when we fall or are bruised.

Fats Help Maintain Cell Function and Provide Protection to the Body

Fats are a critical part of every cell membrane. There, they help determine what substances are transported into and out of the cell and regulate what substances can bind to the cell; thus, fats strongly influence the function of the cell. In addition, fats help maintain cell fluidity and other physical properties of the cell membrane. Fats enable our red blood cells, for example, to be flexible enough to bend and move through the smallest capillaries in our body, delivering oxygen to all our cells.

Stored body fat pads the body and protects our organs, such as the kidneys and liver, when we fall or are bruised. The fat under our skin acts as insulation to help us retain body heat. Although we often think of all body fat as "bad," it does play an important role in keeping our body healthy and functioning properly.

Fats Contribute to the Flavor and Texture of Foods

Dietary fat adds texture and flavor to foods. Fat makes salad dressings smooth and ice cream "creamy," and it gives cakes and cookies their moist, tender texture. Frying foods in fat, as with doughnuts or french fries, gives them a crisp, flavorful coating. On the other hand, foods containing fats, such as cookies, crackers, chips, and breads, become rancid quickly if they are not stored properly. Manufacturers add preservatives to increase the shelf life of foods with fats.

◄ Fat adds texture and flavor to foods.

Fats Help Us Feel Satiated

Fats in foods help us feel *satiated*—satisfied—after a meal. Two factors probably contribute to this effect: first, as noted earlier, fat has a much higher energy density than carbohydrate or protein. An amount of butter weighing the same number of grams as a medium apple would contain 840 kcal! Second, fat takes longer to digest than protein or carbohydrate because more steps are involved in the digestion process. This may help you feel satisfied for a longer period of time because energy is slowly being released into your body.

RECAP Dietary fats provide twice the energy of protein and carbohydrate, at 9 kcal per gram, and the majority of energy required while we are at rest. Fats are also a major fuel source during exercise. Dietary fats help transport the fat-soluble vitamins into the body and help regulate cell function and maintain membrane integrity. Stored body fat in the adipose tissue helps protect vital organs and pad the body. Fats contribute to the flavor and texture of foods and the satiety we feel after a meal.

What Happens to the Fats We Eat?

Because fats are not soluble in water, they cannot enter the bloodstream easily from the digestive tract. Thus, fats must be digested, absorbed, and transported within the body differently than are carbohydrates and proteins, which are water soluble. Let's review the process here (Figure 4.7).

The Mouth and Stomach Have Limited Roles in Fat Digestion

Dietary fats usually come mixed with other foods in our diet, which we chew and then swallow. Water, mucus, and a salivary enzyme called lingual lipase mix with the fats in the mouth, but this enzyme has a limited role in the breakdown of fats until they reach the stomach (Figure 4.7, step 1). Once in the stomach, lingual lipase and gastric lipase, which is secreted by the stomach, can digest about 10% of fats present. But the primary role of the stomach in fat digestion is to mix and break up the fat into droplets (Figure 4.7, step 2). Because they are not soluble in water, these fat droplets typically float on top of the watery digestive juices in the stomach until they are passed into the small intestine.

Fats and oils do not dissolve readily in water.

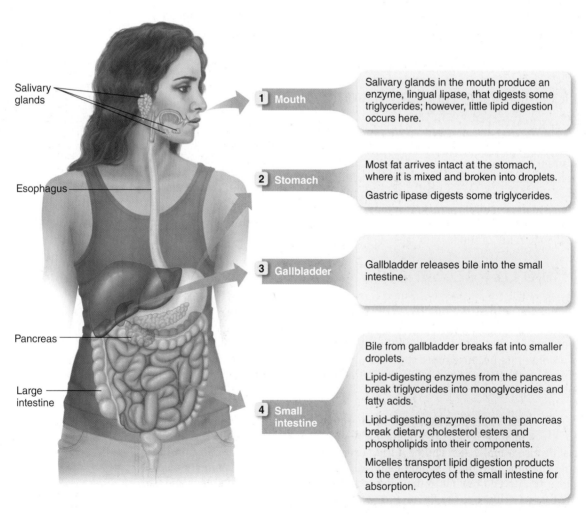

Salivary glands

Esophagus

Pancreas

Large intestine

1 **Mouth**
Salivary glands in the mouth produce an enzyme, lingual lipase, that digests some triglycerides; however, little lipid digestion occurs here.

2 **Stomach**
Most fat arrives intact at the stomach, where it is mixed and broken into droplets.
Gastric lipase digests some triglycerides.

3 **Gallbladder**
Gallbladder releases bile into the small intestine.

4 **Small intestine**
Bile from gallbladder breaks fat into smaller droplets.
Lipid-digesting enzymes from the pancreas break triglycerides into monoglycerides and fatty acids.
Lipid-digesting enzymes from the pancreas break dietary cholesterol esters and phospholipids into their components.
Micelles transport lipid digestion products to the enterocytes of the small intestine for absorption.

Figure 4.7 The process of fat digestion.

The Gallbladder, Liver, and Pancreas Assist in Fat Breakdown

Because fat is not soluble in water, its digestion requires the help of mixing compounds from the gallbladder and digestive enzymes from the pancreas. Recall that the gallbladder is a sac attached to the underside of the liver, and the pancreas is an oblong-shaped organ sitting below the stomach. Both have a duct connecting them to the small intestine.

As fat enters the small intestine from the stomach, the gallbladder contracts and releases a substance called *bile* (Figure 4.7, step 3). Bile is produced in the liver from cholesterol and is stored in the gallbladder until needed. Bile contains salts that are detergents and, much like soap, break up the fat into smaller and smaller droplets. At the same time, lipid-digesting enzymes produced in the pancreas travel through the pancreatic duct into the small intestine. Once bile has broken the fat into small droplets, these pancreatic enzymes take over, breaking up the triglycerides by removing some of the fatty acids from the glycerol backbone. Each triglyceride molecule is eventually broken down into two free fatty acids and one *monoglyceride,* which is the glycerol backbone with one fatty acid still attached.

Most Fat Is Absorbed in the Small Intestine

The free fatty acids and monoglycerides next need to be transported to the cells that line the small intestine (Figure 4.7, step 4), so that they can be absorbed into the body. This trip requires the help of *micelles,* globules of bile and phospholipids that trap the free fatty acids and monoglycerides and transport them to the intestinal cells. Once there, shorter fatty acids can pass directly across the intestinal cell membrane. Longer fatty acids first bind to a special carrier protein and then are absorbed into the cells.

After absorption into the intestinal cells, the shortest fatty acids cross unassisted into the bloodstream and are then transported to the liver. In contrast, the longer fatty acids and monoglycerides are reformulated back into triglycerides. As you know, triglyceride molecules don't mix with water, so they can't cross independently into the bloodstream. Once again, their movement requires special packaging, this time in the form of lipoproteins. A **lipoprotein** is a spherical (round-shaped) compound in which triglycerides cluster deep in the center and phospholipids and proteins, which are water soluble, form the surface of the sphere **(Figure 4.8)**. The specific lipoprotein that transports fat from a meal is called a **chylomicron.** Once chylomicrons are formed, they are transported from the intestinal cells into the lymphatic system, and from there, released into the bloodstream.

Now that you know how fats are absorbed into the body, you may be wondering if there's any way to block the process so you could enjoy french fries and ice cream without getting the Calories. Manufacturers of weight-loss supplements called "fat-blockers" claim their products do precisely this, and current research provides some evidence to back up their claim. The main ingredient in one group of fat-blockers is *chitosan,* a nondigestible substance from marine crustaceans that is said to bind fat.[10] Research has shown that consumption of chitosan can produce modest weight loss: an average of 1.7–3.7 pounds over 8–9 weeks.[11,12,13]

Another fat-blocker, an over-the-counter medication called Alli®, doesn't bind fat but, instead, works to block the enzymes that break it down. Research shows that, like chitosan, Alli® can produce modest weight loss, although only when combined with a low-fat diet.[14] A common side effect of fat blockers is gastrointestinal distress. If you're trying to lose weight, consult your healthcare provider to learn about the options that make the most sense for you.

Fat Is Stored for Later Use

The chylomicrons, which are filled with dietary fat, are transported to the liver, which can release them into the circulating blood where the fatty acids in the

Chitosan, which comes from marine crustaceans, such as these shrimp, is the main ingredient in one group of fat-blockers.

lipoprotein A spherical (round-shaped) compound in which fat clusters in the center and phospholipids and proteins form the outside of the sphere.

chylomicron A lipoprotein produced in the mucosal cell of the intestine; transports dietary fat out of the intestinal tract.

Figure 4.8 Structure of a lipo-protein. Notice that the fat clusters in the center of the molecule and the phospholipids and proteins, which are water soluble, form the outside of the sphere. This enables lipoproteins to transport fats in the bloodstream.

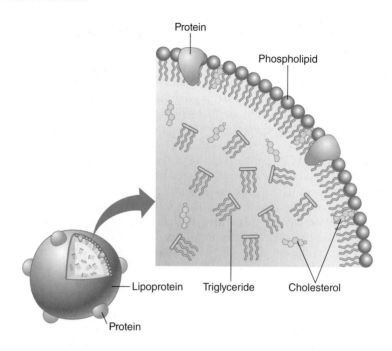

chylomicrons can be taken up by cells. There are three primary fates of this dietary fat:

- If your body needs the fat for energy, it will be quickly transported into your cells and used as fuel.
- The liver can use the fat to make lipid-containing compounds, such as certain hormones and bile.
- Or, the fat can be taken up by the muscle or adipose tissue, where it is repackaged as triglyceride and stored for later use.

If you are physically active, your body will preferentially store this extra fat in the muscle tissue first, so that the next time you go out for a run, the fat is readily available for energy. That's why people who engage in regular physical activity are more likely to have extra fat stored in their muscle tissue and to have less adipose tissue—something many of us would prefer. Of course, fat stored in the adipose tissue can also be used for energy during exercise, but it must be broken down first and then transported to the muscle cells.

RECAP Fat digestion begins when fats are broken into droplets by bile. Pancreatic enzymes then digest the triglycerides into two free fatty acids and one monoglyceride. These are transported into the cells that line the small intestine with the help of micelles. Once inside, triglycerides are reformed and packaged into lipoproteins called chylomicrons. Dietary fat is transported by the chylomicrons to cells within the body that need energy. Fat stored in the muscle tissue is used as a source of energy during physical activity. Excess fat is stored in the adipose tissue and can be used whenever the body needs energy.

How Much Fat Should We Eat?

Without a doubt, Americans agree that dietary fat is bad! Yet, because fat plays such an important role in keeping our body healthy, our diet should include a moderate amount of energy from fat. But what, exactly, is a moderate amount? And what foods contain healthful fats? We'll explore these questions here.

Dietary Reference Intake for Total Fat

The Acceptable Macronutrient Distribution Range (AMDR) for fat is 20% to 35% of total energy intake.[2] For a diet of 2,000 kcal per day, this amounts to 400 to 700 kcal, or approximately 45 to 77 grams of fat. For reference, a tablespoon of butter is 11 grams of fat and about 100 kcal. Within this range of fat intake, it is also recommended that we reduce our intake of saturated and *trans* fatty acids; these changes will lower our risk for heart disease.

Athletes and other physically active people typically need to eat a lower percentage of fat than sedentary people because their carbohydrate and protein needs are higher. It's recommended that athletes consume 20% to 30% of their total energy from fat, 55% to 60% of energy from carbohydrate, and 12% to 15% of energy from protein.[15,16] This level of fat intake represents about 45 to 55 grams per day of fat for an athlete consuming 2,000 kcal per day, and 78 to 97 grams per day of fat for an athlete consuming 3,500 kcal per day.

Although many people trying to lose weight greatly restrict their consumption of fat, this practice may do more harm than good, especially if they are also eating fewer than 1,500 kcal per day. Research suggests that very-low-fat diets (those with less than 15% of energy from fat) do not provide additional health or performance benefits over moderate-fat diets, and are often very difficult to follow.[17] In fact, most people find that they feel better, are more successful in maintaining weight, and are less preoccupied with food if they keep their fat intakes at 20% to 25% of their total energy intake.

Additionally, people trying to reduce their dietary fat often eliminate entire food groups such as meat, dairy, eggs, and nuts. In doing so, they also eliminate important potential sources of protein and many essential vitamins and minerals needed for maintaining good health and an active lifestyle. Diets very low in fat may also be deficient in essential fatty acids.

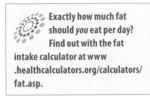

Exactly how much fat should *you* eat per day? Find out with the fat intake calculator at www .healthcalculators.org/calculators/ fat.asp.

Dietary Reference Intakes for Essential Fatty Acids

Dietary Reference Intakes (DRIs) for the two essential fatty acids were set in 2005.[2] The adequate intakes are as follows:

- Linoleic acid: 14 to 17 grams per day for adult men and 11 to 12 grams per day for women 19 years and older. Using the typical energy intakes for adult men and women, this translates into an AMDR of 5% to 10% of total energy.
- Alpha-linolenic acid: 1.6 grams per day for adult men and 1.1 grams per day for adult women. This translates into an AMDR of 0.6% to 1.2% of total energy.

For example, a person consuming 2,000 kcal per day should consume about 11 to 22 grams per day of linoleic acid and about 1.3 to 2.6 grams per day of alpha-linolenic acid.

Although the body converts some alpha-linolenic acid to DHA and EPA, the extent of this conversion is limited. Thus, some public health authorities, such as the World Health Organization, are now making formal recommendations for DHA and EPA specifically. These recommendations typically range from 0.3 to 0.5 grams per day of EPA/DHA, as well as 0.8 to 1.1 grams per day of alpha-linolenic acid.[6]

Most Americans Eat Too Much Saturated and *Trans* Fat

Of the dietary fat we eat, saturated and *trans* fats are the most associated with an increased risk for heart disease. Thus, the recommended intake of saturated fat is less

In the United States, we eat too many saturated and *trans* fats.

than 7–10% of total energy. Unfortunately, Americans' average intake of saturated fats is between 11% and 12% of energy.[18]

The 2010 *Dietary Guidelines for Americans* and the Institute of Medicine recommend that we keep our intake of *trans* fatty acids to an absolute minimum.[1] Determining the actual amount of *trans* fatty acids consumed in America has been hindered by the lack of an accurate and comprehensive database of foods containing *trans* fatty acids. At present, a best guess comes from a recent national survey, which estimated our average intake at 2–3% of our total fat intake.[19,20]

RECAP The Acceptable Macronutrient Distribution Range (AMDR) for total fat is 20% to 35% of total energy. The adequate intake (AI) for linoleic acid is 14 to 17 grams per day for adult men and 11 to 12 grams per day for adult women. The AI for alpha-linolenic acid is 1.6 grams per day for adult men and 1.1 grams per day for adult women. Because saturated and *trans* fatty acids can increase the risk for heart disease, health professionals recommend that we reduce our intake of saturated fat to less than 7–10% of our total energy intake and reduce our intake of *trans* fatty acids to the absolute minimum.

Shopper's Guide: Choosing Foods with Healthful Fats

The last time you popped a frozen dinner into the microwave, did you stop and read the Nutrition Facts Panel on the box? If you had, you might have been shocked to learn how much saturated fat was in the meal. As we discuss here, many processed foods are hidden sources of fat, especially saturated and *trans* fats. In contrast, many whole foods, such as oils, fish, and nuts, are rich sources of the healthful unsaturated fats our body needs.

Visible Versus Invisible Fats

At breakfast this morning, did you add cream to your coffee? Spread butter on your toast? These added fats, such as oils, butter, margarine, cream, shortening, mayonnaise, or salad dressings, are called **visible fats** because we can easily see that we are adding them to our food.

When we add fat to foods ourselves, we know how much we are adding and what kind. When fat is added in the preparation of a frozen dinner or a fast-food burger and fries, we are less aware or unaware of how much or what type of fat is actually there. In fact, unless we read food labels carefully, we might not know that a food contains any fat at all. We call fats in prepared and processed foods **invisible fats** because they are effectively hidden within the food. In fact, their invisibility often tricks us into choosing them over more healthful foods. For example, a slice of yellow cake is much higher in fat (40% of total energy) than a slice of angel food cake (1% of total energy). Yet many people would assume the fat content of these foods is the same, because both are cake. For most of us, the majority of the fat in our diet comes from invisible fat. Foods that can be high in invisible fats are baked goods, regular-fat dairy products, processed meats or meats that are not trimmed, and most convenience and fast foods, such as hamburgers, hot dogs, chips, ice cream, french fries, and other fried foods.

Because high-fat diets have been associated with obesity and heart disease, many Americans have tried to reduce their total fat intake, and food manufacturers are more than happy to provide consumers with low-fat alternatives to their favorite foods. However, these lower-fat foods may not necessarily have fewer

visible fats Fats that we can see in our foods or see added to foods, such as butter, margarine, cream, shortening, salad dressings, chicken skin, and untrimmed fat on meat.

invisible fats Fats that are hidden in foods, such as those found in baked goods, regular-fat dairy products, marbling in meat, and fried foods.

HIGHLIGHT
Low-Fat, Reduced-Fat, Nonfat . . . What's the Difference?

Although most of us enjoy high-fat foods, we also know that eating a lot of fat isn't good for our health or our waistline. Because of this concern, food manufacturers have produced a host of modified fat foods—so you can have your cake and eat it, too! In fact, it's now estimated that there are more than 5,000 different fat-modified foods on the market.[21] This means that there are many similar types of foods that come in a wide range of fat contents. For example, you can purchase full-fat, low-fat, or fat-free milk, ice cream, sour cream, cheese, and yogurt.

Table 4.1 lists a number of full-fat foods with their lower-fat alternatives. If you incorporate these products into your diet on a regular basis, you can significantly reduce the amount of fat you consume, but watch out! You might not be reducing the number of Calories you consume.

For example, drinking nonfat milk (86 Calories and 0.5 grams of fat per serving) instead of whole milk (150 Calories and 8.2 grams of fat per serving) will significantly reduce both fat and energy (Calorie) intake. However, eating fat-free Fig Newton cookies (3 cookies have 204 Calories and 0 grams of fat) instead of regular Fig Newtons (3 cookies have 210 Calories and 4.5 grams of fat) will not significantly reduce your energy intake, even though it will reduce your fat intake.

The Food and Drug Administration and the U.S. Department of Agriculture have set specific regulations on allowable product descriptions for reduced-fat products. The following claims are defined for 1 serving: *Fat-free*: less than 0.5 grams of fat; *low-fat*: 3 grams or less of fat; *reduced or less fat*: at least 25% less fat as compared to a standard serving; *light*: one-third fewer Calories or 50% less fat as compared with a standard serving size.

TABLE 4.1 Comparison of Full-Fat, Reduced-Fat, and Low-Fat Foods

Product and Serving Size	Version	Energy (kcal)	Protein (g)	Carbohydrate (g)	Fat (g)
Milk, 8 oz	Whole, 3.3% fat	150	8.0	11.4	8.2
	2% fat	121	8.1	11.7	4.7
	Skim (nonfat)	86	8.4	11.9	0.5
Mayonnaise, 1 tbsp.	Regular	100	0.0	0.0	11.0
	Light	50	0.0	1.0	5.0
Margarine, corn oil, 1 tbsp.	Regular	100	0.0	0.0	11.0
	Reduced-fat	60	0.0	0.0	7.0
Peanut butter, 1 tbsp.	Regular	95	4.1	3.1	8.2
	Reduced-fat	81	4.4	5.2	5.4
Wheat Thins, 18 crackers	Regular	158	2.3	21.4	6.8
	Reduced-fat	120	2.0	21.0	4.0
Cookies, Oreo, 3 cookies	Regular	160	2.0	23.0	7.0
	Reduced-fat	130	2.0	25.0	3.5
Cookies, Fig Newton, 3 cookies	Regular	210	3.0	30.0	4.5
	Fat-free	204	2.4	26.8	0.0

Data from Food Processor-SQL, Version 9.9, ESHA Research, Salem, OR.

Calories. Review the *Highlight* box (shown above) to learn how to be a better consumer of reduced-fat foods.

Food Sources of Beneficial Fats

In addition to limiting your total fat consumption to no more than 35% of your diet, it's essential to choose healthful forms of fat. Substituting unsaturated fats for saturated or *trans* fats isn't difficult. The *Eating Right All Day* feature highlights some simple menu choices to get you started. See also **Table 4.2** (page 115) which identifies the omega-3 fatty content of various foods. In addition, the following are some general guidelines for finding healthful fats:

Baked goods are often high in invisible fats.

Eating Right All Day

Breakfast
Non-fat yogurt with walnuts instead of bacon and eggs!

Lunch
Veggie pita instead of a ham and cheese sandwich!

Dinner
Grilled salmon instead of steak!

Snack
Whole-grain crackers with peanut butter instead of potato chips!

Eat More Fish   Americans appear to get adequate amounts of omega-6 fatty acids, probably because of the high amount of salad dressings, vegetable and nut oils, margarine, and mayonnaise we eat. In contrast, our consumption of omega-3 fatty acids—and especially EPA/DHA—varies, and can be low in the diets of people who do not eat fish. That's because seafood is one of the most reliable dietary sources of these fatty acids (Table 4.1). So to increase your consumption of EPA/DHA, choose fish or shellfish at least twice a week. At the deli, grab a tuna sandwich instead of roast beef. Out for Mexican food? Order fish tacos. Asian food? Try a stir-fry with prawns. Burgers? A haddock or salmon burger makes a nice change from beef.

You may be aware of warnings associated with eating large amounts of certain types of fish on a regular basis. These include sport-caught fish and predator fish such as shark, swordfish, and king mackerel, which can contain high levels of environmental contaminants, such as mercury and polychlorinated biphenyls (PCBs). Women who are pregnant or breast-feeding, women who may become pregnant, and small children are at particularly high risk for toxicity from these contaminants. Fortunately, many types of fish that provide EPA/DHA are considered safe to consume. These include salmon (except from the Great Lakes region), farmed trout, flounder, sole, mahi mahi, and cooked shellfish.

Choose Plants   Of course, healthful fats include not only the essential fatty acids but also polyunsaturated and monounsaturated fats in general. An easy way to shift your diet toward these healthful fats—without increasing your total fat intake—is to replace animal-based foods with versions derived from plants. For example, drink soy milk or almond milk instead of cow's milk. Order your Chinese take-out with tofu instead of beef. Plant oils are excellent sources of unsaturated fats, so cook with olive, canola, soybean, or walnut oil instead of butter. Use thin slices of avocado in a sandwich in place of cheese, or serve tortilla chips with just guacamole instead of nacho-cheese.

Nuts and seeds provide another way to increase the healthful fats in your diet. They are rich in unsaturated fats and provide protein, minerals, vitamins, and fiber. Yet they are also high in energy: a 1 oz serving of nuts (about 4 tablespoons) contains 160–180 kcal. So eat them in moderation—for instance, by sprinkling a few on your salad, yogrt, or breakfast cereal. Spread a nut butter on your morning toast (try something new, like almond butter), or pack a PB&J instead of a meat sandwich for lunch. Or add some pumpkin or sunflower seeds to raisins and pretzel sticks for a quick trail mix.

TABLE 4.2 Omega-3 Fatty Acid Content of Selected Foods			
	Total Omega-3	DHA*	EPA†
Food Item	g/serving		
Flaxseed oil, 1 tbsp.	7.25	0.00	0.00
Salmon oil (fish oil), 1 tbsp.	4.39	2.48	1.77
Sardine oil, 1 tbsp.	3.01	1.45	1.38
Flaxseed, whole, 1 tbsp.	2.50	0.00	0.00
Herring, Atlantic, broiled, 3 oz	1.83	0.94	0.77
Salmon, Coho, steamed, 3 oz	1.34	0.71	0.46
Canola oil, 1 tbsp.	1.28	0.00	0.00
Sardines, Atlantic, w/bones & oil, 3 oz	1.26	0.43	0.40
Trout, rainbow fillet, baked, 3 oz	1.05	0.70	0.28
Walnuts, English, 1 tbsp.	0.66	0.00	0.00
Halibut, fillet, baked, 3 oz	0.53	0.31	0.21
Shrimp, canned, 3 oz	0.47	0.21	0.25
Tuna, white, in oil, 3 oz	0.38	0.19	0.04
Crab, Alaska King, steamed, 3 oz	0.36	0.10	0.25
Scallops, broiled, 3 oz	0.31	0.14	0.17
Smart Balance Omega-3 Buttery Spread (1 tbsp.)	0.32	0.01	0.01
Tuna, light, in water, 3 oz	0.23	0.19	0.04
Avocado, Calif., fresh, whole	0.22	0.00	0.00
Spinach, ckd, 1 cup	0.17	0.00	0.00
Egglands Best, 1 large egg, with omega-3	0.12	0.06	0.03

*DHA = docosahexaenoic acid.
†EPA = eicosapentaenoic acid.
Data from Food Processor SQL, Version 10.3, ESHA Research, Salem, OR and manufacturer labels.

Opt for Low-Fat   When you are consuming animal-based foods, choose those lower in fat. Select lean meats, poultry, and fish. When preparing these foods at home or ordering them at a restaurant, make sure they're broiled or grilled rather than fried. Select low-fat or nonfat milk and yogurt, and reduce your intake of full-fat cheeses and cheese spreads. When shopping, look for lower-fat versions of all processed foods you buy. Read the *Nutrition Label Activity* feature box (page 116) to learn how to compare the fat content of packaged foods.

Fat Replacers

One way manufacturers lower the fat content of foods such as chips, muffins, cakes, and cookies is by using a *fat replacer*. Since their introduction into the market in the 1990s, fat replacers have mainly been used in snack foods, since it's difficult to simply remove the fat from such products without dramatically changing their taste.

Some fat replacers, such as olestra (brand name Olean), may cause gastrointestinal distress in some people with GI tract sensitivities or if used in large quantities. For that reason, foods containing olestra initially had to include a label warning of potential gastrointestinal side effects. In 2003, the FDA announced that the warning was no longer necessary, as research indicates that olestra causes only mild, infrequent discomfort.

Fat replacers may be helpful in reducing overall fat intake, but they have not helped reduce caloric intake or overall obesity rates.[22] These products, however, may be useful tools for weight loss if they're combined with a well-balanced energy-restricted diet.

Snack foods are the primary target for fat replacers, such as Olean, because it's more difficult to eliminate fat from these types of foods without dramatically changing the taste.

NUTRITION LABEL ACTIVITY

Which Food Has More Fat?

How do you know if a food you're buying is high in fat? One simple way to determine the amount of fat in foods is to read the Nutrition Facts Panel on the label. By becoming a better label reader, you can make more healthful food selections.

Two cracker labels are shown in **Figure 4.9**: one cracker is labeled as "reduced-fat," while the other is not. Because the serving size for these crackers is the same, you can tell which has more fat by comparing the total Calories from fat in each serving.

Look at the first two lines under **Amount Per Serving** and enter the following data:

1. **For the regular wheat crackers, the total Calories per serving = _____.**
2. **The Calories from fat = _____.**
3. **In the regular wheat crackers, about what fraction of total Calories comes from fat? Circle one of the following answers: one-quarter; one-third; one-half.**

4. **For the reduced-fat wheat crackers, the total Calories per serving = _____.**
5. **The Calories from fat = _____.**
6. **In the reduced-fat wheat crackers, about what fraction of total Calories comes from fat? Circle one of the following answers: one-quarter; one-third; one-half.**

(Answers can be found on the Companion Website at www.pearsonhighered.com/thompsonmanore.)

Your answers should indicate that, while the total number of Calories per serving is not very different between the two crackers, the level of fat is quite different.

Occasionally, the Calories from fat per serving are not provided on a food label. In such cases, you can compare products by looking at the *grams* of fat per serving. Here, the regular wheat crackers have 6 grams of fat per serving, whereas the reduced-fat wheat crackers have only 4 grams of fat per serving.

(a)

(b)

⬥ **Figure 4.9** Labels for two types of wheat crackers. **(a)** Regular wheat crackers. **(b)** Reduced-fat wheat crackers.

FOODS YOU DON'T KNOW YOU LOVE YET

Flaxseeds

Flax is a flowering plant grown in many parts of the world for centuries. Its fibers are used in making fabrics, paper, and other products, while its seeds are crushed for their oil. Flaxseed oil provides both omega-6 and omega-3 fatty acids. It is available in many markets today, and it can be consumed directly by teaspoon; mixed into yogurt, puddings, or applesauce; or taken as a capsule. Flaxseeds themselves are largely undigestible, but when ground they provide EFAs as well as fiber and phytochemicals called *lignans*. Ground flaxseeds, like their oil, can be mixed into yogurt and other creamy foods. You can also sprinkle them on breakfast cereal or mix them into the batter of pancakes, breads, and other baked goods for an added nutritional boost.

RECAP Visible fats can be easily recognized, such as fat on meats. Invisible fats are those fats added to food during the manufacturing or cooking process. Common food sources of omega-6 fatty acids include vegetables and vegetable oils, nuts and nut oils, salad dressings, margarine, and mayonnaise. Food sources of omega-3 fatty acids include fish, walnuts, soy milk, and soybean, canola, or flaxseed oil. However, certain fish and shellfish are the best sources of EPA/DHA specifically. Fat replacers are substances used to replace the typical fats found in foods to reduce the amount of fat in the food.

HEALTHWATCH

What Role Do Fats Play in Chronic Disease?

We know that a diet high in saturated and *trans* fatty acids can contribute to chronic diseases, including cardiovascular disease and cancer. But just how significant a factor is diet, and what other factors also play a role?

What Is Cardiovascular Disease?

Cardiovascular disease is a general term used to describe any abnormal condition involving dysfunction of the heart (*cardio* means "heart") and blood vessels. There are many forms of the disease, but the three most common forms are listed here:

- **Coronary heart disease** occurs when blood vessels supplying the heart (the *coronary arteries*) become blocked or constricted; such blockage reduces the flow of blood—and the oxygen and nutrients it carries—to the heart. This can result in chest pain and lead to a heart attack.
- **Stroke** is caused by blockage or rupture of one of the blood vessels supplying the brain (the *cerebral arteries*). When this occurs, the region of the brain depending on that artery for oxygen and nutrients cannot function. As a result, the movement, speech, or other body functions controlled by that part of the brain suddenly stop.

cardiovascular disease A general term referring to abnormal conditions (dysfunction) of the heart and blood vessels; cardiovascular disease can result in heart attack or stroke.

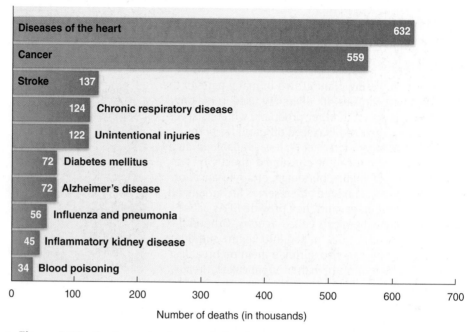

Figure 4.10 Cardiovascular disease, which includes heart disease, is the leading cause of death in the United States.

Data from National Center for Health Statistics. 2009. Heron et al. Final data for 2006. www.cdc.gov/nchs/data/nvse57/nvse57_14.pdf.

- **Hypertension,** also called *high blood pressure*, is a condition that may not cause any immediate symptoms but increases your risk for a heart attack or stroke. If your blood pressure is high, it means the force of the blood flowing through your arteries is above normal.

According to the Centers for Disease Control and Prevention, cardiovascular disease (in its various forms) is the leading cause of death in the United States across racial and ethnic groups, and is a major cause of permanent disability **(Figure 4.10).**[23]

> Use this online risk assessment tool to estimate your 10-year risk of having a heart attack: http://hp2010.nhlbihin.net/atpiii/calculator.asp?usertype=pub.

Dietary Fats Play an Important Role in Cardiovascular Disease

Recall that lipids are transported in the blood by lipoproteins made up of a lipid center and a protein outer coat. Because lipoproteins are soluble in blood, they are commonly called *blood lipids*. In addition to the chylomicrons discussed earlier in this chapter, three lipoproteins are important to consider in any discussion of cardiovascular health and disease:

- very-low-density lipoproteins (VLDLs)
- low-density lipoproteins (LDLs)
- high-density lipoproteins (HDLs)

The density of a lipoprotein refers to its *ratio* of lipid (less dense) to protein (very dense). Thus, a VLDL contains mostly lipid and little protein. The chemical composition of various lipoproteins is compared in **Figure 4.11.** Our blood contains a mixture of these blood lipids according to our diet, our fitness level, and whether we have been eating or fasting. Let's look at each of these blood lipids in more detail to determine how they are linked to heart disease risk.

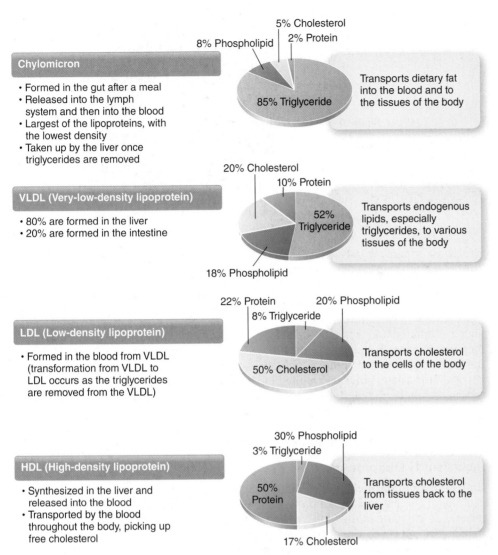

Chylomicron
- Formed in the gut after a meal
- Released into the lymph system and then into the blood
- Largest of the lipoproteins, with the lowest density
- Taken up by the liver once triglycerides are removed

5% Cholesterol
2% Protein
8% Phospholipid
85% Triglyceride
Transports dietary fat into the blood and to the tissues of the body

VLDL (Very-low-density lipoprotein)
- 80% are formed in the liver
- 20% are formed in the intestine

20% Cholesterol
10% Protein
52% Triglyceride
18% Phospholipid
Transports endogenous lipids, especially triglycerides, to various tissues of the body

LDL (Low-density lipoprotein)
- Formed in the blood from VLDL (transformation from VLDL to LDL occurs as the triglycerides are removed from the VLDL)

22% Protein
8% Triglyceride
20% Phospholipid
50% Cholesterol
Transports cholesterol to the cells of the body

HDL (High-density lipoprotein)
- Synthesized in the liver and released into the blood
- Transported by the blood throughout the body, picking up free cholesterol

30% Phospholipid
3% Triglyceride
50% Protein
17% Cholesterol
Transports cholesterol from tissues back to the liver

Figure 4.11 The chemical components of various lipoproteins. Notice that chylomicrons contain the highest proportion of triglycerides, making them the least dense, while HDLs have the highest proportion of protein, making them the most dense.

Very-Low-Density Lipoproteins

Very-low-density lipoproteins (VLDLs) are made up mostly of triglyceride. The liver is the primary source of VLDLs, but they are also produced in the intestines. VLDLs are mainly transport vehicles that carry triglycerides, which are produced in the liver or intestine, to other cells of the body. If their triglyceride load is not needed for fuel, the fatty acids can be released and taken up by the adipose cells for storage.

Diets high in saturated fat, simple sugars, and extra energy tend to increase blood levels of VLDLs, because they increase the production of triglycerides in the liver. Conversely, diets high in omega-3 fatty acids can help reduce VLDL levels because they inhibit the production of triglycerides, which are the primary component of VLDLs. In addition, exercise can reduce VLDLs because the triglycerides transported in the VLDLs can be used for energy instead of remaining to circulate in the blood.

Low-Density Lipoproteins

The lipoproteins that result when VLDLs release their triglyceride load are much higher in cholesterol, phospholipids, and protein and therefore somewhat more dense. These **low-density lipoproteins (LDLs)** circulate in the blood until they are absorbed by the body's cells, thereby delivering their cholesterol to the cells. Diets

very-low-density lipoprotein (VLDL) A large lipoprotein made up mostly of triglyceride. Functions primarily to transport triglycerides from their source to the body's cells, including to adipose tissues for storage.

low-density lipoprotein (LDL) A molecule resulting when a VLDL releases its triglyceride load. Higher cholesterol and protein content makes LDLs somewhat more dense than VLDLs.

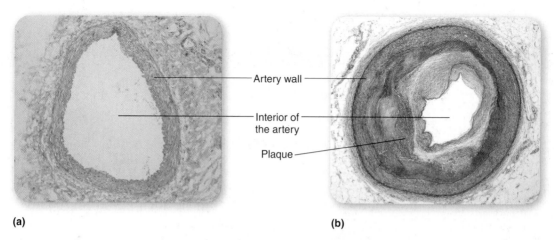

Artery wall

Interior of the artery

Plaque

(a)   (b)

🔺 **Figure 4.12** These light micrographs show a cross section of **(a)** a normal artery containing little cholesterol-rich plaque and allowing adequate blood flow through the heart and **(b)** an artery that is partially blocked with cholesterol-rich plaque, which can lead to a heart attack.

high in saturated and *trans* fats decrease the removal of LDLs by body cells and therefore increase LDL levels in the blood. The more LDLs circulating in the blood, the greater the risk that some of their cholesterol will adhere to the walls of the blood vessels. This causes *scavenger* white blood cells to rush to the site and bind the cholesterol. As more and more cholesterol binds to these cells, they burst to form a fatty patch, known as *plaque*, that eventually hardens, blocking the artery **(Figure 4.12)**. Because high blood levels of LDL-cholesterol increase the risk for heart disease, LDL-cholesterol is often referred to as "bad cholesterol."

High-Density Lipoproteins

High-density lipoproteins (HDLs) are small, dense lipoproteins with a very low cholesterol content and a high protein content. They are produced in the liver, then released to circulate in the blood, picking up cholesterol from dying cells and arterial plaques or transferring it to other lipoproteins. When HDLs deliver their newly acquired cholesterol to the liver, they remove it from the cardiovascular system. That's why high blood levels of HDLs are associated with a lower risk for coronary artery disease and why HDL-cholesterol is often referred to as "good cholesterol." Incidentally, one of the ways in which omega-3 fatty acids decrease our risk for heart disease is by increasing HDL-cholesterol.[6] There is also some evidence that getting regular physical exercise can modestly increase HDL-cholesterol levels.

Total Serum Cholesterol

For a small number of people, the level of dietary cholesterol eaten can influence serum (blood) cholesterol levels. Normally, as the level of dietary cholesterol increases, the body decreases the amount of cholesterol it makes, which keeps the body's level of cholesterol fairly constant. Unfortunately, this feedback mechanism does not work well in everyone. For some people, eating dietary cholesterol doesn't decrease the amount of cholesterol produced in the body, and as a result their total body cholesterol levels rise. This in turn increases the levels of cholesterol in the blood. They would benefit from reducing their intake of dietary cholesterol, by limiting their intake of animal products or selecting low-fat animal products. Research also shows that high intakes of saturated and *trans* fatty acids can increase the total serum cholesterol.

The Role of *Trans* Fatty Acids

Research indicates that *trans* fatty acids can raise blood LDL-cholesterol levels as much as saturated fat.[2,24] Thus, to reduce the risk for heart disease, we must reduce our intake of both high-fat animal products and foods that contain vegetable shortening or partially hydrogenated oil (because these are *trans* fats). Don't forget that foods fried in hydrogenated oils, such as french fries and doughnuts, are high in

high-density lipoprotein (HDL) A small, dense lipoprotein with a very low cholesterol content and a high protein content.

WHAT ABOUT YOU?

Calculate Your Risk for Metabolic Syndrome

When you're young, it's hard to imagine that you could someday develop a chronic disease. Yet many overweight and obese children, teens, and young adults are at risk for *metabolic syndrome*.[25] It's estimated that 47 million adults—25% of the adult U.S. population— already have metabolic syndrome.[26] Could you be at risk?

Recall that metabolic syndrome is a group of risk factors associated with overweight or obesity that increases your risk for type 2 diabetes and cardiovascular disease, including your risk of experiencing a heart attack or stroke. Listed below are the National Institutes of Health criteria for metabolic syndrome.[26] The presence of just three out of these five factors warrants a diagnosis of metabolic syndrome. But even one factor—such as abdominal obesity (excessive body fat stored around your waist and abdomen)—increases your risk. So get out the tape measure and see if your waistline puts you at risk. If it does, have your healthcare provider check your other risk factors to determine if you have metabolic syndrome.

1. *Abdominal obesity*: a waist circumference, measured just above the hip bone, that is greater than or equal to 40 inches for men and 35 inches for women
2. *Elevated blood triglycerides*: blood triglyceride levels greater than or equal to 150 mg/dL
3. *Low HDL-cholesterol*: blood HDL-cholesterol levels less than 40 mg/dL for men and 50 mg/dL for women
4. *Higher than normal blood pressure*: a blood pressure greater than 130/85 mmHg
5. *Elevated blood glucose levels*: a blood glucose level greater than 100 mg/dL

trans fatty acids, so these types of foods should also be avoided. Finally, if you use margarine and shortening, look for products that contain no *trans* fatty acids. Choose olive oil, nut butters, and other healthful fats instead.

Calculate Your Risk for Cardiovascular Disease

A simple laboratory analysis of your blood can reveal your blood lipid levels, specifically your LDL-cholesterol, HDL-cholesterol, and total serum cholesterol. If you do not know this information about yourself, there are easy ways to find out. Many college health centers offer blood lipid screenings at low cost or for free to students. Or the next time you visit your physician, ask to have your blood lipids measured. You should also get your blood pressure checked regularly. Blood pressure screening is often offered at student health centers, at health fairs, and even in many drug stores. It is especially important to take these steps if you have a family history of heart disease. Once you know your blood pressure and blood lipid levels, then you can estimate your risk of developing cardiovascular disease **(Figure 4.13)**. You can also do this quick assessment on family members or friends to help them become more aware of their risk factors for cardiovascular disease.

Your healthcare provider also considers your blood lipid levels when determining your risk for *metabolic syndrome*. As you know, metabolic syndrome is a cluster of factors more likely to be present in people who develop type 2 diabetes and/or cardiovascular disease. See the ***What About You?*** box to learn more about your risk for metabolic syndrome.

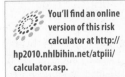

You'll find an online version of this risk calculator at http:// hp2010.nhlbihin.net/atpiii/ calculator.asp.

WHAT IS YOUR AGE?

Female:

Age	Points
20–34	–7
35–39	–3
40–44	0
45–49	3
50–54	6
55–59	8
60–64	10
65–69	12
70–74	14
75–79	16

Male:

Age	Points
20–34	–9
35–39	–4
40–44	0
45–49	3
50–54	6
55–59	8
60–64	10
65–69	11
70–74	12
75–79	13

Enter your points ☐

WHAT IS YOUR TOTAL CHOLESTEROL NUMBER?

Female:

Age	Total Cholesterol					
	<160	160–199	200–239	240–279	≥280	
20–39	0	4	8	11	13	
40–49	0	3	6	8	10	Points
50–59	0	2	4	5	7	
60–69	0	1	2	3	4	
70–79	0	1	1	2	2	

Male:

Age	Total Cholesterol					
	<160	160–199	200–239	240–279	≥280	
20–39	0	4	7	9	11	
40–49	0	3	5	6	8	Points
50–59	0	2	3	4	5	
60–69	0	1	1	2	3	
70–79	0	0	0	1	1	

Enter your points ☐

DO YOU SMOKE?

Nonsmoker, Female:

Age	Points
20–39	0
40–49	0
50–59	0
60–69	0
70–79	0

Nonsmoker, Male:

Age	Points
20–39	0
40–49	0
50–59	0
60–69	0
70–79	0

Smoker, Female:

Age	Points
20–39	9
40–49	7
50–59	4
60–69	2
70–79	1

Smoker, Male:

Age	Points
20–39	8
40–49	5
50–59	3
60–69	1
70–79	1

Enter your points ☐

WHAT IS YOUR HIGH-DENSITY LIPOPROTEIN NUMBER (HDL)?

Female:

HDL (mg/dL)	Points
≥60	–1
50–59	0
40–49	1
<40	2

Male:

HDL (mg/dL)	Points
≥60	–1
50–59	0
40–49	1
<40	2

Enter your points ☐

WHAT IS YOUR TOTAL NUMBER OF POINTS (what is your 10-year risk)?

Female:

Point total	10-Year risk %
<9	<1
9	1
10	1
11	1
12	1
13	2
14	2
15	3
16	4
17	5
18	6
19	8
20	11
21	14
22	17
23	22
24	27
≥25	≥30

Male:

Point total	10-Year risk %
<0	<1
0	1
1	1
2	1
3	1
4	1
5	2
6	2
7	3
8	4
9	5
10	6
11	8
12	10
13	12
14	16
15	20
16	25
≥17	≥30

Enter your 10-year risk percentage ☐

WHAT IS YOUR SYSTOLIC BLOOD PRESSURE (the top number)?

Female:

Systolic BP (mm Hg)	If untreated	If treated
<120	0	0
120–129	1	3
130–139	2	4
140–159	3	5
≥160	4	6

Male:

Systolic BP (mm Hg)	If untreated	If treated
<120	0	0
120–129	0	1
130–139	1	2
140–159	1	2
≥160	2	3

Enter your points ☐

Figure 4.13 Calculation matrix to estimate the 10-year risk for cardiovascular disease for men and women.

Data from National Institutes of Health. 2001. *Third Report of the National Cholesterol Education Program: Detection, Evaluation and Treatment of High Blood Cholesterol in Adults (ATP: III)*. Bethesda, MD: National Cholesterol Education Program, National Heart, Lung, and Blood Institute. www.nhlbi.nih.gov/guidelines/cholesterol/atp3xsum.pdf.

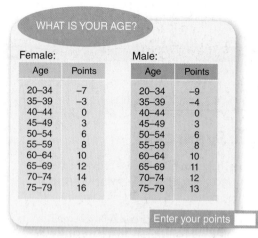
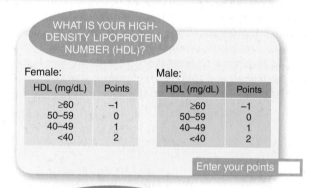
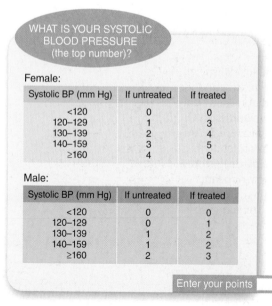

Reduce Your Risk for Cardiovascular Disease

The Centers for Disease Control and Prevention (CDC), the Expert Panel on Detection, Evaluation, and Treatment of High Blood Cholesterol in Adults (ATP III), and the American Heart Association have all made recommendations for diet, physical activity, and lifestyle factors that can improve blood lipid levels and reduce your risk for cardiovascular disease.[4,18] Aim for the recommended levels of LDL-cholesterol, HDL-cholesterol, and triglycerides by making the following dietary changes and incorporating physical activity into your lifestyle:

Foods fried in hydrogenated vegetable oils, such as french fries, are high in *trans* fatty acids and should be avoided.

- *Maintain your total fat intake* to within 20% to 35% of energy, and keep your intake of saturated and *trans* fatty acids low.[2] Polyunsaturated fats (such as soy and canola oil) can comprise up to 10% of total energy intake, while monounsaturated fats (such as olive oil) can comprise up to 20% of total energy intake. For many people, a lower fat intake may help maintain a healthful body weight.
- *Decrease your consumption of saturated fat* to less than 7–10% of total energy intake. Decrease your cholesterol intake to less than 300 mg per day, and keep *trans* fats intake at an absolute minimum. Lowering your consumption of these fats will lower your LDL-cholesterol level. Replace saturated fat (such as, butter, margarine, vegetable shortening, or lard) with more healthful cooking oils, such as olive or canola oil.
- *Increase your consumption of whole grains, fruits, and vegetables*, so that total dietary fiber is 20 to 30 grams per day. Foods high in fiber decrease blood LDL-cholesterol levels.
- *Schedule regular physical checkups* to help monitor your lipid levels and determine if your values are within normal limits.
- *Eat a healthful diet overall.* The relationship between diet and cardiovascular disease is complicated, and is also affected by your genetic risk for this disease. Eating a healthful diet will help you maintain an optimal body weight and keep your blood lipids, glucose, and blood pressure within healthy limits. For example, eat throughout the day instead of getting most of your Calories shortly before you go to bed. Eat foods that are *whole* (such as whole-wheat breads and cereals, fruits and vegetables, and beans and legumes). Limit your intake of sodium, which is often present in high amounts in processed food. Limit your intake of high-sugar foods (for example, sweetened sodas, cookies, and candy). This dietary change will help maintain blood glucose and insulin concentrations within normal ranges. High blood glucose levels are associated with high blood triglycerides.
- *Be active.* Exercise most days of the week for 30 to 60 minutes whenever possible, and make regular exercise a priority. Exercise increases "good" HDL-cholesterol while lowering blood triglyceride levels. Exercise also helps you maintain a healthy body weight, lowers blood pressure, and reduces your risk for diabetes.
- *Maintain a healthy body weight.* Blood lipids and glucose levels typically improve when people who are obese or significantly overweight lose weight and engage in regular physical activity.
- *Avoid using and being exposed to tobacco products.* Research indicates that smokers have a 70% greater chance of developing cardiovascular disease than non-smokers. Without question, stopping smoking or never starting in the first place is one of the best ways to reduce your risk for cardiovascular disease. Former smokers who stop smoking live longer than those who continue to smoke, and a 15-year period of non-smoking will reduce your risk factors for cardiovascular disease to those of a nonsmoker. You should also avoid second-hand smoke.

For more strategies for reducing your risk for cardiovascular disease, check out the accompanying *Game Plan* feature box (page 124).

GAME PLAN
Tips for Heart-Healthy Eating

When shopping for and preparing meals at home, as well as when eating out, try these simple strategies to tip the balance of your diet toward heart-healthy fats.

At Home

☐ Boost the nutrients in your breakfast cereal by adding 1 tablespoon of ground flaxseed meal.

☐ Select whole-grain breads, and try peanut, almond, cashew, or walnut butter as a spread for your toast.

☐ If you normally eat two eggs for breakfast, remove the yolk from one egg for half the cholesterol. Do the same in recipes calling for two eggs.

☐ Select low-fat or nonfat milk, coffee creamers, yogurt, cream cheese, cottage cheese, sour cream, mayonnaise, and salad dressings.

☐ Substitute lower-fat cheeses, such as parmesan, for higher-fat cheeses, such as cheddar.

☐ If you use margarine, choose one made from a high-omega-3 oil, such as canola oil, and is *trans* fat free.

☐ Start meals with a salad dressed with olive oil and vinegar, or a fat-free soup.

☐ Select lean cuts of meat. Load your plate with vegetables, and make meat a "condiment."

☐ Instead of frying meats, fish, and vegetables, bake or broil them.

☐ Trim visible fat from meats and poultry before cooking. Eat poultry without the skin.

☐ Instead of buttering your bread, dip it in a mixture of olive oil with a dribble of balsamic vinegar.

☐ Avoid cookies and crackers. If you must have them, make sure that any you buy are low in saturated fats and free of *trans* fatty acids.

☐ Choose ice milk, sorbet, or low-fat or nonfat yogurt and fruit for dessert instead of high-fat ice cream.

☐ For snacks, munch on air-popped popcorn, raw vegetables, or a mixture of whole and dried fruits, nuts, seeds, and pretzels.

☐ Choose water, skim milk, soy milk, almond milk, or unsweetened beverages over sugar-sweetened beverages.

☐ Read the labels of packaged foods and select low-fat versions whenever possible.

☐ Control your portion size, especially when eating high-fat foods.

Eating Out

☐ When eating out, select a high-omega-3 fatty acid fish, such as salmon, or try a vegetarian entrée made with tofu or tempeh. If you do choose meat, ask for it to be trimmed of fat and broiled rather than fried.

☐ Consider splitting an entrée with a friend and complement it with a side salad.

☐ On your salad, choose olive oil and vinegar instead of a cream-based dressing. Also use olive oil and vinegar instead of butter for your bread.

☐ Order a baked potato or rice instead of french fries or potatoes with cheese toppings.

☐ Skip dessert or choose a fat-free sorbet.

☐ The next time you order a fast-food meal, skip the french fries or order the kid's meal to help your portion control.

☐ Order pizza with vegetable toppings instead of pepperoni or sausage.

☐ Order coffee drinks with skim milk instead of cream or whole milk, and accompany them with a biscotti instead of a brownie.

Does a High-Fat Diet Cause Cancer?

Cancer develops as a result of a poorly understood interaction between the environment and genetic factors. In addition, most cancers take years to develop, so examining the impact of diet on cancer development can be a long and difficult process. However, diet and lifestyle are two of the most important environmental factors that have been identified in the development of cancer.[27,28] Current research shows that obesity and physical inactivity may account for 25% to 30% of several major cancers, including colon cancer and postmenopausal breast cancer.[29] Of course, a diet high in fat can contribute to obesity.

Three types of cancer have been studied extensively for their possible relationship to dietary fat intake: breast cancer, colon cancer, and prostate cancer.

- Breast cancer. Currently, no clinical trials show a link between the amount or type of fat consumed and increased risk for breast cancer.[30,31,32,33]
- Colon cancer. Recent research shows that a typical American diet high in red meat, fat, refined grains, and dessert foods is associated with a greater recurrence of colon cancer compared to a diet high in fruits, vegetables, poultry, and fish.[34] Because we now know that physical activity can reduce the risk for colon cancer, earlier diet and colon cancer studies that did not control for this factor are now being questioned.
- Prostate cancer. As with other cancers, the precise link between dietary fat intake and prostate cancer is still unclear.[29,35] Research shows that there is a consistent link between prostate cancer risk and consumption of animal fats, but not other types of fats. The exact mechanism by which animal fats may contribute to prostate cancer has not yet been identified. Men who consume diets high in animal fat typically have lower intakes of fruits and vegetables.

Until we know more about the link between diet (especially fat) and cancer, the American Institute for Cancer Research recommends the following diet and lifestyle changes to reduce your risks:[28]

- Maintain a healthy body weight.
- Be physically active for at least 30 minutes a day.

▲ Eating whole fruits and vegetables can reduce your risk for some cancers.

NUTRI-CASE JUDY

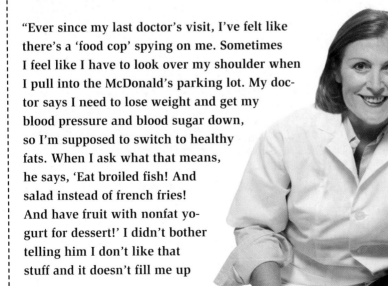

"Ever since my last doctor's visit, I've felt like there's a 'food cop' spying on me. Sometimes I feel like I have to look over my shoulder when I pull into the McDonald's parking lot. My doctor says I need to lose weight and get my blood pressure and blood sugar down, so I'm supposed to switch to healthy fats. When I ask what that means, he says, 'Eat broiled fish! And salad instead of french fries! And have fruit with nonfat yogurt for dessert!' I didn't bother telling him I don't like that stuff and it doesn't fill me up and I don't have the money to buy it or the time to make it! That kind of diet is for movie stars. All the real people I know eat the same way I do."

Think back on what you've learned about the many factors influencing our food choices. Identify at least two factors that might be affecting Judy's choices. Do you agree that the foods Judy's doctor recommended are not for "real people" like Judy? Why or why not?

- Avoid sugary drinks and limit your consumption of energy-dense foods (foods high in sugar and fat).
- Eat a variety of fruits, vegetables, whole grains, and legumes.
- Limit your consumption of red meats (such as beef, pork, and lamb), and avoid processed meats.
- If you drink alcohol, limit it to two drinks/day for men and one drink/day for women.
- Limit your consumption of salty foods and foods processed with salt.
- Don't use or regard supplements as a way to protect against cancer.

RECAP The types of fats we eat can significantly affect our risk for disease. Saturated and *trans* fatty acids increase our risk for heart disease, whereas the omega-3 fatty acids EPA and DHA can reduce our risk. High levels of LDL-cholesterol and low levels of HDL-cholesterol increase your risk for heart disease. Other risk factors for heart disease include being overweight, being physically inactive, smoking, having high blood pressure, and having diabetes. Consuming a healthful diet and making recommended lifestyle choices will also reduce your risk for some cancers.

COOKING 101

Healthful fats are a necessary part of foods and cooking, and help meals taste great! Learn how to prepare a delicious pizza that maximizes healthful fats by watching our new Cooking 101 videos, available on the Companion Website at www.pearsonhighered.com/thompsonmanore.

Chapter Review

What Can I Do Today?

Now that you've read this chapter, try making these three changes:

- Instead of having meat at both lunch and dinner today, choose fish or shellfish. Or, have a vegetarian meal that might include beans, whole grains, or a low-fat cheese.
- If you drink whole milk, switch to low-fat or skim.
- Get at least 30 minutes of physical activity today, and see how it makes you feel.

Test Yourself ANSWERS

1. ⓉＴ The body can manufacture all the cholesterol it needs from nutrients, so we don't need to consume it in our diet. Eating a diet low in saturated fat will also keep intake of dietary cholesterol within recommended levels.

2. Ⓣ Fat is our primary source of energy, both at rest and during low-intensity exercise. Fat is also an important fuel source during prolonged exercise.

3. Ⓣ Foods fried in vegetable shortening can be unhealthful because they are higher in *trans* fatty acids. In addition, fried foods are high in fat and energy and can contribute to overweight and obesity.

4. Ⓣ Certain essential fatty acids, including EPA and DHA, reduce inflammation, blood clotting, and other risk factors associated with heart disease.

5. Ⓕ Cancer develops as a result of a poorly understood interaction between environmental and genetic factors. Researchers are examining the links between the consumption of high dietary fat and certain cancers, but this research is currently inconclusive.

 **NutriTools**   Check out the Companion Website at www.pearsonhighered.com/thompsonmanore, or use MyNutritionLab.com to access interactive animations, including

- Build-a-Pizza
- Know Your Fat Sources

Review Questions

1. Cholesterol is
   a. a form of *trans* fatty acid.
   b. a form of saturated fatty acid.
   c. produced in the liver and small intestine.
   d. found in leafy green vegetables, flaxseeds, and soy.

2. One of the most sensible ways to reduce body fat is to
   a. limit intake of fat to less than 15% of total energy consumed.
   b. exercise regularly.
   c. avoid all consumption of *trans* fatty acids.
   d. restrict total Calories to less than 1,200 per day.

3. Micelles assist in the
   a. transport of dietary fat to the cells of the small intestine.
   b. emulsification of dietary fat in the small intestine.
   c. production of cholesterol in the liver.
   d. storage of excess fat in adipose tissue.

4. The risk for heart disease is lower in people who have high blood levels of
   a. triglycerides.
   b. very-low-density lipoproteins.
   c. low-density lipoproteins.
   d. high-density lipoproteins.

5. Triglycerides with a double carbon bond at one part of the molecule are referred to as
   a. monounsaturated fats.
   b. hydrogenated fats.
   c. saturated fats.
   d. sterols.

6. True or False? The Acceptable Macronutrient Distribution Range (AMDR) for fat is 20% to 35% of total energy.

7. True or False? During exercise, fat cannot be mobilized from adipose tissue for use as energy.

8. True or False? Triglycerides are the same as fatty acids.

9. True or False? *Trans* fatty acids are produced by food manufacturers; they do not occur in nature.

10. True or False? A serving of food labeled *reduced fat* has at least 25% less fat and 25% fewer Calories than a full-fat version of the same food.

Answers to Review Questions are located at the back of this text.

Web Links

www.heart.org/HEARTORG
American Heart Association

www.nhlbi.nih.gov/chd
National Cholesterol Education Program

www.nih.gov
National Institutes of Health (NIH)

www.nlm.nih.gov/medlineplus
MEDLINE Plus Health Information

www.hsph.harvard.edu/nutritionsource
Harvard University's Nutrition Source: Knowledge for Healthy Eating

5
Proteins: Crucial Components of All Body Tissues

Test Yourself

Are these statements true or false? Circle your guess.

1. (T) (F) Protein is a primary source of energy for our body.

2. (T) (F) Amino acid supplements help build muscle mass.

3. (T) (F) Any protein eaten in excess is excreted in your urine.

4. (T) (F) Vegetarian diets are inadequate in protein.

5. (T) (F) Most people in the United States consume more protein than they need.

Test Yourself answers can be found at the end of the chapter.

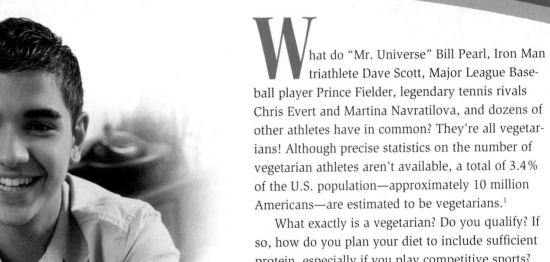

What do "Mr. Universe" Bill Pearl, Iron Man triathlete Dave Scott, Major League Baseball player Prince Fielder, legendary tennis rivals Chris Evert and Martina Navratilova, and dozens of other athletes have in common? They're all vegetarians! Although precise statistics on the number of vegetarian athletes aren't available, a total of 3.4% of the U.S. population—approximately 10 million Americans—are estimated to be vegetarians.[1]

What exactly is a vegetarian? Do you qualify? If so, how do you plan your diet to include sufficient protein, especially if you play competitive sports? Are there real advantages to eating meat, or is plant protein just as good?

It seems as if everybody has an opinion about protein, both how much you should consume and from what sources. In this chapter, we address these and other questions to clarify the importance of protein in the diet and dispel common myths about this crucial nutrient.

Nutrition Online icons are located throughout the chapter, directing you to web links, videos, podcasts, and other useful online resources.

"Where I'm Starting From . . ."

How many grams of protein do you think you need to eat each day?

Do you think you get this amount of protein most days?

Yes or No

How often would you say you go for an entire day without eating meat? (Choose one.)

☐ Every day—I'm a vegetarian.
☐ At least once or twice a week.
☐ Maybe once or twice a month.
☐ Almost never—I don't feel right if I don't eat meat every day.

What Are Proteins?

Proteins are large, complex molecules found in the cells of all living things. Although proteins are best known as part of our muscle mass, they are, in fact, critical components of all tissues of the human body, including our bones and blood. In addition, although our body prefers to use carbohydrates and fats for energy, proteins do provide energy in certain circumstances. These and many more functions of proteins will be discussed later in this chapter.

How Do Proteins Differ from Carbohydrates and Lipids?

Proteins are one of the three macronutrients and are found in a wide variety of foods. Our body is able to manufacture (*synthesize*) all of the macronutrients. But **DNA,** the genetic material in our cells, dictates the structure only of protein molecules, not of carbohydrates or lipids. We'll explore how our body synthesizes proteins and the role that DNA plays in this process shortly.

Another key difference between proteins and the other macronutrients lies in their chemical makeup. In addition to the carbon, hydrogen, and oxygen also found in carbohydrates and lipids, proteins contain a special form of nitrogen that our body can readily use. When we digest protein-containing plant and animal foods, nitrogen is released for use in many important body processes. Carbohydrates and lipids do not provide this critical form of nitrogen.

The Building Blocks of Proteins Are Amino Acids

Proteins are long, chainlike compounds made up of unique molecules called **amino acids.** If you were to imagine proteins as beaded necklaces, each bead would be an amino acid **(Figure 5.1)**. The links that bind the amino acid "beads" to each other are unique chemical bonds called **peptide bonds.**

Most of the proteins in our body are made from varying combinations of just 20 amino acids, identified in **Table 5.1**. By "stringing together" dozens to hundreds of copies of these 20 amino acids in different sequences, our cells manufacture an estimated 10,000 to 50,000 unique proteins.

proteins Large, complex molecules made up of amino acids and found as essential components of all living cells.

DNA A molecule present in the nucleus of all body cells that directs the assembly of amino acids into body proteins.

amino acids Nitrogen-containing molecules that combine to form proteins.

peptide bonds Unique types of chemical bonds in which the amine group of one amino acid binds to the acid group of another in order to manufacture dipeptides and all larger peptide molecules.

TABLE 5.1   Amino Acids of the Human Body

Essential Amino Acids	Nonessential Amino Acids
These amino acids must be obtained from food.	*These amino acids can be manufactured by the body.*
Histidine	Alanine
Isoleucine	Arginine
Leucine	Asparagine
Lysine	Aspartic acid
Methionine	Cysteine
Phenylalanine	Glutamic acid
Threonine	Glutamine
Tryptophan	Glycine
Valine	Proline
	Serine
	Tyrosine

Now let's look at the structure of these amino acid "beads." At the core of every amino acid molecule is a central carbon atom. As you learned in the previous chapter, carbon atoms have four attachment sites. In amino acids, the central carbon's four attachment sites are filled by the following (**Figure 5.2a**):

1. a *hydrogen atom*
2. an *acid group:* all acid groups in amino acids are identical
3. an *amine group:* the word *amine* means "nitrogen-containing," and nitrogen is indeed the essential component of the amine portion of the molecule; like acid groups, all amine groups in amino acids are identical
4. a *side chain:* this is the portion of the amino acid that makes each unique; as shown in Figure 5.2b, variations in the structure of the side chain give each amino acid its distinct properties

Of the 20 amino acids in our body, 9 are classified as essential. This does not mean that they are more important than the 11 nonessential amino acids. Instead, **essential amino acids** are those that our body cannot produce at all or cannot produce in sufficient quantities to meet our physiological needs. Thus, we must obtain essential amino acids from food. If we do not consume enough of the essential amino acids, we lose our ability to make the proteins and other nitrogen-containing compounds our body needs.

Nonessential amino acids are just as important to our body as essential amino acids, but it can make them in sufficient quantities, so we do not need to consume them in our diet. We make nonessential amino acids by combining parts of different amino acids and the breakdown products of carbohydrates and fats.

RECAP Proteins are critical components of all tissues of the human body. Like carbohydrates and lipids, they contain carbon, hydrogen, and oxygen. Unlike the other macronutrients, they also contain nitrogen, and their structure is dictated by DNA. The building blocks of proteins are amino acids. The amine group of the amino acid contains nitrogen. The portion of the amino acid that changes, giving each amino acid its distinct identity, is the side chain. The body cannot make essential amino acids, so we must obtain them from our diet. Our body can make nonessential amino acids from parts of other amino acids, carbohydrates, and fats.

Figure 5.1 Structure of proteins. Proteins are chains of amino acids linked together by special chemical bonds called peptide bonds. This illustration shows a molecule of glucagon, a protein important in regulating blood glucose level. Notice that glucagon contains sixteen different amino acids. Some of these occur more than once, for a total of twenty-nine amino acids in this protein.

How Are Proteins Made?

You are unique because you inherited a unique set of genes from your parents. **Genes** are segments of DNA that carry the instructions for assembling available amino acids into your body's unique proteins. Slight differences in amino acid sequencing lead to slight differences in proteins. These differences in proteins result in the unique physical and physiologic characteristics you possess.

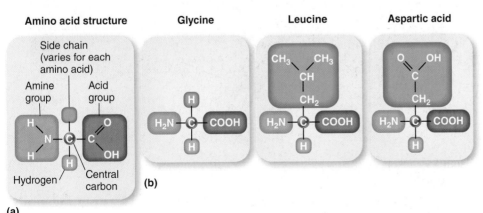

(a) **(b)**

essential amino acids Amino acids not produced by the body that must be obtained from food.

nonessential amino acids Amino acids that can be manufactured by the body in sufficient quantities and therefore do not need to be consumed regularly in our diet.

gene A segment of DNA that carries the instructions for assembling available amino acids into a unique protein.

Figure 5.2 Structure of an amino acid. **(a)** All amino acids contain five parts: a central carbon atom, an amine group around the atom that contains nitrogen, an acid group, a hydrogen atom, and a side chain. **(b)** Only the side chain differs for each of the twenty amino acids, giving each its unique properties.

⬆ Proteins are an integral part of body tissues, including muscle tissue.

Protein Shape Determines Function

Two amino acids joined together form a *dipeptide,* and three amino acids joined together are called a *tripeptide.* The term *oligopeptide* is used to identify a string of four to nine amino acids. Proteins are made up of *polypeptides,* which are chains of ten or more amino acids linked together by peptide bonds. As a polypeptide chain grows longer, it begins to fold into any of a variety of complex shapes that give proteins their sophisticated structure.

The three-dimensional shape of a protein is critically important because it determines that protein's function in the body. For example, the proteins that form tendons are much longer than they are wide. Tendons are connective tissues that attach bone to muscle, and their long, rodlike structure provides strong, fibrous connections. In contrast, the proteins that form red blood cells are globular in shape, and they result in the red blood cells being shaped like flattened disks with depressed centers, similar to a microscopic doughnut **(Figure 5.3).** This structure and the flexibility of the proteins in the red blood cells permit them to change shape and flow freely through even the tiniest blood vessels to deliver oxygen and still return to their original shape.

Proteins can uncoil and lose their shape when they are exposed to heat, acids, bases, heavy metals, alcohol, and other damaging substances. The term used to describe this change in the shape of proteins is *denaturation.* When a protein is denatured, its function is lost. Familiar examples of protein denaturation are the stiffening of egg whites when they are whipped, the curdling of milk when lemon juice or another acid is added, and the solidifying of eggs as they cook. Denaturation also occurs during protein digestion as a response to body heat and stomach acids.

Protein Synthesis Can Be Limited by Missing Amino Acids

Our body synthesizes proteins by selecting the needed amino acids from the pool of all amino acids available at any given time. For protein synthesis to occur, all essential amino acids must be available to the cell. If this is not the case, the amino acid that is missing or in the smallest supply is called the **limiting amino acid.** Without the proper combination and quantity of essential amino acids, protein synthesis slows to the point at which proteins cannot be generated. For instance, the protein hemoglobin contains the essential amino acid histidine. If we do not consume

limiting amino acid The essential amino acid that is missing or in the smallest supply in the amino acid pool and is thus responsible for slowing or halting protein synthesis.

incomplete proteins Foods that do not contain all of the essential amino acids in sufficient amounts to support growth and health.

complete proteins Foods that contain all nine essential amino acids.

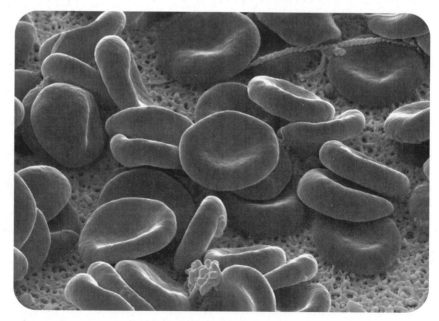

⬆ **Figure 5.3** Protein shape determines function. The globular shape of the protein in red blood cells contributes to the flexible-disk shape of the cells. This in turn enables their passage through the tiniest blood vessels of the body.

enough histidine, our body will be unable to make hemoglobin, and we will lose the ability to transport oxygen to our cells. Without oxygen, our cells cannot function and will eventually die.

Proteins can be described as incomplete or complete:

- **Incomplete proteins** do not contain all of the essential amino acids in sufficient quantities to support growth and health. They are also called *low-quality proteins*. Lentils, for example, are an incomplete protein.
- **Complete proteins** have all nine of the essential amino acids. They are also called *high-quality proteins*. These include proteins derived from animal products, such as egg whites, beef, poultry, fish, and dairy products such as milk and cheese. Soybeans also contain all nine essential amino acids and are the only complete vegetable protein.

◆ Stiffening egg whites denatures some of the proteins within them.

Protein Synthesis Can Be Enhanced by Mutual Supplementation

Many people believe that we must consume meat or dairy products to obtain complete proteins. Not true! Consider a meal of black beans and rice. Black beans are low in the amino acids methionine and cysteine but have adequate amounts of isoleucine and lysine. Rice is low in isoleucine and lysine but contains sufficient methionine and cysteine. By combining black beans and rice, we create a complete protein source.

Mutual supplementation is the process of combining two or more incomplete protein sources to make a complete protein. The foods involved provide **complementary proteins** that, when combined, provide all nine essential amino acids (**Figure 5.4**). Thus, mutual supplementation is important for people who consume no animal products.

mutual supplementation The process of combining two or more incomplete protein sources to make a complete protein.

complementary proteins Two or more foods that together contain all nine essential amino acids necessary for a complete protein. It is not necessary to eat complementary proteins at the same meal.

Combining Complementary Foods

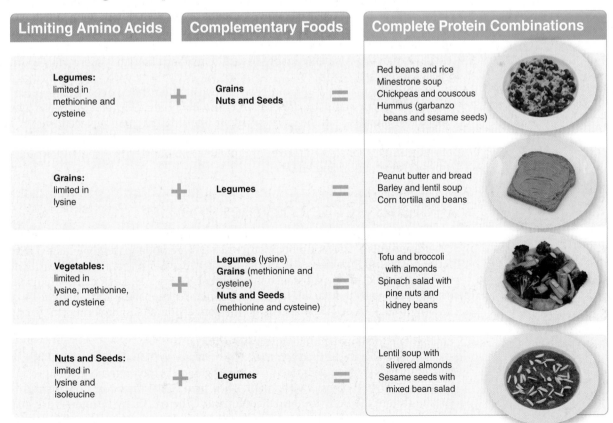

Limiting Amino Acids	Complementary Foods	Complete Protein Combinations
Legumes: limited in methionine and cysteine	**+** **Grains** **Nuts and Seeds**	**=** Red beans and rice Minestrone soup Chickpeas and couscous Hummus (garbanzo beans and sesame seeds)
Grains: limited in lysine	**+** **Legumes**	**=** Peanut butter and bread Barley and lentil soup Corn tortilla and beans
Vegetables: limited in lysine, methionine, and cysteine	**+** **Legumes** (lysine) **Grains** (methionine and cysteine) **Nuts and Seeds** (methionine and cysteine)	**=** Tofu and broccoli with almonds Spinach salad with pine nuts and kidney beans
Nuts and Seeds: limited in lysine and isoleucine	**+** **Legumes**	**=** Lentil soup with slivered almonds Sesame seeds with mixed bean salad

◆ **Figure 5.4** Complementary food combinations.

Complementary proteins do not need to be eaten at the same meal. We maintain a free "pool" of amino acids in the blood; these amino acids come from food and sloughed-off cells. When we eat an incomplete protein, its amino acids join those in the free amino acid pool. These free amino acids can then combine to synthesize complete proteins. However, to maximize protein synthesis, it is wise to eat complementary-protein foods during the same day.

RECAP Amino acids bind together to form proteins. Genes regulate the amino acid sequence, and thus the structure, of all proteins. The shape of a protein determines its function. When a protein is denatured by damaging substances, such as heat and acids, it loses its shape and its function. For protein synthesis to occur, all nine essential amino acids must be available to the cell. A complete protein provides all nine essential amino acids. Mutual supplementation combines two complementary-protein sources to make a complete protein.

Why Do We Need to Eat Proteins?

The functions of proteins in the body are so numerous that only a few can be described in detail here. Note that proteins function most effectively when we also consume adequate amounts of energy as carbohydrates and fat. When there is not enough energy available, the body uses proteins as an energy source, limiting their availability for other functions.

Proteins Contribute to Cell Growth, Repair, and Maintenance

The proteins in our body are dynamic, meaning that they are constantly being broken down, repaired, and replaced. When proteins are broken down, many amino acids are recycled into new proteins. Think about all of the new proteins that are needed to allow an embryo to develop and grow into a 9-month-old fetus. In this case, an entire human body is being made! In fact, a newborn baby has more than 10 trillion body cells.

Even in the mature adult, our cells are constantly turning over, meaning old cells are broken down and parts are used to create new cells. Our red blood cells live for only 3 to 4 months, and the cells lining our intestinal tract are replaced every 3 to 6 days. In addition, cellular damage that occurs must be repaired in order to maintain our health. The constant turnover of proteins from our diet is essential for such cell growth, repair, and maintenance.

Proteins Act as Enzymes and Hormones

You may remember that *enzymes* are small chemicals, usually proteins, that act on other chemicals to speed up body processes but are not apparently changed during those processes. Enzymes can bind substances together or break them apart, and they can transform one substance into another **(Figure 5.5)**. Each cell contains thousands of enzymes that facilitate specific cellular reactions. For example, the enzyme phosphofructokinase (PFK) speeds up the conversion of carbohydrates to energy during physical exercise. Without PFK, we would be unable to generate energy at a fast enough rate to allow us to be physically active.

You may also recall that *hormones* are substances that act as chemical messengers in the body. They are stored in various glands, which release them in response to changes in the body's environment. They then signal the body's organs and tissues to restore the body to normal conditions. Whereas many hormones are made from lipids, some are made from amino acids. These include insulin and glucagon, which play a role in regulating blood glucose levels, and thyroid hormone, which helps control the rate at which glucose is used for fuel.

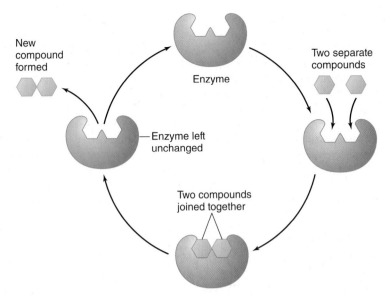

Figure 5.5 Proteins act as enzymes. Enzymes facilitate chemical reactions, such as joining two compounds together.

Proteins Help Maintain Fluid and Electrolyte Balance

For our body to function properly, fluids and *electrolytes* (minerals, such as sodium and potassium, that are able to carry an electrical charge) must be maintained at healthy levels inside and outside cells and within blood vessels. Proteins help maintain fluid and electrolyte balance in two ways:

- They attract fluids. Proteins in the bloodstream, the cells, and the spaces surrounding the cells work together to keep both fluids and electrolytes moving across these spaces.
- They move and retain fluids in the proper quantities to help us maintain both fluid balance and blood pressure.

When protein intake is deficient, the concentration of proteins in the bloodstream is insufficient to draw fluid from the tissues and across the blood vessel walls; fluid then collects in the tissues, causing **edema** **(Figure 5.6)**. In addition to being uncomfortable, edema can lead to serious medical problems.

The conduction of nerve signals and contraction of muscles also depend on a proper balance of electrolytes. If protein intake is deficient, we lose our ability to maintain these functions, resulting in potentially fatal changes in the rhythm of the heart. Other consequences of chronically low protein intakes include muscle weakness and spasms, kidney failure, and, if conditions are severe enough, death.

Proteins Transport Nutrients and Other Substances

Proteins play a key role in transporting nutrients and other important substances throughout the body. Some examples of these **transport proteins** include the following:

- Transport proteins within the cell membrane help maintain fluid and electrolyte balance. These proteins act as pumps to assist in the movement of the electrolytes

edema A disorder in which fluids build up in the tissue spaces of the body, causing fluid imbalances and a swollen appearance.

transport proteins Protein molecules that help transport substances throughout the body and across cell membranes.

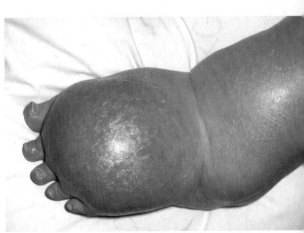

Figure 5.6 Edema can result from deficient protein intake. This foot with edema is swollen because of fluid imbalance.

- sodium and potassium into and out of the cell.
- Transport proteins also carry vitamins and minerals through the bloodstream to the organs and cells that need them. For example, retinol-binding protein transports fat-soluble vitamin A (also called retinol) in the blood.
- Transport proteins also move glucose from the bloodstream into the cells, where it can be used for energy.

Proteins Help Maintain Acid–Base Balance

The body's cellular processes result in the constant production of acids and bases. *Acids* are substances that contain significant amounts of hydrogen, whereas *bases* are low in hydrogen. Some hydrogen is essential to life, but too much can be harmful to body cells. Thus, the body maintains very tight control over the **pH,** or the level of hydrogen (H), in the blood. Proteins are excellent **buffers,** meaning they help maintain proper acid–base balance. They do this by attracting hydrogen and neutralizing it. Proteins can also release hydrogen when the blood becomes too basic. By buffering acids and bases, proteins help maintain acid–base balance.

Proteins Help Maintain a Strong Immune System

Antibodies are special proteins that help our body defend itself against foreign substances. When bacteria, viruses, toxins, and other harmful agents enter the body, the immune system produces antibodies that attach to and neutralize the invaders.

Adequate protein is necessary to support the increased production of antibodies that occurs in response to a cold, the flu, or any other infectious illness. If we do not consume enough protein, our resistance is weakened. On the other hand, eating more protein than we need does not improve immune function.

Proteins Serve as an Energy Source

The body's primary energy sources are carbohydrate and fat. So it's not surprising that both these macronutrients have specialized storage forms that can be used for energy—carbohydrate as glycogen and fat as triglycerides. Proteins do not have a specialized storage form for energy. This means that, when proteins need to be used for energy, they are taken from the blood and body tissues, such as the liver and skeletal muscle.

Adequate intake of carbohydrate and fat spares protein. During times of low carbohydrate and fat intake, the body breaks down proteins into individual amino acids, which are degraded further to provide the building blocks for the production of glucose, which provides needed energy to the brain. This process is called *gluconeogenesis*. In well-nourished people, proteins contribute very little to energy needs. Because we are efficient at recycling amino acids, our protein needs are relatively low compared to our needs for carbohydrate and fat.

pH Stands for "percentage of hydrogen." It is a measure of the acidity—or level of hydrogen—of any solution, including human blood.

buffers Proteins that help maintain proper acid–base balance by attaching to, or releasing, hydrogen ions as conditions change in the body.

antibodies Defensive proteins of the immune system. Their production is prompted by the presence of bacteria, viruses, toxins, or allergens.

NUTRITION
MILESTONE

In **1934**, Dr. Asbjørn Følling, a Norwegian physician and biochemist, examined children with mental retardation who were excreting urine that smelled unusually strong. He found that the urine contained a substance called phenylpyruvic acid, which is produced as a by-product of the breakdown of the amino acid phenylalanine. Although a small amount of this by-product in the urine is normal, a large amount indicates an inability to completely break down phenylalanine. Initially named Følling's disease, this condition is now known as phenylketonuria, or PKU. It is a genetic disorder that causes a deficiency in the enzyme that breaks down phenylalanine. In people with PKU, phenylalanine can build up in the body, causing brain damage, seizures, and psychiatric disorders. As a result of Følling's discovery, healthcare providers now screen the blood of all newborns for PKU. Those newborns found to have PKU are prescribed a diet low in phenylalanine, and they can develop into healthy children and adults.

RECAP Proteins serve many important functions, including (1) enabling growth, repair, and maintenance of body tissues; (2) acting as enzymes and hormones; (3) maintaining fluid and electrolyte balance; (4) transporting nutrients and other substances; (5) maintaining acid–base balance; (6) making antibodies, a component of our immune system; and (7) providing energy when carbohydrate and fat intakes are inadequate. Proteins function best when we also consume adequate amounts of carbohydrate and fat.

What Happens to the Proteins We Eat?

Our body does not directly use proteins from the foods we eat to make the proteins we need. Dietary proteins are first digested and broken into smaller particles, such as amino acids, dipeptides, and tripeptides, so that they can pass through the intestinal lining cells. In this section, we will review how proteins are digested and absorbed. As you read about each step in this process, refer to **Figure 5.7**.

- *Step 1.* The mechanical digestion of proteins in food occurs through chewing, crushing, and moistening the food with saliva. These actions ease swallowing and increase the surface area for more efficient digestion farther down the digestive tract. There is no chemical digestive action on proteins in the mouth.
- *Step 2.* When proteins reach the stomach, they are broken apart by *hydrochloric acid*, which denatures the strands of protein. Hydrochloric acid also converts the

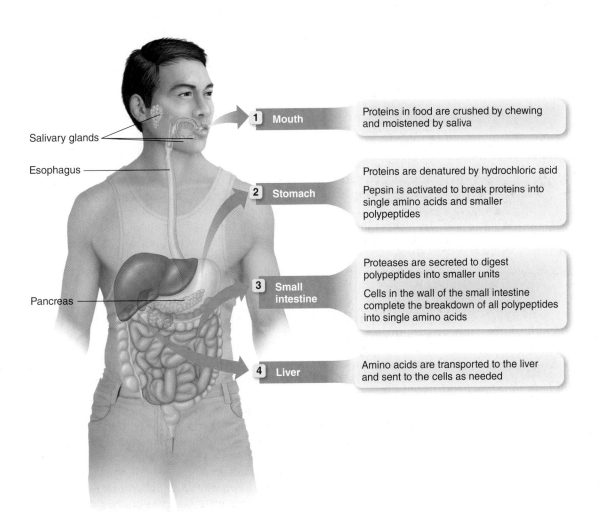

Salivary glands

Esophagus

Pancreas

| 1 | **Mouth** | Proteins in food are crushed by chewing and moistened by saliva |

| 2 | **Stomach** | Proteins are denatured by hydrochloric acid |
| | | Pepsin is activated to break proteins into single amino acids and smaller polypeptides |

| 3 | **Small intestine** | Proteases are secreted to digest polypeptides into smaller units |
| | | Cells in the wall of the small intestine complete the breakdown of all polypeptides into single amino acids |

| 4 | **Liver** | Amino acids are transported to the liver and sent to the cells as needed |

Figure 5.7 The process of protein digestion.

⬆ Meats are highly digestible sources of dietary protein.

inactive enzyme *pepsinogen* into its active form, **pepsin.** Although pepsin is a protein, it is not denatured by stomach acid because it has evolved to work optimally in an acidic environment. Pepsin begins breaking proteins into single amino acids and smaller polypeptides, which then travel to the small intestine for further digestion.

- *Step 3.* In the small intestine, the polypeptides encounter enzymes called **proteases,** which digest them into single amino acids, dipeptides, and tripeptides. The cells in the wall of the small intestine then absorb these molecules. Enzymes in the intestinal cells complete digestion by breaking the dipeptides and tripeptides into single amino acids.
- *Step 4.* The amino acids are transported into the bloodstream to the liver and on to cells throughout our body as needed.

As discussed earlier, the number of essential amino acids in a protein affects its quality: higher-quality-protein foods contain more of the essential amino acids needed to build proteins. Another factor to consider when determining protein quality is *digestibility,* or how efficiently our body can digest and absorb a protein. Animal foods and legumes, including soy products, have high digestibility, and we absorb almost all of their proteins. Grains and many vegetable proteins are less digestible.

RECAP In the stomach, hydrochloric acid denatures proteins and pepsin breaks proteins into single amino acids and smaller polypeptides. In the small intestine, proteases break down polypeptides. Enzymes in the cells in the wall of the small intestine break the remaining peptide fragments into single amino acids, which are then transported to the liver for distribution to the body.

How Much Protein Should We Eat?

Consuming adequate protein is a major concern for many people. In fact, one of the most common concerns among athletes is that their diet is deficient in protein (see the *Nutrition Myth or Fact?* box for a discussion of this topic). In developed nations, concerns about people getting sufficient dietary protein are generally unnecessary, because we can easily consume the protein our body needs by eating an adequate amount and variety of foods. However, many people in developing nations are at risk for protein deficiency. For example, a severe protein deficit in children, called *kwashiorkor,* commonly develops when a toddler is weaned from breast milk and fed a diet that is low in protein and high in diluted starches. *Marasmus* is a disease resulting from severe deficits of all of the energy nutrients, which can occur during periods of famine. (These and other hunger-related diseases are discussed in detail in Chapter 12.)

Recommended Dietary Allowance (RDA) for Protein

How much protein should we eat? **Table 5.2** lists the daily recommendations for protein intake for sedentary adults and for athletes. It also provides a calculation for converting the recommendation, which is stated in grams per kilogram of body weight, into total grams of protein per day. If you are sedentary and weigh 140 pounds, you need about 50 grams of protein a day. If you're an athlete who weighs 140 pounds, you need about 75 to 108 grams. Protein needs are higher for children, adolescents, and pregnant/lactating women because more protein is needed during times of growth and development.

When you consider that a small serving (3 oz) of ground beef or canned tuna provides about 22 to 24 grams of protein and a glass of low-fat milk another 8 grams, you can see how easy it is to meet this recommendation. In fact, it shouldn't surprise

pepsin An enzyme in the stomach that begins the breakdown of proteins into shorter polypeptide chains and single amino acids.

proteases Enzymes that continue the breakdown of polypeptides in the small intestine.

NUTRITION MYTH OR FACT?
Do Athletes Need More Protein Than Inactive People?

At one time, it was believed that the Recommended Dietary Allowance (RDA) for protein, which is 0.8 gram per kilogram of body weight, was sufficient for both inactive people and athletes. Recent studies, however, show that the protein needs of athletes are higher.

Athletes need more protein for several reasons:

- Regular exercise increases the transport of oxygen to body tissues, requiring changes in the oxygen-carrying capacity of the blood. To carry more oxygen, we need to produce more of the protein that carries oxygen in the blood (that is, hemoglobin, which is a protein).

- During intense exercise, we use a small amount of protein directly for energy.

- We also use protein to make glucose to prevent hypoglycemia (low blood sugar) during exercise.

- Regular exercise stimulates tissue growth and causes tissue damage, which must be repaired by additional proteins.

⬆ Some athletes who persistently diet are at risk for low protein intake.

As a result of these increased demands for protein, strength athletes (such as weightlifters) need 1.2 to 1.7 times more protein than the current RDA, and endurance athletes (such as distance runners) need 1.2 to 1.4 times more protein.

Does this mean that, if you are an athlete, you should add more protein to your diet? Not necessarily. Contrary to popular belief, most Americans, including athletes, already consume more than twice the RDA for protein. Thus, they are already more than fulfilling their protein needs. In fact, eating more protein or taking amino acid supplements does not cause muscles to become bigger or stronger. Only regular strength training can achieve these goals. For healthy people, evidence does not support eating more than two times the RDA for protein to increase strength, build muscle, or improve athletic performance. By eating a balanced diet and consuming a variety of foods, athletes can easily meet their protein requirements.

TABLE 5.2 Recommended Protein Intakes

Group	Recommended Protein Intake (g/kg body weight/day)*
Most adults[†]	0.8
Nonvegetarian endurance athletes[‡]	1.2 to 1.4
Nonvegetarian strength athletes[‡]	1.2 to 1.7
Vegetarian endurance athletes[‡]	1.3 to 1.5
Vegetarian strength athletes[‡]	1.3 to 1.8

*To convert body weight to kilograms, divide weight in pounds by 2.2.
Weight (lb) ÷ 2.2 = Weight (kg). For example, 150 lb ÷ 2.2 = 68 kg.
Weight (kg) × recommended protein intake = protein intake (grams per day). For example, for a non-athlete, 68 kg × 0.8 = 54.4 grams per day.
[†]Data from Food and Nutrition Board, Institute of Medicine. 2002. *Dietary Reference Intakes for Energy, Carbohydrate, Fiber, Fat, Fatty Acids, Cholesterol, Protein, and Amino Acids (Macronutrients)*, pp. 465–608. Washington, DC: National Academies Press.
[‡]American College of Sports Medicine, American Dietetic Association, and Dietitians of Canada. 2009. Joint Position Statement. Nutrition and athletic performance. *Med. Sci. Sports Exerc.* 41(3):709–731.

you to learn that most Americans eat 1.5 to 2 times their RDA for protein without any effort!

The recommended percentage of energy that should come from protein is 12% to 20% of your total daily energy intake. Many high-protein, low-carbohydrate diets recommend that a much greater percentage of your diet be derived from protein, but as we discuss next, excessive protein intake has some health costs.

To find out whether you're meeting—or exceeding—your protein needs, complete the calculation in the feature box *What About You?* (page 140).

WHAT ABOUT YOU?

Are You Meeting Your Protein Needs?

Before you can figure out whether you're meeting your protein needs, you have to know what those needs are. Look at Table 5.2 (page 139). Unless you qualify as an endurance or strength athlete, even if you exercise every day, your protein needs are 0.8 gram per kilogram of your body weight. If you're not familiar with the metric system, the following steps will help you translate this recommendation into the number of grams right for you:

1. Start by converting your weight from pounds to kilograms. For example, let's say you weigh 150 pounds. To convert this value to kilograms, divide by 2.2:

    150 pounds ÷ 2.2 pounds/kg = 68 kg.

2. Next, multiply your weight in kilograms by your RDA for protein:

    68 kg × 0.8 g/kg = 54 grams of protein per day.

    If you work out vigorously for an hour or more 5 or 6 days a week, you might want to use a protein intake level of 1 gram per kilogram of body weight. This calculation is easier!

1. Start by converting your weight from pounds to kilograms. For example, let's say you weigh 200 pounds. To convert this value to kilograms, divide by 2.2:

    200 pounds ÷ 2.2 pounds/kg = 91 kg.

2. Next, multiply your weight in kilograms by your RDA for protein:

    91 kg × 1 g/kg = 91 grams of protein per day.

Now that you know how many grams of protein you need each day, you can log on to www.mypyramidtracker.gov to see how much protein you're getting in an average day, and whether that amount meets—or even exceeds—your needs. Or you can get a rough estimate by checking Table 5.3, which identifies grams of protein for many common foods. Circle the foods you eat most days, and add up the protein per serving.

Let's say you need 68 grams of protein per day, as in our first example. You typically eat either a ham or tuna sandwich on whole-wheat bread with a glass of skim milk for lunch. Either of these options would meet more than half of your daily protein needs—in one meal! As you can see, it's easy for most Americans to get enough protein every day.

RECAP The RDA for protein for most nonactive, nonpregnant, nonlactating, nonvegetarian adults is 0.8 gram per kilogram of body weight. Children, pregnant women, nursing mothers, vegetarians, and athletes need slightly more. Most people who eat enough energy and carbohydrates have no problem meeting their RDA for protein.

Too Much Dietary Protein Can Be Harmful

Over the last few decades, many people seeking to lose weight have turned to high-protein diets. Are such diets the key to weight loss? The **Nutrition Myth or Fact?** feature box (page 142) explores this question. One concern associated with such diets is that they may increase the risk for health problems. Three health conditions that have received particular attention are heart disease, bone loss, and kidney disease. Here is the state of current research into these three claims:

- *Heart disease.* High-protein diets composed of predominantly animal sources are associated with higher blood cholesterol levels. This is probably due to the saturated fat in animal products, which is known to increase blood cholesterol levels and the risk for heart disease. Vegetarians have been shown to have a greatly reduced risk for heart disease.[2,3]

- *Bone loss.* Animal foods contain more of the sulfur amino acids (methionine and cysteine). Metabolizing these amino acids makes the blood more acidic, and calcium, which is a base and is the main mineral component of bone, is pulled from the bone into the blood to buffer these acids. Although eating more protein can cause you to excrete more calcium, it is unknown whether high protein intakes actually cause bone loss. We do know that eating too little protein causes bone loss and that adequate protein intakes protect bone.[4,5] Recently, a study found that feeding healthy older women a higher-protein diet caused a slight improvement in calcium retention, which almost fully compensated for the slight increase in calcium excretion that resulted from the diet.[6] Thus, there does not appear to be direct evidence at this time to show that higher protein intakes cause bone loss in healthy people.

- *Kidney disease.* The more protein we eat, the more protein the body has to break down. A waste product of protein digestion is a chemical called *urea*: the kidneys form urea when the nitrogen-containing amine group is removed during amino acid breakdown. A high protein intake can therefore be stressful to kidneys that aren't functioning properly, so people with kidney disease are advised to eat a low-protein diet. On the other hand, experts agree that eating up to 2 grams of protein per kilogram of body weight each day is safe for healthy people. In fact, one study found that athletes consuming up to 2.8 grams of protein per kilogram of body weight per day experienced no reduction in kidney function.[7] Still, people who consume a lot of protein should also consume more fluid to flush the excess urea from their kidneys.

Shopper's Guide: Good Food Sources of Protein

Table 5.3 compares the protein content of a variety of foods. In general, good sources of protein include meats (lean cuts of beef, pork, poultry, and seafood), dairy products (low-fat milk-based products and egg whites), soy products, legumes, nuts, and

The quality of the protein in some legumes is almost equal to that of meat.

TABLE 5.3 Protein Content of Commonly Consumed Foods

Food	Serving Size	Protein (g)	Food	Serving Size	Protein (g)
Beef:			**Beans:**		
Ground, lean, baked (15% fat)	3.0 oz	22.0	Refried	½ cup	7.0
Prime rib, broiled (1/8 in. trim)	3.0 oz	18.0	Kidney, red	½ cup	7.7
Top sirloin, broiled (1/8 in. trim)	3.0 oz	23.0	Black	½ cup	7.0
Poultry:			**Nuts:**	1 oz	6.7
Chicken breast, broiled, no skin (bone removed)	½ breast	29.0	Peanuts, dry roasted		
			Peanut butter, creamy	2 tbsp.	8.0
Chicken thigh, bone and skin removed	1 thigh	13.5	Almonds, blanched	1 oz	6.0
Turkey breast, roasted, Louis Rich	3.0 oz	15.0	**Cereals, Grains, and Breads:**		
Seafood:			Oatmeal, quick instant	1 cup	5.4
Cod, cooked	3.0 oz	19.0	Cheerios	1 cup	3.0
Salmon, Chinook, baked	3.0 oz	22.0	Corn Bran	1 cup	2.0
Shrimp, steamed	3.0 oz	18.0	Grape Nuts	½ cup	6.0
Tuna, in water, drained	3.0 oz	22.0	Raisin Bran	1 cup	5.0
Pork:			Brown rice, cooked	1 cup	5.0
Pork loin chop, broiled	3.0 oz	25.0	Whole-wheat bread	1 slice	2.7
Ham, roasted, lean	3.0 oz	20.0	Bagel, 3½ in. diameter	1 each	7.0
Dairy:			**Vegetables:**		
Whole milk (3.3% fat)	8 fl. oz	7.9	Carrots, raw (7.5 × 1⅛ in.)	1 each	0.7
1% milk	8 fl. oz	8.5	Broccoli, raw, chopped	1 cup	2.6
Skim milk	8 fl. oz	8.8	Collards, cooked from frozen	1 cup	5.0
Low-fat, plain yogurt	8 fl. oz	13.0	Spinach, raw	1 cup	0.9
American cheese, processed	1 oz	6.0			
Cottage cheese, low-fat (2%)	1 cup	27.0			
Soy Products:					
Tofu	3.3 oz	7.0			
Tempeh, cooked	3.3 oz	18.0			
Soy milk beverage	1 cup	7.0			

Data from U.S. Department of Agriculture (USDA). 2010. National Nutrient Database for Standard Reference, Release 23. www.ars.usda.gov/ba/bhnrc/ndl.

NUTRITION MYTH OR FACT?

Are High-Protein Diets the Key to Weight Loss?

The promotional photo shows an enticing plate of fried eggs and sausage, or a juicy steak on the grill. If you're a meat eater and want to lose weight, chances are you've at least flirted with the idea of following a high-protein diet. Do these diets help people shed pounds and maintain their weight loss, and do they improve our health or harm us?

Supporters of high-protein diets propose that our high-simple-carbohydrate diet (including white bread, pasta made from white flour, and particularly refined sugars and high-fructose corn syrup) has caused the alarming rise in obesity in the United States in the past few decades. They claim that high-protein diets, such as the Atkins Diet, result in substantial weight loss. They also say that, despite the high saturated–fat content of animal sources of protein, meat-based high-protein diets do not cause unhealthful changes in blood cholesterol.

Are there any research studies to support these claims? Recently, the results of a few randomized controlled trials studying high-protein diets have been published. These studies have begun to shed some light on the effects of such diets on weight loss and blood lipid levels in obese individuals. One study placed participants on either the Atkins Diet or a low-fat diet plan recommended by the American Heart Association.[8] Participants consuming the Atkins Diet lost considerably more weight than people on the low-fat diet over the first 6 months, but weight loss between the two groups was no longer different after 1 year.[9] More significant, people consuming the Atkins Diet had lower triglyceride levels and had less of a decrease in HDL-cholesterol (the "good cholesterol") than people eating the low-fat diet. In another study conducted over a 1-year period using similar diet plans, the results were quite similar.[10] Two recent reviews of the studies on high-protein, low-carbohydrate diets concluded that there are not enough data currently to make recommendations for or against their use.[11,12] These reviews indicate that the weight loss that occurs with these diets appears to be more associated with a decreased energy intake and longer diet duration and is not necessarily due to the reduced carbohydrate content of the diet.

Detractors of high-protein weight-loss diets contend that the U.S. population is substantially overweight because we eat too many calories, not because we eat too much carbohydrate or too much fat, specifically. Nutrition experts have long agreed that the key to weight loss is eating less energy than you expend. If you eat more energy than you expend, you will gain weight. Thus, any type of diet that contains fewer Calories than the person expends will result in weight loss.

Additionally, there are concerns about potential health risks that are associated with eating a diet that is both low in carbohydrate and high in fat. These risks have prevented many nutrition experts from endorsing high-protein diets for weight loss. These health risks include the following:

- Low blood glucose levels leading to low energy levels, diminished cognitive functioning, and elevated ketones. Despite this concern, recent evidence shows that these risks do not occur in people eating a high-protein diet that is modestly restricted in carbohydrate and fat. However, anyone eating a weight-loss diet can experience low blood glucose and low energy levels, which can prevent some people from exercising regularly.

- Increased risk for heart disease because high-protein diets that rely on animal sources of protein are typically high in saturated fat. It is well established that eating a diet high in saturated fat increases a person's LDL-cholesterol, which in turn increases the risk for heart disease. Nevertheless, research shows that high-protein diets that contain lean meat choices and low-fat dairy products (as recommended in the most recent version of the Atkins Diet) do not cause unhealthful changes in blood lipids. In fact, these types of diets can lead to healthier changes in blood lipids compared to diets higher in carbohydrate.[13]

- Increased risk for some forms of cancer due to eating a diet that is high in fat and low in fiber. Some high-protein diet plans recommend few foods that contain fiber and antioxidants, so many nutrition experts are concerned that eating this type of a diet over many

⬆ Many people will try any diet to lose weight, but is it worth it in the long run?

years will increase a person's risk for some forms of cancer, particularly colon cancer. In a recent study, seventeen obese men ate weight-loss diets high in protein and low in carbohydrate and fiber for 4 weeks.[14] At the end of this study, the men were found to have a decrease in cancer-protective substances and an increase in cancer-promoting substances in their feces. These findings suggest that consuming these types of diets over the long term may increase the risk for cancer and other diseases of the colon. However, revised versions of the Atkins Diet and other high-protein diets promote the consumption of many foods that are high in fiber and antioxidants and lower in saturated fat. The effects of these revised diets on cancer risk have yet to be explored.

Should you adopt a high-protein diet? This is not an easy question to answer. Each of us must decide on the type of diet to consume based on our own needs, preferences, health risks, and lifestyle. At the present time, there is not enough evidence to state with any certainty that high-protein diets are always better than higher-carbohydrate plans, and we still need to learn much more about the safety of eating a high-protein diet over many years. Based on what we currently know, the most sound weight-loss plans are those that are moderately reduced in energy intake and contain ample fruits, vegetables, and whole grains; adequate carbohydrate and lean protein foods; moderate amounts of total fat; and relatively low amounts of saturated fat. It is also important to choose a food plan that you can follow throughout your lifetime. By researching the benefits and risks of various diet plans, you can make an educated decision about the type of diet that will work best to maintain a healthful weight and muscle mass and provide enough energy and nutrients to maintain your lifestyle and your long-term health.

certain whole grains. This wide variety of healthful protein sources makes it easy to *Eat Right All Day*!

Although most people are aware that meats are an excellent source of protein, many are surprised to learn that the quality of the protein in some legumes rivals that of meat. As noted earlier, soy is a complete protein, providing all essential amino acids. For more information about the nutrients in soy, claims regarding its health benefits, and ways to enjoy soy, check out the upcoming *Highlight* box (page 144).

Other legumes include kidney beans, pinto beans, black beans, garbanzo beans (chickpeas), lentils, green peas, black-eyed peas, and lima beans. In addition to being excellent sources of protein, legumes are also high in fiber, iron, calcium, and many of the B-vitamins (although they do not contain vitamin B_{12}). They are also low in saturated fat and have no cholesterol. Because legumes other than soy are deficient in methionine, an essential amino acid, they are often served with grains, which supply it.

Eating legumes regularly, including foods made from soybeans, may help reduce the risk for heart disease by lowering blood cholesterol levels. Diets high in legumes and soy products are also associated with lower rates of some cancers. If you're not used to eating beans and lentils, the *Game Plan* box (page 146) provides tips for incorporating these nourishing foods into your daily diet.

Nuts are another healthful high-protein food. In fact, the USDA Food Patterns counts ⅓ cup of nuts or 2 tablespoons of peanut butter as equivalent to 1 ounce—about one-third of a serving—of meat! Moreover, as you learned previously (see Chapter 4),

Eating Right All Day

Breakfast Whole-grain cereal with soymilk instead of a doughnut!

Lunch Veggie burger instead of a ground beef burger!

Dinner Stir fry chicken instead of fried chicken!

Snack Raw veggies with lowfat dip instead of nachos!

HIGHLIGHT
What's So Great About Soy?

Twenty years ago, if you were able to find a soy-based food in a traditional grocery store in the United States or Canada, it was probably soy milk. Now, it seems there are soy products in almost every aisle, from marinated tofu and tempeh to miso soup to soy-based cheeses, cereals, hot dogs, burgers, frozen dinners, and even tofu ice cream. Why the explosion? What's so great about soy, and should you give it a try?

What Is Soy?

Before we explore the many health claims tied to soy-based foods, let's define some terms. First, all soy-based foods start with soybeans, a staple in many Asian countries. Soybeans provide all essential amino acids and have almost twice as much protein as any other legume (7–10 grams of protein in 1 cup of soy milk). Although they also pack three to ten times as much fat as other beans, almost all of it is unsaturated, and soy has no cholesterol. Soy is also rich in a group of phytochemicals called *isoflavones*. These plant chemicals mimic the effect of the hormone estrogen in the human body. Here are some common varieties of soy-based foods you might find in your local supermarket:

- *Soy milk* is a beverage produced when soybeans are ground with water. Flavorings are added to make the drink palatable, and many brands of soy milk are fortified with calcium.

- *Tofu* is made from soy milk coagulated to form curds. If the coagulant used is calcium sulfate, the resulting product is high in calcium. Tofu is usually sold in blocks, like cheese, and is used as a meat substitute. Although many people object to its bland taste and mushy texture, tofu adapts well to many seasonings, and when drained and frozen before cooking it develops a chewy texture similar to meat. Tofu is also the basis of many processed foods, such as meatless hot dogs and burgers.

- *Tempeh* is a more flavorful and firmer-textured meat substitute made from soybeans fermented with grains. It is often used in stir-fried dishes.

- *Miso* is a paste made from fermented soybeans and grains. It is used sparingly as a base for soups and sauces, as it is very high in sodium.

- *Edamame* are precooked, frozen soybeans eaten as a snack or in salads and other dishes.

Soy May Reduce Your Risk for Chronic Disease

Now let's look at the health claims. Proponents say that a diet high in soy protein can reduce your risk for heart disease, certain types of cancer, and osteoporosis (loss of bone density). Let's review the research behind each of these claims.

Heart Disease

In October 1999, the U.S. Food and Drug Administration (FDA) gave food manufacturers permission to put labels on products high in soy protein stating that a daily diet containing 25 grams of soy protein and low in saturated fat and cholesterol may reduce the risk for heart disease.[15] The FDA reviewed twenty-seven relevant clinical studies before concluding that diets providing four servings a day of soy can provoke a modest reduction in blood levels of LDL-cholesterol. The cholesterol-reducing benefits of soy appear to be linked only to soy-based foods, not supplements. The American Heart Association therefore recommends consuming soy milk and tofu as part of a heart-healthy diet.[16]

Cancer Risk

Many studies suggest that soy protects against prostate cancer, which is the most common cancer in men.[17] Again, although the isoflavones in soy foods appear to exert the protective effect, researchers recommend eating soy foods, not supplements.

Whereas the risk-reducing benefits of soy seem clear in the case of prostate cancer, the claims for soy's effect on breast cancer risk are controversial. Some studies have suggested that the isoflavones in soy may reduce a woman's risk for breast cancer; however, their findings conflict with those of other studies indicating a possible increased risk. The American Cancer Society (ACS) explains that the plant estrogens in soy "may have both a protective role and a stimulatory role in breast cancer cell growth depending on several factors, including at what age they're consumed and whether they're consumed as food or as supplement." Several federally funded studies are currently being conducted to further our understanding of the effect of soy on breast cancer risk, but for now, the ACS recommends consuming naturally occurring soy foods as part of a balanced, plant-based diet.[18]

Bone Loss

Published studies of the effect of soy on bone density, a particular concern for older women, have also been inconclusive. Whereas some suggest that soy can help keep bones strong, others suggest little benefit. A recent review combining the results of ten randomized controlled trials found that consuming soy helped prevent bone loss in the spine in menopausal women.[19] Several new studies investigating the potential link between soy and bone health are underway.

Adding Soy to Your Diet

If you decide that you want to try soy, how do you go about it? A first step for many people is to substitute soy milk for cow's milk on its own, on cereal, in smoothies, or in recipes for baked goods. Different brands of soy milk can have very different flavors, so try a few before you decide you don't like the taste.

Here are some other possibilities for adding soy to your diet:[15]

- Try one of the breakfast cereals made with soy.
- Use soy nut butter (similar to peanut butter), soy deli meats, or soy cheese in sandwiches.
- Try soy sausages, bacon, hot dogs, burgers, ground "beef," and "chicken" patties.
- Toss cubes of prepackaged flavored, baked tofu or tempeh or a handful of edamame into stir-fried vegetables and serve over Chinese noodles or rice.
- Order soy-based dishes, such as spicy bean curd and miso soup, at Asian restaurants.
- Eat roasted soy nuts, edamame, or a soy protein bar for a snack.
- Try soy yogurt and ice cream.

studies show that consuming about 2 to 5 oz of nuts per week significantly reduces people's risk for cardiovascular disease.[20] Although the exact mechanism behind this is not known, nuts contain many nutrients and other substances that are associated with health benefits, including fiber, unsaturated fats, potassium, folate, and plant sterols that inhibit cholesterol absorption.

A new source of non-meat protein that is available on the market is *quorn*, a protein product derived from fermented fungus. It is mixed with a variety of other foods to produce various types of meat substitutes. Other "new" foods high in protein include some very ancient grains! For instance, you may have heard of pastas and other products made with *quinoa*, a plant so essential to the diet of the ancient Incas that they considered it sacred. No wonder: quinoa, cooked much like rice, provides 8 grams of protein in a 1-cup serving. It's highly digestible, and unlike many more familiar grains, provides all nine essential amino acids. See the upcoming feature *Foods You Don't Know You Love Yet* (page 147) for more on quinoa. A similar grain called amaranth also provides complete protein. Teff, millet, and sorghum are grains long cultivated in Africa as rich sources of protein. They are now widely available in the United States. Although these three grains are low in the essential amino acid lysine, combining them with legumes produces a complete-protein meal.

Most other types of grains, as well as fruits and vegetables, are not particularly high in protein; however, these foods provide fiber and many vitamins and minerals and are excellent sources of carbohydrates. Thus, eating fruits, vegetables, and grains can help spare protein for use in building and maintaining our body rather than using it for energy.

Amino Acid Supplements: Any Truth to the Hype?

"Amino acid supplements—you can't gain without them!" This is just one of the countless headlines found in bodybuilding magazines and on Internet sites touting amino acid supplements as the key to achieving power, strength, and performance "perfection." Many athletes who read these claims believe that taking amino acid supplements will boost their energy during performance, replace proteins metabolized

90%

GAME PLAN

Tips for Adding Legumes to Your Daily Diet

They're high in protein and fiber and low in fat, and they fill you up with fewer calories than meat sources of protein. What's more, they taste good! Maybe that's why nutrition experts consider legumes an almost perfect food. From main dishes to snacks, here are some simple ways to add legumes to your daily diet. By the way, some people experience uncomfortable intestinal gas after eating legumes. This is produced when bacteria in the colon break down the starches. If you're one of those people, make sure you soak legumes thoroughly, changing the water once or twice, before cooking. You can also try using enzyme supplements available in most grocery stores, such as Beano. Taken before meals, they reduce the occurrence of intestinal gas.

Breakfast

☐ Instead of cereal, eggs, or a muffin, microwave a frozen bean burrito for a quick, portable breakfast.

☐ Make your pancakes with soy milk or pour soy milk on your cereal.

☐ If you normally have a side of bacon, ham, or sausage with your eggs, have a side of black beans.

Lunch and Dinner

☐ Try a sandwich made with hummus (a garbanzo bean spread), cucumbers, tomato, avocado, and/or lettuce on whole-wheat bread or in a whole-wheat pocket.

☐ Add garbanzo beans, kidney beans, edamame, or fresh peas to tossed salads, or make a three-bean salad with kidney beans, green beans, and garbanzo beans.

☐ Make a side dish using legumes, such as peas, with pearl onions or succotash (lima beans, corn, and tomatoes).

☐ Make black-bean soup, lentil soup, pea soup, minestrone soup, or a batch of dhal (a type of yellow lentil used in Indian cuisine) and serve over brown rice. Top with plain yogurt, a traditional accompaniment in many Asian cuisines.

☐ Make tacos or burritos with black or pinto beans instead of shredded meat.

☐ Make a "meatloaf" using cooked, mashed lentils instead of ground beef.

☐ For fast food at home, keep canned beans on hand. Serve over rice with a salad for a complete and hearty meal.

Snacks

☐ Instead of potato chips or pretzels, try one of the new bean chips.

☐ Dip fresh vegetables in bean dip.

☐ Have hummus on wedges of pita bread.

☐ Add roasted soy "nuts" to your trail mix.

☐ Keep frozen tofu desserts, such as tofu ice cream, in your freezer.

FOODS YOU DON'T KNOW YOU LOVE YET

Quinoa

Quinoa (pronounced KEEN-wa) is a grain-like crop grown for its edible seeds. Quinoa originated in South America, and it is considered a *pseudocereal* or grain, which means it is not a member of the grass family and not considered an actual grain, such as wheat and rice. Quinoa is not only high in protein compared to other grains but is also an excellent plant source

of complete protein and a good source of fiber and minerals, including phosphorus, magnesium, and iron. It is also gluten free, so it's a safe grain choice for people who are allergic to gluten or have celiac disease.

Because quinoa has a bitter coating in its natural state, it needs to be soaked and rinsed prior to cooking. However, many stores sell quinoa that has been pre-rinsed; check the package instructions. Once cooked, quinoa is light and fluffy, with a nutty taste. You can use quinoa as a substitute for rice or couscous in dishes such as stuffing, pilaf, salads, and soups. Quinoa pasta is also available in various shapes. Quinoa can be found in most major supermarkets and health food stores, and it can be bought online through websites such as Amazon.com.

for energy during exercise, enhance muscle growth and strength, and hasten recovery from intense training or injury. Should you believe the hype?

Consider two facts: first, we use very little protein for energy during exercise; second, most Americans already consume more than two times the RDA for protein. Thus, most of us already get more than enough protein to support either strength or endurance exercise training and performance. What about the claims related to muscle building? Although some research has shown that intravenous infusions of various amino acids in the laboratory can stimulate certain hormones that enhance the building of muscle, there is little evidence that taking individual amino acid or protein supplements orally can build muscle or improve strength.[21] So, no matter what the headlines say, the claims for amino acid supplements are unfounded.

What about drawbacks? Amino acid supplements are relatively expensive compared to foods, so using them will put a significant dent in your wallet! More importantly, although it's commonly assumed that taking amino acid supplements is harmless, this is not true. Taking high amounts of cysteine has been shown to cause nausea, dizziness, fatigue, and insomnia.[22] Methionine is considered to be one of the most toxic amino acids and can cause severe nausea, vomiting, and liver dysfunction.[22] The Institute of Medicine recommends that more research be done, as relatively little is known about the adverse effects of taking large amounts of amino acid supplements.[23]

RECAP Eating too much protein may increase your risk for heart disease. Good sources of protein include meats, eggs, dairy products, soy products, legumes, nuts, quorn, and certain grains. Taking amino acid supplements does not enhance muscle building or strength, and taking large amounts of some amino acids can cause harmful side effects.

HEALTHWATCH

Can a Vegetarian Diet Provide Adequate Protein?

Vegetarianism is the practice of restricting the diet to food substances of vegetable origin, including fruits, grains, and nuts. To address the question of whether a vegetarian diet can provide adequate protein, let's begin with a look at the different types of vegetarian diets.

There Are Many Types of Vegetarian Diets

There are almost as many types of vegetarian diets as there are vegetarians. Some people who consider themselves vegetarians regularly eat fish. Others avoid the flesh of animals but consume eggs, milk, and cheese liberally. Still others strictly avoid all products of animal origin, including milk and eggs, and even by-products, such as candies and puddings made with gelatin. A type of "vegetarian" diet receiving significant media attention recently has been the *flexitarian* diet. Flexitarians are considered semivegetarians who eat mostly plant foods, eggs, and dairy but occasionally eat red meat, poultry, and/or fish; hence, they are flexible about occasionally adding some meat-based protein to their diet. Vegetarian diets are also referred to as *plant-based* diets and are recognized for having many health benefits compared to diets that contain more meat and fewer plant-based foods.

vegetarianism The practice of restricting the diet to food substances of plant origin, including vegetables, fruits, grains, and nuts.

Table 5.4 identifies the various types of vegetarian diets, ranging from the broadest to the most restrictive. Notice that the more restrictive the diet, the more challenging it becomes to get adequate dietary protein.

TABLE 5.4	**Terms and Definitions of a Vegetarian Diet**	
Type of Diet	**Foods Consumed**	**Comments**
Semivegetarian (also called a flexitarian or plant-based diet)	Vegetables, grains, nuts, fruits, legumes, eggs, dairy products, and occasionally seafood and/or poultry	Typically excludes or limits red meat; may also avoid other meats.
Pescovegetarian	Similar to a semivegetarian but excludes poultry	*Pesco* means "fish," the only nonplant source of protein in this diet
Lacto-ovo-vegetarian	Vegetables, grains, nuts, fruits, legumes, dairy products (*lacto*), and eggs (*ovo*)	Excludes animal flesh and seafood
Lacto-vegetarian	Similar to a lacto-ovo-vegetarian but excludes eggs	Relies on milk and cheese for animal sources of protein
Ovovegetarian	Vegetables, grains, nuts, fruits, legumes, and eggs	Excludes dairy, flesh, and seafood products
Vegan (also called strict vegetarian)	Only plant-based foods (vegetables, grains, nuts, seeds, fruits, and legumes)	May not provide adequate vitamin B_{12}, zinc, iron, or calcium
Macrobiotic diet	Vegan-type of diet; becomes progressively more strict until almost all foods are eliminated; at the extreme, only brown rice and small amounts of water or herbal tea are consumed	When taken to extremes, can cause malnutrition and death
Fruitarian	Only raw or dried fruit, seeds, nuts, honey, and vegetable oil	Extremely restrictive; deficient in protein, calcium, zinc, iron, vitamin B_{12}, riboflavin, and other nutrients

Why Do People Become Vegetarians?

When discussing vegetarianism, one of the most often-asked questions is why people make this food choice. The most common responses are included here.

Religious, Ethical, and Food-Safety Reasons

Some make the choice for religious or spiritual reasons. Several religions prohibit or restrict the consumption of animal flesh; however, generalizations can be misleading. For example, although certain sects within Hinduism observe nonviolence, including toward animals, scanning the menu at an Indian restaurant will reveal that many Hindus regularly consume small quantities of meat, poultry, and fish. Many Buddhists are vegetarians, as are some Christians, including most Seventh-Day Adventists.

Many vegetarians are guided by their personal philosophy to choose vegetarianism. These people feel that it is morally and ethically wrong to consume animals and any products from animals (such as dairy or egg products) because they view the practices in the modern animal industries as inhumane. They may consume milk and eggs but choose to purchase them only from family farms where they believe animals are treated humanely.

There is also a great deal of concern about meat-handling practices, because outbreaks of foodborne illness occur frequently and can have serious consequences. For example, in recent years, outbreaks of severe bloody diarrhea have been traced to a bacterium called *E. coli* in hamburgers and steaks prepared at home or served in restaurants, in bologna, and in frozen pepperoni pizza. Many people have had to be hospitalized, some with kidney failure, which in a few victims proved fatal. Another concern surrounding beef is the possibility that it is tainted by the microbes that cause a fatal nerve disorder commonly referred to as *mad cow disease*. Contaminated poultry products—from ground turkey to frozen chicken pies and dinners—have also caused disease outbreaks, typically because of a bacterium called *Salmonella*.

Ecological Reasons

Many people choose vegetarianism because of their concerns about the effect of the meat industries on the global environment. They argue that cattle consume large quantities of grain and water, require grazing areas that could be used for plant food production, destroy vulnerable ecosystems (including rain forests), produce wastes that run off into surrounding bodies of water, and belch gases high in methane, which is associated with global warming **(Figure 5.8)**. Meat industry organizations argue that such effects are minor and greatly exaggerated. One area of agreement that has recently emerged focuses the argument not on *whether* we eat meat but on *how much* meat we consume. The environmental damage caused by the raising of livestock is due in part to the large number of animals produced. When a population reduces its consumption of meat, reduced production follows. The United Nations Intergovernmental Panel on Climate Change (IPCC) therefore recommends that we progressively reduce our meat consumption.

Health Benefits

Still others practice vegetarianism because of its health benefits. Research over several years has consistently shown that a varied and balanced vegetarian diet can reduce the risk for many chronic diseases. Its health benefits include the following:[24]

(a)

(b)

Interested in trying a vegetarian diet but don't know where to begin? Check out the Vegetarian Starter Kit from the Physicians Committee for Responsible Medicine, at www.pcrm.org/health/veginfo/vsk/index.html.

Figure 5.8 Both **(a)** livestock production and **(b)** aggressive deforestation contribute to greenhouse gases.

- reduced risk for obesity, type 2 diabetes, high blood pressure, and heart disease, most likely due to the lower saturated-fat content of vegetarian diets
- fewer intestinal problems, most likely due to the higher fiber content of vegetarian diets

- reduced risk for some cancers, particularly colon cancer;[25] many components of a vegetarian diet can contribute to reducing cancer risks, including higher fiber, lower dietary fat, lower consumption of **carcinogens** (cancer-causing agents) that are formed when cooking meat, and higher consumption of soy protein, which may have anticancer properties[26]
- reduced risk for kidney disease, kidney stones, and gallstones; the lower protein content of vegetarian diets, plus the higher intake of legumes and vegetables, may be protective against these conditions.

⬆ A well-balanced vegetarian diet can provide adequate protein and other nutrients.

carcinogens Cancer-causing agents, such as certain pesticides, industrial chemicals, and pollutants.

What Are the Challenges of a Vegetarian Diet?

Although a vegetarian diet can be healthful, it also presents some challenges. With reduced consumption of flesh and dairy products, there is a potential for inadequate intakes of certain nutrients. **Table 5.5** lists the nutrients that can be deficient in a vegan type of diet plan and describes good non-animal sources of these nutrients. Supplementation may be necessary for certain individuals if they cannot include adequate amounts in their diet.

Can a vegetarian diet provide enough protein? Because high-quality protein sources are quite easy to obtain in developed countries, a well-balanced vegetarian diet can provide adequate protein. In fact, the American Dietetic Association and the Dietitians of Canada endorse an appropriately planned vegetarian diet as healthful, nutritionally adequate, and beneficial in reducing and preventing various diseases.[24]

As you can see, the emphasis is on a *balanced* and *adequate* vegetarian diet; thus, it is important for vegetarians to consume soy products, eat complementary proteins, and obtain enough energy from other macronutrients to spare protein from being used as an energy source. Although the digestibility of a vegetarian diet is potentially lower than that of an animal-based diet, there is no separate protein recommendation for vegetarians who consume complementary plant proteins.[27]

TABLE 5.5 Nutrients of Concern in a Vegan Diet		
Nutrient	**Functions**	**Non-Meat/Non-Dairy Food Sources**
Vitamin B_{12}	Assists with DNA synthesis; protection and growth of nerve fibers	Vitamin B_{12}–fortified cereals, yeast, soy products, and other meat analogs; vitamin B_{12} supplements
Vitamin D	Promotes bone growth	Vitamin D–fortified cereals, margarines, and soy products; adequate exposure to sunlight; supplementation may be necessary for those who do not get adequate exposure to sunlight
Riboflavin (vitamin B_2)	Promotes release of energy; supports normal vision and skin health	Whole and enriched grains, green leafy vegetables, mushrooms, beans, nuts, and seeds
Iron	Assists with oxygen transport; involved in making amino acids and hormones	Whole-grain products, prune juice, dried fruits, beans, nuts, seeds, and leafy vegetables (such as spinach)
Calcium	Maintains bone health; assists with muscle contraction, blood pressure, and nerve transmission	Fortified soy milk and tofu, almonds, dry beans, leafy vegetables, calcium-fortified juices, and fortified breakfast cereals
Zinc	Assists with DNA and RNA synthesis, immune function, and growth	Whole-grain products, wheat germ, beans, nuts, and seeds

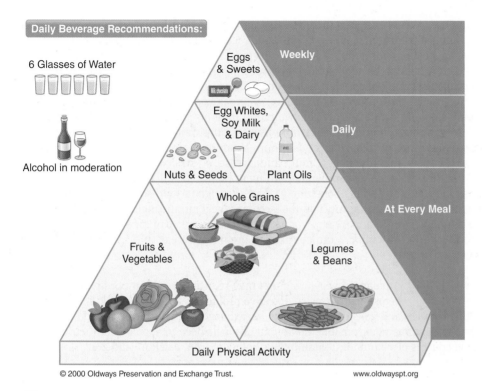

Daily Beverage Recommendations:

6 Glasses of Water

Alcohol in moderation

Eggs & Sweets — Weekly

Egg Whites, Soy Milk & Dairy — Daily

Nuts & Seeds — Plant Oils

Whole Grains

Fruits & Vegetables — Legumes & Beans — At Every Meal

Daily Physical Activity

© 2000 Oldways Preservation and Exchange Trust.   www.oldwayspt.org

Figure 5.9 The Vegetarian Diet Pyramid. This image helps guide users in making general vegetarian food choices at each meal, daily, and weekly.

A Special Food Pyramid Can Help Vegetarians Consume Adequate Nutrients

Vegetarians can use the food pyramid illustrated in **Figure 5.9** to design a diet that contains adequate levels of all the necessary nutrients. Figure 5.9 emphasizes the importance of eating whole grains, fruits, vegetables, and legumes at every meal. Daily foods include nuts and seeds, egg whites, soy milk and dairy products, and

Vegetarians should eat 5 servings of beans, nuts, seeds, eggs, or meat substitutes, such as this tofu, daily.

NUTRI-CASE THEO

"No way would I ever become a vegetarian! The only way to build up your muscles is to eat meat. I was reading in a body-building magazine last week about some guy who doesn't eat anything from animals, not even milk or eggs, and he looked pretty buff—but I don't believe it. They can do anything to photos these days. Besides, during basketball season, I just crave red meat. If I don't have it, I feel sort of like my batteries don't get charged. It's just not practical for a competitive athlete to go without meat."

What two claims does Theo make here about the role of red meat in his diet? Do you think these claims are valid? Why or why not? What facts might be important to consider about the nature of plant and animal proteins?

plant oils. Weekly choices include eggs and sweets. Although this version provides a helpful illustration of the types of foods recommended for vegetarians, it does not give suggestions for daily number of servings.

The American Dietetic Association recommends that vegetarians eat eight or more servings each day of calcium-rich foods.[28] Lacto and lacto-ovo-vegetarians can consume low-fat or nonfat dairy products, whereas vegans and ovovegetarians can consume calcium-fortified soy, rice, or almond milk or calcium-fortified orange juice.

Vegetarians should also consume five servings daily of foods from the legumes, nuts, and other protein-rich foods group. Vitamin B_{12} is found naturally only in animal products, including eggs, milk, and cheese, so strict vegans need to consume fortified plant foods or supplements to meet their needs. In general, it is recommended that vegetarians consume at least three good food sources of vitamin B_{12} each day. Examples appropriate for lacto-ovo-vegetarians include 1 large egg, ½ cup cow's milk, and ¾ cup yogurt, whereas vegans can meet this need with 1 cup fortified soy milk, 1 ounce fortified breakfast cereal, and 1½ ounces fortified meat substitute.

RECAP A balanced vegetarian diet may reduce the risk for obesity, type 2 diabetes, heart disease, digestive problems, some cancers, kidney disease, kidney stones, and gallstones. Although varied vegetarian diets can provide enough protein, vegetarians who consume no animal products need to supplement their diet with good sources of vitamin B_{12}, vitamin D, riboflavin, iron, calcium, and zinc.

COOKING 101

Proteins are among our most important nutrients, whether you're a meat devotee or a committed vegetarian! Check out ways to boost your protein intake and build great meals around "easy eggs" by viewing our new Cooking 101 videos, available on the Companion Website at www.pearsonhighered.com/thompsonmanore.

Chapter Review

What Can I Do **Today?**

Now that you've read this chapter, try making these three changes:

- Try adding soy milk to your break-fast cereal.
- Make it a goal today to consume meals that provide adequate protein from sources low in saturated fats and cholesterol, such as fish, poultry without the skin, lean beef, egg whites, legumes, nuts and nut butters, and tofu.

- If you regularly eat red meat, try re-placing one of your meat choices for the next 7 days with a meat substi-tute, such as quorn, veggie burgers/sausages, or tofu.

Test Yourself ANSWERS

1. **F** Although protein can be used for energy in cer-tain circumstances, fats and carbohydrates are the primary sources of energy for our body.

2. **F** There is no evidence that consuming amino acid supplements assists in building muscle tissue. Consuming adequate energy and exercising muscles, specifically using weight training, build muscle tissue.

3. **F** Excess protein is broken down and its component parts are either stored as fat or used for energy or tissue building and repair. Only the nitrogen component of protein is excreted in the urine.

4. **F** Vegetarian diets can meet and even exceed an individual's protein needs, assuming that adequate energy-yielding macronutrients, a variety of protein sources, and complementary protein sources are consumed.

5. **T** Most people in the United States consume 1.5 to 2 times more protein than they need.

 **NutriTools** Check out the Companion Website at www.pearsonhighered.com/thompsonmanore, or use MyNutritionLab.com, to access interactive animations, including

- Know Your Protein Sources

Review Questions

1. The process of combining peanut butter and whole-wheat bread to make a complete protein is called
   a. deamination.
   b. vegetarianism.
   c. transamination.
   d. mutual supplementation.

2. Which of the following meals is typical of a vegan diet?
   a. rice, pinto beans, acorn squash, soy butter, and almond milk
   b. veggie dog, bun, and a banana blended with yogurt
   c. raw lean beef and green tea
   d. egg salad on whole-wheat toast, broccoli, carrot sticks, and soy milk

3. Proteins are synthesized following instructions dictated by
   a. enzymes.
   b. DNA.
   c. hormones.
   d. ketones.

4. The portion of an amino acid that contains nitrogen is called the
   a. side chain.
   b. amine group.
   c. acid group.
   d. nitrate cluster.

5. Proteins contain
   a. carbon, oxygen, and nitrogen.
   b. oxygen and hydrogen.
   c. carbon, oxygen, hydrogen, and nitrogen.
   d. carbon, oxygen, and hydrogen.

6. True or False? After leaving the small intestine, amino acids are transported to the liver for distribution throughout the body.

7. True or False? When a protein is denatured, its shape is lost but its function is retained.

8. True or False? All hormones are proteins.

9. True or False? Buffers help the body maintain acid–base balance.

10. True or False? Athletes typically require about three times as much protein as nonactive people.

Answers to Review Questions are located at the back of this text.

Web Links

www.eatright.org
American Dietetic Association

www.vrg.org
Vegetarian Resource Group

www.beef.org
National Cattlemen's Beef Association

www.cdc.gov
Centers for Disease Control and Prevention

www.nal.usda.gov/fnic
USDA Food and Nutrition Information Center

6

Vitamins: Micronutrients with Macro Powers

Test Yourself

Are these statements true or false? Circle your guess.

1. **T** **F** Vitamin D is called the "sunshine vitamin" because our body can make it by using energy obtained from sunlight.

2. **T** **F** Taking vitamin C supplements helps prevent colds.

3. **T** **F** The B-vitamins are an important source of energy for our body.

4. **T** **F** Phytochemicals are a small group of plant chemicals that are believed to cause cancer.

5. **T** **F** Taking a daily multivitamin supplement is a waste of money.

Test Yourself answers can be found at the end of the chapter.

Nutrition Online icons are located throughout the chapter, directing you to web links, videos, podcasts, and other useful online resources.

D r. Leslie Bernstein looked in astonishment at the 80-year-old man in his office. A leading gastro-enterologist and professor of medicine at Albert Einstein College of Medicine in New York City, he had admired Pop Katz for years as one of his most healthy patients, a strict vegetarian and athlete who just weeks before had been going on 3-mile runs. Now he could barely stand. He was confused, cried easily, was wandering away from his home, and had lost control of his bladder. Tests showed that he had not had a stroke; did not have a tumor, an infection, or Alzheimer's disease; and had no evidence of exposure to pesticides or other toxins. A neurologist diagnosed dementia, but Bernstein was unconvinced: How could a man who hadn't been sick for 80 years suddenly become demented? Then it struck him: "The man's been a vegetarian for 38 years. No meat. No fish. No eggs. No milk. He hasn't had any animal protein for decades. He has to be B_{12} deficient!"[1]

Bernstein immediately tested Katz's blood, then gave him an injection of vitamin B_{12}. The blood test confirmed Bernstein's hunch: the level of B_{12} in Katz's blood was too low to detect. The morning after his injection, Katz could sit up without help. Within a week of continuing treatment, he could read, play card games, and hold his own in conversations. Unfortunately, some neurological damage remained, including alterations in his personality and an inability to concentrate.

155

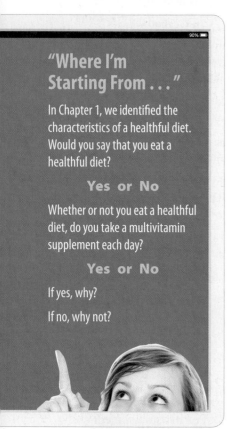

Bernstein notes, "A diet free of animal protein can be healthful and safe, but it should be supplemented periodically with B$_{12}$ by mouth or by injection."[1]

It was not until 1906, when the English biochemist F. G. Hopkins discovered what he called *accessory factors* that scientists began to appreciate the many critical roles of micronutrients in maintaining human health. Vitamin B$_{12}$, for instance, was not even isolated until 1948! In this chapter, we explore the roles vitamins play as tissue guardians, antioxidants, and energy generators. But first, let's take a moment to define exactly what vitamins are.

What Are Vitamins?

Vitamins are compounds that contain carbon and are essential in regulating our body's processes **(Figure 6.1)**. Because our body cannot synthesize most vitamins, we must consume them in our diet. Fortunately, most are found in a variety of foods. Vitamins are classified as either fat soluble or water soluble. Here, we discuss the general properties of these two groups.

Fat-Soluble Vitamins Are Stored in the Body

Vitamins A, D, E, and K are **fat-soluble vitamins.** These vitamins are absorbed in our intestines along with dietary fat. They are then transported to the liver or other organs, where they are either used immediately or stored in fatty tissues for later use. Because we are capable of storing fat-soluble vitamins, we do not have to consume the recommended

Energy Generators
Help convert food into energy

Pantothenic Acid
Niacin
Thiamin
Riboflavin
Folate
Vitamin B$_{12}$
Vitamin B$_6$
Biotin
Vitamin C

Tissue Guardians
Help keep body structures healthy

Vitamin D
Vitamin K
Vitamin C
Vitamin A

Blood Boosters
Help optimize blood health

Vitamin K
Vitamin B$_{12}$
Vitamin B$_6$
Folate

Antioxidants
Help protect against oxidative damage

Beta-Carotene and other Carotenoids
Vitamin E
Vitamin C
Vitamin A

Figure 6.1 The functions of fat-soluble and water-soluble vitamins and related compounds, such as beta-carotene and biotin. Good food sources are also shown for each functional group.

intakes of these nutrients every single day. As long as our diet provides the average amounts recommended over any given time period, we won't develop deficiencies.

Our ability to store fat-soluble vitamins has a distinct disadvantage. If we consume more of these vitamins than our body can use, they can build up to toxic levels in our fatty tissues. Symptoms of toxicity include damage to our hair, skin, bones, eyes, and nervous system. **Megadosing**—that is, taking ten or more times the recommended amount of a nutrient—can even lead to death when it involves the fat-soluble vitamins A and D.

Even though we can store fat-soluble vitamins, deficiencies sometimes occur, especially in people with diseases that prevent the normal absorption of fat and in people who consume very little fat. Using mineral oil as a laxative can result in a significant loss of fat-soluble vitamins in our feces. Deficiencies of fat-soluble vitamins can lead to serious health problems, such as night blindness, fragile bones, and even death in the most severe cases.

The potential for toxicity from supplements is one reason it's wise to get your vitamins from foods whenever possible. Fat-soluble vitamins are found in a variety of fat-containing foods. Meats, dairy products, vegetable oils, avocados, nuts, and seeds are all potentially good sources. **Table 6.1** identifies major functions and recommended intakes.

vitamins Micronutrients that contain carbon and assist us in regulating our body's processes. They are classified as water soluble or fat soluble.

fat-soluble vitamins Vitamins that are not soluble in water but soluble in fat. These include vitamins A, D, E, and K.

megadosing Taking a dose of a nutrient that is ten or more times greater than the recommended amount.

TABLE 6.1 Fat-Soluble Vitamins

Vitamin Name	Primary Functions	Recommended Intake*	Reliable Food Sources	Toxicity/Deficiency Symptoms
A (retinol, retinal, retinoic acid)	Required for ability of eyes to adjust to changes in light; Protects color vision; Assists cell differentiation; Required for sperm production in men and fertilization in women; Contributes to healthy bone; Contributes to healthy immune system	RDA: Men = 900 μg; Women = 700 μg; UL = 3,000 μg/day	Preformed retinol: beef and chicken liver, egg yolks, milk; Carotenoid precursors: spinach, carrots, mango, apricots, cantaloupe, pumpkin, yams	*Toxicity:* fatigue; bone and joint pain; spontaneous abortion and birth defects of fetuses in pregnant women; nausea and diarrhea; liver damage; nervous system damage; blurred vision; hair loss; skin disorders; *Deficiency:* night blindness, xerophthalmia; impaired growth, immunity, and reproductive function
D (cholecalciferol)	Regulates blood calcium levels; Maintains bone health; Assists cell differentiation	RDA (assumes that person does not get adequate sun exposure): Adult aged 19 to 50 = 600 IU/day; Adult aged 50 to 70 = 600 IU/day; Adult aged >70 = 800 IU/day; UL = 4,000 IU/day	Canned salmon and mackerel, milk, fortified cereals	*Toxicity:* hypercalcemia; *Deficiency:* rickets in children; osteomalacia and/or osteoporosis in adults
E (tocopherol)	As a powerful antioxidant, protects cell membranes, polyunsaturated fatty acids, and vitamin A from oxidation; Protects white blood cells; Enhances immune function; Improves absorption of vitamin A	RDA: Men = 15 mg/day; Women = 15 mg/day; UL = 1,000 mg/day	Sunflower seeds, almonds, vegetable oils, fortified cereals	*Toxicity:* rare; *Deficiency:* hemolytic anemia; impairment of nerve, muscle, and immune function
K (phylloquinone, menaquinone, menadione)	Serves as a coenzyme during production of specific proteins that assist in blood coagulation and bone metabolism	AI: Men = 120 μg/day; Women = 90 μg/day	Kale, spinach, turnip greens, brussels sprouts	*Toxicity:* none known; *Deficiency:* impaired blood clotting; possible effect on bone health

*Abbreviations: RDA, Recommended Dietary Allowance; UL, upper limit; AI, Adequate Intake.

TABLE 6.2 **Water-Soluble Vitamins** *Pull out at certain level*

Vitamin Name	Primary Functions	Recommended Intake*	Reliable Food Sources	Toxicity/Deficiency Symptoms
Thiamin (vitamin B_1)	Required as enzyme cofactor for carbohydrate and amino acid metabolism	RDA: Men = 1.2 mg/day Women = 1.1 mg/day	Pork, fortified cereals, enriched rice and pasta, peas, tuna, legumes	*Toxicity:* none known *Deficiency:* beriberi; fatigue, apathy, decreased memory, confusion, irritability, muscle weakness
Riboflavin (vitamin B_2)	Required as enzyme cofactor for carbohydrate and fat metabolism	RDA: Men = 1.3 mg/day Women = 1.1 mg/day	Beef liver, shrimp, milk and other dairy foods, fortified cereals, enriched breads and grains	*Toxicity:* none known *Deficiency:* ariboflavinosis; swollen mouth and throat; seborrheic dermatitis; anemia
Niacin, nicotinamide, nicotinic acid	Required for carbohydrate and fat metabolism Plays role in DNA replication and repair and cell differentiation	RDA: Men = 16 mg/day Women = 14 mg/day UL = 35 mg/day	Beef liver, most cuts of meat/fish/poultry, fortified cereals, enriched breads and grains, canned tomato products	*Toxicity:* flushing, liver damage, glucose intolerance, blurred vision differentiation *Deficiency:* pellagra; vomiting, constipation, or diarrhea; apathy
Pyridoxine, pyridoxal, pyridoxamine (vitamin B_6)	Required as enzyme cofactor for carbohydrate and amino acid metabolism Assists synthesis of blood cells	RDA: Men and women aged 19 to 50 = 1.3 mg/day Men aged >50 = 1.7 mg/day Women aged >50 = 1.5 mg/day UL = 100 mg/day	Chickpeas (garbanzo beans), most cuts of meat/fish/poultry, fortified cereals, white potatoes	*Toxicity:* nerve damage, skin lesions *Deficiency:* anemia; seborrheic dermatitis; depression, confusion, convulsions
Folate (folic acid)	Required as enzyme cofactor for amino acid metabolism Required for DNA synthesis Involved in metabolism of homocysteine	RDA: Men = 400 µg/day Women = 400 µg/day UL = 1,000 µg/day	Fortified cereals, enriched breads and grains, spinach, legumes (lentils, chickpeas, pinto beans), greens (spinach, romaine lettuce), liver	*Toxicity:* masks symptoms of vitamin B_{12} deficiency, specifically signs of nerve damage *Deficiency:* macrocytic anemia; neural tube defects in a developing fetus; elevated homocysteine levels
Cobalamin (vitamin B_{12})	Assists with formation of blood Required for healthy nervous system function Involved as enzyme cofactor in metabolism of homocysteine	RDA: Men = 2.4 µg/day Women = 2.4 µg/day	Shellfish, all cuts of meat/fish/poultry, milk and other dairy foods, fortified cereals	*Toxicity:* none known *Deficiency:* pernicious anemia; tingling and numbness of extremities; nerve damage; memory loss, disorientation, dementia
Pantothenic acid	Assists with fat metabolism	AI: Men = 5 mg/day Women = 5 mg/day	Meat/fish/poultry, shiitake mushrooms, fortified cereals, egg yolk	*Toxicity:* none known *Deficiency:* rare
Biotin	Involved as enzyme cofactor in carbohydrate, fat, and protein metabolism	RDA: Men = 30 µg/day Women = 30 µg/day	Nuts, egg yolk	*Toxicity:* none known *Deficiency:* rare
Ascorbic acid (vitamin C)	Antioxidant in extracellular fluid and lungs Regenerates oxidized vitamin E Assists with collagen synthesis Enhances immune function Assists in synthesis of hormones, neurotransmitters, and DNA Enhances iron absorption	RDA: Men = 90 mg/day Women = 75 mg/day Smokers = 35 mg more per day than RDA UL = 2,000 mg	Sweet peppers, citrus fruits and juices, broccoli, strawberries, kiwi	*Toxicity:* nausea and diarrhea, nosebleeds, increased oxidative damage, increased formation of kidney stones in people with kidney disease *Deficiency:* scurvy; bone pain and fractures, depression, anemia

*Abbreviations: RDA, Recommended Dietary Allowance; UL, upper limit; AI, Adequate Intake.

Water-Soluble Vitamins Should Be Consumed Daily or Weekly

Vitamin C and the B-vitamins (thiamin, riboflavin, niacin, vitamin B_6, vitamin B_{12}, pantothenic acid, biotin, and folate) are the **water-soluble vitamins.** Because they dissolve in water, these vitamins are readily absorbed through the intestinal wall directly into the bloodstream. They then travel to cells, where they are needed.

We cannot store large amounts of water-soluble vitamins, because our kidneys filter out from our bloodstream any that are unneeded. We then excrete them in our urine. Because we do not store large amounts in our tissues, toxicity rarely occurs when we consume these vitamins in our diet. We *can* acquire toxic levels through supplementation, however, if we consume higher amounts than our body can eliminate.

A disadvantage of our inability to store large amounts of water-soluble vitamins is that we need to consume them on a daily or weekly basis. If we do not, deficiency symptoms and even disease can result fairly quickly. Still, most people don't need to use supplements: the water-soluble vitamins are abundant in many foods, including whole grains, fruits, vegetables, meats, and dairy products. **Table 6.2** identifies major functions and recommended intakes.

For a helpful overview of vitamins, check out the FDA video *Fortify Your Knowledge About Vitamins* at www.fda.gov/ForConsumers/ConsumerUpdates/ucm118079.htm.

⬆ Because we cannot store large amounts of water-soluble vitamins, we need to consume foods that contain them, such as fruits and vegetables, daily.

RECAP   Vitamins are carbon-containing compounds that are essential in regulating a multitude of body processes. Vitamins A, D, E, and K are fat soluble and are present in certain fat-containing foods. We store fat-soluble vitamins in the fatty tissues of our body. Water-soluble vitamins include vitamin C and the B-vitamins (thiamin, riboflavin, niacin, vitamin B_6, vitamin B_{12}, pantothenic acid, biotin, and folate). Because these vitamins are soluble in water, the body cannot store large amounts, so it excretes excesses in the urine.

Tissue Guardians: Vitamins A, D, and K

The fat-soluble vitamins A, D, and K are important for the health of certain body tissues. Vitamin A protects the retina of the eyes, vitamin D is required for healthy bone, and vitamin K guards against blood loss. Let's take a closer look at these three fat-soluble vitamins.

Vitamin A Protects Our Sight

Vitamin A is multitalented: its known functions are numerous, and researchers speculate that many are still to be discovered. Most would agree, though, that vitamin A's starring role is in the maintenance of healthy vision. Vitamin A enables us to see images as well as to distinguish different colors. Let's take a closer look at this process.

Light enters our eyes through the cornea, travels through the lens, and then hits the **retina,** a delicate membrane lining the back of the inner eyeball **(Figure 6.2,** page 160). Indeed, the primary form that vitamin A takes in our body is *retinal,* which got its name because it is found in—and is integral to—the retina. When light hits the retina, it reacts with the retinal within it. This reaction sparks the transmission of a signal to the brain that is interpreted as a black-and-white image. If the light hitting the retina is bright enough, retinal can also enable the retina to distinguish the different wavelengths of light as different colors. These processes go on continually, allowing us to perceive moment-by-moment changes in our visual field, such as green and yellow leaves fluttering in the wind.

Our abilities to adjust to dim light and recover from a bright flash of light are also critically dependent on adequate levels of retinal in our eyes. That's why deficiency of vitamin A causes vision disorders, including night blindness, discussed shortly.

water-soluble vitamins Vitamins that are soluble in water. These include vitamin C and the B-vitamins.

retina The delicate, light-sensitive membrane lining the inner eyeball and connected to the optic nerve. It contains retinal.

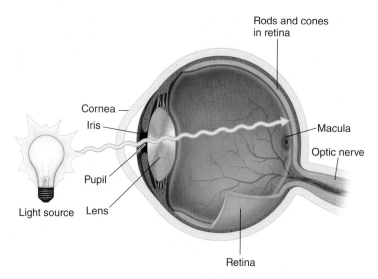

▲ **Figure 6.2** Vitamin A is necessary to maintain healthy vision. Light enters the eye through the cornea, travels through the lens, and hits the retina, located in the back of the eye. The light reacts with the retinal stored in the retina, which allows us to see images.

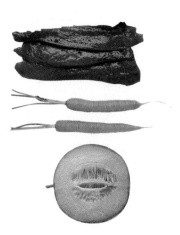

▲ Liver, carrots, and cantaloupe are all good sources of vitamin A.

cell differentiation The process by which immature, undifferentiated cells develop into highly specialized functional cells of discrete organs and tissues.

provitamin An inactive form of a vitamin that the body can convert to an active form. An example is beta-carotene.

carotenoid Fat-soluble plant pigment that the body stores in the liver and adipose tissues. The body is able to convert certain carotenoids to vitamin A.

How Else Do We Use Vitamin A?

Vitamin A also contributes to **cell differentiation,** the process by which immature cells develop into highly specialized cells that perform unique functions. This process is critical to the development of healthy *epithelial tissues* (the skin and the tissues that line the respiratory and gastrointestinal tracts), as well as specialized immune cells called *T lymphocytes,* which help us fight infections.

Vitamin A also

- helps break down old bone tissue, so that new bone can develop,
- is involved in sperm production in men and in fertilization in women, and
- is associated with lower risks of some forms of cancer and heart disease when blood levels of this vitamin are adequate.

Two popular treatments for acne contain derivatives of vitamin A. Retin-A, or tretinoin, is a treatment applied to the skin. Accutane, or isotretinoin, is taken orally. These medications should be used carefully and only under the supervision of a physician. Both medications increase a person's sensitivity to the sun, and it is recommended that exposure to the sun be limited while using them. They also can cause birth defects in infants whose mothers used them while pregnant. It is recommended that a woman discontinue use at least 2 years prior to conceiving, and women of childbearing age who are using one of these medications should use reliable contraceptives to avoid becoming pregnant. Both medications have also been associated with other toxicity problems in some patients. Interestingly, vitamin A itself has no effect on acne; thus, vitamin A supplements are not recommended in its treatment.

What Is the Role of Beta-Carotene?

Beta-carotene is a water-soluble *provitamin* found in many fruits and vegetables. **Provitamins** are inactive forms of vitamins that the body cannot use until they are converted to their active form. Our body converts beta-carotene to an active form of vitamin A called *retinol.* For this reason, beta-carotene is also referred to as a *precursor* of retinol.

Beta-carotene is also classified as a **carotenoid,** one of a group of more than 600 plant pigments that are the basis for the red, orange (think *carrots*), and deep-yellow colors of many fruits and vegetables. (Even dark-green leafy vegetables contain plenty of carotenoids, but the green pigment, chlorophyll, masks their color.)

We are just beginning to learn about the many functions of carotenoids in the body and how they influence our health. We do know that carotenoids

- defend against damage to our cell membranes,
- enhance our immune system,
- protect our skin from the damage caused by the sun's ultraviolet rays, and
- prevent or delay age-related vision impairment.

Interestingly, taking beta-carotene supplements has been shown to increase the risk for lung, prostate, and stomach cancers.[2,3] However, consuming carotenoids in the diet is associated with a decreased risk for cardiovascular disease and certain types of cancer. Still, it's possible to overdo it! Although harmless and reversible, eating large amounts of foods high in beta-carotene can cause a condition referred to as *carotenosis* or *carotenoderma*, which turns the skin yellow or orange. Carotenoids and other beneficial plant chemicals (called *phytochemicals*) are discussed in detail shortly.

Apricots are high in carotenoids.

How Much Vitamin A Should We Consume?

Table 6.1 identifies the RDA for vitamin A. Nutrition scientists do not classify beta-carotene and other carotenoids as micronutrients, as they play no known essential roles in our body and are not associated with any deficiency symptoms. Thus, no formal DRI for beta-carotene has been determined.

Because the body converts vitamin A and beta-carotene into retinol, you may also see the expression *retinol activity equivalents (RAE)* or *retinol equivalents (RE)* for vitamin A on food labels and dietary supplements. Sometimes, the vitamin A content of foods and supplements is expressed in International Units (IU).

We consume vitamin A from animal foods, such as beef liver, chicken liver, eggs, and dairy products. Vitamin A is also available from foods high in beta-carotene and other carotenoids, which the body can convert to vitamin A. These include dark-green, orange, and deep-yellow fruits and vegetables, such as spinach, carrots, mango, and cantaloupe. Common food sources of vitamin A and beta-carotene are also identified in **Figure 6.3**.

Vitamin A is highly toxic, and toxicity symptoms develop after consuming only three to four times the RDA. Toxicity rarely results from food sources, but vitamin A

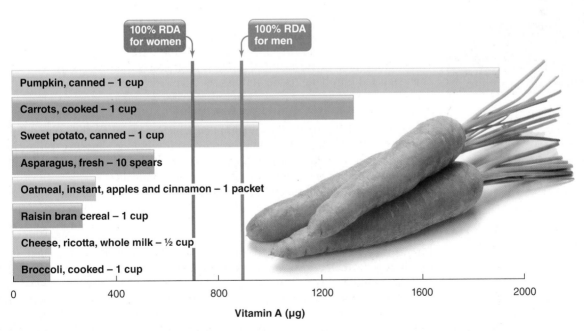

Figure 6.3 Common food sources of vitamin A or beta-carotene. The RDA for vitamin A is 900 µg per day for men and 700 µg per day for women.

Data from U.S. Department of Agriculture, Agricultural Research Service. 2010. USDA Nutrient Database for Standard Reference, Release 23. Nutrient Data Laboratory Home Page. www.ars.usda.gov/ba/bhnrc/ndl.

supplements are known to have caused severe illness and even death. That's why single-nutrient vitamin A supplements should never be taken unless prescribed by your healthcare provider. Consuming excess vitamin A while pregnant can cause serious birth defects and spontaneous abortion. Other toxicity symptoms include fatigue, loss of appetite, blurred vision, hair loss, skin disorders, bone and joint pain, abdominal pain, nausea, diarrhea, and damage to the liver and nervous system. If caught in time, many of these symptoms are reversible once vitamin A supplementation is stopped. However, permanent damage can occur to the liver, eyes, and other organs. Because liver contains such a high amount of vitamin A, children and pregnant women should not consume liver on a daily or weekly basis.

What happens if we don't consume enough vitamin A? **Night blindness,** the inability to see in dim light, is a major vitamin A–deficiency concern in developing nations. Color blindness and other vision impairments can also occur. If night blindness progresses, it can result in irreversible total blindness due to hardening of the cornea (the transparent membrane covering the front of the eye). This is why it is critical to catch night blindness in its early stages and treat it either with the regular consumption of fruits and vegetables that contain beta-carotene or with vitamin A supplementation.

Other deficiency symptoms include impaired immunity, increased risk for illness and infections, reproductive system disorders, and stunted bone growth. According to the World Health Organization, as many as 250,000 to 500,000 vitamin A–deficient children become blind each year, with half of them dying within 1 year of losing their sight.[4]

Vitamin D Guards Our Bones

Vitamin D is different from other nutrients in that it does not always need to come from the diet. This is because our body can synthesize vitamin D using energy from sunlight: when the ultraviolet rays of the sun hit our skin, they react with a cholesterol compound in skin cells. This reaction converts the compound into a precursor of vitamin D, which travels to the liver and then to the kidneys for further conversion into the form of vitamin D our body can use.

Functions of Vitamin D

Vitamin D can be considered not only a nutrient but also a *hormone* because it is made in one part of the body, yet it regulates various activities in other parts of the body. One of its most important functions is to work with other hormones to regulate blood calcium levels. You probably know that calcium is the primary mineral in our bones. According to our body's changing needs for calcium, vitamin D causes more or less calcium to be absorbed from the small intestine and signals the kidneys to excrete more or less in our urine. Vitamin D also assists the process by which calcium is crystallized into bone tissue and assists in cell differentiation.

How Much Vitamin D Should We Consume?

Table 6.1 identifies the RDA for vitamin D, which is based on the assumption that an individual does not get adequate sun exposure. If your exposure to the sun is adequate, then you do not need to consume any vitamin D in your diet. But how do you know whether or not you are getting enough sunshine?

Of the many factors that affect our ability to synthesize vitamin D from sunlight, latitude and time of year are most significant. Individuals living in very sunny climates close to the equator, such as the southern United States and Mexico, may synthesize enough vitamin D from the sun to meet their needs throughout the year—as long as they spend a few minutes out of doors each day with at least their arms and face exposed. However, vitamin D synthesis from the sun is not possible in the winter months in Canada and the northern United States, from northern Pennsylvania in the East to northern California in the West. This is because, at northern latitudes during the winter, the sun never rises high enough in the sky to provide the direct sunlight needed. Thus, people living in northern states and Canada need to consume vitamin D in the winter.

In addition, vitamin D synthesis is decreased in older adults and in people with darkly pigmented skin.[5] These individuals are at increased risk for vitamin D

↥ Vitamin D synthesis from the sun is not possible during most of the winter months for people living in high latitudes. Therefore, many people need to consume vitamin D in their diet, particularly during the winter.

night blindness A vitamin A–deficiency disorder that results in the loss of the ability to see in dim light.

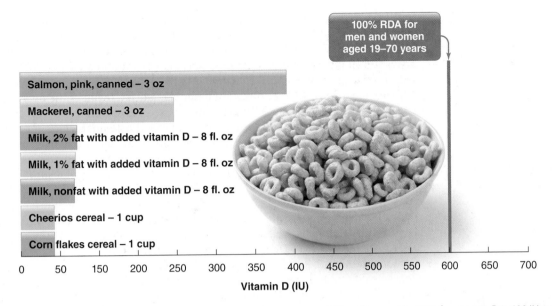

100% RDA for men and women aged 19–70 years

Salmon, pink, canned – 3 oz

Mackerel, canned – 3 oz

Milk, 2% fat with added vitamin D – 8 fl. oz

Milk, 1% fat with added vitamin D – 8 fl. oz

Milk, nonfat with added vitamin D – 8 fl. oz

Cheerios cereal – 1 cup

Corn flakes cereal – 1 cup

0   50   150   200   250   300   350   400   450   500   550   600   650   700

Vitamin D (IU)

◄ **Figure 6.4** Common food sources of vitamin D. For men and women aged 19 to 70 years, the RDA for vitamin D is 600 IU per day. The RDA increases to 800 IU per day for adults over the age of 70 years.

Data from U.S. Department of Agriculture, Agricultural Research Service. 2010. USDA Nutrient Database for Standard Reference, Release 23. Nutrient Data Laboratory Home Page. www.ars.usda.gov/ba/bhnrc/ndl.

deficiency. Recently, a great deal of controversy has been generated regarding the recommendations for vitamin D, with a growing number of nutrition experts calling for substantially higher RDA values due to the relatively poor vitamin D status of many people of all ages and skin tones around the world.[4,6] The Institute of Medicine recently reevaluated the research regarding vitamin D and concluded that there is clear evidence that vitamin D plays a key role in bone health.[9] However, it stated that Americans overall consume enough vitamin D, whereas consuming too much of this nutrient can be harmful.

Most foods naturally contain very little vitamin D. Thus, our primary source of vitamin D in the diet is fortified foods, such as milk. As identified in **Figure 6.4**, other common food sources of vitamin D include fatty fish—such as salmon, mackerel, and sardines—and certain fortified cereals. Because plants contain very little vitamin D, vegetarians who consume no dairy products need to obtain their vitamin D from sun exposure, from fortified soy or cereal products, or from supplements.

We cannot get too much vitamin D from sun exposure, as our skin has the ability to limit its production. The only way we can consume too much vitamin D is through supplementation. Toxicity of vitamin D causes the bones to leach calcium into the bloodstream. High blood calcium concentrations cause weakness, loss of appetite, diarrhea, mental confusion, vomiting, and the formation of calcium deposits in soft tissues, such as the kidneys, liver, and heart.

To learn more about the role of vitamin D, go to www.youtube.com/watch?v=JwPVibQ6_3Y.

What Happens If We Don't Get Enough Vitamin D?

The primary deficiency associated with inadequate vitamin D is loss of bone mass. Calcium is a key component of bones, but when vitamin D levels are inadequate, our intestines can absorb only 10% to 15% of the calcium we consume. Vitamin D–deficiency disease in children, called **rickets,** causes deformities of the skeleton, such as bowed legs and knocked knees **(Figure 6.5)**. Rickets was rampant as late as the early 20th century in northern cities of the United States and Europe. In 1921, rickets was considered the most common nutritional disease of children, affecting approximately 75% of infants in New York City.[10] A common folk remedy for rickets, cod liver oil, was widely known to be effective, but it was not until the discovery of vitamin D in the 1930s that the anti-rickets property of cod liver oil became

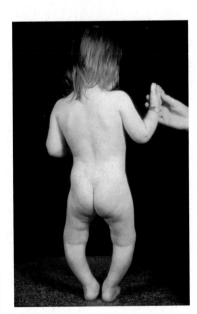

◄ **Figure 6.5** A vitamin D deficiency causes a bone-deforming disease in children called rickets.

rickets A vitamin D–deficiency disease in children. Symptoms include deformities of the skeleton, such as bowed legs and knocked knees.

understood.[11] Rickets still occurs in the United States and throughout the world, especially among dark-skinned toddlers living at northern latitudes who are not fed fatty fish, foods fortified with vitamin D, or supplements.[11] Vitamin D deficiency is also still common among fair-skinned Americans: a recent study found that almost half of white girls aged 9 to 11 years in Maine were deficient in vitamin D at the end of winter, with 17% remaining vitamin D deficient even at the end of summer because they either stayed out of the sun or used sunscreen.[12]

Vitamin D–deficiency disease in adults is called **osteomalacia,** a term meaning "soft bones." With osteomalacia, bones become weak and prone to fractures, and the person typically experiences diffuse bone pain. Today, osteomalacia occurs most often in individuals who have diseases that cause intestinal malabsorption of fat, and thus of the fat-soluble vitamins.

Vitamin D deficiency can also contribute to *osteoporosis*, a condition in which the bones are overly porous and prone to fractures. Although the symptoms of osteomalacia and osteoporosis are similar, the symptoms of osteomalacia are reversed after treatment with vitamin D, whereas many factors are typically involved in the development and treatment of osteoporosis. Recent evidence suggests that vitamin D deficiency may also be associated with an increased risk for some cancers, type 1 diabetes, various forms of arthritis, multiple sclerosis, and infectious diseases, such as tuberculosis,[7] although this evidence is not strong enough to justify increasing the current RDA for vitamin D.[9]

> For more information about the new recommendations for vitamin D, check out this news video: www.youtube.com/watch?v=PHwss_HCh6w.

Now that you've read about the "sunshine vitamin," you might be wondering whether or not you should supplement this nutrient, especially if you live in a northern climate. If so, check out the accompanying **What About You?** feature box (page 165).

Vitamin K Protects Against Blood Loss

Vitamin K is a fat-soluble vitamin required for blood clotting. It acts as a **coenzyme**—that is, a compound that combines with an inactive enzyme to form an active enzyme. **Figure 6.6** illustrates how coenzymes work. As a coenzyme, vitamin K assists in the synthesis of a number of proteins involved in the coagulation of blood. Without adequate vitamin K, blood cannot clot quickly and adequately. This can lead to increased bleeding from even minor wounds, as well as internal hemorrhaging. Vitamin K also acts as a coenzyme to facilitate the production of osteocalcin, a protein associated with bone turnover.

⬅ Green leafy vegetables, including brussels sprouts and turnip greens, are good sources of vitamin K.

osteomalacia Vitamin D–deficiency disease in adults, in which bones become weak and prone to fractures.

coenzyme A compound that combines with an inactive enzyme to form an active enzyme.

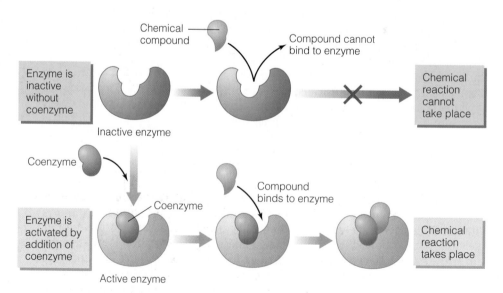

⬅ **Figure 6.6** Coenzymes combine with enzymes to activate them, ensuring that the chemical reactions that depend on these enzymes can occur.

90% 🔋

WHAT ABOUT YOU?

Do You Get Enough Vitamin D?

After reading this chapter, you may wonder whether you're getting enough vitamin D to keep your tissues healthy and strong. Take the following simple quiz to find out. For each question, circle YES or NO.

- I live south of 40° latitude (see **Figure 6.7**) and expose my bare arms and face to sunlight (without sunscreen) for at least a few minutes 2 to 3 days per week all year.

  YES or NO

- I consume a multivitamin supplement or vitamin D supplement that provides at least 600 IU per day.

  YES or NO

- I consume a diet high in fatty fish, fortified milk, and/or fortified cereals that provides at least 600 IU per day.

  YES or NO

If you answered *No* to all three of these statements, you are at high risk for vitamin D deficiency. You are probably getting enough vitamin D if you answered *Yes* to at least one. Notice, though, that if you rely on sun exposure for your vitamin D, you must make sure that you expose your bare skin to sunlight for an adequate length of time. What's adequate varies for each person: the darker your skin tone, the more time you need in the sun. A general guideline is to expose your skin for one-third the amount of time in which you would get sunburned. This means that, if you normally sunburn in 1 hour, you should get 20 minutes of sun two or three times a week. Expose your skin when the sun is high in the sky (generally between the hours of 9 AM and 3 PM). Put on sunscreen only *after* your skin has had its daily dose of sunlight.[5–8]

Remember: if you live in the northern United States or Canada, you cannot get adequate sun exposure

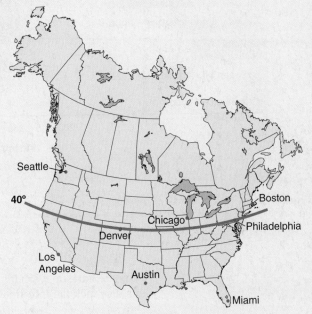

Figure 6.7 This map illustrates the geographical location of 40° latitude in the United States. In southern cities below 40° latitude, such as Los Angeles, Austin, and Miami, the sunlight is strong enough to allow for vitamin D synthesis throughout the year. In northern cities above 40° latitude, such as Seattle, Chicago, and Boston, the sunlight is too weak from about mid-October through mid-March to allow for adequate vitamin D synthesis.

to synthesize vitamin D from approximately October through February, no matter how long you expose your bare skin to the sun. If you are not regularly consuming fortified foods, fatty fish, or cod liver oil, you need to supplement vitamin D during those months.

Our needs for vitamin K are relatively small, as shown in Table 6.1, but vitamin K is found in few foods. Healthful intestinal bacteria produce vitamin K in the large intestine, providing us with an important nondietary source.

Green leafy vegetables are good sources of vitamin K, including collard greens, spinach, broccoli, brussels sprouts, and cabbage (**Figure 6.8**, page 166). Soybean and canola oils are also good sources.

There are no known side effects associated with consuming large amounts of vitamin K from supplements or from food.[10] People with diseases that cause malabsorption of fat can suffer secondarily from a deficiency of vitamin K. In the

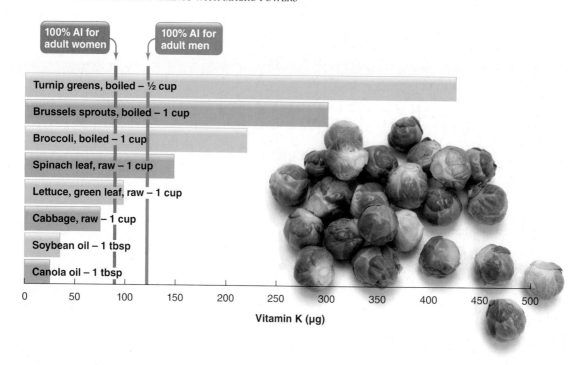

Figure 6.8 Common food sources of vitamin K. The AIs for adult men and women are 120 µg/day and 90 µg/day, respectively.
Data from U.S. Department of Agriculture, Agricultural Research Service. 2010. USDA Nutrient Database for Standard Reference, Release 23. Nutrient Data Laboratory Home Page. www.ars.usda.gov/ba/bhnrc/ndl.

United States, physicians typically give newborns an injection of vitamin K at birth, as they lack the intestinal bacteria necessary to produce this nutrient.

RECAP Vitamin A and its precursor, beta-carotene, are essential for healthy vision, cell differentiation, bone growth, and immune and reproductive functions. Single-nutrient supplementation with vitamin A can lead to life-threatening toxicity. Vitamin D regulates blood calcium levels and maintains bone health. Unless we have adequate sun exposure, we need to consume vitamin D in foods or supplements. Vitamin K is essential for blood clotting.

The Mighty Antioxidants: Vitamins E and C

Fitness and health magazines, supplement companies, and even food manufacturers tout the benefits of antioxidants. But what exactly does this term mean, and why are antioxidant micronutrients important to our health?

What Are Antioxidants, and How Does Our Body Use Them?

Antioxidant vitamins, found in many fresh vegetables, stabilize free radicals.

antioxidant A compound that has the ability to prevent or repair the damage caused by oxidation.

free radical A highly unstable atom with an unpaired electron in its outermost shell.

As we discussed earlier in the text (Chapter 2), chemical reactions occur continuously in our body in order to break down the food we eat and reassemble its smaller molecules into the substances we need to live. Many of these chemical reactions involve the exchange of oxygen. Such reactions are collectively referred to as *oxidation. Anti* means "against"; thus, **antioxidants** are vitamins and minerals that protect our cells against oxidation.

Our cells need the protection of antioxidants because, although necessary to our functioning, oxidation results in the production of harmful by-products called **free radicals.** Why are we concerned with the formation of free radicals? Simply put, it is

HIGHLIGHT
Herbal Supplements: Use with Caution

A common saying in India cautions "A house without ginger is a sick house." Indeed, ginger, garlic, echinacea, and many other herbs have been used by cultures throughout the world for centuries to promote health and ward off disease. The National Center for Complementary and Alternative Medicine (NCCAM) defines an *herb* (also called a *botanical*) as a plant or plant part used for its scent, flavor, and/or therapeutic properties.[13] As you would suspect, with a definition this broad there are hundreds of different herbs on the market. In 2008, U.S. consumers spent $4.8 billion on herbal and botanical supplements.[14]

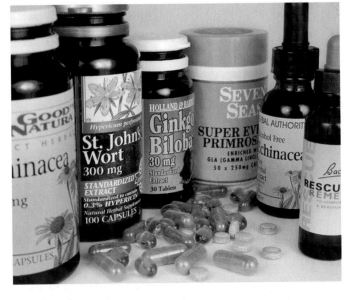

It is clear that some herbs are effective medicines, but for what disorders, in what forms, and at what dosages? And are some herbs promoted as medicines ineffective, or even dangerous? To answer these questions about herbs you might be considering, the NCCAM evaluates dozens of the most commonly used herbs in "Herbs at a Glance" fact sheets, available at its website. See Web Links at the end of this chapter.

There are a number of precautions you should consider before taking herbal supplements. The most essential of these precautions is to consult your healthcare provider before using any herbal supplement. Herbs can act the same way as drugs; therefore, they can cause medical problems if not used correctly or if taken in large amounts. In some cases, people have experienced negative effects, even though they followed the instructions on a supplement label. It's especially important to check with your healthcare provider if you are taking any prescription medications. Some herbal supplements are known to interact with medications in ways that cause health problems.

It is critical to avoid using herbs if you are pregnant or nursing, unless your physician has approved their use. Some can promote miscarriage or birth defects or can enter breast milk. This caution also applies to treating children with herbal supplements.

Finally, be aware that the active ingredients in many herbs and herbal supplements are not known. There may be dozens, even hundreds, of unknown compounds in an herbal supplement. Also, published analyses of herbal supplements have found differences between what's listed on the label and what's in the bottle. This means you may be taking less—or more—of the supplement than what the label indicates or ingesting substances not mentioned on the label. Some herbal supplements have been found to be contaminated with metals, unlabeled prescription drugs, microorganisms, and other substances. An investigation by the United States Government Accountability Office reported in 2010 that nearly all of the herbal supplements it had tested contained traces of lead and other contaminants.[15] Be aware that the word *standardized*, *certified*, or *verified* on a label is no guarantee of product quality; in the United States, these terms have no legal definition for supplements.

---

because of their destabilizing power. Like chemical thieves, free radicals attempt to "steal" parts from stable molecules. When they do, they transform those molecules into new free radicals. This prompts a dangerous chain reaction as the generated free radicals, in turn, damage more and more cells.

One of the most significant sites of free-radical damage is within the lipid portion of the cell membrane. When lipid molecules are damaged by free radicals, they no longer repel water and the cell membrane loses its integrity. It can no longer regulate the movement of fluids and nutrients into and out of the cell. Free radicals also damage our low-density lipoproteins (LDLs), cell proteins, and DNA. Not surprisingly, oxidation is one of the factors thought to cause our body to age. In addition, many diseases are linked to free-radical production, including cancer, heart disease, stroke, and diabetes.

Antioxidant vitamins, especially vitamins E and C, work by stabilizing free radicals, thereby halting the chain reaction of cell membrane injury. When our intake of these vitamins is not sufficient, free-radical damage can be significant. Note that the carotenoids discussed earlier, as well as the mineral selenium, also play roles in antioxidant functioning. In addition, many herbs have a long history of use and of claimed benefits in combating aging and the diseases associated with oxidation, such as hypertension, diabetes, and even cancer. Do herbal supplements promote health and longevity? Are they safe? And exactly what qualifies as an herbal supplement? These questions are explored in the accompanying *Highlight* feature box (page 167).

Want to learn about the recent changes happening in the European Union regarding the regulation of herbal medicines and supplements? Go to www.bbc.co.uk/news/ health-13215010.

⬆ Vegetable oils, nuts, and seeds are good sources of vitamin E.

Vitamin E Maintains Healthy Cells

About 90% of the vitamin E in our body is stored in our adipose (fat) tissues; the rest is found in our cell membranes. In these locations, it protects the fatty components of our cells from oxidation. It also protects LDLs, red blood cells, and the cells of our lungs, which are continuously exposed to oxygen from the air we breathe.

How Else Do We Use Vitamin E?

In addition to its role as an antioxidant, vitamin E serves other roles essential to human health. It is critical for normal fetal and early-childhood development of nerves and muscles and for neuromuscular function throughout life. It protects white blood cells and other components of the immune system, thereby helping defend our body against infection and disease. Vitamin E also improves the absorption of vitamin A if dietary intake of vitamin A is low.

How Much Vitamin E Should We Consume?

Considering the importance of vitamin E to our health, you might think that you need to consume a huge amount daily. In fact, as you can see in Table 6.1, the RDA for vitamin E for men and women is modest.

Vitamin E is widespread in foods **(Figure 6.9)**. Much of the vitamin E we consume comes from vegetable oils and the products made from them. Safflower oil, sunflower oil, canola oil, and soybean oil are good sources. Nuts, seeds, some vegetables, wheat germ, and soybeans also contribute vitamin E to our diet. Cereals are often fortified with vitamin E, and other grain products contribute modest amounts. Animal and dairy products are poor sources of vitamin E.

Vitamin E is destroyed by exposure to oxygen, metals, ultraviolet light, and heat. Although vegetable oils contain vitamin E, heating these oils destroys it. Thus, foods that are deep-fried and processed contain little vitamin E. This includes most fast foods and convenience foods.

Vitamin E toxicities and deficiencies are uncommon. One result of significant vitamin E deficiency is a rupturing of red blood cells that leads to *anemia*, a condition in which our red blood cells cannot carry and transport enough oxygen to our tissues. Anemia in turn causes fatigue, weakness, and a diminished ability to perform physical and mental work. Other symptoms of vitamin E deficiency include loss of muscle coordination and reflexes, impaired vision and speech, and reduced immune function.

Vitamin C Protects Cells and Tissues

⬆ Vitamin C helps protect our lung tissue from airborne pollutants.

Vitamin C is also known as *ascorbic acid*. Like vitamin E, vitamin C is a potent antioxidant, but because it is water soluble, it primarily acts within the fluid

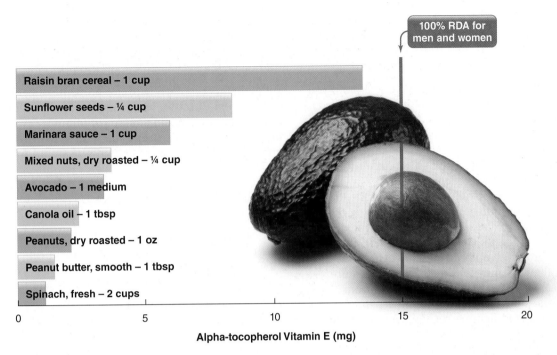

Figure 6.9 Common food sources of vitamin E. The RDA for vitamin E is 15 mg alpha-tocopherol per day for men and women.
Data from U.S. Department of Agriculture, Agricultural Research Service. 2010. USDA Nutrient Database for Standard Reference, Release 23. Nutrient Data Laboratory Home Page. www.ars.usda.gov/ba/bhnrc/ndl.

outside of cells. There, it binds with free radicals, keeping them from destroying cell membranes. It plays a key role in defending our lung tissues from the damage caused by ozone, cigarette smoke, and other airborne pollutants. Indeed, smoking increases a person's need for vitamin C to combat oxidative damage to the lungs. In the stomach, vitamin C reduces the formation of *nitrosamines,* cancer-causing agents found in foods such as cured and processed meats. Vitamin C also regenerates vitamin E after it has been oxidized, enabling vitamin E to "get back to work."

How Else Do We Use Vitamin C?

Another important role of vitamin C is to synthesize **collagen,** a component of bone, teeth, skin, tendons, and blood vessels. Without adequate vitamin C, the body cannot form collagen; thus, bones become brittle, blood vessels leak, wounds fail to heal, and teeth fall out. These symptoms characterize the disease called *scurvy,* which centuries ago was responsible for more than half of the deaths that occurred at sea **(Figure 6.10)**. During long sea voyages, the crew ate all of the fruits and vegetables early in the trip. These foods are high in vitamin C. Later in the voyage, only grain and animal products were available. These foods do not provide vitamin C. In 1740 in England, Dr. James Lind discovered that the consumption of citrus fruits can prevent scurvy. Thus, British sailors were given rations of lime juice, earning them the nickname "limeys."

Vitamin C assists in the synthesis of other important compounds as well, including DNA, neurotransmitters (chemicals that transmit messages via the nervous system), and various hormones. Vitamin C also enhances our immune response and thus protects us from illness and infection. Indeed, you might have heard that vitamin C supplements can prevent the common cold. See the ***Nutrition Myth or Fact?*** box (page 170) to find out if this claim is true.

Finally, vitamin C enhances the absorption of iron. It is recommended that people with low iron stores consume vitamin C–rich foods along with iron sources

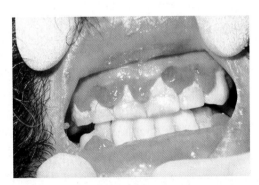

Figure 6.10 Bleeding gums are one symptom of scurvy, the most common vitamin C–deficiency disease.

collagen A protein found in all connective tissues in our body.

NUTRITION MYTH OR FACT?
Can Vitamin C Prevent the Common Cold?

What do you do when it seems as if everyone around you is suffering from a cold? If you are like many people, you drink a lot of orange juice or take vitamin C supplements to ward it off. But do these approaches really help prevent a cold?

It is well known that vitamin C is important for a healthy immune system. Deficiency of vitamin C can seriously weaken the ability of immune cells to detect and destroy invading microbes, increasing our susceptibility to many diseases and illnesses, including the common cold. It's not surprising, then, that many people turn to vitamin C supplements to prevent colds. When they do, they find their local drug store stocking at least a dozen forms of vitamin C, from lozenges to tablets and even packets of powder to mix with water into a cold-fighting cocktail. But do these products work?

Unfortunately, it appears they do not. A recent review of many of the studies of vitamin C and the common cold reported that people who took vitamin C experienced as many colds as people who took a placebo. However, the *duration* of their colds was somewhat reduced—by 8% in adults and 13.6% in children.[16] Timing appeared to be important, though: taking vitamin C after the onset of cold symptoms did not reduce either the duration or the severity of the cold. Interestingly, taking vitamin C supplements regularly did reduce the number of colds experienced by marathon runners, skiers, and soldiers participating in exercises done under extreme environmental conditions.

The amount of vitamin C taken in these studies was at least 200 mg per day, with many using doses as high as 4,000 mg per day (more than forty times the RDA), with no harmful effects noted in those studies that reported adverse events.

In summary, it appears that, for most people, taking vitamin C

supplements regularly will not prevent colds but may reduce their duration. Consuming a healthful diet that includes excellent sources of vitamin C will also help you maintain a strong immune system. Taking vitamin C after the onset of cold symptoms does not appear to help.

So what *can* you do to prevent a cold? The National Institute of Allergy and Infectious Diseases suggests the following:[17]

- Because most cold germs enter the body via the eyes or the nose, try to keep from touching or rubbing your eyes and nose.

- If possible, avoid being close to people who have colds.

- Wash your hands frequently with soap and warm (not hot) water throughout cold season and whenever you have had contact with many people (throughout the workday or school day, when returning home from shopping, and so on). Hand-washing is one of the most effective ways to keep from getting colds or giving them to others. When water isn't available, use an alcohol-based waterless hand sanitizer.

- Cold viruses can live for up to 3 hours on your skin or on objects, such as telephones and desks. Clean environmental surfaces with a virus-killing disinfectant when feasible.

One word of caution: if you're thinking of taking vitamin C supplements, bear in mind that vitamin C enhances the absorption of iron. It is recommended that people with low iron stores consume vitamin C–rich foods along with iron sources to improve absorption of the iron. For people with high iron stores, however, this practice can be dangerous and lead to iron toxicity. Before you begin supplementing, check with your healthcare provider.

to improve absorption. For people with high iron stores, this practice can lead to iron toxicity.

How Much Vitamin C Should We Consume?

The RDA for vitamin C is listed in Table 6.2. Citrus fruits (such as oranges, lemons, and limes), potatoes, strawberries, tomatoes, kiwi fruit, broccoli, spinach and other leafy greens, cabbage, green and red peppers, and cauliflower are excellent sources (**Figure 6.11**). Because heat and oxygen destroy vitamin C, fresh sources of these foods have the highest content. Cooking foods, especially boiling, leaches them of their vitamin C, which is then lost when we strain them. Forms of cooking that are least likely to compromise the vitamin C content of foods include steaming, microwaving, and stir-frying.

Because vitamin C is water soluble, excess amounts are easily excreted and do not lead to toxicity. Even taking megadoses of vitamin C is not fatally harmful. However, side effects of doses exceeding 2,000 mg per day include nausea, diarrhea, abdominal cramps, and nosebleeds and may increase the risk for kidney stones in some people.[18]

Eating Right All Day

Breakfast
Grapefruit juice instead of sweetened coffee!

Lunch
Vegetable soup instead of chicken noodle!

Dinner
Spring rolls instead of sweet & sour pork!

Snack
Grapes instead of M&Ms!

NUTRI-CASE HANNAH

"Since I started college in September, I've had one cold after another. I guess it's being around so many different people every day, plus all the stress. Then a few weeks ago I found this cool orange-tasting vitamin C powder at the health food outlet on campus, and I started mixing it into my orange juice every morning. I guess it's working, because I haven't had a cold since I started using it, but this morning I woke up with stomach cramps and diarrhea, so now I guess I have to worry about a stomach flu. I wish there was a vitamin C powder for that!"

Given what you've learned about the effects of taking vitamin C as a supplement, do you think it's possible that Hannah's vitamin C habit is doing her more harm than good? Why or why not? Explain your answer.

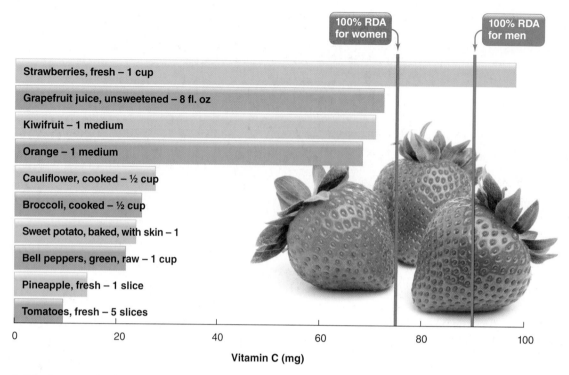

Figure 6.11   Common food sources of vitamin C. The RDA for vitamin C is 90 mg per day for men and 75 mg per day for women.
Data from U.S. Department of Agriculture, Agricultural Research Service. 2010. USDA Nutrient Database for Standard Reference, Release 23. Nutrient Data Laboratory Home Page. www.ars.usda.gov/ba/bhnrc/ndl.

Many fruits, such as these yellow tomatoes, are high in vitamin C.

metabolism The sum of all the chemical and physical processes by which the body breaks down and builds up molecules.

RECAP   Vitamin E protects the fatty portion of our cell membranes from oxidation, enhances immune function, and improves our absorption of vitamin A if dietary intake is low. Vitamin C scavenges free radicals and regenerates vitamin E after it has been oxidized. It is required for the synthesis of collagen and assists in the synthesis of certain hormones, neurotransmitters, and DNA. Vitamin C boosts the absorption of iron.

The Energy Generators: B-Vitamins

Contrary to popular belief, vitamins and minerals do not contain energy (Calories). Only the macronutrients (carbohydrates, fats, and proteins) contain energy. However, vitamins and minerals do assist the body in *generating* energy. **Metabolism** is the sum of all the chemical and physical processes by which the body breaks down and builds up molecules. The B-vitamins play a critical role in energy metabolism, because they assist the chemical reactions that release energy from carbohydrates, fats, and proteins. This group of water-soluble vitamins includes thiamin, riboflavin, vitamin B_6, niacin, folate, vitamin B_{12}, pantothenic acid, and biotin.

How Does Our Body Use B-Vitamins to Produce Energy?

B-vitamins help us access the energy in the food we eat by acting as coenzymes. Recall that a coenzyme is a molecule that combines with an enzyme to activate it and help it do its job (see Figure 6.6). Without the B-vitamins working as coenzymes, we would be unable to produce the energy necessary to stay alive.

For instance, thiamin combines with another enzyme to assist in the breakdown of glucose. Riboflavin is a part of two coenzymes that help break down glucose and fatty acids. The specific functions of each B-vitamin are described in detail next. Their DRIs are identified in Table 6.2 (page 158).

In addition to the B-vitamins and a vitamin-like substance called choline, the minerals iodine, chromium, manganese, copper, and sulfur are also involved in energy metabolism. (Minerals are discussed in Chapter 7.)

Thiamin (Vitamin B$_1$) Helps Metabolize Glucose

Thiamin was the first B-vitamin discovered, hence its designation as vitamin B$_1$. Thiamin is part of a coenzyme that plays a critical role in the breakdown of glucose for energy. It also acts as a coenzyme in the metabolism of a few amino acids. Thiamin is also used in producing DNA and plays a role in the synthesis of neurotransmitters.

Good food sources of thiamin include enriched cereals and grains, whole-grain products, ready-to-eat cereals, and ham and other pork products **(Figure 6.12)**. There are no known adverse effects from consuming excess amounts of thiamin.

Thiamin-deficiency disease is called **beriberi.** In this disease, the body's inability to metabolize energy leads to muscle wasting and nerve damage; in later stages, patients may be unable to move at all. The heart muscle may also be affected, and the patient may die of heart failure. Beriberi occurs when unenriched, processed grains are a primary food source; for instance, it was widespread throughout Asia a century ago when rice was first processed and refined. Rice and many other staples are now enriched with thiamin, and beriberi is rarely seen except among people displaced by wars and natural disasters receiving inadequate food aid. In these populations, symptoms can begin to develop within 2 to 3 months. Beriberi is also seen in people with heavy alcohol consumption and limited food intake.

Riboflavin (Vitamin B$_2$) Helps Break Down Carbohydrates and Fats

Riboflavin is an important component of coenzymes that break down carbohydrates and fats. It is also a part of an antioxidant enzyme that helps cells defend against oxidative damage.

beriberi A disease caused by thiamin deficiency.

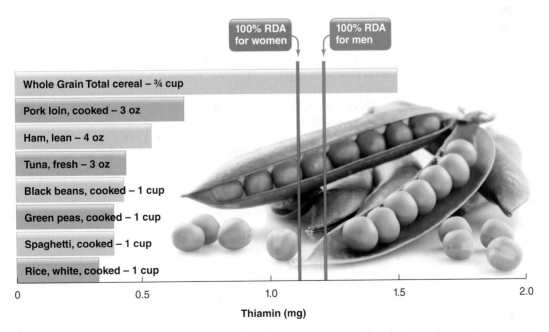

◀ **Figure 6.12** Common food sources of thiamin. The RDA for thiamin is 1.2 mg/day for men and 1.1 mg/day for women 19 years and older.

Data from U.S. Department of Agriculture, Agricultural Research Service. 2010. USDA Nutrient Database for Standard Reference, Release 23. Nutrient Data Laboratory Home Page. www.ars.usda.gov/ba/bhnrc/ndl.

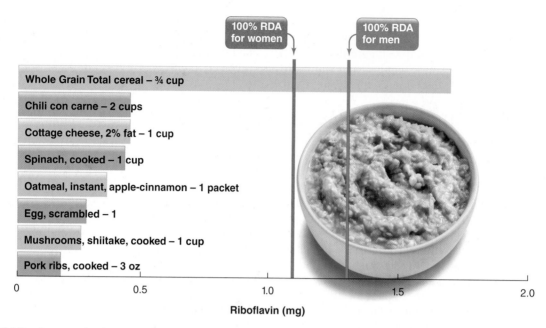

100% RDA for women

100% RDA for men

Whole Grain Total cereal – ¾ cup

Chili con carne – 2 cups

Cottage cheese, 2% fat – 1 cup

Spinach, cooked – 1 cup

Oatmeal, instant, apple-cinnamon – 1 packet

Egg, scrambled – 1

Mushrooms, shiitake, cooked – 1 cup

Pork ribs, cooked – 3 oz

0   0.5   1.0   1.5   2.0

Riboflavin (mg)

🔺 **Figure 6.13**   Common food sources of riboflavin. The RDA for riboflavin is 1.3 mg/day for men and 1.1 mg/day for women 19 years and older.

Data from U.S. Department of Agriculture, Agricultural Research Service. 2010. USDA Nutrient Database for Standard Reference, Release 23. Nutrient Data Laboratory Home Page. www.ars.usda.gov/ba/bhnrc/ndl.

Flavins are yellow pigments, and, indeed, riboflavin is found in egg yolks. Milk is another good source of riboflavin. Because riboflavin is destroyed when it is exposed to light, milk is stored in opaque containers. Other good food sources of riboflavin include yogurt, enriched bread and grain products, ready-to-eat cereals, and organ meats **(Figure 6.13)**.

There are no known adverse effects from consuming excess amounts of riboflavin. Riboflavin deficiency is referred to as **ariboflavinosis.** Symptoms of ariboflavinosis include sore throat, swelling of the mucous membranes in the mouth and throat, lips that are dry and scaly, a purple-colored tongue, and inflamed, irritated patches on the skin. Severe riboflavin deficiency can impair the metabolism of vitamin B$_6$.

Niacin Helps Produce Energy and Build and Repair DNA

As a coenzyme, niacin assists in the metabolism of carbohydrates and fatty acids and thus is essential in helping our body derive the energy from these foods. Niacin also plays an important role in DNA replication and repair and in the process of cell differentiation. Good food sources include meat, fish, poultry, enriched grain products, and tomato paste **(Figure 6.14)**.

NUTRITION
M I L E S T O N E

Pellagra is caused by a niacin deficiency. It commonly occurred in the southern United States and parts of Europe in the early 20th century, and was originally thought to be caused by infection.

In 1914, a physician named Dr. Joseph Goldberger began studying the disease. He noticed that it struck only impoverished people who ate a limited, corn-based diet. Goldberger began conducting experiments to test his theory that pellagra is caused by a nutrient deficiency and eventually hit upon brewer's yeast as a cure. Although Dr. Goldberger lived until 1937, he died without knowing why brewer's yeast works against this disease. Shortly after Goldberger's death, scientists identified the nutrient niacin and discovered its importance to human health. They quickly determined that corn is low in niacin as well as the amino acid tryptophan, a precursor for niacin. In contrast, brewer's yeast—Goldberger's curative—is rich in niacin.

ariboflavinosis A condition caused by riboflavin deficiency.

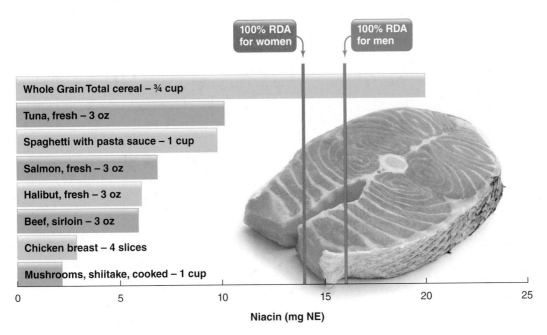

100% RDA for women

100% RDA for men

Whole Grain Total cereal – ¾ cup

Tuna, fresh – 3 oz

Spaghetti with pasta sauce – 1 cup

Salmon, fresh – 3 oz

Halibut, fresh – 3 oz

Beef, sirloin – 3 oz

Chicken breast – 4 slices

Mushrooms, shiitake, cooked – 1 cup

0   5   10   15   20   25

Niacin (mg NE)

🔺 **Figure 6.14** Common food sources of niacin. The RDA for niacin is 16 mg niacin equivalents (NE)/day for men and 14 mg NE/day for women 19 years and older.

Data from U.S. Department of Agriculture, Agricultural Research Service. 2010. USDA Nutrient Database for Standard Reference, Release 23. Nutrient Data Laboratory Home Page. www.ars.usda.gov/ba/bhnrc/ndl.

Megadoses of niacin have been shown to reduce LDL-cholesterol and raise HDL-cholesterol; therefore, some physicians prescribe a pharmacologic form of niacin for patients with unhealthful blood lipid levels. It is typically prescribed in a time-release preparation to prevent an uncomfortable side effect called *flushing*, which is defined as burning, tingling, and itching sensations accompanied by a reddened flush primarily on the face, arms, and chest. Unfortunately, some prescription forms of niacin can cause liver damage. Niacin toxicity can also cause glucose intolerance, blurred vision, and edema of the eyes.

Pellagra results from a severe niacin deficiency. It is characterized by a skin rash, diarrhea, mental impairment, and in severe cases death (**Figure 6.15**). Pellagra is rarely seen in industrialized countries, except in cases of chronic alcoholism. Worldwide, outbreaks of pellagra still occasionally occur, especially among refugees and during emergencies in developing countries.[19]

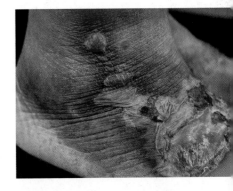

🔺 **Figure 6.15** Pellagra is often characterized by a scaly skin rash.

Vitamin B₆ (Pyridoxine) Helps Manufacture Nonessential Amino Acids

You can think of vitamin B_6 as the "protein vitamin" because it is needed for more than 100 enzymes involved in protein metabolism.[20] Without adequate vitamin B_6, all amino acids become essential and must be consumed in our diet, as our body cannot make them in sufficient quantities. Vitamin B_6 also assists in the synthesis of hemoglobin, a component of red blood cells that transports oxygen, and it helps maintain blood glucose within a normal range. In addition, vitamin B_6 is needed for the synthesis of neurotransmitters, which enable nerve cells to communicate.

Good food sources of vitamin B_6 include enriched ready-to-eat cereals, beef liver, fish, poultry, garbanzo beans, and fortified soy-based meat substitutes (**Figure 6.16**). White potatoes and other starchy vegetables are also good sources.

Vitamin B_6 supplements have been used to treat conditions such as premenstrual syndrome (PMS) and carpal tunnel syndrome. Unfortunately, clinical trials have failed to support any significant benefit of B_6 supplements for these conditions.[20]

pellagra A disease that results from severe niacin deficiency.

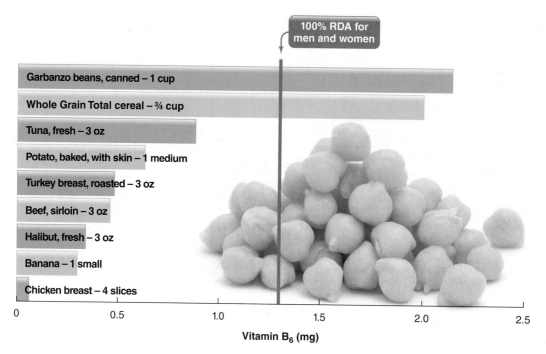

100% RDA for men and women

Garbanzo beans, canned – 1 cup

Whole Grain Total cereal – ¾ cup

Tuna, fresh – 3 oz

Potato, baked, with skin – 1 medium

Turkey breast, roasted – 3 oz

Beef, sirloin – 3 oz

Halibut, fresh – 3 oz

Banana – 1 small

Chicken breast – 4 slices

0   0.5   1.0   1.5   2.0   2.5

Vitamin B$_6$ (mg)

Figure 6.16 Common food sources of vitamin B$_6$. The RDA for vitamin B$_6$ is 1.3 mg/day for men and women aged 19 to 50 years.
Data from U.S. Department of Agriculture, Agricultural Research Service. 2010. USDA Nutrient Database for Standard Reference, Release 23. Nutrient Data Laboratory Home Page. www.ars.usda.gov/ba/bhnrc/ndl.

Because of its critical role in the first few weeks of pregnancy, folate is added to all ready-to-eat cereals.

homocysteine An amino acid that requires adequate levels of folate, vitamin B$_6$, and vitamin B$_{12}$ for its metabolism. High levels of homocysteine in the blood are associated with an increased risk for vascular diseases, such as cardiovascular disease.

What's more, supplementing with B$_6$ can result in nerve damage to the arms and legs: in one study, twenty-three of fifty-eight women taking daily vitamin B$_6$ supplements for PMS had nerve damage.[20]

Vitamin B$_6$ deficiency is rare in the United States except among people who chronically abuse alcohol and children taking the asthma drug theophylline, which decreases body stores of vitamin B$_6$. Deficiency symptoms include anemia, convulsions, depression, confusion, and inflamed, irritated patches on the skin. A deficiency of vitamin B$_6$ may also increase the level of the amino acid **homocysteine** in the blood. High homocysteine levels may damage coronary arteries or promote the formation of clotted arteries, increasing the risk for a heart attack or stroke.[20]

Folate Is Critical During the Earliest Weeks of Pregnancy

All women of childbearing age need to consume adequate folate. This is because folate, which promotes DNA synthesis and cell division, is a critical nutrient during the first few weeks of pregnancy—typically before a woman even knows she is pregnant—when the combined sperm–egg cell is multiplying rapidly to form the primitive tissues of the human body. When folate intake is inadequate in the first weeks of pregnancy, the fetus can develop a *neural tube defect*, a malformation affecting the spinal cord that can cause neurologic problems and impaired movement.

In everyone, folate is essential for healthy blood. Without sufficient folate, the red blood cells become unable to carry sufficient oxygen to all our body cells, and we become weak and exhausted. This condition is called *macrocytic anemia*. Folate is also important in amino acid metabolism. Like B$_6$ deficiency, folate deficiency can cause too high a level of the amino acid homocysteine in the blood, a risk factor for heart disease and stroke.

Because of its critical role during the first few weeks of pregnancy, and the fact that many women of childbearing age do not consume adequate amounts, folate

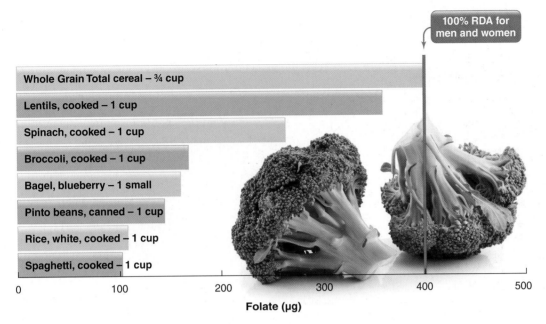

100% RDA for men and women

Whole Grain Total cereal – ¾ cup

Lentils, cooked – 1 cup

Spinach, cooked – 1 cup

Broccoli, cooked – 1 cup

Bagel, blueberry – 1 small

Pinto beans, canned – 1 cup

Rice, white, cooked – 1 cup

Spaghetti, cooked – 1 cup

0   100   200   300   400   500

Folate (µg)

Figure 6.17 Common food sources of folate and folic acid. The RDA for folate is 400 µg/day for men and women.
Data from U.S. Department of Agriculture, Agricultural Research Service. 2010. USDA Nutrient Database for Standard Reference, Release 23. Nutrient Data Laboratory Home Page. www.ars.usda.gov/ba/bhnrc/ndl.

has been added to ready-to-eat cereals and bread products. Thus, these two foods are among the primary sources of folate in the United States. Other good food sources include liver, spinach, lentils, oatmeal, asparagus, and romaine lettuce **(Figure 6.17)**.

Toxicity can occur when taking supplemental folate. One especially frustrating problem with folate toxicity is that it can mask a simultaneous vitamin B_{12} deficiency. As you saw in the chapter-opening case, a delay in the diagnosis of B_{12} deficiency can permanently damage the nervous system. There do not appear to be any clear symptoms of folate toxicity independent from its interaction with vitamin B_{12} deficiency.

Vitamin B_{12} (Cobalamin) Maintains Healthy Nerves and Blood

In the chapter-opening scenario, you saw the effects of vitamin B_{12} deficiency on Mr. Katz's nervous system. His nerve function deteriorated because adequate levels of vitamin B_{12} are necessary to maintain the sheath that coats nerve fibers. When this sheath is damaged or absent, nerves fire inappropriately, causing numerous physical and cognitive problems. Vitamin B_{12} is also part of coenzymes that assist with the formation of blood.

In addition, as with folate and vitamin B_6, adequate levels of vitamin B_{12} are necessary to break down the amino acid homocysteine. When vitamin B_{12} consumption is inadequate, homocysteine levels—and your risk for heart disease or stroke—rise.

Vitamin B_{12} is found only in dairy products, meats, and poultry, so individuals consuming a vegan diet need to eat foods that are fortified with vitamin B_{12} or take vitamin B_{12} supplements or injections **(Figure 6.18)**. As we age, our sources of vitamin B_{12} may need to change. Individuals younger than 51 years are generally able to meet the RDA for vitamin B_{12} by consuming it in foods. However, it is estimated that about 10% to 30% of adults older than 50 have a condition referred to as **atrophic gastritis,** which results in low stomach acid secretion.[21] Because stomach acid separates food-bound vitamin B_{12} from dietary proteins, if the acid content of the stomach is inadequate, the body cannot free up enough vitamin B_{12} from food sources alone. Since atrophic gastritis is estimated to affect almost one-third of the older adult

Turkey contains vitamin B_{12}.

atrophic gastritis A condition that results in low stomach acid secretion, estimated to occur in about 10% to 30% of adults older than 50 years of age.

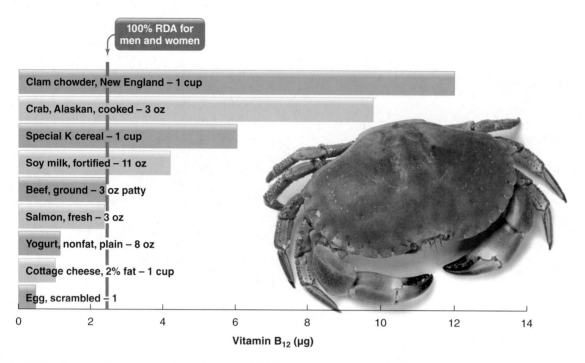

100% RDA for men and women

Food	
Clam chowder, New England – 1 cup	
Crab, Alaskan, cooked – 3 oz	
Special K cereal – 1 cup	
Soy milk, fortified – 11 oz	
Beef, ground – 3 oz patty	
Salmon, fresh – 3 oz	
Yogurt, nonfat, plain – 8 oz	
Cottage cheese, 2% fat – 1 cup	
Egg, scrambled – 1	

Vitamin B₁₂ (μg)

🔺 **Figure 6.18** Common food sources of vitamin B$_{12}$. The RDA for vitamin B$_{12}$ is 2.4 μg/day for men and women.

Data from U.S. Department of Agriculture, Agricultural Research Service. 2010. USDA Nutrient Database for Standard Reference, Release 23. Nutrient Data Laboratory Home Page. www.ars.usda.gov/ba/bhnrc/ndl.

population, it is recommended that people older than 50 years of age consume foods fortified with vitamin B$_{12}$, take a vitamin B$_{12}$–containing supplement, or have periodic B$_{12}$ injections.

Vitamin B$_{12}$ deficiency causes diminished energy and exercise tolerance, fatigue, shortness of breath, and the neurologic symptoms described in the chapter-opening scenario. One of the primary causes of vitamin B$_{12}$ deficiency is a condition called *pernicious anemia.* People with pernicious anemia lack adequate amounts of a protein secreted by the stomach that helps vitamin B$_{12}$ be absorbed into the bloodstream. There are no known adverse effects from consuming excess amounts of vitamin B$_{12}$.

Pantothenic Acid Assists in Building and Breaking Down Fatty Acids

Pantothenic acid is a component of coenzymes that assist with the metabolism of fatty acids. It is also critical for building new fatty acids.

The prefix *pan-* means "widespread," and indeed pantothenic acid is found in a wide variety of foods, from beef, chicken, organ meats, and egg yolk to potatoes, tomato products, and whole grains. There are no known adverse effects from consuming excess amounts of pantothenic acid. Deficiencies of pantothenic acid are very rare.

🔺 Shiitake mushrooms contain pantothenic acid.

Biotin Helps Metabolize All Macronutrients

Biotin is a component of coenzymes that help the body break down all of the macronutrients. It also plays an important role in gluconeogenesis.

The biotin content has been determined for very few foods, and these values are not reported in food composition tables or dietary analysis programs. Biotin appears to be widespread in foods. There are no known adverse effects from consuming excess amounts, and biotin deficiencies are rare.

Choline Is a Vitamin-Like Substance Found in Many Foods

The carbon-containing compound choline, although not classified as a vitamin, is typically grouped with the B-vitamins because of its role in assisting homocysteine metabolism. Choline also accelerates the synthesis and release of *acetylcholine,* a neurotransmitter involved in movement and other functions. It is also necessary for healthy cell membranes, and it plays an important role in the transport and metabolism of fats and cholesterol.

Choline has an AI of 550 mg per day for men ages 19 and older and an AI of 425 mg per day for women ages 19 and older. The choline content of foods is not typically reported in nutrient databases. However, we do know that choline is widespread in foods, especially milk, liver, eggs, and peanuts. Inadequate intakes of choline can eventually lead to liver damage. Excessive intake of supplemental choline results in various toxicity symptoms, including a fishy body odor, vomiting, sweating, diarrhea, and low blood pressure. The UL for choline for adults 19 years of age and older is 3.5 grams/day.

◆ Choline is widespread in foods and can be found in eggs and milk.

RECAP Water-soluble B-vitamins include thiamin, riboflavin, niacin, pyridoxine (vitamin B$_6$), folate, cobalamin (vitamin B$_{12}$), pantothenic acid, and biotin. Acting as coenzymes, the B-vitamins assist in breaking down food to produce energy. They are commonly found in enriched breads and cereals, meats, dairy products, and some fruits and vegetables. B-vitamin toxicity is rare unless a person consumes large doses in supplements. B-vitamin deficiencies are not commonly seen except in individuals with another health problem, such as alcohol abuse. The exceptions are folate deficiency during early pregnancy, which can lead to neural tube defects in the developing fetus, and vitamin B$_{12}$ deficiency, which leads to anemia and nervous system damage and is sometimes seen in older adults with atrophic gastritis and people consuming a vegan diet. Choline is a carbon-containing compound that assists in homocysteine metabolism.

HEALTHWATCH

Do Antioxidants Protect Against Cancer?

Beta-carotene and the antioxidant vitamins E and C protect our cell membranes, proteins, lipoproteins, and DNA from damage by free radicals, so does that mean they protect us against cancer? Before we answer that question, let's take a closer look at precisely what cancer is and how it spreads. **Cancer** is actually a group of diseases that are all characterized by cells that grow "out of control." By this we mean that cancer cells reproduce spontaneously and independently and don't stay within the boundaries of the tissue or organ where they grow. Instead, they aggressively invade tissues and organs, sometimes far away from those in which they originally formed.

Most forms of cancer result in one or more **tumors,** which are masses of immature cells that have no useful function. Although the word *tumor* sounds frightening, it is important to note that not every tumor is *malignant,* or cancerous. Many are *benign* (not harmful) and are made up of cells that will not spread widely.

Figure 6.19 shows how changes to normal cells prompt a series of other changes that can progress into cancer. There are three primary steps of cancer development: initiation, promotion, and progression:

1. *Initiation:* The initiation of cancer occurs when a cell's DNA is *mutated* (changed). This mutation, which can be caused by a variety of factors, including

cancer A group of diseases characterized by cells that reproduce spontaneously and independently and may invade other tissues and organs.

tumor Any newly formed mass of undifferentiated cells.

Figure 6.19 **(a)** Cancer cells develop as a result of a genetic mutation in the DNA of a normal cell. **(b)** The mutated cell replicates uncontrollably, eventually resulting in a tumor. **(c)** If not destroyed or removed, the cancerous tumor metastasizes to other parts of the body.

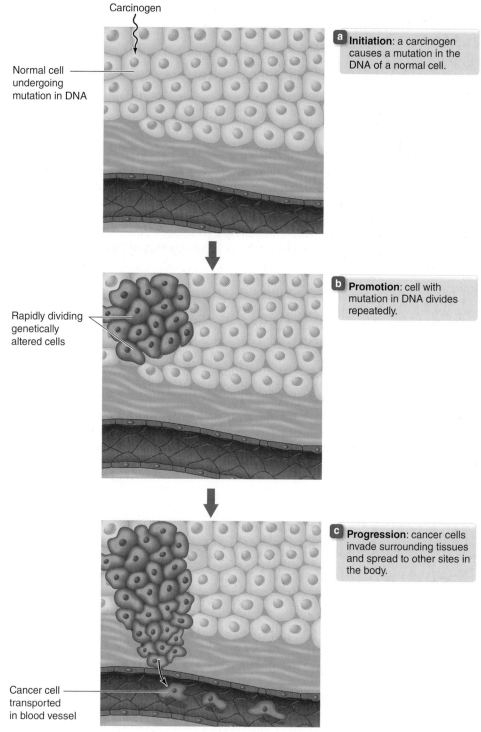

Carcinogen

Normal cell undergoing mutation in DNA

a **Initiation**: a carcinogen causes a mutation in the DNA of a normal cell.

Rapidly dividing genetically altered cells

b **Promotion**: cell with mutation in DNA divides repeatedly.

c **Progression**: cancer cells invade surrounding tissues and spread to other sites in the body.

Cancer cell transported in blood vessel

exposure to a virus, toxic chemical, or other agent, causes permanent changes in the cell. Substances such as toxic chemicals that prompt such cellular mutations are called *carcinogens*.

2. *Promotion:* During this phase, the mutated cell repeatedly divides. The mutated DNA is locked into each new cell's genetic instructions. These cells also continue to divide uninhibited.

3. *Progression:* During this phase, the cancerous cells grow out of control and invade surrounding tissues. These cells then *metastasize* (spread) to other sites

of the body. In the early stages of progression, the immune system can sometimes detect these cancerous cells and destroy them. However, if the cells continue to grow, they develop into malignant tumors, and cancer results.

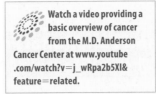

Watch a video providing a basic overview of cancer from the M.D. Anderson Cancer Center at www.youtube .com/watch?v=j_wRpa2b5XI& feature=related.

Many Factors Influence Cancer Risk

In the United States, cancer is the second leading cause of death across all age groups combined, and researchers estimate that about half of all men and one-third of all women will develop cancer during their lifetime. But what causes cancer? Are you and your loved ones at risk? The answer depends on several factors, including your family history of cancer, your exposure to environmental agents, and various lifestyle choices. These are discussed, along with several practical steps you can take to reduce your risk for cancer, in the *Game Plan* feature box (page 184).

Antioxidants Play a Role in Preventing Cancer and Other Diseases

There is a large and growing body of evidence that antioxidants play an important role in preventing cancer, heart disease, and stroke, as well as certain other diseases. How do they do this? Some proposed mechanisms include the following:

- Enhancing the immune system, which assists in the destruction and removal of precancerous cells from the body
- Inhibiting the growth of cancer cells and tumors
- Preventing oxidative damage to the cells' DNA by seeking out and stabilizing free radicals
- Reducing inflammation in blood vessel walls and protecting against the formation and release of blood clots that can cause heart attack and stroke

Eating whole foods high in antioxidant nutrients, such as vitamins E and C and beta-carotene—especially fruits and vegetables—is shown to be associated with decreased cancer risk.[23] Additional studies show that populations eating diets low in antioxidant nutrients have a higher risk for cancer. Other studies show that people who eat more fruits and vegetables have a significantly reduced risk for heart disease and stroke.[24,25] These studies show a strong *association* between diet and disease risk, but they do not prove cause and effect. Nutrition experts agree that there are important interactions between antioxidant nutrients and other substances in foods, such as fiber and phytochemicals (discussed next), which work together to reduce the risk for many diseases.

The benefit of consuming antioxidants in supplement form is not at all clear. Some studies suggest that antioxidant supplements may reduce cancer or heart disease risk, but others are inconclusive or even show increased risk. For example, the Preventive Services Task Force of the U.S. Agency for Healthcare Research and Quality finds that there is insufficient evidence to recommend either for or against the use of supplements of vitamin A, C, or E, or antioxidant combinations, for the prevention of cancer or cardiovascular disease.[26] The SELECT prostate cancer prevention study found that vitamin E and selenium supplements, taken together or alone, did not prevent prostate cancer.[27] The World Cancer Research Fund and American Institute for Cancer Research confirm that, at the present time, dietary supplements cannot be recommended for cancer prevention in the general population and that nutritional needs should be met through diet alone.[28]

How can there be such conflicting evidence on the effectiveness of supplements? The human body is very complex, as are the development and progression of chronic

Eating more fruits and vegetables high in antioxidants has been associated with reduced cancer risk.

HIGHLIGHT

Dietary Supplements and Functional Foods . . . Do We Really Need All These Vitamins?

Dietary supplements are products taken by mouth that contain a "dietary ingredient" intended to supplement the diet. Multivitamin/multimineral supplements, including pills, capsules, liquids, and powders, are the most popular type of dietary supplement sold: approximately 40% of Americans report using them.[29] In addition to using supplements, many Americans are getting even more vitamins from products called *functional foods*. Do we really need all these vitamins? Before we can answer this question, let's look at the rising popularity of functional foods.

Many Functional Foods Provide Extra Vitamins

On her way home from work, Judy stops at the grocery store to pick up a frozen dinner and a six-pack of diet soda. In the beverage aisle, she notices a display promoting her favorite soda— but the packaging says "Now fortified with essential vitamins!" She reads the label and finds that a can of the soda provides 15% of the Daily Value for niacin and vitamins B_6 and B_{12}. Judy hesitates. The soda costs a little more than the version she has always bought before, and she's not even sure what these particular vitamins do. But still, she wonders . . . Maybe it's worth it. Maybe she *does* need some extra vitamins.

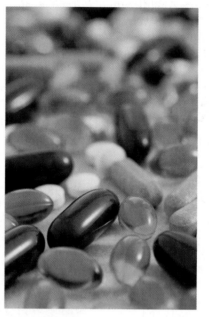

Although Judy doesn't know it, her confusion reflects an ongoing debate between food manufacturers and consumer advocates about the promotion of what are called *functional foods*. The American Dietetic Association defines functional foods as those that "move beyond necessity to provide additional health benefits that may reduce disease risk and/or promote optimal health."[30] Also called *nutraceuticals*, functional foods provide a health benefit beyond the basic benefit of providing nutrients. Functional foods include whole foods, such as nuts, broccoli, and blueberries, as well as processed foods, including fortified, enriched, or enhanced foods.

Examples of such modified foods include calcium-enhanced orange juice, folate-enriched breads, and foods formulated with bioactive ingredients, such as fish oils or phytochemicals. Sometimes, the health-promoting substances are developed in a functional food by altering the way in which the food is produced. For example, eggs with higher levels of omega-3 fatty acids result from feeding hens a special diet. Yogurts can be cultured to promote the reproduction of specific strains of healthful bacteria. And fruits and vegetables can be genetically engineered to contain higher levels of nutrients.

Notice that the benefit associated with functional foods is not always derived from a vitamin. However, vitamin-fortified products do make up a substantial proportion of the functional food market. A stroll through your local grocery store will probably reveal vitamin-enhanced bottled waters, juices, sodas, energy bars, breakfast cereals, and breads, not to mention several shelves of single-vitamin and multivitamin dietary supplements.

Dietary Supplements and Functional Foods Are Not Strictly Regulated

Both dietary supplements and functional foods are categorized by the FDA within the general group of foods, not drugs. This means that, as long as all ingredients are recognized as safe for consumption, the product is allowed on the market. Thus, the regulation of such products is much less rigorous than for drugs. As an informed consumer, you should know the following:

- Supplements and functional foods do not need approval from the FDA before they are marketed.

- The manufacturer is responsible for determining that the product is safe; the FDA does not test it for safety prior to marketing.

- In particular, supplement companies do not have to provide the FDA with any evidence that their supplements are safe, unless the company is marketing a new dietary ingredient that was not sold in the United States prior to 1994.

- There are currently no federal guidelines on practices to ensure the purity, quality, safety, and composition of supplements.

- There are no rules to limit the serving size or amount of a nutrient in any supplement or functional food.

- Once a supplement or functional food is marketed, it is the FDA's responsibility to prove that a product is unsafe before it can be removed from the market.

Over the years, many consumer advocacy groups have petitioned the FDA to reevaluate the way it regulates dietary supplements and functional foods. They contend that many companies are making unsubstantiated health claims for their products, and that the use of such products could have adverse health effects on vulnerable consumers. In response to these and other concerns, the FDA is considering a new regulatory system by which any product bearing health claims would be subject to FDA oversight. But until such a system is in effect, consumers should remain skeptical about the safety and effectiveness of dietary supplements and functional foods.

Extra Vitamins Can Be Helpful or Harmful

It is not always easy to determine who should take multivitamin supplements and/or consume vitamin-fortified foods. Our nutritional needs change throughout our life span, and some of us may need to take supplements at certain times for various conditions. For instance, people at risk for osteoporosis may benefit from taking vitamin D supplements if their sun exposure is inadequate. Certainly, strict vegetarians (vegans) need to supplement their diet with vitamin B_{12}. Thousands of vitamin supplements and vitamin-fortified foods are sold, and it is impossible to discuss here all of the situations in which these products may be helpful. So to keep our discussion brief, let's focus on describing the most obvious situations in which people may or may not benefit from vitamin supplementation.

Who Might Benefit from Taking Micronutrient Supplements?

Foods contain a diverse combination of compounds that are critical to our health and cannot be packaged in a pill. Thus, supplements are not substitutes for whole foods. However, certain groups of people do benefit from taking supplements. Some examples of widely recommended vitamin or mineral supplements include

- a single dose of vitamin K for newborns at birth,
- vitamin D supplements for breastfed infants from birth to age 6 months and iron-fortified cereal for breastfed infants 6 months of age and older,
- Fluoride supplements for children not drinking fluoridated water,
- multivitamin/multimineral supplements for people on prolonged energy-restricted diets and for people with HIV/AIDS or other wasting diseases,
- calcium and vitamin D supplements for people at risk for low bone mass, and
- vitamin B_{12} supplements for elderly people and vegans.

If you identify with one or more of these groups, you should analyze your diet to determine whether you actually need supplements. In addition, it is always a good idea to check with your healthcare provider or a registered dietitian (RD) before taking any supplements.

When Can Taking a Vitamin or Mineral Supplement Be Harmful?

Fortified foods typically contain from 10% to 50% of the DRI for any micronutrients they contain. Even if you eat a breakfast cereal providing 100% of the Daily Value for a certain micronutrient, plus later in the day you eat an energy bar providing 50% of the Daily Value for the same micronutrient, you're unlikely to reach toxic levels unless you are also consuming supplements. Instances in which taking vitamin and mineral supplements is unnecessary or potentially harmful include the following:

- Providing fluoride supplements to children who already drink fluoridated water
- Taking supplements in the belief that they will cure a disease such as cancer, diabetes, or heart disease
- Taking supplements without checking with your healthcare provider to determine their reaction with medications you are taking
- Taking beta-carotene supplements if you are a smoker. Evidence suggests that beta-carotene supplementation may increase the risk for cancer in smokers.[28]
- Taking vitamins and minerals in an attempt to improve physical appearance, athletic performance, or energy level. There is no evidence that vitamin and mineral supplements enhance appearance, athletic performance, or energy level in healthy adults who consume a varied diet with adequate energy.
- Taking supplements in excess of the tolerable upper limit (UL), unless your healthcare provider prescribes them for a diagnosed medical condition. Taking amounts of the fat-soluble vitamin A above the UL can quickly lead to toxicity. In addition, excessive supplementation of some B-vitamins can lead to liver damage or nerve damage, and megadoses of vitamin C can cause severe diarrhea and other symptoms.

As advised by the American Dietetic Association, the ideal nutritional strategy is to eat a healthful diet that contains a variety of foods.[30] If you determine that you still need to supplement and/or consume micronutrient-fortified foods, make sure that together the sources don't provide more than 100% of the recommended levels of any nutrients these products contain. Avoid taking single-nutrient supplements unless advised by your healthcare practitioner.

90% 🔋

GAME PLAN

Simple Steps to Reduce Your Risk for Cancer

Cancer often seems to strike apparently healthy people "out of the blue." Because genetic and certain environmental factors are beyond an individual's control, you may be wondering what, if anything, you can do to reduce your risk. Here are some answers.

Nutritional Factors

☐ Eat a variety of colorful fruits and vegetables daily, as these foods are rich in antioxidant nutrients and phytochemicals.

☐ Choose whole grains in preference to refined grains.

☐ Limit your consumption of saturated and *trans* fats. Some studies suggest that diets high in saturated fat can increase our risk for some cancers.

☐ Limit your consumption of red meats, especially processed meats and meats high in fat.

☐ Limit your consumption of nitrates and nitrites. These chemicals are found in cured meats, such as sausage, ham, bacon, and many lunch meats. They are known carcinogens.

☐ If you eat meat, avoid cooking methods that require high temperatures, such as broiling, frying, and barbecuing. High-temperature cooking methods prompt the development of carcinogens called *heterocyclic amines*, which do not form when meat is cooked more slowly at lower temperatures, such as by roasting or baking.

☐ Maintain a healthful weight. Obesity appears to increase the risk for certain cancers. The exact link between obesity and increased cancer risk is not clear but may be due to hormonal changes that occur with having excess body fat.

Lifestyle Factors

☐ If you smoke cigarettes or cigars or use smokeless tobacco, stop. It is an established fact that these behaviors significantly increase the risk for many forms of cancer. More than forty compounds identified in tobacco and tobacco smoke are known carcinogens.

☐ If you drink alcoholic beverages, limit consumption. Alcohol use is linked with an increased risk for many types of cancer. Alcohol may impair the cell's ability to repair damaged DNA, increasing the possibility of cancer initiation.

☐ Limit your sun exposure and avoid sunburn. Skin cancer is the most common form of cancer in the United States. Most cases are linked to excessive exposure to the ultraviolet (UV) rays of the sun, which can damage the DNA of skin cells. After a few minutes of sun exposure during midday (from about 9 AM to 3 PM) to build up your vitamin D stores, apply sunscreen.

☐ Limit your exposure to environmental and occupational carcinogens. These include such things as secondhand cigarette and cigar smoke and pollutants in the air, the food and water supply, and the workplace.

☐ Adopt a physically active lifestyle. Studies conducted over the past 10 years have shown a possible link between lower cancer risk and higher levels of physical activity. Specifically, the American Cancer Society recommends that you engage in at least moderate activity for 30 minutes or more on 5 or more days of the week.[22]

Some data from American Cancer Society. Cancer Prevention. www.cancer.org.

disease. People differ substantially in their susceptibility for disease and in their response to protective factors. In any research study, it is impossible to control all the factors that may influence the risk for disease, and many unknown factors can affect study outcomes. Still, manufacturers continue to produce products, from pills to fortified waters, that provide supplemental vitamins. Are such products worth their cost? Refer to the *Highlight* box to gain a better understanding of situations that may warrant vitamin supplementation.

For assistance in evaluating and making informed decisions about vitamin supplements, check out the FDA website (see Web Links at the end of this chapter).

Other Dietary Factors May Influence Cancer Risk

Although most of the currently available evidence shows the importance of consuming fruits and vegetables to reduce cancer risk, other dietary factors may also play an important role in cancer prevention.[28] For example, there is growing evidence to suggest that consuming foods high in folic acid may help reduce the risk for cancer of the pancreas. Risks for cancers of the colon and rectum may be reduced by consuming garlic, foods high in dietary fiber, and either milk or calcium.

Being physically active and maintaining a healthy body weight are also recognized as ways to decrease your overall risk for cancer. Are you making dietary and activity choices that help reduce your risk for cancer and other chronic diseases? Take the Living Smart quiz in the *What About You?* feature box (page 186) and find out!

Phytochemicals Appear to Reduce Our Risk for Cancer and Other Diseases

Phytochemicals are naturally occurring chemicals in plants (*phyto* means "plant"), such as the plant pigments that give fruits and vegetables their rich colors. Many research studies suggest that phytochemicals, working together with other nutrients and

FOODS YOU DON'T KNOW YOU LOVE YET

Blueberries

Recently touted as a "superfood," blueberries have received a great deal of attention for their contribution to good health. Blueberries are mostly native to North America, with the state of Maine being the largest producer of wild blueberries in the world. Blueberries are actually the fruit of the flowering blueberry plant, and have a deep purple color when ripe.

Blueberries are packed with antioxidants and phytochemicals, and have been shown to reduce the risk for heart disease, high blood pressure, urinary tract infections, and the cognitive decline that can occur with aging. Frozen blueberries are just as healthy as fresh, and they can be eaten in a fruit salad, with breakfast cereals, in a blended fruit smoothie, as a topping for whole-grain pancakes, or, of course, in blueberry pie. Dried blueberries can be added to trail mix and used as a substitute for raisins in recipes. Sweet with a bit of tartness, blueberries are a delicious addition to a healthy diet.

phytochemicals Chemicals found in plants, such as pigments and other substances, that may reduce our risk for diseases such as cancer and heart disease.

90% 🔋

WHAT ABOUT YOU?

Are You Living Smart?

Cancer often seems to strike apparently healthy people "out of the blue." Because genetic and certain environmental factors are beyond your control, you may be wondering how your diet and level of physical activity might be influencing your risk. If so, take the following quiz and see for yourself! Answer each question Yes or No. Then keep reading to see how you can keep living smart.

1. I eat at least five servings of vegetables and fruits every day.	Yes/No
2. I eat at least three servings of whole-grain bread, rice, pasta, and cereal every day.	Yes/No
3. I drink reduced-fat or fat-free milk and yogurt, and I seldom eat high-fat cheeses.	Yes/No
4. I rarely eat processed and red meat like bacon, hot dogs, sausage, steak, ground beef, pork, or lamb.	Yes/No
5. I take it easy on high-calorie baked goods such as pies, cakes, cookies, sweet rolls, and doughnuts.	Yes/No
6. I rarely add butter, margarine, oil, sour cream, or mayonnaise to foods when I'm cooking or at the table.	Yes/No
7. I rarely (less than twice a week) eat fried foods.	Yes/No
8. I try to maintain a healthful weight.	Yes/No
9. I get at least 30 minutes of moderate to vigorous physical activity on five or more days of the week.	Yes/No
10. I usually take the stairs instead of waiting for an elevator.	Yes/No
11. I try to spend most of my time being active, instead of watching television or sitting at the computer.	Yes/No
12. I never, or only occasionally, drink alcohol.	Yes/No

How Do You Rate?
0–4 Yes answers: Diet Alert!

Your diet is probably too high in fat and too low in plant foods like vegetables, fruits, and grains. You may want to take a look at your eating habits and find ways to make some changes.

**5–8 Yes answers: Not Bad!
You're Halfway There!**

You still have a way to go. Look at your "No" answers to help you decide which areas of your diet need to be improved, or whether your physical activity level should be increased.

**9–12 Yes answers: Good for You!
You're Living Smart!**

Keep up the good habits and keep looking for ways to improve.

fiber in plant-based foods, slow the aging process and reduce the risk for certain forms of cancer, heart disease, stroke, vision impairment, and other diseases. Phytochemicals are found in abundance in fruits, vegetables, whole grains, legumes, seeds, soy products, garlic, onion, and green and black teas. **Figure 6.20** lists many of the phytochemicals that are specifically linked to cancer prevention and identifies their food sources.

Phytochemicals exhibit clear cancer-prevention properties under laboratory conditions. However, we do not know the specific phytochemical content of most foods, and an ideal phytochemical intake in humans has not yet been determined. That said, a growing body of research suggests that the following phytochemicals do play a role in reducing the risk of some forms of cancer:[24]

- Lycopene (found in tomato products, red peppers, pink grapefruit, and watermelon)
- Organosulfur compounds (found in garlic, onions, and cruciferous vegetables)

Phytochemical	Health Claims	Food Source	
Carotenoids: alpha-carotene, beta-carotene, lutein, lycopene, zeaxanthin, etc.	Diets with foods rich in these phytochemicals may reduce the risk for cardiovascular disease, certain cancers (e.g., prostate), and age-related eye diseases (cataracts, macular degeneration).	Red, orange, and deep-green vegetables and fruits, such as carrots, cantaloupe, sweet potatoes, apricots, kale, spinach, pumpkin, and tomatoes	
Flavonoids:[1] flavones, flavonols (e.g., quercetin), catechins (e.g., epigallocatechin gallate or EGCG), anthocyanidins, isoflavonoids, etc.	Diets with foods rich in these phytochemicals are associated with lower risk for cardiovascular disease and cancer, possibly because of reduced inflammation, blood clotting, and blood pressure and increased detoxification of carcinogens or reduction in replication of cancerous cells.	Berries, black and green tea, chocolate, purple grapes and juice, citrus fruits, olives, soybeans and soy products (soy milk, tofu, soy flour, textured vegetable protein), flaxseed, whole wheat	
Phenolic acids:[1] ellagic acid, ferulic acid, caffeic acid, curcumin, etc.	Similar benefits as flavonoids.	Coffee beans, fruits (apples, pears, berries, grapes, oranges, prunes, strawberries), potatoes, mustard, oats, soy	
Phytoestrogens:[2] genistein, diadzein, lignans	Foods rich in these phytochemicals may provide benefits to bones and reduce the risk for cardiovascular disease and cancers of reproductive tissues (e.g., breast, prostate).	Soybeans and soy products (soy milk, tofu, soy flour, textured vegetable protein), flaxseed, whole grains	
Organosulfur compounds: allylic sulfur compounds, indoles, isothiocyanates, etc.	Foods rich in these phytochemicals may protect against a wide variety of cancers.	Garlic, leeks, onions, chives, cruciferous vegetables (broccoli, cabbage, cauliflower), horseradish, mustard greens	

[1] Flavonoids, phenolic acids, and stilbenes are three groups of phytochemicals called phenolics. The phytochemical Resveratrol is a stilbene. Flavonoids and phenolic acids are the most abundant phenolics in our diet.
[2] Phytoestrogens include phytochemicals that have mild or anti-estrogenic action in our body. They are grouped together based on this similarity in biological function, but they also can be classified into other phytochemical groups, such as isoflavonoids.

Figure 6.20 Health claims and food sources of phytochemicals.

- Flavonoids (found in many fruits and vegetables, garlic, green and black teas, and red wine)
- Phytoestrogens (found in whole grains, vegetables, and soy products)

Phytochemicals are thought to slow aging and reduce our risk for various diseases in part by moderating the damage done by free radicals. Some also seem to prevent

90% 🔋

GAME PLAN

Tips for Increasing Your Phytochemical Intake

As we explained, phytochemicals (pronounced "fight-o-chemicals") help your body fight chronic disease. So it makes sense to include an appropriate variety of them in your daily diet. But what's appropriate for you? And how can you select and prepare them in ways that work for your busy lifestyle?

Start by reviewing **Figure 6.20**, which identifies the largest groups of phytochemicals. Because most of these are plant pigments, and many fruits and vegetables contain several different types, you can be sure you are getting a wide variety if you eat 5 to 12 servings of brightly colored fruits and vegetables every day.

Next check out the Fruits & Veggies—More Matters health initiative, which was created by the Centers for Disease Control and Prevention and the Produce for Better Health Foundation to demonstrate that eating more fruits and vegetables can fit in with your busy schedule and help keep you healthy. The initiative offers cooking advice, nutrition information, and shopping and storage tips, and all this and more can be found at www.fruitsandveggiesmorematters.org.

The goal is to eat at least 5 servings of colorful fruits and vegetables each day to help fight cancer, heart disease, and the effects of aging. Here are only a few examples of the wide variety of foods in each group:

☐ Blue-purple foods include eggplant, red onions, purple cabbage, cherries, blackberries, blueberries, raspberries, red grapes, and plums.

☐ Green foods include avocados, broccoli, brussels sprouts, chives, cabbage, collard greens, green peppers, kale, swiss chard, leaf lettuces, spinach, and kiwifruit.

☐ White foods include cauliflower, bok choy, white turnips, mushrooms, garlic, onions, leeks, scallions, and bananas.

☐ Yellow-orange foods include carrots, corn, yellow peppers, pumpkin, butternut and other winter squashes, sweet potatoes, cantaloupe, apricots, oranges, papaya, and mangoes.

☐ Red foods include tomatoes, red peppers, apples, strawberries, pink grapefruit, and watermelon.

When Shopping

☐ Build a rainbow in your shopping cart. That way, you'll have on hand several colorful choices to incorporate into meals and snacks each day.

☐ Because fruits and vegetables are perishable, purchase only an amount of fresh produce that you know you can consume within a few days. Nutrient losses increase with each day of storage.

☐ Purchase some less perishable forms of fruits and vegetables, such as dried fruits, 100% fruit and vegetable juices, soups, canned fruits and vegetables (check for no-sugar and no-sodium added), and frozen vegetables.

fruits & veggies
more matters®

In the Kitchen

☐ Wash fresh fruits and vegetables thoroughly, except for berries, which should be washed immediately before eating to discourage spoilage.

☐ Store tomatoes, garlic, and bananas at room temperature.

☐ Store unripened avocados, pears, and other fruits in a lightly closed paper bag until ripe. Add a banana to the bag to speed ripening time. Once ripe, consume or refrigerate.

☐ Store potatoes and onions in a cool, dark location, such as a cellar or cool cupboard.

☐ Nutrients become depleted when exposed to air, so peel and cut fruits and vegetables only when you are ready to eat them. Many fruits and vegetables have edible peels that contain important nutrients and fiber, so wash them and eat them unpeeled when possible.

☐ To reduce nutrient loss in cooking water, eat vegetables raw, or zap coarsely chopped vegetables in the microwave for 2–4 minutes with approximately 1 tablespoon of water. Alternatively, stir-fry them in a small amount of oil, or steam them in a basket over simmering water. Always cook vegetables for as short a time as necessary to make them palatable.

☐ Store leftovers in an airtight container in the refrigerator. If you don't plan to eat the leftovers within a few days, freeze them.

☐ Top your breakfast cereal with sliced banana, berries, or raisins or other dried fruits.

☐ Make a quick fruit salad with one can of mandarin orange slices, one can of pineapple chunks, a sliced banana, a chopped apple, and some berries, grapes, or raisins. Serve with yogurt.

☐ Add fresh vegetables to salads, soups, homemade pizza, and pasta.

☐ Add dark-green leaf lettuce, tomato, and onion to sandwiches, or make a veggie sandwich using avocado slices in place of meat.

☐ Next time you're at a barbecue, grill fruits or vegetables on skewers.

☐ For homemade salsa, combine chopped tomatoes, avocado, red onions, cilantro (coriander), and lime juice.

☐ For shared meals, try a veggie-burrito buffet: set out a plate of warmed corn or whole-wheat tortillas with bowls of warm black or pinto beans, chopped tomatoes, chopped avocado, chopped black olives, minced onion or scallions, and plain yogurt or nonfat sour cream. Invite your friends to assemble their own!

☐ Make gazpacho! In a blender, combine 1–3 cups tomato juice, chunks of green pepper, red onion, a cucumber with seeds removed (no need to peel), the juice of one lime, a garlic clove, a splash each of red wine vinegar and olive oil, a half teaspoon each of basil and cumin, and salt and pepper to taste. Seed and dice two to three fresh tomatoes and add to blended ingredients. Chill for several hours. Serve very cold.

On the Run

☐ Buy ready-to-eat vegetables, such as baby carrots, cherry tomatoes, and celery sticks, or take a minute to wash and slice a red pepper or broccoli crowns. Toss some in a zip-lock bag to take to school or work.

☐ Throw a single-serving container of unsweetened applesauce, mandarin orange slices, pineapple chunks, or other fruit into your backpack for an afternoon snack. Don't forget the spoon!

☐ Make up small bags of fresh or dried fruits (grapes, raisins, apricots, cherries, prunes, figs, dates, banana chips, and so on) with nuts to take along.

☐ Pack a banana, an apple, a plum, an orange, or other fruit you can eat whole.

☐ Store some juice boxes in your freezer to take along. A frozen juice box will remain cold for several hours.

Data from Some suggestions from Centers for Disease Control and Prevention (CDC) and Produce for Better Health Foundation. at www.fruitsandveggiesmatter.gov and www.fruitsandveggiesmorematters.org; and Phytochemical Information Center. www.pbhfoundation.org.

blood clots from forming or to reduce inflammation in the walls of our blood vessels. Some appear able to reduce the ability of bacteria to cling to our tissues, and some may enhance the body's ability to destroy cancer cells or slow or stop their growth.[31] Precisely how phytochemicals perform these functions in conjunction with other nutrients is the subject of current research, as is the question of whether consuming phytochemicals in supplement form is also protective.

Given the many benefits of phytochemicals, you're probably wondering how to be sure you're getting all you need each day. Check out the *Game Plan* box for information on the number of servings you need, preparation guidelines, and tips for phytochemically charged meals and snacks.

RECAP Cancer is a group of diseases in which genetically mutated cells grow out of control. Tobacco use, sun exposure, nutritional factors, radiation and chemical exposures, and low physical activity levels are related to a higher risk for some cancers. Eating foods high in antioxidants is associated with lower rates of cancer. Phytochemicals are substances in plants that, together with other nutrients and fiber in plant-based foods, appear to reduce our risk for cancer and heart disease.

COOKING 101

Fresh fruits and vegetables look beautiful and provide lots of important vitamins . . . deliciously! Learn how to select and store your fruits and veggies for maximum taste and freshness with our new Cooking 101 videos, available on the Companion Website at **www.pearsonhighered.com/thompsonmanore**.

Chapter Review

What Can I Do **Today?**

Now that you've read this chapter, try making these three changes.

- Try eating at least 2 servings of fruit and 3 servings of vegetables every day for 1 week—if you already eat this amount regularly, try to eat 1 more serving of each.

- Add 1 serving of almonds or sunflower seeds to your next salad.

- For breakfast, eat 1 serving of a high-fiber cereal that is fortified with B-vitamins, and add to that a cup of vitamin D–fortified milk or soy milk.

Test Yourself ANSWERS

1. **T** Our body can use energy from sunlight to convert a cholesterol compound in our skin into vitamin D.

2. **F** Extensive research on vitamin C and colds does not support the theory that taking vitamin C supplements reduces our risk of catching a cold.

3. **F** B-vitamins do not directly provide energy for our body. However, they enable our body to generate energy from carbohydrates, fats, and proteins.

4. **F** Phytochemicals are chemicals that occur naturally in plants and appear to reduce our risk for heart disease, some forms of cancer, and certain other diseases.

5. **T** **F** For an individual who consumes a varied diet that provides adequate energy and nutrients, this statement is true. However, many people do not consume a varied diet that provides adequate levels of micronutrients, and others have health issues that increase their requirements or affect their ability to absorb micronutrients from food. For these individuals, a daily multivitamin supplement is not a waste of money—it's a wise investment in their health.

 **NutriTools** Check out the Companion Website at www.pearsonhighered.com/thompsonmanore, or use MyNutritionLab.com, to access interactive animations, including

- Vitamin Functionality
- Let's Go to Lunch!: Fat-Soluble Vitamins
- Let's Go to Lunch!: Water-Soluble Vitamins
- Nutrients: Vitamin or Mineral?

Review Questions

1. The B-vitamins include
   a. niacin, folate, and selenium.
   b. thiamin, pantothenic acid, and biotin.
   c. beta-carotene, riboflavin, and pyridoxine.
   d. cobalamin, choline, and chromium.

2. Which of the following is a characteristic of vitamin E?
   a. enhances the absorption of iron
   b. can be manufactured from beta-carotene
   c. is a coenzyme involved in the metabolism of carbohydrates and fats
   d. is destroyed by exposure to high heat

3. Which of the following are known carcinogens?
   a. phytochemicals
   b. antioxidants
   c. carotenoids
   d. nitrates

4. Taking daily megadoses of which of the following nutrients may cause death?
   a. vitamin A
   b. vitamin C
   c. vitamin E
   d. riboflavin

5. The vitamin most closely associated with blood clotting is
   a. vitamin A.
   b. vitamin K.
   c. niacin.
   d. vitamin B$_{12}$.

6. True or False? The best way for a woman to reduce her risk of having a baby with a neural tube defect is to begin taking a folate supplement as soon as she learns she is pregnant.

7. True or False? The body absorbs vitamin D from sunlight.

8. True or False? Free-radical formation can occur as a result of normal cellular metabolism.

9. True or False? Pregnant women are advised to consume plenty of beef liver.

10. True or False? High blood levels of the amino acid homocysteine are associated with an increased risk for heart disease.

Answers to Review Questions are located at the back of this text.

Web Links

www.nlm.nih.gov/medlineplus
MEDLINE Plus Health Information

www.cdc.gov
Centers for Disease Control and Prevention

www.fruitsandveggiesmorematters.org
Fruits & Veggies—More Matters

www.cancer.org
American Cancer Society (ACS)

www.fda.gov
Food and Drug Association (FDA)

www.cancer.gov
National Cancer Institute

www.cfsan.fda.gov
Center for Food Safety and Applied Nutrition

www.nccam.nih.gov
National Center for Complementary and Alternative Medicine

www.dietary-supplements.info.nih.gov
Office of Dietary Supplements

7

Minerals: Building and Moving Our Body

As a young woman, Erika Goodman leapt across the stage in leading roles with the Joffrey Ballet, one of the premier dance companies in the world. But at the age of 59, she died after falling in her Manhattan apartment. Goodman had a disease called *osteoporosis,* which means "porous bones." As you might suspect, the less dense the bone, the more likely it is to break; indeed, osteoporosis can cause bones to break during even minor weight-bearing activities, such as carrying groceries. In advanced cases, bones in the hip and spine fracture spontaneously, merely from the effort of holding the body erect.

In this chapter, we discuss the minerals that form our bones and explore how mineral deficiencies lead to bone disease. We also explain how minerals called *electrolytes* provide the electrical charge that enables our body to dance, work, think . . . indeed, to perform any conscious or unconscious activity. Still other minerals work with the B-vitamins to metabolize food into energy and some help transport oxygen within our blood. As you can see, minerals are indispensable to our functioning **(Figure 7.1)**. Still, you don't have to take supplements to get the minerals you need. Just make sure to eat a variety of nutrient-dense foods, especially fruits, vegetables, whole grains, legumes, and low-fat dairy products. Before we discuss individual minerals, let's pause to explore exactly what minerals are.

Nutrition Online icons are located throughout the chapter, directing you to web links, videos, podcasts, and other useful online resources.

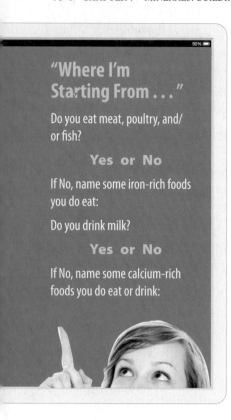

What Are Minerals?

Minerals are solid, crystalline substances that do not contain carbon and are not broken down during digestion. In fact, they can't be created or destroyed by any natural means, including heat, cold, light, chemicals, or mechanical force. Minerals exist not only in foods but also in the environment: the zinc in meats is the same as the zinc in the earth's crust.

One of the most important properties of minerals is their ability to carry an electrical charge. Like magnets, minerals with opposite electrical charges bond tightly together to form durable compounds—for instance, in our bones. The electrical charge of minerals also attracts water, so the minerals inside our cells help them retain the amount of water they need to function. And in both our cells and tissues, the electrical charges of various minerals stimulate our nerves to fire and our muscles to contract.

Minerals are classified according to the amounts we need in our diet and according to how much of the mineral is found in our body. The two categories of minerals in our diet and our body are the major minerals and the trace minerals.

Major Minerals Are Required in Amounts Greater Than 100 mg per Day

Major minerals earned their name from the fact that we need to consume at least 100 mg of each per day in our diet. In addition, the total amount of each major mineral present in the body is at least 5 grams (5,000 mg). For instance, the major

Power Plants
Help convert food into energy
Chromium
Manganese
Sulfur
Selenium
Iodine

Essential Electrolytes
Help maintain hydration and muscle functioning
Phosphorus
Potassium
Sodium
Chloride

Blood Fortifiers
Help maintain healthy blood
Iron
Zinc
Copper

Bone Builders
Help keep bones healthy
Calcium
Phosphorus
Magnesium
Fluoride

▲ **Figure 7.1** The functions of the major and trace minerals. Good food sources are also shown for each functional group.

mineral calcium is a primary component of our bones. In addition to calcium, the major minerals include sodium, potassium, phosphorus, chloride, magnesium, and sulfur. **Table 7.1** identifies the primary functions, recommended intakes, and food sources of these minerals.

Trace Minerals Are Required in Amounts Less Than 100 mg per Day

Trace minerals are those we need to consume in amounts less than 100 mg per day. The total amount of any trace mineral in the body is less than 5 grams (5,000 mg). The trace minerals include selenium, fluoride, iodine, chromium, manganese, iron, zinc, and copper. **Table 7.2** (page 196) identifies major functions, recommended intakes, and food sources of these minerals.

minerals Solid, crystalline substances that do not contain carbon and are not changed by natural processes, including digestion.

major minerals Minerals we need to consume in amounts of at least 100 mg per day, and of which the total amount present in the body is at least 5 grams (5,000 mg).

trace minerals Minerals we need to consume in amounts less than 100 mg per day, and of which the total amount present in the body is less than 5 grams (5,000 mg).

TABLE 7.1	Major Minerals			
Mineral	**Primary Functions**	**Recommended Intake***	**Reliable Food Sources**	**Toxicity/Deficiency Symptoms**
Sodium	Fluid balance Acid–base balance Transmission of nerve impulses Muscle contraction	AI: adults = 1.5 g/day (1,500 mg/day)	Table salt, pickles, most canned soups, snack foods, cured lunch meats, canned tomato products	*Toxicity:* water retention, high blood pressure, loss of calcium *Deficiency:* muscle cramps, dizziness, fatigue, nausea, vomiting, mental confusion
Potassium	Fluid balance Transmission of nerve impulses Muscle contraction	AI: adults = 4.7 g/day (4,700 mg/day)	Most fresh fruits and vegetables: potatoes, bananas, tomato juice, orange juice, melons	*Toxicity:* muscle weakness, vomiting, irregular heartbeat *Deficiency:* muscle weakness, paralysis, mental confusion, irregular heartbeat
Phosphorus	Fluid balance Bone formation Component of ATP, which provides energy for our body	RDA: adults = 700 mg/day	Milk/cheese/yogurt, soy milk and tofu, legumes (lentils, black beans), nuts (almonds, peanuts and peanut butter), poultry	*Toxicity:* muscle spasms, convulsions, low blood calcium *Deficiency:* muscle weakness, muscle damage, bone pain, dizziness
Chloride	Fluid balance Transmission of nerve impulses Component of stomach acid (HCl) Antibacterial	AI: adults = 2.3 g/day (2,300 mg/day)	Table salt	*Toxicity:* none known *Deficiency:* dangerous blood acid–base imbalances, irregular heartbeat
Calcium	Primary component of bone Acid–base balance Transmission of nerve impulses Muscle contraction	RDAs: Adults aged 19–50 = 1,000 mg/day Men aged 51–70 = 1,000 mg/day; men aged >70 = 1,200 mg/day Women aged >50 = 1,200 mg/day UL = 2,500 mg/day	Milk/yogurt/cheese (best-absorbed form of calcium), sardines, collard greens and spinach, calcium-fortified juices	*Toxicity:* mineral imbalances, shock, kidney failure, fatigue, mental confusion *Deficiency:* osteoporosis, convulsions, heart failure
Magnesium	Component of bone Muscle contraction Assists more than 300 enzyme systems	RDAs: Men aged 19–30 = 400 mg/day; men aged >30 = 420 mg/day Women aged 19–30 = 310 mg/day; women aged >30 = 320 mg/day UL = 350 mg/day	Greens (spinach, kale, collard greens), whole grains, seeds, nuts, legumes (navy and black beans)	*Toxicity:* none known *Deficiency:* low blood calcium, muscle spasms or seizures, nausea, weakness, increased risk for chronic diseases (such as heart disease, hypertension, osteoporosis, type 2 diabetes)
Sulfur	Component of certain B-vitamins and amino acids Acid–base balance Detoxification in liver	No DRI	Protein-rich foods	*Toxicity:* none known *Deficiency:* none known

*Abbreviations: RDA, Recommended Dietary Allowance; UL, upper limit; AI, Adequate Intake; DRI, Dietary Reference Intake.

TABLE 7.2   Trace Minerals

Mineral	Primary Functions	Recommended Intake*	Reliable Food Sources	Toxicity/Deficiency Symptoms
Selenium	Required for carbohydrate and fat metabolism	RDA: adults = 55 µg/day UL = 400 µg/day	Nuts, shellfish, meat/fish/poultry, whole grains	*Toxicity:* brittle hair and nails, skin rashes, nausea and vomiting, weakness, liver disease *Deficiency:* specific forms of heart disease and arthritis, impaired immune function, muscle pain and wasting, depression, hostility
Fluoride	Development and maintenance of healthy teeth and bones	RDAs: Men = 4 mg/day Women = 3 mg/day UL: 2.2 mg/day for children aged 4 to 8; children aged >8 = 10 mg/day	Fish, seafood, legumes, whole grains, drinking water (variable)	*Toxicity:* fluorosis of teeth and bones *Deficiency:* dental caries, low bone density
Iodine	Synthesis of thyroid hormones Temperature regulation Reproduction and growth	RDA: Adults = 150 µg/day UL = 1,100 µg/day	Iodized salt, saltwater seafood	*Toxicity:* goiter *Deficiency:* goiter, hypothyroidism, cretinism in infant of mother who is iodine deficient
Chromium	Glucose transport Metabolism of DNA and RNA Immune function and growth	AI: men aged 19–50 = 35 µg/day; men aged >50 = 30 µg/day Women aged 19–50 = 25 µg/day; women aged >50 = 20 µg/day	Whole grains, brewer's yeast	*Toxicity:* None known *Deficiency:* Elevated blood glucose and blood lipids, damage to brain and nervous system
Manganese	Assists many enzyme systems Synthesis of protein found in bone and cartilage	AIs: Men = 2.3 mg/day Women = 1.8 mg/day UL = 11 mg/day for adults	Whole grains, nuts, leafy vegetables, tea	*Toxicity:* impairment of neuromuscular system *Deficiency:* impaired growth and reproductive function, reduced bone density, impaired glucose and lipid metabolism, skin rash
Iron	Component of hemoglobin in blood cells Component of myoglobin in muscle cells Assists many enzyme systems	RDAs: Adult men = 8 mg/day Women aged 19–50 = 18 mg/day; women aged >50 = 8 mg/day	Meat/fish/poultry (best-absorbed form of iron), fortified cereals, legumes, spinach	*Toxicity:* nausea, vomiting, and diarrhea; dizziness, confusion; rapid heartbeat, organ damage, death *Deficiency:* iron-deficiency microcytic anemia (small red blood cells), hypochromic anemia
Zinc	Assists more than 100 enzyme systems Immune system function Growth and sexual maturation Gene regulation	RDAs: Men = 11 mg/day Women = 8 mg/day UL = 40 mg/day	Meat/fish/poultry (best-absorbed form of zinc), fortified cereals, legumes	*Toxicity:* nausea, vomiting, diarrhea, headaches, depressed immune function, reduced absorption of copper *Deficiency:* growth retardation, delayed sexual maturation, eye and skin lesions, hair loss, increased incidence of illness and infection
Copper	Assists many enzyme systems Iron transport	RDA: Adults = 900 µg/day UL = 10 mg/day	Shellfish, organ meats, nuts, legumes	*Toxicity:* nausea, vomiting, diarrhea, liver damage *Deficiency:* anemia, reduced levels of white blood cells, osteoporosis in infants and growing children

*Abbreviations: RDA, Recommended Dietary Allowance; UL, upper limit; AI, Adequate Intake.

Most Ultra-Trace Minerals Are of Uncertain Status

ultra-trace minerals Minerals we need to consume in amounts less than 1 mg/d (mg per day) of body weight.

A number of **ultra-trace minerals** are found in our body, including boron, molybdenum, nickel, silicon, and others. They are classified as ultra-trace because researchers estimate that we have a dietary requirement of less than 1 mg/d (mg per day) of body weight for these minerals.[1] Of those just listed, only molybdenum is considered essential for human health.[1] This mineral is important for key enzymes within the body, and it has an RDA of 45 µg/day for adults 19 to 70 years of age. Rich sources of molybdenum are legumes, grains, and nuts.[1] Many other ultra-trace minerals are thought to be important for health, but their exact role in the body is still not clear, and they have no DRI.

RECAP Minerals are solid, crystalline substances that do not contain carbon and are not changed by any natural means. We need to consume at least 100 mg per day of the major minerals, which include sodium, potassium, phosphorus, chloride, calcium, magnesium, and sulfur. We need to consume less than 100 mg per day of the trace minerals, which include selenium, fluoride, iodine, chromium, manganese, iron, zinc, and copper. Ultra-trace minerals are required in amounts lower than 1 mg/d (mg per day) of body weight.

Many different foods provide minerals.

Essential Electrolytes: Sodium, Potassium, Chloride, and Phosphorus

The interior of all body cells contains fluid, and many cells anchored together in a fluid bath make up body tissues. Dissolved in these cellular and tissue fluids are four major minerals: sodium, potassium, chloride, and phosphorus. There, these minerals are referred to as **electrolytes,** because they form charged particles called **ions,** which carry an electrical current. This electricity is the "spark" that stimulates nerves to transmit impulses, so electrolytes are critical to nervous system functioning. Serious electrolyte disturbances can lead to seizures, loss of consciousness, and cardiac arrest.

Electrolytes are also critical to maintaining our fluid balance; that is, they keep our cells from becoming swollen with too much fluid or dehydrated from too little. Two qualities help electrolytes work together to control fluid balance: First, they all strongly attract water. Second, they are not able to move freely from one side of the cell membrane to the other. Instead, potassium and phosphate tend to remain inside our cells, and sodium and chloride tend to remain outside, in the tissue spaces. Although none of the electrolytes can move freely across the cell membrane, water can. Thus, the equal attraction for water of the electrolytes on either side of the cell membrane keeps our body in fluid balance **(Figure 7.2)**.

When our electrolytes go out of balance, body fluids soon go out of balance as well. For instance, imagine a shipwrecked sailor in a lifeboat. With no fresh water to drink, he drinks seawater, which is, of course, high in sodium. This heavy load of sodium remains in the tissue spaces outside his cells, where it strongly attracts water. Because the level of electrolytes inside the cells has not been increased, there is now a much greater concentration of electrolytes outside the cells. This higher concentration

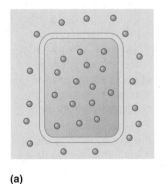
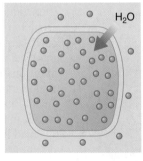
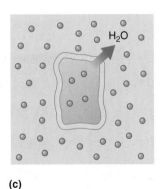

(a)   (b)   (c)

Figure 7.2 The health of the body's cells depends on maintaining the proper balance of fluids and electrolytes on both sides of the cell membrane. **(a)** The concentration of electrolytes is the same on both sides of the cell membrane. **(b)** The concentration of electrolytes is much greater inside the cell, drawing water into the cell and making it swell. **(c)** The concentration of electrolytes is much greater outside the cell, drawing water out of the cell and making it shrink.

electrolyte A (mineral) substance that dissolves in solution into positively and negatively charged ions and is thus capable of carrying an electrical current.

ion An electrically charged particle.

Many popular snack foods are high in sodium.

of electrolytes pulls water out of the cells into the tissue spaces (Figure 7.2c). This leaves the cells dehydrated. The sailor's body then excretes the salty tissue fluid as urine, decreasing the total amount of water in his body. If the sailor continues to drink seawater, he will become so dehydrated that he will die.

Similarly, food poisoning, eating disorders, and other illnesses involving repeated vomiting and diarrhea can threaten the delicate balance of fluid inside and outside our cells. With diarrhea or vomiting, the body loses a great deal of fluid from the intestinal tract and the tissue spaces outside the cells. This heavy fluid loss causes the electrolyte concentration outside the cells to become very high. In response, a great deal of the interior fluid of the cells flows out. The resulting fluid and electrolyte imbalance alters the flow of electrical impulses through the heart, causing an irregular heart rate that can lead to death if left untreated.

The recommended intakes of the electrolytes and other major minerals are identified in Table 7.1.

RECAP The major minerals sodium, potassium, chloride, and phosphorus are called electrolytes, because when they dissolve in water they form electrically charged particles called ions, which can carry an electrical current. Electrolytes assist in nerve transmission and regulation of fluid balance. Repeated diarrhea or vomiting can threaten fluid balance.

Eating Right All Day

Breakfast
Whole-grain waffle with jam instead of a ham & cheese omlette!

Lunch
Spinach salad instead of canned spinach!

Dinner
Veggie pizza instead of pepperoni!

Snack
Unsalted almonds instead of corn chips!

Sodium Is Part of Table Salt

Many people equate sodium with table salt, but in truth, those crystals in your salt shaker are made up of both sodium and chloride. Over the past 20 years, researchers have linked high sodium intake to an increased risk for high blood pressure. Because of this link, many people have come to believe that sodium is harmful to the body. This simply is not true: sodium is an essential nutrient that the body needs to survive. We'll explore the link between sodium and high blood pressure shortly.

Why Do We Need Sodium?

Sodium is a major mineral with many functions. As discussed, it helps cells maintain proper fluid balance. It also helps regulate blood pressure and acid–base balance, plays a leading role in the transmission of nerve signals, and is an important component of gastric secretions. Finally, sodium assists in the absorption of certain nutrients, such as glucose.

In addition to its functions in the body, sodium in table salt enhances the flavor of foods. It is also a powerful antimicrobial: for thousands of years, it has been used to preserve meats and other foods.

How Much Sodium Should We Consume?

Virtually all of the sodium we consume in our diet is absorbed by the body. To give

TABLE 7.3 High-Sodium Foods and Lower-Sodium Alternatives

High-Sodium Food	Sodium (mg)	Lower-Sodium Food	Sodium (mg)
Dill pickle (1 large, 4 in.)	1,181	Low-sodium dill pickle (1 large, 4 in.)	12
Ham, cured, roasted (3 oz)	1,128	Pork, loin roast (3 oz)	48
Corn beef (3 oz)	1,110	Beef chuck roast, cooked (3 oz)	40
Tomato juice, regular (1 cup)	680	Tomato juice, lower-sodium (1 cup)	141
Tomato sauce, canned (1/2 cup)	642	Fresh tomato (1 medium)	6
Canned cream corn (1 cup)	730	Cooked corn, fresh (1 large ear), boiled	0
Tomato soup, canned (1 cup)	675	Low-sodium tomato soup, canned (1 cup)	60
Potato chips, salted (1 oz)	149	Baked potato, unsalted (1 medium)	17
Saltine crackers (4 each)	256	Saltine crackers, unsalted (4 each)	92

Data from U.S. Department of Agriculture, Agricultural Research Service. 2010. USDA Nutrient Database for Standard Reference, Release 23. Nutrient Data Laboratory Home Page. www.ars.usda.gov/services/docs.htm?docid=20958.

you a sense of how little sodium we need each day, consider that the AI (1,500 mg) is a little more than half a teaspoon! Most people in the United States greatly exceed this amount, consuming between 3,000 and 6,000 mg of sodium per day.[2]

Sodium is found naturally in many foods, and processed foods typically contain added sodium. Try to guess which of the following foods contains the most sodium: 1 cup of tomato juice, 1 oz of potato chips, or four saltine crackers. Now look at **Table 7.3** to find the answer. Are you surprised to discover that, of these three food items, the tomato juice has the most sodium? Lots of processed foods, such as lunch meats, canned soups and beans, vegetable juices, and prepackaged rice and pasta dishes, are very high in sodium, as are many snack foods and fast foods, not to mention many dishes served in college cafeterias!

Does Sodium Play a Role in High Blood Pressure?

Consuming excessive sodium causes water retention (bloating), as water is drawn out of the interior of cells to dilute the sodium in the tissue fluids. A high level of sodium in the tissue fluid of the bloodstream (called *plasma*) similarly attracts water, and when it does, the total volume of blood circulating in the blood vessels increases. This, in turn, increases the level of pressure inside the blood vessels. This condition, commonly called high blood pressure, is clinically known as *hypertension*. Although it is one of the major chronic diseases in the United States, hypertension often causes no symptoms. Instead, it's typically diagnosed when a routine blood pressure screening reveals above-average readings. Early detection and treatment is essential, because hypertension is a warning sign that the person is at an increased risk for a heart attack or stroke.

When we define hypertension as blood pressure above the average range, what exactly do we mean? Well, blood pressure measurements are recorded in millimeters of mercury (mm Hg) in two phases, systolic and diastolic:

- *Systolic blood pressure* represents the pressure exerted in our arteries at the moment that the heart contracts, sending blood into our blood vessels. Optimal systolic blood pressure is *less than* 120 mm Hg.
- *Diastolic blood pressure* represents the pressure in our arteries between contractions, when our heart is relaxed. Optimal diastolic blood pressure is *less than* 80 mm Hg.

For example, a healthy blood pressure reading might be 110 mm Hg systolic and 70 mm Hg diastolic—which a clinician would report to you as "110 over 70 mm Hg." *Prehypertension* is defined as a systolic blood pressure between 120 and 139 mm Hg, or a diastolic blood pressure between 80 and 89 mm Hg. So "120 over 85 mm Hg" indicates prehypertension. You would be diagnosed with true hypertension if your systolic blood pressure were greater than or equal to 140 mm Hg or your diastolic blood pressure were greater than or equal to 90 mm Hg.

Hypertension is more common in people who consume high-sodium diets, but whether high-sodium diets can actually *cause* hypertension is the subject of some

Almost all sodium is consumed through table salt.

⬆ Tomato juice is an excellent source of potassium. Make sure you choose the low-sodium variety!

controversy. In most people who consume too much sodium, the body can make adjustments to compensate and the kidneys will excrete the excess sodium in the urine. But in some individuals, the body is unable to compensate for a high sodium intake and blood pressure increases.

Research into hypertension funded by the National Institutes of Health (NIH) has led to the development of the DASH Diet, an eating plan shown to reduce hypertension. DASH stands for "Dietary Approaches to Stop Hypertension" and in-cludes recommendations for consuming 8 to 10 servings of fruits and vegetables daily, as well as limiting dietary sodium; for example, the lowest-sodium version of the DASH Diet recommends 1,500 mg of sodium per day. The DASH Diet has been shown to significantly reduce blood pressure, with the greatest reductions in people following the lowest-sodium version.[3]

>
> To download a brief guide to the DASH Diet, including a sample meal plan and more, go to www.nhlbi.nih.gov/health/public/heart/hbp/dash/dash_brief.pdf.

Because sodium is so abundant, it's easy to overdo it. Check out the low-sodium choices in the *Eating Right All Day* feature (page 198). Each of those choices would be appropriate on the DASH Diet.

Also, if you're interested in reducing your sodium intake, what's the best way to start? Check out the *Game Plan* feature box (page 202).

Potassium Helps Maintain Healthful Blood Pressure

The major mineral potassium is a component of all living cells and is found in both plants and animals. About 85% of dietary potassium is absorbed, and as with sodium, the kidneys work to regulate its level in the blood. Most excretion of potassium occurs in the urine, with some excretion in the feces.

Potassium is a primary electrolyte within cells, where it balances the sodium outside the cell membrane to maintain proper fluid balance. It also plays a role in regulating the transmission of nerve impulses and assists in maintaining blood pressure. In contrast to a high-sodium diet, eating a diet high in potassium actually helps maintain a lower blood pressure.

The best sources of potassium are fresh foods, particularly fresh fruits and veg-etables (**Figure 7.3**). Processing foods gener-ally increases their sodium and decreases their potassium. You can boost your potas-sium intake by eating more fresh fruits, vegetables, and whole grains and reduce your sodium intake by avoiding processed foods. Most salt substitutes are made from potassium chloride, and these products con-tain relatively high amounts of potassium.

People with healthy kidneys are able to excrete excess potassium effectively, so toxicity in healthy people is rare. Because potassium is widespread in many foods, a dietary potassium deficiency is also rare. However, potassium deficiency is not un-common among people who have serious medical disorders, including kidney dis-ease. Extreme dehydration, vomiting, and diarrhea can also cause deficiency, as can abuse of alcohol or laxatives, and use of

NUTRITION
MILESTONE

Sodium does not occur by itself in nature. Instead, it forms compounds, such as table salt, baking soda, and lye. So how and when did it come to be recognized as an independent mineral?

In the early **1800s**, the English chemist Sir Humphry Davy began experimenting with a new device—a forerunner of our modern battery—that could generate an electrical current. He used the device to run an electrical current through a variety of chemical compounds, thereby forcing a chemical reaction that wouldn't otherwise have occurred. He discovered that the cur-rent caused the compounds to break down into their component minerals.

In 1807, Davy used his technique to separate the components of a powdery salt commonly called potash. In doing so, he isolated potassium. Shortly there-after, he used the same technique on lye and isolated sodium, which until that time had not been considered distinct from potassium. The following year, he succeeded in isolating calcium and mag-nesium. For these reasons, Davy is con-sidered a pioneer of electrochemistry.

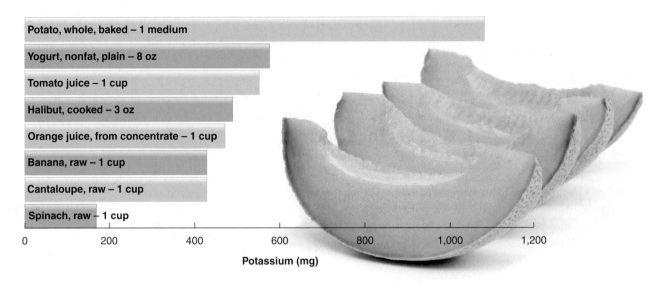

Potato, whole, baked – 1 medium

Yogurt, nonfat, plain – 8 oz

Tomato juice – 1 cup

Halibut, cooked – 3 oz

Orange juice, from concentrate – 1 cup

Banana, raw – 1 cup

Cantaloupe, raw – 1 cup

Spinach, raw – 1 cup

0   200   400   600   800   1,000   1,200

Potassium (mg)

Figure 7.3 Common food sources of potassium. The AI for potassium is 4.7 grams/day (or, 4700 mg/d).
Data from U.S. Department of Agriculture, Agricultural Research Service. 2007. USDA Nutrient Database for Standard Reference, Release 22. Nutrient Data Laboratory Home Page. www.ars.usda.gov/ba/bhnrc/ndl.

Low-fat milk and other dairy products are a good source of phosphorus.

certain types of diuretics (medications that increase the body's excretion of fluid). Symptoms of potassium deficiency include confusion, loss of appetite, and muscle weakness. Severe deficiency results in fatal changes in heart rate; many deaths attributed to extreme dehydration or to an eating disorder are caused by abnormal heart rhythms due to potassium deficiency.

Chloride and Phosphorus Also Assist Fluid Balance

Chloride is a major mineral that we obtain almost exclusively from consuming sodium chloride, or table salt. It should not be confused with *chlorine*, which is a poisonous gas used to kill bacteria and other germs in our water supply.

Coupled with sodium in the fluid outside cells, chloride assists with the maintenance of fluid balance and in the transmission of nerve impulses. Chloride is also a part of hydrochloric acid in the stomach, which aids in digesting food, and it assists white blood cells during an immune response to help kill bacteria.

Although chloride is found in some fruits and vegetables, our primary dietary sources are table salt and the salt in processed foods. There is no known toxicity symptom, and deficiency is rare except during conditions of severe dehydration and frequent vomiting.

Phosphorus is pooled with potassium in the fluid inside cells, where it helps maintain proper fluid balance. As we discuss later in this chapter, phosphorus also plays a critical role in bone formation.

RECAP Sodium is a major mineral and is prominent in the fluid outside of cells. It helps regulate fluid balance, blood pressure, and nerve function. Excessive sodium intake has been related to hypertension. Potassium is a major mineral in the fluid within cells, and it balances sodium in body fluids. Chloride and phosphorus are major minerals that also help maintain fluid balance.

Our body contains very little chromium. Asparagus is a good dietary source of this trace mineral.

Mineral Power Plants: Chromium, Manganese, Sulfur, Iodine, and Selenium

Many minerals help our body access the nutrients in foods by assisting their transport into cells or by helping the enzymes that break down foods into energy. Others assist in the production of hormones that regulate metabolic processes. These minerals are discussed here, and their recommended intakes are listed in Tables 7.1 and 7.2.

GAME PLAN

Tips for Sparing the Salt

If you've decided to try to reduce your intake of sodium, you're probably thinking that the first step is to hide the salt shaker. You're right—limiting the salt you add to foods *is* important! You can train your taste buds to prefer less salt by gradually reducing the amount you use over a period of several weeks to months. If you try this, you might be surprised at how quickly chips, soups, and other foods you once enjoyed start to taste much too salty.

Still, the majority of the sodium in our diet comes from processed food—in other words, from salt that you might not even realize is there. So the next step in reducing your sodium consumption is to shop for fresh, whole foods and cook them with less salt. Here are some tips to get you started.

When Shopping

Next time you stock up on processed foods, keep the following shopping tips in mind:

☐ Look for the words "low sodium" on the label, as well as a sodium amount no higher than 200 mg per serving on the Nutrition Facts Panel.

☐ When possible, choose low-sodium alternatives to the following high-sodium foods:
- canned beans, soups, gravies, pasta sauces, soy sauce, other sauces, vegetables, and vegetable juices
- packaged pasta dishes, rice dishes, and potato dishes
- frozen entrées, frozen dinners, frozen pizza, and other frozen meals
- smoked meats and fish
- cheese
- pickles, olives, three-bean salad, salad dressing
- snack foods such as crackers, cookies, potato chips, pretzels, popcorn, and salted nuts

When Cooking

When you have time for a home-cooked meal, take these steps to limit your sodium intake:

☐ Challenge yourself to use primarily fresh ingredients. For instance, try preparing pasta with fresh tomatoes, instead of prepared pasta sauce.

☐ When using canned beans, rinse them with cold water before heating.

☐ Experiment with salt substitutes.

☐ Substitute herbs or spices for salt. The following are particularly useful in low-sodium cooking:
- *basil, oregano, or thyme:* fish, lamb, soups, and sauces
- *black pepper, cayenne pepper, or chili powder:* soups, casserole, cheese sauces, baked egg dishes, barbequed poultry, and lean meats
- *cumin or curry:* meat, chicken, fish, stews, lentils, and beans
- *garlic:* lean meats, fish, poultry, soups, salads, vegetables, and pasta dishes
- *lemon or lime juice:* fish, poultry, salads, vegetables, and sauces

☐ Add ginger or chilies to a stir-fry.

☐ Use cooking wine for meat, poultry, or fish.

☐ Avoid using the "salt" version of any spice, such as garlic salt.

At the Table

☐ Put the salt shaker out of reach.

☐ Limit your use of condiments such as catsup, mustard, or pickles.

☐ When eating out, ask that your food be prepared without salt.

☐ Don't order soup in a restaurant. Many are loaded with sodium.

☐ If you order a salad, skip the prepared dressing; use lemon juice and olive oil instead.

NUTRITION MYTH OR FACT?

Do Chromium Supplements Enhance Body Composition?

Chromium supplements, typically in the form of chromium picolinate, are popular with bodybuilders and weight lifters. That's because their manufacturers claim that chromium increases muscle mass and muscle strength and decreases body fat. What's behind this claim?

More than 20 years ago, a study of chromium supplementation found that chromium use in both untrained men and football players decreased body fat and increased muscle mass.[4] This finding caused a surge in popularity of chromium supplements. In the meantime, the next study of chromium supplementation found no effects of chromium on muscle mass, body fat, or muscle strength.[5]

These contradictory reports led many scientists to closely examine the two studies and to design more sophisticated studies to assess the effect of chromium on body composition. There were a number of flaws in the methodology of the early studies. One major concern was that the chromium status of the research participants prior to the study was not measured or controlled. Chromium deficiency at the onset of the study could cause a more positive reaction to

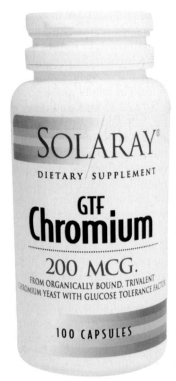

chromium than would be expected in people with normal chromium status.

A second major concern was that body composition was measured in these studies using the skinfold technique, in which calipers are used to measure the thickness of the skin and fat at various sites on the body. While this method gives a good general estimate of body fat in young, lean, healthy people, it is not sensitive to small changes in muscle mass. Thus, subsequent studies of chromium used more sophisticated methods of measuring body composition.

The results of subsequent research studies have consistently shown that chromium supplementation has no effect on muscle mass, body fat, or muscle strength in a variety of groups, including untrained college males and females, obese females, collegiate wrestlers, and older men and women.[6–13] However, despite the overwhelming evidence to the contrary, many supplement companies continue to claim that chromium supplements enhance strength and muscle mass and reduce body fat. These claims result in millions of dollars of sales each year. Don't be fooled: chromium supplementation is nothing more than an expensive nutrition myth.

Chromium and Manganese Are Important in Metabolism

Chromium is a trace mineral that plays an important role in the breakdown of carbohydrates. It does this by enhancing the ability of insulin to transport glucose from the bloodstream into cells. Chromium also assists in the metabolism of RNA and DNA, in immune function, and in growth. You may be interested to learn that the chromium in our body is the same metal used in the chrome plating for cars!

Chromium supplements have been marketed with claims that they reduce body fat and enhance muscle mass. This marketing has targeted bodybuilders and other athletes interested in improving their body composition. Refer to the *Nutrition Myth or Fact?* box to find out if taking supplemental chromium is effective in improving body composition. There appears to be no toxicity related to consuming chromium supplements, and chromium deficiency appears to be uncommon in the United States.

A trace mineral, manganese is involved in energy metabolism and in the formation of urea, the primary component of urine. It also assists in the synthesis of bone tissue and cartilage, a tissue supporting our joints. Manganese also helps protect the body from oxidative damage.

Sulfur Is a Component of Other Nutrients

Sulfur is a major mineral and a component of the B-vitamins thiamin and biotin. In addition, as part of the amino acids methionine and cysteine, sulfur helps the body's

Raspberries are one of the many foods that contain manganese.

proteins maintain their three-dimensional shapes. The liver requires sulfur to assist in the detoxification of alcohol and various drugs, and sulfur helps maintain acid–base balance.

Our body is able to make all the sulfur we need using the amino acids in the protein-containing foods we eat; as a result, we do not need to consume sulfur in the diet, and there is no DRI for it. There are no known toxicity or deficiency symptoms associated with sulfur.

Iodine and Selenium Help Make Thyroid Hormone

Iodine and selenium are trace minerals necessary for the synthesis of thyroid hormones. The body requires thyroid hormones to grow, reproduce, regulate body temperature, and maintain resting metabolic rate.

Very few foods naturally contain iodine. Saltwater fish do have high amounts, because marine animals concentrate iodine from seawater. In foods, iodine is mostly found in the form of iodide. Good sources include iodized salt and breads made with iodized salt, as well as milk and other dairy products. In the United States, iodine has been added to salt since early in the 20th century to combat iodine deficiency resulting from the poor iodine content of soils in this country. Approximately ½ teaspoon of iodized salt meets the entire adult RDA for iodine.

If you consume either too much or too little iodine, your body will stop manufacturing thyroid hormones, leading to *hypothyroidism*, or low levels of thyroid hormones. This causes enlargement of the thyroid gland, called **goiter,** which occurs when the thyroid gland attempts to produce more thyroid hormones **(Figure 7.4).** Other symptoms of hypothyroidism are decreased body temperature, inability to tolerate cold, weight gain, fatigue, and sluggishness. If a woman experiences iodine deficiency during pregnancy, her infant has a high risk of being born with a form of mental retardation referred to as **cretinism.** In addition to mental retardation, people with cretinism may suffer from stunted growth, deafness, and muteness.

The body's selenium is contained in amino acids. In addition to its role in the production of thyroid hormones, selenium works as an antioxidant to spare vitamin E and prevent oxidative damage to cell membranes. Its role in preventing heart disease and certain types of cancer is under investigation.

Selenium is found in varying amounts in soil and thus in foods. Organ meats and nuts are good sources, but the selenium content of fruits and vegetables depends on the level in the soil in which they are grown. Selenium toxicity is rare.[14] Deficiency is associated with rare forms of heart disease and arthritis. See **Figure 7.5** for a list of common food sources of selenium.

Figure 7.4 Goiter, or enlargement of the thyroid gland, occurs with both iodine toxicity and deficiency.

goiter A condition marked by enlargement of the thyroid gland, which can be caused by iodine toxicity or deficiency.

cretinism A form of mental retardation that occurs in people whose mothers experienced iodine deficiency during pregnancy.

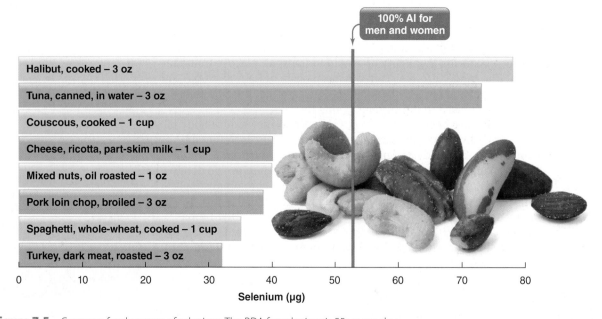

Figure 7.5 Common food sources of selenium. The RDA for selenium is 55 µg per day.
Data from U.S. Department of Agriculture, Agricultural Research Service. 2009. USDA Nutrient Database for Standard Reference, Release 22. Nutrient Data Laboratory Home Page. www.ars.usda.gov/ba/bhnrc/ndl.

RECAP Chromium enhances the ability of insulin to transport glucose from the bloodstream into cells. Manganese is involved in energy metabolism and in the formation of urea, the primary component of urine. Sulfur is a major mineral and a component of the B-vitamins thiamin and biotin. Iodine and selenium assist in the synthesis of thyroid hormones, and selenium has antioxidant properties.

The Blood Fortifiers: Iron, Zinc, and Copper

Without healthy blood to transport nutrients and oxygen to our cells and to remove cellular wastes, we could not survive. Our health and our ability to perform daily activities are compromised if the quantity and quality of our blood are diminished.

Blood is made up of four components **(Figure 7.6)**:

- Red blood cells (*erythrocytes*) are the cells that transport oxygen.
- White blood cells (*leukocytes*) protect us from infection and illness.
- Platelets are cell fragments that assist in the formation of blood clots and help stop bleeding.
- Plasma is the fluid portion of the blood and enables blood to flow easily through the blood vessels.

In addition to vitamin K, the micronutrients recognized as playing a critical role in maintaining blood health include iron, zinc, and copper. Recommended intakes of these three minerals are identified in Table 7.2.

Iron Is a Key Component of Hemoglobin

Iron is a trace mineral that is needed in very small amounts in our diet; nevertheless, it is present in every one of the millions of red blood cells in a single drop of blood.

Why Do We Need Iron?

Iron is critical to healthy blood because it is a key component of **hemoglobin,** which is the oxygen-carrying protein in our red blood cells. As shown in **Figure 7.7** (page 206), the hemoglobin molecule consists of four protein strands studded with four iron-containing **heme** groups. Hemoglobin depends on the iron in its heme groups to carry oxygen. In the bloodstream, iron acts as a shuttle, picking up oxygen from the air we breathe,

Wheat is a rich source of selenium.

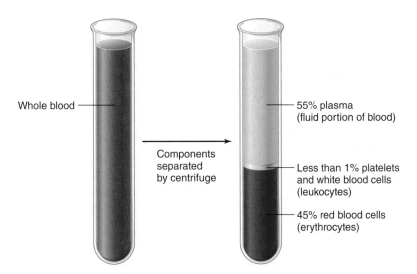

Whole blood

Components separated by centrifuge

55% plasma (fluid portion of blood)

Less than 1% platelets and white blood cells (leukocytes)

45% red blood cells (erythrocytes)

Figure 7.6 Blood has four components, which are visible when the blood is drawn into a test tube and spun in a centrifuge. The bottom layer is the red blood cells. The milky layer above the red blood cells contains the white blood cells and the platelets. The yellow fluid on top is the plasma.

hemoglobin The oxygen-carrying protein found in our red blood cells; almost two-thirds of all the iron in our body is found in hemoglobin.

heme The iron-containing molecule found in hemoglobin.

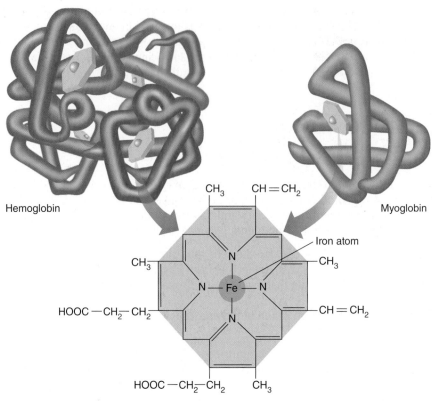

Heme portion containing iron (Fe)

⬆ **Figure 7.7** Iron is contained in the heme portion of hemoglobin and myoglobin.

binding it during its transport in the bloodstream, and then dropping it off again in our tissues.

In addition to being a part of hemoglobin, iron is a component of **myoglobin,** an oxygen-binding protein that functions similarly to hemoglobin but is found in muscle cells. As a part of myoglobin, iron assists in the transport of oxygen into muscle cells, which need oxygen to function.

Finally, iron is found in the body in certain enzymes. As a component of enzymes, it assists energy production from carbohydrates, fats, and protein. Also, iron is part of an antioxidant enzyme system that fights free radicals. Interestingly, excessive iron in the body can also promote the production of free radicals.

What Factors Affect Iron Absorption?

The type of iron in the foods you eat is a major factor influencing your iron absorption—and therefore how much you need to eat. Two types of iron are found in foods:

- **Heme iron** is a part of hemoglobin and myoglobin and is found only in animal-based foods, such as meat, fish, and poultry. Heme iron is readily absorbed by the body. Thus, animal-based foods are reliable sources of iron.
- **Non-heme iron** is not a part of hemoglobin or myoglobin. It is not easily absorbed by the body. Whereas animal-based foods contain both heme and non-heme iron, all of the iron found in plant-based foods is non-heme iron. This means that plant-based foods are less reliable than animal-based foods as sources of readily absorbed iron.

Consumption of certain substances in the same food or meal can enhance the absorption of non-heme iron:

- Meat, poultry, and fish contain a special factor that enhances the absorption of the non-heme iron in these foods, as well as in other foods eaten at the same meal.

myoglobin An iron-containing protein similar to hemoglobin, except that it is found in muscle cells.

heme iron Iron that is part of hemoglobin and myoglobin; found only in animal-based foods, such as meat, fish, and poultry.

non-heme iron The form of iron that is not a part of hemoglobin or myoglobin; found in animal- and plant-based foods.

- Consumption of vitamin C (ascorbic acid) can greatly increase the body's absorption of non-heme iron. Thus, the non-heme iron in a bean burrito will be more fully absorbed if the burrito includes chopped tomatoes. Similarly, drinking a glass of orange juice with your breakfast cereal will increase the absorption of the non-heme iron in the cereal.

Incidentally, cooking food in a cast-iron pan significantly increases the iron content of the food, as the iron in the pan is absorbed into the food during the cooking process.

Chemicals in certain foods impair iron absorption. These include phytates, which are binding factors found in legumes, rice, and whole grains, and polyphenols, chemicals present in black tea, coffee, and red wine. Soybean protein and calcium also inhibit iron absorption; thus, it is best to avoid drinking soy milk or cow's milk or taking calcium supplements when eating iron-rich foods.

Because of these dietary factors, it is estimated that only about 10% of the iron consumed in a vegan diet is absorbed by the body, whereas absorption averages 18% for a mixed Western diet.[15] For this reason, iron requirements are 1.8 times higher for vegetarians than for those who eat a mixed diet. This also means that people who eliminate meat, poultry, and fish from their diet are at a higher risk for anemia than those who eat animal-based foods. This risk is compounded for menstruating females; thus, supplementation or careful meal planning in consultation with a registered dietitian is advised.

⬆ Cooking foods in cast-iron pans significantly increases their iron content.

What Are Iron Needs and Sources?

The iron requirement for young women is higher than for young men because of the iron in the blood women lose during menstruation each month. Those at the highest risk for iron-deficiency anemia in the United States are toddlers and menstruating girls and women, among whom the prevalence is approximately 2% to 5%.[16] Pregnancy is also a time of very high iron needs, and the RDA for pregnant women is 27 mg per day. A number of other circumstances significantly affect iron requirements. These are identified in **Table 7.4**.

Good food sources of heme iron include meats, poultry, and fish, especially clams and oysters. Enriched breakfast cereals and breads and some vegetables and legumes

TABLE 7.4 Special Circumstances Affecting Iron Status

Circumstances That Improve Iron Status	Circumstances That Diminish Iron Status
Use of oral contraceptives—use of oral contraceptives reduces menstrual blood loss in women.	**Use of hormone replacement therapy**—use of hormone replacement therapy in postmenopausal women can cause uterine bleeding, increasing iron requirements.
Breastfeeding—breastfeeding delays resumption of menstruation in new mothers and, so, reduces menstrual blood loss. It is therefore an important health measure, especially in developing nations.	**Eating a vegetarian diet**—vegetarian diets, particularly vegan diets, contain no sources of heme iron. Due to the low absorbability of non-heme iron, vegetarians have iron requirements that are 1.8 times higher than those of nonvegetarians.
Consumption of iron-containing foods and supplements	**Intestinal parasitic infection**—approximately 1 billion people suffer from intestinal parasite infection. Many of these parasites cause intestinal bleeding and occur in countries in which iron intakes are inadequate. Iron-deficiency anemia is common in people with intestinal parasitic infection.
	Blood donation—blood donors have lower iron stores than nondonors; people who donate frequently, particularly premenopausal women, may require iron supplementation to counter the iron losses that occur with blood donation.
	Intense endurance exercise training—people engaging in intense endurance exercise appear to be at risk for poor iron status due to many factors, including suboptimal iron intake and increased iron loss in sweat and increased fecal losses.

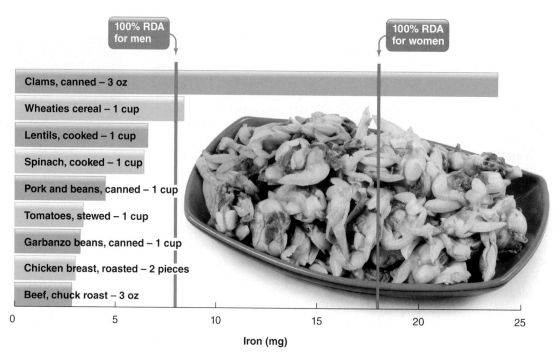

100% RDA for men

100% RDA for women

- Clams, canned – 3 oz
- Wheaties cereal – 1 cup
- Lentils, cooked – 1 cup
- Spinach, cooked – 1 cup
- Pork and beans, canned – 1 cup
- Tomatoes, stewed – 1 cup
- Garbanzo beans, canned – 1 cup
- Chicken breast, roasted – 2 pieces
- Beef, chuck roast – 3 oz

0   5   10   15   20   25

Iron (mg)

Figure 7.8 Common food sources of iron. The RDA for iron is 8 mg/day for men and 18 mg/day for women aged 19 to 50 years.
Data from U.S. Department of Agriculture, Agricultural Research Service. 2009. USDA Nutrient Database for Standard Reference, Release 22. Nutrient Data Laboratory Home Page. www.ars.usda.gov/ba/bhnc/ndl.

are good sources of non-heme iron. Your body's ability to absorb this non-heme iron can be enhanced by eating these foods with small amounts of meat, fish, or poultry or eating them with vitamin C–rich foods or beverages. **Figure 7.8** identifies common food sources of iron. For a delicious full-day's menu of iron-rich foods, see the ***Eating Right All Day*** feature (page 209).

What Happens If We Consume Too Much or Too Little Iron?

Some iron-containing supplements resemble colorful candies, and accidental iron overdose is the most common cause of poisoning deaths in children younger than 6 years of age in the United States.[17] It is important for parents to take the same precautions with dietary supplements that they would take with other drugs, keeping them in a locked cabinet or well out of reach of children. Symptoms of iron toxicity include nausea, vomiting, diarrhea, dizziness, confusion, and rapid heartbeat. If iron toxicity is not treated quickly, significant damage to the heart, central nervous system, liver, and kidneys can result in death.

Adults who take iron supplements even at prescribed doses commonly experience constipation. Taking vitamin C with the iron supplement not only enhances absorption but also can help reduce constipation.

Iron deficiency is the most common nutrient deficiency in the world. It results in **iron-deficiency anemia,** a disorder in which the red blood cells do not contain enough hemoglobin to deliver to the body's cells and tissues all the oxygen they need. Symptoms include exhaustion, increased risk for infection, and impaired thinking. Severe, chronic iron deficiency can cause premature death. People at particularly high risk include infants and young children, menstruating girls and women, and pregnant women. Sensible choices for meals and snacks can help you get all the iron you need all day—and avoid deficiency.

iron-deficiency anemia A disorder in which the production of normal, healthy red blood cells decreases and hemoglobin levels are inadequate to fully oxygenate the body's cells and tissues.

RECAP Iron is a trace mineral that, as part of the hemoglobin protein, transports oxygen in our blood. Meat, fish, and poultry are good sources of heme iron, which is more absorbable than non-heme iron. Iron deficiency is the most common nutrient deficiency in the world.

Zinc Assists the Work of Many Different Enzymes

Zinc is a trace mineral that assists the work of approximately 100 different enzymes involved in many different tasks, including metabolism, the production of hemoglobin, and the activation of vitamin A in the retina of the eye. Zinc is also critical for normal growth. In fact, zinc deficiency was discovered in the early 1960s when researchers were trying to determine the cause of severe growth retardation in a group of Middle Eastern men.

Zinc also supports the proper development and functioning of the immune system. This role in immune functioning is behind the development of zinc lozenges, which manufacturers say help fight the common cold. See the ***Nutrition Myth or Fact?*** box (page 211) to find out whether these are effective.

As with iron, our need for zinc is relatively small, but our absorption is variable. High non-heme iron intake can inhibit zinc absorption. This is a serious concern for anyone taking iron supplements (which are composed of non-heme iron), but especially for pregnant women, in whom zinc is essential for normal fetal growth. Thus, consultation with a registered dietitian may be advisable. Zinc absorption is also a concern for many vegetarians, whose diets are typically rich in non-heme iron. In addition, vegetarians tend to consume plentiful whole grains and beans: these foods contain phytates and fiber, both of which also inhibit zinc absorption. When whole grains are made into bread using yeast, the yeast produces an enzyme that breaks down the phytates. Thus, the zinc in whole-grain breads is more available for absorption than that found in breakfast cereals. In contrast, high intakes of heme iron appear to have no effect on zinc absorption, and dietary protein, especially animal-based protein, enhances zinc absorption.

Good food sources of zinc include red meats, some seafood, whole-grain breads, and enriched foods. As shown in **Figure 7.9** (page 210), zinc is significantly more absorbable from animal-based foods; thus, zinc deficiency is a concern for vegetarians.

Zinc toxicity is unlikely unless a person is consuming zinc in supplements and in highly fortified foods. Toxicity symptoms include intestinal pain and cramps, nausea, vomiting, loss of appetite, diarrhea, and headaches. Excessive zinc supplementation has also been shown to depress immune function. High intakes of zinc can also reduce the absorption of copper.

In addition to growth retardation, symptoms of zinc deficiency include diarrhea, delayed sexual maturation and impotence, eye and skin lesions, hair loss, and impaired appetite. Because zinc is critical to a healthy immune system, zinc deficiency also results in increased incidence of infections and illnesses.

Eating Right All Day

Breakfast
Whole-grain iron-fortified toast with orange juice instead of white toast with coffee!

Lunch
Pasta with clams and tomatoes instead of mac & cheese!

Dinner
Beef stew with vegetables instead of a burger with fries!

Snack
Low-cal nutrition bar instead of a chocolate bar!

Zinc can be found in pork and beans.

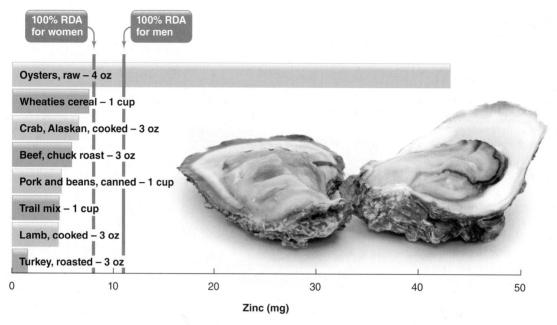

▲ Lobster is a food source of copper.

Figure 7.9 Common food sources of zinc. The RDA for zinc is 11 mg/day for men and 8 mg/day for women. Data from U.S. Department of Agriculture, Agricultural Research Service. 2009. USDA Nutrient Database for Standard Reference, Release 22. Nutrient Data Laboratory Home Page. www.ars.usda.gov/ba/bhncr/ndl.

Copper Helps Transport Iron and Build Tissues

Copper is a component of *ceruloplasmin,* a protein that is critical for the proper transport of iron. If ceruloplasmin levels are inadequate, iron accumulation results and can lead to iron toxicity. Copper also contributes to blood tissue, collagen, and the tissue surrounding nerve fibers. It is part of several enzyme systems and contributes to chemicals called *neurotransmitters,* which are important for transmitting nerve signals.

Copper is a trace mineral, and our need for it is very small. Nevertheless, high intakes of zinc or iron can reduce copper absorption and, subsequently, copper status. Food sources of copper include organ meats, seafood, nuts, seeds, and whole-grain products. The long-term effects of copper toxicity are not well studied in humans. Copper deficiency is rare.

RECAP Zinc is a trace mineral that is a part of almost 100 enzymes that affect virtually every body system. Zinc plays a critical role in hemoglobin synthesis, physical growth, sexual maturation, and immune function and assists in fighting the oxidative damage caused by free radicals. Copper is a trace mineral that is important in the transport of iron. It also contributes to several tissues and is part of several enzyme systems.

The Bone Builders: Calcium, Phosphorus, Magnesium, and Fluoride

Contrary to what most people think, our skeleton is not an inactive collection of bones that simply holds the body together. Bones are living organs that contain several tissues, including bone tissue, nerves, cartilage, and connective tissue, with blood vessels supplying vital nutrients.

Bones have many functions. Structurally, they provide physical support and attachments for muscle movement, and they protect our most vulnerable tissues.

NUTRITION MYTH OR FACT?
Do Zinc Lozenges Help Fight the Common Cold?

The common cold has plagued human beings since the beginning of time. Children suffer from 6 to 10 colds each year, and adults average 2 to 4 per year. Although colds are typically benign, they result in significant absenteeism from school and work and cause discomfort and stress. It is estimated that more than 200 different viruses can cause a cold, so developing vaccines or treatments for colds is extremely challenging. Nevertheless, researchers continue to attempt to search for a cure for the common cold.

The role of zinc in the health of our immune system is well known. When zinc was specifically shown to inhibit the reproduction of viruses that cause the common cold, some researchers began speculating that taking zinc supplements might reduce the length and severity of colds.[18] Consequently, zinc lozenges were formulated as a means of providing potential relief from cold symptoms. These lozenges are readily found in most drugstores.

Does taking zinc in lozenge form actually reduce the length and severity of a cold? During the past 25 years, numerous research studies have been conducted to try to answer this question. Unfortunately, the results of these studies have been mixed.[19] A recent study examined thirteen randomized controlled trials with over 966 participants.[20] They found a reduction in the severity and duration of the common cold with zinc lozenges or syrups (30–160 mg/day) if administered within 24–48 hours of the onset of the cold. Overall, the duration of the cold was reduced by about 1 day. Assessment of the severity of cold symptoms is more difficult because there is no objective measure. However, the study found that severity scores were very modestly reduced with supplementation. However, study participants reported significant negative effects from zinc supplementation as well, including a bad taste and nausea.

Unfortunately, we will probably never know the true effect of zinc lozenges on colds for the following reasons:

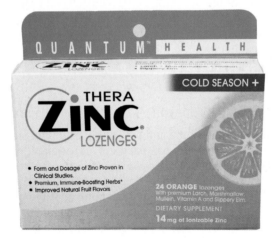

Zinc lozenges come in various formulations and dosages.

- *It is difficult to truly "blind" participants to the treatment.* Because zinc lozenges have a unique taste, it may be difficult to truly "blind" the research participants as to whether they are getting zinc lozenges or a placebo. Knowing which lozenge they are taking could lead participants to report biased results.

- *Self-reported symptoms are subject to inaccuracy.* Many studies had the research participants self-report changes in symptoms, which may be inaccurate and influenced by mood and other emotional factors.

- *A wide variety of viruses cause the common cold.* Because more than 200 viruses can cause a cold, it is highly unlikely that zinc can combat all of them. It is possible that people who do not respond favorably to zinc lozenges are suffering from a cold virus that does not respond to zinc.

- *Zinc formulations and dosages differ.* The type of zinc formulation and the dosages of zinc consumed by study participants differ across studies, which may determine how quickly the zinc ions are delivered to the tissues in the mouth. These differences most likely have contributed to various responses across studies. It is estimated that, for zinc to be effective, at least 80 mg of zinc should be consumed each day and that people should begin using zinc lozenges within 24 to 48 hours of the onset of cold symptoms. Also, sweeteners and flavorings found in many zinc lozenges, such as citric acid, sorbitol, and mannitol, may bind the zinc and inhibit its ability to be absorbed into the body, limiting its effectiveness.

Have you ever tried zinc lozenges, and did you find them effective? Even if you were certain you could reduce the length of your cold by 1 day by taking zinc lozenges, next time you felt a cold coming on, would you try them?

One word of caution: if you decide to use zinc lozenges, more is not better. Excessive or prolonged zinc supplementation can depress immune function and cause other mineral imbalances. Check the label of the product you are using, and do not exceed its recommended dosage or duration of use.

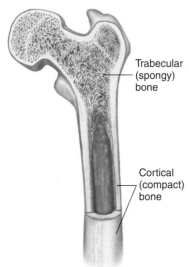

Trabecular (spongy) bone

Cortical (compact) bone

▲ **Figure 7.10** The structure of bone. Notice the difference in density between the trabecular (spongy) bone and the cortical (compact) bone.

cortical bone A dense bone tissue that makes up the outer surface of all bones as well as the entirety of most small bones of the body; also called compact bone.

trabecular bone A porous bone tissue found within the ends of the long bones, as well as inside the spinal vertebrae, flat bones (breastbone, ribs, and most bones of the skull), and bones of the pelvis; also called spongy bone.

bone density The degree of compactness of bone tissue, reflecting the strength of the bones. *Peak bone density* is the point at which a bone is strongest.

remodeling The two-step process by which bone tissue is recycled; includes the breakdown of existing bone and the formation of new bone.

osteoclasts Cells that break down the surface of bones by secreting enzymes and acids that dig grooves into the bone matrix.

osteoblasts Cells that prompt the formation of new bone matrix by laying down the collagen-containing component of bone, which is then mineralized.

Think of the hard shell that our skull forms around our delicate brain tissue, or the bony cage of ribs that protects the heart. Bones also act as "mineral banks," storing calcium, phosphorus, magnesium, and fluoride. When these minerals are needed for body processes, bone is broken down, so that they can be released into our bloodstream. Also, did you know that most of our blood cells are formed deep within bones?

Given the importance of bones, it is critical we keep them strong. In addition to vitamin D, four minerals—calcium, phosphorus, magnesium, and fluoride—help us maintain strong bones.

Bones Are Made of Minerals and Proteins

We tend to think of bones as totally rigid, but if they were, how could we play basketball or even carry an armload of books up a flight of stairs? Bones need to be both strong and flexible, so that they can resist the crunching, stretching, and twisting that occur throughout our daily activities. Fortunately, the composition of bone is ideally suited for its complex job. About 65% of bone tissue is made up of an assortment of minerals (mostly calcium and phosphorus) that provide hardness. These minerals form tiny crystals that cluster around *collagen fibers*—protein fibers that provide strength, durability, and flexibility. Collagen fibers are phenomenally strong; they are actually stronger than steel fibers of similar size. They enable bones to bear weight while responding to demands for movement.

If you examine a bone very closely, you will notice two distinct types of tissue (**Figure 7.10**): cortical bone and trabecular bone. **Cortical bone,** which is also called *compact bone,* is very dense. It composes approximately 80% of the skeleton. The outer surface of all bones is cortical; in addition, many small bones of the body, such as the bones of the wrists, hands, and feet, are made entirely of cortical bone.

In contrast, **trabecular bone** makes up only 20% of the skeleton. It is found in the ends of the long bones (such as the bones of the arms and legs) and inside the spinal vertebrae, skull, pelvis, and several other bones. Trabecular bone is sometimes referred to as *spongy bone,* because to the naked eye it looks like a sponge. The microscope reveals that trabecular bone is, in fact, aligned in a precise network of columns that protects the bone from extreme stress. You can think of trabecular bone as the bone's scaffolding.

How Do Bones Stay Healthy?

Although the shape and size of bones do not significantly change after puberty, **bone density**—the compactness and strength of bones—continues to develop into early adulthood. *Peak bone density* is the point at which bones are strongest because they are at their highest density. About 90% of a woman's bone density is built by 17 years of age. For men, peak bone density occurs during their twenties. However, male or female, before we reach the age of 30 years, our bones have reached peak density, and by age 40, our bone density has begun its irreversible decline.

Just as other body cells die off and are continually replaced, bone mass is regularly recycled. This process, called **remodeling,** involves two steps: the breakdown of existing bone and the formation of new bone (**Figure 7.11**). Bone is broken down by cells called **osteoclasts,** which erode the bone surface by secreting enzymes and acids that dig grooves into the bone matrix (Figure 7.11a). New bone is formed through the action of cells called **osteoblasts,** or "bone builders" (Figure 7.11b). These cells work to synthesize new bone matrix in the eroded areas.

In young, healthy adults, bone building and bone breakdown occur at equal rates, resulting in bone mass being maintained. Around 40 years of age, bone breakdown begins to outpace bone formation, and this imbalance results in a gradual loss in bone density.

Achieving a high peak bone density requires adequate intake of the four minerals discussed in this section, and recommended intakes are identified in Tables 7.1 and 7.2. Adequate protein and vitamins D and K are also essential. In addition to

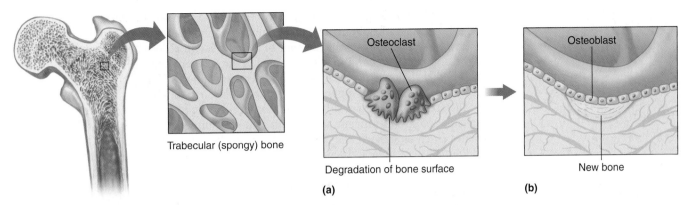

Trabecular (spongy) bone

Osteoclast

Degradation of bone surface

(a)

Osteoblast

New bone

(b)

◆ **Figure 7.11** Bone remodeling involves breakdown and formation. **(a)** Osteoclasts break down bone, releasing minerals, which are then transported to the bloodstream. **(b)** Osteoblasts work to build new bone by filling the pit formed by the erosion process with new bone.

nutrients, healthy bone density requires regular weight-bearing exercise, such as weight lifting, strength training, rope jumping, tennis, jogging and walking, and even jumping jacks, all of which appropriately stress the bones and stimulate their growth.

RECAP Bones are composed of mineral crystals that cluster around collagen fibers. Bone tissue is recycled through a process called remodeling, in which osteoclasts break down old bone and osteoblasts lay down new bone.

Calcium Is a Key Component of Bones

Calcium is by far the most abundant major mineral in the body, composing about 2% of our entire body weight! Not surprisingly, it plays many critical roles in maintaining overall function and health.

Why Do We Need Calcium?

Calcium has four primary roles in the body. First, it provides structure to the bones and teeth. About 99% of the calcium in the body is stored in the bones, packed into crystals built up on the collagen foundation. The remaining 1% is found in the blood and soft tissues.

Calcium is alkaline, or basic, and because of this property it plays a critical role in assisting with acid–base balance. If the blood becomes acidic, osteoclasts begin to break down bone. This releases calcium into the bloodstream, making it more alkaline. It's important to consume enough dietary calcium to make sure it balances the calcium taken from the bones.

Calcium is also critical for the normal transmission of nerve impulses. When it flows into nerve cells, it stimulates the release of neurotransmitters, chemicals that transfer nerve impulses across the gap (synapse) separating one nerve cell from the next. Without adequate calcium, the ability of nerves to transmit messages is inhibited. Not surprisingly, when blood calcium levels fall dangerously low, a person can experience seizures.

A fourth role of calcium is to assist in muscle contraction. Contraction of muscles is stimulated when calcium flows into the muscle cell. Muscles relax when calcium is pumped back outside the muscle cell.

Other roles of calcium include the maintenance of healthy blood pressure, the initiation of blood clotting, and the regulation of various hormones and enzymes. As you can see, calcium is a versatile micronutrient.

◆ Although spinach contains high levels of calcium, binding factors in the plant prevent much of its absorption.

How Much Calcium Is Absorbed?

The term **bioavailability** refers to the degree to which the body can absorb and use any given nutrient. Healthy men and non-pregnant women, across a wide age range, absorb about 30% of the calcium they consume; however, absorption may decrease slightly

bioavailability The degree to which our body can absorb and use any given nutrient.

with age.[21] This decrease in calcium absorption with aging and the need to maintain bone as one ages explain the higher calcium recommendations for older adults.

The body is limited in the amount of calcium it can absorb at any one time, and as the amount of calcium in a single meal or supplement goes up, the fraction that is absorbed goes down. Thus, it is important to consume calcium-rich foods throughout the day, rather than relying on a single high-dose supplement.

Dietary factors can also affect the absorption of calcium. Binding factors, such as phytates and oxalates, occur naturally in some calcium-rich seeds, nuts, grains, and vegetables (such as spinach and Swiss chard). Such factors can limit calcium absorption. Additionally, consuming calcium at the same time as iron, zinc, magnesium, or phosphorus has the potential to interfere with the absorption and use of all of these minerals. Finally, because vitamin D is necessary for the absorption of calcium, lack of vitamin D severely limits the bioavailability of calcium. To learn more about how calcium absorption rates vary for select foods, see the ***Nutrition Label Activity*** box (page 215).

Dairy products are among the most common and best-absorbed sources of calcium in the U.S. diet. Skim milk, low-fat cheeses, and nonfat yogurt are excellent sources of calcium, and they are low in fat and energy. Cottage cheese is one dairy product that is a relatively poor source of calcium, most of which is lost in processing. Other food sources of absorbable calcium are canned fish with bones (providing that you eat the bones) and green leafy vegetables, such as kale, turnip greens, collard greens, broccoli, and Chinese cabbage (bok choy). These vegetables contain low levels of oxalates. Many beverages are fortified with calcium. For example, you can buy calcium-fortified orange juice, fruit punch, soy milk, almond milk, and rice milk. Some dairies have even boosted the amount of calcium in their brand of milk. See **Figure 7.12** for other common food sources of calcium.

How Can You Estimate Your Daily Calcium Intake?

Many people in the United States do not meet the DRI for calcium because they consume very few dairy-based foods and calcium-rich vegetables. At particular risk are

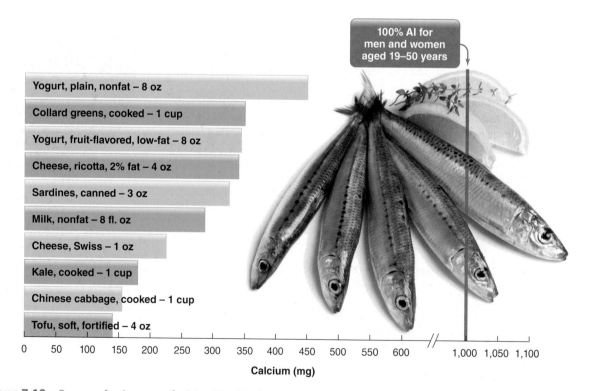

⬥ **Figure 7.12**   Common food sources of calcium. The RDA for calcium is 1,000 mg/day for men and women aged 19 to 50.

Data from U.S. Department of Agriculture, Agricultural Research Service. 2009. USDA Nutrient Database for Standard Reference, Release 22. Nutrient Data Laboratory Home Page. www.ars.usda.gov/ba/bhnrc/ndl.

NUTRITION LABEL ACTIVITY
How Much Calcium Am I Really Consuming?

As you have learned in this chapter, we do not absorb 100% of the calcium contained in foods. This is particularly true for individuals who eat lots of foods high in fiber, oxalates, and phytates, such as whole grains and certain vegetables. So if you want to design an eating plan that contains adequate calcium, it's important to understand how the rate of calcium absorption differs for the foods you include.

Although the absorption rate of calcium has not been determined for all foods, estimates have been established for common foods that are considered good sources of calcium. The accompanying table shows some of these foods, their calcium content per serving, their calcium absorption rate, and the estimated amount of calcium absorbed.

As you can see from this table, many dairy products have a similar calcium absorption rate, just over 30%. Interestingly, many green, leafy vegetables have a higher absorption rate of around 60%; however, because a typical serving of these foods contains less calcium than a

▲ Low-fat and nonfat yogurts are excellent sources of calcium.

serving of dairy foods, you would have to eat more vegetables to get the same calcium as you would from a standard serving of dairy foods. Note the relatively low absorption rate for spinach, even though it contains a relatively high amount of calcium. This is due to the high levels of oxalates in spinach, which bind with calcium and reduce its bioavailability.

Remember that the DRIs for calcium take these differences in absorption rate into account. Thus, the 300 mg of calcium in a glass of milk counts as 300 mg toward your daily calcium goal. In general, you can trust that dairy products such as milk and yogurt (but not cottage cheese) are good, absorbable sources of calcium, as are most dark green, leafy vegetables. Other dietary sources of calcium with good absorption rates include calcium-fortified orange juice, soy milk, almond milk, and rice milk; tofu processed with calcium; and fortified breakfast cereals.[22] Armed with this knowledge, you will be better able to select food sources that can optimize your calcium intake and support your bone health.

Food	Serving Size	Calcium per Serving (mg)*	Absorption Rate (%)†	Estimated Amount of Calcium Absorbed (mg)
Yogurt, plain skim milk	8 fl. oz	452	32	145
Milk, skim	1 cup	306	32	98
Milk, 2%	1 cup	285	32	91
Kale, frozen, cooked	1 cup	179	59	106
Turnip greens, boiled	1 cup	197	52	103
Broccoli, frozen, chopped, cooked	1 cup	61	61	37
Cauliflower, boiled	1 cup	20	69	14
Spinach, frozen, cooked	1 cup	291	5	14

*Data from U.S. Department of Agriculture, Agricultural Research Service. 2009. USDA National Nutrient Database for Standard Reference, Release 22. www.ars.usda.gov/ba/bhnrc/ndl.
†Weaver, C. M., W. R. Proulx, and R. Heaney. 1999. Choices for achieving adequate dietary calcium with a vegetarian diet. *Am. J. Clin. Nutr.* 70(suppl.):543S–548S; Weaver, C. M., and K. L. Plawecki. 1994. Dietary calcium: adequacy of a vegetarian diet. *Am. J. Clin. Nutr.* 59(suppl.):1238S–1241S.

menstruating women and girls. There are quick, simple tools available to assist you in estimating your daily calcium intake.

What Happens If We Consume Too Much or Too Little Calcium?

In general, consuming extra calcium from food sources does not lead to significant toxicity symptoms in healthy people, because much of the excess calcium is excreted in urine and feces. However, excessive intake of calcium from supplements can lead to various mineral imbalances because calcium interferes with the absorption of other minerals, including iron, zinc, and magnesium. It can

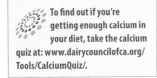

To find out if you're getting enough calcium in your diet, take the calcium quiz at: www.dairycouncilofca.org/Tools/CalciumQuiz/.

▲ Kale is a good source of calcium.

also cause constipation, as the body attempts to eliminate the excess calcium via the feces. Severe hypercalcemia (excessive calcium in the blood) can lead to death.

There are no short-term symptoms associated with consuming too little calcium. When dietary calcium is low, the body maintains blood calcium levels by taking calcium from the bones. The long-term consequence of inadequate calcium intake is osteoporosis. This disease is discussed in more detail shortly. To keep your bones as dense as possible, it's important to make calcium-rich menu choices, that are also low in fat and Calories, throughout the day.

RECAP Calcium is the most abundant mineral in the body and a significant component of bones. Bone calcium is used to maintain normal blood calcium if dietary intake is inadequate. Calcium is also necessary for normal nerve and muscle function. Dairy foods, calcium-fortified juices and soy milk, and some dark-green leafy vegetables are excellent sources of calcium.

🔺 Phosphorus, in the form of phosphoric acid, is a major component of soft drinks.

Phosphorus Is Part of the Mineral Complex of Bone

As we mentioned earlier, the major mineral phosphorus works with potassium inside cells to help maintain proper fluid balance. It also plays a critical role in bone formation, as it is a part of the mineral crystals that provide the hardness of bone. About 85% of the body's phosphorus is stored in bones, with the rest stored in soft tissues, such as muscles and organs.

Additionally, phosphorus is a primary component of adenosine triphosphate (ATP), the energy molecule. It also helps activate and deactivate enzymes and is a component of the genetic material in the cells (including both DNA and RNA), cell membranes, and lipoproteins.

Phosphorus is widespread in many foods and is found in high amounts in foods that contain protein **(Figure 7.13)**. Milk, meats, and eggs are good sources. Phosphorus

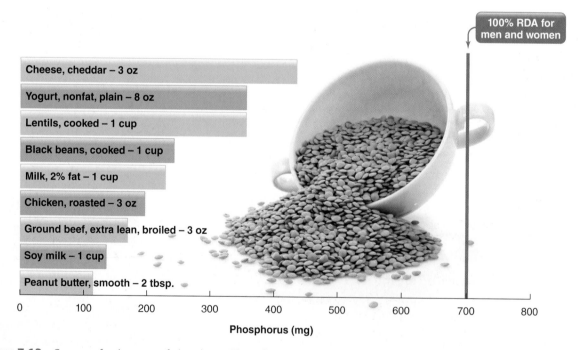

100% RDA for men and women

Cheese, cheddar – 3 oz

Yogurt, nonfat, plain – 8 oz

Lentils, cooked – 1 cup

Black beans, cooked – 1 cup

Milk, 2% fat – 1 cup

Chicken, roasted – 3 oz

Ground beef, extra lean, broiled – 3 oz

Soy milk – 1 cup

Peanut butter, smooth – 2 tbsp.

0   100   200   300   400   500   600   700   800

Phosphorus (mg)

🔺 **Figure 7.13**   Common food sources of phosphorus. The AI for phosphorus is 700 mg/day.
Data from U.S. Department of Agriculture, Agricultural Research Service. 2009. USDA Nutrient Database for Standard Reference, Release 22. Nutrient Data Laboratory Home Page. www.ars.usda.gov/ba/bhnrc/ndl.

is also added to many processed foods, where it enhances smoothness, binding, and moisture retention. In the form of phosphoric acid, it is also a major component of soft drinks. Many researchers have linked the consumption of soft drinks to poor bone density. The most likely explanation for this link appears to be the *milk-displacement effect;* that is, soft drinks take the place of milk in our diet, depriving us of calcium and vitamin D.[23]

Severely high levels of phosphorus in the blood can cause muscle spasms and convulsions. Phosphorus deficiencies are rare but can occur in people who abuse alcohol, in premature infants, and in elderly people with a poor diet.

Magnesium Is Found in Bones and Soft Tissues

Magnesium is a major mineral. About 50% to 60% of the magnesium in the body is found in bones, and the rest is in soft tissues. Magnesium influences the crystallization of bone through its regulation of calcium balance and its interactions with vitamin D and parathyroid hormone.

Magnesium assists more than 300 enzyme systems with roles in the production of ATP, as well as DNA and protein synthesis and repair. It also supports muscle contraction and blood clotting.

Magnesium is found in green leafy vegetables, such as spinach, and in whole grains, seeds, and nuts. Other good sources include seafood, beans, and some dairy products **(Figure 7.14)**. The magnesium content of drinking water varies considerably: the "harder" the water, the higher its content of magnesium.

Considering magnesium's role in bone formation, it is not surprising that long-term magnesium deficiency is associated with osteoporosis. Magnesium deficiency can also cause muscle cramps, spasms or seizures, nausea, weakness, irritability, and confusion. It may result from kidney disease, chronic diarrhea, or chronic alcohol abuse but is uncommon in healthy adults, except those who regularly consume too much fiber. As you know, dietary fiber is important to health; however, fiber binds magnesium, reducing the ability of the small intestine to absorb it. Thus, magnesium deficiency can occur in people who consume a diet with excessive fiber. To avoid

🔺 Trail mix with chocolate chips, nuts, and seeds is one common food source of magnesium.

🔺 **Figure 7.14** Common food sources of magnesium. For adult men 19 to 30 years of age, the RDA for magnesium is 400 mg/day; the RDA increases to 420 mg per day for men 31 and older. For adult women 19 to 30 years of age, the RDA for magnesium is 310 mg per day; this value increases to 320 mg per day for women 31 and older.

Data from U.S. Department of Agriculture, Agricultural Research Service. 2009. USDA Nutrient Database for Standard Reference, Release 22. Nutrient Data Laboratory Home Page. www.ars.usda.gov/ba/bhnrc/ndl.

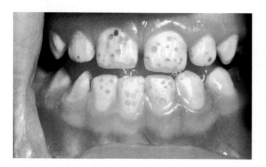

▲ Figure 7.15 Consuming too much fluoride causes fluorosis, leading to staining and pitting of the teeth.

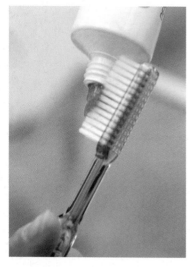

▲ Fluoride is available through fluoridated water and dental products.

fluorosis A condition marked by staining and pitting of the teeth; caused by an abnormally high intake of fluoride.

osteoporosis A disease characterized by low bone mass and deterioration of bone tissue, leading to increased bone fragility and fracture risk.

magnesium deficiency, consume the recommended amount of fiber each day (19 to 38 grams per day, depending on life stage and gender).

Magnesium toxicity is rare except in people consuming high-potency supplements. Symptoms of magnesium toxicity include diarrhea, nausea, and abdominal cramps. In extreme cases, toxicity can result in acid–base imbalances, massive dehydration, cardiac arrest, and death.

Fluoride Supports Our Teeth and Bones

Fluoride is a trace mineral. About 99% of the fluoride in the body is stored in teeth and bones. During the development of both baby teeth and permanent teeth, fluoride combines with calcium and phosphorus to make teeth more resistant to destruction by acids and bacteria. Thus, teeth that have been treated with fluoride are better protected against dental caries (cavities) than teeth that have not been treated. Fluoride also stimulates new bone growth, and it is currently being researched as a potential treatment for osteoporosis.

The two primary sources of fluoride for people in the United States are fluoridated water and fluoridated dental products, such as toothpastes and mouthwashes. Fluoride supplements are available only by prescription, and they are generally given only to children who do not have access to fluoridated water. Tea also contains significant amounts of fluoride independent of whether it was made with fluoridated water. There is epidemiological evidence that people who habitually consume tea (for more than 6 years) have significantly higher bone density values than people who are not habitual tea drinkers.[24]

Consuming too much fluoride increases the protein content of tooth enamel, resulting in a condition called **fluorosis.** Because increased protein makes the enamel more porous, the teeth become stained and pitted **(Figure 7.15)**. Teeth seem to be at highest risk for fluorosis during the first 8 years of life. Mild fluorosis generally causes white patches on the teeth. However, neither mild nor moderate fluorosis appears to impair tooth function.[21]

The primary result of fluoride deficiency is an increased risk for dental caries.[21] Adequate fluoride intake appears necessary at an early age and throughout adult life to reduce the risk for tooth decay. Inadequate fluoride intake may also be associated with lower bone density, but there is not enough research currently available to support the widespread use of fluoride to prevent osteoporosis.

RECAP The major mineral phosphorus helps maintain fluid balance and bone health and is found in many high-protein foods. Magnesium is a major mineral important for bone health, energy production, and muscle function and is found in a wide variety of foods. Fluoride is a trace mineral that supports the health of teeth and bones. Primary sources of fluoride are fluoridated dental products and fluoridated water.

HEALTHWATCH

Are You at Risk for Osteoporosis?

Of the many disorders associated with poor bone health, the most prevalent one in the United States is **osteoporosis.** The bone tissue of a person with osteoporosis is more porous and thinner than that of a person with healthy bone. These structural changes weaken the bone, leading to a significantly reduced ability to bear weight and a high risk for fractures **(Figure 7.16)**.

Osteoporosis is the single most important cause of fractures of the hip and spine in older adults. These fractures are extremely painful and can be debilitating, with many individuals requiring nursing home care. In addition, they cause an increased risk for infection and other illnesses that can lead to premature death, as we saw with dancer Erika Goodman in our chapter-opening story. In fact, about 24% of older adults who suffer a hip fracture die within 1 year after the fracture occurs.[25] Osteoporosis of the spine also causes a generalized loss of height and can be disfiguring: gradual compression fractures in the vertebrae of the upper back lead to a shortening and rounding of the spine called *kyphosis*, commonly referred to as *dowager's hump* **(Figure 7.17)**.

Unfortunately, osteoporosis is a common disease: worldwide, one in three women and one in five men over the age of 50 are affected, and in the United States, more than 10 million people have been diagnosed.[26,27]

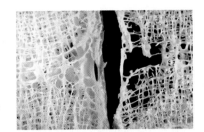

Figure 7.16 The vertebra of a person with osteoporosis (right) is thinner and more collapsed than the vertebra of a healthy person (left), in which the bone is more dense and uniform.

Risk Factors for Osteoporosis

The following factors influence the risk for osteoporosis:

- *Age.* Bone density declines with age, so low bone mass and osteoporosis are significant health concerns for both older men and women. Reproductive hormones in men and women play important roles in promoting the deposition of new bone and limiting the activity of osteoclasts. With aging, the production of reproductive hormones decreases. This makes bone more sensitive to osteoclasts, and a gradual loss of bone mass occurs. Although both men and women are affected, the change is more dramatic in women, who can lose 20% of their bone mass during the first 5 to 7 years following menopause.[25] In addition, reduced levels of physical activity in older people and a decreased ability to metabolize vitamin D with age exacerbate hormone-related bone loss.

- *Gender.* About 80% of Americans with osteoporosis are women. This greater prevalence is due not only to women's more dramatic age-related decline in reproductive hormones. It's also explained by the fact that women have a lower bone density than men to begin with, and they live longer than men. Secondary factors include social pressure on girls to be thin, which can lead to extreme dieting. This in turn can result in poor nutrition and amenorrhea (no menstrual period), which reduces the positive impact of reproductive hormones on bone. Extreme dieting is particularly harmful in adolescence, when bone mass is building and adequate consumption of nutrients is critical. In contrast, men experience pressure to "bulk up," typically by lifting weights. This puts healthful stress on the bones, resulting in increased density.

Figure 7.17 Gradual compression of the vertebrae in the upper back causes a shortening and rounding of the spine called *kyphosis*.

- *Genetics.* A family history of osteoporosis increases the risk for this disease. Particularly at risk are Caucasian women of low body weight who have a first-degree relative (mother or sister) with osteoporosis. Asian women are also at high risk.

- *Smoking.* Cigarette smoking is known to decrease bone density because of its effects on the hormones that influence bone remodeling; thus, cigarette smoking increases the risk for osteoporosis.

- *Nutrition.* Nutritional factors that appear to affect the risk for osteoporosis include total energy intake, protein, calcium, vitamin D, and fruits and vegetables.[28] Excess dieting and inadequate energy also appear to be bad for bone. There seems to be an interaction between dietary calcium and protein, in that adequate amounts of each nutrient are needed together to support bone health. Also, diets high in fruits and vegetables are associated with improved bone health.[29,30] This is most likely due to the fact that fruits and vegetables are good sources of the nutrients that play a role in bone and collagen health, including magnesium, vitamin C, and vitamin K. Finally, chronic alcohol abuse is detrimental to bone health and is associated with high rates of fractures.[28]

Smoking increases the risk for osteoporosis and resulting fractures.

FOODS YOU DON'T KNOW YOU LOVE YET

Kefir

A slightly tart, fermented beverage, kefir (commonly pronounced KEE-fer) is like a drinkable yogurt . . . only some claim it's better! That's because—depending on the way it's formulated—it can contain more strains of helpful bacteria in a greater quantity than is found in traditional yogurts, as well as beneficial yeasts that can compete with species that cause illness. Its curd size is smaller than that of yogurt, so people may find it even easier to digest. Moreover, some brands of kefir provide more calcium than the same-size serving of milk or yogurt and are rich in magnesium, phosphorus, and several vitamins, making kefir an excellent choice for supporting bone health. Kefir is sold in most large supermarkets in plain or fruit flavors. It's naturally thick, so you can blend it with chunks of banana, strawberries, or other sweet fruits for a delicious and easy smoothie.

Regular weight-bearing exercise, such as jogging, can help increase and maintain our bone mass.

- *Physical activity.* Regular exercise is highly protective against bone loss and osteoporosis. Athletes are consistently shown to have denser bones than non-athletes, and regular participation in a variety of weight-bearing exercises, such as walking, jogging, tennis, and strength training, can help increase and maintain bone mass. Exercise causes the muscles to contract and pull on bones; this stresses bone tissue in a healthful way that stimulates increases in bone density. Intense physical activity can be harmful, however, in people who are not eating enough to maintain a healthful body weight.

NUTRI-CASE GUSTAVO

"When my wife, Antonia, broke her hip, I was shocked. You see, the same thing happened to her mother, but she was an old lady by then! Antonia's only 68, and she still seems young and beautiful—at least to me! As soon as she's better, her doctor wants to do some kind of scan to see how thick her bones are. But I don't think she has that disease everyone talks about! She's always watched her weight and keeps active with our kids and grandchildren.

It's true she drinks coffee and diet colas, not milk, but that's not enough to make a person's bones fall apart, is it?"

What lifestyle factors increase Antonia's risk for osteoporosis? What risk factors are in her favor? Given what Gustavo has said about his wife's nutrition and lifestyle, do you think he should encourage her to have a bone density scan? Why or why not?

90% ▭

WHAT ABOUT YOU?

Calculate Your Risk for Osteoporosis

One in two women and one in four men will develop osteoporosis in their lifetime.[25] But if you know you're at risk, you can take the steps identified in this chapter, such as increasing your weight-bearing exercise and making sure you get enough calcium and vitamin D, to maintain the maximum amount of bone mass possible. That's why it's important to assess your risk.

Following is a questionnaire adapted from the National Osteoporosis Foundation to determine your risk of developing osteoporosis. For each question, circle the appropriate answer. The more Yes answers you have, the greater the likelihood that you're in a higher risk group than the general population.

- Do you have a small, thin bone structure and/or are you Caucasian or Asian?

  YES or NO

- Are you underweight?

  YES or NO

- Have you or a member of your immediate family broken a bone as an adult?

  YES or NO

- If you are female, have your periods stopped for more than 12 months (other than because of pregnancy)?

  YES or NO

- Have you taken high doses of thyroid medications or used glucocorticoids (for example, prednisone, cortisone) for more than 3 months?

  YES or NO

- Do you suffer frequently from diarrhea (caused by such chronic problems as celiac disease or irritable bowel syndrome)?

  YES or NO

- Is your diet low in dairy products and other sources of calcium?

  YES or NO

- Do you lead a sedentary lifestyle (engage in little physical activity most days)?

  YES or NO

- Do you smoke cigarettes?

  YES or NO

- Do you drink more than one alcoholic beverage per day (women) or two alcoholic beverages per day (men)?

  YES or NO

If you answered Yes to any of these questions, it does not mean you have osteoporosis.[25] It does, however, suggest that you should discuss the quiz results with your doctor, who will advise you as to whether or not you should take a bone density test.

Do you have a greater than average risk for osteoporosis? What about your older relatives? See the *What About You?* feature box (above).

Treatments for Osteoporosis

Although there is no cure for osteoporosis, a variety of treatments can slow and even reverse bone loss. First, individuals with osteoporosis are encouraged to consume a diet that provides adequate calcium, vitamin D, vitamin K, and other bone-building nutrients and to exercise regularly. Studies have shown that the most effective exercise programs include weight-bearing exercises such as jogging, stair climbing, and resistance training.[31]

In addition, several medications are available that slow or stop bone breakdown but do not affect bone formation. This results in an overall reduction or cessation

in the rate of bone loss. *Hormone replacement therapy (HRT)* has been used for the prevention of osteoporosis in women but is controversial. *HRT* reduces bone loss, increases bone density, and reduces the risk for hip and spinal fractures. However, side effects include breast tenderness, changes in mood, vaginal bleeding, and an increased risk for gallbladder disease. In addition, a recent study found that one type of HRT increases a woman's risk for heart disease, stroke, and breast cancer. Thus, a woman's decision regarding appropriate therapy must weigh the benefits of HRT in reducing fracture risk with the drawbacks of increased risk for other diseases.

> Think osteoporosis is just "an old woman's disease"? This interview with teens may change your mind: check out www.webmd.com/video/teen-osteoporosis-screening.

RECAP Osteoporosis increases the risk for fractures and premature death from subsequent illness. Factors that increase the risk for osteoporosis include genetics, being female, being of the Caucasian or Asian race, cigarette smoking, alcohol abuse, a sedentary lifestyle, and diets low in calcium and vitamin D. Medications are available for the prevention and treatment of osteoporosis.

COOKING 101

Deep-colored, leafy greens and a host of other vegetables (and fruits) provide essential minerals and can be combined in endless ways to make great salads! Learn how to put together a nutritious salad you'll love by viewing our new Cooking 101 videos, available on the Companion Website at www.pearsonhighered.com/thompsonmanore.

Chapter Review

What Can I Do **Today?**

Now that you've read this chapter, try making these three changes:

- Today, try eating 8 to 10 servings of fruits and vegetables, as recommended in the DASH diet plan.

- Three times today, choose a beverage that provides calcium, such as calcium-fortified orange juice, milk, a yogurt smoothie, a coffee latte, or calcium-fortified soy, almond, or rice milk.
- Exercise for at least 30 minutes today!

Test Yourself ANSWERS

1. **F** In the typical American diet, the majority of sodium comes from salt (sodium chloride) added to processed foods and restaurant foods.

2. **F** Iodine is added to many—but not all—salts sold in the United States. Look for the word *iodized* on the label.

3. **T** Worldwide, iron deficiency is particularly common in infants, children, and women of childbearing age.

4. **F** Osteoporosis is more common among elderly women, but elderly men are also at increased risk, and some women develop osteoporosis in their middle-adult years. Young women who suffer from an eating disorder and menstrual cycle irregularity, referred to as the *female athlete triad,* also commonly develop osteoporosis.

5. **T** Cigarette smoking has a detrimental effect on the hormones that influence the density of our bones. People who smoke have an increased risk for osteoporosis and fractures.

 **NutriTools**

Check out the Companion Website at www.pearsonhighered.com/thompsonmanore, or use MyNutritionLab.com, to access interactive animations, including

- Know Your Calcium Sources
- Know Your Iron Sources
- Mineral Functionality
- Let's Go to Lunch!: Minerals
- Nutrients: Vitamin or Mineral?

Review Questions

1. Which of the following is true of the cell membrane?
   a. It is freely permeable to water and all electrolytes.
   b. It is freely permeable to all electrolytes but not to water.
   c. It is freely permeable to water but not to all electrolytes.
   d. It is impermeable.

2. Which of the following statements about iron is true?
   a. Iron is stored primarily in the heart muscle and skeletal muscles.
   b. Iron is a component of hemoglobin, myoglobin, and certain enzymes.
   c. Iron is a component of red blood cells, white blood cells, platelets, and plasma.
   d. Iron needs are higher for elderly women than for young women.

3. Three important nutrients found in many brands of table salt sold in the United States are
   a. sodium, chloride, and iodine.
   b. sodium, potassium, and iodine.
   c. sodium, potassium, and chlorine.
   d. sodium, calcium, and magnesium.

4. Which of the following statements about trabecular bone is true?
   a. It accounts for about 80% of the skeleton.
   b. It forms the core of all bones.
   c. It is also called compact bone.
   d. It provides the scaffolding for cortical bone.

5. Calcium is necessary for several body functions, including
   a. hemoglobin production, nerve-impulse transmission, and immune responses.
   b. the structure of cartilage, nerve-impulse transmission, and muscle contraction.
   c. the structure of bone and blood, immune responses, and muscle contraction.
   d. the structure of bone, nerve-impulse transmission, and muscle contraction.

6. True or False? The process by which bone is formed through the action of osteoblasts and is broken down through the action of osteoclasts is called *remodeling*.

7. True or False? Red blood cells contain iron.

8. True or False? There is no DRI for sulfur.

9. True or False? Both zinc deficiency and zinc toxicity are characterized by reduced immune function.

10. True or False? Although osteoporosis can lead to painful and debilitating fractures, it is not associated with an increased risk for premature death.

Answers to Review Questions are located at the back of this text.

Web Links

www.americanheart.org/HEARTORG
American Heart Association

www.anemia.com
Anemia Lifeline

www.nof.org
National Osteoporosis Foundation

www.niams.nih.gov/Health_Info/Bone
National Institutes of Health: Osteoporosis and Related Bone Diseases—National Resource Center

8

Fluid Balance, Water, and Alcohol

I n April 2007, David Rogers, a healthy 22-year-old fitness instructor, was running in the London Marathon. Thrilled to be competing in his first marathon, he waved to his parents as he ran and leaped in the air for joy. But just after crossing the finish line in 3 hours and 50 minutes, David collapsed. He was rushed to the hospital, comatose, where he died the next morning. Despite the 73°F heat on the day of the race, the official cause of death was not dehydration. Instead, it was hyponatremia—too little sodium in the blood. Simply put, David died from drinking too much water.

Hyponatremia usually results from a problem called *water intoxication*. Victims have included college students participating in fraternity initiation rituals in which they're forced to drink excessive water, dieters who drink very large amounts of water and restrict their sodium intake, and people participating in endurance activities, such as cyclists, triathletes, hikers—and of course, marathon runners. According to a study of runners in a 2002 Boston Marathon (where 28-year-old runner Cynthia Lucero died of hyponatremia), 13% developed the condition by the end of the race.[1]

What causes hyponatremia, and how does it differ from dehydration? Are you at risk for either condition? Do sports beverages offer any protection against these fluid imbalances? If at the start of a track event on a hot, humid afternoon, a fellow runner confided that he went on a drinking binge the night before,

Nutrition Online icons are located throughout the chapter, directing you to web links, videos, podcasts, and other useful online resources.

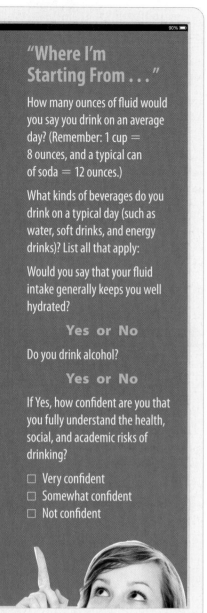

◆ As we age, our body water content decreases: approximately 75% of an infant's body weight is composed of water, whereas an elderly adult's is only 50%, or less.

and had vomited twice that morning, would you urge him to tell his coach—and if so, why?

You've learned that electrolytes are minerals that help keep body fluid in balance inside and outside our cells. Together with the water and other fluids you drink, they keep the body properly hydrated. We discuss this process in this chapter and take a look at some disorders that can occur when our body fluids are out of balance. We also discuss the effects of alcohol, including the benefits of moderate consumption and the problems of alcohol abuse.

What Are Fluids, and What Are Their Functions?

You know that water, orange juice, blood, and urine are all fluids, but what makes them so? A **fluid** is a substance characterized by its ability to move freely and changeably, adapting to the shape of any container that holds it. This might not seem important, but as you'll learn in this chapter, the fluid within our cells and tissues is critical to the body's functioning.

Water is the main component of all body fluids. A colorless, odorless, and tasteless liquid, pure water is made up of a precise ratio of hydrogen and oxygen (H_2O). Pure water is the main component of milk, juices, mineral water, and thousands of other beverages we drink and is found, in varying amounts, in all foods. Water is one of the six nutrient groups, and is essential to life.

Body Fluid Is the Liquid Portion of Cells and Tissues

Between 50% and 70% of a healthy adult's body weight is water. Think about it: if you weigh 150 pounds, then about 75 to 105 pounds of your body isn't solid, but fluid! When we cut a finger, we can see some of this fluid dripping out as blood, but blood alone certainly can't account for 105 pounds! So where is all this fluid hiding?

About two-thirds of the body's fluid, known as *intracellular fluid*, is held within the walls of our cells **(Figure 8.1a)**. Every cell in the body contains fluid. When cells lose their fluid, they shrink and die. On the other hand, when cells take in too much fluid, they swell and burst. This is why appropriate fluid balance—which we'll discuss throughout this chapter—is so critical to life.

The remaining third of the body's fluid is known as *extracellular fluid* because it flows outside of the cells. There are two types. Interstitial fluid (tissue fluid) flows between the cells that make up a particular tissue or organ (Figure 8.1b). The rest of the body's extracellular fluid flows within blood vessels or lymphatic vessels. The fluid portion of blood is called *plasma*. It transports blood cells within the body's arteries, veins, and capillaries (Figure 8.1c). The fluid in lymphatic vessels is simply called lymphatic fluid.

Not every tissue in the body contains the same amount of fluid. Lean tissues, such as muscle, are more than 70% fluid by weight, whereas fat tissue is between 10% and 20% fluid. Body fluid also varies according to gender. Men have more lean tissue and thus a higher percentage of total weight as body fluid than women. Our percentage of weight as body fluid also decreases as we age, from about 75% in infants to generally less than 50% in older adults. This decrease is related to the loss of lean tissue that typically occurs as we age.

Fluids Serve Many Critical Functions

Fluids not only quench our thirst; the water they contain performs a number of functions that are critical to support life.

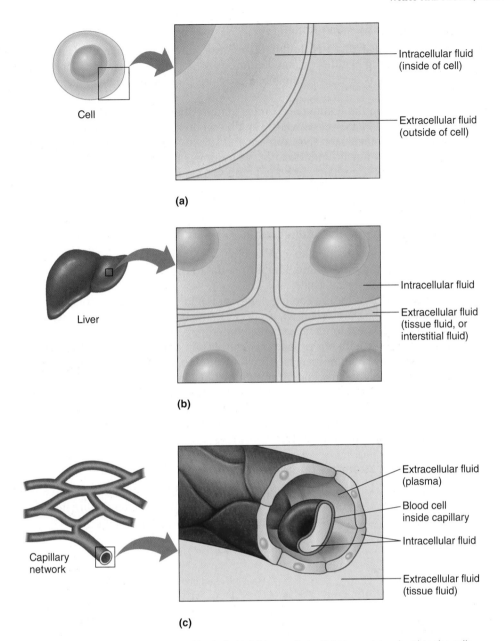

Cell

Intracellular fluid (inside of cell)

Extracellular fluid (outside of cell)

(a)

Liver

Intracellular fluid

Extracellular fluid (tissue fluid, or interstitial fluid)

(b)

Capillary network

Extracellular fluid (plasma)

Blood cell inside capillary

Intracellular fluid

Extracellular fluid (tissue fluid)

(c)

Figure 8.1 The components of body fluid. **(a)** Intracellular fluid is contained within the cells that make up our body tissues. Extracellular fluid is external to cells. **(b)** Interstitial fluid is external to tissue cells, and **(c)** plasma is external to blood cells.

Fluids Dissolve and Transport Substances

As noted earlier, water is an essential nutrient. It is an excellent **solvent,** which means it is capable of dissolving a variety of substances. Water-soluble substances, such as glucose, amino acids, minerals, and water-soluble vitamins, are easily transported in the bloodstream. In contrast, lipids do not dissolve in water. To overcome this chemical incompatibility, fats, cholesterol, and fat-soluble vitamins are either attached to or surrounded by water-soluble proteins so that they, too, can be transported in the blood.

The body also uses water to transport and excrete metabolic wastes, excess micronutrients, and other unwanted substances. The kidneys filter these substances from the blood and dilute them with water to create urine, which is stored in the bladder until it flows out of the body.

fluid A substance composed of molecules that move past one another freely. Fluids are characterized by their ability to conform to the shape of whatever container holds them.

solvent A substance that is capable of mixing with and breaking apart a variety of compounds. Water is an excellent solvent.

Fluids Account for Blood Volume

Blood volume is the amount of fluid in blood; thus, appropriate fluid levels are essential to maintaining healthful blood volume. When blood volume is inappropriately low, blood pressure is also low. Low blood pressure can cause people to feel tired, confused, or dizzy.

In contrast, when the volume of blood is inappropriately high, it exerts greater pressure against the blood vessel walls. High blood pressure (called *hypertension*) is an important risk factor for heart disease and stroke. You can't develop hypertension by drinking too much fluid, because your kidneys normally excrete excess fluid in your urine. But if you retain more fluid than your kidneys can excrete, your blood pressure will rise. Excessive sodium consumption can cause fluid retention and hypertension in some salt-sensitive people.

Fluids Help Maintain Body Temperature

Just as overheating is disastrous to a car engine, a high internal temperature can cause the body to stop functioning. Fluids are vital to the body's ability to maintain its temperature within a safe range.

Two factors account for the cooling power of fluids. First, it takes a lot of external energy to raise the temperature of water. Because the body contains a lot of water, it takes sustained high heat to increase body temperature.

Second, body fluids are our primary coolant. When our temperature rises and our body needs to release heat, it increases the flow of blood from vessels in the warm body core to vessels lying just under the skin. At the same time, the sweat glands secrete more sweat—which is mainly water—from the skin. As this sweat evaporates off the skin's surface, heat is released into the environment, and the skin and underlying blood are cooled (**Figure 8.2**). This cooler blood flows back to the body's core and reduces internal body temperature.

Fluids Protect and Lubricate Body Tissues

Water is a major part of the fluids that protect tissues. The cerebrospinal fluid that surrounds the brain and spinal column acts as a shock absorber, protecting them from damage, and amniotic fluid protects a fetus in a mother's womb.

▲ A hiker needs to consume adequate amounts of water to prevent heat illness under hot and dry conditions.

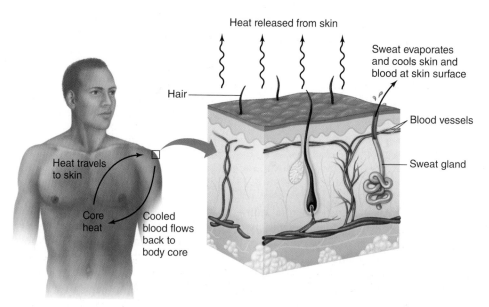

▲ **Figure 8.2**   Evaporative cooling occurs when heat is transported from the body core through the bloodstream to the surface of the skin. When a person sweats, water evaporates into the air and carries away heat. This cools the skin and underlying blood, which then circulates back to the body core, reducing body temperature.

blood volume The amount of fluid in blood.

Body fluids also act as lubricants. Fluid within our joints facilitates smooth joint motion. Fluid covering the lungs allows for their friction-free expansion and retraction within the chest cavity. Tears cleanse and lubricate the eyes. Saliva moistens the food we eat, and the mucus lining the digestive tract facilitates the smooth movement of nutrients.

RECAP Water is an essential nutrient. Between about 50% and 70% of a healthy adult's body weight is water. About two-thirds of the body's fluid is held within the walls of our cells (intracellular fluid), and the remaining third flows outside of cells (extracellular fluid). Fluids serve many important functions, including dissolving and transporting substances, accounting for blood volume, regulating body temperature, and protecting and lubricating body tissues.

How Does Our Body Maintain Fluid Balance?

Our body maintains a healthy balance of fluid by a series of mechanisms that prompt us to drink and retain fluid when we are dehydrated, and to excrete fluid as urine when we consume more than we need.

The Thirst Mechanism Prompts Us to Drink Fluids

Imagine that, at lunch, you ate a ham sandwich and a bag of salted potato chips. Now it's almost time for your afternoon class to end, and suddenly you are very thirsty. The last 5 minutes of class are a torment, and when the instructor ends the session you dash to the nearest drinking fountain. What prompted you to feel so thirsty?

The body's command center for fluid intake is a cluster of nerve cells in the same part of the brain related to food intake—the *hypothalamus*. Within the hypothalamus is a group of cells, known as the **thirst mechanism,** that causes you to consciously desire fluids. The thirst mechanism prompts us to feel thirsty when it detects either of two conditions:

- *An increased concentration of sodium and other dissolved substances in the blood.* Remember that ham sandwich and those potato chips? Both these foods are salty, and eating them temporarily increases the concentration of sodium in the blood.
- *A decrease in blood volume and blood pressure.* This can occur in different circumstances, such as when we lose fluid during profuse sweating, or because of traumatic injury that causes heavy blood loss, or simply when our fluid intake is too low.

Once the hypothalamus detects such changes, it stimulates the release of a hormone that signals the kidneys to reduce urine flow and return more water to the bloodstream. Water is drawn out of the salivary glands in the mouth in an attempt to further dilute the concentration of substances in the blood; this leaves less water available to make saliva and causes the mouth and throat to become dry. Together, these mechanisms help us retain fluid, prevent a further loss of fluid, and avoid dehydration.

Although you might think you can rely on the thirst mechanism to accurately signal when you need to drink more fluids, there are times when thirst is actually not the best predictor of fluid imbalance. Most people tend to drink only until they are no longer thirsty, but the amount of fluid they consume may not be enough to achieve fluid balance. This is particularly true when body water is rapidly lost, such as during intense exercise in the heat. Also, in older adults, the thirst mechanism is not as accurate as in younger adults. Because the thirst mechanism has these limitations, it is important that you drink regularly throughout the day, even if you don't feel particularly thirsty.

thirst mechanism A cluster of nerve cells in the hypothalamus that stimulate our conscious desire to drink fluids in response to an increase in the concentration of salt in our blood or a decrease in blood pressure and volume.

Figure 8.3 Water content of different foods. Much of your daily water intake comes from the foods you eat.
Data from U.S. Department of Agriculture, Agricultural Research Service. 2009. USDA National Nutrient Database for Standard Reference, Release 22. Nutrient Data Laboratory Home Page.
www.ars.usda.gov/ba/bhnrc/ndl.

Fruits and vegetables are delicious sources of water.

metabolic water The water formed as a by-product of our body's metabolic reactions.

diuretic A substance that increases fluid loss via the urine. Common diuretics include alcohol and some prescription medications for high blood pressure and other disorders.

We Gain Fluids Through Intake and Metabolism

The fluid we need each day comes from the drinks and foods we consume, as well as the body's production of metabolic water. Of course, you know that beverages are mostly water, but it isn't as easy to see the water content of foods. For example, iceberg lettuce is about 96% water, and even almonds contain a small amount of water (Figure 8.3).

Metabolic water is the water formed as a by-product of the body's breakdown of fat, carbohydrate, and protein. The water that is formed during these metabolic reactions contributes about 10% to 14% of the total water our body needs each day.

We Lose Fluids Through Urine and Feces, Sweat, Evaporation, and Exhalation

Our kidneys absorb from the bloodstream any water that the body does not need. They then send the fluid, in the form of dilute urine, to the bladder for storage until we urinate. A small amount of water is also lost each day in the feces. However, when someone experiences severe diarrhea, water loss in the feces can be as high as several quarts per day.

We also lose fluid via sweat. Fluid loss in sweat is much higher during physical labor or exercise, and when we are in a hot environment. In fact, some large football players can lose more than 8 quarts of fluid per day as sweat![2]

Water is also continuously evaporated from our skin, even when we are not obviously sweating. Finally, water is continuously exhaled from the lungs as we breathe.

Figure 8.4 shows the estimated amounts and categories of water sources and losses for a woman expending about 2,500 kcal of energy per day. It shows that her fluid losses of 3,000 ml (3 L, or just over 12 cups) per day are matched by her intake of about

- 2,200 ml (2.2 L, or about 9 cups) of fluid in beverages,
- an additional 500 ml (about 2 cups) of fluid in foods, and
- an additional 300 ml (about 1.3 cups) of metabolic water.

So, this woman would need to drink about 9 cups of water to meet her needs.

The consumption of **diuretics**—substances that increase fluid loss via the urine—can result in dangerously excessive fluid loss. Some prescription medications have a diuretic effect, and many over-the-counter weight-loss products are really just

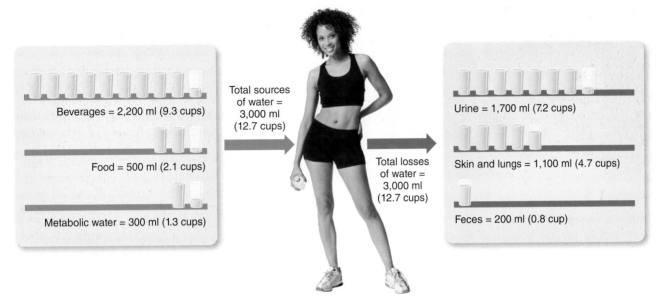

Beverages = 2,200 ml (9.3 cups)

Food = 500 ml (2.1 cups)

Metabolic water = 300 ml (1.3 cups)

Total sources of water = 3,000 ml (12.7 cups)

Total losses of water = 3,000 ml (12.7 cups)

Urine = 1,700 ml (7.2 cups)

Skin and lungs = 1,100 ml (4.7 cups)

Feces = 200 ml (0.8 cup)

➤ **Figure 8.4** Amounts and categories of water sources and losses for a woman expending 2,500 kcal per day.

diuretics. Alcohol also has a strong diuretic effect. In the past, it was believed that caffeine-containing beverages, such as coffee, tea, and cola, acted as diuretics, but more recent research suggests that caffeinated drinks do not in fact have a significant impact on the hydration status of adults.[3] Although more research on this aspect needs to be done, it's probably safe to count caffeinated beverages toward your daily fluid requirements. Later in this chapter, we identify ways to determine whether or not you are adequately hydrated.

RECAP The thirst mechanism prompts us to feel thirsty when it detects an increased concentration of sodium and other dissolved substances in the blood. It is also triggered by low blood volume or blood pressure. A healthy fluid level is maintained in the body by balancing intake with excretion. Primary sources of fluids include beverages, foods, and the production of metabolic water in the body. Fluid losses occur through urine, feces, sweating, evaporation from the skin, and exhalation from the lungs.

How Much Fluid Do You Need—and What Kinds?

You need to drink enough fluid every day so that your body can sweat, breathe, and produce urine and feces without drawing water from your cells. But how much is "enough"—for you? The DRI guidelines from the Institute of Medicine recommend that men consume approximately 3,000 ml (about 13 cups) of fluids daily from water and other beverages, with an additional 700 ml of water from food. Women should consume about 2,200 ml (9 cups) of fluid, as well as 500 ml of water from food.[3] Still, fluid requirements are highly individualized. For example, a male athlete training in a hot environment may need to drink up to 10 liters (about 42 cups) of fluid per day, whereas a petite, sedentary woman who works in a temperature-controlled office building may require only about 2 liters (8 cups) per day.

Mineral, Fizzy, or Tap: Water Is a Healthful Choice

All beverages provide water, but plain drinking water hydrates your body more efficiently than juices, sodas, and other beverages and does not contribute to weight

▲ Numerous varieties of drinking water are available to consumers.

gain. There are so many types of drinking water available in the United States; how can we distinguish among them? Here's a quick list:

- *Carbonated water* contains carbon dioxide gas. There are two types: in *sparkling water,* the carbon dioxide occurs naturally, whereas in *soda water,* the carbon dioxide is added by the manufacturer. Carbonated water is usually available in a variety of flavors and may or may not contain added sugar.
- *Mineral water* contains varying levels of minerals. While many people enjoy the unique taste of mineral water, a number of brands contain high amounts of sodium so should be avoided by people who are trying to reduce their sodium intake.
- *Distilled water* is processed in such a way that all dissolved minerals are removed. Although this type of water is sodium free, some people complain that it has a "flat" taste.
- *Tap water* comes from municipal water systems and is pumped to homes, offices, and public places. It often contains chlorine, which is used as an antimicrobial, and may be fluoridated.
- *Well water* is used by many people in rural areas who do not have access to community water supplies. This water varies in quality; it can be more pure and better tasting than municipal water, or it can be dangerously high in lead, arsenic, or other impurities. Water-quality testing is important for people who rely on well water for their drinking water.

Bottled water has been one of the most lucrative products marketed by the beverage industry for the past 20 years. Americans consume about 35 gallons of bottled water per person per year, which translates to 85 million bottles of water per day in the United States alone.[4] This meteoric rise in bottled water production and consumption is most likely due to its convenience, the health messages related to drinking more water, and the public's fears related to the safety of tap water. However, in recent years environmental concerns about impacts of the production and disposal of plastic water bottles have slowed sales to some extent.

Is bottled water really safer or more healthful than tap water? Do environmental concerns about the effects of widespread consumption of bottled water outweigh the health benefits? See the **Nutrition Myth or Fact?** box on bottled water for answers (page 233).

All Beverages Are Not Created Equal

Many beverages contain important nutrients in addition to their water content, while others provide water and refined sugar but very little else. Let's review the health benefits and potential concerns of some of the most popular beverages on the market.

Milk and Milk Substitutes

Low-fat and skim milk are healthful choices, because they contain protein, calcium, phosphorus, vitamin D, and usually vitamin A. Many brands of milk are now "specialized" and provide additional calcium, vitamin E, essential fatty acids, or other nutrients. Calcium-fortified soy milk, rice milk, and almond milk are also good sources of protein and calcium. When buying flavored milks, check the Nutrition Facts Panel for the sugar content. Some brands of chocolate milk, for example, can contain 6 or more teaspoons of refined sugar in a single cup!

Beverages Containing Caffeine

Coffee without cream or nondairy creamer can be a healthful choice if consumed in moderation. As mentioned earlier, recent research suggests that its caffeine content does not significantly decrease the body's hydration status, and the calcium in coffee drinks made with milk, such as café con leche and café latte, can be significant.

▲ Bottled water is very popular, but how does it really compare to tap water?

NUTRITION MYTH OR FACT?

Is Bottled Water Safer Than Tap Water?

Bottled water has become increasingly popular during the past 20 years. It is estimated that Americans drink almost 9 billion gallons of bottled water each year.[4,5] Many people prefer the taste of bottled water to that of tap water. They also feel that bottled water is safer than tap water. Is this true?

The water we drink in the United States generally comes from two sources: surface water and groundwater.

- *Surface water* comes from lakes, rivers, and reservoirs. Common contaminants of surface water include runoff from highways, pesticides, animal wastes, and industrial wastes. Many of the cities across the United States get their water from surface-water sources.
- *Groundwater* comes from spaces between underground rock formations called *aquifers.* Many people who live in rural areas consume groundwater pumped from a well as their main water source. Hazardous substances leaking from waste sites, dumps, landfills, and oil and gas pipelines can contaminate groundwater. Groundwater can also be contaminated by naturally occurring substances, such as arsenic or high levels of iron in soil.

The most common chemical used to treat and purify our water is *chlorine,* which is effective in killing many dangerous microbes. Water treatment plants also routinely check water supplies for hazardous chemicals, minerals, and other contaminants. Because of these efforts, the United States has one of the safest water systems in the world.

The Environmental Protection Agency (EPA) sets and monitors the standards for our municipal water systems. The EPA does not monitor water from private wells, but it publishes recommendations for well owners to help them maintain a safe water supply. Local water regulatory agencies, such as cities and counties, must provide an annual report on specific water contaminants to all households served by that agency.

In contrast, the Food and Drug Administration (FDA) regulates bottled water. It does not require that bottled water meet higher quality standards than public water. Despite many people's assumptions, bottled water is taken from either surface-water or groundwater sources, the same as tap water. However, bottled water is often treated and filtered differently than tap water, which changes its taste and appearance.

Although bottled water may taste better to some than tap water, there is actually no evidence that it is safer to drink. Look closely at the label of your favorite bottled water. If the label states "From a public water source," it has come directly from the tap! Some types of bottled water may contain more minerals than tap water, but there are no other additional nutritional benefits of drinking bottled water. *Micron filtration* and *reverse osmosis* are two treatments that are very effective against the most common waterborne disease–causing microorganisms. Purification of bottled water by filtration, carbon-filtration, particle-filtration, or treatment with ultraviolet light or ozone may be less effective, since these methods have not been proven to be effective against the most common disease-producing microbes.

Should you spend money on bottled water? The answer depends on personal preference and your source of drinking water. If you live in an area where you don't have reliable access to safe drinking water, bottled water may be your only safe water source. Whenever you choose to drink bottled water, look for brands that carry the trademark of the International Bottled Water Association (IBWA). This association follows the regulations of the FDA.

Be wary of vending machines dispensing filtered water where you can fill your own bottles. These machines may not be cleaned, and the filters may not be changed on a regular basis, so before using them, contact the vendor to determine how often and how they are serviced. If you get your water from a water cooler, make sure the cooler is cleaned once per month according to the manufacturer's instructions.

If you use a special or additional filtration system at home, be familiar with the specific contaminants it removes from your water, and make sure you change the filters regularly as recommended by the manufacturer. Be cautious of companies making claims about impurities in your tap water. If a private company tests your water and reports contamination, confirm those results with your local water agency. It could save you hundreds or thousands of dollars on an unnecessary or ineffective home water-purifying system.

For more information on drinking water safety, go to the EPA website at www.epa.gov. For information on bottled water, search the FDA website at www.fda.gov.

Coffee is known to provide several types of phytochemicals that may lower the risk for certain chronic diseases, such as type 2 diabetes and heart disease. There is also growing evidence that people who drink coffee have a lower risk for stroke, although not all research supports this finding. Although some people are sensitive to the caffeine in coffee, in moderation it is a safe and potentially healthful source of fluid.

Tea is second only to water as the most commonly consumed beverage in the world. With the exception of herbal teas, all forms of tea come from the same plant, *Camellia sinesis*. These include the following:

- *Black tea* is produced in Asia, India, Turkey, and parts of Africa. It's the most highly processed tea (the tea leaves are fully fermented), and it has the highest level of caffeine (about half the level in the same amount of brewed coffee).
- *Oolong* is a Chinese tea, the leaves of which are withered in the sun and are only partially fermented. Thus, oolong tea has less caffeine than black tea.
- *Green tea* leaves have been dried and steamed but not fermented. Their caffeine content is lower than that of oolong.
- *White tea* is made only from the buds or first leaves of the tea plant. As with green tea, these are dried but not fermented. White tea has the least caffeine of all non-herbal teas.

If consumed without added sugar, tea is an excellent source of fluid that may have unexpected long-term health benefits. For example, all of the listed teas provide *phytochemicals*. Green and white teas have much higher levels, including antioxidant-rich polyphenols, than black and oolong teas. These antioxidants are thought to contribute to the health-promoting qualities of tea, including decreased risk for heart disease, diabetes, and certain cancers; decreased levels of LDL cholesterol; and increased levels of HDL cholesterol. Some research suggests that green and white teas may also have anti-bacterial and antiviral effects.

Chocolate- and cocoa-based beverages also provide small amounts of caffeine, although the levels are much lower than those found in coffee, tea, or colas. Dark chocolate is rich in antioxidants known as flavanols, which may lower risk for heart attacks and stroke. Hot chocolate made with dark cocoa powder and skim or low-fat milk is a nutritious and satisfying drink.

Beverages with Added Sugars

Sugar is added to many juice drinks, sweetened teas, flavored waters, and sodas. Many are sweetened with high-fructose corn syrup (HFCS), the potential health consequences of which are the subject of significant debate. Other beverage companies sweeten their products with so-called fruit juice concentrate; although it sounds like a healthy option, this concentrate is little more than pure sugar, with none of the fiber or other nutrients that make fruit nutritious. Honey is another popular source of added sugar, but it is also very low in nutrient value.

As package sizes increase, the Calorie count for sweetened drinks can be unexpectedly high. For example, you may think that cranberry juice cocktail is a healthful beverage, but did you know that one 8-ounce serving contains more than 7 teaspoons of sugar? If you were to drink a 24-ounce bottle, you'd consume more than 300 Calories! In the past, few people realized how many Calories were in the beverages they drank. Public health experts believe that this ignorance has contributed to the growing problem of obesity. Recently, most large manufacturers of non-alcoholic beverages have committed to the "Clear on Calories" campaign, which requires that they list Calorie content on the front of the product. All beverages packaged in containers 20 fl. oz or smaller will display the total Calories per package, not just per serving. Now, when consumers buy a 20 oz bottle of sweetened tea, they'll know they're getting, for example, 250 Calories if they drink the whole bottle.

▲ Consuming coffee drinks in moderation can be a healthful choice for adults, and the calcium content in caffeinated drinks made with milk can be significant. Avoid using cream or nonfat creamers and opt for low- or nonfat milk.

To watch a video of the American Beverage Association's Clear on Calories ad, go to www.ameribev .org/nutrition—science/clear-on-calories/ads—multimedia/.

FOODS YOU DON'T KNOW YOU LOVE YET

Rooibos Tea

Also called red tea, rooibos (pronounced ROY-bos) is a ruddy tea with a naturally sweet, nutty flavor. The plant it comes from, *Aspalathus linearis*, is grown only in a small region of South Africa, but over the past decade rooibos has become increasingly available in markets throughout the United States. Sold both loose and in tea bags, it's prepared like black tea, and many people drink it with lemon. The increasing popularity of rooibos is due in part to its health benefits: it contains no caffeine and is rich in antioxidant phytochemicals. Traditionally, South Africans have used rooibos tea as a treatment for allergies, asthma, and skin inflammation.

Designer Waters

Flavored waters, made with or without added sugars, are widely available, as are so-called designer or enhanced waters. Many of these drinks are made with added nutrients and herbs and are labeled with structure–function claims stating, for example, that drinking the product will enhance memory, delay aging, boost energy levels, or strengthen the immune response. Notice, however, that the label also includes a disclaimer, such as "This statement has not been evaluated by the FDA. This product is not intended to diagnose, treat, cure, or prevent any disease." The FDA requires this disclaimer whenever a manufacturer makes a structure–function claim. In other words, manufacturers must acknowledge that the statements made on the labels of these fortified waters are not, in fact, based on research or reliable sources.

Actually, the level of nutrients is typically so much lower than what can be obtained from foods that such beverages rarely have much of an impact on health or well-being. Moreover, waters made with HFCS, honey, or other sweeteners can add more than 300 Calories to your diet.

Energy Drinks

Energy drinks represent another popular beverage option, with over $9 billion in sales in 2011. These products advertise their ability to provide a boost, jump start, buzz, punch, or rocket-powered blast! As many as half of all adolescents and young adults consume energy drinks, yet nutrition experts and consumer groups have raised significant concerns about them.[6] Many of these drinks contain more than three times the amount of caffeine in a comparable serving of cola, and a few contain up to ten times the caffeine found in cola. Energy drinks often contain guarana seed extract as well: guarana seeds contain more caffeine than coffee beans, so their "extract" is simply a potent source of additional caffeine. Some also contain taurine, an amino acid associated with muscle contraction.

There is little research on the effects of these ingredients, either alone or in combination with one another. What we do know is that their combined effects can significantly increase blood pressure and heart rate. Mood swings, behavioral disorders, insomnia, dizziness, tremors, seizures, caffeine dependency, dehydration, and other problems have also been linked to consumption of these beverages. Over 5,000 cases of caffeine overdose were reported in 2007; nearly

"Energy drinks" are a popular segment of the beverage market, but many contain caffeine and other substances that can cause harmful effects.

half of those affected were younger than 19 years of age.[6] Although the FDA limits the amount of caffeine in soft drinks, it has no legal authority to regulate the ingredients, including caffeine, in energy drinks, which are classified as dietary supplements, not foods.

To watch a video on the dangers of energy drinks, go to www.cbsnews.com/video/watch/?id=1596076n.

Sports Beverages

A final fluid option is that of a traditional sports beverage, which provides water, electrolytes, and a source of carbohydrate, although some products now offer low-/no-sugar options. Because of the potential for fluid and electrolyte imbalances during rigorous exercise, many athletes drink sports beverages instead of plain water before, during, and after workouts. Recently, sports beverages have also become popular with recreationally active people and non-athletes. Is it really necessary or helpful for people to consume these beverages? See the *Highlight* feature box on sports beverages (page 237) to learn whether they are right for you.

As you can see, American consumers have a wide range of beverage choices available to them. Poor choices can increase your total caloric intake and lower your daily intake of nutrients.[7] Over the past 40 years, the caloric contributions of beverages to total energy intake have almost doubled. In 1965, fewer than 12% of Americans' Calories came from beverages; in 2002, that ratio increased to 21% of total calories.[8] Pure drinking water remains Calorie and additive free, is highly effective in quenching thirst and maintaining hydration status, and poses no health threat. For most of us, water really is the perfect beverage choice.

RECAP Although fluid requirements are highly individualized, men require approximately 3.0 liters (13 cups) of fluids daily, and women approximately 2.2 liters (9 cups). All beverages provide water, and some—such as mineral waters, milk, and calcium-fortified drinks—provide other important nutrients as well. Some beverages contain unnecessary and potentially harmful ingredients and should be consumed in limited amounts. Pure water remains the best beverage choice for most people.

HEALTHWATCH

Can Too Little or Too Much Fluid Intake Be Deadly?

Fluid imbalances can be serious, even fatal. Dehydration, heatstroke, and hyponatremia are fluid imbalances that produce negative health effects, and each is explained in this section.

Dehydration Is Common with Exercise in Hot Weather

Dehydration is a serious health problem that results when fluid losses exceed fluid intake. It occurs most often as a result of heavy exercise and/or exposure to high environmental temperatures, when loss of body water via sweating and breathing is increased.

Both the elderly and the very young have increased risk for dehydration. The thirst mechanism becomes less sensitive with age, so elderly people can fail to drink

dehydration A serious condition of depleted body fluid that results when fluid excretion exceeds fluid intake.

HIGHLIGHT
Sports Beverages: Help or Hype?

Once considered specialty products used exclusively by elite athletes, sports beverages have become popular everyday choices for both active and nonactive people. The market for these drinks has become so lucrative that many of the large soft drink companies now produce them. This surge in popularity leads us to ask three important questions:

- Do sports beverages benefit highly active athletes?
- Do sports beverages benefit recreationally active people?
- Do nonactive people benefit from consuming sports beverages?

The first question is relatively easy to answer. Sports beverages were originally developed to meet the unique fluid, electrolyte, and carbohydrate needs of competitive athletes. Highly active people need to replenish both fluids and electrolytes to avoid both dehydration and hyponatremia (low blood sodium). Sports beverages can particularly benefit athletes who exercise in the heat and are thus at an even greater risk for loss of water and electrolytes through respiration and sweat. The carbohydrates in sports beverages provide energy during relatively intense exercise bouts lasting more than 1 hour. Thus, competitive athletes are able to exercise longer, maintain a higher intensity, and improve performance times when they drink a sports beverage during exercise.

In addition, sports beverages may help athletes consume more energy than they could by eating solid foods and water alone. Some competitive athletes train or compete for 6 to 8 hours each day on a regular basis. It is virtually impossible for them to consume enough solid foods to support this intense level of exercise.

Do recreationally active people or those working in a physically demanding job benefit from drinking sports beverages? The answer depends on the duration and intensity of exercise,

the environmental conditions of temperature and humidity, and the individual's level of physical fitness. Here are some situations in which drinking a sports beverage is appropriate:

- before exercise or manual labor if you're concerned that dehydration might occur, especially if you are already feeling dehydrated
- during exercise or manual labor if you have recently had diarrhea or vomiting
- during exercise or manual labor in high heat and/or high humidity
- during exercise or manual labor at high altitude and in cold environments; these conditions increase fluid and electrolyte losses
- during continuous, vigorous exercise or labor lasting longer than 60 minutes in any climate
- between exercise bouts when it is difficult to consume food, such as between multiple soccer matches during a tournament

Recently, sports beverages have become very popular with people who do little or no regular exercise or manual labor. However, there's no evidence that people who do not exercise get any benefits from consuming sports beverages. Even if they live in a hot climate, they should be able to replenish the fluid and electrolytes they lose during sweating by drinking water and other beverages and eating a normal diet.

When inactive people drink sports beverages, a common consequence is inappropriate weight gain. Drinking 12 fl. oz (1.5 cups) of Gatorade adds 90 Calories to a person's daily energy intake. Many inactive people consume two to three times this amount each day, increasing their risk for overweight or obesity—with no benefit to their health.

---

adequate amounts of fluid. Older adults also have less body water than younger adults, so fluid imbalances can occur more quickly. On the other end, because a large proportion of infants' body weight is water, they need to drink a relatively large amount of fluid for their body size. Infants also excrete urine at a higher rate, cannot tell us when they are thirsty, and have a greater ratio of body surface area to body core, causing them to respond more dramatically to heat and cold and to lose more body water than an older child or adult. For these reasons, fluid losses, such as with diarrhea or vomiting, must be closely monitored in infants.

In all people, relatively small losses in body water, equal to a 1% to 2% change in body weight, result in symptoms that include thirst, discomfort, and loss of

⬆ Vigorous exercise causes significant losses of water and electrolytes, which must be replenished to optimize performance and health.

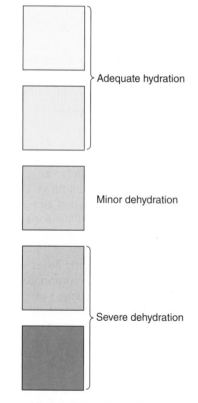

⬆ **Figure 8.5** Urine color chart. Color variations indicate levels of hydration.

heatstroke A potentially fatal response to high temperature characterized by failure of the body's heat-regulating mechanisms commonly called *sunstroke*.

appetite. More severe water losses can cause nausea, flushed skin, and problems with mental concentration. Losses of body water greater than 8% of body weight can result in delirium, coma, and death.

Earlier we discussed the importance of fluid replacement when you are exercising. How can you tell whether you're drinking enough fluid before, during, and after athletic competitions or exercise sessions? First, you can measure your body weight before and after each session, using the same scale, unclothed or just in your underwear. Whether you've lost 2 ounces or 2 pounds of body weight during your session, you need to consume enough water and other fluids to regain that weight before you exercise again.

A second way to monitor your fluid levels is to observe the color of your urine **(Figure 8.5)**. If you are properly hydrated, your urine should be clear to pale yellow in color, similar to diluted lemonade. Urine that is medium to dark yellow, similar in color to apple juice, indicates inadequate fluid intake. Very dark or brown urine, such as the color of a cola beverage, is a sign of severe dehydration and indicates potential muscle breakdown and kidney damage. People should strive to maintain a urine color that is clear or pale yellow.

How should you replace fluid you've lost during exercise or competition? Begin physical activity in a well-hydrated state by slowly drinking water or sport beverages at least 4 hours before the activity. During a session, prevent dehydration by drinking water or sports beverages as needed. A marathon runner may need to drink 400 to 800 ml (1½ to 3 cups) of a sports beverage per hour during the race; however, a player in a casual tennis match may require much less. Most people can restore fluid and electrolyte balance after activity through normal meals, snacks, and beverages. But if your weight or the color of your urine indicates that you are significantly dehydrated, one guideline is to drink about 1,500 ml (about 6 cups) for each kilogram of body weight lost.[2]

Heatstroke

People who work outdoors in the heat, such as farm workers, highway or construction workers, and soldiers, are particularly vulnerable to dangerous fluid loss. So are athletes who train or compete in hot weather. Between 2005 and 2009, 18 U.S. athletes, many in middle school or high school, died of **heatstroke.**[9]

Heatstroke occurs when the body cannot release enough heat in the form of sweat to keep the body temperature within a safe range. The body's ability to cool itself via sweating requires that the sweat be able to evaporate: this means that the air around us needs to be somewhat dry. Thus, evaporative cooling is less effective in a humid environment. Heavy clothing, such as a military or football uniform, special padding, and helmet, significantly reduces the body's ability to dissipate heat. Body composition also plays a role: larger people with a lot of muscle mass produce more body heat. In addition, people with high levels of body fat have an extra layer of insulation that makes it difficult to dissipate body heat both at rest and during exercise.

Symptoms of heatstroke include a rapid pulse, deep breathing, hot and dry skin, high temperature, and loss of consciousness. Heatstroke is a medical emergency: to prevent death, immediate care is essential. If you're working, training, or competing in the heat and someone collapses, call 911. If possible, immerse the victim in an ice bath if she or he is conscious and can be constantly supervised. Otherwise, apply ice packs to the victim's armpits and groin area, and sponge or spray the person's body continually with cold water until help arrives.

You can reduce your own risk for heat stroke by maintaining a healthy fluid balance before, during, and after exercise or manual labor. If you're training, competing, or working in a hot environment and begin to feel dizzy, light-headed, disoriented, or nauseated, stop immediately. Find a cool place to rest, consume cool beverages (such as water or a sports beverage), and ask someone to notify your trainer, coach, or employer that you need assistance.

Water Intoxication

Is it possible to drink too much water? **Water intoxication,** also called *overhydration*, can occur, but it is rare. In non-athletes, it generally occurs only in people with health problems that cause the kidneys to retain too much water or during dangerous activities, such as hazing rituals and the use of certain illegal drugs. It is more common in endurance athletes, such as long-distance runners and triathletes, because kidney function is reduced during intense exercise. When athletes drink too much water and do not replace adequate sodium during a long event, their body can retain too much fluid, resulting in a dangerous dilution of blood sodium called *hyponatremia.*

As noted at the beginning of this chapter, hyponatremia can be fatal. Warning signs of hyponatremia include continuing thirst despite fluid intake, nausea, headache, inability to concentrate, and confusion. These symptoms indicate the need for immediate medical assistance.

Athletes who train or compete in hot weather are vulnerable to dangerous fluid loss.

RECAP Dehydration, heatstroke, and water intoxication can occur when water and electrolyte losses are not balanced with water and electrolyte replacement. These conditions can occur in manual laborers and in athletes training or competing in hot weather, and it can be fatal.

How Much Alcohol Is Safe to Drink?

Alcohol is the common name for a beverage made from fermented fruits, vegetables, and grains. Alcoholic beverages include beer, wine, and distilled spirits, such as whiskey. Although alcohol is an energy-rich compound providing 7 kcal per gram, it is not considered a nutrient because, instead of being essential to our body's functioning, it can significantly impair functioning.

Alcohol Consumption Is Described as Drinks per Day

Alcohol consumption is typically described in terms of *drinks per day*. A **drink** is defined as the amount of a beverage that provides ½ fl. oz of alcohol. Typically, that's equivalent to 1½ oz of distilled spirits (80-proof vodka, gin, whiskey, rum, scotch), 5 oz of wine, or 12 oz of beer or a wine cooler.[10] These amounts are shown in **Figure 8.6** (page 240).

Beers, wines, and distilled spirits contain different percentages of alcohol by volume. Beers range from about 3% to 4% alcohol for light beers to 5% or 6% for regular beers, and as much as 7% for stout beers, malt liquor, and other specialty beers. Most wines contain from 9% to 15% alcohol. The alcohol content of distilled spirits is directly related to its **proof:** 100-proof liquor is 50% alcohol, whereas 80-proof liquor is 40% alcohol. Some fruit-flavored alcohol drinks (sometimes called *alcopops)* can contain as much as 12% alcohol. Many are packaged in 23 oz cans. Thus, people who drink the entire can are consuming not one drink but more than four! No wonder some public health authorities refer to such drinks as "a binge in a can."

The 2010 Dietary Guidelines for Americans advise, "If alcohol is consumed, it should be consumed in moderation—up to one drink per day for women and two drinks per day for men—and only by adults of legal drinking age."[11] It's important to understand that these are *daily* guidelines; a person who drinks no alcoholic beverages Sunday through Friday, but has seven drinks on Saturday night, would not be classified as a moderate drinker! The 2010 Guidelines also identify specific groups who should not consume any alcohol at all:[11]

- women who are or may become pregnant
- anyone younger than the legal drinking age

water intoxication Dilution of body fluid that results when water intake or retention is excessive; it can lead to hyponatremia; also called *overhydration.*

alcohol A beverage made from fermented fruits, vegetables, or grains.

drink The amount of an alcoholic beverage that provides approximately ½ fl. oz of pure ethanol.

proof A measure of the alcohol content of a liquid. For example, 100-proof liquor is 50% alcohol by volume, whereas 80-proof liquor is 40% alcohol by volume.

Figure 8.6 What does one drink look like? The National Institute on Alcohol Abuse and Alcoholism lists "one drink" as 5 oz of wine, 12 oz of beer or wine cooler, or 1½ oz of distilled spirits.

- people who cannot control their alcohol intake or keep it within moderate levels
- people taking medications that can interact with alcohol
- people who drive, operate machinery, or engage in other tasks requiring attention and coordination

In the United States, fewer than half of all adults regularly consume alcohol. Of the adults who drink, almost 30% report binge drinking within the past month, often on several occasions. About 40% of Americans are lifetime or current abstainers (defined as having no alcoholic drinks within the previous 12 months); women are twice as likely as men to be lifetime abstainers.[12]

Alcohol Absorption Rates Vary

Alcohol, which does not require digestion, is absorbed from both the stomach and the small intestine. From there, it's transported to the liver, where it is subsequently metabolized or, if consumed in excess, released into the bloodstream and rapidly distributed throughout the body.

The rate at which we absorb alcohol varies. If consumed without food, alcohol is absorbed from the stomach almost immediately. Eating a meal or snack with some fat, protein, and fiber before or with alcohol intake will slow gastric emptying and delay the intestinal absorption of alcohol. Carbonated alcoholic beverages are absorbed more rapidly than noncarbonated, resulting in the infamous intoxicating effect of champagne and sparkling wines. Women often absorb 30–35% more of a given amount of alcohol than do men of the same size, which may explain why women are often more susceptible to its effects.

In a healthy adult, the liver breaks down alcohol at a fairly constant rate, equal to about one drink per hour. If someone drinks more than that, such as three drinks in an hour, the excess alcohol is released back into the bloodstream, where it is distributed to all body tissues and fluids, including the brain and liver.

> Trace the flow of alcohol through the body and see how it affects your organs and body systems. Click to get started at www.collegedrinkingprevention.gov/CollegeStudents/interactive-Body.aspx.

Despite popular notions, there is no effective way to speed up the breakdown of alcohol: it doesn't help to walk around, consume coffee or energy drinks, or use commercial herbal or nutrient supplements. The keys to avoiding intoxication are to consume alcohol slowly, to have no more than one drink per hour, and to drink alcoholic beverages only after or while eating a meal or large snack.

Blood Alcohol Concentration (%)	Typical Response
TABLE 8.1	**Effects of Blood Alcohol Concentration (BAC) on Brain Activity**
0.02–0.05	Feeling of relaxation; euphoria; relief
0.06–0.10	Impaired judgment, fine motor control, and coordination; loss of normal emotional control; legally drunk in many states (at the upper end of the range)
0.11–0.15	Impaired reflexes and gross motor control; staggered gait; legally drunk in all states; slurred speech
0.16–0.20	Impaired vision; unpredictable behavior; further loss of muscle control
0.21–0.35	Total loss of coordination; in a stupor
0.40 and above	Loss of consciousness; coma; suppression of respiratory response; death

As a person's alcohol intake increases over time, the liver metabolizes alcohol more efficiently and blood alcohol levels rise more slowly. This metabolic tolerance to alcohol explains why people who chronically abuse alcohol must consume larger and larger amounts before becoming intoxicated. Over time, some may need to consume twice as much alcohol as when they first started to drink in order to reach the same state of intoxication.

Of the alcohol we consume, a small amount, typically less than 10%, is excreted through the urine, breath, and sweat. As the blood alcohol concentration increases, so does the level of alcohol in breath vapor; this relationship forms the basis of the common Breathalyzer testing done by law enforcement agencies. It may surprise you to learn that your driving ability becomes impaired at quite low levels of alcohol consumption. For example, certain driving skills are reduced by blood alcohol concentrations (BAC) as low as 0.02%, despite the fact that most states in the U.S. do not charge drivers with a DUI/DWI offense if their BAC is below 0.08%.[13] **Table 8.1** identifies typical responses of individuals at varying BAC levels.

◆ Contrary to popular notions, coffee will not speed the breakdown of alcohol.

RECAP Alcohol provides 7 kcal per gram but is not a nutrient because it is not essential to body functioning. Alcohol intake is classified in terms of "drinks per day." A drink is defined as the amount of a beverage that provides ½ fl. oz of alcohol. Fewer than half of Americans regularly consume alcohol. Alcohol absorption can be slowed by the consumption of a meal or large snack. The liver breaks down absorbed alcohol at a steady rate of approximately one drink per hour; there is no effective way to speed up this process.

Moderate Alcohol Consumption Has Health Benefits and Risks

The psychological benefits of moderate alcohol consumption are well known: it can relieve tension and anxiety while increasing a sense of relaxation and self-confidence. But moderate alcohol consumption has health benefits as well. It has been linked to a reduced risk for cardiovascular disease and certain types of strokes.[14,15] Moderate alcohol intake increases levels of protective HDL-cholesterol and reduces the risk for clot formation in the arteries.[16] Although many people believe these benefits come only from red wines, recent studies suggest that intakes of white wine, distilled spirits, or even beer have similar effects.[16]

In the elderly, moderate alcohol consumption may stimulate appetite and improve dietary intake. Some, but not all, research suggests that moderate alcohol consumption may lower risk for cognitive impairment and other forms of dementia, particularly in nonsmoking women.[17] As research in this area continues, healthcare providers will develop a clearer picture of which groups of people might benefit from moderate alcohol intake.

◆ Drinking beverages that contain alcohol causes an increase in water loss, because alcohol is a diuretic.

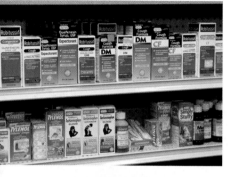

← Alcohol can interfere with and increase the risks of using various over-the-counter and prescription medications.

Despite such benefits, moderate drinking can also be risky. A person's genetic background, state of health, use of medicines, and age all influence the short- and long-term responses to alcohol intake, even at moderate levels. For example, some studies have reported an increased risk for breast cancer among women consuming even low to moderate levels of alcohol,[18] and others have reported an increased risk of developing high blood pressure (hypertension) among men consuming as little as two drinks per day.[19] In addition, alcohol consumption interferes with the absorption and utilization of thiamin, folate, and vitamin B_6, increasing the risk for nutrient deficiency.

In some drinkers, moderate alcohol intake may increase total energy intake and risk for overweight or obesity; because alcoholic beverages don't trigger the normal satiety response, most people fail to compensate for the Calories by eating less food. In addition, moderate alcohol consumption stimulates appetite over the short term, increasing total energy intake.[20]

Drinking alcohol while taking any one of more than 150 medications can also cause problems.[21,22] For example, if you are taking antihistamines for an allergy, alcohol will increase their sedative effect, making you extremely drowsy. And you can develop serious liver damage if you are taking large doses of the painkiller acetaminophen (sold in many over-the-counter remedies, such as Tylenol), even if you are drinking only moderately.

RECAP Moderate alcohol consumption is associated with health benefits as well as potential risks. Every person will have a unique metabolic and behavioral response to a given alcohol exposure and must carefully weigh the pros and cons of alcohol consumption.

Excessive Alcohol Consumption Leads to Serious Health Problems

Alcohol is a drug. It exerts a narcotic effect on virtually every part of the brain, acting as a sedative and depressant. Alcohol suppresses the area of the brain that controls reasoning and judgment, causes blurred vision and slurred speech, and impairs fine and gross motor skills (see Table 8.1). It also interferes with normal sleep patterns and reduces sexual function.

← Drinking too much, too often, and inappropriately are signs of alcohol abuse.

Excessive alcohol consumption negatively affects not only the drinker's physiology but his or her mood and behavior as well. Many people who drink to excess experience mood swings, irritability, or intense anger, whereas others experience sadness or lethargy. Did you know that about 25% of college students report academic consequences of their drinking, such as missing class, falling behind, and getting poor grades?[23] In addition, alcohol impairs judgment, making a person more likely to perform or become the victim of vandalism, physical or sexual assault, and other crimes. Intoxication significantly increases the likelihood that a person will engage in unprotected sex, which in turn puts them at risk for sexually transmitted infections and unplanned pregnancy. And, like many drugs, it can be highly addictive.

In the absence of addiction, excessive alcohol consumption is often called as *alcohol abuse* or "problem drinking." It is characterized by drinking too *much*, too *often* or *inappropriately* (such as when pregnant, prior to driving a motor vehicle, between classes, or to quell negative emotions). Although the legal drinking age in the United States is 21 years, 20% of adolescents report such problem drinking—specifically, getting drunk six or more times each year and/or experiencing negative consequences as a result of their drinking. Another 31% of college students also self-report alcohol abuse.

How much alcohol do you drink, and should you be concerned about it? Check out the ***What About You?*** feature box (page 243) to help you decide.

Binge Drinking

binge drinking The consumption of five or more alcoholic drinks on one occasion.

Binge drinking, defined as consuming five or more alcoholic drinks on one occasion, is a common type of alcohol abuse, especially on college campuses. The rate of binge drinking is highest (51%) among those 18 to 20 years of age; more men report binge drinking than women.[24] About 90% of the alcohol consumed by those under

90% 🔋

WHAT ABOUT YOU?

Should You Be Concerned About How Much Alcohol You Drink?

As discussed in this chapter, alcohol contributes to societal violence as well as personal illness, disability, and death.

Answer the following questions, provided by the National Institute on Alcohol Abuse and Alcoholism (NIAAA), to help you find out if you have a drinking problem. For each question, circle Yes or No.

- Have you ever felt you should cut down on your drinking?
  YES or NO
- Have people annoyed you by criticizing your drinking?
  YES or NO
- Have you ever felt bad or guilty about your drinking?
  YES or NO
- Do you drink alone when you feel angry or sad?
  YES or NO
- Has your drinking ever made you late for school or work?
  YES or NO
- Have you ever had a drink first thing in the morning to steady your nerves or to get rid of a hangover?
  YES or NO
- Do you ever drink after promising yourself you won't?
  YES or NO

One "yes" answer suggests a possible alcohol problem. More than one "yes" answer means it is highly likely that a problem exists.

If you think you might have an alcohol problem, it's important to see a doctor or other healthcare provider right away. She or he can help you determine if a drinking problem exists and plan the best course of action. If your doctor tells you to cut down on or stop drinking, these steps from the NIAAA can help you:

1. Write down your reasons for cutting down or stopping, such as complying with drinking-age laws or campus zero-tolerance policies, improving your health or grades, or getting along better with friends.
2. Also write down your goal (for example, *I will stop drinking alcohol as of today, May 18, 2011*).
3. To help you achieve your goal, keep a diary listing every time you have a drink, the amount and type, and what circumstances (such as peer pressure, loneliness) prompted you to drink.
4. Make sure there is no alcohol in your house, dorm room, apartment, car, locker, and so forth. Instead, keep non-alcoholic beverages that you enjoy well stocked wherever you go.
5. Learn how to say NO. You don't have to drink when other people drink. Practice ways to say no politely. For instance, you can tell people that you feel better when you drink less, or that you are watching your weight. Stay away from people who harass you about not drinking.
6. Get support. Tell your family and trusted friends about your plan to cut down or stop drinking, and ask them for support in reaching your goal. Or contact your local chapter of Alcoholics Anonymous.

age 21 is in the form of bingeing. In other words, among those too young to legally consume alcohol, it is typically an "all or nothing" situation. Many rituals associated with student life, including acceptance into a fraternity or sorority, sports events, and 21st-birthday rituals, involve binge drinking.

The negative effects of binge drinking range from being debilitating to life threatening. They include impaired motor control, disorientation, impaired judgment, memory loss, dehydration, nausea, vomiting, loss of bowel control, and accidental and intentional injuries. When alcohol intake is so high that it overwhelms the liver's ability to clear the alcohol from the blood, alcohol poisoning, a potentially fatal consequence of binge drinking, can occur. Alcohol poisoning depresses the areas of the brain that regulate breathing and cardiac function, resulting in respiratory and heart failure, then death.

Most binge drinkers lose consciousness before alcohol poisoning becomes fatal, but immediate medical care is still essential. That's because any alcohol in the stomach and intestines will continue to seep into the bloodstream, further elevating the person's BAC. As this toxic level of alcohol circulates throughout the body, it can cause brain damage or death. In addition, extremely intoxicated people can vomit while they're unconscious. If the vomit blocks their breathing passages, they can choke to death. If it is inhaled into their lungs, they can develop a life-threatening form of pneumonia. For these reasons, a person who passes out after binge drinking should *never* be left alone to "sleep it off," but should be turned on his or her side and carefully watched for vomiting; cold, clammy, or bluish skin; and slow or irregular breathing patterns. If any of these signs are present, seek emergency medical care immediately.

Chronic Alcohol Abuse

Chronic alcohol abuse, defined as excessive intake over a period of several months to years, impairs brain function in a number of ways. In adolescence and young adulthood, the brain is still developing, and alcohol abuse during these years can actually change brain structure and function.[25] This may impair the development of intellect and abstract reasoning, diminish memory, and interfere with behavioral and emotional regulation. Even after becoming sober, many people who have chronically abused alcohol often continue to experience ongoing memory and learning problems.

Chronic alcohol abuse can also lead to *alcoholism* (also known as *alcohol dependence*), a disease characterized by the following four symptoms, described by the National Institute on Alcohol Abuse and Alcoholism (NIAAA):

- *craving:* a strong need, or urge, to drink alcoholic beverages
- *loss of control:* not being able to stop drinking once drinking has begun
- *physical dependence:* the development of withdrawal symptoms, such as nausea, sweating, shakiness, and anxiety after stopping alcohol intake
- *tolerance:* the need to drink larger and larger amounts of alcohol to get the same "high" or pleasurable sensations associated with alcohol intake

In addition, chronic alcohol abuse severely damages the liver. As the primary site of alcohol metabolism, the liver is extremely vulnerable to the toxic effects of alcohol. Liver cells are damaged or destroyed during excessive and binge-drinking episodes. If alcohol abuse persists, liver function continues to decline. *Fatty liver* is an early and reversible sign of damage. If drinking continues, the person may develop alcohol-related **hepatitis,** which causes loss of appetite, nausea and vomiting, abdominal pain, jaundice, and, on occasion, mental confusion. **Cirrhosis** of the liver is a chronic condition that develops after many years of alcohol abuse. It is characterized by scarring of liver tissue, impaired blood flow through the liver, and a life-threatening impairment of liver function **(Figure 8.7).** Moreover, chronic alcohol abuse is associated with an increased risk for a several cancers, including cancer of the mouth, esophagus, and gastrointestinal tract.

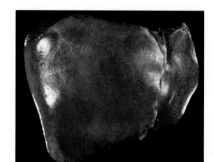

(a)

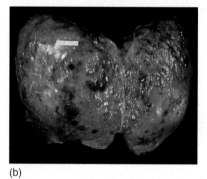

(b)

Figure 8.7 Cirrhosis of the liver, caused by chronic alcohol abuse. **(a)** A healthy liver. **(b)** A liver damaged by cirrhosis.

hepatitis Inflammation of the liver; can be caused by a virus or a toxic agent, such as alcohol.

cirrhosis End-stage liver disease characterized by significant abnormalities in liver structure and function; may lead to complete liver failure.

Alcohol Consumption Greatly Increases the Risk for Accidental Death

Although the rate of alcohol-related traffic deaths has decreased by almost 25% over the past decade, the number remains unacceptably high. In 2009, more than 10,000 people died in automobile crashes involving a drunk driver, nearly one-third of all automotive fatalities.[26] It is estimated that as many as 6,000 Americans under the age of 21 die each year from alcohol-related accidents, homicides, and suicides. Alcohol has also been implicated in 40% of all suicide attempts, 54% of all violent crimes, 60% of all emergency room admissions, and 80% of all domestic disputes.

Reading about these problems of alcohol consumption may prompt you to think about someone you know who abuses or is addicted to alcohol. If so, the *Game Plan*

For a list of DWI/DUI laws in all fifty states, go to the Insurance Institute for Highway Safety's web page at www.iihs.org/laws/dui.aspx.

feature (page 246) has guidelines for helping someone with an alcohol problem get treatment.

Strategies for Limiting Alcohol Intake

As you can see, drinking too much alcohol is dangerous for many reasons. So, if you often drink "to get drunk," a reasonable question to ask yourself is, *Why*? How does binge drinking fit in with your goals for yourself, your academic career, your future? Does it reflect a conscious choice, or do you feel pressured into it? If you do it to relieve stress, is there a less dangerous way to achieve that goal—maybe a martial arts class or an intense session of power yoga? If you decide that you want to drink socially, but avoid intoxication, here are some tips for staying in control:

Excessive alcohol consumption greatly increases the risks for car accidents and other traumatic injuries.

- Take steps ahead of time to keep within your limits. For example:
  - If you're going to a bar, take only enough money to buy two beers and two sodas.
  - Have a meal or snack containing protein before you leave home; having food in your stomach delays its emptying. This gives your stomach more time to break down the alcohol.
  - Have a "No thanks" line ready. Chances are, at some point during the evening, someone is going to offer you a drink when you're at your limit. Rehearsing a polite but firm response in advance—even something as simple as "No thanks, I'm good"—can help you side-step peer pressure.
- When you get to the bar, club, or party, make your first beverage a large glass of sparkling water, iced tea, diet soda, juice, or non-alcoholic beer. Once your thirst has been satisfied, you'll naturally drink less. After that, rotate between alcoholic and non-alcoholic drinks.
- If you're mixing a drink for yourself, use less liquor and dilute it with large amounts of diet soda, water, or juice. If you're in a bar, order your mixed drink yourself, and ask the bartender to make it weak.
- Whether or not your drink is diluted, sip slowly to allow your liver time to keep up with your alcohol intake.
- Stay occupied by dancing, sampling the food, watching the game, or talking with friends.

Another smart strategy is to volunteer to be the designated driver. You'll have a "free pass" for the night in terms of saying no to alcohol.

NUTRI-CASE THEO

"I was driving home from a post-game party last night when I was pulled over by the police. The officer said I seemed to be driving 'erratically' and asked me how many drinks I'd had. I told him I'd only had three beers and explained that I was pretty tired from the game. Then, just to prove I was fine, I offered to count backwards from a hundred, but I must have sounded sober, because he didn't make me do it. I can't believe he thought I was driving drunk! Still, maybe three beers after a game really is too much."

Do you think it is physically possible that Theo's driving might have been impaired, even though he had consumed only three beers? Before you answer, consider that Theo weighs around 170 lb during practice season and that he had just played a long basketball game. What other information would be important to find out to help you answer this question?

90% 🔋

GAME PLAN

Strategies for Helping Someone with an Alcohol Problem Get Treatment

If you know someone who abuses alcohol by drinking too much, too often, or inappropriately or who experiences symptoms of alcoholism, what should you do? The National Institute on Alcoholism and Alcohol Abuse (NIAAA) suggests the following steps to help someone with an alcohol problem get treatment:

☐ *Stop all "cover ups."* Family members and friends often make excuses to others to hide the fact that their loved one is drinking. If you've been doing this, stop. It is important that the person experience the full consequences of drinking.

☐ *Time your intervention.* The best time to talk to the drinker is shortly after an alcohol-related problem has occurred—such as a serious argument or an accident. Choose a time when he or she is sober, both of you are fairly calm, and you have a chance to talk in private.

☐ *Be specific.* Tell the person that you are worried about his or her drinking. Use examples of the ways in which the drinking has caused problems, including the most recent incident.

☐ *State the results.* Explain to the person what you will do if he or she doesn't go for help—not to punish the drinker but to protect yourself from his or her problems. What you say may range from refusing to go with the person to any social activity where alcohol will be served, to moving out of shared housing. Don't make any threats you are not prepared to carry out.

☐ *Get help.* Gather information in advance about treatment options on your campus or in your community. If the person is willing to get help, call immediately for an appointment. Offer to go with the person on the first visit.

☐ *Call on a friend.* If the person still refuses to get help, ask others to talk with him or her using the steps just described. A friend who is a recovering alcoholic may be particularly persuasive, but any person who is caring and nonjudgmental may help. The intervention of more than one person, more than one time, is often necessary to coax the person to seek help.

☐ *Find strength in numbers.* If the intervention of individual people does not persuade the person to seek help, consider joining together to confront them. This approach should be tried only under the guidance of a healthcare professional who is experienced in this kind of group intervention.

☐ *Get support.* It's important to remember that you are not alone. Support groups offered on many campuses and communities include Al-Anon, which holds regular meetings for adult partners and friends of people with a drinking problem, and Alateen, which is geared to children of alcoholics. These groups help friends and family members understand that they are not responsible for the person's drinking and that they need to take care of themselves, regardless of whether the person chooses to get help.

RECAP Alcohol abuse (also called problem drinking) occurs when a person drinks too much, too often, or inappropriately. Binge-drinking is the consumption of five or more drinks on one occasion. It can cause alcohol poisoning, which can be fatal. Chronic alcohol abuse can result in significant cognitive, emotional, and behavioral deficits and can lead to alcoholism. It can also severely damage the liver and increase the risk for certain cancers. Alcohol consumption, particularly in underage drinkers, is strongly associated with traumatic death.

HEALTHWATCH

Fetal Alcohol Syndrome Is Caused by Maternal Consumption of Alcohol

Alcohol is a known *teratogen* (a substance capable of causing birth defects). When a pregnant woman consumes alcohol, it quickly crosses the placenta into the fetal bloodstream. Since the immature fetal liver cannot effectively metabolize alcohol, it builds up in the fetal blood and tissues, increasing the risk for a variety of birth defects. The effects of maternal alcohol intake are dose-dependent: the more the mother drinks, the greater the potential harm to the fetus.

The term **fetal alcohol spectrum disorders (FASD)** is an umbrella term used to describe the range of complications that can develop when a pregnant woman consumes alcohol.[27] FASD includes fetal alcohol syndrome (FAS), alcohol-related neurodevelopmental disorder (ARND), and alcohol-related birth defects (ARBD). It is estimated that more than 40,000 babies are born each year with some type of FASD, at a cost of up to $6 billion per year.[28]

Fetal alcohol syndrome (FAS) is the most severe form of FASD and is characterized by malformations of the face, limbs, heart, and nervous system (**Figure 8.8**). Newborn and infant death rates are high, and those who survive typically have emotional, behavioral, social, learning, and developmental problems throughout life. FAS is one of the most common causes of mental retardation in the United States and is the only one that is completely preventable.

FAS is usually recognized at birth, due in large part to the characteristic facial features of affected infants. In contrast, **alcohol-related neurodevelopmental disorder (ARND)** is a more subtle consequence of maternal alcohol consumption. ARND results in various developmental and behavioral problems, such as hyperactivity, attention deficit disorder, and impaired learning. **Alcohol-related birth defects (ARBD)** is diagnosed when an infant is born with abnormalities in the heart, kidney, skeletal system, hearing, and/or vision as a result of maternal alcohol consumption. Infants and children with ARND and ARBD do not have the characteristic facial features seen in FAS.[27]

Can pregnant women safely consume small amounts of alcohol? Although some pregnant women do have an occasional alcoholic drink with no apparent ill effects, the fact is there is no amount of alcohol

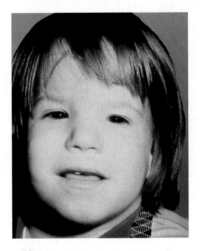

Figure 8.8 The facial features characteristic of children with fetal alcohol syndrome (FAS) include a short nose with a low, wide bridge; drooping eyes with an extra skinfold; and a flat, thin upper lip. Behavioral problems and learning disorders are also characteristic. The effects of FAS are irreversible.

fetal alcohol spectrum disorders (FASD) An umbrella term describing the range of effects that can occur in the child of a woman who drinks during pregnancy. Fetal alcohol syndrome (FAS), alcohol-related neurodevelopmental disorder (ARND), and alcohol-related birth defects (ARBD) are components of FASD.

fetal alcohol syndrome (FAS) A cluster of birth defects in the children of a mother who consumed alcohol during pregnancy, including facial deformities, impaired growth, and a spectrum of mild to severe cognitive, emotional, and physical problems.

NUTRITION
MILESTONE

It's clear from historical records that, for centuries, physicians have recognized that the children born to alcoholic mothers suffer a variety of physical and cognitive defects. However, it wasn't until the late **1960s** that researchers began to study these children. One of the first was a pediatric resident in Seattle, Dr. Christy Ulleland, who in a study of infants diagnosed with "failure to thrive" noted they were all born to alcoholic mothers. Two medical doctors and a psychologist then became involved in Ulleland's research and noticed characteristic physical flaws, and learning and behavioral problems, among the children. Their study results, published in a British medical journal in 1973, brought fetal alcohol syndrome to the attention of the world.

that is known to be safe. The 2010 Dietary Guidelines for Americans specifically state that "women who are pregnant or who may be pregnant" should not drink alcohol. The Guidelines confirm that "no safe level of alcohol consumption during pregnancy has been established."[11]

Breastfeeding women should also be very cautious about their use of alcohol, which rapidly enters breast milk at levels similar to those in the mother's bloodstream. In addition to inhibiting the mother's milk supply, alcohol that passes into breast milk can make the baby sleepy, depress its central nervous system, and, over time, slow the child's motor development. During the initial stages of breastfeeding, when the infant nurses nearly around the clock, alcohol consumption should be completely avoided. When feedings become less frequent, after about 3 months of age, an occasional glass of wine or beer is considered safe, as long as there is sufficient time (approximately 4 hours) before the next feeding. This will allow time for the alcohol to be metabolized by the mother and will lower maternal blood levels, thus limiting alcohol from entering the breast milk.[11] Another option is for the mother to express breast milk before consuming alcohol and save it for a later feeding.

RECAP Alcohol is a known teratogen (substance capable of causing birth defects). Fetal alcohol syndrome is a condition characterized by malformations of the face, limbs, heart, and nervous system in infants born to mothers who abuse alcohol during pregnancy. Alcohol-related neurodevelopmental disorder and alcohol-related birth defects can also occur if a woman drinks during her pregnancy. No amount of alcohol during pregnancy is considered safe.

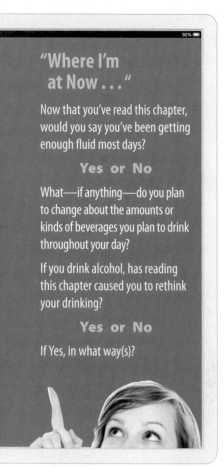

COOKING 101

Keeping your body well-hydrated can be easy and delicious if you know the essentials! Find out how to boost your fluids and treat yourself with soothing teas (hot or cold) by checking out our new Cooking 101 videos, available on the Companion Website at **www.pearsonhighered.com/thompsonmanore**.

alcohol-related neurodevelopmental disorder (ARND) A condition in which children have problems with learning and behavior—leading to poor school performance and difficulties with attention, judgment, and impulse control—as a result of maternal alcohol consumption.

alcohol-related birth defects (ARBD) Heart, kidney, bone, and other defects that develop as a result of maternal consumption of alcohol during pregnancy.

Chapter Review

What Can I Do **Today?**

Now that you've read this chapter, try making these three changes.

- Track your fluid intake. Are you drinking enough to stay optimally hydrated?
- Choose healthful beverages! For one full day, try avoiding all sweetened

drinks and stick to plain water, coffee, tea, 100% fruit juice, nonfat milk, calcium-fortified soy milk, rice milk, almond milk, or orange juice. Then see if you can make it a habit to limit the amount of sweetened drinks you consume on average.

- If you drink alcohol, keep your intake moderate: no more than one standard-size drink for women, and two for men, per day.

Test Yourself ANSWERS

1. **T** Between approximately 50% and 70% of our body weight consists of water.

2. **F** Our thirst mechanism signals that we need to replenish fluids, but it is not sufficient to ensure we are completely hydrated.

3. **F** Persistent vomiting can lead to long-term health consequences and even death.

4. **T** According to the National Institute on Alcohol Abuse and Alcoholism, a part of the National Institutes of Health, alcohol consumption is responsible for more deaths of young people annually than any other factor, in part because of its role in motor vehicle accidents, drownings, and homicides.

5. **T** Carbonated alcoholic beverages, such as champagne, are absorbed more rapidly than noncarbonated varieties of alcohol.

Review Questions

1. Which of the following people probably has the greatest percentage of body fluid?
   a. a female adult who is slightly overweight
   b. a male adult who is obese
   c. an elderly male of average weight
   d. a healthy infant of average weight

2. Plasma is one example of
   a. fluid outside our cells.
   b. fluid inside our cells.
   c. an electrolyte.
   d. metabolic water.

3. Pale urine typically indicates
   a. water intoxication.
   b. kidney failure.
   c. adequate hydration.
   d. dehydration.

4. One gram of alcohol provides
   a. 9 kcal of energy.
   b. 8 kcal of energy.
   c. 7 kcal of energy.
   d. varying amounts of energy, according to the type of drink (beer, wine, or spirits).

5. Excessive alcohol consumption
   a. increases risk for suicide and violent crimes.
   b. is implicated in one-third of all traffic fatalities.
   c. interferes with the absorption of some B-vitamins.
   d. All of the above are true.

6. True or False? Blood volume decreases when the amount of fluid in blood decreases.

7. True or False? A decreased concentration of electrolytes in our blood stimulates the thirst mechanism.

8. True or False? The 2010 Dietary Guidelines for Americans define "moderate" alcohol intake as no more than three drinks per day.

9. True or False? Technically speaking, an 8 oz (1-cup, or 250 ml) glass of wine is one drink.

10. True or False? An individual who chronically abuses alcohol requires larger and larger amounts to experience intoxication.

Answers to Review Questions are located at the back of this text.

Web Links

www.epa.gov
U.S. Environmental Protection Agency (EPA)

www.fda.gov
U.S. Food and Drug Administration (FDA)

www.collegedrinkingprevention.gov
College Drinking: Changing the Culture

www.aa.org
Alcoholics Anonymous, Inc. (AA)

www.al-anon.alateen.org
Al-Anon Family Group Headquarters, Inc.

9
Achieving and Maintaining a Healthful Body Weight

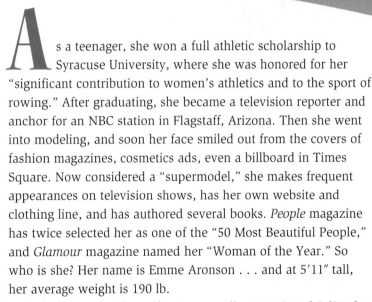

A s a teenager, she won a full athletic scholarship to Syracuse University, where she was honored for her "significant contribution to women's athletics and to the sport of rowing." After graduating, she became a television reporter and anchor for an NBC station in Flagstaff, Arizona. Then she went into modeling, and soon her face smiled out from the covers of fashion magazines, cosmetics ads, even a billboard in Times Square. Now considered a "supermodel," she makes frequent appearances on television shows, has her own website and clothing line, and has authored several books. *People* magazine has twice selected her as one of the "50 Most Beautiful People," and *Glamour* magazine named her "Woman of the Year." So who is she? Her name is Emme Aronson . . . and at 5'11" tall, her average weight is 190 lb.

Emme describes herself as "very well-proportioned." (See her photo on page 253.) She focuses not on maintaining a certain weight but instead on keeping healthy and fit. A cancer survivor, she follows a nutritious diet and works out regularly. Observing that "We live in a society that is based on the attainment of un-realistic beauty," Emme works hard to get out the message that self-esteem should not be contingent on size. On news programs and talk shows, at high schools and on college campuses, she speaks out against weight-based discrimination and promotes acceptance of body diversity.

Are you happy with your weight, shape, body composition, and fitness? If not, what needs to change—your diet, the amount or type of physical

Nutrition Online icons are located throughout the chapter, directing you to web links, videos, podcasts, and other useful online resources.

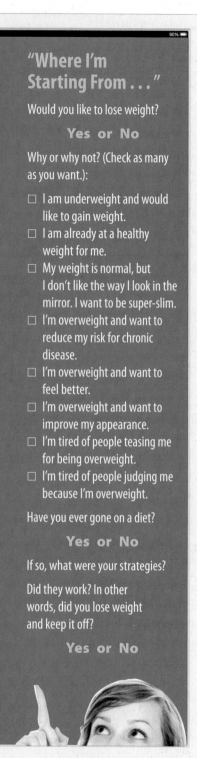

90% 🔋

"Where I'm Starting From . . ."

Would you like to lose weight?

Yes or No

Why or why not? (Check as many as you want.):

☐ I am underweight and would like to gain weight.

☐ I am already at a healthy weight for me.

☐ My weight is normal, but I don't like the way I look in the mirror. I want to be super-slim.

☐ I'm overweight and want to reduce my risk for chronic disease.

☐ I'm overweight and want to feel better.

☐ I'm overweight and want to improve my appearance.

☐ I'm tired of people teasing me for being overweight.

☐ I'm tired of people judging me because I'm overweight.

Have you ever gone on a diet?

Yes or No

If so, what were your strategies?

Did they work? In other words, did you lose weight and keep it off?

Yes or No

body mass index (BMI) A measurement representing the ratio of a person's body weight to his or her height.

underweight Having too little body fat to maintain health, causing a person to have a weight for a given height that is below an acceptably defined standard.

activity you do, or maybe just your attitude? How much control do we have over our body weight? To what extent are our size and shape due to genetics? What influence does society—including food advertising—have? And if you decide that you do need to lose weight, what's the best way to do it? In this chapter, we will explore these questions and provide some answers.

Is Your Body Weight Healthful?

As you begin to think about achieving and maintaining a healthful weight, it's important to make sure you understand what a healthful body weight actually is and the various methods you can use to figure out if your own weight is healthful.

Understand What a Healthful Body Weight Really Is

We can define a healthful weight as all of the following:[2]

- A weight that is appropriate for your age and physical development
- A weight that is based on your genetic background and family history of body shape and weight
- A weight that you can achieve and sustain without severely curtailing your food intake or constantly dieting
- A weight that is compatible with normal blood pressure, lipid levels, and glucose tolerance
- A weight that promotes good eating habits and allows you to participate in regular physical activity
- A weight that is acceptable to you

As you can see, a healthful weight is not one at which a person must be extremely thin or overly muscular. In addition, there is no one body type that can be defined as healthful. Thus, achieving a healthful body weight should not be dictated by the latest fad or current societal expectations of what is acceptable.

Various methods are available to help you determine whether you are currently maintaining a healthful body weight. Let's review a few of these methods.

Determine Your Body Mass Index

Body mass index (BMI) is a commonly used comparison of a person's body weight to his or her height. You can calculate your BMI using the following equation:

$$\text{BMI (kg/m}^2\text{)} = \text{weight (kg)/height (m)}^2$$

For those less familiar with the metric system, there is an equation to calculate BMI using weight in pounds and height in inches:

$$\text{BMI (kg/m}^2\text{)} = [\text{weight (lb)/height (in.)}^2] \times 703$$

A less exact but practical method is to use the graph in **Figure 9.1**, which shows approximate BMI values for your height and weight and whether your BMI is in a healthful range.

Your body mass index provides an important clue to your overall health. Physicians, nutritionists, and other scientists classify BMI accordingly:

> You can also calculate your BMI more precisely on the Internet using the BMI calculator found at www.nhlbisupport.com/bmi/.

- **Underweight** is defined as having too little body fat to maintain health, causing a person to have a weight that is below an acceptably defined standard for a given height. A person having a BMI less than 18.5 kg/m^2 is considered underweight.
- **Normal weight** is defined as having an adequate but not excessive level of body fat for health. It ranges from 18.5 to 24.9 kg/m^2.

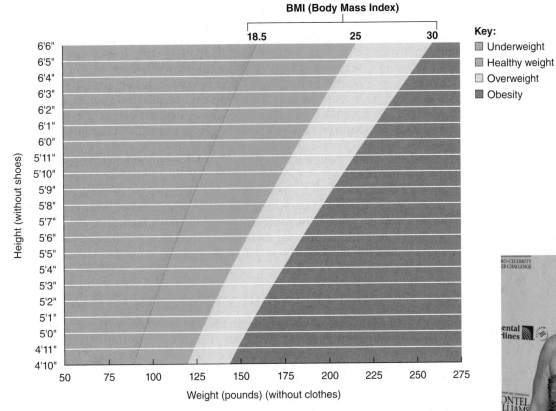

▲ Figure 9.1 Measure your body mass index (BMI) using this graph. To determine your BMI, find the value for your height on the left and follow this line to the right until it intersects with the value for your weight on the bottom axis. The area on the graph where these two points intersect is your BMI.

▲ Fashion model Emme's weight is healthful for her.

- **Overweight** is defined as having a moderate amount of excess body fat, resulting in a person having a weight that is greater than some accepted standard for a given height but is not considered obese. Having a BMI between 25.1 and 29.9 kg/m^2 indicates that a person is overweight.
- **Obesity** is defined as having an excess of body fat that adversely affects health, resulting in a person having a weight that is substantially greater than some accepted standard for a given height. A BMI value between 30 and 39.9 kg/m^2 is consistent with obesity.
- **Morbid obesity** is defined as a BMI greater than or equal to 40 kg/m^2; in this case, the person's body weight exceeds 100% of normal, putting him or her at very high risk for serious health consequences.

Research studies show that a person's risk for type 2 diabetes, high blood pressure, heart disease, and many other diseases increases significantly when BMI is above a value of 30. On the other hand, being underweight and having a very low BMI, below 18.5, are also associated with an increased risk for health problems. In the Healthwatch sections later in this chapter, we discuss obesity issues in more detail, as well as disordered eating, which is commonly a factor in underweight. All of these conditions can cause severe, even life-threatening illness.

Although calculating BMI can be very helpful in estimating disease risk, this method is limited when used with children, teens, and adults over age 65. It is also of limited value for people who have a disproportionately higher muscle mass for a given height. For example, one of Theo's friends, Randy, is a weight lifter. Randy is 5'7" and weighs 200 lb. Using Figure 9.1, you can see that Randy's BMI is over 30, placing him in the high-risk category for many diseases. But is Randy really overweight? To answer that question, an assessment of body composition is necessary.

normal weight Having an adequate but not excessive level of body fat for health.

overweight Having a moderate amount of excess body fat, resulting in a person having a weight for a given height that is greater than an accepted standard but is not considered obese.

obesity Having an excess of body fat that adversely affects health, resulting in a person having a weight for a given height that is substantially greater than an accepted standard.

morbid obesity A condition in which a person's body weight exceeds 100% of normal, putting him or her at very high risk for serious health consequences.

A healthful body weight is one that is appropriate for your age, your physical development, your heredity, and other factors

Measure Your Body Composition

There are many methods available to assess your **body composition,** or the amount of body fat (*adipose tissue*) and lean body mass (*lean tissue*) you have. **Figure 9.2** lists and describes some of the more common methods. It is important to remember that measuring body composition only provides an estimate of your body fat and lean body mass, meaning that you cannot measure your exact level of these tissues. Because the range of error of these methods can be 3% to more than 20%, body composition results should not be used as the only indicator of health status.

Let's return to Randy, whose BMI is over 30. Is he obese? Randy trains with weights 4 days per week, rides an exercise bike for about 30 minutes per session three times per week, and does not take drugs, smoke cigarettes, or drink alcohol. Through his local gym, Randy contacted a technician who assesses body composition. The results of his skinfold measurements show that his body fat is 9%. This value is within the healthful range for men. Randy is an example of a person whose BMI appears to be very high but who is not actually obese.

Assess Your Fat Distribution Pattern

To complete your evaluation of your current body weight, it's important to consider the way fat is distributed throughout your body. This is because your fat distribution pattern is known to affect your risk for various diseases. **Figure 9.3** (page 256) shows two types of fat patterning:

- In *apple-shaped fat patterning,* or upper-body obesity, fat is stored mainly around the waist. Apple-shaped patterning is known to significantly increase a person's risk for many chronic diseases, such as type 2 diabetes, heart disease, and high blood pressure. It is thought that this patterning causes problems with the metabolism of fat and carbohydrate, leading to unhealthful changes in blood cholesterol, insulin, glucose, and blood pressure. Men tend to store fat in the apple-shaped pattern.
- In *pear-shaped fat patterning,* or lower-body obesity, fat is stored mainly around the hips and thighs. This pattern does not seem to significantly increase a person's risk for chronic diseases. Premenopausal women tend to store fat in the pear-shaped pattern; postmenopausal women tend to store fat in the apple-shaped pattern.

You can use the following three-step method to determine your type of fat patterning:

1. Ask a friend to measure the circumference of your natural waist—that is, the narrowest part of your torso as observed from the front (**Figure 9.4a**, page 256).
2. Then have that friend measure your hip circumference at the maximal width of the buttocks as observed from the side (Figure 9.4b).
3. Then divide the waist value by the hip value. This measurement is called your *waist-to-hip ratio.* For example, if your natural waist is 30 inches and your hips are 40 inches, then your waist-to-hip ratio is 30 divided by 40, which equals 0.75.

Once you figure out your ratio, how do you interpret it? An increased risk for chronic disease is associated with the following waist-to-hip ratios:

- In men, a ratio higher than 0.90
- In women, a ratio higher than 0.80

These ratios suggest an apple-shaped fat distribution pattern. In addition, waist circumference alone can indicate your risk for chronic disease. For males, your risk of chronic disease is increased if your waist circumference is above 40 inches (102 cm). For females, your risk is increased at measurements above 35 inches (88 cm).

body composition The ratio of a person's body fat to lean body mass.

Method	Limitations

Underwater weighing:
Considered the most accurate method. Estimates body fat within a 2–3% margin of error. This means that if your underwater weighing test shows you have 20% body fat, this value could be no lower than 17% and no higher than 23%. Used primarily for research purposes.

- Must be comfortable in water.
- Requires trained technician and specialized equipment.
- Does not work well with obese people.
- Must abstain from food for at least 8 hours and from exercise for at least 12 hours prior to testing.

Skinfolds:
Involves "pinching" a person's fold of skin (with its underlying layer of fat) at various locations of the body. The fold is measured using a specially designed caliper. When performed by a skilled technician, it can estimate body fat with an error of 3–4%. This means that if your skinfold test shows you have 20% body fat, your actual value could be as low as 16% or as high as 24%.

- Less accurate unless technician is well trained.
- Proper prediction equation must be used to improve accuracy.
- Person being measured may not want to be touched or to expose their skin.
- Cannot be used to measure obese people, as their skinfolds are too large for the caliper.

Bioelectrical impedance analysis (BIA):
Involves sending a very low level of electrical current through a person's body. As water is a good conductor of electricity and lean body mass is made up of mostly water, the rate at which the electricity is conducted gives an indication of a person's lean body mass and body fat. This method can be done while lying down, with electrodes attached to the feet, hands, and the BIA machine. Hand-held and standing models (which look like bathroom scales) are now available. Under the best of circumstances, BIA can estimate body fat with an error of 3–4%.

- Less accurate.
- Body fluid levels must be normal.
- Proper prediction equation must be used to improve accuracy.
- Should not eat for 4 hours and should not exercise for 12 hours prior to the test.
- No alcohol should be consumed within 48 hours of the test.
- Females should not be measured if they are retaining water due to menstrual cycle changes.

Dual-energy x-ray absorptiometry (DXA):
The technology is based on using very-low-level x-rays to differentiate among bone tissue, soft (or lean) tissue, and fat (or adipose) tissue. It involves lying for about 30 minutes on a specialized bed fully clothed, with all metal objects removed. The margin of error for predicting body fat ranges from 2% to 4%.

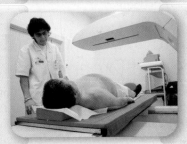

- Expensive; requires trained technician with specialized equipment.
- Cannot be used to measure extremely tall, short, or obese people, as they do not fit properly within the scanning area.

Bod Pod:
A machine that uses air displacement to measure body composition. This machine is a large, egg-shaped chamber made from fiberglass. The person being measured sits inside, wearing a swimsuit. The door is closed and the machine measures how much air is displaced. This value is used to calculate body composition. It appears promising as an easier and equally accurate alternative to underwater weighing in many populations, but it may overestimate body fat in some African-American men.

- Expensive.
- Less accurate in some populations.

Figure 9.2 Overview of various body composition assessment methods.

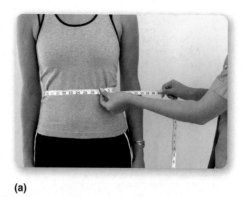 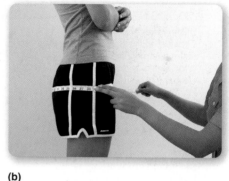

(a) **(b)**

▲ **Figure 9.4** Determining your type of fat patterning. **(a)** Measure the circumference of your natural waist. **(b)** Measure the circumference of your hips at the maximal width of the buttocks as observed from the side. Dividing the waist value by the hip value gives you your waist-to-hip ratio.

RECAP Body mass index, body composition, the waist-to-hip ratio, and waist circumference are tools that can help you evaluate the health impact of your current body weight. None of these methods is completely accurate, but most can be used appropriately as general health indicators.

What Makes Us Gain and Lose Weight?

Have you ever wondered why some people are thin and others are overweight, even though they seem to eat about the same diet? If so, you're not alone. For hundreds of years, researchers have puzzled over what makes us gain and lose weight. In this section, we explore some information and current theories that may shed light on this question.

We Gain or Lose Weight When Our Energy Intake and Expenditure Are Out of Balance

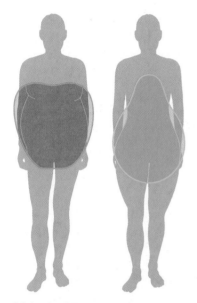

(a) Apple-shaped fat patterning　**(b) Pear-shaped fat patterning**

▲ **Figure 9.3** Fat distribution patterns. **(a)** An apple-shaped fat distribution pattern increases an individual's risk for many chronic diseases. **(b)** A pear-shaped distribution pattern does not seem to be associated with an increased risk for chronic disease.

Fluctuations in body weight are a result of changes in our **energy intake,** or the food we eat, and our **energy expenditure,** or the amount of energy we expend at rest, as a result of eating, and as a result of the physical activity we do. This relationship between what we eat and what we do is defined by the energy balance equation:

Energy balance occurs when energy intake = energy expenditure

This means that our energy is balanced when we consume the same amount of energy that we expend each day. **Figure 9.5** shows how our weight changes when we change either side of this equation. From this figure, you can see that, in order to lose body weight, we must expend more energy than we consume. In contrast, to gain weight, we must consume more energy than we expend. Finding the proper balance between energy intake and expenditure allows us to maintain a healthful body weight.

Energy Intake Is from Foods and Beverages

energy intake The amount of food a person eats; in other words, it is the number of kilocalories consumed.

energy expenditure The energy the body expends to maintain its basic functions and to perform all levels of movement and activity.

Energy intake is the amount of energy in the food and beverages we consume each day. This value includes the carbohydrate, fat, protein, and alcohol that each contains; vitamins, minerals, and water have no energy value, so they contribute zero kilocalories to our energy intake. Our daily energy intake is expressed as *kilocalories per day* (*kcal/day*).

You have several options for determining how much energy you consume. For packaged foods, read the "Calories" line on the Nutrition Facts Panel, and make sure

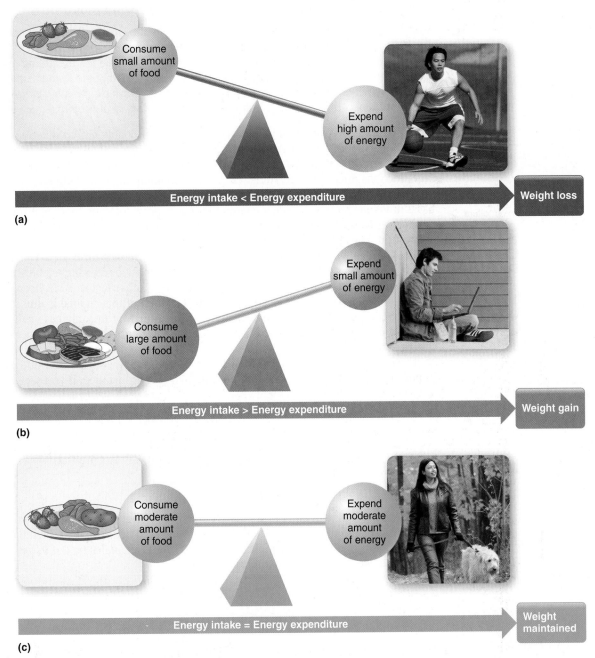

Consume
small amount
of food

Expend
high amount
of energy

Energy intake < Energy expenditure   **Weight loss**

(a)

Expend
small amount
of energy

Consume
large amount
of food

Energy intake > Energy expenditure   **Weight gain**

(b)

Consume
moderate
amount
of food

Expend
moderate
amount
of energy

Energy intake = Energy expenditure   **Weight
maintained**

(c)

🔺 **Figure 9.5** Energy balance is the relationship between the food we eat and the energy we burn each day. **(a)** Weight loss occurs when food intake is less than energy output. **(b)** Weight gain occurs when food intake is greater than energy output. **(c)** We maintain our body weight when food intake equals energy output.

you adjust the value to the serving size you consume. For instance, if a serving is listed as half a cup but you routinely have a full cup, you need to double the value. To locate specific nutrient values for numerous fresh foods, including fruits, vegetables, meats, and many other foods, see the detailed Food Composition Table supplement that accompanies this text.

When our total daily energy intake exceeds the amount of energy we expend, we gain weight. An excess intake of approximately 3,500 kilocalories will result in a gain of 1 lb. Without exercise or other increased physical activity, this gain will likely be fat.

🔺 The energy provided by a bowl of oatmeal is derived from its protein, carbohydrate, and fat content.

Energy Expenditure Includes More Than Just Physical Activity

Energy expenditure (also known as *energy output*) is the energy the body expends to maintain its basic functions and to perform all levels of movement and activity. We can calculate how much energy we expend in a typical 24-hour period by adding together estimates of the energy we use during rest, as a result of eating food, and as a result of physical activity. These three factors are referred to as our *basal metabolic rate (BMR)*, the *thermic effect of food (TEF)*, and the *energy cost of physical activity* **(Figure 9.6)**.

Basal Metabolic Rate Is Energy Output at Rest You probably don't think about it, but your body expends a lot of energy just to maintain your functioning, even while you're sleeping. Your **basal metabolic rate (BMR)** is the energy you expend for *basal*, or *resting*, functions, including breathing, circulation, maintaining body temperature, synthesis of new cells and tissues, secretion of hormones, and nervous system activity. These basal functions require so much energy that the *majority* of your energy output each day (about 60–75%) is a result of your BMR.[3] This means that 60% to 75% of your energy output goes to keeping you alive, aside from any physical activity.

BMR varies widely among people. The primary influence on BMR is the amount of lean body mass: people with a higher lean body mass have a higher BMR, because it takes more energy to support lean tissue. Age is another factor: BMR decreases approximately 3% to 5% per decade after age 30. Much of this change is due to the loss of lean body mass resulting from inactivity. Thus, much of this decrease can be prevented with regular physical activity. Several other factors that can affect a person's BMR are listed in **Table 9.1**.

How can you estimate your BMR? Begin by converting your current body weight in pounds to kilograms, by dividing pounds by 2.2. For instance, if you weigh 175 lb, your weight in kilograms is 79.5:

$$175 \text{ lb}/2.2 = 79.5 \text{ kg}$$

If you're a male, you can assume that your weight in kilograms roughly matches the kilocalories (kcal) you expend per hour: that is, 79.5 kcal per hour. Thus, your BMR for a 24-hour day is

$$79.5 \text{ kcal per hour} \times 24 \text{ hours} = 1,908$$

Females have less lean body mass on average than males, so their BMR is considered about 90% of the BMR for males of the same weight. Thus, if you're a woman who weighs 175 lb, you'll need to multiply the 1,908 BMR for males by 0.9 to get your final value. Here's the full equation for women:

$$175 \text{ lb}/2.2 = 79.5 \text{ kg}$$

$$1,908 \times 0.9 = 1,717 \text{ BMR for women}$$

The Thermic Effect of Food Is the Energy Expended to Process Food The **thermic effect of food** is the energy we expend to digest food and to absorb, transport,

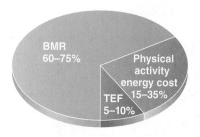

Components of energy expenditure

Figure 9.6 The components of energy expenditure include basal metabolic rate (BMR), the thermic effect of food (TEF), and the energy cost of physical activity. BMR accounts for 60% to 75% of our total energy output, whereas TEF and physical activity together account for 25% to 40%.

basal metabolic rate (BMR) The energy the body expends to maintain its fundamental physiologic functions.

thermic effect of food The energy expended as a result of processing food consumed.

TABLE 9.1	Factors Affecting Basal Metabolic Rate (BMR)	
Factors That Increase BMR	**Factors That Decrease BMR**
Higher lean body mass	Lower lean body mass
Greater height (more surface area)	Lower height
Younger age	Older age
Elevated levels of thyroid hormone	Depressed levels of thyroid hormone
Stress	Starvation or fasting
Male gender	Female gender
Pregnancy and lactation	
Certain drugs, such as stimulants, caffeine, and tobacco	

metabolize, and store the nutrients. The thermic effect of food is equal to about 5% to 10% of the energy content of a meal. Thus, if a meal contains 500 kcal, the thermic effect of processing that meal is about 25 to 50 kcal. Interestingly, our body uses less energy to digest, transport, and store fat and relatively more to process protein and carbohydrate.

The Energy Cost of Physical Activity Is Highly Variable The **energy cost of physical activity** represents about 15% to 35% of our total energy output each day. This is the energy that we expend due to any movement or work above basal levels. This includes low-intensity activities such as sitting, standing, and walking and higher-intensity activities such as running, skiing, and bicycling. One of the most obvious ways to increase how much energy we expend as a result of physical activity is to do more activities for a longer period of time.

> To determine how much energy you consumed in one meal or on 1 day, log on to www.choosemyplate.gov, click on "Analyze My Diet," and enter the foods and beverages into the MyPyramid Tracker (see the box on the right side of the home page).

Table 9.2 lists the energy cost of certain activities. As you can see, activities that involve moving our larger muscle groups (or more parts of the body) require more energy. The amount of energy we expend during activities is also affected by our body size. This is why the kilocalories of energy in the third column of Table 9.2 are expressed per pound of body weight.

TABLE 9.2	**Energy Costs of Various Physical Activities**	
Activity	**Intensity**	**Kilocalories Used per Pound per Hour**
Sitting, quietly watching television	Light	0.48
Sitting, reading	Light	0.62
Sitting, studying (including reading or writing)	Light	0.86
Cooking or food preparation (standing or sitting)	Light	0.95
Walking, shopping	Light	1.09
Walking, 2 mph (slow pace)	Light	1.20
Cleaning (dusting, straightening up, vacuuming, changing linen, carrying out trash)	Moderate	1.20
Stretching—Hatha yoga	Moderate	1.20
Weight lifting (free weights, Nautilus, or universal type)	Light or moderate	1.42
Bicycling <10 mph	Leisure (work or pleasure)	1.90
Walking, 4 mph (brisk pace)	Moderate	2.40
Aerobics	Low impact	2.40
Weight lifting (free weights, Nautilus, or universal type)	Vigorous	2.86
Bicycling 12 to 13.9 mph	Moderate	3.82
Running, 5 mph (12 minutes per mile)	Moderate	3.82
Running, 6 mph (10 minutes per mile)	Moderate	4.77
Running, 8.6 mph (7 minutes per mile)	Vigorous	6.68

From Ainsworth B. E., W. L. Haskell, M. C. Whitt, M. L. Irwin, A. M. Swartz, S. J. Strath, W. L. O'Brien, D. R. Bassett, Jr., K. H. Schmitz, P. O. Emplaincourt, D. R. Jacobs, Jr., and A. S. Leon. 2000. Compendium of physical activities: an update of activity codes and MET intensities. From *Med. & Sci. in Sports & Exer.*, January 2000. Copyright © 2000 by Wolters Kluwer Health. Reprinted with permission.

energy cost of physical activity The energy expended on body movement and muscular work above basal levels.

The energy balance equation is just the beginning of the story, as research is revealing that the same energy intake and energy expenditure might lead to different results in weight loss or gain in different people. Why? Let's look at some genetic and physiologic factors that might contribute to these variations in weight change.

How Many Kilocalories Do You Need?

Given everything we've discussed so far, you're probably asking yourself, How much should I eat? This question is not always easy to answer, as our energy needs fluctuate from day to day according to our activity level, the environmental conditions, and other factors, such as the amount and type of food we eat and our intake of caffeine. So how can you make a general estimate of how many kilocalories your body needs per day?

A simple way to estimate your total daily kilocalorie needs is to multiply your BMR by a varying amount according to how active you are. The following formula is a simplified version of activity factors measured during a 1919 study of basal metabolism, and these factors are still in use today.[4] As with the formula for BMR, these activity factors do not account for wide variations in body composition, such as those that occur in the very old, the very muscular, or the obese. Those who are very muscular typically need more kilocalories than the formula suggests, and the elderly and obese need fewer. The formula is as follows:

- If you do little or no exercise or physical labor, multiply your BMR by 1.2.
- If you participate in moderate exercise or labor three to five times a week, multiply your BMR by 1.5.
- If you participate in intense exercise or labor six to seven times a week, multiply your BMR by 1.75.

For example, let's say that Rashid is a male student who weighs 160 lb. To calculate his BMR, he divides his weight in pounds by 2.2 to determine his weight in kilograms, then multiplies that number by 24 hours:

$$160 \text{ lb}/2.2 = 72.72 \text{ kg} \times 24 = 1{,}745$$

Rashid's BMR is 1,745. He does no regular exercise and spends his waking hours pretty much sitting in classes, studying, watching television, working a part-time job at a computer, driving to and from school, and so forth. Let's see how many kilocalories he needs per day to maintain his current weight and level of activity:

$$\text{BMR of } 1{,}745 \times 1.2 = 2{,}094 \text{ kcal per day}$$

If Rashid wants to lose weight, he needs to increase his level of physical activity or consume fewer than 2,094 kcal a day. Even if he doesn't want to lose weight, Rashid should begin a program of physical activity, at least 30 minutes a day most days of the week, to promote his wellness.

For a more precise estimate of your kilocalorie needs, you can use Table 9.2 to calculate the actual kilocalories you expend in physical activity on any given day. Then add that to your BMR. Precise calculations of energy expenditure are nearly impossible in real life, however. That's because we don't really spend long stretches of time sitting completely still, or performing exactly the same activity at exactly the same pace. For instance, while you were quietly studying for an hour, did you fidget, or get up and stretch, or rush downstairs to answer the door? Despite its limitations, estimating the energy you use during various activities can give you a general sense of the number of kilocalories you expend on an average day and perhaps provide you with an incentive to increase your physical activity.

RECAP The energy balance equation relates food intake to energy expenditure. Eating more energy than you expend causes weight gain, whereas eating less energy than you expend causes weight loss. The three components of this equation are basal metabolic rate, the thermic effect of food, and the energy cost of physical activity. A simple way to estimate daily energy needs is to calculate your BMR and then multiply it by a number reflecting your daily activity level.

↞ Brisk walking is a great way to expend energy.

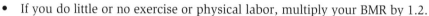

Genetic Factors Affect Body Weight

Our genetic background influences our height, weight, body shape, basal metabolic rate, and other aspects of our physiology (how the body functions). A classic study shows that the body weights of adults who were adopted as children are similar to the weights of their biological parents, not their adoptive parents.[5] **Figure 9.7** shows that about 25% of our body fat is accounted for by genetic influences. Some proposed theories linking genetics with body weight are the thrifty gene theory and the set-point theory.

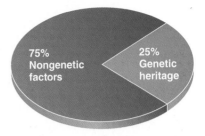

Percent (%) contribution to body fat

◀ **Figure 9.7** Research indicates that about 25% of our body fat is accounted for by our genetic heritage. However, nongenetic factors, such as diet and exercise, play a much larger role.

The Thrifty Gene Theory

The **thrifty gene theory** suggests that some people possess a gene (or genes) that causes them to be energetically thrifty. This means that, both at rest and during activity, these people expend less energy than those who do not possess this gene. The proposed purpose of this gene is to protect a person from starving to death during times of extreme food shortages. This theory has been applied to some Native American tribes, as these societies were exposed to centuries of feast and famine. Those with a thrifty metabolism survived when little food was available, and this trait was passed on to future generations. Although an actual thrifty gene (or genes) has not yet been identified, researchers continue to study this explanation as a potential cause of obesity.

If this theory is true, think about how people who have this thrifty gene might respond to today's environment. Low levels of physical activity, inexpensive food sources that are high in fat and energy, and excessively large serving sizes are the norm in our society. People with a thrifty metabolism would experience more weight gain than those without the gene, and their body would be more resistant to weight loss. Theoretically, having thrifty genetics appears advantageous during times of minimal food resources; however, this state could lead to very high levels of obesity in times of plenty.

The Set-Point Theory

The **set-point theory** suggests that our body is designed to maintain our weight within a narrow range, or at a "set point." In many cases, our body appears to respond in such a way as to maintain our current weight. When we dramatically reduce energy intake (such as with fasting or strict diets), our body responds with physiologic changes that cause our BMR to drop. This causes a significant slowing of our energy output. In addition, being physically active while fasting or strictly dieting is difficult because we just don't have the energy for it. These two mechanisms of energy conservation may contribute to some of the rebound weight gain many dieters experience after they quit dieting.

Conversely, overeating in some people may cause an increase in BMR and is thought to be associated with an increased thermic effect of food, as well as an increase in spontaneous movements, or fidgeting. This in turn increases energy output and prevents weight gain. These changes may explain why some people fail to gain as much weight as might be expected from eating excess food. We don't eat exactly the same amount of food each day; some days we overeat, and other days we eat less. When you think about how much our daily energy intake fluctuates (about 20% above and below our average monthly intake), our ability to maintain a certain weight over long periods of time suggests that there is some evidence to support the set-point theory.

Can we change our set point? It appears that, when we maintain changes in our diet and activity level over a long period of time, weight change does occur. This is obvious in the case of obesity, since many people become obese during middle adulthood, and they are not able to maintain the lower body weight they had as a younger adult. Also, many people do successfully lose weight and maintain that weight loss over long periods of time. Thus, the set-point theory cannot entirely account for our body's resistance to weight loss.

thrifty gene theory A theory that suggests that some people possess a gene (or genes) that causes them to be energetically thrifty, resulting in their expending less energy at rest and during physical activity.

set-point theory A theory that suggests that the body raises or lowers energy expenditure in response to increased and decreased food intake and physical activity. This action maintains an individual's body weight within a narrow range.

RECAP Many factors affect our ability to gain and lose weight. Our genetic background influences our height, weight, body shape, and metabolic rate. The thrifty gene theory suggests that some people possess a thrifty gene, or set of genes, that causes them to expend less energy than people who do not have this gene. The set-point theory suggests that our body is designed to maintain weight within a narrow range.

Physiologic Factors Influence Body Weight

Numerous physiologic factors affect body weight and contribute to the complexities of weight regulation.

Hunger and Satiety

Hunger is an innate, physiologic drive for food triggered by physiologic changes, such as low blood glucose. The part of the brain referred to as the hypothalamus plays an important role in hunger regulation. Special hypothalamic cells referred to as *feeding cells* respond to conditions of low blood glucose, causing hunger and driving a person to eat. Once the food is digested, blood glucose increases. Now, other centers in the hypothalamus are triggered, and the desire to eat is reduced. The state reached in which there is no longer a desire to eat is referred to as *satiety*. It may be that some people have an insufficient satiety mechanism, which prevents them from feeling full after a meal, allowing them to overeat.

Proteins

Leptin is a protein that is produced by adipose cells and functions as a hormone. First discovered in mice, leptin acts to reduce food intake and cause a decrease in body weight and body fat. A gene called the *ob* gene (obesity gene) codes for the production of leptin. Obese mice were found to have a genetic mutation in the *ob* gene. This mutation reduces the ability of adipose cells to synthesize leptin in sufficient amounts; therefore, food intake increases dramatically, energy output is reduced, and weight gain occurs.

When these findings were first published, a great deal of excitement was generated about how leptin might decrease obesity in humans. Unfortunately, studies have shown that, although obese mice respond positively to leptin injections, obese humans do not. Instead, they tend to have very high amounts of leptin in their body and are insensitive to leptin's effects. In truth, we have just begun to learn about leptin and its role in the human body. Researchers are currently studying its role in starvation and overeating, and it appears it might play a role in cardiovascular and kidney complications that result from obesity and related diseases.

In addition to leptin, numerous proteins affect the regulation of appetite and storage of body fat. Primary among these is *ghrelin*, a protein synthesized in the

NUTRITION
MILESTONE

Prior to 1994, very little was known about the physiology of weight control. But in that year, Dr. Jeffrey Friedman, a molecular geneticist at Rockefeller University, published results that advanced our understanding dramatically. Friedman and his research team identified a gene in obese mice and humans that codes for a hormone he later named leptin, after the Greek word *leptos* meaning "thin." They found that leptin regulates food intake and energy expenditure and plays key roles in reproductive and immune function. Mice that do not produce leptin are massively obese, weighing up to three times more than their normal littermates. Dr. Friedman showed that injecting obese mice with leptin causes a substantial increase in physical activity and dramatic weight loss. Friedman subsequently discovered that the majority of obese humans have very high levels of circulating leptin—but are resistant to its effects. Moreover, diet-induced weight loss was found to reduce leptin levels, a fact that may help explain why maintaining weight loss is so difficult. Friedman's research team is now exploring whether or not administering leptin while obese patients are dieting can help them avoid this response.

leptin A hormone produced by body fat that acts to reduce food intake, causing a decrease in body weight and body fat.

stomach. It acts as a hormone and plays an important role in appetite regulation through its actions in the hypothalamus. Ghrelin stimulates appetite and increases food intake. *Peptide YY*, or *PYY*, is a protein produced in the gastrointestinal tract. It is released after a meal, in amounts proportional to the energy content of the meal. In contrast with ghrelin, PYY decreases appetite and inhibits food intake in animals and humans.

Uncoupling proteins have recently become the focus of research into body weight. These proteins are found in the mitochondria of our cells; mitochondria work to generate energy and are found in skeletal muscle cells and adipose cells. Some research suggests that uncoupling proteins uncouple certain steps in the production of energy; when this occurs, the process produces heat instead of energy. This production of heat increases energy expenditure and results in less storage of excess energy. Thus, a person with more uncoupling proteins or a higher activity of these proteins would be more resistant to weight gain and obesity.

One type of uncoupling protein is found exclusively in **brown adipose tissue,** a type of adipose tissue that has more mitochondria than white adipose tissue. It is found in significant amounts in animals and newborn humans. It was traditionally thought that adult humans have very little brown adipose tissue. However, recent evidence suggests that humans may have substantially more brown adipose tissue than previously assumed[6] and that people with higher BMI values have lower amounts of brown adipose tissue.[7] These findings suggest a possible role of brown adipose tissue in obesity. The roles of brown adipose tissue and uncoupling proteins in human obesity are currently being researched.

Other Physiologic Factors

Various other physiologic factors are known to increase satiety (or decrease food intake). These include hormones such as serotonin and cholecystokinin (CCK). Changes that occur after we consume a meal also increase satiety, including an increase in blood glucose levels, stomach expansion, and nutrient absorption from the small intestine.

Factors that can decrease satiety (or increase food intake) include hormones such as beta-endorphins, neuropeptide Y, an amino acid–containing compound produced in the hypothalamus, and decreased blood glucose levels, such as the decrease that occurs after an overnight fast.

Cultural and Economic Factors Affect Food Choices and Body Weight

Both cultural and economic factors can contribute to obesity. Cultural factors (including religious beliefs and learned food preferences) affect our food choices and eating patterns. In addition, the customs of many cultures put food at the center of celebrations of festivals and holidays, and overeating is tacitly encouraged. In addition, because both parents work outside the home in most American families, more people are embracing the "fast-food culture," preferring and almost exclusively choosing highly processed and highly Caloric fast foods from restaurants and grocery stores.

Coinciding with these cultural influences on food intake are cultural factors that promote inactivity. These include the shift from manual labor to more sedentary jobs and increased access to labor-saving devices in all areas of our lives. Even seemingly minor changes—such as texting someone in your dorm instead of walking down the hall to chat or walking through an automated door instead of pushing a door open—add up to a lower expenditure of energy by the end of the day. Research with sedentary ethnic minority women in the United States indicates that other common barriers to increasing physical activity include lack of personal motivation, no physically active role models to emulate, acceptance of larger body size, exercise being considered culturally unacceptable, and fear for personal safety in both rural and urban settings.[8,9] In short, cultural factors influence both food consumption and levels of physical activity and can contribute to weight gain.

Behaviors learned as a child can affect adulthood weight and physical activity patterns.

brown adipose tissue A type of adipose tissue that has more mitochondria than white adipose tissue, and which can increase energy expenditure by uncoupling certain steps in the energy production process. It is found in significant amounts in animals and newborn humans.

NUTRITION MYTH OR FACT?
Does It Cost More to Eat Right?

The shelves of American supermarkets are filled with an abundance of healthful food options: organic meats and produce, exotic fish, out-of-season fresh fruits and vegetables that are flown in from warmer climates, whole-grain breads and cereals, and low-fat and low-sodium options of traditional foods. With all of this choice, it would seem easy for anyone to consume healthful foods throughout the year. But a closer look at the prices of these foods suggests that, for many, they simply are not affordable. This raises the question "Does eating right have to be expensive?"

It is a fact that organic foods are more expensive than non-organic options. However, there is little evidence indicating that organic foods are actually more healthful choices than non-organic foods. In addition, some of the lowest-cost foods currently available in stores are also some of the most nutritious: these include beans, lentils, and other legumes, seasonal fruits, root vegetables (such as potatoes and winter squashes), cooking oils high in mono- and polyunsaturated fats, and frozen as well as canned fruits and vegetables, which are generally just as nutritious as fresh options. Thus, people can still eat healthfully on a tight budget.

Here are some more tips to help you save money when shopping for healthful foods:

- Buy whole grains, such as cereals, brown rice, and pastas in bulk—they store well for longer periods and provide a good base for meals and snacks.
- Buy frozen vegetables on sale and stock up—these are just as healthful as fresh vegetables, require less preparation, and are typically cheaper.

- If lower-sodium options of canned vegetables are too expensive, buy the less expensive regular option and drain the juice from the vegetables before cooking.
- Consume leaner meats and in smaller amounts—by eating less, you'll not only save money but reduce your total intake of energy and fat while still obtaining the nutrients that support good health.
- Choose frozen fish or canned salmon or tuna packed in water as an alternative to fresh fish.
- Avoid frozen or dehydrated prepared meals. They are usually expensive; high in sodium, saturated fats, and energy; and low in fiber and other important nutrients.
- Buy generic or store brands of foods—be careful to check the labels to ensure that the foods are similar in nutrient value to the higher-priced options.
- Cut coupons from local newspapers and magazines, and watch the sale circulars, so that you can stock up on healthful foods you can store.
- Consider cooking more meals at home; you'll have more control over what goes into your meals and you'll be able to cook larger amounts and freeze leftovers for future meals.

As you can see, eating healthfully does not have to be expensive. However, it helps to become a savvy consumer by reading food labels, comparing prices, and gaining the skills and confidence to cook at home. The information shared throughout this text should help you acquire these skills, so that you can eat healthfully even on a limited budget!

Economic status is related to health status, particularly in developed countries such as the United States: people of lower economic status have higher rates of obesity and related chronic diseases than people with higher incomes.[10] In addition to the impact of one's income on access to healthcare, economic factors strongly impact our food choices and eating behaviors. It is a common belief that healthful foods are expensive and that only wealthy people can afford to purchase them. While it is true that certain foods considered more healthful, such as organic foods, imported fruits and vegetables, many fish, and leaner selections of some meats, can be costly, does healthful eating always have to be expensive? Refer to the **Nutrition Myth or Fact?** feature box (shown above) to learn more about whether a healthful diet can also be an affordable one.

Psychological and Social Factors Influence Behavior and Body Weight

Appetite is considered a psychological drive to eat, being stimulated by learned preferences for food and particular situations that promote eating. Thus, appetite can be experienced in the absence of hunger. People may also follow social cues related to the timing and size of meals. Mood can also affect appetite, as some people will eat more or less if they feel depressed or happy. As you can imagine, appetite leads many people to overeat.

Some Social Factors Promote Overeating

Social factors can encourage us to overeat or to choose high-Calorie foods. For example, experiencing pressure from family members to eat the way they do, choosing the same foods and the same cooking methods, or being told as a child to "clean your plate" can be a significant barrier to weight loss. Family parties, company picnics, a barbecue with friends, and other social occasions can also provide excuses to overeat. Do you eat differently when you attend a Super Bowl party? It's often hard to resist nachos, burgers, hot dogs, pizza, and many other foods that taste great but are relatively high in fat and energy. The pressure to overeat on such occasions is high.

▲ Fast foods may be inexpensive and filling, but most are high in saturated fat, salt, and sugar.

We also have numerous opportunities to overeat because of easy access to foods high in fat and energy throughout our normal daily routine. For instance, how many fast-food venues are on your college campus? How many vending machines do you pass every day?

Furthermore, it probably hasn't escaped you that food manufacturers are producing products in ever-larger serving sizes. For instance, in 2005, the Mars candy company introduced a supersize version of M&M's candy, with each piece about 55% larger than the standard-size M&M's. Other supersize examples include the Monster Thickburger from Hardee's restaurant, the Full House XL pizza from Pizza Hut, and the extra large Slurpee from 7-Eleven.[11] Serving sizes have become so large that many Americans are suffering from "portion distortion" **(Figure 9.8)**.

> To test your understanding of a serving size, take the "Portion Distortion" interactive quiz from the National Institutes of Health at http://hp2010.nhlbihin.net/portion.

Even foods we have traditionally considered healthful, such as peanut butter, yogurt, and milk, are often filled with added sugars and other ingredients that are high in energy. For instance, one national brand of yogurt packs 20 grams of sugar—that's 5 teaspoons—into a small (4.5 oz) serving.

The more often we eat out, the less control we have over the energy and nutrient content of our meals. This makes it easy to overeat. A report from the National Restaurant Association states that the typical American individual buys a snack or meal away from home an average of almost six times per week, and annual spending on food away from home is $1,078 per person.[12] College students may go for weeks without eating a single home-cooked meal. Although typically inexpensive, the meals served at many of the diners, fast-food restaurants, and cafeterias favored by students offer large serving sizes high in Calories, saturated and *trans* fats, and simple sugars and low in fiber-rich carbohydrates and omega fatty acids. As a result, in 2011 the FDA proposed regulations that would require the posting of Calorie information for menu items in any restaurant chain with 20 or more locations and for foods in vending machines.[13] If these proposed regulations are approved, this change could take effect by 2012. Whether or not you know the precise Calorie count for restaurant items, you can eat out healthfully—if you're smart about it! The *Game Plan* box (page 266) identifies some tactics for eating smart when eating out.

Some Social Factors Promote Inactivity

Social factors can also cause people to be less physically active. For instance, we don't even have to spend time or energy preparing food anymore, as everything either is ready to serve or requires just a few minutes to cook in a microwave oven. Other social factors restricting physical activity include living in an unsafe community, watching a lot

20 Years Ago

Today

8 fluid ounces, 42 Calories

16 fluid ounces, 350 Calories

▲ **Figure 9.8** A cup of coffee has increased from 8 fl. oz to 16 fl. oz over the past 20 years and now commonly contains Calorie-dense flavored syrup as well as steamed whole milk.

90%

GAME PLAN
Tactics for Eating Smart When Eating Out

During the past 20 years, there has been phenomenal growth in the restaurant industry, particularly in the fast-food market. During this period, rates of obesity increased dramatically. The lunches in Figure 9.9 are both from popular fast-food restaurants, McDonald's and Subway. The lunch on the left, a Big Mac hamburger with extra-large french fries and an apple pie, provides 1,429 Calories and contains 47% of its total energy as fat. In contrast, the Subway meal of one 6" cold-cut trio sandwich, a granola bar with chocolate chips, and a medium apple provides 610 Calories and contains 31% of its total energy as fat.

The energy provided by the McDonald's lunch is enough to support an entire day's needs for a small, sedentary woman! Similar meals at other fast-food restaurants are also high in Calories, total fat, and sodium. This example makes it easier to see how a person can become overweight or obese consuming meals like this on a regular basis. The lesson? Seemingly small choices, such as what type of fast food to choose for lunch, can make a big difference to your waistline.

Does this mean that eating out—especially fast food—cannot be a part of a healthful diet? Not if you make smart choices.

Try these tactics the next time you eat out:

☐ Avoid all-you-can-eat buffet-style restaurants.

☐ Choose lower-fat versions of your favorite meals. Even fast-food restaurants typically offer "lite" or lower-fat menu items.

☐ Order a healthful appetizer as your entreé.

☐ If a child-size portion is available for your menu choice, order it.

☐ Share your meal with a friend. Many restaurant meals are large enough for two people.

☐ Order any meat item grilled or broiled. Avoid fried foods.

☐ Instead of a hamburger, choose a chicken burger, fish burger, or veggie burger.

☐ Order a meatless dish filled with vegetables and whole grains. Avoid dishes with cream sauces or a lot of cheese.

☐ Order broth-based soups instead of cream-based soups.

☐ Instead of french fries, order a salad and choose low-fat or nonfat dressing.

☐ Order beverages with few or no Calories, such as water, tea, or diet drinks, or order skim milk. Also request skim milk in lattés, cappuccinos, and other coffee drinks. Beware of milkshakes! A McDonald's chocolate milkshake comes in at 422 Calories!

☐ Also watch out for "yogurt parfaits" now offered at several fast-food restaurants. Many are loaded with saturated fat, simple sugars, and Calories.

☐ Skip dessert or share one dessert with a lot of friends! Another healthful alternative is to order fresh fruit for dessert.

☐ Don't feel you have to eat everything you are served. If you're full, stop!

About 1,430 Calories (kcal)	About 610 Calories (kcal)

McDonald's Big Mac hamburger
French fries, extra large
3 tbsp. ketchup
Apple pie

Subway cold-cut trio 6"sandwich
Granola bar, hard, with
    chocolate chips, 1 bar (24 g)
1 fresh medium apple

⬆ **Figure 9.9** The energy density of two fast-food meals. The meal on the left is higher in total Calories and fat; the one on the right is the preferred choice for someone trying to lose weight.

of television, living in an area with harsh weather conditions, and coping with family, community, and work responsibilities that do not involve physical activity. Many overweight people identify such factors as major barriers to maintaining a healthful body weight, and research seems to confirm their influence.

Certainly, social factors are contributing to decreased physical activity among children. There was a time when children played outdoors regularly and physical education was offered daily in school. Today, many children cannot play outdoors due to safety concerns and lack of recreational facilities, and few schools have the resources to offer regular physical education to children.

Another social factor promoting inactivity in both children and adults is the increasing dominance of technology in our choices of entertainment. Instead of participating in sports or gathering for a dance at the community hall, we go to the movies or stay at home watching television, surfing the Internet, and playing with video games and other hand-held devices. By reducing energy expenditure, these behaviors contribute to weight gain. For instance, a study of 11- to 13-year-old schoolchildren found that children who watched more than 2 hours of television per night were more likely to be overweight or obese than children who watched less than 2 hours per night. Similarly, adults who reported an increase in television watching of 20 hours per week (approximately 3 hours per day) over a 9-year period had a significant increase in waist circumference, indicating significant weight gain.[14]

Social Pressures Can Promote Underweight

On the other hand, social pressures to maintain a lean body are great enough to encourage some people to undereat, or to avoid foods they perceive as "bad," especially fats. Our society ridicules, and often ostracizes, overweight people, many of whom face discrimination in many areas of their lives, including employment. A recent study found that children who are obese are 60% more likely to experience bullying than children of normal weight.[15] Moreover, media images of waiflike fashion models and men in tight jeans with muscular chests and abdomens encourage many people—especially adolescents and young adults—to skip meals, resort to crash diets, and exercise obsessively. Even some people of normal body weight push themselves to achieve an unrealistic and unattainable weight goal, in the process threatening their health and even their lives (see the Healthwatch section later in this chapter for the consequences of disordered eating). It should be clear that how a person gains, loses, and maintains body weight is a complex matter. Most people who are overweight have tried several weight-loss programs but have been unsuccessful in maintaining long-term weight loss. A significant number of these people have consequently given up all weight-loss attempts. Some even suffer from severe depression related to their body weight. Should we condemn these people as failures and continue to pressure them to lose weight? Should people who are overweight but otherwise healthy (for example, having low blood pressure, cholesterol, triglycerides, and glucose levels) be advised to lose weight? As we continue to search for ways to help people achieve and maintain a healthful body weight, our society must take measures to reduce the social pressures facing people who are overweight or obese.

RECAP Physiologic factors, such as hunger, leptin, ghrelin, peptide YY, uncoupling proteins, and various hormones, impact body weight by their effects on satiety, appetite, and energy expenditure. Cultural and economic factors can significantly influence the amounts and types of food we eat. Psychological and social factors influencing weight include the ready availability of large portions of high-energy foods and a lack of physical activity. Social pressures against people who are overweight can drive them to use harmful methods to achieve an unrealistic body weight.

How Can You Achieve and Maintain a Healthful Body Weight?

Now that you understand what constitutes a healthful body weight, how are you feeling about yours? You might decide that you'd like to lose weight, but are you really committed to making the changes required? To find out, check out the **What About You?** box. If your results suggest that you are, then take heart. Losing weight and maintaining that loss are goals well within your reach using three primary strategies:

- Gradual reduction in energy intake
- Incorporation of regular and appropriate physical activity
- Application of behavior modification techniques

In this section, we first discuss popular diet plans, which may or may not incorporate these strategies. We then explain how to design a personalized weight-loss program that includes all three of them.

If You Decide to Follow a Popular Diet Plan, Choose One Based on the Three Strategies

If you'd like to lose weight, the information ahead will help you design your own personalized diet plan. If you'd feel more comfortable following an established plan, however, many are available. How can you know whether or not it is based on sound dietary principles, and whether its promise of long-term weight loss will prove true for *you*? Look to the three strategies just identified: Does the plan promote gradual reductions in energy intake? Does it advocate increased physical activity? Does it include strategies for modifying your eating and activity-related behaviors? Reputable diet plans incorporate all of these strategies. Unfortunately, many dieters are drawn to fad diets, which do not.

Avoid Fad Diets

Beware of fad diets! They are simply what their name implies—fads that do not result in long-term, healthful weight changes. To be precise, fad diets are programs that enjoy short-term popularity and are sold based on a marketing gimmick that appeals to the public's desires and fears. Of the hundreds of such diets on the market today, most will "die" within a year, only to be born again as a "new and improved" fad diet. The goal of the person or company designing and marketing a fad diet is to make money.

How can you tell if the program you are interested in qualifies as a fad diet? Check out the **Highlight** feature box on fad diets (page 272) for some telltale signs.

Diets Focusing on Macronutrient Composition May or May Not Work for You

It is well recognized that achieving a negative energy balance is the major factor in successful weight loss. The impact of the macronutrient composition of a diet is currently a topic of considerable debate. The three main types of weight-loss diets that

WHAT ABOUT YOU?
Are You Really Ready to Lose Weight?

How well do your attitudes equip you for a weight-loss program? For each question, circle the answer that best describes your attitude. As you complete sections 2–5, tally your score and analyze it according to the scoring guide.

1 Diet history

A. How many times in the last year have you been on a diet?

0 times	1–3 times	4–10 times	11–20 times	More than 20 times

B. What is the most weight you lost on any of these diets?

0 lb	1–5 lb	6–10 lb	11–20 lb	More than 20 lb

C. How long did you stay at the new lower weight?

Less than 1 mo	2–3 mo	4–6 mo	6–12 mo	Over 1 yr

D. Why do you think you started to regain the weight?

E. Put a check mark by each dieting method you have tried:

_____ skipping breakfast
_____ skipping lunch or dinner
_____ taking over-the-counter appetite suppressants
_____ counting calories
_____ cutting out most fats
_____ cutting out most carbohydrates
_____ increasing regular exercise
_____ taking weight-loss supplements
_____ cutting out all snacks
_____ using meal replacements, such as Slim Fast
_____ taking prescription appetite suppressants
_____ taking laxatives
_____ inducing vomiting
_____ other _____

2 Readiness to start a weight-loss program

If you are thinking about starting a weight-loss program, answer questions A–F.

A. How motivated are you to lose weight?

1	2	3	4	5
Not at all motivated	Slightly motivated	Somewhat motivated	Quite motivated	Extremely motivated

B. How certain are you that you will stay committed to a weight-loss program long enough to reach your goal?

1	2	3	4	5
Not at all certain	Slightly certain	Somewhat certain	Quite certain	Extremely certain

C. Taking into account other stresses in your life (school, work, and relationships), to what extent can you tolerate the effort required to stick to your diet plan?

1	2	3	4	5
Cannot commit	Can commit somewhat	Uncertain	Can commit well	Can commit easily

D. Assuming you should lose no more than 1 to 2 pounds per week, have you allotted a realistic amount of time for weight loss?

1	2	3	4	5
Very unrealistic	Somewhat unrealistic	Moderately unrealistic	Somewhat realistic	Very realistic

E. While dieting, do you fantasize about eating your favorite foods?

1	2	3	4	5
Always	Frequently	Occasionally	Rarely	Never

F. While dieting, do you feel deprived, angry, upset?

1	2	3	4	5
Always	Frequently	Occasionally	Rarely	Never

Total your scores from questions A–F and circle your score category.

6 to 16: This may not be a good time for you to start a diet. Inadequate motivation and commitment and unrealistic goals could block your progress. Think about what contributes to your lack of readiness. What are some of the reasons you aren't prepared to make a meaningful change? Consider changing these factors before undertaking a diet.

17 to 23: You may be nearly ready to begin a program but should think about ways to boost your readiness.

24 to 30: The path is clear—you can decide how to lose weight in a safe, effective way.

(Continued)

(Continued)

3 Hunger, appetite, and eating

Think about your hunger and the cues that stimulate your appetite or eating, and then answer questions A–C.

A. When food comes up in conversation or in something you read, do you want to eat, even if you are not hungry?

1	2	3	4	5
Never	Rarely	Occasionally	Frequently	Always

B. How often do you eat for a reason other than physical hunger?

1	2	3	4	5
Never	Rarely	Occasionally	Frequently	Always

C. When your favorite foods are in the house, do you succumb to eating them between meals?

1	2	3	4	5
Never	Rarely	Occasionally	Frequently	Always

Total your scores from questions A–C and circle your score category.

3 to 6: You might occasionally eat more than you should, but it is due more to your own attitudes than to temptation and other environmental cues. Controlling your own attitudes toward hunger and eating may help you.

7 to 9: You may have a moderate tendency to eat just because food is available. Losing weight may be easier for you if you try to resist external cues and eat only when you are physically hungry.

10 to 15: Some or much of your eating may be in response to thinking about food or exposing yourself to temptations to eat. Think of ways to minimize your exposure to temptations, so that you eat only in response to physical hunger.

4 Controlling overeating

How good are you at controlling overeating when you are on a diet? Answer questions A–C.

A. A friend talks you into going out to a restaurant for a midday meal instead of eating a brown-bag lunch. As a result, you would

1	2	3	4	5
Eat much less	Eat somewhat less	Eat no differently	Eat somewhat more	Eat much more

B. You "break" your diet by eating a fattening, "forbidden" food. As a result, for the day, you would

1	2	3	4	5
Eat much less	Eat somewhat less	Eat no differently	Eat somewhat more	Eat much more

C. You have been following your diet faithfully and decide to test yourself by taking a bite of something you consider a treat. As a result, for the day, you would

1	2	3	4	5
Eat much less	Eat somewhat less	Eat no differently	Eat somewhat more	Eat much more

Total your scores from questions A–C and circle your score category.

3 to 7: You recover rapidly from mistakes. However, if you frequently alternate between out-of-control eating and very strict dieting, you may have a serious eating problem and should get professional help.

8 to 11: You do not seem to let unplanned eating disrupt your program. This is a flexible, balanced approach.

12 to 15: You may be prone to overeating after an event breaks your control or throws you off track. Your reaction to these problem-causing events could use improvement.

5 Emotional eating

Consider the effects of your emotions on your eating behaviors, and answer questions A–C.

A. Do you eat more than you would like to when you have negative feelings, such as anxiety, depression, anger, or loneliness?

1	2	3	4	5
Never	Rarely	Occasionally	Frequently	Always

B. Do you have trouble controlling your eating when you have positive feelings (for instance, do you celebrate feeling good by eating)?

1	2	3	4	5
Never	Rarely	Occasionally	Frequently	Always

C. When you have unpleasant interactions with others in your life or after a difficult day at work, do you eat more than you'd like?

1	2	3	4	5
Never	Rarely	Occasionally	Frequently	Always

Total your scores from questions A–C and circle your score category.

3 to 8: You do not appear to let your emotions affect your eating.

9 to 11: You sometimes eat in response to emotional highs and lows. Monitor this behavior to learn when and why it occurs, and be prepared to find alternative activities to respond to your emotions.

12 to 15: Emotional ups and downs can stimulate your eating. Try to deal with the feelings that trigger the eating and find other ways to express them.

6 Exercise patterns and attitudes

Exercise is key for weight loss. Think about your attitudes toward it, and answer questions A–D.

A. How often do you exercise?

1	2	3	4	5
Never	Rarely	Occasionally	Somewhat frequently	Frequently

B. How confident are you that you can exercise regularly?

1	2	3	4	5
Not at all confident	Slightly confident	Somewhat confident	Highly confident	Completely confident

C. When you think about exercise, do you develop a positive or a negative picture in your mind?

1	2	3	4	5
Completely negative	Somewhat negative	Neutral	Somewhat positive	Completely positive

D. How certain are you that you can work regular exercise into your daily schedule?

1	2	3	4	5
Not at all certain	Slightly certain	Somewhat certain	Quite certain	Extremely certain

Total your scores from questions A–D and circle your score category.

4 to 10: You're probably not exercising as regularly as you should. Determine whether it is your attitude about exercise or your lifestyle that is blocking your way; then change what you must and put on those walking shoes!

11 to 16: You need to feel more positive about exercise, so that you can do it more often. Think of ways to be more active that are fun and fit your lifestyle.

17 to 20: The path is clear for you to be active. Now think of ways to get motivated.

From "When and How to Diet," by Kelly D. Bronwell, *Psychology Today* (June 1989). Copyright © 1989 by Sussex Publishers, Inc, Reprinted by permission.

have been most seriously and comprehensively researched all encourage increased consumption of certain macronutrients and restrict the consumption of others. Provided here is a brief review of these three main types and their general effects on weight loss and health parameters.[17]

Diets High in Carbohydrate and Moderate in Fat and Protein   Balanced high-carbohydrate, moderate-fat and -protein diets typically contain 55–60% of total energy intake as carbohydrate, 20–30% of total energy intake as fat, and 15–20% of energy intake as protein. These diets include Weight Watchers, Jenny Craig, and others that follow the general guidelines of the DASH Diet and the USDA Food Guide. All of these diet plans emphasize that weight loss occurs when energy intake is lower than energy expenditure. The goal is gradual weight loss, or about 1 to 2 lb of body weight per week. Typical suggested energy deficits are between 500 and 1,000 kcal per day. It is recommended that women eat no less than 1,000 to 1,200 kcal per day and that men consume no less than 1,200 to 1,400 kcal per day. Regular physical activity is encouraged.

To date, these types of low-energy diets have been researched more than any others. A substantial amount of high-quality scientific evidence (from randomized, controlled trials) indicates that they are effective in decreasing body weight. In addition, the people who lose weight on these diets also decrease their LDL-cholesterol and triglyceride levels and decrease their blood pressure. The diets are nutritionally adequate if the individual's food choices follow the USDA Food Patterns. If the individual's food choices are not varied and balanced, the diets may be low in nutrients such as fiber, zinc, calcium, iron, and vitamin B_{12}. Under these circumstances, supplementation is needed.

Diets Low in Carbohydrate and High in Fat and Protein   Low-carbohydrate, high-fat and -protein diets cycle in and out of popularity on a regular basis. By definition, these types of diets generally contain less than 100 grams of carbohydrate per day, about 55–65% of total energy intake as fat, and the balance of daily energy intake as protein. Examples of these types of diets include Dr. Atkins' Diet Revolution, the Carbohydrate Addict's Diet, Life Without Bread, Sugar Busters, and Protein Power. These diets minimize the role of restricting total energy intake on weight loss. They instead advise participants to restrict carbohydrate intake, proposing that carbohydrates are addictive and that they cause significant overeating, insulin surges leading to excessive fat storage, and an overall metabolic imbalance that leads to obesity. The goal is to reduce carbohydrates enough to cause ketosis, which decreases blood glucose and insulin levels and can reduce appetite.

"Low-carb" diets may lead to weight loss but are nutritionally inadequate and can have negative side effects.

HIGHLIGHT
The Anatomy of Fad Diets

Fad diets are weight-loss programs that enjoy short-term popularity and are sold based on a marketing gimmick that appeals to the public's desires and fears. In addition, the goal of the person or company designing and marketing the diet is not to improve public health but to make money. How can you tell if the program you are interested in is a fad diet? Here are some telltale signs:

- The promoters of the diet claim that the program is new, improved, or based on some new discovery; however, no scientific data are available to support these claims.

- The program is touted for its ability to result in rapid weight loss or body-fat loss, usually more than 2 lb per week, and may claim that weight loss can be achieved with little or no physical exercise.

- The diet includes special foods and supplements, many of which are expensive and/or difficult to find or can be purchased only from the diet promoter. Common recommendations for these diets include avoiding certain foods, eating only a special combination of certain foods, and including magic foods in the diet that "burn" fat and speed up metabolism.

- The diet includes a rigid menu that must be followed daily or allows only a few, select foods each day.

Alternatively, the diet focuses on one macronutrient group (such as protein) and severely restricts the others (such as carbohydrate and fat). Variety and balance are discouraged, and certain foods (such as all dairy products or all foods made with refined flour) are entirely forbidden.

- Many fad diets identify certain foods and/or supplements as critical to the success of the diet and usually claim that these substances can cure or prevent a variety of health ailments or that the diet can stop the aging process.

It is estimated that we currently spend more than $33 billion on fad diets each year.[16] The success of fad diets typically lies in the ability of diet promoters to persuade people that they can lose weight quickly with no significant change in their lifestyle. Fad diets also tend to appeal to goals many people share, such as becoming more attractive or stronger, reducing the effects of aging (such as wrinkles and loose skin), and enjoying better health. In a world where many people feel they have to meet a certain physical standard to be valued, these types of diets flourish. Unfortunately, the only people who usually benefit from them are their marketers, who can become very wealthy promoting programs that are highly ineffectual.

The current, limited evidence suggests that individuals in both free-living and experimental conditions do lose weight with these diets. In addition, it appears that people who lose weight may also experience positive metabolic changes, such as decreased blood lipid levels, decreased blood pressure, and decreased blood glucose and insulin. However, the amount of weight loss and improvements in metabolic health measured with these diets are no greater than those seen with higher-carbohydrate diets. Also, our current, limited research into long-term compliance, potential health risks, and side effects has made these diets controversial. (Refer to Chapter 5, page 144, Highlight box on high-protein diets.)

Low-fat and very-low-fat diets emphasize eating foods higher in complex carbohydrates and fiber.

Low-Fat and Very-Low-Fat Diets Low-fat diets contain 11–19% of total energy as fat, whereas very-low-fat diets contain less than 10% of total energy as fat. Both of these types of diets are high in carbohydrate and moderate in protein. Examples include Dr. Dean Ornish's Program for Reversing Heart Disease and the New Pritikin Program. These diets do not focus on total energy intake but emphasize eating foods higher in complex carbohydrates and fiber. Consumption of sugar and white flour is very limited. The Ornish diet is vegetarian, whereas the Pritikin diet allows 3.5 oz of lean meat per day. Regular physical activity is a key component of these diets.

These programs were not originally designed for weight loss but, rather, were developed to decrease or reverse heart disease. Also, these diets are not popular with consumers, who view them as too restrictive and difficult to follow. Thus, there are limited data on their effects. However, high-quality evidence suggests that people following these diets do lose weight, and some data suggest that these diets may also decrease blood pressure and blood levels of LDL-cholesterol, triglycerides, glucose, and insulin. Few side effects have been reported on these diets; the most common is flatus, which typically decreases over time. Low-fat diets are low in vitamin B_{12}, and very-low-fat diets are low in essential fatty acids, vitamins B$_{12}$ and E, and zinc. Thus, supplementation is needed. These types of diets are not considered safe for people with diabetes who are insulin dependent (either type 1 or type 2) or for people with carbohydrate-malabsorption illnesses.

If You Decide to Design Your Own Diet Plan, Include the Three Strategies

As we noted earlier, a healthful and effective weight-loss plan involves a modest reduction in energy intake, incorporating physical activity into each day, and practicing changes in behavior that can help you reduce your energy intake and increase your energy expenditure. To further assist you, guidelines for a sound weight-loss plan are identified in the *Game Plan* box (pages 274–275). Following are some guidelines for designing your own personalized diet plan that incorporates these strategies.

Set Realistic Goals

The first key to safe and effective weight loss is setting realistic goals related to how much weight to lose and how quickly (or slowly) to lose it. Although making gradual changes in body weight is frustrating for most people, this slower change is much more effective in maintaining weight loss over the long term. Ask yourself the question "How long did it take me to gain this extra weight?" If you are like most people, your answer is that it took 1 or more years, not just a few months. A fair expectation for weight loss is similarly gradual: experts recommend a pace of about 0.5 to 2 pounds per week. A weight-loss plan should never provide less than a total of 1,200 kcal per day unless you are under a physician's supervision. Your weight-loss goals should also take into consideration any health-related concerns you have. After checking with your physician, you may decide initially to set a goal of simply maintaining your current weight and preventing additional weight gain. After your weight has remained stable for several weeks, you might then write down realistic goals for weight loss.

Goals that are more likely to be realistic and achievable share the following characteristics:

- *They are specific.* Telling yourself "I will eat less this week" is not helpful because the goal is not specific. An example of a specific goal is "I will eat only half of my restaurant entrée tonight and take the rest home and eat it tomorrow for lunch."
- *They are reasonable.* If you are not presently physically active, it would be unreasonable to set of a goal of exercising for 30 minutes every day. A more reasonable goal would be to exercise for 15 minutes per day, 3 days per week. Once you've achieved that goal, you can increase the frequency, intensity, and time of exercise according to the improvements in fitness that you have experienced.
- *They are measurable.* Effective goals are ones you can measure. An example is "I will lose at least half a pound by May 1st" or "I will substitute drinking water for my regular soft drink at lunch each day this week." Recording your specific, measurable goals will help you better determine whether you are achieving them.

By monitoring your progress regularly, you can determine whether you are meeting your goals or whether you need to revise them based on accomplishments or challenges that arise.

Eat Smaller Portions of Lower-Fat Foods

Two of the biggest weight-loss challenges are understanding what a healthful portion size is and then reducing the portion sizes of the foods and beverages we consume. Recent studies indicate that, when children and adults are presented with large portion sizes of foods and beverages, they eat more energy overall and do not respond to cues of fullness.[19,20] Thus, it has been suggested that effective weight-loss strategies include reducing both the portion size and the energy density of foods consumed and replacing energy-dense beverages with low-Calorie or non-Calorie beverages.[20]

GAME PLAN

Steps Toward Sustained Weight Loss

Now that you know how to spot a fad diet, you may be wondering what makes a weight-loss plan sound. That is, what should you do to lose weight and keep it off while staying well nourished and healthy? An expert panel from the National Institutes of Health recommends the following steps toward weight loss that lasts.[18]

Dietary Recommendations

☐ Aim for a weight loss of 0.5 to 2 lb per week. Remember that 1 lb of fat is equal to about 3,500 kilocalories.

☐ To achieve this rate of weight loss, reduce your current energy intake by approximately 250 to 1,000 kilocalories a day. A weight-loss plan should never provide less than a total of 1,200 kilocalories a day.

☐ Aim for a total fat intake of 15% to 25% of total energy intake, and choose unsaturated rather than saturated or *trans* fats.

☐ Limit your intake of simple sugars.

☐ Consume 25 to 35 grams of fiber a day.

☐ Consume 1,000 to 1,500 mg of calcium a day.

☐ Select leaner cuts of meat (such as the white meat of poultry and extra-lean ground beef) and reduced-fat or skim dairy products.

☐ Select lower-fat food-preparation methods (baking, broiling, and grilling instead of frying).

☐ Save high-fat, high-Calorie snack foods for occasional special treats.

Steps for Increasing Your Physical Activity

☐ Try to do a minimum of 30 minutes of moderate physical activity most, preferably all, days of the week. Moderate physical activity includes walking, jogging, riding a bike, roller blading, and so forth.

☐ Ideally, do 45 minutes or more of moderate physical activity at least 5 days per week.

☐ Keep clothes and equipment for physical activity in convenient places.

☐ Move throughout the day, such as by taking stairs, pacing while talking on the phone, or doing sit-ups while watching television.

☐ Join an exercise class, mall-walking group, running club, yoga group, or any other group of people who are physically active.

☐ Use the "buddy" system by exercising with a friend or relative and calling this support person when you need an extra boost to stay motivated.

☐ Prioritize exercise by writing it down, along with your classes and other engagements, in your daily planner.

Steps for Modifying Your Food-Related Behavior

☐ Eat only at set times in one location. Do not eat while studying, working, driving, watching television, and so forth.

☐ Keep a log of what you eat, when, and why. Note any triggers you discover, and list ways to avoid them.

☐ Avoid shopping when you are hungry.

☐ Avoid buying problem foods—that is, foods you have difficulty eating in moderate amounts.

☐ Avoid purchasing high-fat, high-sugar food from vending machines and convenience stores.

☐ At fast-food restaurants, choose small portions of foods lower in fat and simple sugars.

☐ Follow the serving sizes indicated as part of the USDA Food Patterns atMyPlate.gov.

☐ Serve your food portions on smaller dishes, so that they appear larger.

☐ Avoid feelings of deprivation by eating small, regular meals throughout the day.

☐ Whether at home or dining out, share food with others.

☐ Prepare healthful snacks to take with you, so that you won't be tempted by foods from vending machines, fast-food restaurants, and so forth.

☐ Chew food slowly, taking at least 20 minutes to eat a full meal and stopping at once if you begin to feel full.

☐ Reward yourself for positive behaviors by getting a massage, buying new clothes, or going to a movie or concert.

☐ Set reasonable goals, and don't punish yourself if you deviate from your plan (and you will—everyone does). Ask others to avoid responding to any slips you make.

Joining an exercise class can help you increase your physical activity.

Data from National Heart, Lung, and Blood Institute Expert Panel, National Institutes of Health. 1998. *Clinical Guidelines on the Identification, Evaluation, and Treatment of Overweight and Obesity in Adults.* Washington, DC: Government Printing Office.

To help you get started, here are some specific suggestions from the Weight-Control Information Network:[21]

- Follow the amounts recommended in the USDA Food Patterns (Chapter 1, pages 15–22). Making this change involves understanding what constitutes a portion, and measuring foods to determine whether they meet or exceed the recommended amounts.
- To help increase your understanding of the portion sizes of packaged foods, measure out the amount of food that is identified as 1 serving on the Nutrition Facts Panel, and eat it from a plate or bowl instead of straight out of the box or bag.
- Try using smaller dishes, bowls, and glasses. This will make your portion appear larger, and you'll be eating or drinking less.
- When cooking at home, put a serving of the entrée on your plate; then freeze any leftovers in single-serving containers. This way, you won't be tempted to eat the whole batch before the food goes bad, and you'll have ready-made servings for future meals.
- To help you fill up, take second helpings of plain vegetables. That way, dessert may not seem so tempting!
- When buying snacks, go for single-serving, prepackaged items. If you buy larger bags or boxes, divide the snack into single-serving bags.
- When you have a treat, such as ice cream, measure out ½ cup, eat it slowly, and enjoy it!

Now that you have your portion sizes under control, what can you do to reduce the saturated fat and energy content of the portions you *do* eat? Remember that people trying to lose weight should aim for a total fat intake of 15–25% of total energy intake and a saturated fat intake of 10% or below. This goal can be achieved by eliminating extra fats, such as butter, cheese sauces, and mayonnaise, and snack foods, such as ice cream, doughnuts, and cakes. Save these foods as occasional special treats. Select lower-fat versions of the foods listed in the USDA Food Patterns (ChooseMyPlate.gov). This means selecting leaner cuts of meat (such as the white meat of poultry and extra-lean ground

FOODS YOU DON'T KNOW YOU LOVE YET

Air-Popped Popcorn

Popcorn is one of the most popular snacks in the United States. What would a night at the movies be without it? Unfortunately, the versions sold in movie theaters typically contain alarmingly high levels of fat, salt, and Calories. A quick Internet search reveals that even a small size at the nation's largest movie theater chains can pack between 400 and 700 Calories! Even microwave popcorns can contain excessive fat and salt, and many of the lower-fat brands contain *trans* fats. But have you ever tried popcorn in its natural state? Without all the additives, popcorn is naturally low in fat and high in fiber, and contains no salt or sugar.

You can make a healthy popcorn snack by air-popping it—no fancy gadget required! Just put 1/8 cup (2 tablespoons) of popcorn kernels into a brown paper lunch bag. Fold the bag two or three times at the top, about an inch per fold, and set it upright on your microwave turntable. Pop for about 2 minutes, but watch and listen closely: as soon as the popping slows down, stop the microwave. Otherwise, you risk burned popcorn and a smoky kitchen! Many options are also available today from manufacturers who offer fat- and salt-free air-popped popcorn in pre-measured amounts. Always be sure to tilt the bag away from you when you open it, as hot steam will escape. if you wish, add a small amount of melted butter (100 Calories per tablespoon) and a pinch of salt for flavoring. For more zest, try instead adding a little parmesan cheese, or even garlic or chili powder. Some people also enjoy it plain. Air-popped popcorn can be a delicious, low-Calorie, healthful snack!

---

beef) and reduced-fat or skim dairy products and using lower-fat preparation methods (such as baking and broiling instead of frying). It also means switching from a sugar-filled beverage to a low-Calorie or non-Calorie beverage during and between meals.

In addition, try to increase the number of times each day that you choose foods that are relatively low in energy density. This includes salads (with low- or non-Calorie dressings), fruits, vegetables, and soups (broth-based). These foods are low in energy and high in fiber, water, and nutrients. Because they contain relatively more water and fiber than more energy-dense foods, they can help you feel satiated without having to consume large amounts of energy.

Figure 9.10 illustrates two sets of meals, one higher in energy and one lower in energy. You can see from this figure that simple changes to a meal, such as choosing lower-fat dairy products, smaller portion sizes, and foods that are relatively less dense in energy, can reduce energy intake without sacrificing taste, pleasure, or nutritional quality!

Participate in Regular Physical Activity

The Dietary Guidelines for Americans places strong emphasis on the role of physical activity in maintaining a healthful weight. Why is being physically active so important for achieving changes in body weight and for maintaining a healthful body weight? Of course, we expend extra energy during physical activity, but there's more to it than that, because exercise alone (without a reduction of energy intake) does not result in dramatic decreases in body weight. Instead, one of the most important reasons for being regularly active is that it helps us maintain or increase our lean body mass and our BMR. In contrast, energy restriction alone causes us to lose lean body mass. As you've learned, the more lean body mass we have, the more energy we expend over the long term.

About 3,300 Calories (kcal)/day

Breakfast:
1½ cups Fruit Loops cereal
1 cup 2% milk
1 cup orange juice
2 slices white toast
1 tbsp. butter (on toast)

Lunch:
McDonald's Big Mac
   hamburger
French fries, extra large
3 tbsp. ketchup
Apple pie

Dinner:
4.5 oz ground beef (80% lean,
   crumbled), cooked
2 medium taco shells
2 oz cheddar cheese
2 tbsp. sour cream
4 tbsp. store-bought salsa
1 cup shredded lettuce
½ cup refried beans
6 Oreos

About 1,700 Calories (kcal)/day

Breakfast:
1½ cups Cheerios cereal
1 cup skim milk
½ fresh pink grapefruit

Lunch:
Subway cold-cut trio 6"
   sandwich
Granola bar, hard, with
   chocolate chips, 1 bar (24 g)
1 fresh medium apple

Dinner:
5 oz ground turkey, cooked
2 soft corn tortillas
3 oz low-fat cheddar cheese
4 tbsp. store-bought salsa
1 cup shredded lettuce
1 cup cooked mixed veggies
3 Oreos

Figure 9.10 The energy density of two sets of daily meals. The meals on the left are higher in total kilocalories and fat, whereas those on the right are the preferred choice for someone trying to lose weight.

The National Weight Control Registry is an ongoing project documenting the habits of people who have lost at least 30 pounds and kept their weight off for at least 1 year. Of the 784 people studied thus far, the average weight loss was 66 pounds, and the group maintained the minimum weight-loss criteria of 30 pounds for more than 5 years.[22] Almost all of the people (89%) reported changing both physical activity and dietary intake to lose weight and maintain weight loss. No one form of exercise seemed to be most effective, but many people reported doing some form of aerobic exercise (such as bicycling, walking, running, aerobic dance, step aerobics, or hiking) and weight lifting at least 45 minutes most days of the week. In fact, on average, this group expended more than 2,800 kcal each week through physical activity! Although very few weight-loss studies have documented long-term maintenance of weight loss, those that have find that only people who are regularly active are able to maintain most of their weight loss.

In addition to expending energy and maintaining lean body mass and BMR, regular physical activity improves our mood, results in a higher quality of sleep, increases self-esteem, and gives us a sense of accomplishment. All of these changes enhance our ability to engage in long-term healthful lifestyle behaviors.

Incorporate Appropriate Behavior Modifications into Daily Life

Successful weight loss and long-term maintenance of a healthful weight require people to modify their behaviors. Some of the behavior modifications related to food and physical activity have been discussed in the previous sections. Here are a few more practical changes you can make to help you lose weight and keep it off:

- Shop for food only when you are not hungry.
- Avoid buying problem foods—that is, foods that you may have difficulty eating in moderate amounts.

Participating in regular and appropriate physical activity is one of the main components of a weight-change plan.

- Avoid purchasing high-fat, high-sugar food from vending machines and convenience stores.
- Avoid feelings of deprivation by eating small, regular meals throughout the day.
- Eat only at set times in one location. Do not eat while studying, working, driving, watching television, and so forth.
- Slow down while eating.
- Keep a log of what you eat, when, and why. Try to identify social or emotional cues that cause you to overeat, such as getting a poor grade on an exam or feeling lonely.

Then strategize about other ways to cope, such as calling or texting a sympathetic friend.

- Save high-fat, high-Calorie snack foods, such as ice cream, doughnuts, and cake, for occasional special treats.
- Whether at home or dining out, share food with others.
- Prepare healthful snacks to take with you, so that you won't be tempted by foods from vending machines, fast-food restaurants, and so forth.
- Chew food slowly, taking at least 20 minutes to eat a full meal and stopping at once if you begin to feel full.
- Always use appropriate utensils.
- Leave food on your plate, or store it for the next meal.
- Don't punish yourself for deviating from your plan (and you probably will—almost everyone does). Ask your friends and family to be supportive and not dwell on the occasional slip-up.

RECAP Achieving and maintaining a healthful body weight involves gradual reductions in energy intake, such as by eating smaller portion sizes and limiting dietary fat; incorporating regular physical activity; and applying appropriate behavior modification techniques. Fad diets do not incorporate these strategies and do not result in long-term, healthful weight change. Diets based on macronutrient composition may promote long-term weight loss, but some have unhealthful side effects.

HEALTHWATCH

How Can You Avoid Obesity?

At the beginning of this chapter, we defined obesity as having an amount of excess body fat that adversely affects health, resulting in a person having a weight for a given height that is substantially greater than some accepted standard. People with a BMI between 30 and 39.9 are considered obese. Morbid obesity occurs when a person's body weight exceeds 100% of normal. People who are morbidly obese have a BMI greater than or equal to 40.

Both overweight and obesity are now considered an epidemic in the United States. Obesity rates have increased more than 50% during the past 20 years, and it is now estimated that 34.2% of adults 20 years and older are overweight, and another 33.8% are obese.[23]

Why Is Obesity Harmful?

The alarming rise in obesity is a major health concern because it is linked to many chronic diseases and complications:

- Hypertension
- Dyslipidemia, including elevated total cholesterol, triglycerides, and LDL-cholesterol and decreased HDL-cholesterol
- Type 2 diabetes
- Heart disease
- Stroke

- Gallbladder disease
- Osteoarthritis
- Sleep apnea
- Certain cancers, such as colon, breast, endometrial, and gallbladder
- Menstrual irregularities and infertility
- Gestational diabetes, premature fetal deaths, neural tube defects, and complications during labor and delivery
- Depression
- Alzheimer's disease, dementia, and cognitive decline

Abdominal obesity, specifically a large amount of visceral fat that is stored deep within the abdomen (**Figure 9.11**), is one of five risk factors collectively referred to as *metabolic syndrome*. As we discussed earlier in this text (see Chapters 3 and 4), a diagnosis of metabolic syndrome is typically made if a person has three or more of the factors, and it increases one's risk for heart disease, type 2 diabetes, and stroke. These risk factors include

- abdominal obesity (defined as a waist circumference greater than or equal to 40 inches for men and 35 inches for women),
- higher-than-normal triglyceride levels (greater than or equal to 150 mg/dL),
- lower-than-normal HDL-cholesterol levels (less than 40 mg/dL in men and 50 mg/dL in women),
- elevated blood pressure (greater than or equal to 130/85 mm Hg), and
- fasting blood glucose levels greater than or equal to 100 mg/dL, including people with diabetes.[24]

People with metabolic syndrome are twice as likely to develop heart disease and five times as likely to develop type 2 diabetes than people without metabolic syndrome. About 25% of adults in the United States have metabolic syndrome, and rising obesity rates are contributing to increased rates.[25]

Obesity is also associated with an increased risk for premature death: mortality rates for people with a BMI of 30 kg/m² or higher are 50–100% above the rates for those with a BMI between 20 and 25 kg/m². This increased risk for premature death is reflected in national mortality statistics: of the ten leading causes of death in the United States, three—heart disease, stroke, and diabetes—are strongly associated with obesity. In addition, obesity increases the risk that other health problems—from infections to traumatic injuries—will be more severe.

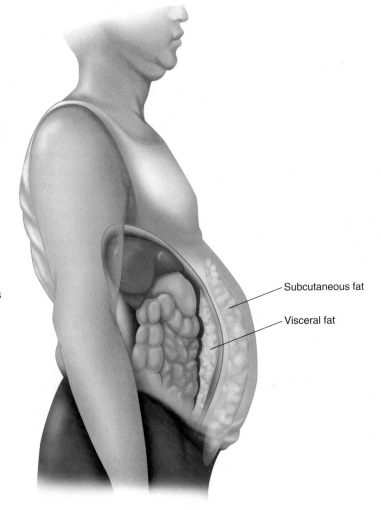

Subcutaneous fat

Visceral fat

Figure 9.11 Abdominal obesity, specifically a high amount of visceral fat stored deep within the abdomen, is one of the risk factors for metabolic syndrome.

Watch a video explaining the health risks of obesity from the Howard Hughes Medical Center, at www.hhmi.org/biointeractive/media/health_problems-sm.mov.

Why Do People Become Obese?

Obesity is known as a **multifactorial disease,** meaning that there are many things that cause it. This makes obesity extremely difficult to treat. Although it is certainly true that obesity, like overweight, is caused by eating more energy than is expended, it is also true that some people are more susceptible to becoming obese than others, and some are more resistant to weight loss and maintaining weight loss. Research on the causes and best treatments of obesity is ongoing, but let's explore some current theories.

multifactorial disease Any disease that may be attributable to one or more of a variety of causes.

Genetic and Physiologic Factors Influence Obesity Risk

Because our genetic background influences our height, weight, body shape, and metabolic rate, it also affects our risk for obesity. Some obesity experts point out that, if proved, the existence of a thrifty gene or genes (discussed earlier) would show that obese people have a genetic tendency to expend less energy, both at rest and during physical activity. Other researchers are working to determine whether the set-point theory can partially explain why many obese people are very resistant to weight loss. As we learn more about genetics, we will gain a greater understanding of the role that our genetic background plays in the development and treatment of obesity.

Also recall that several physiologic factors influence an individual's experience of hunger and satiation. These include the proteins leptin, ghrelin, PYY, and uncoupling proteins. Other physiologic factors, such as beta-endorphins, neuropeptide Y, and decreased blood glucose, can reduce satiety or increase hunger, theoretically promoting overeating and weight gain.

Childhood Overweight and Obesity Are Linked to Adult Obesity

The prevalence of overweight in children and adolescents is increasing at an alarming rate (**Figure 9.12**). There was a time when having extra "baby fat" was considered good for the child. It was assumed that childhood overweight and obesity were temporary, and that the child would grow out of it. Although it is important for children to have a certain minimum level of body fat to maintain health and to grow properly, researchers are now concerned that obesity is harming children's health and increasing their risk for obesity in adulthood.

Health data demonstrate that obese children are already showing signs of chronic disease while they are young, including elevated blood pressure, high cholesterol levels, and changes in insulin and glucose metabolism that may increase their risk for type 2 diabetes (formerly known as *adult onset diabetes*). In some instances, children

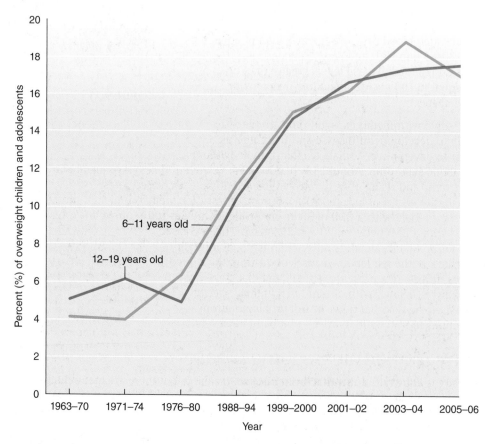

Figure 9.12 Increases in childhood and adolescent overweight from 1963 to 2006.
Data from Centers for Disease Control and Prevention, National Center for Health Statistics. 2007. Prevalence of Overweight Among Children and Adolescents: United States, 2003–2004. www.cdc.gov/nchs/products/pubs/pubd/hestats/overweight/overwght_child_03.htm.

as young as 5 years of age have been diagnosed with type 2 diabetes. Unfortunately, many of these children are likely to maintain these disease risk factors into adulthood.

Does being an obese child guarantee that obesity will be maintained during adulthood? The odds are not good. Although some children who are obese grow up to attain a normal body weight, the majority—about 70%—of children who are obese maintain their higher weight as adults.[26] Obviously, this has important consequences for their lifelong health.

Having either one or two overweight parents increases the risk for obesity by two to four times.[27] This may be explained in part by genetics and in part by unhealthful eating patterns or lack of physical activity within the family. We know that children who eat healthful diets that do not contain a lot of excess fat and sugar and are very physically active are unlikely to become obese. In contrast, children who eat a lot of foods that contain excess fat and sugar and spend most of their time on the computer or in front of the television are more likely to be obese. When these patterns are carried into adolescence and adulthood, the obesity is likely to persist.

Social Factors Appear to Influence Obesity Risk

Poverty has been linked to obesity. One reason for this may be that high-Calorie processed foods cost less and are easier to find and prepare than more healthful foods, such as fresh fruits and vegetables. Other reasons may include reduced access to safe places to walk, hike, or engage in other forms of physical activity, not to mention the cost of membership in a health club, gym, or commercial weight-loss program. Poverty also typically reduces access to high-quality healthcare, including health education and other types of preventive care.

Our social ties may also have a subtle influence on our risk for obesity. Although their data have been challenged, researchers from Harvard Medical School evaluated a social network of more than 12,000 people and concluded that an individual's risk of becoming obese increases significantly—by 37% to 57%—if the person has a spouse, sibling, or friend who has become obese.[28]

Physical Factors Can Contribute to Obesity

An abnormally low level of thyroid hormone, or an elevated level of the hormone cortisol, can lead to weight gain and obesity. A physician can check a patient's blood for levels of these hormones. Certain prescription medications, including steroids used for asthma and other disorders, seizure medications, and some antidepressants, can slow basal metabolic rate or stimulate appetite, leading to weight gain.[29]

Does Obesity Respond to Treatment?

Ironically, up to 40% of women and 25% of men are dieting at any given time. How can obesity rates be so high when there are so many people dieting? Although relatively few studies have tracked weight-loss maintenance, evidence from one study suggests that only about 20% of obese people are successful at long-term weight loss.[30] In this study, success was defined as losing at least 10% of initial body weight and maintaining the loss for at least 1 year. The results suggest that about 80% of obese people who are dieting fail to lose weight or to keep it off. Although these statistics might suggest that obesity somehow resists intervention, that's not the case. Bearing in mind that 20% of people do succeed in long-term weight loss, the question becomes "How do they do it?"

Lifestyle Changes Can Help

The first line of defense in treating obesity consists of a lower-energy diet and regular physical activity. People who are overweight or obese should work with a healthcare practitioner or registered dietitian (RD) to design and maintain a diet in which they consume 500 to 1,000 fewer kilocalories per day.[18]

Physical activity should be increased gradually, so that the person can build to a program in which he or she is exercising at least 30 minutes per day, five times per week. The Institute of Medicine[31] concurs that 30 minutes a day, five times a week is the minimum amount of physical activity needed, but up to

Adequate physical activity is instrumental in preventing childhood obesity.

Want to learn more about the complexities that contribute to obesity? Check out the Foresight Obesity Project Systems Atlas at http://issuu .com/shiftn/docs/obesity_atlas.

60 minutes per day may be necessary for many people to lose weight and sustain a body weight in the healthy range over the long term.

Counseling and support groups can help people maintain these dietary and activity changes. Behavior therapy can be particularly helpful in challenging clients to examine the underlying thought patterns, situations, and stressors undermining their efforts at weight loss.

Weight Loss Can Be Enhanced with Prescribed Medications

Healthful weight loss takes time, effort, and consistency. Many people are looking for a "magic bullet" that will enable them to lose weight quickly and easily. Other people have tried to follow lifestyle recommendations for years without success. In response to these challenges, prescription weight-loss medications have been developed. These should be used only with proper supervision from a medical doctor. One reason physician involvement is so critical is that many drugs developed for weight loss have side effects that range from unpleasant to dangerous. Some have even proven deadly.

Just two prescription weight-loss drugs are currently available: sibutramine and orlistat. However, the long-term safety and effectiveness of both are the subject of controversy. Sibutramine (brand name Meridia) is an appetite suppressant that can cause increased heart rate and blood pressure in some people. Orlistat (brand name Xenical) is a drug that inhibits the absorption of dietary fat from the intestinal tract, which can result in modest weight loss in some people. The side effects of orlistat range from diarrhea and fecal incontinence to liver failure.

Again, these medications should be used only while under a physician's supervision, so that progress and health risks can be closely monitored. They are most effective when combined with a program that supports energy restriction, regular exercise, and increased physical activity throughout each day.

Surgery Can Be Used to Treat Morbid Obesity

For people who are morbidly obese, surgery may be recommended. Generally, surgery is advised for people with a BMI greater than or equal to 40 or people with a BMI greater than or equal to 35 who have other life-threatening conditions, such as diabetes, hypertension, or elevated cholesterol levels. Any surgical procedure is more risky for people who are obese, so weight-loss surgery is considered a last resort, to be used only for obese people who have not been able to lose weight by less drastic means. Three common types of weight-loss surgery are vertical banded gastroplasty, gastric bypass, and gastric banding **(Figure 9.13)**:

- *Vertical banded gastroplasty* involves partitioning a small section of the stomach, via surgical staples and a band, to reduce total food intake.

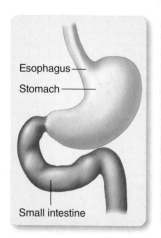

(a) Normal anatomy

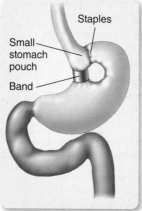

(b) Vertical banded gastroplasty

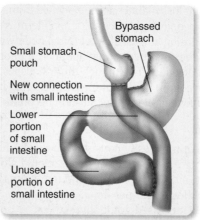

(c) Gastric bypass

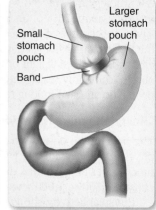

(d) Gastric banding

◆ **Figure 9.13** Various forms of surgery alter the **(a)** normal anatomy of the gastrointestinal tract to promote weight loss. **(b)** Vertical banded gastroplasty, **(c)** gastric bypass surgery, and **(d)** gastric banding are three surgical procedures used to reduce morbid obesity.

- *Gastric bypass surgery* involves attaching the lower part of the small intestine to a greatly reduced stomach, so that most of the food consumed bypasses the stomach and all of it bypasses the duodenum. This results in significantly less absorption of food.
- *Gastric banding* is a relatively new procedure, in which stomach size is reduced using an adjustable constricting band, thus restricting food intake.

Are surgical procedures successful in reducing obesity? About one-third to one-half of people who receive obesity surgery lose significant amounts of weight and keep this weight off for at least 5 years. The reasons that one-half to two-thirds do not experience long-term success include that some people are unable to consistently eat less over time, even with a smaller stomach. For others, staples and gastric bands loosen and stomach pouches enlarge. And in some instances, people do not survive the surgery.

Liposuction is a cosmetic surgical procedure that removes fat cells from localized areas in the body. It is not recommended or typically used to treat obesity or morbid obesity. The procedure is not without risks; blood clots, skin and nerve damage, adverse drug reactions, pain, and perforation injuries can and do occur as a result of liposuction. It can also result in deformations in the area where the fat is removed, and in one recent study, after a year all of the fat removed from the thighs and buttocks of participants returned but was redistributed to the abdominal area.[32] Also, the millions of fat cells that remain in the body after liposuction enlarge if the person continues to overeat. In addition, although liposuction may reduce the fat content of a localized area, it does not reduce a person's risk for the diseases that are more common among overweight or obese people. Therefore, this procedure is not the solution to long-term weight loss. Only energy restriction and exercise can reduce body fat and the risks for chronic diseases.

Liposuction removes fat cells from specific areas of the body.

RECAP Obesity is caused by many factors, including genetics, a history of childhood obesity, overconsumption of energy (consuming too many kilocalories), and lack of adequate physical activity. Treatments for obesity and morbid obesity include low-energy, low-fat diets in combination with regular physical activity; weight-loss prescription medications; and weight-loss surgery.

What If You Are Underweight?

With so much emphasis in the United States on obesity and weight loss, some find it surprising that many people are trying to gain weight. These include people who are clinically underweight—that is, people with a BMI of less than 18.5. Being underweight can be just as unhealthful as being obese, as underweight increases the risk for infections, osteoporosis, and other diseases and can even be fatal. In addition, many athletes want to gain weight in order to increase their strength and power for competition.

To gain weight, people must eat more energy than they expend. Although overeating large amounts of high-saturated-fat foods (such as bacon, sausage, and cheese) can cause weight gain, doing this without exercising is not considered healthful because most of the weight gained is fat, and high-fat diets increase our risks for cardiovascular and other diseases. Unless there are medical reasons to eat a high-fat diet, it is recommended that people trying to gain weight eat a diet that is relatively low in dietary fat (less than 35% of total Calories) and relatively high in complex carbohydrates (55% of total Calories). The following are recommendations for weight gain:

- Eat a diet that includes about 500 to 1,000 kcal per day more than is needed to maintain current body weight. Although we don't know precisely how much extra energy is needed to gain 1 lb, a common estimate is about 3,500 kcal. Thus, eating 500 to 1,000 kcal per day in excess should result in a gain of 1 to 2 lb of weight each week.
- Eat a diet that contains about 55% of total energy from carbohydrate, 25% to 35% of total energy from fat, and 10% to 20% of total energy from protein.
- Eat frequently, including meals and numerous snacks throughout the day. Many underweight people do not take the time to eat often enough.

Eating frequent nutrient- and energy-dense snacks can help promote weight gain.

- Avoid the use of tobacco products, as they depress appetite and increase metabolic rate, which prevent weight gain. In addition, they increase our risks for lung, mouth, esophageal, and other cancers.
- Exercise regularly, and incorporate weight lifting or some other form of resistance training into your exercise routine. This form of exercise is most effective in increasing muscle mass. Performing aerobic exercise (such as walking, running, bicycling, or swimming) at least 30 minutes a day for 3 days per week will help maintain a healthy cardiovascular system.

The key to gaining weight is to eat frequent meals throughout the day and to select energy-dense foods. When selecting foods that are higher in fat, make sure you select foods higher in polyunsaturated and monounsaturated fats (such as peanut butter, olive and canola oils, and avocados). Smoothies and milkshakes made with low-fat milk or yogurt are another great way to take in a lot of energy. Eating fruit or raw vegetables with peanut butter, hummus, guacamole, or cream cheese and including salad dressings on your salad are other ways to increase the energy density of foods. The biggest challenge to weight gain is setting aside time to eat; by packing a lot of foods to take with you throughout the day, you can increase your opportunities to eat more.

RECAP Weight gain can be achieved by eating about 500 to 1,000 kcal per day more than is needed to maintain present weight and by performing weight lifting and aerobic exercise. Eating frequent, healthy meals and snacks throughout the day and avoiding the use of tobacco products are important strategies.

HEALTHWATCH

Disordered Eating: Are You at Risk?

disordered eating A general term used to describe a variety of abnormal or atypical eating behaviors that are used to keep or maintain a lower body weight.

eating disorder A clinically diagnosed psychiatric disorder characterized by severe disturbances in body image and eating behaviors.

anorexia nervosa A serious, potentially life-threatening eating disorder that is characterized by self-starvation, which eventually leads to a deficiency in the energy and essential nutrients the body requires to function normally.

bulimia nervosa A serious eating disorder characterized by recurrent episodes of binge eating and recurrent inappropriate compensatory behaviors in order to prevent weight gain, such as self-induced vomiting, fasting, excessive exercise, or misuse of laxatives, diuretics, enemas, or other medications.

body image A person's perception of his or her body's appearance and functioning.

Disordered eating is a general term used to describe a variety of atypical eating behaviors that people use to achieve or maintain a lower body weight. These behaviors may be as simple as going on and off diets or as extreme as refusing to eat any fat. Such behaviors don't usually continue for long enough to make the person seriously ill, nor do they significantly disrupt the person's normal routine.

In contrast, some people restrict their eating so much or for so long that they become dangerously underweight. These people have an **eating disorder,** a recognized psychiatric condition that involves extreme body dissatisfaction and long-term eating patterns that negatively affect body functioning. The two more commonly diagnosed eating disorders are anorexia nervosa and bulimia nervosa. **Anorexia nervosa** is a potentially life-threatening eating disorder that is characterized by self-starvation, which eventually leads to a severe nutrient deficiency. In contrast, **bulimia nervosa** is characterized by recurrent episodes of extreme overeating and compensatory behaviors to prevent weight gain, such as self-induced vomiting, misuse of laxatives, fasting, or excessive exercise. Both disorders will be discussed in more detail shortly.

Eating Behaviors Occur on a Continuum

When does normal dieting cross the line into disordered eating? Eating behaviors occur on a *continuum*, a spectrum that can't be divided neatly into parts. An example is a rainbow—where exactly does the red end and the orange begin? Thinking about eating behaviors as a continuum makes it easier to understand how a person can progress from relatively normal eating behaviors to a pattern that is disordered. For instance, let's say that for several years you've skipped breakfast in favor of a midmorning snack, but now you find yourself avoiding the cafeteria until early afternoon. Is this normal? To answer that question, you'd need to consider your feelings about food and your **body image**—the way you perceive your body.

Take a moment to consider the statements in the ***What About You?*** feature box (page 285). It will help clarify how you feel about your body and whether or not you're at risk for an eating disorder.

WHAT ABOUT YOU?

Are You at Risk for an Eating Disorder?

Take a look at the Eating Issues and Body Image Continuum (Figure 9.14). Which of the five columns best describes your feelings about food and your body? If you identify with the statements on the left side of the continuum, you probably have few issues with food or body image. Most likely, you accept your body size and view food as a normal part of maintaining your health and fueling your daily physical activity.

As you progress to the right side of the continuum, food and body image become bigger issues, with food restriction becoming the norm. If you identify with the statements on the far right, you are probably afraid of eating and dislike your body. If so, you should consult a healthcare professional as soon as possible. The earlier you seek treatment, the more likely you can take ownership of your body and develop a healthful approach to food.

FOOD IS NOT AN ISSUE	CONCERNED/WELL	FOOD PREOCCUPIED/OBSESSED	DISRUPTIVE EATING PATTERNS	EATING DISORDERED
• I am not concerned about what others think regarding what and how much I eat. • When I am upset or depressed I eat whatever I am hungry for without any guilt or shame. • I feel no guilt or shame no matter how much I eat or what I eat. • Food is an important part of my life but only occupies a small part of my time. • I trust my body to tell me what and how much to eat.	• I pay attention to what I eat in order to maintain a healthy body. • I may weigh more than what I like, but I enjoy eating and balance my pleasure with eating with my concern for a healthy body. • I am moderate and flexible in goals for eating well. • I try to follow Dietary Guidelines for healthy eating.	• I think about food a lot. • I feel I don't eat well most of the time. • It's hard for me to enjoy eating with others. • I feel ashamed when I eat more than others or more than what I feel I should be eating. • I am afraid of getting fat. • I wish I could change how much I want to eat and what I am hungry for.	• I have tried diet pills, laxatives, vomiting, or extra time exercising in order to lose or maintain my weight. • I have fasted or avoided eating for long periods of time in order to lose or maintain my weight. • I feel strong when I can restrict how much I eat. • Eating more than I wanted to makes me feel out of control.	• I regularly stuff myself and then exercise, vomit, or use diet pills or laxatives to get rid of the food or calories. • My friends/family tell me I am too thin. • I am terrified of eating fat. • When I let myself eat, I have a hard time controlling the amount of food I eat. • I am afraid to eat in front of others.

BODY OWNERSHIP	BODY ACCEPTANCE	BODY PREOCCUPIED/OBSESSED	DISTORTED BODY IMAGE	BODY HATE/DISASSOCIATION
• Body image is not an issue for me. • My body is beautiful to me. • My feelings about my body are not influenced by society's concept of an ideal body shape. • I know that the significant others in my life will always find me attractive. • I trust my body to find the weight it needs to be at so I can move and feel confident about my physical body.	• I base my body image equally on social norms and my own self-concept. • I pay attention to my body and my appearance because it is important to me, but it only occupies a small part of my day. • I nourish my body so it has the strength and energy to achieve my physical goals. • I am able to assert myself and maintain a healthy body without losing my self-esteem.	• I spend a significant amount time viewing my body in the mirror. • I spend a significant amount time comparing my body to others. • I have days when I feel fat. • I am preoccupied with my body. • I accept society's ideal body shape and size as the best body shape and size. • I believe that I'd be more attractive if I were thinner, more muscular, etc.	• I spend a significant amount of time exercising and dieting to change my body. • My body shape and size keep me from dating or finding someone who will treat me the way I want to be treated. • I have considered changing or have changed my body shape and size through surgical means so I can accept myself. • I wish I could change the way I look in the mirror.	• I often feel separated and distant from my body—as if it belongs to someone else. • I hate my body and I often isolate myself from others. • I don't see anything positive or even neutral about my body shape and size. • I don't believe others when they tell me I look OK. • I hate the way I look in the mirror.

▲ **Figure 9.14** The Eating Issues and Body Image Continuum. The progression from normal eating (far left) to eating disorders (far right) occurs on a continuum.
From Smiley, King, and Avey. University of Arizona Campus Health Service. Original Continuum by C. Shisslak. Preventive Medicine and Public Health. Copyright ©1997 Arizona Board of Regents. Reprinted by permission.

Many Factors Contribute to Disordered Eating Behaviors

The factors that result in the development of disordered eating are very complex, but research indicates that a number of psychological, interpersonal, social, and biological factors may contribute in any particular individual.

Influence of Family

Research suggests that family conditioning, structure, and patterns of interaction can influence the development of an eating disorder. Based on observational studies, compared with families without a member with an eating disorder, families with an anorexic member show more rigidity in their family structure, have less clear interpersonal boundaries, and tend to avoid open discussions on topics of disagreement. Conversely, families with a member diagnosed with bulimia nervosa tend to have a less stable family organization and to be less nurturing, more angry, and more disruptive.[33] In addition, childhood physical or sexual abuse can increase the risk for an eating disorder.[34]

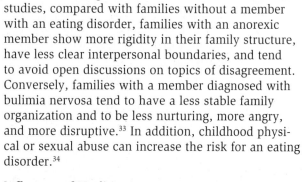

🔊 **Figure 9.15** Photos of celebrities and models are often airbrushed, or altered to "enhance" physical appearance. Unfortunately, many people believe that these are accurate portrayals and strive to reach unrealistic levels of physical beauty.

Influence of Media

As media saturation has increased over the last century, so has the incidence of eating disorders among white women.[35] Every day, we are confronted with advertisements in which computer-enhanced images of lean, beautiful women promote everything from beer to cars **(Figure 9.15)**. Most adult men and women understand that these images are unrealistic, but adolescents, who are still developing a sense of their identity and body image, lack the same ability to distance themselves from what they see.[36] Because body image influences eating behaviors, it is likely that the barrage of media models is contributing to the increase in eating disorders. However, scientific evidence demonstrating that the media are *causing* this increase is difficult to obtain.

Influence of Social and Cultural Values

Eating disorders are significantly more common in white females in Western societies than in other women worldwide. This may be due in part to the white Western culture's association of slenderness with health, wealth, and high fashion **(Figure 9.16)**. In contrast, until recently, the prevailing view in developing societies has been that excess body fat is desirable as a sign of health and material abundance.

The members of society with whom we most often interact—our family members, friends, classmates, and co-workers—also influence the way we see ourselves. Their comments about our body weight or shape can be particularly hurtful—enough so to cause some people to start down the path of disordered eating. For example, people with bulimia nervosa (commonly referred to as just *bulimia*) have reported that they perceived greater pressure from their peers to be thin than did controls, and research shows that peer teasing about weight increases body dissatisfaction and eating disturbances.[37] Thus, our comments to others about their weight do count.

🔊 **Figure 9.16** The preferred look among runway models can require extreme emaciation, often achieved by self-starvation and/or drug abuse.

Influence of Personality

A number of studies suggest that people with anorexia nervosa (commonly referred to as just *anorexia*) exhibit increased rates of obsessive-compulsive behaviors and perfectionism. They also tend to be socially inhibited, compliant, and emotionally restrained.[38] Unfortunately, many studies observe these behaviors only in individuals who are very ill and in a state of starvation, which may affect personality. Thus, it is difficult to determine if personality is the cause or the effect of the disorder.

In contrast to people with anorexia, people with bulimia tend to be more impulsive, have low self-esteem, and demonstrate an extroverted, erratic personality style that seeks attention and admiration. In these people, negative moods are more likely to cause overeating than food restriction.[38]

Influence of Genetic Factors

Overall, the diagnosis of anorexia nervosa or bulimia nervosa is several times more common in siblings and other blood relatives who also have the diagnosis than in the general population.[39] This observation might imply the existence of an "eating disorder gene"; however, it is difficult to separate the genetic factors from the environmental factors within families.

RECAP Eating behaviors occur along a continuum. *Disordered eating* is a general term that describes a variety of atypical eating behaviors people use to achieve or maintain a lower body weight; whereas an *eating disorder* is a recognized psychiatric condition that involves extreme body dissatisfaction and long-term eating patterns that negatively affect body functioning. The development of disordered eating behaviors and eating disorders may be influenced by family environment, the media, society, culture, personality, and genetics.

Anorexia Nervosa Is a Potentially Deadly Eating Disorder

According to the American Psychiatric Association, 90% to 95% of people with anorexia nervosa are young girls or women.[39] Approximately 0.5% to 1% of American females develops anorexia, and between 5% and 20% of these will die from complications of the disorder within 10 years of initial diagnosis.[34] These statistics make anorexia the most common and deadly psychiatric disorder diagnosed in women and the leading cause of death in females between the ages of 15 and 24 years.[34] As the statistics indicate, anorexia also occurs in males, but the prevalence is much lower than in females.[40]

Signs and Symptoms of Anorexia Nervosa

The classic sign of anorexia nervosa is an extremely restrictive eating pattern that leads to self-starvation **(Figure 9.17)**. These individuals may fast completely, restrict energy intake to only a few kilocalories per day, or eliminate all but one or two food groups from their diet. They also have an intense fear of weight gain, and even small amounts (for example, 1–2 lb) trigger high stress and anxiety.

In women, **amenorrhea** (experiencing no menstrual periods for at least 3 months) is a common feature of anorexia. It occurs when a young woman consumes insufficient energy to maintain normal body functions. The signs of an eating disorder such as anorexia may be somewhat different in men. For more information, see the *Highlight* feature box on eating disorders in men (page 288).

Health Risks of Anorexia Nervosa

Left untreated, anorexia nervosa eventually leads to a deficiency in energy and other nutrients that are required by the body to function normally. The body will then use stored fat and lean tissue (such as organ and muscle tissue) as an energy source to maintain brain tissue and vital body functions. The body will also shut down or reduce nonvital body functions to conserve energy. Electrolyte imbalances can lead to

▲ **Figure 9.17** People with *anorexia nervosa* experience an extreme drive for thinness, resulting in potentially fatal weight loss.

Have you ever wondered what it's like to experience the negative effects of anorexia nervosa? Watch a CBS News interview with a survivor at www .cbsnews.com/video/watch/?id =5284619n.

amenorrhea The absence of menstruation. In females who had previously been menstruating, the absence of menstrual periods for 3 or more months.

HIGHLIGHT
Eating Disorders in Men: Are They Different?

Like many people, you might find it hard to believe that men develop eating disorders or, if they do, their disorders must be somehow "different," right? To explore this question, let's take a look at what research has revealed about similarities and differences between men and women with eating disorders.

Comparing Men and Women with Eating Disorders

Until about a decade ago, little research was conducted on eating disorders in males. Recently, however, eating disorder experts have begun to examine the gender-differences debate in detail and have discovered that eating disorders in males are largely similar to eating disorders in females. But some differences *do* exist.

Women with eating disorders say they *feel* fat even though they typically are of normal weight or even underweight before they develop the disorder. In contrast, men who develop eating disorders are more likely to have actually *been* overweight or even obese.[40,41] Thus, male fears of "getting fat again" are based on reality. In addition, men with disordered eating are less concerned about actual body weight (scale weight) than females but are more concerned about body composition (percentage of muscle mass compared with fat mass).

Whereas dieting itself is a common trigger for eating disorders in both males and females, research suggests that the factors *initiating* the dieting behavior differ.[42] There appear to be four reasons that males diet: to improve athletic performance, to avoid being teased for being fat, to avoid obesity-related illnesses observed in male family members, and to improve a homosexual relationship.[43] Similar factors are rarely reported by women.

The methods that men and women use to achieve weight loss also appear to differ. Males are more likely to use excessive exercise as a means of weight control, whereas females use more passive methods, such as severe energy restriction, vomiting, and laxative abuse. These weight-control differences may stem from the societal biases surrounding dieting and male behavior; that is, dieting is considered to be more "acceptable" for women, whereas the overwhelming sociocultural belief is that "real men don't diet."[41]

Muscle Dysmorphia: A Disorder Unique to Men

As we noted earlier, eating behavior and body image are

⬆ Men are more likely than women to exercise excessively in an effort to control their weight.

closely related. Recently, some psychologists who work with men have identified a disorder called *muscle dysmorphia (MD)*, which has been classified variously as an eating disorder or as a body-image disorder. Men with MD are distressed by the idea that they are not sufficiently lean and muscular, spend long hours lifting weights, and follow an extremely specialized diet. The disorder has also been called *reverse anorexia nervosa*, and indeed, men with MD perceive themselves as small and frail even though they are actually quite large and muscular. Frequently, men with MD abuse anabolic steroids, but no matter how "buff" or "chiseled" they become, their anatomy cannot match their ideal.[43] Additionally, whereas people with anorexia eat little of anything, men with MD tend to consume excessive amounts of high-protein foods and dietary supplements, such as protein powders.

Men with MD share some characteristics with men and women with true anorexia nervosa. For instance, they also report "feeling fat" and engage in behaviors indicating an obsession with appearance (such as looking in the mirror). They also express significant discomfort with the idea of having to expose their body to others (for example, take off their clothes in the locker room), and they have increased rates of mental illness.[44]

The following are outward signs that someone may be struggling with MD:

- A rigid and excessive schedule of weight training
- Strict adherence to a high-protein, muscle-enhancing diet
- Use of anabolic steroids, protein powders, or other muscle-enhancing drugs or supplements
- Poor attendance at work, school, or sports activities because of interference with a rigid weight-training schedule
- Avoidance of social engagements where the person will not be able to follow his strict diet
- Avoidance of situations in which the person would have to expose his body to others
- Frequent and critical self-evaluation of body composition

Although muscle dysmorphia isn't typically life-threatening, it can certainly cause distress and despair. Therapy—especially participation in an all-male support group—can help.

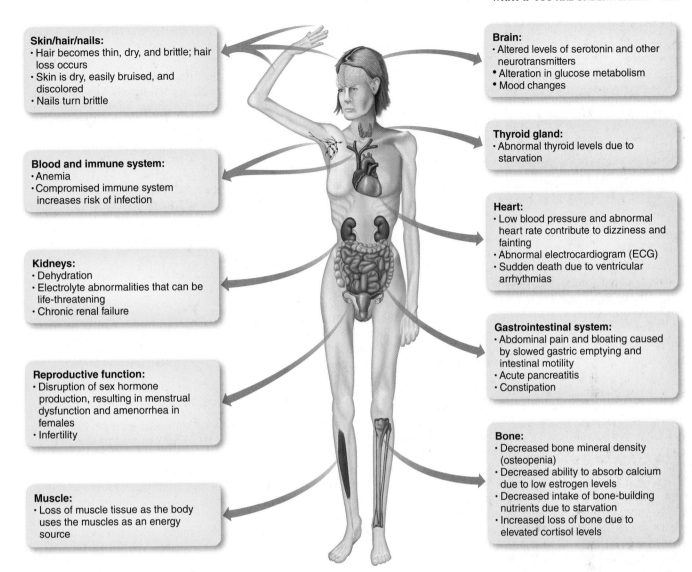

Skin/hair/nails:
- Hair becomes thin, dry, and brittle; hair loss occurs
- Skin is dry, easily bruised, and discolored
- Nails turn brittle

Blood and immune system:
- Anemia
- Compromised immune system increases risk of infection

Kidneys:
- Dehydration
- Electrolyte abnormalities that can be life-threatening
- Chronic renal failure

Reproductive function:
- Disruption of sex hormone production, resulting in menstrual dysfunction and amenorrhea in females
- Infertility

Muscle:
- Loss of muscle tissue as the body uses the muscles as an energy source

Brain:
- Altered levels of serotonin and other neurotransmitters
- Alteration in glucose metabolism
- Mood changes

Thyroid gland:
- Abnormal thyroid levels due to starvation

Heart:
- Low blood pressure and abnormal heart rate contribute to dizziness and fainting
- Abnormal electrocardiogram (ECG)
- Sudden death due to ventricular arrhythmias

Gastrointestinal system:
- Abdominal pain and bloating caused by slowed gastric emptying and intestinal motility
- Acute pancreatitis
- Constipation

Bone:
- Decreased bone mineral density (osteopenia)
- Decreased ability to absorb calcium due to low estrogen levels
- Decreased intake of bone-building nutrients due to starvation
- Increased loss of bone due to elevated cortisol levels

Figure 9.18 The impact of *anorexia nervosa* on the female body.

heart failure and death. **Figure 9.18** highlights many of the health problems that occur in people with anorexia nervosa.

Bulimia Nervosa Is Characterized by Bingeing and Purging

Bulimia nervosa (commonly referred to as just *bulimia*) is an eating disorder characterized by repeated episodes of **binge eating** followed by some form of **purging**. While binge eating, the person feels a loss of self-control, including an inability to end the binge once it has started.[45] At the same time, the person feels a sense of euphoria not unlike a drug-induced high. A *binge* is usually defined as a quantity of food that is large for the person and for the amount of time in which it is eaten **(Figure 9.19)**. For example, a person may eat a dozen brownies with 2 quarts of ice cream in 30 minutes.

The prevalence of bulimia is higher than that of anorexia; bulimia is estimated to affect 1% to 4% of women. Like anorexia, bulimia is found predominately in women: six to ten females are diagnosed for every one male. The mortality rate for bulimia is lower than for anorexia, with 1% of patients dying within 10 years of diagnosis.[34]

Although the prevalence of bulimia nervosa is much higher in women, rates for men are significant in some predominately "thin-build" sports in which participants are encouraged or required to maintain a low body weight (such as horse racing,

binge eating Consumption of a large amount of food in a short period of time, usually accompanied by a feeling of loss of self-control.

purging An attempt to rid the body of unwanted food by vomiting or other compensatory means, such as excessive exercise, fasting, or laxative abuse.

Figure 9.19 People with *bulimia nervosa* consume relatively large amounts of food in very brief periods of time.

wrestling, crew, and gymnastics). Individuals in these sports typically do not have all the characteristics of bulimia nervosa, however, and the purging behaviors they practice typically stop once the sport is discontinued.

A person with bulimia typically purges after most episodes, but not necessarily on every occasion, and the weight gained as a result of binge eating can be significant. Methods of purging include vomiting, laxative or diuretic abuse, enemas, fasting, and excessive exercise. For example, after a binge, a runner may increase her daily mileage to equal the "calculated" energy content of the binge.

Signs and Symptoms of Bulimia Nervosa

In addition to the recurrent and frequent binge-eating and purging episodes, the National Institute of Mental Health has identified the following signs and symptoms of bulimia nervosa:

- Chronically inflamed and sore throat
- Swollen glands in the neck and below the jaw
- Worn tooth enamel and increasingly sensitive and decaying teeth as a result of exposure to stomach acids
- Gastroesophageal reflux disorder
- Intestinal distress and irritation from laxative abuse
- Severe dehydration from purging of fluids

Health Risks of Bulimia Nervosa

The destructive behaviors of bulimia nervosa can lead to illness and even death. The following are the most common health consequences associated with bulimia:

- Electrolyte imbalance typically caused by dehydration and the loss of potassium and sodium from the body with frequent vomiting. This can lead to irregular heartbeat and even heart failure and death.
- Gastrointestinal problems: inflammation, ulceration, and possible rupture of the esophagus and stomach from frequent bingeing and vomiting. Chronic irregular bowel movements and constipation may result in people with bulimia who chronically abuse laxatives.
- Dental problems: tooth decay and staining from stomach acids released during frequent vomiting

Binge-Eating Disorder Can Cause Significant Weight Gain

When was the last time a friend or relative confessed to you about "going on an eating binge"? Most likely, they explained that the behavior followed some sort of stressful event, such as a problem at work, the break-up of a relationship, or a poor grade on an exam. Many people have one or two binge episodes every year or so, in response to stress. But in people with **binge-eating disorder,** the behavior occurs an average of twice a week or more and is not usually followed by purging. This lack of compensation for the binge distinguishes binge-eating disorder from bulimia nervosa and explains why the person tends to gain a lot of weight.

The prevalence of binge-eating disorder is estimated to be 2% to 3% of the adult population and 8% of the obese population. In contrast to anorexia and bulimia, binge-eating disorder is also quite common in men. Our current food environment, which offers an abundance of good-tasting, cheap food any time of the day, makes it difficult for people with binge-eating disorder to avoid food triggers.

Night-Eating Syndrome Is Linked to Insomnia

Night-eating syndrome was first described in a group of patients who were not hungry in the morning but spent the evening and night eating and reported having insomnia. It is associated with obesity because, although night eaters don't binge, they do consume significant energy, and they don't compensate for the excess energy intake.

People with night-eating syndrome consume most of their daily energy between 8 PM and 6 AM.

binge-eating disorder A disorder characterized by binge eating an average of twice a week or more, typically without compensatory purging.

night-eating syndrome A disorder characterized by intake of the majority of the day's energy between 8:00 PM and 6:00 AM. Individuals with this disorder also experience mood and sleep disorders.

The distinguishing characteristic of night-eating syndrome is time: most of the day's energy intake occurs between 8:00 PM and 6:00 AM. Night eating is also characterized by insomnia and a depressed mood. In short, night eaters appear to have a unique combination of three disorders: an eating disorder, a sleep disorder, and a mood disorder.[46] The obesity that may develop in night eaters also increases the risk for sleep apnea (a type of chronic snoring), which can further disrupt the night eater's already abnormal sleeping pattern.

The Female Athlete Triad Consists of Three Disorders

Female athlete triad is a term used to describe a serious syndrome that consists of three clinical conditions in some physically active females: low energy availability (inadequate energy intake to maintain menstrual function—with or without eating disorders), menstrual dysfunction, and low bone density **(Figure 9.20)**.[47] Sports that emphasize leanness or a thin body build may place a young girl or a woman at risk for the female athlete triad. These include figure skating, gymnastics, and diving. Classical ballet dancers are also at increased risk for the disorder.

Active women experience the general social and cultural demands placed on women to be thin, as well as pressure from their coach, teammates, judges, and/or spectators to meet weight standards or body-size expectations for their sport. Failure to meet these standards can result in severe consequences, such as being cut from the team, losing an athletic scholarship, or experiencing decreased participation with the team.

As the pressure to be thin mounts, active women may engage in disordered eating behaviors. Low energy availability combined with high levels of physical activity can disrupt the menstrual cycle and result in amenorrhea. Female athletes with menstrual dysfunction also typically have reduced levels of the reproductive hormones estrogen and progesterone. When estrogen levels in the body are low, it is difficult for bone to retain calcium, and gradual loss of bone mass occurs. Thus, many female athletes are at increased risk for fractures.

Menstrual dysfunction

Low bone density

Low energy availability

◆ **Figure 9.20** The female athlete triad is a syndrome consisting of three coexisting disorders: low energy availability (with or without eating disorders), menstrual dysfunction (such as amenorrhea), and low bone density. Energy availability is defined as *dietary energy intake* (how much energy you take in through foods) minus *exercise energy expenditure* (how much energy you expend through exercise).

female athlete triad A serious syndrome that consists of three clinical conditions in some physically active females: low energy availability (with or without eating disorders), menstrual dysfunction, and low bone density.

NUTRI-CASE LIZ

"I used to dance with a really cool modern company, where everybody looked sort of healthy and 'real.' No waifs! When they folded after Christmas, I was really bummed, but this spring, I'm planning to audition for the City Ballet. My best friend dances with them, and she told me that they won't even look at anybody over 100 pounds. So I've had to put myself on a pretty strict diet. Most days, I come in under 1,200 Calories, although some days I cheat and then I feel so out of control. Last week, my dance teacher stopped me after class and asked me whether or not I was menstruating. I thought that was a pretty weird question, so I just said sure, but then when I thought about it, I realized that I've been so focused and stressed out lately that I really don't know! The audition is only a week away, so I'm going on a juice fast this weekend. I've just got to make it into the City Ballet!"

What factors increase Liz's risk for the female athlete triad? If you were to explain to her about osteoporosis, stress fractures, and increased injuries, do you think it would change her disordered eating behaviors? Why or why not? What, if anything, do you think Liz's dance teacher should do? Why is intervention even necessary, since the audition is only a week away?

"Where I'm at Now . . ."

Now that you've read this chapter, do you feel that weight loss is an important goal for you?

Yes or No

If so, what strategies do you plan to use? (Check as many as you want.):

☐ I'll follow an established diet plan.
☐ I'll join a support group.
☐ I'll just eat smaller portions.
☐ Il fix my own meals and snacks more often.
☐ I'll increase my physical activity.
☐ I'll keep a log of what I eat, when, and why.
☐ I'll ask my doctor if weight-loss medications are right for me.

Treatment for Disordered Eating Requires a Multidisciplinary Approach

As with any health problem, prevention is the best treatment for disordered eating. People having trouble with eating and body image issues need help to deal with these issues before they develop into something more serious.

Treating anyone with disordered eating requires a multidisciplinary approach. In addition to a physician and psychologist, a nutritionist, the person's coach (if an athlete), and family members and friends all must work together. Patients who are severely underweight, display signs of malnutrition, are medically unstable, or are suicidal may require immediate hospitalization. Conversely, patients who are underweight but are still medically stable may enter an outpatient program designed to meet their specific needs. Some outpatient programs are extremely intensive, requiring patients to come in each day for treatment, whereas others are less rigorous, requiring only weekly visits for meetings with a psychiatrist or eating disorder specialist.

RECAP Anorexia nervosa is a potentially life-threatening disorder in which a person refuses to maintain a minimally normal body weight. Bulimia nervosa is characterized by binge eating followed by purging. In contrast, in binge-eating disorder, no purging typically occurs, and significant weight gain is likely. Night-eating syndrome is a combination of an eating disorder, a sleep disorder, and a mood disorder. The female athlete triad is a syndrome consisting of low energy availability, menstrual dysfunction, and low bone density. Treatment of eating disorders requires a multidisciplinary approach. Severely malnourished patients require hospitalization as a life-saving measure.

COOKING 101

A great way to maintain a healthful body weight is to prepare easy, satisfying snacks that help you beat cravings and meet your goals. Find out how to get creative and make delicious small servings in our new Cooking 101 videos, available on the Companion Website at www.pearsonhighered.com/thompsonmanore.

Chapter Review

What Can I Do **Today?**

Now that you've read this chapter, try making these three changes:

- Calculate your body mass index from your current height and weight, and measure your waist-to-hip ratio to determine if your body weight and shape are in the healthy range.
- If you need to lose weight, list three realistic, measurable goals you can begin to work toward today to help you achieve a healthy weight.
- If you eat out today, whether in the campus cafeteria or at your favorite fast-food restaurant, choose a healthier, low-Calorie meal as an alternative to your usual meal.

Test Yourself ANSWERS

1. **F** Health can be defined in many ways. A person who is overweight but exercises regularly and has no additional risk factors for various diseases (such as unhealthful blood lipid levels or smoking) is considered healthy.

2. **F** According to the Centers for Disease Control and Prevention, the United States has an overall obesity rate of 33.8%.

3. **T** Being underweight increases our risk for illness and premature death and in many cases can be just as unhealthful as being obese.

4. **F** Body composition assessments can help provide a general idea of your body fat levels, but most methods are not extremely accurate.

5. **F** Males also are diagnosed with eating disorders, but the incidence is much lower than for females.

Review Questions

1. The ratio of a person's body weight to height is represented as his or her
   a. body composition.
   b. basal metabolic rate.
   c. bioelectrical impedance.
   d. body mass index.

2. The body's total daily energy expenditure includes
   a. basal metabolic rate, thermal effect of food, and effect of physical activity.
   b. basal metabolic rate, movement, temperature regulation, and sleeping.
   c. effect of physical activity, standing, and sleeping.
   d. body mass index, thermal effect of food, and effect of physical activity.

3. All people gain weight when they
   a. eat a high-fat diet (> 35% fat).
   b. take in more energy than they expend.
   c. fail to exercise.
   d. take in less energy than they expend.

4. The set-point theory proposes that
   a. obese people have a gene not found in slender people that regulates their weight, so that it always hovers near a given set point.
   b. obese people have a gene that causes them to be energetically thrifty.
   c. all people have a genetic set point for their body weight.
   d. all people have a hormone that regulates their weight, so that it always hovers near a given set point.

5. Obesity increases the risk for
   a. heart disease.
   b. type 2 diabetes.
   c. premature death.
   d. all of the above.

6. True or False? Pear-shaped fat patterning is more likely to contribute to health problems than apple-shaped fat patterning.

7. True or False? One pound of fat is equal to about 3,500 kilocalories.

8. True or False? People with binge-eating disorder typically purge to compensate for the binge.

9. True or False? One recommendation for weight gain is to avoid both aerobic and resistance exercise for the duration of the weight-gain program.

10. True or False? The risks of gastric surgery in people who are obese are very high.

Answers to Review Questions are located at the back of this text.

Web Links

www.ftc.gov/bcp/edu/pubs/consumer/health/hea05.pdf
Partnership for Healthy Weight Management, PDF Publication

www.oa.org
Overeaters Anonymous

www.obesity.org
American Obesity Association

www.harriscentermgh.org
Harris Center, Massachusetts General Hospital's center for eating disorders

www.anad.org
National Association of Anorexia Nervosa and Associated Disorders

www.nationaleatingdisorders.org
National Eating Disorders Association

10
Nutrition and Physical Activity: Keys to Good Health

I n the summer of 2009, Millie Bolton of Ohio and Glenn Dody of Arizona each took the gold medal for the 400-meter dash in track and field at the National Senior Games. Bolton clocked 2 minutes, 31 seconds, and Dody's time was 1 minute, 42 seconds. If these performance times don't amaze you, perhaps they will when you consider these athletes' ages: both were competing in the class for 85- to 89-year-olds!

There's no doubt about it: regular physical activity dramatically improves our strength, stamina, health, and longevity. But what qualifies as "regular physical activity"? In other words, how much do we need to do to reap the benefits? And if we do become more active, does our diet have to change, too?

A nourishing diet and regular physical activity are like teammates, interacting in a variety of ways to improve our strength and stamina and increase our resistance to many chronic diseases and acute illnesses. In this chapter, we define physical activity, identify its many benefits, and discuss the nutrients needed to maintain an active life.

Nutrition Online

icons are located throughout the chapter, directing you to web links, videos, podcasts, and other useful online resources.

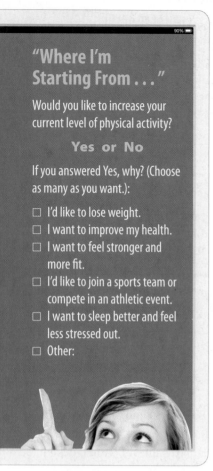

"Where I'm Starting From . . ."

Would you like to increase your current level of physical activity?

Yes or No

If you answered Yes, why? (Choose as many as you want.):

☐ I'd like to lose weight.
☐ I want to improve my health.
☐ I want to feel stronger and more fit.
☐ I'd like to join a sports team or compete in an athletic event.
☐ I want to sleep better and feel less stressed out.
☐ Other:

physical activity Any movement produced by muscles that increases energy expenditure; includes occupational, household, leisure-time, and transportation activities.

leisure-time physical activity Any activity not related to a person's occupation; includes competitive sports, recreational activities, and planned exercise training.

exercise A subcategory of leisure-time physical activity; any activity that is purposeful, planned, and structured.

physical fitness The ability to carry out daily tasks with vigor and alertness, without undue fatigue, and with ample energy to enjoy leisure-time pursuits and meet unforeseen emergencies.

aerobic exercise Exercise that involves the repetitive movement of large muscle groups, increasing the body's use of oxygen and promoting cardiovascular health.

resistance training Exercise in which our muscles act against resistance.

stretching Exercise in which muscles are gently lengthened using slow, controlled movements.

Why Engage in Physical Activity?

The term **physical activity** describes any movement produced by muscles that increases energy expenditure. Different categories of physical activity include occupational, household, leisure-time, and transportation.[1] **Leisure-time physical activity** is any activity not related to a person's occupation that includes competitive sports, planned exercise training, and recreational activities, such as hiking, walking, and bicycling. **Exercise** is therefore considered a subcategory of leisure-time physical activity and refers to activity that is purposeful, planned, and structured.[2]

Physical Activity Increases Our Fitness

A lot of people are looking for a "magic pill" that will help them maintain weight loss, reduce their risk for diseases, make them feel better, and improve their quality of sleep. Although many people are not aware of it, regular physical activity is this "magic pill." That's because it promotes **physical fitness:** the ability to carry out daily tasks with vigor and alertness, without undue fatigue, and with ample energy to enjoy leisure-time pursuits and meet unforeseen emergencies.[1]

The four components of physical fitness are cardiorespiratory fitness, which is the ability of the heart, lungs, and blood vessels to supply working muscles; musculoskeletal fitness, which is fitness of the muscles and bones; flexibility; and body composition **(Table 10.1)**.[3] Notice that these are achieved through three types of exercise:

- **Aerobic exercise** involves the repetitive movement of large muscle groups, which increases the body's use of oxygen and promotes cardiovascular health. In your daily life, you get aerobic exercise when you walk to school, work, or a bus stop or take the stairs to a third-floor classroom.
- **Resistance training** is a form of exercise in which our muscles work against resistance, such as against handheld weights. Carrying grocery bags or books and moving heavy objects are everyday activities that make our muscles work against resistance.
- **Stretching** exercises are those that increase flexibility, as they involve lengthening muscles using slow, controlled movements. You can perform stretching exercises even while you're sitting in a classroom by flexing, extending, and rotating your neck, limbs, and extremities.

> Sitting too long, studying for tomorrow's exam? Stretching can help! Learn some simple stretches by watching the how-to video collection from the Mayo Clinic at www.mayoclinic.com/health/office-stretches/MY00921.

TABLE 10.1	**The Components of Fitness**
Fitness Component	**Examples of Activities One Can Do to Achieve Fitness in Each Component**
Cardiorespiratory	Aerobic-type activities, such as walking, running, swimming, cross-country skiing
Musculoskeletal fitness:	Resistance training, weight lifting, calisthenics, sit-ups, push-ups
Muscular strength	Weight lifting or related activities using heavier weights with few repetitions
Muscular endurance	Weight lifting or related activities using lighter weights with more repetitions
Flexibility	Stretching exercises, yoga
Body composition	Aerobic exercise, resistance training

Physical Activity Reduces Our Risk for Chronic Disease

In addition to contributing to our fitness, physical activity can reduce our risk for certain diseases. Specifically, the health benefits of physical activity:

- *Reduces our risks for, and complications of, heart disease, stroke, and high blood pressure.* Regular physical activity increases high-density lipoprotein (HDL) cholesterol (the "good" cholesterol) and lowers triglycerides in the blood, improves the strength of the heart, helps maintain healthy blood pressure, and limits the progression of atherosclerosis ("hardening of the arteries").
- *Reduces our risk for obesity.* Regular physical activity maintains lean body mass and promotes more healthful levels of body fat, may help in appetite control, and increases energy expenditure and the use of fat as an energy source.
- *Reduces our risk for type 2 diabetes.* Regular physical activity enhances the action of insulin, which improves the cells' uptake of glucose from the blood, and it can improve blood glucose control in people with diabetes, which in turn reduces the risk for, or delays the onset of, diabetes-related complications.
- *May reduce our risk for colon cancer.* Although the exact role that physical activity may play in reducing colon cancer risk is still unknown, we do know that regular physical activity enhances gastric motility, which reduces the transit time of potentially cancer-causing agents through the gut.
- *Reduces our risk for osteoporosis.* Regular physical activity, especially weight-bearing exercise, increases bone density and enhances muscular strength and flexibility, thereby reducing the likelihood of falls and the incidence of fractures and other injuries when falls occur.

Regular physical activity is also known to improve our sleep patterns, reduce our risk for upper respiratory infections by improving immune function, and reduce anxiety and mental stress. It can also be effective in treating mild and moderate depression.

Most Americans Are Inactive

Until quite recently, humans were very physically active. This was not by choice, but because their survival depended on it. Prior to the industrial age, humans expended a considerable amount of energy each day, foraging and hunting for food, planting and harvesting food, preparing food once it was acquired, and securing shelter. In addition, their diet was composed primarily of small amounts of lean meats and naturally grown vegetables and

With the help of a nutritious diet, many people are able to remain physically active—and even competitive—throughout adult life.

NUTRITION
MILESTONE

1953 Although the benefits of exercise have been touted throughout history, it wasn't until 1953 that a significant link between physical health and exercise was confirmed. After returning from military service in World War II, Dr. Jeremiah Morris and other public health researchers in the United Kingdom became aware of the growing modern epidemic of coronary heart disease. Some evidence suggested that a person's occupation may play a key role in their risk for having a heart attack. Dr. Morris was able to prove his hypothesis in a landmark paper, published in *The Lancet*, which discussed his research on London transport employees.

This study showed that the heart attack rates of the bus drivers (who sat most of the day) were more than twice as high as those of conductors (who ran up and down the stairs of double-decker buses all day). He documented the waist circumferences of the bus employees via their pant waistband sizes, which indicated that the physically active conductors had a significantly lower risk for heart attack, no matter what the size of their waist! Dr. Morris is recognized as the father of physical activity epidemiology, and he continued to be an active exerciser and public health researcher until his death in 2009 at the age of 99.

⬆ Moderate physical activity, such as gardening, helps maintain overall health.

fruits. This lifestyle pattern contrasts considerably with today's lifestyles, which are characterized by sedentary jobs, easy access to an overabundance of energy-dense foods, and few opportunities for or little interest in expending energy through occupational or recreational activities.

Given these changes, it isn't surprising that most people find the "magic pill" of regular physical activity difficult to swallow. Despite the plethora of benefits derived from being regularly active, most people in the United States are physically inactive. The Centers for Disease Control and Prevention report that almost 38% of all U.S. adults do not do enough physical activity to meet national health recommendations, and 25% of adults in the United States admit to doing no leisure-time physical activity at all **(Figure 10.1)**.[4,5] These statistics are reflected in the high rates of obesity, heart disease, and type 2 diabetes in industrialized countries.

This trend toward inadequate physical activity levels is also occurring in young people. Among high school students, only 11.4% of girls and 24.8% of boys are meeting the recommended 60 minutes per day on 5 or more days per week.[6] Although physical education (PE) is part of the mandated curriculum in most states, only 33% of high school students attend PE classes daily,[6] and only 6.4% of middle schools offer daily PE for the entire school year.[7] Since our habits related to eating and physical activity are formed early in life, it is imperative that we provide opportunities for children and adolescents to engage in regular, enjoyable physical activity every day. An active lifestyle during childhood increases the likelihood of a healthier life as an adult.

RECAP Physical activity is any movement produced by muscles that increases energy expenditure. Physical fitness is the ability to carry out daily tasks with vigor and alertness, without undue fatigue, and with ample energy to enjoy leisure-time pursuits and meet unforeseen emergencies. Physical activity provides a multitude of health benefits, including reducing our risks for obesity and many chronic diseases and relieving anxiety and stress. Despite the many health benefits of physical activity, most people in the United States, including many children, are inactive.

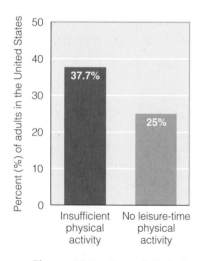

⬆ **Figure 10.1** Rates of physical inactivity in the United States. Almost 38% of the U.S. population does not do enough physical activity to meet national health recommendations, and 25% report doing no leisure-time physical activity.
Data from Centers for Disease Control and Prevention [CDC]. 2010. U.S. Physical Activity Statistics, 2007. http://apps.nccd.cdc.gov/PASurveillance/StateSumResultV.asp; and CDC. 2010. 1988–2008 No Leisure-Time Physical Activity Trend Chart. www.cdc.gov/nccdphp/dnpa/physical/stats/leisure_time.htm.

What Is a Sound Fitness Program?

Several widely recognized qualities of a sound fitness program, as well as guidelines to help you design one that is right for you, are explored in this section. Keep in mind that people with heart disease, high blood pressure, diabetes, obesity, osteoporosis, asthma, or arthritis should get approval to exercise from their healthcare practitioner prior to starting a fitness program. In addition, a medical evaluation should be conducted before starting an exercise program for an apparently healthy but currently inactive man 40 years or older or woman 50 years or older.

A Sound Fitness Program Meets Your Personal Goals

A fitness program that is ideal for you is not necessarily right for everyone. Before designing or evaluating any program, it is important to define your personal fitness goals. Do you want to prevent osteoporosis, diabetes, or another chronic disease that runs in your family? Do you simply want to increase your energy and stamina? Or do you intend to compete in athletic events? Each of these scenarios requires a unique fitness program. This concept is referred to as the *specificity principle*: specific actions yield specific results.

Training is generally defined as activity leading to skilled behavior. Training is very specific to any activity or goal. For example, if you wanted to train for athletic competition, a traditional approach that includes planned, purposive exercise sessions under the guidance of a trainer or coach would be beneficial. If you wanted to achieve cardiorespiratory fitness, you would likely be advised to participate in an aerobics class at least three times a week or jog for at least 20 minutes three times a week.

In contrast, if your goal were simply to maintain your overall health, you could do better to follow the 1996 report of the Surgeon General on achieving health through regular physical activity.[1] This report emphasizes that significant health benefits, such as reducing your risk for certain chronic diseases, can be achieved by participating in a moderate amount of physical activity (such as 30 minutes of gardening, housework, brisk walking, or bike riding) on most, if not all, days of the week. The 2010 Dietary Guidelines for Americans also recommend engaging in at least 30 minutes of moderate physical activity most days of the week. If 30 minutes at one time seems daunting, note that health benefits occur even when the time spent performing the physical activities is cumulative (for example, brisk walking for 10 minutes three times a day). Although these guidelines are appropriate for achieving health benefits, they are not necessarily of sufficient intensity and duration to improve physical fitness.

A Sound Fitness Program Is Varied, Consistent . . . and Fun!

One of the most important goals for everyone is fun; unless you enjoy being active, you may find it very difficult to maintain your physical fitness. What activities do you consider fun? If you enjoy the outdoors, hiking, camping, fishing, and rock climbing are potential activities for you. If you would rather exercise with friends between classes, walking, climbing stairs, jogging, roller-blading, or bicycle riding may be more appropriate. Or you may prefer to use the programs and equipment at your local fitness club or purchase your own treadmill and free weights.

Variety is critical to maintaining your fitness. Although some people enjoy doing similar activities day after day, most of us get bored with the same fitness routine. Incorporating a variety of activities into your fitness program will help maintain your interest and increase your enjoyment while promoting the different types of fitness identified in Table 10.1.

Variety can be achieved by

- combining aerobic exercise, resistance training, and stretching;
- combining indoor and outdoor activities throughout the week;
- taking different routes when you walk or jog each day;
- watching a movie, reading a book, or listening to music while you ride a stationary bicycle or walk on a treadmill; or
- participating in different activities each week, such as walking, dancing, bicycling, yoga, weight lifting, swimming, hiking, and gardening.

This "smorgasbord" of activities can increase your fitness without leading to monotony and boredom.

A useful tool has been developed to help you increase the variety of your physical activity choices **(Figure 10.2**, page 300). The **Physical Activity Pyramid** recommends the types and amounts of activity you should do weekly to increase your physical activity level. The bottom of the pyramid describes activities that should be done every day, including walking more, taking the stairs instead of the elevator, and working in your garden. Aerobic types of exercises (such as bicycling and brisk walking) and recreational activities (such as soccer, tennis, and basketball) should be done three to five times each week, for at least 20 or 30 minutes. Flexibility, strength, and leisure activities should be done two to three times a week. The top of the pyramid emphasizes things we should do less often, including watching TV, playing computer games, and sitting for more than 30 minutes at one time.

It is important to understand that you cannot do just one activity to achieve overall fitness because every activity is specific to a certain fitness component. Look back at Table 10.1, and notice the different activities listed as examples for the various components. For instance, participating in aerobic-type activities will improve cardiorespiratory fitness but will do little to improve muscular strength. To achieve that goal, you

▲ Hiking is a leisure-time activity that can contribute to your physical fitness. An important component for any activity is how much you enjoy doing it.

Map your walking, running, or cycling route and share it with friends—or check out dozens of fitness loops right in your neighborhood at www.livestrong.com/loops/.

Physical Activity Pyramid A visual pyramid, similar to the previous USDA Food Guide Pyramid, that makes recommendations for the types and amounts of activity that should be done weekly to increase physical activity levels.

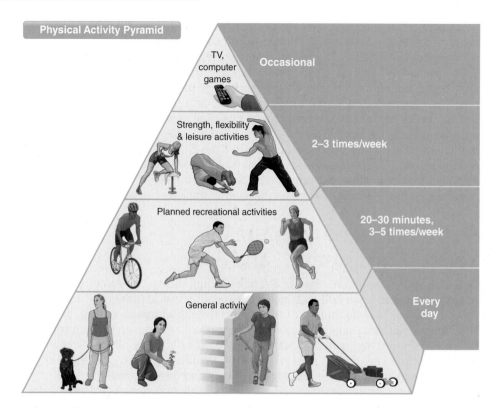

▲ **Figure 10.2** You can use this Physical Activity Pyramid as a visual guide to increase your level of physical activity.

Data from Corbin, C. B., and R. D. Pangrazi. 1998. Physical Activity Pyramid rebuffs peak experience. *ACSM Health Fitness J.* 2[1]. Copyright © 1998.

must participate in some form of resistance training. Flexibility is achieved by participating in stretching activities. By following the recommendations put forth in the Physical Activity Pyramid, you can achieve physical fitness in all components.

RECAP A sound fitness program must meet your personal fitness goals, such as reducing your risks for disease or preparing for competition in athletic events. It should also be fun and include activities you enjoy. Variety and consistency are important to help you maintain interest and achieve physical fitness in all components.

A Sound Fitness Program Appropriately Overloads the Body

In order to improve your fitness, you must place an extra physical demand on your body. This is referred to as the **overload principle.** A word of caution is in order here: *the overload principle does not advocate subjecting your body to inappropriately high stress,* because this can lead to exhaustion and injuries. In contrast, an appropriate overload on various body systems will result in healthy improvements in fitness.

To achieve an appropriate overload, you should consider three factors, collectively known as the **FIT principle:**

- Frequency
- Intensity
- Time of activity

overload principle The principle of placing an extra physical demand on your body in order to improve your fitness level.

FIT principle The principle used to achieve an appropriate overload for physical training; stands for frequency, intensity, and time of activity.

You can use the FIT principle to design either a general physical fitness program or a performance-based exercise program. **Figure 10.3** shows how the FIT principle can be applied to a cardiorespiratory and muscular fitness program.

Let's consider each of the FIT principle's three factors in more detail.

	Frequency	Intensity	Time
Cardiorespiratory fitness	3–5 days per week	64–90% maximal heart rate	At least 20 consecutive minutes
Muscular fitness	2–3 days per week	70–85% maximal weight you can lift	1–3 sets of 8–12 lifts* for each set *A minimum of 8–10 exercises involving the major muscle groups such as arms, shoulders, chest, abdomen, back, hips, and legs, is recommended.
Flexibility	2–4 days per week	Stretching through full range of motion	2–4 repetitions per stretch* *Hold each stretch for 15–30 seconds.

Figure 10.3 Using the FIT principle to achieve cardiorespiratory and musculoskeletal fitness and flexibility.

Frequency

Frequency refers to the number of activity sessions per week. Depending on your goals for fitness or health, the frequency of your activities will vary. To achieve and maintain cardiorespiratory fitness, you should train more than 2 days per week. Training 3 to 5 days per week appears optimal. On the other hand, training more than 5 days per week does not cause significant gains in fitness but can substantially increase your risk for injury. In contrast, only 2 to 3 days a week are needed to achieve musculoskeletal fitness.

Intensity

Intensity refers to the amount of effort expended, or how difficult the activity is to perform. We can describe the intensity of activity as low, moderate, or vigorous:

- **Low-intensity activities** are those that cause very mild increases in breathing, sweating, and heart rate.
- **Moderate-intensity activities** cause moderate increases in breathing, sweating, and heart rate. For instance, you can carry on a conversation, but not continuously.
- **Vigorous-intensity activities** produce significant increases in breathing, sweating, and heart rate, so that talking is difficult when exercising.

Traditionally, heart rate has been used to indicate level of intensity during aerobic activities. You can calculate the range of exercise intensity that is appropriate for you by estimating your **maximal heart rate,** which is the rate at which your heart beats during maximal-intensity exercise. Maximal heart rate is estimated by subtracting your age from 220.

frequency The number of activity sessions per week you perform.

intensity The amount of effort expended during the activity, or how difficult the activity is to perform.

low-intensity activities Activities that cause very mild increases in breathing, sweating, and heart rate.

moderate-intensity activities Activities that cause noticeable increases in breathing, sweating, and heart rate.

vigorous-intensity activities Activities that produce significant increases in breathing, sweating, and heart rate; talking is difficult when exercising at a vigorous intensity.

maximal heart rate The rate at which your heart beats during maximal-intensity exercise.

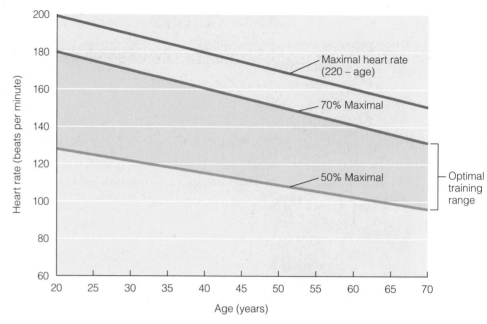

⬆ **Figure 10.4** This heart rate training chart can be used to estimate your aerobic exercise intensity. The top line indicates the predicted maximal heart rate value for a person's age (220 – age). The shaded area represents the heart rate values that fall between 50% and 70% of maximal heart rate, which is the range generally recommended to achieve aerobic fitness.

⬆ Testing in a fitness lab is the most accurate way to determine maximal heart rate.

Figure 10.4 shows an example of a heart rate training chart, which you can use to estimate the intensity of your own workout. The Centers for Disease Control and Prevention makes the following recommendations:[8]

• To achieve moderate-intensity physical activity, your target heart rate should be 50–70% of your estimated maximal heart rate. Older adults and anyone who has been inactive for a long time may want to exercise at the lower end of the moderate-intensity range.
• To achieve vigorous-intensity physical activity, your target heart rate should be 70–85% of your estimated heart rate. Those who are physically fit or are striving for a more rapid improvement in fitness may want to exercise at the higher end of the vigorous-intensity range.
• Competitive athletes generally train at a higher intensity, around 80–95% of their maximal heart rate.

Although the calculation of *220 minus age* has been used extensively for years to predict maximal heart rate, it was never intended to accurately represent everyone's true maximal heart rate or to be used as the standard of aerobic training intensity. The most accurate way to determine your own maximal heart rate is to complete a maximal exercise test in a fitness laboratory; however, this test is not commonly conducted with the general public and can be very expensive. Although not completely accurate, the estimated maximal heart rate method can still be used to give you a general idea of your aerobic training range.

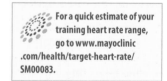

For a quick estimate of your training heart rate range, go to www.mayoclinic .com/health/target-heart-rate/ SM00083.

So what is your maximal heart rate and training range? To find out, try the easy calculation in the **What About You?** feature box (page 303).

Time of Activity

time of activity The amount of time that a given exercise session lasts, not including warm-up and cool-down periods.

Time of activity refers to how long each session lasts. To achieve general health, you can do multiple short bouts of activity that add up to 30 minutes each day. However, to achieve higher levels of fitness, it is important that the activities be done for at least 20 to 30 consecutive minutes.

WHAT ABOUT YOU?

What's Your Maximal Heart Rate and Training Range?

90% 🔋

You can estimate your maximal heart rate by using the following easy calculation:

your maximal heart rate = 220 minus your age

Let's say you are 20 years old:

your maximal heart rate = 220 − 20
= 200 beats per minute (bpm)

Now let's calculate your training range. As we said in the text, for non-athletes this number is 50% to 70% of your maximal heart rate. If you want to work out at the lower end of your range, you should multiply your maximal

heart rate by 50%. If your maximal heart rate is 200, your equation is

lower end of your training range
= 200 bpm × 0.50 = 100 bpm

If you want to work out at the higher end of your range, you should multiply your maximal heart rate by 70%:

higher end of your training range
= 200 bpm × 0.70 = 140 bpm

Thus, your training range is between 100 and 140 bpm.

For example, let's say you want to compete in triathlons. To be successful during the running segment of the triathlon, you will need to be able to run at least 5 miles. Thus, it is appropriate for you to train so that you can complete 5 miles during one session and still have enough energy to swim and bicycle during the race. You will need to consistently train at a distance of 5 miles; you will also benefit from running longer distances.

A Sound Fitness Plan Includes Warm-Up and Cool-Down Periods

To properly prepare for and recover from an exercise session, warm-up and cool-down activities should be performed. **Warm-up,** also called preliminary exercise, includes general activities, such as gentle aerobics, calisthenics, and then stretching followed by specific activities that prepare you for the actual activity, such as jogging or swinging a golf club. Your warm-up should be brief (5 to 10 minutes), gradual, and sufficient to increase muscle and body temperature but should not cause fatigue or deplete energy stores.

Warming up prior to exercise is important, as it properly prepares your muscles for exertion by increasing blood flow and body temperature. It enhances the body's flexibility and may also help prepare you psychologically for the exercise session or athletic event.

Cool-down activities are done after the exercise session. The cool-down should be gradual and allow your body to slowly recover. Your cool-down should include some of the same activities you performed during the exercise session, but at a low intensity, and you should allow ample time for stretching. Cooling down after exercise assists in the prevention of injury and may help reduce muscle soreness.

Now that you know the benefits of regular physical activity and the characteristics of a sound fitness plan, how do you get started? If you haven't been active until now, it's important to set realistic goals you can achieve in a short period of time—for instance, "I want to perform at least 30 minutes of physical activity each day on at least 5 days next week." For tips on incorporating physical activity into your daily life, check out the *Game Plan* feature box (page 304).

Stretching should be included in the warm-up before, and the cool-down after, exercise.

warm-up Activities that prepare you for an exercise session, including stretching, calisthenics, and movements specific to the exercise you are about to engage in; also called preliminary exercise.

cool-down Activities done after an exercise session is completed; they should be gradual and allow your body to slowly recover from exercise.

90% 🔋

GAME PLAN

Tips for Increasing Your Physical Activity

There are 1,440 minutes in every day. Spend just 30 of those minutes in physical activity, and you'll be taking an important step toward improving your health. Here are some tips for working activity into your daily life:

☐ Walk as often and as far as possible: park your car farther away from your dorm, a lecture hall, or shops; walk to school or work; go for a brisk walk between classes; get on or off the bus one stop away from your destination. And don't be in such a rush to reach your destination—take the long way and burn a few more Calories.

☐ Take the stairs instead of the elevator.

☐ Exercise while watching television—for example by doing sit-ups, stretching, or using a treadmill or stationary bike.

☐ While talking on your cell phone, memorizing vocabulary terms, or practicing your choral part, don't stand still—pace!

☐ Turn on some music and dance!

☐ Get an exercise partner: join a friend for walks, hikes, cycling, skating, tennis, or a fitness class.

☐ Take up a group sport.

☐ Register for a class from the physical education department in an activity you've never tried before, maybe yoga or fencing.

☐ Register for a dance class, such as jazz, tap, or ballroom.

☐ Use the pool, rock-climbing wall, or other facilities at your campus fitness center, or join a health club, gym, or YMCA/YWCA in your community.

☐ Join an activity-based club, such as a skating, tennis, or hiking club.

☐ Play golf without using a golf cart—choose to walk and carry your clubs instead.

☐ Choose a physically active vacation that provides daily activities combined with exploring new surroundings.

If you have been inactive for a while, use a sensible approach by starting out slowly. Gradually build up the time you spend doing the activity by adding a few minutes every few days until you reach 30 minutes a day. As this 30-minute minimum becomes easier, gradually increase the length of time you spend in activity, the intensity of the activities you choose, or both.

RECAP To improve fitness, you must place an appropriate overload on your body. Follow the FIT principle: *FIT* stands for frequency, intensity, and time of activity. Frequency is the number of activity sessions per week. Intensity is how difficult the activity is to perform. Time of activity is how long each activity session lasts. Warm-up exercises prepare the muscles for exertion by increasing blood flow and temperature. Low-intensity cool-down activities help prevent injury and may help reduce muscle soreness.

What Fuels Our Activities?

In order to perform exercise, or muscular work, we must be able to generate energy. The common currency of energy for virtually all cells in the body is **adenosine triphosphate (ATP).** As you might guess from its name, a molecule of ATP includes an organic compound called adenosine and three phosphate groups **(Figure 10.5).** When one of the phosphates is cleaved, or broken away, from ATP, energy is released. The products remaining after this reaction are adenosine diphosphate (ADP) and an independent inorganic phosphate group (P_i). In a mirror image of this reaction, the body regenerates ATP by adding a phosphate group back to ADP. In this way, we continually provide energy to our cells.

The amount of ATP stored in a muscle cell is very limited; it can keep the muscle active for only about 1 to 3 seconds. When more energy is needed, a high-energy compound called **creatine phosphate (CP)** can be broken down to support the regeneration of ATP. Because this reaction can occur in the absence of oxygen, it is referred to as **anaerobic** (meaning "without oxygen").

Muscle tissue contains about four to six times as much CP as ATP, but that is still not enough to fuel long-term activities. CP is used the most during very intense, short bouts of activity, such as lifting, jumping, and sprinting. Together, our stores of ATP and CP can support a *maximal* physical effort for only about 3 to 15 seconds. As a result, we rely on other energy sources, such as carbohydrate and fat, to support activities of longer duration **(Figure 10.6,** page 306).

The Breakdown of Carbohydrates Provides Energy for Brief and Long-Term Exercise

During activities lasting about 30 seconds to 3 minutes, our body needs an energy source that can be used quickly to produce ATP. The breakdown of carbohydrates, specifically glucose, provides this quick energy in a process called **glycolysis.** The most common source of glucose during exercise comes from glycogen stored in our muscles and glucose found in our blood. As shown in **Figure 10.7** (page 307), for every glucose molecule that goes through glycolysis, two ATP molecules are produced. The primary end product of glycolysis is **pyruvic acid.**

When oxygen availability is limited in the cell, pyruvic acid is converted to **lactic acid** (see the blue section of Figure 10.7). For years, it was assumed that lactic acid was a useless, even potentially toxic by-product of high-intensity exercise. We now know that lactic acid is an important intermediate of glucose breakdown and that it plays a critical role in supplying fuel for working muscles, the heart, and resting tissues. But does it cause muscle fatigue and soreness? See the *Nutrition Myth or Fact?* box (page 308).

The major advantage of glycolysis is that it is the fastest way that we can regenerate ATP for exercise, other than the ATP–CP system. However, this high rate of

adenosine triphosphate (ATP) The common currency of energy for virtually all cells of the body.

creatine phosphate (CP) A high-energy compound that can be broken down for energy and used to regenerate ATP.

anaerobic Means "without oxygen"; refers to metabolic reactions that occur in the absence of oxygen.

glycolysis The breakdown of glucose; yields two ATP molecules and two pyruvic acid molecules for each molecule of glucose.

pyruvic acid The primary end product of glycolysis.

lactic acid A compound that results when pyruvic acid is metabolized.

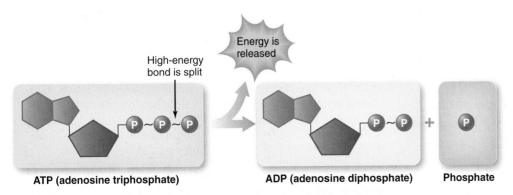

Figure 10.5 Structure of adenosine triphosphate (ATP). Energy is produced when ATP is split into adenosine diphosphate (ADP) and inorganic phosphate (P_i).

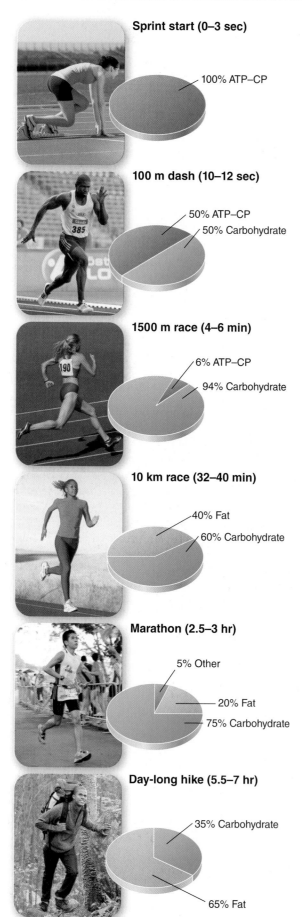

Sprint start (0–3 sec)

100% ATP–CP

100 m dash (10–12 sec)

50% ATP–CP
50% Carbohydrate

1500 m race (4–6 min)

6% ATP–CP
94% Carbohydrate

10 km race (32–40 min)

40% Fat
60% Carbohydrate

Marathon (2.5–3 hr)

5% Other
20% Fat
75% Carbohydrate

Day-long hike (5.5–7 hr)

35% Carbohydrate
65% Fat

ATP production can be sustained for only a brief period of time, generally less than 3 minutes. To continue to exercise, we must rely on the aerobic energy system to provide adequate ATP.

In the presence of oxygen, pyruvic acid can go through additional metabolic pathways. Although this process is slower than glycolysis, the breakdown of one glucose molecule going through aerobic metabolism yields thirty-six to thirty-eight ATP molecules for energy (recall that glycolysis yields only two). Thus, this aerobic process supplies eighteen times more energy! Another advantage of the aerobic process is that it does not result in significant production of metabolic by-products that contribute to muscle fatigue, which means that a low-intensity activity can be performed for hours. Aerobic metabolism of glucose is the primary source of fuel for our muscles during activities lasting from 3 minutes to 4 hours (see Figure 10.6).

We can store only a limited amount of glycogen in our body. An average, well-nourished man who weighs about 154 pounds (70 kg) can store about 200 to 500 grams of muscle glycogen, which is equal to 800 to 2,000 kilocalories of energy. Although trained athletes can store more muscle glycogen than the average person, even their body does not store enough glycogen to provide an unlimited energy supply for long-term activities. Thus, we also need a fuel source that is very abundant and can be broken down under aerobic conditions, so that it can support activities of lower intensity and longer duration. This fuel source is fat.

The Aerobic Breakdown of Fats Supports Exercise of Low Intensity and Long Duration

The triglyceride molecule is the primary storage form of fat in our cells. Its three fatty acid molecules provide much of the energy we need to support long-term activity.

There are two major advantages of using fatty acids as a fuel. First, fat is a very abundant energy source, even in lean people. For example, a man who weighs 154 lb (70 kg) who has a body fat level of 10% has approximately 15 lb of body fat, which is equivalent to more than 50,000 kcal of energy! This is significantly more energy than can be provided by muscle glycogen (800 to 2,000 kcal). Second, fat provides 9 kcal of energy per gram, whereas carbohydrate provides only 4 kcal per gram, which means that fat supplies more than twice as much energy per gram as carbohydrate. The primary disadvantage of using fat as a fuel is that the breakdown process is relatively slow; thus, fat is used predominantly as a fuel source during activities of lower intensity and longer duration. Fat is also our primary energy source during rest, sitting, and standing in place.

What specific activities are primarily fueled by fat? Walking long distances uses fat stores, as do other low- to moderate-intensity forms of exercise. Fat is also an important fuel source during endurance events such as marathons (26.2 miles) and ultramarathons (49.9 miles). Endurance exercise training

◀ **Figure 10.6** The relative contributions of ATP–CP, carbohydrate, and fat to activities of varying durations and intensities.

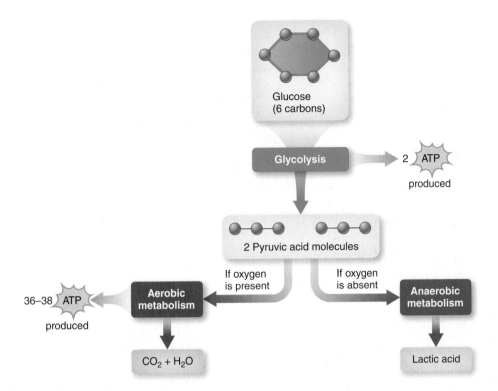

Figure 10.7 The breakdown of one molecule of glucose, or the process of glycolysis, yields two molecules of pyruvic acid and two ATP molecules. The further metabolism of pyruvic acid in the presence of insufficient oxygen (anaerobic process) results in the production of lactic acid. The metabolism of pyruvic acid in the presence of adequate oxygen (aerobic process) yields thirty-six to thirty-eight molecules of ATP.

improves our ability to use fat for energy, which may be one reason that endurance athletes tend to have lower body fat levels than people who do not exercise.

Our body is continually using some combination of carbohydrate and fat for energy. At rest, we use very little carbohydrate, relying mostly on fat. However, this does not mean that we can reduce our body fat by resting and doing very little activity! To lose weight and reduce body fat, a person needs to exercise regularly and reduce energy intake, so that a negative energy balance results. During maximal exercise (at 90% to 100% effort), we are using virtually all carbohydrate. However, most activities we do each day involve some use of both fuels.

When it comes to eating properly to support regular physical activity or exercise training, the nutrient to focus on is carbohydrate. This is because most people store more than enough fat to support exercise, whereas our storage of carbohydrate is limited. It is especially important that we maintain adequate stores of glycogen for moderate to intense exercise.

Amino Acids Are Not Major Sources of Fuel During Exercise

Proteins, or more specifically amino acids, are not major energy sources during exercise. Amino acids can be used directly for energy if necessary, but they are more often used to make glucose to maintain our blood glucose levels during exercise. Amino acids also help build and repair tissues after exercise. Depending on the intensity and duration of the activity, amino acids may contribute about 1% to 6% of the energy needed.[9]

Given this, why are so many people concerned about their protein intake? Our muscles are not stimulated to grow when we eat extra dietary protein. Only appropriate physical training can stimulate our muscles to grow and strengthen. Thus, although we need enough dietary protein to support activity and recovery, consuming very high amounts does not provide an added benefit. The protein needs of

NUTRITION MYTH OR FACT?
Does Lactic Acid Cause Muscle Fatigue and Soreness?

Theo and his teammates won their basketball game last night, but just barely. With two of the players sick, Theo got more court time than usual, and when he got back to the dorm, he could hardly get his legs to carry him up the stairs. This morning, Theo's muscles ache all over, and he wonders if a buildup of lactic acid is to blame.

Lactic acid is a by-product of glycolysis. For many years, both scientists and athletes believed that lactic acid caused both muscle fatigue and soreness. Does recent scientific evidence support this belief?

The exact causes of muscle fatigue are not known, and there appear to be many contributing factors. Recent evidence suggests that fatigue may be due not only to the accumulation of many acids and other metabolic by-products, such as inorganic phosphate,[10] but also to the depletion of creatine phosphate and changes in calcium in the cells that affect muscle contraction. Depletion of muscle glycogen, liver glycogen, and blood glucose, as well as psychological factors, can all contribute to fatigue.[11] Thus, it appears that lactic acid contributes to fatigue but does not cause it independently.

So what causes muscle soreness? As with fatigue, there are probably many factors. It is hypothesized that soreness usually results from microscopic tears in the muscle fibers as a result of strenuous exercise. This damage triggers an inflammatory reaction, which causes an influx of fluid and various chemicals to the damaged area. These substances work to remove damaged tissue and initiate tissue repair, but they may also stimulate pain. However, it appears highly unlikely that lactic acid is an independent cause of muscle soreness.

Recent studies indicate that lactic acid is produced even under aerobic conditions! This means it is produced at rest as well as during exercise at any intensity. The reasons for this constant production of lactic acid are still being studied. What we do know is that lactic acid is an important fuel for resting tissues, for working cardiac and skeletal muscles, and even for the brain both at rest and during exercise.[12,13] We also know that endurance training improves the muscles' ability to use lactic acid for energy. Thus, contrary to being a waste product of glucose metabolism, lactic acid is actually an important energy source for muscle cells during rest and exercise.

---

athletes are only slightly higher than the needs of non-athletes, and most of us eat more than enough protein to support even the highest requirements for competitive athletes! Thus, there is generally no need for recreationally active people or even competitive athletes to consume protein or amino acid supplements.

RECAP Adenosine triphosphate, or ATP, is the common energy source for all cells of the body. ATP and creatine phosphate stored in our muscle cells can fuel only brief spurts of activity. To support activities that last longer, energy is produced from the breakdown of glucose. Fat is broken down slowly to support activities of low intensity and long duration. Amino acids help build and repair tissues after exercise but contribute only 1% to 6% of the energy needed during exercise. We generally consume more than enough protein in our diet to support regular exercise and do not need protein or amino acid supplements.

What Kind of Diet Supports Physical Activity?

Lots of people wonder, "Do my nutrient needs change if I become more physically active?" The answer to this question depends on the type, intensity, and duration of the activity in which you participate. It is not necessarily true that our requirement for every nutrient is greater if we are physically active.

People who are performing moderate-intensity daily activities for health can follow the dietary guidelines put forth in the USDA Food Patterns. For smaller or less active people, the lower end of the range of recommendations for each food group may be appropriate. For larger or more active people, the higher end of the

↞ Small, healthful snacks can help you meet daily energy demands.

TABLE 10.2	Suggested Intakes of Nutrients to Support Vigorous Exercise	
Nutrient	**Functions**	**Suggested Intake**
Energy	Supports exercise, activities of daily living, and basic body functions	Depends on body size and the type, intensity, and duration of activity For many female athletes: 1,800 to 3,500 kcal/day For many male athletes: 2,500 to 7,500 kcal/day
Carbohydrate	Provides energy, maintains adequate muscle glycogen and blood glucose; high-complex-carbohydrate foods provide vitamins and minerals	45% to 65% of total energy intake Depending on sport and gender, should consume 6–10 grams of carbohydrate per kg of body weight per day
Fat	Provides energy, fat-soluble vitamins, and essential fatty acids; supports production of hormones and transport of nutrients	20% to 35% of total energy intake
Protein	Helps build and maintain muscle; provides building material for glucose; is an energy source during endurance exercise; aids recovery from exercise	10% to 35% of total energy intake Endurance athletes: 1.2–1.4 grams per kg body weight Strength athletes: 1.2–1.7 grams per kg body weight
Water	Maintains temperature regulation (adequate cooling); maintains blood volume and blood pressure; supports all cell functions	Consume fluid before, during, and after exercise Consume enough to maintain body weight Consume at least 8 cups (64 fl. oz) of water daily to maintain regular health and activity Athletes may need up to 10 liters (170 fl. oz) every day; more is required if exercising in a hot environment
B-vitamins	Is critical for energy production from carbohydrate, fat, and protein	May need slightly more (one to two times the RDA) for thiamin, riboflavin, and vitamin B_6
Calcium	Builds and maintains bone mass; assists with nervous system function, muscle contraction, hormone function, and transport of nutrients across cell membrane	Meet the current RDA: 14–18 years: 1,300 mg/day 19–50 years: 1,000 mg/day 51–70 years, men: 1,000 mg/day 51–70 years, women: 1,200 mg/day >70 years: 1,200 mg/day
Iron	Is primarily responsible for the transport of oxygen in blood to cells; assists with energy production	Consume at least the RDA: Men: 14–18 years: 11 mg/day 19 years and older: 8 mg/day Women: 14–18 years: 15 mg/day 19–50 years: 18 mg/day 51 years and older: 8 mg/day

range is suggested. Modifications may be necessary for people who exercise vigorously every day, particularly for athletes training for competition. **Table 10.2** provides an overview of the nutrients that can be affected by regular, vigorous exercise training. Each of these nutrients is described in more detail in this section.[14]

Vigorous Exercise Increases Energy Needs

Athletes generally have higher energy needs than moderately physically active or sedentary people. The amount of extra energy needed to support regular training is determined by the type, intensity, and duration of the activity. In addition, the energy needs of male athletes are higher than those of female athletes because male athletes weigh more, have more muscle mass, and expend more energy during activity. This is relative, of course: a large woman who trains 3 to 5 hours each day will probably need more energy than a small man who trains 1 hour each day. The energy needs of athletes can range from only 1,500 to 1,800 kcal/day for a small female gymnast to more than 7,500 kcal/day for a male cyclist competing in the Tour de France cross-country cycling race.

Figure 10.8 (page 310) shows an example of 1 day's meals and snacks that total 1,800 kcal and 4,000 kcal, with the carbohydrate content of these foods meeting more

Eating for Athletes: Meeting High Energy Demands

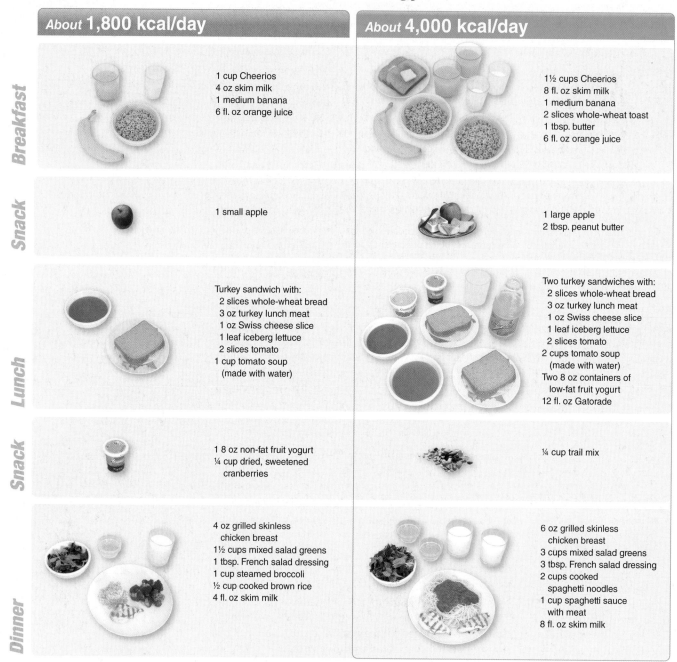

	About **1,800 kcal/day**	*About* **4,000 kcal/day**
Breakfast	1 cup Cheerios 4 oz skim milk 1 medium banana 6 fl. oz orange juice	1½ cups Cheerios 8 fl. oz skim milk 1 medium banana 2 slices whole-wheat toast 1 tbsp. butter 6 fl. oz orange juice
Snack	1 small apple	1 large apple 2 tbsp. peanut butter
Lunch	Turkey sandwich with: 2 slices whole-wheat bread 3 oz turkey lunch meat 1 oz Swiss cheese slice 1 leaf iceberg lettuce 2 slices tomato 1 cup tomato soup (made with water)	Two turkey sandwiches with: 2 slices whole-wheat bread 3 oz turkey lunch meat 1 oz Swiss cheese slice 1 leaf iceberg lettuce 2 slices tomato 2 cups tomato soup (made with water) Two 8 oz containers of low-fat fruit yogurt 12 fl. oz Gatorade
Snack	1 8 oz non-fat fruit yogurt ¼ cup dried, sweetened cranberries	¼ cup trail mix
Dinner	4 oz grilled skinless chicken breast 1½ cups mixed salad greens 1 tbsp. French salad dressing 1 cup steamed broccoli ½ cup cooked brown rice 4 fl. oz skim milk	6 oz grilled skinless chicken breast 3 cups mixed salad greens 3 tbsp. French salad dressing 2 cups cooked spaghetti noodles 1 cup spaghetti sauce with meat 8 fl. oz skim milk

🔺 **Figure 10.8** High-carbohydrate (approximately 60% of total energy) meals and snacks that contain approximately 1,800 kcal per day (on left) and 4,000 kcal per day (on right). Athletes must plan their diet carefully to meet energy demands, particularly those with very high energy needs.

grazing The practice of consistently eating small meals throughout the day; done by many athletes to meet their high-energy demands.

than 60% of total energy intake. As you can see, athletes who need 4,000 kcal per day need to consume very large quantities of food. However, the heavy demands of daily physical training, work, school, and family responsibilities often leave these athletes with little time to eat adequately. Thus, many athletes meet their energy demands by planning regular meals and snacks and **grazing** (eating small meals throughout the day) consistently. They may also take advantage of the energy-dense snack foods and meal replacements specifically designed for athletes participating in vigorous training. These steps help athletes maintain their blood glucose levels and energy stores.

If an athlete is losing body weight, his or her energy intake is inadequate. Conversely, weight gain may indicate that energy intake is too high. Weight maintenance is generally recommended to maximize performance. If weight loss is warranted, food intake should be lowered no more than 200 to 500 kcal/day, and athletes should try to lose weight prior to the competitive season, if at all possible. Weight gain may be necessary for some athletes and can usually be accomplished by consuming 500 to 700 kcal/day more than needed for weight maintenance. The extra energy should come from a healthy balance of carbohydrate (45% to 60% of total energy intake), fat (20% to 35% of total energy intake), and protein (10% to 35% of total energy intake).

Many athletes are concerned about their weight. Jockeys, boxers, wrestlers, judo athletes, and others are required to "make weight"—to meet a predefined weight category. Others, such as distance runners, gymnasts, figure skaters, and dancers, are required to maintain a very lean figure for performance and aesthetic reasons. These athletes tend to eat less energy than they need to support vigorous training, which puts them at risk for inadequate intakes of all nutrients. These athletes are also at a higher risk of suffering from health consequences resulting from poor energy and nutrient intake, including eating disorders, osteoporosis, menstrual disturbances (in women), dehydration, heat and physical injuries, and even death. It is also important to understand that athletes should not adopt low-carbohydrate diets in an attempt to lose weight. As we discuss next, carbohydrates are a critical energy source for maintaining exercise performance.

Carbohydrate Needs Increase for Many Active People

Carbohydrate (in the form of glucose) is one of the primary sources of energy for a body in training. Both endurance athletes and strength athletes require adequate carbohydrate to maintain their glycogen stores and provide quick energy.

How Much of an Athlete's Diet Should Be Carbohydrates?

You may recall that the AMDR for carbohydrates is 45% to 65% of total energy intake. Athletes should consume carbohydrate intakes within this recommended range. Although high-carbohydrate diets (greater than 60% of total energy intake) have been recommended in the past, this percentage value may not be appropriate for all athletes.

When Should Carbohydrates Be Consumed?

It is important for athletes not only to consume enough carbohydrate to maintain glycogen stores but also to time their intake optimally. Our body stores glycogen very rapidly during the first 24 hours of recovery from exercise, with the highest storage rates occurring during the first few hours.[15] Higher carbohydrate intakes during the first 24 hours of recovery from exercise are associated with higher amounts of glucose being stored as muscle glycogen. It is recommended that a daily carbohydrate intake of approximately 6 to 10 grams of carbohydrate per kg of body weight will optimize muscle glycogen stores in many athletes. However, this need may be much greater in athletes who are training heavily daily, as they have less time to recover and require more carbohydrate to support both training and storage needs.

If an athlete has to perform or participate in training bouts that are scheduled less than 8 hours apart, he or she should try to consume enough carbohydrate in the few hours following training to allow for ample glycogen storage. However, with a longer recovery time (generally 12 hours or more), the athlete can eat when he or she chooses, and glycogen levels should be restored as long as the total carbohydrate eaten is sufficient.

Interestingly, studies have shown that muscle glycogen can be restored to adequate levels in the muscle whether the food is eaten in small, multiple snacks or in larger meals,[15] although some studies show enhanced muscle glycogen storage during the first 4 to 6 hours of recovery when athletes are fed large amounts of carbohydrate every 15 to 30 minutes.[16,17] There is also evidence that consuming high glycemic-index

Fruit and vegetable juices can be good sources of carbohydrates.

foods during the immediate postrecovery period results in higher glycogen storage than is achieved as a result of eating low glycemic-index foods. This may be due to a greater malabsorption of the carbohydrate in low glycemic-index foods, as these foods contain more indigestible forms of carbohydrate.[15]

What Food Sources of Carbohydrate Support Are Good for Athletes?

What are good carbohydrate sources to support vigorous training? In general, fiber-rich, less-processed carbohydrate foods, such as whole grains and cereals, fruits, vegetables, and juices, are excellent sources that also supply fiber, vitamins, and minerals. Guidelines recommend that intake of simple sugars be less than 10% of total energy intake, but some athletes who need very large energy intakes to support training may need to consume more. In addition, as previously mentioned, glycogen storage can be enhanced by consuming foods with a high glycemic index immediately postrecovery. Thus, there are advantages to consuming a wide variety of carbohydrate sources.

As a result of time constraints, many athletes have difficulties consuming enough food to meet carbohydrate demands. Sports drinks and energy bars have been designed to help athletes increase their carbohydrate intake. **Table 10.3** identifies some energy bars and other simple, inexpensive snacks and meals that provide 50 to 100 grams of carbohydrate.

When Does Carbohydrate Loading Make Sense?

As you know, carbohydrate is a critical energy source to support exercise—particularly endurance-type activities—yet we have a limited capacity to store them. So it's not surprising that discovering ways to maximize our storage of carbohydrates has been at the forefront of sports nutrition research for many years. The practice of **carbohydrate loading,** also called *glycogen loading,* involves altering both exercise duration and carbohydrate intake to maximize the amount of muscle glycogen. **Table 10.4** provides a schedule for carbohydrate loading for an endurance athlete.

carbohydrate loading The practice of altering training and carbohydrate intake so that muscle glycogen storage is maximized; also known as *glycogen loading.*

TABLE 10.3 Carbohydrate and Total Energy in Various Foods

Food	Amount	Carbohydrate (grams)	Energy from Carbohydrate (%)	Total Energy (kcal)
Sweetened applesauce	1 cup	50	97	207
Large apple	1 each	50	82	248
with Saltine crackers	8 each			
Whole-wheat bread	1-oz. slice	50	71	282
with jelly	4 tsp			
and skim milk	12 fl. oz			
Spaghetti (cooked)	1 cup	50	75	268
with tomato sauce	¼ cup			
Brown rice (cooked)	1 cup	100	88	450
with mixed vegetables	½ cup			
and apple juice	12 fl. oz			
Grape Nuts cereal	½ cup	100	84	473
with raisins	3/8 cup			
and skim milk	8 fl. oz			
Clif Bar (chocolate chip)	2.4 oz	45	72	250
Meta-Rx (fudge brownie)	3.53 oz	48	60	320
Power Bar (chocolate)	2.25 oz	42	75	225
PR Bar Ironman	2 oz	24	42	230

Data from "Carbohydrate and Total Energy in Various Foods and Sports Bars" adapted from *Sport Nutrition for Health and Performance,* by Manore and J. Thompson. Copyright © 2000. Published by Human Kinetics.

TABLE 10.4	**Recommended Carbohydrate-Loading Procedure for Endurance Athletes**	
Days Prior to Event	**Exercise Duration (minutes) at 70% Maximal Effort**	**Carbohydrate Content of Diet (grams per kg of body weight)**
6	90	5
5	40	5
4	40	5
3	20	10
2	20	10
1	Rest	10
Day of race	Competition	Precompetition food and fluid

From *Sports Nutrition: A Practice Manual for Professionals* 4th edition. Copyright © 2006 by American Dietetic Association. Reprinted with permission.

Athletes who may benefit from carbohydrate loading are those competing in marathons, ultramarathons, long-distance swimming, cross-country skiing, and tri-athlons. Athletes who compete in baseball, American football, 10K runs, walking, hiking, weight lifting, and most swimming events will not gain any performance benefits from this practice, nor will people who regularly participate in moderately intense physical activities to maintain fitness.

It is important to emphasize that, even in endurance events, carbohydrate loading does not always improve performance. There are many adverse side effects of this prac-tice, including extreme gastrointestinal distress, particularly diarrhea. We store water along with the extra glycogen in our muscles, which leaves many athletes feeling heavy and sluggish. Athletes who want to try carbohydrate loading should experiment prior to competition to determine whether it is an acceptable and beneficial approach for them.

↟ Carbohydrate loading may benefit endurance athletes, such as cross-country skiers.

RECAP The type, intensity, and duration of activities we participate in determine our nutrient needs. Men generally need more energy than women be-cause of their greater muscle mass and higher body weight. In general, athletes should consume at least 45% to 60% of their total energy as carbohydrate. Consuming car-bohydrate sources within the first few hours of recovery can maximize carbohydrate storage rates. Carbohydrate loading involves altering physical training and the diet so that the storage of muscle glycogen is maximized in an attempt to enhance endurance performance.

Moderate Fat Consumption Is Enough to Support Most Activities

Fat is an important energy source for both moderate physical activity and vigorous endurance training. When athletes reach a physically trained state, they are able to use more fat for energy; in other words, they become better "fat burners." This can also occur in people who are not athletes but who regularly participate in aerobic-type fitness activities. This training effect occurs for a number of reasons, including an increase in the number and activity of various enzymes involved in fat metabolism, an improved ability of the muscles to store fat, and an improved ability to extract fat from the blood for use during exercise. By using fat as a fuel, athletes can spare car-bohydrate, so that they can use it during prolonged, intense training or competition.

Many athletes concerned with body weight and physical appearance believe they should eat less than 15% of their total energy intake as fat, but this is inadequate for vigorous activity. Instead, a fat intake of 20% to 35% of total energy intake is gener-ally recommended for most athletes, with less than 10% of total energy intake as saturated fat. The same recommendations are put forth for non-athletes. Fat provides not only energy but also the fat-soluble vitamins and essential fatty acids that are critical to maintaining general health. If fat consumption is too low, inadequate levels of these nutrients can eventually prove detrimental to training and performance.

Athletes who have chronic disease risk factors, such as high blood lipids, high blood pressure, or unhealthful blood glucose levels, should work with their physician to adjust their intake of fat and carbohydrate according to their health risks.

Many Athletes Have Increased Protein Needs

The protein intakes suggested for active people range from 0.8 to 1.7 grams/kg body weight. At the lower end of this range are people who exercise four to five times a week for 30 minutes or less. At the upper end are athletes who train five to seven times a week for more than an hour a day. Studies do not support the contention that consuming more than 2 grams of protein per kilogram of body weight improves protein synthesis, muscle strength, or performance.[13]

Most inactive people and many athletes in the United States consume more than enough protein to support their needs.[14] However, some athletes do not consume enough protein, including those with very low energy intakes, vegetarians or vegans who do not consume high-protein food sources, and young athletes who are growing and are not aware of their higher protein needs.

In 1995, Dr. Barry Sears published *The Zone: A Dietary Road Map,* a book that claims numerous benefits of a high-protein, low-carbohydrate diet for competitive athletes.[18] Since that time, Sears has published more than a dozen spin-offs, all of which recommend the consumption of a 40-30-30 diet, or one composed of 40% carbohydrate, 30% fat, and 30% protein. Dr. Sears claims that high-carbohydrate diets impair athletic performance because of the unhealthful effects of insulin. These claims have not been supported by research, and in fact, many of Dr. Sears's claims are not consistent with human physiology. The primary problem with the Zone Diet for athletes is that it is too low in both energy and carbohydrate to support training and performance.

High-quality protein sources include lean meats, poultry, fish, eggs, low-fat dairy products, legumes, and soy products. By following their personalized MyPlate food patterns, people of all fitness levels can consume more than enough protein without the use of supplements or specially formulated foods.

RECAP Athletes and other physically active people use more fat for energy. A dietary fat intake of 20% to 35% is generally recommended, with less than 10% of total energy intake as saturated fat. Protein needs can be somewhat higher for athletes, but most people in the United States already consume more than twice their daily needs. Although low-carbohydrate, high-protein diets have been marketed to athletes, they are generally too low in carbohydrate and total energy to support training and competition.

FOODS YOU DON'T KNOW YOU LOVE YET

Star Fruit

There's a new "star" in the fruit galaxy—the star fruit! Also known as carambola, the star fruit is native to the Philippines, Indonesia, India, and Sri Lanka. As it thrives in warm, humid conditions, star fruit are now grown in the United States in Florida and Hawaii. Its name reflects its unique shape, with ridges running down its sides, which cause it to look like a star when cut in cross section. There are both tart and sweet types of star fruit, and they taste like a combination of lemons, pineapples, and plums. Star fruit are an excellent source of water and vitamin C, and they are naturally low in fat and sodium. To enjoy star fruit, no peeling is necessary— simply wash them, remove any damaged areas, slice crosswise to get the star shape, and enjoy!

Regular Exercise Increases Our Need for Fluids

During vigorous physical activity, adequate fluid intake is critical to replace losses and keep the body cool.

Cooling Mechanisms

Heat production can increase by fifteen to twenty times during heavy exercise! The primary way in which we dissipate this heat is through sweating, which is also called **evaporative cooling.** When body temperature rises, more blood (which contains water) flows to the surface of the skin. In this way, heat is carried from the core of our body to the surface of our skin. By sweating, the water (and body heat) leaves our body, and the air around us picks up the evaporating water from our skin, cooling our body.

Dehydration and Heat-Related Illnesses

Heat illnesses occur because, when we exercise in the heat, our muscles and skin constantly compete for blood flow. When there is no longer enough blood flow to simultaneously provide adequate blood to our muscles and our skin, muscle blood flow takes priority and evaporative cooling is inhibited. Exercising in heat plus humidity is especially dangerous because, whereas the heat dramatically raises body temperature, the high humidity inhibits evaporative cooling; that is, the environmental air is already so saturated with water that it is unable to absorb the water in sweat. Body temperature becomes dangerously high, and heat illness is likely.

Dehydration significantly increases the risk for heat illnesses. **Figure 10.9** identifies the symptoms of dehydration during heavy exercise.

Heat illnesses include heat syncope, heat cramps, heat exhaustion, and heatstroke:

- **Heat syncope** is dizziness that occurs when people stand for too long in the heat and the blood pools in their lower extremities. It can also occur when people stop suddenly after a race or stand suddenly from a lying position.
- **Heat cramps** are muscle spasms that can occur during exercise or several hours after strenuous exercise or manual labor. They are most commonly felt in the legs, arms, or abdomen after a person cools down. They occur when sweat losses and fluid intakes are high, urine volume is low, and sodium intake is inadequate to replace losses.
- **Heat exhaustion** and **heatstroke** occur on a continuum, with unchecked heat exhaustion leading to heatstroke. Early signs of heat exhaustion include excessive sweating, cold and clammy skin, rapid but weak pulse, weakness, nausea,

evaporative cooling Another term for sweating, which is the primary way in which we dissipate heat.

heat syncope Dizziness that occurs when people stand for too long in the heat, stop suddenly after a race, or stand suddenly from a lying position; results from blood pooling in the lower extremities.

heat cramps Muscle spasms that occur several hours after strenuous exercise; most often occur when sweat losses and fluid intakes are high, urine volume is low, and sodium intake is inadequate.

heat exhaustion A heat illness characterized by excessive sweating, weakness, nausea, dizziness, headache, and difficulty concentrating. Unchecked heat exhaustion can lead to heatstroke.

heatstroke A potentially fatal heat illness characterized by hot, dry skin; rapid heart rate; vomiting; diarrhea; body temperature greater than or equal to 104°F; hallucinations; and coma.

Symptoms of Dehydration During Heavy Exercise:
- Decreased exercise performance
- Increased level in perceived exertion
- Dark yellow or brown urine color
- Increased heart rate at a given exercise intensity
- Decreased appetite
- Decreased ability to concentrate
- Decreased urine output
- Fatigue and weakness
- Headache and dizziness

Figure 10.9 Symptoms of dehydration during heavy exercise.

Water is essential for maintaining fluid balance and preventing dehydration.

dizziness, headache, and difficulty concentrating. As this condition progresses, consciousness becomes impaired. Signs that a person is progressing to heatstroke are hot, dry skin; rapid and strong pulse; vomiting; diarrhea; a body temperature greater than or equal to 104°F; hallucinations; and coma. Prompt medical care is essential to save the person's life.

Guidelines for Proper Fluid Replacement

How can we prevent dehydration and heat illnesses? Obviously, adequate fluid intake is critical before, during, and after exercise. Unfortunately, our thirst mechanism cannot be relied upon to signal when we need to drink. If we rely only on our feelings of thirst, we will not consume enough fluid to support exercise.

General fluid replacement recommendations are based on maintaining body weight. Athletes who are training and competing in hot environments should weigh themselves before and after the training session or event and should regain the weight lost over the subsequent 24-hour period. They should avoid losing more than 2–3% of body weight during exercise, as performance can be impaired with fluid losses as small as 1% of body weight.

Table 10.5 reviews the guidelines for proper fluid replacement. For activities lasting less than 1 hour, plain water is generally adequate to replace fluid losses. However,

---

TABLE 10.5   Guidelines for Fluid Replacement

Activity Level	Environment	Fluid Requirements (liters per day)
Sedentary	Cool	2–3
Active	Cool	3–6
Sedentary	Warm	3–5
Active	Warm	5–10

Before Exercise or Competition

- Drink adequate fluids during 24 hours before the event; should be able to maintain body weight.
- Slowly drink about 0.17 to 0.24 fl. oz per kg body weight of water or a sports drink at least 4 hours before exercise or an event, to allow time for excretion of excess fluid prior to the event.
- Slowly drink another 0.10 to 0.17 fl. oz per kg body weight about 2 hours before the event.
- Consuming beverages with sodium and/or small amounts of salted snacks at a meal will help stimulate thirst and retain fluids consumed.

During Exercise or Competition

- Drink early and regularly throughout the event to sufficiently replace all water lost through sweating.
- The amount and rate of fluid replacement depend on a person's rate of sweating and the exercise duration, weather conditions, and opportunities to drink.
- Fluids should be cooler than the environmental temperature and flavored to enhance taste and promote fluid replacement.

During Exercise or Competition That Lasts More Than 1 Hour

- Fluid replacement beverage should contain 5–10% carbohydrate to maintain blood glucose levels; sodium and other electrolytes should be included in the beverage in amounts of 0.5–0.7 gram of sodium per liter of water to replace the sodium lost by sweating.

Following Exercise or Competition

- Consume about 3 cups of fluid for each pound of body weight lost.
- Fluids after exercise should contain water to restore hydration status, carbohydrates to replenish glycogen stores, and electrolytes (for example, sodium and potassium) to speed rehydration.
- Consume enough fluid to permit regular urination and to ensure the urine color is very light or light yellow in color; drinking about 125–150% of fluid loss is usually sufficient to ensure complete rehydration.

In General

- Products that contain fructose should be limited, as these may cause gastrointestinal distress.
- Caffeine and alcohol should be avoided, as these products increase urine output and reduce fluid retention.
- Carbonated beverages should be avoided, as they reduce the desire for fluid intake due to stomach fullness.

Data from Murray, R. 1997. Drink more! Advice from a world class expert. *ACSM's Health Fitness J.* 1:19–23; American College of Sports Medicine. 2007. Position stand, exercise and fluid replacement. *Med. Sci. Sports Exerc.* 39(2):377–390; and Casa, D. J., L. E. Armstrong, S. K. Hillman, S. J. Montain, R. V. Reiff, B. S. E. Rich, W. O. Roberts, and J. A. Stone. 2000. National Athletic Trainers' Association position statement: fluid replacement for athletes. *J. Athletic Training.* 35:212–224.

for training and competition lasting longer than 1 hour in any weather, sports beverages containing carbohydrate and electrolytes are recommended. These beverages are also recommended for people who will not drink enough water because they don't like the taste. If drinking these beverages will promote adequate hydration, they are appropriate to use.

Inadequate Intakes of Some Vitamins and Minerals Can Diminish Health and Performance

When people train vigorously for athletic events, their requirements for certain vitamins and minerals may be altered. Many highly active people do not eat enough food or a variety of foods that allows them to consume enough of these nutrients, yet it is imperative that active people do their very best to eat an adequate, varied, and balanced diet to try to meet their increased needs.

Drinking sports beverages during training and competition lasting more than 1 hour replaces fluid, carbohydrates, and electrolytes.

B-Vitamins

The B-vitamins are directly involved in energy metabolism. There is reliable evidence that—as a population—active people may require slightly more thiamin, riboflavin, and vitamin B_6 than the current RDA because of increased production of energy and inadequate dietary intake in some active people.[19] However, these increased needs are easily met by consuming adequate energy and plentiful fiber-rich carbohydrates. Active people at risk for poor B-vitamin status are those who consume inadequate energy or who consume mostly refined-carbohydrate foods, such as soda pop and sugary snacks. Vegan athletes and active people may be at risk for inadequate intake of vitamin B_{12}; food sources enriched with this nutrient include soy and cereal products.

Calcium

Calcium supports proper muscle contraction and ensures bone health. Calcium intakes are inadequate for most women in the United States, including both sedentary and active women. This is most likely due to the failure to consume foods that are high in calcium, particularly dairy products. Although vigorous training does not appear to increase our need for calcium, we need to consume enough calcium to support bone health. If we do not, stress fractures and severe loss of bone can result.

Some female athletes suffer from a syndrome known as the female athlete triad (see Chapter 9). In the female athlete triad, nutritional inadequacies cause irregularities in the menstrual cycle and hormonal disturbances that can lead to a significant loss of bone mass. Thus, for female athletes, consuming the recommended amounts of calcium is critical. For female athletes who are physically small and have lower energy intakes, calcium supplementation may be needed to meet current recommendations.

Iron

Iron, a part of the hemoglobin molecule, is critical for the transport of oxygen in our blood to our cells and working muscles. Iron is also involved in energy production. Research has shown that active people lose more iron in the sweat, feces, and urine than do inactive people and that endurance runners lose iron when their red blood cells break down in their feet due to the high impact of running.[20] Female athletes and non-athletes lose more iron than male athletes because of menstrual blood losses, and females in general tend to eat less iron in their diet. Vegetarian athletes and active people may also consume less iron. Thus, many athletes and active people are at higher risk for iron deficiency. Depending on its severity, poor iron status can impair athletic performance and our ability to maintain regular physical activity.

A phenomenon known as *sports anemia* was identified in the 1960s. Sports anemia is not true anemia, but a transient decrease in iron stores that occurs at the start of an exercise program for some people, as well as in some athletes who increase their training intensity. Exercise training increases the amount of water in our blood (called *plasma volume*); however, the amount of hemoglobin does not increase until later into the training period. Thus, the iron content in the blood appears to be low but instead is falsely depressed due to increases in plasma volume. Sports anemia, since it is not true anemia, does not affect performance.

In general, it appears that physically active females are at relatively high risk of suffering from the first stage of iron depletion, in which iron stores are low.[21,22] Because of this, it is suggested that blood tests of iron stores and monitoring of dietary iron intakes be routinely done for active females.[19] In some cases, iron needs cannot be met through the diet and supplementation is necessary. Iron supplementation should be done with a physician's approval and proper medical supervision.

RECAP Regular exercise increases fluid needs. Fluid is critical to cool our internal body temperature and prevent heat illnesses. Dehydration is a serious threat during exercise in extreme heat and high humidity. Active people may need more thiamin, riboflavin, and vitamin B_6 than inactive people. Exercise itself does not increase our calcium needs, but many women, including active women, do not consume enough calcium. Some female athletes suffer from the female athlete triad, a condition that involves the interaction of low energy availability, menstrual dysfunction, and bone loss. Many active people require more iron, particularly female athletes and vegetarian athletes.

HEALTHWATCH

Are Ergogenic Aids Necessary for Active People?

Many competitive athletes and even some recreationally active people search continually for that something extra that will enhance their performance. **Ergogenic aids** are substances used to improve exercise and athletic performance. For example, nutrition supplements can be classified as ergogenic aids, as can anabolic steroids and other pharmaceuticals. Interestingly, people report using ergogenic aids not only to enhance athletic performance but also to improve their physical appearance, prevent or treat injuries and diseases, and help them cope with stress. Some people even report using them because of peer pressure!

As you have learned in this chapter, adequate nutrition is critical to athletic performance and to regular physical activity, and products such as sports bars and beverages can help athletes maintain their competitive edge. However, as we will explore shortly, many ergogenic aids are not effective, some are dangerous, and most are very expensive. For the average consumer, it is virtually impossible to track the latest research findings for these products. In addition, many have not been adequately studied, and unsubstantiated claims surrounding them are rampant. So how can you become a more educated consumer?

Be on the lookout for the common deceptive practices used to sell ergogenic aids and nutritional supplements.[23,24] These practices are identified in the *Highlight* feature box (page 319). For example, in many cases, research done on a product is misrepresented or is conducted by an inexperienced or biased investigator. Some companies claim that research is being conducted but state that the findings cannot be shared with the public. This is a warning sign, as there is no need to hide research findings. The use of a celebrity spokesperson is also very common, as celebrity testimonials help sell products. However, many celebrities do not actually use the product they are being paid to endorse. Finally, it is critical to realize that a patent on a product does not guarantee the effectiveness or safety of that product. Patents are granted solely to distinguish differences among products; indeed, they can be granted on a product that has never been scientifically tested for effectiveness or safety.

> Want to learn what the U.S. Food and Drug Administration is doing to crack down on fraudulent health claims and the companies that make them? Click on www.fda.gov/ Drugs/EmergencyPreparedness/ BioterrorismandDrugPreparedness/ ucm137261.htm.

ergogenic aids Substances used to improve exercise and athletic performance.

HIGHLIGHT
Nine Deceptive Practices Used to Market Ergogenic Aids

1. *General misrepresentation of research:*
   - Published research is taken out of context, or findings are applied in an unproven manner.
   - Claims that the product is university-tested may be true, but the investigator may be inexperienced or the manufacturer may control all aspects of the study.
   - Research may not have been done, but the company falsely claims that it has.

2. *Company claims that research is currently being done:* Although many companies claim they are doing properly controlled research, when asked to provide specific information about this research, many are unable to do so.

3. *Company claims that research is not available for public review:* Consumers have a right to obtain proof of performance claims, and there is no rationale to support hiding research findings.

4. *Testimonials:* Celebrities who endorse a product may be doing so only for the money. Testimonials can be bought, exaggerated, and even faked. If the product does work for one celebrity, its perceived effectiveness may be due to the placebo effect. The **placebo effect** means that, even though a product has been proved to have no physiologic benefits, a person believes so strongly in the product that his or her performance improves. It is estimated that there is a 40% chance that any substance will enhance mental or physical performance through the placebo effect.

5. *Patents:* These are granted to indicate distinguishable differences among products. Patents do not indicate the effectiveness or safety of a product and can be issued without any research on a product.

6. *Inappropriately referenced research:*
   - References may include poorly designed and inadequately controlled studies.
   - The company may refer to research that was published in another country and is not accessible in the United States or may base claims on unsubstantiated rumors or unconfirmed reports.
   - The company may cite outdated research that has not been validated or may fail to quote studies that do not support its claims.

7. *Media approaches:* Advertising modes include infomercials and mass-media marketing videos. Although the Federal Trade Commission (FTC) regulates false claims in advertising, products are generally investigated only if they pose significant danger to the public.

8. *Mail-order or Internet-based fitness evaluations and genetic testing:* Companies may use these to attract consumers to their products. Most of these evaluations are not specific enough to be useful to the consumer, and their accuracy is highly questionable.

9. *Anabolic measurements:* Some companies perform in-house tests of hair and blood to give consumers information on protein balance. Often, these tests are used inappropriately and only to sell the ergogenic products. The test results may be inaccurate or may indicate nutritional deficiencies that can be remedied with proper nutrition.

Data from Lightsey, D. M., and J. R. Attaway. 1992. Nine deceptive tactics used in marketing purported ergogenic aids. *Natl. Strength Cond. Assoc. J.* 14:26–31.

New ergogenic aids are introduced virtually every month. It is therefore not possible to discuss every available product here. However, a brief review of a number of currently popular ergogenic aids is provided.

Anabolic Products Are Promoted as Muscle and Strength Enhancers

Many ergogenic aids are said to be **anabolic,** meaning that they build muscle and increase strength. Most anabolic substances promise to increase testosterone, which is the hormone associated with male sex characteristics that increases muscle size and strength. Although some anabolic substances are effective, they are generally associated with harmful side effects.

Anabolic Steroids

Anabolic steroids are testosterone-based drugs known to be effective in increasing muscle size, strength, power, and speed. They have been used extensively by strength and power athletes; however, they are illegal in the United States, and their use is

placebo effect Improved performance based on the belief that a product is beneficial, although the product has been proved to have no physiologic benefits.

anabolic The term used for a substance that builds muscle and increases strength.

Anabolic substances are often marketed to people trying to increase muscle size, but they carry risks for harmful side effects.

banned by all major collegiate and professional sports organizations, in addition to both the U.S. and the International Olympic Committees. Proven long-term and irreversible effects of steroid use include infertility; early closure of the plates of the long bones, resulting in permanently shortened stature; shriveled testicles, enlarged breast tissue (that can be removed only surgically), and other signs of "feminization" in men; enlarged clitoris, facial hair growth, and other signs of "masculinization" in women; increased risk for certain forms of cancer; liver damage; unhealthful changes in blood lipids; hypertension; severe acne; hair thinning or baldness; and depression, delusions, sleep disturbances, and extreme anger (so-called roid rage).

Androstenedione and Dehydroepiandrosterone

Androstenedione ("andro") and dehydroepiandrosterone (DHEA) are precursors of testosterone. Manufacturers of these products claim that taking them will increase testosterone levels and muscle strength. Androstenedione became very popular after baseball player Mark McGwire claimed he used it during the time he was breaking home run records. A national survey found that, in 2002, about one of every forty high-school seniors had used it in the past year.[25] Contrary to popular claims, recent studies have found that neither androstenedione nor DHEA increases testosterone levels, and androstenedione has been shown to increase the risk for heart disease in men aged 35 to 65 years.[26] There are no studies that support claims that these products improve strength or increase muscle mass.

Gamma-Hydroxybutyric Acid

Gamma-hydroxybutyric acid, or GHB, is a central nervous system depressant. It was once promoted as an alternative to anabolic steroids for building muscle. The production and sale of GHB were never approved in the United States; however, it was illegally produced and sold on the black market as a dietary supplement. For many users, GHB caused only dizziness, tremors, or vomiting, but others experienced severe side effects, including seizures, respiratory depression, sedation, and coma. Many people were hospitalized, and some died.

In 2001, the federal government placed GHB on the Controlled Substances list, making its manufacture, sale, and possession illegal. A form of GHB is available by prescription for the treatment of narcolepsy, a rare sleep disorder, but extra paperwork is required by the prescribing physician, and prescriptions are closely monitored. After the ban, a similar product (gamma-butyrolactone, or GBL) was marketed in its place. This product was also found to be dangerous and was removed from the market by the FDA. Recently, another replacement product called BD (also known as 1,4-butanediol) was also banned by the FDA because it has caused at least seventy-one deaths, with forty more under investigation. BD is an industrial solvent and is listed on ingredient labels as tetramethylene glycol, butylene glycol, or sucol-B. Side effects include wild, aggressive behavior; nausea; incontinence; and sudden loss of consciousness.

Creatine

Creatine is a supplement that has become wildly popular with strength and power athletes. Creatine, or creatine phosphate, is found in meat and fish and stored in our muscles. As described earlier, our body uses creatine phosphate (CP) to regenerate ATP. It is theorized that creatine supplements make more CP available to replenish ATP, which prolongs a person's ability to train and perform in short-term, explosive activities, such as weight lifting and sprinting. Between 1994 and 2011, more than 1,700 research articles related to creatine and exercise in humans were published. Creatine does not seem to enhance performance in aerobic-type events but has been shown to enhance sprint performance in swimming, running, and cycling.[27–30] Other studies have shown that creatine increases the amount of work performed and the amount of strength gained during resistance exercise.[29,31,32]

In January 2001, the *New York Times* reported that the French government had claimed that creatine use could lead to cancer.[33] The news spread quickly across national and international news organizations and over the Internet. Subsequently, these claims were found to be false, as there are no studies in humans that suggest an increased risk for cancer with creatine use. In fact, numerous studies show an anticancer effect.[34,35] Although side effects such as dehydration, muscle cramps, and gastrointestinal disturbances have been reported with creatine use, there is very little information on how the long-term use of creatine affects health. Further research is needed to determine the effectiveness and safety of creatine use over prolonged periods of time.

Protein and Amino Acid Supplements

Protein and amino acid supplements have long been popular and are widely available in health food stores and on the Internet. Examples of these products include various protein powders and individual amino acids, such as glutamine and arginine. Although manufacturers claim that these products build muscle mass and enhance strength, research indicates that they do not.[19,36,37]

Some Products Are Said to Optimize Fuel Use During Exercise

Certain ergogenic aids are said to increase energy levels and improve athletic performance by optimizing our use of fat, carbohydrate, and protein. The products reviewed here include caffeine, ephedrine, carnitine, chromium, and ribose.

Caffeine

Caffeine is a stimulant that makes us feel more alert and energetic, decreasing feelings of fatigue during exercise. In addition, caffeine has been shown to increase the use of fat as a fuel during endurance exercise, which spares muscle glycogen and improves performance.[38,39] Energy drinks that contain high amounts of caffeine, such as Red Bull, have become popular with athletes and many college students. These

NUTRI-CASE JUDY

"I can't remember a time in my life when I wasn't trying to lose weight. But nothing ever works, and when I go off a diet, I always end up fatter than I started out! These last couple of years I'd sort of given up, but last week I had my annual checkup and my doctor confirmed what I already knew—I'm obese! The doctor also said my weight is contributing to my high blood sugar, and that my blood pressure is high, too. As a nurse's aide, I see every day the health problems caused by obesity. Still, knowing how bad it is doesn't help me lose the weight and keep it off. So we talked about some "slow and steady" strategies for losing weight: I promised I'd do a better job of watching my diet, take my medications as prescribed, and start working out at the new fitness center here at the hospital. I checked it out on my lunch break today, and I guess it's OK. They have a couple of treadmills and stationary bikes right in front of a big TV, so you can watch the soaps while you work out. Still, I'm not really sure what I'm supposed to do or how many times a week or for how long. I mean, if I only had to lose 5 pounds, that would be easy. But I've got to lose 50! And I only get half an hour for lunch!"

Imagine that you were a trainer at the Valley Hospital employee fitness center and Judy told you about her weight-loss and health goals. Applying the FIT principle, recommend an initial physical activity program that can get Judy started on improving her health that includes an appropriate

- number of times per 5-day work week,
- intensity,
- duration of activity, and
- variety of activities.

drinks should be avoided during exercise, however, as severe dehydration can result from the combination of fluid loss from exercise and caffeine consumption. Research also indicates that energy drinks are associated with serious side effects in children, adolescents, and young adults with conditions such as seizures, diabetes, and mood and behavior disorders.[40] It should be recognized that caffeine is a controlled or restricted drug in the athletic world, and athletes can be banned from Olympic competition if their urine caffeine levels are too high. However, the amount of caffeine that is banned is quite high, and athletes would need to consume caffeine in pill form to reach this level. Side effects of caffeine use include increased blood pressure, increased heart rate, dizziness, insomnia, headache, and gastrointestinal distress.

Ephedrine

Ephedrine is made from the herb *Ephedra sinica* (Chinese ephedra).

Ephedrine, also known as ephedra, Chinese ephedra, or *ma huang*, is a strong stimulant marketed as a weight-loss supplement and energy enhancer. In reality, many products sold as Chinese ephedra (or herbal ephedra) contain ephedrine from the laboratory and other stimulants, such as caffeine. The use of ephedra does not appear to enhance athletic performance, but supplements containing both caffeine and ephedra have been shown to prolong the amount of exercise that can be done until exhaustion is reached.[41] Ephedra is known to reduce body weight and body fat in sedentary women, but its impact on weight loss and body fat levels in athletes is unknown. Side effects of ephedra use include headache, nausea, nervousness, anxiety, irregular heart rate, and high blood pressure, and at least seventeen deaths have been attributed to its use.[42] It is currently illegal to sell ephedra-containing supplements in the United States.

Carnitine

Carnitine is a compound made from amino acids that is found in the membrane of mitochondria. Carnitine helps shuttle fatty acids into the mitochondria, so that they can be used for energy. It has been proposed that exercise training depletes our cells of carnitine and that supplementation should restore carnitine levels, thereby enabling us to improve our use of fat as a fuel source. Thus, carnitine is marketed not only as a performance-enhancing substance but also as a fat burner. Research studies of carnitine supplementation do not support these claims, as neither the transport of fatty acids nor their oxidation appears to be enhanced with supplementation.[43,44] The use of carnitine supplements has not been associated with significant side effects.

Chromium

Chromium is a trace mineral that enhances insulin's action of increasing the transport of amino acids into the cell. It is found in whole-grain foods, cheese, nuts, mushrooms, and asparagus. It is theorized that many people are chromium deficient and that supplementation will enhance the uptake of amino acids into muscle cells, which will increase muscle growth and strength. Like carnitine, chromium is marketed as a fat burner, as it is speculated that its effect on insulin stimulates the brain to decrease food intake.[42] Chromium supplements are available as chromium picolinate and chromium nicotinate. Early studies of chromium supplementation showed promise, but more recent, better-designed studies do not support any benefit of chromium supplementation for muscle mass, muscle strength, body fat, or exercise performance.[45]

Ribose

Ribose is a five-carbon sugar that is critical to the production of ATP. Ribose supplementation is claimed to improve athletic performance by increasing work output and by promoting a faster recovery time from vigorous training. Although ribose has been shown to improve exercise tolerance in patients with heart disease,[46] several studies have reported that ribose supplementation has no impact on athletic performance.[47–49]

From this review of ergogenic aids, you can see that most are not effective in enhancing athletic performance or in optimizing muscle strength or body composition. It is important to be a savvy consumer when examining these products to make sure you are not wasting your money or putting your health at risk by using them.

RECAP Ergogenic aids are substances used to improve exercise and athletic performance. Anabolic steroids are effective in increasing muscle size, power, and strength, but they are illegal and can cause serious health problems. Androstenedione and dehydroepiandrosterone are precursors of testosterone; neither has been shown to effectively increase testosterone levels, strength, or muscle mass. GHB and its derivatives are illegal substances associated with dangerous sedation and death. Creatine supplements are popular and can enhance sprint performance in swimming, running, and cycling. Protein and amino acid supplements do not increase muscle growth or strength. Caffeine is a stimulant that increases the use of fat during exercise; its use in the athletic world is controlled. Ephedrine is a stimulant that has potentially fatal side effects. Carnitine, chromium, and ribose are marketed as ergogenic aids but studies do not support their effectiveness.

COOKING 101

E ating well and being active are keys to good health. Lean meats, prepared healthfully, are an excellent way to fuel your body. Another delicious, easy way to stay energized and get essential nutrients is through fabulous smoothies! Learn about these and other tips in our new Cooking 101 videos, available on the Companion Website at **www.pearsonhighered.com/thompsonmanore**.

"Where I'm at Now . . ."

Now that you've read this chapter, do you feel that increased physical activity is an important goal for you?

Yes or No

If Yes, jot down here a specific, measurable goal that is personalized to you and that you are confident you can begin to meet starting today:

Chapter Review

What Can I Do **Today?**

Now that you've read this chapter, try making these three changes:

- For 1 day, leave your car parked at home and try walking, cycling, or taking public transportation to school or work.

- Exercise for at least 30 minutes today. Before you do, estimate your training heart rate range. During your workout, keep track of your heart rate and try to keep it within your target training range.

- Use the Physical Activity Pyramid to design an activity plan that will help you increase your daily level of physical activity.

Test Yourself ANSWERS

1. (T) Almost 38% of Americans do not do enough physical activity, and another 25% report doing no physical activity at all, not even on the job.

2. (F) Walking, water aerobics, heavy gardening, and other forms of moderate physical activity do yield significant health benefits if you engage in these activities for approximately 30 minutes a day most days of the week.

3. (F) Our muscles are not stimulated to grow when we eat extra protein, whether as food or as supplements.

Weight-bearing exercise appropriately stresses the body and produces increased muscle mass and strength.

4. (T) Most ergogenic aids are ineffective, or they do not produce the results that are advertised. Some, such as anabolic steroids and ephedra, are banned because of their serious side effects.

5. (F) Carbohydrate loading may help improve performance for endurance events such as marathons and triathlons, but it does not improve performance in nonendurance types of athletic events, such as a 1,500-meter run.

Review Questions

1. For achieving and maintaining physical fitness, the intensity range during exercise typically recommended is
   a. 25% to 50% of your estimated maximal heart rate.
   b. 35% to 75% of your estimated maximal heart rate.
   c. 50% to 70% of your estimated maximal heart rate.
   d. 75% to 95% of your estimated maximal heart rate.

2. The amount of ATP stored in a muscle cell can keep a muscle active for about
   a. 1 to 3 seconds.   c. 1 to 3 minutes.
   b. 10 to 30 seconds.   d. 1 to 3 hours.

3. To support a daylong hike, the body predominantly uses which nutrient for energy?
   a. carbohydrate   c. amino acids
   b. fat   d. lactic acid

4. Creatine
   a. seems to enhance performance in aerobic-type events.
   b. appears to increase a person's risk for bladder cancer.
   c. seems to increase strength gained in resistance exercise.
   d. is stored in the liver.

5. Athletes participating in an intense athletic competition lasting more than 1 hour should drink
   a. beverages containing caffeine.
   b. beverages containing carbohydrates and electrolytes.
   c. plain, room-temperature water.
   d. nothing.

6. True or False? A sound fitness program overloads the body.

7. True or False? A dietary fat intake of 10% to 15% is generally recommended for active people.

8. True or False? Carbohydrate loading involves altering the duration and intensity of exercise and the intake of carbohydrate such that the storage of fat is minimized.

9. True or False? Sports anemia is a chronic decrease in iron stores that occurs in some athletes who have been training intensely for several months to years.

10. True or False? *FIT* stands for frequency, intensity, and time of activity.

Answers to Review Questions are located at the back of this text.

Web Links

www.americanheart.org
American Heart Association

www.acsm.org
American College of Sports Medicine

www.webmd.com
WebMD Health

www.win.niddk.nih.gov/publications/physical.htm
Physical Activity and Weight Control

www.dietary-supplements.info.nih.gov
NIH Office of Dietary Supplements

11
Nutrition Throughout the Life Cycle

O n Sunday afternoons, the Harris family gathers for dinner at the Long Beach apartment of their 88-year-old great-great-grandmother, Anabelle. Anabelle is as thin as a rail, as are her 70-year-old daughter and 67-year-old son. But when her granddaughters, who are cooking the family meal, send everyone to the table, a change becomes evident. Almost all of Anabelle's grandchildren and their spouses are overweight, as are most of her great-grandchildren. Even her "darling" 2-year-old great-great-granddaughter, Tina-Marie, is chubby. Anabelle worries about everyone's weight. One of her grandsons had a heart attack last year. During her pregnancy with Tina-Marie, Anabelle's great-granddaughter developed gestational diabetes, and several other family members have been diagnosed with type 2 diabetes. Anabelle's family isn't alone in their weight problems: more than 32% of American children and adolescents (age 2 to 19 years)

Nutrition Online icons are located throughout the chapter, directing you to web links, videos, podcasts, and other useful online resources.

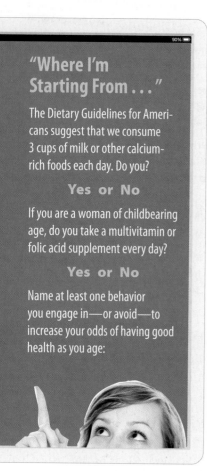

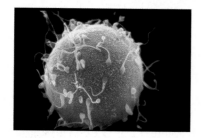

⬆ During conception, a sperm fertilizes an egg.

conception The uniting of an ovum (egg) and sperm to create a fertilized egg.

teratogen Any substance that can cause a birth defect.

are overweight or obese,[1] along with more than 68% of American adults.[2] And type 2 diabetes occurs in about 7% of all American adults and is on the rise.

Why have rates of obesity and its associated chronic diseases skyrocketed in the past 10 years, and what can be done to promote weight management across the life span? How do our nutrient needs change as we grow and age, and what other nutrition-related concerns develop in each life stage? This chapter will help you answer these questions.

Starting Out Right: Healthful Nutrition in Pregnancy

From conception through infancy, adequate nutrition is essential for tissue formation and growth, including neurologic development. Our ability to reach peak physical and intellectual potential as adults is in part determined by the nutrition we receive during fetal development and the first year of life.

Why Is Nutrition Important Before Conception?

Several factors make nutrition important even before **conception**—the point at which a woman's ovum (egg) is fertilized with a man's sperm. Three of the factors discussed in the following paragraphs affect the health of the offspring, and two influence maternal health.

First, some deficiency-related problems develop extremely early in the pregnancy, typically before the mother even realizes she is pregnant. The consequences of these nutrient deficiencies can be lifelong for the child. An adequate and varied preconception diet reduces the risk for such problems, providing "insurance" during those first few weeks of life. For example, inadequate maternal folate intake during the first 28 days after conception—typically before the woman realizes she is pregnant—may cause the fetal spinal cord tissues to fail to close, resulting in problems ranging from paralysis to an absence of brain tissue. For this reason, all women capable of becoming pregnant are encouraged to consume 400 μg of folic acid daily from fortified foods, such as cereals, or supplements, in addition to natural sources of folate from a varied, healthful diet. Note that consuming adequate folate should be a health habit that is established *before* a woman attempts to conceive.

Second, adopting a healthful diet and lifestyle prior to conception optimizes fetal health and development. Women must avoid alcohol, illegal drugs, and other known **teratogens** (substances that cause birth defects). Women should also consult their healthcare provider about their consumption of caffeine, prescription medications, herbs, and supplements. Smoking increases the risk for a low-birth-weight baby and infant mortality, so women should quit smoking before getting pregnant.

Third, the mother's health prior to conception greatly influences the future health of her child. The offspring of women who are obese at the time of conception are at much higher risk for obesity and birth defects, such as cleft lip or palate and heart defects.[3] Children of diabetic women are much more likely to develop type 2 diabetes, high blood pressure, and unhealthful blood lipid levels as adults compared to the offspring of non-diabetic women. Additionally, certain nutrient deficiencies in a pregnant woman may alter the genetic profile of her child.

Before conception, a woman who consumes a healthful diet and engages in regular physical activity will have the greatest opportunity to achieve and maintain an optimal body weight prior to pregnancy. Women with a healthy pre-pregnancy weight have the best chance of an uncomplicated pregnancy and delivery, with low risk for negative outcomes, such as prolonged labor and cesarean section. Women who are underweight or overweight prior to conception are at greater risk for pregnancy-related complications.

Finally, maintaining a balanced and nourishing diet before conception reduces a woman's risk of developing a health problem during her pregnancy. Although some problems are beyond the woman's control, others, from iron-deficiency anemia to high blood pressure, are less likely in women following a healthful diet.

The man's nutrition and lifestyle prior to pregnancy are important as well, because malnutrition contributes to abnormalities in sperm. Here are some findings:

- Men with high intakes of saturated fat produce fewer sperm compared to men with low intakes of saturated fat. In contrast, higher intakes of omega-3 and omega-6 polyunsaturated fats have been shown to improve sperm structure and motility.[4]
- Men with high folate intake have fewer sperm defects compared to those with lower intakes.[5]
- Antioxidants, such as vitamins C and E, have been linked to improved sperm motility.
- Men who abuse alcohol, smoke, or use illegal drugs are more likely to produce defective sperm than men who avoid such practices.

Why Is Nutrition Important During Pregnancy?

A balanced, nourishing diet throughout pregnancy provides the nutrients needed to support fetal growth and development without depriving the mother of the nutrients she needs to maintain her own health. It also minimizes the risks of excessive weight gain.

In clinical practice, the calculation of weeks in a pregnancy begins with the date of the first day of a woman's last menstrual period. A full-term pregnancy lasts 38 to 42 weeks and is divided into three **trimesters,** with each trimester lasting about 13 to 14 weeks.

The first trimester (approximately weeks 1 to 13) begins when the ovum and sperm unite to form a single, fertilized cell. Over the next few weeks, layers of cells develop into the distinct tissues of the developing **embryo.**

By about week 8, the embryo's tissues and organs have differentiated dramatically. A primitive skeleton and muscles have begun to develop. A primitive heart has begun to beat, and distinct digestive organs are forming. During the next few weeks, the embryo continues to grow and change dramatically into a recognizable human **fetus.**

Given such remarkable development, it isn't surprising that the embryo is most vulnerable to teratogens during the first trimester (**Figure 11.1**, page 328). Alcohol, illegal drugs, medications, supplements, cigarette smoking, microbes, and radiation can interfere with embryonic development and cause birth defects. In addition, deficiencies of nutrients such as folate can harm the embryo. In some cases, the damage is so severe that the pregnancy is naturally terminated in a **spontaneous abortion** (also called a *miscarriage*), most commonly in the first trimester.

It is also during the first trimester that the **placenta** forms, the organ that provides nutrients to the fetus and removes wastes. The placenta is connected to the fetus via the **umbilical cord,** an extension of fetal blood vessels emerging from the fetus's navel (see the top photo in Figure 11.1).

During the second trimester (approximately weeks 14 to 27 of pregnancy), the fetus grows to approximately 10 inches and gains about 2 lb. Bones become harder and organ systems continue to develop and mature.

During the third trimester (approximately week 28 to birth), the fetus gains nearly half its body length and three-quarters of its body weight! At the time of birth, an average baby is approximately 18 to 22 inches long and about 7.5 lb. Brain growth (which continues to be rapid for the first 2 years of life) is also quite remarkable.

Generally, a birth weight of at least 5.5 lb is considered a marker of a successful pregnancy. An undernourished mother is likely to give birth to a **low-birth-weight** infant. Any infant weighing less than 5.5 lb at birth is considered to be of low birth weight and is at increased risk for infection, learning disabilities, impaired physical development, and death in the first year of life. Although nutrition is not the only factor contributing to maturity and birth weight, its role cannot be overstated.

trimester Any one of three stages of pregnancy, each lasting 13 to 14 weeks.

embryo The human growth and developmental stage lasting from the third week to the end of the eighth week after fertilization.

fetus The human growth and developmental stage lasting from the beginning of the ninth week after conception to birth.

spontaneous abortion The natural termination of a pregnancy and expulsion of the fetus and pregnancy tissues because of a genetic, developmental, or physiologic abnormality that is so severe that the pregnancy cannot be maintained; also known as *miscarriage*

placenta A pregnancy-specific organ formed from both maternal and embryonic tissues. It is responsible for oxygen, nutrient, and waste exchange between mother and fetus.

umbilical cord The cord containing arteries and veins that connects the baby (from the navel) to the mother via the placenta.

low birth weight A weight of less than 5.5 lb at birth.

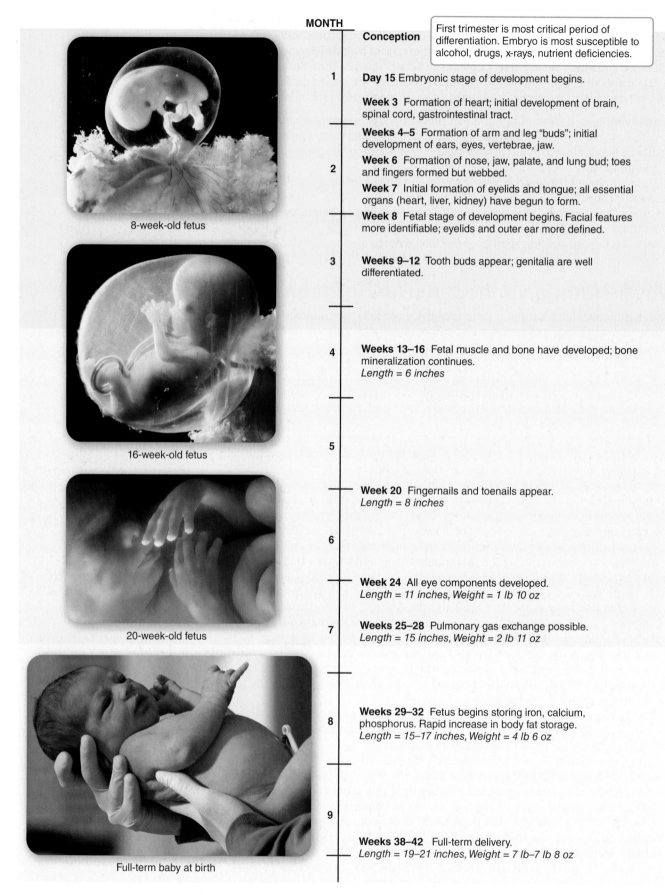

MONTH

Conception

> First trimester is most critical period of differentiation. Embryo is most susceptible to alcohol, drugs, x-rays, nutrient deficiencies.

1

Day 15 Embryonic stage of development begins.

Week 3 Formation of heart; initial development of brain, spinal cord, gastrointestinal tract.

Weeks 4–5 Formation of arm and leg "buds"; initial development of ears, eyes, vertebrae, jaw.

2

Week 6 Formation of nose, jaw, palate, and lung bud; toes and fingers formed but webbed.

Week 7 Initial formation of eyelids and tongue; all essential organs (heart, liver, kidney) have begun to form.

Week 8 Fetal stage of development begins. Facial features more identifiable; eyelids and outer ear more defined.

8-week-old fetus

3

Weeks 9–12 Tooth buds appear; genitalia are well differentiated.

4

Weeks 13–16 Fetal muscle and bone have developed; bone mineralization continues.
Length = 6 inches

16-week-old fetus

5

Week 20 Fingernails and toenails appear.
Length = 8 inches

6

Week 24 All eye components developed.
Length = 11 inches, Weight = 1 lb 10 oz

20-week-old fetus

7

Weeks 25–28 Pulmonary gas exchange possible.
Length = 15 inches, Weight = 2 lb 11 oz

8

Weeks 29–32 Fetus begins storing iron, calcium, phosphorus. Rapid increase in body fat storage.
Length = 15–17 inches, Weight = 4 lb 6 oz

9

Weeks 38–42 Full-term delivery.
Length = 19–21 inches, Weight = 7 lb–7 lb 8 oz

Full-term baby at birth

Figure 11.1 A timeline of embryonic and fetal development.

RECAP Nutrition is critical both before and during pregnancy. A full-term pregnancy lasts from 38 to 42 weeks and is traditionally divided into trimesters lasting 13 to 14 weeks. During the first trimester, cells differentiate and divide rapidly to form the various tissues of the human body. The fetus is especially vulnerable during this time. The second and third trimesters are characterized by profound growth and maturation. An adequate birth weight is at least 5.5 lb.

How Much Weight Should a Pregnant Woman Gain?

Recommendations for weight gain vary according to a woman's weight *before* she became pregnant. As you can see in **Table 11.1**, the average recommended weight gain for women of normal pre-pregnancy weight is 25 to 35 lb; underweight women should gain a little more than this amount, and overweight and obese women should gain somewhat less.[6] Adolescents, who may not have completed their own growth, are advised to gain at the upper end of these ranges, as they are at high risk of delivering low-birth-weight and premature infants. Small women, 5'2" or shorter, should aim for a total weight gain at the lower end of these ranges. Women who are pregnant with twins are advised to gain 37 to 54 lb if they were of normal pre-pregnancy weight, less if they became pregnant while overweight or obese.

Women who gain too little weight during their pregnancy increase their risk of having a preterm or low-birth-weight baby. They also risk dangerously depleting their own nutrient reserves. Gaining *too much* weight during pregnancy increases the risk that the fetus will be large, and large babies have increased risks for trauma during vaginal delivery and for cesarean birth. Also, a high birth weight has been linked to increased risk for childhood and adolescent obesity.[7] In addition, the more weight gained during pregnancy, the more difficult it is for the mother to return to her pre-pregnancy weight and the more likely it is that her weight gain will be permanent.

In addition to the amount of weight, the *pattern* of weight gain is important. During the first trimester, a woman of normal weight should gain no more than 3 to 5 lb. During the second and third trimesters, an average of about 1 lb a week is considered healthful. Overweight and obese women are advised to gain only about ½ pound per week.[6]

Women should never diet during pregnancy, even if they begin the pregnancy overweight, as this can lead to nutrient deficiencies for both the mother and the fetus. Instead, women concerned about their weight should consult their physician or a registered dietitian experienced in working with prenatal populations.

Of the total weight gained in pregnancy, 10 to 12 lb are accounted for by the fetus itself, the amniotic fluid, and the placenta (**Figure 11.2**, page 330). Another 3 to 8 lb represent a natural increase in the volume of the mother's blood and extracellular fluid. A woman can expect to be about 10 to 12 lb lighter immediately after the birth and, within about 2 weeks, another 5 to 8 lb lighter because of fluid loss.

After the first 2 weeks, losing the remainder of the pregnancy weight depends on more energy being expended than is taken in. Appropriate physical activity can help women lose those extra pounds. Also, because the production of breast milk requires significant energy, breastfeeding helps many new mothers lose the remaining weight.

⬆ Following a physician-approved exercise program helps pregnant women maintain a positive body image and prevent excess weight gain.

TABLE 11.1 Recommended Weight Gain for Women During Pregnancy[6]		
Pre-Pregnancy Weight Status	**Body Mass Index (kg/m²)**	**Recommended Weight Gain (lb)**
Normal	18.5–25.0	25–35
Underweight	<18.5	28–40
Overweight	25.1–29.9	15–25
Obese	≥30.0	11-20

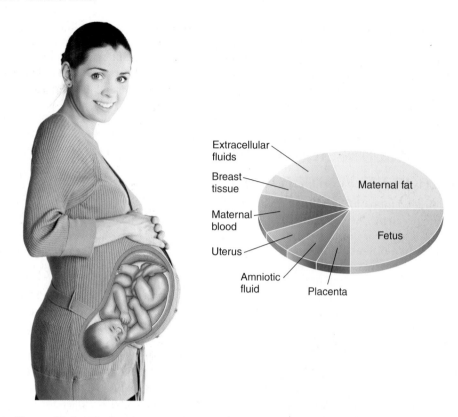

Figure 11.2 The weight gained during pregnancy is distributed between the mother's own tissues and the pregnancy-specific tissues.

What Are a Pregnant Woman's Nutrient Needs?

The requirements for nearly all nutrients increase during pregnancy to accommodate the growth and development of the fetus without depriving the mother of the nutrients she needs to maintain her own health. The DRI tables located in the end pages of this textbook identify the DRIs for pregnant women in three age groups.

Macronutrient Needs of Pregnant Women

During the first trimester, a woman should maintain approximately the same Calorie intake as during her nonpregnant days. Instead of eating more, she should attempt to maximize the nutrient density of what she eats. For example, she should drink low-fat milk; calcium-fortified soy, almond, or rice milk; or orange juice rather than soft drinks.

During the last two trimesters of pregnancy, energy needs increase by about 350 to 450 kcal/day. For a woman normally consuming 2,000 kcal/day, an extra 400 kcal represents only a 20% increase in energy intake, a goal that can be met more easily than many pregnant women realize. For example, 1 cup of low-fat yogurt and two pieces of whole-wheat toast spread with a tablespoon of peanut butter is about 400 kcal. At the same time, some vitamin and mineral needs increase by 50% or more, so again, the key for getting adequate micronutrients while not consuming too many extra Calories is choosing nutrient-dense foods.

During pregnancy, protein needs increase to about 1.1 grams per day per kilogram of body weight, an increase of about 25 grams of protein per day. Many women already eat this much protein every day. If not, however, it does not take much food to add 25 grams of protein. Remember that yogurt and toast with peanut butter we just mentioned? This light meal provides the additional 25 grams of protein most women need.

Pregnant women should aim for a carbohydrate intake of at least 175 grams per day.[8] Glucose is the primary metabolic fuel of the developing fetus; thus, pregnant women need to consume healthful sources of carbohydrate, such as whole-grain breads, cereals, and grains, throughout the day. The guideline for the percentage of daily Calories that comes from fat does not change during pregnancy. Pregnant women should be aware that, because new tissues and cells are being built, adequate consumption of dietary fat is even more important than in the nonpregnant state. Like anyone else, pregnant women should limit their intakes of saturated and *trans* fats because of their negative impact on cardiovascular health.

An omega-3 polyunsaturated fatty acid known as *docosahexaenoic acid (DHA)* has been found to be uniquely critical for both neurologic and eye development. Because the fetal brain grows dramatically during the third trimester, DHA is especially important in the mother's diet at this time. Good sources of DHA are oily fish, such as anchovies, mackerel, salmon, and sardines. It is also found in lower amounts in tuna, chicken, and eggs (some eggs are DHA-enhanced by feeding hens a DHA-rich diet).

Pregnant women who eat fish should be aware of the potential for mercury contamination, as even a limited intake of mercury during pregnancy can impair a fetus's developing nervous system. Large fish, such as swordfish, shark, tile fish, and king mackerel, have high levels of mercury and should be avoided. The Food and Drug Administration recommends that women who are pregnant or breastfeeding should eat at least 12 oz of most other types of fish, such as salmon, mackerel, sardines, and tuna, per week, as long as it is adequately cooked.[9]

Micronutrient Needs of Pregnant Women

The needs for certain micronutrients increase during pregnancy. See **Table 11.2** for an overview of these changes. The key micronutrients are discussed in this section.

⬆ Spinach is a good source of folate.

Folate As noted earlier, adequate folate is critical during the first 28 days after conception, when it is required for the formation and closure of the **neural tube**—an embryonic structure that eventually becomes the brain and spinal cord. Folate deficiency is associated with neural tube defects such as **spina bifida (Figure 11.3**, page 332) and **anencephaly,** a fatal defect in which there is a partial absence of brain tissue.[10] To reduce the risk for a neural tube defect, all women capable of becoming pregnant are encouraged to consume 400 µg of folic acid per day from supplements, fortified foods, or both in addition to a variety of foods naturally high in folate. Adequate folate intake does not guarantee normal neural tube development, as the precise cause of neural tube defects is unknown, and in some cases there is a genetic component.

Of course, folate remains very important even after the neural tube has closed. Folate deficiency can result in macrocytic anemia (a condition in which blood cells do not mature properly) and has been associated with low birth weight, preterm delivery, and failure of the fetus to grow properly. The RDA for folate for pregnant women is 600 µg/day, a full 50% increase over the RDA for a nonpregnant female.[10]

Vitamin B$_{12}$ Vitamin B$_{12}$ (cobalamin) is vital during pregnancy because it regenerates the active form of folate. The RDA for vitamin B$_{12}$ for pregnant women is shown in Table 11.2. It can easily be obtained from animal food sources; however, deficiencies

TABLE 11.2	Nutrient Recommendations for Pregnant Adult Women		
Micronutrient	**Pre-Pregnancy**	**Pregnancy**	**% Increase**
Folate	400 µg/day	600 µg/day	50
Vitamin B$_{12}$	2.4 µg/day	2.6 µg/day	8
Vitamin C	75 mg/day	85 mg/day	13
Vitamin A	700 µg/day	770 µg/day	10
Vitamin D	15 µg/day	15 µg/day	0
Calcium	1,000 mg/day	1,000 mg/day	0
Iron	18 mg/day	27 mg/day	50
Zinc	8 mg/day	11 mg/day	38
Sodium	1,500 mg/day	1,500 mg/day	0
Iodine	150 µg/day	220 µg/day	47

neural tube Embryonic tissue that forms a tube, which eventually becomes the brain and spinal cord.

spina bifida An embryonic neural tube defect that occurs when the spinal vertebrae fail to completely enclose the spinal cord, allowing it to protrude.

anencephaly A fatal neural tube defect in which there is a partial absence of brain tissue, most likely caused by failure of the neural tube to close.

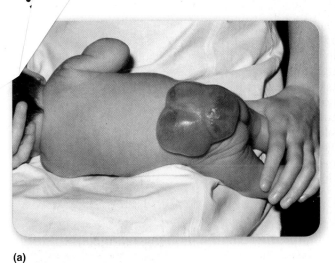

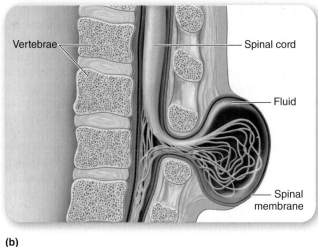

(a)   **(b)**

Figure 11.3 Spina bifida, a common neural tube defect. **(a)** An external view of an infant with spina bifida. **(b)** An internal view of the protruding spinal cord tissue and fluid-filled sac.

have been observed in vegan women. Fortified foods and supplementation provide these women with the necessary B_{12}.

Vitamin C Vitamin C is needed for the synthesis of collagen, a component of skin, blood vessels, tendons, and bones. As shown in Table 11.2, the RDA for vitamin C during pregnancy is increased by a little more than 10% over the RDA for nonpregnant women. Women who smoke during pregnancy should consume even higher levels, because smoking lowers both serum and amniotic fluid levels of vitamin C.

Vitamin A As seen in Table 11.2, vitamin A needs increase during pregnancy, and deficiency has been linked to low birth weight and preterm delivery. However, the consumption of excessive amounts of vitamin A, particularly during the first trimester, increases the risk for the birth of an infant with cleft lip or palate, heart defects, and abnormalities of the central nervous system.[11] A well-balanced diet supplies sufficient vitamin A, so supplementation even at low levels is not recommended. However, high intakes of beta-carotene (which is converted to vitamin A in the body) from plant foods have not been associated with birth defects.

Vitamin D Despite the role of vitamin D in calcium absorption, the RDA for this nutrient does not increase during pregnancy. However, pregnant women with darkly pigmented skin and/or limited sun exposure who do not regularly drink milk now will benefit from vitamin D supplementation. Most prenatal vitamin supplements now contain 15 µg/day (600 IU) of vitamin D, which is considered safe and acceptable. Vitamin D can be highly toxic, however, so excessive intakes must be avoided.[12]

Calcium Growth of the fetal skeleton requires calcium. However, the RDA for calcium does not change during pregnancy; it remains at 1,300 mg/day for pregnant adolescents and 1,000 mg/day for adult pregnant women for two reasons. First, pregnant women absorb calcium from their diet more efficiently than nonpregnant women. Second, the extra demand for calcium has not been found to cause permanent demineralization of the mother's bones or to increase fracture risk, so there is no rationale for recommending a higher intake.[12]

Meats provide protein and heme iron, which are important for both maternal and fetal nutrition.

Iron Iron is important in the formation of red blood cells, which transport oxygen throughout the body. During pregnancy, the demand for red blood cells increases to accommodate the needs of the expanded maternal blood volume, growing uterus, placenta, and fetus.[11] Thus, more iron is needed (see Table 11.2). Fetal demand for iron increases even further during the last trimester, when the fetus stores iron in the liver for use during the first few months of life. This iron storage is protective because breast milk is low in iron.

Severely inadequate iron intake certainly has the potential to harm the fetus, resulting in an increased rate of low birth weight, preterm birth, stillbirth, and death of the newborn in the first weeks after birth. However, in most cases, the fetus builds adequate stores by "robbing" maternal iron, prompting iron-deficiency anemia in the mother. During pregnancy, maternal iron deficiency causes pallor and exhaustion, but at birth it endangers her life: anemic women are more likely to die during or shortly after childbirth because they are less able to tolerate blood loss and fight infection. To ensure adequate iron during pregnancy, an iron supplement (as part of, or distinct from, a total prenatal supplement) is routinely prescribed during the last two trimesters.

Zinc   Because zinc has critical roles in DNA and protein synthesis, it is very important that adequate zinc status be maintained during pregnancy to facilitate proper growth and development of both maternal and fetal tissues. The RDA for zinc for adult pregnant women is 11 mg per day and increases to 12 mg per day for pregnant adolescents (see Table 11.2).[11]

Sodium and Iodine   The AI for sodium does not change during pregnancy.[13] Although too much sodium is associated with fluid retention and bloating, as well as high blood pressure, increased body fluids are a normal and necessary part of pregnancy, and some sodium is needed to maintain fluid balance.

As shown in Table 11.2, iodine needs increase significantly during pregnancy, but the RDA is easy to achieve by using a modest amount of iodized salt in cooking.

Do Pregnant Women Need Supplements?

Prenatal multivitamin and mineral supplements are not strictly necessary during pregnancy, but most healthcare providers recommend them. Meeting all the nutrient needs would otherwise take careful and somewhat complex dietary planning. Prenatal supplements are especially good insurance for vegans, adolescents, and others whose diet is low in one or more micronutrients. It is important that pregnant women understand, however, that supplements are to be taken *in addition to,* not as a substitute for, a nutrient-rich diet.

Fluid Needs of Pregnant Women

Fluid plays many vital roles during pregnancy. It allows for the necessary increase in the mother's blood volume, acts as a lubricant, aids in regulating body temperature, and is necessary for many metabolic reactions. Fluid that the mother consumes also

It's important that pregnant women drink about 10 cups of fluid a day.

NUTRI-CASE GUSTAVO

"I don't believe in taking vitamins. If you eat good food, you get everything you need, and it's the way nature intended it. My daughter kept nagging at my wife and me to start taking B-vitamins. She said when people get to be our age they have problems with their nerves and their blood pressure if they don't. I didn't fall for it, but my wife did, and then her doctor told her she needed calcium pills and vitamin D, too. The kitchen counter is starting to look like a medicine chest! You know what I think? I think this whole vitamin thing is just a hoax to get you to empty your wallet."

Would you support Gustavo's decision to avoid taking a B-vitamin supplement? Given what you have learned in previous Nutri-Cases about Gustavo's wife, would you support or oppose her taking a vitamin B, calcium, or vitamin D supplement? Explain your choices.

helps maintain the **amniotic fluid** that surrounds, cushions, and protects the fetus in the uterus. The AI for fluid intake is approximately 2.3 liters (10 cups) of fluid as beverages, including drinking water.[13]

RECAP During the last two trimesters of pregnancy, energy needs increase by about 350 to 450 kcal/day. Pregnant women should consume enough energy from nutrient-dense foods to support an appropriate weight gain, typically 25 to 35 lb. Protein, carbohydrates, and fats provide the building blocks for fetal growth. Folate deficiency has been associated with neural tube defects. Most healthcare providers recommend prenatal supplements as well as an iron supplement for pregnant women. More fluid is needed during pregnancy to provide for increased maternal blood volume and amniotic fluid.

Nutrition-Related Concerns for Pregnant Women

Conditions involving a particular nutrient, such as neural tube defects and iron-deficiency anemia, have already been discussed. The following are some of the most common discomforts and disorders of pregnant women that are related to their general nutrition.

Morning Sickness

More than half of all pregnant women experience **morning sickness,** or *nausea and vomiting of pregnancy (NVP)*. It is thought to be prompted at least in part by the effect of pregnancy-related hormones on the brain stem and gastrointestinal (GI) tract. The symptoms vary from occasional mild queasiness to constant nausea with bouts of vomiting. In truth, "morning sickness" is not an appropriate name because about 80% of pregnant women report that their symptoms last all day. Except in severe cases, the mother and fetus do not suffer lasting harm. However, some women experience such frequent vomiting that they require hospitalization.

There is no cure for morning sickness. However, some women find it helpful to snack lightly throughout the day rather than consuming three larger meals. Greasy and high-fat foods should be avoided, as should strong cooking odors. Some women find that cold or room-temperature foods are less likely to cause nausea. Alternative therapies such as meditation, biofeedback, and acupressure wrist bands may also help.

Food Cravings

It seems as if nothing is more stereotypical about pregnancy than the image of a frazzled husband getting up in the middle of the night to run to the convenience store to get his pregnant wife some pickles and ice cream. This image, although humorous, is

NUTRITION
MILESTONE

The Fetal Environment and Adult Health

1986 During World War II, parts of England, Wales, and other European countries experienced widespread famine, leading to high rates of premature births and low-birth-weight infants. Decades later, however, the infants born during this time of deprivation matured into adults who were actually developing obesity, type 2 diabetes, heart disease, and other complications at rates *higher* than among adults of normal birth weight. Dr. David Barker, a British cardiologist, first published the epidemiological evidence of this phenomenon in 1986, in an article proposing a theory now referred to as the "developmental origins of adult disease." Barker and other researchers have since then published many additional studies documenting this phenomenon. As a result, the hypothesis has become generally accepted and is now thought to be somewhat broader in its implications: fetal exposure to excessive or inadequate nutrients has now been linked to an individual's risk for diseases as diverse as heart disease, osteoporosis, and depression, probably through changes in gene activity. The term *life cycle* accurately reflects the impact that the fetal environment has for decades to come.

amniotic fluid The watery fluid contained in the innermost membrane of the sac containing the fetus. It cushions and protects the growing fetus.

morning sickness Varying degrees of nausea and vomiting associated with pregnancy, most commonly in the first trimester.

HIGHLIGHT
The Danger of Nonfood Cravings

A few weeks after her nurse told her she was pregnant, Darlene started feeling "funny." She'd experience bouts of nausea lasting several hours every day, and her appetite seemed to disappear. At the grocery store, she'd wander through the aisles with an empty cart, confused about what foods she should be choosing for her growing baby and unable to find anything that appealed to her. Eventually, she'd return home with a few things: frozen prepared macaroni and cheese, cereal bars, orange and grape soda—and a large bag of ice. She took cupfuls of ice from the soda machine at the assembly plant where she worked and ate it throughout the day. Each weekend, she went through more than a boxful of popsicles to "settle her stomach." Even her favorite strawberry ice cream no longer appealed to her.

At Darlene's next checkup, her nurse became concerned because she had lost weight. "I want to eat the stuff like in those pictures you gave me," Darlene confessed, "but I don't like it very much." She was too embarrassed to admit to anyone, even the nurse, that the only thing she really wanted to eat was ice.

Some people contend that a pregnant woman with unusual food cravings is intuitively seeking needed nutrients. Arguing against this theory is the phenomenon of *pica*—the craving and consumption of nonfood material, which often occurs during pregnancy. A woman with pica may crave ice, clay, dirt, chalk, coffee grounds, baking soda, laundry starch, or any other substance. The cause of these nonfood cravings is not known; however, people with developmental disabilities are at increased risk.[14] Underlying biochemical disorders (such as decreased activity of neurotransmitters in the brain), lower socioeconomic status, and family stress have also been implicated, as have cultural factors. For example, in the United States, pica is more common among pregnant African American women than women from other racial or ethnic groups. The practice of eating clay has been traced to central Africa, and researchers theorize that people taken from central Africa and sent as slaves to the United States brought the practice with them. In addition, nutrient deficiencies have been associated with pica, although it is not at all clear that nutrient deficiencies cause it. In fact, the inhibition of nutrient absorption caused by the ingestion of clay and other substances may produce nutrient deficiency.

No matter the cause, pica is dangerous. Consuming ice can lead to inadequate weight gain if, as with Darlene, the ice substitutes for food. The ingestion of clay, starch, and other substances can not only inhibit absorption of nutrients but also cause constipation, intestinal blockage, and even excessive weight gain. Women with pica are known to be at risk for high lead exposure, which may impair the neurodevelopment of the fetus and increase the risk for pregnancy-related complications.[15] The ingestion of certain substances, such as dish-washing liquid, can lead to such severe vomiting and diarrhea that the individual experiences electrolyte disturbances that lead to seizures or death.

Some pregnant women with pica find food items they can substitute for the craved nonfood—for instance, peanut butter for clay or nonfat powdered milk for starch. If a woman experiences pica, she should talk with her healthcare provider immediately to identify strategies to avoid consuming dangerous substances and to consume healthful foods that will support the optimal growth and development of her fetus.

---

far from reality. Although some women have specific cravings, most crave a type of food (such as "something sweet" or "something salty") rather than a particular food.

Most cravings are, of course, for edible substances. But a surprising number of pregnant women crave nonfoods, such as laundry starch, chalk, and clay. This craving, called **pica,** is the subject of the *Highlight* feature box (shown above).

Gestational Diabetes

Gestational diabetes, which occurs in approximately 7% of all U.S. pregnancies, is defined as any degree of glucose intolerance that begins or is first diagnosed during pregnancy. It is usually a temporary condition in which a pregnant woman is unable to produce sufficient insulin or becomes insulin resistant, resulting in elevated levels of blood glucose. Obesity is a risk factor. Because of the high rate of obesity among young women and the implementation of new diagnostic criteria, it is expected that the number of women developing gestational diabetes will increase in the next few years.

As many as 10% of women with gestational diabetes develop type 2 diabetes shortly after the birth, and 35% to 60% will become diabetic over the next 10 to 20 years. Fortunately, gestational diabetes has no short-term ill effects on the fetus if blood glucose levels are strictly controlled through diet, physical activity, and/or

pica An abnormal craving to eat something not fit for food, such as clay, chalk, paint, or other nonfood substances.

gestational diabetes In a pregnant woman, insufficient insulin production or insulin resistance that results in consistently high blood glucose levels; the condition typically resolves after birth occurs.

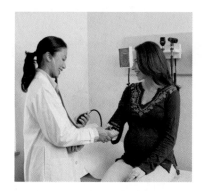

◄ Pregnant women should have their blood pressure measured to test for gestational hypertension.

medication. Over the long term, however, the offspring of women with gestational diabetes may remain at higher risk for type 2 diabetes and other disorders. If blood glucose is not adequately controlled, gestational diabetes can result in a type of maternal high blood pressure, discussed in the next section. It can also result in a baby that is too large as a result of receiving too much glucose across the placenta during fetal life. Infants who are overly large are at risk for early birth and trauma during vaginal birth and may need to be delivered by cesarean section.

Hypertensive Disorders of Pregnancy

About 7% to 8% of U.S. pregnant women develop some form of hypertension, or high blood pressure, yet it accounts for almost 15% of pregnancy-related deaths. A woman who develops high blood pressure during pregnancy, with no other complications, is diagnosed with *gestational hypertension.* A more complex and severe hypertensive disorder during pregnancy is *preeclampsia,* in which the elevated blood pressure is accompanied by sudden weight gain and loss of protein in the urine. If left untreated, hypertensive disorders during pregnancy can lead to seizures and kidney failure that are life-threatening for both the mother and the fetus.

No one knows exactly what causes hypertensive disorders during pregnancy, but deficiencies in dietary protein, vitamin C, vitamin E, calcium, and magnesium seem to increase the risk. Pregnant adolescents and women who are pregnant for the first time are at higher risk, as are African American and low-income women. Management focuses mainly on blood pressure control. Typical treatment includes medication and close medical oversight. In nearly all women without a history of hypertension, blood pressure returns to normal within about a day after childbirth.

Adolescent Pregnancy

Although the rate of adolescent pregnancies in the United States has declined by almost one-third since 1991, approximately 377,000 U.S. teenagers, ages 15 to 19 years, gave birth in 2008.[16] Adolescents who become pregnant face greater nutritional challenges than adult women for several reasons:

- An adolescent's body is still changing and growing: peak bone mass has not yet been reached, and full stature may not have been attained. This demand for tissue growth keeps nutrient needs during adolescence very high. Iron-deficiency anemia is a common complication among pregnant adolescents, increasing the risk for preterm birth and other complications. **Table 11.3** summarizes the differences in nutrient requirements between pregnant and nonpregnant adolescents.
- Many adolescents have not yet established healthful eating patterns. The added burden of pregnancy on an adolescent body can create a nutrient demand that is very difficult to meet.
- Pregnant adolescents are less likely than older women to receive early and regular prenatal care.

TABLE 11.3	Differences in Nutrient Recommendations Between Nonpregnant and Pregnant Adolescents		
Nutrient	**Nonpregnant Adolescent**	**Pregnant Adolescent**	**% Increase**
Folate	400 µg/day	600 µg/day	50
Vitamin B12	2.4 µg/day	2.6 µg/day	8
Vitamin C	65 mg/day	80 mg/day	23
Vitamin A	700 µg/day	750 µg/day	7
Vitamin D	15 µg/day	15 µg/day	0
Calcium	1,300 mg/day	1,300 mg/day	0
Iron	15 mg/day	27 mg/day	80
Zinc	9 mg/day	12 mg/day	33
Iodine	150 µg/day	220 µg/day	47

- Pregnant adolescents are more likely to smoke and less likely to understand the medical consequences of prenatal smoking, alcohol consumption, and drug abuse.
- Pregnant adolescents with excessive prenatal weight gain are more likely to retain the excess weight postnataly than are adult women, increasing their risk for adult obesity.

These factors make adolescent mothers more likely than older mothers to have preterm births, low-birth-weight babies, and other complications. In addition, the rate of infant mortality is higher among infants born to adolescent mothers.

Vegetarianism

With the possible exception of iron and zinc, vegetarian women who consume dairy products and eggs (lacto-ovo-vegetarians) have no nutritional concerns beyond those encountered by every pregnant woman. In contrast, women who are vegan need to be more vigilant than usual about their intake of nutrients that are derived primarily or wholly from animal products. These include vitamin D (unless regularly exposed to sunlight throughout the pregnancy), vitamin B_6, vitamin B_{12}, calcium, iron, and zinc. Supplements and/or fortified foods containing these nutrients are usually necessary.

Consumption of Caffeine

Caffeine readily crosses the placenta and thus quickly reaches the fetus, but at what dose and to what extent it causes fetal harm is still a subject of controversy and study. Current thinking holds that women who consume less than about 200 mg of caffeine per day (the equivalent of one to two 8-ounce cups of coffee) are not harming the fetus. Evidence suggests that consuming higher daily doses of caffeine (the higher the dose, the more compelling the evidence) may slightly increase the risk for miscarriage, preterm delivery, and low birth weight. It is sensible, then, for pregnant women to limit daily caffeine intake to no more than the equivalent of one 12-ounce cup of coffee.[17]

Consumption of Alcohol

Alcohol is a known teratogen that readily crosses the placenta and accumulates in the fetal bloodstream. The immature fetal liver cannot readily metabolize alcohol, and its presence in fetal blood and tissues is associated with a variety of birth defects, including *fetal alcohol syndrome* (see Chapter 8). According to the March of Dimes, approximately 40,000 babies are born in the United States each year with some type of alcohol-induced damage.[18]

Heavy drinking during the first trimester typically results in fetal malformations such as heart defects and facial abnormalities. Because many women do not even realize they are pregnant until several weeks after conception, public health officials recommend not only that pregnant women abstain from all alcoholic beverages but also that women who are trying to become pregnant or suspect they may be pregnant abstain.

Smoking

Despite the well-known consequences of cigarette smoking and the growing social stigma associated with smoking during pregnancy, 15.3% of pregnant U.S. women smoke.[19] The rate of smoking among pregnant teens age 15 to 17 is higher (20.6%).

Several components and metabolites of tobacco are toxic to the fetus, including lead, cyanide, nicotine, and carbon monoxide. Fetal nourishment, growth, and development may be impaired by reduced oxygen levels in fetal blood and reduced placental blood flow.

Maternal smoking greatly increases the risk for miscarriage, stillbirth, placental abnormalities, poor fetal growth, preterm delivery, and low birth weight. The effects of maternal smoking continue after birth: sudden infant death syndrome and respiratory illnesses occur with greater frequency in the children of smokers than the children of nonsmokers.

Cigarette smoking may interfere with nutrient metabolism.

Legal and Illegal Drugs

The U.S. Food and Drug Administration (FDA) rigorously tests prescription and over-the-counter medications for safety and effectiveness; however, little is known about the effects of many of these drugs on fetal development. In general, pregnant women should consult their healthcare provider about continuing to use any medication, especially in the first trimester.

In 2009, 4.5% of pregnant women in the United States used illicit drugs. Any drug abuse is likely to be harmful to a developing fetus. Most drugs pass through the placenta into the fetal bloodstream and accumulate in the blood and tissues. Many decrease oxygen delivery to the fetus, causing respiratory distress and, in some cases, fetal death by suffocation. Some impair placental blood flow, thereby reducing the transfer of nutrients from the mother to the developing fetus. Many newborns suffer from withdrawal symptoms, and developmental disabilities, including learning and attention deficits, can continue throughout life.[20] All women are strongly advised to stop taking illegal drugs *before* becoming pregnant. If a woman using illegal drugs discovers she is pregnant, she should seek healthcare immediately.

Herbal Supplements

Many pregnant women feel that, as "natural" products, herbals are safe. This is a dangerous assumption. Herbal supplements typically are not tested for purity, safety, or effectiveness. Pregnant women should always consult with their healthcare provider before using any type of herbal product.

Food Safety

Because of the risk for foodborne illness, pregnant women should avoid a few specific foods. These include unpasteurized milk; raw or partially cooked eggs; raw or undercooked meat, fish, or poultry; unpasteurized juices; and raw sprouts. Soft cheeses, such as Brie, feta, Camembert, Roquefort, and Mexican-style cheeses, also called *queso blanco* or *queso fresco*, should be avoided unless they are clearly labeled as made with pasteurized milk.

As discussed earlier, fish is an excellent source of the omega-3 essential fatty acid DHA and, in appropriate amounts, is a healthful addition to a balanced prenatal diet. However, certain types of fish should be avoided because of their high mercury content.[9] All fish should be thoroughly cooked to kill any disease-causing bacteria or parasites. Pregnant women should avoid sushi and other raw fish, as well as raw oysters and clams.

Maintaining Fitness

Exercise can help keep a woman physically fit during pregnancy. Other benefits of exercise during pregnancy include the following:

- Exercise is a great mood booster, helping women feel more in control of their changing body and reducing postpartum depression.
- Expending additional energy through exercise compensates for extra energy consumed when a ravenous appetite kicks in.
- Regular moderate exercise reduces the risk for gestational diabetes, helps keep blood pressure down, and confers all the cardiovascular benefits that it does to nonpregnant individuals.[21,22]
- Regular exercise can shorten the duration of active labor.
- A woman who exercises throughout pregnancy will have an easier time resuming a fitness routine and losing weight after the birth.

If a woman was not active prior to pregnancy, she should begin an exercise program slowly and progress gradually under the guidance of her healthcare provider. If a woman was physically active before pregnancy, she can continue as before within comfort and reason. Brisk walking, hiking, swimming, and water aerobics are excellent choices. Women who have been avid runners before pregnancy

▲ During pregnancy, women should adjust their physical activity to comfortable, low-impact exercises.

To view a slide show of pregnancy exercises, go to www.mayoclinic.com/health/pregnancy-exercises/MY01424.

can often continue; however, they should consult their healthcare provider about the distance and intensity of their runs as the pregnancy progresses.

RECAP Pregnant women may experience a variety of nutrition-related concerns during pregnancy, from morning sickness to gestational diabetes. These can seriously affect maternal and fetal health. As adolescents' bodies are still growing and developing, their nutrient needs during pregnancy become so high that adequate nourishment for the mother and baby becomes difficult. Women who follow a vegan diet usually need to consume multivitamin and mineral supplements during pregnancy. Caffeine intake should not exceed one 12-ounce cup of coffee per day. Any use of alcohol, illegal drugs, and tobacco can be dangerous to the woman and her fetus. Pregnant women should avoid certain foods associated with foodborne illness. Exercise (provided the mother has no contraindications) can enhance the health of a pregnant woman.

Nutrition in Infancy

In the first year of life, infants generally grow about 10 inches and triple their weight—a growth rate more rapid than will ever occur again. At the same time, their limited physical activity means that the majority of their energy expenditure is to support growth.

What Are the Benefits of Breastfeeding?

Throughout most of human history, infants have thrived on only one food: breast milk. Breastfeeding is universally recognized as the ideal method of infant feeding because of the nutritional quality and health benefits of breast milk.[23] However, the technique requires patience and practice. La Leche League International is an advocacy group for breastfeeding: its publications, website, and local meetings are all valuable resources for breastfeeding mothers and their families. Many hospitals and HMOs also offer breastfeeding classes.

Nutritional Quality of Breast Milk

During pregnancy, the woman's body is prepared to produce breastmilk by the development of the milk-producing glands, called *alveoli* (**Figure 11.4**). At birth, changing hormone levels stimulate milk production. In the first few days after birth, the breast milk is called **colostrum.** This yellowish fluid is rich in protein, vitamins A and E, and antibodies that help protect the newborn from infection. It also contains a factor that promotes the growth of helpful intestinal bacteria and has a laxative effect, which helps the newborn expel the sticky first stool.

Within 2 to 4 days, colostrum is replaced by mature breast milk. The amount and types of proteins in breast milk are ideally suited to the human infant: they are easily digested in the infant's immature GI tract, reducing the risk for gastric distress; they prevent the growth of harmful bacteria; and they include antibodies that help prevent infection while the infant's immune system is still immature.

The primary carbohydrate in breast milk is lactose, a disaccharide composed of glucose and galactose. The galactose component is important in nervous system development. Lactose provides energy and promotes the growth of beneficial

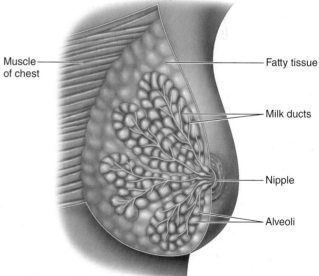

Muscle of chest — Fatty tissue — Milk ducts — Nipple — Alveoli

Figure 11.4 Anatomy of the breast. During pregnancy, hormones secreted by the placenta prepare the breast for lactation.

colostrum The first fluid made and secreted by the breasts from late in pregnancy to about a week after birth. It is rich in immune factors and protein.

⬆ Breastfeeding has important benefits for both the mother and the infant.

gut bacteria. It also aids in the absorption of calcium. Breast milk has more lactose than cow's milk does.

As with protein, the amount and types of fat in breast milk are ideally suited to the human infant. The fats in breast milk, especially omega-3 DHA and omega-6 arachidonic acid (ARA), have been shown to be essential for the growth and development of the infant's nervous system and the retina of the eyes. Many people are surprised to learn that the fat content of breast milk is higher than that of whole cow's milk. The energy provided by these fats, however, supports the rapid rate of growth during the first year of life.

The fat content of breast milk changes according to the age of the infant, providing a ratio of fatty acids unique to the growing infant's needs. The fat content also changes during the course of every feeding: the milk that is initially released is watery and is thought to satisfy the infant's initial thirst. As the feeding progresses, the milk acquires more fat, until the very last 5% or so of the milk produced is similar to cream. This milk is thought to satiate the infant. Breast milk is also relatively high in cholesterol, which supports the rapid growth and development of the brain and nervous system.

In terms of micronutrients, breast milk is a good source of readily absorbed calcium and magnesium. It is low in iron, but the iron it does contain is easily absorbed (recall that the fetus stores iron in preparation for the first few months of life). Most experts agree that breast milk can meet the iron needs of full-term healthy infants for the first 6 months, after which iron-rich foods are needed.

Because its nutrient composition changes as the baby grows, breast milk alone is entirely sufficient to sustain an infant for the first 6 months of life. Throughout the next 6 months of infancy, as solid foods are gradually introduced, breast milk remains the baby's primary source of superior-quality nutrition. The American Academy of Pediatrics (AAP) encourages exclusive breastfeeding (no food or other source of nourishment) for the first 6 months of life, continuing breastfeeding for at least the first year of life and, if acceptable within the family unit, into the second year of life or longer.[23]

Immunologic Benefits for Breast-Fed Infants

Immune factors from the mother, including antibodies and immune cells, are passed directly from the mother to the newborn through breast milk. These factors provide important disease protection for the infant while its immune system is still immature. It has been shown that breast-fed infants have a lower incidence of bacterial infections. Breast-fed infants also demonstrate an enhanced immune response to polio, tetanus, and diphtheria immunizations. It has been estimated that, if 90% of U.S. infants were exclusively breasted for six months, medical expenses would be decreased by $13 billion per year and over 900 infant deaths would be prevented.[24]

In addition, breast milk is nonallergenic, and breastfeeding is associated with a reduced risk for atopic dermatitis, wheezing, asthma, and cow's milk allergies during infancy,[25] childhood, and adulthood. Breast-fed babies also die less frequently from **sudden infant death syndrome (SIDS)** and have a decreased chance of developing diabetes, overweight and obesity, hypercholesterolemia, and chronic digestive disorders.

Physiologic Benefits for the Mother

Breastfeeding causes uterine contractions that quicken the return of the uterus to pre-pregnancy size and reduce bleeding. Many women also find that breastfeeding helps them lose the weight they gained during pregnancy, particularly if they breastfeed for more than 6 months.

Breastfeeding also suppresses **ovulation,** lengthening the time between pregnancies and giving a mother's body the chance to recover before she conceives again. Ovulation may not cease completely, however, so it is still possible to become pregnant while breastfeeding. The benefits of breastfeeding are summarized in **Table 11.4.**

sudden infant death syndrome (SIDS) A condition marked by the sudden death of a previously healthy infant; the most common cause of death in infants more than 1 month of age.

ovulation The release of an ovum (egg) from a woman's ovary.

TABLE 11.4   Benefits of Breastfeeding

Benefits to Infant	Benefits to Mother	Benefits to Family/Society
Provides superior level and balance of nutrients for infant growth, health, and development	Increases level of oxytocin, resulting in less postpartum bleeding and more rapid return of uterus to pre-pregnant state	Reduces healthcare costs and employee absenteeism for care attributable to infant/child illness
Decreases incidence and severity of a wide range of infectious diseases, including diarrhea, bacterial meningitis, and respiratory infections	Delays resumption of menstrual periods, causing reduced menstrual blood loss over the months after the birth and preserving maternal iron	Decreases family food expenditures: cost of purchasing extra food for lactating mother is less than half the cost of purchasing infant formula
Is associated with decreased risk for both type 1 and type 2 diabetes	Delays resumption of ovulation and thereby increases spacing between pregnancies	Decreases environmental burden for production and transport of formula, bottles, artificial nipples, and so on
Has possible protective effect against sudden infant death syndrome (SIDS), several chronic digestive diseases, leukemia, lymphoma, Hodgkin disease, asthma, and allergies	Promotes an earlier return to pre-pregnancy weight	Reduces caregiver time away from infant/siblings to prepare infant food: breast milk requires no preparation and is always the perfect temperature
Is associated with reduced risk for childhood and adulthood overweight and obesity	Improves bone remineralization in months after birth	
Is associated with enhanced cognitive development	Reduces the woman's risk for ovarian cancer and premenopausal breast cancer	

Data from: American Academy of Pediatrics, Section on Breastfeeding. February 2005. Policy Statement: Breastfeeding and the use of human milk. *Ped.* 115(2):496–506. In addition to these benefits, the La Leche League and other breastfeeding advocacy organizations identify emotional and psychological benefits of skin-to-skin suckling.

Effects of Drugs and Other Substances on Breast Milk

Many substances make their way into breast milk. Among them are illegal and prescription drugs, over-the-counter drugs, and even substances from foods the mother eats. All illegal drugs should be assumed to pass into breast milk and should be avoided by breastfeeding mothers. Prescription drugs vary in the degree to which they pass into breast milk. Breastfeeding mothers should inform their healthcare provider that they are breastfeeding. In some cases, a woman may be advised to switch to formula feeding while she is taking a certain medication.

Caffeine, alcohol, and nicotine all rapidly enter breast milk. Caffeine can make the baby agitated and fussy, whereas alcohol can make the baby sleepy, depress the central nervous system, and, over time, slow motor development, in addition to inhibiting the mother's milk supply. Nicotine interferes with infant sleep patterns, and maternal smoking increases the risk for respiratory illness in the infant.[26]

Food components that pass into the breast milk may not seem harmful; however, some substances that the mother eats, such as chemicals found in garlic, onions, peppers, broccoli, and cabbage, are distasteful enough to the infant to prevent proper feeding. Although some high-risk babies may have allergic reactions to foods the mother has eaten, such as wheat, cow's milk, or eggs, there is no strong evidence that limiting maternal food choices during lactation provides additional protection against infant allergies.

Although environmental contaminants can enter the breast milk, the benefits of breastfeeding almost always outweigh potential risks. Fresh fruits and vegetables should be thoroughly washed and peeled to minimize exposure to pesticide and fertilizer residues. The mother's exposure to solvents, paints, gasoline fumes, furniture strippers, and similar products should also be limited.

The human immunodeficiency virus, HIV, which causes AIDS, can be transmitted from mother to baby through breast milk. Thus, HIV-positive women in the United States and Canada are encouraged to feed their infants formula.[27] Women with tuberculosis should not breastfeed until they have completed at least 2 weeks of specialized therapy. Women with cancer should avoid breastfeeding while on chemotherapy.

What Are a Breastfeeding Woman's Nutrient Needs?

You might be surprised to learn that breastfeeding requires even more energy and nutrients than pregnancy! This is because breast milk has to supply an adequate amount of all of the nutrients an infant needs to grow and develop. The current DRIs during breastfeeding (also called *lactation*) are listed in tables at the back of this textbook.

Nutrient Recommendations for Breastfeeding Women

It's estimated that milk production requires about 700 to 800 kcal/day. It is generally recommended that breastfeeding women aged 19 years and above consume 330 kcal/day above their pre-pregnancy energy needs during the first 6 months of breastfeeding and 400 additional kcal/day during the second 6 months.[8] This additional energy is sufficient to support adequate milk production. At the same time, the remaining energy deficit helps women gradually lose any excess fat and body weight gained during pregnancy. It is critical that breastfeeding women avoid severe energy restriction, as this practice can result in decreased milk production.

> Visit the La Leche League home page, where you'll find answer pages, podcasts, and links to breastfeeding families, at www.llli.org.

Of the macronutrients, carbohydrate and protein needs are increased. An additional 15 to 25 grams of protein/day and 80 grams of carbohydrate/day above pre-pregnancy requirements are recommended.

Although the needs for several vitamins and minerals increase over the requirements of pregnancy, the DRI for iron decreases significantly—to just 9 mg/day. This is because iron is not a significant component of breast milk and breastfeeding usually suppresses menstruation for at least a few months, reducing iron losses. The recommended calcium intake for a lactating woman is the same as for all women between the ages of 19 and 50 years—that is, 1,000 mg/day. Because of their own continuing growth, however, teen mothers who are breastfeeding should continue to consume 1,300 mg/day.[12]

Do Breastfeeding Women Need Supplements?

If a breastfeeding woman appropriately increases her energy intake and does so with nutrient-dense foods, her nutrient needs can usually be met without supplements. However, there is nothing wrong with taking a basic multivitamin for insurance, as long as it is not considered a substitute for proper nutrition. Breastfeeding women should consume omega-3 fatty acids either in fish or supplements to support the infant's developing nervous system, and women who don't consume dairy products should monitor their calcium and vitamin D intakes carefully. Women following a vegan diet should consume a vitamin B_{12} supplement or include B_{12}–fortified foods in their diets.

Fluid Recommendations for Breastfeeding Women

Because extra fluid is expended with every feeding, lactating women need to consume about an extra quart (about 1 litre) of fluid per day. The AI for fluid recommends about 13 cups of beverages to facilitate milk production and prevent dehydration.[13]

What Is "Successful" Breastfeeding?

A woman can be confident that she is successfully breastfeeding when:

- The infant gains an appropriate amount of weight, as monitored by a healthcare provider,

- The infant produces four to six wet diapers a day and has one to two bowel movements (often soft) per day,
- Maternal breasts are firm prior to the feeding and softer after the baby has nursed, and
- The infant is relaxed or sleepy after the feeding.

Women should nurse "on demand" and not set a predefined, fixed schedule. Most newborns nurse every 2 to 3 hours, with the interval increasing as the infant ages. Blankets, large scarves or shawls, or breastfeeding blouses can be used to help preserve modesty and comfort for women nursing in public. Women who must be physically apart from their infant can manually express milk into sterile bottles or use an electric or hand pump. Lactation support groups, such as La Leche League, and professional lactation consultants can provide help to any woman seeking guidance and assurance.

What Is the Nutritional Quality of Infant Formula?

Women with certain infectious diseases are advised not to breastfeed, as are women using certain prescription medications and women who abuse drugs.[23] Other women choose not to breastfeed for other reasons. If breastfeeding is not feasible, several types of commercial formulas provide nutritious alternatives. Most formulas are based on cow's milk that is modified to make it more appropriate for human infants. Soy-based formulas are a viable alternative for infants who are lactose intolerant (although this is rare in infants) or who cannot tolerate the proteins in cow's milk–based formulas. Soy formulas may also satisfy the requirements of families who are strict vegans. However, soy-based formulas are not without controversy. Because soy contains isoflavones, or plant forms of estrogens, there is some concern over the effects these compounds have on growing infants. In addition, soy itself is a common allergen.

Cow's milk should *not* be introduced to infants under 1 year of age. Cow's milk is too high in protein, and the protein is difficult to digest; its poor digestibility may contribute to gastrointestinal bleeding. In addition, cow's milk has too much sodium, too little iron, and a poor balance of other vitamins and minerals for infants. Goat's milk, soy milk, almond milk, and rice milk are also inappropriate for infants.

When feeding an infant formula, parents and caretakers need to pay close attention to their infant's cues for hunger and fullness. Although most parents instinctively recognize when their baby needs to eat, it is often harder for them to know when to stop. Some infants turn their head away from the nipple or tightly close their lips; others simply nod off or fall asleep. Older infants may actually push away the bottle or initiate playlike behaviors.

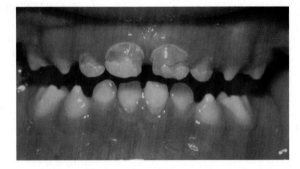

Figure 11.5 Leaving a baby alone with a bottle can result in the tooth decay of baby bottle syndrome.

Once the baby's teeth start coming in, he or she should not be allowed to fall asleep while sucking on the bottle. This practice allows the formula to pool around the teeth and, without the normal release of saliva that occurs when the baby is awake, can lead to a form of severe dental decay known as *baby bottle syndrome* **(Figure 11.5)**.

What Are an Infant's Nutrient Needs?

Three characteristics of infants combine to make their nutritional needs unique. These are (1) their high energy needs compared to their body weight; (2) their immature digestive tracts and kidneys; and (3) their small body size. The DRIs for infants are based on the nutrient values of breast milk and are listed in the tables at the back of this textbook.

Macronutrient Needs of Infants

Infants grow rapidly and need to consume about 40 to 50 kcal/pound of body weight per day. About 40% to 50% of an infant's caloric intake should come from fat. Intakes below this level can be harmful before the age of 2 years. Omega-6 and omega-3 fatty acids are essential for the rapid brain growth, retinal maturation, and nervous system development that happen in the first 1 to 2 years of life.

Although carbohydrate and protein are also essential for infant growth and development, no more than 20% of an infant's daily energy requirement should come from protein. Immature kidneys are not able to process and excrete the excess nitrogen from higher-protein diets.

Micronutrient Needs of Infants

Breast milk and commercial formulas provide most of the vitamins and minerals infants need. However, several micronutrients may warrant supplementation.

All infants are routinely given an injection of vitamin K shortly after birth. This provides vitamin K until the infant's intestines can develop their own healthful bacteria, which then provide the needed vitamin K.

Breast milk is low in vitamin D, and deficiencies of this nutrient are common in breastfed infants with darkly pigmented skin and those with limited sunlight exposure. Breastfed infants are commonly prescribed a vitamin D supplement, even in sunny climates.[23] Vitamin D deficiency is increasingly common in infants, particularly dark-skinned infants and those with low sun exposure.

Breastfed infants also require additional iron beginning no later than 6 months of age because the infant's iron stores become depleted and breast milk is a poor source of iron. Iron is extremely important for mental and physical development and the prevention of iron-deficiency anemia. Infant rice cereal fortified with iron, an excellent choice as a first food, can serve as an additional iron source, as can puréed meats.

Depending on the fluoride content of the household water supply, breastfed infants over the age of 6 months may need a fluoride supplement. Most brands of bottled water have low levels of fluoride, and many home water treatment systems remove fluoride. On the other hand, fluoride toxicity may be a risk for infants simultaneously exposed to fluoridated toothpaste and rinses, fluoridated water, and fluoride supplements.

There are special conditions in which additional supplements may be needed for breastfed infants. For example, a vegan mother's breast milk may be low in vitamin B_{12}, and a supplement of this vitamin should be given to the baby.

Many formulas are already fortified with iron and vitamin D. Thus, infants who are fed formula typically need no additional iron or vitamin D supplement.

Fluid Recommendations for Infants

Fluid is critical for everyone, but for infants the balance is more delicate for two reasons. First, infants have a relative large body surface area, so they proportionally lose more water through evaporation than adults. Second, their kidneys are immature and unable to concentrate urine. Hence, they are at increased risk for dehydration. An infant needs about 2 fl. oz of fluid per pound of body weight, and either breast milk or formula is almost always adequate in providing this amount. Experts recently confirmed that "infants exclusively fed human milk do not require supplemental water."[13] The practice common among some low-income families of diluting infant formula with extra water is extremely dangerous. Overhydration can cause nutrient imbalances, such as hyponatremia (low blood sodium), as well as inadequate weight gain and failure to thrive.

RECAP Breast milk provides superior nutrition and heightened immunity for infants. Mothers who breastfeed experience the benefit of increased post-pregnancy weight loss and suppressed ovulation. If breastfeeding is not feasible, several types of commercial formulas provide nutritious alternatives. Vitamin D supplements may be recommended for exclusively breastfed infants; iron and fluoride supplements may be prescribed for infants older than 6 months of age.

When Do Infants Begin to Need Solid Foods?

Before 4 to 6 months of age, most infants are not physically or developmentally able to consume solid food. The suckling response, present at birth, depends on a particular movement of the tongue that draws liquid out of a breast or bottle. When very young infants are spoon-fed solid food, this tongue movement, known as the *extrusion reflex*, causes most of the food to be pushed back out of the mouth. This reflex action must begin to subside before solid foods can be successfully introduced, typically after 4 to 6 months of age.

In addition, to minimize the risk of choking or gagging, the infant must have gained muscular control of the head and neck. The infant must also be able to sit up (with or without support).

An infant is also not ready for solid foods until the digestive system has matured. Infants are able to digest and absorb lactose from the time of their birth; however, they lack adequate levels of the enzyme amylase, for the digestion of starch, until the age of 3 to 4 months. If an infant is fed solid foods too soon, starches remain undigested, contributing to diarrhea and bloating, and proteins can be absorbed intact and undigested, setting the stage for allergies. In addition, the kidneys must have matured so that they are better able to process electrolytes and nitrogen waste products, as well as properly concentrate urine.

When deciding which foods to introduce first, parents must consider their infant's nutrient needs and the risk for an allergic reaction. At about 6 months of age, infant iron stores become depleted; thus, the first food introduced is often iron-fortified infant cereal. Rice cereal rarely triggers an allergic response and is easy to digest. Cereal and other solid foods should always be fed to the infant from a spoon, not placed into a bottle.

Parents should not introduce another new food for at least 4 to 5 days in order to carefully watch for signs of a food allergy or intolerance, including a rash, unexplained diarrhea, runny nose, or wheezing. If all goes well with the rice cereal, another single-grain cereal (other than wheat, which is highly allergenic) can be introduced, or the family may choose to introduce a different single-item food, such as a strained vegetable or meat. Some nutritionists recommend meat because it is a good source of iron and zinc, whereas others encourage the introduction of vitamin C–rich vegetables. It is wise to introduce strained vegetables before fruits because, once a child becomes accustomed to the sweetness of bananas, peaches, and other fruits, the relative blandness of most vegetables may be less appealing.

Commercial baby foods are convenient and are typically made without added salt or sugar; however, homemade baby foods are usually cheaper and reflect the food patterns of the family. Gradually, a variety of foods should be introduced to the infant by the end of the first year. Throughout the first year, solid foods should only be a supplement to, not a substitute for, breast milk or formula.

◄ The extrusion reflex will push solid food out of an infant's mouth.

What Not to Feed an Infant

The following foods should *never* be offered to an infant:

- *Foods that could cause choking.* Foods such as grapes, chunks of hot dogs, nuts, popcorn, raw carrots, raisins, and hard candies cannot be chewed adequately by infants and can cause choking.
- *Corn syrup and honey.* These may contain spores of the bacterium *Clostridium botulinum*. These spores can produce a toxin that can be fatal. Children older than 1 year can safely consume these substances because their digestive tract is mature enough to kill any *C. botulinum* spores.
- *Goat's milk.* Goat's milk is notoriously low in many nutrients that infants need, such as folate, vitamin C, vitamin D, and iron.
- *Cow's milk.* For infants under 1 year, cow's milk is too concentrated in minerals and protein and contains too few carbohydrates to meet infant energy needs. Children can begin to consume whole cow's milk after their first birthday.
- *Large quantities of fruit juices.* Fruit juices are poorly absorbed in the infant digestive tract, causing diarrhea if consumed in excess. It is considered safe for infants older than 6 months to consume 4 to 8 oz of pure fruit juice (no sweeteners added) per day, with no more than 2 to 4 oz given at a time.
- *Too much salt and sugar.* Infant foods should not be seasoned with salt or other seasonings. Cookies, cakes, and other excessively sweet, processed foods should be avoided.
- *Too much breast milk or formula.* As nutritious as breast milk and formula are, once infants reach the age of 6 months, solid foods should be introduced gradually.

Six months of age is a critical time; it is when a baby's iron stores begin to be depleted. Overreliance on breast milk or formula can result in a condition known as *milk anemia*.

RECAP In the absence of breastfeeding, commercial formulas provide adequate nutrition for infants. Solid foods can gradually be introduced into an infant's diet at 4 to 6 months of age, beginning with rice cereal, then moving to single-item vegetables or meats. Parents should avoid foods that represent a choking hazard, foods containing honey or corn syrup, cow's and goat's milk, and foods and beverages high in salt and sugar.

Nutrition-Related Concerns for Infants

Nutrition is one of the biggest concerns of new parents. Infants cannot speak, and their cries are sometimes indecipherable. Feeding time can be frustrating for parents, especially if the child is not eating, not growing appropriately, or has problems such as diarrhea, vomiting, or persistent skin rashes. Following are some nutrition-related concerns for infants.

Allergies

As noted earlier, breastfeeding minimizes the risk for allergy development, as does delaying the introduction of solid foods until 4 to 6 months of age. One of the most common allergies in infants is to the proteins in cow's milk–based formulas. Egg whites, peanuts and other nuts, wheat, soy, and citrus are other common allergens.

As stated, every food should be introduced in isolation, so that any allergic reaction can be identified and the particular food avoided. If there is a strong family history of food allergies, parents should be particularly watchful when introducing new foods to their infant and should examine food and beverage labels closely for offending ingredients.

Colic

← Colicky babies will begin crying for no apparent reason, even if they otherwise appear well nourished and happy.

Perhaps nothing is more frustrating to new parents than the relentless crying spells of some infants, typically referred to as **colic**. In this condition, infants who appear happy, healthy, and well nourished suddenly begin to cry or even shriek and continue for hours, no matter what their caregiver does to console them. The spells tend to occur at the same time of day, typically late in the afternoon or early in the evening, and often occur daily for a period of several weeks. Overstimulation of the nervous system, feeding too rapidly, swallowing of air, and intestinal gas pain are considered possible culprits, but the precise cause is unknown. For breastfed infants, colic spells are sometimes reduced when the mother switches to a bland diet. For formula-fed infants, a change in the type of formula sometimes helps.

Gastroesophageal Reflux

Particularly common in preterm infants, gastroesophageal reflux occurs in about 3% of newborns. Typically, as the gastrointestinal tract matures within the first 12 months of life, this condition resolves. Caretakers should avoid overfeeding the infant, keep the infant upright after each feeding, and watch for choking or gagging. Some infants improve when fed whey-enriched formulas.

Iron-Deficiency Anemia

colic A condition in infants marked by unconsolable crying for unknown reasons that lasts for hours at a time.

As stated earlier, full-term infants are born with sufficient iron stores to last for approximately the first 6 months of life. In older infants and toddlers, however, iron is the mineral most likely to be deficient. Iron-deficiency anemia causes pallor, lethargy, and impaired growth. Iron-fortified formula and cereals are good sources of this mineral. Overconsumption of cow's milk remains a common cause of anemia among U.S. infants and children.

Dehydration

Whether the cause is diarrhea, vomiting, prolonged fever, or inadequate fluid intake, dehydration is extremely dangerous to infants and if left untreated can quickly result in death. Treatment includes providing fluids, a task that is difficult if vomiting is occurring. In some cases, the physician may recommend that a pediatric electrolyte solution, readily available at most grocery and drug stores, be administered on a temporary basis. In more severe cases, hospitalization and the administration of intravenous fluids may be necessary.

RECAP The risk for food allergies can be reduced by breastfeeding and delaying the introduction of solid foods until the infant is at least 4 to 6 months of age. Infants with colic or gastroesophageal reflux present special challenges, but both conditions generally improve over time. Iron-deficiency anemia is easily prevented through the use of iron-fortified cereals. Dehydration is extremely dangerous to infants, and prompt fluid/electrolyte replacement is essential.

Nutrition for Toddlers

The rapid growth rate of infancy begins to slow during toddlerhood—the period from 12 to 36 months of age. During the second and third years of life, a toddler will grow a total of about 5.5 to 7.5 inches and gain an average of 9 to 11 lb. However, toddlers expend significant energy to fuel their increasing levels of activity. **Table 11.5** identifies the nutrient recommendations for toddlers, children, and adolescents.

What Are a Toddler's Nutrient Needs?

A healthy toddler generally requires about 1,000 kcal per day. Toddlers need more fat than adults, up to 40% of total Calories, and should not be given low-fat or skim milk or other dairy products until at least age 2. Toddlers' protein and carbohydrate needs increase modestly; most of the carbohydrates they eat should be complex, and refined carbohydrates should be kept to a minimum. As toddlers grow, their micronutrient needs increase.

Toddlers sometimes become so busy playing that they ignore or fail to recognize the thirst sensation, so caregivers need to make sure an active toddler is drinking

Toddlers expend significant amounts of energy actively exploring their world.

TABLE 11.5	**Nutrient Recommendations for Children and Adolescents**			
Nutrient	**Toddlers (1 to 2 years)**	**Children (3 to 8 years)**	**Children (9 to 13 years)**	**Adolescents (14 to 18 years)**
Carbohydrate	130 grams/day	130 grams/day	130 grams/day	130 grams/day
Fat	No DRI	No DRI	No DRI	No DRI
Protein	1.10 grams/kg body weight per day	0.95 gram/kg body weight per day	0.95 gram/kg body weight per day	0.85 gram/kg body weight per day
Vitamin A	300 µg/day	400 µg/day	600 µg/day	Boys = 900 µg/day Girls = 700 µg/day
Vitamin C	15 mg/day	25 mg/day	45 mg/day	Boys = 75 mg/day Girls = 65 mg/day
Vitamin E	6 mg/day	7 mg/day	11 mg/day	15 mg/day
Calcium	500 mg/day	800 mg/day	1,300 mg/day	1,300 mg/day
Iron	7 mg/day	10 mg/day	8 mg/day	Boys = 11 mg/day Girls = 15 mg/day
Zinc	3 mg/day	5 mg/day	8 mg/day	Boys = 11 mg/day Girls = 9 mg/day
Fluid	1.3 liters/day	1.7 liters/day	Boys = 2.4 liters/day Girls = 2.1 liters/day	Boys = 3.3 liters/day Girls = 2.3 liters/day

↰ Most toddlers are delighted by food prepared in a fun way.

adequately. The recommended total fluid intake for toddlers is about 4 cups of beverages.[13] Suggested beverages include plain water, milk and soy milk, and diluted fruit juices.

Given their typically erratic eating habits, toddlers can develop nutrient deficiencies. That's why many pediatricians recommend a multivitamin and mineral supplement formulated especially for toddlers.

Encouraging Nutritious Food Choices with Toddlers

Toddlers tend to be choosy about what they eat. Some avoid entire food groups groups, such as all meats or vegetables. Others will abruptly refuse all but one or two favorite foods (such as peanut butter on crackers) for several days or longer. Still others eat in extremely small amounts, seemingly satisfied by a single slice of apple or two bites of toast. These behaviors concern many parents, but as long as healthful food is abundant and choices are varied, toddlers have the ability to match their intake with their needs. Parents who offer only foods of high nutritional quality can feel confident that their toddlers are getting the nutrition they need, even if their choices seem odd or erratic on any particular day. Food should never be "forced" on a child; doing so sets the stage for eating and control issues later in life.[28]

Toddlers' stomachs are still very small and they cannot consume all of the Calories they need in three meals. They need several small meals and snacks and should eat every 2 to 3 hours. One proven feeding technique is to create a snack tray filled with small portions of nutritious food choices and leave it within reach of the child's play area. The child can then "graze" while he or she plays. A snack tray plus a spill-proof cup of water is particularly useful on car trips.

Firm, raw foods, such as nuts, carrots, grapes, raisins, and cherry tomatoes, are difficult for a toddler to chew, as are cooked, cut-up hot dogs. Such foods pose a choking hazard. Foods should be soft and sliced into strips or wedges that are easy for children to grasp. As the child develops more teeth and becomes more coordinated, food choices can become more varied.

Foods prepared for toddlers should also be fun. Parents can use cookie-cutters to turn a peanut butter sandwich into a pumpkin face or arrange cooked peas or carrot slices to look like a smiling face on top of mashed potatoes. Juice and low-fat yogurt can be frozen into "popsicles" or blended into "milkshakes."

Even at mealtime, portion sizes should be small. One tablespoon of a food for each year of age constitutes a serving throughout the preschool years **(Figure 11.6)**. Realistic portion sizes can give toddlers a sense of accomplishment when they "eat it all up" and lessen parents' fears that their child is not eating enough.

Introduce new foods gradually. Most toddlers are leery of new foods, spicy foods, hot (temperature) foods, mixed foods (such as casseroles), and foods with strange textures. A helpful rule is to require the child to eat at least one bite of a new food: if the child does not want the rest, nothing negative should be said and the child should be praised just for the willingness to try. Parents should reintroduce the food a few weeks later because, over time, toddlers will often accept foods they once rejected.

Nutrition-Related Concerns for Toddlers

↰ **Figure 11.6** Portion sizes for preschoolers should be much smaller than those for older children. Use the following guideline: 1 tablespoon of food for each year of age equals 1 serving. For example, 2 tbsp. of rice, 2 tbsp. of black beans, and 2 tbsp. of chopped tomatoes is appropriate for a 2-year-old toddler.

As during infancy, new foods should be presented one at a time, and the toddler should be monitored for allergic reactions for 4 to 5 days before introducing additional new foods. Although many food allergies subside as a child ages, toddlers remain at risk.

For toddlers, a lacto-ovo-vegetarian diet in which dairy foods and eggs are included can be as wholesome as a diet including meats

NUTRITION MYTH OR FACT?
Are Vegan Diets Inappropriate for Young Children?

The wisdom of feeding a vegan diet to young children is a subject of controversy. Many who support veganism feel that the consumption of any type of animal product is immoral, that feeding animal products to children fosters a lifetime of obesity and chronic disease, and that eating animal products wastes natural resources and contributes to climate change. In contrast, opponents contend that feeding a vegan diet to young children deprives them of a healthful level of nutrients that can only be obtained if the child consumes animal products. Some people even suggest that veganism for young children is, in essence, a form of child abuse.

As with many controversies, there are valid concerns on both sides. For example, there have been documented cases of children failing to thrive, and even dying, on extreme vegan diets.[29] Cases have been cited of vitamin B_{12}, calcium, zinc, and vitamin D deficiencies in vegan children. These nutrients are found primarily or almost exclusively in animal products, and deficiencies can have serious and lifelong consequences. For example, not all of the neurologic impairments caused by a vitamin B_{12} deficiency can be reversed.

However, most examples of nutrition-related illness in vegan children stem from a lack of education and/or extremism. Informed parents following responsible vegan diets are rarely involved. Still, veganism is not a lifestyle one can safely undertake without a thorough education. Parents must understand the need for supplementation of those nutrients not available in plant foods. They also must recognize how difficult it is for a young child to maintain iron status without consuming sources of heme iron, which are totally absent in a vegan diet. Parents also need to understand that typical vegan diets are high in fiber and low

in fat, and that this combination can lead to inadequate weight gain and impaired growth in young children. Moreover, certain staples of the vegan diet, such as wheat, soy, and nuts, commonly provoke allergic reactions in children; when this happens, finding a plant-based substitute that contains adequate nutrients can be challenging.

Both the American Dietetic Association and the American Academy of Pediatrics have stated that a vegan diet can promote normal growth and development—*provided* that adequate supplements and/or fortified foods are consumed. However, most healthcare organizations stop short of outright endorsement of a vegan diet for young children. The reasons for caution include the following:

- Some vegan parents are not adequately educated on meal planning and the need to include supplements to ensure adequate levels of all nutrients.
- Most young children are picky eaters and hesitate to eat certain food groups, particularly vegetables.
- The high fiber content of vegan diets may not be appropriate for very young children.
- Young children have small stomachs and are often not able to consume enough plant-based foods to ensure adequate intakes of all nutrients and energy.

Because of these concerns, most nutrition experts advise parents to take a more moderate approach, one that emphasizes plant foods but also includes some animal-based foods, such as fish, dairy, and/or eggs. Once children reach school age, the benefits of a well-planned vegan diet (low fat, abundant fiber, antioxidant rich) will promote good health as they progress into adulthood.

---

and fish. However, because meat is an excellent source of zinc and heme iron, the most bioavailable form of iron, families who do not serve meat must be careful to include enough zinc and iron from other sources in their child's diet, such as fortified cereals.

In contrast, a vegan diet, in which no foods of animal origin are consumed, poses several potential nutritional risks for toddlers. For this reason, the practice of feeding children a vegan diet is highly controversial. See the **Nutrition Myth or Fact?** feature box (shown above) for more information about this issue.

RECAP Toddlers are highly active and need to consume enough energy to fuel their growth and activity. Total energy, fat, and protein requirements are higher for toddlers than for infants. Until age 2, healthy toddlers of appropriate weight should drink whole milk to meet calcium requirements and sustain adequate fat intake. Toddlers require small, frequent, nutritious meals and snacks, and food should be cut in small pieces, so that it is easy to handle, chew, and swallow. Because toddlers are becoming more independent and can self-feed, parents need to be alert for choking and should watch for allergies and monitor weight gain. Feeding vegan diets to toddlers is controversial because it poses potential deficiencies for several nutrients.

◆ Foods that may cause allergies, such as peanuts and citrus fruits, should be introduced to toddlers one at a time.

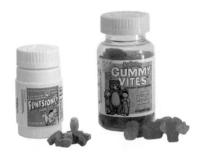

⬥ Many children's multivitamins appear in whimsical shapes or bright colors.

Nutrition Throughout Childhood

Children experience an average growth of 2 to 4 inches per year throughout childhood. Between the ages of 3 and 13, children begin to make some of their own food choices. The impact of these decisions on children's health can be profound, so age-appropriate nutrition education is critical.

What Are a Child's Nutrient Needs?

By age 3, children exposed to a wide variety of foods typically have developed a varied diet. Nevertheless, children cannot be expected to consume all of the nutrients they need in three meals. Thus, nutrient-dense snacks continue to be important. Table 11.5 identifies the nutrient needs of children ages 3 to 8 and 9 to 13.

Macronutrient Recommendations for Children

Fat remains a key macronutrient in childhood, and children's fat intakes should be around 25% to 35% of total energy.[8] A diet lower in fat is not recommended for healthy children of school age, as they are still growing, developing, and maturing.

Total need for protein increases, but the need for carbohydrate remains the same as for toddlers. Fiber-rich carbohydrates are important, and simple sugars should come from fruits and fruit juices, with refined-carbohydrate items (such as cakes, cookies, and candies) saved for occasional indulgences.

Micronutrient Recommendations for Children

Children who fail to consume the recommended 5 or more servings of fruits and vegetables each day may become deficient in vitamins A, C, and E. Minerals of concern continue to be calcium, iron, and zinc, which come primarily from animal-based foods (see Table 11.5). Notice that calcium needs increase dramatically in children age 9 to 13 years to allow for increased bone growth and density.

If there is any doubt that a child's nutrient needs are not being met for any reason (for instance, breakfasts are skipped, lunches are traded, or parents lack money for nourishing food), a vitamin/mineral supplement that provides no more than 100% of the daily value for the micronutrients may help correct any existing deficit.

Fluid Recommendations for Children

Fluid recommendations for children are shown in Table 11.5. The exact amount of fluid a child needs varies according to their level of physical activity and the weather conditions. Under most circumstances, water is the beverage of choice; sports beverages, fruit drinks, and sodas provide excess Calories that can, over time, contribute to inappropriate weight gain.

⬥ Fluid intake is important for children, who may become so involved in their play that they ignore the sensation of thirst.

Encouraging Nutritious Food Choices with Children

Most children can understand that some foods will "help them grow up healthy and strong" and that other foods will not. Because children want to grow as quickly as possible, parents can capitalize on this natural desire and, using age-appropriate language, encourage children to eat foods high in fiber-rich carbohydrates, protein, and micronutrients.

However, peer pressure can be extremely difficult for both parents and their children to deal with during this life stage. If a popular child is eating chips and drinking sugared soft drinks, it may be hard for a child to eat a tuna-on-whole-wheat sandwich, apple, and milk without embarrassment.

Even as children age, parents remain powerful role models and should "set the tone" with their own healthful eating and activity patterns. Parents can take advantage of online tools, such as the MyPyramid.gov site, where a child can print out a personalized pyramid and the MyPyramid for Kids poster (**Figure 11.7**), which

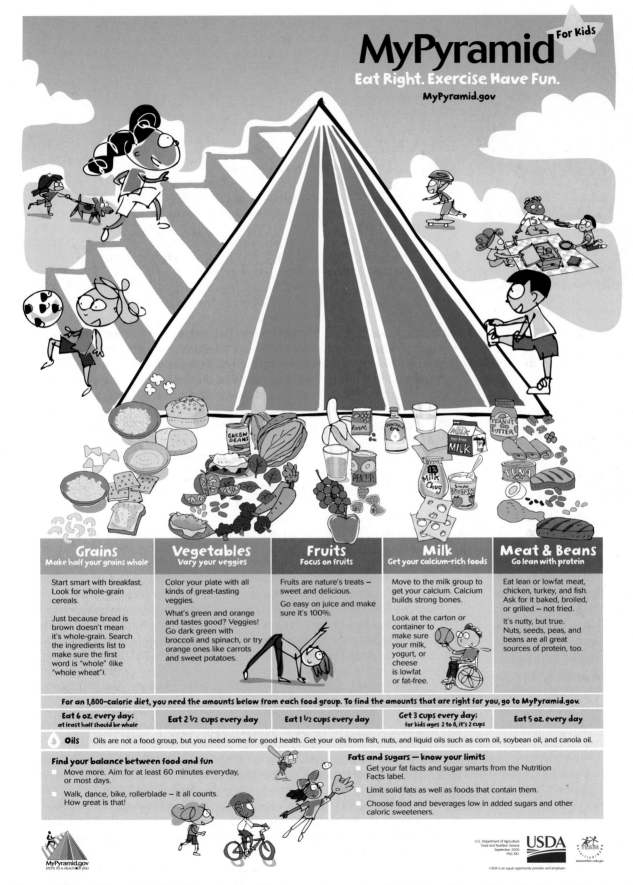

Figure 11.7 MyPyramid for Kids. This symbol modifies the previous version of the MyPyramid graphic to reflect the nutritional needs of children ages 6 to 11 and encourages them to "Eat Right. Exercise. Have Fun."

School-age children may receive a standard school lunch, but many choose less healthful foods when given the opportunity.

provides age-appropriate nutrition information that reminds children to "Eat Right. Exercise. Have Fun."

Parents can also continue to involve children in food choices.[28] For instance, children can grow foods in small container gardens, develop their own shopping list with nutritious favorites, and help with age-appropriate food-preparation activities. If children have input into what is going into their body, they are more likely to take an active role in their health.

What Is the Effect of School Attendance on Nutrition?

Children's school attendance can affect their nutrition in several ways. First, in the hectic time between waking and getting out the door, many children minimize or skip breakfast completely. Students who eat breakfast perform better on school-work, have improved attention spans, and demonstrate fewer behavioral problems than their peers who skip breakfast.[30–31] Public schools are required to offer low-cost school breakfasts that are free of charge to low-income families. Taking advantage of these breakfasts can help children avoid hunger in the classroom. We discuss the benefits of eating breakfast in more detail in the upcoming *Nutrition Myth or Fact?* box (page 356).

Another consequence of attending school is that, with no one monitoring what they eat, children do not always consume adequate amounts of food. They may spend their lunchtime conversing or playing with friends rather than eating. If they purchase a school lunch, they might not like the foods being served, or their peers might influence them to skip certain foods with comments such as "This broccoli is nasty!" Even homemade lunches that contain nutritious foods may be left uneaten or traded for less nutritious fare.

Are school lunches nutritious? On the surface, the answer to this question is yes. All school lunches must meet certain nutrition requirements set forth by federal guidelines, but not for each individual meal.[32] Thus, over the course of a week, the school lunches that students actually eat tend to be higher in fat and lower in key nutrients because students choose foods they like, such as pizza, hamburgers, hot dogs, and french fries, instead of veggie lasagna, lentil soup, a baked potato, or carrots. In addition, some schools actually have fast-food restaurants selling their food in competition with the school lunch program! School nutrition professionals are actively working to increase students' intakes of fruits, vegetables, and whole grains, as well as their physical activity.[33] Especially when supported by parents, these efforts can help reduce children's risk for obesity and enhance their lifelong health.[32]

Despite recent federal and state legislation, along with new industry-sponsored initiatives to limit the sales of snack foods, some schools still provide vending machines filled with foods and beverages that are high in energy, sugar, and fat. Eating too many of these foods, either in place of or in addition to lunch, can lead to overweight and nutrient imbalances. Nutrition standards have recently been developed to encourage schools to sell only those foods and beverages that promote a healthful diet.[34]

Nutrition-Related Concerns for Children

Two significant nutrition-related concerns for children are food insecurity and overweight. Surprisingly, these can occur simultaneously.

Childhood Food Insecurity

Although most children in the United States grow up with an abundant and healthful supply of food, a small but persistent percentage of children are faced with food insecurity and hunger. *Food insecurity* occurs when a family is not able to ensure a predictable supply of safe and nutritious food or is unable to acquire food in a socially acceptable manner; in other words, the parents might have to steal food, forage for food in trash receptacles, or beg for food. Approximately 11% of U.S.

households with children can be classified as food insecure, including about 1% with very low food security.[35] Households experiencing food insecurity limit the variety of foods offered to their children, are not always able to afford foods for balanced meals, and indicate that, at times, their children don't get enough to eat because of lack of money.

The effects of food insecurity can be very harmful to young children. Impaired nutrient status can blunt children's immune responses, making them more susceptible to common childhood illnesses. Poorly nourished preschoolers often fail to achieve their full growth potential, falling off their normal growth curve. Iron-deficiency anemia can develop, and deficiencies of vitamin D and/or calcium can keep children from attaining optimal bone density. Poverty is also a risk factor for overweight and obesity: families with little money to spend on food typically buy the lowest-cost options—usually foods low in nutrients but high in Calories.

One of the options for families facing food insecurity is government programs, such as WIC (Women, Infants, and Children); the Supplementary Nutrition Assistance Program (SNAP), previously known as the Food Stamp program; and school breakfast and lunch programs. Private and church-based food pantries and kitchens also can provide a narrow range of foods for a limited period of time but cannot be relied on to consistently meet the nutritional needs of young children and their families.

Obesity Watch: Encouraging an Active Lifestyle

As with adults, the problem of overweight and obesity in children is now approaching epidemic proportions in the United States. Nationwide, about 36% of U.S. children between 6 and 11 years of age are overweight or obese (BMI for age ≥85th percentile), as are 34% of 12- to 19-year-olds.[1] These children are at higher risk for several health problems: overweight can worsen asthma, contribute to the development of type 2 diabetes, cause sleep apnea, impair the child's mobility, and lead to intense teasing, low self-esteem, and social isolation.

Experts agree that the main culprits in childhood obesity are similar to those involved in adult obesity: eating too much and moving around too little. Thus, they recommend a two-pronged approach: establishing healthful eating practices that work for the whole family and increasing physical activity.

Because of the high nutrient needs of children, restrictive diets are not advised. Rather, parents should strive to consistently provide nutritious food choices. Families should also sit down together to a shared family meal each evening. The television should be off throughout dinner to encourage slow eating and true enjoyment of the food.

To encourage activity throughout the day, parents should limit their own and their children's sitting time to no more than 2 hours per day. Time spent watching television, playing video games, or working on a computer not only reduces the time available for physical activity but can increase energy intake: children often snack excessively on high-calorie, low-nutrient snack foods during sedentary activities. Both the federal government and the food industry have begun limiting the types and numbers of food advertisements targeting children. Marketing restrictions would apply not only to traditional television and magazine ads but would also include online games, movies, social media, and fast-food restaurants.[36]

Parents should encourage children to replace sedentary activities with shared activities, such as ball games, bike rides, and hikes, or one of the newly developed electronic game systems that offer virtual tennis, dancing, and other simulations. Over time, overweight children who are active can "catch up" to their weight as they grow taller without restricting their intake of healthful foods. Increased activity also helps young children acquire motor skills and muscle strength and develop self-esteem as they feel themselves becoming faster, stronger, and more skilled.

The Institute of Medicine recommends that children engage in physical activity for at least an hour each day.[8] Children should be exposed to a variety of activities, so that they move different muscles, play at various intensities, avoid boredom, and find out what they like and don't like to do. The American Dietetic Association has used an activity pyramid for kids to help guide children toward a physically active lifestyle **(Figure 11.8)**.

Active, healthy-weight children are less likely to become overweight adults.

▶ **Figure 11.8** The Kids' Activity Pyramid gives guidelines for the duration, intensity, and frequency of various types of activities that are appropriate for children ages 2 to 11 years.
Copyright © 1996 Park Nicollet HealthSource™, Park Nicollet Institute. Reprinted by permission.

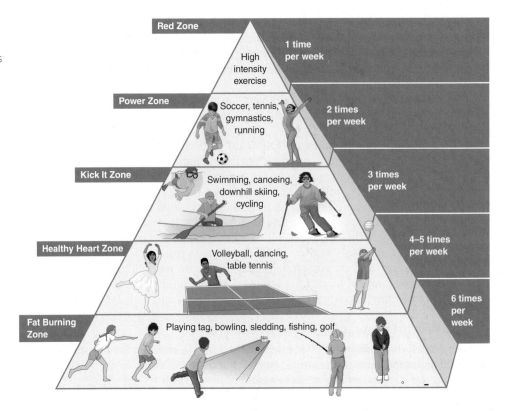

RECAP Children experience an average growth of 2 to 4 inches per year. They need a lower percentage of fat Calories than toddlers but slightly more than adults (25% to 35% of energy). Micronutrient needs increase because of growth and maturation. Children can become easily dehydrated, especially during vigorous activity in warm weather. Peer pressure influences children's nutritional choices. Involving children in food growing, purchasing, and preparation can help. School meals must meet federal nutrition guidelines, but the foods that children actually choose to eat can be high in saturated fat, sugar, and energy and low in nutrients. Food insecurity and obesity are significant nutritional concerns for U.S. children.

Nutrition for Adolescents

The adolescent years begin with the onset of **puberty,** the period in life in which secondary sexual characteristics develop and there is the capacity for reproducing. Adolescence is characterized by increasing independence and self-reliance. All teens deal with their emerging sexuality, and some experiment with behaviors, such as smoking and drinking, that lie outside their traditional cultural or social boundaries. During this stage, they may ignore their parents' attempts to improve their diet, or they may adopt a diet that is much more healthful than that of their parents.

Adolescent Growth and Activity Patterns

The nutritional needs of adolescents are influenced by their rapid growth in height, increased weight, changes in body composition, and individual levels of physical activity. Both boys and girls experience *growth spurts,* or periods of accelerated growth, during which their height increases by an average of 20% to 25%. Growth spurts for girls tend to begin around 10 to 11 years of age, and they typically grow a total of 2 to 8 inches. Growth spurts for boys begin around 12 to 13 years of age, and they tend to grow by 4 to 12 inches.

The average weight gained by girls and boys during this time is 35 and 45 lb, respectively. The weight gained by girls and boys is dramatically different in terms of its composition. Girls tend to gain significantly more body fat than boys, who tend to gain more muscle mass.

puberty The period of life in which secondary sexual characteristics develop and people are biologically capable of reproducing.

The physical activity levels of adolescents are highly variable. Many are physically active in sports or other organized physical activities, whereas others become less interested in sports and more interested in intellectual or artistic pursuits. This variability results in highly individual energy needs.

What Are an Adolescent's Nutrient Needs?

The nutrient needs of adolescents are influenced by rapid growth and sexual maturation, in addition to the demands of physical activity.

Energy and Macronutrient Recommendations for Adolescents

Adolescents need a significant amount of energy to maintain their health, support their dramatic growth and maturation, and fuel their physical activity. Still, adolescence is often a time in which overweight begins. Dieting to lose weight should be undertaken only under the guidance of a physician or registered dietitian, and fad diets should be strictly avoided.

Because adolescents are at risk for the same chronic diseases as adults, they are advised to consume 25% to 35% of total energy from fat and to consume no more than 10% of total energy from saturated fat.[8] Adolescents should consume about 45% to 65% of their total energy as carbohydrate, and most carbohydrate should come from fiber-rich sources.[8] The RDA for protein for adolescents is similar to that of adults, at 0.85 gram of protein per kilogram of body weight per day.[8] This amount is assumed to be sufficient to support health and to cover the additional needs of growth and development during the adolescent stage.

Micronutrient Recommendations for Adolescents

Micronutrients of particular concern for adolescents include calcium, iron, and vitamin A. Adequate calcium intake is critical to achieve peak bone density. The RDA for calcium remains high throughout adolescence and can be difficult to consume for teens who do not drink milk or calcium-fortified beverages.[12]

As shown in Table 11.5, the iron needs of adolescents are relatively high to replace the blood lost during menstruation in girls and to support the growth of muscle mass in boys.[11] If energy intake is adequate and adolescents consume animal products each day, they should be able to meet their iron needs. However, some young people adopt a vegetarian lifestyle during this life stage, or they consume foods that have limited nutrient density. Both of these situations can prevent adolescents from meeting the RDA for iron.

Vitamin A is critical to support the rapid growth and development that occurs during adolescence. Consuming at least 5 servings of fruits and vegetables each day can help teens meet their RDA (see Table 11.5).[11]

If an adolescent is unable or unwilling to eat adequate amounts of nutrient-dense foods, a multivitamin and mineral supplement that provides no more than 100% of the Daily Value for the micronutrients can be beneficial. As with younger children and adults, a supplement should not be considered a substitute for a healthful diet.

Fluid Recommendations for Adolescents

The AI for total fluid for adolescent boys is about 11 cups as beverages, including water. The AI for girls is about 8 cups as beverages. Boys are generally more active than girls and have more lean tissue, so they require a higher fluid intake. Highly active adolescents who are exercising in the heat may have higher fluid needs than the AI and should drink often to avoid dehydration.[13]

Encouraging Nutritious Food Choices with Adolescents

Adolescents make most of their own food choices, and many are buying and preparing a significant amount of the foods they consume. Although parents can still be effective role models, adolescents are generally strongly influenced by their peers, the mass media, and their own developing sense of what foods compose a healthful diet.

Many adolescent diets lack adequate amounts of vegetables, fruits, low-fat dairy, and whole grains. Many teens eat on the run at fast-food restaurants, convenience stores,

NUTRITION MYTH OR FACT?

Is Breakfast the Most Important Meal of the Day?

What did you eat for breakfast this morning? Whole-grain cereal with low-fat milk? A strawberry toaster pastry? Nothing? What does it matter, anyway? Sure, you've heard the saying that breakfast is the most important meal of the day, but that's just a myth—isn't it? As long as you eat a nutritious meal at lunch and dinner, why should skipping breakfast matter?

Over the past two decades, dozens of published studies have pointed to the importance of a healthful breakfast. Most of these studies cite two key health benefits: First, breakfast supports our physical and mental functioning. Second, it helps us maintain a healthful weight. Let's examine the evidence for each of these claims.

The word *breakfast* was initially used as a verb meaning "to break the fast"—that is, to end the hours of fasting that naturally occur during a night of sleep. When we fast, our body breaks down stored nutrients to provide energy to fuel the resting body. First, cells break down glycogen stores in the muscle tissues and liver, using the "freed" glucose for energy. These stores last about 12 hours. But people who skip breakfast fast much longer than that: if they finish dinner around 7:00 PM and don't eat again until noon the next day,

◆ Breakfast doesn't have to be boring! A breakfast burrito with scrambled eggs, low-fat cheese, and vegetables served in a whole-grain tortilla provides energy and nutrients to start your day off right.

they're going without fuel for 17 hours! Long before this point, essentially all the stored glycogen is used up, and the body turns to fatty acids and amino acids for fuel.

If you're like most people, when your blood glucose is low, you experience not only hunger but also weakness, shakiness, irritability, and poor concentration. So it's not surprising that children and teens who skip breakfast don't function as well—either physically or academically—as their breakfast-eating peers.[30–31] Recent research supports the following conclusions:[38,39]

- Missing breakfast and experiencing hunger impair children's ability to learn. These children exhibit slower memory recall, score lower on cognitive tests, have more behavioral and emotional problems, and are more likely to have to repeat a grade than children who arrive at school in a well-nourished state.

- Eating breakfast at school helps children perform better on demanding mental tasks and improves their attention and memory. Children who eat a complete breakfast make fewer mistakes and work faster in math and vocabulary.

- Breakfast improves students' behavior, including improving their reaction to frustration, reducing disciplinary office referrals, decreasing tardiness, and increasing school attendance rates.

- Children who skip breakfast "up-regulate" their appetites, leading to overeating later in the day. Teens who eat breakfast are more likely to have a BMI and body fat within the healthy range than those who tend to skip breakfast.[40,41]

Skeptics say the studies' conclusions suggest an *association* between eating breakfast and health benefits, but not a *cause*. They say, for example, that the same parents who insist that their kids eat a healthful breakfast are likely to be those who also make sure their kids get adequate sleep, help with their kids' homework, and monitor their TV watching.

What do you think? Is breakfast the most important meal of the day? And what—if anything—will you be having for breakfast tomorrow?

and vending machines, where these healthful foods may not be available. In addition, many teens skip meals. For instance, adolescent girls often skip breakfast because they believe it might make them fat. In reality, teens who start their day with cereal have a better diet and weight/body fat measures compared to those who skip breakfast.[37] Other teens skip breakfast because they're rushing to get to school. Whatever the reason, many nutrition experts believe that adolescents who skip breakfast are hurting both their performance in school and their health. Is breakfast the most important meal of the day? Check out the **Nutrition Myth or Fact?** feature box (shown above) to find the answer.

Parents and school food service programs can capitalize on adolescents' preferences for pizza, burgers, spaghetti, and sandwiches by providing more healthful versions of these foods, as well as appealing vegetable-based sides. In addition, stocking the refrigerator with raw fruits and vegetables that are already cleaned and sliced may encourage adolescents to eat more of these foods as between-meal snacks. Teens should also be encouraged to consume adequate milk and other calcium-enriched beverages.

Nutrition-Related Concerns for Adolescents

Obesity prevention continues to be a concern during adolescence. Additional concerns are disordered eating, low bone density, acne, and the use of alcohol and tobacco products.

Obesity Watch: Balancing Food and Physical Activity

Although expected and healthful, weight gain during adolescence can become excessive, increasing the risk for the early onset of type 2 diabetes, hypertension, and high blood lipid levels. A teen's energy intake must be balanced with adequate physical activity. Adolescent girls and boys average about 8 to 11 hours of physical activity per week, with lower activity patterns after age 13.[42] Daily physical education in school and opportunities to participate in regular physical activity in the community can help reduce the prevalence of overweight and obesity among adolescents.

Disordered Eating and Eating Disorders

An initially healthful concern about body image and weight can turn into a dangerous obsession during this emotionally challenging life stage. Clinical eating disorders frequently begin during adolescence and occur in boys as well as girls. Parents, teachers, and friends should be aware of the warning signs, which include rapid and excessive weight loss, a preoccupation with weight and body image, going to the bathroom regularly after meals, and signs of frequent vomiting or laxative use (see Chapter 9).

Bone-Density Watch

Early adolescence, 13 to 15 years of age, is a crucial time for ensuring adequate dietary calcium in order to maximize bone mineral density and reduce the risk for osteoporosis. Meeting the adolescent RDA for calcium (1,300 mg/day) requires a daily consumption of at least 4 servings (4 cups) of milk or other dairy foods, calcium-fortified foods and beverages, or supplements. It is extremely challenging to meet this RDA from plant-based foods alone. However, 16-year-old girls and boys consume an average of only 1.5 and 2 cups of milk per day, respectively.[43] Although not the only factor, dairy consumption is strongly linked to improved bone health among adolescents.[44]

Adolescent Acne and Diet

The hormonal changes that occur during puberty are largely responsible for the acne flare-ups that plague 80% to 90% of adolescents.[45] Emotional stress, genetic factors, and personal hygiene are most likely secondary contributors. But what about foods? Current research does not support a link between acne and consumption of chocolate, salt, or fats. There is some evidence that high glycemic index diets and an increased intake of cow's milk (skim, low-fat, or full-fat) may be associated with an increase in acne prevalence, severity, or duration.[45] On the other hand, a healthful diet, rich in fruits, vegetables, whole grains, and lean meats, provides nutrients to optimize skin health and maintain an effective immune system.

Prescription medications, including a vitamin A derivative called Accutane, effectively control severe forms

The nutrient needs of adolescents are affected by their activity levels.

FOODS YOU DON'T KNOW YOU LOVE YET

Milk Alternatives

Y ou know you need to replenish your body's stores of calcium every day, throughout the day, but you've also learned in this chapter that the proteins in cow's milk are a common allergen, and that the consumption of cow's milk might be associated with acne flare-ups. So now what? Milk alternatives to the rescue! Soy milk, almond milk, and rice milk—all of which are available in most larger grocery stores nationwide—are plant-based beverages that typically are enriched with as much calcium (not to mention vitamin D) as a glass of cow's milk. Many brands are also enriched with vitamin B_{12}, making them ideal for people following a vegan diet. They're also low in saturated fat and cholesterol free, and they come in a variety of flavors, from vanilla to coffee.

of acne. Neither Accutane nor any other prescription vitamin A derivative should be used by women who are pregnant or who may become pregnant. Accutane is a known teratogen, causing severe fetal malformations. Women of childbearing age who want to treat their acne with vitamin A–derivative prescription drugs must register in a risk management program developed by the FDA. Accutane has also been associated with depression, psychosis, suicidal thoughts or actions, aggressive or violent behavior, and other mood disorders.[46] For these reasons, the drug should be considered only for teens who have severe, disfiguring acne, and anyone using it should be monitored closely for signs of depression, irritability, and other emotional changes.

Use of Alcohol and Tobacco

Many adolescents experiment with alcohol and tobacco. (The risks of alcohol consumption are discussed in Chapter 8.) Cigarette smoking diminishes appetite, interferes with nutrient metabolism, reduces physical fitness, damages the lungs, increases the incidence of respiratory illness, and promotes addiction to nicotine. Most people who begin smoking during adolescence continue to smoke in adulthood, increasing their risks for lung cancer, heart disease, osteoporosis, and emphysema.

RECAP Adolescents experience rapid increases in height, weight, and lean body mass and fat mass, so their energy needs can be very high. Because many adolescents fail to eat a variety of nutrient-dense foods, their intakes of some nutrients may be deficient. Calcium is needed to optimize bone growth and to achieve peak bone density, and iron needs are increased due to increased muscle mass in boys and the onset of menstruation in girls. Obesity can occur during adolescence because of increased appetite and food intake and decreased physical activity. Disordered eating behaviors typically develop in adolescence. Consumption of alcohol and cigarette smoking are additional risks.

Nutrition for Older Adults

The U.S. population is getting older each year. In 2008, about 39 million people aged 65 and older lived in the United States, representing about 13% of the population.[47] It is estimated that, by the year 2030, the elderly will account for about 20% of Americans, or more than 72 million adults.

In 2009, the average U.S. **life expectancy,** which is the average number of years that a person can be expected to live, reached 78.2 years.[48] Whereas some research-

life expectancy The expected number of years remaining in one's life, typically stated from the time of birth.

ers have argued that the growing rate of obesity and its medical consequences will drive down U.S. life expectancy over the next several decades, others refute this claim, saying that future advances in healthcare will balance this factor.

Life span is the age to which the longest-living member of the species has lived. Madame Jeanne Calment, born in 1875, survived to the age of 122 and is generally acknowledged as having lived longer than anyone else in the world. Researchers have made great progress toward understanding the aging of humans, but much remains unknown. Scientists can't even agree on why we age or when the aging process begins. Some believe aging is programmed into our genes, whereas others view aging as the consequence of progressive cellular damage.[49] As the debate continues, however, gerontologists agree that humans can positively influence the aging process through personal choices, such as eating a nourishing diet, participating in regular physical activity, and avoiding smoking and substance abuse.

⬆ Older adults have unique nutritional needs.

Physiologic Changes That Accompany Aging

Aging is natural and inevitable; however, the changes that typically accompany aging are at least partly within our control. For instance, decreased muscle strength is partly due to low physical activity levels. Older adults who regularly participate in strengthening exercises and aerobic-type activities experience less muscle atrophy and weakness.

For most of us, eating is a social and pleasurable process; the sights, sounds, odors, and textures associated with food are integral to the stimulation and continuation of appetite. With age comes the decline of taste, odor, and tactile and visual perception: the more each of these functions becomes impaired, the greater is the potential impact on the person's food intake. For example, the loss of visual acuity may result in difficulty reading food labels, including nutrient information and "pull dates" for perishable foods. Driving skills decline, limiting the ability of some older Americans to get to markets that sell healthful, affordable foods. Older adults may no longer be able to read their favorite recipes or distinguish the small markings on temperature knobs on ovens and stoves. Their diet may thus consist of a few foods that are easy to prepare, such as cereal with milk and sandwiches with cold cuts, and may lack the variety necessary to prevent nutrient deficiencies.

With increasing age, salivary production declines. Thus, teeth are more susceptible to decay, chewing and swallowing become more difficult, and the risk for choking increases. Achlorhydria, a severe reduction in gastric acid production, limits the absorption of minerals such as calcium, iron, and zinc and food sources of folic acid and vitamin B_{12}. Lack of intrinsic factor reduces the absorption of vitamin B_{12}, whether from food or supplements. Older adults may also experience a delay in gastric emptying, resulting in a prolonged sense of fullness and a reduced appetite. Because only about 30% of older adults retain an "adequate" level of lactase activity, many restrict their milk intake and fail to consume adequate calcium.

⬆ A variety of gastrointestinal and other physiologic changes can lead to weight loss in older adults.

Age-Related Changes in Body Composition

With aging, muscle mass declines. It has been estimated that women and men lose 20% to 25% of their lean body mass, respectively, as they age from 35 to 70 years. Decreased production of certain hormones and chronic diseases contribute to this loss of muscle, as do poor diet and an inactive lifestyle. Along with adequate dietary intake, regular physical activity, including strength or resistance training, can help older adults maintain or enhance their muscle mass and strength.

Body fat increases from young adulthood through middle age, peaking at approximately 55 to 65 years of age. It remains somewhat stable through about age 70 and then tends to decline. With aging, body fat shifts from subcutaneous stores, just below the skin, to internal or visceral fat stores. Maintaining an appropriate energy intake and remaining physically active can help keep body fat at a healthy level.

Bone mineral density declines with age, increasing the risk for fracture. Among older women, the onset of menopause leads to a sudden and dramatic loss of bone due to the lack of estrogen. Although less dramatic, bone loss in elderly males also

life span The highest age reached by any member of a species; currently, the human life span is 122 years.

occurs, due in part to decreasing levels of testosterone. A nourishing diet with adequate protein, calcium, phosphorus, and vitamin D and regular weight-bearing activity can reduce these losses.

Age-Related Changes in Organ Function

With increasing age, the kidneys lose their ability to concentrate waste products, leading to an increase in urine output and greater risk for dehydration. Bladder control also often declines. The aged liver is less efficient at breaking down drugs and alcohol, and the aged heart lacks the endurance to sustain a sudden increase in physical activity. In most instances, older adults can adapt to these age-related changes through minor lifestyle adjustments, such as reducing their alcohol consumption and gradually increasing their physical activity.

The number of neurons in the brain decreases with age, impairing memory, reflexes, coordination, and learning ability. Although many people believe that dementia is an inevitable part of the aging process, this is not true: diet, physical activity, intellectual stimulation, social contact, and other factors can help preserve the health of the brain as well as the body.

Factors That Accelerate the Aging Process

It is never too late to change our personal habits. Many older adults can enhance their remaining years by paying close attention to their diet, activity, and personal health practices.

The Genetics of Aging

There is no doubt that genes exert tremendous influence on the aging process. Siblings of centenarians, those who live to be at least 100 years old, are four times more likely to live into their nineties than others. The brother of Madame Calment, previously mentioned as the world's oldest human, survived to the age of 97. A number of studies currently underway suggest that our genetic makeup influences our cellular aging and life span.

The Biochemistry of Aging

As cells age, they undergo many changes in structure and function.[49] Some cells, such as skeletal and cardiac muscle, atrophy (decrease in size), whereas others, including fat cells, enlarge. Many gerontologists have linked the aging process to a progressive accumulation of free radicals, known to damage DNA and various cell proteins. Others cite a progressive failure in DNA repair. Still others point to an abnormal attachment of glucose to proteins in our tissues. Cell membrane function certainly declines with age, allowing waste products to accumulate within the cell and preventing the normal uptake of nutrients and oxygen.

⬆ A less physically active lifestyle will lead to lower total energy requirements in older adults.

Lifestyle and Environmental Influences on Aging

The way we live greatly influences the way we age. Whereas **chronologic age** is immovable, **biologic age** is largely due to our personal choices. Accelerated or unsuccessful aging is marked by premature loss of function, high rates of disability, and multiple disease complications. It is now possible to estimate how long you are likely to live by answering a series of scored questions related to smoking habits, sun exposure, family history, weight status, alcohol consumption, food choices, and other factors.

Are you curious about your longevity? Take the interactive life expectancy quiz at http://preventdisease.com/ healthtools/articles/health_age .shtml to get a prediction!

chronologic age Age as defined by calendar years, from date of birth.

biologic age Physiologic age as determined by health and functional status; often estimated by scored questionnaires.

RECAP The physiologic changes that occur with aging include sensory declines, loss of muscle mass and lean tissue, increased fat mass, decreased bone density, and impaired ability to absorb and metabolize various nutrients. Body organs lose functional capacity and are less tolerant of stressors. Many of these changes influence the nutritional needs of older adults and their ability to consume a healthful diet.

What Are an Older Adult's Nutrient Needs?

The requirements for many nutrients are the same for older adults as for young and middle-aged adults. A few nutrient requirements increase, and a few are actually lower. **Table 11.6** identifies the nutrient recommendations important to older adults.

Energy and Macronutrient Recommendations for Older Adults

The energy needs of older adults are lower than those of younger adults. This decrease is primarily due to a loss of muscle mass and lean tissue, which results in a lower basal metabolic rate, and a less physically active lifestyle, which lowers total energy requirements. Some of this decrease in energy expenditure is an inevitable response to aging, but some of the decrease can be delayed or minimized by staying physically active. Because their energy needs are lower, older adults need to pay particularly close attention to consuming a diet high in nutrient-dense foods but not too high in energy in order to avoid weight gain. Refer to the nearby *Highlight* feature box (page 362) to learn more about the theory of caloric restriction, which proposes that energy-restricted diets may significantly prolong our life span.

TABLE 11.6 Nutrient Recommendations of Importance with Increased Age	
Key Nutrient Recommendations	**Rationale**
Vitamin D *Increased need* for vitamin D from 15 μg/day for young adults to 10 μg/day for all adults up to 70 years of age, and to 20 μg/day for adults over age 70	Decreased bone density Decreased ability to synthesize vitamin D in our skin Decreased absorption of dietary calcium
Calcium *Increased need* for calcium from 1,000 mg/day for young adults to 1,200 mg/day for adults 51 years of age and older	Decreased bone density Decreased absorption of dietary calcium
B-Vitamins *Increased need* for vitamin B_6 and need for vitamin B_{12} *as a supplement or from fortified foods*	Lower levels of stomach acid Decreased absorption of food B_{12} from gastrointestinal tract Increased need to reduce homocysteine levels and to optimize immune function
Fiber *Decreased need* for fiber from 38 grams/day for young men to 30 grams/day for men 51 years and older; decreases for women are from 25 grams/day for young women to 21 grams/day for women 51 years and older	Decreased energy intake
Iron *Decreased need* for iron from 18 mg/day for young women to 8 mg/day for women 51 years and older; no change for men 51 years and older	Cessation of menstruation in women; some loss of muscle and lean tissue in both men and women, although the loss of muscle mass in men is not enough to change iron guidelines Intake of heme iron from meats/fish/poultry may be limited because of their expense and the difficulty of chewing certain cuts of meat
Zinc No change in recommendations; however, special attention to adequacy may be important for older adults	Optimizes immune function Enhances wound healing Intake from meats and poultry may be limited because of their expense and the difficulty of chewing certain cuts of meat
Vitamins C and E No change in recommendations; however, special attention to adequacy may be important for older adults	Counteract the increased oxidative stress of chronic diseases and the aging process
Vitamin A No change in recommendations; however, older adults are at higher risk for vitamin A toxicity	Inappropriately high use of vitamin A supplements may increase risk for bone fractures, liver damage, and neurologic problems

HIGHLIGHT

Can We Live Longer by Eating a Low-Energy Diet?

How old do you want to live to be—80 years, 90, 100? If you were to discover that you could live more than a century by eating about one-third less than your current energy intake and still be healthy as you age, would you do it? Believe it or not, some people already are.

Research shows that feeding certain species of small animals a low-energy diet, a practice referred to as *caloric restriction,* can significantly extend their life span.[50] Until recently, we did not know if the same effect would be seen in larger animals, including humans. But preliminary studies suggest that the practice can improve various metabolic, hormonal, and functional measures of human health, which might then translate into an extended life span in humans as well.[51]

How can caloric restriction prolong our life span? It is thought that the reduction in metabolic rate that occurs with restricting energy intake results in a much lower production of free radicals, which then reduces oxidative damage. Caloric restriction improves insulin sensitivity and triggers hormonal changes that reduce the risk for chronic diseases, such as heart disease and diabetes. Some of the effects of prolonged caloric restriction reported in some, but not all, human studies include[50,51]

⬆ Maintaining a calorically restricted diet that is also highly nutritious requires significant meal planning and preparation.

- decreased insulin levels, improved insulin sensitivity, and decreased fasting blood glucose;
- decreased core body temperature and blood pressure;
- decreased energy expenditure;
- decreased oxidative stress and reduced DNA damage;
- decreased fat mass and lean body mass; and
- decreased serum LDL- and total cholesterol and increased serum HDL-cholesterol.

Scientists are currently measuring *markers* of the aging process, such as hormones or metabolites, in short-term research projects. Long-term studies that could fully answer this question will likely never be conducted because of ethical and logistical concerns. Institutional committees that review research studies are hesitant to approve caloric-restriction research in humans not only because of this logistical problem but also because of the considerable potential for malnutrition in study participants.

To meet the caloric-restriction levels studied in animals, an average, healthy adult would need to consume 30% to 40% less energy than usual. If you normally eat about 2,000 kcal/day, this reduction would limit you to about 1,200 to 1,400 kcal/day. Although this reduction may not seem excessive, it would be very difficult to achieve over a lifetime! You must also keep in mind that this diet must be of *extraordinarily high nutritional quality*. This would require meticulous planning of meals, preparation of most (if not all) of your own foods, limited options for eating meals outside the home, and the challenge of working the demands of your special diet around the eating behaviors of family members and friends. In addition, people who report following a caloric-restriction program often complain of being hungry, feeling cold, and losing their libido (sex drive).[51]

Considering the potential benefits and risks of caloric restriction, do you think it is worth following this type of diet? Are you willing to make the sacrifices and lifestyle changes required, even though no one knows for sure whether this practice can prolong your life? If it is found that caloric restriction does increase longevity, should it be recommended for all people? This debate will continue as more research is conducted, possibly for generations to come.

The DRIs for total fat, protein, and carbohydrate for older adults are the same as those for adults of all ages.[8] After age 50, however, fiber needs decrease slightly: 30 grams of fiber per day for men and 21 grams per day for women is assumed sufficient to reduce the risks for constipation and diverticular disease, to maintain healthful blood levels of glucose and lipids, and to provide good sources of nutrient-dense, low-energy foods.

Micronutrient Recommendations for Older Adults

The vitamin and mineral recommendations that change for older adults are identified in Table 11.6. Although zinc recommendations are the same for all adults, zinc is a critical nutrient for optimizing immune function and wound healing in older adults. Intakes of both zinc and iron can be inadequate in older adults who eat less red meat, poultry, and fish.

Vitamin A requirements are also the same for adults of all ages; however, older adults should be careful not to consume more than the RDA, as absorption of vitamin A is actually greater in older adults. Thus, this group is at greater risk for vitamin A toxicity, which can cause liver damage, neurologic problems, and increased risk for bone fracture. However, consuming foods high in beta-carotene does not lead to vitamin A toxicity.

Older adults need to pay close attention to consuming adequate amounts of the B-vitamins, particularly vitamin B_{12}, vitamin B_6, and folate. Inadequate intakes of these vitamins increases blood levels of homocysteine, an amino acid that some researchers have linked to increased risk for heart disease and dementia. Older adults need larger amounts of vitamin B_6 in their diet, and they should get most of their vitamin B_{12} from supplements or fortified foods.[10]

Fluid Recommendations for Older Adults

The AI for fluid is the same for older and younger adults.[13] Many elderly people do not perceive thirst as effectively as do younger adults and can develop dehydration. Some older adults intentionally limit their beverage intake because they have urinary incontinence or do not want to be awakened for nighttime urination. This practice can endanger their health, so it is important for these individuals to seek treatment for the incontinence and continue to drink plenty of fluids. Notice that fluids are the foundation of the Tufts Modified MyPyramid for older adults, shown in **Figure 11.9**. At least eight 1-cup (8 oz) servings of water or other fluid are recommended.

Older adults need the same amount of fluids as other adults.

Modified MyPyramid for Older Adults

2007© TUFTS UNIVERSITY

Figure 11.9 The Tufts Modified MyPyramid for Older Adults highlights the need for fluids and supplemental vitamins B_{12} and D.

RECAP Older adults have lower energy needs due to their loss of lean tissue and lower physical activity levels. Fat, protein, and carbohydrate recommendations are the same as for younger adults, but their fiber needs decrease slightly. Micronutrients of concern for older adults include calcium, vitamin D, zinc, vitamin B_{12}, vitamin B_6, and folate. Older adults are at increased risk for dehydration, so ample fluid intake should be encouraged.

▲ Older adults should participate in regular physical activity to maintain a healthful weight and reduce the risk for low bone mass.

Healthy Eating Tips for Older Adults

For some older adults, planning healthy meals is a challenge. Limited resources, energy, knowledge, and interest all work against them when answering that age-old question "What's to eat?" Here are a few suggestions on how to improve the diet of your grandparents or other older adults:

- Encourage them to stock up on healthful ready-to-eat foods, such as pre-packaged salads, frozen low-fat entrées, ready-made grilled chicken, pre-cut fruits and vegetables, and low-sodium soups.
- Suggest that they eat their main meal when their appetite is strongest. For many, that means a substantial breakfast or lunch, with a smaller dinner.
- Provide visual cues to a healthy diet, such as a healthy foods shopping list print-out from http://nutrition.about.com/library/ngrocery_list.htm.
- Collect examples of simple but healthy menus and recipes from consumer magazines and put them into a binder. Use highlighters to emphasize the meals that include their favorite foods.
- Join your grandparents for lunch and dinner as often as possible. Most older adults eat better when there is someone to socialize with during meals.

Nutrition-Related Concerns for Older Adults

Older adults have a number of unique medical, social, and nutritional concerns that are closely interrelated.

Overweight and Underweight: A Delicate Balancing Act

Not surprisingly, overweight and obesity are of concern to older adults. In the United States, 78% of men and 69% of women age 60 years and older are overweight or obese. Within those groups, rates of obesity alone range from 34% to 37%.[2] The elderly population as a whole has a high risk for heart disease, hypertension, type 2 diabetes, and cancer, and these diseases are more prevalent in people who are overweight or obese. It is estimated that older adults who were overweight or obese at age 65 incur up to 17% higher medical expenses over their lifetime compared to those of normal weight at age 65.[52]

Although some healthcare providers question the value of attempting obesity treatment among older adults, even moderate weight loss in obese elderly people can improve their physical functioning. The preferred interventions are the same as for younger adults: the use of dietary modifications to achieve an energy deficit while retaining adequate nutrient intakes, gradual and medically appropriate initiation of physical activity, and culturally appropriate behavior modification. Although there is limited information on the effectiveness and safety of weight-loss drugs in the elderly, at least one study of older adults (65 years and above) suggested that long-term drug therapy for obesity was both effective and well tolerated.[53] Obesity and increasing age independently increase the risk for surgical complications; thus, older adults are usually not viewed as appropriate candidates for weight-loss surgery, such as gastric bypass. Despite these concerns, nearly 5% of patients having weight-loss surgery are 65 years or older. Older adults did have a longer hospitalization following surgery compared to younger adults, but there was no increase in major surgical complications with increasing age.[54]

Underweight may actually be more risky for older adults than overweight, as mortality rates are higher in underweight elderly. Many older adults lose weight as a result of illness, medication, loss of ability to perform self-care, tooth loss or mouth pain, alcoholism, smoking, or economic hardship. In addition, depression and reduced social contact, which can develop after the death of family members and friends or when adult children move out of the area, can cause older adults to lose the desire to prepare nourishing meals for themselves. Impaired vision can make it difficult to read labels and recipes, and a reduced sense of taste can contribute to loss of appetite. Dementia can cause older adults to forget to eat, to eat only an extremely limited diet, or to store foods inappropriately (for example, meats or milk in a cabinet rather than in the refrigerator). Any of these factors can result in underweight and frailty, significantly increasing the person's risk for serious illness, injuries (such as fractures), and death.

Osteoporosis

Osteoporosis is a complex disease that develops over an extended period of time and manifests in the elderly in fractures of the hip, wrist, and spine. It is estimated that 50% of Americans over the age of 50 will have an osteoporosis-related bone fracture in their lifetime. As many as 38% of elderly male hip fracture patients will die of complications related to the fracture.[55]

Age-Related Eye Disorders

Cataracts, a cloudiness of the eye lens that impairs vision, develop in almost 70% of adults in their eighties. *Macular degeneration,* deterioration of the retina of the eye that causes a loss or distortion of vision, is the most common cause of blindness in U.S. elderly individuals. Sunlight exposure and smoking increase the risk for each condition.

Recent research suggests, but does not prove, that dietary choices may slow the progress of these degenerative eye diseases. For example, vitamins C and E, zinc, and two phytochemicals, lutein and zeaxanthin, may provide protection against these diseases. Although the research is not yet conclusive, older adults can benefit by eating foods rich in these nutrients, primarily richly colored fruits and vegetables, nuts, and whole grains.

Use of Medications and Supplements

The average number of filled prescriptions for older Americans in the year 2009 was thirty-one.[56] Although the elderly account for less than 15% of the U.S. population, they experience almost 40% of the adverse drug effects, in part because of **polypharmacy,** the use of three or more drugs at the same time. These drugs can interact with one another in a way that is harmful to the consumer.

Drugs can also interact adversely with nutrients. Some medications affect appetite, either increasing or decreasing food intake, and others alter nutrient digestion and absorption. Several drugs negatively impact the activation or metabolism of nutrients such as vitamin D, folate, and vitamin B_6, whereas others increase the kidneys' excretion of nutrients. Conversely, nutrient intake can affect the action of certain drugs. For example, excessive vitamin K can block the action of anticoagulant drugs. **Table 11.7** summarizes a few of the more common drug–nutrient interactions that place older adults at risk.

TABLE 11.7 Examples of Common Drug–Nutrient Interactions	
Category of Drug	**Common Nutrient/Food Interactions**
Antacids	May decrease the absorption of iron, calcium, folate, and vitamin B_{12}
Antibiotics	May reduce the absorption of calcium, fat-soluble vitamins; reduce the production of vitamin K by gut bacteria
Anticonvulsants	Interfere with activation of vitamin D
Anticoagulants ("blood thinners")	Oppose the clotting activity of vitamin K
Antidepressants	May cause weight gain as a result of increased appetite
Antiretroviral agents (treatment of HIV/AIDS)	Reduce the absorption of most nutrients
Aspirin	Lowers blood folate levels; increases loss of iron due to GI bleeding
Diuretics	Some types may increase urinary loss of potassium, sodium, calcium, and magnesium; some cause retention of potassium and other electrolytes
Laxatives	Increase fecal excretion of dietary fat, fat-soluble vitamins, calcium, and other minerals

polypharmacy The concurrent use of three or more medications.

Supplement usage continues to grow among all segments of the U.S. population, including the elderly. The Institute of Medicine, in establishing the DRI for vitamin B_{12}, specifically stated that adults over the age of 50 years should obtain most of their B_{12} "by consuming foods fortified with B_{12} or a B_{12}-containing supplement."[10] The Tufts Modified Pyramid for older adults recommends calcium and vitamin D supplements as well (Figure 11.9). Older adults should consult their healthcare provider about the need for other single-nutrient or multivitamin/mineral supplements.

What Social Programs Provide Food to Older Adults in Need?

Approximately 8% of older adults living alone experience food insecurity at some point during any given year. The most common cause of food insecurity and hunger among older adults is lack of income and poverty.[35] Older adults in poverty may live in areas with few or no supermarkets, may not be able to afford transportation to buy healthful food, and may fear leaving their home to shop for groceries. Low-income elderly households may lack working refrigerators and/or stoves, limiting the types of foods they can buy, store, and prepare.

The federal government has developed an extensive network of food and nutrition services for older Americans. Many of them are coordinated with state and local governments, as well as nonprofit or community organizations. They include the following:

- *Supplemental Nutrition Assistance Program (SNAP):* Commonly known as "food stamps," this USDA program is designed to meet the basic nutritional needs of eligible households or individuals. Older adults account for about 17% of all household recipients. Participants are provided with a monthly allotment, typically in the form of a prepaid debit card. There are very few restrictions on the foods that can be purchased under this plan. Among the elderly living alone, the benefit provides about $130 per month.
- *Child and Adult Care Program:* This program provides healthful meals and snacks to older and functionally impaired adults in qualified adult day-care settings.
- *Commodity Supplemental Food Program:* Unlike food stamps, this program is not intended to provide a complete array of foods. Instead, specific commodity foods are distributed, including cereals, peanut butter, dry beans, rice or pasta, and canned juice, fruits, vegetables, meat, poultry, and tuna. On occasion, other surplus foods are distributed.
- *Seniors' Farmers' Market Nutrition Program:* This program, sponsored by the U.S. Department of Agriculture, provides coupons to low-income seniors, so that they can buy eligible foods at farmers' markets, roadside stands, and community-supported agricultural programs. Seniors benefit from the nutritional advantages of fresh produce and are often able to increase the variety of the foods they eat.
- *Nutrition Services Incentive Program:* The Department of Health and Human Services, through the Administration on Aging, provides cash and USDA commodity foods to individual state agencies for meals for senior citizens. There are no income criteria; any person 60 years or above (and spouse, even if younger) can take part in this program. Meals, designed to provide one-third of the RDA for key nutrients, are served at senior centers and other locations in the community. Some centers provide "bag dinners" for evening meals, and others send home meals on Fridays for use over the weekend. This program also provides nutrition and health education and usually offers transportation to and from the meal site. For qualified elders, meals can be delivered to their homes through the Meals on Wheels program.

Participation in nutrition programs for the elderly improves the dietary quality and nutrient intakes of older adults. Unfortunately, many of these programs have long waiting lists and are unable to meet the current demands of their communities. With the ever-increasing number of elderly people, legislators must continue to commit adequate funding for these essential services.

⬆ For homebound disabled and older adults, community programs such as Meals on Wheels provide nourishing, balanced meals as well as vital social contact.

RECAP Both overweight and underweight can contribute to poor health in older adults. Osteoporosis is increasingly common in both men and women in this age group, as are fracture-related deaths. Risk for eye disorders may be reduced by intakes of antioxidants and phytochemicals. An older adult's nutrition can influence the effectiveness of certain medications, and some drugs affect nutrient status. A number of social services are available to older adults who are unable to secure a healthful diet.

COOKING 101

Eating well in settings with limited space, equipment, or time can be a challenge! Simple and convenient foods can help make that easier, but check out creative ways to make the most of your resources and become a real cook (even in a small kitchen!) in our new Cooking 101 videos, available on the Companion Website at www.pearsonhighered.com/thompsonmanore.

"Where I'm at Now . . ."

Now that you've read this chapter, identify three servings of calcium-rich foods you plan to consume each day to build and maintain healthy bones:

1. _____
2. _____
3. _____

Jot down the reason women of childbearing age need to consume at least 400 µg/day of folic acid, whether or not they plan on becoming pregnant:

You should now understand how lifestyle choices can increase your odds of good health as you age. Of the following behaviors, which do you plan to make a part of your life? (Check as many as you want.):

☐ Consume a nutritious diet.
☐ Maintain a healthful weight.
☐ Participate in regular physical activity.
☐ Avoid smoking.
☐ Avoid substance abuse.
☐ Consume alcohol in moderation, if at all.
☐ Other: I plan to. . . .

Chapter Review

What Can I Do Today?

Now that you've read this chapter, try making these three changes:

- If you are a woman of childbearing age, whether or not you plan to become pregnant, make sure you are consuming 400 µg of folic acid per day from supplements, fortified foods, or both.
- Eat a nourishing breakfast.
- If you smoke, stop today. Half of all smoking-related deaths occur in middle age (ages 35 through 69), resulting in an average loss of 20 to 25 years of normal life expectancy.

Test Yourself ANSWERS

1. **F** More than half of all pregnant women experience morning sickness, and food cravings or aversions are also common.

2. **F** Most infants do not have a physiologic need for solid food until about 6 months of age.

3. **F** As a percentage of total Calories, young toddlers have a higher need for fat than do older children or adults, so nonfat dairy foods are not appropriate choices.

4. **T** Hormonal changes, emotional stress, genetic factors, and personal hygiene are the most likely contributors to adolescent acne.

5. **T** About 11% of American households with children are unable to acquire adequate, nutritious food throughout the year.

Review Questions

1. Folate deficiency in the first weeks after conception has been linked with which of the following problems in newborns?
   a. high blood pressure
   b. neural tube defects
   c. abnormally high birth weight
   d. poor bone mineralization

2. Which of the following nutrients should be added to the diet of breast-fed infants when they are around 6 months of age?
   a. fiber   c. iron
   b. fat   d. vitamin C

3. The RDA for calcium for adolescents is
   a. less than that for young children.
   b. less than that for adults.
   c. less than that for pregnant adults.
   d. greater than that for children, adults, and pregnant adults.

4. Which of the following nutrients is needed in increased amounts in older adulthood?
   a. fiber   c. carbohydrate
   b. vitamin D   d. vitamin A

5. Why are older adults often at risk for inappropriate weight loss?
   a. Certain drugs interfere with normal appetite.
   b. Depression and social isolation decrease food intake.
   c. Many elderly people have limited incomes and have no transportation to shop for healthful foods.
   d. All of the above are correct.

6. True or False? Major developmental errors and birth defects are most likely to occur in the third trimester of pregnancy.

7. True or False? For infants, honey is a safer choice of sweetener than white sugar.

8. True or False? Toddlers are too young to be influenced by their parents' examples.

9. True or False? The rate of obesity among adolescents has increased in the past decade.

10. True or False? Sensory deficits, such as impaired vision, can contribute to nutrient deficiencies.

Answers to Review Questions are located at the back of this text.

Web Links

www.aap.org
American Academy of Pediatrics

www.marchofdimes.com
March of Dimes

www.diabetes.org
American Diabetes Association

www.llli.org
La Leche League

www.nofas.org
National Organization on Fetal Alcohol Syndrome

www.teamnutrition.usda.gov/kids-pyramid.html
MyPyramid for Kids

www.aarp.org
American Association for Retired Persons

www.aoa.gov
The Department of Health, and Human Services Administration on Aging

www.nihseniorhealth.gov
The National Institutes of Health, SeniorHealth

www.livingto100.com
The Living to 100 Healthspan Calculator

12

Nutrition Issues: The Safety and Security of the World's Food Supply

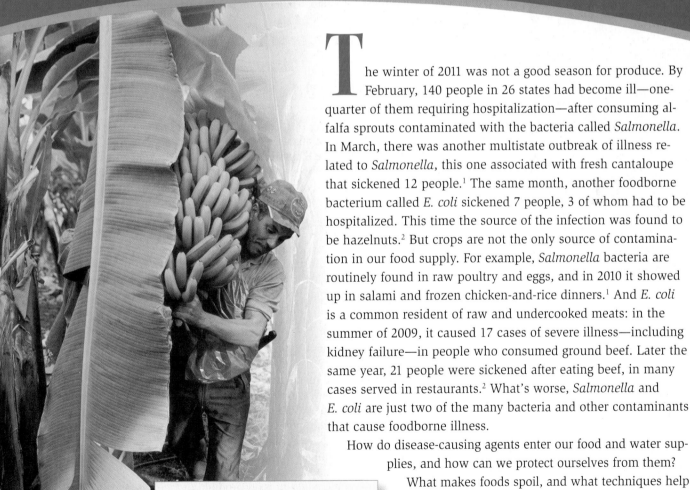

The winter of 2011 was not a good season for produce. By February, 140 people in 26 states had become ill—one-quarter of them requiring hospitalization—after consuming alfalfa sprouts contaminated with the bacteria called *Salmonella*. In March, there was another multistate outbreak of illness related to *Salmonella*, this one associated with fresh cantaloupe that sickened 12 people.[1] The same month, another foodborne bacterium called *E. coli* sickened 7 people, 3 of whom had to be hospitalized. This time the source of the infection was found to be hazelnuts.[2] But crops are not the only source of contamination in our food supply. For example, *Salmonella* bacteria are routinely found in raw poultry and eggs, and in 2010 it showed up in salami and frozen chicken-and-rice dinners.[1] And *E. coli* is a common resident of raw and undercooked meats: in the summer of 2009, it caused 17 cases of severe illness—including kidney failure—in people who consumed ground beef. Later the same year, 21 people were sickened after eating beef, in many cases served in restaurants.[2] What's worse, *Salmonella* and *E. coli* are just two of the many bacteria and other contaminants that cause foodborne illness.

How do disease-causing agents enter our food and water supplies, and how can we protect ourselves from them? What makes foods spoil, and what techniques help keep foods fresh longer? Are pesticides and food additives helpful or harmful, and are organic

Nutrition Online

icons are located throughout the chapter, directing you to web links, videos, podcasts, and other useful online resources.

foods more nutritious? Is there anything we can do to increase everyone's access to safe, adequate, and wholesome foods, not only throughout the United States but also in other nations? We explore these and other questions in this chapter.

Why Is Foodborne Illness a Critical Concern?

Foodborne illness is a term used to encompass any symptom or disorder that arises from ingesting food or water contaminated with disease-causing (*pathogenic*) microscopic organisms (called *microorganisms*), their toxic secretions, or chemicals (such as mercury or pesticides). You probably refer to foodborne illness as *food poisoning*.

Foodborne Illness Affects Millions of Americans Annually

According to the Centers for Disease Control and Prevention (CDC), approximately 48 million Americans—1 out of every 6—report experiencing foodborne illness each year. Of these, 128,000 are hospitalized and 3,000 die.[3] The people most at risk for serious foodborne illness include

- developing fetuses, infants, and young children, as their immune system is immature;
- people who are very old or have a chronic illness, as their immune system may be compromised;
- people with acquired immunodeficiency syndrome (AIDS); and
- people who are receiving immune-system-suppressing drugs, such as transplant recipients and cancer patients.

Although the statistics may seem frightening, most experts consider our food supply safe. That's partly because not all cases of food contamination make all people sick; in fact, even virulent strains cause illness in only a small percentage of people. For example, in a *Salmonella* outbreak traced to the Peanut Corporation of America (PCA) in early 2009, more than 700 people became ill, but thousands are assumed to have eaten the tainted products.[4] Moreover, modern science and technology have given us a wide array of techniques to preserve foods. We discuss these later in this chapter.

Finally, food safety in the United States is monitored by several government agencies. In addition to the CDC, mentioned earlier, the United States Department of Agriculture (USDA), Food and Drug Administration (FDA), and Environmental Protection Agency (EPA) monitor and regulate food production and preservation. Information about these agencies and how to access them appear in **Table 12.1** (page 372).

Food Production Is Increasingly Complex

Despite safeguards, foodborne illness has emerged as a major public health threat in recent years. One reason is that more foods are mass-produced than ever before, with a combination of ingredients from a much greater number of sources, including fields, feedlots, and a variety of processing facilities all over the world. These various sources can remain hidden not only to consumers but even to food companies using the ingredients.

Contamination can occur at any point from farm to table **(Figure 12.1)**, and when it does, it can be difficult to trace. For example, in the PCA outbreak, many of the manufacturers of the recalled cookies and other products could not identify the source of their peanut ingredients.

At the same time, federal oversight of food production facilities decreased in the last decades of the 20th century. Thirty-five years ago, the FDA inspected about half of the nation's food-processing facilities annually. By 2008, the inspection rate had dropped below 5%. Not surprisingly, in 2009, the CDC warned that, after decades of steady progress, the safety of the nation's food supply was no longer improving and, in the case of *Salmonella*, infections were creeping upward.[5] The same year,

foodborne illness An illness transmitted by food or water contaminated by a pathogenic microorganism, its toxic secretions, or a toxic chemical.

Farms

Animals raised for meat can harbor harmful microorganisms, and crops can be contaminated with pollutants from irrigation, runoff from streams, microorganisms or toxins in soil, or pesticides. Contamination can also occur during animal slaughter or from harvesting, sorting, washing, packing, and/or storage of crops.

Processing

Some foods, such as produce, may go from the farm directly to the market, but most foods are processed. Processed foods may go through several steps at different facilities. At each site, people, equipment, or environments may contaminate foods. Federal safeguards, such as cleaning protocols, testing, and training, can help prevent contamination.

Transportation

Foods must be transported in clean, refrigerated vehicles and containers to prevent multiplication of microorganisms and microbial toxins.

Retail

Employees of food markets and restaurants may contaminate food during storage, preparation, or service. Conditions such as inadequate refrigeration or heating may promote multiplication of microorganisms or microbial toxins. Establishments must follow FDA guidelines for food safety and pass local health inspections.

Table

Consumers may contaminate foods with unclean hands, utensils, or surfaces. They can allow the multiplication of microorganisms and microbial toxins by failing to follow the food-safety guidelines for storing, preparing, cooking, and serving foods discussed in this chapter.

◀ **Figure 12.1** Food is at risk for contamination at any of the five stages from farm to table, but following food safety guidelines can reduce the risks.

TABLE 12.1	Government Agencies That Regulate Food Safety		
Name of Agency	**Year Established**	**Role in Food Regulations**	**Website**
U.S. Department of Agriculture (USDA)	1785	Oversees safety of meat, poultry, and eggs sold across state lines; also regulates which drugs can be used to treat sick cattle and poultry	www.usda.gov
U.S. Food and Drug Administration (FDA)	1862	Regulates food standards of food products (except meat, poultry, and eggs) and bottled water; regulates food labeling and enforces pesticide use as established by EPA	www.fda.gov
Centers for Disease Control and Prevention (CDC)	1946	Works with public health officials to promote and educate the public about health and safety; able to track information needed in identifying foodborne illness outbreaks	www.cdc.gov
Environmental Protection Agency (EPA)	1970	Regulates use of pesticides and which crops they can be applied to; establishes standards for water quality	www.epa.gov

President Barack Obama announced the creation of a Food Safety Working Group to sponsor changes in food-safety laws. The U.S. Congress responded by crafting a new food safety bill, the Food Safety Modernization Act, which was passed into law in January 2011. Among its provisions are the following:[6]

- new requirements for actions food processors must take to prevent contamination
- new requirements for food importers to verify the safety of food from their suppliers
- new FDA enforcement tools, including mandatory recall authority
- a new, more rigorous inspection schedule

RECAP Foodborne illness affects 48 million Americans a year. Contamination can occur at any point from farm to table. The Centers for Disease Control and Prevention, the Food and Drug Administration, the United States Department of Agriculture, and the Environmental Protection Agency monitor and regulate food production and preservation. The Food Safety Modernization Act of 2011 increased the oversight of food production by federal agencies and authorized the FDA to swiftly recall contaminated foods from the market.

What Causes Most Foodborne Illness?

The consumption of food containing pathogenic microorganisms—those capable of causing disease—results in *food infections*. *Food intoxications* result from consuming food in which microorganisms have secreted harmful substances called *toxins*. Naturally occurring plant and marine toxins also contaminate food. Finally, chemical residues in foods, such as pesticides and pollutants in soil or water, can cause illness. Residues are discussed later in this chapter.

Several Types of Microorganisms Contaminate Foods

The microorganisms that most commonly cause food infections are bacteria and viruses; however, other tiny organisms and nonliving particles can also contaminate foods.

Bacteria are microorganisms that lack a true cell nucleus and reproduce either by division or by forming spores. Many thrive in the intestines of birds and mammals, including poultry, pigs, and cattle, so foodborne infection often results from consuming undercooked or raw meats, foods contaminated with juices from raw meats, or produce, milk, or water contaminated with infected animal feces. Bacteria cause about 39% of all foodborne illnesses.[3] A few of the most common culprits are identified in **Table 12.2**. Of these, the bacterium responsible for the most illnesses, hospitalizations, and deaths is *Salmonella* (**Figure 12.2**).[3]

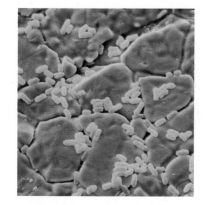

▲ **Figure 12.2** *Salmonella* is a species of bacteria responsible for about 11% of cases of foodborne illness, 35% of hospitalizations, and 28% of deaths. Infection can cause fever, diarrhea, and abdominal cramps, and cells of some strains of *Salmonella* can perforate the intestines and invade the blood.

bacteria Microorganisms that lack a true nucleus and reproduce by division or by forming spores.

TABLE 12.2 Common Bacterial Causes of Foodborne Illness

Bacteria	Incubation Period	Duration	Symptoms	Foods Most Commonly Affected	Usual Sources of Contamination	Steps for Prevention
Salmonella (more than 2,300 types)	12–24 hours	4–7 days	Diarrhea Abdominal pain Chills Fever Vomiting Dehydration	Raw or undercooked eggs, poultry, and meat Raw milk and dairy products Seafood Fruits and vegetables	Intestinal tract and feces of poultry *Salmonella enteritidis* in raw shell eggs	Cook foods thoroughly. Avoid cross-contamination. Use sanitary practices.
Clostridium perfringens	6–24 hours	1 day	Abdominal cramps Diarrhea	Beef Poultry Gravies Dried foods Cooked foods prepared in large quantities Leftovers	Widely found in environment and in intestinal tracts of animals and humans Can survive in little or no oxygen	Cook foods thoroughly. Serve hot. Refrigerate leftovers promptly. Reheat leftovers thoroughly before serving.
Campylobacter jejuni	1–7 days	7–10 days	Fever Headache and muscle pain followed by diarrhea (sometimes bloody) Nausea Abdominal cramps	Raw and undercooked meat, poultry, or shellfish Raw eggs Cake icing Untreated water Unpasteurized milk	Intestinal tracts of animals and birds Raw milk Untreated water and sewage sludge	Only drink pasteurized milk. Cook foods properly. Avoid cross-contamination.
Escherichia coli (O157:H7 and other strains that can cause human illness)	2–4 days	5–10 days	Diarrhea (may be bloody) Abdominal cramps Nausea Can lead to kidney and blood complications	Contaminated water Raw milk Raw or rare ground beef, sausages Unpasteurized apple juice or cider Uncooked fruits and vegetables	Intestinal tracts of cattle Raw milk Unchlorinated water	Thoroughly cook meat. Avoid cross-contamination.
Staphylococcus	1–6 hours	2–3 days	Severe nausea and vomiting Abdominal cramps Diarrhea	Custard- or cream-filled baked goods Ham Poultry Dressings, sauces, and gravies Eggs Mayonnaise-based salads	Human skin Infected cuts Pimples Noses and throats	Refrigerate foods. Use sanitary practices.
Listeria monocytogenes	2 days–3 weeks	None reported	Fever Muscle aches Nausea Diarrhea Headache, stiff neck, confusion, loss of balance, or convulsions if infection spreads to nervous system. Infections during pregnancy can lead to miscarriage or stillbirth	Uncooked meats and vegetables Soft cheeses Lunch meats and hot dogs Unpasteurized milk	Intestinal tract and feces of animals Soil and manure used as fertilizer Raw milk	Thoroughly cook all meats. Wash produce before eating. Avoid cross-contamination. Avoid unpasteurized milk and foods made with unpasteurized milk. People at high risk should • not eat hotdogs or lunch meats unless they are reheated until steaming hot; • avoid getting fluid from hotdog packages on foods, utensils, and surfaces; • wash hands after handling hotdogs or lunch meats; and • avoid eating refrigerated smoked seafood unless it is cooked.

Data from Iowa State University Extension, Food Safety and Quality Project. 2000. Safe Food: It's Your Job Too! www.extension.iastate.edu/foodsafety/Lesson/L1.html; U.S. Food and Drug Administration (FDA). How Can I Prevent Foodborne Illness? www.cfsan.fda.gov/~dms/qa-fdb1.html; and Centers for Disease Control and Prevention (CDC), Division of Bacterial and Mycotic Diseases. 2005. Disease Information, Foodborne Illness. www.cdc.gov/ncidod/dbmd/diseaseinfo/foodborneinfections_g.htm.

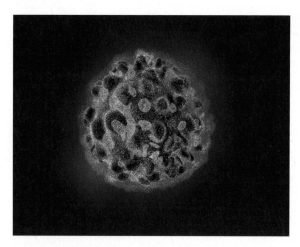

◆ **Figure 12.3** Norovirus is the leading cause of foodborne infection in the U.S. It is responsible for more foodborne illness than all other viruses, bacteria, and parasites combined.

◆ **Figure 12.4** Tapeworms have long, wormlike bodies and hooks and suckers, which help them attach to human tissues.

viruses A group of infectious agents that are much smaller than bacteria, lack independent metabolism, and are incapable of growth or reproduction outside of living cells.

parasite A microorganism that simultaneously derives benefit from and harms its host.

helminth A multicellular microscopic worm.

protozoa Single-celled, mobile microorganisms.

fungi Plantlike, spore-forming organisms that can grow as either single cells or multicellular colonies.

Viruses are much smaller than bacteria, and they can't survive apart from living cells. Just one type, called norovirus, causes nearly all foodborne viral illness in the United States and 58% of all foodborne illness from any known cause **(Figure 12.3)**.[7] Norovirus is so common and contagious that many people refer to it simply as "the stomach flu." Norovirus illness typically comes on suddenly as *gastroenteritis*, inflammation of the lining of the stomach and intestines, and results in stomach cramps, vomiting, and diarrhea. In healthy people, the symptoms typically resolve spontaneously in a day or two. Raw foods can harbor norovirus, and it can spread from person to person. Infected food-service workers can contaminate foods during preparation or serving if they have the virus on their hands. This was the suspected mode of transmission of a norovirus outbreak in 2009 at the University of Michigan that sickened eight people who ate at the same university cafeteria.[8] Hepatitis A and hepatitis E viruses also commonly contaminate foods during harvesting, processing, or preparation. They can cause acute liver damage and even death.

Parasites are microorganisms that simultaneously derive benefit from and harm their host. They are responsible for only about 2% of foodborne illnesses. The following are the most common culprits:

- **Helminths** are multicellular worms, such as tapeworms **(Figure 12.4)**, flukes, and roundworms. They reproduce by releasing their eggs into vegetation or water. Animals, including fish, then consume the contaminated matter. The eggs hatch inside their host, and larvae develop in the host's tissue. The larvae can survive in the flesh long after the host is killed for food. Thoroughly cooking beef, pork, or fish destroys the larvae. In contrast, people who eat contaminated foods either raw or undercooked consume living larvae, which then mature into adult worms in their small intestine. Some worms cause mild symptoms, such as nausea and diarrhea, but others can grow large enough to cause intestinal obstruction or even death.
- **Protozoa** are single-celled organisms that commonly cause waterborne illness. One of the most common culprits worldwide is *Giardia duodenalis*, which causes a diarrheal illness called *giardiasis*.[9] *Giardia* lives in the intestines of infected animals and humans and is passed into the environment from their stools. People typically consume *Giardia* by swallowing contaminated water (in lakes, streams, rivers, swimming pools, and so on) or by eating contaminated food. Symptoms include diarrhea, stomach cramps, and upset stomach, usually beginning within 1 to 2 weeks of being infected and generally lasting 2 to 6 weeks.

Fungi are plantlike, spore-forming organisms that can grow as either single cells or multicellular colonies. Two types of fungi are yeasts, which are globular, and molds, which are long and thin. Less than 1% of foodborne illnesses are caused by fungi.[3] This is due in part to the fact that very few species of fungi cause serious disease in people with healthy immune systems, and those that do cause disease in humans are not typically foodborne.[10] In addition, unlike bacterial growth, which is invisible and often tasteless, fungal growth typically makes food look and taste so unappealing that we immediately discard it **(Figure 12.5)**.

A foodborne illness in beef cattle that has had front-page exposure in recent years is mad cow disease, or *bovine spongiform encephalopathy* (*BSE*). This neurological disorder is caused by a **prion,** a proteinaceous infectious particle that is self-replicating. Prions are normal proteins of animal tissues that can misfold and become infectious. When they do, they can transform other normal proteins into abnormally shaped prions until they eventually cause illness.

The human form of BSE can develop in people who consume contaminated meat or tissue. If you eat beef, are you at risk? Check out the ***Nutrition Myth or Fact?*** feature box (page 376).

Some Microorganisms Release Toxins

The microorganisms just discussed cause illness by directly infecting and destroying body cells. In contrast, other bacteria and fungi secrete chemicals, called **toxins,** that are responsible for serious and even life-threatening illnesses. These toxins bind to body cells and can cause a variety of symptoms, such as diarrhea, vomiting, organ damage, convulsions, and paralysis. Toxins can be categorized depending on the type of cell they bind to; the two primary types of toxins associated with foodborne illness are neurotoxins, which damage the nervous system and can cause paralysis, and enterotoxins, which target the gastrointestinal system and generally cause severe diarrhea and vomiting.

Figure 12.5 Molds rarely cause human illness, in part because they look so unappealing that we throw the food away.

One of the most common and deadly neurotoxins is produced by the bacterium *Clostridium botulinum.* The botulism toxin blocks nerve transmission to muscle cells and causes paralysis, including of the muscles required for breathing. Common sources of contamination are foods in damaged (split, pierced, or bulging) cans, foods improperly canned at home, and raw honey. However, improperly heated commercial canned goods can also contain the toxin: in March 2011, a food producer voluntarily recalled thousands of cases of canned beets because of concerns about *C. botulinum.*

Some fungi produce poisonous chemicals called *mycotoxins.* (The prefix *myco-* means "fungus.") These toxins are typically found in grains stored in moist environments. In some instances, moist conditions in the field encourage fungi to reproduce and release their toxins on the surface of growing crops. Long-term consumption of mycotoxins can cause organ damage or cancer.

Some Toxins Occur Independently of Microorganisms

Some toxins develop in foods independently of microorganisms. For example, a highly visible fungus that causes food intoxication is the poisonous mushroom. Most mushrooms are not toxic, but a few, such as the deathcap mushroom (*Amanita phalloides*), can be fatal. Some poisonous mushrooms are quite colorful **(Figure 12.6)**, a fact that helps explain why the victims of mushroom poisoning are often children.[10]

In February 2010, scientists predicted that a severe "red tide" could threaten the New England shellfish industry and cause paralysis in anyone consuming mussels or clams.[12] Red tides are caused by an excessive production of certain species of toxic algae, whose bloom turns ocean waters red. Humans don't consume these marine toxins directly, but they can accumulate in mussels, clams, and other seafoods. When humans consume the seafood, which typically looks, smells, and tastes normal, illness results.[13]

Figure 12.6 Some mushrooms, such as this fly agaric, contain toxins that can cause illness or even death.

Ciguatoxins are among the most common marine toxins. They are produced by microscopic sea plants called *dinoflagellates*, which are consumed by small fish. The toxins become progressively more concentrated as larger fish eat these small fish, and high concentrations can be present in grouper, sea bass, snapper, and a number of other large fish from tropical regions. Symptoms of ciguatoxin poisoning include nausea, vomiting, diarrhea, headache, itching, a "pins-and-needles" feeling, and even nightmares or hallucinations, but the illness is rarely fatal and typically resolves within a few weeks.[13]

Potatoes that have turned green contain the toxin solanine, which forms during the greening process. The green color is actually due to chlorophyll, a harmless pigment that forms when the potatoes are exposed to light. Although the production of solanine occurs simultaneously with the production of chlorophyll, the two processes are separate and unrelated.[14] There is a potential for toxicity from consuming potatoes with a very high solanine content. You can avoid the greening of potatoes by storing them for only short periods in a dark cupboard or brown paper bag in a cool area. Wash the potato to expose its color, and cut away and discard any green areas.

prion A protein that misfolds and becomes infectious; prions are not living cellular organisms or viruses.

toxin Any harmful substance; in microbiology, a chemical produced by a microorganism that harms tissues or causes harmful immune responses.

NUTRITION MYTH OR FACT?

Mad Cow Disease: Is It Safe to Eat Beef?

Mad cow disease is a fatal brain disorder in cattle caused by a *prion*, which is an abnormally folded, infectious protein. Prions influence other proteins to take on their abnormal shape, and these abnormal proteins cause brain damage. Mad cow disease is also called *bovine spongiform encephalopathy (BSE)*. The disease eats away at a cow's brain, leaving it full of spongelike holes. Eventually, the brain can no longer control vital life functions and the cow literally "goes mad." Unfortunately, people who eat meat from infected cattle will also be infected. Symptoms may take years to appear, but eventually the person may develop the human form of mad cow disease, called *variant Creutzfeldt-Jakob disease (vCJD)*. This disease has killed at least 168 people in Great Britain, as well as people in France and other nations.[11] So if you eat beef, are you at risk?

Scientists are not certain how the prions are introduced to cattle. They think that cattle become infected by eating feed containing tissue from the brains and spinal cords of other infected cattle. Decades ago in Great Britain and Europe, it was common practice to feed livestock with meal made from other animals. This practice has ceased.

The effect of mad cow disease on the European beef market was staggering, with beef consumption dropping 25–70% in certain countries. In addition, ranchers were forced to slaughter almost 5 million cattle.

For many years, experts in North America believed BSE to be a problem limited to Europe. But

then, eight cases of BSE were found in cows in Canada from 2003 to 2006. And in December 2003, the first case of mad cow disease was reported in the United States, shocking those who believed the U.S. food supply to be safe from this disease. These discoveries prompted many countries to immediately ban importation of Canadian and American beef. In the United States, the federal government and beef industry took quick action to restore confidence in the beef supply. Steps included the destruction of any potentially infected beef, as well as changes in feeding practices, including the use of meal made from soybeans and increased enforcement of a ban on the use of meal made with animal by-products. In addition, for many years in the United States, cattle have been slaughtered at an early age. Because BSE takes years to develop, this step reduces the likelihood of advanced infection.

So is it safe to eat beef? The U.S. Department of Agriculture, the FDA, the National Institutes of Health, and the Centers for Disease Control and Prevention are working together to eliminate the use of animal-based feed and to enhance technology that can track signs of BSE and act quickly if it reappears. The U.S. beef industry is highly motivated to comply with safety regulations, since reduced beef intake translates into millions of dollars in lost income. Although it may not be possible to guarantee the safety of U.S. beef, adherence to strict safety standards should minimize the risk and keep beef safe for human consumption.

⬆ Sea bass may look appealing, but like several other large predatory tropical fish, it can be contaminated with a high concentration of marine toxins.

The Body Responds to Contaminants with Acute Illness

Many contaminants are killed in the mouth by antimicrobial enzymes in saliva or in the stomach by hydrochloric acid. Any that survive these chemical assaults usually trigger vomiting and/or diarrhea as the gastrointestinal tract attempts to expel them. Simultaneously, the white blood cells of the immune system are activated, and a generalized inflammatory response causes the person to experience nausea, fatigue, fever, and muscle aches. Depending on the state of one's health, the precise microorganism or toxin involved, and the "dose" ingested, the symptoms can range from mild to severe, including double vision, loss of muscle control, and excessive or bloody diarrhea. As noted earlier, some cases, if left untreated, can result in death.

To diagnose a foodborne illness, a specimen—usually blood or stool—must be analyzed. Treatment usually involves keeping the person hydrated and comfortable, as most foodborne illness tends to be self-limiting; the person's vomiting and/or diarrhea, though unpleasant, rid the body of the offending agent. In more severe cases, hospitalization may be necessary.

In the United States, all confirmed cases of foodborne illness must be reported to the state health department, which in turn reports these illnesses to the CDC in Atlanta, Georgia. The CDC monitors its reports for indications of epidemics of foodborne illness and assists local and state agencies in controlling such outbreaks.

Certain Conditions Help Microorganisms Multiply in Foods

Given the correct environmental conditions, microorganisms can thrive in many types of food. Four factors affect the survival and reproduction of food microorganisms:

- *Temperature.* Many microorganisms capable of causing human illness thrive at warm temperatures, from about 40°F to 140°F (4°C to 60°C). You can think of this range of temperatures as the **danger zone (Figure 12.7)**. These microorganisms can be destroyed by thoroughly heating or cooking foods, and their reproduction can be slowed by refrigeration and freezing. We identify safe cooking and food-storage temperatures later in this chapter.
- *Humidity.* Many microorganisms require a high level of moisture; thus, foods such as boxed dried pasta do not make suitable microbial homes, although cooked pasta left at room temperature would prove hospitable.
- *Acidity.* Most microorganisms have a preferred range of acidity, or pH, in which they thrive. For instance, *Clostridium botulinum* thrives in alkaline environments. It cannot grow or produce its toxin in acidic environments, so the risk for botulism is decreased in citrus fruits, pickles, and tomato-based foods. In contrast, alkaline foods, such as fish and most vegetables—including beets—are a magnet for *C. botulinum.*
- *Oxygen content.* Many microorganisms require oxygen to function; thus, food-preservation techniques that remove oxygen, such as industrial canning and bottling, keep foods safe for consumption. Because *C. botulinum* thrives in an oxygen-free environment, the canning process heats foods to an extremely high temperature to destroy this organism. In the recall of canned beets mentioned earlier, the producer's concern was that the food had not been heated high enough prior to canning.

In addition, microorganisms need an entryway into a food. Just as our skin protects our body from microbial invasion, the peels, rinds, and shells of many foods seal off access to the nutrients within. Eggshells are a good example of a natural food barrier. Once such a barrier is removed, however, the food loses its primary defense against contamination.

RECAP Food infections result from the consumption of food containing living microorganisms, such as bacteria, whereas food intoxications result from consuming food in which microorganisms have secreted toxins. Some plants and animals can also develop toxins. The body has several defense mechanisms that help rid us of offending microorganisms or their toxins. In order to reproduce in foods, microorganisms require a precise range of temperature, humidity, acidity, and oxygen content.

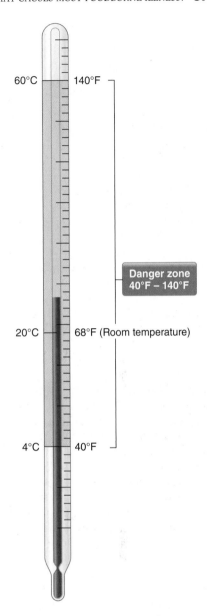

◆ Figure 12.7 The danger zone is a range of temperature at which many pathogenic microorganisms thrive. Notice that "room temperature" (about 68°F) is within the danger zone!

danger zone Range of temperature (about 40°F to 140°F, or 4°C to 60°C) at which many microorganisms capable of causing human disease thrive.

⬆ Peels protect foods against contamination; however, you should still wash the fruit before peeling.

Keep Food Safe From Bacteria

⬆ **Figure 12.8** Fight BAC! is the food-safety logo of the U.S. Department of Agriculture.

How Can You Prevent Foodborne Illness?

The United States Department of Agriculture's FightBAC! logo identifies four basic rules for food safety, each of which is explored in detail shortly **(Figure 12.8)**:

1. Clean. Wash your hands and kitchen surfaces often.
2. Separate. Keep foods separate to prevent **cross-contamination,** that is, the spread of microorganisms from one food to another. This commonly occurs when raw foods, such as chicken and vegetables, are cut using the same knife, prepared on the same cutting board, or stored on the same plate.
3. Chill. Refrigerate or freeze foods to prevent microorganisms from growing.
4. Cook. Thoroughly cook and reheat foods to their proper temperatures.

Wash Your Hands and Kitchen Surfaces Often

One of the easiest and most effective ways to prevent foodborne illness is to wash your hands. Scrub for at least 20 seconds with a mild soap before rinsing under warm, running water. Although you should wash dishes in hot water, it's too harsh for normal hand washing: it causes the surface layer of the skin to break down, increasing the risk that microorganisms will be able to penetrate your skin. Always wash[15]

- before and after handling food;
- after using the bathroom, changing a diaper, or tending to a sick person;
- after blowing your nose, coughing, or sneezing; and
- after handling pets.

Remove any rings or bracelets before you begin, because jewelry can harbor bacteria. Also, keep your sleeves rolled up. Make sure to wash the areas underneath your fingernails and between your fingers. Rinse your hands thoroughly, rubbing them together, and then dry on a clean towel or use paper towels.

Clean tools and a clean work area are also essential in reducing cross-contamination. Wash utensils, containers, and cutting boards in the dishwasher or with hot, soapy water (wear gloves!) before and after contact with food. If a cutting board, plate, countertop, or other surface has held raw meat, poultry, or seafood, sanitize it with a solution of ¾ teaspoon of chlorine bleach to 1 quart of water.[15] Flood the surface with the bleach solution and allow it to stand for several minutes before rinsing it with clean water. Then dry it with paper towels or allow it to air dry. It's also important to wash faucets, cabinet knobs, and other areas you have touched.

Consider using paper towels to clean kitchen surfaces. When done, throw them away immediately. If you use cloth towels, wash them often in the hot cycle of your washing machine, along with aprons and cloth napkins. Wash sponges in the dishwasher each time you run it, or put them in boiling water for 3 minutes to sterilize them on a routine basis. Replace them frequently.[15]

Separate Foods to Avoid Cross-Contamination

Raw meat, poultry, and seafood harbor an array of microbes and can easily contaminate other foods through direct contact, as well as by the juices they leave behind on surfaces (including hands). Avoid contact between foods that have already been cooked or that won't be cooked, such as salad ingredients, and raw foods or their juices. Also avoid placing cooked or ready-to-eat foods on a plate or other surface that previously held raw meat, seafood, or poultry. When preparing meals with a

cross-contamination Contamination of one food by another via the unintended transfer of microorganisms through physical contact.

marinade, reserve some of the fresh marinade in a clean container; then add the raw ingredients to the remainder. In this way, some uncontaminated marinade will be available if needed later in the cooking process. Raw food should always be marinated in the refrigerator.

Store Foods in the Refrigerator or Freezer

The third rule for keeping food safe from bacteria is to promptly refrigerate or freeze it. Remember the danger zone: microorganisms that cause foodborne illness can reproduce in temperatures above 40°F. So to keep them from multiplying in your food, keep it cold. Refrigeration (at or below 40°F) and freezing (at or below 0°F)[16] do not kill all microorganisms, but cold temperatures diminish their ability to reproduce in quantities large enough to cause illness. Also, many naturally occurring enzymes that cause food spoilage are deactivated at cold temperatures.

Shopping for Perishable Foods

When shopping for food, purchase refrigerated and frozen foods last. Many grocery stores are actually designed so that these foods are in the last aisles. Put packaged meat, poultry, or fish into a plastic bag before placing it in your shopping cart. This prevents drippings from those foods from coming into contact with others in your cart. Also, if you use cloth shopping bags, wash them often in hot water.[15]

When choosing perishable foods, check the "sell by" or "best used by" date on the label. The "sell by" date indicates the last day a product can be sold and still maintain its quality during normal home storage and consumption. The "best used by" date tells you how long a product will maintain optimum quality before eating.[17] If the stamped date has passed, don't purchase the item and notify the store manager. These foods should be promptly removed from the shelves.

Do not purchase foods with damaged packaging. Dented, leaking, or bulging cans, cracked jars, and jars with loose or bulging lids are especially dangerous, as they could harbor potentially deadly *C. botulinum* toxin. Report any damaged packaging to the store manager. If you do inadvertently purchase food in such a container, or find that the container spurts liquid when you open it, throw it out immediately. *Never* taste the food, as even a tiny amount of botulism toxin can be deadly.[18]

Watch for unsanitary practices and conditions inside the store. For example, the displaying of food products such as cooked shrimp on the same bed of ice as raw seafood is not safe, nor is slicing cold cuts with the same knife used to trim raw meat. Report such unsanitary practices or conditions to your local health authorities.

After you purchase perishable foods, get them home and into the refrigerator or freezer within 1 hour. If your trip home will be longer than an hour, take along a cooler to transport them in.

Refrigerating Foods at Home

As soon as you get home from shopping, put meats, eggs, cheeses, milk, and any other perishable foods in the refrigerator. Store meat, poultry, and seafood in the back of the refrigerator away from the door, so that they stay cold, and on the lowest shelf, so that their juices do not drip onto any other foods. If you are not going to use raw poultry, fish, or ground beef within 2 days of purchase, store it in the freezer. Other foods will keep a little longer. A guide for storing foods in your refrigerator is provided in **Figure 12.9** (page 280).

Avoid overstocking your refrigerator or freezer. Air needs to circulate around food to cool it quickly and continuously. After a meal, refrigerate leftovers promptly—even if still hot—to discourage microbial growth. The standard rule is to refrigerate leftovers within *2 hours* of serving. If the temperature is 90°F or higher, such as at a picnic, then foods should be refrigerated within 1 hour.[16] A larger quantity of food takes longer to cool and will allow more microorganisms to thrive, so divide and conquer: separate large amounts of leftovers into shallow containers for quicker cooling.[16] Finally, avoid keeping leftovers for more than a few days. See Figure 12.9 for storage times for specific types of leftovers. If you don't plan to finish a dish within that time frame, freeze it.

One of the most effective strategies for preventing foodborne illness is simply to wash your hands thoroughly.

The "sell by" date tells the store how long to display the product for sale.

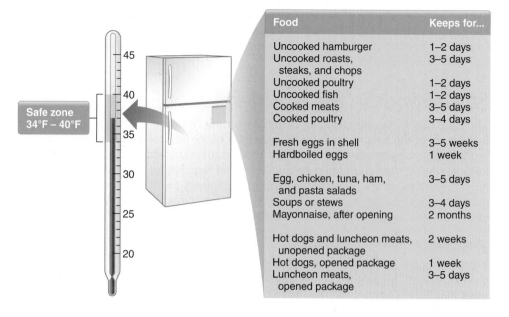

Figure 12.9 While it's important to keep a well-stocked refrigerator, it's also important to know how long foods will keep. Data from U.S. Department of Agriculture, Food Safety and Inspection Service. November 2005. Fact Sheets. Safe Food Handling. Refrigeration and Food Safety. www.fsis.usda.gov/Fact_Sheets/Refrigeration_&_Food_Safety/index.asp.

Food	Keeps for...
Uncooked hamburger	1–2 days
Uncooked roasts, steaks, and chops	3–5 days
Uncooked poultry	1–2 days
Uncooked fish	1–2 days
Cooked meats	3–5 days
Cooked poultry	3–4 days
Fresh eggs in shell	3–5 weeks
Hardboiled eggs	1 week
Egg, chicken, tuna, ham, and pasta salads	3–5 days
Soups or stews	3–4 days
Mayonnaise, after opening	2 months
Hot dogs and luncheon meats, unopened package	2 weeks
Hot dogs, opened package	1 week
Luncheon meats, opened package	3–5 days

Safe zone 34°F – 40°F

Freezing and Thawing Foods

The temperature in your freezer should be set at 0°F. Use a thermometer and check it periodically. If your electricity goes out, avoid opening the freezer until the power is restored. When the power does come back on, check the temperature on the top shelf. If it is at or below 40°F, the food should still be safe to eat, or refreeze. Food should also be safe if it is still partially frozen or has ice crystals. Discard any food that has been warmer than 40°F for more than 2 hours.[18]

As with refrigeration, smaller packages will freeze more quickly. So rather than attempting to freeze an entire casserole or a whole batch of homemade spaghetti sauce, divide the food into multiple small portions in freezer-safe containers; then freeze.

Sufficient thawing will ensure adequate cooking throughout, which is essential to preventing foodborne illness. Thaw poultry on the bottom shelf of the refrigerator, in a large bowl to catch its juices. **Table 12.3** shows recommended poultry thawing times based on weight. Never thaw frozen meat, poultry, or seafood on a kitchen counter or in a basin of warm water. Room temperatures allow growth of bacteria on the surface of food, although the inside may still be frozen. A microwave is also

TABLE 12.3   A Guide to Thawing Poultry

Method Needed	Size of Poultry	Approximate Length of Time
Refrigerator	1–3 pounds, small chickens, pieces	1 day
	3–6 pounds, large chickens, ducks, small turkeys	2 days
	6–12 pounds, large turkeys	3 days
	12–16 pounds, whole turkey	3–4 days
	16–20 pounds, whole turkey	4–5 days
Microwave (read instructions)	1–3 pounds, small chickens, pieces	8–15 minutes* (standing time 10 minutes)
	3–6 pounds, large chickens, ducks, small turkeys	15–30 minutes* (standing time 20 minutes)

*Approximate, read microwave's instructions.
Note: Turkeys purchased stuffed and frozen with the USDA or state mark of inspection on the packaging are safe because they have been processed under controlled conditions. These turkeys *should not* be thawed before cooking. Follow package directions for safe handling. Data from R. W. Lacey. 1994. Hard to Swallow: A Brief History of Food. Cambridge: Cambridge University Press, pp. 85–187; U.S. Department of Agriculture, Food Safety and Inspection Service. 2000. Turkey Basics: Safe Thawing. www.fsis.usda.gov/Fact_Sheets/Poultry_Preparation_Fact_Sheets/index.asp.

useful for thawing if the food is to be cooked immediately, but be sure to follow your microwave's instructions carefully.

Dealing with Molds in Refrigerated Foods

Have you ever taken cheese out of the refrigerator and noticed that it had a fuzzy, blue growth on it? This is mold, a type of fungus. Some molds like cool temperatures. For instance, when acidic foods, such as leftover applesauce or spaghetti sauce, are refrigerated, they readily support the growth of mold. So how did the mold get into the closed, refrigerated jar? Mold spores are common in the atmosphere, and they randomly land on food in open containers at your home. If the temperature and acidity of the food are hospitable, they will grow.

If the surface of a small portion of a solid food, such as hard cheese, becomes moldy, it is generally safe to cut off that section down to about an inch and eat the unspoiled portion. However, if soft cheese, sour cream, yogurt, tomato sauce, applesauce, or another soft or fluid product becomes moldy, discard it.

Cook Foods Thoroughly

Thoroughly cooking food is a sure way to kill the intestinal worms discussed earlier and many other microorganisms. The appropriate internal temperatures for the doneness of meat, poultry, seafood, and eggs vary **(Figure 12.10)**.

Tips for Cooking Meat, Poultry, Fish, and Eggs

The color of cooked meat can be deceiving. Grilled meat and poultry often brown very quickly on the outside but may not be thoroughly cooked on the inside. The only way to be sure meat is thoroughly cooked is to test it with a food thermometer. Test your food in several places to be sure it has cooked evenly, and remember to wash the thermometer after each use. See the **Game Plan** feature box (page 382) for more tips about grilling and barbequing.

Microwave cooking is convenient, but you need to be sure your food is thoroughly and evenly cooked and that there are no cold spots in the food where bacteria can thrive. For best results, cover food, stir often, and rotate for even cooking.[18] If you are microwaving meat or poultry, use a thermometer to check internal temperatures in several spots, because temperatures vary more in microwave cooking than in conventional ovens.

Raw and semi-raw (such as marinated or partly cooked) fish delicacies, including sushi and sashimi, may be tempting, but their safety cannot be guaranteed. Always cook fish thoroughly. When done, fish should be opaque and flake easily with a fork. If you're wondering how sushi restaurants can guarantee the safety of their food, the short answer is they can't. All fish to be used for sushi must be flash frozen at −31°F (−35°C) or below for 15 hours or be regularly frozen to −4°F (−20°C) or below for 7 days.[19] Although this effectively kills any parasites that are in the fish, it does not kill bacteria or viruses. Thus, eating raw seafood remains risky, and the FDA advises that pregnant women and others at increased risk for foodborne illness avoid it.[20]

You may have memories of licking cake batter off a spoon when you were a kid, but such practices are no longer considered safe. That's because most cake batter contains raw eggs, one of the most common sources of *Salmonella*. Between May and September of 2010, for example, over 1,600 cases of *Salmonella* infection were associated with contaminated eggs.[21] The USDA recommends that you cook eggs until firm. If you are using eggs in a casserole or custard, make sure that the internal temperature reaches at least 160°F.

Protect Yourself from Toxins in Foods

Killing microorganisms with heat is an important step in keeping food safe, but it won't protect you against their toxins. That's because many toxins are unaffected by heat and are capable of causing severe illness even when the microorganisms that produced them have been destroyed. For example, let's say you prepare a casserole for a team picnic. Too bad you forget to wash your hands before serving it

Food Safety and Inspection Service, USDA

Figure 12.10 The United States Department of Agriculture's "Thermy" provides temperature guidelines for safely cooking foods at home.
To visit the Thermy website for current recommendations, see Web Links at the back of this chapter.
Data from www.fsis.usda.gov/oa/thermy/poster.pdf.

GAME PLAN

Food-Safety Tips for Your Next Barbecue

It's the end of the term and you and your friends are planning a lakeside barbecue to celebrate! Here are some tips from the Center for Food Safety and Applied Nutrition at the U.S. Food and Drug Administration for preventing foodborne illness at any outdoor gathering.

☐ **Wash your hands, utensils, and food-preparation surfaces.** Even in outdoor settings, food safety begins with hand washing. Take along a water jug, some soap, and paper towels or a box of moist disposable towelettes. Keep all utensils and platters clean when preparing foods.

☐ **Keep foods cold during transport.** Use coolers with ice or frozen gel packs to keep food at or below 40°F. It's easier to maintain a cold temperature in small coolers.

⬆ At a barbecue, it's essential to heat foods to the proper temperature.

Consider packing three: put beverages in one cooler, washed fruits and vegetables and containers of potato salad in another, and wrapped, frozen meat, poultry, and seafood in another. Keep coolers in the air-conditioned passenger compartment of your car, rather than in a hot trunk.

☐ **Grill foods thoroughly.** Use a food thermometer to be sure the food has reached an adequate internal temperature before serving.

☐ **Avoid cross-contamination.** When taking food from the grill to the table, never use the same platter or utensils that previously held raw meat or seafood!

☐ **Keep hot foods hot.** Keep grilled food hot until it is served by moving it to the side of the grill, just away from the coals, so that it stays at or above 135°F. If grilled food isn't going to be eaten right away, wrap it well and place it in an insulated container.

☐ **Keep cold foods cold.** Cold foods, such as chicken salad, should be kept in a bowl of ice during your barbecue. Drain off water as the ice melts and replace the ice frequently. Don't let any perishable food sit out longer than 2 hours. In temperatures above 90°F, don't let food sit out for more than 1 hour.

Data from U.S. Food and Drug Administration, Center for Food Safety and Applied Nutrition. 2007. Food Facts. Eating Outdoors. Handling Food Safely.

to your teammates, because you contaminate the casserole with the bacterium *Staphylococcus aureus*, which is commonly found on moist skinfolds.[10] You and your friends go off and play soccer, leaving the food in the sun, and a few hours later you take the rest of the casserole home. At supper, you heat the leftovers thoroughly, thinking that this will kill any bacteria that multiplied while it was left out. That night you experience nausea,

 To listen to any of dozens of podcasts on food safety at home, go to www.fsis.usda.gov/News_&_Events/Food_Safety_at_Home_Podcasts/index.asp?src_location=content&src_page=FSEd.

severe vomiting, and abdominal pain. What happened? While your food was left out, the bacteria from your hands multiplied in the casserole and produced a toxin (Figure 12.11). When you reheated the food, you killed the microorganisms, but their toxin was unaffected by the heat. When you then ate the food, the toxin made you sick. Fortunately, in the case of *S. aureus*, symptoms typically resolve on their own in healthy people in about 24 hours.

Be Choosy When Eating Out—
Close to Home or Far Away

When choosing a place to eat out, avoid restaurants that don't look clean. Grimy tabletops and dirty restrooms indicate indifference to hygiene. On the other hand, cleanliness of areas used by the public doesn't guarantee that the kitchen is clean. That is why health inspections are important. Public health inspectors randomly visit and inspect the food-preparation areas of all businesses that serve food, whether

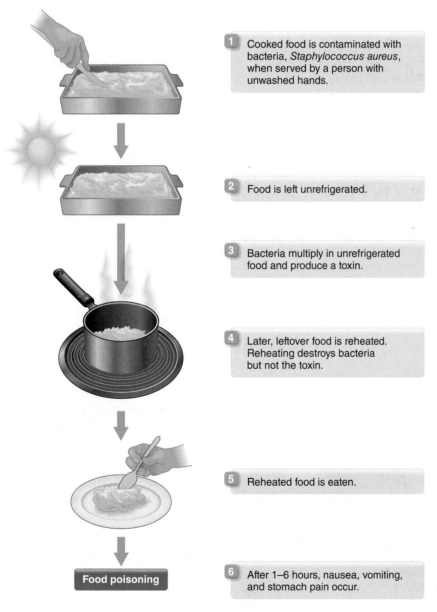

1. Cooked food is contaminated with bacteria, *Staphylococcus aureus*, when served by a person with unwashed hands.

2. Food is left unrefrigerated.

3. Bacteria multiply in unrefrigerated food and produce a toxin.

4. Later, leftover food is reheated. Reheating destroys bacteria but not the toxin.

5. Reheated food is eaten.

Food poisoning

6. After 1–6 hours, nausea, vomiting, and stomach pain occur.

Figure 12.11 Food contamination can occur long after the microorganism itself has been destroyed.

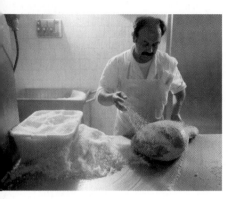

⬆ A worker salting a Parma ham.

eaten in or taken out. You can usually find the results of these inspections by contacting your local health department or by checking the inspection results posted in the restaurant.

Another way to protect yourself when dining out is by ordering foods to be cooked thoroughly. If you order a hamburger and it arrives pink in the middle, or scrambled eggs and they arrive runny, send the food back to be cooked thoroughly.

When planning a trip, tell your physician your travel plans and ask about vaccinations needed or any medications that you should take along in case you get sick. Pack a waterless antibacterial hand cleanser and use it frequently. When dining, select foods and beverages carefully. All raw food has the potential for contamination.

Tap water is seldom a safe option, even if chlorinated, because chlorine doesn't kill all the organisms that can cause disease. In regions where hygiene and sanitation are suspect, consume only canned, bottled, or boiled beverages, such as tea. Ask for drinks without ice, because freezing contaminated water does not kill all microorganisms.

> Find more information about how to ensure food and water safety when traveling by visiting the CDC's website: wwwnc.cdc.gov/travel/content/safe-food-water.aspx.

RECAP Foodborne illness can be prevented at home by following four tips: *Clean*: wash your hands and kitchen surfaces often. *Separate*: isolate foods to prevent cross-contamination. *Chill*: store foods in the refrigerator or freezer. *Cook*: heat foods long enough and at the correct temperatures to ensure proper cooking. When eating out, avoid restaurants that don't look clean, and ask that all food be cooked thoroughly. When traveling, avoid all raw foods unless thoroughly washed in bottled or boiled water, and choose beverages that are boiled, bottled, or canned, without ice.

How Is Food Spoilage Prevented?

processed foods Foods that are manipulated mechanically or chemically.

Any food that has been harvested and that people aren't ready to eat must be preserved in some way or, before long, it will degrade enzymatically and become home to a variety of microorganisms. Even **processed foods**—foods that are manipulated mechanically or chemically—have the potential to spoil.

NUTRI-CASE THEO

"I got really sick yesterday after eating lunch in the cafeteria. I had a turkey sandwich, potato salad, and a cola. A few hours later, in the middle of basketball practice, I started to shake and sweat. I felt really nauseated and barely made it to the bathroom before vomiting. Then I went back to my dorm room and crawled into bed. This morning I still feel a little sick to my stomach, and sort of weak. I asked some of my friends who ate in the cafeteria yesterday if they got sick, and none of them did, but I still think it was the food. I'm going off-campus for lunch from now on!"

Do you think that Theo's illness was foodborne? If so, what food(s) do you most suspect? What do you think of his plan to go off-campus for lunch from now on?

Natural Methods Are Effective in Preserving Foods

The most ancient methods of preserving foods include salting, sugaring, drying, and smoking, all of which draw the water out of the plant or animal cells. By dehydrating the food, these methods make it inhospitable to microorganisms and dramatically slow the action of enzymes that would otherwise degrade the food:

- *Salt* is often used for curing meats and fish. A good example is the Parma ham from Italy, which is cured with sea salt.
- *Sugar* is used to preserve foods such as fruits. Before families had electric refrigerators and freezers, they used sugaring to preserve summer's fruit harvest for winter consumption in the form of jellies and jams.
- *Drying* is used for fruits, herbs, and spices, and the modern technique of *freeze-drying* is used to preserve coffee, tea, and powdered milk.
- For centuries, meats, poultry, and fish would be hung near a campfire or chimney, so that the smoke of the fire permeated the food, drying it. Unfortunately, *smoking* does not guarantee that a food is safe to eat. Contamination of smoked fish, for example, is common.

Another natural method of food preservation is *cooling*, which works by slowing the reproduction of bacteria. Long before the invention of refrigerators, people stored foods in underground cellars, caves, running streams, and even "cold pantries"—north-facing rooms of the house that were kept dark and unheated and often were stocked with ice. The forerunner of our refrigerator, the "ice box," was developed in the early 1800s, and in cities and towns the local "iceman" made rounds, delivering ice to homes.

⬆ Before the modern refrigerator, an "iceman" would deliver ice to homes and businesses.

Technical Advances Have Improved Food Safety

Several techniques have helped food producers preserve the integrity of their products during the days, weeks, and months between harvesting and consumption:

- *Canning.* French inventor Nicolas Appert developed the canning process in the late 1700s. It involves washing and blanching the food, placing it in cans, siphoning out the air, sealing the cans, and then heating them to a very high temperature. Canned food has an average shelf life of at least 2 years from the date of purchase.
- *Pasteurization.* The technique called **pasteurization** exposes a beverage or other food to heat high enough to destroy microorganisms but for a short enough period of time that the taste and quality of the food are not affected. For example, in *flash pasteurization*, milk or other liquids are heated to 162°F (72°C) for 15 seconds.
- **Irradiation** is a process that exposes foods to gamma rays from radioactive metals. Energy from the rays penetrates food and its packaging, killing or disabling microorganisms in the food. The process does not cause foods to become radioactive! A few nutrients, including thiamin and vitamins A, E, and K, are lost, but these losses are also incurred

NUTRITION
MILESTONE

In **1859**, French chemist and microbiologist Louis Pasteur boiled a meat broth in a flask that had a long, slender, curved neck that allowed air, but not dust, access to the broth. The flask remained free of contamination by microorganisms. However, when the neck of the flask was changed so that dust could enter, the broth quickly became contaminated. This experiment disproved a belief held for 2,000 years that life could arise spontaneously from inanimate matter. Just 3 years later, in 1862, Pasteur showed that the growth of microorganisms is responsible for spoiling beverages such as beer, wine, and milk. He heated milk to a very high temperature, theorizing that the heat would kill any microorganisms present. The experiment was a success, and the technique, called pasteurization, bears his name.

⬆ Canning food involves several steps to ensure all microorganisms in the food are killed.

pasteurization A form of sterilization using high temperatures for short periods of time.

irradiation A sterilization process in which food is exposed to gamma rays or high-energy electron beams to kill microorganisms. Irradiation does not impart any radiation to the food being treated.

⬆ **Figure 12.12** The U.S. Food and Drug Administration requires the Radura—the international symbol of irradiated food—to be displayed on all irradiated food sold in the United States.

in conventional processing and preparation. Although irradiated food has been shown to be safe, the FDA requires that all irradiated foods be labeled with a "radura" symbol and a caution against irradiating the food again **(Figure 12.12)**.

- *Aseptic packaging.* You probably know aseptic packaging best as "juice boxes." Food and beverages are first heated, then cooled, then placed in sterile containers. The process uses less energy than traditional canning, and the cartons use less material than any comparable container. By eliminating the need for refrigeration or preservatives, aseptic packaging also reduces subsequent energy use.[22]

- *Modified atmosphere packaging.* In this process, the oxygen in a package of food is replaced with an inert gas, such as nitrogen or carbon dioxide. This prevents a number of chemical reactions that spoil food, and it slows the growth of bacteria that require oxygen. The process can be used with a variety of foods, including meats, fish, vegetables, and fruits.

- *High-pressure processing* is a technique in which the food to be preserved is subjected to an extremely high pressure. This inactivates most bacteria while retaining the food's quality and freshness.

Some cans, plastics, and other types of packaging have been found to contain a chemical called bisphenol A (BPA), which has been linked to certain types of cancer, reproductive system problems, and even heart disease. In 2010, the FDA announced that it was conducting research into BPA and supporting industry efforts to remove it from all packaging. In the meantime, you should avoid carrying, storing, or microwaving foods and liquids in containers with the recycling code 3 or 7.[23]

RECAP Salting, sugaring, drying, smoking, and cooling have been used for centuries to preserve food. Canning, pasteurization, irradiation, and several packaging techniques are used to preserve a variety of foods during shipping, as well as on grocer and consumer shelves.

What Are Food Additives, and Are They Safe?

Have you ever picked up a loaf of bread and started reading its ingredients? You'd expect to see flour, yeast, water, and some sugar, but what are all those other items? They are collectively called *food additives*, and they are in almost every processed food. **Food additives** are not foods in themselves but, rather, natural or synthetic chemicals added to foods to enhance them in some way. More than 3,000 different food additives are currently used in the United States. **Table 12.4** identifies only a few of the most common.

Food Additives Include Nutrients and Preservatives

Vitamins and minerals are added to foods as nutrients and as preservatives. Vitamin E is usually added to fat-based products to keep them from going rancid, and vitamin C is used as an antioxidant in many foods. Iodine is added to table salt to help decrease the incidence of goiter, a condition that causes the thyroid gland to enlarge. Vitamin D is added to milk, and calcium is added to soy milk, rice milk, almond milk, and some juices to help prevent osteoporosis. Folate is added to cereals, breads, and other foods to help prevent certain types of birth defects.

The following two preservatives have raised health concerns:

- *Sulfites.* A small segment of the population is sensitive to sulfites, preservatives used in many beers and wines and some other processed foods. These people can

⬆ Aseptic packaging allows foods to be stored unrefrigerated for several months without spoilage.

food additive A substance or mixture of substances intentionally put into food to enhance its appearance, safety, palatability, and quality.

TABLE 12.4	Examples of Common Food Additives
Food Additive	**Foods Found In**
Coloring Agents	
Beet extract	Beverages, candies, ice cream
Beta-carotene	Beverages, sauces, soups, baked goods, candies, macaroni and cheese mixes
Caramel	Beverages, sauces, soups, baked goods
Tartrazine	Beverages, cakes and cookies, ice cream
Preservatives	
Alpha-tocopherol (vitamin E)	Vegetable oils
Ascorbic acid (vitamin C)	Breakfast cereals, cured meats, fruit drinks
BHA	Breakfast cereals, chewing gum, oils, potato chips
BHT	Breakfast cereals, chewing gum, oils, potato chips
Calcium proprionate/sodium proprionate	Bread, cakes, pies, rolls
EDTA	Beverages, canned shellfish, margarine, mayonnaise, processed fruits and vegetables, sandwich spreads
Propyl gallate	Mayonnaise, chewing gum, chicken soup base, vegetable oils, meat products, potato products, fruits, ice cream
Sodium benzoate	Carbonated beverages, fruit juice, pickles, preserves
Sodium chloride (salt)	Most processed foods
Sodium nitrate/sodium nitrite	Bacon, corned beef, lunch meats, smoked fish
Sorbic acid/potassium sorbate	Cakes, cheese, dried fruits, jellies, syrups, wine
Sulfites (sodium bisulfite, sulfur dioxide)	Dried fruits, processed potatoes, wine
Texturizers, Emulsifiers, and Stabilizers	
Calcium chloride	Canned fruits and vegetables
Carageenan/pectin	Ice cream, chocolate milk, soy milk, frostings, jams, jellies, cheese, salad dressings, sour cream, puddings, syrups
Cellulose gum/guar gum/gum arabic/locust gum/xanthan gum	Soups and sauces, gravies, sour cream, ricotta cheese, ice cream, syrups
Gelatin	Desserts, canned meats
Lecithin	Mayonnaise, ice cream
Humectants	
Glycerin	Chewing gum, marshmallows, shredded coconut
Propylene glycol	Chewing gum, gummy candies

experience asthma, headaches, or other symptoms after eating food containing the offending preservatives.

- *Nitrites.* Commonly used to preserve processed meats, nitrites can be converted to *nitrosamines* during the cooking process. Nitrosamines have been found to be carcinogenic in animals, so the FDA has required all foods with nitrites to contain additional antioxidants to decrease the formation of nitrosamines.

Other Food Additives Include Flavorings, Colorings, and Other Agents

Flavoring agents are used to replace the natural flavors lost during food processing. In contrast, *flavor enhancers* have little or no flavor of their own but accentuate the

↞ Many foods, such as ice cream, contain colorings.

natural flavor of foods. One of the most common flavor enhancers used is monosodium glutamate (MSG). In some people, MSG causes symptoms such as headaches, difficulty breathing, and heart palpitations.

Common food colorings include beet juice, which imparts a red color; beta-carotene, which gives a yellow color; and caramel, which adds brown color. The coloring tartrazine (FD&C Yellow #5) causes an allergic reaction in some people, and its use must be indicated on the product packaging.

Texturizers are added to foods to improve their texture. Emulsifiers help keep fats evenly dispersed within foods. Stabilizers give foods "body" and help them maintain a desired texture or color. Humectants keep foods such as marshmallows, chewing gum, and shredded coconut moist and stretchy. Desiccants prevent moisture absorption from the air; for example, they are used to prevent table salt from forming clumps.[24]

Are Food Additives Safe?

Federal legislation was passed in 1958 to regulate food additives. The Delaney Clause, also enacted in 1958, states, "No additive may be permitted in any amount if tests show that it produces cancer when fed to man or animals or by other appropriate tests." Before a new additive can be used in food, the producer of the additive must demonstrate its safety to the FDA by submitting data on its reasonable safety. The FDA determines the additive's safety based on these data.

Also in 1958, the U.S. Congress recognized that many substances added to foods would not require this type of formal review by the FDA prior to marketing and use, as their safety had already been established through long-term use or because their safety had been recognized by qualified experts through scientific studies. These substances are exempt from the more stringent testing criteria for new food additives and are referred to as substances that are **Generally Recognized as Safe (GRAS).** The GRAS list identifies substances that have either been tested and determined by the FDA to be safe and approved for use in the food industry or are deemed safe as a result of consensus among experts qualified by scientific training and experience.

↞ Mayonnaise contains emulsifiers to prevent separation of fats.

In 1985, the FDA established the Adverse Reaction Monitoring System (ARMS). Under this system, the FDA investigates complaints from consumers, physicians, and food companies about food additives.

Want to look up the unfamiliar ingredients listed on the packages of your favorite foods? Check out the FDA database at www.fda.gov/Food/FoodIngredientsPackaging/GenerallyRecognizedasSafeGRAS/GRASSubstancesSCOGSDatabase/default.htm.

RECAP   Food additives are chemicals intentionally added to foods to enhance their color, flavor, texture, nutrient density, moisture level, or shelf life. Although there is continuing controversy over food additives in the United States, the FDA regulates additives used in our food supply and considers safe those it approves.

How Is Genetic Modification Used in Food Production?

Generally Recognized as Safe (GRAS) List established by Congress to identify substances used in foods that are generally recognized as safe based on a history of long-term use or on the consensus of qualified research experts.

genetic modification The process of changing an organism by manipulating its genetic material.

In **genetic modification,** also referred to as *genetic engineering,* the genetic material, or DNA, of an organism is altered to bring about specific changes in its seeds or offspring. Selective breeding is one example of genetic modification; for example, Brahman cattle, which have poor-quality meat but high resistance to heat and humidity, are bred with English shorthorn cattle, which have good meat but low resistance to heat and humidity. The outcome of this selective breeding process is Santa Gertrudis cattle, which have the desired characteristics of higher-quality meat and resistance to heat and humidity. Although selective breeding is effective and has helped increase crop yields and improve the quality and quantity of our food supply,

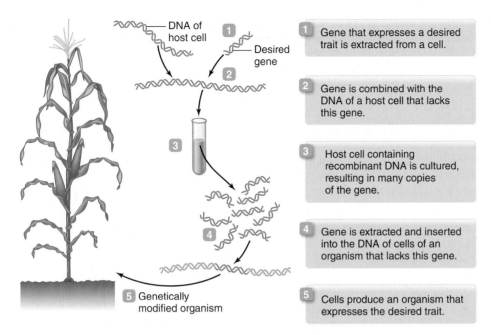

— DNA of host cell
1
— Desired gene
2

3

4

5 Genetically modified organism

1 Gene that expresses a desired trait is extracted from a cell.

2 Gene is combined with the DNA of a host cell that lacks this gene.

3 Host cell containing recombinant DNA is cultured, resulting in many copies of the gene.

4 Gene is extracted and inserted into the DNA of cells of an organism that lacks this gene.

5 Cells produce an organism that expresses the desired trait.

◆ **Figure 12.13** Recombinant DNA technology involves producing plants and other organisms that contain modified DNA, which enables them to express desirable traits that are not present in the original organism.

it is a relatively slow and imprecise process, as a great deal of trial and error typically occurs before the desired characteristics are achieved.

Recently, advances in biotechnology have moved genetic modification beyond selective breeding. These advances include the manipulation of the DNA of living cells of one organism to produce the desired characteristics of a different organism. Called **recombinant DNA technology,** the process commonly begins when scientists isolate from an animal, a plant, or a microbial cell a particular segment of DNA—one or more genes—that codes for a protein conferring a desirable trait, such as salt tolerance in tomato plants **(Figure 12.13).** Scientists then splice the DNA into a "host cell," usually a microorganism. The cell is cultured to produce many copies—a *gene library*—of the beneficial gene. Then, many scientists can readily obtain the gene to modify other organisms that lack the desired trait—for example, traditional tomato plants. The modified DNA causes the plant's cells to build the protein of interest, and the plant expresses the desired trait. The term *genetically modified organism* (*GMO*) refers to any organism in which the DNA has been altered using recombinant DNA technology.

In agriculture, GMOs are used to induce resistance to herbicides and pesticides. For example, genetically modified corn crops can be sprayed with chemicals that kill weeds without harming the corn. Genetic modification can also increase resistance to insects or viruses that cause disease in plants. Scientists can also insert a gene to make crops more tolerant of environmental conditions, such as drought or poor soil. Another use is to increase the nutritional value of a crop. For instance, researchers have modified soybeans and canola to increase their content of monounsaturated fatty acids.

Since 1994, hundreds of plants and animals have been genetically modified and incorporated into our current food market. The U.S. Department of Agriculture reports that 52% of all corn crops and 87% of all soybean crops grown in the United States are genetically engineered varieties.[25]

The relative benefits and harm of genetic modification have been debated worldwide. For information about this debate, see the ***Highlight*** feature box (page 390).

◆ Corn is one of the most widely cultivated genetically modified crops.

RECAP In genetic modification, the genetic material, or DNA, of an organism is altered to enhance certain qualities. In agriculture, genetic modification is often used to improve crop protection or to increase nutrients in the resulting food. Genetic modification is also used in animals and microorganisms.

recombinant DNA technology A type of genetic modification in which scientists combine DNA from different sources to produce a transgenic organism that expresses a desired trait.

HIGHLIGHT

Genetically Modified Organisms: A Blessing or a Curse?

Genetic modification is a process in which entirely new organisms are created by splicing genes from one species into another. Supporters envision an ever-expanding role for genetic modification in food production. The following are just a few of the potential benefits they see resulting from the application of this technology:

- enhanced taste and nutritional quality of food

- crops that grow faster, have higher yields, can be grown in inhospitable soils, and have increased resistance to pests, disease, herbicides, and spoilage

- increased production of high-quality meat, eggs, and milk

- improved animal health due to increased disease resistance and overall hardiness

- environmentally responsible outcomes, such as the use of less harmful herbicides and insecticides; the conservation of soil, water, and energy; and more efficient food processing

- increased food security for countries struggling with food insecurity and starvation

Despite these potential benefits, there is significant opposition to genetic engineering. Detractors cite a wide range of concerns, including the following:

- gene transfer from GM foods to cells of the body or to bacteria in the gastrointestinal tract, which could adversely affect human health; for example, if antibiotic-resistant genes were transferred, susceptibility to infectious disease could increase[26]

- unintentional transfer of genes to nontarget species through cross-pollination, which could result in undesirable plants, such as superweeds that are tolerant to conventional herbicides or a food tainted with nonfood-grade ingredients; the risk of such transfer is real, as was shown when traces of a type of maize that was approved for use only in animal feed appeared in maize products for human consumption in the United States[26]

- loss of biodiversity of plants and animals

- increased risk of either creating a new allergen or causing allergic reactions in susceptible individuals

- development of new diseases that can attack plants, animals, and humans

- production of bacteria that are resistant to all antibiotics

- potential for only a few food companies and countries to control the majority of world food production; for example, the seed industry has become increasingly concentrated as large bioengineering firms have bought up smaller seed companies, then increased seed prices for crops such as corn and soybeans[27]

- inadequate or nonexistent labeling laws that prevent consumers from knowing if they are consuming foods that are genetically modified

- creation of biological weapons and increased risk of bioterrorism

Some who oppose genetic engineering believe that it is unnatural and unethical to alter the genes of any organism. Most opponents base their concern on the fact that the potential long-term risks and dangers are unknown and may far outweigh the potential short-term benefits.

Genetically modified organisms are welcomed in some countries but outlawed in others. Six countries grow almost 100% of the world's genetically modified crops: the United States (59%), Argentina (20%), Canada (6%), Brazil (6%), China (5%), and Paraguay (2%).[28] Even though the United States and Canada are among the top three, regions within these countries have succeeded in banning the production of GMOs. These include several counties in California, including Mendocino, Trinity, and Marin, and the Canadian province of Prince Edward Island.

The European Union (EU) has strict regulations regarding GMOs, including having mechanisms in place to track GMO products through production and distribution chains and to monitor any effect of GMOs on the environment. All foods produced for human consumption and all animal feed products that contain GMOs must be clearly labeled. In addition, any foods that are produced from GMO ingredients must be clearly labeled, even if the final food product does not contain the DNA or protein of the original GMO. Currently, only two biotech crops—corn and potatoes—are approved for cultivation in the EU,[29] and only fifteen genetically modified foods are marketed in the EU. Companies that wish to market GMOs and genetically modified foods in the EU must submit an application that includes a full environmental risk assessment and a safety assessment. This report is then reviewed by the designated government agencies and a decision is made regarding the application.

Do you support the cultivation and distribution of genetically modified foods, both in the United States and around the world? Do you have any reservations about buying and consuming genetically modified foods? As GMOs and genetically modified foods have been available for only a few years, it will take more time to understand their impact on the world.

Many people oppose the genetic engineering of foods for environmental, health, or economic reasons.

Do Residues Harm Our Food Supply?

Food **residues** are chemicals that remain in foods despite cleaning and processing. Three types of residues of global concern are persistent organic pollutants, pesticides, and hormones and antibiotics used in animals. Although residues can cause nerve damage, skin rashes, and other health problems, the most common concern related to residues is an increased risk for cancer.

One of the ways mercury is released into the environment is by burning fossil fuels.

Persistent Organic Pollutants Can Cause Illness

Many different chemicals are released into the atmosphere as a result of industry, agriculture, automobile emissions, and improper waste disposal. These chemicals, collectively referred to as **persistent organic pollutants (POPs),** eventually enter the food supply through the soil or water. If a pollutant gets into the soil, a plant can absorb the chemical into its structure and pass it on as part of the food chain. Animals can also absorb the pollutant into their tissues or consume it when feeding on plants growing in the polluted soil. Fat-soluble pollutants are especially problematic, as they tend to accumulate in the animal's body tissues and are then absorbed by humans when the animal is used as a food source **(Figure 12.14)**.

POP residues have been found in virtually all categories of foods, including baked goods, fruit, vegetables, meat, poultry, fish, and dairy products. It is believed that all living organisms carry a measurable level of POPs in their tissues.[30]

residues Chemicals that remain in the foods we eat despite cleaning and processing.

persistent organic pollutants (POPs) Chemicals released into the environment as a result of industry, agriculture, or improper waste disposal; automobile emissions also are considered POPs.

Mercury and Lead Are Nerve Toxins

Mercury, a naturally occurring element, is found in soil, rocks, and water. It is also released into the air by pulp and paper processing and the burning of garbage and

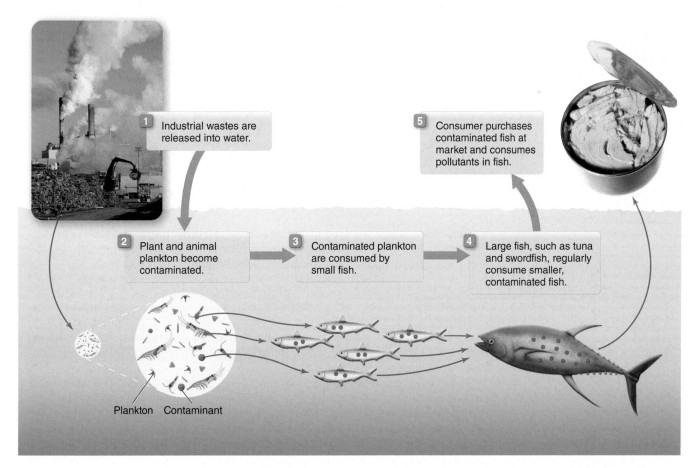

1 Industrial wastes are released into water.

5 Consumer purchases contaminated fish at market and consumes pollutants in fish.

2 Plant and animal plankton become contaminated.

3 Contaminated plankton are consumed by small fish.

4 Large fish, such as tuna and swordfish, regularly consume smaller, contaminated fish.

Plankton   Contaminant

Figure 12.14   Bioaccumulation of persistent organic pollutants in the food supply.

⬆ Antique porcelain is often coated with lead-based glaze.

fossil fuels. As mercury falls from the air, it finds its way to streams, rivers, lakes, and the ocean, where it accumulates. Fish absorb mercury as they feed on aquatic organisms, and this mercury is passed on to us when we consume the fish. As mercury accumulates in the body, it has a toxic effect on the nervous system.

Large predatory fish, such as swordfish, shark, King mackerel, and tilefish, tend to contain the highest levels of mercury.[31] Because mercury is especially toxic to the developing nervous system of fetuses and growing children, pregnant and breastfeeding women and young children are advised to avoid eating these types of fish. Canned tuna, salmon, cod, pollock, sole, shrimp, mussels, and scallops do not contain high levels of mercury and are safe to consume; however, the FDA recommends that pregnant women and young children eat no more than two servings (12 oz) per week of any type of fish.[31]

Lead can also be found naturally in the soil, water, and air. It also occurs as industrial waste from leaded gasoline, lead-based paints, and lead-soldered cans, now outlawed but decomposing in landfills. Some ceramic mugs and other dishes are fired with lead-based glaze. Thus, residues can build up in foods. Excessive lead exposure can cause learning and behavioral impediments in children and cardiovascular and kidney disease in adults.

Dioxins Are Carcinogens

Dioxins are industrial pollutants typically formed as a result of combustion processes, such as waste incineration or the burning of wood, coal, or oil. There is concern that long-term exposure to dioxins can result in an increased risk for cancer and other disorders.[32] Dioxins enter the soil and can persist in the environment for years. Thus, even though dioxin levels have been declining for the last 30 years, largely as a result of increased regulation, some of the dioxins emitted decades ago will still be in the environment years from now. Because dioxins easily accumulate in the fatty tissues of animals, over 95% of dioxin exposure in humans occurs through dietary intake of animal fats.[32] The Environmental Protection Agency (EPA) is working to further reduce levels of all types of dioxins.

Pesticides Protect Against Crop Losses

Pesticides are a family of chemicals used in both fields and farm storage areas to decrease the destruction and crop losses caused by weeds, animals, insects, and fungi. Pesticides also help reduce the potential spread of disease by decreasing the level of microorganisms on crops. They increase overall crop yield and allow for greater crop diversity. The three most common types of pesticides used in food production are

- *herbicides,* which are used to control weeds and other unwanted plant growth,
- *insecticides,* which are used to control insects that can infest crops, and
- *fungicides,* which are used to control plant-destroying fungal growth.

Some pesticides used today are naturally derived and/or have a low impact on the environment. These include **biopesticides,** which are species-specific and work to suppress a pest's population, not eliminate it. For example, pheromones are a biopesticide that disrupts insect mating by attracting males into traps. Biopesticides also do not leave residues on crops—most degrade rapidly and are easily washed away with water.

In contrast, pesticides made from petroleum-based products can leave residues on foods. The liver is responsible for detoxifying these chemicals. But if the liver is immature, as in a fetus, an infant, or a child, or is stressed by disease or other toxins, such as excessive alcohol, then it cannot effectively remove pesticide residues. These residues have the potential to accumulate and cause nerve damage, cancer, birth defects, and other problems. It is therefore essential to wash all produce carefully.

> For a guide to safe seafood consumption, download the Natural Resources Defense Council's wallet card at www.nrdc.org/health/effects/mercury/walletcard.PDF.

pesticides Chemicals used either in the field or in storage to decrease destruction by predators or disease.

biopesticides Primarily insecticides, these chemicals use natural methods to reduce damage to crops.

The EPA is responsible for regulating the labeling, sale, distribution, use, and disposal of all pesticides in the United States. Before a pesticide can be accepted by the EPA for use, it must be determined that it performs its intended function with minimal impact to the environment. Once the EPA has certified a pesticide, states can set their own regulations for its use. The following are some tips from the EPA for reducing your level of exposure to pesticides:[33]

- Wash and scrub all fresh fruits and vegetables thoroughly under running water.
- Peel fruits and vegetables whenever possible, and discard the outer leaves of leafy vegetables, such as cabbage and lettuce. Trim the excess fat from meat and remove the skin from poultry and fish because some pesticide residues collect in the fat.
- Eat a variety of foods from various sources, as this can reduce the risk of exposure to a single pesticide.
- Consume more organically grown foods.
- If you garden, avoid using fertilizers and pesticides to keep these chemicals out of your groundwater as well as your foods.
- Filter your tap water, whether it comes from a municipal water system or a well, to reduce your exposure to pesticides, fertilizers, and other contaminants.

For a list of the "Dirty Dozen"—the twelve foods most likely to contain high levels of pesticide residue—go to the Environmental Working Group's website and download its Shopper's Guide to Pesticides at www .foodnews.org/walletguide.php.

Growth Hormones and Antibiotics Are Used in Animals

Introduced in the U.S. food supply in 1994, **recombinant bovine growth hormone (rBGH)** is a genetically engineered growth hormone. It is used in beef herds to induce animals to grow more muscle tissue and less fat. It is also injected into a third of U.S. dairy cows to increase milk output.

Although the FDA has allowed the use of rBGH in the United States, both Canada and the European Union have banned its use for two reasons:

- The available evidence shows an increased risk for mastitis (inflamed udders), in dairy cows injected with rBGH.[34] Farmers treat mastitis with antibiotics, promoting the development of strains of pathogenic bacteria that are resistant to antibiotics.
- The milk of cows receiving rBGH has higher levels of a hormone called insulin-like growth factor (IGF-1). This hormone can pass into the bloodstream of humans who drink milk from cows that receive rBGH, and some studies have shown that an elevated level of IGF-1 in humans may increase the risk for certain cancers. However, the evidence from these studies is inconclusive.[34]

The American Cancer Society suggests that more research is needed to help better appraise these health risks. In the meantime, consumer concerns about rBGH have caused a significant decline in sales of milk from cows treated with rBGH.[34]

Antibiotics are used not only in dairy cows but also in other animals raised for food. For example, they are routinely added to the feed of swine to reduce the number of disease outbreaks in overcrowded pork-production facilities. Many researchers are concerned that cows, pigs, and other animals treated with antibiotics are becoming significant reservoirs for the development of a particularly virulent antibiotic-resistant strain of bacteria known as methicillin-resistant *Staphylococcus aureus* (MRSA).[35] Infection with MRSA can cause symptoms ranging from a "flesh-eating" skin rash to death: the CDC reports that, in 2005, MRSA was responsible for more than 18,000 deaths in the United States.[36] In a study conducted on hog farms in Illinois and Iowa, 100% of the swine aged 9 and 12 weeks tested positive for MRSA, and the prevalence among their workers was 64%.[35]

You can reduce your exposure to antibiotics, growth hormones, and toxic runoff from livestock feedlots by choosing organic eggs, milk, yogurt, and cheeses and by eating free-range meat from animals raised without the use of these chemicals. You can also reduce your risk by eating vegetarian and vegan meals more often.

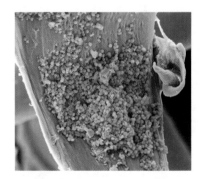

The resistant strain of bacteria responsible for methicillin-resistant *Staphylococcus aureus* (MRSA).

recombinant bovine growth hormone (rBGH) A genetically engineered hormone injected into dairy cows to enhance their milk output.

RECAP Persistent organic pollutants (POPs) of concern include mercury, lead, and dioxins. Pesticides are used to prevent or reduce food crop losses but are potential toxins; therefore, it is essential to wash all produce carefully. Use of recombinant bovine growth hormone (rBGH) and antibiotics raises concerns about bovine and human health.

What's Behind the Rising "Food Movement"?

In 1993, four children in Washington State died after eating fast-food hamburgers contaminated with *E. coli*. Though certainly not the first food-safety incident to capture public attention, it marked a turning point, after which Americans increasingly questioned the assumption that all of our food is always entirely safe to eat. A national debate about food safety and food politics began; a series of investigative news articles, books, and films explored not only the health risks but also the environmental and social costs of contemporary methods of food production. Advocates for public health, animal welfare, farmland preservation, the rights of farmworkers, and environmental quality all came together in a common cause. The food movement was born. Although a comprehensive discussion of the food movement isn't possible here, let's take a brief look at some of its most recognizable aspects.

Organic Agriculture Reduces the Use of Pesticides

The term *organic* describes foods that are grown without the use of toxic and persistent fertilizers and pesticides, genetic engineering, or irradiation. A recent national survey indicates that approximately 3.5% of all food products sold in the United States are now organic. Between 1990 and 2008, sales of organic products in the United States skyrocketed from $1 billion to $23 billion.[37]

To Be Labeled Organic, Foods Must Meet Federal Standards

In 2002, the National Organic Program (NOP) of the USDA established organic standards that provide uniform definitions for all organic products. Any product claiming to be organic must comply with the following definitions:

- *100% organic:* products containing only organically produced ingredients, excluding water and salt
- *organic:* products containing 95% organically produced ingredients by weight, excluding water and salt, with the remaining ingredients consisting of those products not commercially available in organic form
- *made with organic ingredients:* a product containing more than 70% organic ingredients

If a processed product contains less than 70% organically produced ingredients, then those products cannot use the term *organic* in the principal display panel, but ingredients that are organically produced can be specified on the ingredients statement on the information panel. Products that are "100% organic" and "organic" may display the USDA organic seal (**Figure 12.15**).

Farms certified as organic must pass an inspection by a government-approved certifier who verifies that the farmer is following all USDA organic standards.[38] Organic farming methods are strict and require farmers to find natural alternatives to many common problems, such as weeds and insects. Contrary to common belief, organic farmers can use pesticides as a final option for pest control when all other methods have failed or are known to be ineffective, but they are restricted to a limited number that have been approved for use. Organic farmers emphasize the use of renewable resources and the conservation of soil and water. Once a crop is harvested, a winter crop (usually a legume) is planted to help fix nitrogen in the soil and decrease erosion, which also lessens the need for fertilizers.

Figure 12.15 The USDA organic seal identifies foods that are at least 95% organic.

FOODS YOU DON'T KNOW YOU LOVE YET

Tofu

If you're a vegetarian, you probably eat tofu several times a week. If not, you're in for a pleasant surprise. Tofu is made by coagulating soy milk, forming curds, so it's 100% plant food, yet it provides 9 grams of protein per 4 oz serving, making it a nutritious substitute for meat. What's more, tofu is free from the dioxins, hormones, and antibiotics that can exist as residues in animal-based foods. In addition, it's highly versatile to prepare (it can be baked, braised, broiled, etc.), and very tasty! Tofu serves as the backbone of many delicious Chinese dishes, as just one example, and its smooth natural flavor works well with many different spices and sauces.

You can find tofu in almost any market, and a quick Internet search will reveal thousands of ways to prepare it. Or buy a four-pack of frozen, ready-made tofu burgers. Add veggies and a whole-grain bun for a high-protein, low-fat, residue-free meal!

Organic meat, poultry, eggs, and dairy products come from animals fed only organic feed, and if the animals become ill, they are removed from the others until well again. None of these animals are given growth hormones to increase their size or ability to produce milk.

Studies Comparing Organic and Conventionally Grown Foods Are Limited

Over the past decade, several studies indicated that some organically grown fruits and vegetables are higher in vitamins E and C and in certain antioxidant phytochemicals than their non-organic counterparts.[39-41] However, a 2009 systematic review of 162 studies published from 1958 through 2008 found no nutritional superiority of organically produced foods over foods conventionally produced. The study's lead author concluded that there is currently no evidence to support the selection of organic foods for nutritional superiority.[42] Still, you might decide to choose organic produce if you are concerned about reducing your exposure to pesticides.

Sustainable Agriculture Preserves Natural Resources

According to the EPA, one definition of **sustainability** is the ability to meet, or satisfy, basic economic, social, and security needs now and in the future without undermining the natural resource base and environmental quality on which life depends.[43] Whereas some people view sustainability as a lofty but impractical ideal, others point out that it's a necessary condition of human survival. Notice that organic farms typically practice sustainable agriculture. The following are a few more examples of the many ways that individuals, communities, and corporations are putting sustainability into practice:

- *Family farms.* The number of farms in the United States is increasing for the first time in decades. The USDA's most recent Census of Agriculture showed a 4% increase in the number of farms between 2002 and 2007—a net increase of more than 75,000 farms.[44] And many of the new farmers are young adults taking advantage of programs offering land, financial support, and mentoring.
- *Community supported agriculture (CSA).* In CSA programs, a farmer sells a certain number of "shares" to the public. Shares typically consist of

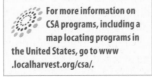 For more information on CSA programs, including a map locating programs in the United States, go to www.localharvest.org/csa/.

sustainability The ability to meet or satisfy basic economic, social, and security needs now and in the future without undermining the natural resource base and environmental quality on which life depends.

a box of produce from the farm on a regular basis, such as once weekly through-out the growing season. Farmers get cash early on, as well as guaranteed buy-ers. Consumers get fresh, locally grown food. Together, farmers and consumers develop ongoing relationships as they share the bounty in a good year, as well as the losses when weather extremes or blight reduces yield. Although there is no national database on CSA programs, the organization LocalHarvest lists over 4,000.[45]

- *Farmers' markets.* There are now more than 6,000 farmers' markets in the United States, more than double the number 10 years ago.[46] Along with CSAs, farmers' markets represent a growing trend toward the consumption of "local food"—that is, food grown within a few hundred miles of the consumer. Supporters claim that consuming local food limits energy use and greenhouse gas emissions from trans-portation (so-called food miles) and that these foods are fresher and nutritionally superior. Although researchers agree that the lowest environmental impact is associated with consuming foods harvested in-season from a local farm, this is not possible year-round in the many regions of the world with short growing seasons. In such cases, the resource costs of both greenhouse cultivation and long-term storage of foods may exceed the energy costs of transported foods.[47]

> Find a farmers' market near you! Go to the USDA's Farmers' Market Search page at http://apps.ams.usda.gov/FarmersMarkets/Default.aspx.

- *Urban agriculture.* Urban agriculture is on the rise. From Pittsburgh to San Francisco, city governments are changing zoning codes to encourage the cultiva-tion of vegetable gardens on rooftops, in abandoned parking lots, and even as part of the landscaping on municipal properties.[48]
- *Corporate involvement.* Whereas many smaller natural-food companies have long made sustainable agriculture part of their company identity, only recently has the food movement moved into corporate America. In 2010, the world's largest retailer, Walmart, unveiled a set of global sustainable agriculture goals the com-pany intends to reach by the year 2015. Those goals include selling $1 billion in foods from small and mid-size local farms and providing training in sustainable farming practices to 1 million farmers.[49] In early 2011, McDonald's Corporation announced its own new sustainable agriculture commitment, and other retailers and restaurant chains are expected to follow suit.

Public health experts point out that these efforts to promote sustainability also have the potential to reduce the number of so-called food deserts—areas such as some inner-city neighborhoods and isolated rural regions where people lack access to affordable, nutritious food.

RECAP The USDA regulates organic farming standards and inspects and certifies farms that follow all USDA organic standards. The USDA organic seal identifies foods that are at least 95% organic. The goal of sustainable agriculture initia-tives, such as community supported agriculture and farmers' markets, is to satisfy food needs without depleting natural resources or environmental quality.

Malnutrition Is a Global Concern

Malnutrition is a state of poor nutritional health. It includes deficiencies of one or more nutrients, such as protein or iron, as well as *undernutrition*, an inadequate intake of energy. In some parts of the world, undernutrition is *endemic* (common throughout a region for many years) because of wars, floods, droughts, or farming practices that make widespread crop failure common. Chronically undernourished adults and children appear wasted, with a low body weight for their height. In addi-tion, they are often shorter than would be expected for their age, a condition known as stunting. In some impoverished regions, entire populations can be both wasted and stunted.

malnutrition A state of poor nutritional health.

Malnutrition Occurs in the Absence of Food Security

Malnutrition is more likely to develop in people who lack **food security**—that is, daily access to food with enough energy and nutrient quality to support a healthy, active life. The food is available because the people grow it themselves or because they have enough money to buy it from a vendor accessible to them. In 2009, food security was enjoyed by 85.3% of the U.S. population **(Figure 12.16)**; most individuals in developed nations enjoy food security.[50]

In contrast, 14.7% of Americans experienced food insecurity in 2009. As shown in Figure 12.16, 9% had *low food security*; that is, they were uncertain of having or being able to acquire enough food to meet their needs. Another 5.7% experienced *very low food security*, meaning that they lacked enough food to meet the energy needs of one or more household members.[50] In 2009, over 12 million adults and 5 million children lived in homes with very low food security. Families consisting of a single mother with children are most at risk: in 2009, over 36% of these families experienced food insecurity.[50] Other at-risk groups in the United States are the homeless, the unemployed, migrant laborers, and other unskilled workers in minimum-wage jobs.

These statistics are disheartening, but food insecurity is even more prevalent— and more severe—worldwide. The Food and Agriculture Organization of the United Nations (FAO) estimates that, in 2009, more than 1 billion of the world's people were not just food insecure but undernourished and hungry.[51] The FAO described the situation in developing nations a crisis **(Figure 12.17)**: all but about 15 million of the world's chronically hungry people live in the developing world.[51]

Food-insecure households (14.7%)

Households with low food security (9.0%)

Households with very low food security (5.7%)

Food-secure households (85.3%)

U.S. households by food security status, 2009

Figure 12.16 Food security status of U.S. households in 2009.
Data from Economic Research Service (ERS), using data from the 2009 Current Population Survey Food Security Supplement. www.ers.gov/Briefing/FoodSecurity/food_security_2009_ers.jpg.

Several Factors Contribute

For most of us, the words *world hunger* tend to conjure up images of **famine**—widespread food shortage—caused by natural disasters, such as flood or drought. It's true that such disasters can destroy substantial amounts of local crops in a short time, resulting in hunger. But many other factors also contribute, including the following:

- *Overpopulation.* When resources such as fertile land or irrigation systems are insufficient to support the number of people living in a region, food shortages may be common.

food security A situation in which a person has daily access to a supply of safe foods with enough energy and sufficiently rich nutrient quality to promote a healthy, active life.

famine A widespread and severe food shortage that causes starvation and death in a large portion of a population in a region.

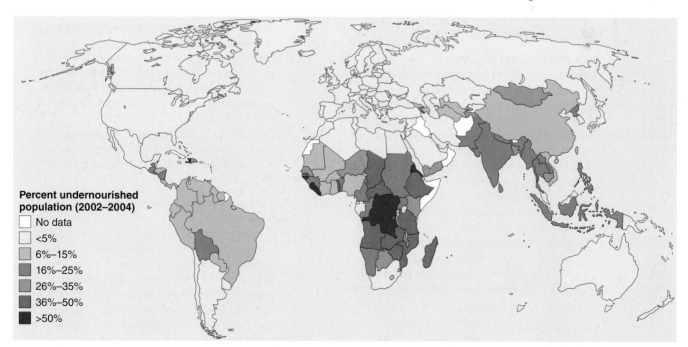

Percent undernourished population (2002–2004)
- No data
- <5%
- 6%–15%
- 16%–25%
- 26%–35%
- 36%–50%
- >50%

Figure 12.17 Undernutrition is most prevalent in parts of sub-Saharan Africa and Southeast Asia.

From "Undernourished Population (2002–2004)" by the Food and Agriculture Organization of the United Nations. Copyright © 2004 by the Food and Agricultural Organiztion of the United Nations. Reprinted by permission.

90% 🔋

WHAT ABOUT YOU?

Do Your Actions Contribute to Global Food Security?

Have you ever wondered whether your actions inadvertently contribute to the problem of world hunger? Or whether any efforts you make in your home or community can help feed people thousands of miles away? If so, you might want to reflect on your behaviors in each of three roles you play every day: consumer, student, and citizen of the world.

In your role as a Consumer, ask yourself:

☐ **What kinds of food products do I buy?**
Your purchases influence the types of foods that are manufactured and sold, and buying fewer processed foods saves energy.

1. Choose fresh, locally grown, organic foods more often to support local sustainability.
2. Choose whole or less processed versions of packaged foods (such as peanut butter made solely from ground peanuts or plain yogurt from a local dairy), rather than versions of foods made with high-fructose corn syrup, dyes, and other additives. This encourages increased production of the less processed foods.
3. Limit purchases of nutrient-poor foods and beverages to discourage their profitability. Also limit high-Calorie fast-food meals.

☐ **How often do I eat vegetarian?**
Vegetarian foods can be produced with less energy than animal-based foods; plus, livestock production contributes much higher levels of greenhouse gases to the environment. So every time you eat vegetarian, you save global energy and contribute to reductions in global warming.

1. Experiment with some recipes in a vegetarian cookbook. Try making at least one new vegetarian meal each week.
2. Introduce friends and family members to your new vegetarian dishes.
3. When eating out, choose restaurants that provide vegetarian menu choices. If the campus cafeteria or a favorite restaurant has no vegetarian choices, request that one or more be added to the menu.

☐ **How much do I eat?**
Eating just the Calories you need to maintain a healthy weight provides more of the global harvest for others and will likely reduce your use of limited medical resources.

1. To raise your consciousness about the physical experience of hunger, consider fasting for 1 day. If health or other reasons prevent you from fasting safely, try keeping silent during each meal throughout 1 day, so that you can more fully appreciate the food you're eating and reflect on those who do not enjoy food security.
2. For 1 week, keep track of how much food you throw away, and why. Do you put more food on your plate than you can eat? Do you allow foods stored in your refrigerator to spoil?

In your role as a Student, ask yourself:

☐ **How can I use what I have learned about nutrition to help feed my neighbors and the world?**

1. Join the National Student Campaign Against Hunger and Homelessness. If your campus doesn't have a branch, start one!
2. Research what local produce is available in each season. Write an article for your school newspaper, listing what is in season each month of the year and include two healthy, low-cost recipes using vegetables and fruits that are in season during the month your article will be published.
3. Create an entertaining skit or puppet show that encourages young children to eat healthful foods. Offer to entertain on the weekends at your local library, day-care center, or after-school community program.
4. Begin or join a food cooperative, community garden, or shared farming program. Donate a portion of your produce each week to a local food pantry.

☐ **What careers could I consider to promote global food security?**

1. If you are interested in teaching, you could become a member of the Peace Corps and teach nutrition in developing countries. If you want to teach in the United States, see the Feeding Minds Fighting Hunger website (listed in Web Links) for information on teaching young people about global nutrition.
2. If you are interested in science, you could help develop higher-yielding crops, better irrigation methods, or projects to improve food or water safety.

3. If you plan a career in business, you could enter the food industry and help market healthful, affordable foods.
4. If you pursue a career in healthcare, you could join an international medical corps working among the poor.

In your role as a World Citizen, ask yourself:

☐ **How can I improve the nutrition of people in my own community?**
   1. You can volunteer at a local soup kitchen, homeless shelter, food bank, or community garden.
   2. To combat obesity in your community, you can help increase opportunities for physical activity. Start a walking group, or volunteer to coach children in your favorite sport.

☐ **How can I improve the nutrition of people in developing nations?**
   1. Donate time or money to one of the international agencies that work to provide relief from famine or chronic hunger. Check out options for charitable contributions and volunteer efforts at www.charitynavigator.org.
   2. Research the global effects of protectionist agricultural subsidies in the United States and Europe; then write letters to your school or community newspaper, your elected officials, and political action groups, expressing your concerns.
   3. Research the human rights records of international food companies whose products you buy. If you don't like what you find out, switch brands and write to the company and tell them why you did.
   4. Vote for elected officials who support policies that help impoverished Americans and promote agricultural equity around the world.

- *War.* Famine is often a product of war, which can drive people from their homes, interfere with planting or harvesting, or interrupt transportation of food when roads, bridges, or rail lines are blocked or destroyed by explosives.
- *Poor farming practices.* Traditional farming methods, such as growing the same crop year after year, can deplete the soil of nutrients and reduce crop yield. The use of land for cash crops, such as cotton or tobacco, reduces the land available for food crops.
- *Lack of infrastructure.* Many developing countries lack roads and rail lines for transporting food to rural areas, as well as electricity for refrigeration to store foods.
- *Impact of disease.* People who are ill are less able to work their own land or keep a job that would provide cash to buy food. For example, the AIDS epidemic has devastated families and communities, increasing the risk for chronic hunger in many developing regions.
- *Unequal distribution.* The world produces a surplus of food. Unequal distribution of that food occurs because of poverty, as well as cultural biases that favor males, young adults, or particular ethnic or religious groups.

What Can Be Done?

To combat malnutrition and achieve global food security, long-term solutions are critical. We discuss some of the most effective here.

Global Solutions

Among the most important long-term solutions for improving the survival and health of children worldwide are programs that encourage breastfeeding. This is because breast milk provides optimal nutrition for the newborn and contains antibodies that protect against infections, including infectious diarrhea. In contrast, feeding infants with formula increases the infant's risk for diarrhea if the powder is mixed with

An Indian farmer inspects what is left of his crop during a drought.

unsanitary water. The World Health Organization (WHO) sponsors programs to encourage breastfeeding throughout the developing world.

Campaigns to increase the immunization of children are also helping reduce the rate of infectious disease in children worldwide. At the same time, supplying local health agencies with oral rehydration therapy, a simple solution of fluids and electrolytes that can be administered to children with diarrhea, is helping reduce deaths from dehydration.

Many international organizations help improve the nutrient status of the poor by enabling them to produce their own foods. For example, both USAID and the Peace Corps have agricultural education programs, the World Bank provides loans to fund small business ventures, and many nonprofit and nongovernmental organizations support community and family farms. Many international programs provide training and support in methods of sustainable agriculture.

Local Solutions

In the United States, several government programs help low-income citizens acquire food over extended periods of time. Among these are the Supplemental Nutrition Assistance Program (SNAP—commonly referred to as food stamps), which helps low-income individuals of all ages; the Special Supplemental Nutrition Program for Women, Infants, and Children (WIC), which helps pregnant women and children up to age 5; the National School Lunch and National School Breakfast Programs, which help low-income schoolchildren; and the Summer Food Service Program, which helps low-income children during the summer.

The U.S. Department of Agriculture also sponsors programs to distribute emergency foods and surplus commodity foods to qualifying families. Foods may be distributed through charitable organizations or local or county agencies. Another USDA program, called Harvest for the Hungry, supports *gleaning*—a practice of gathering the fruits and vegetables remaining in orchards and fields after harvesting. Many local groups also practice gleaning and distribute the foods to area food pantries.

Get Involved!

Several times each year, college students from hundreds of campuses all over the United States gather to fight hunger. Members of the National Student Campaign Against Hunger and Homelessness, they hold Hunger Clean-Ups, staff relief agencies, solicit donations of food and money, and promote community activism. Their organization is just one of dozens in which you can get involved. For more information, see Web Links at the end of this chapter. In addition, the **What About You?** feature box (page 398) challenges you to find out how your actions affect global food security.

RECAP Food security is daily access to a supply of adequate, safe, and nutritious food. Although the world produces a surplus of food, almost 15% of American households experience food insecurity, and about 1 billion people throughout the world experience undernutrition and hunger. Strategies for relieving malnutrition include international, national, and private efforts.

HEALTHWATCH

What Diseases Commonly Result from Malnutrition?

Malnutrition can cause a wide variety of disorders. Of these, some of the most common are the following:

- *Infection.* Malnutrition and nutrient deficiency make children more vulnerable to fatal infections. In impoverished nations, pneumonia and infectious diarrhea are the leading causes of death among children under 5 years of age.[52] Malnutrition reduces a child's general health and immune resistance, increasing the likelihood that the child will not survive infection. On the other hand, infections exacerbate malnutrition by decreasing appetite and causing vomiting and diarrhea. A vicious cycle of malnutrition, infection, worsening malnutrition, and increased vulnerability to infection develops. Infection also increases the mortality rate of women during childbirth, as well as their newborns. In 2009, infant-mortality rates varied from 5 per 1,000 in developed nations to 84 per 1,000 in developing nations where malnutrition is endemic.[53]

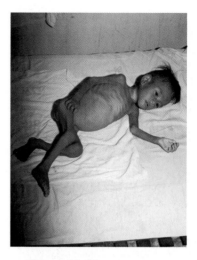

- *Marasmus* is a disease of children that results from grossly inadequate food intake **(Figure 12.18)**. Essentially, children with marasmus starve to death. These children have anemia, minimal fat stores, and severe muscle wasting. Over time, they experience stunting, as well as impaired brain development. Their weakened immune systems make them vulnerable to death from infectious disease. Other causes of death include dehydration and heart failure from a weakened heart muscle.

⬆ **Figure 12.18** Marasmus results from a grossly inadequate intake of energy and other nutrients.

- *Kwashiorkor* is a protein-deficiency disease of toddlers who have recently been weaned because a sibling has been born and is monopolizing breastfeeding **(Figure 12.19)**. Typically, the breast milk is replaced with a watery, cereal-based porridge with inadequate amounts of poor-quality protein and marginal amounts of total energy. The low level of protein in the child's blood is inadequate to keep fluids from seeping into the tissue spaces, and the child develops edema. This can make a child with kwashiorkor appear adequately nourished. The child's belly may also be swollen because of intestinal parasites. The child experiences severe wasting of muscle tissue, becomes inactive and apathetic, has little appetite, and easily succumbs to infection.

- *Night blindness* is caused by a lack of sufficient vitamin A in the diet. When the deficiency continues, permanent blindness results. Because vitamin A is also critical for immune function, about half of affected children die of infection within a year of becoming blind.

⬆ **Figure 12.19** Kwashiorkor occurs in toddlers denied breast milk and fed a watery cereal that provides inadequate protein.

- *Iron-deficiency anemia.* Iron deficiency is the world's most common nutrient deficiency. The WHO estimates that more than 30% of the world's population is anemic due to inadequate iron intake.[54] Malaria and worm infections also contribute to iron deficiency. Because iron deficiency affects so many people—increasing the risk for infection, premature birth, and low birth weight; rendering children less able to learn; impairing the ability of adults to work; and increasing the likelihood that women will die in childbirth—it is a global public health problem of unparalleled importance.

- *Iodine deficiency.* The most common cause of preventable brain damage in children is low iodine intake during the mother's pregnancy and the early childhood years.[55] Since 1993, the WHO has been leading a worldwide public health drive to iodize salt. This effort has halved the number of countries with endemic iodine deficiency; however, 54 countries are still iodine deficient.[55]

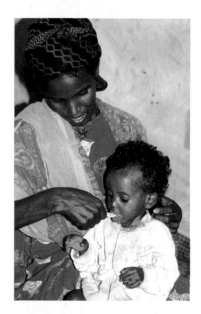

In addition to these disorders, chronic diseases such as heart disease and type 2 diabetes are increasing in developing nations as well as in those—such as Brazil, India, and China—transitioning out of poverty. As we have discussed throughout this book, overweight and obesity are risk factors for these diseases. As an increasing percentage of the population becomes food secure, there is a greater variety and abundance of high-Calorie food, including more high-fat, high-sugar, processed food. At the same time, the population has greater access to motorized transportation and labor-saving devices, as well as sedentary forms of entertainment. These trends have combined to contribute to an alarming increase in the prevalence of obesity and associated chronic diseases. The WHO estimates that in developing nations 115 million people now suffer from obesity-related disease.[56]

⬆ In developing nations, providing vitamin A supplements to children under age 5 has significantly reduced mortality.

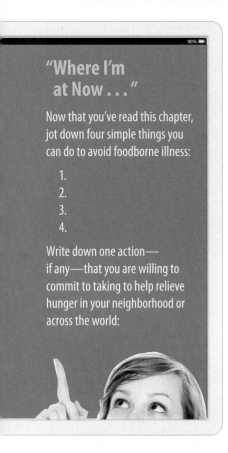

⬆ Overnutrition is becoming a global concern now that low-cost,
energy-dense foods are becoming widely available.

RECAP Malnutrition increases the risk for infection, the primary cause of death in undernourished children. Marasmus is a disease of children that results from grossly inadequate intakes of all nutrients, whereas kwashiorkor is linked to inadequate protein intake. Vitamin A deficiency causes permanent blindness and increased vulnerability to infection. Iron deficiency increases the risk for infection, impaired development, and premature death, and iodine deficiency can cause brain damage. Developing nations are also beginning to experience an epidemic of obesity.

COOKING 101

An important part of developing healthful habits is understanding the essentials of food handling and basic techniques for keeping a well-run kitchen! Learn more about safe food preparation, handling and clean-up tips in our new Cooking 101 videos, available on the Companion Website at **www.pearsonhighered .com/thompsonmanore**.

Chapter Review

What Can I Do **Today?**

Now that you've read this chapter, try making these three changes.

- Before every meal, whether you're preparing it yourself or eating out, wash your hands!

- Tape a copy of Figure 12.9 onto your fridge; then throw out any leftovers that are no longer safe to eat.

- Take a donation of cash or canned goods to your local food bank.

Test Yourself ANSWERS

1. **(F)** Freezing destroys some microorganisms but only inhibits the ability of other microorganisms to reproduce. When the food is thawed, these cold-tolerant microorganisms resume reproduction.

2. **(F)** A majority of cases of foodborne illness are caused by just one species of virus, called norovirus. Bacteria also commonly cause foodborne illness.

3. **(T)** Although some studies have found higher levels of vitamins E and C and certain antioxidant phytochemicals

in organic foods, there are not enough studies published on this topic to state with confidence that organic foods are consistently more nutritious than non-organic foods.

4. **(T)** In both 2008 and 2009, the last 2 years for which research is available, nearly 15% of Americans experienced food insecurity.

5. **(F)** Iron deficiency is the most common nutrient deficiency in the world, affecting more than 30% of the world's population.

Review Questions

1. The temperature in your refrigerator should be at or below
   a. 0°F.
   b. 20°F.
   c. 40°F.
   d. 60°F.

2. Foods that are labeled *100% organic*
   a. contain only organically produced ingredients, excluding water and salt.
   b. may display the EPA's organic seal.
   c. were produced without the use of pesticides.
   d. contain foods from plant sources only.

3. Of the following techniques for food preservation, which has the least effect on taste?
   a. sugaring
   b. smoking
   c. salting
   d. pasteurization

4. Which of the following childhood illnesses has been linked to inadequate intake of dietary protein?
   a. cretinism
   b. malaria
   c. night blindness
   d. kwashiorkor

5. More than 100 million people in developing countries are now experiencing chronic diseases related to
   a. infection.
   b. obesity.
   c. natural disasters.
   d. overpopulation.

6. True or False? You prepare a potato, egg, and red onion salad with mayonnaise at 10:00 AM for a 2:00 PM barbecue. It is safe to leave the salad at room temperature until the barbecue.

7. True or False? Children with night blindness have an increased risk for premature death.

8. True or False? In the United States, farms certified as organic are allowed to use pesticides under certain conditions.

9. True or False? Irradiation makes foods radioactive.

10. True or False? The world has a surplus of food.

Answers to Review Questions are located at the back of this text.

Web Links

www.foodsafety.gov
Foodsafety.gov

www.fightbac.org
Partnership for Food Safety Education

www.epa.gov/pesticides
U.S. Environmental Protection Agency: Pesticides

www.ams.usda.gov
USDA National Organic Program

www.feedingminds,org
The Feeding Minds, Fighting Hunger Initiative

www.ota.com
Organic Trade Association

www.unicef.org
United Nations Children's Fund

www.who.int/nutrition/en
World Health Organization: Nutrition

www.studentsagainsthunger.org
National Student Campaign Against Hunger and Homelessness

www.fsis.usda.gov/food_safety_education/thermy/index.asp.
USDA "Thermy" webpage

APPENDICES

THE USDA FOOD GUIDE EVOLUTION

Early History of Food Guides

Did you know that in the United States food guides in one form or another have been around for over 125 years?

That's right. Back in 1885 a college chemistry professor named Wilber Olin (W. O.) Atwater helped bring the fledgling science of nutrition to a broader audience by introducing scientific data boxes that became the basis for the first known U.S. food guide. Those early dietary standards focused on defining the nutritional needs of an "average man" in terms of his daily consumption of proteins and calories. These became food composition tables defined in three sweeping categories; protein, fats and carbohydrate; mineral matter; and fuel values. As early as 1902, Atwater advocated for three foundational nutritional principles that we still support today; the concepts of variety, proportionality, and moderation in food choices and eating.

These ideas were adapted a few years later by a nutritionist named Caroline Hunt, who developed a food "buying" guide divided into five categories: meats and proteins; cereals and starches; vegetables and fruits; fatty foods; and sugar, based on a 2,800 calorie-per-day diet.

Starting in 1930s and 1940s, on through the following 30 years to the early 1970s, these concepts were further developed and experimented with, evolving from 12 food groups to a "Basic Seven" group approach, to the "Basic Four," and from there to a "Hassel-Free" construct that briefly increased the number of groups up to five. While all these approaches had drawbacks and received critical scrutiny, they were nonetheless important and necessary attempts to provide Americans with reliable guidelines based on the best scientific data and practices available at the time.

The USDA Food Guide Pyramid

Beginning around the early 1980s these concepts began to assume forms we've become familiar with today. In the process, important philosophical goals became attached to the development of a comprehensive guide. These core values included the following goals for a guide:

- it must encompass a broad focus on **overall health**;
- it should emphasize the use of **current research**;
- it should be an approach that includes the **total diet**, rather than parts or pieces;
- it should be **useful**;
- it should be **realistic**;
- it should be **flexible**;
- it should be **practical**;
- and it must be **evolutionary**, in that it should be able to adapt to new information that comes to light.

Additionally, the essential steps needed to develop a modern food guide became articulated. These are readily apparent in the first USDA Food Guide Pyramid released in 1992, which attempted for the first time to create a graphic representation of the guidelines. The steps required the inclusion of:

- Nutritional Goals
- Food Groups
- Serving Sizes
- Nutrient Profiles
- Numbers of Servings, including addressing the needs to for adequacy and moderation.

Remarkably, W. O. Atwater's early principles of *variety, proportionality, and moderation* remain relevant and appropriate to our modern graphic guidelines. The attempts to develop a conceptual framework for selecting the types and amounts of food that can support a nutritionally sound diet continue to evolve. Nutritionists and other health professionals are still working to find better ways to communicate to a large and diverse audience how to translate recommendations for nutrient intake into recommendations on which food to eat, and in what amounts.

Let's take a look at the evolution of the modern Food Guide over the past quarter-century:

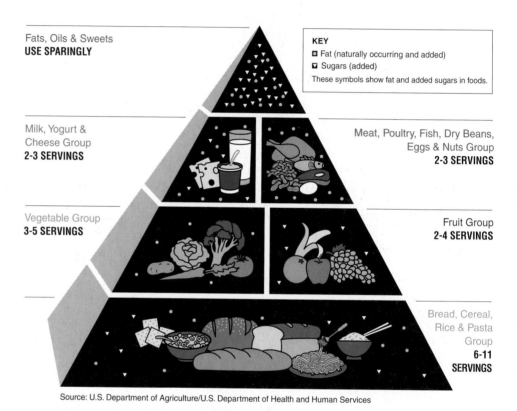

Source: U.S. Department of Agriculture/U.S. Department of Health and Human Services

🔺 **Figure A.1** The 1992 Food Guide Pyramid. This representation of the USDA guidelines took several years to develop and attempted to convey in a single image all the key aspects of a nutritional guide.

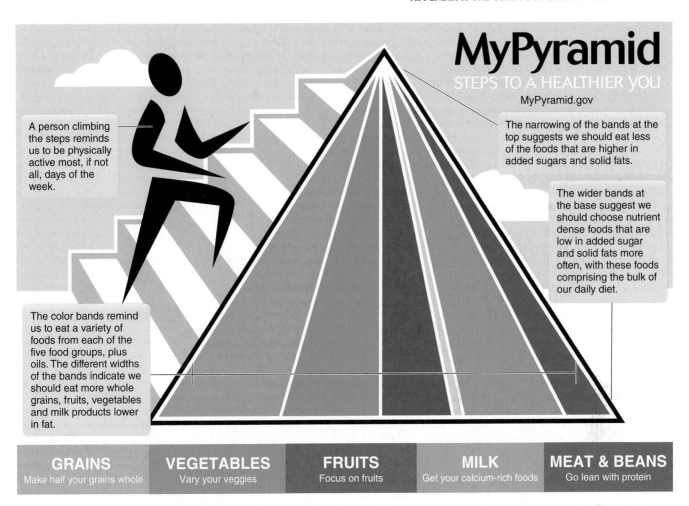

Figure A.2 The USDA revised the food guide pyramid in 2005 to address concerns regarding the recommendations and ease-of-use for a general audience. They put forth the MyPyramid Food Guidance System, which continues with the "pyramid" concept, but in a simpler presentation.

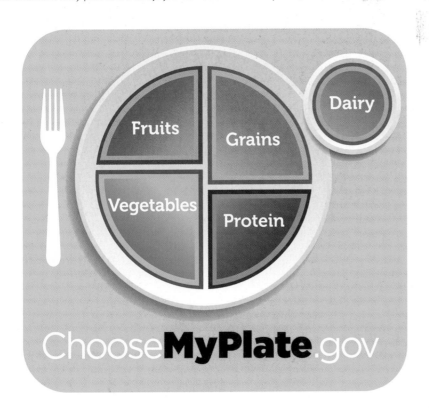

Figure A.3 In May 2011 the USDA made a dramatic change by withdrawing the pyramid concept and focusing instead on conveying core information in a simple, direct, and easy-to-follow way, as MyPlate. In MyPlate, the icons are intended as healthy eating reminders, rather than as specific messages encompassing detailed information.

Data adapted from www.nal.usda.gov/fnic/history/hist.htm and http://www.choosemyplate.gov/downloads/MyPlate/ABriefHistoryOfUSDAFoodGuides.pdf

CALCULATIONS AND CONVERSIONS

Calculation and Conversion Aids

Commonly Used Metric Units

millimeter (mm): one-thousandth of a meter (0.001)
centimeter (cm): one-hundredth of a meter (0.01)
kilometer (km): one-thousand times a meter (1,000)
kilogram (kg): one-thousand times a gram (1,000)
milligram (mg): one-thousandth of a gram (0.001)
microgram (µg): one-millionth of a gram (0.000001)
milliliter (ml): one-thousandth of a liter (0.001)

International Units

Some vitamin supplements may report vitamin content as International Units (IU).

To convert IU to

- Micrograms of vitamin D (cholecalciferol), divide the IU value by 40 or multiply by 0.025.
- Milligrams of vitamin E (alpha-tocopherol), divide the IU value by 1.5 if vitamin E is from natural sources. Divide the IU value by 2.22 if vitamin E is from synthetic sources.
- Vitamin A: 1 IU = 0.3 µg retinol or 3.6 µg beta-carotene.

Retinol Activity Equivalents

Retinol Activity Equivalents (RAE) are a standardized unit of measure for vitamin A. RAE account for the various differences in bioavailability from sources of vitamin A. Many supplements will report vitamin A content in IU, as just shown, or Retinol Equivalents (RE).

1 RAE = 1 µg retinol
12 µg beta-carotene
24 µg other vitamin A carotenoids

To calculate RAE from the RE value of vitamin carotenoids in foods, divide RE by 2.

For vitamin A supplements and foods fortified with vitamin A, 1 RE = 1 RAE.

Folate

Folate is measured as Dietary Folate Equivalents (DFE). DFE account for the different factors affecting bioavailability of folate sources.

1 DFE = 1 µg food folate
0.6 µg folate from fortified foods
0.5 µg folate supplement taken on an empty stomach
0.6 µg folate as a supplement consumed with a meal

To convert micrograms of synthetic folate, such as that found in supplements or fortified foods, to DFE:

$$\text{µg synthetic} \times \text{folate } 1.7 = \text{µg DFE}$$

For naturally occurring food folate, such as spinach, each microgram of folate equals 1 microgram DFE:

$$\text{µg folate} = \text{µg DFE}$$

Conversion Factors

Use the following table to convert U.S. measurements to metric equivalents:

Original Unit	Multiply By	To Get
ounces avdp	28.3495	grams
ounces	0.0625	pounds
pounds	0.4536	kilograms
pounds	16	ounces
grams	0.0353	ounces
grams	0.002205	pounds
kilograms	2.2046	pounds
liters	1.8162	pints (dry)
liters	2.1134	pints (liquid)
liters	0.9081	quarts (dry)
liters	1.0567	quarts (liquid)
liters	0.2642	gallons (U.S.)
pints (dry)	0.5506	liters
pints (liquid)	0.4732	liters
quarts (dry)	1.1012	liters
quarts (liquid)	0.9463	liters
gallons (U.S.)	3.7853	liters
millimeters	0.0394	inches
centimeters	0.3937	inches
centimeters	0.03281	feet
inches	25.4000	millimeters
inches	2.5400	centimeters
inches	0.0254	meters
feet	0.3048	meters
meters	3.2808	feet
meters	1.0936	yards
cubic feet	0.0283	cubic meters
cubic meters	35.3145	cubic feet
cubic meters	1.3079	cubic yards
cubic yards	0.7646	cubic meters

Length: U.S. and Metric Equivalents

¼ inch = 0.6 centimeter
1 inch = 2.5 centimeters
1 foot = 0.3048 meter
30.48 centimeters
1 yard = 0.91144 meter
1 millimeter = 0.03937 inch
1 centimeter = 0.3937 inch
1 decimeter = 3.937 inches
1 meter = 39.37 inches
1.094 yards
1 micrometer = 0.00003937 inch

Weights and Measures

Food Measurement Equivalencies from U.S. to Metric

Capacity

$\frac{1}{5}$ teaspoon = 1 milliliter
$\frac{1}{4}$ teaspoon = 1.25 milliliters
$\frac{1}{2}$ teaspoon = 2.5 milliliters
1 teaspoon = 5 milliliters
1 tablespoon = 15 milliliters
1 fluid ounce = 28.4 milliliters
$\frac{1}{4}$ cup = 60 milliliters
$\frac{1}{3}$ cup = 80 milliliters
$\frac{1}{2}$ cup = 120 milliliters
1 cup = 225 milliliters
1 pint (2 cups) = 473 milliliters
1 quart (4 cups) = 0.95 liter
1 liter (1.06 quarts) = 1,000 milliliters
1 gallon (4 quarts) = 3.84 liters

Weight

0.035 ounce = 1 gram
1 ounce = 28 grams
$\frac{1}{4}$ pound (4 ounces) = 114 grams
1 pound (16 ounces) = 454 grams
2.2 pounds (35 ounces) = 1 kilogram

U.S. Food Measurement Equivalents

3 teaspoons = 1 tablespoon
$\frac{1}{2}$ tablespoon = 1$\frac{1}{2}$ teaspoons
2 tablespoons = $\frac{1}{8}$ cup
4 tablespoons = $\frac{1}{4}$ cup
5 tablespoons + 1 teaspoon = $\frac{1}{3}$ cup
8 tablespoons = $\frac{1}{2}$ cup
10 tablespoons + 2 teaspoons = $\frac{2}{3}$ cup
12 tablespoons = $\frac{3}{4}$ cup
16 tablespoons = 1 cup
2 cups = 1 pint
4 cups = 1 quart
2 pints = 1 quart
4 quarts = 1 gallon

Volumes and Capacities

1 cup = 8 fluid ounces
$\frac{1}{2}$ liquid pint
1 milliliter = 0.061 cubic inch
1 liter = 1.057 liquid quarts
0.908 dry quart
61.024 cubic inches
1 U.S. gallon = 231 cubic inches
3.785 liters
0.833 British gallon
128 U.S. fluid ounces
1 British Imperial gallon = 277.42 cubic inches
1.201 U.S. gallons
4.546 liters
160 British fluid ounces

1 U.S. ounce, liquid or fluid = 1.805 cubic inches
29.574 milliliters
1.041 British fluid ounces
1 pint, dry = 33.600 cubic inches
0.551 liter
1 pint, liquid = 28.875 cubic inches
0.473 liter
1 U.S. quart, dry = 67.201 cubic inches
1.101 liters
1 U.S. quart, liquid = 57.75 cubic inches
0.946 liter
1 British quart = 69.354 cubic inches
1.032 U.S. quarts, dry
1.201 U.S. quarts, liquid

Energy Units

1 kilocalorie (kcal) = 4.2 kilojoules
1 millijoule (MJ) = 240 kilocalories
1 kilojoule (kJ) = 0.24 kcal
1 gram carbohydrate = 4 kcal
1 gram fat = 9 kcal
1 gram protein = 4 kcal

Temperature Standards

	°Fahrenheit	°Celsius
Body temperature	98.6°	37°
Comfortable room temperature	65–75°	18–24°
Boiling point of water	212°	100°
Freezing point of water	32°	0°

Temperature Scales

To Convert Fahrenheit to Celsius:

$$[(°F - 32) \times 5]/9$$

1. Subtract 32 from °F.
2. Multiply (°F − 32) by 5; then divide by 9.

To Convert Celsius to Fahrenheit:

$$[(°C \times 9)/5] + 32$$

1. Multiply °C by 9; then divide by 5.
2. Add 32 to (°C × 9/5).

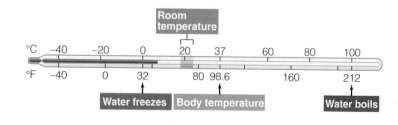

FOODS CONTAINING CAFFEINE

Source: Data from USDA Nutrient Database for Standard Reference, Release 22.

Beverages

Food Name	Serving	Caffeine/Serving (mg)
Beverage mix, chocolate flavor, dry mix, prepared w/milk	1 cup (8 fl. oz)	7.98
Beverage mix, chocolate malt powder, fortified, prepared w/milk	1 cup (8 fl. oz)	5.3
Beverage mix, chocolate malted milk powder, no added nutrients, prepared w/milk	1 cup (8 fl. oz)	7.95
Beverage, chocolate syrup w/o added nutrients, prepared w/milk	1 cup (8 fl. oz)	5.64
Beverage, chocolate syrup, fortified, mixed w/milk	1 cup milk and 1 tbsp. syrup	2.63
Cocoa mix w/aspartame and calcium and phosphorus, no sodium or vitamin A, low kcal, dry, prepared	6 fl. oz water and 0.53 oz packet	5
Cocoa mix w/aspartame, dry, low kcal, prepared w/water	1 packet dry mix with 6 fl. oz water	1.92
Cocoa mix, dry mix	1 serving (3 heaping tsp. or 1 envelope)	5.04
Cocoa mix, dry, w/o added nutrients, prepared w/water	1 oz packet with 6 fl. oz water	4.12
Cocoa mix, fortified, dry, prepared w/water	6 fl. oz H_2O and 1 packet	6.27
Cocoa, dry powder, high-fat or breakfast, plain	1 piece	6.895
Cocoa, hot, homemade w/whole milk	1 cup	5
Coffee liqueur, 53 proof	1 fl. oz	9.048
Coffee liqueur, 63 proof	1 fl. oz	9.05
Coffee w/cream liqueur, 34 proof	1 fl. oz	2.488
Coffee mix w/sugar (cappuccino), dry, prepared w/water	6 fl. oz H_2O and 2 rounded tsp. mix	74.88
Coffee mix w/sugar (French), dry, prepared w/water	6 fl. oz H_2O and 2 rounded tsp. mix	51.03
Coffee mix w/sugar (mocha), dry, prepared w/water	6 fl. oz and 2 round tsp. mix	33.84
Coffee, brewed	1 cup (8 fl. oz)	94.8
Coffee, brewed, prepared with tap water, decaffeinated	1 cup (8 fl. oz)	2.37
Coffee, instant, prepared	1 cup (8 fl. oz)	61.98
Coffee, instant, regular, powder, half the caffeine	1 cup (8 fl. oz)	30.99
Coffee, instant, decaffeinated	1 cup (8 fl. oz)	1.79
Coffee and cocoa (mocha) powder, with whitener and low-calorie sweetener	1 cup	405.48
Coffee, brewed, espresso, restaurant-prepared	1 cup (8 fl. oz)	502.44
Coffee, brewed, espresso, restaurant-prepared, decaffeinated	1 cup (8 fl. oz)	2.37
Energy drink, with caffeine, niacin, pantothenic acid, vitamin B_6	1 fl. oz	9.517
Milk beverage mix, dairy drink w/aspartame, low kcal, dry, prep	6 fl. oz	4.08
Milk, lowfat, 1% fat, chocolate	1 cup	5
Milk, whole, chocolate	1 cup	5
Soft drink, cola w/caffeine	1 fl. oz	2
Soft drink, cola, w/higher caffeine	1 fl. oz	8.33
Soft drink, cola or pepper type, low kcal w/saccharin and caffeine	1 fl. oz	3.256
Soft drink, cola, low kcal w/saccharin and aspartame, w/caffeine	1 fl. oz	4.144
Soft drink, lemon-lime soda, w/caffeine	1 fl. oz	4.605
Soft drink, low kcal, not cola or pepper, with aspartame and caffeine	1 fl. oz	4.44
Soft drink, pepper type, w/caffeine	1 fl. oz	3.07
Tea mix, instant w/lemon flavor, w/saccharin, dry, prepared	1 cup (8 fl. oz)	16.59
Tea mix, instant w/lemon, unsweetened, dry, prepared	1 cup (8 fl. oz)	26.18
Tea mix, instant w/sugar and lemon, dry, no added vitamin C, prepared	1 cup (8 fl. oz)	28.49
Tea mix, instant, unsweetened, dry, prepared	1 cup (8 fl. oz)	30.81
Tea, brewed	1 cup (8 fl. oz)	47.36
Tea, brewed, prepared with tap water, decaffeinated	1 cup (8 fl. oz)	2.37
Tea, instant, unsweetened, powder, decaffeinated	1 tsp.	1.183
Tea, instant, w/o sugar, lemon-flavored, w/added vitamin C, dry prepared	1 cup (8 fl. oz)	26.05
Tea, instant, with sugar, lemon-flavored, decaffeinated, no added vitamin	1 cup	9.1

Cake, Cookies, and Desserts

Food Name	Serving	Caffeine/Serving (mg)
Brownie, square, large (2-3/4" × 7/8")	1 piece	1.12
Cake, chocolate pudding, dry mix	1 oz	1.701
Cake, chocolate, dry mix, regular	1 oz	3.118
Cake, German chocolate pudding, dry mix	1 oz	1.985
Cake, marble pudding, dry mix	1 oz	1.985
Candies, chocolate-covered, caramel with nuts	1 cup	35.34
Candies, chocolate-covered, dietetic or low-calorie	1 cup	16.74
Candy, milk chocolate w/almonds	1 bar (1.45 oz)	9.02
Candy, milk chocolate w/rice cereal	1 bar (1.4 oz)	9.2
Candy, raisins, milk-chocolate-coated	1 cup	45
Chocolate chips, semisweet, mini	1 cup chips (6 oz package)	107.12
Chocolate, baking, unsweetened, square	1 piece	22.72
Chocolate, baking, Mexican, square	1 piece	2.8
Chocolate, sweet	1 oz	18.711
Cookie Cake, Snackwell Fat Free Devil's Food, Nabisco	1 serving	1.28
Cookie, Snackwell Caramel Delights, Nabisco	1 serving	1.44
Cookie, chocolate chip, enriched, commercially prepared	1 oz	3.118
Cookie, chocolate chip, homemade w/margarine	1 oz	4.536
Cookie, chocolate chip, lower-fat, commercially prepared	3 pieces	2.1
Cookie, chocolate chip, refrigerated dough	1 portion, dough spooned from roll	2.61
Cookie, chocolate chip, soft, commercially prepared	1 oz	1.985
Cookie, chocolate wafers	1 cup, crumbs	7.84
Cookie, graham crackers, chocolate-coated	1 oz	13.041
Cookie, sandwich, chocolate, cream-filled	3 pieces	3.9
Cookie, sandwich, chocolate, cream-filled, special dietary	1 oz	0.85
Cupcake, chocolate w/frosting, low-fat	1 oz	0.86
Doughnut, cake, chocolate w/sugar or glaze	1 oz	0.284
Doughnut, cake, plain w/chocolate icing, large (3-1/2")	1 each	1.14
Fast food, ice cream sundae, hot fudge	1 sundae	1.58
Fast food, milk beverage, chocolate shake	1 cup (8 fl. oz)	1.66
Frosting, chocolate, creamy, ready-to-eat	2 tbsp. creamy	0.82
Frozen yogurt, chocolate	1 cup	5.58
Fudge, chocolate w/nuts, homemade	1 oz	1.984
Granola bar, soft, milk-chocolate-coated, peanut butter	1 oz	0.85
Granola bar, w/coconut, chocolate-coated	1 cup	5.58
Ice cream, chocolate	1 individual (3.5 fl. oz)	1.74
Ice cream, chocolate, light	1 oz	0.85
Ice cream, chocolate, rich	1 cup	5.92
M&M's Peanut Chocolate	1 cup	18.7
M&M's Plain Chocolate	1 cup	22.88
Milk chocolate	1 cup chips	33.6
Milk-chocolate-coated coffee beans	1 NLEA serving	48
Milk dessert, frozen, fat-free milk, chocolate	1 oz	0.85
Milk shake, thick, chocolate	1 fl. oz	0.568
Pastry, éclair/cream puff, homemade, custard-filled w/chocolate	1 oz	0.567
Pie crust, chocolate-wafer-cookie-type, chilled	1 crust, single 9"	11.15
Pie, chocolate mousse, no bake mix	1 oz	0.284
Pudding, chocolate, instant dry mix prepared w/reduced-fat (2%) milk	1 oz	0.283
Pudding, chocolate, regular dry mix prepared w/reduced-fat (2%) milk	1 oz	0.567
Pudding, chocolate, ready-to-eat, fat-free	4 oz can	2.27
Syrups, chocolate, genuine chocolate flavor, light, Hershey	2 tbsp.	1.05
Topping, chocolate-flavored hazelnut spread	1 oz	1.984
Yogurt, chocolate, nonfat milk	1 oz	0.567
Yogurt, frozen, chocolate, soft serve	0.5 cup (4 fl. oz)	2.16

Starch List

1 starch choice = 15 g carbohydrate, 0–3 g protein, 0–1 g fat, and 80 cal

Icon Key

☺ = More than 3 g of dietary fiber per serving.

❗ = Extra fat, or prepared with added fat. (Count as 1 starch + 1 fat.)

❗ = 480 mg or more of sodium per serving.

Food	Serving Size
Bread	
Bagel, 4 oz	¼ (1 oz)
❗ Biscuit, 2½" across	1
Bread	
☺ reduced-calorie	2 slices (1½ oz)
white, whole-grain, pumpernickel, rye, unfrosted raisin	1 slice (1 oz)
Chapatti, small, 6" across	1
❗ Cornbread, 1¾" cube	1 (1½ oz)
English muffin	½
Hot dog bun or hamburger bun	½ (1 oz)
Naan, 8" by 2"	¼
Pancake, 4" across, ¼" thick	1
Pita, 6" across	½
Roll, plain small	1 (1 oz)
❗ Stuffing, bread	⅓ cup
❗ Taco shell, 5" across	2
Tortilla	
Corn, 6" across	1
Flour, 6" across	1
Flour, 10" across	⅓ tortilla
❗ Waffle, 4"-square or 4" across	1
Cereals and Grains	
Barley, cooked	⅓ cup
Bran, dry	
☺ oat	¼ c
☺ wheat	½ c
☺ Bulgur (cooked)	½ c
Cereals	½ c
☺ bran	½ c
cooked (oats, oatmeal)	½ c
puffed	1½ c
shredded wheat, plain	½ c
sugar-coated	½ c
unsweetened, ready-to-eat	¾ c
Couscous	⅓ c
Granola	
low-fat	¼ c
❗ regular	¼ c
Grits, cooked	½ c

Food	Serving Size
Kasha	½ c
Millet, cooked	⅓ c
Muesli	¼ c
Pasta, cooked	⅓ c
Polenta, cooked	⅓ c
Quinoa, cooked	⅓ c
Rice, white or brown, cooked	⅓ c
Tabbouleh (tabouli), prepared	½ c
Wheat germ, dry	3 tbs
Wild rice, cooked	½ c
Starchy Vegetables	
Cassava	⅓ c
Corn	½ c
on cob, large	½ cob (5 oz)
☺ Hominy, canned	¾ c
☺ Mixed vegetables with corn, peas, or pasta	1 c
☺ Parsnips	½ c
☺ Peas, green	½ c
Plantain, ripe	⅓ c
Potato	
baked with skin	¼ large (3 oz)
boiled, all kinds	½ c or ½ medium (3 oz)
❗ mashed, with milk and fat	½ c
French fried (oven-baked)	1 cup (2 oz)
☺ Pumpkin, canned, no sugar added	1 c
Spaghetti/pasta sauce	½ c
☺ Squash, winter (acorn, butternut)	1 c
☺ Succotash	½ c
Yam, sweet potato, plain	½ c
Crackers and Snacks	
Animal crackers	8
Crackers	
❗ round-butter type	6
saltine-type	6
❗ sandwich-style, cheese or peanut butter filling	3
❗ whole-wheat regular	2–5 (¾ oz)
☺ whole-wheat lower fat or crispbreads	2–5 (¾ oz)
Graham crackers, 2½" square	3

Food	Serving Size	Food	Serving Size
Matzoh	¾ oz	**Beans, Peas, and Lentils**	
Melba toast, about 2" by 4" piece	4 pieces	*(Count as 1 starch + 1 lean meat)*	
Oyster crackers	20	☺ Baked beans	⅓ c

Crackers and Snacks

Food	Serving Size
Popcorn	3 c
! ☺ with butter	3 c
☺ no fat added	3 c
☺ lower fat	3 c
Pretzels	¾ oz
Rice cakes, 4" across	2
Snack chips	
fat-free or baked (tortilla, potato), baked pita chips	15–20 (¾ oz)
! regular (tortilla, potato)	9–13 (¾ oz)

Food	Serving Size
☺ Beans, cooked (black, garbanzo, kidney, lima, navy, pinto, white)	½ c
☺ Lentils, cooked (brown, green, yellow)	½ c
☺ Peas, cooked (black-eyed, split)	½ c
∥ ☺ Refried beans, canned	½ c

Fruit List

1 fruit choice = 15 g carbohydrate, 0 g protein, 0 g fat, and 60 cal
Weight includes skin, core, seeds, and rind.

Icon Key
☺ = More than 3 g of dietary fiber per serving.
! = Extra fat, or prepared with added fat.
∥ = 480 mg or more of sodium per serving.

Food	Serving Size	Food	Serving Size
Apples		Grapes, small	17 (3 oz)
unpeeled, small	1 (4 oz)	Honeydew melon	1 slice or 1 c cubed (10 oz)
dried	4 rings	☺ Kiwi	1 (3½ oz)
Applesauce, unsweetened	½ c	Mandarin oranges, canned	¾ c
Apricots		Mango, small	½ fruit (5½ oz) or ½ c
canned	½ c	Nectarine, small	1 (5 oz)
dried	8 halves	☺ Orange, small	1 (6½ oz)
! fresh	4 whole (5½ oz)	Papaya	½ fruit or 1 c cubed (8 oz)
Banana, extra small	1 (4 oz)	Peaches	
∥ Blackberries	¾ c	canned	½ c
Blueberries	¾ c	fresh, medium	1 (6 oz)
Cantaloupe, small	⅓ melon or 1 c cubed (11 oz)	Pears	
Cherries		canned	½ c
sweet, canned	½ c	fresh, large	½ (4 oz)
sweet, fresh	12 (3 oz)	Pineapple	
Dates	3	canned	½ c
Dried fruits (blueberries, cherries, cranberries, mixed fruit, raisins)	2 tbs	fresh	¾ c
Figs		Plums	
dried	1½	canned	½ c
☺ fresh	1½ large or 2 medium (3½ oz)	dried (prunes)	3
Fruit cocktail	½ c	small	2 (5 oz)
Grapefruit		☺ Raspberries	1 c
large	½ (11 oz)	☺ Strawberries	1¼ c whole berries
sections, canned	¾ c		

Food	Serving Size	Food	Serving Size
☺ Tangerines, small ....2 (8 oz)		Grape juice ....¹/₃ c	
Watermelon ....1 slice or 1¼ c cubes (13½ oz)		Grapefruit juice ....¹/₂ c	
		Orange juice ....¹/₂ c	
Fruit Juice		Pineapple juice...................................¹/₂ c	
Apple juice/cider ....¹/₂ c		Prune juice ....¹/₃ c	
Fruit juice blends, 100% juice ....¹/₃ c			

Milk and Yogurts

1 milk choice = 12 g carbohydrate and 8 g protein

Food	Serving Size	Count As
Fat-Free or Low-Fat (1%)		
(0–3 g fat per serving, 100 calories per serving)		
Milk, buttermilk, acidophilus milk, Lactaid ....1 c		1 fat-free milk
Evaporated milk ....¹/₂ c		1 fat-free milk
Yogurt, plain or flavored with an artificial sweetener ....²/₃ c (6 oz)		1 fat-free milk
Reduced-Fat (2%)		
(5 g fat per serving, 120 calories per serving)		
Milk, acidophilus milk, kefir, Lactaid ....1 c		1 reduced-fat milk
Yogurt, plain ....²/₃ c (6 oz)		1 reduced-fat milk
Whole		
(8 g fat per serving, 160 calories per serving)		
Milk, buttermilk, goat's milk ....1 c		1 whole milk
Evaporated milk ....¹/₂ c		1 whole milk
Yogurt, plain ....8 oz		1 whole milk
Dairy-Like Foods		
Chocolate milk		
fat-free ....1 c		1 fat-free milk + 1 carbohydrate
whole ....1 c		1 whole milk + 1 carbohydrate
Eggnog, whole milk	½ c	1 carbohydrate + 2 fats
Rice drink		
flavored, low-fat ....1 c		2 carbohydrates
plain, fat-free ....1 c		1 carbohydrate
Smoothies, flavored, regular ....10 oz		1 fat-free milk + 2½ carbohydrates
Soy milk		
light ....1 c		1 carbohydrate + ½ fat
regular, plain ....1 c		1 carbohydrate + 1 fat
Yogurt		
and juice blends ....1 c		1 fat-free milk + 1 carbohydrate
low carbohydrate (less than 6 g carbohydrate per choice) ....²/₃ c (6 oz)		½ fat-free milk
with fruit, low-fat ....²/₃ c (6 oz)		1 fat-free milk + 1 carbohydrate

Sweets, Desserts, and Other Carbohydrates List

1 other carbohydrate choice = 15 g carbohydrate and variable protein, fat, and calories.

Icon Key

▮ = 480 mg or more of sodium per serving.

Food	Serving Size	Count As
Beverages, Soda, and Energy/Sports Drinks		
Cranberry juice cocktail	½ c	1 carbohydrate
Energy drink	1 can (8.3 oz)	2 carbohydrates
Fruit drink or lemonade	1 c (8 oz)	2 carbohydrates
Hot chocolate		
regular	1 envelope added to 8 oz water	1 carbohydrate + 1 fat
sugar-free or light	1 envelope added to 8 oz water	1 carbohydrate
Soft drink (soda), regular	1 can (12 oz)	2½ carbohydrates
Sports drink	1 cup (8 oz)	1 carbohydrate
Brownies, Cake, Cookies, Gelatin, Pie, and Pudding		
Brownie, small, unfrosted	1¼" square, ⅞" high (about 1 oz)	1 carbohydrate + 1 fat
Cake		
angel food, unfrosted	1½ of cake (about 2 oz)	2 carbohydrates
frosted	2" square (about 2 oz)	2 carbohydrates + 1 fat
unfrosted	2" square (about 2 oz)	1 carbohydrate + 1 fat
Cookies		
chocolate chip	2 cookies (2¼" across)	1 carbohydrate + 2 fats
gingersnap	3 cookies	1 carbohydrate
sandwich, with creme filling	2 small (about ⅔ oz)	1 carbohydrate + 1 fat
sugar-free	3 small or 1 large (¾ oz–1 oz)	1 carbohydrate + 1–2 fats
vanilla wafer	5 cookies	1 carbohydrate + 1 fat
Cupcake, frosted	1 small (about 1¾ oz)	2 carbohydrates + 1–1½ fats
Fruit cobbler	½ c (3½ oz)	3 carbohydrates + 1 fat
Gelatin, regular	½ c	1 carbohydrate
Pie		
commercially prepared fruit, 2 crusts	⅙ of 8" pie	3 carbohydrates + 2 fats
pumpkin or custard	⅛ of 8" pie	1½ carbohydrates + 1½ fats
Pudding		
regular (made with reduced-fat milk)	½ c	2 carbohydrates
sugar-free, or sugar-free and fat-free (made with fat-free milk)	½ c	1 carbohydrate
Candy, Spreads, Sweets, Sweeteners, Syrups, and Toppings		
Candy bar, chocolate/peanut	2 "fun size" bars (1 oz)	1½ carbohydrates + 1½ fats
Candy, hard	3 pieces	1 carbohydrate
Chocolate "kisses"	5 pieces	1 carbohydrate + 1 fat
Coffee creamer		
dry, flavored	4 tsp	½ carbohydrate + ½ fat
liquid, flavored	2 tbsp	1 carbohydrate
Fruit snacks, chewy (pureed fruit concentrate)	1 roll (¾ oz)	1 carbohydrate
Fruit spreads, 100% fruit	1½ tbs	1 carbohydrate
Honey	1 tbsp	1 carbohydrate

Food	Serving Size	Count As
Jam or jelly, regular	1 tbs	1 carbohydrate
Sugar	1 tbs	1 carbohydrate
Syrup		
chocolate	2 tbs	2 carbohydrates
light (pancake type)	2 tbs	1 carbohydrate
regular (pancake type)	1 tbs	1 carbohydrate

Condiments and Sauces

Food	Serving Size	Count As
Barbeque sauce	3 tbs	1 carbohydrate
Cranberry sauce, jellied	¼ c	1½ carbohydrates
Gravy, canned or bottled	½ c	½ carbohydrate + ½ fat
Salad dressing, fat-free, low-fat, cream-based	3 tbs	1 carbohydrate
Sweet and sour sauce	3 tbs	1 carbohydrate

Doughnuts, Muffins, Pastries, and Sweet Breads

Food	Serving Size	Count As
Banana nut bread	1" slice (1 oz)	2 carbohydrates + 1 fat
Doughnut		
cake, plain	1 medium, (1½ oz)	1½ carbohydrates + 2 fats
yeast type, glazed	3¾" across (2 oz)	2 carbohydrates + 2 fats
Muffin (4 oz)	¼ muffin (1 oz)	1 carbohydrate + ½ fat
Sweet roll or Danish	1 (2½ oz)	2½ carbohydrates + 2 fats

Frozen Bars, Frozen Dessert, Frozen Yogurt, and Ice Cream

Food	Serving Size	Count As
Frozen pops	1	½ carbohydrate
Fruit juice bars, frozen, 100% juice	1 bar (3 oz)	1 carbohydrate
Ice cream		
fat-free	½ c	1-½ carbohydrates
light	½ c	1 carbohydrate + 1 fat
no sugar added	½ c	1 carbohydrate + 1 fat
regular	½ c	1 carbohydrate + 2 fats
Sherbet, sorbet	½ c	2 carbohydrates
Yogurt, frozen		
fat-free	⅓ c	1 carbohydrate
regular	½ c	1 carbohydrate + 0–1 fat

Granola Bars, Meal Replacement Bars/Shakes, and Trail Mix

Food	Serving Size	Count As
Granola or snack bar, regular or low-fat	1 bar (1 oz)	1½ carbohydrates
Meal replacement bar	1 bar (1⅓ oz)	1½ carbohydrates + 0–1 fat
Meal replacement bar	1 bar (2 oz)	2 carbohydrates + 1 fat
Meal replacement shake, reduced-calorie	1 can (10–11 oz)	1½ carbohydrates + 0–1 fat
Trail mix		
candy/nut-based	1 oz	1 carbohydrates + 2 fats
dried-fruit-based	1 oz	1 carbohydrate + 1 fat

Nonstarchy Vegetable List

1 vegetable choice = 5 g carbohydrate, 2 g protein, 0 g fat, 25 cal

Icon Key

☺ = More than 3 g of dietary fiber per serving.

▮ = 480 mg or more of sodium per serving.

Amaranth or Chinese spinach	Kohlrabi
Artichoke	Leeks
Artichoke hearts	Mixed vegetables (without corn, peas, or pasta)
Asparagus	Mung bean sprouts
Baby corn	Mushrooms, all kinds, fresh
Bamboo shoots	Okra
Beans (green, wax, Italian)	Onions
Bean sprouts	Oriental radish or daikon
Beets	Pea pods
▮ Borscht	☺ Peppers (all varieties)
Broccoli	Radishes
☺ Brussels sprouts	Rutabaga
Cabbage (green, bok choy, Chinese)	▮ Sauerkraut
☺ Carrots	Soybean sprouts
Cauliflower	Spinach
Celery	Squash (summer, crookneck, zucchini)
☺ Chayote	Sugar pea snaps
Coleslaw, packaged, no dressing	☺ Swiss chard
Cucumber	Tomato
Eggplant	Tomatoes, canned
Gourds (bitter, bottle, luffa, bitter melon)	▮ Tomato sauce
Green onions or scallions	▮ Tomato/vegetable juice
Greens (collard, kale, mustard, turnip)	Turnips
Hearts of palm	Water chestnuts
Jicama	Yard-long beans

Meat and Meat Substitutes List

Icon Key

ǃ = Extra fat, or prepared with added fat. (Add an additional fat choice to this food.)

▮ = 480 mg or more of sodium per serving (based on the sodium content of a typical 3 oz serving of meat, unless 1 or 2 is the normal serving size).

Food	Amount	Food	Amount
Lean Meats and Meat Substitutes		*Fish, fresh or frozen, plain:* catfish, cod, flounder,	
(1 lean meat choice = 7 g protein, 0–3 g fat, 45 calories)		haddock, halibut, orange roughy, salmon,	
		tilapia, trout, tuna ....1 oz	
Beef: Select or Choice grades trimmed of fat:		▮ *Fish, smoked:* herring or salmon (lox) ....1 oz	
ground round, roast (chuck, rib, rump),		*Game:* buffalo, ostrich, rabbit, venison ....1 oz	
round, sirloin, steak (cubed, flank,		▮ Hot dog with 3 g of fat or less per oz (8 dogs	
porterhouse, T-bone), tenderloin ....1 oz		per 14 oz package) (*Note: May be high in*	
▮ Beef jerky ....1 oz		*carbohydrate.*) 1	
Cheeses with 3 g of fat or less per oz ....1 oz		*Lamb:* chop, leg, or roast ....1 oz	
Cottage cheese ....¼ cup		*Organ meats:* heart, kidney, liver (*Note: May*	
Egg substitutes, plain ....¼ cup		*be high in cholesterol*) ....1 oz	
Egg whites 2			

Food	Amount
Oysters, fresh or frozen . . . . .6 medium	
Pork, lean	
❙ Canadian bacon . . . . .1 oz	
rib or loin chop/roast, ham, tenderloin . . . . . .1 oz	
Poultry without skin: Cornish hen, chicken,	
domestic duck or goose (well drained of fat),	
turkey . . . . .1 oz	
Processed sandwich meats with 3 g of fat or less	
per oz: chipped beef, deli thin-sliced meats,	
turkey ham, turkey kielbasa, turkey pastrami . . .1 oz	
Salmon, canned . . . . .1 oz	
Sardines, canned . . . . .2 medium	
❙ Sausage with 3 g or less fat per oz . . . . .1 oz	
Shellfish: clams, crab, imitation shellfish, lobster,	
scallops, shrimp . . . . .1 oz	
Tuna, canned in water or oil, drained . . . . .1 oz	
Veal: Lean chop, roast . . . . .1 oz	

Medium-Fat Meat and Meat Substitutes
(1 medium-fat meat choice = 7 g protein, 4–7 g fat, and 75 calories)

Food	Amount
Beef: corned beef, ground beef, meatloaf,	
Prime grades trimmed of fat (prime rib),	
short ribs, tongue . . . . .1 oz	
Cheeses with 4–7 g of fat per oz: feta, mozzarella,	
pasteurized processed cheese spread,	
reduced-fat cheeses, string . . . . .1 oz	
Egg (*Note:* High in cholesterol, limit to 3 per week.) . . .1	
Fish, any fried product . . . . .1 oz	
Lamb: ground, rib roast . . . . .1 oz	
Pork: cutlet, shoulder roast .1 oz	

Food	Amount
Poultry: chicken with skin; dove, pheasant,	
wild duck, or goose; fried chicken;	
ground turkey . . . . .1 oz	
Ricotta cheese . . . . .2 oz or ¼ c	
❙ Sausage with 4–7 g fat per oz . . . . .1 oz	
Veal: Cutlet (no breading) . . . . .1 oz	

High-Fat Meat and Meat Substitutes[a]
(1 high-fat meat choice = 7 g protein, 8+ g fat, 100 calories)

Food	Amount
Bacon	
❙ pork . . . . .2 slices (16 slices per lb or 1 oz each, before cooking)	
❙ turkey . . . . .3 slices (½ oz each before cooking)	
Cheese, regular: American, bleu, brie, cheddar,	
hard goat, Monterey Jack, queso, Swiss . . . . . . .1 oz	
❙ ❗ *Hot dog:* beef, pork, or combination	
(10 per lb-sized package) 1	
❙ *Hot dog:* turkey or chicken (10 per lb-sized	
package) 1	
Pork: ground, sausage, spareribs . . . . .1 oz	
Processed sandwich meats with 8 g of fat or	
more per oz: bologna, pastrami, hard salami . . .1 oz	
❙ *Sausage with 8 g of fat or more per oz:*	
bratwurst, chorizo, Italian, knockwurst,	
Polish, smoked, summer . . . . .1 oz	

[a]These foods are high in saturated fat, cholesterol, and calories and may raise blood cholesterol levels if eaten on a regular basis. Try to eat 3 or fewer servings from this group per week.

Plant-Based Proteins

Because carbohydrate and fat content varies among plant-based proteins, you should read the food label.

Icon Key

☺ = More than 3 g of dietary fiber per serving; 7g protein; calories vary.

❙ = 480 mg or more of sodium per serving (based on the sodium content of a typical 3-oz serving of meat, unless 1 or 2 oz is the normal serving size).

Food	Amount	Count As
"Bacon" strips, soy-based	3 strips	1 medium-fat meat
☺ Baked beans	⅓ c	1 starch + 1 lean meat
☺ *Beans, cooked:* black, garbanzo, kidney, lima, navy, pinto, white	½ c	1 starch + 1 lean meat
☺ "Beef" or "sausage" crumbles, soy-based	2 oz	½ carbohydrate + 1 lean meat
"Chicken" nuggets, soy-based	2 nuggets (1½ oz)	½ carbohydrate + 1 medium-fat meat
☺ Edamame	½ c	½ carbohydrate + 1 lean meat
Falafel (spiced chickpea and wheat patties)	3 patties (about 2 inches across)	1 carbohydrate + 1 high-fat meat
Hot dog, soy-based	1 (1½ oz)	½ carbohydrate + 1 lean meat
☺ Hummus	⅓ c	1 carbohydrate + 1 high-fat meat

Food	Amount	Count As
☺ Lentils, brown, green, or yellow	½ c	1 carbohydrate + 1 lean meat
☺ Meatless burger, soy-based	3 oz	½ carbohydrate + 2 lean meats
☺ Meatless burger, vegetable- and starch-based	1 patty (about 2½ oz)	1 carbohydrate + 2 lean meats
Nut spreads: almond butter, cashew butter, peanut butter, soy nut butter	1 tbs	1 high-fat meat
☺ *Peas, cooked:* black-eyed and split peas	½ c	1 starch + 1 lean meat
▯☺ Refried beans, canned	½ c	1 starch + 1 lean meat
"Sausage" patties, soy-based	1 (1½ oz)	1 medium-fat meat
Soy nuts, unsalted	¾ oz	½ carbohydrate + 1 medium-fat meat
Tempeh	¼ cup	1 medium-fat meat
Tofu	4 oz (½ cup)	1 medium-fat meat
Tofu, light	4 oz (½ cup)	1 lean meat

Fat List

1 fat choice = 5 g fat, 45 cal

Icon Key

▯ = 480 mg or more of sodium per serving.

Food	Serving Size	Food	Serving Size
Unsaturated Fats— Monounsaturated Fats		Nuts	
Avocado, medium	2 tbs (1 oz)	Pignolia (pine nuts)	1 tbs
Nut butters (trans fat-free): almond butter, cashew butter, peanut butter (smooth or crunchy)	1½ tsp	walnuts, English	4 halves
Nuts		*Oil:* corn, cottonseed, flaxseed, grape seed, safflower, soybean, sunflower	1 tsp
almonds	6 nuts	*Oil:* made from soybean and canola oil—Enova	1 tsp
Brazil	2 nuts	Plant stanol esters	
cashews	6 nuts	light	1 tbs
filberts (hazelnuts)	5 nuts	regular	2 tsp
macadamia	3 nuts	Salad dressing	
mixed (50% peanuts)	6 nuts	▯ reduced-fat (*Note: May be high in carbohydrate.*)	2 tbs
peanuts	10 nuts	▯ regular	1 tbs
pecans	4 halves	Seeds	1 tbs
pistachios	16 nuts	flaxseed, whole	1 tbs
Oil: canola, olive, peanut	1 tsp	pumpkin, sunflower	1 tbs
Olives		sesame seeds	1 tbs
black (ripe)	8 large	Tahini or sesame paste	2 tsp
green, stuffed	10 large	**Saturated Fats**	
Polyunsaturated Fats		Bacon, cooked, regular or turkey	1 slice
Margarine: lower-fat spread (30% to 50% vegetable oil, *trans* fat-free)	1 tbs	Butter	
Margarine: stick, tub (*trans* fat-free), or squeeze (*trans* fat-free)	1 tsp	reduced-fat	1 tbs
Mayonnaise		stick	1 tsp
reduced-fat	1 tbs	whipped	2 tsp
regular	1 tsp	Butter blends made with oil	
Mayonnaise-style salad dressing		reduced-fat or light	1 tbs
reduced-fat	1 tbs	regular	1½ tsp
regular	2 tsp	Chitterlings, boiled	2 tbs (½ oz)
		Coconut, sweetened, shredded	2 tbs

Food	Serving Size	Food	Serving Size
Coconut milk		Lard	1 tsp
light	$^1/_3$ c	*Oil:* coconut, palm, palm kernel	1 tsp
regular	1$^1/_2$ tbs	Salt pork	$^1/_4$ oz
Cream		Shortening, solid	1 tsp
half and half	2 tbs	Sour cream	
heavy	1 tbs	reduced-fat or light	3 tbs
light	1$^1/_2$ tbs	regular	2 tbs
whipped	2 tbs		
whipped, pressurized	$^1/_4$ c		
Cream cheese			
reduced-fat	1$^1/_2$ tbs ($^3/_4$ oz)		
regular	1 tbs ($^1/_2$ oz)		

Free Foods List

A *free food* is any food or drink that has less than 20 calories and 5 g or less of carbohydrate per serving. Foods with a serving size listed should be limited to three servings per day. Foods listed without a serving size can be eaten as often as you like.

Icon Key

▮ = 480 mg or more of sodium per serving.

Food	Serving Size	Food	Serving Size
Low Carbohydrate Foods		Salad dressing	
Cabbage, raw	$^1/_2$ c	fat-free or low-fat	1 tbs
Candy, hard (regular or sugar-free)	1 piece	fat-free, Italian	2 tbs
Carrots, cauliflower, or green beans, cooked	$^1/_4$ c	Sour cream, fat-free, reduced-fat	1 tbs
Cranberries, sweetened with sugar substitute	$^1/_2$ c	Whipped topping	
Cucumber, sliced	$^1/_2$ c	light or fat-free	2 tbs
Gelatin		regular	1 tbs
dessert, sugar-free		**Condiments**	
unflavored		Barbecue sauce	2 tsp
Gum		Catsup (ketchup)	1 tbs
Jam or jelly, light or no sugar added	2 tsp	Honey mustard	1 tbs
Rhubarb, sweetened with sugar substitute	$^1/_2$ c	Horseradish	
Salad greens		Lemon juice	
Sugar substitutes (artificial sweeteners)		Miso	1$^1/_2$ tsp
Syrup, sugar-free	2 tbs	Mustard	
Modified Fat Foods		Parmesan cheese, freshly grated	1 tbs
with Carbohydrate		Pickle relish	1 tbs
Cream cheese, fat-free	1 tbs ($^1/_2$ oz)	Pickles	
Creamers		▮ dill	1$^1/_2$ medium
nondairy, liquid	1 tbs	sweet, bread and butter	2 slices
nondairy, powdered	2 tsp	sweet, gherkin	$^3/_4$ oz
Margarine spread		Salsa	$^1/_4$ c
fat-free	1 tbs	▮ Soy sauce, regular or light	1 tbs
reduced-fat	1 tsp	Sweet and sour sauce	2 tsp
Mayonnaise		Sweet chili sauce	2 tsp
fat-free	1 tbs	Taco sauce	1 tbs
reduced-fat	1 tsp	Vinegar	
Mayonnaise-style salad dressing		Yogurt, any type	2 tbs
fat-free	1 tbs		
reduced-fat	1 tsp		

Drinks/Mixes

Any food on this list—without serving size listed—can be consumed in any moderate amount.

Icon Key

‖ = 480 mg or more of sodium per serving.

‖ Bouillon, broth, consommé		Diet soft drinks, sugar-free
Bouillon or broth, low sodium		Drink mixes, sugar-free
Carbonated or mineral water		Tea, unsweetened or with sugar substitute
Club soda		Tonic water, diet
Cocoa powder, unsweetened (1 tbs)		Water
Coffee, unsweetened or with sugar substitute		Water, flavored, carbohydrate free

Seasonings

Any food on this list can be consumed in any moderate amount.

Flavoring extracts (for example, vanilla, almond, peppermint)	Spices
Garlic	Hot pepper sauce
Herbs, fresh or dried	Wine, used in cooking
Nonstick cooking spray	Worcestershire sauce
Pimento	

Combination Foods List

Icon Key

☺ = More than 3 g of dietary fiber per serving.

‖ = 600 mg or more of sodium per serving (for combination food main dishes/meals).

Food	Serving Size	Count As
Entrées		
‖ Casserole type (tuna noodle, lasagna, spaghetti with meatballs, chili with beans, macaroni and cheese)	1 c (8 oz)	2 carbohydrates + 2 medium-fat meats
‖ Stews (beef/other meats and vegetables)	1 c (8 oz)	1 carbohydrate + 1 medium-fat meat + 0–3 fats
Tuna salad or chicken salad	½ c (3½ oz)	½ carbohydrate + 2 lean meats + 1 fat
Frozen Meals/Entrées		
‖☺ Burrito (beef and bean)	1 (5 oz)	3 carbohydrates + 1 lean meat + 2 fats
‖ Dinner-type meal	generally 14–17 oz	3 carbohydrates + 3 medium-fat meats + 3 fats
‖ Entrée or meal with less than 340 calories	about 8–11 oz	2–3 carbohydrates + 1–2 lean meats
Pizza		
‖ cheese/vegetarian thin crust	¼ of 12" (4½ to 5 oz)	2 carbohydrates + 2 medium-fat meats
‖ meat topping, thin crust	¼ of 12" (5 oz)	2 carbohydrates + 2 medium-fat meats, + 1½ fats
‖ Pocket sandwich	1 (4½ oz)	3 carbohydrates + 1 lean meat + 1–2 fats
‖ Pot pie	1 (7 oz)	2½ carbohydrates + 1 medium-fat meat + 3 fats
Salads (Deli-Style)		
Coleslaw	½ c	1 carbohydrate + 1½ fats
Macaroni/pasta salad	½ c	2 carbohydrates + 3 fats
‖ Potato salad	½ c	1½ carbohydrates + 1–2 fats
Soups		
‖ Bean, lentil, or split pea	1 cup	1 carbohydrate + 1 lean meat

Food	Serving Size	Count As
▮ Chowder (made with milk)	1 c (8 oz)	1 carbohydrate + 1 lean meat + 1½ fats
▮ Cream (made with water)	1 c (8 oz)	1 carbohydrate + 1 fat
▮ Instant	6 oz prepared	1 carbohydrate
▮ with beans or lentils	8 oz prepared	2½ carbohydrates + 1 lean meat
▮ Miso soup	1 c	½ carbohydrate + 1 fat
▮ Oriental noodle	1 c	2 carbohydrates + 2 fats
Rice (congee)	1 c	1 carbohydrate
▮ Tomato (made with water)	1 c (8 oz)	1 carbohydrate
▮ Vegetable beef, chicken noodle, or other broth-type	1 c (8 oz)	1 carbohydrate

Fast Foods List[a]

Icon Key
☺ = More than 3 g of dietary fiber per serving.
▮ = Extra fat, or prepared with added fat.
▮ = 600 mg or more sodium per serving (for fast food main dishes/meals).

Food	Serving Size	Exchanges per Serving
Breakfast Sandwiches		
▮ Egg, cheese, meat, English muffin	1 sandwich	2 carbohydrates + 2 medium-fat meats
▮ Sausage biscuit sandwich	1 sandwich	2 carbohydrates + 2 high-fat meats + 3½ fats
Main Dishes/Entrees		
▮ ☺ Burrito (beef and beans)	1 (about 8 oz)	3 carbohydrates + 3 medium-fat meats + 3 fats
▮ Chicken breast, breaded and fried	1 (about 5 oz)	1 carbohydrate + 4 medium-fat meats
Chicken drumstick, breaded and fried	1 (about 2 oz)	2 medium-fat meats
▮ Chicken nuggets	6 (about 3½ oz)	1 carbohydrate + 2 medium-fat meats + 1 fat
▮ Chicken thigh, breaded and fried	1 (about 4 oz)	½ carbohydrate + 3 medium-fat meats + 1½ fats
▮ Chicken wings, hot	6 (5 oz)	5 medium-fat meats + 1½ fats
Oriental		
▮ Beef/chicken/shrimp with vegetables in sauce	1 c (about 5 oz)	1 carbohydrate + 1 lean meat + 1 fat
▮ Egg roll, meat	1 (about 3 oz)	1 carbohydrate + 1 lean meat + 1 fat
Fried rice, meatless	½ c	1½ carbohydrates + 1½ fats
▮ Meat and sweet sauce (orange chicken)	1 c	3 carbohydrates + 3 medium-fat meats + 2 fats
▮☺ Noodles and vegetables in sauce (chow mein, lo mein)	1 c	2 carbohydrates + 1 fat
Pizza		
▮ Cheese, pepperoni, regular crust	⅛ of 14" (about 4 oz)	2½ carbohydrates + 1 medium-fat meat + 1½ fats
▮ Cheese/vegetarian, thin crust	¼ of 12" (about 6 oz)	2½ carbohydrates + 2 medium-fat meats + 1½ fats
Sandwiches		
▮ Chicken sandwich, grilled	1	3 carbohydrates + 4 lean meats
▮ Chicken sandwich, crispy	1	3½ carbohydrates + 3 medium-fat meats + 1 fat
Fish sandwich with tartar sauce	1	2½ carbohydrates + 2 medium-fat meats + 2 fats
Hamburger		
▮ large with cheese	1	2½ carbohydrates + 4 medium-fat meats + 1 fat
regular	1	2 carbohydrates + 1 medium-fat meat + 1 fat
▮ Hot dog with bun	1	1 carbohydrate + 1 high-fat meat + 1 fat
Submarine sandwich		
▮ less than 6 grams fat	6" sub	3 carbohydrates + 2 lean meats
▮ regular	6" sub	3½ carbohydrates + 2 medium-fat meats + 1 fat

[a]The choices in the Fast Foods list are not specific fast food meals or items, but are estimates based on popular foods. You can get specific nutrition information for almost every fast food or restaurant chain. Ask the restaurant or check its website for nutrition information about your favorite fast foods.

Food	Serving Size	Exchanges per Serving
Taco, hard or soft shell (meat and cheese)	1 small	1 carbohydrate + 1 medium-fat meat + 1½ fats
Salads		
Salad, main dish (grilled chicken type, no dressing or croutons)	Salad	1 carbohydrate + 4 lean meats
Salad, side, no dressing or cheese	Small (about 5 oz)	1 vegetable
Sides/Appetizers		
French fries, restaurant style	Small	3 carbohydrates + 3 fats
Medium		4 carbohydrates + 4 fats
Large		5 carbohydrates + 6 fats
Nachos with cheese	Small (about 4½ oz)	2½ carbohydrates + 4 fats
Onion rings	1 serving (about 3 oz)	2½ carbohydrates + 3 fats
Desserts		
Milkshake, any flavor	12 oz	6 carbohydrates + 2 fats
Soft-serve ice cream cone	1 small	2½ carbohydrates + 1 fat

Alcohol List

In general, 1 alcohol choice (½ oz absolute alcohol) has about 100 calories.

Alcoholic Beverage	Serving Size	Count As
Beer		
light (4.2%)	12 fl. oz.	1 alcohol equivalent + ½ carbohydrate
regular (4.9%)	12 fl. oz.	1 alcohol equivalent + 1 carbohydrate
Distilled spirits: vodka, rum, gin, whiskey, 80 or 86 proof	1½ fl. oz.	1 alcohol equivalent
Liqueur, coffee (53 proof)	1 fl. oz.	1 alcohol equivalent + 1 carbohydrate
Sake	1 fl. oz.	½ alcohol equivalent
Wine		
dessert (sherry)	3½ fl. oz.	1 alcohol equivalent + 1 carbohydrate
dry, red or white (10%)	5 fl. oz.	1 alcohol equivalent

CDC Growth Charts: United States
Stature-for-age percentiles: Boys, 2 to 20 years

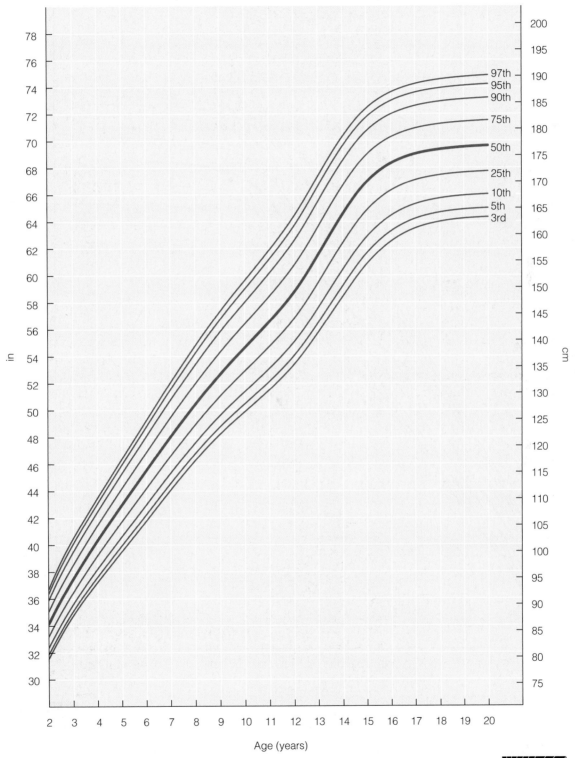

Age (years)

Published May 30, 2000.
Source: Developed by the National Center for Health Statistics
              in collaboration with the National Center for Chronic
              Disease Prevention and Health Promotion (2000).

SAFER · HEALTHIER · PEOPLE™

CDC Growth Charts: United States
Stature-for-age percentiles: Girls, 2 to 20 years

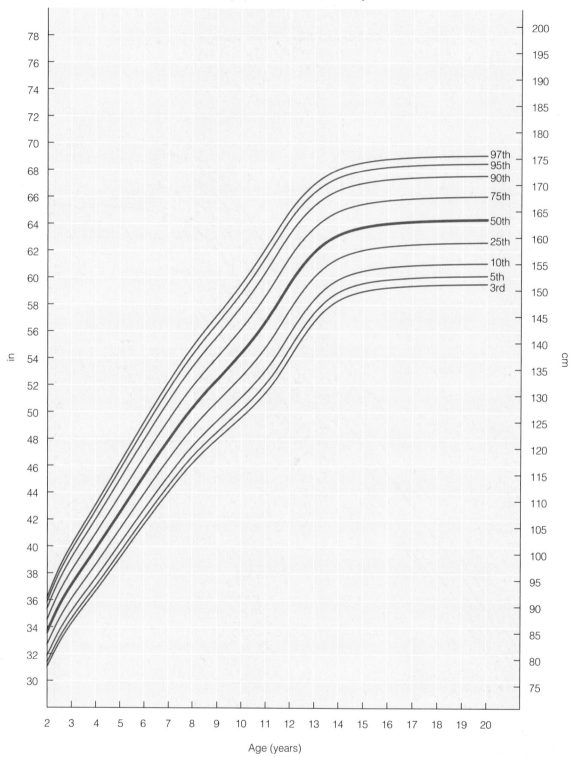

Age (years)

Published May 30, 2000.
Source: Developed by the National Center for Health Statistics
in collaboration with the National Center for Chronic
Disease Prevention and Health Promotion (2000).

SAFER · HEALTHIER · PEOPLE™

Academic Journals

International Journal of Sport Nutrition and Exercise Metabolism
Human Kinetics
P.O. Box 5076
Champaign, IL 61825-5076
(800) 747-4457
www.humankinetics.com/IJSNEM

Journal of Nutrition
Department of Nutrition
Pennsylvania State University
126-S Henderson Building
University Park, PA 16802-6504
(814) 865-4721
www.nutrition.org

Nutrition Research
Elsevier: Journals Customer Service
6277 Sea Harbor Drive
Orlando, FL 32887
(877) 839-7126
www.journals.elsevierhealth.com/periodicals/NTR

Nutrition
Elsevier: Journals Customer Service
6277 Sea Harbor Drive
Orlando, FL 32887
(877) 839-7126
www.journals.elsevierhealth.com/periodicals/NUT

Nutrition Reviews
International Life Sciences Institute
Subscription Office
P.O. Box 830430
Birmingham, AL 35283
(800) 633-4931
www.ingentaconnect.com/content/ilsi/nure

Obesity Research
North American Association for the Study
of Obesity (NAASO)
8630 Fenton Street, Suite 918
Silver Spring, MD 20910
(301) 563-6526
www.nature.com/oby/index.html

International Journal of Obesity
Journal of the International Association for
the Study of Obesity
Nature Publishing Group
The Macmillan Building
4 Crinan Street
London N1 9XW
United Kingdom
www.nature.com/ijo

Journal of the American Medical Association
American Medical Association
P.O. Box 10946
Chicago, IL 60610-0946
(800) 262-2350
www.jama.ama-assn.org

New England Journal of Medicine
10 Shattuck Street
Boston, MA 02115-6094
(617) 734-9800
www.nejm.org

American Journal of Clinical Nutrition
The American Journal of Clinical Nutrition
9650 Rockville Pike
Bethesda, MD 20814-3998
(301) 634-7038
www.ajcn.org

Journal of the American Dietetic Association
Elsevier, Health Sciences Division
Subscription Customer Service
6277 Sea Harbor Drive
Orlando, FL 32887
(800) 654-2452
www.adajournal.org

Aging

Administration on Aging
U.S. Health & Human Services
200 Independence Avenue, SW
Washington, DC 20201
(877) 696-6775
www.aoa.gov

American Association of Retired Persons (AARP)
601 E. Street, NW
Washington, DC 20049
(888) 687-2277
www.aarp.org

Health and Age
Sponsored by the Novartis Foundation for Gerontology &
The Web-Based Health Education Foundation
Robert Griffith, MD
Executive Director
573 Vista de la Ciudad
Santa Fe, NM 87501
www.healthandage.com

National Council on the Aging
300 D Street, SW, Suite 801
Washington, DC 20024
(202) 479-1200
www.ncoa.org

International Osteoporosis Foundation
5 Rue Perdtemps
1260 Nyon
Switzerland
41 22 994 01 00
www.iofbonehealth.org

National Institute on Aging
Building 31, Room 5C27
31 Center Drive, MSC 2292
Bethesda, MD 20892
(301) 496-1752
www.nia.nih.gov

Osteoporosis and Related Bone Diseases
National Resource Center
2 AMS Circle
Bethesda, MD 20892-3676
(800) 624-BONE
www.hiams.nih.gov/health_info/bone/

American Geriatrics Society
The Empire State Building
350 Fifth Avenue, Suite 801
New York, NY 10118
(212) 308-1414
www.americangeriatrics.org

National Osteoporosis Foundation
1232 22nd Street, NW
Washington, DC 20037-1292
(202) 223-2226
www.nof.org

Alcohol and Drug Abuse

National Institute on Drug Abuse
6001 Executive Boulevard, Room 5213
Bethesda, MD 20892-9561
(301) 443-1124
www.nida.nih.gov/nidahome.html

National Institute on Alcohol Abuse and Alcoholism
5635 Fishers Lane, MSC 9304
Bethesda, MD 20892-9304
www.niaaa.nih.gov

Alcoholics Anonymous
Grand Central Station
P.O. Box 459
New York, NY 10163
www.aa.org

Narcotics Anonymous
P.O. Box 9999
Van Nuys, CA 91409
(818) 773-9999
www.na.org

National Council on Alcoholism and Drug Dependence
20 Exchange Place, Suite 2902
New York, NY 10005
(212) 269-7797
www.ncadd.org

National Clearinghouse for Alcohol and Drug Information
11420 Rockville Pike
Rockville, MD 20852
(800) 729-6686
www.store.samhsa.gov/home

Canadian Government

Health Canada
A.L. 0900C2
Ottawa, ON
K1A 0K9
(613) 957-2991
www.hc-sc.gc.ca/english

National Institute of Nutrition
408 Queen Street, 3rd Floor
Ottawa, ON K1R 5A7
(613) 235-3355
www.nin.ca/public_html

Agricultural and Agri-Food Canada
Public Information Request Service
Sir John Carling Building
930 Carling Avenue
Ottawa, ON K1A 0C5
(613) 759-1000
www.agr.gc.ca

Bureau of Nutritional Sciences
Sir Frederick G. Banting Research Centre
Tunney's Pasture (2203A)
Ottawa, ON K1A 0L2
(613) 957-0352
www.hc-sc.gc.ca/food-aliment/ns-sc/e_nutrition.html

Canadian Food Inspection Agency
59 Camelot Drive
Ottawa, ON K1A 0Y9
(613) 225-2342
www.inspection.gc.ca/english/toce.shtml

Canadian Institute for Health Information
CIHI Ottawa
377 Dalhousie Street, Suite 200
Ottawa, ON K1N 9N8
(613) 241-7860
www.cihi.ca

Canadian Public Health Association
1565 Carling Avenue, Suite 400
Ottawa, ON K1Z 8R1
(613) 725-3769
www.cpha.ca

Canadian Nutrition and Professional Organizations

Dietitians of Canada
480 University Avenue, Suite 604
Toronto, ON M5G 1V2
(416) 596-0857
www.dietitians.ca

Canadian Diabetes Association
National Life Building
1400-522 University Avenue
Toronto, ON M5G 2R5
(800) 226-8464
www.diabetes.ca

National Eating Disorder Information Centre
CW 1-211, 200 Elizabeth Street
Toronto, ON M5G 2C4
(866) NEDIC-20
www.nedic.ca

Canadian Pediatric Society
100-2204 Walkley Road
Ottawa, ON K1G 4G8
(613) 526-9397
www.cps.ca

Canadian Dietetic Association
480 University Avenue, Suite 604
Toronto, ON M5G 1V2
(416) 596-0857
www.dietitians.ca

Disordered Eating

American Psychiatric Association
1000 Wilson Boulevard, Suite 1825
Arlington, VA 22209
(703) 907-7300
www.psych.org

National Institute of Mental Health
Office of Communications
6001 Executive Boulevard, Room 8184, MSC 9663
Bethesda, MD 20892
(866) 615-6464
www.nimh.nih.gov

*National Association of Anorexia Nervosa
and Associated Disorders (ANAD)*
Box 7
Highland Park, IL 60035
(847) 831-3438
www.anad.org

National Eating Disorders Association
603 Stewart Street, Suite 803
Seattle, WA 98101
(206) 382-3587
www.nationaleatingdisorders.org

Eating Disorder Referral and Information Center
2923 Sandy Pointe, Suite 6
Del Mar, CA 92014
(858) 792-7463
www.edreferral.com

Anorexia Nervosa and Related Eating Disorders, Inc. (ANRED)
E-mail: jarinor@rio.com
www.anred.com

Overeaters Anonymous
P.O. Box 44020
Rio Rancho, NM 87174
(505) 891-2664
www.oa.org

Exercise, Physical Activity, and Sports

American College of Sports Medicine (ACSM)
P.O. Box 1440
Indianapolis, IN 46206-1440
(317) 637-9200
www.acsm.org

American Physical Therapy Association (ASNA)
1111 North Fairfax Street
Alexandria, VA 22314
(800) 999-APTA
www.apta.org

Gatorade Sports Science Institute (GSSI)
617 West Main Street
Barrington, IL 60010
(800) 616-GSSI
www.gssiweb.com

National Coalition for Promoting Physical Activity (NCPPA)
1010 Massachusetts Avenue, Suite 350
Washington, DC 20001
(202) 454-7518
www.ncppa.org

*Sports, Wellness, Eating Disorder and Cardiovascular
Nutritionists (SCAN)*
P.O. Box 60820
Colorado Springs, CO 80960
(719) 635-6005
www.scandpg.org

President's Council on Physical Fitness and Sports
Department W
200 Independence Avenue, SW
Room 738-H
Washington, DC 20201-0004
(202) 690-9000
www.fitness.gov

American Council on Exercise
4851 Paramount Drive
San Diego, CA 92123
(858) 279-8227
www.acefitness.org

The International Association for Fitness Professionals (IDEA)
10455 Pacific Center Court
San Diego, CA 92121
(800) 999-4332, ext. 7
www.ideafit.com

Food Safety

Food Marketing Institute
655 15th Street, NW
Washington, DC 20005
(202) 452-8444
www.fmi.org

Agency for Toxic Substances and Disease Registry (ATSDR)
ORO Washington Office
Ariel Rios Building
1200 Pennsylvania Avenue, NW
M/C 5204G
Washington, DC 20460
(888) 422-8737
www.atsdr.cdc.gov

Food Allergy and Anaphylaxis Network
11781 Lee Jackson Highway, Suite 160
Fairfax, VA 22033-3309
(800) 929-4040
www.foodallergy.org

Foodsafety.gov
www.foodsafety.gov

The USDA Food Safety and Inspection Service
Food Safety and Inspection Service
United States Department of Agriculture
Washington, DC 20250
www.fsis.usda.gov

Consumer Reports
Web Site Customer Relations Department
101 Truman Avenue
Yonkers, NY 10703
www.consumerreports.org

Center for Science in the Public Interest: Food Safety
1875 Connecticut Avenue, NW
Washington, DC 20009
(202) 332-9110
www.cspinet.org/foodsafety

Center for Food Safety and Applied Nutrition
5100 Paint Branch Parkway
College Park, MD 20740
(888) SAFEFOOD
www.cfsan.fda.gov

Food Safety Project
Dan Henroid, MS, RD, CFSP
HRIM Extension Specialist and Website Coordinator
Hotel, Restaurant and Institution Management
9e MacKay Hall
Iowa State University
Ames, IA 50011
(515) 294-3527
www.extension.iastate.edu/foodsafety

Organic Consumers Association
6101 Cliff Estate Road
Little Marais, MN 55614
(218) 226-4164
www.organicconsumers.org

Infancy and Childhood

Administration for Children and Families
370 L'Enfant Promenade, SW
Washington, DC 20447
www.acf.hhs.gov

The American Academy of Pediatrics
141 Northwest Point Boulevard
Elk Grove Village, IL 60007
(847) 434-4000
www.aap.org

Kidnetic.com
E-mail: contactus@kidnetic.com
www.kidnetic.com

Kidshealth: The Nemours Foundation
12735 West Gran Bay Parkway
Jacksonville, FL 32258
(866) 390-3610
www.kidshealth.org

National Center for Education in Maternal and Child Health
Georgetown University
Box 571272
Washington, DC 20057
(202) 784-9770
www.ncemch.org

Birth Defects Research for Children, Inc.
930 Woodcock Road, Suite 225
Orlando, FL 32803
(407) 895-0802
www.birthdefects.org

USDA/ARS Children's Nutrition Research Center at Baylor College of Medicine
1100 Bates Street
Houston, TX 77030
www.bcm.edu

Keep Kids Healthy.com
www.keepkidshealthy.com

International Agencies

UNICEF
3 United Nations Plaza
New York, NY 10017
(212) 326-7000
www.unicef.org

World Health Organization
Avenue Appia 20
1211 Geneva 27
Switzerland
41 22 791 21 11
www.who.int/en

The Stockholm Convention on Persistent Organic Pollutants
11–13 Chemin des Anémones
1219 Châtelaine
Geneva, Switzerland
41 22 917 8191
www.chm.pops.int

Food and Agricultural Organization of the United Nations
Viale delle Terme di Caracalla
00100 Rome, Italy
39 06 57051
www.fao.org

International Food Information Council Foundation
1100 Connecticut Avenue, NW
Suite 430
Washington, DC 20036
(202) 296-6540

Pregnancy and Lactation

San Diego County Breastfeeding Coalition
c/o Children's Hospital and Health Center
3020 Children's Way, MC 5073
San Diego, CA 92123
(800) 371-MILK
www.breastfeeding.org

National Alliance for Breastfeeding Advocacy
Barbara Heiser, Executive Director
9684 Oak Hill Drive
Ellicott City, MD 21042-6321
OR
Marsha Walker, Executive Director
254 Conant Road
Weston, MA 02493-1756
www.naba-breastfeeding.org

American College of Obstetricians and Gynecologists
409 12th Street, SW,
P.O. Box 96920
Washington, DC 20090
www.acog.org

La Leche League
1400 N. Meacham Road
Schaumburg, IL 60173
(847) 519-7730
www.lalecheleague.org

National Organization on Fetal Alcohol Syndrome
900 17th Street, NW
Suite 910
Washington, DC 20006
(800) 66 NOFAS
www.nofas.org

March of Dimes Birth Defects Foundation
1275 Mamaroneck Avenue
White Plains, NY 10605
(888) 663-4637
www.marchofdimes.org

Professional Nutrition Organizations

Association of Departments and Programs of Nutrition (ANDP)
Dr. Marilynn Schnepf, ANDP Chair
316 Ruth Leverton Hall
Nutrition and Health Sciences
University of Nebraska–Lincoln
Lincoln, NE 68583-0806
www.fshn.hs.iastate.edu/andp

North American Association for the Study of Obesity (NAASO)
8630 Fenton Street, Suite 918
Silver Spring, MD 20910
(301) 563-6526
www.obesity.org

American Dental Association
211 East Chicago Avenue
Chicago, IL 60611-2678
(312) 440-2500
www.ada.org

American Heart Association
National Center
7272 Greenville Avenue
Dallas, TX 75231
(800) 242-8721
www.heart.org/HEARTORG

American Dietetic Association (ADA)
120 South Riverside Plaza, Suite 2000
Chicago, IL 60606-6995
(800) 877-1600
www.eatright.org

The American Society for Nutrition (ASN)
9650 Rockville Pike, Suite L-4500
Bethesda, MD 20814-3998
(301) 634-7050
www.nutrition.org

The Society for Nutrition Education
7150 Winton Drive, Suite 300
Indianapolis, IN 46268
(800) 235-6690
www.sne.org

American College of Nutrition
300 S. Duncan Avenue, Suite 225
Clearwater, FL 33755
(727) 446-6086
www.americancollegeofnutrition.org

American Obesity Association
1250 24th Street, NW, Suite 300
Washington, DC 20037
(800) 98-OBESE

American Council on Health and Science
1995 Broadway
Second Floor
New York, NY 10023
(212) 362-7044
www.acsh.org

American Diabetes Association
ATTN: National Call Center
1701 North Beauregard Street
Alexandria, VA 22311
(800) 342-2383
www.diabetes.org

Institute of Food Technologies
525 W. Van Buren, Suite 1000
Chicago, IL 60607
(312) 782-8424
www.ift.org

ILSI Human Nutrition Institute
One Thomas Circle, Ninth Floor
Washington, DC 20005
(202) 659-0524
www.ilsi.org

Trade Organizations

American Meat Institute
1700 North Moore Street
Suite 1600
Arlington, VA 22209
(703) 841-2400
www.meatami.com

National Dairy Council
10255 W. Higgins Road, Suite 900
Rosemont, IL 60018
(312) 240-2880
www.nationaldairycouncil.org

United Fresh Fruit and Vegetable Association
1901 Pennsylvania Ave. NW, Suite 1100
Washington, DC 20006
(202) 303-3400
www.unitedfresh.org

U.S.A. Rice Federation
Washington, DC
4301 North Fairfax Drive, Suite 425
Arlington, VA 22203
(703) 236-2300
www.usarice.com

U.S. Government

The USDA National Organic Program
Agricultural Marketing Service
USDA-AMS-TMP-NOP
Room 4008-South Building
1400 Independence Avenue, SW
Washington, DC 20250-0020
(202) 720-3252
www.ams.usda.gov

U.S. Department of Health and Human Services
200 Independence Avenue, SW
Washington, DC 20201
(877) 696-6775
www.hhs.gov

Food and Drug Administration (FDA)
5600 Fishers Lane
Rockville, MD 20857
(888) 463-6332
www.fda.gov

Environmental Protection Agency
Ariel Rios Building
1200 Pennsylvania Avenue, NW
Washington, DC 20460
(202) 272-0167
www.epa.gov

Federal Trade Commission
600 Pennsylvania Avenue, NW
Washington, DC 20580
(202) 326-2222
www.ftc.gov

Office of Dietary Supplements
National Institutes of Health
6100 Executive Boulevard, Room 3B01, MSC 7517
Bethesda, MD 20892
(301) 435-2920
www.ods.od.nih.gov

Nutrient Data Laboratory Homepage
Beltsville Human Nutrition Center
10300 Baltimore Avenue
Building 307-C, Room 117
BARC-East
Beltsville, MD 20705
(301) 504-8157
www.nal.usda.gov/fnic/foodcomp

National Digestive Disease Clearinghouse
2 Information Way
Bethesda, MD 20892-3570
(800) 891-5389
www.digestive.niddk.nih.gov

The National Cancer Institute
NCI Public Inquiries Office
Suite 3036A
6116 Executive Boulevard, MSC 8322
Bethesda, MD 20892-8322
(800) 4-CANCER
www.cancer.gov

The National Eye Institute
31 Center Drive, MSC 2510
Bethesda, MD 20892-2510
(301) 496-5248
www.nei.nih.gov

The National Heart, Lung, and Blood Institute
Building 31, Room 5A52
31 Center Drive, MSC 2486
Bethesda, MD 20892
(301) 592-8573
www.nhlbi.nih.gov

Institute of Diabetes and Digestive and Kidney Diseases
Office of Communications and Public Liaison
NIDDK, NIH, Building 31, Room 9A04
Center Drive, MSC 2560
Bethesda, MD 20892
(301) 496-4000
www.niddk.nih.gov

National Center for Complementary and Alternative Medicine
NCCAM Clearinghouse
P.O. Box 7923
Gaithersburg, MD 20898
(888) 644-6226
www.nccam.nih.gov

U.S. Department of Agriculture (USDA)
14th Street, SW
Washington, DC 20250
(202) 720-2791
www.usda.gov

Centers for Disease Control and Prevention (CDC)
1600 Clifton Road
Atlanta, GA 30333
(404) 639-3311/Public Inquiries: (800) 311-3435
www.cdc.gov

National Institutes of Health (NIH)
9000 Rockville Pike
Bethesda, MD 20892
(301) 496-4000
www.nih.gov

Food and Nutrition Information Center
Agricultural Research Service, USDA
National Agricultural Library, Room 105
10301 Baltimore Avenue
Beltsville, MD 20705-2351
(301) 504-5719
www.nal.usda.gov/fnic

National Institute of Allergy and Infectious Diseases
NIAID Office of Communications and Public Liaison
6610 Rockledge Drive, MSC 6612
Bethesda, MD 20892
(301) 496-5717
www.niaid.nih.gov

Weight and Health Management
The Vegetarian Resource Group
P.O. Box 1463, Dept. IN
Baltimore, MD 21203
(410) 366-VEGE
www.vrg.org

American Obesity Association
1250 24th Street, NW
Suite 300
Washington, DC 20037
(202) 776-7711
www.obesity.org

Anemia Lifeline
(888) 722-4407
www.anemia.com

The Arc
(301) 565-3842
E-mail: info@thearc.org
www.thearc.org

Bottled Water Web
P.O. Box 5658
Santa Barbara, CA 93150
(805) 879-1564
www.bottledwaterweb.com

The Food and Nutrition Board
Institute of Medicine
500 Fifth Street, NW
Washington, DC 20001
(202) 334-2352
www.iom.edu

The Calorie Control Council
www.caloriecontrol.org

TOPS (Take Off Pounds Sensibly)
4575 South Fifth Street
P.O. Box 07360
Milwaukee, WI 53207
(800) 932-8677
www.tops.org

Shape Up America!
15009 Native Dancer Road
N. Potomac, MD 20878
(240) 631-6533
www.shapeup.org

World Hunger

Center on Hunger, Poverty, and Nutrition Policy
Tufts University
Medford, MA 02155
(617) 627-3020
www.tufts.edu/nutrition

Freedom from Hunger
1644 DaVinci Court
Davis, CA 95616
(800) 708-2555
www.freedomfromhunger.org

Oxfam International
1112 16th Street, NW, Suite 600
Washington, DC 20036
(202) 496-1170
www.oxfam.org

WorldWatch Institute
1776 Massachusetts Avenue, NW
Washington, DC 20036
(202) 452-1999
www.worldwatch.org

Food First
398 60th Street
Oakland, CA 94618
(510) 654-4400
www.foodfirst.org

The Hunger Project
15 East 26th Street
New York, NY 10010
(212) 251-9100
www.thp.org

U.S. Agency for International Development
Information Center
Ronald Reagan Building
Washington, DC 20523
(202) 712-0000
www.usaid.gov

REFERENCES

Chapter 1

1. Institute of Medicine, Food and Nutrition Board. 2003. *Dietary Reference Intakes: Applications in Dietary Planning.* Washington, DC: National Academies Press.

2. U.S. Department of Agriculture and U.S. Department of Health and Human Services. 2010. *Dietary Guidelines for Americans, 2010.* 7th edn. Washington, DC: U.S. Government Printing Office.

3. Young, L. R., and M. Nestle. 1998. Variations in perceptions of a "medium" food portion: implications for dietary guidance. *J. Am. Diet. Assoc.* 98:458–459.

4. Young, L. R., and M. Nestle. 2002. The contribution of expanding portion sizes to the U.S. obesity epidemic. *American Journal of Public Health.* 92(2):246–249.

5. Food and Nutrition Information Center. 2010. Dietary Guidance. Ethnic/Cultural Food Pyramid. www.fnic.nal .usda.gov/nal_display/index.

6. Winterfeldt, E. A., M. L. Bogle, and L. L. Ebro. 2005. *Dietetics. Practice and Future Trends.* 2nd edn. Sudbury, MA: Jones and Bartlett.

7. Agricultural Research Service. June 6, 2008. Founding American Nutrition Science. ARS Timeline. www.ars .usda.gov/is/timeline/nutrition.htm.

8. Rising, K., P. Bacchetti, and L. Bero. 2008. Reporting bias in drug trials submitted to the Food and Drug Administration: review of publication and presentation. *PLoS Medicine.* 5(11):e217. Doi:10.1371/journal. pmed.0050217.

9. Schott, G., H. Pachl, U. Limbach, U. Gundert-Remy, W. Ludwig, and K. Lieb. 2010. The financing of drug trials by pharmaceutical companies and its consequences: Part 1. A qualitative, systematic review of the literature on possible influences on the findings, protocols, and quality of drug trials. *Deutsch Aerzteblatt International.* 107(16):279–285.

Chapter 2

1. Paddon-Jones, D., E. Westman, R. D. Mattes, R. R. Wolfe, A. Astrup, and M. Westerterp-Plantenga. 2008. Protein, weight management, and satiety. *Am. J. Clin. Nutr.* 87(5):1558S–1561S.

2. Halton, T. L., and F. B. Hu. 2004. The effects of high-protein diets on thermogenesis, satiety, and weight loss: a critical review. *J. Am. Coll. Nutr.* 23(5):373–385.

3. Watters, E. 2006. DNA is not destiny. *Discover,* 32–75.

4. The NCMHD Center of Excellence for Nutritional Genomics. http://nutrigenomics.ucdavis.edu.

5. Johnson, N., and J. Kaput. 2003. Nutrigenomics: an emerging scientific discipline. *Food Technology.* 57(4):60–67.

6. Grierson, B. 2003. What your genes want you to eat. *New York Times,* May 4.

7. Wallace, K. 2007. Diet, exercise may lower colon cancer risk [television broadcast]. CBS News, March 15.

8. Kaput, J., and R. Rodriguez. 2004. Nutritional genomics: the next frontier in the postgenomic era. *Physiological Genomics.* 16:166–177.

9. Kerr, M. 2003. Probiotics significantly reduce symptoms of IBS, ulcerative colitis. Medscape Medical News. www .medscape.com/viewarticle/455964_print.

10. Kopp-Hoolihan, L. 2001. Prophylactic and therapeutic uses of probiotics: a review. *J. Am. Diet. Assoc.* 101: 229–238, 241.

11. Saier, M. H., Jr., and N. M. Mansour. 2005. Probiotics and prebiotics in human health. *J. Mol. Microbiol. Bio-technol.* 10(1):22–25.

12. Doron, S., and S. L. Gorbach. 2006. Probiotics: their role in the treatment and prevention of diseases. *Expert Rev. Anti-Infect. Ther.* 4(2):261–275.

13. Ezendam, J., and H. van Loveren. 2006. Probiotics: immunomodulation and evaluation of safety and efficacy. *Nutr. Rev.* 64(1):1–14.

14. Sanders, M. E., D. C. Walker, K. M. Walker, K. Aoyama, and T. R. Klaenhammer. 1996. Performance of commercial cultures in fluid milk applications. *J. Dairy Sci.* 79: 943–955.

15. National Digestive Diseases Information Clearinghouse (NDDIC). 2003. Heartburn, hiatal hernia, and gastroesophageal reflux disease (GERD). NIH Publication No. 03-0882. http://digestive.niddk.nih.gov/ddiseases/ pubs/gerd/index.htm.

16. Bauman, R. 2011. *Microbiology,* 3rd edn. San Francisco: Pearson Benjamin Cummings.

17. Chan, F. K. L., and W. K. Leung. 2002. Peptic-ulcer disease. *Lancet.* 360:933–941.

18. National Digestive Diseases Information Clearinghouse (NDDIC). 2010. NSAIDs and peptic ulcers. NIH Publication No. 10-4644. http://digestive.niddk.nih.gov/ ddiseases/pubs/nsaids/index.htm.

19. U.S. Food and Drug Administration (FDA). January 27, 2011. Food Allergies: What You Need to Know. www.fda .gov/Food/ResourcesForYou/Consumers/ucm079311.htm.

20. National Institute of Allergy and Infectious Diseases: NIAID-Sponsored Expert Panel. 2010. Guidelines for the diagnosis and management of food allergy in the United States. *Journal of Allergy and Clinical Immunology.* 126(6)(suppl.):S1–S58. www.jacionline.org/article/ S0091-6749(10)01566-6/fulltext.

21. National Digestive Diseases Information Clearinghouse (NDDIC). September 2008. Celiac Disease. NIH Publication No. 08-4269. http://digestive.niddk.nih.gov.

22. National Digestive Diseases Information Clearinghouse (NDDIC). January 2011. Diarrhea. NIH Publication No. 11-2749. http://digestive.niddk.nih.gov/ddiseases/ pubs/diarrhea/index.htm.

23. National Digestive Diseases Information Clearinghouse (NDDIC). September 2007. Irritable bowel syndrome. NIH Publication No. 07-693. http://digestive.niddk.nih.gov/ ddiseases/pubs/ibs/index.htm.

24. National Institutes of Health. March 12, 2002. Celiac Disease Meeting Summary. DDICC Meeting Minutes. http://digestive.niddk.nih.gov/federal/ddicc/ minutes_3-12-02.pdf.

Chapter 3

1. Sears, B. 1995. *The Zone. A Dietary Road Map.* New York: HarperCollins.
2. Steward, H. L., M. C. Bethea, S. S. Andrews, and L. A. Balart. 1995. *Sugar Busters! Cut Sugar to Trim Fat.* New York: Ballantine Books.
3. Atkins, R. C. 1992. *Dr. Atkins' New Diet Revolution.* New York: M. Evans & Company.
4. U.S. Department of Agriculture and U.S. Department of Health and Human Services. 2010. *Dietary Guidelines for Americans, 2010,* 7th edn. Washington, DC: U.S. Government Printing Office.
5. Institute of Medicine, Food and Nutrition Board. 2002. *Dietary Reference Intakes for Energy, Carbohydrates, Fiber, Fat, Protein and Amino Acids (Macronutrients).* Washington, DC: The National Academy of Sciences.
6. International Food Information Council Foundation. 2009. Facts About Low-Calorie Sweeteners. www.foodinsight .org/Content/6/LCS%20Fact%20Sheet_11-09.pdf.
7. Spiers, P. A., L. Sabounjian, A. Reiner, D. K. Myers, J. Wurtman, and D. L. Schomer. 1998. Aspartame: neuropsychologic and neurophysiologic evaluation and chronic effects. *Am. J. Clin. Nutr.* 68:531–537.
8. National Cancer Institute. 2009. Artificial Sweeteners and Cancer. www.cancer.gov/cancertopics/factsheet/Risk/ artificial-sweeteners.
9. Howard, B. V., and J. Wylie-Rosett. 2002. Sugar and cardiovascular disease. A statement for healthcare professionals from the Committee on Nutrition of the Council on Nutrition, Physical Activity, and Metabolism of the American Heart Association. *Circulation.* 106:523–527.
10. Meyer, K. A., L. H. Kushi, D. R. Jacobs, J. Slavin, T. A. Sellers, and A. R. Folsom. 2000. Carbohydrates, dietary fiber, and incident of type 2 diabetes in older women. *Am. J. Clin. Nutr.* 71:921–930.
11. Troiano, R. P., R. R. Briefel, M. D. Carroll, and K. Bialostosky. 2000. Energy and fat intakes of children and adolescents in the United States: data from the National Health and Nutrition Examination Surveys. *Am. J. Clin. Nutr.* 72:1343S–1353S.
12. Ludwig, D. S., K. E. Peterson, and S. L. Gortmaker. 2001. Relation between consumption of sugar-sweetened drinks and childhood obesity: a prospective, observational analysis. *Lancet.* 357:505–508.
13. National Diabetes Information Clearinghouse (NDIC). 2011. National Diabetes Statistics 2011. Diagnosed Diabetes. National Institutes of Health Publication No. 11-3892. http://diabetes.niddk.nih.gov/dm/pubs/ statistics/index.htm.
14. Huang, T., T.-K., Kempf, A. M., Strother, M. L., Li, C., Lee, R. E., Harris, K. J., and Kaur, H. 2004. Overweight and components of the metabolic syndrome in college students. *Diab. Care.* 27(12):3000–3001.
15. Pan, X.-P., G.-W. Li, Y.-H. Hu, J. X. Wang, W. Y. Yang, Z. X. An, Z. X. Hu, J. Lin, J. Z. Xiao, H. B. Cao, P. A. Liu, X. G. Jiang, Y. Y. Jiang, J. P. Wang, H. Zheng, H. Zhang, P. H. Bennett, and B. V. Howard. 1997. Effects of diet and exercise in preventing NIDDM in people with impaired glucose tolerance. *Diabetes Care.* 20:537–544.
16. American College of Sports Medicine and American Diabetes Association. 2010. Joint position stand. Exercise and type 2 diabetes. *Med. Sci. Sports Exerc.* 42(12):2282–2303.

Chapter 4

1. U.S. Department of Agriculture (USDA) and the Department of Health and Human Services (DHHS). 2010. Dietary Guidelines for Americans. www.cnpp.usda.gov/ dietaryguidelines.htm.
2. Institute of Medicine, Food and Nutrition Board. *2005. Dietary Reference Intakes for Energy, Carbohydrate, Fiber, Fat, Fatty Acids, Cholesterol, Protein, and Amino Acids (Macronutrients).* Washington, DC: National Academies Press.
3. Angell, S. Y., L. D. Silver, G. P. Goldstein, C. M. Johnson, D. R. Deitcher, T. T. Frieden, and M. T. Bassett. 2009. *Annals of Internal Medicine.*151(2):129–134.
4. Lichtenstein, A. H., et al. 2006. Diet and lifestyle recommendations revision 2006. A scientific statement from the American Heart Association Nutrition Committee. *Circulation.* 114:82–96.
5. Jones, P. J. H., and S. Kubow. 2006. Lipids, sterols, and their metabolites. In: Shils M. E., M. Shike, A. C. Ross, B. Caballero, and R. J. Cousins, eds. *Modern Nutrition in Health and Disease, 10th edn.* Baltimore, MD: Lippincott Williams & Wilkins.
6. Kris-Etherton, P. M., W. S. Harris, and L. J. Appel. 2002. Fish consumption, fish oil, omega-3 fatty acids and cardiovascular disease. *Circulation.* 106:2747–2757.
7. Din, J. N., D. E. Newby, and A. D. Flapan. 2004. Omega 3 fatty acids and cardiovascular disease—fishing for a natural treatment. *British Med. J.* 328(3):30–35.
8. Wijendran, V., and K. C. Hayes. 2004. Dietary n-6 and n-3 fatty acid balance and cardiovascular health. *Annu. Rev. Nutr.* 24:597–615.
9. Jebb, S. A., A. M. Prentice, G. R. Goldberg, P. R. Murgatroyd, A. E. Black, and W. A. Coward. 1996. Changes in macronutrient balance during over- and underfeeding assessed by 12-d continuous whole-body calorimetry. *Am. J. Clin. Nutr.* 64:259–266.
10. Ormrod, D. J., C. C. Holmes, and T. E. Miller. 1998. Dietary chitosan inhibits hypercholesterolaemia and atherogenesis in the apolipoprotein E–deficient mouse model of atherosclerosis. *Atherosclerosis.* 138(2):329–334.
11. Mhurchu, C. N., C. Dunshea-Mooij, D. Bennet, and A. Rodgers. 2005a. Effect of chitosan on weight loss in overweight and obese individuals: a systemic review of randomized control trials. *Obesity Rev.* 6:35–42.
12. Mhurchu, C. N., C. A. Dunshea-Mooij, D. Bennett, and A. Rodgers. 2005b. Chitosan for overweight or obesity. Cochrane database of systematic reviews (Online) (Cochrane Database Syst Rev) 2005(3): CD003892. 2005b.
13. Pittler, M. H., and E. Ernst. 2004 Dietary supplements for body-weight reduction: a systematic review. *Am. J. Clin. Nutr.* 79(4):529–536.
14. Mayo Clinic. 2010. Alli Weight-Loss Pill: Does It Work? MayoClinic.com, www.mayoclinic.com/health/alli/ WT00030.
15. Rodriguez, N. R., N. M. DiMarco, and S. Langley S. 2009. Position of the American Dietetic Association, Dietitians of Canada, and the American College of Sports Medicine: nutrition and athletic performance. *J. Am. Diet. Assoc.* 109:509–527.
16. Manore, M. M., S. I. Barr, and G. E. Butterfield. 2000. Position of the American Dietetic Association, Dietitians of Canada, and the American College of Sports

Medicine: nutrition and athletic performance. *J. Am. Diet. Assoc.* 100:1543–1556.

17. Lichtenstein, A. H., and L. Van Horn. 1998. Very low fat diets. *Circulation.* 98:935–939.

18. Expert Panel on Detection, Evaluation, and Treatment of High Blood Cholesterol in Adults, National Institutes of Health. 2001. Executive summary of the Third Report of the National Cholesterol Education Program (NCEP) Expert Panel on Detection, Evaluation, and Treatment of High Blood Cholesterol in Adults (Adult Treatment Panel III). *JAMA.* 285(19):2486–2509.

19. Teegala, S. M., W. C. Willett, and D. Mazaffarian. 2009. Consumption and health effects of trans fatty acids: a review. *JAOAC International.* 92(5):1250–1257.

20. Allison, D. B., S. K. Egan, L. M. Barraj, C. Caughman, M. Infante, and J. T. Heimbach. 1999. Estimated intakes of trans fatty and other fatty acids in the U.S. population. *J. Am. Diet. Assoc.* 99:166–174.

21. Kennedy, E., and D. Bowman. Assessment of the effect of fat-modified foods on dietary quality in adults, 19–50 years, using data from the Continuing Survey of Food Intake by Individuals. *JADA.* 2110:101(4):455–460.

22. Melanson, K., and J. Dwyer. 2002. Popular diets for treatment of overweight and obesity. In: Wadden, T. A., and A. J. Stunkard, eds., *Handbook of Obesity Treatment.* New York: Guilford Press.

23. National Center for Chronic Disease Prevention and Health Promotion (NCCDPHP). 2010. Heart Disease and Stroke Prevention. Addressing the Nation's Leading Killers: At a Glance 2010. www.cdc.gov/chronicdisease/resources/publications/AAG/dhdsp.htm.

24. Oomen, C. M., M. C. Ocké, E. J. Feskens, M. A. van Erp-Baart, F. J. Kok, and D. Kromhout. 2001. Association between trans fatty acid intake and 10-year risk of coronary heart disease in the Zutphen Elderly Study: a prospective population-based study. *Lancet.* 357(9258):746–751.

25. Tailor, A. M., P. H. M. Peeters, T. Norat, P. Vineis, and D. Romaguera. 2010. An update on the prevalence of the metabolic syndrome in children and adolescents. *International Journal of Pediatric Obesity.* 5:202–213.

26. National Institutes of Health, National Heart, Lung, and Blood Institute. 2010. What Is Metabolic Syndrome? www.nhlbi.nih.gov/health/dci/Diseases/ms/ms_whatis.html.

27. Kim, Y. I. 2001. Nutrition and cancer. In: Bowman, B. A., and R. M. Russell, eds., *Present Knowledge in Nutrition,* 8th edn. Washington, DC: International Life Sciences Institute Press.

28. American Institute for Cancer Research (AICR), World Cancer Research Fund, 2007. Food, Nutrition, Physical Activity, and the Prevention of Cancer: A Global Perspective. www.aicr.org.

29. American Cancer Society (ACS). December 2011. What Are the Risk Factors for Prostate Cancer? www.cancer.org/Cancer/ProstateCancer/.

30. Pierce, J. P., et al. 2007. Influence of a diet very high in vegetables, fruit and fiber and low in fat on prognosis following treatment for breast cancer. The Women's Healthy Eating and Living (WHEL) Randomized Trial. *JAMA.* 298(3):289–298.

31. Prentice, R. L., et al. 2006. Low-fat dietary pattern and risk of invasive breast cancer. The Women's Health Initiative randomized controlled dietary modification trial. *JAMA.* 295:629–642.

32. Willette, W. C., and M. J. Stamper. 2006. Foundations of a healthy diet. In: Shils, M. E., M. Shike, A. C. Ross, B. Caballero, and R. J. Cousins, eds., *Modern Nutrition in Health and Disease,* 10th edn. Baltimore, MD: Lippincott Williams & Wilkins.

33. Alexander, D. D., L. M. Morimoto, P. J. Mink, and K. A. Lowe. 2010. Summary and meta-analysis of prospective studies of animal fat intake and breast cancer. *Nutrition Research Reviews.* 23(1):169–179.

34. Meyerhart, J. A., et al. 2007. Association of dietary patterns with cancer recurrence and survival in patients with stage III colon cancer. *JAMA.* 298(7):754–764.

35. Ma, R. W., and K. Chapman. 2009. A systemic review of the effect of diet in prostate cancer prevention and treatment. *Journal of Human Nutrition and Dietetics.* 22(3):187–199.

Chapter 5

1. Vegetarian Resource Group. 2009, June 3. How many vegetarians are there? *Vegetarian Journal.* www.vrg.org/press/2009poll.htm.

2. Leitzmann, C. 2005. Vegetarian diets: what are the advantages? *Forum Nutr.* 57:147–156.

3. Szeto, Y. T., T. C. Kwok, and I. F. Benzie. 2004. Effects of a long-term vegetarian diet on biomarkers of antioxidant status and cardiovascular risk. *Nutrition.* 20(10):863–866.

4. Munger, R. G., J. R. Cerhan, and B. C.-H. Chiu. 1999. Prospective study of dietary protein intake and risk of hip fracture in postmenopausal women. *Am. J. Clin. Nutr.* 69:147–152.

5. Alekel, D. L., A. St. Germain, C. T. Peterson, K. B. Hanson, J. W. Stewart, and T. Toda. 2000. Isoflavone-rich soy protein isolate attenuates bone loss in the lumbar spine of perimenopausal women. *Am. J. Clin. Nutr.* 72:844–852.

6. Hunt, J. R., L. K. Johnson, and Z. K. Fariba Roughead. 2009. Dietary protein and calcium interact to influence calcium retention: a controlled feeding study. *Am. J. Clin. Nutr.* 89:1357–1365.

7. Poortmans, J. R., and O. Dellalieux. 2000. Do regular high-protein diets have potential health risks on kidney function in athletes? *Int. J. Sport Nutr.* 10:28–38.

8. Samaha, F. F., N. Iqbal, P. Seshadri, K. L. Chicano, D. A. Daily, J. McGrory, T. Williams, M. Williams, E. J. Gracely, and L. Stern. 2003. A low-carbohydrate as compared with a low-fat diet in severe obesity. *N. Engl. J. Med.* 348:2074–2081.

9. Stern, L., N. Iqbal, P. Seshadri, K. L. Chicano, D. A. Daily, J. McGrory, M. Williams, E. J. Gracely, and F. F. Samaha. 2004. The effects of low-carbohydrate versus conventional weight loss diets in severely obese adults: one-year follow-up of a randomized trial. *Ann. Intern. Med.* 140:778–785.

10. Foster, G. D., H. R. Wyatt, J. O. Hill, B. G. McGuckin, C. Brill, B. S. Mohammed, P. O. Szapary, D. J. Rader, J. S. Edman, and S. Klein. 2003. A randomized trial of a low-carbohydrate diet for obesity. *N. Engl. J. Med.* 348:2082–2090.

11. Bravata, D. M., L. Sanders, J. Huang, H. M. Krumholz, I. Olkin, C. D. Gardner, and D. M. Bravata. 2003. Efficacy and safety of low-carbohydrate diets. A systematic review. *JAMA.* 289:1837–1850.

12. Brehm, B. J., and D. A. D'Alessio. 2008. Benefits of high-protein weight loss diets: enough evidence for practice? *Curr. Opin. Endocrinol. Diabetes Obes.* 15:416–421.

13. Clifton, P. M., K. Bastiaans, and J. B. Keogh. 2009. High protein diets decrease total and abdominal fat and improve CVD risk profile in overweight and obese men and women with elevated triacylglycerol. *Nutr. Metab. Cardiovas. Dis.* 19:548–554.

14. Russell, W. R., S. W. Gratz, S. H. Duncan, G. Holtrop, J. Ince, L. Scobbie, G. Duncan, A. M. Johnstone, G. E. Lobley, R. John Wallace, G. G. Duthie, and H. J. Flint. 2011. High-protein, reduced-carbohydrate weight-loss diets promote metabolite profiles likely to be detrimental to colonic health. *Am. J. Clin. Nutr.* 93(5):1062–1072.

15. Henkel, J. 2000. Soy: health claims for soy protein, questions about other components. *FDA Consumer Magazine*, May–June. www.fda.gov/fdac/features/2000/300_soy.html.

16. American Heart Association. 2005. Choosing a Heart-Healthy Diet. www.americanheart.org/presenter.jhtml?identifier=353.

17. Centers for Disease Control and Prevention. (2010, June 7). Cancer and Men. www.cdc.gov/Features/CancerAndMen/.

18. American Cancer Society. 2007. Can Phytoestrogens Reduce Breast Cancer Risk and Treat Menopause? www.cancer.org/docroot/MED/content/MED_2_1x_Can_Phytoestrogens_Reduce_Cancer_Risk_and_Treat_Menopause.asp.

19. Ma, D.-F., L.-Q. Qin, P.-Y. Wang, and R. Katoh. 2008. Soy isoflavone intake increases bone mineral density in the spine of menopausal women: meta-analysis of randomized-controlled trials. *Clin. Nutr.* 27(1):57–64.

20. Albert, C. M., J. M. Gaziano, W. C. Willett, J. E. Mason, and C. H. Hennekens. 2002. Nut consumption and decreased risk of sudden cardiac death in the Physicians' Health Study. *Arch. Intern. Med.* 162:1382–1387.

21. Manore, M. M., N. L. Meyer, and J. Thompson. 2009. *Sport Nutrition for Health and Performance*, 2nd edn. Champaign, IL: Human Kinetics.

22. Garlick, P. J. 2004. The nature of human hazards associated with excessive intake of amino acids. *J. Nutr.* 134:1633S–1639S.

23. Institute of Medicine, Food and Nutrition Board. 2005. *Dietary Reference Intakes for Energy, Carbohydrate, Fiber, Fat, Fatty Acids, Cholesterol, Protein, and Amino Acids (Macronutrients)*. Washington, DC: National Academies Press.

24. Messina, M., and V. Messina. 1996. *The Dietitian's Guide to Vegetarian Diets*. Gaithersburg, MD: Aspen.

25. American Dietetic Association; Dietitians of Canada. 2003. Position of the American Dietetic Association and Dietitians of Canada: vegetarian diets. *J. Am. Diet. Assoc.* 103(6):748–765.

26. Messina, M. J. 1999. Legumes and soybeans: overview of their nutritional profiles and health effects. *Am. J. Clin. Nutr.* 70 (suppl.):439S–450S.

27. Institute of Medicine, Food and Nutrition Board. 2002. *Dietary Reference Intakes for Energy, Carbohydrate, Fiber, Fat, Fatty Acids, Cholesterol, Protein, and Amino Acids (Macronutrients)*. Washington, DC: National Academies Press.

28. Messina V., V. Melina, and A. Reed Mangels. 2003. A new food guide for North American vegetarians. *J. Am. Diet. Assoc.* 103(6):771–775.

Chapter 6

1. Bernstein, L. 2000. Dementia without a cause: lack of vitamin B_{12} can cause dementia. *Discover*, February 21.

2. Albanes, D., O. P. Heinonen, J. K. Huttunen, P. R. Taylor, J. Virtamo, B. K. Edwards, J. Haapakoski, M. Rautalahti, A. M. Hartman, J. Palmgren, and P. Greenwald. 1995. Effects of alpha-tocopherol and beta-carotene supplements on cancer incidence in the Alpha-Tocopherol Beta-Carotene Cancer Prevention Study. *Am. J. Clin. Nutr.* 62(suppl.):1427S–1430S.

3. Omenn, G. S., G. E. Goodman, M. D. Thornquist, J. Balmes, M. R. Cullen, A. Glass, J. P. Keogh, F. L. Meyskens, B. Valanis, J. H. Williams, S. Barnhart, and S. Hammar. 1996. Effects of a combination of beta carotene and vitamin A on lung cancer and cardiovascular disease. *New Engl. J. Med.* 334:1150–1155.

4. World Health Organization (WHO). 2008. Micronutrient Deficiencies. Vitamin A Deficiency. www.who.int/nutrition/topics/vad/en/.

5. Lim, H. W., B. A. Gilchrest, K. D. Cooper, H. A. Bischoff-Ferrari, D. S. Rigel, W. H. Cyr, S. Miller, et al. 2005. Sunlight, tanning booths, and vitamin D. *J. Am. Acad. Dermatol.* 52:868–876.

6. Heaney, R. P. 2005. The vitamin D requirement in health and disease. *J. Steroid Biochem. Molec. Biol.* 97:13–19.

7. Heaney, R. P. 2007. The case for improving vitamin D status. *J. Steroid Biochem. Molec. Biol.* 103:635–641.

8. Holick, M. F. 2006. Resurrection of vitamin D deficiency and rickets. *J. Clin. Invest.* 116:2062–2072.

9. Institute of Medicine, Food and Nutrition Board. 2010. *Dietary Reference Intakes for Calcium and Vitamin D.* Washington, DC: National Academies Press.

10. Centers for Disease Control and Prevention. 1999. Achievements in public health, 1900–1999: safer and healthier foods. *Morbidity and Mortality Weekly Report (MMWR).* 48(40):905–913. www.cdc.gov/mmwr/preview/mmwrhtml/mm4840a1.htm.

11. Rajakumar, K. 2003. Vitamin D, cod-liver oil, sunlight, and rickets: a historical perspective. *Pediatrics.* 112(2):e132–e135. http://pediatrics.aappublications.org/cgi/content/full/112/2/e132.

12. Sullivan, S. S., C. J. Rosen, W. A. Halteman, T. C. Chen, and M. F. Holick. 2005. Adolescent girls in Maine are at risk for vitamin D insufficiency. *J. Am. Diet. Assoc.* 105:971–974.

13. National Center for Complementary and Alternative Medicine. 2011. Dietary and Herbal Supplements. http://nccam.nih.gov/health/supplements/.

14. Nutrition Business Journal. 2009. 2009 U.S. Nutrition Industry Overview. Vol XIV, No 6/7, June/July. ©Penton Media, Inc.

15. U.S. Government Accountability Office. 2010. Herbal Dietary Supplements: Examples of Deceptive or

Questionable Marketing Practices and Potentially Dangerous Advice. GAO-10-662T. www.gao.gov/new.items/d10662t.pdf.

16. Hemilä, H., E. Chalker, B. Treacy, and B. Douglas. 2007. Vitamin C for preventing and treating the common cold. *Cochrane Database of Systematic Reviews*. Issue 3. Art. No. CD000980. DOI: 10.1002/14651858.CD000980.pub3.

17. National Institute of Allergy and Infectious Diseases. December 2004. The Common Cold. www.niaid.nih.gov/factsheets/cold.htm.

18. Massey, L. K., M. Liebman, and S. A. Kynast-Gales. 2005. Ascorbate increases human oxaluria and kidney stone risk. *J. Nutr.* 135:1673–1677.

19. Institute of Medicine, Food and Nutrition Board. 2001. *Dietary Reference Intakes for Vitamin A, Vitamin K, Arsenic, Boron, Chromium, Copper, Iodine, Iron, Manganese, Molybdenum, Nickel, Silicon, Vanadium, and Zinc.* Washington, DC: National Academies Press.

20. Office of Dietary Supplements (ODS). 2005. Dietary Supplement Fact Sheet: Vitamin B$_6$. http://ods.od.nih.gov/factsheets/vitaminb6.assumption.

21. Institute of Medicine, Food and Nutrition Board. 1998. *Dietary Reference Intakes for Thiamin, Riboflavin, Niacin, Vitamin B$_6$, Folate, Vitamin B$_{12}$, Pantothenic Acid, Biotin, and Choline.* Washington, DC: National Academies Press.

22. American Cancer Society. 2008. ACS Guidelines on Nutrition and Physical Activity for Cancer Prevention. www.cancer.org.

23. Greenwald, P., C. K. Clifford, and J. A. Milner. 2001. Diet and cancer prevention. *Eur. J. Cancer.* 37:948–965.

24. Joshipura, K. J., F. B. Hu, J. E. Manson, M. J. Stampfer, E. B. Rimm, F. E. Speizer, et al. 2001. The effect of fruit and vegetable intake on risk for coronary heart disease. *Ann. Intern. Med.* 134:1106–1114.

25. Liu, S., I.-M. Lee, U. Ajani, S. R. Cole, J. E. Buring, and J. E. Manson. 2001. Intake of vegetables rich in carotenoids and risk of coronary heart disease in men: The Physicians' Health Study. *Int. J. Epidemiol.* 30:130–135.

26. Agency for Healthcare Research and Quality (AHRQ), U.S. Preventive Services Task Force (USPSTF). 2003. Routine Vitamin Supplementation to Prevent Cancer and Cardiovascular Disease. www.ahrq.gov/clinic/3rduspstf/vitamins/vitaminsrr.htm.

27. National Center for Complementary and Alternative Medicine. 2008. Consumer Advisory: Vitamin E Supplements. http://nccam.nih.gov/news/alerts/vitamine/vitamine.htm.

28. World Cancer Research Fund/American Institute for Cancer Research (AICR). 2007. *Food, Nutrition, Physical Activity, and the Prevention of Cancer: A Global Perspective.* Washington, DC: AICR.

29. Gahche, J., R. Bailey, V. Burt, J. Hughes, E. Yetley, J. Dwyer, M. F. Picciano, M. McDowell, and C. Sempos. 2011. Dietary Supplement Use Among U.S. Adults Has Increased Since NHANES III (1988–1994). NCHS Data Brief. Number 61. www.cdc.gov/nchs/data/databriefs/db61.htm.

30. American Dietetic Association. 2009. Position of the American Dietetic Association: functional foods. *J. Am. Diet. Assoc.* 109(4):735–746.

31. Phytochemical Information Center. 2005. 5 a Day. Eat Your Colors, Get Your Phytochemicals. www.5aday.com/html/phytochem/colors.php.

Chapter 7

1. Eckhert, C. D. 2006. Other trace elements. In: Shils, M. E., M. Shike, A. C. Ross, B. Caballero, and R. J. Cousins, eds. *Modern Nutrition in Health and Disease,* 10th edn. Philadelphia: Lippincott Williams & Wilkins, pp. 338–350.

2. Institute of Medicine, Food and Nutrition Board. 2010. *Strategies to Reduce Sodium Intake in the United States.* Washington, DC: National Academies Press.

3. Sacks, F. M., L. P. Svetkey, W. M. Vollmer, L. J. Appel, G. A. Bray, D. Harsha, E. Obarzanek, P. R. Conlin, E. R. Miller III, D. G. Simons-Morton, N. Karanja, and P.-H. Lin. 2001. Effects on blood pressure of reduced dietary sodium and the Dietary Approaches to Stop Hypertension (DASH) diet. *N. Engl. J. Med.* 344:3–10.

4. Evans, G. W. 1989. The effect of chromium picolinate on insulin controlled parameters in humans. *Int. J. Biosoc. Med. Res.* 11:163–180.

5. Hasten, D. L., E. P. Rome, D. B. Franks, and M. Hegsted. 1992. Effects of chromium picolinate on beginning weight training students. *Int. J. Sports Nutr.* 2:343–350.

6. Lukaski, H. C., W. W. Bolonchuk, W. A. Siders, and D. B. Milne. 1996. Chromium supplementation and resistance training: effects on body composition, strength, and trace element status of men. *Am. J. Clin. Nutr.* 63:954–965.

7. Hallmark, M. A., T. H. Reynolds, C. A. DeSouza, C. O. Dotson, R. A. Anderson, and M. A. Rogers. 1996. Effects of chromium and resistive training on muscle strength and body composition. *Med. Sci. Sports Exerc.* 28:139–144.

8. Pasman, W. J., M. S. Westerterp-Plantenga, and W. H. Saris. 1997. The effectiveness of long-term supplementation of carbohydrate, chromium, fibre and caffeine on weight maintenance. *Int. J. Obesity Related Metab. Disorders.* 21:1143–1151.

9. Walker, L. S., M. G. Bemben, D. A. Bemben, and A. W. Knehans. 1998. Chromium picolinate effects on body composition and muscular performance in wrestlers. *Med. Sci. Sports Exerc.* 30:1730–1737.

10. Campbell, W. W., L. J. Joseph, S. L. Davey, D. Cyr-Campbell, R. A. Anderson, and W. J. Evans. 1999. Effects of resistance training and chromium picolinate on body composition and skeletal muscle in older men. *J. Appl. Physiol.* 86:29–39.

11. Volpe, S. L., H. W. Huang, K. Larpadisorn, and I. I. Lesser. 2001. Effect of chromium supplementation and exercise on body composition, resting metabolic rate and selected biochemical parameters in moderately obese women following an exercise program. *J. Am. Coll. Nutr.* 20:293–306.

12. Campbell, W. W., L. J. O. Joseph, R. A. Anderson, S. L. Davey, J. Hinton, and W. J. Evans. 2002. Effects of resistive training and chromium picolinate on body composition and skeletal muscle size in older women. *Int. J. Sports Nutr. Ex. Metab.* 12:125–135.

13. Vincent, J. B. 2003. The potential value and toxicity of chromium picolinate as a nutritional supplement, weight loss agent and muscle development agent. *Sports Med.* 33:213–230.

14. Office of Dietary Supplements. 2009. Dietary Supplement Fact Sheet: Selenium. http://ods.od.nih.gov/factsheets/selenium/.

15. Institute of Medicine, Food and Nutrition Board. 2001. *Dietary Reference Intakes for Vitamin A, Vitamin K, Arsenic, Boron, Chromium, Copper, Iodine, Iron, Manganese, Molybdenum, Nickel, Silicon, Vanadium, and Zinc.* Washington, DC: National Academies Press.

16. Centers for Disease Control and Prevention (CDC). 2002. Iron Deficiency—United States, 1999–2000. *Morbidity and Mortality Weekly Report.* 51(40):871–920. www.cdc.gov/mmwr/PDF/wk/mm5140.pdf.

17. U.S. Food and Drug Administration. 1997. Preventing iron poisoning in children. *FDA Backgrounder.* www.fda.gov/opacom/backgrounders/ironbg.html.

18. Prasad, A. 1996. Zinc: the biology and therapeutics of an ion. *Ann. Intern. Med.* 125:142–143.

19. Jackson J. L., E. Lesho, and C. Peterson. 2000. Zinc and the common cold: a meta-analysis revisited. *J. Nutr.* 130:1512S–1515S.

20. Sigh, M., and R. R. Das. 2011. Zinc for the common cold. *Cochrane Database of Systematic Reviews.* Issue 2. Art. No.: CD001364. DOI: 10.1002/14651858. CD001364.pub3.

21. Institute of Medicine, Food and Nutrition Board. 2011. *Dietary Reference Intakes for Calcium, Phosphorus, Magnesium, Vitamin D, and Fluoride.* Washington, DC: National Academies Press.

22. Keller, J. L., A. J. Lanou, and N. D. Barnard. 2002. The consumer cost of calcium from food supplements. *J. Am. Diet. Assoc.* 102: 1669–1671.

23. Heaney, R. P., and K. Rafferty. 2001. Carbonated beverages and urinary calcium excretion. *Am. J. Clin. Nutr.* 74: 343–347.

24. Wu, C. H., Y. C. Yang, W. J. Yao, F. H. Lu, J. S. Wu, and C. J. Chang. 2002. Epidemiological evidence of increased bone mineral density in habitual tea drinkers. *Arch. Intern. Med.* 162:1001–1006.

25. National Osteoporosis Foundation (NOF). 2011. Fast Facts. www.nof.org/node/40.

26. International Osteoporosis Foundation. 2004. By 2020, One in Two Americans over Age 50 Will Be at Risk for Fractures from Osteoporosis or Low Bone Mass. Press release issued by the Office of the U.S. Surgeon General, Thursday, October 14, 2004. www.osteofound.org/press_centre/pr_2004_10_14.html.

27. International Osteoporosis Foundation. 2010. The Facts About Osteoporosis and Its Impact. www.iofbonehealth.org/facts-and-statistics.html#factsheet-category-14.

28. National Institutes of Health. 2011. Osteoporosis Handout on Health. www.niams.nih.gov/Health_Info/Bone/Osteoporosis/osteoporosis_hoh.asp#5.

29. Tucker, K. L., M. T. Hannan, H. Chen, L. A. Cupples, P. W. F. Wilson, and D. P. Kiel. 1999. Potassium, magnesium, and fruit and vegetable intakes are associated with greater bone mineral density in elderly men and women. *Am. J. Clin. Nutr.* 69:727–736.

30. Tucker, K. L., H. Chen, M. T. Hannan, L. A. Cupples, P. W. F. Wilson, D. Felson, and D. P. Kiel. 2002. Bone mineral density and dietary patterns in older adults: The Framingham Osteoporosis Study. *Am. J. Clin. Nutr.* 76:245–252.

31. South-Pal, J. E. 2001. Osteoporosis: part II. Nonpharmacologic and pharmacologic treatment. *Am. Fam. Physician.* 63:1121–1128.

Chapter 8

1. Almond, C. S. D., et al. 2005. Hyponatremia among runners in the Boston Marathon. *N. Engl. J. Med.* 352:1150–1156.

2. Sawka, M. N., L. M. Burke, E. R. Eichner, R. J. Maughan, S. J. Montain, and N. S. Stachenfeld. 2007. American College of Sports Medicine position stand: exercise and fluid replacement. *Med. Sci. Sports. Exerc.* 39(2):377–390.

3. Institute of Medicine, Food and Nutrition Board. 2004. *Dietary Reference Intakes: Water, Potassium, Sodium, Chloride, and Sulfate.* Washington, DC: National Academies Press.

4. NPR Author Interview. May 10, 2010. War on Tap: Americans Obsession with Bottled Water, by Peter Gleick. www.npr.org/templates/story/story.php?storyId=126833795.

5. International Bottled Water Association. 2008. Consumers Vote for Bottled Water as Their "Number One" Beverage for a Healthy Lifestyle. www.bottledwater.org/public/2007_releases/2007-06-28_survey.htm.

6. Seifert, S. M., J. L. Schaechter, E. R. Hershorin, and S. E. Lipshultz. 2011. Health effects of energy drinks on children, adolescents, and young adults. *Pediatrics.* 127:511–528.

7. Centers for Disease Control and Prevention. 2011. Rethink Your Drink. www.cdc.gov/healthyweight/healthy_eating/drinks.html.

8. Duffey, K. J., and B. M. Poplin. 2007. Shifts in patterns and consumption of beverages between 1965 and 2002. *Obesity.* 15:2739–2747.

9. National Center for Catastrophic Sports Injury at UNC at Chapel Hill. http://ksi.uconn.edu/pdf%20linked/NCCSRecent%20Data%20on%20Heat%20Illness.pdf.

10. Centers for Disease Control and Prevention. 2010. FAQs: Alcohol and Public Health. www.cdc.gov/alcohol/faqs.htm.

11. U.S. Department of Agriculture and U.S. Department of Health and Human Services. 2010. *Dietary Guidelines for Americans, 2010,* 7th edn. Washington, DC: U.S. Government Printing Office.

12. Schoenborn, C. A., and P. F. Adams. 2010. Health behaviors of adults: United States, 2005–2007. *Vital Health Stat.* 10(245).

13. Insurance Institute for Highway Safety, Highway Loss Data Institute. 2011. DUI/DWI Laws. www.iihs.org/laws/dui.aspx.

14. Patra, J., B. Taylor, H. Irving, M. Roerecke, D. Baliunas, S. Mohapatra, and J. Rehm. 2010. Alcohol consumption and the risk of morbidity and mortality for different stroke types—a systemic review and meta-analysis. *BMC Public Health.* 10:258–269.

15. Ronksley, P. E., S. E. Brien, B. J. Turner, K. J. Mukamal, and W. A. Ghali. 2011. Association of alcohol consumption with selected cardiovascular disease outcomes: a systematic review and meta-analysis. *Brit. Med. J.l.* 342:d671doi:10.1136/bmj.d671. www.bmj.com/content/342/bmj.d671.full.

16. Brien, S. E., P. E. Ronksley, B. J. Turner, K. J. Mukamal, and W. A. Ghali. 2011. Effect of alcohol consumption on biological markers associated with risk of coronary heart disease: systematic review and meta-analysis of interventional studies. *Brit. Med.l Jl.*

342:d636doi:10.1136/bmj.d363. www.bmj.com/content/342/bmj.d636.long.

17. García, A. M., N. Ramón-Bou, and M. Porta. 2010. Isolated and joint effects of tobacco and alcohol consumption on risk of Alzheimer's disease. *J. Alzheimers Dis.* 20: 577–586.

18. Li, C. I., R. T. Chlebowski, M. Freiberg, K. C. Johnson, L. Kuller, D. Lane, L. Lessin, M. J. O'Sullivan, J. Wactawski-Wende, S. Yasmeen, and R. Prentice. 2010. Alcohol consumption and risk of postmenopausal breast cancer by subtype: the Women's Health Initiative Observational Study. *J. National Cancer Institute.* doi: 10.1093/jnci/djq316. http://jnci.oxfordjournals.org/content/early/2010/08/23/jnci.djq316.abstract.

19. Sesso, H. D., N. R. Cook, J. E. Buring, J. E. Manson, and J. M. Gaziano. 2008. Alcohol consumption and the risk of hypertension in women and men. *Hypertension.* 51:1080–1087.

20. Caton, S. J., M. Ball, A. Ahern, and M. M. Hetherington. 2004. Dose-dependent effects of alcohol on appetite and food intake. *Physiol. Behav.* 81:51–58.

21. National Institute on Alcohol Abuse and Alcoholism (NIAAA). 2008. Alcohol and other drugs. *Alcohol Alert.* 76:1–6. http://pubs.niaaa.nih.gov/publications/AA76/AA76.pdf.

22. National Institute on Alcohol Abuse and Alcoholism (NIAAA). 2007. Harmful Interactions: Mixing Alcohol with Medicines. NIH Publication No. 03-5329. http://pubs.niaaa.nih.gov/publications/medicine/medicine.htm.

23. U.S. Department of Education. Consequences of High Risk Drinking: Academic Performance. www.higheredcenter.org/high-risk/alcohol/consequences/academic-performance.

24. Centers for Disease Control and Prevention. 2010. Fact Sheets: Binge Drinking. www.cdc.gov/alcohol/fact-sheets/binge-drinking.htm.

25. Clark, D. B., D. L. Thatcher, and S. F. Tapert. 2008. Alcohol, psychological dysregulation, and adolescent brain development. *Alcoholism: Clin. and Exper. Res.* 32:375–385.

26. National Highway Traffic Safety Administration. 2010. U.S. Transportation Secretary LaHood Views Demonstration of New In-Vehicle Technology Targeted Toward Habitual Drunk Drivers. www.nhtsa.gov/PR/DOT-12-11.

27. Centers for Disease Control and Prevention. 2010. Fetal Alcohol Spectrum Disorders. www.cdc.gov/ncbddd/fasd/facts.html.

28. U.S. Department of Health and Human Services, Center for Substance Abuse Prevention. 2007. *Fetal Alcohol Spectrum Disorders by the Numbers*. DHHS Publication No. (SMA) 06-4236.

Chapter 9

1. Emme. 2009. Bio profile. http://emmestyle.com/about.

2. Manore, M. M, N. L. Meyer, and J. Thompson. 2009. *Sport Nutrition for Health and Performance,* 2nd edn. Champaign, IL: Human Kinetics.

3. Ravussin, E., S. Lillioja, T. E. Anderson, L. Christin, and C. Bogardus. 1986. Determinants of 24-hour energy expenditure in man: methods and results using a respiratory chamber. *J. Clin. Invest.* 78:1568–1578.

4. Harris, J., and F. Benedict. 1919. *A Biometric Study of Basal Metabolism in Man.* Washington, DC: Carnegie Institute of Washington.

5. Stunkard, A. J., T. I. A. Sørensen, C. Hanis, T. W. Teasdale, R. Chakraborty, W. J. Schull, and F. Schulsinger. 1986. An adoption study of human obesity. *N. Engl. J. Med.* 314:193–198.

6. Virtanen, K. A., M. E. Lidell, J. Orava, M. Heglind, R. Westergren, T. Niemi, M. Taittonen, J. Laine, N-J. Savito, S. Enerbäck, and P. Nuutila. 2009. Functional brown adipose tissue in healthy adults. *N. Engl. J. Med.* 360(15):1518–1525.

7. Cypess, A. M., S. Lehman, G. Williams, I. Tal, D. Rodman, A. B. Goldfine, F. C. Kuo, E. L. Palmer, Y-H. Tseng, A. Doria, G. M. Kolodny, and C. R. Kahn. 2009. Identification and importance of brown adipose tissue in adult humans. *N. Engl. J. Med.* 360(15):1509–1517.

8. Eyler, A. E., D. Matson-Koffman, D. Rohm-Young, S. Wilcox, J. Wilbur, J. L. Thompson, B. Sanderson, and K. R. Evenson. 2003. Quantitative study of correlates of physical activity in women from diverse racial/ethnic groups: the Women's Cardiovascular Health Network Project. *Am. J. Prev. Med.* 25(3Si):93–103.

9. Eyler, A. E., D. Matson-Koffman, J. R. Vest, K. R. Evenson, B. Sanderson, J. L. Thompson, J. Wilbur, S. Wilcox, and D. Rohm-Young. 2002. Environmental, policy, and cultural factors related to physical activity in a diverse sample of women: the Women's Cardiovascular Health Network Project—summary and discussion. *Women and Health.* 36:123–134.

10. Pickett, K. E., S. Kelly, E. Brunner, T. Lobstein, and R. G. Wilkinson. 2005. Wider income gaps, wider waistbands? An ecological study of obesity and income inequality. *J. Epidemiol. Community Health.* 59:670–674.

11. Elliott, S. 2005. Calories? Hah! Munch some mega M&M's. *The New York Times*, August 5, p. C5.

12. National Restaurant Association. 2007. Restaurant Industry to Continue to Be Major Driver in Nation's Economy Through Sales, Employment Growth in 2008. www.restaurant.org/pressroom/pressrelease.cfm?ID=1535.

13. U.S. Food and Drug Administration. April 1, 2011. FDA Proposes Draft Menu and Vending Machine Labeling Requirements, Invites Public to Comment on Proposals. www.fda.gov/NewsEvents/Newsroom/PressAnnouncements/ucm249471.htm.

14. Koh-Banerjee, P., N. F. Chu, D. Spiegelman, B. Rosner, G. Colditz, W. Willett, and E. Rimm. 2003. Prospective study of the association of changes in dietary intake, physical activity, alcohol consumption, and smoking with 9-y gain in waist circumference among 16,587 U.S. men. *Am. J. Clin. Nutr.* 78:719–27.

15. Lumeng, J. C., P. Forrest, D. P. Appugliese, N. Kaciroti, R. F. Corwyn, and R. H. Bradley. 2010. Weight status as a predictor of being bullied in third through sixth grades. *Pediatrics.* 125(6):e1301–e1307.

16. American Dietetic Association. 2002. Position of the American Dietetic Association: food and nutrition misinformation. *J. Am. Diet. Assoc.* 102(2):260–266.

17. Freedman, M. R., J. King, and E. Kennedy. 2001. Popular diets: a scientific review. *Obes. Res.* 9(suppl. 1):1S–40S.

18. National Institutes of Health. National Heart, Lung, and Blood Institute. 1998. Clinical Guidelines on the

Identification, Evaluation, and Treatment of Overweight and Obesity in Adults. Executive Summary. www.nhlbi .nih.gov/guidelines/obesity/ob_exsum.pdf.

19. Ello-Martin, J. A., J. H. Ledikwe, and B. J. Rolls. 2005. The influence of food portion size and energy density on energy intake: implications for weight management. *Am. J. Clin. Nutr.* 82(suppl.):236S–241S.

20. Flood, J. E., L. S. Roe, and B. J. Rolls. 2006. The effect of increased beverage portion size on energy intake at a meal. *J. Am. Diet. Assoc.* 106:1984–1990.

21. National Institute of Diabetes and Digestive and Kidney Diseases. Weight-control Information Network. 2009. Just Enough for You. About Food Portions. www.win.niddk .nih.gov/publications/just_enough.htm.

22. Klem, M. L., R. R. Wing, M. T. McGuire, H. M. Seagle, and J. O. Hill. 1997. A descriptive study of individuals successful at long-term maintenance of substantial weight loss. *Am. J. Clin. Nutr.* 66: 239–246.

23. Flegal, K. M, M. D. Carroll, C. L. Ogden, and L. R. Curtin. 2010. Prevalence and trends in obesity among U.S. adults, 1999–2008. *JAMA.* 303(3):235–241.

24. Grundy, S. M., B. Hansen, S. C. Smith, J. I. Cleeman, and R. A. Kahn. 2004. Clinical management of metabolic syndrome: report of the American Heart Association/ National Heart, Lung, and Blood Institute/American Diabetes Association Conference on Scientific Issues Related to Management. *Circulation,* 109:551–556.

25. Department of Health and Human Services. National Institutes of Health. National Heart, Lung and Blood Institute. 2010. Diseases and Conditions Index. Metabolic Syndrome. What Is Metabolic Syndrome? www.nhlbi.nih .gov/health/dci/Diseases/ms/ms_whatis.html.

26. Torgan, C. 2002. Childhood Obesity on the Rise. The NIH Word on Health. www.nih.gov/news/WordonHealth/ jun2002/childhoodobesity.htm.

27. Dietz, W. H. 1994. Critical periods in childhood for the development of obesity. *Am. J. Clin. Nutr.* 59:955–959.

28. Christakis, N. A., and J. H. Fowler. 2007. The spread of obesity in a large social network over 32 years. *N. Engl. J. Med.* 357(4):370–379.

29. National Institute of Diabetes and Digestive and Kidney Diseases. Weight-Control Information Network. 2008. Understanding Adult Obesity. NIH Publication No. 06–3680 www.win.niddk.nih.gov/publications/ understanding.htm#environmental.

30. Wing, R. R., and S. Phelan. 2005. Long-term weight loss maintenance. *Am. J. Clin. Nutr.* 82(1):222S–225S.

31. Institute of Medicine. Food and Nutrition Board. 2002. *Dietary Reference Intakes for Energy, Carbohydrate, Fiber, Fat, Fatty Acids, Cholesterol, Protein, and Amino Acids (Macronutrients).* Washington, DC: National Academies Press.

32. Hernandez, T. L., J. M. Kittelson, C. K. Law, L. L. Ketch, N. R. Stob, R. C. Lindstrom, A. Scherzinger, E. R. Stamm, and R. H. Eckel. 2011. Fat redistribution following suction lipectomy: defense of body fat and patterns of restoration. *Obesity.* Epublication ahead of print, doi:10.1038/ oby.2011.64.

33. Vandereycken, W. 2002. Families of patients with eating disorders. In: Fairburn, D. G., and K. D. Brownell, eds. *Eating Disorders and Obesity: A Comprehensive Handbook,* 2nd edn. New York Guilford Press, pp. 215–220.

34. Patrick, L. 2002. Eating disorders: a review of the literature with emphasis on medical complication and clinical nutrition. *Altern. Med. Rev.* 7(3):184–202.

35. Striegel-Moore, R. H., and L. Smolak. 2002. Gender, ethnicity, and eating disorders. In: Fairburn, D. G., and K. D. Brownell, eds. *Eating Disorders and Obesity: A Comprehensive Handbook,* 2nd edn. New York: Guilford Press, pp. 251–255.

36. Steinberg, L. 2002. *Adolescence,* 6th edn. New York: McGraw-Hill.

37. Stice, E. 2002. Sociocultural influences on body image and eating disturbances. In: Fairburn, D. G., and K. D. Brownell, eds. *Eating Disorders and Obesity: A Comprehensive Handbook,* 2nd edn. New York: Guilford Press, pp. 103–107.

38. Wonderlich, S. A. 2002. Personality and eating disorders. In: Fairburn, D. G., and K. D. Brownell, eds. *Eating Disorders and Obesity: A Comprehensive Handbook,* 2nd edn. New York: Guilford Press, pp. 204–209.

39. American Psychiatric Association (APA). 1994. *Diagnostic and Statistical Manual of Mental Disorders (DSM-IV,* 4th edn. Washington, DC: APA.

40. Robb, A. S., and M. J. Dadson. 2002. Eating disorders in males. *Child Adolesc. Psychiatric. Clin. N. Am.* 11:399–418.

41. Beals, K. A. 2004. *Disordered Eating in Athletes: A Comprehensive Guide for Health Professionals.* Champaign, IL: Human Kinetics.

42. Andersen, A. E. 1992. Eating disorders in male athletes: a special case? In: Brownell, K. D., J. Rodin, and J. H. Wilmore, eds. *Eating, Body Weight and Performance in Athletes: Disorders of Modern Society.* Philadelphia: Lea and Febiger, pp. 172–188.

43. Rohman, L. 2009. The relationship between anabolic androgenic steroids and muscle dysmorphia: a review. *Eat. Disord.* 17(3):187–199.

44. Pope, H. G., K. A. Phillips, and R. Olivardia. 2000. *The Adonis Complex: The Secret Crisis of Male Body Obsession.* New York: Free Press.

45. Garfinkel, P. E. 2002. Classification and diagnosis of eating disorders. In: Fairburn D. G., and K. D. Brownell, eds. *Eating Disorders and Obesity: A Comprehensive Handbook,* 2nd edn. New York: Guilford Press, pp. 155–161.

46. Stunkard, A. J. 2002. Night eating syndrome. In: Fairburn, D. G., and K. D. Brownell, eds. *Eating Disorders and Obesity: A Comprehensive Handbook,* 2nd edn. New York: Guilford Press, pp. 183–187.

47. Nattiv, A., A. B. Loucks, M. M. Manore, C. F. Sanborn, J. Sundgot-Borgen, and M. P. Warren. 2007. The female athlete triad. *Med. Sci. Sports Exerc.* 39(10):1867–1882.

Chapter 10

1. U.S. Department of Health and Human Services. 1996. *Physical Activity and Health: A Report of the Surgeon General.* Atlanta: U.S. Department of Health and Human Services, Centers for Disease Control and Prevention, National Centers for Chronic Disease Prevention and Health Promotion.

2. Caspersen, C. J., K. E. Powell, and G. M. Christensen. 1985. Physical activity, exercise, and physical fitness: definitions and distinctions for heath-related research. *Public Health Rep.* 100:126–131.

3. Heyward, V. H. 2010. *Advanced Fitness Assessment and Exercise Prescription,* 6th edn. Champaign, IL: Human Kinetics.

4. Centers for Disease Control and Prevention. 2010. U.S. Physical Activity Statistics. http://apps.nccd.cdc.gov/PASurveillance/StateSumResultV.asp.

5. Centers for Disease Control and Prevention. 2010. No Leisure-Time Physical Activity Trend Chart. www.cdc.gov/nccdphp/dnpa/physical/stats/leisure_time.htm.

6. Centers for Disease Control and Prevention. 2010. Youth risk behavior surveillance—United States, 2009. *MMWR.* 59(SS-5):1–142.

7. Pate, R. R., M. G. Davis, T. N. Robinson, E. J. Stone, T. L. McKenzie, and J. C. Young. 2006. Promoting physical activity in children and youth. A leadership role for schools: a scientific statement from the American Heart Association Council on Nutrition, Physical Activity and Metabolism (Physical Activity Committee) in collaboration with the Councils on Cardiovascular Disease in the Young and Cardiovascular Nursing. *Circulation.* 114:1214–1224.

8. Centers for Disease Control and Prevention. 2010. Physical Activity for Everyone. Target Heart Rate and Estimated Maximum Heart Rate. www.cdc.gov/physicalactivity/everyone/measuring/heartrate.html.

9. Tarnopolsky, M. 2010. Protein and amino acid needs for training and bulking up. In: Burke, L., and V. Deakin, eds. *Clinical Sports Nutrition,* 3rd edn. New York: McGraw-Hill, pp. 61–95.

10. Westerblad, H., D. G. Allen, and J. Lännergren. 2002. Muscle fatigue: lactic acid or inorganic phosphate the major cause? *News Physiol. Sci.* 17(1):17–21.

11. Brooks, G. A., T. D. Fahey, T. P. White, and K. M. Baldwin. 2000. *Exercise Physiology: Human Bioenergetics and Its Applications.* Mountain View, CA: Mayfield.

12. Brooks, G. A. 2009. Cell–cell and intracellular lactate shuttles. *J. Physiol.* 587(23):5591–5600.

13. Van Hall G., M. Stromstad, P. Rasmussen, O. Jans, M. Zaar, C. Gam, B. Quistorff, N. H. Secher, and H. B. Nielsen. 2009. Blood lactate is an important energy source for the human brain. *J. Cerebral Blood Flow & Metab.* 29(6):1121–1129.

14. American College of Sports Medicine, American Dietetic Association, and Dietitians of Canada. 2009. Nutrition and athletic performance. Joint position statement. *Med. Sci. Sports Exerc.* 41:709–731.

15. Burke, L. 2010. Nutrition for recovery after training and competition. In: Burke, L., and V. Deakin, eds. *Clinical Sports Nutrition,* 4th edn. New York: McGraw-Hill, pp. 358–392.

16. Van Loon, L. J. C., W. H. M. Saris, M. Kruijshoop, and A. J. M. Wagenmakers. 2000. Maximizing postexercise muscle glycogen synthesis: carbohydrate supplementation and the application of amino acid or protein hydrolysate mixtures. *Am. J. Clin. Nutr.* 72:106–111.

17. Jentjens, R. L., L. J. C. van Loon, C. H. Mann, A. J. M. Wagenmakers, and A. E. Jeukendrup. 2001. Addition of protein and amino acids to carbohydrates does not enhance postexercise muscle glycogen synthesis. *J. Appl. Physiol.* 91:839–846.

18. Sears, B. 1995. *The Zone: A Dietary Road Map.* New York: HarperCollins.

19. Manore, M. M., N. L. Meyer, and J. Thompson. 2009. *Sport Nutrition for Health and Performance.* 2nd edn. Champaign, IL: Human Kinetics.

20. Weaver, C. M., and S. Rajaram. 1992. Exercise and iron status. *J. Nutr.* 122:782–787.

21. Haymes, E. M. 1998. Trace minerals and exercise. In: Wolinsky, I., ed. *Nutrition and Exercise and Sport.* Boca Raton, FL: CRC Press, pp. 1997–2218.

22. Haymes, E. M., and P. M. Clarkson. 1998. Minerals and trace minerals. In: Berning J. R., and S. N. Steen, eds. *Nutrition and Sport and Exercise.* Gaithersburg, MD: Aspen, pp. 77–107.

23. Lightsey, D. M., and J. R. Attaway. 1992. Deceptive tactics used in marketing purported ergogenic aids. *Natl. Strength Cond. Assoc. J.* 14:26–31.

24. Federal Trade Commission (FTC). 2009. Facts for Consumers. 'Miracle' Health Claims: Add a Dose of Skepticism. www.ftc.gov/bcp/edu/pubs/consumer/health/hea07.shtm.

25. Food and Drug Administration (FDA). 2004. HHS Launches Crackdown on Products Containing Andro. www.fda.gov/NewsEvents/Newsroom/PressAnnouncements/2004/ucm108262.htm.

26. Broeder, C. E., J. Quindry, K. Brittingham, et al. 2000. The Andro Project: physiological and hormonal influences of androstenedione supplementation in men 35 to 65 years old participating in a high-intensity resistance training program. *Arch. Intern. Med.* 160:3093–3104.

27. Balsom, P. D., K. Söderlund, B. Sjödin, and B. Ekblom. 1995. Skeletal muscle metabolism during short duration high-intensity exercise: influence of creatine supplementation. *Acta Physiol. Scand.* 1154:303–310.

28. Grindstaff, P. D., R. Kreider, R. Bishop, M. Wilson, L. Wood, C. Alexander, and A. Almada. 1997. Effects of creatine supplementation on repetitive sprint performance and body composition in competitive swimmers. *Int. J. Sport Nutr.* 7:330–346.

29. Kreider, R. B., M. Ferreira, M. Wilson, et al. 1998. Effects of creatine supplementation on body composition, strength, and sprint performance. *Med. Sci. Sports Exerc.* 30:73–82.

30. Tarnopolsky, M. A., and D. P. MacLennan. 2000. Creatine monohydrate supplementation enhances high-intensity exercise performance in males and females. *Int. J. Sport Nutr. Exerc. Metab.* 10:452–463.

31. Kreider, R., M. Ferreira, M. Wilson, and A. L. Almada. 1999. Effects of calcium beta-hydroxy-beta-methylbutyrate (HMB) supplementation during resistance-training on markers of catabolism, body composition and strength. *Int. J. Sports Med.* 20(8):503–509.

32. Volek, J. S., N. D. Duncan, S. A. Mazzetti, et al. 1999. Performance and muscle fiber adaptations to creatine supplementation and heavy resistance training. *Med. Sci. Sports Exerc.* 31:1147–1156.

33. Reuters. 2001. Creatine use could lead to cancer, French government reports. *The New York Times,* January 25.

34. Jeong, K. S., S. J. Park, C. S. Lee, et al. 2000. Effects of cyclocreatine in rat hepatocarcinogenesis model. *Anticancer Res.* 20(3A):1627–1633.

35. Ara, G., L. M. Gravelin, R. Kaddurah-Daouk, and B. A. Teicher. 1998. Antitumor activity of creatine analogs produced by alterations in pancreatic hormones and glucose metabolism. *In Vivo.* 12:223–231.

36. Finn, K. J., R. Lund, and M. Rosene-Treadwell. 2003. Glutamine supplementation did not benefit athletes during short-term weight reduction. *J. Sports Sci. Med.* 2:163–168.

37. Campbell, B. I., P. M. La Bounty, and M. Roberts. 2004. The ergogenic potential of arginine. *J. Int. Soc. Sports Nutr.* 1(2):35–38.

38. Anderson, M. E., C. R. Bruce, S. F. Fraser, N. K. Stepto, R. Klein, W. G. Hopkins, and J. A. Hawley. 2000. Improved 2000-meter rowing performance in competitive oarswomen after caffeine ingestion. *Int. J. Sport Nutr. Exerc. Metab.* 10:464–475.

39. Spriet, L. L., and R. A. Howlett. 2000. Caffeine. In: Maughan, R. J., ed. *Nutrition in Sport.* Oxford: Blackwell Science, pp. 379–392.

40. Seifert, S. M., J. L. Schaechter, E. R. Hershorin, and S. E. Lipshultz. 2011. Health effects of energy drinks on children, adolescents, and young adults. *Pediatrics.* 127(3):511–528.

41. Bucci, L. 2000. Selected herbals and human exercise performance. *Am. J. Clin. Nutr.* 72:624S–636S.

42. Williams, M. H. 1998. *The Ergogenics Edge.* Champaign, IL: Human Kinetics.

43. Hawley, J. A. 2002. Effect of increased fat availability on metabolism and exercise capacity. *Med. Sci. Sports Exerc.* 34(9):1485–1491.

44. Heinonen, O. J. 1996. Carnitine and physical exercise. *Sports Med.* 22:109–132.

45. Vincent, J. B. 2003. The potential value and toxicity of chromium picolinate as a nutritional supplement, weight loss agent and muscle development agent. *Sports Med.* 33(3):213–230.

46. Pliml, W., T. von Arnim, A. Stablein, H. Hofmann, H. G. Zimmer, and E. Erdmann. 1992. Effects of ribose on exercise-induced ischaemia in stable coronary artery disease. *Lancet.* 340(8818):507–510.

47. Earnest, C. P., G. M. Morss, F. Wyatt, A. N. Jordan, S. Colson, T. S. Church, Y. Fitzgerald, L. Autrey, R. Jurca, and A. Lucia. 2004. Effects of a commercial herbal-based formula on exercise performance in cyclists. *Med. Sci. Sports Exerc.* 36(3):504–509.

48. Hellsten, Y., L. Skadhauge, and J. Bangsbo. 2004. Effect of ribose supplementation on resynthesis of adenine nucleotides after intense intermittent training in humans. *Am. J. Physiol. Regul. Integr. Comp. Physiol.* 286:R182–R188.

49. Kreider, R. B., C. Melton, M. Greenwood, C. Rasmussen, J. Lundberg, C. Earnest, and A. Almada. 2003. Effects of oral D-ribose supplementation on anaerobic capacity and selected metabolic markers in healthy males. *Int. J. Sport Nutr. Exerc. Metab.* 13(1):76–86.

Chapter 11

1. Ogden, C. L., M. D. Carroll, L. R. Curtin, M. M. Lamb, and K. M. Flegal. 2010. Prevalence of high body mass index in U.S. children and adolescents, 2007–2008. *JAMA.* 303:242–249.

2. Flegal, K. M., M. D. Carroll, C. L. Ogden, and L. R. Curtin. 2010 Prevalence and trends in obesity among U.S. adults, 1999–2008. *JAMA.* 303:235–241.

3. Stothard, K. J., P. W. G. Tennant, R. Bell, and J. Rankin. 2009. Maternal overweight and obesity and the risk of congenital anomalies: a systematic review and meta-analysis. *JAMA.* 301:636–650.

4. Attaman, J. A. 2010. Dietary Fats and Semen Quality Among Men Attending a Fertility Clinic. American Society for Reproductive Medicine 66th Annual Meeting, Abstract O-168. October 26, 2010.

5. Young, S. S., B. Eskenazi, F. M. Marchetti, G. Block, and A. J. Wyrobek. 2008. The association of folate, zinc, and antioxidant intake with sperm aneuploidy in healthy non-smoking men. *Human Reproduction.* 23:1014–1022.

6. Rasmussen, K. M., and A. L. Yaktine, eds., Committee to Reexamine IOM Pregnancy Weight Guidelines; Institute of Medicine; National Research Council. 2009. *Weight Gain During Pregnancy: Reexamining the Guidelines.* Washington, DC: National Academies Press.

7. Wrotniak, B. H., J. Shults, S. Butts, and N. Stettler. 2008. Gestational weight gain and risk of overweight in the offspring at age 7 in a multicenter, multiethnic cohort study. *Am. J. Clin. Nutr.* 87:1818–1824.

8. Institute of Medicine, Food and Nutrition Board. 2002. *Dietary Reference Intakes for Energy, Carbohydrate, Fiber, Fat, Fatty Acids, Cholesterol, Protein, and Amino Acids.* Washington, DC: National Academies Press.

9. U.S. Food and Drug Administration. 2009. What You Need to Know About Mercury in Fish and Shellfish. www.fda.gov/food/resourcesforyou/consumers/ucm110591.htm.

10. Institute of Medicine, Food and Nutrition Board. 1998. *Dietary Reference Intakes for Thiamin, Riboflavin, Niacin, Vitamin B_6, Folate, Vitamin B_{12}, Pantothenic Acid, Biotin, and Choline.* Washington, DC: National Academies Press.

11. Institute of Medicine, Food and Nutrition Board. 2001. *Dietary Reference Intakes for Vitamin A, Vitamin K, Arsenic, Boron, Chromium, Copper, Iodine, Iron, Manganese, Molybdenum, Nickel, Silicon, Vanadium, and Zinc.* Washington, DC: National Academies Press.

12. Institute of Medicine, Food and Nutrition Board. 2011. *Dietary Reference Intakes for Calcium and Vitamin D.* Washington, DC: National Academies Press.

13. Institute of Medicine, Food and Nutrition Board. 2004. *Dietary Reference Intakes for Water, Potassium, Sodium, Chloride, and Sulfate.* Washington, DC: National Academies Press.

14. Matson, J. L., B. Belva, M. A. Hattier, and M. L. Matson. 2011. Pica in persons with developmental disabilities: characteristics, diagnosis, and assessment. *Research in Autism Spectrum Disorders.* Doi:10.1016/j.rasd.2011.02.006.

15. Kuehn, B. M. 2011. CDC advises pregnancy lead screening that targets populations at risk. *JAMA.* 305:347. www.nlm.nih.gov/medlineplus/ency/article/001538.htm.

16. Martin, J. A., B. E. Hamilton, P. D. Sutton, S. J. Ventura, T. J. Mathews, and M. J. K. Osterman. 2010. Births: final data for 2008. National Vital Statistics Reports 59(1). Hyattsville, MD: National Center for Health Statistics.

17. March of Dimes. 2010. Caffeine in Pregnancy. www.marchofdimes.com/nutrition_caffeine.html.

18. March of Dimes. 2008. Drinking Alcohol During Pregnancy. www.marchofdimes.com/alcohol_indepth.html.

19. Substance Abuse and Mental Health Services Administration. 2010. *Results from the 2009 National Survey on Drug Use and Health: National Findings, Tobacco Use.* (PDF–1.17 MB) Rockville, MD: Substance Abuse and Mental Health Services Administration, Office of Applied Studies.

20. Davidson, M., M. London, and P. Ladewig, P. (2012). *Olds' Maternal-Newborn Nursing and Women's Health,* 9th edn. Upper Saddle River, NJ: Pearson.

21. American College of Obstetricians and Gynecologists. 2003. Exercise During Pregnancy. www.acog.org/publications/patient_education/bp119.cfm.

22. Gavard, J. A., and R. Arrtal. 2008. Effect of exercise on pregnancy outcome. *Clin. Obst. & Gyn.* 51:467–480.

23. American Academy of Pediatrics. 2005. Policy statement: breastfeeding and the use of human milk. *Pediatrics.* 115(2):496–506.

24. Bartick, M., and A. Reinhold. 2010. The burden of suboptimal breastfeeding in the United States: a pediatric cost analysis. *Pediatrics.* 125:e1048–e1056.

25. Thygarajan, A., and A. W. Burks. 2008. American Academy of Pediatrics recommendations on the effects of early nutritional interventions on the development of atopic disease. *Curr. Opin. Pediatr.* 20:698–702.

26. Mennella, J. A., L. M. Yourshaw, and L. K. Morgan. 2007. Breastfeeding and smoking: short-term effects on infant feeding and sleep. *Pediatrics.* 120:497–502.

27. U.S. Department Health and Human Services. 2011. AIDS Info: HIV Infected Women and Their Babies After Birth. www.aidsinfo.nih.gov/contentfiles/hivpositivewomenandtheirbabies_fs_en.pdf.

28. Satter, E. 2005. *Your Child's Weight: Helping Without Harming, Birth Through Adolescence.* Madison, WI: Kelcy Press.

29. Stern, R. 2007. Diet from hell. *Phoenix New Times,* May 10, 2007. www.phoenixnewtimes.com/2007-05-10/news/diet-from-hell/.

30. Benton, D. 2010. The influence of dietary status on the cognitive performance of children. *Molecular Nutr. Food Res.* 54:457–470.

31. Hoyland, A., L. Dye, and C. L. Lawton. 2009. A systematic review of the effect of breakfast on the cognitive performance of children and adolescents. *Nutr. Res. Rev.* 22:220–243.

32. Story, M. 2009. The Third School Nutrition Dietary Assessment Study: findings and policy implications for improving the health of U.S. children. *J. Am. Diet Assoc.* 109:S7–S13.

33. Miller, C. H. 2009. A practice perspective on the Third School Nutrition Dietary Assessment Study. *J. Am. Diet. Assoc.* 109:S14–S17.

34. Stallings, V. A., and A. L. Yaktine, eds. 2007. *Nutrition Standards for Foods in Schools: Leading the Way Toward Healthier Youth.* Washington, DC: National Academies Press.

35. Nord, M., A. Coleman-Jensen, M. Andrews, and S. Carlson. 2010. *Household Food Security in the United States, 2009.* ERS Report Summary. Economic Research Report No. (ERR-108). Washington, DC: Economic Research Service.

36. Neuman, W. 2011. U.S. seeks new limits on food ads for children. *The New York Times,* April 29. www.nytimes.com/2011/04/29/business/29label.html.

37. Deshmukh-Taskar, P. R., T. A. Nicklas, C. E. O'Neil, D. R. Keast, J. D. Radcliffe, and A. Cho, S. 2010. The relationship of breakfast skipping and type of breakfast consumption with nutrient intake and weight status in children and adolescents: the National Health and Nutrition Examination Survey 1999–2006. *J. Am. Diet. Assoc.* 110:869–878.

38. Food Research & Action Center. 2010. Breakfast in the Classroom Bibliography. http://frac.org/wp-content/uploads/2010/10/bic_bibliography.pdf.

39. Giovannini, M., C. Agonstoni, and R. Shamir. 2010. Symposium overview: do we all eat breakfast and is it important? *Crit. Revs. in Food Sci. and Nut.* 50:97–99.

40. Fiore, H., S. Travis, A. Whalen, P. Auinger, and S. Ryan. 2006. Potentially protective factors associated with healthful body mass index in adolescents with obese and nonobese parents: a secondary data analysis of the Third National Health and Nutrition Examination Survey, 1988–1994. *J. Am. Diet Assoc.* 106:55–64.

41. Alexander, K. E., E. E. Ventura, D. Spruijt-Metz, M. J. Weigensberg, M. I. Goran, and J. N. Davis. 2009. Association of breakfast skipping with visceral fat and insulin indices in overweight Latino youth. *Obesity.* 17:1528–1533.

42. Kahn, J. A., B. Huang, M. W. Gillman, A. E. Field, S. B. Austin, G. A. Colditz, and A. L. Frazier. 2008. Patterns and determinants of physical activity in U.S. adolescents. *J. Adolescent Health.* 42:369–377.

43. Larson, L. I., D. Neumark-Sztainer, L. Harnack, M. Wall, M. Story, and M. E. Eisenberg. 2009. Calcium and dairy intake: longitudinal trends during the transition to young adulthood and correlates of calcium intake. *J. Nutr. Educ. Behav.* 41:254–260.

44. Moore, L. L., M. L. Bradless, A. S. Di Gao, and M. R. Singer. 2008. Effects of average childhood dairy intake on adolescent bone health. *J. Pediatr.* 153:667–673.

45. Spencer, E. H., H. R. Ferdowsian, and N. D. Barnard. 2009. Diet and acne: a review of the evidence. *Int. J. of Derm.* 48:339–347.

46. U.S. Food and Drug Administration. 2010. Isotretinoin (Marketed as Accutane) Capsule Information. www.fda.gov/Drugs/DrugSafety/PostmarketDrugSafetyInformationforPatientsandProviders/ucm094305.htm.

47. Federal Interagency Forum on Aging-Related Statistics. 2010. *Older Americans 2010: Key Indicators of Well-Being.* Washington, DC: U.S. Government Printing Office.

48. www.cdc.gov/nchs/data/nvsr/nvsr59/nvsr59_04.pdf.

49. Jin, K. 2010. Modern biological theories of aging. *Aging Dis.* 1:72–74.

50. Fontana, L., L. Partridge, and V. D. Longo. 2010. Extending healthy life span—from yeast to humans. *Science.* 328:321–326.

51. Speakman, J. 2010. Can calorie restriction increase the human lifespan? *Experimental Biology.*

52. Ogden, C. L., M. D. Carroll, L. R. Curtin, M. A. McDowell, C. J. Tabak, and K. M. Flegal. 2006. Prevalence of overweight and obesity in the United States, 1999–2004. *JAMA.*295:1549–1555.

53. Horie, N. C., C. Cercato, M. C. Mancini, and A. Halpern. 2010. Long-term pharmacotherapy for obesity in elderly patients: a retrospective evaluation of medical records from a specialized obesity outpatient clinic. *Drugs & Aging.* 27:497–506.

54. Dorman, R. B., A. Abraham, W. B. Al-Refaie, H. M. Parsons, S. Ikramuddin, and E. Habermann. 2011. Bariatric surgery outcomes in the elderly population: an ACS NSQUI study. *Gastroenterology.* 140:S24. www.ssat.com/cgi-bin/abstracts/11ddw/O24.cgi.

55. Nelson, H. D., E. M. Haney, T. Dana, C. Bougatsos, and R. Chou. 2010. Screening for osteoporosis: an update for the U.S. Preventive Services Task Force. *Anls. of Int. Med.* 153:99–111.

56. Kaiser Family Foundation. 2009. Retail Prescription Drugs Filled at Pharmacies (Annual per Capita by Age), 2009. www.statehealthfacts.org/comparetable.jsp?ind=268&cat.

Chapter 12

1. Centers for Disease Control and Prevention (CDC). 2011. Salmonella. www.cdc.gov/salmonella/.

2. Centers for Disease Control and Prevention. 2011. *E. coli.* www.cdc.gov/ecoli/.

3. Scallan, E., R. M. Hockstra, F. J. Angulo, R. V. Tauxe, M-A. Widdowso, S. L. Roy, et al. 2011. Foodborne illness acquired in the United States—major pathogens. *Emerg. Infect. Dis.* DOI: 10.3201/eid1701.P11101.

4. Centers for Disease Control and Prevention. 2009. Investigation Update: Outbreak of *Salmonella typhimurium* Infections, 2008–2009. www.cdc.gov/salmonella/typhimurium/update.html.

5. Centers for Disease Control and Prevention. 2009. Annual Report Indicates Salmonella Continues to Show Least Improvement. www.cdc.gov/media/pressrel/2009/r090409.htm.

6. Hamburg, M. A. 2011. Food Safety Modernization Act: Putting the Focus on Prevention. www.whitehouse.gov/blog/2011/01/03/food-safety-modernization-act-putting-focus-prevention.

7. Hall, A. J. 2011. Norovirus in the News. www.foodsafety.gov/blog/norovirus.html.

8. Norovirus Blog. January 14, 2009. Michigan Continues to Be a Hotspot for Norovirus. www.noroblog.com/2009/01/articles/norovirus-outbreaks/michigan-continues-to-be-a-hotspot-for-norovirus/.

9. U.S. Department of Agriculture (USDA) Food Safety and Inspection Service. 2001. Parasites and Foodborne Illness. http://origin-www.fsis.usda.gov/Fact_Sheets/Parasites_and_Foodborne_Illness/index.asp.

10. Bauman, R. W. 2009. *Microbiology.* San Francisco: Pearson Benjamin Cummings.

11. International Society for Infectious Diseases. 2010. Prion Disease Update 2010. *March 4, 2010.* http://promedmail.oracle.com/pls/otn/pm?an=20100304.0709.

12. Preidt, R. 2010. Predicted "Red Tide" Could Make Shellfish a Dangerous Dish. National Library of Medicine's MedlinePlus: HealthDay. www.nlm.nih.gov/medlineplus/print/news/fullstory_95794.html.

13. Centers for Disease Control and Prevention, Division of Bacterial and Mycotic Diseases (DFBMD). 2005. Marine Toxins. www.cdc.gov/ncidod/dbmd/diseaseinfo/marinetoxins_g.htm.

14. Pavlista, A. D. 2001. Green potatoes: The problem and solution. NebGuide. The University of Nebraska–Lincoln Cooperative Extension. http://ianrpubs.unl.edu/horticulture/g1437.htm.

15. U.S. Department of Agriculture. 2010. Fight Bac Fact Sheet: Clean. www.fightbac.org/storage/documents/flyers/clean_fightbac_factsheet_2010_bw_pdf.

16. U.S. Department of Agriculture. 2010. Fight Bac Fact Sheet: Chill. www.fightbac.org/storage/documents/flyers/chill_%20fightbac_factsheet_2010_color.pdf.

17. U.S. Department of Agriculture. 2007. Food Product Dating. Fact Sheets: Food Labeling. www.fsis.usda/gov/Factsheets/Food_Product_Dating/index.asp.

18. U.S. Department of Agriculture. 2011. Food Safety and Inspection Service: Common Questions: Food Safety. www.fsis.usda.gov/help/faqs_hotline_preparation/index.asp#10.

19. Food and Drug Administration (FDA). 2003. *Anisakis simplex* and Related Worms. Foodborne Pathogenic Microorganisms and Natural Toxins Handbook. www.cfsan.fda.gov/~mow/chap25.html.

20. Food and Drug Administration. 2009. Food Safety for Moms-to-Be. www.fda.gov/Food/ResourcesForYou/HealthEducators/ucm081785.htm.

21. FoodSafety.gov. 2011. Eggs and Egg Products. www.foodsafety.gov/keep/types/eggs/index.html.

22. Aseptic Packaging Council. 2005. The Award-Winning, Earth Smart Packaging for a Healthy Lifestyle. www.aseptic.org/main.shtml.

23. U.S. Department of Health and Human Services (USDHHS). 2010. Bisphenol A (BPA) Information for Parents. www.hhs.gov/safety/bpa/.

24. Center for Science in the Public Interest (CSPI). 2005. Food Safety. Chemical Cuisine. CSPI's Guide to Food Additives. www.cspinet.org/reports/chemcuisine.htm.

25. U.S. Department of Agriculture. 2005. Economic Research Service. Data: Adoption of Genetically Engineered Crops in the U.S. www.ers.usda.gov/Data/BiotechCrops/.

26. World Health Organization (WHO). 2010. Twenty Questions on Genetically Modified (GM) Foods. www.who.int/foodsafety/publications/biotech/20questions/en/.

27. Neuman, W. 2010. Justice Dept. Tells Farmers It Will Press Agriculture Industry on Antitrust. *The New York Times*, March 12. www.nytimes.com/2010/03/13/business/13seed.html.

28. James, C. 2004. Preview: Global Status of Commercialized Biotech/GM Crops: 2004. ISAAA Briefs No. 32. Ithaca, NY: International Service for the Acquisition of Agri-biotech Applications.

29. Kanter, J. 2010. E.U. Clears Biotech Potato for Cultivation. *The New York Times,* March 3. www.nytimes.com/2010/03/03/business/global/03potato.html.

30. Schafer, K. S., and S. E. Kegley. 2002. Persistent toxic chemicals in the U.S. food supply. *J. Epidemiol. Community Health.* 56:813–817.

31. Food and Drug Administration. 2009. What You Need to Know About Mercury in Fish and Shellfish. www.fda.gov/Food/ResourcesForYou/Consumers/ucm110591.htm.

32. U.S. Food and Drug Administration. 2009. Questions and Answers About Dioxins. www.fda.gov/Food/FoodSafety/FoodContaminantsAdulteration/ChemicalContaminants/DioxinsPCBs/ucm077524.htm.

33. Environmental Protection Agency (EPA). 2005. Pesticides and Food: Healthy, Sensible Food Practices. www.epa.gov/pesticides/food/tips.htm.

34. American Cancer Society. 2011. Recombinant Bovine Growth Hormone. www.cancer.org/cancer/cancercauses/

othercarcinogens/athome/recombinant-bovine-growth-hormone.

35. Smith, T. C., M. J. Male, A. L. Harper, J. S. Kroeger, G. P. Tinkler, et al. 2009. Methicillin-resistant *Staphylococcus aureus* (MRSA) strain ST398 is present in midwestern U.S. swine and swine workers. PLoS ONE 4(1):e4258. Doi: 10.1371/journal.pone.0004258.

36. Centers for Disease Control and Prevention. 2007. Invasive MRSA. www.cdc.gov/ncidod/dhqp/ar_mrsa _Invasive_FS.html.

37. Organic Trade Association. 2009. OTA's 2009 Organic Industry Survey. www.ota.com/pics/documents/01a _OTAExecutiveSummary.pdf.

38. U.S. Department of Agriculture. Agricultural Marketing Service. National Organic Program. 2010. Understanding Organic. www.ams.usda.gov/AMSv1.0/ ams.fetchTemplateData.do?template=TemplateA&l eftNav=NationalOrganicProgram&page=NOPUnde rstandingOrganic&description=Understanding%20 Organic&acct=nopgeninfo.

39. Asami, D. K., Y. J. Hong, D. M. Barrett, and A. E. Mitchell. 2003. Comparison of the total phenolic and ascorbic acid content of freeze-dried and air-dried marionberry, strawberry, and corn grown using conventional, organic, and sustainable agricultural practices. *J. Agric. Food Chem.* 51(5):1237–1241.

40. Carbonaro, M., M. Mattera, S. Nicoli, P. Bergamo, and M. Cappelloni. 2002. Modulation of antioxidant compounds in organic vs conventional fruit (peach, Prunus persica L., and pear, Pyrus communis L.). *J. Agric. Food Chem.* 50(19):5458–5462.

41. Grinder-Pedersen, L., S. E. Rasmussen, S. Bügel, L. O. Jørgensen, D. Vagn Gundersen, and B. Sandström. 2003. Effect of diets based on foods from conventional versus organic production on intake and excretion of flavonoids and markers of antioxidative defense in humans. *Agric. Food Chem.* 51(19):5671–5676.

42. Dangour, A. D., S. K. Dodhia, A. Hayter, E. Allen, K. Lock, and R. Uauy. 2009. Nutritional quality of organic foods: a systematic review. *Am. J. of Clin. Nut.* Doi:10.3945/ajcn.2009.28041. www.ajcn.org/cgi/content/ abstract/ajcn.2009.28041v1.

43. Environmental Protection Agency. 2011. What Is Sustainability? www.epa.gov/sustainability/basicinfo.htm.

44. U.S. Department of Agriculture. 2008. 2007 Census of Agriculture. www.agcensus.usda.gov/Publications/2007/ Online_Highlights/Fact_Sheets/farm_numbers.pdf.

45. LocalHarvest. 2011. Community Supported Agriculture. www.localharvest.org/csa/.

46. U.S. Department of Agriculture 2010. Farmers Market Growth: 1994–2010. www.ams.usda.gov/AMSv1.0/ ams.fetchTemplateData.do?template=TemplateS&navID =WholesaleandFarmersMarkets&leftNav=WholesaleandF armersMarkets&page=WFMFarmersMarketGrowth&descri ption=Farmers%20Market%20Growth&acct=frmrdirmkt.

47. Edwards-Jones, G. 2010. Does eating local food reduce the environmental impact of food production and enhance consumer health? *Proceed. of the Nut. Soc.* 69:582–591.

48. Bittman, M. 2011. Food: six things to feel good about. *The New York Times,* http://opinionator.blogs. nytimes.com/2011/03/22/food-six-things-to-feel-good-about/?emc=eta1.

49. Walmart. 2010. Walmart Sustainable Agriculture: Fact Sheet. http://graphics8.nytimes.com/packages/pdf/ opinion/Fact_Sheet_Walmart_Sustainable.pdf.

50. U.S. Department of Agriculture Economic Research Service. 2011. Food Security in the United States: Key Statistics and Graphics. www.ers.usda.gov/Briefing/ FoodSecurity/stats_graphs.htm.

51. Food and Agriculture Organization (FAO), FAO Media Centre. 2009. The State of Food Insecurity in the World 2009. www.fao.org/news/story/en/item/36207/icode/.

52. World Health Organization (WHO). 2003. *The World Health Report: Shaping the Future.* Geneva, Switzerland: WHO.

53. UNICEF. 2009. The State of the World's Children 2009. www.unicef.org/sowc09/press/fastfacts.php.

54. World Health Organization. 2011. Micronutrient Deficiencies: Iron Deficiency Anaemia. www.who.int/ nutrition/topics/ida/en/index.html.

55. World Health Organization. 2011. Micronutrient Deficiencies: Iodine Deficiency Disorders. www.who.int/ nutrition/topics/idd/en/.

56. World Health Organization. 2011. Nutrition: Controlling the Global Obesity Epidemic. www.who.int/nutrition/ topics/obesity/en/index.html.

ANSWERS TO REVIEW QUESTIONS

Chapter 1

1. **d.** all of the above.
2. **b.** provides enough of the energy, nutrients, and fiber to maintain a person's health.
3. **c.** Being physically active each day.
4. **b.** eating more dark green and orange vegetables.
5. **b.** vitamin A, vitamin C, sodium, iron, and calcium.
6. False. Vitamins do not provide any energy, although many vitamins are critical to the metabolic processes that assist us in generating energy from carbohydrates, fats, and proteins.
7. True.
8. True. There is some evidence that drinking alcoholic beverages in moderation is associated with cardiovascular health benefits. However, because drinking in excess can lead to significant health and social problems, the Dietary Guidelines for Americans recommend that, if someone does drink alcoholic beverages, he or she should do so in moderation.
9. False. Although eating a variety of foods is one component of a healthful diet, it is not the only factor to ensure that one's diet is healthful. Other factors to consider include adequacy, moderation, and balance.
10. True.

Chapter 2

1. **b.** chemicals that help speed up body processes.
2. **d.** emulsifies fats.
3. **c.** hypothalamus.
4. **a.** seepage of gastric acid into the esophagus.
5. **c.** small intestine.
6. False. Cells are the smallest units of life. Atoms are the smallest units of matter in nature.
7. True.
8. True.
9. False. Vitamins and minerals are not really "digested" the same way that macronutrients are. These compounds do not have to be broken down because they are small enough to be readily absorbed by the small intestine. For example, fat-soluble vitamins, such as vitamins A, D, E, and K, are soluble in lipids and are absorbed into the intestinal cells along with the fats in our foods. Water-soluble vitamins, such as the B-vitamins and vitamin C, typically undergo some type of active transport process that helps assure the vitamin is absorbed by the small intestine. Minerals are absorbed all along the small intestine, in some cases in the large intestine as well, by a wide variety of mechanisms.
10. False. People with irritable bowel syndrome may experience constipation, diarrhea, or a combination of both.

Chapter 3

1. **b.** the potential of foods to raise blood glucose and insulin levels.
2. **d.** carbon, hydrogen, and oxygen.
3. **d.** sweetened soft drinks.
4. **a.** monosaccharides.
5. **c.** type 2 diabetes.
6. False. Although in the past this was true, recently there has been a significant increase in the incidence of type 2 diabetes among children and teens.
7. True.

8. False. A person with lactose intolerance has a difficult time tolerating milk and other dairy products. This person does not have an allergy to milk, as he or she does not exhibit an immune response indicative of an allergy. Instead, this person does not digest lactose completely, which causes intestinal distress and symptoms such as gas, bloating, diarrhea, and nausea.
9. False. Plants store glucose as starch.
10. False. Salivary amylase breaks starches into maltose and shorter polysaccharides.

Chapter 4

1. **c.** synthesized in the liver and small intestine.
2. **b.** exercise regularly.
3. **a.** transport of dietary fat to the wall of the small intestine.
4. **d.** high-density lipoproteins.
5. **a.** monounsaturated fats.
6. True.
7. False. Fat is an important source of energy during rest and during exercise, and adipose tissue is our primary storage site for fat. We rely significantly on the fat stored in our adipose tissue to provide energy during rest and exercise.
8. False. A triglyceride is a lipid comprised of a glycerol molecule and three fatty acids. Thus, fatty acids are a component of triglycerides.
9. False. Although most *trans* fatty acids result from the hydrogenation of vegetable oils by food manufacturers, a small amount of *trans* fatty acids are found in cow's milk.
10. False. A serving of food labeled *reduced fat* has at least 25% less fat than a standard serving, but it may not have fewer Calories than a full-fat version of the same food.

Chapter 5

1. **d.** mutual supplementation.
2. **a.** rice, pinto beans, acorn squash, soy butter, and almond milk.
3. **b.** DNA.
4. **b.** amine group.
5. **c.** carbon, oxygen, hydrogen, and nitrogen.
6. True.
7. False. Both shape and function are lost when a protein is denatured.
8. False. Some hormones are made from lipids.
9. True.
10. False. Depending on the type of sport, athletes may require the same or up to two times as much protein as nonactive people.

Chapter 6

1. **b.** thiamin, pantothenic acid, and biotin.
2. **d.** is destroyed by exposure to high heat.
3. **d.** nitrates.
4. **a.** vitamin A.
5. **b.** vitamin K.
6. False. Neural tube defects occur during the first 4 weeks of pregnancy; this is often before a woman even knows she is pregnant. Thus, the best way for a woman to protect her fetus against neural tube defects is to make sure she is consuming adequate folate before she is pregnant.

7. False. Our body makes vitamin D by converting a cholesterol compound in our skin to the active form of vitamin D that we need to function. We do not absorb vitamin D from sunlight, but when the ultraviolet rays of the sun hit our skin, they react to eventually form calcitriol, which is considered the primary active form of vitamin D in our body.
8. True.
9. False. Pregnant women should not consume beef liver very often, as it can lead to vitamin A toxicity and potentially serious birth defects.
10. True.

Chapter 7

1. **c.** It is freely permeable to water but not to all electrolytes.
2. **b.** Iron is a component of hemoglobin, myoglobin, and certain enzymes.
3. **a.** sodium, chloride, and iodine.
4. **d.** It provides the scaffolding for cortical bone.
5. **d.** structure of bone, nerve transmission, and muscle contraction.
6. True.
7. True.
8. True.
9. True.
10. False. The fractures that result from osteoporosis cause an increased risk for infection and other related illnesses that can lead to premature death.

Chapter 8

1. **d.** a healthy infant of average weight.
2. **a.** fluid outside our cells.
3. **c.** adequate hydration.
4. **c.** 7 kcal of energy.
5. **d.** All of the above are true.
6. True.
7. False. Our thirst mechanism is triggered by an increase in the concentration of electrolytes in our blood.
8. False. The recommendations state, "If you don't drink, don't start. If you do drink, do so in moderation."
9. False. One "drink" of wine is equivalent to 5 oz of wine.
10. True.

Chapter 9

1. **d.** body mass index.
2. **a.** basal metabolic rate, thermal effect of food, and effect of physical activity.
3. **b.** take in more energy than they expend.
4. **c.** all people have a genetic set point for their body weight.
5. **d.** disordered eating, menstrual dysfunction, and osteoporosis.
6. False. It is the apple-shaped fat patterning, or excess fat in the trunk region, that is known to increase a person's risk for many chronic diseases.
7. True.
8. False. People with binge-eating disorder typically do not purge to compensate for the binge; thus, these individuals are usually overweight or obese.

9. False. Healthful weight gain includes eating more energy than you expend and exercising both to maintain aerobic fitness and to build muscle mass.
10. True.

Chapter 10

1. **c.** 64% to 90% of your estimated maximal heart rate.
2. **a.** 1 to 3 seconds.
3. **b.** fat.
4. **c.** seems to increase strength gained in resistance exercise.
5. **b.** beverages containing carbohydrates and electrolytes.
6. True.
7. False. A dietary fat intake of 20% to 25% is typically recommended.
8. False. Carbohydrate loading involves altering the duration and intensity of exercise and the intake of carbohydrate such that the storage of carbohydrate is maximized.
9. False. Sports anemia is not true anemia, but a transient decrease in iron stores that occurs at the start of an exercise program. This is a result of an initial increase in plasma volume (water in our blood) that is not matched by an increase in hemoglobin.
10. True.

Chapter 11

1. **b.** neural tube defects.
2. **c.** iron.
3. **d.** greater than that for children, adults, and pregnant adults.
4. **b.** vitamin D.
5. **d.** all of the above.
6. False. These issues are most likely to occur in the first trimester of pregnancy.
7. False. Honey may contain spores of the bacterium *Clostridium botulinum*, which can be fatal for infants.
8. False. Toddlers are greatly influenced by their parents' own examples of eating and are influenced by the foods parents choose for them to eat.
9. True.
10. True.

Chapter 12

1. **b.** a flavor enhancer used in a variety of foods.
2. **a.** contain only organically produced ingredients, excluding water and salt.
3. **d.** pasteurization.
4. **d.** kwashiorkor.
5. **a.** the nutrition transition.
6. False. Bacteria that cause foodborne illnesses multiply rapidly at room temperature. Foods should be refrigerated promptly to keep microbes from multiplying.
7. True. It is easier for them to be infected (low vitamin A) and harder for them to fight off the infection.
8. True.
9. False. Irradiation kills the microbes that can cause foodborne illness or leaves them unable to reproduce.
10. True.

GLOSSARY

A

absorption The physiologic process by which molecules of food are taken from the GI tract into the body.

acceptable daily intake (ADI) An estimate made by the Food and Drug Administration of the amount of a non-nutritive sweetener that someone can consume each day over a lifetime without adverse effects.

Acceptable Macronutrient Distribution Range (AMDR) A range of intakes for a particular energy source that is associated with reduced risk for chronic disease while providing adequate intake of essential nutrients.

added sugars Sugars and syrups that are added to food during processing or preparation.

adenosine triphosphate (ATP) The common currency of energy for virtually all cells of the body.

adequate diet A diet that provides enough energy, nutrients, and fiber to maintain a person's health.

Adequate Intake (AI) A recommended average daily nutrient intake level based on observed or experimentally determined estimates of nutrient intake by a group of healthy people.

aerobic exercise Exercise that involves the repetitive movement of large muscle groups, increasing the body's use of oxygen and promoting cardiovascular health.

alcohol A beverage made from fermented fruits, vegetables, or grains.

alcohol-related birth defects (ARBD) Heart, kidney, bone, and other defects that develop as a result of maternal consumption of alcohol during pregnancy.

alcohol-related neurodevelopmental disorder (ARND) A condition in which children have problems with learning and behavior—leading to poor school performance and difficulties with attention, judgment, and impulse control—as a result of maternal alcohol consumption.

alpha-linolenic acid An essential fatty acid found in leafy green vegetables, flaxseed oil, soy oil, fish oil, and fish products; an omega-3 fatty acid.

amenorrhea The absence of menstruation. In females who had previously been menstruating, the absence of menstrual periods for 3 or more months.

amino acids Nitrogen-containing molecules that combine to form proteins.

amniotic fluid The watery fluid contained in the innermost membrane of the sac containing the fetus. It cushions and protects the growing fetus.

anabolic The term used for a substance that builds muscle and increases strength.

anaerobic Means "without oxygen"; refers to metabolic reactions that occur in the absence of oxygen.

anencephaly A fatal neural tube defect in which there is a partial absence of brain tissue, most likely caused by failure of the neural tube to close.

anorexia nervosa A serious, potentially life-threatening eating disorder that is characterized by self-starvation, which eventually leads to a deficiency in the energy and essential nutrients the body requires to function normally.

antibodies Defensive proteins of the immune system. Their production is prompted by the presence of bacteria, viruses, toxins, or allergens.

antioxidant A compound that has the ability to prevent or repair the damage caused by oxidation.

appetite A psychological desire to consume specific foods.

ariboflavinosis A condition caused by riboflavin deficiency.

atrophic gastritis A condition that results in low stomach acid secretion, estimated to occur in about 10% to 30% of adults older than 50 years of age.

B

bacteria Microorganisms that lack a true nucleus and reproduce by division or by forming spores.

balanced diet A diet that contains the combinations of foods that provide the proper proportion of nutrients.

basal metabolic rate (BMR) The energy the body expends to maintain its fundamental physiologic functions.

beriberi A disease caused by thiamin deficiency.

bile Fluid produced by the liver and stored in the gallbladder that emulsifies fats in the small intestine.

binge drinking The consumption of five or more alcoholic drinks on one occasion.

binge eating Consumption of a large amount of food in a short period of time, usually accompanied by a feeling of loss of self-control.

binge-eating disorder A disorder characterized by binge eating an average of twice a week or more, typically without compensatory purging.

bioavailability The degree to which our body can absorb and use any given nutrient.

biologic age Physiologic age as determined by health and functional status; often estimated by scored questionnaires.

biopesticides Primarily insecticides, these chemicals use natural methods to reduce damage to crops.

blood volume The amount of fluid in blood.

body composition The ratio of a person's body fat to lean body mass.

body image A person's perception of his or her body's appearance and functioning.

body mass index (BMI) A measurement representing the ratio of a person's body weight to his or her height.

bone density The degree of compactness of bone tissue, reflecting the strength of the bones. *Peak bone density* is the point at which a bone is strongest.

brown adipose tissue A type of adipose tissue that has more mitochondria than white adipose tissue, and which can increase energy expenditure by uncoupling certain steps in the energy production process. It is found in significant amounts in animals and newborn humans.

buffers Proteins that help maintain proper acid–base balance by attaching to, or releasing, hydrogen ions as conditions change in the body.

bulimia nervosa A serious eating disorder characterized by recurrent episodes of binge eating and recurrent inappropriate compensatory behaviors in order to prevent weight gain, such as self-induced vomiting, fasting, excessive exercise, or misuse of laxatives, diuretics, enemas, or other medications.

C

cancer A group of diseases characterized by cells that reproduce spontaneously and independently and may invade other tissues and organs.

carbohydrate One of the three macronutrients, a compound made up of carbon, hydrogen, and oxygen. It is derived from plants and provides energy.

carbohydrate loading The practice of training and carbohydrate intake so that muscle glycogen storage is maximized; also known as *glycogen loading.*

carbohydrates The primary fuel source for our bodies, particularly for the brain and for physical exercise.

carcinogens Cancer-causing agents, such as certain pesticides, industrial chemicals, and pollutants.

cardiovascular disease A general term referring to abnormal conditions (dysfunction) of the heart and blood vessels; cardiovascular disease can result in heart attack or stroke.

carotenoid Fat-soluble plant pigment that the body stores in the liver and adipose tissues. The body is able to convert certain carotenoids to vitamin A.

celiac disease A genetic disorder characterized by an inability to absorb a protein called gluten. This causes an inflammatory immune response that damages the lining of the small intestine.

cell The smallest unit of matter that exhibits the properties of living things, such as growth, reproduction, and the taking in of nutrients.

cell differentiation The process by which immature, undifferentiated cells develop into highly specialized functional cells of discrete organs and tissues.

cell membrane The boundary of an animal cell that separates its internal cytoplasm, nucleus, and other structures from the external environment.

chronologic age Age as defined by calendar years, from date of birth.

chylomicron A lipoprotein produced in the mucosal cell of the intestine; transports dietary fat out of the intestinal tract.

chyme Semifluid mass consisting of partially digested food, water, and gastric juices.

cirrhosis End-stage liver disease characterized by significant abnormalities in liver structure and function; may lead to complete liver failure.

coenzyme A compound that combines with an inactive enzyme to form an active enzyme.

colic A condition in infants marked by unconsolable crying for unknown reasons that lasts for hours at a time.

collagen A protein found in all connective tissues in our body.

colostrum The first fluid made and secreted by the breasts from late in pregnancy to about a week after birth. It is rich in immune factors and protein.

complementary proteins Two or more foods that together contain all nine essential amino acids necessary for a complete protein. It is not necessary to eat complementary proteins at the same meal.

complete proteins Foods that contain all nine essential amino acids.

complex carbohydrate A nutrient compound consisting of long chains of glucose molecules, such as starch, glycogen, and fiber.

conception The uniting of an ovum (egg) and sperm to create a fertilized egg.

constipation A condition characterized by the absence of bowel movements for a period of time that is significantly longer than normal for the individual. When a bowel movement does occur, stools are usually small, hard, and difficult to pass.

cool-down Activities done after an exercise session is completed; they should be gradual and allow your body to slowly recover from exercise.

cortical bone A dense bone tissue that makes up the outer surface of all bones as well as the entirety of most small bones of the body; also called compact bone.

creatine phosphate (CP) A high-energy compound that can be broken down for energy and used to regenerate ATP.

cretinism A form of mental retardation that occurs in people whose mothers experienced iodine deficiency during pregnancy.

cross-contamination Contamination of one food by another via the unintended transfer of microorganisms through physical contact.

cytoplasm The fluid within an animal cell, enclosed by the cell membrane.

D

danger zone Range of temperature (about 40°F to 140°F, or 4°C to 60°C) at which many microorganisms capable of causing human disease thrive.

dehydration A serious condition of depleted body fluid that results when fluid excretion exceeds fluid intake.

diabetes A serious, chronic disease in which the body can no longer regulate glucose.

diarrhea A condition characterized by the frequent passage of loose, watery stools.

dietary fiber The type of fiber that occurs naturally in foods.

Dietary Guidelines for Americans A set of principles developed by the U.S. Department of Agriculture and the U.S. Department of Health and Human Services to assist Americans in designing a healthful diet and lifestyle.

Dietary Reference Intakes (DRIs) A set of nutritional reference values for the United States and Canada that apply to healthy people.

digestion The process by which foods are broken down into their component molecules, both mechanically and chemically.

disaccharide A carbohydrate compound consisting of two sugar molecules joined together.

disordered eating A general term used to describe a variety of abnormal or atypical eating behaviors that are used to keep or maintain a lower body weight.

diuretic A substance that increases fluid loss via the urine. Common diuretics include alcohol and some prescription medications for high blood pressure and other disorders.

DNA A molecule present in the nucleus of all body cells that directs the assembly of amino acids into body proteins.

docosahexaenoic acid (DHA) A type of omega-3 fatty acid that can be made in the body from alpha-linolenic acid and found in our diet primarily in marine plants and animals; together with EPA, it appears to reduce our risk for a heart attack.

drink The amount of an alcoholic beverage that provides approximately ½ fl. oz of pure ethanol.

E

eating disorder A clinically diagnosed psychiatric disorder characterized by severe disturbances in body image and eating behaviors.

edema A disorder in which fluids build up in the tissue spaces of the body, causing fluid imbalances and a swollen appearance.

eicosapentaenoic acid (EPA) A type of omega-3 fatty acid that can be made in the body from alpha-linolenic acid and found in our diet primarily in marine plants and animals.

electrolyte A (mineral) substance that dissolves in solution into positively and negatively charged ions and is thus capable of carrying an electrical current.

elimination The process by which the undigested portions of food and waste products are removed from the body.

embryo The human growth and developmental stage lasting from the third week to the end of the eighth week after fertilization.

empty Calories Calories from solid fats and/or added sugars which provide few or no nutrients.

energy cost of physical activity The energy expended on body movement and muscular work above basal levels.

energy expenditure The energy the body expends to maintain its basic functions and to perform all levels of movement and activity.

energy intake The amount of food a person eats; in other words, it is the number of kilocalories consumed.

enzymes Chemicals, usually proteins, that act on other chemicals to speed up body processes.

ergogenic aids Substances used to improve exercise and athletic performance.

esophagus Muscular tube of the GI tract connecting the back of the mouth to the stomach.

essential amino acids Amino acids not produced by the body that must be obtained from food.

essential fatty acids (EFAs) Fatty acids that must be consumed in the diet because they cannot be made by our body. The two essential fatty acids are linoleic acid and alpha-linolenic acid.

Estimated Average Requirement (EAR) The average daily nutrient intake level estimated to meet the requirement of half of the healthy individuals in a particular life stage and gender group.

Estimated Energy Requirement (EER) The average dietary energy intake that is predicted to maintain energy balance in a healthy adult.

evaporative cooling Another term for sweating, which is the primary way in which we dissipate heat.

exercise A subcategory of leisure-time physical activity; any activity that is purposeful, planned, and structured.

F

famine A widespread and severe food shortage that causes starvation and death in a large portion of a population in a region.

fats An important energy source for our body at rest and during low-intensity exercise.

fat-soluble vitamins Vitamins that are not soluble in water but soluble in fat. These include vitamins A, D, E, and K.

fatty acids Long chains of carbon atoms bound to each other as well as to hydrogen atoms.

female athlete triad A serious syndrome that consists of three clinical conditions in some physically active females: low energy availability (with or without eating disorders), menstrual dysfunction, and low bone density.

fetal alcohol spectrum disorders (FASD) An umbrella term describing the range of effects that can occur in the child of a woman who drinks during pregnancy. Fetal alcohol syndrome (FAS), alcohol-related neurodevelopmental disorder (ARND), and alcohol-related birth defects (ARBD) are components of FASD.

fetal alcohol syndrome (FAS) A cluster of birth defects in the children of a mother who consumed alcohol during pregnancy, including facial deformities, impaired growth, and a spectrum of mild to severe cognitive, emotional, and physical problems.

fetus The human growth and developmental stage lasting from the beginning of the ninth week after conception to birth.

fiber The nondigestible carbohydrate parts of plants that form the support structures of leaves, stems, and seeds.

fiber-rich carbohydrates A group of foods containing either simple or complex carbohydrates that are rich in dietary fiber. These foods, which include most fruits, vegetables, and whole grains, are typically fresh or only moderately processed.

FIT principle The principle used to achieve an appropriate overload for physical training; stands for frequency, intensity, and time of activity.

fluid A substance composed of molecules that move past one another freely. Fluids are characterized by their ability to conform to the shape of whatever container holds them.

fluorosis A condition marked by staining and pitting of the teeth; caused by an abnormally high intake of fluoride.

food additive A substance or mixture of substances intentionally put into food to enhance its appearance, safety, palatability, and quality.

food allergy An inflammatory reaction caused by an immune system hypersensitivity to a protein component of a food.

foodborne illness An illness transmitted by food or water contaminated by a pathogenic microorganism, its toxic secretions, or a toxic chemical.

food intolerance A cluster of GI symptoms that occurs following consumption of a particular food but is not caused by an immune system response.

food security A situation in which a person has daily access to a supply of safe foods with enough energy and sufficiently rich nutrient quality to promote a healthy, active life.

free radical A highly unstable atom with an unpaired electron in its outermost shell.

frequency The number of activity sessions per week you perform.

fructose The sweetest natural sugar; a monosaccharide that occurs in fruits and vegetables. Also called *fruit sugar*.

functional fiber The nondigestible forms of carbohydrate that are extracted from plants or manufactured in the laboratory and have known health benefits.

fungi Plantlike, spore-forming organisms that can grow as either single cells or multicellular colonies.

G

galactose A monosaccharide that joins with glucose to create lactose, one of the three most common disaccharides.

gallbladder A sac of tissue beneath the liver that stores bile and secretes it into the small intestine.

gastric juice Acidic liquid secreted within the stomach that contains hydrochloric acid, pepsin, and other chemicals.

gastroesophageal reflux disease (GERD) A more painful type of gastroesophageal reflux that occurs more than twice per week.

gastrointestinal (GI) tract A long, muscular tube consisting of several organs: the mouth, esophagus, stomach, small intestine, and large intestine.

gene A segment of DNA that carries the instructions for assembling available amino acids into a unique protein.

Generally Recognized as Safe (GRAS) List established by Congress to identify substances used in foods that are generally recognized as safe based on a history of long-term use or on the consensus of qualified research experts.

genetic modification The process of changing an organism by manipulating its genetic material.

gestational diabetes In a pregnant woman, insufficient insulin production or insulin resistance that results in consistently high blood glucose levels; the condition typically resolves after birth occurs.

glucagon A hormone secreted by the alpha cells of the pancreas in response to decreased blood levels of glucose; causes breakdown of liver stores of glycogen into glucose.

gluconeogenesis The generation of glucose from the breakdown of proteins.

glucose The most abundant sugar molecule; a monosaccharide generally found in combination with other sugars. The preferred source of energy for the brain and an important source of energy for all cells.

glycemic index A value that rates the potential of a given food to raise blood glucose and insulin levels.

glycemic load The amount of carbohydrate contained in a given food, multiplied by its glycemic index value.

glycerol An alcohol composed of three carbon atoms; it is the backbone of a triglyceride molecule.

glycogen A polysaccharide stored in animals; the storage form of glucose in animals.

glycolysis The breakdown of glucose; yields two ATP molecules and two pyruvic acid molecules for each molecule of glucose.

goiter A condition marked by enlargement of the thyroid gland, which can be caused by iodine toxicity or deficiency.

grazing The practice of consistently eating small meals throughout the day; done by many athletes to meet their high-energy demands.

H

healthful diet A diet that provides the proper combination of energy and nutrients and is adequate, moderate, balanced, and varied.

heat cramps Muscle spasms that occur several hours after strenuous exercise; most often occur when sweat losses and fluid intakes are high, urine volume is low, and sodium intake is inadequate.

heat exhaustion A heat illness characterized by excessive sweating, weakness, nausea, dizziness, headache, and difficulty concentrating. Unchecked heat exhaustion can lead to heatstroke.

heatstroke A potentially fatal response to high temperature characterized by failure of the body's heat-regulating mechanisms; commonly called *sunstroke*.

heat syncope Dizziness that occurs when people stand for too long in the heat, stop suddenly after a race, or stand suddenly from a lying position; results from blood pooling in the lower extremities.

helminth A multicellular microscopic worm.

heme The iron-containing molecule found in hemoglobin.

heme iron Iron that is part of hemoglobin and myoglobin; found only in animal-based foods, such as meat, fish, and poultry.

hemoglobin The oxygen-carrying protein found in our red blood cells; almost two-thirds of all the iron in our body is found in hemoglobin.

hepatitis Inflammation of the liver; can be caused by a virus or a toxic agent, such as alcohol.

high-density lipoprotein (HDL) A small, dense lipoprotein with a very low cholesterol content and a high protein content.

homocysteine An amino acid that requires adequate levels of folate, vitamin B_6, and vitamin B_{12} for its metabolism. High levels of homocysteine in the blood are associated with an increased risk for vascular diseases, such as cardiovascular disease.

hormone A chemical messenger that is secreted into the bloodstream by one of the many glands of the body.

hunger A physiologic sensation that prompts us to eat.

hydrogenation The process of adding hydrogen to unsaturated fatty acids, making them more saturated and therefore more solid at room temperature.

hypoglycemia A condition marked by blood glucose levels that are below normal fasting levels.

hypothalamus A brain region where sensations such as hunger and thirst are regulated.

I

impaired fasting glucose Fasting blood glucose levels that are higher than normal but not high enough to lead to a diagnosis of type 2 diabetes; also called *pre-diabetes*.

incomplete proteins Foods that do not contain all of the essential amino acids in sufficient amounts to support growth and health.

insoluble fibers Fibers that do not dissolve in water.

insulin A hormone secreted by the beta cells of the pancreas in response to increased blood levels of glucose; facilitates uptake of glucose by body cells.

intensity The amount of effort expended during the activity, or how difficult the activity is to perform.

invisible fats Fats that are hidden in foods, such as those found in baked goods, regular-fat dairy products, marbling in meat, and fried foods.

ion An electrically charged particle.

iron-deficiency anemia A disorder in which the production of normal, healthy red blood cells decreases and hemoglobin levels are inadequate to fully oxygenate the body's cells and tissues.

irradiation A sterilization process in which food is exposed to gamma rays or high-energy electron beams to kill microorganisms. Irradiation does not impart any radiation to the food being treated.

irritable bowel syndrome (IBS) A bowel disorder that interferes with normal functions of the colon. IBS causes abdominal cramps, bloating, and constipation or diarrhea.

L

lactic acid A compound that results when pyruvic acid is metabolized.

lactose A disaccharide consisting of one glucose molecule and one galactose molecule; also called *milk sugar*. Found in milk, including human breast milk.

lactose intolerance A disorder in which the body does not produce sufficient lactase enzyme and therefore cannot digest foods that contain lactose, such as cow's milk.

large intestine Final organ of the GI tract consisting of the cecum, colon, rectum, and anal canal and in which most water is absorbed and feces are formed.

leisure-time physical activity Any activity not related to a person's occupation; includes competitive sports, recreational activities, and planned exercise training.

leptin A hormone produced by body fat that acts to reduce food intake, causing a decrease in body weight and body fat.

life expectancy The expected number of years remaining in one's life, typically stated from the time of birth.

life span The highest age reached by any member of a species; currently, the human life span is 122 years.

limiting amino acid The essential amino acid that is missing or in the smallest supply in the amino acid pool and is thus responsible for slowing or halting protein synthesis.

linoleic acid An essential fatty acid found in vegetable and nut oils; also known as omega-6 fatty acid.

lipids A diverse group of organic substances that are insoluble in water; lipids include triglycerides, phospholipids, and sterols.

lipoprotein A spherical (round-shaped) compound in which fat clusters in the center and phospholipids and proteins form the outside of the sphere.

liver The largest organ of the GI tract and one of the most important organs of the body. Its functions include production of bile and processing of nutrient-rich blood from the small intestine.

low birth weight A weight of less than 5.5 lb at birth.

low-density lipoprotein (LDL) A molecule resulting when a VLDL releases its triglyceride load. Higher cholesterol and protein content makes LDLs somewhat more dense than VLDLs.

low-intensity activities Activities that cause very mild increases in breathing, sweating, and heart rate.

M

macronutrients Nutrients that our bodies need in relatively large amounts to support normal function and health. Carbohydrates, fats, and proteins are macronutrients.

major minerals Minerals we need to consume in amounts of at least 100 mg per day, and of which the total amount present in the body is at least 5 grams (5,000 mg).

malnutrition A state of poor nutritional health.

maltose A disaccharide consisting of two molecules of glucose. Does not generally occur independently in foods but results as a by-product of digestion. Also called *malt sugar*.

maximal heart rate The rate at which your heart beats during maximal-intensity exercise.

megadosing Taking a dose of a nutrient that is ten or more times greater than the recommended amount.

metabolic water The water formed as a by-product of our body's metabolic reactions.

metabolism The sum of all the chemical and physical processes by which the body breaks down and builds up molecules.

micronutrients Nutrients needed in relatively small amounts to support normal health and body functions. Vitamins and minerals are micronutrients.

minerals Solid, crystalline substances that do not contain carbon and are not changed by natural processes, including digestion.

moderate-intensity activities Activities that cause noticeable increases in breathing, sweating, and heart rate.

moderation Eating the right amounts of foods to maintain a healthy weight and to optimize our body's functioning.

monosaccharide The simplest of carbohydrates; consists of one sugar molecule, the most common form of which is glucose.

monounsaturated fatty acid (MUFA) A fatty acid that has two carbons in the chain bound to each other with one double bond; these types of fatty acids are generally liquid at room temperature.

morbid obesity A condition in which a person's body weight exceeds 100% of normal, putting him or her at very high risk for serious health consequences.

morning sickness Varying degrees of nausea and vomiting associated with pregnancy, most commonly in the first trimester.

multifactorial disease Any disease that may be attributable to one or more of a variety of causes.

mutual supplementation The process of combining two or more incomplete protein sources to make a complete protein.

myoglobin An iron-containing protein similar to hemoglobin, except that it is found in muscle cells.

N

neural tube Embryonic tissue that forms a tube, which eventually becomes the brain and spinal cord.

night blindness A vitamin A–deficiency disorder that results in the loss of the ability to see in dim light.

night-eating syndrome A disorder characterized by intake of the majority of the day's energy between 8:00 PM and 6:00 AM. Individuals with this disorder also experience mood and sleep disorders.

nonessential amino acids Amino acids that can be manufactured by the body in sufficient quantities and therefore do not need to be consumed regularly in our diet.

non-heme iron The form of iron that is not a part of hemoglobin or myoglobin; found in animal- and plant-based foods.

non-nutritive sweeteners Manufactured sweeteners that provide little or no energy; also called *alternative sweeteners*.

normal weight Having an adequate but not excessive level of body fat for health.

nutrient density The relative amount of nutrients per amount of energy (or number of Calories).

nutrients   Chemicals found in foods that are critical to human growth and function.

nutrition   The scientific study of food and how food nourishes the body and influences health.

Nutrition Facts Panel   The label on a food package that contains the nutrition information required by the FDA.

nutritive sweeteners   Sweeteners, such as sucrose, fructose, honey, and brown sugar, that contribute calories (energy).

O

obesity   Having an excess of body fat that adversely affects health, resulting in a person having a weight for a given height that is substantially greater than an accepted standard.

organ   A body structure composed of two or more tissues and performing a specific function—for example, the esophagus.

organism   A complete and independent living being.

osteoblasts   Cells that prompt the formation of new bone matrix by laying down the collagen-containing component of bone, which is then mineralized.

osteoclasts   Cells that break down the surface of bones by secreting enzymes and acids that dig grooves into the bone matrix.

osteomalacia   Vitamin D–deficiency disease in adults, in which bones become weak and prone to fractures.

osteoporosis   A disease characterized by low bone mass and deterioration of bone tissue, leading to increased bone fragility and fracture risk.

ounce-equivalent (oz-equivalent)   A term used to define a serving size that is 1 ounce, or equivalent to an ounce, for the grains section and the protein foods section of MyPlate.

overload principle   Placing an extra physical demand on your body in order to improve your fitness level.

overweight   Having a moderate amount of excess body fat, resulting in a person having a weight for a given height that is greater than an accepted standard but is not considered obese.

ovulation   The release of an ovum (egg) from a woman's ovary.

P

pancreas   Gland located behind the stomach that secretes digestive enzymes.

pancreatic amylase   An enzyme secreted by the pancreas into the small intestine that digests any remaining starch into maltose.

parasite   A microorganism that simultaneously derives benefit from and harms its host.

pasteurization   A form of sterilization using high temperatures for short periods of time.

pellagra   A disease that results from severe niacin deficiency.

pepsin   An enzyme in the stomach that begins the breakdown of proteins into shorter polypeptide chains and single amino acids.

peptic ulcer   An area of the GI tract that has been eroded away by the acidic gastric juice of the stomach. The two main causes of peptic ulcers are an *H. pylori* infection or use of nonsteroidal anti-inflammatory drugs.

peptide bonds   Unique types of chemical bonds in which the amine group of one amino acid binds to the acid group of another in order to manufacture dipeptides and all larger peptide molecules.

percent daily values (%DV)   Information on a Nutrition Facts Panel that tells you how much a serving of food contributes to your overall intake of nutrients listed on the label. The information is based on an energy intake of 2,000 Calories per day.

peristalsis   Waves of squeezing and pushing contractions that move food in one direction through the length of the GI tract.

persistent organic pollutants (POPs)   Chemicals released into the environment as a result of industry, agriculture, or improper waste disposal; automobile emissions also are considered POPs.

pesticides   Chemicals used either in the field or in storage to decrease destruction by predators or disease.

pH   Stands for "percentage of hydrogen." It is a measure of the acidity—or level of hydrogen—of any solution, including human blood.

phospholipid   A type of lipid in which a fatty acid is combined with another compound that contains phosphate; unlike other lipids, phospholipids are soluble in water.

photosynthesis   The process by which plants use sunlight to fuel a chemical reaction that combines carbon and water into glucose, which is then stored in their cells.

physical activity   Any movement produced by muscles that increases energy expenditure; includes occupational, household, leisure-time, and transportation activities.

Physical Activity Pyramid   A visual pyramid, similar to the previous USDA Food Guide Pyramid, that makes recommendations for the types and amounts of activity that should be done weekly to increase physical activity levels.

physical fitness   The ability to carry out daily tasks with vigor and alertness, without undue fatigue, and with ample energy to enjoy leisure-time pursuits and meet unforeseen emergencies.

phytochemicals   Chemicals found in plants, such as pigments and other substances, that may reduce our risk for diseases such as cancer and heart disease.

pica   An abnormal craving to eat something not fit for food, such as clay, chalk, paint, or other nonfood substances.

placebo effect   Improved performance based on the belief that a product is beneficial, although the product has been proved to have no physiologic benefits.

placenta   A pregnancy-specific organ formed from both maternal and embryonic tissues. It is responsible for oxygen, nutrient, and waste exchange between mother and fetus.

polypharmacy   The concurrent use of three or more medications.

polysaccharide   A complex carbohydrate consisting of long chains of glucose.

polyunsaturated fatty acids (PUFAs)   Fatty acids that have more than one double bond in the chain; these types of fatty acids are generally liquid at room temperature.

prion   A protein that misfolds and becomes infectious; prions are not living cellular organisms or viruses.

processed foods   Foods that are manipulated mechanically or chemically.

proof   A measure of the alcohol content of a liquid. For example, 100-proof liquor is 50% alcohol by volume, whereas 80-proof liquor is 40% alcohol by volume.

proteases   Enzymes that continue the breakdown of polypeptides in the small intestine.

proteins   Large, complex molecules made up of amino acids and found as essential components of all living cells.

protozoa   Single-celled, mobile microorganisms.

provitamin   An inactive form of a vitamin that the body can convert to an active form. An example is beta-carotene.

puberty   The period of life in which secondary sexual characteristics develop and people are biologically capable of reproducing.

purging   An attempt to rid the body of unwanted food by vomiting or other compensatory means, such as excessive exercise, fasting, or laxative abuse.

pyruvic acid   The primary end product of glycolysis.

Q

quackery   The promotion of an unproven remedy, such as a supplement or other product or service, usually by someone unlicensed and untrained.

R

recombinant bovine growth hormone (rBGH)
A genetically engineered hormone injected into dairy cows to enhance their milk output.

recombinant DNA technology   A type of genetic modification in which scientists combine DNA from different sources to produce a transgenic organism that expresses a desired trait.

Recommended Dietary Allowance (RDA)   The average daily nutrient intake level that meets the nutrient requirements of 97% to 98% of healthy individuals in a particular life stage and gender group.

remodeling   The two-step process by which bone tissue is recycled; includes the breakdown of existing bone and the formation of new bone.

residues   Chemicals that remain in the foods we eat despite cleaning and processing.

resistance training   Exercise in which our muscles act against resistance.

retina   The delicate, light-sensitive membrane lining the inner eyeball and connected to the optic nerve. It contains retinal.

rickets   A vitamin D–deficiency disease in children. Symptoms include deformities of the skeleton, such as bowed legs and knocked knees.

S

saliva   A mixture of water, mucus, enzymes, and other chemicals that moistens the mouth and food, binds food particles together, and begins the digestion of carbohydrates.

salivary amylase   An enzyme in saliva that breaks starch into smaller particles and eventually into the disaccharide maltose.

salivary glands   A group of glands found under and behind the tongue and beneath the jaw that release saliva continually as well as in response to the thought, sight, smell, or presence of food.

saturated fatty acid (SFA)   A fatty acid that has no carbons joined together with a double bond; these types of fatty acids are generally solid at room temperature.

set-point theory   A theory that suggests that the body raises or lowers energy expenditure in response to increased and decreased food intake and physical activity. This action maintains an individual's body weight within a narrow range.

simple carbohydrate   A monosaccharide or disaccharide, such as glucose; commonly called *sugar*.

small intestine   The largest portion of the GI tract, where most digestion and absorption take place.

soluble fibers   Fibers that dissolve in water.

solvent   A substance that is capable of mixing with and breaking apart a variety of compounds. Water is an excellent solvent.

sphincter   A tight ring of muscle separating organs of the GI tract that opens in response to nerve signals, indicating that food is ready to pass into the next section.

spina bifida   An embryonic neural tube defect that occurs when the spinal vertebrae fail to completely enclose the spinal cord, allowing it to protrude.

spontaneous abortion   The natural termination of a pregnancy and expulsion of the fetus and pregnancy tissues because of a genetic, developmental, or physiologic abnormality that is so severe that the pregnancy cannot be maintained; also known as *miscarriage*.

starch   A polysaccharide stored in plants; the storage form of glucose in plants.

sterol   A type of lipid found in foods and the body that has a ring structure; cholesterol is the most common sterol that occurs in our diet.

stomach   A J-shaped organ where food is partially digested, churned, and stored until released into the small intestine.

stretching   Exercise in which muscles are gently lengthened using slow, controlled movements.

sucrose   A disaccharide composed of one glucose molecule and one fructose molecule. It is sweeter than lactose or maltose.

sudden infant death syndrome (SIDS)   A condition marked by the sudden death of a previously healthy infant; the most common cause of death in infants more than 1 month of age.

sustainability   The ability to meet or satisfy basic economic, social, and security needs now and in the future without undermining the natural resource base and environmental quality on which life depends.

system   A group of organs that work together to perform a unique function—for example, the gastrointestinal system.

T

teratogen   Any substance that can cause a birth defect.

thermic effect of food   The energy expended as a result of processing food consumed.

thirst mechanism   A cluster of nerve cells in the hypothalamus that stimulate our conscious desire to drink fluids in response to an increase in the concentration of salt in our blood or a decrease in blood pressure and volume.

thrifty gene theory   A theory that suggests that some people possess a gene (or genes) that causes them to be energetically thrifty, resulting in their expending less energy at rest and during physical activity.

time of activity   The amount of time that a given exercise session lasts, not including warm-up and cool-down periods.

tissue   A sheet or other grouping of like cells that performs like functions—for example, muscle tissue.

Tolerable Upper Intake Level (UL)   The highest average daily nutrient intake level likely to pose no risk of adverse health effects to almost all individuals in a particular life stage and gender group.

total fiber   The sum of dietary fiber and functional fiber.

toxin   Any harmful substance; in microbiology, a chemical produced by a microorganism that harms tissues or causes harmful immune responses.

trabecular bone   A porous bone tissue found within the ends of the long bones, as well as inside the spinal vertebrae, flat bones (breastbone, ribs, and most bones of the skull), and bones of the pelvis; also called spongy bone.

trace minerals   Minerals we need to consume in amounts less than 100 mg per day, and of which the total amount present in the body is less than 5 grams (5,000 mg).

transport proteins   Protein molecules that help transport substances throughout the body and across cell membranes.

triglyceride   A molecule consisting of three fatty acids attached to a three-carbon glycerol backbone.

trimester   Any one of three stages of pregnancy, each lasting 13 to 14 weeks.

tumor   Any newly formed mass of undifferentiated cells.

type 1 diabetes   The form of diabetes in which the body cannot produce enough insulin.

type 2 diabetes   The form of diabetes in which body cells progressively become less responsive to insulin, or the body does not produce enough insulin.

U

ultra-trace minerals   Minerals we need to consume in amounts less than 1 mg/d (mg per day) body weight.

umbilical cord   The cord containing arteries and veins that connects the baby (from the navel) to the mother via the placenta.

underweight   Having too little body fat to maintain health, causing a person to have a weight for a given height that is below an acceptably defined standard.

V

variety   Eating different foods each day.

vegetarianism   The practice of restricting the diet to food substances of plant origin, including vegetables, fruits, grains, and nuts.

very-low-density lipoprotein (VLDL)   A large lipoprotein made up mostly of triglyceride. Functions primarily to transport triglycerides from their source to the body's cells, including to adipose tissues for storage.

vigorous-intensity activities   Activities that produce significant increases in breathing, sweating, and heart rate; talking is difficult when exercising at a vigorous intensity.

viruses   A group of infectious agents that are much smaller than bacteria, lack independent metabolism, and are incapable of growth or reproduction outside of living cells.

visible fats   Fats that we can see in our foods or see added to foods, such as butter, margarine, cream, shortening, salad dressings, chicken skin, and untrimmed fat on meat.

vitamins   Micronutrients that contain carbon and assist us in regulating our body's processes. They are classified as water soluble or fat soluble.

W

warm-up   Activities that prepare you for an exercise session, including stretching, calisthenics, and movements specific to the exercise you are about to engage in; also called *preliminary exercise.*

water intoxication   Dilution of body fluid that results when water intake or retention is excessive; it can lead to hyponatremia; also called *overhydration.*

water-soluble vitamins   Vitamins that are soluble in water. These include vitamin C and the B-vitamins.

wellness   A multidimensional, lifelong process that includes physical, emotional, and spiritual health.

INDEX

CREDITS

Photo Credits

Feature boxes

"Where I'm Starting From . . ." boxes: Krystian Kaczmarski/iStock-photo; Game Plan boxes: Aldo Murillo/iStockphoto; What About You? boxes: ranplett/iStockphoto; Nutri-Case boxes, Gustavo: Ned Frisk Photography/Corbis; Nutri-Case boxes, Liz: Rubberball/Getty Images, Inc.; Nutri-Case boxes, Judy: George Doyle & claran Griffin/Stockbte/Getty Images, Inc.; Nutri-Case boxes, Theo: Stockbyte/Getty Images, inc.; Nutri-Case boxes, Hannah: PhotoDisc/Getty Images, Inc.

Chapter 1

Opening Photo: Agencja FREE / Alamy; **fig. 1.1:** Wrangel/Dreamstime; **p. 3** Brian Chase/Bvdc/Dreamstime; **p. 6:** Tom Stewart/CORBIS; **p. 7:** Bluehill/Dreamstime; **p. 8:** Scott Rothstein/Webking/Dreamstime; **p. 9 left:** Photosani/Shutterstock; **p. 9 right:** forest badger/Shutterstock; **p. 10:** Comstock Images/Thinkstock; **p. 11:** Kzenon/Shutterstock; **fig. 1-7a-j:** Creative Digital Visions; **p. 13 top:** ALEXANDER WALTER/Getty Images, Inc.; **p. 13 bottom:** Andrew Whittuck/Dorling Kindersley; **p. 14:** Adams Picture Library/Alamy; **p. 15:** Steve Terrill/CORBIS- NY; **fig. 1-9a:** ALEAIMAGE/iStock-photo; **fig. 1-9b:** Kelly Cline/iStockphoto; **fig. 1-9c:** Lew Robertson/iStockphoto; **fig. 1-9d:** Morgan Lane Photography/Shutterstock; **fig. 1-9e:** Natalia Mylova/Fotolia; **fig. 1-11a-c:** Kristin Piljay; **fig. 1-12a left:** Image Source Pink/Alamy; **fig. 1-12a right:** Envision/CORBIS; **fig. 1-12b:** Photodisc/Getty Images; **p. 19:** istockphoto/Thinkstock; **p. 27:** Radius Images/Alamy

Chapter 2

Opening Photo: Jamie Grill/Getty Images, Inc.; **p. 39:** Howard Kingsnorth/ Getty Images, Inc.; **fig. 2.2:** Jon Riley/Stone/Getty Images; **p. 40:** Jean Luc Morales/Getty Images, Inc.; **p. 42:** photomadnz/Alamy; **p. 44:** Randy L. Jirtle; **p. 46:** JONELLE WEAVER/Getty Images, Inc.; **fig. 2-11a:** Steve Gschmeissner/Photo Researchers, Inc.; **fig. 2-11b:** Steve Gschmeissner/Science Photo Library/Alamy; **p. 53:** Bruce Shippee/Shutterstock; **p. 54:** SPL/Photo Researchers, Inc.; **p. 57:** Getty Images Inc.; **fig. 2-15a:** MedicalRF.com/Alamy Images; **fig. 2-15b:** Dr. E. Walker/Science Photo Library/Photo Researchers, Inc.; **p. 60:** David Murray and Jules Selmes (c) Dorling Kindersley; **p. 61 top:** Cordelia Molloy/Photo Researchers, Inc.; **p. 61 bottom:** iStockphoto; **p. 62:** Shutterstock; **p. 63:** Susan Van Etten/PhotoEdit Inc.

Chapter 3

Opening Photo: Datacraft Co., Ltd./Corbis; **p. 69:** Brocreativ/Shutterstock; **p. 70 left:** Foodcollection/Getty Images Inc.; **p. 70 right:** Rimglow/Dreamstime; **p. 71:** Monkey Business Images/Shutterstock; **fig. 3-5a:** Rebecca Ellis/iStockphoto; **fig. 3-5b:** Ben Beltman/iStock-photo; **p. 74:** George Doyle/Stockbyte/Thinkstock; **fig. 3-6a:** Richard Smith/Masterfile; **fig. 3-6b:** Doug Menuez /Photodisc/Getty Images; **fig. 3-6c:** technotr/iStockphoto; **p. 75:** Peter Weber/Shutterstock; **p. 77:** Dorling Kindersley; **p. 81 top left:** Steve Shott/Dorling Kindersley; **p. 81 top right:** Ryan McVay/Getty Images Inc.; **p. 81 bottom:** Ian O'Leary/Dorling Kindersley; **p. 82:** Joe Raedl /Getty Images, Inc.; **p. 83:** Kristin Piljay; **p. 84:** Photodisc/getty Images Inc.; **p. 86:** Dorling Kindersley; **p. 87 top left:** john shepherd/iStockphoto; **p. 87 top right:** DUSAN ZIDAR/Shutterstock; **p. 87 middle left:** Dorling Kindersley; **p. 87 middle right:** Bgphoto/Dreamstime LLC; **p. 87 bottom:** Dorling Kindersley; **fig. 3-13:** Alexandr Vlassyuk/Dreamstime; **p. 88:** AGE Fotostock America, Inc.; **fig. 3-16:** Volkan Taner/iStockphoto; **p. 93 top:** Shutterstock; **p. 93 bottom:** Bon Appetit/Alamy

Chapter 4

Opening Photo: Rubberball/Mike Kemp/Getty Images; **p. 99:** Dorling Kindersley; **p. 101 top:** Sailorr/Dreamstime; **p. 101 bottom:** Fotolia; **p. 102:** Akira Ono/AP Wide World Photos; **p. 103:** Comstock/Thinkstock; **p. 104:** Lyudmila Suvorova/iStockphoto; **fig. 4-6:** Myrleen Ferguson Cate/PhotoEdit Inc.; **p. 106 middle:** Andersen Floss/Photodisc/Getty Images, Inc.; **p. 106 bottom:** Doug Pensinger/Getty Images, Inc.; **p. 107 top:** Odd Anderdsen/Agence France Presse/Getty Images; **p. 107 bottom:** Danny E. Hooks/Shutterstock; **p. 108:** Kip Peticolas/Fundamental Photographs, NYC; **p. 109:** Alex Potemkin/iStockphoto.com; **p. 111:** James Leynse/Bettmann/CORBIS; **fig. 4-14:** Wilmy van Ulft/Shutterstock; **p. 114 top left:** Shutterstock; **p. 114 top right:** istockphoto/Thinkstock; **p. 114 bottom left:** Jacek Chabraszewski/Shutterstock; **p. 114 bottom right:** Scott Karcich/Dreamstime LLC -Royalty Free; **fig. 4-9a-b:** Foodfolio/Alamy Images; **p. 117:** Shutterstock; **fig. 4-12a:** SCIENCE PHOTO LIBRARY/Photo Researchers, Inc.; **fig. 4-12b:** Wikipedia, The Free Encyclopedia; **p. 123:** Rich Kareckas/AP Wide World Photos; **p. 125:** United States Department of Agriculture

Chapter 5

Opening Photo: MBI/Alamy; **fig. 5-3:** Andrew Syed/Photo Researchers, Inc.; **p. 132:** Shutterstock; **p. 133:** Nicholas Rjabow/iStock-photo; **fig. 5-6:** Medical on Line/Alamy; **p. 138:** Ian O'Leary/Dorling Kindersley; **p. 139:** Lionel Cironneau/AP Wide World Photos; **p. 141:** Ranald MacKechnie/Dorling Kindersley; **p. 142:** Ryan McVay/Getty Images, Inc.; **p. 143 top left:** Barbara Petrick/Dreamstime; **p. 143 top right:** stockstudios/Shutterstock; **p. 143 bottom left:** Lauri Patterson/iStockphoto; **p. 143 bottom right:** Elena Elisseeva/Dreamstime; **p. 147:** Shutterstock; **fig. 5-8a:** Glowimages/Getty Images Royalty Free; **fig. 5-8b:** Kevin Schafer/Danita Delimont Photography; **p. 150:** Shutterstock; **p. 151:** Dorling Kindersley

Chapter 6

Opening Photo: Dan Kenyon/Getty Images, Inc.; **fig. 6-1 bottom left:** ikola Bilic/Shutterstock; **fig. 6-1 bottom left inset:** matka_Wariatka/Shutterstock; **fig. 6-1 bottom right:** Milos Luzanin/shutterstock; **fig. 6-1 bottom right inset:** GoodMood Photo/Shutterstock; **fig. 6-1 top left:** Pixelman/Shutterstock; **fig. 6-1 top right:** Lyudmila Suvorova/iStockphoto; **fig. 6-1 top right inset:** Lepas/Shutterstock; **fig. 6-1 top left inset:** J. T. Lewis/Shutterstock; **p. 159:** JLP/Sylvia Torres/CORBIS; **p. 160:** Dorling Kindersley; **fig. 6-3:** Leonid Nyshko/iStock-photo; **p. 161:** Ian O'Leary/Dorling Kindersley; **p. 162:** Peter Turnley/CORBIS; **fig. 6-4:** Jiri Hera/Shutterstock; **fig. 6-5:** Biophoto Associates/Photo Researchers, Inc.; **p. 164 top:** Philip Dowell /Dorling Kindersley; **p. 164 bottom:** Dorling Kindersley; **fig. 6-8:** vm/iStock-photo; **p. 166:** Philip Wilkins/Dorling Kindersley; **p. 167:** Cordelia Molloy/Photo Researchers, Inc.; **p. 168 top:** Valentyn Volkov/Shutterstock; **p. 168 bottom:** Walter Bibikow/Alamy Images; **fig. 6-9:** eyewave/iStockphoto; **fig. 6-10:** Medical-on-Line/Alamy Images; **p. 170:** Steve Gorton/Dorling Kindersley; **p. 171 top left:** Paul Blundell/Alamy Images; **p. 171 top right:** foodfolio/Alamy Images; **p. 171 bottom left:** Le Do/iStockphoto; **p. 171 bottom right:** Stock Foundry/Alamy Images; **fig. 6-11:** Uyen Le/iStockphoto; **p.172:**

Pollok/Taxi/Getty Images; **p. 363:** Deborah Jaffe/FoodPix/Creatas/ Getty Images; **p. 364:** Donna Day/Image Bank/Getty Images; **p. 366:** Karen Preuss/The Image Works

Chapter 12

Opening Photo: Getty Images; **fig. 12-1a:** Exactostock/Superstock; **fig. 12-1b:** Fotolia; **fig. 12-1c:** David Wei/Alamy Images; **fig. 12-1d:** Frank Rumpenhorst/Newscom; **fig. 12-1e:** Huntstock, Inc./Alamy Images; **fig. 12-2:** Dr. Tony Brain/Photo Researchers, Inc.; **fig. 12-3:** DocCheck Medical Services GmbH / Alamy; **fig. 12-4:** Andrew Syred/ Photo Researchers, Inc.; **fig. 12-5:** Matt Meadows/Photolibrary; **fig. 12-6:** Neil Fletcher / Dorling Kindersley; **p. 376 box:** Stockfood/

Getty Images; **p. 376 bottom:** Jean-Louis Vosgien/Shutterstock; **p. 378:** Vanessa Davies / Dorling Kindersley; **p. 379 top:** Shutterstock; **p. 379 bottom:** Shutterstock; **p. 382:** Alan Richardson; **p. 384:** Owen Franken/CORBIS; **p. 385 top:** New York Times Co./Hulton Archives Photos/Getty Images, Inc.; **p. 385 bottom:** Getty Images; **p. 386:** Lon C. Diehl/PhotoEdit Inc.; **p. 388:** AbleStock.com/Thinkstock; **p. 389:** image100/Corbis; **p. 390:** Toby Talbot/AP Wide World Photos; **fig. 12-14 left:** Carl Walsh/Aurora Photos, Inc.; **fig. 12-14 right:** Brian Hagiwara/Foodpix/Getty Images; **p. 391:** Corbis; **p. 392:** Red Cover/ Alamy Images; **p. 393:** Paul Gunning/Photo Researchers, Inc.; **p. 395:** iStockphoto; **p. 399:** Reuters/ CORBIS; **fig. 12-18:** Paul Almasy / CORBIS; **fig. 12-19:** AP Wide World Photos; **p. 401:** NEIL COOPER/ Alamy Images; **p. 402:** David Turnley/CORBIS

Text Credits

Chapter 5

fig. 5.9: "Vegetarian Diet Pyramid." Copyright © 2000 Oldways Preservation & Exchange Trust. www.oldwayspt.org. Reprinted with permission

Chapter 7

feature: Game Plan: Tips for Sparing the Salt, **p. 202.** From Spice Up Your Meals and Lower Your Salt Intake. Copyright © 2004 by American Dietertic Association. Reprinted with permission; **fig. 7.9:** Hemoglobin illustrations by Irving Geis. Copyright © 2011 by Howard Hughes Medical Institute. Not to be reprinted without permission

DIETARY REFERENCE INTAKES: RDA, AI*

Life-Stage Group	Calcium (mg/d)	Phosphorus (mg/d)	Magnesium (mg/d)	Iron (mg/d)	Zinc (mg/d)	Selenium (µg/d)	Iodine (µg/d)	Copper (µg/d)	Manganese (mg/d)	Fluoride (mg/d)	Chromium (µg/d)	Molybdenum (µg/d)
Infants												
0–6 mo	200*	100*	30*	0.27*	2*	15*	110*	200*	0.003*	0.01*	0.2*	2*
7–12 mo	260*	275*	75*	11	3	20*	130*	220*	0.6*	0.5*	5.5*	3*
Children												
1–3 y	700	460	80	7	3	20	90	340	1.2*	0.7*	11*	17
4–8 y	1000	500	130	10	5	30	90	440	1.5*	1*	15*	22
Males												
9–13 y	1300	1250	240	8	8	40	120	700	1.9*	2*	25*	34
14–18 y	1300	1250	410	11	11	55	150	890	2.2*	3*	35*	43
19–30 y	1000	700	400	8	11	55	150	900	2.3*	4*	35*	45
31–50 y	1000	700	420	8	11	55	150	900	2.3*	4*	35*	45
51–70 y	1000	700	420	8	11	55	150	900	2.3*	4*	30*	45
>70 y	1200	700	420	8	11	55	150	900	2.3*	4*	30*	45
Females												
9–13 y	1300	1250	240	8	8	40	120	700	1.6*	2*	21*	34
14–18 y	1300	1250	360	15	9	55	150	890	1.6*	3*	24*	43
19–30 y	1000	700	310	18	8	55	150	900	1.8*	3*	25*	45
31–50 y	1000	700	320	18	8	55	150	900	1.8*	3*	25*	45
51–70 y	1200	700	320	8	8	55	150	900	1.8*	3*	20*	45
>70 y	1200	700	320	8	8	55	150	900	1.8*	3*	20*	45
Pregnancy												
≤18 y	1300	1250	400	27	12	60	220	1000	2.0*	3*	29*	50
19–30 y	1000	700	350	27	11	60	220	1000	2.0*	3*	30*	50
31–50 y	1000	700	360	27	11	60	220	1000	2.0*	3*	30*	50
Lactation												
≤18 y	1300	1250	360	10	13	70	290	1300	2.6*	3*	44*	50
19–30 y	1000	700	310	9	12	70	290	1300	2.6*	3*	45*	50
31–50 y	1000	700	320	9	12	70	290	1300	2.6*	3*	45*	50

Note: This table is adapted from the DRI reports; see www.nap.edu. It lists Recommended Dietary Allowances (RDAs), with Adequate Intakes (AIs) indicated by an asterisk (*). RDAs and AIs may both be used as goals for individual intake. RDAs are set to meet the needs of almost all (97% to 98%) individuals in a group. For healthy breast-fed infants, the AI is the mean intake. The AI for other life-stage and gender groups is believed to cover the needs of all individuals in the group, but lack of data prevents being able to specify with confidence the percentage of individuals covered by this intake. From Dietary Reference Intakes series. Copyright © 2011 by the National Academy of Sciences. Reprinted by permission of the National Academy of Sciences. Courtesy of the National Academies Press, Washington, DC.

DIETARY REFERENCE INTAKES: RDA, AI*

Vitamins

Life-Stage Group	Vitamin A (µg/d)a	Vitamin D (IU/d)b	Vitamin E (mg/d)c	Vitamin K (µg/d)	Thiamin (mg/d)	Riboflavin (mg/d)	Niacin (mg/d)d	Pantothenic Acid (mg/d)	Biotin (µg/d)	Vitamin B6 (mg/d)	Folate (µg/d)e	Vitamin B12 (µg/d)	Vitamin C (mg/d)	Choline (mg/d)
Infants														
0–6 mo	400*	400*	4*	2.0*	0.2*	0.3*	2*	1.7*	5*	0.1*	65*	0.4*	40*	125*
7–12 mo	500*	400*	5*	2.5*	0.3*	0.4*	4*	1.8*	6*	0.3*	80*	0.5*	50*	150*
Children														
1–3 y	300	600	6	30*	0.5	0.5	6	2*	8*	0.5	150	0.9	15	200*
4–8 y	400	600	7	55*	0.6	0.6	8	3*	12*	0.6	200	1.2	25	250*
Males														
9–13 y	600	600	11	60*	0.9	0.9	12	4*	20*	1.0	300	1.8	45	375*
14–18 y	900	600	15	75*	1.2	1.3	16	5*	25*	1.3	400	2.4	75	550*
19–30 y	900	600	15	120*	1.2	1.3	16	5*	30*	1.3	400	2.4	90	550*
31–50 y	900	600	15	120*	1.2	1.3	16	5*	30*	1.3	400	2.4	90	550*
51–70 y	900	600	15	120*	1.2	1.3	16	5*	30*	1.7	400	2.4	90	550*
>70 y	900	800	15	120*	1.2	1.3	16	5*	30*	1.7	400	2.4	90	550*
Females														
9–13 y	600	600	11	60*	0.9	0.9	12	4*	20*	1.0	300	1.8	45	375*
14–18 y	700	600	15	75*	1.0	1.0	14	5*	25*	1.2	400	2.4	65	400*
19–30 y	700	600	15	90*	1.1	1.1	14	5*	30*	1.3	400	2.4	75	425*
31–50 y	700	600	15	90*	1.1	1.1	14	5*	30*	1.3	400	2.4	75	425*
51–70 y	700	600	15	90*	1.1	1.1	14	5*	30*	1.5	400	2.4	75	425*
>70 y	700	800	15	90*	1.1	1.1	14	5*	30*	1.5	400	2.4	75	425*
Pregnancy														
≤18 y	750	600	15	75*	1.4	1.4	18	6*	30*	1.9	600	2.6	80	450*
19–30 y	770	600	15	90*	1.4	1.4	18	6*	30*	1.9	600	2.6	85	450*
31–50 y	770	600	15	90*	1.4	1.4	18	6*	30*	1.9	600	2.6	85	450*
Lactation														
≤18 y	1200	600	19	75*	1.4	1.4	17	7*	35*	2.0	500	2.8	115	550*
19–30 y	1300	600	19	90*	1.4	1.4	17	7*	35*	2.0	500	2.8	120	550*
31–50 y	1300	600	19	90*	1.4	1.4	17	7*	35*	2.0	500	2.8	120	550*

Note: This table is adapted from the DRI reports; see www.nap.edu. It lists Recommended Dietary Allowances (RDAs), with Adequate Intakes (AIs) indicated by an asterisk (*). RDAs and AIs may both be used as goals for individual intake. RDAs are set to meet the needs of almost all (97% to 98%) individuals in a group. For healthy breast-fed infants, the AI is the mean intake. The AI for other life-stage and gender groups is believed to cover the needs of all individuals in the group, but lack of data prevents being able to specify with confidence the percentage of individuals covered by this intake.

a Given as retinal activity equivalents (RAE).
b Also known as calciferol. The DRI values are based on the absence of adequate exposure to sunlight.
c Also known as α-tocopherol.
d Given as niacin equivalents (NE), except for infants 0–6 months, which are expressed as preformed niacin.
e Given as dietary folate equivalents (DFE).

DIETARY REFERENCE INTAKES: RDA, AI,* (AMDR)

	Macronutrients					
Life-Stage Group	Carbohydrate— Total Digestible (g/d)	Total Fiber (g/d)	Total Fat (g/d)	n-6 Polyunsaturated fatty acids (linoleic acid) (g/d)	n-3 Polyunsaturated Fatty acids (?-linoleic acid) (g/d)	Protein and Amino Acids (grams/d)[a]
Infants						
0–6 mo	60* (ND[b])[c]	ND	31*	4.4* (ND)	0.5* (ND)	9.1* (ND)
7–12 mo	95* (ND)	ND	30*	4.6* (ND)	0.5* (ND)	13.5 (ND)
Children						
1–3 y	130 (45–65)	19*	(30–40)	7* (5–10)	0.7* (0.6–1.2)	13 (5–20)
4–8 y	130 (45–65)	25*	(25–35)	10* (5–10)	0.9* (0.6–1.2)	19 (10–30)
Males						
9–13 y	130 (45–65)	31*	(25–35)	12* (5–10)	1.2* (0.6–1.2)	34 (10–30)
14–18 y	130 (45–65)	38*	(25–35)	16* (5–10)	1.6* (0.6–1.2)	52 (10–30)
19–30 y	130 (45–65)	38*	(20–35)	17* (5–10)	1.6* (0.6–1.2)	56 (10–35)
31–50 y	130 (45–65)	38*	(20–35)	17* (5–10)	1.6* (0.6–1.2)	56 (10–35)
51–70 y	130 (45–65)	30*	(20–35)	14* (5–10)	1.6* (0.6–1.2)	56 (10–35)
>70 y	130 (45–65)	30*	(20–35)	14* (5–10)	1.6* (0.6–1.2)	56 (10–35)
Females						
9–13 y	130 (45–65)	26*	(25–35)	10* (5–10)	1.0* (0.6–1.2)	34 (10–30)
14–18 y	130 (45–65)	26*	(25–35)	11* (5–10)	1.1* (0.6–1.2)	46 (10–30)
19–30 y	130 (45–65)	25*	(20–35)	12* (5–10)	1.1* (0.6–1.2)	46 (10–35)
31–50 y	130 (45–65)	25*	(20–35)	12* (5–10)	1.1* (0.6–1.2)	46 (10–35)
51–70 y	130 (45–65)	21*	(20–35)	11* (5–10)	1.1* (0.6–1.2)	46 (10–35)
>70 y	130 (45–65)	21*	(20–35)	11* (5–10)	1.1* (0.6–1.2)	46 (10–35)
Pregnancy						
≤18 y	175 (45–65)	28*	(20–35)	13* (5–10)	1.4* (0.6–1.2)	71 (10–35)
19–30 y	175 (45–65)	28*	(20–35)	13* (5–10)	1.4* (0.6–1.2)	71 (10–35)
31–50 y	(45–65)	28*	(20–35)	13* (5–10)	1.4* (0.6–1.2)	71 (10–35)
Lactation						
≤18 y	210 (45–65)	29*	(20–35)	13* (5–10)	1.3* (0.6–1.2)	71 (10–35)
19–30 y	210 (45–65)	29*	(20–35)	13* (5–10)	1.3* (0.6–1.2)	71 (10–35)
31–50 y	210 (45–65)	29*	(20–35)	13* (5–10)	1.3* (0.6–1.2)	71 (10–35)

Note: This table is adapted from the DRI reports; see www.nap.edu. It lists Recommended Dietary Allowances (RDAs), with Adequate Intakes (AIs) indicated by an asterisk (*), and Acceptable Macronutrient Distribution Range (AMDR) data provided in parentheses. RDAs and AIs may both be used as goals for individual intake. RDAs are set to meet the needs of almost all (97% to 98%) individuals in a group. For healthy breast-fed infants, the AI is the mean intake. The AI for other life-stage and gender groups is believed to cover the needs of all individuals in the group, but lack of data prevents being able to specify with confidence the percentage of individuals covered by this intake.

[a] Based on 1.5 g/kg/day for infants, 1.1 g/kg/day for 1–3 y, 0.95 g/kg/day for 4–13 y, 0.85 g/kg/day for 14–18 y, 0.8 g/kg/day for adults, and 1.1 g/kg/day for pregnant (using pre-pregnancy weight) and lactating women.

[b] ND = Not determinable due to lack of data of adverse effects in this age group and concern with regard to lack of ability to handle excess amounts. Source of intake should be food only to prevent high levels of intake.

[c] Data in parentheses are Acceptable Macronutrient Distribution Range (AMDR). This is the range of intake for a particular energy source that is associated with reduced risk for chronic disease while providing intakes of essential nutrients. If an individual consumes in excess of the AMDR, there is a potential of increasing the risk for chronic diseases and/or insufficient intakes of essential nutrients. From "Dietary Reference Intakes for Energy, Carbohydrates, Fiber, Fat, Fatty Acids, Cholesterol, Protein, and Amino Acids (Macronutrients)" 2005. Copyright © 2005 by the National Academy of Sciences. Reprinted with permission by the National Academy of Sciences, courtesy of the National Academies Press, Washington, DC.